J.K. LASSER'S™

YOUR
INCOME
TAX 2003

Prepared by the

J.K. LASSER INSTITUTE™

John Wiley & Sons, Inc.

New York • Chichester • Weinheim • Brisbane • Singapore • Toronto

Staff for This Book

J.K. Lasser Editorial
Elliott Eiss, Member of the New York Bar, Editorial Director of the J.K. Lasser Institute™
Donna LeValley, Member of the New York Bar, Contributing Editor
Angelo C. Jack, Associate Managing Editor
Chino T. Panz, Production Assistant
Bill Hamill, Production Assistant
Carolyn Francis, Copyediting and Proofreading
Helen Chin, Indexing

John Wiley & Sons, Inc.

John Wiley & Sons, Inc.
111 River Street
Hoboken, NJ

Publisher's Note: *Your Income Tax* is published in recognition of the great need for useful information regarding the income tax laws for the millions of men and women who must fill out returns. We believe the research and interpretation by the J.K. Lasser Institute™ of the nation's tax laws will be of help to taxpayers. Taxpayers are cautioned, however, that this book is sold with the understanding that the publisher and the contributors to this book are not engaged in rendering legal, accounting, or other professional services herein. Taxpayers with specific tax problems are urged to seek the professional advice of a tax accountant, lawyer, or preparer.

The publisher and contributors to this book specifically disclaim any responsibility for any liability, loss, or risk (financial, personal, or otherwise) that may be claimed or incurred as a consequence, directly or indirectly, of the use and/or application of any of the contents of this book.

For general information on our other products and services, or technical support, please contact our Customer Care Department within the United States at 800-762-2974, outside the United States at 317-572-3993 or fax 317-572-4002.

Wiley also publishes its books in a variety of electronic formats. Some content that appears in print may not be available in electronic books.

For more information about Wiley products, visit our web site at www.wiley.com.

ISBN 0-471-22825-7

Manufactured in the United States of America

10 9 8 7 6 5 4 3 2 1

Sixty-Sixth Edition

How to Use *Your Income Tax 2003*

Tax alert symbols. Throughout the text of *Your Income Tax*, these special symbols alert you to advisory tips about filing your return and tax planning opportunities:

Filing Tip or Filing Instruction . . . . . . A **Filing Tip** or **Filing Instruction** helps you prepare your 2002 return.

Planning Reminder . . . . A **Planning Reminder** highlights year-end tax strategies for 2002 or planning opportunities for 2003 and later years.

Caution . . . . A **Caution** points out potential pitfalls to avoid and areas where IRS opposition may be expected.

Law Alert . . . . A **Law Alert** indicates recent changes in the tax law and pending legislation before Congress.

Court Decision . . . . A **Court Decision** highlights key rulings from the Tax Court and other federal courts.

IRS Alert . . . . An **IRS Alert** highlights key rulings and announcements from the IRS.

The federal income tax law, despite efforts at simplification, remains a maze of statutes, regulations, rulings, and court decisions written in technical language covering thousands and thousands of pages. For over 65 years, J.K. Lasser's™ *Your Income Tax* has aided and guided millions of taxpayers through this complex law. Every effort has been made to provide a direct and easy-to-understand explanation that shows how to comply with the law and at the same time take advantage of tax-saving options and plans.

The 2003 edition of *Your Income Tax*—our 66th edition—continues this tradition.
To make maximum use of this tax guide, we suggest that you use these aids:

Contents at a glance. Page v shows the nine major parts of the book and directly leads you to each part.

Contents chapter by chapter. The contents, on **pages vii–xxiii** list the chapters in *Your Income Tax*. References direct you to sections within a particular chapter. Thus a reference to *21.1* directs you to Chapter 21 and then to section 1 within that chapter. Section and page references are provided in the index at the back of the book.

What's New for 2002. Pages xxv-xxviii alert you to tax developments that may affect your 2002 tax return.

Looking Ahead to Tax Changes for Years After 2002. Pages xxix–xxx provide an overview of the tax law changes for years after 2002 .

Filing tax basics. Pages 1–7 alert you to filing requirements, filing addresses shown on a map of IRS Service Centers, and a calendar with 2003 filing deadlines.

Glossary of tax terms. The tax law is a technical subject with its own particular terminology. Many of the major tax terms are defined in this special glossary starting on **page 761**.

Contents at a Glance

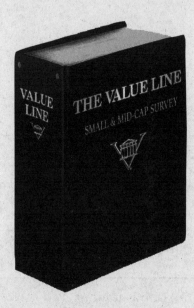

Contents Chapter by Chapter

PART 6   BUSINESS TAX PLANNING   597

What's New for 2002

For an update on tax developments and a free download
of the Supplement to this book, visit us online at
www.jklasser.com.

Item	Highlight
Tax rates and brackets	The 10% rate is in the tax tables and rate schedules, and the top four tax rates are reduced by another .5% to 27%, 30%, 35%, and 38.6%. The 15% rate remains unchanged.
Standard deduction	Basic standard deduction increased to $4,700 for singles, $6,900 for heads of household, $3,925 for married persons filing separately, and $7,850 for joint returns and qualifying widow(er)s; *see* Chapter 13.
Personal exemptions	Personal exemption deduction is $3,000 (up from $2,900), subject to the phase-out rules for high-income taxpayers; *see 21.1* and *21.16*.
Bonus first-year depreciation	Bonus depreciation allows an additional first-year deduction equal to 30% of the basis of qualifying property placed into service after September 10, 2001. This is in addition to any first-year expensing; *see 42.20*. Regular first-year expensing limit on business equipment placed in service in 2002 is $24,000; *see 42.3*.
Bonus first-year auto depreciation limit	Bonus depreciation allows an additional first-year deduction of 30% of the basis of an automobile placed into service after September 10, 2001 provided the auto is used more than 50% for business. If the bonus is claimed for the car, the depreciation ceiling is increased from $3,060 to $7,660; *see 43.4*. If business use is 50% or less or the bonus allowance is not claimed, the first-year depreciation limit for 2002 is $3,060; *see 43.4*.
Net operating losses (NOLs)	A five-year carryback period is allowed for NOLs incurred in 2002 and 2001. The five-year period may be waived if it is more advantageous to use the regular carryback period; *see 40.18*.
Student-loan interest deduction	Maximum deduction remains $2,500. However, the 60-month deduction limit has been repealed. Those prevented from deducting student loan interest before 2002 due to the 60-month limitation may now deduct interest payments made on the same loan after 2001. The deduction phase-out range is increased to MAGI of $50,000–$65,000 for singles and to MAGI of $100,000–$130,000 for joint filers; *see 38.6*.
Traditional IRA and Roth IRA contribution limits	The maximum annual contribution for traditional and Roth IRAs increased by $1,000 to $3,000. Individuals age 50 and over can make an additional $500 contribution, raising their maximum contribution limit for 2002 to $3,500; *see 8.2*.

Item	Highlight
Traditional IRA deduction phaseout	For 2002, deductions for active plan participants are phased out if MAGI exceeds $34,000 if single or $54,000 if married filing jointly (up from $33,000 and $53,000, respectively); see 8.4.
New life expectancy tables to compute IRA minimum distributions	The IRS released final regulations for figuring required minimum distributions after age 70 1/2 from traditional IRAs, and issued revised life expectancy tables to be used for making the computation; see 8.13 and 8.14.
IRS can waive 60-day rollover period	The IRS has the discretion to waive the 60-day deadline where illness, institutional error, or other events beyond taxpayer control result in the failure to complete a rollover within 60 days.
Retirement savings credit	For 2002 through 2006, low-to-moderate-income taxpayers may receive a tax credit for retirement contributions to traditional and Roth IRAs, and 401(k), 403(b), governmental 457, SIMPLE, or SEP plans. A credit of 10%, 20%, or 50% may be allowed for contributions up to $2,000, depending on income. The credit will not be available to joint filers with MAGI over $50,000, heads of household with MAGI over $37,500 and single persons, qualified widow(er)s, or married persons filing separately with MAGI over $25,000. Dependents, workers under age 18, and full-time students are also ineligible; see 22.5.
Coverdell ESA (education IRA) contributions	The annual contribution limit jumps from $500 to $2,000 per beneficiary. For married persons filing jointly, the contribution phase-out range increases to MAGI of $190,000–$220,000, double the range for single filers. Contributions for 2002 can be made until April 15, 2003. For special needs children, contributions to a Coverdell ESA may continue after the beneficiary reaches age 18, and the account does not have to be emptied at age 30; see 38.11.
Coverdell ESA (education IRA) distributions	The definition of eligible educational expenses that may be paid tax free by a Coverdell ESA is expanded to include kindergarten through high school costs; see 38.12.
College tuition deduction	An above-the-line deduction for up to $3,000 of college tuition and related fees is allowed to unmarried filers with MAGI up to $65,000 and joint filers with MAGI up to $130,000. The deduction is not allowed if a Hope or lifetime learning credit is claimed for the same student for the same year; see 38.13.
Qualified tuition programs	Distributions from state-maintained qualified tuition programs are tax free if used for qualified expenses; see 38.5.
Coordination of education benefits	Tax-free treatment can be claimed for a distribution from a Coverdell ESA, or a qualified tuition plan in the same year as an education credit is claimed for the same student, provided the distribution is not used to cover the same expenses used to figure the credit; see 38.5, 38.7, 38.12.

Item	Highlight
Employer-provided tuition assistance	The $5,250 exclusion from income for employer-provided tuition assistance applies to all years after 2001 and is now available for graduate-level courses; *see 3.6.*
Itemized deduction reduction	Itemized deductions such as mortgage interest, taxes, and miscellaneous expenses are reduced by 3% of the amount of your 2002 adjusted gross income over $137,700 ($68,650) if married filing separately; *see 13.7.*
Estimated tax safe harbor	Safe harbor tests for figuring the estimated tax penalty for 2002 and estimated payments for 2003 are discussed at *27.1.*
FICA and self-employment tax base	For 2002, wages and self-employment earnings of up to $84,900 (from $80,400) are subject to the 6.2% Social Security tax; *see 26.10* and *45.4.*
Elective deferrals	The deferral limit for 401(k), 403(b), and SEP plans increases by $500 to $11,000 and the deferral limit for a governmental Section 457 plans increases from $8,500 to $11,000. The deferral limit for SIMPLE plans increases to $7,000. For those age 50 and over an additional $1,000 deferral may be made to a 401(k), 403(b), SEP, or governmental Section 457 plan if the plan allows the contribution. For a SIMPLE plan the additional deferral limit is $500; *see 7.17* and *7.18.*
Higher deductible contribution limits for SEP and Keogh plans	The maximum deductible contribution rate for profit-sharing plans increases from 15% to 25%. The compensation limit increases to $200,000 and the dollar limit on contributions to $40,000 assuming the plan is amended in 2002 to implement the increases; *see 41.5.*
Expanded rollover options	Eligible rollover distributions from a traditional IRA, qualified plan, 403(b) plan, or governmental Section 457 plan may be rolled over to any of such plans. After-tax contributions may also be rolled into a qualified defined contribution plan or traditional IRA; *see 7.8.*
Faster vesting for matching contributions	For plan years beginning after 2001, plans must offer 100% vesting of employer matching funds in three years or must vest 20% per year starting in the second year of service.
IRS business mileage rate	The business mileage rate for 2002 is 36.5 cents per mile; *see 43.1.*
Personal tax credits	Nonrefundable personal tax credits, such as the child tax credit, dependent care credit, and the education credits, can reduce alternative minimum tax (AMT) as well as regular income tax on 2002 returns.
Foreign earned income exclusion	Exclusion for 2002 is $80,000 (up from $78,000); *see 36.1.*

Item	Highlight
Adoption Credit	The credit for non-special needs adoptions is made permanent and the maximum credit for all adoptions increases to $10,000. The phaseout of the credit begins at MAGI of $150,000 (instead of $75,000) and is complete at $190,000 or more.
Earned income credit (EIC)	Increased credit and phase-out limits; *see 25.12–25.14.*
Estate tax exclusion	In addition to the top rate coming down 5% to 50%, the per-estate exclusion amount is increased to $1 million; *see 39.5.*
Estate tax credit for state death taxes	The federal estate tax credit for state death taxes is reduced by 25%, the first step in phasing it out by 2005; *see 39.5.*
Continuing care facility	The loan threshold for taxing imputed interest on entrance fees to qualified facilities is $148,800 (up from $144,100); *see 34.11.*
Health Reimbursement Accounts (HRAs)	Employer established health-care reimbursement accounts, generally used in conjunction with high-deductible insurance, allow employees to receive tax-free reimbursements for deductibles and other costs that would qualify for an itemized medical deduction. Unused portions may be carried forward to later years; *see 3.2.*
Victims and Survivors of Terrorist Attacks	Special tax breaks for the families of those killed in the September 11th attacks, anthrax attacks, and the Oklahoma City bombing include: income tax forgiveness, special estate tax rates, and tax-free payments from various sources. Other survivors are also eligilble for tax-free payments. For further details, *see 35.9.*
Cash-method accounting safe harbor increased	The IRS will allow business taxpayers with average annual gross receipts of $10 million or less for the three prior tax years to use the cash method of accounting; *see 40.3.*
New York Liberty Zone	Businesses located in the area on or south of Canal Street, and on or south of East Broadway and Grand Street where these intersect with Canal Street are eligible for special tax breaks. These breaks include an increased Work Opportunity Credit *(see 40.23)* and increased first-year expensing limit of $59,000. An additional first-year depreciation deduction of 30% is allowed for Liberty Zone property that does not qualify for the general 30% depreciation bonus; *see 42.3 and 42.20.*
Educator expense deduction	For 2002 and 2003, teachers and other professionals who work at least 900 hours in a public or private elementary or secondary school may deduct up to $250 of out-of-pocket costs for books, supplies, computer equipment, software, and other classroom materials; *see 12.2.*

Looking Ahead to Tax Changes for Years After 2002

Item	Highlight
Tax rates	The rates for 2003 remain 10%, 15%, 27%, 30%, 35%, and 38.6%. In 2004 and 2005 rates over the 15% rate will fall to 26%, 29%, 34%, and 37.6%. In 2006, another reduction will lower the top four rates to 25%, 28%, 33%, and 35%. The amount of income subject to those rates will continue to be adjusted annually for inflation. The 15% rate will not change; however, the bracket will be expanded for inflation and, starting in 2005, the amount of taxable income subject to the 15% rate will be increased for married couples filing jointly under the marriage penalty relief provisions (*see* below). The amount of income subject to the 10% rate will not change until 2008, when it will apply to the first $14,000 on joint returns (up from $12,000), $7,000 for single filers and married persons filing separately (up from $6,000); it will remain $10,000 for heads of household.
IRA contributions	The annual limit for 2003–2004 traditional and Roth IRA contributions is $3,000. The limit increases to $4,000 for 2005–2007. It will increase again in 2008 to $5,000. After 2008, the $5,000 figure will be indexed for inflation. The annual contribution limit for workers 50 and over is increased by an additional $500 for 2003 through 2005 and $1,000 in 2006 and later years.
AMT exemptions	Unless new legislation is enacted, the increased AMT exemptions allowed for 2001–2004 will not apply starting in 2005; the exemption amounts will return to 2001 levels.
Child tax credit	The credit for 2003–2004 is $600. The credit will increase to $700 for 2005–2008, to $800 for 2009, and to $1,000 for 2010 and later years. In addition, the refundable portion of the credit will increase in 2005 to 15% (from 10%) of earned income exceeding $10,000 (as adjusted for inflation).
Adoption credit	The maximum $10,000 adoption credit amount and $150,000 phase-out threshold may be adjusted for inflation beginning in 2003. For a special needs adoption finalized after 2002, qualifying expenses are "grossed up" to $10,000 if expenses for all years are under $10,000, ensuring that the maximum $10,000 credit is received for the year the adoption is finalized.
College tuition deduction	The deduction is scheduled to last for only four years, from 2002 through 2005 (unless it is extended by an act of Congress). The maximum deduction allowed in 2003 is $3,000 for unmarried filers with MAGI of no more than $65,000 and for joint filers with MAGI of no more than $130,000. Subject to the $65,000 or $130,000 MAGI limit, the maximum deduction increases to $4,000 for 2004–2005. A reduced deduction limit of $2,000 applies to unmarried filers with MAGI of no more than $80,000 and joint filers with MAGI of no more than $160,000 in 2004 and 2005.

Item	Highlight
Dependent care credit	The limit on expenses eligible for the credit increases from $2,400 for one dependent and $4,800 for two or more dependents to $3,000 and $6,000, respectively, in 2003. The maximum credit will increase from 30% to 35% of expenses.
Estate tax rates and exclusion amounts	*See 39.5* for a year-by-year chart of the estate tax rate cuts and expanded exclusion amounts leading up to repeal of the estate tax in 2010.
Estate tax credit for state death tax phased out	The state death tax credit allowed for federal estate tax purposes under pre-2002 law will be reduced by 50% in 2003 and 75% in 2004. In 2005 the credit is repealed and replaced with an estate tax deduction for any state death tax actually paid.
Estate tax family-owned business deduction	The deduction is repealed for estates of individuals dying after 2003.
Qualified tuition plan distributions	Starting in 2004, distributions from a qualified tuition program established by a private college or university are tax free if used for qualified higher education expenses.
Elective deferrals	The deferral limit for 401(k), 403(b), SEP, and governmental Section 457 plans is $12,000 in 2003. The limit increases by $1,000 per year until it reaches $15,000 in 2006. The deferral limit for SIMPLE plans in 2003 is $8,000. The limit increases by $1,000 each year until 2005, when it reaches $10,000. If the plan allows additional contributions for those age 50 and over, an additional $2,000 for 2003, $3,000 for 2004, $4,000 for 2005, and $5,000 for 2006 may be made to a 401(k), 403(b), SEP, or governmental 457 plan. For SIMPLE plans, the additional amount is half as much.
Optional Roth 401(k) or 403(b)	If your plan permits, starting in 2006 you may treat elective deferrals as after-tax Roth contributions to be held in a separate account. As under Roth IRA rules, tax-free distributions can be made after a five-year waiting period if you are at least age $59^1/_2$.
Exemption phaseout and itemized deduction reduction	The 3% reduction to itemized deductions and the personal exemption phaseout for high-income taxpayers will be phased out. These deduction limitations will be reduced by one-third in 2006–2007, by two-thirds in 2008–2009, and fully repealed in 2010.
Marriage penalty relief—standard deduction	Between 2005 and 2009, the basic standard deduction will be increased on joint returns until it is double that of single filers. It will increase to 174% of a single taxpayer's deduction in 2005, 184% in 2006, 187% in 2007, 190% in 2008, and 200% in 2009 and later years.
Marriage penalty relief—15% bracket for joint returns	Between 2005 and 2008, the end point of the 15% bracket for joint filers will be expanded until it is double the end point of the 15% bracket for single filers. It will be 180% of the bracket for single filers in 2005, 187% in 2006, 193% in 2007, and 200% in 2008 and after.

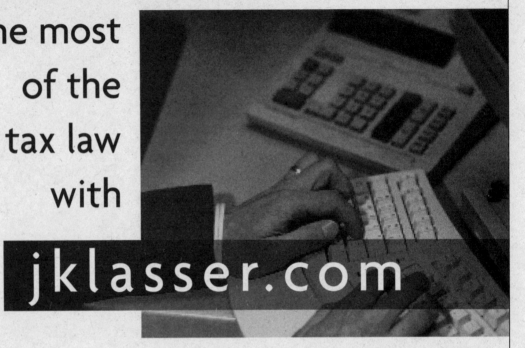

Part 1

Filing Basics

In this part, you will learn these income tax basics:

- Whether you must file a return
- When and where to file your return
- Which tax form to file
- What filing status you qualify for
- When filing separately is an advantage for married persons
- How to qualify as head of household
- How filing rules for resident aliens and nonresident aliens differ
- How to claim personal exemption deductions for yourself, your spouse, and your dependents.

Do You Have To File a 2002 Tax Return?

If you are—	You must file if gross income is at least—
Single	
Under age 65	$7,700
Age 65 or older on or before January 1, 2003	8,850
Married and living together at the end of 2002	
Filing a joint return—both spouses under age 65	13,850
Filing a joint return—one spouse age 65 or older	14,750
Filing a joint return—both spouses age 65 or older	15,650
Filing a separate return (any age)	3,000
Married and living apart at the end of 2002	
Filing a joint or separate return	3,000
Head of a household maintained for a child or other relative *(see 1.12)*	
Under age 65	9,900
Age 65 or older on or before January 1, 2003	11,050
Widowed in 2001 or 2000 and have a dependent child *(see 1.11)*	
Under age 65	10,850
Age 65 or older on or before January 1, 2003	11,750

Marital status. For 2002 tax purposes, marital status is generally determined as of December 31, 2002. Thus, if you were divorced or legally separated during 2002, you are not considered married for 2002 tax purposes, and you must use the filing threshold for single persons unless you qualify as a head of household *(1.12),* or you remarried in 2002 and are filing a joint return with your new spouse.

If your spouse died in 2002 and you were living together on the date of death, use the filing threshold shown for married persons living together at the end of 2002. If you were not living together on the date of death, the $3,000 filing threshold applies, unless you remarried during 2002 and are filing jointly with your new spouse.

Age 65. Whether you are age 65 or older is generally determined as of the end of the year, but if your 65th birthday is on January 1, 2003, you are treated as being age 65 for 2002 tax purposes.

Gross income. Gross income is generally all the income that you received in 2002, except for items specifically exempt from tax.

Include wages, tips, self-employment income (Chapter 45), taxable scholarships (Chapter 38), taxable interest and dividends (Chapter 4), capital gains (Chapter 5), taxable pensions and annuities (Chapter 7), rents (Chapter 9), and trust distributions (Chapter 11). Home sale proceeds that are tax free (Chapter 29) and tax-free foreign earned income (Chapter 36) *are* considered gross income for purposes of the filing test.

Exclude tax-exempt interest (Chapter 4), tax-free fringe benefits (Chapter 3), qualifying scholarships (Chapter 38), and life insurance (Chapter 33). Also exclude Social Security benefits *unless* you are married filing separately and you lived with your spouse at any time during 2002.

Other situations when you must file. Even if you are not required to file under the gross income tests, you must file a 2002 return if:

- You are self-employed and you owe self-employment tax because your net self-employment earnings for 2002 are $400 or more (Chapter 45), *or*
- You are entitled to a refund of taxes withheld from your wages or a refund based on the earned income credit for working families (Chapter 25), *or*
- You received any earned income credit payments in advance from your employer (Chapter 25), *or*
- You owe any special tax such as alternative minimum tax (Chapter 23), IRA penalty (Chapter 8), and FICA on tips (Chapter 26), *or*
- You are a nonresident alien with a U.S. business or have tax liability not covered by withholding; *see* Form 1040NR.

Filing tests for dependents. If you can be claimed as a dependent by your parent, or by any other taxpayer, see the rules on the next page to determine if you must file a return.

Filing Tests for Dependents: 2002 Returns

The income threshold for filing a tax return is generally lower for an individual who may be claimed as a dependent than for a nondependent. If your 2002 gross income was $3,000 or more, you may be claimed as a dependent only by your parent, and only if you were either under age 19 or a full-time student under age 24. This income test and the other tests for depenf nts ar e explained in Chapter 21.

If, under the tests in Chapter 21, you may be claimed as a dependent by someone else, use the chart on this page to determine if you must file a 2002 return. Include as unearned income taxable interest and dividends, capital gains, pensions, annuities, unemployment compensation, and distributions of unearned income from a trust. Earned income includes wages, tips, self-employment income, and taxable scholarships or fellowships (Chapter 38). Gross income is the total of unearned and earned income.

For married dependents, the filing requirements in the chart assume that the dependent is filing a separate return and not a joint return (Chapter 1). Generally, a married person who files a joint return may not be claimed as a dependent by a third party who provides support.

If you are the parent of a dependent child who was under age 14 on January 1, 2003, and who had only investment income, you may elect to report the child's income on your own return instead of filing a separate return for the child; *see 24.5* for the election rules.

For purposes of the following chart, a person is treated as being age 65 (or older) if his or her 65th birthday is on or before January 1, 2003. Blindness is determined as of December 31, 2002.

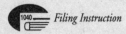

Filing Instruction

File for Refund of Withholdings

Even if you are not required to file a return under the income tests on this page, you should file to obtain a refund of federal tax withholdings. Also see page 3 for other situations when you must file.

File a Return for 2002 If You Are a—

Single dependent. Were you **either** age 65 or older **or** blind?

☐ **No.** You must file a return if **any** of the following apply:
- Your **unearned income** was over $750.
- Your **earned income** was over $4,700.
- Your **gross income** was more than the **larger** of—
  - $750 **or**
  - Your earned income (up to $4,450) plus $250.

☐ **Yes.** You must file a return if **any** of the following apply:
- Your unearned income was over $1,900 ($3,050 if 65 or older **and** blind).
- Your earned income was over $5,850 ($7,000 if 65 or older **and** blind).
- Your gross income was more than—

The larger of:	Plus	This amount:
• $750 **or** • Your earned income (up to $4,450) plus $250	}	$1,150 ($2,300 if 65 or older **and** blind)

Married dependent. Were you **either** age 65 or older **or** blind?

☐ **No.** You must file a return if **any** of the following apply:
- Your unearned income was over $750.
- Your earned income was over $3,925.
- Your gross income was at least $5 and your spouse files a separate return and itemizes deductions.
- Your gross income was more than the **larger** of—
  - $750 **or**
  - Your earned income (up to $3,675) plus $250.

☐ **Yes.** You must file a return if **any** of the following apply:
- Your unearned income was over $1,650 ($2,550 if 65 or older **and** blind).
- Your earned income was over $4,825 ($5,725 if 65 or older **and** blind).
- Your gross income was at least $5 and your spouse files a separate return and itemizes deductions.
- Your gross income was more than—

The larger of:	Plus	This amount:
• $750 **or** • Your earned income (up to $3,675) plus $250	}	$900 ($1,800 if 65 or older **and** blind)

Where To File

If you are filing—	File with the Internal Revenue Service Center—
Form 1040, 1040A, or 1040EZ	For your place of legal residence. If you received an IRS packet of forms with a pre-addressed envelope, use it unless you have moved. If you do not have an envelope, mail your return to the Service Center shown on the map below for your residence.
A partnership (Form 1065) or S corporation (Form 1120S) return	For the location of your principal place of business; follow the Form 1065 or 1120S instructions.
As a U.S. citizen working abroad	File Form 1040, 1040A, or 1040EZ at Philadelphia, PA 19255-0215.
As a service member in the Armed Forces	For the place you are stationed. If you are overseas and have an APO or FPO address, file Form 1040, 1040A, or 1040EZ with the Service Center at Philadelphia, PA 19255-0215.

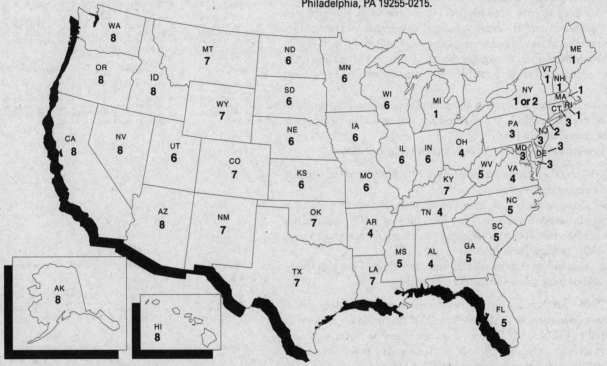

Key to Service Center Map

Key	Form 1040 Mailing Address—*	Key	Form 1040 Mailing Address—*
1.	Internal Revenue Service, Andover, Massachusetts 05501-0102 if making a payment; otherwise 05501-0002. New York residents file here if they reside outside of New York City or counties of Nassau, Rockland, Suffolk, or Westchester.	4.	Internal Revenue Service, Memphis, Tennessee 37501-0102 if making a payment; otherwise 37501-0002.
2.	Internal Revenue Service, Holtsville, New York 00501-0102 if making a payment; otherwise 00501-0002. New York residents in New York City or counties of Nassau, Rockland, Suffolk, or Westchester file here.	5.	Internal Revenue Service, Atlanta, Georgia 39901-0102 if making a payment; otherwise 39901-0002.
3.	Internal Revenue Service, Philadelphia, Pennsylvania 19255-0102 if making a payment; otherwise 19255-0002. Residents of the District of Columbia file here.	6.	Internal Revenue Service, Kansas City, Missouri 64999-0102 if making a payment; otherwise 64999-0002.
		7.	Internal Revenue Service, Austin, Texas 73301-0102 if making a payment; otherwise 73301-0002.
		8.	Internal Revenue Service, Fresno, California 93888-0102 if making a payment; otherwise 93888-0002.

__Filing Form 1040A or 1040EZ:__ If you are filing Form 1040A, the last four digits of the zip codes for the IRS Service Centers are 0015 (no payment) or 0115 (payment). For Form 1040EZ the last four digits are 0014 (no payment) or 0114 (payment). Check your tax form instructions and the Supplement for any late changes to the addresses or zip codes on this page.

Filing Deadlines (on or Before)

January 15, 2003—Pay the balance of your 2002 estimated tax. If you do not meet this date, you may avoid an estimated tax penalty for the last quarter by filing your 2002 return and paying the balance due by January 31, 2003.

Farmers and fishermen: File your single 2002 estimated tax payment by this date. If you do not, you may still avoid an estimated tax penalty by filing a final tax return and paying the full tax by March 3, 2003.

January 31, 2003—Make sure you have received a Form W-2 from each employer for whom you worked in 2002.

April 15, 2003—File your 2002 tax return and pay the balance of your tax. If you cannot meet the April 15 deadline, you may obtain an automatic four-month filing extension by filing Form 4868 (on paper or electronically). However, even if you get an extension, interest will still be charged for taxes not paid by April 15, and late payment penalties will be imposed unless at least 90% of your tax liability is paid by this date. If you cannot pay the full amount of tax you owe when you file your return, you can file Form 9465 to request an installment payment arrangement.

If on this date you are a U.S. citizen or resident living and working abroad or in military service outside the U.S. or Puerto Rico, you have an automatic two-month filing extension until June 16, 2003.

Pay the first installment of your 2003 estimated tax by this date.

June 16, 2003—Pay the second installment of your 2003 estimated tax. You may amend your estimate at this time.

If on April 15 you were a U.S. citizen or resident living and working abroad or in military service outside the U.S. or Puerto Rico, file your 2002 return and pay the balance due. You may obtain an additional two-month filing extension until August 15, 2003, by filing Form 4868.

If you are a nonresident alien who did not have tax withheld from your wages, file Form 1040NR by this date and pay the balance due.

August 15, 2003—File your 2002 return if you received an automatic four-month filing extension using Form 4868. Also file your 2002 return and pay the balance due if on April 15 you were a U.S. citizen or resident living and working abroad or in military service outside the U.S. or Puerto Rico, and by June 16 you qualified for an additional two-month extension by filing Form 4868.

September 15, 2003—Pay the third installment of your 2003 estimated tax. You may amend your estimate at this time.

December 31, 2003—If self-employed, this is the last day to set up a Keogh plan for 2003.

January 15, 2004—Pay the balance of your 2003 estimated tax.

April 15, 2004—File your 2003 return and pay the balance of your tax. Pay the first installment of your 2004 estimated tax by this date.

15th day of the 4th month after the fiscal year ends—File your fiscal year return and pay the balance of the tax due. If you cannot meet the filing deadline, apply for an automatic four-month filing extension on Form 4868.

Choosing Which Tax Form To File

There are three individual tax forms: Form 1040, Form 1040A, and Form 1040EZ. Use the simplified Form 1040EZ or Form 1040A only if you find the return will save you time and not cause you to give up tax-saving deductions or credits that are only available if you file Form 1040. To help you make your selection, fill in the following chart.

By checking the box that indicates your tax status, income, expenses, and credit items, you will be guided in choosing which form to use.

Item—	Form 1040EZ—	Form 1040A—	Form 1040—
Single	X[1,2]	X[1]	X
Head of household		X[1]	X
Married filing jointly	X[1,2]	X[1]	X
Married filing separately		X[1]	X
Widow or widower		X[1]	X
Exemption for dependents		X	X
Wages, salary	X	X	X
Interest	X[3]	X	X
Ordinary dividends		X	X
Unemployment compensation	X	X	X
Self-employment income			X
Pension-annuity		X	X
IRA distributions		X	X
Rents and royalties			X
Gains and losses from property sales			X
Capital gain distributions from mutual funds		X[5]	X
Alimony			X
State tax refunds			X
Social Security benefits		X	X
IRA deduction		X	X
Alimony paid			X
Student loan interest		X	X
Tuition and fees deduction		X	X
Educator expenses		X	X
Moving expenses			X
Self-employed health insurance			X
50% of self-employment tax			X
Archer MSA deduction			X
Penalty for early withdrawal of savings			X
Deduction for Keogh, SEP, and SIMPLE plans			X
Employee business expenses			X
State and local income taxes			X
Real estate taxes			X
Home mortgage interest, investment and business interest			X
Charitable contributions			X
Medical and dental expenses			X
Casualty and theft losses			X
Miscellaneous deductions (investment expenses, tax preparation)			X
Credit for child and dependent care		X	X
Earned income credit	X[4]	X	X
Credit for elderly and totally disabled		X	X
Child tax credit		X	X
Additional child tax credit		X	X
Adoption credit		X	X
Retirement savings contributions credit		X	X
Education credits		X	X
All other credits			X
Estimated tax payments and estimated tax penalty		X	X
Advance earned income credit (EIC) payments		X	X
Self-employment tax			X
Roth conversion IRA			X
Penalty tax on an IRA			X
Alternative minimum tax			X
Social Security tax on tips not reported to your employer			X
Uncollected Social Security tax on tips shown on your Form W-2			X
"Kiddie" tax on child's return		X	X
"Kiddie" tax on parent's return			X
Household employee taxes			X
All other taxes or penalties			X

[1] Taxable income less than $50,000.

[2] Under age 65 and not blind on January 1, 2003.

[3] Up to $400.

[4] If you did not receive any advance earned income credit payments.

[5] If you do not need Schedule D of Form 1040 for any other transaction.

Chapter 1

Filing Status

The filing status you use when you file your return determines the tax rates that will apply to your taxable income; *see 1.2*. Filing status also determines the standard deduction you may claim if you do not itemize deductions *(see 13.1)* and your ability to claim certain other deductions, credits, and exclusions.

This chapter explains the five different filing statuses: single, married filing jointly, married filing separately, head of household, and qualifying widow(er). If you are married, filing a joint return is generally advantageous, but there are exceptions discussed in *1.3*. If you are unmarried and are supporting a child who lives with you, you may qualify as a head of household *(see 1.12)*, which will enable you to use more favorable tax rates than those allowed for single taxpayers. If you were widowed in either 2001 or 2000 and in 2002 a dependent child lived with you, you may be able to file as a qualifying widow(er) for 2002, which allows you to use joint return rates.

Special filing situations, such as for children, nonresident aliens, and deceased individuals, are also discussed in this chapter.

Your personal or family status also determines the number of personal exemptions you may claim on your return. For 2002, each personal exemption you claim is the equivalent of a $3,000 deduction. Exemptions for children, parents, and other dependents are allowed if the tests in Chapter 21 are met.

Importance of Filing Status

1.1 Which Filing Status Should You Use?

Your filing status generally depends on whether you are married at the end of the year, and, if unmarried, whether you maintain a household for a qualifying dependent. The five filing statuses are: single, married filing jointly, married filing separately, head of household, and qualifying widow or widower.

If you are *married at the end of the year*, you may file jointly *(1.4)* or separately *(1.3)*. If you lived apart from your spouse for the last half of 2002 and your child lived with you, you may qualify as an "unmarried" head of household *(see 1.12)*, which allows you to apply more favorable tax rates than you could as a married person filing separately.

If you are *unmarried at the end of the year*, your filing status is single unless you meet the tests for a head of household or qualifying widow(er). Generally, you are a head of household if you pay more than 50% of the household costs for a relative who lives with you, or a parent, whether or not he or she lives with you; *see 1.12*. You generally are a qualifying widow(er) if you were widowed in 2000 or 2001 and in 2002 you pay more than 50% of the household costs for you and your dependent child; *see 1.11*. The tax rates for heads of households and for qualifying widow(er)s are more favorable than those for single taxpayers; *see 1.2*.

The filing status you use determines the tax rates that apply to your taxable income, as shown in *1.2*, as well as the standard deduction you may claim *(see 13.1)* if you do not itemize deductions. Certain other deductions, credits, or exclusions are also affected by filing status. For example, if you are married, certain tax benefits are only allowed if you file jointly, but more deductions overall may be allowed in certain cases if you file separately; *see 1.3*. The deduction for personal exemptions is phased out for high income taxpayers at levels based upon filing status; *see 21.16*.

Marital status determined at the end of the year. If you are divorced during the year under a final decree of divorce or separate maintenance, you are treated as unmarried for that whole year, assuming you have not remarried before the end of the year. For the year of the divorce, file as a single person unless you care for a child and qualify as a head of household under the rules at *1.12*.

If at the end of the year you are living apart from your spouse, or you are separated under a provisional decree that has not yet been finalized, you are not considered divorced. If you care for a child and meet the other tests at *1.12*, you may file as an unmarried head of household. Otherwise, you must file a joint return or as a married person filing separately.

If at the end of the year you live together in a common law marriage that is recognized by the law of the state in which you live or the state where the marriage began, you are treated as married.

If your spouse dies during the year, you are treated as married for that entire year and may file a joint return for you and your deceased spouse, assuming you have not remarried before year's end; *see 1.10*.

1.2 Tax Rates Based on Filing Status

The most favorable tax brackets apply to married persons filing jointly and qualifying widow(er)s *(see 1.11)*, who also use the joint return rates. The least favorable brackets are those for married persons filing separately, but filing separately is still advisable for married couples in certain situations, as discussed in *1.3*. The table on the next page compares 2002 tax rate brackets.

If you are unmarried at the end of the year, do not assume that your filing status is single. If your child lives with you in a home you maintain, you generally may file as a head of household *(see 1.12)*, which allows you to use more favorable tax rates than a single person. If you were widowed in either of the two prior years and maintain a household for your dependent child, you generally may file as a qualified widow(er), which allows you to use favorable joint return rates; *see 1.11*.

If you are married at the end of the year but for the second half of the year you lived with your child apart from your spouse, and you and your spouse agree not to file jointly, you may use head of household tax rates, which are more favorable than those for married persons filing separately.

Applying the tax table or tax rate schedule. If your taxable income is less than $100,000, you will look up your tax in the tax tables, which are shown in Part 8 of this book. If your taxable income is $100,000 or more, you figure your tax using the tax rate schedules, also in Part 8. Chapter 22 has examples applying the tax tables or rate schedules to determine regular income tax liability.

Taxable Income Brackets for 2002

	10% bracket ends at—	15% bracket ends at—	27% bracket ends at—	30% bracket ends at—	35% bracket ends at—	38.6% bracket applies to—
Married filing separately	$ 6,000	$ 23,350	$ 56,425	$ 85,975	$ 153,525	over $ 153,525
Single	6,000	27,950	67,700	141,250	307,050	over 307,050
Head of household	10,000	37,450	96,700	156,600	307,050	over 307,050
Married filing jointly or Qualifying widow(er)	12,000	46,700	112,850	171,950	307,050	over 307,050

Married Taxpayers

1.3 Filing Separately Instead of Jointly

Filing a joint return saves taxes for a married couple where one spouse earns all, or substantially all, of the taxable income. If both you and your spouse earn taxable income, you should figure your tax on joint and separate returns to determine which method provides the lower tax.

Separate returns may save taxes where filing separately allows you to claim more deductions. On separate returns, larger amounts of medical expenses, casualty losses, or miscellaneous deductions may be deductible because lower adjusted gross income floors apply. Unless one spouse earns substantially more than the other, separate and joint tax rates are likely to be the same, regardless of the type of returns filed. The Example on page 13 illustrates how filing separately can save you taxes.

Suspicious of your spouse's tax reporting? If you suspect that your spouse is evading taxes and may be liable on a joint return, you may want to file a separate return. By filing separately, you avoid liability for unpaid taxes due on a joint return, plus interest and penalties.

If you do file jointly and the IRS tries to collect tax due on the joint return from you personally, you may be able to avoid liability under the innocent spouse rules *(see 1.7)*. If you are no longer married to or are separated from the person with whom you jointly filed, you may be able to elect separate liability treatment *(see 1.8)*.

Standard deduction restriction on separate returns. Keep in mind that if you and your spouse file separately, both must either itemize or claim the standard deduction, which is $3,925 in 2002 for married persons filing separately *(13.3)*. Thus, if one spouse itemizes, the other spouse must also itemize even if he or she would get a larger deduction by taking the $3,925 standard deduction.

Joint return required for certain benefits. Also be aware that certain tax benefits may be claimed by married persons only if they file jointly.

If you want to take advantage of the $25,000 rental loss allowance *(10.2)* or the credit for the elderly (Chapter 34), you must file jointly unless you live apart for the whole year. You must file jointly to claim an IRA deduction for a nonworking spouse *(8.3)*. A joint return is also required to claim the Hope Credit or Lifetime Learning Credit (Chapter 38). You must file jointly to claim the dependent care credit or the earned income credit (Chapter 25), unless you live apart for the last six months of the year. Furthermore, if you receive Social Security benefits, 85% of your benefits are generally subject to tax on a separate return; *see* Chapter 34.

Filing Status If Married at the End of 2002

Filing Jointly	*Filing Separately*	*Living Apart From Spouse: Filing as Unmarried Head of Household*
Filing jointly allows the use of joint return rates.	Filing separately, instead of jointly, may be advisable where you and your spouse each earn taxable income and have separate deductions, as explained at *1.3.* You are required to use tax rates for married persons filing separately in these cases:	If you lived apart from your spouse during the last half of 2002, and your child lived with you for most of the year, you may qualify for tax purposes as "unmarried" and use head of household tax rates, which are lower than rates for married persons filing separately.

Filing jointly allows the use of joint return rates.

You may file a joint return if you are legally married on the last day of 2002.

You need not live together provided you are legally married. A couple legally separated under a final decree of divorce or separate maintenance as of the end of 2002 may not file a joint return.

You may file jointly if your spouse died during 2002; *see 1.10.*

If one spouse is a nonresident alien, you may file jointly only if you elect to be taxed on your worldwide income; *see 1.5.*

You *must* file jointly to contribute to a traditional IRA on behalf of a nonworking spouse *(8.3).* Roth IRA contributions generally may not be made by a married person filing separately because of an extremely low phase-out range *(8.20).* You must file jointly to convert a traditional IRA to a Roth IRA *(8.21).* To claim the credit for the elderly (Chapter 34), you must file jointly unless you lived apart for the entire year or qualify as head of household. You must file jointly to claim the dependent care credit or the earned income credit (Chapter 25) unless you live apart and qualify as a head of household.

On a joint return, each spouse is liable for the entire tax. If one spouse does not pay, the other spouse may be liable even though all of the income was earned by the spouse who failed to pay the tax. An "innocent" spouse who files a joint return may be relieved of penalties and tax liability in certain circumstances; *see 1.7.*

For community property rules, *see 1.6.*

Filing separately, instead of jointly, may be advisable where you and your spouse each earn taxable income and have separate deductions, as explained at *1.3.* You are required to use tax rates for married persons filing separately in these cases:

1. Your spouse files a separate return. If you are experiencing marital discord, you may be forced to file separately unless your spouse consents to a joint return.

2. Someone else claims you or your spouse as a dependent; *see 21.13.*

3. You and your spouse have different tax reporting years. If you report on the calendar year but your spouse reports on a fiscal year, you must file separately unless you get permission from the IRS to change your reporting year (Form 1128). This bar to joint filing does not apply when your tax years begin on the same day but one or both end because of the death of either or both spouses. A spouse who has never filed a tax return may elect to use the other spouse's tax year as his or her first tax year; then they can file a joint return. A husband and wife can file a joint return even if they had different tax years before their marriage.

4. You or your spouse is a nonresident alien and you do not make an election to be taxed on your worldwide income; *see 1.5.*

If you lived apart from your spouse during the last half of 2002, and your child lived with you for most of the year, you may qualify for tax purposes as "unmarried" and use head of household tax rates, which are lower than rates for married persons filing separately.

The following four tests must be met for you to file separately from your spouse as a head of household:

1. Your spouse was not a member of your household during the last six months of 2002.

2. You maintain your home as the principal place of abode for your child, adopted child, or stepchild for more than half of 2002. However, a foster child must be a member of your household for the entire year.

3. You are entitled to claim the child as a dependent. Ignore this test if the noncustodial spouse claims the exemption for the child under the rules of *21.11.*

4. You provide over half of the cost of supporting the household.

See 1.12 for further details.

Filing Status If Not Married at the End of 2002

Single	*Head of Household*	*Qualifying Widow(er)*

If you are not married at the end of 2002, use the rate for single individuals, unless you qualify as a surviving spouse or a head of household.

If you are widowed, you are "unmarried" and use rates for single individuals regardless of the number of years you were married. There is an exception for recent widows or widowers supporting children, as explained in the "qualifying widow(er)" column.

If at the end of the year you are not married, you may use special head of household rates if you meet these tests:

1. You maintain a household for more than half of 2002 for your child or grandchild, or for a dependent relative. The household must be your home and the main residence of your relative except that a dependent parent need not live with you. However, you must maintain a dependent parent's separate household for the entire year to claim head of household status based on that support.

2. You pay more than one-half the cost of supporting the household.

3. You are a U.S. citizen or resident alien during the entire tax year.

These rules are explained in detail in *1.12.*

If you are a widow or widower and your spouse died in 2000 or 2001, you may use 2002 joint return tax rates if you meet these four tests:

1. You maintain your home as the main home of your child for the entire year and you furnish over half the cost of maintaining the household.

2. You are entitled to claim the child as a dependent; *see 21.1.*

3. In the year your spouse died, you could have filed a joint return.

4. You did not remarry before January 1, 2003.

If you meet these tests, your filing status is qualifying widow or widower; *see 1.11.*

EXAMPLE

Mike Palmer's 2002 adjusted gross income (AGI) is $73,650 and his wife Fran has AGI of $50,000. Neither of them can claim exemptions for dependents. Mike has medical expenses of $7,150; Fran's are $1,000. Mike has an $8,865 casualty loss *(18.12)* on property owned in his name. He also has unreimbursed miscellaneous expenses of $2,773 and Fran has $500. Mike has deductible mortgage interest expenses of $5,000 and Fran has $2,000. Mike's deductible state and local taxes are $2,499; Fran's are $1,000. If they file separately and Mike itemizes deductions, Fran must also itemize even if the standard deduction would give her a larger deduction; *see 13.3*.

As the example worksheet below shows, filing separate returns saves Mike and Fran an overall $858, because they can deduct more on separate returns. If they filed jointly they would have received no deduction for medical expenses and casualty losses because the deductions would have been eliminated by the higher adjusted gross income floors. If they file separately, the 3% reduction of itemized deductions *(13.7)* applies to Mike but not Fran because only Mike's AGI exceeds the $68,650 threshold. If they file jointly, the 3% reduction does not apply because their AGI is below the $137,300 threshold for joint returns. The phaseout of personal exemptions *(21.16)* does not apply regardless of how they file.

Item		Mike (Separately)	Fran (Separately)	Joint Return
1.	**AGI**	**$ 73,650**	**$ 50,000**	**$ 123,650**
2.	Medical expenses	7,150	1,000	8,150
	Less 7¹/₂% of AGI	5,524	3,750	9,274
	Allowable medical	1,626	0	0
3.	Taxes	2,499	1,000	3,499
4.	Mortgage interest	5,000	2,000	7,000
5.	Casualty loss	8,865	0	8,865
	Less 10% of AGI	7,365		12,365
	Allowable casualty	1,500		0
6.	Miscellaneous expenses	2,773	500	3,273
	Less 2% of AGI	1,473	1,000	2,473
	Allowable miscellaneous	1,300	0	800
7.	**Total itemized** *(Lines 2–6)*	**11,925**	**3,000**	**11,299**
	Less 3% reduction	150*	0	0
8.	**Net itemized**	**11,775**	**3,000**	**11,299**
9.	Personal exemptions	3,000	3,000	6,000
10.	**Net itemized plus exemptions**	**14,775**	**6,000**	**17,299**
11.	Taxable income *(Line 1 minus Line 10)*	58,875	44,000	106,351
12.	**Tax liability**	**12,868**	**8,785**	**22,511**
	Total tax filing separately			21,653
	Savings from filing separately			*858*

* $150 reduction = 3% × $5,000 ($73,650 AGI – $68,650 floor; see 13.7)

1.4 Filing a Joint Return

If you are married at the end of the year, you may file a joint return with your spouse. For federal tax purposes, a marriage means only a legal union between a man and woman as husband and wife. Filing jointly saves taxes for many married couples, but if you and your spouse both earn taxable income, in some cases overall tax liability is reduced by filing separately; *see 1.3*.

You may not file a 2002 joint return if you were divorced under a decree of divorce or separate maintenance that is *final* by the end of the year. You may file jointly if you separated during 2002 under an interlocutory (temporary or provisional) decree or order, so long as a final divorce decree was not entered by the end of the year. If during the period that a divorce decree is interlocutory you are permitted to remarry in another state, the IRS recognizes the new marriage and allows a joint return to be filed with the new spouse. However, courts have refused to allow a joint return where a new marriage took place in Mexico during the interlocutory period in violation of California law.

Planning Reminder

Switching From Separate to Joint Return

If you and your spouse file separate returns, you have three years from the due date (without extensions) to change to a joint return. If a joint return is filed, you may not change to separate returns once the due date has passed. The filing of separate or joint estimated tax installments (Chapter 27) does not commit you to a similar tax return.

Filing Tip

Can Filing Separately Avoid Exemption Phaseout or Itemized Deduction Reduction?

Filing separately will sometimes allow either you or your spouse to avoid part of the personal exemption phaseout *(21.16)* or the 3% reduction to specified itemized deductions *(13.7)*. If you file jointly and have total 2002 adjusted gross income (AGI) exceeding $206,000, the exemption phaseout applies. If you file separately, the phaseout does not apply to the spouse reporting separate AGI of $103,000 or less. On the other hand, where your joint AGI is $206,000 or less, a spouse reporting AGI over $103,000 on a separate return will be subject to the phaseout although no phaseout would apply on a joint return.

If for 2002 you itemize deductions, the deductions for taxes, mortgage interest, charitable donations, and miscellaneous deductions are reduced by 3% of AGI exceeding $137,300 on a joint return, or exceeding $68,650 on a separate return. If you file separately, the reduction does not apply on a separate return showing AGI of $68,650 or less. Where joint AGI is $137,300 or less, a spouse filing separately with separate AGI over $68,650 is subject to the 3% reduction although no reduction would apply on a joint return.

Both spouses generally liable on joint return but "innocent" spouse may be relieved of liability. When you and your spouse file jointly, each of you may generally be held individually liable for the entire tax due, plus interest and any penalties. The IRS may try to collect the entire amount due from you even if your spouse earned all of the income reported on the joint return, or even if you have divorced under an agreement that holds your former spouse responsible for the taxes on the joint returns you filed together. However, there are exceptions to this joint liability rule for "innocent" spouses and for divorced or separated persons.

You may be able to obtain *innocent spouse* relief where tax on your joint return was understated without your knowledge because your spouse omitted income or claimed erroneous deductions or tax credits. In such a case, you may make an innocent spouse election within two years from the time the IRS begins a collection effort from you for taxes due on the return. *See 1.7* for details on the innocent spouse rules.

Furthermore, if you are divorced, legally separated, living apart or the spouse with whom you filed jointly has died, you may be able to avoid tax on the portion of a joint return deficiency that is allocable to your ex-spouse by making an election within two years of the time the IRS begins collection efforts against you. *See 1.8* for details on this separate liability election. You may make the separate liability election even if you apply for innocent spouse relief. In some cases, it may be easier to qualify for relief under the separate liability rules than under the innocent spouse rules because innocent spouse relief may be denied if you had "reason to know" that tax was understated on the joint return, whereas the IRS must show that you had "actual knowledge" of the omitted income or erroneous deductions or credits to deny a separate liability election.

Signing the joint return. Both you and your spouse must sign the joint return. Under the following rules, if your spouse is unable to sign, you may sign for him or her.

If, because of illness, your spouse is physically unable to sign the joint return, you may, with the oral consent of your spouse, sign his or her name on the return followed by the words "By _____, Husband (or Wife)." You then sign the return again in your own right and attach a signed and dated statement with the following information: (1) the type of form being filed, (2) the tax year, (3) the reason for the inability of the sick spouse to sign, and (4) that the sick spouse has consented to your signing.

To sign for your spouse in other situations, you need authorization in the form of a power of attorney, which must be attached to the return. IRS Form 2848 may be used.

If your spouse does not file, you may be able to prove you filed a joint return even if your spouse did not sign and you did not sign as your spouse's agent where:

- You intended it to be a joint return—your spouse's income was included (or the spouse had no income).
- Your spouse agreed to have you handle tax matters and you filed a joint return.
- Your answers to the questions on the tax return indicate you intended to file a joint return.
- Your spouse's failure to sign can be explained.

> **EXAMPLE**
>
> The Hills generally filed joint returns. In one year, Mr. Hill claimed joint return filing status and reported his wife's income as well as his own; in place of her signature on the return, he indicated that she was out of town caring for her sick mother. She did not file a separate return. The IRS refused to treat the return as joint. The Tax Court disagreed. Since Mrs. Hill testified that she would have signed had she been available, her failure to do so does not bar joint return status. The couple intended to make a joint return at the time of filing.

Filing Tip

Spouse in Combat Zone

If your spouse is in a combat zone or a qualified hazardous duty area *(35.4)*, you can sign a joint return for your spouse. Attach a signed explanation to the return.

Filing Tip

Election To File a Joint Return

Where a U.S. citizen or resident is married to a nonresident alien, the couple may file a joint return if both elect to be taxed on their worldwide income. The requirement that one spouse be a U.S. citizen or resident need be met only at the close of the year. Joint returns may be filed in the year of the election and all later years until the election is terminated.

1.5 Nonresident Alien Spouse

If either you or your spouse was a nonresident alien *(1.16)* during any part of the year, a joint return may be filed only if both of you make a special election to be taxed on your worldwide income. Thus, if you are a U.S. citizen and your spouse is a nonresident alien at the beginning of the year who becomes a resident during the year, the special election to file jointly must be made.

If the election is not made, you may be able to claim your nonresident alien spouse as an exemption on a return filed as married filing separately, but only if the spouse had no income and could not be claimed as a dependent by another taxpayer; *see 21.2.* If the alien spouse becomes a resident before the beginning of the next tax year, you may file jointly for that year.

A couple who make the election must keep books and records of their worldwide income and give the IRS access to such books and records. If either spouse does not provide the necessary information to the IRS, the election is terminated. Furthermore, the election is terminated if either spouse revokes it or dies; revocation before the due date of the return is effective for that return. The election automatically terminates in the year following the year of the death of either spouse. However, if the survivor is a U.S. citizen or resident and has a qualifying child, he or she may be able to use joint return rates as a qualifying widow or widower in the two years following the year of the spouse's death; see 1.11. The election to file jointly also terminates if the couple is legally separated under a decree of divorce or separate maintenance. Termination is effective as of the beginning of the taxable year of the legal separation. If neither spouse is a citizen or resident for any part of the taxable year, an election may not be made and an existing election is suspended. If an election is suspended it may again become effective if either spouse becomes a U.S. citizen or resident. Once the election is terminated, neither spouse may ever again make the election to file jointly.

Electing to file a joint return does not terminate the special withholding on the nonresident alien's income.

1.6   Community Property Rules

If you live in Arizona, California, Idaho, Louisiana, Nevada, New Mexico, Texas, Washington, or Wisconsin, the income and property you and your spouse acquire during the marriage is generally regarded as community property. Community property means that each of you owns half of the community income and community property, even if legal title is held by only one spouse. But note that there are some instances in which community property rules are disregarded for tax purposes; these instances are clearly highlighted in the pertinent sections of this book.

Separate property may still be owned. Property owned before marriage generally remains separate property; it does not become community property when you marry. Property received during the marriage by one spouse as a gift or an inheritance from a third party is generally separate property. In some states, if the nature of ownership cannot be fixed, the property is presumed to be community property.

In some states, income from separate property may be treated as community property income. In other states, income from separate property remains the separate property of the individual owner.

Divorce or separation. If you and your spouse divorce, your community property automatically becomes separate property. A separation agreement or a decree of legal separation or of separate maintenance may or may not end the marital community, depending on state law.

Community income rules may not apply to separated couples. If a husband and wife in a community property state file separate returns, each spouse must generally report one-half of the community income. However, a spouse may be able to avoid reporting income earned by his or her spouse if they live apart during the entire calendar year and do not file a joint return.

To qualify, one or both spouses must have earned income for the year and none of that earned income may be transferred, directly or indirectly, between the spouses during the year. One spouse's payment to the other spouse solely to support the couple's dependent children is not a disqualifying transfer. If the separated couple qualifies under these tests, community income is allocated as follows:

- Earned income (excluding business or partnership income) is taxed to the spouse who performed the personal services.
- Business income (other than partnership income) is treated as the income of the spouse carrying on the business.
- Partnership income is taxed to the spouse entitled to a distributive share of partnership profits.

Innocent spouse rules apply to community property. As discussed above, community property rules may not apply to earned income where spouses live apart for the entire year and file separate returns. In addition, a spouse who files a separate return may be relieved of tax liability on community income that is attributable to the other spouse if he or she does not know (or have reason to know) about the income and if it would be inequitable under the circumstances for him or her to be taxed on such income. Even if you fail to qualify for such relief because you knew (or had reason to know) about the income, the IRS may relieve you of liability if it would be inequitable to hold you liable.

Filing Tip

Nonresident Alien Becomes Resident

Where one spouse is a U.S. citizen or resident and the other is a nonresident alien who becomes a resident during the tax year, the couple may make a special election to file a joint return for that year and be taxed on their worldwide income. Thereafter, neither spouse may make the election again even if married to a new spouse. Tests for determining status as a resident or nonresident alien are at 1.18.

Filing Tip

Claiming Dependents on Separate Returns

Married parents in community property states who plan to file separate returns should be aware that neither parent may be able to claim an exemption for a dependent child. Where all of the couple's income is considered community income, each parent on a separate return is treated as having provided exactly one-half of the child's support, regardless of who actually paid it. Since neither parent has provided more than one-half of the support, neither can claim the child as a dependent.

To avoid this result, parents whose sole income is community income and who want to file separately should consider signing a multiple support agreement, Form 2120, designating which parent may claim the exemption.

The IRS may disregard community property rules and tax income to a spouse who treats such income as if it were solely his or hers and who fails to notify the other spouse of the income before the due date of the return (including extensions).

Relief from liability on joint return. If you file jointly, you may elect to avoid liability under the innocent spouse rules discussed at *1.7* and the separate liability rules at *1.8*. In applying those rules, items that would otherwise be allocable solely to your spouse will not be partly allocated to you merely because of the community property laws.

Death of spouse. The death of a spouse dissolves the community property relationship, but income earned and accrued from community property before death is community income.

Moving from a community property to a common law (separate property) state. Most common law states (those which do not have community property laws) recognize that both spouses have an interest in property accumulated while residing in a community property state. If the property is not sold or reinvested, it may continue to be treated as community property. If you and your spouse sell community property after moving to a common law state and reinvest the proceeds, the reinvested proceeds are generally separate property, which you may hold as joint tenants or in another form of ownership recognized by common law states.

Moving from a common law to a community property state. Separate property brought into a community property state generally retains its character as separately owned property. However, property acquired by a couple after moving to a community property state is generally owned as community property. In at least one state (California), personal property that qualifies as community property is treated as such, even though it was acquired when the couple lived in a common law state.

Supporting a dependent with separate rather than community income. Filing a Form 2120 multiple support agreement is not necessary where either parent can prove that he or she has income that is considered separate income rather than community income; that parent may be able to satisfy the more-than-50% support test. In certain community property states, the law may provide that income of a husband and wife living apart is considered separate income rather than community income.

Avoiding or Limiting Liability on Joint Returns

1.7 Innocent Spouse Rules

Whether you are still married to the spouse with whom you filed the joint return or you have since divorced or separated, you are liable as an individual for any tax due unless you qualify for relief.

If you are still married and living with the same spouse, the only way to avoid personal liability on the joint return is to qualify as an innocent spouse under the rules in this section, or to apply for equitable relief from the IRS, discussed at *1.9*.

If you are divorced, legally separated, living apart, or your spouse has died, you may either seek relief under the innocent spouse rules below or you may be able to elect separate liability treatment as discussed at *1.8* or seek equitable relief *(1.9)* from the IRS.

Qualifying tests for innocent spouse election. You must satisfy *all* of the following conditions to qualify for innocent spouse relief:

1. The tax shown on the joint return was understated due to the omission of income by your spouse, or erroneous deductions or credits claimed by your spouse.

2. When signing the joint return, you did not know and had no reason to know that tax on the return was understated.

    According to the IRS and Tax Court, where your claim for innocent spouse relief is based on the omission of income by your spouse, knowledge of the underlying transaction that produced the omitted income (such as a retirement distribution received by your spouse or an investment held by your spouse in his own name) is enough to bar your claim, even if you did not know that the amount of taxable income reported on the joint return was incorrect. The Courts of Appeal for both the Fifth Circuit and the District of Columbia Circuit agree with the Tax Court that knowledge of the underlying transaction that produced the omitted income defeats a claim for innocent spouse relief.

 Caution

Knowledge May Bar Innocent Spouse Relief

The IRS may try to defeat your claim for innocent spouse relief on the grounds that you knew, or should have known, that tax was understated on the joint return.

In cases arising under prior law where the requested innocent spouse relief was based on improper deductions or tax credits attributed to the other spouse, the Tax Court held that knowledge of the underlying transaction was enough to bar innocent spouse relief. However, in such erroneous deduction (or credit) cases, most appeals courts held that relief should be denied under the knowledge test only if, given all the facts and circumstances, the spouse seeking relief knew or had reason to know that the deduction would result in a tax understatement, and this depends on his or her education level and involvement in the couple's financial affairs.

Although the "knowledge" test continues to be a significant hurdle, partial relief may be available. If you knew or had reason to know that there was "some" tax understatement on the return but were unaware of the extent of the understatement, innocent spouse relief is available for the liability attributable to the portion of the understatement that you did not know about or have reason to know about.

3. Taking all the circumstances into account, it would be inequitable to hold you liable for the tax. This test also applied under prior law. In deciding the "equity" issue, the IRS and courts consider the extent to which you benefitted from the tax underpayment, beyond receiving normal support. Thus, it is possible to be held liable for a tax understatement that you did not know about or have reason to know about, on the grounds that you benefitted from the underpayment in the form of a high standard of living. The IRS will also consider whether you later divorced or were deserted by your spouse.

4. You file an innocent spouse election with the IRS on Form 8857.

Election must be filed on Form 8857 to obtain relief. You must file an election on Form 8857 to claim innocent spouse relief. You do this by attaching a statement explaining why you qualify; follow the Form 8857 instructions. The election must be made no later than two years from the date that the IRS first begins collection activity (such as IRS garnishment of your wages) against you for tax due on the joint return. If the election is not made by the end of that two-year period, you will not be granted innocent spouse relief even if you meet the above qualification tests.

If collection activities against you began before July 22, 1998, the two-year period for making the election ends two years after the first collection activity occurring after July 22, 1998.

Tax Court appeal. If the IRS denies an election for innocent spouse relief, you have 90 days to petition the Tax Court for review under the rules discussed at the end of *1.8*.

Did your spouse fail to pay the tax due on a correct return? Innocent spouse relief applies to tax understatements; that is, where the amount of tax shown on a joint return is incorrect. If the proper amount of tax liability is shown on the return but not paid, innocent spouse relief is not available. However, the IRS can provide equitable relief where innocent spouse relief is unavailable and it would be unfair to hold you liable. *See 1.9.*

1.8 Separate Liability Election for Former Spouses

If the IRS attempts to collect the taxes due on a joint return from you and you have since divorced or separated, you may be able to avoid or at least limit your liability by filing a separate liability election on Form 8857. If you qualify, you will be liable only for the part of the tax liability (plus interest and any penalties) that is allocable to you. If you make the election and a tax deficiency is entirely allocable to your former spouse under the rules discussed below, you will not have to pay any part of it. However, you may *not* avoid liability for any part of a tax deficiency allocable to the other spouse if you had actual knowledge of the income or expense item that gave rise to the tax deficiency that the IRS is trying to collect. *See* below for details of the knowledge test.

Furthermore, you may not avoid liability to the extent that certain disqualified property transfers were made between you and the other spouse. An election may be completely denied for both spouses if transfers were made as part of a fraudulent scheme.

As with innocent spouse relief *(1.7)*, the separate liability election applies only to tax understatements where the proper tax liability was *not* shown on the joint return. If the proper liability was shown but not paid, equitable relief *(1.9)* may be requested.

 Law Alert

IRS Must Notify Non-Electing Spouse

After the filing of Form 8857, the IRS is required to notify the non-electing spouse (or former spouse) of an electing spouse's request for relief and allow the non-electing spouse an opportunity to participate in the determination.

 Planning Reminder

Deadline for Innocent Spouse Election

You have until two years from the date that the IRS first attempts to collect tax from you on the joint return to make an innocent spouse election.

Are you eligible for the separate liability election? You may make the separate liability election on Form 8857 if at the time of the election:

1. You are divorced or legally separated from the spouse with whom you filed the joint return, *or*
2. You have not lived with your spouse (with whom you filed the return) at any time in the 12-month period ending on the date you file the election, *or*
3. The spouse with whom you filed the joint return has died.

If you qualify under any of the above, you may make the separate liability election on Form 8857 by attaching a statement that identifies which items giving rise to the tax understatement are allocable to you and which are allocable to the other spouse. You do not have to actually compute your separate liability, however. You may make the separate liability election in addition to the innocent spouse election *(1.7)*.

Timing of the election. The separate liability election must be filed with the IRS on Form 8857 no later than two years after the IRS begins collection activities against you. If collections began before July 22, 1998 (when the law took effect), the two-year election period ends two years after the date of the first IRS collection action after July 22, 1998.

Actual knowledge of the item allocable to the other spouse bars relief. If you elect separate liability treatment and the IRS shows that at the time you signed the joint return you had actual knowledge of an erroneous item (omitted income or improper deduction or credit) that would otherwise be allocated to the other spouse, you may *not* avoid liability for the portion of a deficiency attributable to that item. However, if you signed the return under duress, separate liability is not barred despite your knowledge.

The actual knowledge test is intended by Congress to be more favorable to the taxpayer than the "had reason to know" test under the innocent spouse rules *(1.7)*. Congressional committee reports state that the IRS is required to prove that an electing spouse had actual knowledge of an erroneous deduction and may not infer such knowledge. According to the Tax Court, the IRS must prove actual knowledge by a "preponderance of the evidence." If the IRS proves actual knowledge of an erroneous item, that item is treated as allocable to both spouses, so the IRS can collect that portion of the deficiency from either spouse.

However, there is a controversy as to how to apply the actual knowledge test. Taxpayers and commentators have argued that Congress intended separate liability relief to be available to a spouse unless she or he knew that the tax return was incorrect. The IRS position is that relief is barred to a spouse who had knowledge of the income or expenditure that gave rise to the tax deficiency, even if the electing spouse did not know that the entry on the return was incorrect. The Tax Court, the Fifth Circuit, and the District of Columbia Circuit agree with the IRS in cases involving omitted income; *see* Example 1 below.

In erroneous deduction cases, the Tax Court definition of "actual knowledge" is not as clear, but it has indicated that it will look at whether the electing spouse was aware of the "factual circumstances" that made the item nondeductible. If the electing spouse knew the factual basis for denial of the deduction, separate liability relief will be denied. In cases involving limited partnership tax-shelter deductions, the IRS may be unable to prove that an electing spouse had such disqualifying knowledge, but relief may still be partially denied if the spouse received a tax benefit from the deductions; *see* Example 3 below.

 Caution

Actual Knowledge Bars Relief

The separate liability election generally allows you to avoid liability for the portion of a tax deficiency that is allocable to the other spouse. Such relief is unavailable, however, to the extent that you had actual knowledge of the omitted income or deducted item that gave rise to the tax deficiency.

The IRS admitted in a report to Congress that it was having difficulty applying the actual knowledge test. The IRS stated that it would support a Congressional repeal of the standard, even if this would result in an increased number of claims for relief.

EXAMPLES

1. Cheshire knew that her husband had received an early retirement distribution. She knew that the distribution had been deposited into their joint account and used to pay off a mortgage, buy a truck, pay other family expenses and provide start-up capital for the husband's business. Cheshire's husband falsely told her that a CPA had determined that most of his retirement distribution was not taxable. After they divorced, Cheshire made a separate liability election to avoid tax on the unreported income. She claimed that she was entitled to relief because she did not know that the taxable amount of the retirement distribution had been misstated on their joint return. The Tax Court held that she could not obtain relief because she knew about the retirement distribution. It is immaterial that she did not know that the reporting of the distribution on the tax return was incorrect. The Court of Appeals for the Fifth Circuit affirmed. The District of Columbia Circuit has also denied a wife's claim for relief because she had actual knowledge of her husband's retirement income.

2. You file a joint return on which you report wages of $150,000 and your husband reports $30,000 of self-employment income. The IRS examines your return and determines that your husband failed to report $20,000 of income, resulting in a $9,000 deficiency. You file a separate liability election with the IRS after obtaining a divorce.

Assume that the IRS proves that you had actual knowledge of $5,000 of the unreported income but not the other $15,000. You are liable for 25% of the deficiency, or $2,250, allocable to the $5,000 of income that you knew about ($2,250 = $5,000 × $20,000 × $9,000). Your former spouse is liable for the entire deficiency since the unreported income was his. The IRS can collect the entire deficiency from him, or can collect $2,250 from you and the balance from him.

3. Mora's husband arranged an investment in a cattle-breeding tax shelter partnership. He put the partnership in both of their names, although Mora did not sign any of the partnership papers. On their joint returns, they claimed partnership losses which turned out to be inflated; deductions were based on overvalued cattle. After their divorce, the IRS disallowed the partnership losses and Mora elected separate liability relief. The IRS refused, claiming that she participated in making the investment so the claimed losses were allocable to her as well as her husband. The Tax Court held that Mora was not involved in making the investment and so the partnership losses are allocable to the husband unless Mora knew the factual basis for the denial of the deductions or she received a tax benefit from the deductions. She did not know about the overvaluation of the cattle, which was the factual basis for the IRS's denial of the deductions. In fact, the IRS conceded that neither spouse understood the nature of their investment or the basis of the deductions. This may often be the case where passive investors claim deductions passed through to them by a limited partnership. For this reason, the IRS argued that the "knowledge of the factual basis" test makes it too easy for limited partnership investors to obtain relief. The Tax Court responded that the law does not distinguish between passive and active investments and there is no policy reason for the courts to create a distinction. Furthermore, although the husband also lacked knowledge of the factual basis for the disallowance of the losses, he cannot avoid liability for the deficiency since the erroneous deductions would be allocable to him on a separate return.

Despite Mora's "win" on the actual knowledge issue, she remained partially liable for the deficiency because she received a tax benefit from the erroneous deductions. Under the tax benefit rule discussed below, the deductions first offset the income that would have been reported by the husband had he filed a separate return. The balance of the deductions benefitted Mora by reducing her separate return income. If she benefitted from 25% of the deductions, she would remain liable for 25% of the deficiency.

Allocating tax liability between spouses. Generally, if you make a separate liability election, you are liable only for the portion of the tax due on the joint return that is allocable to you, determined as if you had filed a separate return. If erroneous items (omitted income or improper deductions or credits) are allocable to the other spouse but you had actual knowledge of the items as discussed above, you cannot avoid liability and the IRS remains able to collect the tax due from either of you. Where deductions are allocable to the other spouse and you are not barred from relief by the actual knowledge test, you can still be held partially liable if you received a tax benefit from the deductions; *see* the discussion of the tax benefit rule below.

In general, the allocation of a tax deficiency depends on which spouse's "items" gave rise to the deficiency. The items may be omitted income or disallowed deductions or credits. Items are generally allocated to the spouse who would have reported them on a separate return. If a deficiency is based on unreported income, the deficiency is allocated to the spouse who earned the income. Income from a jointly owned business is allocated equally unless you provide evidence that more should be allocated to the other spouse. Similarly, if a deficiency is based on the denial of personal deductions, the deficiency is allocated equally between you unless you show that a different allocation is appropriate. A deficiency based on the denial of business deductions is allocated according to your respective ownership shares in the business. If the IRS can show fraud, it can reallocate joint return items.

On Form 8857, you do *not* have to figure the portion of the deficiency for which you are liable. The IRS will figure your separate liability (and any related interest and penalties). However, you can use a worksheet in IRS Publication 971 to figure your separate liability.

EXAMPLES

1. After you obtain a divorce, the IRS examines a joint return you filed with your former husband and assesses a tax deficiency attributable to income he failed to report. If you did not know about the omitted income and timely elect separate liability treatment, you are not liable for any part of the tax deficiency, which is entirely allocable to your former husband who earned the income. You are not liable even if the IRS is unable to collect the tax from your former husband and you have substantial assets from which the tax could be paid.

2. The IRS assesses a joint return deficiency attributable to $35,000 of income that your former spouse failed to report and $15,000 of disallowed deductions that you claimed. Both of you may make the separate liability election and limit your respective liabilities.

    If you make the election, your liability will be limited to 30% of the deficiency, as your disallowed deductions of $15,000 are 30% of the $50,000 of items causing the deficiency. If your former husband makes the election, he will be liable for the remaining 70% of the deficiency (his $35,000 of unreported income is 70% of the $50,000 of items causing the deficiency).

    If either of you does not make the election, the non-electing person could be held liable for 100% of the deficiency unless innocent spouse relief is available or the IRS grants equitable relief.

Tax benefit rule limits relief based on erroneous deductions or credits. The tax benefit limitation is an exception to the general rule that allocates items between the spouses as if separate returns had been filed. If you received a tax benefit from an erroneous deduction or credit that is allocable to the other spouse, you remain liable for the proportionate part of the deficiency. You are treated as having received a tax benefit if the disallowed deduction exceeded the income that would have been reported by the other spouse on a hypothetical separate return.

EXAMPLE

On a joint return, you report wages of $100,000 and your husband reports $15,000 of self-employment income. You divorce the following year. The IRS examines the return and disallows a $20,000 business expense deduction claimed by your former husband, resulting in a $5,600 tax deficiency. Of the $20,000 deduction, $15,000 is allocable to your former husband as that amount offset his entire income. The $5,000 balance offset your separate income and thereby gave you a tax benefit. Your former husband will be liable for 75% of the deficiency ($4,200) and you will be liable for the 25% balance ($1,400).

If your former husband had reported income of $30,000 instead of $15,000, you would not be liable for any part of the deficiency under the tax benefit rule. The deduction is attributed entirely to his income, so the entire deficiency is allocated to him.

These allocations assume that the IRS does not show that you had "actual knowledge" (see above) of the deductions attributable to your former husband. To the extent you had such knowledge, the deductions are allocable to both of you, so both of you remain liable for that part of the deficiency.

Planning Reminder

Unpaid Tax on Correct Return

The separate liability election is not available where the proper amount of tax was reported on a joint return but your spouse did not pay the tax. However, equitable relief *(1.9)* may be available in this type of tax underpayment situation.

Transfers intended to avoid tax. You may be held liable for more than your allocable share of a deficiency if a disqualified asset transfer was made to you by your spouse with a principal purpose of avoiding tax. Transfers made to you within the one-year period preceding the date on which the IRS sends the first letter of proposed deficiency are presumed to have a tax avoidance purpose unless they are pursuant to a divorce decree or decree of separate maintenance. You may rebut the presumption by showing that tax avoidance was not the principal purpose of the transfer. If the tax avoidance presumption is not rebutted, the transfer is considered a disqualified transfer and the value of the transferred asset adds to your share of the liability as otherwise determined under the above election rules.

If the IRS proves that you and your former spouse transferred assets between you as part of a fraudulent scheme, neither of you will be allowed to make the separate liability election; both of you will remain individually liable for the entire joint return deficiency.

Appeal to Tax Court. You may petition the Tax Court if the IRS disputes your election or your allocation of liability. The petition must be filed within 90 days of the date on which the IRS mails a determination to you by registered or certified mail if the IRS mailing is within six months of the filing of the election. If an IRS notice is not mailed within the six-month period, a Tax Court petition may be filed without waiting for an IRS response or, if you do wait, you have until 90 days after the date the IRS mails the notice to file the petition.

The IRS may not take any collection action against you during the 90-day period and if the Tax Court petition is filed, the suspension lasts until a final court decision is made.

1.9   Equitable Relief

The IRS may grant equitable relief for liability on a joint return where innocent spouse relief *(1.7)* and separate liability *(1.8)* are not available. For example, the separate liability election and inno-cent spouse relief are not available where the proper amount of tax was reported on a joint return but your spouse failed to pay the tax owed. If you signed a correct return on which tax was owed and, without your knowledge, your spouse used the funds intended for payment of the tax for other purposes, the IRS may grant you equitable relief. A request for equitable relief is made on Form 8857. The IRS may also grant equitable relief in cases where the proper amount of tax was under-stated on the joint return if it would be inequitable to hold you liable.

The IRS has set the following conditions for granting equitable relief:

1. Relief is not available under the innocent spouse or separate liability election rules.
2. The request is made on Form 8857 no later than two years after the IRS began collection pro-ceedings against you, or within two years following the date of the first IRS collection action after July 22, 1998, if collection efforts began before that date.
3. Taxes are unpaid when the request for relief is made; refunds will only be granted in limited situations.
4. You and your spouse did not file the joint return or transfer assets to one another in order to avoid paying taxes or with fraudulent intent.

Tax underpayment. The IRS will ordinarily grant equitable relief to a divorced or separated individual who would face economic hardship if forced to pay unpaid joint return liability. The spouse requesting relief must be able to show that at the time the joint return was signed, it was reasonable to believe that the other spouse would pay the reported liability. The unpaid liability must be allocable to the other spouse.

Equitable relief in other cases where it would be inequitable to hold you liable. According to the IRS, factors weighing in favor of equitable relief are: you are divorced, legally sepa-rated, or living apart from the other spouse; you would suffer economic hardship if relief was not granted; you were abused by the other spouse; the other spouse was legally obligated to pay the out-standing liability by a divorce decree or agreement; the liability is solely attributable to the other spouse.

The IRS will treat these factors as weighing against equitable relief: the unpaid tax or item giv-ing rise to the deficiency was attributable to you; you knew or had reason to know when the return was signed of the item giving rise to the liability or that the reported liability would not be paid; you significantly benefitted, beyond normal support, from the unpaid liability or items giving rise to the deficiency; you are legally obligated to pay the liability by a divorce decree or agreement; you did not make a good faith effort to comply with the federal tax laws in the tax years following the year for which relief is sought.

How Widows and Widowers File

1.10   Death of Your Spouse in 2002

If your spouse died in 2002, you are considered married for the whole year. If you did not remarry in 2002, you may file a 2002 joint return for you and your deceased spouse. Generally, you file a joint return with the executor or administrator. But you alone may file a joint return if you are otherwise entitled to file jointly and:

1. The deceased did not file a separate return, and
2. Someone other than yourself has not been appointed as executor or administrator before the due date for filing the return. An executor or administrator appointed after the joint return is filed may revoke the joint return within the one-year period following the due date.

If you do file jointly, you include on the return all of your income and deductions for the full year and your deceased spouse's income and deductions *up to the date of death (see 1.14).*

For 2003 and 2004, you may be able to file as a qualifying widow(er) if a dependent child lives with you; *see 1.11.*

 *Filing Instruction*

Reporting Income of Deceased Spouse

If your spouse died during the year and you are filing a joint return, include his or her income earned through the date of death.

Planning Reminder

Possible Estate Insolvency

If you will be appointed executor or administrator and are concerned about estate insolvency, it may be advisable to hedge as follows: (1) File separate returns. If it is later seen that a joint return is preferable, you have three years to change to a joint return. (2) File jointly but postpone being appointed executor or administrator until after the due date of the joint return. In this way, the joint return may be disaffirmed if the estate cannot cover its share of the taxes.

Joint return barred. As a surviving spouse, you may not file a joint return for you and your deceased spouse if:

1. You remarry before the end of the year of your spouse's death. In this case you may file jointly with your new spouse. A final return for the deceased spouse must be filed by the executor or administrator using the filing status of married filing separately.
2. You or your deceased spouse has a short year because of a change in annual accounting period.
3. Either of you was a nonresident alien at any time during the tax year; but *see 1.5*.

Executor or administrator may revoke joint return. If an executor or administrator is later appointed, he or she may revoke a joint return that you alone have filed by filing a separate return for the decedent. Even if you have properly filed a joint return for you and the deceased spouse (as just discussed), the executor or administrator is given the right to revoke the joint return. But a state court held that a co-executrix could not refuse to sign a joint return where it would save the estate money.

To revoke the joint return, the executor must file a separate return within one year of the due date (including extensions). The executor's separate return is treated as a late return; interest charges and a late filing penalty apply. The joint return that you filed is deemed to be your separate return. Tax on that return is recalculated by excluding items belonging to your deceased spouse.

Signing the return. A joint return reporting your deceased spouse's income should list both of your names. Where there is an executor or administrator, the return is signed by you as the surviving spouse and the executor or administrator in his or her official capacity. If you are the executor or administrator, sign once as surviving spouse and again as the executor or administrator. Where there is no executor or administrator, you sign the return, followed by the words, "taxpayer and surviving spouse."

Surviving spouse's liability. If a joint return is filed and the estate cannot pay its share of the joint income tax liability, you, as the surviving spouse, may be liable for the full amount. Once the return is filed and the filing date passes, you can no longer change the joint return election and file a separate return unless an administrator or executor is appointed after the due date of the return.

In that case, as previously discussed, the executor may disaffirm the joint return.

1.11 Qualifying Widow(er) Status If Your Spouse Died in 2001 or 2000

If your spouse died in either 2000 or 2001 and you meet the following three requirements, your 2002 filing status is *qualifying widow or widower*, which allows you to use joint return rates on an individual return.

1. You did not remarry before 2003 (if you did remarry, you may file a 2002 joint return with your new spouse).
2. You may claim as your dependent (*see* Chapter 21) in 2002 a child, stepchild, adopted child, or foster child who lived with you during 2002 and you paid over half the cost of maintaining your home. The child must live with you for the entire year, not counting temporary absences such as to attend school or take a vacation.
3. You were able to file jointly in the year of your spouse's death, even if you did not do so.

If you meet all these tests and do not itemize deductions (Schedule A, Form 1040), use the standard deduction for married couples filing jointly *(13.1)*. Use the 2002 tax table or rate schedule for qualifying widows or widowers, the same schedule used by married couples filing jointly; *see 1.2*.

Spouse's death before 2000. If your spouse died before 2000 and you did not remarry before 2003, you may be able to use head of household rates for 2002 if you qualify under the rules discussed in *1.12*.

Filing as Head of Household

1.12 Qualifying as Head of Household

You can file as "head of household" for 2002 if you are unmarried at the end of 2002 and you maintained a household for your dependent child, parent, or other qualifying relative. You must be a U.S. citizen or resident *(see 1.18)* for the entire year. Tax rates are lower for a head of household than for a person filing as single *(see 1.2)* and the standard deduction is higher *(see* Chapter 13). If you are married but for the last half of 2002 you lived apart from your spouse, you may be treated as unmarried and able to qualify for head of household tax rates and standard deduction, which are more favorable than those for a married person filing separately; *see* Test 1 below.

Test 1. Are you unmarried?

You are "unmarried" for 2002 head of household purposes if you are any one of the following:

- *Single as of the end of 2002.*
- *A widow or widower and your spouse died before 2002.* If a dependent child lives with you, *see 1.11* to determine if you may use the even more advantageous filing status of qualifying widow(er). If your spouse died in 2002, you are treated as married and cannot qualify as a 2002 head of household, but a joint return may be filed; *see 1.10.*
- *Legally separated or divorced under a final court decree as of the end of 2002.* A custody and support order does not qualify as a legal separation. A provisional decree (not final), such as a support order *pendente lite* (while action is pending) or a temporary order, has no effect for tax purposes until the decree is made final.
- *Married but living apart from your spouse.* You are considered unmarried for 2002 head of household purposes if your spouse was not a member of your household during the last six months of 2002, you file separate returns, and you maintain a household for more than half the year for a dependent child, stepchild, or adopted child. A foster child qualifies if he or she is a member of your household for the whole year. You must be able to claim the child as a dependent unless your spouse (the non-custodial parent) has the right to the exemption under the rules of *21.11.*
- *Married to an individual who was a nonresident alien during any part of 2002 and you do not elect to file a joint return reporting your joint worldwide income (1.5).*

Test 2: Did you maintain a home for a qualifying relative?

You must pay more than half of the costs of maintaining a household for a qualifying relative, and unless he or she is your parent, that relative must live with you in that home for more than half the year, or for the whole year in the case of a foster child. Your parent does not have to live with you, but you must pay more than half the costs of your parent's household, whether your parent lives alone, with someone else, or in a senior citizen residence.

Relative generally must be your dependent.

The table on the following page shows the relatives who may qualify you to claim head of household status. As the table shows, the relative generally must qualify as your dependent under the tests at *21.1,* except for children and grandchildren who are unmarried as of the end of the year. If the relative is your dependent only because you have a multiple support agreement *(21.10),* you may *not* claim head of household status.

Although a *married* child generally must be your dependent to be treated as a qualifying relative, there is an exception if you are a divorced or separated parent and you waive the exemption for the married child in favor of the other parent, or the other parent may claim the exemption under a pre-1985 agreement *(see 21.11).*

If you are married, live apart from your spouse for the last six months of the year and maintain a home for a child, stepchild, adopted child, or foster child, the child, *whether married or unmarried,* must be your dependent unless you have waived the exemption in favor of the other parent or the other parent is entitled to the exemption under a pre-1985 agreement *(21.11).*

> **EXAMPLE**
>
> Your mother lived with your sister in your sister's apartment, which cost $7,000 to maintain in 2002. Of this amount, you contributed $4,000 and your sister $3,000. Your mother has no income and did not contribute any funds to the household. You qualify as head of household: For 2002, you paid over half the cost of maintaining the home for your mother, who also qualifies as a dependent on your return. A child or dependent relative other than your parent would have to live with you to enable you to file as head of household.

Filing Tip

Advantages of Head of Household Status

Tax rates are lower for a head of household than for those filing as single. The standard deduction is also higher. For a married person who lived apart from his or her spouse during the last half of the year, qualifying as a head of household allows use of tax rates that are more favorable than those for married persons filing separately.

Filing Tip

Child May Be Head of Household

You may qualify as a head of household for filing purposes even if you are not head of the family. For example, a son who earns more than his father and contributes more than half of the cost of maintaining the family may qualify as a head of household. That the father, not the son, exercises family control does not matter. The important factor is a dollar test: whether the head of household for tax purposes contributed more than half the cost of maintaining the household that is his or her home and the principal home of the qualifying dependents.

QUALIFYING RELATIVES FOR HEAD OF HOUSEHOLD PURPOSES

Relationship	Does the Relative Have To Be Your Dependent?	Does the Relative Have To Live With You?
Unmarried child, stepchild or adopted child	No*	Yes
Unmarried foster child	Yes	Yes
Unmarried grandchild or great-grandchild	No	Yes
Married child, stepchild, adopted child, foster child, grandchild, or great-grandchild	Yes*	Yes
Parent	Yes	No
Step-parent	Yes	Yes
Grandparent	Yes	Yes
Brother, sister, half-brother, half-sister, stepbrother, stepsister	Yes	Yes
Father-in-law, mother-in-law	Yes	Yes
Son-in-law, daughter-in-law	Yes	Yes
If related by blood: uncle, aunt, niece, nephew	Yes	Yes

*See the text under "Relative generally must be your dependent," above, for a contrary rule that may apply in the case of divorced or legally separated parents, or parents living apart during the last half of the year.

 *Caution*

Multiple Support Agreement

You are *not* eligible for head of household status if the qualifying relative is your dependent only because you are allowed to claim the exemption under a multiple support agreement (Form 2210; *see 21.10*).

Two-family house. A mother was allowed head of household status by the Tax Court in the following case. She and her unmarried daughter rented one floor of a multilevel home. A married daughter lived on a different floor with her family. Parts of the home were shared. According to the court, the mother was a head of household, based on support of her unmarried daughter. Although she did not pay more than half of the total household expenses, she paid more than half the expenses attributable to her and her unmarried daughter.

Do you have to live in the home you maintain? You generally must pay more than half of the cost of a home that is your qualifying relative's principal residence for more than half the year. If your parent is the qualifying relative and he or she does not live with you, the home must be the parent's principal residence for the entire year. If the relative is not your parent, then, according to the IRS, the home you maintain for the relative must also be your principal residence for more than half the year. Some courts have held that the taxpayer must live for a "substantial" period of time in the same house as the dependent. An appeals court in one case allowed a mother to claim head of household status where she maintained a home for a child in one state and had her principal residence in another state. However, the Tax Court has upheld the IRS position; *see* the following Example.

EXAMPLE

Doctors advised McDonald that her mentally ill son might become self-sufficient if he lived in a separate residence, but one nearby enough for her to provide supervision. She took the advice and kept up a separate home for her son that was about a mile from her own home. She frequently spent nights at his home and he at hers. The Tax Court agreed with the IRS that McDonald could not file as head of household since her principal residence was not the same as her son's.

Costs of maintaining the household. You must pay for *more than half* of the property taxes, mortgage interest, rent, utility charges, upkeep and repairs, domestic help, property insurance, and food eaten in the household. Do not consider the rental value of the lodgings provided the dependent or clothing, education costs, medical expenses, vacation costs, life insurance premiums, transportation costs, and the value of your work around the house. However, these expenses may be considered in figuring your support contribution in determining whether you may claim the child or other relative as a dependent; *see 21.7*.

Household Costs for the Year

1. Property taxes $ _____
2. Mortgage interest   _____
3. Rent paid   _____
4. Property insurance   _____
5. Utilities   _____
6. Domestic help   _____
7. Repairs and upkeep   _____
8. Food eaten in the home   _____
9. Total of Lines 1–8   _____
10. 50% of Line 9 $ _____

If you paid more than the amount on Line 10, you "maintain" the household for purposes of Test 2 on page 23.

Temporary absences disregarded. In determining whether you and a dependent relative lived together for more than half the year, temporary absences are ignored if the absence is due to illness, or being away at school, on a business trip, on vacation, serving in the military, or staying with a parent under a child custody agreement. The IRS requires that it be reasonable to expect your qualifying child or dependent to return to your household after such a temporary absence, and that you continue to maintain the household during the temporary absence. Under this rule, you would lose the right to file as head of household if your dependent moved into his or her own permanent residence before the end of the year.

You may claim head of household status when your qualifying relative is confined to a hospital or a sanitarium and his or her absence is temporary and you continue to maintain a household in expectation of his or her return.

Death or birth during the year. In the year a qualifying relative is born or dies, meeting the residence test for the portion of the year the dependent is alive allows you to claim head of household status.

Tax Returns for Children

1.13 Filing for Your Child

The income of your minor child is *not* included on your return unless you make a special election to report a child's investment income under the rules of *24.5*. A minor is considered a taxpayer in his or her own right. If the child is required to file a return but is unable to do so because of age or for any other reason, the parent or guardian is responsible for filing the return.

A tax return must be filed for a dependent child who had more than $750 of investment income and no earned income (for personal services) for 2002. If your child had only earned income (for personal services) and no investment income, a tax return must be filed if the earned income exceeded $4,700. *See* page 4 for further filing threshold rules.

If the child is unable to sign the return, the parent or guardian should sign the child's name in the proper place, followed by the words, "by [signature], parent [or guardian] for minor child." A parent is liable for tax due on pay earned by the child for services, but not on investment income.

A child who is not required to file a return should still do so for a refund of taxes withheld.

Social Security numbers. A parent or guardian must obtain a Social Security number for a child before filing the child's first income tax return. The child's Social Security number must also be provided to banks, brokers, and other payers of interest and dividends to avoid penalties and backup withholding; *see 26.12*. To obtain a Social Security number, file Form SS-5 with your local Social Security office. If you have applied for a Social Security number but not yet received it by the filing due date, write "applied for" on the tax return in the space provided for the number.

Whether or not you are filing a return for a child, you must obtain and report on your return a Social Security number for a child whom you are claiming as a dependent; *see 21.15*.

 Filing Tip

Kiddie Tax for Children Under Age 14

Children who are under age 14 at the end of 2002 generally must use Form 8615 to figure their 2002 tax if they had more than $1,500 of investment income; *see 24.3*. On Form 8615, the investment earnings over $1,500 are taxed at the parent's top tax rate. However, in certain cases under the rules of *24.5*, parents may elect to report their children's investment income on their own return using Form 8814.

Wages you pay your children. You may deduct wages paid to your children in your business. Keep records showing that their activities are of a business rather than personal nature.

Withholding for children. Children with wages are generally subject to withholding and should file Form W-4 with their employer. An exemption from withholding may be claimed only in limited cases. The child must certify on Form W-4 that he or she had no federal tax liability in the prior year and expects no liability in the current year for which the withholding exemption is sought. For example, in 2002, a child with investment income exceeding $250 who expected to be claimed as another taxpayer's dependent could claim an exemption from withholding only if the expected amount of investment income plus wages was $750 or less (this amount may change annually).

Wages you pay to your own children under age 18 for working in your business are not subject to FICA taxes (Social Security and Medicare); *see 26.10*.

Filing for a Deceased or Incompetent Person

1.14 Return for Deceased

When a person dies, another tax-paying entity is created—the decedent's estate. Until the estate is fully distributed, it will generally earn income for which a return must be filed. For example, Carlos Perez dies on June 30, 2002. The wages and bank interest he earned through June 30 are reported on his final income tax return, Form 1040, which is due by April 15, 2003. Income earned on the bank account after June 30 is attributed to the estate, or to the beneficiary if the right to the account passes by law directly to the beneficiary. Income received by the estate is reported on Form 1041, the income tax return for the estate, if the estate has gross income of $600 or more.

What income tax returns must be filed on behalf of the deceased? If the individual died after the close of the taxable year but before the income tax return was filed, the following must be filed:

1. Income tax return for the prior year;
2. Final income tax return, covering earnings in the period from the beginning of the taxable year to the date of death; *and*
3. Estate income tax return, covering earnings in the period after the decedent's death.

If the individual died after filing a return for the prior tax year, then only 2 and 3 are filed.

 *Filing Instruction*

IRD Not Included on Decedent's Final Return

Do not report on the decedent's final return income that is received after his or her death, or accrues after or because of death if the decedent used the accrual method. This income is considered "income in respect of a decedent," or IRD. IRD is taxed to the estate or beneficiary receiving the income in the year of the receipt. On the decedent's final return, only deductible expenses paid up to and including the date of death may be claimed. If the decedent reported on the accrual basis, those deductions accruable up to and including the date of death are deductible. If a check for payment of a deductible item was delivered or mailed before the date of the decedent's death, a deduction is allowable on the decedent's last return, even though the check was not cashed or deposited until after the decedent's death. If the check was not honored by the bank, the item is not deductible.

> **EXAMPLE**
>
> Steven Jones died on January 31, 2003, before he could file his 2002 tax return. The 2002 income tax return must be filed by April 15, 2003, unless an extension is obtained. A final income tax return to report earnings from January 1, 2003, through January 31, 2003, will have to be filed on April 15, 2004. Jones's estate will have to file an income tax return on Form 1041 to report earnings and other income that were not earned by Jones before February 1, 2003, unless the gross income of the estate is under $600.

Who is responsible for filing? The executor, administrator, or other legal representative is responsible for filing all returns. For purposes of determining whether a final income tax return for the decedent is due, the annual gross income test at page 3 is considered in full. You do not prorate it according to the part of the year the decedent lived. A surviving spouse may assume responsibility for filing a joint return for the year of death if no executor or administrator has been appointed and other tests are met *(1.10)*. However, if a legal representative has been appointed, he or she must give the surviving spouse consent to file a joint return for the year of the decedent's death. In one case, a state court held that a co-executrix could not refuse consent and was required to sign a joint return where it would save the estate money.

How do you report the decedent's income and deductions? You follow the method used by the decedent during his or her life, either the cash method or the accrual method, to account for the income up to the date of death. The income does not have to be put on an annual basis. Each item is taxed in the same manner as it would have been taxed had the decedent lived for the entire year.

If the decedent owned U.S. Savings Bonds, *see 4.29*.

When one spouse dies in a community property state *(1.6)*, how should the income from the community property be reported during the administration of the estate? The IRS says that half the income is the estate's and the other half belongs to the surviving spouse.

Deductible expenses paid (or accrued under the accrual method) by the decedent before death are claimed on the final return.

Medical expenses of the decedent. If the estate pays the decedent's personal medical expenses (not those for the decedent's dependents) within one year of the date of death, the expenses can be deducted on the decedent's final return, subject to the regular 7.5% of adjusted gross income floor *(17.8)*. However, the expenses are not deductible for income tax purposes if they are deducted for estate tax purposes. To deduct such medical expenses on the decedent's final return, a statement must be attached to the final return affirming that no estate tax deduction has been taken and that the rights to the deduction have been waived.

Partnership income. The death of a partner closes the partnership tax year for that partner. The final return for the partner must include his or her distributive share of partnership income and deductions for the part of the partnership's tax year ending on the date of death. Thus, if a partner dies on July 26, 2002, and the partnership's taxable year ends December 31, 2002, the partner's final 2002 return must include partnership items for January 1, 2002 through July 26, 2002. Partnership items for the balance of 2002 must be reported by the partner's executor or other successor in interest on the estate's income tax return.

Exemptions allowed on a final return. These are generally the same exemptions the decedent would have had if he or she had not died. You do not reduce the exemptions because of the shorter taxable year. If the deceased had contributed more than one-half of a dependent's annual support, a dependency exemption is claimed on his or her final return.

Estimated taxes. No estimated tax need be paid by the executor after the death of an unmarried individual; the entire tax is paid when filing the final tax return. But where the deceased and a surviving spouse paid estimated tax jointly, the rule is different. The surviving spouse is still liable for the balance of the estimated tax unless an amended estimated tax voucher is filed. Further, if the surviving spouse plans to file a joint return *(1.10)* that includes the decedent's income, estimated tax payments may be required; *see* Chapter 27.

Where the estate has gross income, estimated tax installments are not required on Form 1041-ES for the first two years after the decedent's death.

Signing the return. An executor or administrator of the estate signs the return. If it is a joint return, *see 1.10.*

When a refund is due on a final return. The decedent's final return may also be used as a claim for a refund of an overpayment of withheld or estimated taxes. Form 1310 may be used to get the refund, but the form is not required if you are a surviving spouse filing a joint return for the year your spouse died. If you are an executor or administrator of the estate and you are filing Form 1040, 1040A, or 1040EZ for the decedent, you do not need Form 1310, but you must attach to the return a copy of the court certificate showing your appointment as personal representative.

Itemized deduction for IRD subject to estate tax. Items of gross income that the decedent had a right to receive but did not receive before death (or accrue if under the accrual method) are subject to income tax when received by the estate or beneficiary. This "income in respect of a decedent," or IRD, is also included in the decedent's estate for estate tax purposes. If estate tax is paid, an individual beneficiary may claim an itemized deduction for an allocable share of the estate tax paid on IRD items; *see 11.17* for deduction details.

1.15 Return for an Incompetent Person

A legal guardian of an incompetent person files Form 1040 for an incompetent whose gross income meets the filing tests on page 3. Where a spouse becomes incompetent, the IRS says the other spouse may file a return for the incompetent without a power of attorney, if no legal guardian has been appointed. For example, during the period an individual was in a mental hospital, and before he was adjudged legally incompetent, his wife continued to operate his business. She filed an income tax return for him and signed it for him although she had no power of attorney. The IRS accepted the return as properly filed. Until a legal guardian was appointed, she was charged with the care of her husband and his property.

 *Planning Reminder*

Promptly Closing the Estate
To expedite the closing of the decedent's estate, an executor or other personal representative of the decedent may file Form 4810 for a prompt assessment. Once filed, the IRS has 18 months to assess additional taxes. Without making the request, the IRS has three years from the due date of the return to make assessments. Form 4810 must be filed separately from the final return.

The IRS has accepted a joint return filed by a wife in her capacity as legal guardian for her missing husband. However, the Tax Court has held that where one spouse is mentally incompetent, a joint return may not be filed because the incompetent spouse was unable to consent to a joint return; an appeals court agreed.

How Resident and Nonresident Aliens File

1.16 How a Nonresident Alien Is Taxed

A *nonresident* alien is generally taxed only on income from U.S. sources. A nonresident alien's income that is *effectively connected* with a U.S. business and capital gains from the sale of U.S. real estate are subject to tax at regular U.S. rates. Other capital gains are not taxed unless a nonresident alien has a U.S. business or is in the U.S. for 183 days during the year. Generally, investment income of a nonresident alien from U.S. sources that is *not effectively connected* with a U.S. business is subject to a 30% tax rate (or lower rate if provided by treaty).

Nonresident aliens who are required to file must do so on Form 1040NR. If you are a nonresident alien, get a copy of IRS Publication 519, U.S. Tax Guide for Aliens. It explains how nonresident aliens pay U.S. tax.

Dual status. In the year a person arrives in or departs from the U.S., both resident and nonresident status may apply.

> **EXAMPLE**
> On May 1, 2002, Leon Marchand arrived on a non-immigrant visa and was present in the U.S. for the rest of the year. From January 1 to April 31, 2002, he is a nonresident; from May 1 to the end of the year, he is a resident, under the 183-day test *(1.18)*. Despite "dual status," he does not file two returns. Since he is a U.S. resident on the last day of the year, he files Form 1040 and reports income on the basis of his status for each part of the year. The income for the nonresident portion of the year should be shown on a separate schedule.

Certain restrictions apply to dual status taxpayers. For example, a joint return may not be filed, unless you and your spouse agree to be taxed as U.S. residents for the entire year.

For details on filing a return for a dual status year, *see* IRS Publication 519 and the instructions to Form 1040NR.

1.17 How a Resident Alien Is Taxed

A resident alien *(1.18)* is taxed on worldwide income from all sources, just like a U.S. citizen. The exclusion for foreign earned income may be claimed if the foreign physical presence test is satisfied or if the bona fide residence test is met by an individual residing in a treaty country; *see 36.5*. A resident alien may generally claim a foreign tax credit; *see 36.14*. A resident alien's pension from a foreign government is subject to regular U.S. tax. A resident alien working in the United States for a foreign government is not taxed on the wages if the foreign government allows a similar exemption to U.S. citizens.

1.18 Who Is a Resident Alien?

The following tests determine whether an alien is taxed as a U.S. resident. Intent to remain in the U.S. is not considered.

You are treated as a resident alien and taxed as a U.S. resident for 2002 tax purposes if you meet either of the following tests:

1. You have been issued a "green card," which grants you the status of lawful permanent resident. If you were outside the U.S. for part of 2002 and then became a lawful permanent resident, *see* the rules for dual tax status on the following page.
2. You meet a 183-day substantial presence test. Under this test, you are treated as a U.S. resident if you were in the U.S. for at least 31 days during the calendar year and have been in the U.S. for at least 183 days within the last three years (the current year and the two preceding calendar years). The 183-day test is complicated and there are several exceptions.

Caution

Who Is a Resident?
An alien's mere presence in the U.S. does not make him or her a "resident." An alien is generally treated as a "resident" only if he or she is a lawful permanent resident who has a "green card" or meets a substantial presence test; *see 1.18*.

To determine if you meet the 183-day test for 2002, the following cumulative times are totaled. Each day in the U.S. during 2002 is counted as a full day. Each day in 2001 counts as $\frac{1}{3}$ of a day; each day in 2000 counts as $\frac{1}{6}$ of a day. Note that you must be physically present in the U.S. for at least 31 days in the current year. If you are not, the 183-day test does not apply.

Other exceptions to the substantial presence test are: commuting from Canada or Mexico; keeping a tax home and close contacts or connections in a foreign country; having a diplomat, teacher, trainee, or student status; being a professional athlete temporarily in the U.S. to compete in a charitable sports event; or being confined in the U.S. for certain medical reasons. These exceptions are explained in the following paragraphs.

Commute from Mexico or Canada. If you regularly commute to work in the U.S. from Mexico or Canada, commuting days do not count as days of physical presence for the 183-day test.

Tax home/closer connection exception. If you are in the United States for less than 183 days during 2002, show that you had a closer connection with a foreign country than with the U.S., and keep a tax home there for the year, you generally will not be subject to tax as a U.S. resident even if you meet the substantial presence test. Under this exception, it is possible to have a U.S. abode and a tax home in a foreign country. A tax home is usually where a person has his or her principal place of business; if there is no principal place of business, it is the place of regular abode. Proving a tax home alone is not sufficient; the closer connection relationship must also be shown.

To claim the closer connection exception, you must file Form 8840 explaining the basis of your claim. The tax home/closer connection exception does not apply to an alien who is present for 183 days or more during a year or who has applied for a "green card." A relative's application is not considered as the alien's application.

Exempt-person exception. Days of presence in the U.S. are not counted under the 183-day test if you are considered an exempt person such as a teacher, trainee, student, foreign-government-related person, or professional athlete temporarily in the U.S. to compete in a charitable sports event.

To exclude days of presence as a teacher, trainee, student, or professional athlete, you must file Form 8843 with the IRS.

A foreign-government-related person is any individual temporarily present in the U.S. who (1) has diplomatic status or a visa that the Secretary of the Treasury (after consultation with the Secretary of State) determined represents full-time diplomatic or consular status; or (2) is a full-time employee of an international organization; or (3) is a member of the immediate family of a diplomat or international organization employee.

A teacher or trainee is any individual other than a student who is temporarily present in the U.S. under a "J" or "Q" visa and who substantially complies with the requirements for being so present.

A student is any individual who is temporarily present in the U.S. under either an "F," "J," "M," or "Q" visa and who substantially complies with the requirements for being so present.

The exception generally does not apply to a teacher or trainee who has been exempt as a teacher, trainee, or student for any part of two of the six preceding calendar years. However, if during the period you are temporarily present in the U.S. under an "F," "J," "M," or "Q" visa and all of your compensation is received from outside the U.S., you may qualify for the exception if you were exempt as a teacher, trainee, or student for less than four years in the six preceding calendar years. The exception also does not apply to a student who has been exempt as a teacher, trainee, or student for more than five calendar years, unless you show that you do not intend to reside permanently in the U.S. and that you have substantially complied with the requirements of the student visa providing for temporary presence in the U.S.

Medical exception. If you plan to leave but cannot physically leave the U.S. because of a medical condition that arose in the U.S., you may be treated as a nonresident, even if present here for more than 183 days during the year. You must file Form 8843 to claim the medical exception.

Tax treaty exceptions. The lawful permanent residence test and the substantial physical presence test do not override tax treaty definitions of residence. Thus, you may be protected by a tax treaty from being treated as a U.S. resident even if you would be treated as a resident under either test.

Dual tax status in first year of residency. If you first became a lawful permanent resident of the U.S. (received a green card) during 2002 and were not a U.S. resident during 2001, your period of U.S. residency begins with the first day in 2002 that you are present in the U.S. with the status of lawful permanent resident. Before that date, you are a nonresident alien. This means that

Planning Reminder

Is 2002 Your First Year of Residency?

If you were not a resident during 2001 but in 2002 you satisfy both the lawful resident (green card) test and the 183-day presence test, your residence begins on the earlier of the first day you are in the U.S. while a lawful permanent resident and the first day of physical presence.

if you become a lawful permanent resident after January 1, 2002, you have a dual status tax year. On Form 1040, you attach a separate schedule showing the income for the part of the year you are a nonresident. Form 1040NR (or 1040 NR-EZ) may be used as the statement. Write "Dual-Status Return" or "Dual-Status Statement" across the top.

To figure tax for a dual status year, *see* IRS Publication 519 and the instructions to Form 1040NR.

You also may have a dual status year if you were not a U.S. resident in 2001, and in 2002 you are a U.S. resident under the 183-day presence test. Your period of U.S. residency starts on the first day in 2002 for which you were physically present; before that date you are treated as a nonresident alien. However, if you meet the 183-day presence test (but not the green card test) and also spent 10 or fewer days in the U.S. during a period in which you had a closer connection to a foreign country than to the U.S., you may disregard the 10-day period. The purpose of this exception is to allow a brief presence in the U.S. for business trips or house hunting before the U.S. residency period starts.

> **EXAMPLES**
>
> 1. Manuel Riveras, who has never before been a U.S. resident, lives in Spain until May 15, 2002. He moves to the U.S. and remains in the U.S. through the end of the year, thereby satisfying the physical presence test. On May 15, he is a U.S. resident. However, for the period before May 15, he is taxed as a nonresident.
>
> 2. Same facts as in Example 1, but Riveras attends a meeting in the U.S. on February 2 through 8. On May 15, he moves to the U.S.; May 15, not February 2, is the starting date of the residency. During February, he had closer connection to Spain than to the U.S. Thus, his short stay in February is an exempt period.

First-year choice. If you do not meet either the green card test or the 183-day substantial presence test for the year of your arrival in the U.S. or for the immediately preceding year, but you do meet the substantial presence test for the year immediately following the year of your arrival, you may elect to be treated as a U.S. resident for part of the year of your arrival. To do this, you must (1) be present in the U.S. for at least 31 consecutive days in the year of your arrival; and (2) be present in the U.S. for at least 75% of the number of days beginning with the first day of the 31-consecutive-day period and ending with the last day of the year of arrival. For purposes of this 75% requirement, you may treat up to five days of absence from the U.S. as days of presence within the U.S.

Do not count as days of presence in the U.S. days for which you are an *exempt individual* as discussed earlier.

You make the first-year election to be treated as a U.S. resident by attaching a statement to Form 1040 for the year of your arrival. A first-year election, once made, may not be revoked without the consent of the IRS.

If you make the election, your residence starting date for the year of your arrival is the first day of the earliest 31-consecutive-day period of presence that you use to qualify for the choice. You are treated as a U.S. resident for the remainder of the year.

Last year of residence. You are no longer treated as a U.S. resident as of your *residency termination date.* If you do not have a green card but are a U.S. resident for the year under the 183-day presence test, and you leave the U.S. during that year, your residency termination date is the last day you are present in the U.S., provided that: (1) after leaving the U.S. you had a closer connection to a foreign country than to the U.S. and had your tax home in that foreign country for the rest of the year, and (2) you are not treated as a U.S. resident for any part of the next calendar year.

If during the year you give up your green card (lawful permanent resident status) and meet tests (1) and (2), your residency termination date is the first day that you are no longer a lawful permanent resident. If during the year you meet both the green card test and the 183-day presence test and meet tests (1) and (2), your residency termination date is the *later* of the last day of U.S. presence or the first day you are no longer a lawful permanent resident. If tests (1) and (2) are not met, the residency termination date is the last day of the calendar year. In the year of your residency termination date, the filing rules for dual status taxpayers in this section apply.

1.19 When an Alien Leaves the United States

Current law generally requires an alien who leaves the U.S., regardless of how long the trip is, to obtain a "sailing" or "departure" permit, technically known as a "certificate of compliance." The permit states that you have fulfilled your income tax obligations to the U.S. Without it, unless you are excused from obtaining one, you will be required at your point of departure to file a tax return and pay any tax due or post a bond. Diplomats, employees of international organizations or foreign governments, and students are generally exempt from the permit requirement. If a permit is required, Form 1040-C or in some cases a shorter Form 2063 must be filed with the IRS. *See* Publication 519 for further details.

1.20 Expatriation Tax

Special tax rules apply to U.S. citizens who renounce their citizenship and long-term residents who end their residency if tax avoidance is one of their principal purposes for leaving. For a 10-year period, such individuals are subject to regular U.S. tax on income and gains from U.S. sources. A long-term resident is someone who was a lawful permanent resident (with a green card) in at least eight of the last 15 years ending with the last year of residency.

The law presumes a tax avoidance purpose in certain cases. For 2002, tax avoidance is presumed if (1) the departing individual's average net income tax for the last five years before losing citizenship or terminating residency was more than $120,000 or (2) net worth when citizenship or residency ended was $599,000 or more. These dollar amounts are subject to annual adjustments for inflation. To rebut the presumption of a tax avoidance purpose, a ruling request may be submitted to the IRS.

All individuals who lose their citizenship or who end long-term residency must file Form 8854 with a consular office or federal court; *see* IRS Publication 519.

 *Planning Reminder*

Departure Permit

An alien planning to leave the U.S. should obtain a copy of Form 1040-C from the IRS to review his or her tax reporting obligations.

PART 2

Reporting Your Income

In this part, you will learn what income is taxable, what income is tax free, and how to report income on your tax return.

Pay special attention to—

- Form W-2, which shows your taxable wages and provides other important information on fringe benefits received (Chapter 2).
- Tax-free fringe benefit plans available from your employer (Chapter 3).
- Reporting rules for interest and dividend income (Chapter 4).
- Reporting gains and losses from sales of property (Chapter 5).
- Rules for tax-free exchanges of like-kind property (Chapter 6).
- Planning for retirement distributions. Lump-sum distributions from employer plans may qualify for special averaging or tax-free rollover (Chapter 7).
- IRA contributions and distributions. Penalties for distributions before age 59 $\frac{1}{2}$ and after age 70 $\frac{1}{2}$ may be avoided by advance planning (Chapter 8).
- Restrictions on rental losses where a rented residence is used personally by you or by family members during the year (Chapter 9).
- Passive activity restrictions. Losses from rentals or passive business operations are generally not allowed, but certain real estate professionals are exempt from the loss restrictions, and for others, a special rental loss allowance of up to $25,000 may be available (Chapter 10).
- Reporting refunds of state and local taxes. A refund of previously deducted taxes is generally taxable unless you had no benefit from the deduction (Chapter 11).
- Cancellation of debts. When your creditor cancels debts you owe, you generally have taxable income, but there are exceptions for debts discharged while you are bankrupt or insolvent (Chapter 11).
- Damages received in court proceedings. Learn when these are tax free and when taxable (Chapter 11).

Chapter 2

Taxable Wages, Salary, and Other Compensation

Except for tax-free fringe benefits (*see* Chapter 3), practically everything you receive for your work or services is taxed, whether paid in cash, property, or services. Your employer will generally report your taxable compensation on Form W-2 and other information returns, such as Form 1099-R for certain retirement payments. Do not reduce the amount you report on your return by withholdings for income taxes, Social Security taxes, union dues, or U.S. Savings Bond purchases. Your Form W-2 does not include in taxable pay your qualifying salary-reduction contributions to a retirement plan, although the amount may be shown on the form.

Attach Copy B of Form W-2 to your return; do not attach Forms 1099 unless there are withholdings.

Unemployment benefits are fully taxable. The benefits are reported to the IRS on Form 1099-G. You do not have to attach your copy of Form 1099-G to your return.

Income and expenses from self-employment are discussed in Chapter 40.

Key to Your Form W-2 for 2002 Wages and Tips

Amount in—	What You Should Know—
Box 1	**Taxable wages and tips.** Your taxable wages and tips are listed in Box 1. Taxable fringe benefits that may be shown in Box 14 will also be included in Box 1 as other compensation. The value of tax-free fringe benefits is not shown on Form W-2. Mileage or *per diem* travel allowances will not be reported in Box 1 as taxable wages unless they exceed the IRS rate. *See* the discussion of Box 14, below. Do not decrease the amount shown in Box 1 by the amount your employer withholds for income taxes, Social Security taxes, disability insurance payments, hospitalization insurance premiums, U.S. Savings Bonds, union dues, or payments to a creditor who has attached your salary. Box 1 does not include salary reduction contributions to a retirement plan. Compensation shown in Box 1 must be reported on Line 7 of Form 1040 or 1040A, or Line 1 of Form 1040EZ.
Box 2	**Federal tax withholdings.** This is the amount of federal income tax withheld from your pay. Enter the amount on Line 62 of Form 1040, Line 39 of Form 1040A, or on Line 7 of Form 1040EZ. If the withheld amount plus your estimated tax installments exceeds your tax liability, you are entitled to a refund for the excess payments.
Boxes 3, 4, and 7	**Social Security withholdings.** Withholdings for Social Security coverage are at a rate of 6.2% on up to $84,900 of 2002 wages and tips. If your wages were $84,900 or more, Box 4 should show the maximum tax of $5,263.80. If you worked for more than one employer and a total of more than $5,263.80 was withheld for Social Security taxes, you claim the excess as a tax payment on your tax return; *see 26.10.* Wages subject to Social Security withholdings are shown in Box 3. Elective salary deferrals to a 401(k) plan or SIMPLE plan are included; Social Security withholding applies, although the deferrals are not subject to income tax and are not included in Box 1. Amounts deferred under a nonqualified deferred compensation plan or Section 457 plan are reported here. Similarly, employer payments of qualified adoption expenses (Chapter 3) are included in Box 3 although not included in Box 1 taxable wages. Tips you reported to your employer are shown separately in Box 7. The total of Boxes 3 and 7 should not exceed $84,900.
Boxes 5–6	**Medicare tax withholdings.** Wages, tips, elective salary deferrals, and employer-paid adoption expenses subject to Social Security tax (Boxes 3 and 7) are also subject to a 1.45% Medicare tax, except that there is no wage base limit for Medicare tax. Thus, the Medicare wages shown in Box 5 are not limited to the $84,900 maximum for Boxes 3 and 7. For example, if your wages were $100,000, the amount shown in Box 3 (Social Security wages) would be $84,900, but in Box 5, the full $100,000 would be reported. In Box 6, total Medicare withholdings are reported. On wages of $100,000, the Medicare tax would be $1,450 (1.45% × $100,000).
Box 8	**Allocated tips.** If you worked in a restaurant employing at least 10 people, your employer will report in Box 8 your share of 8% of gross receipts unless you reported tips at least equal to that share *(26.8)*. The amount shown here is not included in Box 1 wages, but you must add it to wages on Line 7 of Form 1040; you cannot file Form 1040A or 1040EZ.
Box 9	**Advance earned income payment.** If you filed a Form W-5 asking for a part of the credit to be added to your wages, the amount of the advance is shown in Box 9. You report the advance as a tax liability when you file Form 1040 or 1040A. *See* Chapter 25 for details on claiming the earned income credit for 2002, and for advance earned income payments.
Box 10	**Dependent care benefits.** Reimbursements from your employer for dependent care expenses and the value of employer-provided care services under a qualifying plan *(3.4)* are included in Box 10. Amounts in excess of $5,000 are also included as taxable wages in Boxes 1, 3, and 5. Generally, amounts up to $5,000 are tax free, but you must determine the amount of the exclusion on Form 2441 if you file Form 1040, or on Schedule 2 if you file Form 1040A. The tax-free amount reduces expenses eligible for the dependent care credit; *see* Chapter 25.
Box 11	**Nonqualified plan distributions.** Distributions shown in Box 11 are from a nonqualified deferred compensation plan, or a nongovernmental Section 457 plan *(7.21)*. Do not report these distributions separately since they have already been included as taxable wages in Box 1.
Box 12	**Elective deferrals to retirement plans.** If you made elective salary deferrals to an employer retirement plan, your contribution (including any excess over the annual deferral limit) is shown in Box 12. Deferrals to a 401(k) plan *(7.18)* should be labeled with Code D. For example, if you made elective pre-tax salary deferrals of $4,500 to a 401(k) plan, your employer would enter D 4,500.00 in Box 12. Code E is used for deferrals to a 403(b) tax-sheltered annuity plan *(7.20)*, Code F for deferrals to a simplified employee pension *(8.16)*, Code G for deferrals (including non-elective as well as elective) to a Section 457 plan *(7.21)*, Code H for elective deferrals to a pension plan created before June 25, 1959, and funded only by employee contributions, and Code S for salary-reduction deferrals to a SIMPLE IRA *(8.18)*.

Key to Your Form W-2 for 2002 Wages and Tips

Amount in—	What You Should Know—
Box 12	***Travel allowance reimbursements.*** If you received a flat mileage allowance from your employer for business trips *(20.33)*; or a *per diem* travel allowance to cover meals, lodging, and incidentals *(20.32)*; and the allowance exceeded the IRS rate, the amount up to the IRS rate (the nontaxable portion) is shown in Box 12 using Code L. The excess is included as taxable wages in Box 1. ***Group-term life insurance over $50,000.*** The cost of coverage over $50,000 is taxable. It is shown in Box 12 using Code C. It is also included in Box 1 wages, Box 3 Social Security wages, and Box 5 Medicare wages and tips. If you are a retiree or other former employee who received group-term coverage over $50,000, any uncollected Social Security tax is shown using Code M and uncollected Medicare tax using Code N. The uncollected amount must be reported on Line 61 of Form 1040 (total tax); write "uncollected tax" next to it. ***Nontaxable sick pay.*** If you contributed to a sick pay plan, an allocable portion of benefits received is tax free and is shown using Code J. ***Uncollected Social Security and Medicare taxes on tips.*** If your employer could not withhold sufficient Social Security on tips, the uncollected amount is shown using Code A. For uncollected Medicare tax, Code B is used. This amount must be reported on Line 61 of Form 1040 (total tax); write "uncollected tax" next to it. ***Excess golden parachute payments.*** If you received an "excess parachute payment as wages," Code K identifies the 20% penalty tax on the excess payment that was withheld by the employer. This withheld amount is included in Box 2, but you also must add it as an additional tax on Line 61 (total tax) of Form 1040. ***Moving expense reimbursements.*** Tax-free employer reimbursements to you for deductible moving expenses (Chapter 12) are shown with Code P. ***Employer contributions to medical savings account (Archer MSA).*** Total employer contributions to an MSA are shown with Code R. Contributions exceeding the excludable limit (Chapter 3) are included as taxable wages in Boxes 1, 3, and 5. ***Employer-financed adoption benefits.*** With Code T, your employer shows qualified adoption expenses paid by the employer *(3.5)* or pre-tax contributions you made to an adoption plan account under a cafeteria plan *(3.13)*. ***Nonstatutory stock option exercised.*** If you exercised a nonstatutory stock option in 2002, your employer may indicate with Code V the taxable "spread" (excess of fair market value of stock over exercise price). This is optional for 2002. Whether or not the income from exercising the option is separately reported in Box 12 (with Code V), the income should be included in Boxes 1, 3 (up to $84,900 Social Security wage ceiling), and 5.
Box 13	***Statutory employee.*** If this box is checked you get a tax break. You report your wage income and deductible job expenses on Schedule C *(see 40.6)*. This treatment allows you to avoid the 2% of adjusted gross income (AGI) floor that applies to job expenses reported on Schedule A. *See 40.6.* Your earnings are not subject to income tax withholding, but are subject to Social Security and Medicare taxes. ***Retirement plan.*** If the box "retirement plan" is checked, this indicates that you were an active participant in an employer plan at some point during the year. As an active participant, you may be unable to make deductible IRA contributions for 2002; IRA deductions for 2002 start to phase out if your AGI exceeds $34,000 (single) or $54,000 (married filing jointly); *see* Chapter 8.
Box 14	***Taxable fringe benefits and miscellaneous payments.*** Your employer may use Box 14 to report fringe benefits or deductions from your pay, such as union dues, educational assistance, health insurance premiums, or voluntary after-tax contributions to profit-sharing or pension plans. If you received taxable fringe benefits, your employer has the option to show the amount in Box 14. The lease value of using a company car *(3.7)* must be included in Box 14 if your employer pays the entire cost of the car. Do not separately report the Box 14 amount as income, since it has already been included in Box 1 as taxable wages.
Boxes 17 and 19	***State and local taxes.*** If you itemize, deduct on Schedule A state and local tax withholdings shown in Boxes 17 and 19.

Sample Form W-2

You should receive your Form W-2 for 2002 from your employer by January 31, 2003.
Note: Boxes 3 and 5 below include the wages in Box 1 plus $2,400
401(k) elective deferral shown in Box 12 with Code D; *see* the
Key to Your Form W-2 on the preceding pages.

a Control number				Safe, accurate, FAST! Use	IRS e-file	Visit the IRS Web Site at www.irs.gov.

OMB No. 1545-0008

b Employer identification number 08-X1X0X1X	1 Wages, tips, other compensation 37,600	2 Federal income tax withheld 5,776

c Employer's name, address, and ZIP code	3 Social security wages 40,000	4 Social security tax withheld 2,480

Finkle Construction Company

5532 Glasgow Plaza

City, State XX111

	5 Medicare wages and tips 40,000	6 Medicare tax withheld 580
	7 Social security tips	8 Allocated tips

d Employee's social security number 0X1 - XX - 1X00	9 Advance EIC payment	10 Dependent care benefits

e Employee's first name and initial Last name	11 Nonqualified plans	12a See instructions for box 12 D 2,400

13 Statutory employee ☐ Retirement plan ☒ Third-party sick pay ☐	12b

Mary Moll

176 Garden Road

City State 1XXX1

14 Other	12c
	12d

f Employee's address and ZIP code

15 State State	Employer's state ID number 11-X1X0X1X	16 State wages, tips, etc. 37,600	17 State income tax 1,880	18 Local wages, tips, etc. 37,600	19 Local income tax 1,000	20 Locality name

Form **W-2** **Wage and Tax Statement**   **2002**   Department of the Treasury—Internal Revenue Service

Copy B To Be Filed with Employee's FEDERAL Tax Return.   (Rev. February 2002)
This information is being furnished to the Internal Revenue Service.

Reporting Compensation

2.1 Salary and Wage Income

The key to reporting your pay is Form W-2, sent to you by your employer. It lists your taxable wages, which may include not only your regular pay, but also other taxable items, such as taxable fringe benefits. A guide to the important information listed on Form W-2 is on pages 36 and 37.

Your employer reports your taxable pay under a simple rule. Unless the item is specifically exempt from tax, you are taxed on practically everything you receive for your work whether paid in cash, property, or services. Taxed pay includes:

Back pay	Honoraria
Bonuses	Jury fees
Commissions	Royalties
Director's fees	Salaries
Sick pay	Severance pay
Employee prizes or awards	Dismissal pay
Expense allowances or reimbursements under	Tips
non-accountable plans	Vacation pay
	Wages

The items that the law specifically excludes from tax are discussed in Chapter 3. The most common tax-free benefits are employer-paid premiums for health and accident plans and certain group-term life insurance plans for coverage up to $50,000.

Withholdings for retirement plans. Amounts withheld from wages as your contribution to your pension or profit-sharing account are generally taxable as compensation unless they are tax-deferred elective deferrals under the limits allowed for Section 401(k) plans *(7.18)*, simplified employee pension plans *(8.16)*, SIMPLE IRAs *(8.18)*, or tax-sheltered annuity plans *(7.20)*. Elective deferrals are reported in Box 12 of Form W-2.

Wages withheld for compulsory forfeitable contributions to a nonqualified pension plan are not taxable if these conditions exist:

1. The contribution is forfeited if employment is terminated prior to death or retirement.
2. The plan does not provide for a refund of employee contributions and, in the administration of the plan, no refund will be made. Where only part of the contribution is subject to forfeiture, the amount of withheld contribution not subject to forfeiture is taxable income.

You should check with your employer to determine the status of your contributions.

Assigning your pay. You may not avoid tax on income you earned by assigning the right to payment to another person. For example, you must report earnings that you donate to charity, even if they are paid directly by your employer to a charity. If you claim itemized deductions, you may claim a contribution deduction for the donation; *see* Chapter 14. Assignments of income-generating intellectual property are held taxable to the assignee. However, if the assignor retained power or control of the property, the assignor could be held liable for the tax according to the 8th Circuit.

The IRS allowed an exception for doctors working in a clinic. The doctors were not taxed on fees for treating patients with limited income (teaching cases) where they were required to assign the fees to a foundation.

Salary advances. Salary paid in advance for services to be rendered in the future is generally taxable in the year received if it is subject to your free and unrestricted use.

Child's wages. A parent is not taxed on wages paid for a child's services even if payment is made to the parent. However, a parent is taxed on income from work contracted for by the parent even if the child assists in the labor. For example, a parent whose children helped her with part-time work at home claimed that the children should be taxed on 70% of the income since they did 70% of the work. The IRS claimed that the parent was taxable on all the income because she, not the children, was the true earner, and the Tax Court agreed. Although the company knew that the children were doing part of the work, it had no agreement with them.

Employee leave-sharing plan. Some companies allow employees to contribute their unused leave into a "leave fund" for use by other employees who have suffered medical emergencies. If you use up your regular leave and benefit from additional leave that has been donated to the plan, the benefit is taxable and will be reported as wages on Form W-2.

Caution

Severance Pay Taxable

You must pay tax on severance pay received upon losing a job. The severance pay is taxable even if you signed a waiver releasing your former employer from potential future damage claims. The waiver does not change the nature of the payments from taxable pay to tax-free personal injury damages; *see 11.7*.

Filing Instruction

Tips

Tips you receive are taxable income. You must report tips to your employer so your employer can withhold FICA and income tax from your regular pay to cover the tips; *see 26.8*.

Court Decision

Tax on Assigned Contingent Fee
An attorney who took a medical malpractice case on a contingent fee basis agreed to split the net fee with his ex-wife pursuant to their divorce agreement. After a favorable settlement, the attorney's take was approximately $40,000 after expenses, half of which went to his ex-wife. Each paid tax on his or her share. The attorney argued that his partial assignment of the fee could shift the tax liability because collection was contingent on the outcome of the lawsuit. However, the IRS and the Tax Court held that the attorney was liable for the tax on the entire contingent fee, and an appeals court agreed. The attorney transferred only the right to receive income. Although his fee was contingent upon the successful outcome of the case, once the fee materialized, it was indisputably compensation for his personal services.

"Golden parachute" payments. Golden parachute arrangements are agreements to pay key employees additional compensation upon a change in company control. If you receive such a payment, part of it may be deemed to be an "excess payment" under a complex formula in the law. You must pay a 20% penalty tax on the "excess" amount in addition to regular income tax on the total. The 20% penalty should be identified on Form W-2 with Code K in Box 12; *see* the Key to Your Form W-2 at the beginning of this chapter.

If the golden parachute payment was reported on Form 1099-MISC as non-employee compensation, it will be included in the total compensation shown in Box 7. If you are self-employed, report the total compensation on Schedule C *(40.6)* and compute self-employment tax on Schedule SE *(45.3)*. Any "excess parachute payment" should be separately labeled in Box 13 of Form 1099-MISC as "EPP." Multiply the "EPP" by 20% and report it on Line 61 (total tax) of Form 1040.

2.2 Constructive Receipt of Year-End Paychecks

As an employee, you use the cash-basis method of accounting. This means that you report all income items in the year they are actually received and deduct expenses in the year you pay them.

You are also subject to the "constructive receipt rule," which requires you to report income not actually received but which has been credited to your account, subject to your control, or put aside for you. Thus, if you received a paycheck on December 31, 2002, you must report the pay on your 2002 return, even though you do not cash or deposit it to your account until 2003. This is true even if you receive the check after banking hours and cannot cash or deposit it until the next year. The Tax Court has also ruled that receipt by an agent (e.g., an attorney) is constructive receipt by the principal. In one case, a woman argued that alimony received by her in 1991 was taxable in 1991. Because the funds were given to her attorney on December 27, 1990, the Tax Court held that she was in constructive receipt of the funds and that they were taxable in 1990.

If your employer does not have funds in the bank and asks you to hold the check before depositing it, you do not have taxable income until the check is cashed. If services rendered in 2002 are paid for by check dated for 2003, the pay is taxable in 2003.

The IRS has ruled that an employee who is not at home on December 31 to take delivery of a check sent by certified mail must still report the check in that year. However, where an employee was not at home to take certified mail delivery of a year-end check that she did not expect to receive until the next year, the Tax Court held that the funds were taxable when received in the following year.

2.3 Pay Received in Property Is Taxed

Your employer may pay you with property instead of cash. You report the fair market value of the property as wages.

> **EXAMPLE**
> For consulting services rendered, Kate Chong receives a check for $10,000 and property with a fair market value of $5,000. She reports $15,000 as wages.

If you receive your company's stock as payment for your services, you include the value of the stock as pay in the year you receive it. However, if the stock is nontransferable or subject to substantial risk of forfeiture, you do not have to include its value as pay until the restrictions no longer apply. You must report dividends on the restricted stock in the year you receive the income.

If you receive your employer's note that has a fair market value, you are taxed on the value of the note less what it would cost you to discount it. If the note bears interest, report the full face value. But do not report income if the note has no fair market value. Report income on the note only when payments are made on it.

A debt cancelled by an employer is taxable income.

Salespeople employed by a dealer have taxable income on receipt of "prize points" redeemable for merchandise from a distributor.

2.4 Gifts From Employers

A payment may be called a gift but still be taxable income. Any payment made in recognition of past services or in anticipation of future services or benefits is taxable even if the employer is not obligated to make the payment. Exceptions for employee achievement awards are discussed at *3.10*.

To prove a gift is tax free, you must show that the employer acted with pure and unselfish motives of affection, admiration, or charity. This is difficult to do, given the employer-employee relationship. A gift of stock by majority stockholders to key employees has been held to be taxable.

2.5 When Commissions Are Taxed

Earned commissions are taxable in the year they are credited to your account and subject to your drawing, whether or not you actually draw them.

On your 2002 tax return, you do not report commissions that were earned in 2002 but cannot be computed or collected until a later year.

> **EXAMPLE**
>
> Arno Jeffers earns commissions based on a percentage of the profits from realty sales. In 2002 he draws $10,000 from his account. However, at the end of 2002 the full amount of his commissions is unknown because profits for the year have not been figured. In January 2003, his 2002 commissions are computed to be $15,000, and the $5,000 balance is paid to him. The $5,000 is taxable in 2003 even though earned in 2002.

Advances against unearned commissions. Under standard insurance industry practice, an agent who sells a policy does not earn commissions until premiums are received by the insurance company. However, the company may issue a cash advance on the commissions before the premiums are received. Agents have claimed that they may defer reporting the income until the year the premiums are earned. The IRS, recognizing that in practice companies rarely demand repayment, requires that advances be included in income in the year received if the agent has full control over the advanced funds. A repayment of unearned commissions in a later year is deducted on Schedule A; *see 2.9.*

Salespeople have been taxed on commissions received on property bought for their personal use. In one case, an insurance agent was taxed on commissions paid to him on his purchase of an insurance policy. In another case, a real estate agent was taxed on commissions he received on his purchase of land. A salesman was also taxed for commissions waived on policies he sold to friends, relatives, and employees.

Kickback of commissions. An insurance agent's kickback of his or her commission is taxable where agents may not under local law give rebates or kickbacks of premiums to their clients. The commissions are income and may not be offset with a business expense deduction; illegal kickbacks may not be deducted.

However, in one case, a federal appeals court allowed an insurance broker to avoid tax when he did not charge clients the basic first-year commission. The clients paid the broker the net premium (gross premium less the commission), which he remitted to the insurance company. The IRS and Tax Court held that the commissions were taxable despite the broker's voluntary waiver of his right to them. He could not deduct them because his discount scheme violated state anti-rebate law (Oklahoma). On appeal, the broker won. The Tenth Circuit Court of Appeals held that since the broker never had any right to commissions under the terms of the contracts he structured with his clients, he was not taxed on the commissions. The court cautioned that if the broker had remitted the full premium (including commission) to the insurance company and then reimbursed the client after having received the commission from the company, the commission probably would have been taxable.

2.6 Unemployment Benefits Are Taxable

All unemployment benefits you receive in 2002 from a state agency or the federal government are treated as taxable income. You should receive Form 1099-G, showing the amount of the payments. Report the payments separately from wages on Line 19 of Form 1040, Line 13 of Form 1040A, or Line 3 of Form 1040EZ.

Supplemental unemployment benefits paid from company-financed funds are taxable as wages and not reported as unemployment compensation. Such benefits are usually paid under guaranteed annual wage plans made between unions and employers.

Unemployment benefits from a private or union fund to which you voluntarily contribute dues are taxable as "other" income on Form 1040, but only to the extent the benefits exceed your contributions to the fund. Your contributions to the fund are not deductible.

Worker's compensation payments are not taxable; *see 2.14.*

Taxable unemployment benefits include federal trade readjustment allowances (1974 Trade Act), airline deregulation benefits (1978 Airline Deregulation Act), and disaster unemployment assistance (1974 Disaster Relief Act).

 Caution

Earned Commissions Credited to Your Account

You may not postpone tax on earned commissions credited to your account in 2002 by not drawing them until 2003 or a later year. However, where a portion of earned commissions is not withdrawn because your employer is holding it to cover future expenses, you are not taxed on the amount withheld.

Repaid settlement benefits. If you had to repay supplemental unemployment benefits to receive trade readjustment allowances (1974 Trade Act), taxable unemployment benefits are reduced by repayments made in the same year. If you repay the benefits in a later year, the benefits are taxed in the year of receipt and a deduction may be claimed in the later year. If the repayment is $3,000 or less, the deduction is added to your other adjustments to income on Line 35 of Form 1040. If the repayment exceeds $3,000, a deduction or a credit may be claimed under the rules at *2.9*.

2.7 Strike Pay Benefits and Penalties

Strike and lockout benefits paid out of regular union dues are taxable as wages unless the payment qualifies as a gift, as discussed below. However, if you have made voluntary contributions to a strike fund, benefits you receive from the fund are tax free up to the amount of your contributions and are taxable to the extent they exceed your contributions.

Strike benefits as tax-free gifts. Here are factors indicating that benefits are gifts: Payments are based on individual need; they are paid to both union and non-union members; and no conditions are imposed on the strikers who receive benefits.

If you receive benefits under conditions by which you are to participate in the strike and the payments are tied to your scale of wages, the benefits are taxable.

> **EXAMPLE**
>
> A striking union pilot claimed that strike benefits were tax-free gifts because they were funded by assessments paid by other union pilots who were not on strike. The IRS and Tax Court held that the benefits were taxable. They were not gifts because they were not motivated by a "detached and disinterested generosity." The union was promoting its own self-interest by giving pilots an incentive to support the strike. The non-striking pilots contributed to the strike fund as an obligation of union membership. The strikers were eligible for benefits only if they agreed to perform any strike activities requested by the union, did not fly for airlines in dispute with the union, and did not take actions that could adversely affect the outcome of the dispute.

Strike pay penalties. Pay penalties charged to striking teachers are not deductible. State law may prohibit public school teachers from striking and charge a penalty equal to one day's pay for each day spent on strike. For example, when striking teachers returned to work after a one-week strike, a penalty of one week's salary was deducted from their pay. Although they did not actually receive pay for the week they worked after the strike, they earned taxable wages. Furthermore, the penalty is not deductible. No deduction is allowed for a fine or penalty paid to a government for the violation of a law.

2.8 Deferring Tax on Pay

If you want to avoid current tax on pay, you may contract with your employer to defer pay to future years. To reduce possible IRS opposition, it is advisable to enter into a deferral compensation arrangement before the year in which the services are to be performed; for example, agree in 2003 to defer pay for 2004 services to 2005 or later years. Furthermore, to defer pay to a future period, you must take some risk. You cannot have any control over your deferred pay account. If you have control over the pay account, you will be treated by the IRS as in "constructive receipt," and thus taxable on employer contributions when made. If you are not confident of your employer's ability to pay in the future, you should not enter into a deferred pay plan.

Before agreeing to a deferral arrangement, consider the possibility that you may be subject to a higher tax on deferred pay than if you had received and paid tax currently on the income.

A deferred pay plan is generally not advisable where a projection of future income shows that there probably will be no substantial income decline, and/or the tax bracket differentials will not be wide. An after-tax dollar in hand for current use is preferable to an expected tax saving that may not materialize.

Qualified salary-reduction plans. An employee is not taxed on qualified 401(k) plan salary reductions, even though the employee had the option to take the cash; *see 7.17*. Qualified salary reductions under a simplified employee pension (SEP) plan *(8.15)*, SIMPLE IRA *(8.17)*, or tax-sheltered annuity plan *(7.20)* are also not taxed, even though you could have received cash currently.

Caution

Law Violation Not Deductible

No deduction is allowed for a fine or penalty paid to a government for the violation of a law.

Caution

Deferring Your Pay But Assuming Risk

To avoid current tax on pay, you may contract with your employer to defer pay to future years. You are not allowed to have control of the deferred amounts. Remember to consider that tax rates could be higher in the future and you may be subject to a higher tax on the deferred pay.

Rabbi trusts. If IRS tests are met, employer contributions to a "rabbi trust" are not taxed until distributions from the trust are received or made available. The trust must be irrevocable and the trust assets must be subject to the claims of the employer's creditors in the event of insolvency or bankruptcy. Employees and their beneficiaries have no preferred claim on the trust assets. *See* a model rabbi trust agreement in Revenue Procedure 92-64.

Employer's contributions to nonqualified plan. If your employer pays into a nonqualified plan for you, you generally must include the contributions in your income as wages for the tax year in which the contributions are made. However, if your interest is subject to a substantial risk of forfeiture (you have a good chance of losing it) at the time of the contribution, you do not have to include the value of your interest in your income until it is no longer subject to a substantial risk of forfeiture.

2.9   Did You Return Wages Received in a Prior Year?

Did you return income in 2002 such as salary or commissions that you reported in a prior taxable year because it appeared you had an unrestricted right to them in the earlier year? If so, you may deduct the repayment as a miscellaneous itemized deduction. If the repayment of wages exceeds $3,000, the deduction is claimed on Line 27 of Schedule A and is not subject to the 2% adjusted gross income (AGI) floor *(19.1)*. However, the law is not clear on the issue of whether a deduction of $3,000 or less is subject to the 2% floor; the IRS takes the position that the 2% floor applies.

Option of tax credit or deduction for repayments over $3,000. If your repayment of wages exceeded $3,000, you may claim the repayment as an itemized deduction, *or* you may claim a tax credit, based upon a recomputation of the prior year's tax; *see* the Filing Instruction on this page.

Repayment of supplemental unemployment benefits. Where repayment is required to qualify for trade readjustment allowances, you may deduct the repayment from gross income. Claim the deduction on Line 35 of Form 1040, and to the left of the line write "subpay TRA." The deduction is allowed even if you do not itemize. If repayment exceeds $3,000, you have the choice of a deduction or claiming a tax credit based on a recomputation of your tax for the year supplemental unemployment benefits were received, as explained in the Filing Instruction on this page.

Repayment of disallowed travel and entertainment expenses. If a "hedge" agreement between you and your company requires you to repay salary or travel and entertainment ("T & E") expenses if they are disallowed to the company by the IRS, you may claim a deduction in the year of repayment. According to the IRS, you may not recalculate your tax for the prior year and claim a tax credit under the rules of Section 1341. However, an appeals court rejected the position taken by the IRS and allowed a tax recomputation under Section 1341 to an executive who returned part of a disallowed salary under the terms of a corporate by-law.

2.10   Waiver of Executor's and Trustee's Commissions

Commissions received by an executor for services performed are taxable as compensation. An executor may waive commissions without income or gift tax consequences by giving a principal legatee or devisee a formal waiver of the executor's right to commissions within six months after the initial appointment or by not claiming commissions at the time of filing the usual accountings.

The waiver may not be recognized if the executor takes any action that is inconsistent with the waiver. An example of an inconsistent action would be the claiming of an executor's fee as a deduction on an estate, inheritance, or income tax return.

A *bequest* received by an executor from an estate is tax free if it is not compensation for services.

2.11   Insurance Plans May Be Tax Free

Company-financed insurance gives employees benefits at low or no tax cost.

Group life insurance. Group insurance plans may furnish not only life insurance protection but also accident and health benefits. Premium costs are low and tax deductible to the company while tax free to you unless you have nonforfeitable rights to permanent life insurance, or, in the case of group-term life insurance, your coverage exceeds $50,000; *see 3.3*. Even where your coverage exceeds $50,000, the tax incurred on your employer's premium payment is generally less than what you would have to pay privately for similar insurance.

It may be possible to avoid estate tax on the group policy proceeds if you assign all of your ownership rights in the policy, including the right to convert the policy, and if the beneficiary is other than your estate. Where the policy allows assignment of the conversion right, in addition to all other rights, and state law does not bar the assignment, you are considered to have made a complete assignment of the group insurance for estate tax purposes.

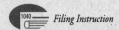

Filing Instruction

Repayments Exceeding $3,000

If a repayment of wages in 2002 exceeds $3,000, a special law (Code Section 1341) gives this alternative: Instead of claiming an itemized deduction from 2002 income, you may recompute your tax for the prior year as if the wages had not been reported. The difference between the actual tax paid in the prior year and the recomputed tax may be claimed as a credit on your 2002 return. The credit is claimed on Line 68 of Form 1040; write next to the line "IRC 1341." If you claim the repayment as a miscellaneous itemized deduction, enter it on Line 27 of Schedule A, where it is not subject to the 2% floor. Choose either the credit or the itemized deduction, whichever gives you the larger tax reduction.

Caution

Charitable Split-Dollar Insurance

In a charitable split-dollar insurance plan, you give money to a charity, which invests in a life insurance policy and splits the proceeds with your beneficiaries. Taxpayers have attempted to deduct the initial "donations," but the tax law was changed to disallow the deduction.

The IRS has ruled that where an employee assigns a group life policy and the value of the employee's interest in the policy cannot be ascertained, there is no taxable gift. This is so where the employer could simply have stopped making payments. However, there is a gift by the employee to the assignee to the extent of premiums paid by the employer. Depending on the assignee, the gift may be a present interest qualifying for the $11,000 annual exclusion discussed at *33.1*.

Split-dollar insurance. Where you want more insurance than is provided by a group plan, your company may be able to help you get additional protection through a split-dollar insurance plan. Under the basic split-dollar plan, your employer purchases permanent cash value life insurance on your life and pays all or part of the annual premium. At your death, your employer is entitled to part of the proceeds equal to the premiums he or she paid. You have the right to name a beneficiary to receive the remaining proceeds which, under most policies, are substantial compared with the employer's share. The IRS has ruled that you must report as taxable income an amount equal to the one-year term cost of the declining life insurance protection to which you are entitled, less any portion of the premium provided by you.

Equity split-dollar arrangements allow employees to retain the right to the cash surrender value in excess of the premiums paid by the employer. Historically, the annual growth in cash value has not been treated as a taxable benefit to employees.

In proposed regulations, the IRS previewed new rules that it intends to promulgate in final regulations. The IRS plans to provide different tax rules for split-dollar arrangements, depending on whether the employee or the employer owns the insurance policy. If the employee is the owner, the employer's premium payments will be treated as loans and the imputed interest will be taxed to the employee. If the employer owns the policy, the employee will be taxed on the value of the life insurance protection. The IRS will apply the proposed rules only to split-dollar arrangements entered into after the date final regulations are published and to prior arrangements materially modified after that date. However, the proposed rules may be relied upon before finalization of the regulations if all parties to the arrangement treat the arrangement consistently. Notice 2002-8 provides guidance for arrangements entered into before the release of the final regulations. An IRS table in Notice 2002-8 may be used to value the insurance coverage provided under arrangements entered into before future guidance is issued. However, if the arrangement was entered into before January 28, 2002, it may be possible to use lower insurance company rates or prior IRS rates. In addition, a transition rule in Notice 2002-8 allows split-dollar arrangements entered into before January 28, 2002, to be terminated or converted to a loan before 2004 without imposition of tax on the built-up cash value. *See* the *Supplement* for further developments.

2.12 Educational Benefits for Employees' Children

Private foundations. The IRS has published guidelines under which a private foundation established by an employer may make tax-free grants to children of employees. An objective, nondiscriminatory program must be adopted. If the guidelines are satisfied, employees are not taxed on the benefits provided to their children. Advance approval of the grant program must be obtained from the IRS.

IRS guidelines require that:

- Grant recipients must be selected by a scholarship committee that is independent of the employer and the foundation. Former employees of the employer or the foundation are not considered independent.
- Eligibility for the grants may be restricted to children of employees who have been employed for a minimum of up to three years, but eligibility may not be related to the employee's position, services, or duties.
- Once awarded, a grant may not be terminated if the parent leaves his job with the employer, regardless of the reason for the termination of employment. If a one-year grant is awarded or a multi-year grant is awarded subject to renewal, a child who reapplies for a later grant may not be considered ineligible because his parent no longer works for the employer.
- Grant decisions must be based solely upon objective standards unrelated to the employer's business and the parent's employment such as prior academic performance, aptitude tests, recommendations from instructors, financial needs, and conclusions drawn from personal interviews.
- Recipients must be free to use the grants for courses that are not of particular benefit to the employer or the foundation.

 Caution

Primary Purpose Determination
If all guidelines other than the percentage test are satisfied, the IRS will determine whether the primary purpose of the program is to educate the children. If it is, the grants will be considered tax-free scholarships or fellowships; if it is not, the grants are taxed to the parent-employees as extra compensation.

- The grant program must not be used by the foundation or employer to recruit employees or induce employees to continue employment.
- There must be no requirement or suggestion that the child or parent is expected to render future employment services.

The grant program must also meet a percentage test. The number of grants awarded in a given year to children of employees must not exceed (1) 25% of the number of employees' children who were eligible, applied for the grants, and were considered by the selection committee in that year; or (2) 10% of the number of employees' children who were eligible during that year, whether or not they applied. Renewals of grants are not considered in determining the number of grants awarded.

Educational benefit trusts and other plans. A medical professional corporation set up an educational benefit plan to pay college costs for the children of "key" employees. Children enrolled in a degree program within two years of graduating from high school could participate in the plan. If an eligible employee quit for reasons other than death or permanent disability, his or her children could not longer receive benefits except for expenses actually incurred before termination. The company made annual contributions to a trust administered by a bank. According to the IRS, amounts contributed to the trust were a form of pay to qualified employees, because the contributions were made on the basis of the parents' employment and earnings records, not on the children's need, merit, or motivation. However, the employees could not be taxed when the funds were deposited because the children's right to receive benefits was conditioned upon each employee's future performance of services and was subject to a substantial risk of forfeiture. Tax is not incurred until a person has a vested right to receive benefits; here, vesting did not occur until a child became a degree candidate and incurred educational expenses while his or her parent was employed by the corporation. Once the child's right to receive a distribution from the plan became vested, the parent of the child could be taxed on the amount of the distribution. The company could deduct the same amount.

The Tax Court and appeals court have upheld the IRS position in similar cases.

Disability and Workers' Compensation

2.13 Sick Pay Is Taxable

Sick pay received from an employer is generally taxable as wages unless it qualifies as workers' compensation under the rules at *2.14*. Payments received under accident or health plans are generally tax free *(3.2)*, unless they constitute excess reimbursements, as discussed at *17.4*. Payments from your employer's plan for certain serious permanent injuries are tax free; *see 3.2*.

Disability pensions are discussed at *2.15*.

Sick pay received from your employer is subject to income tax withholding as if it were wages. Sick pay from a third party such as an insurance company is not subject to withholdings unless you request it on Form W-4S.

2.14 Workers' Compensation Is Tax Free

You do not pay tax on workers' compensation payments for job-related injuries or illness. However, your employer might continue paying your regular salary but require you to turn over your workers' compensation payments. Then you are taxed on the difference between what was paid to you and what you returned.

> **EXAMPLE**
>
> John Wright was injured while at work and was out of work for two months. His company continues to pay his weekly salary of $475. He also receives workers' compensation of $100 a week from the state, which is tax free. He gives the $100 back to his employer. The balance of $375 a week is considered taxable wages.

To qualify as tax-free workers' compensation, the payments must be made under the authority of a *law* (or regulation having the force of a law) that provides compensation for on-the-job injury or illness. Payments made under a labor agreement do *not* qualify as tax-free workers' compensation; *see* the Examples below.

 Caution

Job-Related Injury or Illness

Not all payments for job-related illness or injury qualify as tax-free workers' compensation. Unless the statute or regulation authorizing your disability payment restricts awards to on-the-job injury or illness, your payment is taxable. Even if your payments are in fact based upon job-related injury or illness, they are taxed if other individuals can receive payments from the plan for disabilities that are not work related; *see* Example 1 on the following page.

A retirement pension or annuity does *not* qualify for tax-free treatment if benefits are based on age, length of service, or prior plan contributions. Such benefits are taxable even if retirement was triggered by a work-related injury or sickness.

State law may impose a penalty for unreasonable delay in paying a worker's compensation award. If the penalty is considered to have the remedial purpose of facilitating the injured employee's return to work, the IRS may treat the amount as part of the original tax-free compensation award.

Court Decision

Is Sick Leave Tax-Free Workers' Compensation?

According to the Tax Court, sick leave may qualify as tax-free workers' compensation if it is paid under a specific workers' compensation statute or similar government regulation that authorizes the sick leave payment for job-related injuries or illness; *see* Examples 2, 4, and 5 on this page.

EXAMPLES

1. Kane, a federal district judge, suffered from sleep apnea, a condition characterized by a cessation of breathing during sleep, which was aggravated by the stress of his judicial work. He received a retirement disability payment of $65,135.

   A federal appeals court held that the payment was taxable because it was paid under a statute which did not specifically require that the payments be for work-related injuries. Here, the federal law under which the judge received his payments provided benefits for all permanent disabilities, whether or not job related.

2. A teacher, injured while working, received full salary during a two-year sick leave. She argued that the payments, made under board of education regulations, were similar to workers' compensation and thus tax free. The IRS disagreed; the regulations were not the same as a workers' compensation statute. The Tax Court supported the teacher. The payments were made because of job-related injuries and were authorized by regulations having the force of law.

3. A disabled New York City policeman argued that sick leave payments in 1978 under a union labor contract were tax-free workers' compensation because his disability was work related. However, the IRS, Tax Court, and an appeals court disagreed. The payments were made under a labor contract and not a workers' compensation statute or pursuant to government regulations. Furthermore, even if authorized by a statute or regulations, the officer's sick leave would be taxable since under the labor contract, officers received sick pay whether or not their injury or illness was work related.

   A change in New York City law now qualifies sick leave payments to firefighters and police officers for line-of-duty injuries as tax-free workers' compensation.

4. The IRS, relying on the court decision in Example 2, claimed that a police officer in Lynbrook, N.Y., was subject to tax on line-of-duty disability pay because the payment was under a labor agreement with the Police Benevolent Association (PBA). The Tax Court supported the police officer's claim that the payments were authorized by a specific New York State law requiring full salary for job-related police injuries. The PBA agreement did not affect the officer's rights to those state law payments. Lynbrook treated the case as a workers' compensation claim and in fact received reimbursement from the state workers' compensation board for the payments made to the officer.

5. A Los Angeles sheriff injured on the job retired on disability and, under the Los Angeles workers' compensation law, was allowed to elect sick pay in lieu of the regular workers' compensation amount because the sick pay was larger. The IRS argued that the sheriff had merely received taxable sick pay because he would have received the same amount as sick pay if his injuries had been suffered in a personal accident. However, the Tax Court allowed tax-free treatment. The sick leave was paid under a workers' compensation law that applied solely to work-related injuries. The fact that sick leave may also have been available to other employees under other laws does not mean that it may not be included as an option under a workers' compensation statute.

   The IRS announced that it does not agree with the Tax Court's decision allowing full tax-free treatment. According to the IRS, benefits up to the regular workers' compensation amount should be tax free but excess amounts should be taxed.

Effect of workers' compensation on Social Security. In figuring whether Social Security benefits are taxable *(34.2)*, workers' compensation that reduces Social Security or equivalent Railroad Retirement benefits is treated as a Social Security (or Railroad Retirement) benefit received during the year. Thus, the workers' compensation may be indirectly subject to tax as discussed at *34.2*.

2.15 Disability Pensions

Disability pensions financed by your employer are reported as wage income unless they are for severe permanent physical injuries that qualify for tax-free treatment under the rules at *3.2* or they are tax-free government payments as discussed in this section.

If you receive little or no Social Security and your other income is below a specified threshold, you may be eligible to claim a tax credit for disability payments received while you are under the age of 65 and permanently and totally disabled; *see 34.7.*

Taxable disability pensions are reported as wages until you reach the minimum retirement age under the employer's plan. After reaching minimum retirement age, payments are reported as a pension under the rules of *7.25.*

Federal government services. Certain disability pensions from the military or federal government agencies are tax free. Military disability benefits from the Veterans Administration are tax free, as are payments for combat and terrorist attack–related injuries. Other disability pensions for personal injuries or sickness resulting from active service in the armed forces are taxable if you joined the service after September 24, 1975.

Military disability payments are tax free if before September 25, 1975, you were entitled to military disability benefits or if on that date you were a member of the armed forces (or reserve unit) of the U.S. or any other country or were under a binding written commitment to become a member. A similar tax-free rule applies to disability pensions from the following government agencies if you were entitled to the payments before September 25, 1975, or were a member of the service (or committed to joining) on that date: The Foreign Service, Public Health Service, or National Oceanic and Atmospheric Administration. The exclusion for pre–September 25, 1975, service applies to disability pensions based upon percentage of disability. However, if a disability pension was based upon years of service, you do not pay tax on the amount that would be received based upon percentage of disability.

Veterans Administration benefits. Disability pensions from the Veterans Administration (now called the Department of Veterans Affairs) are tax free. Military retirees who receive disability benefits from other government sources are not taxed on amounts equal to the benefits they would be entitled to receive from the VA. If you retire from the military and are later given a retroactive award of VA disability benefits, retirement pay during the retroactive period is tax free (other than a lump-sum readjustment payment upon retirement) to the extent of the VA benefit.

Pension based on combat-related injuries. Tax-free treatment applies to payments for combat-related injury or sickness that is incurred as a result of any one of the following activities: (1) as a direct result of armed conflict; (2) while engaged in extra-hazardous service, even if not directly engaged in combat; (3) under conditions simulating war, including maneuvers or training; or (4) that is caused by an instrumentality of war, such as weapons.

Terrorist attacks or U.S. military actions. For tax years ending after September 10, 2001, tax-free treatment applies to disability payments received by any individual for injuries incurred as the direct result of a terrorist attack against the United States or its allies. The exclusion also applies to disability income received as a direct result of a military action involving U.S. Armed Forces in response to aggression against the United States or its allies. Under prior law, an exclusion was allowed only to U.S. government civilian employees injured in a terrorist attack outside the United States while performing official duties.

 Filing Tip

Military Disability Tax Free
Military disability benefits from the Veterans Administration are tax free.

 Law Alert

Terrorist Attacks
For tax years ending after September 10, 2001, tax-free treatment applies to disability payments resulting from terrorist attacks inside as well as outside the United States, and anyone, not just a U.S. government civilian employee, is eligible.

Stock Plans and Options

2.16 Stock Appreciation Rights (SARs)

SARs are a form of cash bonus tied to an increase in the price of employer stock. Each SAR entitles an employee to receive cash equal to the excess of the fair market value of one share on the date of exercise over the value on the date the SAR was granted.

> **EXAMPLE**
> When a stock is worth $30 a share, you get 100 SARs exercisable within five years. Two years later, when the stock price increases to $50 a share, you exercise the SAR and receive $2,000. You are taxed when you receive the cash.

Watch SAR Expiration Date

If the rights increase in value, keep a close watch on the expiration date. Do not let them expire before exercise. If you do, not only will you lose income but you will be taxed on income you never received. According to the IRS, an employee who does not exercise the SARs is taxed as if they have been exercised immediately before they expire. The IRS claims that an employee has constructive receipt of income immediately before they expire. At that time, the amount of gain realized from the SARs is fixed because the employee can no longer benefit from future appreciation in value.

Caution

Possible AMT Liability for ISO

If you exercise an incentive stock option and your rights in the acquired stock are transferrable and not subject to a substantial risk of forfeiture, you have to treat as an adjustment for alternative minimum tax purposes *(23.2)* the excess of the fair-market value of the stock when the option was exercised over the option price. Unless you sell the stock by the end of that year, you must report an AMT adjustment based on the value of the stock when the option was exercised, even if the value later declines substantially. You avoid the AMT adjustment if you sell the stock in the same year the option was exercised. If your rights in the stock are restricted in the year you exercise the option, the AMT adjustment applies for the year the restrictions are lifted. *See 23.2* for further details.

An employee may realize taxable income when he or she becomes entitled to the maximum SAR benefit allowed by the company plan. For example, in 1998, when company stock is worth $30, an employee is granted 100 SARs exercisable within five years. By exercising the SARs, the employee may receive cash equal to the appreciation up to $20 per share. If the stock appreciates to $50 per share in 2003, the employee realizes taxable income of $2,000 ($20 per share × 100) in 2003, even if he or she does not exercise the SARs. The reason is that once the stock value appreciates to $50, the maximum SAR benefit of $20 is realized.

Performance shares. The company promises to make an award of stock in the future, at no cost to you, if the company's earnings reach a set level. You are taxed on the receipt of stock (unless the stock is restricted, as discussed in *2.17*).

2.17 Stock Options

Employees receiving statutory stock options do not incur regular income tax liability either at the time the option is granted or when the option is exercised. However, the option spread is generally subject to AMT; *see 23.2.* Statutory options include incentive stock options (ISOs) and options under an employee stock purchase plan (ESPP). Receipt of a nonqualified stock option generally results in an immediate tax.

Incentive stock options (ISOs). A corporation may provide its employees with incentive stock options to acquire its stock (or the stock of its parent or subsidiaries). For regular income tax purposes, ISOs meeting tax law tests are not taxed when granted or exercised. Income or loss is not reported until you sell the stock acquired from exercising the ISO. The option must be exercisable within 10 years of the date it is granted and the option price must be at least equal to the fair market value of the stock when the option is granted. If the fair market value of stock for which ISOs may first be exercised in a particular year by an employee exceeds $100,000 (valued at date of grant), the excess is not considered a qualifying ISO. An ISO may be exercised by a former employee within three months of the termination of employment; if exercised after three months, income is realized under the rules for nonqualified options, discussed on the next page.

AMT consequences of exercising ISO. Although you do not realize taxable income for regular tax purposes when you exercise an ISO, you may incur a substantial liability for alternative minimum tax (AMT). *See* the Caution on the lower left and *23.2.*

Gain or loss on sale of ISO stock. If the stock acquired by the exercise of the ISO is held for more than one year after acquisition and more than two years after the ISO was granted, you have long-term capital gain or loss *(5.3)* on the sale, equal to the difference between the selling price of the stock and the option price you paid when you exercised the ISO.

If you sell *before* meeting the one-year and two-year holding period tests, a gain on the sale is generally treated as ordinary wage income to the extent of the option spread—the excess of the value of the stock when you exercised the ISO over the option price. Any gain in excess of the spread is reported as capital gain. In figuring the capital gain, cost basis for the stock is increased by the amount treated as wages. If the fair market value of the stock declines between the date the option was exercised and the date the stock is sold, the amount that must be treated as wages is generally reduced. The ordinary income (wages) is limited to the actual gain on the stock sale where the gain is less than the option spread at exercise. However, the reduction to ordinary income does *not* apply on a sale of the stock to a related person or if replacement shares are purchased within the wash-sale period *(30.6)* because the reduction applies only if a loss "would be" recognized if sustained (actual loss is not required for limitation to apply so long as a loss "would be" recognized).

If you have a loss on the sale of stock acquired by exercising an ISO, it is a capital loss and there is no ordinary wage income to report.

Employee stock purchase plans (ESPPs). These plans allow employees to buy their company's stock, usually at a discount. The plan must be nondiscriminatory and meet tax law tests on option terms. Options granted under qualified plans are not taxed until you sell the shares acquired from exercising the option.

If you sell the stock more than one year after exercising the option and also more than two years after the option was granted, gain on the sale is capital gain unless the option was granted at a discount. If at the time the option was granted the fair market value of the stock exceeded the option price, then when you sell the stock, gain is ordinary wage income to the extent of that discount. Any excess gain is long-term capital gain. A loss on the sale is long-term capital loss.

If you sell the acquired stock before meeting the one-year and two-year holding period tests, you must report as ordinary wage income the option spread—the excess of the value of the stock when you exercised the option over the option price. This amount must be reported as ordinary income even if it exceeds the gain on the sale (which would occur if the sale price were lower than the exercise price). Add the ordinary income amount to your cost basis for the stock. If the increased basis is less than the selling price, the difference is capital gain. You have a capital loss if the increased basis exceeds the selling price.

EXAMPLES

1. You were granted an incentive stock option (ISO) on March 5, 2000, to buy 1,000 shares of your employer company's stock at its then fair market value of $10 a share. You exercised the option on January 12, 2001, when the market price for the stock was $15 a share. You sold the stock on January 18, 2002, for $20 a share. Although you held the stock for more than one year, you did not sell more than two years after the date the option was granted. Therefore, part of your gain on the sale in 2002 is ordinary wage income. You have ordinary wage income of $5,000, equal to the option spread ($15,000 value on January 12, 2001, minus $10,000 option price) and $5,000 of long-term capital gain.

Selling price ($20 × 1,000 shares)	$20,000
Less: Cost of stock ($10 exercise price × 1,000 shares)	10,000
Gain	10,000
Less: Ordinary wage income	5,000
($15,000 value – $10,000 option price)	
Capital gain ($20,000 sales price – basis of $15,000	$5,000
($10,000 cost + $5,000 treated as wages))	

2. You are granted an option to buy 1,000 shares from your employer's ESPP for $20 a share at a time when the market price is $22 a share. You exercise the option 14 months later when the value of the stock is $23 a share. You sell the stock for $30 a share 18 months after exercising the option. You meet the one-year and two-year holding period tests but because the option was granted at a discount, part of the gain on the sale is treated as ordinary income.

Selling price ($30 × 1,000 shares)	$30,000
Less: Cost of stock ($20 × 1,000 shares)	20,000
Gain	10,000
Less: Ordinary wage income	2,000
($22,000 value at grant – $20,000 option price)	
Capital gain ($30,000 sales price – basis of $22,000	$8,000
($20,000 cost + $2,000 treated as wages)	

3. Same facts as in Example 2, except that you sold the stock only six months after you exercised the ESPP option. Since the one-year holding period test was not met, $3,000 of your $10,000 gain is taxed as ordinary wage income. The $3,000 ordinary income equals the option spread between the $23,000 value of the stock when you exercised the option and the $20,000 option price. You also have a $7,000 short-term capital gain: $30,000 sales price – $23,000 basis ($20,000 cost + $3,000 treated as wages).

Nonqualified stock options. Where a nonqualified option (technically called a "nonstatutory" option) has no ascertainable fair market value, which is almost certainly the case for options that are not actively traded on a public exchange, no income is realized on the receipt of the option. Income will not be realized until the year the option is exercised, assuming you are vested in the stock in the year you receive it. If the stock is *not* vested when you exercise the option, income is deferred until the vesting year, under the restricted property rules at *2.18.* In the year that you become vested in the stock, you must report as ordinary wage income the value of the stock (as of the vesting date), minus the amount you paid. If you receive vested stock when the option is exercised, you are taxed on the difference between the fair market value of the stock when you exercise the option and the option price. For example, in 2002, you exercise a nonqualified stock option to buy 1,000 shares of your employer's stock at $10 a share when the stock has a value of $30 a share. Your rights to the stock are vested when you buy it. When you exercise the option you are treated as receiving wages of $20,000, equal to the option spread ($30,000 value – $10,000 cost). This in-

 Caution

Tax Due on Option Exercise

Determine the amount of cash you will need to make the purchases and meet your tax liability before you exercise a nonqualified option and receive vested stock. If you receive vested stock when you exercise the option, you will realize wage income equal to the excess of the value of the stock over the option price. In addition to the cash to buy the stock, you will need cash to pay the tax on the wage income. The tax is due even if you plan to hold onto the stock before selling.

come is subject to withholding taxes that you will have to pay out-of-pocket at the time of exercise unless the withholding can be taken from regular cash wages. Your cost basis for the shares is increased by the ordinary income reported for exercising the option. If you hold the shares for more than one year after exercising the option and then sell them for $35,000 ($35 a share × 1,000 shares), you will have a $5,000 long-term capital gain ($35,000 – $30,000 increased basis).

If in a rare case a nonqualified stock option has an ascertainable fair market value, the value of the option less any amount you paid is taxable under the restricted property rules *(2.18)* as ordinary wage income in the first year that your right to the option is freely transferable or not subject to a substantial risk of forfeiture. A Section 83(b) election *(2.18)* may *not* be made for the nonqualified option. For other details and requirements, *see* IRS Regulation Section 1.83-7.

Nonqualified stock options may be granted in addition to or in place of incentive stock options. There are no restrictions on the amount of nonqualified stock options that may be granted.

When sale of stock is treated as grant of option. If company stock is purchased on the basis of the executive's promissory note and he or she is not personally liable, the company can recover only its stock in the event of default on the note. If the stock value drops, he or she may walk away from the deal with no personal risk. According to an IRS regulation, the deal may be viewed as an option arrangement. Application of the IRS regulation would give the executive ordinary taxable income when the stock is purchased if the value of the stock at the time of purchase exceeds the purchase price. For example, on July 3, 2000, a corporation sells 100 shares of its stock to an executive. The stock has a fair market value on that date of $25,000 and the executive executes a nonrecourse note secured by the stock in that amount, plus 8% annual interest. An annual payment of $5,000 of principal, plus interest, is required beginning the following year. In 2001, the executive collects the dividends, votes the stock, and pays the interest on the note but no principal. In 2002, when the stock has appreciated in value to $30,000, the executive pays off the note. Under the IRS regulation, the executive would realize ordinary income upon payment of the nonrecourse note to the extent of the difference between the amount paid ($25,000 in 2002) and the value of the stock ($30,000).

2.18 Restricted Stock

If in return for performing services you buy or receive company stock (or other property) subject to restrictions, special tax rules apply. Stock subject to restrictions is taxed as pay in the first year in which it is substantially vested, meaning that it is either transferable or not subject to a substantial risk of forfeiture. A risk of forfeiture exists where your rights are conditioned upon the future performance of substantial services. Generally, taxable income is the difference between the amount, if any, that you pay for the stock and its value at the time the risk of forfeiture is removed. The valuation at the time the forfeiture restrictions lapse is not reduced because of restrictions imposed on the right to sell the property. However, restrictions that will never lapse do affect valuation.

SEC restrictions on insider trading are considered a substantial risk of forfeiture, so that there is no tax on the receipt of stock subject to such restrictions. However, the SEC permits insiders to immediately resell stock acquired through exercise of an option granted at least six months earlier. As the stock acquired through such options is not subject to SEC restrictions, the executive is subject to immediate tax upon exercise of an option held for at least six months.

If the stock is subject to a restriction on transfer to comply with SEC pooling-of-interests accounting rules, the stock is considered to be subject to a substantial restriction.

Non-employees. The tax rules for restricted property are not restricted to employees. They also apply to independent contractors who are compensated for services with restricted stock or other property.

Election to include value of restricted stock in income when received (Section 83(b) election). Although restricted stock is generally not taxable until the year in which it is substantially vested, you may elect to be taxed in the year you receive it on the unrestricted value (as of the date the stock is received), less any payment you made. This election, called a Section 83(b) election, must be made by filing a statement with the IRS no later than 30 days after the date the stock is transferred to you. The election may not be revoked without the consent of the IRS.

Planning Reminder

Electing Immediate Tax on Restricted Stock

If you expect restricted stock to appreciate, consider making an election (Section 83(b) election) to be immediately taxed on the value of the restricted stock, minus your cost. If you make the election, any appreciation in value that has accrued since the election was made will not be taxable when the stock becomes substantially vested. Tax on appreciation will not be due until the stock is sold.

If you make the election, you are treated as an investor and later appreciation in value is not taxed as pay when your rights to the stock become vested. To figure capital gain or loss when you sell the stock, your cost basis for the stock is increased by the amount of income you reported as pay under the election. If you forfeit the stock after the election is made, a capital loss *(5.4)* is allowed for your cost minus any amount realized on the forfeiture.

EXAMPLES

1. In 2002, when your employer's stock has a market value of $100 a share, your employer allows you to buy 100 shares at $10 a share, or $1,000. Under the terms of your purchase, you must resell the stock to your employer at $10 a share if you leave your job within five years. Because your rights to the stock are subject to a substantial risk of forfeiture, you do not have to include any amount as income in 2002 when you buy it. Assume that in 2007, when the restrictions are lifted, the stock is selling for $200 a share. In 2007, you will have to report $19,000 as ordinary wage income ($20,000 unrestricted value – $1,000 you paid).

2. Same facts as in Example 1, except that within 30 days after you receive the stock, you file a Section 83(b) election with the IRS. With the election, you have wage income for 2002 of $9,000, the value of the stock when you received it ($10,000 for 100 shares) minus your cost ($1,000).

   A signed election statement must be filed with the IRS Service Center where you file your return no later than 30 days after the date you received the stock. The statement must include the following: your name, address, Social Security number, the year for which you are making the election, a description of the stock and the restrictions on the stock, the date you received the stock, the fair market value of the stock at receipt (ignoring restrictions unless they never lapse), your cost, if any, for the stock, and a statement that you have provided a copy of the statement to your employer.

   You will not have to report any income when the stock vests in 2007. If after vesting you sell the shares for $20,000, you will have a long-term capital gain of $10,000 ($20,000 – $10,000 increased basis ($1,000 cost plus $9,000 wage income from election)).

Chapter 3

Fringe Benefits

Employer-furnished fringe benefits are exempt from tax if the tests discussed in this chapter are met.

The most common tax-free benefits are accident and health plans, group-term life insurance plans, dependent care plans, education assistance plans, tuition reduction plans, adoption benefit plans, cafeteria plans, and plans providing employees with discounts, no-additional-cost services, or employer-subsidized meal facilities.

Employees of qualifying small employers who have medical coverage through a high-deductible plan may be able to set up a medical savings account (MSA) to pay for medical costs not covered by insurance; *see 3.1*.

Highly compensated individuals may be taxed on certain benefits from such plans if nondiscrimination rules are not met.

Key to Fringe Benefits

Fringe Benefit—	Tax Pointer—
Adoption benefits	Employer payments to a third party or reimbursements to you in 2002 for qualified adoption expenses are generally tax free up to a limit of $10,000. The exclusion is phased out if modified adjusted gross income is between $150,000 and $190,000; *see 3.5* for further details.
Athletic facilities	The fair market value of athletic facilities, such as gyms, swimming pools, golf courses, and tennis courts, is tax free if the facilities are on property owned or leased by the employer (not necessarily the main business premises) and substantially all of the use of the facilities is by employees, their spouses, and dependent children. Such facilities must be open to all employees on a nondiscriminatory basis in order for the company to deduct related expenses.
Child or dependent care plans	The value of day-care services provided or reimbursed by an employer under a written, nondiscriminatory plan is tax free up to a limit of $5,000, or $2,500 for married persons filing separately. Expenses are excludable if they would qualify for the dependent care credit; *see* Chapter 25. On your tax return, you must report employer-provided benefits to figure the tax-free exclusion. Tax-free employer benefits reduce eligibility for the dependent care tax credit; *see 3.4.*
De minimis *(minor)* fringe benefits	These are small benefits that are administratively impractical to tax, such as occasional supper money and taxi fares for overtime work, company parties or picnics, and occasional theater or sporting event tickets; *see 3.9.*
Discounts on company products and services	Services from your employer that are usually sold to customers are tax free if your employer does not incur additional costs in providing them to you; *see 3.15.* Merchandise discounts and other discounted services are also eligible for a tax-free exclusion; *see 3.16.*
Education plans	An up-to-$5,250 exclusion applies to employer-financed undergraduate and graduate courses.
Employee achievement awards	Achievement awards are taxable unless they qualify under special rules for length of service or safety achievement; *see 3.10.*
Group-term life insurance	Premiums paid by employers are not taxed if policy coverage is $50,000 or less; *see 3.3.*
Health and accident plan benefits	Premiums paid by an employer are tax free. Benefits under an employer plan are also generally tax free; *see 3.1* and *3.2.*
Interest-free or low-interest loans	Interest-free loans received from your employer may be taxed; *see 4.31.*
Retirement planning advice	Starting in 2002, retirement income planning advice and information may be provided tax free to employees (and their spouses) so long as the employer maintains a qualified plan. The exclusion does not apply to tax preparation, accounting, legal, or brokerage services.
Transportation benefits	Within limits, employer-provided parking benefits and transit passes are tax free; *see 3.7.*
Tuition reductions	Tuition reductions for courses below the graduate level are generally tax free. Graduate students who are teaching or research assistants are not taxed on tuition reduction unless the reduction is compensation for teaching services; *see 3.6.*
Working condition benefits	Benefits provided by your employer that would be deductible if you paid the expenses yourself are a tax-free working condition fringe benefit. Company cars are discussed at *3.7* and other working condition benefits at *3.8.*

Health, Accident, and Group Insurance and Death Benefits

3.1 Tax-Free Health and Accident Coverage Under Employer Plans

You are not taxed on *contributions* or *insurance premiums* your employer makes to a health, hospitalization, or accident plan to cover you, your spouse, or your dependents. If you are temporarily laid off and continue to receive health coverage, the employer's contributions during this layoff period are tax free. If you are retired, you do not pay tax on insurance paid by your former employer. Medical coverage provided to the family of a deceased employee is tax free since it is treated as a continuation of the employee's fringe-benefit package.

If your employer provides health and accident coverage to your live-in companion, the coverage is taxable to you where the companion is not recognized as a "spouse" under state law or "dependent" status is barred (even if support and household membership tests in Chapter 21 are met) because the relationship violates local law. Furthermore, under the 1996 Defense of Marriage Act, a gay or lesbian companion is not treated as a spouse for federal tax purposes.

If you are age 65 or older, Medicare premiums paid by your employer are not taxed. If you retire and have the option of receiving continued coverage under the medical plan or a lump-sum payment covering unused accumulated sick leave instead of coverage, the lump-sum amount is reported as income at the time you have the option to receive it. If you elect continued coverage, the amount reported as income may be deductible as medical insurance if you itemize deductions; *see 17.5*.

Health Reimbursement Arrangements (HRAs). Employer contributions to health reimbursement arrangements (HRAs) are not taxed to the employees. The contributions must be paid by the employer and not provided by salary reduction. As discussed at *3.2*, HRA contributions can be used to reimburse the medical costs of employees, their spouses, and their dependents, and unused expenses may be carried forward to later years.

Long-term care coverage. An employee is not taxed on employer-provided long-term care coverage that pays benefits in the event the employee becomes *chronically ill*, as defined at *17.15*. However, the coverage is taxable if provided through a cafeteria plan *(3.13)* and reimbursements of long-term care expenses may not be made through a flexible spending arrangement *(3.14)*.

Hiring spouse allows self-employed individual to obtain tax breaks. A self-employed person is not considered an "employee" and thus is generally not eligible for tax-free health coverage or reimbursements *(3.2)* of medical expenses. However, the benefit of a 100% deduction plus tax-free coverage and reimbursements can be obtained by a married self-employed person who hires his or her spouse and provides family coverage to the employee-spouse under an accident and health plan purchased in the name of the business. By covering the spouse, the employer-spouse can then obtain personal coverage under the plan as a member of the employee's family. As long as the employee-spouse is a bona fide employee, and not a self-employed co-owner of the business, the cost of the family's coverage is not taxed to the employee-spouse. Any reimbursements received by the employee-spouse for his or her medical expenses, or those of the employer-spouse or their dependents, are tax-free under the exclusion rules discussed at *3.2*. The employer-spouse can deduct 100% of the coverage costs, including reimbursements, as a business deduction on Schedule C; *see 40.6*.

Medical Savings Account Contributions for Employees of Small Employers Offering High-Deductible Plans

Self-employed individuals and employees of eligible small employers (*see* below) who have health insurance coverage under a high-deductible plan may set up a medical savings account (Archer MSA) that can be used to pay unreimbursed medical costs. The tax consequences for a self-employed individual are illustrated at *17.17*. If you are an eligible employee, your employer may make contributions to your Archer MSA that are tax free to you, subject to the limits discussed below. If the employer does not contribute, you may make deductible contributions up to the same limits; *see* Chapter 12 for claiming the deduction. An Archer MSA may be set up with an insurance company, bank, or any institution qualified to offer IRAs. Distributions from Archer MSAs are discussed at *3.2*.

The law authorizing Archer MSAs is scheduled to expire at the end of 2003.

Law Alert

Medicare MSA

If you are enrolled in Medicare, you may elect an MSA option. Contact your local Social Security office for details.

Filing Tip

Deducting Archer MSA Contributions

If you work for a qualifying small employer who has a high-deductible health plan, you may make deductible contributions to a medical savings account (Archer MSA) only if the employer does not contribute to your account for the year. Report your contributions on Form 8853, and claim the deduction directly from gross income on Line 27 of Form 1040. *See also 17.17.*

Archer MSA eligibility for employees. To be eligible for an Archer MSA, you must be under age 65 and work for a "small" employer, one that had an average of 50 or fewer employees during either of the two preceding years. You must be covered by a high-deductible health plan, which for 2002 must have a deductible of: (1) at least $1,650 and no more than $2,500 for individual coverage or (2) at least $3,300 and no more than $4,950 for family coverage.

The IRS has ruled that a high-deductible family plan may not set a lower deductible for individual family members. For example, a plan does not qualify in 2002 if it sets an overall annual family deductible of $3,300 but allows an individual who incurs expenses exceeding $1,650 to receive benefits.

The plan must limit out-of-pocket costs for covered expenses. For 2002, the out-of-pocket limit is $3,300 for single coverage and $6,050 for family coverage. Premiums are not subject to the limit.

Generally, you are not eligible for an Archer MSA if you have any other health insurance in addition to the high-deductible plan coverage, except for policies covering only disability, vision or dental care, long-term care, or accidental injuries, or plans that pay a flat amount during hospitalization.

Medicare + Choice Medical Savings Accounts (M+C MSAs). If you are eligible for Medicare benefits and have a high-deductible health plan that has been approved by Medicare, you may set up an M+C MSA at an approved financial institution. The Medicare program makes a tax-free contribution each year to your M+C MSA. Earnings in the account accumulate tax free. Medicare also pays the premium for your high-deductible health plan. The contributions and earnings in the M+C MSA may be withdrawn without tax to pay qualified medical costs not covered by Medicare.

Employer contribution limits. Your employer's contributions to your Archer MSA are tax free up to an annual limit of 65% of the plan deductible if you have individual coverage and 75% of the deductible for family coverage. The limit is reduced on a monthly basis if you are not covered for the entire year. For example, if for all of 2002 you were covered by a qualifying family coverage high-deductible plan with a $4,900 annual deductible, the maximum tax-free contribution is $3,675 (75% of $4,900). If you had coverage for only 10 months, the limit would be $3,062 ($^{10}/_{12} \times$ $3,675). All employer contributions to your Archer MSA are reported in Box 12 of Form W-2 (Code R). If the contributions exceed the tax-free limit, the excess is reported in Box 1 of Form W-2 as taxable wages.

If your employer makes any contributions to your account, you may not make any contributions for that year. In addition, if you and your spouse have family coverage under a high-deductible plan and your spouse's employer contributes to his or her Archer MSA, you cannot contribute to your Archer MSA. If your employer (or spouse's employer) does not contribute, you may make deductible contributions up to the above employer contribution limits. Your deduction is claimed on Line 27 of Form 1040. Contributions exceeding the annual limit are subject to a 6% penalty.

Self-employed also eligible. A self-employed person may make deductible contributions to an Archer MSA up to the employer contribution limits discussed above; *see* Chapter 17 for deduction details.

Access and Portability Rules for Group Health Plans

Generally, a group health plan may not bar eligibility to an employee and his or her dependents because of health status or medical history. A plan may exclude coverage for specified conditions or procedures, or limit such coverage, but only if there is no discrimination among similarly situated employees based on health-related factors. Employers are subject to daily penalties if they do not comply with the rules, but small employers with an average of no more than 50 employees in the preceding year are exempt.

Pre-existing conditions can bar coverage only in limited circumstances. Coverage may be denied for a condition that was diagnosed or treated within six months before enrollment. However, the exclusion cannot last more than 12 months, or 18 months for those who enroll late, and the 12-or-18-month period must be reduced by creditable coverage the employee had before enrollment in the new plan if there was no break in the prior coverage of more than 62 days. Coverage may not be denied to women pregnant on the enrollment date. Newborn children who are enrolled within 30 days of birth must be covered and if the parent changes jobs and enrolls in a new plan without a break in coverage of more than 62 days, the new plan may not exclude the child. A similar protective rule applies to adopted children under age 18 who are enrolled within 30 days of the adoption.

 *Court Decision*

COBRA Required Despite Other Coverage

The Supreme Court has held that an employer may not deny continuing care coverage to a former employee who on the date of election has coverage under his or her spouse's group health plan.

Caution

Cost of Continuing Coverage
If you leave your job and elect continuing health coverage, you may be charged a premium of 102% of the regular cost of similar coverage under the plan. If the COBRA coverage period is extended because you are disabled, you may be charged 150% of the regular premium during the extended period.

Continuing coverage for group health plans (COBRA coverage). Employers are subject to daily penalties unless they offer continuing group health and accident coverage to employees who leave the company and to spouses and dependent children who would lose coverage in the case of divorce or the death of the employee. The employer may charge the employee or beneficiary a premium of up to 102% of the regular premium imposed under the plan for the applicable (individual or family) coverage. The employer must wait at least 45 days after continuing coverage is elected to require payment of premiums.

Continuing coverage rules do not apply to small employers who in the previous calendar year had fewer than 20 employees on a typical day, or government agencies and churches. For other employers, continuing coverage must be offered in these situations:

1. An employee with coverage who voluntarily or involuntarily leaves the company—unless termination is for gross misconduct. Employees who would lose coverage because of a reduction in hours must also be offered continuing coverage. Continuing coverage must also be offered for the employee's spouse and dependent children who were covered before the employee's termination or reduction in hours. If accepted, the coverage must last for at least 18 months. Within this period, an employee who elects continuing coverage is protected against the possibility of a coverage gap if he or she joins a new company that limits group health coverage for pre-existing conditions; the old employer's continuing coverage must remain available.

   Extended coverage may apply to disabled individuals. The coverage period is extended from 18 months to 29 months for individuals who notify the plan administrator within 60 days of a determination under Title II or XVI of the Social Security Act that they are disabled. The coverage extension applies if the disability exists at any time during the first 60 days of continuing coverage. During the extended coverage period, the maximum premium that can be charged is increased from 102% to 150% of the applicable premium.

2. On the death of a covered employee, continuing coverage must be offered to the surviving spouse and dependent children who are beneficiaries under the plan on the day before the death. Coverage must be for at least 36 months.

3. If a covered employee obtains a divorce or legal separation, continuing coverage must be offered to the spouse and dependent children for at least 36 months.

4. If a covered employee becomes eligible for Medicare benefits, continuing coverage under the employer's plan must be offered to the employee's spouse and dependent children for at least 36 months.

5. If a dependent child becomes ineligible under the plan upon reaching a certain age, continuing coverage must be offered for at least 36 months.

6. If an employee with health coverage takes unpaid leave under the Family and Medical Leave Act of 1993 (FMLA) upon the birth or adoption of a child or to deal with a serious family illness, and the employee does not return to work following the leave, continuing coverage must be offered as of the last day of the leave. Continuing coverage must also be offered to the employee's spouse and dependent children if they would otherwise lose coverage.

Employers must provide written notice of the continuing coverage option. If one of the previously discussed qualifying events occurs, the eligible employees, spouses, and/or dependent children generally have 60 days to elect continuing coverage.

3.2 Payments From Employer Health and Accident Plans May Be Tax Free

There are two general categories of tax-free benefits paid from employer-financed health and accident plans: (1) reimbursements of medical expenses, and (2) payments for permanent physical injuries. In addition, payments from a long-term care insurance contract or Archer MSA may be tax free. Details on these categories are below.

Benefits that are not within one of the tax-free categories are *fully taxable* if: (1) your employer paid all the premiums, and (2) you were not required to report the premiums as taxable income. If you and your employer each paid part of the premiums and you were not taxed on your employer's payment, the portion of the benefits allocable to the employer's contribution is taxed to you. You are not taxed on benefits to the extent that you paid the premiums with after-tax contributions. Examples of figuring the taxable portion of the benefits are at *17.4*.

Tax-Free Reimbursements for Medical Expenses

Reimbursements of medical expenses *(17.2)* for yourself, your spouse, or any dependent are tax free. Payment does not have to come directly to you to be tax free; it may go directly to your medical care providers. Reimbursements made under a qualifying health reimbursement arrangement (HRA) qualify for tax-free treatment; *see* below.

Tax-free treatment applies only for reimbursed expenses, not amounts you would have received anyway, such as sick leave that is not dependent on actual medical expenses. Medical insurance premiums financed with pre-tax salary-reduction contributions are treated as your employer's payment, not yours, so a reimbursement from the employer is taxable. Only after-tax payments may be reimbursed tax free.

Reimbursements for cosmetic surgery do *not* qualify for tax-free treatment, unless the surgery is for disfigurement related to congenital deformity, disease, or accidental injury.

Reimbursements for your *dependents'* medical expenses are tax free, even if you may not claim them as personal exemptions because their gross income exceeds the annual ceiling for dependents ($3,000 for 2002) or they file a joint return. Furthermore, if you are divorced and your children have health coverage under your plan, reimbursements of their expenses are not taxable to you, even if your ex-spouse claims them as dependents; *see 21.11*.

A qualifying dependent does *not* include a live-in mate where the relationship violates local law.

If the reimbursement is for medical expenses you deducted in a previous year, the reimbursement may be taxable. *See 17.4* for the rules on reimbursements of deducted medical expenses.

If you receive payments from more than one policy and the total exceeds your actual medical expenses, the excess is taxable if your employer paid the entire premium; *see* the Examples in *17.4*.

Health Insurance Reimbursements (HRAs). During 2002, the IRS gave its approval to health reimbursement arrangements (HRAs). Employer contributions are used to reimburse out-of-pocket medical expenses of employees, their spouses, and their dependents. Former employees including retired employees, and spouses and dependents of deceased employees can be covered. Self-employed individuals are not eligible.

Employees are not taxed on HRA reimbursements for qualifying medical expenses (eligible for itemized deduction; *see 17.2*), but long-term care services generally cannot be reimbursed. For contributions and reimbursements *(see 3.1)* to be tax free, employees must not receive cash or any benefit (taxable or nontaxable) from an HRA other than reimbursement for medical expenses. Contributions not used for reimbursements in a coverage year can be carried forward to a subsequent year. Nondiscrimination rules apply to self-insured HRAs. For further HRA details, *see* IRS Notice 2002-45 and Revenue Ruling 2002-41.

Self-employed health plan for spouse. As discussed in *3.1*, if a self-employed person hires his or her spouse and provides family coverage under a health plan purchased in the name of the business, the employee-spouse may be reimbursed tax-free for medical expenses incurred by both spouses and their dependent children.

Executives taxed in discriminatory self-insured medical reimbursement plans. Although reimbursements from an employer plan for medical expenses of an employee and his or her spouse and dependents are generally tax free, this exclusion does not apply to certain highly compensated employees and stockholders if the plan is self-insured and it discriminates on their behalf. A plan is self-insured if reimbursement is not provided by an unrelated insurance company. If coverage is provided by an unrelated insurer, these discrimination rules do not apply. If a self-insured plan is deemed discriminatory, rank-and-file employees are not affected; only highly compensated employees are subject to tax.

Highly compensated participants subject to these rules include employees owning more than 10% of the employer's stock, the highest paid 25% of all employees (other than employees who do not have to be covered under the law), and the five highest paid officers.

If highly compensated employees are entitled to reimbursement for expenses not available to other plan participants, any such reimbursements are taxable to them. For example, if only the five highest paid officers are entitled to dental benefits, any dental reimbursements they receive are taxable. However, routine physical exams may be provided to highly compensated employees (but not their dependents) on a discriminatory basis. This exception does not apply to testing for, or treatment of, a specific complaint.

Caution

Reimbursed Cosmetic Surgery

An employer's reimbursement of expenses for cosmetic surgery is taxable unless the employee had surgery to correct disfigurement from an accident, disease, or congenital deformity.

IRS Alert

Health Reimbursement Arrangements (HRAs)

The IRS has given employers the go-ahead to set up health reimbursement arrangements. Employer contributions to an HRA can be used to reimburse the out-of-pocket medical costs of employees, their spouses, and dependents. Contributions to and reimbursements from a qualifying HRA are not taxed to the employees. Unused amounts can be carried forward for reimbursement use in later years.

If highly compensated participants are entitled to a higher reimbursement limit than other participants, any excess reimbursement over the lower limit is taxable to the highly compensated participant. For example, if highly compensated employees are entitled to reimbursements up to $5,000 while all others have a $1,000 limit, a highly compensated employee who receives a $4,000 reimbursement must report $3,000 ($4,000 received minus the $1,000 lower limit) as income.

A separate nondiscrimination test applies to plan *eligibility*. The eligibility test requires that the plan benefit: (1) 70% or more of all employees or (2) 80% or more of employees eligible to participate, provided that at least 70% of all employees are eligible. A plan not meeting either test is considered discriminatory unless proven otherwise. In applying these tests, employees may be excluded if they have less than three years of service, are under age 25, do part-time or seasonal work, or are covered by a union collective bargaining agreement. A fraction of the benefits received by a highly compensated individual from a nonqualifying plan is taxable. The fraction equals the total reimbursements to highly compensated participants divided by total plan reimbursements; benefits available only to highly compensated employees are disregarded. For example, assume that a plan failing the eligibility tests pays total reimbursements of $50,000, of which $30,000 is to highly compensated participants. A highly compensated executive who is reimbursed $4,500 for medical expenses must include $2,700 in income:

$$\frac{30,000}{50,000} \times 4,500 = 2,700$$

Taxable reimbursements are reported in the year during which the applicable plan year ends. For example, in early 2003 you are reimbursed for a 2002 expense from a calendar-year plan. If under plan provisions the expenses are allocated to the 2002 plan year, the taxable amount should be reported as 2002 income. If the plan does not specify the plan year to which the reimbursement relates, the reimbursement is attributed to the plan year in which payment is made.

Tax-Free Payments for Permanent Physical Injuries

Payments from an employer plan are tax free if they are for the permanent loss of part of the body, permanent loss of use of part of the body, or for permanent disfigurement of yourself, your spouse, or a dependent. To be tax free, the payments must be based on the kind of injury and have no relation to the length of time you are out of work or prior years of service. If the employer's plan does not specifically allocate benefits according to the nature of the injury, the benefits are taxable even if an employee is in fact permanently disabled.

> **EXAMPLE**
> After he loses a foot in an accident, Marc Jones receives $50,000 as specified in his employer's plan. The payment is tax free as it does not depend on how long Jones is out from work.

An appeals court held that severe hypertension does not involve loss of a bodily part or function and thus does not qualify for the exclusion.

Disability payments from profit-sharing plan. The Tax Court has held that a profit-sharing plan may provide benefits that qualify for the exclusion for permanent disfigurement or permanent loss of bodily function. The plan must clearly state that its purpose is to provide qualifying tax-free benefits, and a specific payment schedule must be provided for different types of injuries. Without such provisions, payments from the plan are treated as taxable retirement distributions.

Long-Term Care or Archer MSA Payments

Tax-free benefits from qualifying long-term care policy. Payments from a qualifying long-term care policy (meeting the tests in *17.15*) are tax free if they reimburse long-term care expenses. If payments are received in 2002 under a *per diem* plan that provides a flat daily amount, the tax-free limit is $210 per day unless you can show that you had actual expenses for long-term services equal to part or all of the excess over the $210 limit. *See 17.15* for further details.

Tax-free benefits from Archer MSA. If you work for a small-business employer and have a qualifying Archer MSA *(3.1)*, earnings accumulate in the account tax free. Withdrawals are tax free if used to pay deductible medical costs for you, your spouse, or dependents. Withdrawals used for any other purpose are taxable and a taxable distribution before age 65 or becoming disabled is also subject to a 15% penalty. *See 17.17* for further details.

Permanent Physical Injuries
An employer's payment for permanent disfigurement or permanent loss of bodily function is tax free if the payment is based solely on the nature of the injury. Whether or not you qualify for this exclusion, you may deduct as an itemized deduction any unreimbursed medical expense you have in connection with these injuries subject to the 7.5% adjusted gross income floor; *see 17.1* for details.

3.3   Group-Term Life Insurance Premiums

You are not taxed on your employer's payments of premiums on a policy of up to $50,000 on your life. You are taxed only on the cost of premiums for coverage of over $50,000 as determined by the IRS rates shown in the table below. On Form W-2 your employer should include the taxable amount as wages in Box 1 and separately label the amount in Box 12 with Code C. You may not avoid tax by assigning the policy to another person.

If two or more employers provide you with group-term insurance coverage, you get only one $50,000 exclusion. You must figure the taxable cost for coverage over $50,000 by using the IRS rates below.

Regardless of the amount of the policy, you are not taxed if, for your entire tax year, the beneficiary of the policy is a tax-exempt charitable organization or your employer.

Your payments reduce taxable amount. If you pay part of the cost of the insurance, your payment reduces dollar for dollar the amount includible as pay on Form W-2.

Retirees. If you retired before 1984 at normal retirement age or on disability and are still covered by a company group-term life insurance policy, you are not taxed on premium payments made by your employer even if coverage is over $50,000. If you retired after 1983 because of disability and remain covered by your company's plan, you are not taxed even if coverage exceeds $50,000. Furthermore, if you retired after 1983 and are not disabled, you may qualify for tax-free coverage over $50,000 if the following tests are met:

1. The insurance is provided under a plan existing on January 1, 1984, or under a comparable successor plan;
2. You were employed during 1983 by the company having the plan, or a predecessor employer; and
3. You were age 55 or over on January 1, 1984.

However, even if the three tests are met, you may be taxed under the rule below for discriminatory plans if you retired after 1986 and were a key employee.

Key employees taxed under discriminatory plans. The $50,000 exclusion is not available to key employees unless the group plan meets nondiscrimination tests for eligibility and benefits. For 2002, key employees include those who during the year were: (1) more-than-5% owners; (2) more-than-1% owners earning over $150,000; and (3) officers with compensation over $130,000. If the plan discriminates, a key employee's taxable benefit is based on the larger of (1) the actual cost of coverage or (2) the amount for coverage using the IRS rate table below.

The nondiscrimination rules also apply to former employees who were key employees when they separated from service. The discrimination tests are applied separately with respect to active and former employees.

Group-term life insurance for dependents. Employer-paid coverage for your spouse or dependents is a tax-free *de minimis* fringe benefit *(3.9)* if the policy is $2,000 or less. For coverage over $2,000, you are taxed on the excess of the cost (determined under the IRS table below) over your after-tax payments for the insurance, if any.

Filing Instruction

Uncollected Social Security and Medicare

You must pay with Form 1040 (Line 61) your share of Social Security and Medicare taxes on group-term life insurance over $50,000. The taxable amounts are shown in Box 12 of Form W-2, with Codes M and N.

Taxable Monthly Premiums for Group-Term Insurance Coverage Over $50,000	
Age—*	Monthly cost for each $1,000 of coverage over $50,000—
Under 25	$0.05
25–29	0.06
30–34	0.08
35–39	0.09
40–44	0.10
45–49	0.15
50–54	0.23
55–59	0.43
60–64	0.66
65–69	1.27
70 and over	2.06

* Age is determined at end of year.

Permanent life insurance. If your employer pays premiums on your behalf for permanent non-forfeitable life insurance, you report as taxable wages the cost of the benefit, less any amount you paid. A permanent benefit is an economic value that extends beyond one year and includes paid-up insurance or cash surrender value, but does not include, for example, the right to convert or continue life insurance coverage after group coverage is terminated. Where permanent benefits are combined with term insurance, the permanent benefits are taxed under formulas found in IRS regulations.

Dependent Care, Adoption Benefits, and Educational Assistance

Caution

Figuring Tax-Free Exclusion for Employer-Provided Dependent Care

You cannot assume that your employer-provided dependent care benefit is completely tax free merely because your employer has not included any part of it in Box 1 of Form W-2 as taxable wages. Although up to $5,000 of benefits are generally tax free, the tax-free amount is reduced where you or your spouse earn less than $5,000 or where you file separately from your spouse. You must show the amount of your qualifying dependent care expenses and figure the tax-free exclusion on Form 2441 if you file Form 1040, or on Schedule 2 of Form 1040A.

3.4   Dependent Care Assistance

The value of qualifying day-care services provided by your employer under a written, nondiscriminatory plan is generally not taxable up to a limit of $5,000, or $2,500 if you are filing separately. The same tax-free limits apply if you make pre-tax salary deferrals to a flexible spending account for reimbursing dependent care expenses *(3.14)*. However, you may not exclude from income more than your earned income. If you are married and your spouse earns less than you do, your tax-free benefit is limited to his or her earned income. If your spouse does not work, all of your benefits are taxable unless he or she is a full-time student or is disabled. If a full-time student or disabled, your spouse is treated as earning $200 a month if your dependent care expenses are for one dependent, or $400 a month if the expenses are for two or more dependents.

Expenses are excludable from income only if they would qualify for the dependent care credit; *see* Chapter 25. If you are being reimbursed by your employer, the exclusion is not allowed if dependent care is provided by a relative who is your dependent (or your spouse's dependent) or by your child under the age of 19. You must give your employer a record of the care provider's name, address, and tax identification number. The identifying information also must be listed on your return.

Reporting employer benefits on your return. Your employer will show the total amount of your dependent care benefits in Box 10 of your Form W-2. Any benefits over $5,000 will also be included as taxable wages in Box 1 of Form W-2 and as Social Security wages (Box 3) and Medicare wages (Box 5).

If you file Form 1040, you must report the benefits on Part III of Form 2441. If you file Form 1040A, you report the employer benefits on Schedule 2. On these forms, you determine both the tax-free and taxable (if any) portions of the employer-provided benefits. If any part is taxable, that amount must be included on Line 7 of your return as wages and labeled "DCB."

Follow IRS instructions for identifying the care provider (employer, babysitter, etc.) on Form 2441 or on Schedule 2 of Form 1040A.

The tax-free portion of employer benefits reduces eligibility for the dependent care credit; see *Chapter 25.*

3.5   Adoption Benefits

If your employer pays or reimburses you in 2002 for qualifying adoption expenses under a written, nondiscriminatory plan, up to $10,000 may be tax free (*see* below). Employer-provided adoption assistance may be for any child under age 18, or a person physically or mentally incapable of self-care. If you have other qualifying adoption expenses, you may also be able to claim a tax credit up to a separate $10,000 limit; both the exclusion and the credit may be claimed for the same adoption if they are not for the same expenses. The exclusion and the credit are subject to similar limitations, including a phaseout based on income. *See* Chapter 25 for a full discussion of the credit.

The $10,000 exclusion limit is not an annual limit; it applies to each effort to adopt an eligible child even if the effort lasts longer than one year. The exclusion applies to adoption fees, attorney fees, court costs, travel expenses, and other expenses directly related to a legal adoption. Expenses for adopting your spouse's child and the costs of a surrogate-parenting arrangement do *not* qualify. Starting in 2003, the full $10,000 exclusion limit is available for the adoption of a "special needs" child even if actual adoption expenses are less than $10,000. If the adoption extends over more than one year, the exclusion is limited to actual expenses in the year or years before the adoption is finalized. In the year the adoption is finalized, the portion of the $10,000 exclusion that has not previously been used is available even if the total expenses for all years are under $10,000. A "special needs" designation is made when a state determines that adoption assistance is required to place a child (U.S. citizen or resident) with adoptive parents because of special factors, such as the child's physical condition.

If you are adopting a child who is not a U.S. citizen or resident when the adoption effort begins, the exclusion is available only in the year the adoption becomes final. For example, if in 2002 your employer pays for expenses of adopting a foreign child but the adoption has not become final by the end of the year, you must report the employer's payment as wage income for 2002. You will claim the exclusion on Form 8839 in the year the adoption is final.

Reporting employer benefits and claiming the exclusion on your 2002 return. You must file Form 8839 to report your employer's payments and to figure the tax-free and taxable portions of the benefits. The employer's payments will be included in Box 12 of Form W-2 (Code T). This total includes pre-tax salary reduction contributions that you made to a cafeteria plan *(3.13)* to cover such expenses.

If you are married, you generally must file a joint return to exclude the benefits as income. However, if you are legally separated or if you lived apart from your spouse for the last six months of the year, the exclusion may be available on a separate return; *see* Form 8839 for details.

On 2002 tax returns, the allowable exclusion is phased out if your modified adjusted gross income (MAGI) is between $150,000 and $190,000 (including the employer's adoption assistance and adding back certain tax-free income from foreign sources). Figure the tax-free amount on Form 8839. If your modified adjusted income for 2002 is $190,000 or more, employer-paid adoption expenses are fully taxable.

3.6 Education Assistance Plans

If your employer pays for job-related courses, the payment is tax free to you provided that the courses do not satisfy the employer's minimum education standards and do not qualify you for a new profession. If these tests are met, the employer's education assistance is a tax-free working condition fringe benefit *(3.8)*.

Even if not job related, your employer's payment for courses is tax free up to $5,250, provided the assistance is under a qualifying Section 127 plan meeting nondiscriminatory tests. Starting in 2002, graduate courses qualify for the exclusion as well as undergraduate courses.

Tuition reductions. Employees and retired employees of educational institutions, their spouses, and their dependent children are not taxed on tuition reductions for *undergraduate* courses provided the reduction is not payment for teaching or other services. However, an exclusion is allowed starting in 2002 for tuition reductions under the National Health Services Corps Scholarship Program and the Armed Forces Health Professions Scholarship Program despite the recipient's service obligation. Widows or widowers of deceased employees or of former employees also qualify. Officers and highly paid employees may claim the exclusion only if the employer plan does not discriminate on their behalf. The exclusion applies to tuition for undergraduate education at any educational institution, not only the employer's school.

Graduate students who are teaching or research assistants at an educational institution are not taxed on tuition reductions for courses at that school if the tuition reduction is in addition to regular pay for the teaching or research services or the reduction is provided under the National Health Services Corps Scholarship Program or the Armed Forces Health Professions Scholarship Program. The graduate student exclusion for tuition reductions applies only to teaching and research assistants, and not to faculty or other staff members (or their spouses and dependents) who take graduate courses and also do research for or teach at the school. However, if the graduate courses are work related, a tuition reduction for faculty and staff may qualify as a tax-free working condition fringe benefit *(3.8)*.

 Filing Tip

Claiming Credit and Exclusion
If you paid adoption expenses in 2002 that were not reimbursed by your employer, and the adoption was final in 2002, you may be able to claim the adoption credit; *see* Chapter 25.

 Law Alert

Graduate Courses
Starting in 2002, your employer's payment of graduate school expenses qualifies for the up-to-$5,250 exclusion.

Company Cars, Working Condition and *De Minimis* Benefits, and Employee Achievement Awards

3.7 Company Cars, Parking, and Transit Passes

The costs of commuting to a regular job site are not deductible *(20.2)*, but employees who receive transit passes or travel to work on an employer-financed van get a tax break by not having to pay tax on some or all of such benefits. Where a company car is provided, the value of personal use is generally taxable, as discussed below.

Company cars. The use of a company car is tax free under the working condition fringe benefit rule *(3.8)*, provided you use the car for business. If you use the car for personal driving, you may be taxed on the value of such personal use. Your company has the responsibility of calculating taxable income based on IRS tables that specify the value of various priced cars. For certain cars, a flat mileage allowance may be used to measure personal use. You are also required to keep for your employer a mileage log or similar record to substantiate your business use. Your employer should tell you what type of records are required.

Regardless of personal use, you are not subject to tax for a company vehicle that the IRS considers to be of limited personal value. These are ambulances or hearses; flatbed trucks; dump, garbage, or refrigerated trucks; one-passenger delivery trucks (including trucks with folding jump seats); tractors, combines, and other farm equipment; or forklifts. Also not taxable is personal use of school buses, passenger buses (seating at least 20), and moving vans where such personal use is restricted; and police or fire vehicles, or an unmarked law enforcement vehicle, where personal use is authorized by a government agency.

Demonstration cars. The value of a demonstration car used by a full-time auto salesperson is tax free as a working condition fringe benefit if the use of the car facilitates job performance and if there are substantial personal-use restrictions, including a prohibition on use by family members and for vacation trips. Furthermore, mileage outside of normal working hours must be limited and personal driving must generally be restricted to a 75-mile radius around the dealer's sales office.

Chauffeur services. If chauffeur services are provided for both business and personal purposes, you must report as income the value of the personal services. For example, if the full value of the chauffeur services is $30,000 and 30% of the chauffeur's workday is spent driving on personal trips, then $9,000 is taxable (30% of $30,000) and $21,000 is tax free.

If an employer provides a bodyguard-chauffeur for business security reasons, the entire value of the chauffeur services is considered a tax-free working condition fringe benefit if: (1) the automobile is specially equipped for security and (2) the bodyguard is trained in evasive driving techniques and is provided as part of an overall 24-hour-a-day security program. If the value of the bodyguard-chauffeur services is tax free, the employee is still taxable on the value of using the vehicle for commuting or other personal travel.

How your employer reports taxable automobile benefits. Social Security and Medicare tax must be withheld. Income tax withholding is not required, but your employer may choose to withhold income tax. If income tax is *not* withheld, you must be notified of this fact so that you may consider the taxable benefits when determining whether to make estimated tax installments; *see* Chapter 27. Whether or not withholdings are taken, the taxable value of the benefits is entered on your Form W-2 in Box 14 or on a separate Form W-2 for fringe benefits.

A special IRS rule allows your employer to include 100% of the lease value of using the car on Form W-2, even if you used the car primarily for business. Your employer must specifically indicate on Form W-2 (Box 14) or on a separate statement if 100% of the lease value has been included as income on your Form W-2. If it has, you should compute a deduction on Form 2106 for the business-use value of the car. However, this deduction, plus any unreimbursed car operating expenses, may be claimed only as a miscellaneous itemized deduction on Schedule A subject to the 2% AGI floor; *see 19.1.*

Company planes. Under rules similar to those for company cars, employees who use a company airplane for personal trips are taxable on the value of the flights, as determined by the employer using IRS tables.

Planning Reminder

Year-End Benefits
Your employer may decide to treat fringe benefits provided during the last two months of the calendar year as if they were paid during the following year. If this election is made for a company car in 2002, only the value of personal use from January through October is taxable in 2002; personal use in November and December is taxable in 2003. If your employer elects this special year-end rule, you should be notified near the end of the year or when you receive Form W-2.

Qualified Transportation Benefits

Your employer may provide you with transportation benefits that are tax free within certain limits. There are two categories of qualified benefits: (1) transit passes and commuter transportation in a van, bus, or similar highway vehicle are considered together, and (2) parking.

Transit passes and commuter transportation are subject to a *combined* tax-free limit of $100 a month in 2002. The tax-free exclusion for qualified parking in 2002 is $185 a month. You may receive benefits from each category so long as the applicable monthly limit is not exceeded. If the benefits exceed the monthly limit, the excess is treated as wages subject to income tax, Social Security, and Medicare tax.

The benefits may be provided through a salary-reduction arrangement. An irrevocable salary-reduction election may be made prospectively for a monthly amount of transportation benefits. The salary reduction for any month may not exceed the total limit for both categories, which for 2002 was $285, $100 for transit passes and commuter vehicles, plus $185 for parking. Unused salary reductions may be carried over to later months and from year to year.

Cash reimbursements of qualified transportation benefits are generally tax free if provided under a bona fide reimbursement arrangement. However, for transit passes, vouchers, not reimbursements, are the preferred method. A cash reimbursement for a transit pass is taxable if vouchers (or similar items) are readily available to the employer for distribution to employees. "Ready availability" is determined under tests in IRS regulations. Cash advances for either category of benefits are taxable.

Additional details on the two categories of qualified transportation benefits are in the following paragraphs.

Employer-provided transit passes and van pooling. For regular employees, up to $100 a month is tax free in 2002 for the combined value of employer-provided transit passes plus commuting on an employer's van or bus. For example, if in 2002 the monthly value of a transit pass was $125, $25 per month was treated as taxable wages. If the value of benefits was less than $100 in any month, the unused exclusion cannot be carried over to later months. For years after 2002, the $100 monthly exclusion limit may be increased for inflation.

Qualifying transit passes include tokens, fare cards, or vouchers for mass transit or private transportation businesses using highway vehicles seating at least six passengers.

Qualifying van or bus pool vehicles must seat at least six passengers and be used at least 80% of the time for employee commuting; on average, the number of employees must be at least half the seating capacity.

The exclusion applies only to regular employees. For partners, more than 2% S corporation shareholders, and independent contractors who are provided transit passes, the IRS allows up to $21 per month as a tax-free *de minimis* benefit. If the monthly value exceeds $21, the full value is taxable and not just the excess over $21.

Parking provided by employer. For regular employees, the value of employer-provided parking spots or subsidized parking is tax free in 2002 up to a limit of $185 per month. Parking must be on or near the employer's premises, at a mass transit facility such as a train station or car pooling center. The value of parking benefits exceeding $185 per month is taxable in 2002. For years after 2002, the $185 monthly cap may be adjusted for inflation.

The tax will generally apply to employees working in major urban business districts where parking is costly, or in suburban areas where commercial lots are available.

According to the IRS, parking benefits are to be valued according to the regular commercial price for parking at the same or nearby locations. For example, if an employer in a rural or suburban location provides free parking for employees and there are no commercial parking lots in the area, the employee parking is tax free. Where free parking is available to both business customers and employees, the employee parking is considered to have "zero" value unless the employee has a *reserved* parking space that is closer to the business entrance than the spaces allotted to customers.

If the value of the right of access to a parking space exceeds $185 in a month, an employee will be taxed on the excess for 2002 even if he or she actually uses the space for only a few days during the month.

If the employee pays a reduced monthly price for parking in 2002, there is a taxable benefit for that month only if the price paid plus the $185 exclusion is less than the value of the parking.

 Planning Reminder

Transportation Benefits

If your employer offers you the choice of receiving parking, transit pass, or van pooling benefits instead of cash salary as part of a "cafeteria" plan *(3.13)* and you elect the benefits rather than the cash, you are not taxed, provided the value does not exceed the monthly tax-free limit.

 Law Alert

Transit Passes and Van Pooling

For 2002, the combined monthly tax-free limit for transit passes and van pooling increased to $100 per month (from $65 per month in 2001).

Commuter parking benefits for self-employed partners or more than 2% S corporation share-holders do not qualify for an exclusion and are fully taxable. However, parking benefits provided by the employer while the employee is away from the regular office, such as on one-day business trips to other company locations, are generally treated as tax-free working condition fringe benefits *(3.8)* or *de minimis* benefits *(3.9)*. Parking benefits provided to independent contractors are also generally tax free *de minimis* benefits.

3.8 Working Condition Fringe Benefits

An employer-provided benefit that would be deductible by you if you paid for it yourself *(19.3)* is a tax-free working condition fringe benefit. Under IRS regulations, such benefits include:

Company car or plane. The value of a company car or plane is tax free to the extent that you use it for business; *see 3.7* for more on company cars.

Employer-paid business subscriptions or reimbursed membership dues in professional associations.

Product testing. This is a limited exclusion for employees who test and evaluate company manufactured goods away from company premises.

Employer-provided education assistance. Employer-paid undergraduate and graduate courses may be a tax-free working condition fringe benefit if the courses maintain or improve job skills but are not needed to meet your employer's minimum educational requirements and do not prepare you for a new profession.

Job-placement assistance. According to the IRS, job placement services are tax free so long as they are geared to helping the employees find jobs in the same line of work and the employees do not have an option to take cash instead of the benefits. The employer must also have a business purpose for providing such assistance, such as maintaining employee morale.

For tax-free treatment, there is no nondiscrimination requirement; different types of job placement assistance may be offered, or no assistance at all, in the case of discharged employees with readily transferable skills. Tax-free benefits include the value of counseling on interviewing skills and resume preparation. Executives may be given secretarial support and the use of a private office during the job search.

Job placement benefits received as part of a severance pay arrangement are taxable to the extent that cash could have been elected. An offsetting deduction can be claimed only as a miscellaneous itemized deduction subject to the 2% of adjusted gross income floor *(19.3)*.

3.9 *De Minimis* Fringe Benefits

Small benefits that would be administratively impractical to tax are considered tax-free *de minimis* (minor) fringe benefits. Examples are personal use of company copying machines, company parties, or tickets for the theater or sporting events. Other *de minimis* benefits include:

Company eating facility. The value of meals received by employees on workdays at a subsidized eating facility is a tax-free *de minimis* fringe benefit if the facility is located on or near the business premises and the annual revenue from meal charges equals or exceeds the facility's direct operating costs. Revenue is treated as equal to operating costs for meals that are tax-free to employees under the employer convenience test discussed at *3.11*.

Highly compensated employees or owners with special access to executive dining rooms may not exclude the value of their meals as a *de minimis* fringe benefit; however, the meals may be tax free under the rules in *3.11* if meals must be taken on company premises for business reasons.

Commuting under unsafe circumstances. If you are asked to work outside your normal working hours and due to unsafe conditions your employer provides transportation such as taxi fare, the first $1.50 per one-way commute is taxable but the excess over $1.50 is a tax-free *de minimis* benefit. This exclusion is not available to certain highly compensated employees and officers, corporate directors, or owners of 1% or more of the company.

Even when working their regular shift, hourly employees who are not considered highly compensated are taxed on only $1.50 per one-way commute if their employer pays for car service or taxi fare because walking or taking public transportation to or from work would be unsafe. The excess value of the transportation over $1.50 is tax free. These rules can apply to day-shift employees who work overtime as well as night-shift employees working regular hours so long as transportation is provided because of unsafe conditions.

Planning Reminder

Occasional Overtime Meal Money or Cab Fare

If you work overtime and occasionally receive meal money or cab fare home, the amount is tax free. The IRS has not provided a numerical standard for determining when payments are "occasional."

3.10 Employee Achievement Awards

Achievement awards are taxable unless they meet special rules for awards of tangible personal property (such as a watch, television, or golf clubs) given to you in recognition of length of service or safety achievement. Cash awards, gift certificates, and similar items are taxable.

As a general rule, if your employer is allowed to deduct the cost of a tangible personal property award, you are not taxed. The employer's deduction limit, and therefore the excludable limit for you, is $400 for awards from nonqualified plans and $1,600 for awards from qualified plans or from a combination of qualified and nonqualified plans. If your employer's deduction is less than the item's cost, you are taxed on the greater of: (1) the difference between the cost and your employer's deduction, but no more than the award's fair market value; or (2) the excess of the item's fair market value over your employer's deduction. Deduction tests for achievement awards are discussed at *20.25*. Your employer must tell you if the award qualifies for full or partial tax-free treatment.

An award will not be treated as a tax-free safety achievement award if employee safety achievement awards (other than those of *de minimis* value) were granted during the year to more than 10% of employees (not counting managers, administrators, clerical employees, or other professional employees). An award made to a manager, administrator, clerical employee, or other professional employee for safety achievement does not qualify for tax-free treatment.

Tax-free treatment also does not apply when you receive an award for length of service during the first five years of employment or when you previously received such awards during the last five years, unless the prior award qualified as a *de minimis* fringe benefit.

Caution

Underpriced Award Items

If the value of an achievement award item is disproportionately high compared to the employer's cost, the IRS may conclude that the award is disguised compensation, in which case the entire value would be taxable.

Meals and Lodging

3.11 Employer-Furnished Meals or Lodging

The value of employer-furnished *meals* is not taxable if furnished on your employer's business premises for the employer's convenience. The value of *lodging* is not taxable if, as a condition of your employment, you must accept the lodging on the employer's business premises for the employer's convenience.

Business premises test. The IRS generally defines business premises as the place of employment, such as a company cafeteria in a factory for a cook or an employer's home for a household employee. The Tax Court has a more liberal view, extending the area of business premises beyond the actual place of business in such cases as these:

- A house provided a hotel manager, although located across the street from the hotel. The IRS has agreed to the decision.
- A house provided a motel manager, two blocks from the motel. However, a court of appeals reversed the decision and held in the IRS's favor.
- A rented hotel suite that is used daily by executives for a luncheon conference.

Convenience of employer test. The employer convenience test requires proof that an employer provides the free meals or lodging for a business purpose other than providing extra pay. In the case of meals, the employer convenience test is deemed to be satisfied for *all* meals provided on employer premises if a qualifying business purpose is shown for more than 50% of the meals. If meals and lodging are described in a contract or state statute as extra pay, this does not bar tax-free treatment provided they are *also* furnished for other substantial, noncompensatory business reasons; for example, you are required to be on call 24 hours a day, or there are inadequate eating facilities near the business premises.

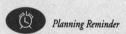

Planning Reminder

Meal Exclusion

You may be able to avoid tax on meals that you receive on your employer's premises even if your meals do not satisfy the employer convenience test. If more than half of the employees to whom meals are furnished on the employer's business premises are furnished the meals for the employer's convenience, *all* of the on-premises meals are treated as being furnished for the employer's convenience.

EXAMPLES

1. A Las Vegas casino operator provided free cafeteria meals to employees, who were required to remain on casino premises during their entire shift. A federal appeals court (Ninth Circuit) held that the casino's "stay-on-premises" requirement constituted a legitimate business reason for the meals and thus all of the employee meals were tax free under the employer convenience test. The court refused to second guess the casino's business decision that a "stay-on-premises" policy was necessary for security and logistics reasons. Once that policy was adopted, the casino employees had no choice but to eat on the premises. The IRS responded to the decision by announcing that it would not challenge "employer convenience" treatment in similar cases where employees are precluded from obtaining a meal off-premises within a normal meal period.

Court Decision

House One Block Away

Two federal courts held that a school superin-tendent received tax-free lodging where the home was one block away from the school and separated by a row of other houses. This met the business premises test. The IRS disagrees with the result and says that it will continue to litigate similar cases arising outside the Eighth Circuit in which the case arose. The Eighth Circuit includes the states of Arkansas, Iowa, Minnesota, Missouri, Nebraska, and North and South Dakota.

2. A waitress who works from 7 a.m. to 4 p.m. is furnished two meals a day without charge. Her employer encourages her to have her breakfast at the restaurant before working, but she is required to have her lunch there. The value of her breakfast and lunch is not taxable under IRS regulations because it is furnished during her work period or imme-diately before or after the period. But say she is also allowed to have free meals on her days off and a free supper on the days she works. The value of these meals is taxable; they are not furnished during or immediately before or after her work period.
3. A hospital maintains a cafeteria on its premises where all of its employees may eat during their working hours. No charge is made for these meals. The hospital furnishes meals to have the employees available for emergencies. The employees are not re-quired to eat there. Since the hospital furnishes the meals in order to have employees available for emergency call during meal periods, the meals are not income to any of the hospital employees who obtain their meals at the hospital cafeteria.
4. To assure bank teller service during the busy lunch period, a bank limits tellers to 30 minutes for lunch and provides them with free meals in a cafeteria on the premises so they can eat within this time period. The value of the meals is tax free.

Meal charges. Your company may charge for meals on company premises and give you an op-tion to accept or decline the meals. However, by law, the IRS must disregard the charge and option factors in determining whether meals that you buy are furnished for noncompensatory business reasons. If such business reasons exist, the convenience-of-employer test is satisfied. If such reasons do not exist, the value of the meals may be tax free as a *de minimis* benefit *(3.9)*; otherwise, the value of the meal subsidy provided by the employer is taxable.

Where your employer provides meals on business premises at a fixed charge that is subtracted from your pay whether you accept the meals or not, the amount of the charge is excluded from your taxable pay. If the meal is provided for the employer's convenience, as in the previous Examples, the value of the meals received is also tax free. If it is not provided for the employer's convenience, the value is taxable whether it exceeds or is less than the amount charged.

Lodging must be condition of employment. This test requires evidence that the lodg-ing is necessary for you to perform your job properly, as where you are required to be available for duty at all times. The IRS may question the claim that you are required to be on 24-hour duty. For example, at one college, rent-free lodgings were provided to teaching and administra-tive staff members, maintenance workers, dormitory parents who supervised and resided with students, and an evening nurse. The IRS ruled that only the lodgings provided to the dorm par-ents and the nurse met the tax-free lodging tests because for the convenience of the college, they had to be available after regular school hours to respond to emergencies.

If you are given the choice of free lodging at your place of employment or a cash allowance, the lodging is not considered to be a condition of employment, and its value is taxable.

If the lodging qualifies as tax free, so does the value of employer-paid utilities such as heat, electric-ity, gas, water, sewerage, and other utilities. Where these services are furnished by the employer and their value is deducted from your salary, the amount deducted is excluded from taxable wages on Form W-2. But if you pay for the utilities yourself, you may not exclude their cost from your income.

Caution

Housing as Job Requirement

If housing is provided to some employees with a certain job and not others, the IRS may hold that the lodging is not a condition of employ-ment. For example, the IRS taxed medical resi-dents on the value of hospital lodging where other residents lived in their own apartments.

EXAMPLE

Tyrone Jones is employed at a construction project at a remote job site. His pay is $800 a week. Because there are no accessible places near the site for food and lodging, the em-ployer furnishes meals and lodging for which it charges $240 a week, which is taken out of Jones's pay. Jones reports only the net amount he receives—$560 a week. The value of the meals and lodging is a tax-free benefit.

Groceries. An employer may furnish unprepared food, such as groceries, rather than prepared meals. Courts are divided on whether the value of the groceries is excludable from income. One court allowed an exclusion for the value of nonfood items, such as napkins and soap—as well as for groceries—furnished to a doctor who ate at his home on the hospital grounds so that he would be available for emergencies.

Cash allowances. A cash allowance for meals and lodging is taxable.

Are Your Board and Lodging Tax Free?

Yes—	No—
Hotel executives, managers, housekeepers, and auditors who are required to live at the hotel.	You have a choice of accepting cash or getting the meals or lodging. For example, under a union contract you get meals, but you may refuse to take them and get an automatic pay increase.
Domestics, farm laborers, fishermen, canners, seamen, servicemen, building superintendents, and hospital and sanitarium employees who are required to have meals and lodging on employer premises.	A state hospital employee is given a choice. He or she may live at the institution rent free or live elsewhere and get extra pay each month. Whether he or she stays at the institution or lives outside, the extra pay is included in his or her income.
Restaurant and other food service employees who have meals furnished during or immediately before or after working hours.	A waitress, on her days off, is allowed to eat free meals at the restaurant where she works.
Employees who must be available during meal periods for emergencies.	
Employees who, because of the nature of the business, must be given short meal periods.	
Workers who must use company-supplied facilities in remote areas.	
Park employees who voluntarily live in rent-free apartments provided by a park department in order to protect the park from vandalism.	
Your employer gives you a cash allowance for your meals or lodgings.	

Caution

Partners Are Not Employees

The IRS does not consider partners or self-employed persons as employees and so does not allow them to exclude the value of partnership-provided meals and lodging.

Faculty lodging. Teachers and other employees (and their spouses and dependents) of an educational institution, including a state university system or academic health center, do not have to pay tax on the value of school-provided lodging if they pay a minimal rent. The lodging must be on or near the campus. The minimal required rent is the smaller of: (1) 5% of the appraised value of the lodging; or (2) the average rental paid for comparable school housing by persons who are neither employees nor students. Appraised value must be determined by an independent appraiser and the appraisal must be reviewed annually.

For purposes of the 5% minimum rent rule, academic health centers include medical teaching hospitals and medical research organizations with regular faculties and curricula in basic and clinical medical science and research.

EXAMPLE

Carol Eng, a professor, pays annual rent of $6,000 for university housing appraised at $100,000. The average rent for comparable university housing paid by non-employees and non-students is $7,000. She does not have to pay any tax on the housing since her rental payments exceed 5% of the appraised housing value (5% of $100,000, or $5,000). If her rent was $4,000, she would have to report income of $1,000 ($5,000 minimum required rent – $4,000).

Peace Corps and VISTA volunteers. Peace Corps volunteers working overseas may exclude subsistence allowances from income under a specific code provision. The law does not provide a similar exclusion for the small living expense allowances received by VISTA volunteers.

3.12 Minister's Rental or Housing Allowance

A duly ordained minister pays no tax on the rental value of a home provided as part of his or her pay. If a minister is provided with an allowance rather than a home itself, the allowance is generally tax free if used to pay rent, to make a down payment to buy a house, to pay mortgage installments, or for utilities, interest, tax, and repair expenses of the house. However, a 2002 law limits the allowance exclusion to the fair rental value of the home; *see* below. A rabbi or cantor is treated the same as a minister for purposes of the allowance or in-kind housing exclusion.

Mortgage Interest and Taxes

If you itemize deductions on Schedule A (Form 1040), deduct payments for qualifying home mortgage interest *(15.1)* and real estate taxes *(16.6)* on your home even if you use a tax-free housing allowance to finance the payments.

The church or local congregation must officially designate the part of the minister's compensation that is a rental or housing allowance. To qualify for tax-free treatment, the designation must be made in advance of the payments. Official action may be shown by an employment contract, minutes, a resolution, or a budget allowance.

New law limits housing allowance to rental value but constitutional challenge remains. The IRS argued in one case (the *Warren* case) that a minister's housing allowance was taxable to the extent that it exceeded the rental value of his home. Nearly all of the minister's compensation, over $263,000 for a three-year period, had been designated by his church as a housing allowance. The annual rental value of the home was $58,000–$59,000 a year. The Tax Court held that the annual tax-free amount was not limited to the rental value of the home. A Court majority allowed a full exclusion for amounts used to pay the costs of the mortgage, real estate taxes and utilities, insurance, furnishings, and repairs. Three dissenting judges agreed with the IRS that the exclusion should be limited to rental value. When the IRS appealed to the Ninth Circuit Court of Appeals, the appeals court questioned the constitutionality of the allowance on Establishment of Religion grounds, although the IRS had not raised the constitutional issue. However, the IRS agreed to drop its appeal after Congress enacted the Clergy Housing Allowance Clarification Act of 2002, which was signed into law on May 20, 2002.

The law effectively sides with the IRS by limiting the exclusion to the fair rental value of the minister's home, including furnishings and appurtenances such as a garage, plus the cost of utilities. The new law applies to allowances for 2002, and also to allowances claimed on pre-2002 returns filed after April 16, 2002.

Who qualifies for tax-free allowance? Tax-free treatment is allowed to ordained ministers, rabbis, and cantors who receive housing allowances as part of their compensation for ministerial duties. Retired ministers qualify if their allowance is furnished in recognition of past services.

The IRS has allowed the tax-free exclusion to ministers working as teachers or administrators for a parochial school, college, or theological seminary which is an integral part of a church organization. A traveling evangelist was allowed to exclude rental allowances from out-of-town churches to maintain his permanent home. Church officers who are not ordained, such as a "minister" of music (music director) or "minister" of education (Sunday School director), do not qualify.

The IRS has generally barred an exclusion to ordained ministers working as executives of nonreligious organizations even where services or religious functions are performed as part of the job. The Tax Court has focused on the duties performed. A minister employed as a chaplain by a municipal police department under church supervision was allowed a housing exclusion, but the exclusion was denied to a minister-administrator of an old-age home that was not under the authority of a church and a rabbi who worked for a religious organization as director of inter-religious affairs.

Allowance subject to self-employment tax. Although parsonage allowances are not taxable income, they are reported as self-employment income for Social Security purposes; *see* Chapter 45. If you do not receive a cash allowance, report the rental value of the parsonage as self-employment income. Rental value is usually equal to what you would pay for similar quarters in your locality. Also include as self-employment income the value of house furnishings, utilities, appurtenances supplied—such as a garage—and the value of meals furnished that meet the rules at *3.11*.

Cafeteria Plans and Flexible Spending Arrangements

3.13 Cafeteria Plans Provide Choice of Benefits

Estimating FSA Contributions

Because of the "use-it-or-lose-it" rule for FSA contributions, make a conservative estimate of your expenses when you make your election. This is particularly true for medical expenses, which are generally difficult to project in advance.

"Cafeteria plans" is a nickname for plans that give an employee a choice of selecting either cash or at least one qualifying nontaxable benefit. You are not taxed when you elect qualifying nontaxable benefits, although cash could have been chosen instead. A cafeteria plan may offer tax-free benefits such as group health insurance or life insurance coverage, long-term disability coverage, dependent care or adoption assistance, medical expense reimbursements, or parking benefits. Long-term care insurance may *not* be offered through a cafeteria plan under current law.

Employees may be offered a premium-only plan (POP), which allows them to purchase group health insurance coverage or life insurance on a pre-tax basis using salary-reduction contributions.

Under a flexible spending arrangement (FSA), employees may be allowed to make tax-free salary-reduction contributions to a medical or dependent care reimbursement plan; *see 3.14*.

A qualified cafeteria plan must be written and not discriminate in favor of highly compensated employees and stockholders. If the plan provides for health benefits, a special rule applies to determine whether the plan is discriminatory. If a plan is held to be discriminatory, the highly compensated participants are taxed to the extent they could have elected cash. Furthermore, if key employees *(3.3)* receive more than 25% of the "tax-free" benefits under the plan, they are taxed on the benefits.

3.14 Flexible Spending Arrangements

A flexible spending arrangement (FSA) allows employees to get reimbursed for medical or dependent care expenses from an account they set up with pre-tax dollars. Under a typical FSA, you agree to a salary reduction that is deducted from each paycheck and deposited in a separate account. The salary-reduction contributions are not included in your taxable wages reported on Form W-2. As expenses are incurred, you are reimbursed from the account.

Funds from a *health* FSA may be used to reimburse you for expenses that you could claim as a medical expense deduction *(17.2)* such as the annual deductible under your employer's regular health plan, co-payments you must make to physicians or for prescriptions, and any other expenses that your health plan does not cover. These may include eye examinations, eyeglasses, routine physicals, and orthodontia work for you and your dependents. However, a health FSA may *not* be used to pay for health insurance premiums, including premiums for coverage under a plan of your spouse or dependent. Also, expenses for long-term care services *cannot* be reimbursed under a health FSA.

The tax advantage of an FSA is that your salary-reduction contributions are not subject to federal income tax or Social Security taxes, allowing your medical or dependent care expenses to be paid with pre-tax rather than after-tax income. The salary deferrals are also exempt from state and local taxes except in New Jersey and Pennsylvania; check with the administrator of your employer's plan.

In the case of a health FSA, paying medical expenses with pre-tax dollars allows you to avoid the 7.5% adjusted gross income (AGI) floor *(17.1)* that limits itemized deductions for medical costs.

However, to get these tax advantages, you must assume some risk. Under a "use-it-or-lose-it" rule, if your out-of-pocket expenses for the year are less than your contributions, the balance is forfeited, as discussed below.

FSA election to contribute generally irrevocable. The IRS has imposed restrictions on FSAs that make them unattractive for many employees. An election to set up an FSA for a given year must be made before the start of that year. You elect how much you want to contribute during the coming year and that amount will be withheld from your pay in monthly installments.

Once the election for a particular year takes effect, you may not discontinue contributions to your account or increase or decrease a coverage election unless there is a change in family or work status that qualifies under IRS regulations.

Use-it-or-lose-it rule. Only expenses incurred during the plan year may be reimbursed, and a "use-it-or-lose-it" rule applies: any unused account balance at the end of the plan year is forfeited. Unused amounts may not be refunded to you or carried over to the next year. There is a grace period, generally until April 15 of the following year, to submit reimbursement claims for expenses incurred during the previous year.

Although there are some differences in the reimbursement rules for health-care and dependent care FSAs, as discussed below, the "use-it-or-lose-it" feature applies to both.

Health-care FSA. At any time during the year, you may receive reimbursements up to your designated limit, even though your payments into the FSA account up to that point may add up to less. For example, if you elect to make salary-reduction contributions of $100 per month to a health-care FSA and you incur $500 of qualifying medical expenses in January, you may get the full $500 reimbursement even though you have paid only $100 into the plan. Your employer may not require you to accelerate contributions to match reimbursement claims.

You may *not* receive tax-free reimbursements for cosmetic surgery expenses unless the surgery is necessary to correct a deformity existing since birth or resulting from a disease or from injury caused by an accident. Nonqualifying reimbursements are taxable.

Employees on medical or family leave. Employees who take unpaid leave under the Family and Medical Leave Act (FMLA) to deal with medical emergencies or care for a newborn child may either continue or revoke their coverage during FMLA leave. If the coverage continues, the maximum reimbursement selected by such an employee must be available at all times during the leave period. If

Filing Instruction

Tax-Free Dependent Care Reimbursements

Whether all or only part of your dependent care FSA reimbursements are tax free is figured on Part III of Form 2441 if you file Form 1040. If you file Form 1040A, the calculation is made on Part III of Schedule 2.

Filing Instruction

Dependent Care Reimbursements Affect Credit

Reimbursements received tax free from your dependent care FSA reduce the expense base for figuring the dependent care credit; *see* Chapter 25.

the coverage is terminated, the employee must be reinstated under the FSA after returning from the leave, but no reimbursement claims may be made for expenses incurred during the leave.

Dependent care FSA. You may contribute to a dependent care FSA if you expect to have expenses qualifying for the dependent care tax credit discussed in Chapter 25, but if you contribute to a dependent care FSA, *any tax-free reimbursement from the account reduces the expenses eligible for the credit; see 25.7.* If you are married, both you and your spouse must work in order for you to receive tax-free reimbursements from an FSA, unless your spouse is disabled or a full-time student; *see 3.4.*

The maximum tax-free reimbursement under the FSA is $5,000, but if either you or your spouse earns less than $5,000, the tax-free limit is the lesser earnings. If your spouse's employer offers a dependent care FSA, total tax-free reimbursements for both of you are limited to $5,000. Furthermore, if you are considered a highly compensated employee, your employer may have to lower your contribution ceiling below $5,000 to comply with nondiscrimination rules.

Unlike health FSAs, an employer may limit reimbursements from a dependent care FSA to your account balance. For example, if you contribute $400 a month to the FSA and in January you pay $1,500 to a day-care center for your child, your employer may reimburse you $400 a month as contributions are made to your account.

Free or Low-Cost Company Products or Services

Caution

Highly Compensated Employees

Highly compensated employees can receive tax-free company services only if the same benefits are available to other employees on a nondiscriminatory basis. For 2002, highly compensated employees include employees owning more than a 5% interest in 2002 or 2001, and employees who in 2001 had compensation over $90,000. Employers have the option of including only the top-paid 20% in the over-$90,000 category. The $90,000 compensation threshold may be increased for 2003.

Line of Business Rule

The line of business limitation discussed at *3.15* for no-additional-cost services also applies to qualified employee discounts. Thus, if a company operates an airline and a hotel, employees who work for the airline may generally not receive tax-free hotel room discounts. However, if a special election was made by the company, employees may receive tax-free benefits from any line of business in existence before 1984.

3.15 Company Services Provided at No Additional Cost

Employees are not taxed on the receipt of services usually sold by their employer to customers where the employer does not incur additional costs in providing them to the employees. Examples are free or low-cost flights provided by an airline to its employees; free or discount lodging for employees of a hotel; and telephone service provided to employees of telephone companies. These tax-free fringes also may be provided to the employee's spouse and dependent children; retired employees, including employees retired on disability; and widows or widowers of deceased or retired employees. Tax-free treatment also applies to free or discount flights provided to parents of airline employees. Benefits provided by another company under a reciprocal arrangement, such as standby tickets on another airline, may also qualify as tax free.

The employer must have excess service capacity to provide the service and not forego potential revenue from regular customers. For example, airline employees who receive free reserved seating on company planes must pay tax on the benefit because the airline is foregoing potential revenue by reserving seating that could otherwise be sold.

Line of business limitations. If a company has two lines of business, such as an airline and a hotel, an employee of the airline may not receive tax-free benefits provided by the hotel. However, there are exceptions. An employee who provides services to both business lines may receive benefits from both business lines. Benefits from more than one line in existence before 1984 may also be available under a special election made by the company for 1985 and later years. Your employer should notify you of this tax benefit.

3.16 Discounts on Company Products or Services

The value of discounts on company products is a tax-free benefit if the discount does not exceed the employer's gross profit percentage. For example, if a company's profit percentage is 40%, the maximum tax-free employee discount for merchandise is 40% of the regular selling price. If you received a 50% discount, then 10% of the price charged customers would be taxable income. The employer has a choice of methods for figuring profit percentage.

Discounts on services that are not tax free under *3.15* for no-additional-cost services qualify for an exclusion, limited to 20% of the selling price charged customers. Discounts above 20% are taxable. An insurance policy is treated as a service. Thus, insurance company employees are not taxed on a discount of up to 20% of the policy's price.

Some company products do not qualify for the exclusion. Discounts on real estate and investment property such as securities, commodities, currency, or bullion are taxable. Interest-free or low-interest loans given by banks or other financial institutions to employees are not excludable. Such loans are subject to tax under the rules discussed at *4.31*.

Highly compensated employees are subject to the nondiscrimination rules discussed at *3.15* for no-additional-cost services.

Chapter 4

Dividend and Interest Income

Dividends and interest that are paid to you in 2002 are reported by the payer to the IRS on Forms 1099.

You will receive copies of:

- Forms 1099-DIV, for dividends
- Forms 1099-INT, for interest
- Forms 1099-OID, for original issue discount

Report the amounts shown on the Forms 1099 on your tax return. The IRS uses the Forms 1099 to check the income you report. If you fail to report income reported on Forms 1099, you will receive a statement asking for an explanation and a bill for the tax deficiency. If you receive a Form 1099 that you believe is incorrect, contact the payer for a corrected form.

Do not attach your copies of Forms 1099 to your return. Keep them with a copy of your tax return.

OMB No. 1545-0074 Page **2**

Name(s) shown on Form 1040. Do not enter name and social security number if shown on other side. | Your social security number

Enrique and Noelle Ballesteros | 0X1 00 XXZZ

Schedule B—Interest and Ordinary Dividends

Attachment Sequence No. **08**

Part I Interest

(See page B-1 and the instructions for Form 1040, line 8a.)

1 List name of payer. If any interest is from a seller-financed mortgage and the buyer used the property as a personal residence, see page B-1 and list this interest first. Also, show that buyer's social security number and address ▶

	Amount
Local Bank	410
National Bank	1,000
Municipal Bonds	390
Total	1,800
less: tax exempt interest	(390)

Note. If you received a Form 1099-INT, Form 1099-OID, or substitute statement from a brokerage firm, list the firm's name as the payer and enter the total interest shown on that form.

2 Add the amounts on line 1	2	1,410
3 Excludable interest on series EE and I U.S. savings bonds issued after 1989 from Form 8815, line 14. You **must** attach Form 8815	3	- 0 -
4 Subtract line 3 from line 2. Enter the result here and on Form 1040, line 8a ▶	4	1,410

Note. If line 4 is over $400, you must complete Part III.

Part II Ordinary Dividends

(See page B-1 and the instructions for Form 1040, line 9.)

5 List name of payer. Include only ordinary dividends. If you received any capital gain distributions, see the instructions for Form 1040, line 13 ▶

	Amount
Car Company	200
Drug Company	250
City Electric	275
Very Mutual Fund	500

Note. If you received a Form 1099-DIV or substitute statement from a brokerage firm, list the firm's name as the payer and enter the ordinary dividends shown on that form.

6 Add the amounts on line 5. Enter the total here and on Form 1040, line 9 . ▶	6	1,225

Note. If line 6 is over $400, you must complete Part III.

Part III Foreign Accounts and Trusts

(See page B-2.)

You must complete this part if you **(a)** had over $400 of taxable interest or ordinary dividends; **(b)** had a foreign account; or **(c)** received a distribution from, or were a grantor of, or a transferor to, a foreign trust.

	Yes	No
7a At any time during 2002, did you have an interest in or a signature or other authority over a financial account in a foreign country, such as a bank account, securities account, or other financial account? See page B-2 for exceptions and filing requirements for Form TD F 90-22.1		X
b If "Yes," enter the name of the foreign country ▶		
8 During 2002, did you receive a distribution from, or were you the grantor of, or transferor to, a foreign trust? If "Yes," you may have to file Form 3520. See page B-2		X

For Paperwork Reduction Act Notice, see Form 1040 instructions. | Schedule B (Form 1040) 2002

Key to Dividend Reporting

Type of Dividend Payment—	How and Where To Report—
Cash dividends	Dividends paid out of a corporation's earnings and profits are taxable. The corporation will report taxable dividends to you on Form 1099-DIV (or an equivalent statement). On Form 1040, report ordinary dividends on Line 9; Schedule B must be filed where the total exceeds $400. If you file Form 1040A, report ordinary dividends on Line 9, and if the total exceeds $400, complete Part II of Schedule 1. Dividends may not be reported on Form 1040EZ.
Dividends on accounts in credit unions, cooperative banks, savings and loan associations, mutual savings banks, and building and loan associations	Distributions from these financial institutions are called "dividends" but are actually interest and are reported to you on Form 1099-INT.
Life insurance policy dividends	Dividends on individual life insurance policies are actually a refund of your premiums and are not taxed unless they exceed the total premiums paid.
Money-market mutual-fund dividends	Dividends paid by a money-market mutual fund are reported on Form 1099-DIV. Report ordinary dividends on Line 9 of Form 1040, and include them on Schedule B if the total exceeds $400. On Form 1040A, report ordinary dividends on Line 9, and fill out Part II of Schedule 1 if the total exceeds $400. Do not confuse money-market funds managed by mutual funds with bank money-market accounts. Bank money-market accounts pay interest reported on Form 1099-INT, not dividends.
Mutual-fund distributions	Mutual funds may pay several kinds of distributions. On Form 1099-DIV, the fund will report ordinary dividends in Box 1, including net short-term capital gains distributions. Long-term capital gain distributions are reported in Box 2a of Form 1099-DIV. Nontaxable distributions are listed in Box 3. Form 1099-DIV for 2002 will include dividends declared in October, November, or December of 2002, even if not actually paid to you until January 2003. How to report these dividends on your return is detailed in *4.3* and *32.5*.
Nominee distribution—joint accounts	If you receive dividends on stock held as a nominee for someone else, or you receive a Form 1099-DIV that includes dividends belonging to another person, such as a joint owner of the account, you are considered to be a "nominee recipient." If the other owner is someone other than your spouse, you should file a separate Form 1099-DIV showing you as the payer and the other owner as the recipient of the allocable income. Give the owner a copy of Form 1099-DIV by January 31, 2003, so the dividends can be reported on his or her 2002 return. File the Form 1099-DIV, together with a Form 1096 ("Transmittal of Information Return"), with the IRS by February 28, 2003; the deadline is March 31, 2003, if filing electronically. On your Schedule B (Form 1040) or Schedule I (Form 1040A), you list on Line 5 the ordinary dividends reported to you on Form 1099-DIV. Several lines above Line 6, subtract the nominee distribution (the amount allocable to the other owner) from the total dividends. Thus, the nominee distribution is not included in the taxable dividends shown on Line 6, of Schedule B or Schedule I.
Return of capital distributions	A distribution that is not paid out of earnings is a nontaxable return of capital, that is, a partial payback of your investment. The company will report the distribution on Form 1099-DIV as a nontaxable distribution. You must reduce the cost basis of your stock by the nontaxable distribution. If your basis is reduced to zero by a return of capital distributions, any further distributions are taxable as capital gains, which you report on Schedule D of Form 1040. Form 1040A or Form 1040EZ may not be used.
Stock dividends and stock splits	If you own common stock and receive additional shares of the same company as a dividend, the dividend is generally not taxed. A dividend is taxed where you had the option to receive cash instead of stock, or if the stock is of another corporation. Preferred shareholders are generally taxed on stock dividends. Taxable stock dividends are discussed at *4.7* and *4.8*. Your corporation will determine whether stock dividends are taxable and report the taxable amount on Form 1099-DIV. If you receive additional shares as part of a stock split, the receipt of new shares is not taxable; although you own more shares, your ownership percentage has not changed.

Reporting Dividends

4.1 Reporting Corporate Dividends

Dividends paid out of current or accumulated earnings of a corporation are subject to tax. Most dividends fall into this class, except for stock dividends and stock rights on common stock, which are generally not taxed; *see 4.6.*

Dividends that are paid to you during 2002 are reported to the IRS by the company on Form 1099-DIV. The IRS uses this information as a check on your reporting of dividends. You receive a copy of Form 1099-DIV. You do not have to attach it to your tax return.

Publicly held corporations generally inform stockholders of the tax consequences of stock dividends and other distributions. Keep such letters with your tax records. You may also want to consult investment publications such as Moody's or Standard & Poor's annual dividend record books for details of dividend distributions and their tax treatment.

4.2 Dividends From a Partnership, S Corporation, Estate, or Trust

You report dividend income you receive as a member of a partnership, stockholder in an S corporation, or as a beneficiary of an estate or trust. The fiduciary of the estate or trust should advise you of the dividend income to be reported on your return.

A distribution from a partnership or S corporation is reported as a dividend only if it is portfolio income derived from nonbusiness activities. Your allowable share of the dividend will be shown on the Schedule K-1 you receive from the partnership or S corporation.

4.3 How Mutual-Fund Distributions Are Taxed

Mutual funds (open-ended, regulated investment companies) pay their shareholders several kinds of dividends and other distributions. Whether the distribution is received by you or reinvested by the fund, you must report it on your return.

The fund will send you Form 1099-DIV (or a similar written form), giving you a breakdown of the type of dividends and distributions paid during the taxable year. In Box 1, the fund reports ordinary dividends, including short-term capital gains. Total capital gain distributions (long term) are reported in Box 2a. Boxes 1 and 2a include dividends and distributions that you reinvested instead of receiving in cash. Nontaxable distributions are reported in Box 3. In the case of a non-publicly offered fund, your share of fund expenses is included as an ordinary dividend in Box 1, and separately shown in Box 5 for itemized deduction purposes *(see 19.24).*

Dividends from a fund's foreign investments are included in the appropriate boxes of Form 1099-DIV, and the fund will indicate in Boxes 6 and 7 any foreign tax paid, which you may claim as a tax credit or deduction; *see 36.14.*

Form 1099-DIV for 2002 will include a dividend received in January 2003 so long as it was declared and was payable in October, November, or December of 2002.

See *Chapter 32 for a closer look at the types of distributions reported on Form 1099-DIV, as well as the rules for figuring gain or loss when you sell mutual-fund shares.*

4.4 Real Estate Investment Trust (REIT) Dividends

Dividends from a real estate investment trust (REIT) are shown on Form 1099-DIV. Ordinary dividends reported in Box 1 are fully taxable. Dividends designated by the trust as capital gain distributions in Box 2a are reported by you as long-term capital gains regardless of how long you have held your trust shares. A loss on the sale of REIT shares held for six months or less is treated as a long-term capital loss to the extent of any capital gain distribution received before the sale plus any undistributed capital gains. However, this long-term loss rule does not apply to sales under periodic redemption plans.

4.5 Taxable Dividends of Earnings and Profits

You pay tax on dividends only when the corporation distributing the dividends has earnings and profits. Publicly held corporations will tell you whether their distributions are taxable. If you hold stock in a close corporation, you may have to determine the tax status of its distribution. You need to know earnings and profits at two different periods:

1. Current earnings and profits as of the *end of the current taxable year*. A dividend is considered to have been made from earnings most recently accumulated.
2. Accumulated earnings and profits as of the *beginning of the current year*. However, when current earnings and profits are large enough to meet the dividend, you do not have to make this computation. It is only when the dividends exceed current earnings (or there are no current earnings) that you match accumulated earnings against the dividend.

The tax term "accumulated earnings and profits" is similar in meaning to the accounting term "retained earnings." Both stand for the net profits of the company after deducting distributions to stockholders. However, "tax" earnings may differ from "retained earnings" for the following reason: Reserve accounts, the additions to which are not deductible for income tax purposes, are ordinarily included as tax earnings.

EXAMPLES

1. During 2002, Corporation A paid dividends of $25,000. At the beginning of 2002 it had accumulated earnings of $50,000. It lost $25,000 during 2002. You are fully taxed on your dividend income in 2002 because the corporation's net accumulated earnings and profits exceed its dividends.
2. At the end of 2001, Corporation B had a deficit of $200,000. Earnings for 2002 were $100,000. In 2002, it paid stockholders $25,000. The dividends are taxed; earnings exceeded the dividends.

4.6 Stock Dividends on Common Stock

If you own common stock in a company and receive additional shares of the same company as a dividend, the dividend is generally not taxable; *see 30.3* and *30.4* for the method of computing cost basis of stock dividends and rights and sales of such stock.

Exceptions to tax-free rule. A stock dividend on common stock is taxable when (1) you may elect to take either stock or cash; (2) there are different classes of common stock, one class receiving cash dividends and another class receiving stock; or (3) the dividend is of convertible preferred stock; *see 4.8* for further details on taxable stock dividends.

Fractional shares. If a stock dividend is declared and you are only entitled to a fractional share, you may be given cash instead. To save the trouble and expense of issuing fractional shares, many companies directly issue cash in lieu of fractional shares or they set up a plan, with shareholder approval, for the fractional shares to be sold and the cash proceeds distributed to the shareholders. Your company should tell you how to report the cash payment. According to the IRS, you are generally treated as receiving a tax-free dividend of fractional shares, followed by a taxable redemption of the shares by the company. You report on Schedule D capital gain or loss equal to the excess of the cash over the basis of the fractional share; long- or short-term treatment depends on the holding period of the original stock. In certain cases, a cash distribution may be taxed as an ordinary dividend and not as a sale reported on Schedule D; your company should tell you if this is the case.

Stock rights. The rules that apply to stock dividends also apply to distributions of stock rights. If you, as a common stockholder, receive rights to subscribe to additional common stock, the receipt of the rights is not taxable provided the terms of the distribution do not fall within the taxable distribution rules discussed in *4.8*.

4.7 Dividends Paid in Property

A dividend may be paid in property such as securities of another corporation or merchandise. You report as income the fair market value of the property. A dividend paid in property is sometimes called a *dividend in kind*.

EXAMPLE

You receive one share of X corporation stock as a dividend from the G company of which you are a stockholder. You received the X stock when it had a market value of $25; you report $25, the value of the property received. The $25 value is also your basis for the stock.

Corporate benefits. On an audit, the IRS may charge that a benefit given to a shareholder-employee is a taxable dividend.

 Filing Tip

Stock Splits Are Not Taxed

The receipt of stock under a stock split is not taxable. Stock splits resemble the receipt of stock dividends, but they are not dividends. They do not represent a distribution of surplus as in the case of stock dividends. The purpose of a stock split is generally to reduce the price of individual shares in order to increase their marketability. The basis of the old holding is divided among all the shares in order to find the basis for the new shares; *see 30.4*.

CORRECTED (if checked)			
PAYER'S name, street address, city, state, ZIP code, and telephone no. **Very Mutual Fund** **155 East 38th Street** **City, State 010X0**	1 Ordinary dividends $ **500**	OMB No. 1545-0110 20**02** Form **1099-DIV**	**Dividends and Distributions**
	2a Total capital gain distr. $ **310**		
	2b 28% rate gain $		
PAYER'S Federal identification number **X1 - 01X0110**	RECIPIENT'S identification number **00X - 1X - 0X00**	2c Qualified 5-year gain $	2d Unrecap. sec. 1250 gain $	**Copy B** **For Recipient**
RECIPIENT'S name **Noelle Ballesteros**		2e Section 1202 gain $	3 Nontaxable distributions $	This is important tax information and is being furnished to the Internal Revenue Service. If you are required to file a return, a negligence penalty or other sanction may be imposed on you if this income is taxable and the IRS determines that it has not been reported.
Street address (including apt. no.) **21 Chauncy Street**		4 Federal income tax withheld $	5 Investment expenses $	
City, state, and ZIP code **City, State 111X0**		6 Foreign tax paid $	7 Foreign country or U.S. possession	
Account number (optional)		8 Cash liquidation distr. $	9 Noncash liquidation distr. $	

Form **1099-DIV**   (keep for your records)   Department of the Treasury - Internal Revenue Service

4.8 Taxable Stock Dividends

The most frequent type of stock dividend is not taxable: the receipt by a common stockholder of a corporation's own common stock as a dividend; see 4.6.

Taxable stock dividends. The following stock dividends are taxable:

- Stock dividends paid to holders of preferred stock. However, no taxable income is realized where the conversion ratio of convertible preferred stock is increased only to take account of a stock dividend or split involving the stock into which the convertible stock is convertible.
- Stock dividends elected by a shareholder of common stock who had the choice of taking stock, property, or cash. A distribution of stock that was immediately redeemable for cash at the stockholder's option was treated as a taxable dividend.
- Stock dividends paid in a distribution where some shareholders receive property or cash and other shareholders' proportionate interests in the assets or earnings and profits of the corporation are increased.
- Distributions of preferred stock to some common shareholders and common stock to other common shareholders.
- Distributions of convertible preferred stock to holders of common stock, unless it can be shown that the distribution will not result in the creation of disproportionate stock interests.

Constructive stock dividends. You may not actually receive a stock dividend, but under certain circumstances, the IRS may treat you as having received a taxable distribution. This may happen when a company increases the ratio of convertible preferred stock.

4.9 Who Reports the Dividends

Stock held by broker in street name. If your broker holds stock for you in a street name, dividends earned on this stock are received by the broker and credited to your account. You report all dividends credited to your account in 2002. The broker is required to file an information return on Form 1099 (or similar form) showing all such dividends.

If your statement shows only a gross amount of dividends, check with your broker if any of the dividends represented nontaxable returns of capital.

Dividends on stock sold or bought between ex-dividend date and record date. Record date is the date set by a company on which you must be listed as a stockholder on its records to receive the dividend. However, in the case of publicly traded stock, an ex-dividend date, which usually precedes the record date by several business days, is fixed by the exchange to determine who is entitled to the dividend.

 Planning Reminder

Dividend Reinvestment in Company Stock

Your company may allow you either to take cash dividends or automatically reinvest the dividends in company stock. If you elect the stock plan, and pay fair market value for the stock, the full cash dividend is taxable.

If the plan lets you buy the stock at a discount, the amount of the taxable dividend is the fair market value of the stock on the dividend payment date plus any service fee charged for the acquisition. The basis of the stock is also the fair market value at the dividend payment date. The service charge may be claimed as an itemized deduction subject to the 2% adjusted gross income floor; see 19.24. If at the same time you also have the option to buy additional stock at a discount and you exercise the option, you have additional dividend income for the difference between the fair market value of the optional shares and the discounted amount you paid for the shares.

If you buy stock before the ex-dividend date, the dividend belongs to you and is reported by you. If you buy on or after the ex-dividend date, the dividend belongs to the seller.

If you sell stock before the ex-dividend date, you do not have a right to the dividend. If you sell on or after the ex-dividend date, you receive the dividend and report it as income.

The dividend declaration date and date of payment do not determine who receives the dividend.

Nominees or joint owners. If you receive ordinary dividends on stock held as a nominee for another person, other than your spouse, give that owner a Form 1099-DIV and file a copy of that return with the IRS, along with a Form 1096 ("Transmittal of U.S. Information Return"). The actual owner then reports the income. List the nominee dividends on Schedule B of Form 1040 (or Schedule 1, Form 1040A) along with your other dividends, and then subtract the nominee dividends from the total.

Follow the same procedure if you receive a Form 1099-DIV for an account owned jointly with someone other than your spouse. Give the other owner a Form 1099-DIV, and file a copy with the IRS, along with a Form 1096. The other owner then reports his or her share of the joint income. On your return, you list the total dividends shown on Forms 1099-DIV and avoid tax by subtracting from the total the nominee dividends reported to the other owner.

EXAMPLE

You receive Form 1099-DIV showing dividends of $960 including a $200 nominee distribution. You prepare a Form 1099-DIV for the actual owner showing the $200 distribution, and file a copy of the form with the IRS, plus Form 1096. When you file your return, report the nominee distribution along with other ordinary dividends on Schedule B of Form 1040 and then subtract it from the total.

Dividend Income	Amount
Mutual Fund	$ 310
Computer Inc.	450
Utility Inc.	200
Subtotal	$ 960
Less: Nominee distribution	(200)
Net dividends	$ 760

4.10 Year Dividends Are Reported

Dividends are generally reported on the tax return for the year in which the dividend is credited to your account or when you receive the dividend check.

Dividends received from a corporation in a year after the one in which they were declared, when you held the stock on the record date, are taxed in the year they are received; *see* Example 4 below.

EXAMPLES

1. A corporation declares a dividend payable on December 27, 2002. It follows a practice of paying dividends by checks that are mailed so that stockholders do not receive them until January 2003. You report this dividend on your 2003 return.
2. On December 27, 2002, a dividend is declared by a mutual fund. You receive it in January 2003. The dividend is taxable in 2002, when declared, and not 2003, when received.
3. On December 27, 2002, a dividend is credited by a corporation to a stockholder's account and made immediately available. The dividend is taxable in 2002, as the crediting is considered constructive receipt in 2002, even though the dividend is not received until 2003 or a later year.
4. You own stock in a corporation. In April 2002, the corporation declared a dividend, but it provided that the dividend will be paid when it gets the cash. It finally pays the dividend in September 2003; the dividend is taxable in 2003.

 Caution

Year-End Dividend From Mutual Fund

A dividend declared and made payable in October through December by a mutual fund or REIT is taxable in the year it is declared, even if it is not paid until January of the following year.

4.11 Distribution Not Out of Earnings: Return of Capital

A return of capital or "nontaxable distribution" reduces the cost basis of the stock. If your shares were purchased at different times, reduce the basis of the oldest shares first. When the cost basis is reduced to zero, further returns of capital are taxed as capital gains on Schedule D. Whether the gain is short term or long term depends on the length of time you have held the stock. The company paying the dividend will usually inform you of the tax treatment of the payment.

Life insurance dividends. Dividends on insurance policies are not true dividends. They are returns of premiums you previously paid. They reduce the cost of the policy and are not subject to tax until they exceed the net premiums paid for the contract. Interest paid or credited on dividends left with the insurance company is taxable. Dividends on VA insurance are tax free, as is interest on dividends left with the VA.

Where insurance premiums were deducted as a business expense in prior years, receipts of insurance dividends are included as business income. Dividends on capital stock of an insurance company are taxable.

Filing Tip

Insurance Premium Refund

Dividends on insurance policies are actually returns of premiums you previously paid. They are not subject to tax until they exceed the net premiums paid for the contract.

Reporting Interest Income

4.12 Reporting Interest on Your Tax Return

You must report all taxable interest. If you earn over $400 of taxable interest, you list the payers of interest on Part I of Schedule B if you file Form 1040, or on Part I of Schedule 1 if you file Form 1040A. Form 1040EZ may not be used if your taxable interest exceeds $400. You must also list tax-exempt interest on your return even though it is not taxable.

You must also list interest that has been shown on Forms 1099 in your name although it may not be taxable to you. For example, you may have received interest as a nominee or as accrued interest on bonds bought between interest dates. In these cases, list the amounts reported on Form 1099 along with your other interest income on Schedule B if you file Form 1040, or Schedule 1 if you file Form 1040A. On a separate line, label the amount as "Nominee distribution," or "Accrued interest," and subtract it from the total interest shown. Accrued interest is discussed at *4.15* and in the "Who Reports Interest Income" chart on page 80. Nominee distributions are discussed further in the chart on page 80.

If you received interest on a frozen account *(4.13)*, include the interest from Form 1099 on Schedule B if you file Form 1040, or on Schedule 1 if you use Form 1040A. On a separate line, write "frozen deposits" and subtract the amount from the total interest reported.

You generally do not have to list the payers of interest if your interest receipts are $400 or less. However, complete Part I of Schedule B if you have to reduce the interest shown on Form 1099 by nontaxable amounts such as accrued interest, tax-exempt interest, nominee distributions, frozen deposit interest, amortized bond premium, or excludable interest on savings bonds used for tuition.

Joint accounts. If you receive a Form 1099-INT for interest on an account you own with someone other than your spouse, you should file a nominee Form 1099-INT with the IRS to indicate that person's share of the interest, together with Form 1096 ("Transmittal of Information Return"). Give a copy of the Form 1099-INT to the other person. When you file your own return, you report the total interest shown on Form 1099-INT and then subtract the other person's share so you are taxed only on your portion of the interest; *see* the Example below.

Do not follow this procedure if you contributed all of the funds and set up the joint account merely as a "convenience" account to allow the other person to automatically inherit the account when you die. In this case, you report all of the interest income.

Filing Instruction

Tax-Exempt Interest

Tax-exempt interest, such as from municipal bonds, must be reported on your return although it is not taxable. Report it on Line 8b of Form 1040 or Form 1040A. On Part I of Schedule B of Form 1040 or Schedule 1 of Form 1040A, report the tax-exempt interest on Line 1 but then subtract it from a subtotal of the total interest so that it is not included in the amount shown on Line 2 of the schedule.

> **EXAMPLE**
>
> Your Social Security number is listed on a bank account owned jointly with your sister. You each invested 50% of the account principal and have agreed to share the interest income. You receive a Form 1099-INT for 2002 reporting total interest of $1,500 on the account. By January 31, 2003, prepare and give to your sister another Form 1099-INT that identifies you as the payer and her as the recipient of her share, or $750 interest. Send a copy of the Form 1099-INT and a Form 1096 to the IRS no later than February 28, 2003 (March 31, if filing electronically). Your sister will report the $750 interest on her return. On your Form 1040, report the full $1,500 interest on Line 1 of Schedule B, along with your other interest income. Above Line 2, subtract the $750 belonging to your sister to avoid being taxed on that amount; label the subtraction "Nominee distribution."

4.13 Interest on Frozen Accounts Not Taxed

If you have funds in a bankrupt or insolvent financial institution that freezes your account by limiting withdrawals, you do not pay tax on interest allocable to the frozen deposits. The interest is taxable when withdrawals are permitted. Officers and owners of at least a 1% interest in the financial institution, or their relatives, may not take advantage of this rule and must still report interest on frozen deposits.

On Part I of Schedule B of Form 1040 or on Schedule 1 of Form 1040A, report the full amount shown on Form 1099-INT, even if the interest is on a "frozen" deposit. Then, on a separate line, subtract the amount allocable to the frozen deposit from the total interest shown on the Schedule; label the subtraction "frozen deposits." Thus, the interest on the frozen deposit is not included on the line of your return showing taxable interest.

Refund opportunity. If you reported interest on a frozen deposit on a tax return for 1999–2001, you may file a refund claim for the tax paid on the interest; *see* Chapter 49.

4.14 Interest Income on Debts Owed to You

You report interest earned on money that you loan to another person. If you are on the cash basis, you report interest in the year you actually receive it or when it is considered received under the "constructive receipt rule." If you are on the accrual basis, you report interest when it is earned, whether or not you have received it.

See 4.31 for minimum interest rates required for loans and *4.18* when OID rules apply.

Where partial payment is being made on a debt, or when a debt is being compromised, the parties may agree in advance which part of the payment covers interest and which covers principal. If a payment is not identified as either principal or interest, the payment is first applied against interest due and reported as interest income to the extent of the interest due.

Interest income is not realized when a debtor gives you a new note for an old note where the new note includes the interest due on the old note.

If you give away a debtor's note, you report as income the collectible interest due at the date of the gift. To avoid tax on the interest, the note must be transferred before interest becomes due.

4.15 Reporting Interest on Bonds Bought or Sold

When you buy or sell bonds between interest dates, interest is included in the price of the bonds. If you are the buyer, you do not report as income the interest that accrued before your date of purchase. The seller reports the accrued interest. Reduce the basis of the bond by the accrued interest reported by the seller. The following Examples illustrate these rules.

Filing Tip

Lost Deposits

If you lose funds because of a financial institution's bankruptcy or insolvency, and you can reasonably estimate such a loss, you may deduct the loss as a nonbusiness bad debt, as a casualty loss, or as a miscellaneous itemized deduction; *see 18.5.*

Filing Tip

Accrued Interest

When you buy bonds between interest payment dates and pay accrued interest to the seller, this interest is taxable to the seller. The accrued interest is included on the Form 1099-INT you receive, but you should subtract it from your taxable interest; *see* Example 1 on this page.

> **EXAMPLES**
>
> 1. *Purchase.* On April 30, you buy for $5,200 a $5,000 corporate bond bearing interest at 5% per year, payable January 1 and July 1. The purchase price of the bond included accrued interest of $88.33 for the period January 1–April 30.
>
> | | |
> |---|---|
> | Interest received on 7/1 | $125.00 |
> | *Less:* Accrued interest | 83.33 |
> | Taxable interest | $ 41.67 |
>
> Form 1099 sent to you includes the $83.33 of accrued interest. On Schedule B of Form 1040, you report the total interest of $125 received on July 1 and then on a separate line subtract the accrued interest of $83.33. Write "Accrued Interest" on the line where you show the subtraction.
>
> Your basis for the bond is $5,117 ($5,200 – $83.33) for purposes of figuring gain or loss on a later sale of the bond.
>
> 2. *Sale.* On April 30, you sell for $5,200 a $5,000 5% bond with interest payable January 1 and July 1. The sales price included interest of $83.33 accrued from January 1–April 30. Your cost for the bond was $5,000. On your return, you report interest of $83.33 and capital gain of $117.
>
> | | |
> |---|---|
> | You receive | $ 5,200.00 |
> | *Less:* Accrued interest | 83.33 |
> | Sales proceeds | $ 5,116.67 |
> | *Less:* Your cost | 5,000.00 |
> | Capital gain | $ 116.67, or $117 |

Who Reports Interest Income

If interest is—	It is reported by—
Joint account interest	The person whose Social Security number is reported to the bank (or other payer) on Form W-9 when the account is opened. If the other owner is not your spouse and you receive a Form 1099-INT for the interest, you should report all the income on your return and also file a nominee Form 1099-INT with the other owner to indicate the other owner's share of the interest. These rules are discussed in the next item. Do not file a nominee form if you contributed all the funds and named a joint owner so that he or she may automatically inherit the account. You report all the interest.
Nominee distribution	If you receive a Form 1099-INT that includes interest belonging to someone other than you or your spouse, file a nominee Form 1099-INT with the IRS to indicate that person's income, and give a copy to that person. Complete a Form 1099-INT on which you are listed as the payer and the other person is listed as the recipient. Give the Form 1099-INT to the other owner by January 31, 2003. File Form 1099-INT plus Form 1096 ("Transmittal of Information Return") with the IRS by February 28, 2003, or March 31, 2003, if filed electronically. On your own Form 1040 or Form 1040A, you list the nominee interest, along with the other interest reported to you on Forms 1099-INT. Then subtract the nominee interest from the total. *See 4.12* for an example of nominee reporting.
Accrued interest on a bond bought between interest payment dates	Interest accrued between interest payment dates is part of the purchase price of the bond. This amount is taxable to the seller as explained at *4.15.* If you purchased a bond and received a Form 1099-INT that includes accrued interest on a bond, include the interest on Line 1 of Schedule B, Form 1040, and then on a separate line above Line 2 subtract the accrued interest from the Line 1 total.
Custodian account of a minor (Uniform Transfers to Minors Act)	The interest is taxable to the child. If a child who was under age 14 as of January 1, 2003, had net investment income for 2002 exceeding $1,500, the excess is subject to tax at the parent's top tax rate; *see 24.3.*

☐ CORRECTED (if checked)

National Bank
45 Sunnyside Drive
City, State 010XX

OMB No. 1545-0112
2002
Interest Income
Form **1099-INT**

PAYER'S Federal identification number **0X-XX100X1** | RECIPIENT'S identification number **0X1-00-XXZZ**

1 Interest income not included in box 3 $ **1,000**

Copy B For Recipient

RECIPIENT'S name **Enrique Ballesteros**
Street address **21 Chauncy Street**
City, state, ZIP **City, State 111X0**

2 Early withdrawal penalty $
3 Interest on U.S. Savings Bonds and Treas. obligations $
4 Federal income tax withheld $
5 Investment expenses $
6 Foreign tax paid $
7 Foreign country or U.S. possession

Form **1099-INT** (keep for your records) Department of the Treasury - Internal Revenue Service

Key to Interest Income Rules

Item—	Pointer—
Forms 1099-INT	Forms 1099-INT, sent by payers of interest income, simplify the reporting of interest income. The forms give you the amount of interest to enter on your tax return. Although they are generally correct, you should check for mistakes, notify payers of any error, and request a new form marked "corrected." If tax was withheld *(26.12)*, claim this tax as a payment on your tax return. The IRS will check interest reported on your return against the Forms 1099-INT sent by banks and other payers.
Deposits in a savings account	Interest credited to your account in 2002 is taxable for 2002. This is true for a "passbook" savings account even though you do not present your passbook to credit the interest. Dividends on accounts in these institutions are reported as interest: mutual savings banks; cooperative banks; domestic building and loan associations; and domestic and federal savings and loan associations.
Savings certificates, deferred interest	The interest element on certificates of deposit and similar plans of more than one year is treated as original issue discount (OID) and is taxable on an annual basis. The bank notifies you of the taxable OID amount on Form 1099-OID. If you discontinue a savings plan before maturity, you may have a loss deduction for forfeited interest, which is listed on Form 1099-INT or Form 1099-OID; *see 4.16*. Tax on interest can be deferred on a savings certificate with a term of one year or less. Interest is taxable in the year it is available for withdrawal without substantial penalty. Where you invest in a six-month certificate before July 1, the entire amount of interest is paid six months later and is taxable in the year of payment. However, when you invest in a six-month certificate after June 30, only interest actually paid or made available for withdrawal without substantial penalty is taxable in the year of issuance. The balance is taxable in the year of maturity. You can defer interest to the following year by investing in a six-month certificate after June 30, provided the payment of interest is specifically deferred to the year of maturity by the terms of the certificate. Similarly, interest may be deferred to the following year by investing in longer term certificates of up to one year, provided that the crediting of interest is specifically deferred until the year of maturity.
U.S. Savings Bonds— Series E, EE	The increase in redemption value of these Savings Bonds is interest income, but if you choose to defer the interest, you do not have to report the annual increase in value until the year in which you cash the bond or the year in which the bond finally matures, whichever is earlier; *see 4.28*.
U.S. Savings Bonds— Series H, HH	Semiannual interest on these bonds is taxable when received.
U.S. Treasury bills	If your T-bill matured in 2002, report as interest the difference between the amount received at redemption and your cost. If in 2002 you sold a bill before maturity, you may have a capital loss, or a gain that is partly interest income and partly capital gain; *see 4.27*.
Zero Coupon Bonds	The interest element is treated as original issue discount (OID) and is taxable annually. You receive a Form 1099-OID reporting the taxable amount.
Interest on funds invested abroad	Interest must be reported in U.S. dollars. If foreign tax has been paid, you may be entitled to a deduction or credit; *see 36.14. See also 36.12* for blocked currency reporting rules.
Bearer or coupon bonds	Interest coupons due and payable in 2002 are taxable for 2002 regardless of when presented for collection. For example, a coupon due January 2002 and presented for payment in 2001 is taxable in 2002. Similarly, a December 2002 coupon presented for payment in 2003 is taxable in 2002.
Corporate obligations in registered form	You report interest when it is received or made available to you. *See 4.15* on how to treat interest when you buy or sell bonds between interest dates.
Interest on state and local government obligations	Although you may receive a Form 1099-INT for interest on state or municipal bonds, you do not pay federal tax on the interest. You are required to list the tax-exempt interest on your tax return, although it is not taxable. The interest may be subject to state income tax.
Borrowing to meet minimum deposit requirements for savings certificates	Interest expenses may be deductible as itemized investment interest deductions *(15.10)*. Report the full amount of interest income listed on Form 1099-INT, even if you do not take interest deductions.
Insurance proceeds	You report interest paid on insurance proceeds left with an insurance company or included in installment payments. Exception: A surviving spouse of an insured who died before October 23, 1986 is not taxed on up to $1,000 a year of interest included in installment payments.
Interest on prepaid premium	Taxable interest is reported by insurance company on Form 1099-INT.
Interest on tax refunds	Interest on tax refunds is fully taxable.
Bank gifts	To attract new deposits, banks and thrifts may offer cash, televisions, toasters, and the like as inducements. The gifts are taxable as interest and reported on Form 1099-INT.
Interest on withdrawn life insurance dividends	If you can withdraw the interest annually, you report the interest in the year it is credited to your account. However, if, under the terms of the insurance policy, the interest can be withdrawn only on the anniversary date of the policy (or some other specified date), then you report the interest in the year in which the anniversary date of the policy (or some other specified date) falls. Interest on GI insurance dividends on deposit with the Department of Veterans Affairs (VA) is not taxable.

Redemptions, bankruptcy, reorganizations. On a redemption, interest received in excess of the amount due at that time is not treated as interest income but as capital gain.

> **EXAMPLE**
>
> You hold a $5,000 9% bond with interest payable January 1 and July 1. The company can call the bonds for redemption on any interest date. In May, the company announces it will redeem the bonds on July 1. But you may present the bond for redemption beginning with June 1 and it will be redeemed with interest to July 1. On June 1 you present the bond and receive $5,225 – $5,000 principal, $187.50 interest to June 1, and $37.50 extra interest to July 1. The $37.50 is treated as a capital gain; the $187.50 is interest.

Taxable interest may continue on bonds after the issuer becomes bankrupt, if a guarantor continues to pay the interest when due. The loss on the bonds will occur only when they mature and are not redeemed or when they are sold below your cost. In the meantime, the interest received from the guarantor is taxed.

Bondholders exchanging their bonds for stock, securities, or other property in a tax-free reorganization, including a reorganization in bankruptcy, have interest income to the extent the property received is attributable to accrued but unpaid interest; *see* Internal Revenue Code Section 354(a)(2)(B).

Bonds selling at a flat price. When you buy bonds with defaulted interest at a "flat" price, a later payment of the defaulted interest is not taxed. It is a tax-free return of capital that reduces your cost of the bond. This rule applies only to interest in default at the time the bond is purchased. Interest that accrues after the date of your purchase is taxed as ordinary income.

4.16 Forfeiture of Interest on Premature Withdrawals

Banks usually impose an interest penalty if you withdraw funds from a savings certificate before the specified maturity date. You may lose interest if you prematurely withdraw funds in order to switch to higher paying investments, or if you need the funds for personal use. In some cases, the penalty may exceed the interest earned so that principal is also forfeited to make up the difference.

If you are penalized, you must still report the full amount of interest credited to your account. However, on Form 1040, you may deduct the full amount of the penalty-forfeited principal as well as interest. The deductible penalty/forfeited amount is shown in Box 2 of Form 1099-INT sent to you. You may claim the deduction even if you do not itemize deductions. On Form 1040, enter the deduction on Line 32, marked "Penalty on early withdrawal of savings."

Loss on redemption before maturity of a savings certificate. If you redeem a long-term (more than one year) savings certificate for a price less than the stated redemption price at maturity, you are allowed a loss deduction for the amount of original issue discount (OID) reported as income but not received. The deductible amount is shown in Box 3 of Form 1099-OID. Claim the deduction on Line 32 of Form 1040. The basis of the obligation is reduced by the amount of the deductible loss.

Do not include in the computation any amount based on a fixed rate of simple or compound interest that is actually payable or is treated as constructively received at fixed periodic intervals of one year or less.

Caution

CD Early Withdrawal

If you are penalized for making an early withdrawal from a certificate of deposit, you may lose part of your interest or principal. You must report the full amount of interest credited to your account, but you may deduct the full amount of the penalty/forfeited principal as well as interest on Line 32 of Form 1040.

Premiums and Discounts on Bonds

4.17 Amortization of Bond Premium

Bond premium is the extra amount paid for a bond in excess of its principal or face amount when the value of the bond has increased due to falling interest rates. Investors may elect to amortize the premium on a taxable bond by deducting it over the life of the bond. Amortizing the premium annually is usually advantageous because it gives an annual deduction to offset the interest income from the bond. Basis of the bond is reduced by the amortized premium. If you claim amortization deductions and hold the bond to maturity, basis is reduced by the entire amortized premium and you have neither gain nor loss at redemption.

You may not claim a deduction for a premium paid on a *tax-exempt* bond; however, you must still decrease your basis by the premium.

Dealers in bonds may not deduct amortization but must include the premium as part of cost.

Capital loss alternative to amortizing premium. If you do not elect to amortize the premium on a taxable bond, you will realize a capital loss when the bond is redeemed at par or you sell it for less than you paid for it. For example, you bought a $1,000 corporate bond for $1,300 and did not amortize the $300 premium; you will realize a $300 capital loss when the bond is redeemed at par: $1,000 proceeds less $1,300 cost basis ($1,000 face value plus $300 premium). You could realize a capital gain if you sell the bond for more than the premium price you paid.

Determining the amortizable amount for the year. The annual amortizable premium is based on the constant yield method if the bond was issued after September 27, 1985. This method is the same as the optional constant yield method for reporting market discount discussed at *4.20*. *See* IRS Publication 1212 or consult a tax professional for making the complex computations.

For bonds issued before September 28, 1985, a monthly straight-line method or a yield method based upon IRS Revenue Ruling 82-10 could be used.

For taxable bonds subject to a call before maturity, the amortization computation is based on the earlier call date if that results in a smaller amortization deduction.

Amortization election made after the year you acquire a bond. An election to amortize premium on a taxable bond does not have to be made in the year you acquire the bond. Attach a statement to the tax return for the first year to which you want the election to apply. If the election is made after the year of acquisition, the premium allocable to the years prior to the year of election is not amortizable; the unamortized amount is included in your cost basis for the bond and will result in a capital loss when the bond is redeemed at par or sold prior to maturity for less than basis.

How to deduct amortized premium on taxable bonds acquired after 1987. The premium amortization for such bonds offsets your interest income from the bonds; *see* the Filing Tip on this page. Any excess of the allocable premium over interest income may be fully deducted as a miscellaneous deduction (not subject to the 2% floor) on Line 27 of Schedule A (Form 1040). However, the miscellaneous deduction is limited to the excess of total interest inclusions on the bonds in prior years over total bond premium deductions in the prior years.

How to deduct premium amortization on taxable bonds acquired after October 22, 1986, but before 1988. The method of claiming amortized premium on taxable bonds acquired after October 22, 1986, but before 1988 depends on whether you made an election to amortize premium for any taxable bond before 1998. If the election was first made for 1998 or a later year, the allocable premium amortization for the bonds offsets interest income on your return. If a pre-1998 election to amortize was made, the allocable premium is treated as investment interest deductible on Line 13 of Schedule A (Form 1040), subject to the deduction limits at *15.10*.

How to deduct premium amortization on taxable bonds acquired before October 23, 1986. For bonds acquired before October 23, 1986, the allocable premium is fully deductible on Line 27 of Schedule A (Form 1040) as a miscellaneous deduction not subject to the 2% floor *(19.1)*.

Effect of amortization election on other taxable bonds you acquire. If you elect to amortize the premium for one bond, you must also amortize the premium on all similar bonds owned by you at the beginning of the tax year, and also to all similar bonds acquired thereafter. An election to amortize may not be revoked without IRS permission. If you file your return without claiming the deduction, you may not change your mind and make the election for that year by filing an amended return or refund claim.

Callable bonds. On taxable bonds, amortization is based either on the maturity or earlier call date, depending on which date gives a smaller yearly deduction. This rule applies regardless of the issue date of the bond. If the bond is called before maturity, you may deduct as an ordinary loss the unamortized bond premium in the year the bond is redeemed.

Convertible bonds. A premium paid for a convertible bond that is allocated to the conversion feature may not be amortized; the value of the conversion option reduces basis in the bond.

Premium on tax-exempt bonds. You may not take a deduction for the amortization of a premium paid on a tax-exempt bond. When you dispose of the bond, you amortize the premium for the period you held the bond and reduce the basis of the bond by the amortized amount. If the bond has call dates, the IRS may require the premium to be amortized to the earliest call date.

Planning Reminder

Amortized Premium Reduces Basis

You reduce the cost basis of the bond by the amount of the premium taken as a deduction.

If you hold the bond to maturity, the entire premium is amortized and you have neither gain nor loss on redemption of the bond. If before maturity you sell the bond at a gain (selling price exceeds your basis for the bond), you realize long-term capital gain if you held the bond long term. A sale of the bond for less than its adjusted basis gives a capital loss.

Filing Tip

How To Deduct Amortized Premium

If you paid a premium on a taxable bond during 2002, you offset interest income on the bond by the amortized premium. You must file Form 1040 and show the reduction on Schedule B. Report the full interest from the bond on Line 1 of Schedule B, along with the rest of your interest income. On a separate line, subtract the amortized premium from a subtotal of the other interest. Label the subtraction "ABP Adjustment."

This interest offset rule applies to all taxable bonds acquired at a premium after 1987; *see* this page for bonds acquired before 1988.

4.18 Discount on Bonds

There are two types of bond discounts: original issue discount and market discount.

Market discount. Market discount arises when the price of a bond declines because its interest rate is less than the current interest rate. For example, a bond originally issued at its face amount of $1,000 declines in value to $900 because the interest payable on the bond is less than the current interest rate. The difference of $100 is called market discount. The tax treatment of market discount is explained in *4.20.*

Original issue discount (OID). OID arises when a bond is issued for a price less than its face or principal amount. OID is the difference between the principal amount (redemption price at maturity) and the issue price. For publicly offered obligations, the issue price is the initial offering price to the public at which a substantial amount of such obligations were sold. All obligations that pay no interest before maturity, such as zero coupon bonds, are considered to be issued at a discount. For example, a bond with a face amount of $1,000 is issued at an offering price of $900. The $100 difference is OID.

Generally, part of the OID must be reported as interest income each year you hold the bond, whether or not you receive any payment from the bond issuer. This is also true for certificates of deposit (CDs), time deposits, and similar savings arrangements with a term of more than one year, provided payment of interest is deferred until maturity. OID is reported to you by the issuer (or by your broker if you bought the obligation on a secondary market) on Form 1099-OID; *see 4.19* for reporting OID.

Exceptions to OID. OID rules do *not* apply to: (1) obligations with a term of one year or less held by *cash-basis taxpayers*; *see 4.21*; (2) tax-exempt obligations, except for certain stripped tax-exempts; *see 4.26*; (3) U.S. Savings Bonds; (4) an obligation issued by an individual before March 2, 1984; and (5) loans of $10,000 or less from individuals who are not professional money lenders, provided the loans do not have a tax avoidance motivation.

Filing Tip

When OID May Be Ignored

You may disregard OID that is less than one-fourth of one percent (.0025) of the principal amount multiplied by the number of full years from the date of original issue to maturity. On most long-term bonds, the OID will exceed this amount and must be reported.

EXAMPLES

1. A 10-year bond with a face amount of $1,000 is issued at $980. One-fourth of one percent (.0025) of $1,000 times 10 is $25. As the $20 OID is less than $25, it may be ignored for tax purposes.
2. Same facts as in Example 1, except that the bond is issued at $950. As OID of $50 is more than the $25, OID must be reported under the rules explained at *4.19.*

Bond bought at premium or acquisition premium. You do not report OID as ordinary income if you buy a bond at a premium. You buy at a premium where you pay more than the total amount payable on the bond after your purchase, not including qualified stated interest. When you dispose of a bond bought at a premium, the difference between the sale or redemption price and your basis is a capital gain or loss; *see 4.17.*

If you do not pay more than the total due at maturity, you do not have a premium, but there is "acquisition premium" if you pay more than the adjusted issue price. This is the issue price plus previously accrued OID but minus previous payments on the bond other than qualified stated interest. The acquisition premium reduces the amount of OID you must report as income. The rules for computing the reduction to OID depend on when the bond was purchased. For bonds purchased after July 18, 1984, OID is reduced by a fraction, the numerator of which is the acquisition premium; the denominator is the OID remaining after your purchase date to the maturity date. *See* IRS Publication 1212 for further details on how to make the computation.

4.19 How To Report Original Issue Discount (OID) on Your Return

The issuer of the bond (or your broker) will make the OID computation and report in Box 1 of Form 1099-OID the OID for the actual dates of your ownership during the calendar year. However, the amount shown in Box 1 of Form 1099-OID must be adjusted if you bought the obligation at a premium or acquisition premium, if the obligation is a stripped bond or stripped coupon, or if you received Form 1099-OID as a nominee for someone else.

If you did not receive a Form 1099-OID, contact the issuer or check IRS Publication 1212 for OID amounts.

Premium. If you paid a premium *(see 4.18)* for a bond originally issued at discount, you do not have to report any OID as income. Report the amount shown on Form 1099-OID and then subtract it as discussed in the Filing Tip on this page.

Acquisition premium. The amount that is shown in Box 1 of Form 1099-OID is not correct if you pay an acquisition premium *(see 4.18)* because such premium reduces the amount of OID you must report as income. *See* IRS Publication 1212 to recompute OID. On your return, report the amount shown on Form 1099-OID and then reduce it, as discussed in the Filing Tip on this page.

Stripped bonds or coupons. The amount that is shown in Box 1 of Form 1099-OID may not be correct for a stripped bond or coupon; *see 4.22.* If it is incorrect, adjust it following the rules in Publication 1212 and report the proper amount, as discussed in the Filing Tip on this page.

Nominee. If you receive a Form 1099-OID for an obligation owned by someone else, other than your spouse, you must file another Form 1099-OID for that owner. The OID computation rules shown in IRS Publication 1212 should be used to compute the other owner's share of OID. You file the other owner's Form 1099-OID and a transmittal Form 1096 with the IRS, and give the other owner a copy of the Form 1099-OID. On your own tax return, report the amount shown on the Form 1099-OID you received and then reduce it, as discussed in the Filing Tip on this page.

Periodic interest reported on Form 1099-OID. If in addition to OID there is regular interest payable on the bond, such interest will be reported in Box 2 of Form 1099-OID. Report the full amount as interest income if you held the bond for the entire year. If you acquired the bond or disposed of it during the year, *see 4.15* for figuring the interest allocable to your ownership period.

REMICS. If you are a regular interest holder in a REMIC (real estate mortgage investment conduit), Box 1 of Form 1099-OID shows the amount of OID you must report on your return and Box 2 includes periodic interest other than OID. If you bought the regular interest at a premium or acquisition, the OID shown on Form 1099-OID must be adjusted as discussed above. If you are a regular interest holder in a single-class REMIC, Box 2 also includes your share of the REMIC's investment expenses. These expenses should be listed in a separate statement and are deductible on Schedule A as a miscellaneous itemized deduction subject to the 2% adjusted gross income floor; *see 19.24.*

4.20 Reporting Income on Market Discount Bonds

Market discount arises where the price of a bond declines below its face amount because it carries an interest rate that is below the current rate of interest.

When you realize a profit on the sale of a market discount bond, the portion of the profit equal to the accrued discount must be reported as ordinary interest income rather than as capital gain. Alternatively, an election may be made to report the accrued market discount annually instead of in the year of disposition.

These rules apply to taxable as well as tax-exempt *bonds bought after April 30, 1993.* However, there are these exceptions: (1) bonds with a maturity date of up to one year from date of issuance; (2) certain installment obligations; and (3) U.S. Savings Bonds. Furthermore, you may treat as zero any market discount that is less than one-fourth of one percent (.0025) of the redemption price multiplied by the number of full years after you acquire the bond to maturity. Such minimal discount will not affect capital gain on a sale.

Bonds bought before May 1, 1993. A *tax-exempt* bond bought before May 1, 1993, is not subject to the market discount rules; *see* the Planning Reminder on this page. For *taxable* bonds bought before May 1, 1993, application of the market discount rules depends on the issue date.

If you bought a *taxable* bond before May 1, 1993, the market discount interest income rule applies if the bond was issued *after* July 18, 1984. If the bond was issued before July 19, 1984, the market discount interest income rule does *not* apply; however, a portion of the gain on disposition can still be treated as interest income if you borrowed money to purchase or carry a market discount bond acquired after July 18, 1984. As discussed in the next paragraph, interest deductions for such loans are restricted and in the year you sell the bond, gain is treated as interest income to the extent of the deferred interest that is deductible in the year of disposition.

 Filing Tip

Reporting OID and Recomputed OID

If you are reporting the full amount of OID from Box 1 of Form 1099-OID include the amount as interest on your Form 1040, 1040A, or 1040EZ. However, if, as discussed in *4.19*, you are reporting less OID than the amount shown in Box 1 of Form 1099-OID, you must file Form 1040 and fill out Schedule B. Include the full amount shown in Box 1 of Form 1099-OID on Line 1 of Schedule B, along with other interest income. Make a subtotal of the Line 1 amounts and subtract from it the OID you are not required to report. Write "OID Adjustment" on the line where you show the subtraction, or "Nominee distribution," if that is the reason for the reduction. If you are reporting more OID than the amount shown in Box 1 of Form 1099-OID, add the additional amount to the subtotal of the interest on Line 1 of Schedule B, and label it "OID Adjustment."

Your basis for the obligation is increased by the taxable OID for purposes of figuring gain on a sale or redemption; *see 4.23.*

 *Planning Reminder*

Older Tax-Exempts

Tax-exempt bonds bought before May 1, 1993, are *not* subject to the market discount interest income rule; all the gain at disposition is capital gain.

Deferral of interest deduction and ordinary income at disposition if you borrow to buy market discount bonds after July 18, 1984. If you took such a loan, and your interest expense exceeds the income earned on the bond (including OID income, if any), the excess may not be currently deducted to the extent of the market discount allocated to the days you held the bond during the year. The limitation on the interest deduction applies to bonds you acquire after July 18, 1984, regardless of the issue date of the bond. The allocation of market discount is based on either the ratable accrual method or constant yield method; *see* below.

You can avoid this interest deduction limitation if you elect to report the market discount annually as interest income; *see* below for "How to figure accrued market discount."

In the year you dispose of the bond, you may deduct the interest expenses that were disallowed in prior years because of the above limitations. *Gain* on the disposition is interest income to the extent of the deferred interest you may deduct in the year of disposition; the balance is capital gain.

You may choose to deduct disallowed interest in a year before the year of disposition if you have net interest income from the bond. Net interest income is interest income for the year (including OID) less the interest expense incurred during the year to purchase or carry the bond. This election lets you deduct any disallowed interest expense to the extent it does not exceed the net interest income of that year. The balance of the disallowed interest expense is deductible in the year of disposition.

EXAMPLE

In 2002, you borrowed to buy a market discount bond. During 2002, your interest expense is $1,000. Income from the bond is $900 and ratable market discount allocated to the annual holding period is $75. On Form 4952 (Investment Interest Expense Deduction), $925 of interest ($1,000 – $75) is reported as investment interest; *see 15.10*.

A similar interest deduction limitation will apply every year you hold the bond, assuming you do not elect to report the market discount annually.

In the year you dispose of the bond, interest deferred under the limitation will be deductible, subject to the investment interest limits of *15.10*. Gain on the disposition will be treated as interest income to the extent of this deferred interest deduction.

Filing Instruction

Discount Bonds Held to Maturity
If you do not report the discount annually and hold a bond until maturity, the discount is reported as interest income in the year of redemption; *see* Example 2 on the following page. However, you have the option of reporting the market discount annually instead of at sale.

How to figure accrued market discount. Where the market discount rules apply, gain is taxed as ordinary interest income to the extent of the market discount accrued to the date of sale. There are two methods for figuring the accrued market discount. The basic method, called the *ratable accrual method*, is figured by dividing market discount by the number of days in the period from the date you bought the bond until the date of maturity. This daily amount is then multiplied by the number of days you held the bond to determine your accrued market discount; *see* Example 1 below.

Instead of using the ratable accrual method to compute accrual of market discount you may elect to figure the accrued discount for any bond under an optional *constant yield* (economic accrual) method. If you make the election, you may not change it. The constant yield method initially provides a smaller accrual of market discount than the ratable method, but it is more complicated to figure. It is generally the same as the constant yield method used in IRS Publication 1212 to compute taxable OID *(4.19)*. For accruing market discount, treat your acquisition date as the original issue date and your basis for the market discount bond (immediately after you acquire it) as the issue price when applying the formula in Publication 1212.

Reporting discount annually. Rather than report market discount in the year you sell the bond, you may elect, in the year you acquire the bond, to report market discount currently as interest income. You may use either the ratable accrual method, as in Example 3 below, or the elective constant yield method discussed earlier. Your election to report annually applies to all market discount bonds subject to the interest income rule that you later acquire. You may not revoke the election without IRS consent. If the election is made, the interest deduction deferral rule discussed earlier does not apply. Furthermore, the election could provide a tax advantage if you sell the bond at a profit and you can benefit from lower tax rates applied to net long-term capital gains.

EXAMPLES

1. You buy a taxable bond at a market discount of $200. There are 1,000 days between the date of your purchase and the maturity date. The daily accrual rate is 20 cents. You hold the bond for 600 days before selling it for a price exceeding what you paid for the bond. Under the ratable accrual method, up to $120 of your profit is market discount taxable as interest income (600 × $0.20).

2. You paid $9,100 for a $10,000 bond maturing in 2003. If you hold the bond to maturity, you will receive $10,000, giving you a gain of $900, equal to the market discount. The entire $900 market discount will be taxable as interest income in 2003 when the bond is redeemed.

3. In 2002, you buy at a $200 discount a bond that was issued after July 18, 1984. There are 1,000 days between the date of your purchase and the maturity date, so that daily accrual is 20 cents. You elect to report the market discount currently using the ratable accrual method. If you held the bond for 112 days in 2002, on your 2002 return you report $22 as interest income (112 × $0.20).

Partial principal payments on bonds acquired after October 22, 1986. If the issuer of a bond (acquired by you after October 22, 1986) makes a partial payment of the principal (face amount), you must include the payment as ordinary interest income to the extent it does not exceed the accrued market discount on the bond. *See* IRS Publication 550 for options on determining accrued market discount. A taxable partial principal payment reduces the amount of remaining accrued market discount when figuring your tax on a later sale or receipt of another partial principal payment.

Market discount on a bond originally issued at a discount. A bond issued at original issue discount may later be acquired at a market discount because of an increase in interest rates. If you acquire at market discount an OID bond issued after July 18, 1984, the market discount is the excess of: (1) the issue price of the bond plus the total original issue discount includible in the gross income of all prior holders of the bond over (2) what you paid for the bond.

Exchanging a market discount bond in corporate mergers or reorganizations. If you hold a market discount bond and exchange it for another bond as part of a merger or other reorganization, the new bond is subject to the market discount rules when you sell it. However, under an exception, market discount rules will not apply to the new bond if the old market discount bond was issued before July 19, 1984, and the terms of interest rates of both bonds are identical.

4.21 Discount on Short-Term Obligations

Short-term obligations (maturity of a year or less from date of issue) may be purchased at a discount from face value. If you are on the cash basis, you report the discount as interest income in the year the obligation is paid. The interest is reported on Form 1099-INT.

EXAMPLE

In May 2001, you paid $920 for a short-term note with a face amount of $1,000. In January 2002, you receive payment of $1,000 on the note. On your 2002 tax return, you report $80 as interest.

Discount must be currently reported by dealers and accrual-basis taxpayers. Discount allocable to the current year must be reported as income by accrual-basis taxpayers, dealers who sell short-term obligations in the course of business, banks, regulated investment companies, common trust funds, certain pass-through entities, and for obligations identified as part of a hedging transaction. Current reporting also applies to persons who separate or strip interest coupons from a bond and then retain the stripped bond or stripped coupon; the accrual rule applies to the retained obligation.

For short-term nongovernmental obligations, OID is generally taken into account instead of acquisition discount, but an election may be made to report the accrued acquisition discount. *See* IRS Publication 550 for details.

Basis in the obligation is increased by the amount of acquisition discount (or OID for nongovernmental obligations) that is currently reported as income.

 Filing Tip

Discount on Short-Term Government Obligations

For short-term governmental obligations (other than tax-exempts), the acquisition discount is accrued in daily installments under the ratable method, unless an election is made to use the constant yield method.

Interest deduction limitation for cash-basis investors. A cash-basis investor who borrows funds to buy a short-term discount obligation may not fully deduct interest on the loan unless an election is made to report the accrued acquisition discount as income. If the election is not made, a complicated formula limits deductible interest to the excess of the interest expense for the year over the taxable interest from the bond during the year less (1) the portion of the discount allocated to the days you held the bond during the year, and (2) the portion of interest not taxable for the year under your method of accounting. Any interest expense disallowed under this limitation is deductible in the year in which the obligation is disposed.

The interest deduction limitation does *not* apply if you elect to include in income the accruable discount under the ratable accrual method or constant yield method discussed in *4.20*. The election applies to all short-term obligations acquired during the year and also in all later years.

Gain or loss on disposition of short-term obligations for cash-basis investors. If you have a gain on the sale or exchange of a discounted short-term *governmental* obligation (other than tax-exempt local obligations), the gain is ordinary income to the extent of the ratable share of the acquisition discount received when you bought the obligation. Follow the computation shown in *4.27* for Treasury bills to figure this ordinary income portion. Any gain over this ordinary income portion is short-term capital gain; a loss would be a short-term capital loss.

Gain on short-term *nongovernmental* obligations is treated as ordinary income up to the ratable share of OID. The formula for figuring this ordinary income portion is similar to that shown in *4.27* for short-term governmental obligations, except that the denominator of the fraction is days from original issue to maturity, rather than days from acquisition. A constant yield method may also be elected to figure the ordinary income portion. Gain above the computed ordinary income amount is short-term capital gain (*see* Chapter 5). For more information, *see* IRS Publication 550.

4.22 Stripped Coupon Bonds and Stock

Brokers holding coupon bonds may separate or strip the coupons from the bonds and sell the bonds or coupons to investors. Examples include zero-coupon instruments sold by brokerage houses that are backed by U.S. Treasury bonds (such as CATS and TIGRS).

The U.S. Treasury also offers its version of zero coupon instruments, with the name STRIPS, which are available from brokers and banks.

Brokers holding preferred stock may strip the dividend rights from the stock and sell the stripped stock to investors.

If you buy a stripped bond or coupon, the spread between the cost of the bond or coupon and its higher face amount is treated as original issue discount (OID). This means that you annually report a part of the spread as interest income. For a stripped bond, the amount of the original issue discount is the difference between the stated redemption price of the bond at maturity and the cost of the bond. For a stripped coupon, the amount of the discount is the difference between the amount payable on the due date of the coupon and the cost of the coupon. The rules for figuring the amount of OID to be reported annually are in IRS Publication 1212. *See 4.19* for reporting OID.

If you strip a coupon bond, interest accrual and allocation rules prevent you from creating a tax loss on a sale of the bond or coupons. You are required to report interest accrued up to the date of the sale and also add the amount to the basis of the bond. If you acquired the obligation after October 22, 1986, you must also include in income any market discount that accrued before the date you sold the stripped bond or coupons. The method of accrual depends on the date you bought the obligation; *see* IRS Publication 1212. The accrued market discount is also added to the basis of the bond. You then allocate this basis between the bond and the coupons. The allocation is based on the relative fair market values of the bond and coupons at the date of sale. Gain or loss on the sale is the difference between the sales price of the stripped item (bond or coupons) and its allocated basis. Furthermore, the original issue discount rules apply to the stripped item which you keep (bond or coupon). Original issue discount for this purpose is the difference between the basis allocated to the retained item and the redemption price of the bond (if retained) or the amount payable on the coupons (if retained). You must annually report a ratable portion of the discount.

4.23 Sale or Retirement of Bonds and Notes

Gain or loss on the sale, redemption, or retirement of debt obligations issued by a government or corporation is generally capital gain or loss.

A redemption or retirement of a bond at maturity must be reported as a sale on Schedule D of Form 1040 *(5.8)* although there may be no gain or loss realized.

Caution

Recomputing Form 1099-OID Amount

Do not report the amount shown in Box 1 of Form 1099-OID for a stripped bond or coupon; that amount must be recomputed under complicated rules described in IRS Publication 1212. *See 4.19* for reporting the recomputed OID on your return.

Corporate bonds with OID issued after 1954 and before May 28, 1969, and government bonds with OID issued before July 2, 1982. If the bonds were originally issued at a discount (OID), you report your ratable monthly share of the OID element as ordinary income when the bonds are sold or redeemed; any gain exceeding OID is reported as capital gain. However, if there was an intention to call before maturity, gain is ordinary income to the full extent of the OID. A loss is a capital loss. IRS Publication 1212 has examples for figuring the amount taxable as ordinary income.

Corporate bonds with OID issued after May 27, 1969, and government bonds with OID issued after July 1, 1982. The accrued amount of OID is reported annually as interest income *(see 4.19)* and added to basis; this includes the accrued OID for the year the bond is sold. If the bonds are sold or redeemed before maturity, you realize capital gain for the proceeds over the adjusted basis (as increased by accrued OID) of the bond, provided there was no intention to call the bond before maturity. If at the time of original issue there was an intention to call the obligation before maturity, the entire OID that has not yet been included in your income is taxable as ordinary income; the balance is capital gain.

Market discount on bonds is taxable under the rules at *4.20*.

Tax-exempts. *See 4.26* for discount on tax-exempt bonds.

Obligations issued by individuals. If you hold an individual's note issued after March 1, 1984, for over $10,000, accrued OID must be reported annually *(4.19)* and added to basis. Gain on your sale of the note is subject to the rules discussed above for corporate and government OID bonds.

If the note is $10,000 or less (when combined with other prior outstanding loans from the same individual), OID is not reported annually provided you are not a professional lender and tax avoidance was not a principal purpose of the loan. On a sale of the note at a gain, your ratable share of the OID is taxed as ordinary income; any balance is capital gain. A loss is a capital loss.

Tax-Free Interest on State and Local Government Obligations

4.24 State and City Interest Generally Tax Exempt

Generally, you pay no tax on interest on bonds or notes of states, cities, counties, the District of Columbia, or a possession of the United States. This includes bonds or notes of port authorities, toll road commissions, utility services activities, community redevelopment agencies, and similar bodies created for public purposes. Bonds issued after June 30, 1983, must be in registered form for the interest to be tax exempt. Interest on federally guaranteed obligations is generally taxable, but *see* exceptions at *4.25*.

Check with the issuer of the bond to verify the tax-exempt status of the interest.

Private activity bonds. Interest on so-called private activity bonds is generally taxable *(see 4.25)*, but there are certain exceptions. For example, interest on the following bonds is tax exempt even if the bond may technically be in the category of private activity bonds; qualified student loan bonds; exempt facility bonds; qualified small issue bonds; qualified mortgage bonds and qualified veterans' mortgage bonds; qualified redevelopment bonds; and qualified 501(c)(3) bonds issued by charitable organizations and hospitals.

However, while interest on such bonds is not subject to regular tax, interest that you receive on such bonds issued after August 7, 1986, is considered a tax preference item that may be subject to alternative minimum tax; *see* Chapter 23.

Check with the issuer for the tax status of a private activity bond.

4.25 Taxable State and City Interest

Interest on certain state and city obligations is taxable. These taxable obligations include federally guaranteed obligations, mortgage subsidy bonds, private activity bonds, and arbitrage bonds.

Federally guaranteed obligations. Interest on state and local obligations issued after April 14, 1983, is generally taxable if the obligation is federally guaranteed, but there are exceptions allowing tax exemptions for obligations guaranteed by the Federal Housing Administration, Department of Veterans Affairs, Bonneville Power Authority, Federal Home Loan Mortgage Corporation, Federal National Mortgage Association, Government National Mortgage Corporation, Resolution Funding Corporation, and Student Loan Marketing Association.

 Filing Tip

Reporting on Schedule B or Schedule 1
On your 2002 return, you must list the amount of tax-exempt interest received during the year although it is not taxable. On Form 1040, you list the tax-exempt interest on Line 8b. On Form 1040A, you list the amount on Line 8b. On Form 1040EZ, you write "TEI" and then the amount of tax-exempt interest to the right of the last word on Line 2, but do not include it in the taxable interest shown on Line 2.

Mortgage subsidy bonds. Interest on bonds issued by a state or local government after April 24, 1979, may not be tax exempt if funds raised by the bonds are used for home mortgages. There are exceptions for certain qualified mortgage bonds and veterans' bonds. Check on the tax-exempt status of mortgage bonds with the issuing authority.

Private activity bonds. Generally, a private activity bond is any bond where more than 10% of the issue's proceeds are used by a private business whose property secures the issue, or if at least 5% of the proceeds (or $5 million if less) are used for loans to parties other than governmental units. Interest on such bonds is generally taxable, but there are exceptions as discussed in *4.24*. Check on the tax status of the bonds with the issuing authority.

4.26 Tax-Exempt Bonds Bought at a Discount

Original issue discount (OID) on tax-exempt obligations is not taxable, and on a sale or redemption, gain attributed to OID is tax exempt. Gain attributed to market discount is capital gain or ordinary income depending on whether the bond was purchased before May 1, 1993, or on or after that date; *see 4.20*.

Original issue discount tax-exempt bond. This arises when a bond is issued for a price less than the face amount of the bond. The discount is considered tax-exempt interest. Thus, if you are the original buyer and hold the bond to maturity, the entire amount of the discount is tax free. If before maturity you sell a bond that was issued before September 4, 1982, and acquired before March 2, 1984, your part of the OID is tax free. On a disposition of a tax-exempt bond issued after September 3, 1982, and acquired after March 1, 1984, you must add to basis accrued OID before determining gain or loss. OID must generally be accrued using a constant yield method; *see* IRS Publication 1212.

When bonds issued after June 8, 1980, are redeemed before maturity, the portion of the original issue discount earned to the date of redemption is tax-free interest; the balance is capital gain. Bonds issued with an intention to redeem before maturity are not subject to this rule; all interest is tax exempt.

Amortization of premiums is discussed at *4.17*.

Market discount tax-exempts. A market discount arises when a bond originally issued at not less than par is bought at below par because its market value has declined. If *before* May 1, 1993, you bought at a market discount a tax-exempt bond which you sell for a price exceeding your purchase price, the excess is capital gain. If the bond was held long term, the gain is long term. A redemption of the bond at a price exceeding your purchase price is similarly treated.

However, for market discount tax-exempt bonds purchased *after* April 30, 1993, the ordinary income rules discussed at *4.20* apply.

Stripped tax-exempt obligations. OID is not currently taxed on a stripped tax-exempt bond or stripped coupon from the bond if you bought it before June 11, 1987. However, for any stripped bond or coupon you bought or sold after October 22, 1986, OID must be accrued and added to basis for purposes of figuring gain or loss on a disposition. Furthermore, if you bought the stripped bond or coupon after June 10, 1987, part of the OID may be taxable; *see* Publication 1212 for figuring the tax-free portion.

Interest on Treasury Securities and U.S. Savings Bonds

4.27 Treasury Bills, Notes, and Bonds

Interest on securities issued by the federal government is fully taxable on your federal return. However, interest on federal obligations is not subject to state or local income taxes. Interest on Treasury bills, notes, and bonds is reported on Form 1099-INT. *See 30.14* and *30.17* for investment information on Treasury securities.

Treasury bonds and notes. Treasury notes have maturities of two to 10 years. Treasury bonds have maturities of over 10 years. You report the fixed or coupon interest as interest income in the year the coupon becomes due and payable. Treasury bonds and notes are capital assets; gain or loss on their sale, exchange, or redemption is reported as capital gain or loss on Schedule D; *see* Chapter 5. If you purchased a federal obligation below par (at a discount) after July 1, 1982, *see 4.19* for the rules on reporting original issue discount. If you purchased a Treasury bond or note above par (at a premium), you may elect to amortize the premium; *see 4.17*. If you do not elect to amortize and you hold the bond or note to maturity, you have a capital loss.

Caution

Arbitrage Bonds

These are state and local bonds issued after October 9, 1969, used to provide funds for reinvestment in higher yielding instruments except where the bond proceeds are part of a required reserve or replacement fund or are being invested temporarily before the purposes of a bond issue can be fulfilled. Interest on arbitrage bonds is taxable.

Planning Reminder

Tax Deferral: T-Bill Maturing Next Year

If you are a cash-basis taxpayer, you may postpone the tax on Treasury bill interest by selecting a Treasury bill maturing next year. Income is not recognized until the date on which the Treasury bill is paid at maturity, unless it has been sold or otherwise disposed of earlier.

Treasury bills. These are short-term U.S. obligations issued at a discount with maturities of four weeks, 13 weeks, or 26 weeks. On a bill held to maturity, you report as interest income the difference between the discounted price and the amount you receive on a redemption of the bills at maturity.

Treasury bills are capital assets and a loss on a disposition before maturity is taxed as a capital loss. If you are a cash-basis taxpayer and have a gain on a sale or exchange, ordinary income is realized up to the amount of the ratable share of the discount received when you bought the obligation. This amount is treated as interest income and is figured as follows:

$$\frac{\text{Days T-bill was held}}{\text{Days from acquisition to maturity}} \qquad \times \qquad \begin{array}{c}\text{T-bill's value at}\\ \text{maturity } \textit{minus} \text{ your cost}\end{array}$$

Any gain over this amount is capital gain; *see* the Example below. Instead of using the above fractional computation for figuring the ordinary income portion of the gain, an election may be made to apply the constant yield method. This method follows the OID computation rules shown in IRS Publication 1212 for obligations issued after 1984, except that the acquisition cost of the Treasury bill would be treated as the issue price in applying the Publication 1212 formula.

Accrual-basis taxpayers and dealers who are required to currently report the acquisition discount element of Treasury bills using either the ratable accrual method or the constant yield method *(4.20)* do not apply the above formula on a sale before maturity. In figuring gain or loss, the discount included as income is added to basis.

EXAMPLE

You buy at original issue a 26-week $10,000 Treasury bill (182-day maturity) for $9,800. You sell it 95 days later for $9,900. Your entire $100 gain ($9,900 – $9,800) is taxed as interest income as it is less than the $104 treated as interest income under the ratable daily formula:

$$\frac{\text{95 days held}}{\begin{array}{c}\text{182 days from}\\ \text{acquisition to maturity}\end{array}} \quad \times \quad \text{\$200 discount} = \text{\$104}$$

Interest deduction limitation. Interest incurred on loans used to buy Treasury bills is deductible by a cash-basis investor only to the extent that interest expenses exceed the following: (1) the portion of the acquisition discount allocated to the days you held the bond during the year; and (2) the portion of interest not taxable for the year under your method of accounting. The deferred interest expense is deductible in the year the bill is disposed of. If an election is made to report the acquisition discount as current income under the rules in *4.21* for governmental obligations, the interest expense may also be deducted currently. The election applies to all future acquisitions.

4.28 Interest on U.S. Savings Bonds

Savings Bond Tables: The Supplement will contain redemption tables showing the 2002 year-end values of Series E and EE U.S. Savings Bonds.

Series E and EE Bonds. Series EE bonds have been available since 1980; before 1980, Series E bonds were issued. Both Series E and Series EE bonds may be cashed for what you paid for them plus an increase in their value over stated periods of time. *See 30.21* for investment information on U.S. Savings Bonds.

The increase in redemption value is taxable as interest, but you do not have to report the increase in value each year on your federal return. You may defer *(4.29)* the interest income until the year in which you cash the bond or the year in which the bond finally matures, whichever is earlier. But if you want, you may report the annual increase by merely including it on your tax return. If you use the accrual method of reporting, you must include the interest each year as it accrues. Savings bond interest is not subject to state or local taxes.

If you initially choose to defer the reporting of interest and later want to switch to annual reporting, you may do so. You may also change from the annual reporting method to the deferral method. *See 4.29* for rules on changing reporting methods.

 Filing Tip

Savings Bond in Child's Name
If your child is the sole registered owner of a U.S. savings bond, you may make an election on behalf of your child to report the savings bond interest annually if your child is unable to file his or her own return. The interest may be offset by the child's standard deduction. To make the election, report the accumulated bond interest and add a statement that the interest will be reported each year. In a later year, the child may change from annual reporting to the deferral method under the rules discussed in *4.29*.

Election for Children Under 14

Where the kiddie tax for children under age 14 *(24.3)* does not apply, making the election to report the interest annually may be advisable, such as where the child has little or no other income and the bond interest can be offset by personal deductions. For example, a dependent child is not allowed to claim a personal exemption, but he or she may claim a standard deduction for 2002 of at least $750; *see 13.5.* If the election to report the savings bond interest currently was made for 2002, up to $750 of the interest would be offset by the standard deduction, assuming the child had no other income.

Series I bonds. "I bonds," first offered in 1998, are inflation-indexed bonds issued at face amount *(see 30.22)*. As with EE bonds, you may defer the interest income (the increase in redemption value each year is interest) until the year in which the bond is redeemed or matures, whichever is earlier; *see 4.29.*

Education funding. If you buy EE or I bonds to pay for educational expenses and you defer the reporting of interest *(4.29)*, you may be able to exclude the accumulated interest from income when you redeem the bonds. *See* Chapter 38.

Bonds registered in name of child. Interest on U.S. savings bonds bought for and registered in the name of a child will be taxed to the child, even if the parent paid for the bonds and is named as beneficiary. Unless an election is made to report the increases in redemption value annually, the accumulated interest will be taxable to the child in the year he or she redeems the bond, or if earlier, when the bond finally matures. However, if the interest is reported annually by a child under age 14, or the child is under age 14 in the year bonds are redeemed, the interest may be subject to tax at the parent's top rate under the "kiddie tax"; *see* Chapter 24. For example, if a child under age 14 has 2002 investment income over $1,500, the excess is taxed at the parent's top tax rate on the child's 2002 return; *see 24.3.* To avoid kiddie tax, savings bond interest may be deferred, as discussed in *4.29.*

Bonds must be reissued to make gift. Assume you have bought E or EE bonds and had them registered in joint names of yourself and your daughter. The law of your state provides that jointly owned property may be transferred to a co-owner by delivery or possession. You deliver the bonds to your daughter and tell her they now belong to her alone. According to Treasury regulations, this is not a valid gift of the bonds. The bonds must be surrendered and reissued in your daughter's name.

If you do not have the bonds reissued and you die, the bonds are taxable to your estate. Ownership of the bonds is a matter of contract between the United States and the bond purchaser. The bonds are nontransferable. A valid gift cannot be accomplished by manual delivery to a donee unless the bonds also are surrendered and registered in the donee's name in accordance with Treasury regulations.

Series HH. These bonds are issued only in exchange for E or EE bonds, or for Freedom Shares. They are issued at face value and pay semiannual interest that is taxable when received.

To be exchanged for HH bonds, the E or EE bonds must have a redemption value of at least $500. If the total value is not a multiple of $500, you will receive cash for the difference. You report the cash received as interest income to the extent of the unreported interest earned on the EE bonds exchanged.

For example, if you trade EE bonds with a redemption value of $3,723.35 for HH bonds, you get $3,500 in HH bonds and cash of $223.35. Report the cash as interest income to the extent it is unreported interest on the EE bonds exchanged.

Series H. These bonds were available before 1980. They were bought at face value and pay semiannual interest that is taxable when received. If you obtained Series H bonds in an exchange for Series E bonds, and you did not report the E bond interest annually, you do not have to report the interest due on the old E bonds until the H bonds are redeemed or mature, whichever occurs first. H bonds issued after January 1957 cease earning interest when they mature in 30 years. At maturity, or on a disposal before maturity, you must report as interest the accumulated interest from any exchanged E bonds.

Freedom Shares. These savings notes were available between 1967 and 1970, with maturities of 30 years.

4.29 Deferring U.S. Savings Bond Interest

You do not have to make a special election on your tax return in order to defer the interest on Series E, EE, or I savings bonds. You may simply postpone reporting the interest until the year you redeem the bond or the year in which it reaches final maturity, whichever is earlier. If you choose to defer the interest, you may decide in a later year to begin annual reporting of the increase in value. You may also switch from annual reporting to the deferral method. These options are discussed in this section.

Changing from deferral to annual reporting. If you have deferred reporting of annual increases in value and want to elect to report annual increases on your 2002 return, make sure you report as 2002 interest income the total of all prior and 2002 increases in value. But next year, report only the increases accruing then, plus increases accruing on bonds newly purchased. Suppose you do not include the annual increase on your 2002 return and later change your mind. If the due date of the return has passed, it is too late to make the election. You may not file an amended return reporting the increase in value for 2002. You have to wait until next year's return to make the election.

Changing from annual reporting to deferral. If you have been reporting annual increases in value, you may change your method and elect to defer interest reporting until the bonds mature or are redeemed. You make the election by attaching to your federal income tax return for the year of the change a statement that meets the conditions of IRS Revenue Procedure 99-49; *see* IRS Publication 550 for details.

Extended maturity periods. E bonds may be held for additional periods of maturity after their initial maturity dates. Bonds held for additional periods increase in value and may be cashed in at any time. If you chose to postpone paying tax on accumulated interest, you may continue to postpone the tax during the extended period. You would then report the entire accumulated interest at the final maturity date or in the year you redeem the bond, whichever occurs earlier.

Co-Owners of E and EE Bonds. How to report interest on the bond depends on how it was bought or issued:

1. You paid for the entire bond: Either you or the co-owner may redeem it. You are taxed on all the interest, even though the co-owner cashes the bond and you receive no proceeds. If the other co-owner does cash in the bond, he or she will receive a Form 1099-INT reporting the accumulated interest. However, since that interest is taxable to you, the co-owner should give you a nominee Form 1099-INT, as explained in the rules for nominee distributions on page 80 in the chart "Who Reports Interest Income."
2. You paid for only part of the bond: Either of you may redeem it. You are taxed on that part of the interest which is in proportion to your share of the purchase price. This is so even though you do not receive the proceeds.
3. You paid for part of the bond, and then had it reissued in another's name. You pay tax only on the interest accrued while you held the bond. The new co-owner picks up his or her share of the interest accruing afterwards.
4. You and another person were named co-owners on a bond bought as a gift by a third party. You are taxed on 50% of the interest income; your co-owner is taxed on the remaining half.

Changing the form of registration. Changing the form of registration of an E or EE bond may result in tax. Assume you use your own funds to purchase a bond issued in your name, payable on your death to your son. Later, at your request, a new bond is issued in your son's name only. The increased value of the original bond up to the date it was redeemed and reissued in your son's name is taxed to you as interest income.

The Examples below show changes in registration that do not result in an immediate tax.

EXAMPLES
1. Jones buys an E bond and has it registered in his name and in the name of his son as co-owner. Jones has the bonds reissued solely in his own name; he is not required to report the accumulated interest at that time.
2. You and your spouse each contributed an equal amount toward the purchase of a $1,000 E bond, which was issued to you as co-owners. You later have the bond reissued as two $500 bonds, one in your name and one in your spouse's name. Neither of you has to report the interest earned to the date of reissue. But if you bought the $1,000 bond entirely with your own funds, you report half the interest earned to the date of reissue.
3. You add another person's name as co-owner to facilitate a transfer of the bond on death. The change in registration does not result in a tax.

Transfer to a spouse. Interest on U.S. Savings Bonds transferred to a spouse in a divorce or settlement may result in tax to the transferor; *see 6.7.*

Transfer to a trust. If you transfer U.S. Savings Bonds to a trust giving up all rights of ownership, you are taxed on the accumulated interest to date of transfer. If, however, you are considered to be the owner of the trust and the interest earned before and after the transfer is taxable to you, you may continue to defer reporting the interest.

 Filing Tip

Form 1099-INT When Savings Bond Is Cashed

When you cash in an E or EE bond, you receive Form 1099-INT that lists as interest the difference between the amount received and the amount paid for the bond. The form may show more taxable interest than you are required to report because you have regularly reported the interest or a prior owner reported the interest. Report the full amount shown on Form 1099-INT on Schedule B if you file Form 1040, or on Part I of Schedule 1 if you file Form 1040A, along with your other interest income. Enter a subtotal of the total interest and then, on a separate line, reduce the subtotal by the savings bond interest that was previously reported and identify the reduction as "Previously Reported U.S. Savings Bond Interest." The interest is exempt from state and local taxes.

 Caution

When Accumulated Interest Becomes Taxable

You may not indefinitely defer the tax on E bond interest. E bonds cease earning interest once the bonds reach their final maturity date. For example, bonds issued during 1962 ceased earning interest in 2002, 40 years from the date of issuance. On your 2002 return, you must pay tax on all the accumulated interest on bonds issued in 1962 unless the bonds are traded for new HH bonds in multiples of $500. E bonds issued in 1972 also reach final maturity in 2002, 30 years from the date of issuance. Exchanging E bonds for HH bonds will continue the tax deferral on E bond interest. *See 30.21* for a listing of final maturity dates.

Filing Tip

Deduction for Estate Tax Paid on Interest

Where an estate tax has been paid on bond interest accrued during the owner's lifetime, the new bondholder may claim the estate tax as a miscellaneous itemized deduction in the year that he or she pays tax on the accumulated interest. The deduction is not subject to the 2% adjusted gross income floor *(11.16)*.

Caution

Get Professional Advice To Draft Loan Agreement

Given the complexity of the imputed interest rules and exceptions, you and your tax advisor should carefully review regulations to the Internal Revenue Code Section 7872 when drafting a loan agreement.

Transfer to a charity. Tax on the accumulated E or EE bond interest is not avoided by having the bonds reissued to a philanthropy. Further, tax may not be deferred by first converting E bonds to HH bonds and then reissuing the HH bonds in the philanthropy's name. The IRS held that by having the bonds reissued in the philanthropy's name, the owner realized taxable income on the accumulated bond interest.

Transfer of an E or EE bond at death. If an owner does not report E or EE bond interest annually and dies before redeeming the bond, the income tax liability on the interest accumulated during the deceased's lifetime becomes the liability of the person who acquires the bond, unless an election is made to report the accrued interest in the decedent's final income tax return; *see 1.14.* If the election is not made on the decedent's final return, the new owner may choose to report the accumulated interest annually, or defer reporting it until the bond is redeemed or reaches final maturity, whichever is earlier. If the election is made on the decedent's final return, the new owner is taxable only on interest earned after the date of death.

Minimum Interest for Loans and Seller-Financed Debt

4.30 Minimum Interest Rules

The law requires a minimum rate of interest to be charged on loan transactions unless a specific exception covers the transaction. Where minimum interest is not charged, the law imputes interest as if the parties agreed to the charge.

The rules are complicated and have been subject to several revisions. There are different minimum interest rates and reporting rules depending on the nature of the transaction. The following discussion provides the important details for understanding the rules. For specific cases and computations, we suggest that you consult IRS regulations for details not covered in this book.

There are two broad classes of transactions:

Loans. These are generally covered by Internal Revenue Code Section 7872. Below-market or low-rate interest loans are discussed at *4.31.*

Seller-financed sales of property. These are covered by either Internal Revenue Code Section 1274 or Section 483. Seller-financed sales are discussed at *4.32.* If parties fail to charge the minimum required interest rate, the same minimum rate is imputed by law.

4.31 Interest-Free or Below-Market-Interest Loans

For many years, the IRS tried to tax interest-free or below-market interest loans. However, court decisions supported taxpayers who argued that such loans did not result in taxable income or gifts. To reverse these decisions, the IRS convinced Congress to pass a law imposing tax on interest-free or low-interest loans made by individuals and businesses. You may not make interest-free or low-interest loans to a relative who uses the loan for personal or investment purposes without adverse income tax consequences, unless the exception discussed in this section for $10,000 or $100,000 loans applies.

How the imputed interest rules work. If interest at least equal to the applicable federal rate set by the IRS is not charged, the law generally treats a below-market interest loan as two transactions:

1. The law assumes that the lender has transferred to the borrower an amount equal to the "foregone" interest element of the loan. In the case of a loan between individuals, such as a parent and child, the lender is subject to gift tax on this element; in the case of a stockholder borrowing from a company, the element is a taxable dividend; in the case of a loan made to an employee, it is taxable pay.
   Note: For *gift tax* purposes *(33.1)*, a term loan is treated as if the lender gave the borrower the excess of the amount of the loan over the present value of payments due during the loan term. Demand loans are treated as if the lender gave the borrower annually the amount of the foregone interest.

2. The law assumes that imputed interest equal to the applicable federal rate is paid by the borrower to the lender. The borrower may be able to claim a deduction for the interest if the loan is used to buy a home and the loan is secured by the residence *(15.1)*, or the loan is used to buy investment property *(15.10)*.

In applying the imputed interest rules, all loans to or from a husband are combined with all loans to or from his wife; they are treated as one person.

With gift loans between individuals, interest computed during the borrower's taxable year is treated for both the lender and the borrower as transferred on the last day of the borrower's taxable year. Treasury regulations to Section 7872 provide rules for figuring "foregone" interest. Where a demand loan is in effect for the entire calendar year, a "blended annual rate" issued by the IRS to simplify reporting may be used to compute the imputed interest. The blended annual rate is announced by the IRS each July. For 2002, the blended rate is 2.78%. The blended rate is not available if the loan was not outstanding for the entire year or if the loan balance fluctuated; computations provided by Treasury regulations must be used.

Charging the applicable federal rate avoids the imputed interest rules. Gift loans qualifying for the $10,000 and $100,000 exceptions are not subject to imputed interest rules. For other loans, the rules imputing income to you as the lender may be avoided by charging interest at least equal to the applicable federal rate. Applicable federal rates are set by the IRS monthly and published in the Internal Revenue Bulletin; you can also get the rates from your local IRS office. For a term loan, the applicable rate is the one in effect as of the day on which the loan is made, computed semiannually. The short-term rate applies to loans of three years or less; the mid-term rate to loans over three and up to nine years; the long-term rate applies to loans over nine years. For a demand loan, the applicable federal rate is the short-term rate in effect at the start of each semiannual period (January and July).

Different computations for different types of loans. There are two general classes of loans: (1) Gift loans, whether term or demand, and nongift demand loans, and (2) nongift term loans.

The distinction is important for figuring and reporting imputed interest. For example, in the case of nongift term loans, the imputed interest element is treated as original issue discount; *see 4.19.*

Gift loans and nongift loans payable on demand. As a lender, you are taxable on the "foregone interest," that is, the interest that you would have received had you charged interest at the applicable federal rate over any interest actually charged. The borrower may be able to claim an interest deduction if the funds are used to buy investment property; *see 15.10.*

Nongift term loans. A term loan is any loan not payable on demand. As a lender of a nongift term loan, you are taxable on any excess of the loan principal over the present value of all payments due under the loan. The excess is treated as original issue (OID) which you report annually as interest income; *see 4.19.*

Reporting imputed interest. Imputed interest is generally treated as transferred by the lender to the borrower and retransferred by the borrower to the lender on December 31 in the calendar year of imputation and is reported under the regular accounting method of the borrower and lender.

> **EXAMPLE**
>
> On January 1, 2002, Jones Company makes a $200,000 interest-free demand loan to Frank, an executive. The loan remains outstanding for the entire 2002 calendar year. Jones Company has a taxable year ending September 30. Frank is a calendar year taxpayer. For 2002, the imputed compensation payment and the imputed interest payment are treated as made on December 31, 2002.

Certain Loans Are Exempt From Imputed Interest Rules

The $10,000 gift loan exception. In the case of a gift loan to an individual, no interest is imputed to any day on which the aggregate outstanding amount of all loans between the parties is not over $10,000, provided the loan is not attributed to the purchase or carrying of income-producing assets. If the exception applies, there are no income tax or gift tax consequences to the loan.

The $100,000 gift loan exception. Imputed interest rates do not apply to an interest-free or low-interest loan of up to $100,000 if the borrower's net investment income is $1,000 or less; *see* the Planning Reminder on this page.

 *Planning Reminder*

Gift Loans up to $100,000

If you give a child or other relative an interest-free loan to buy a home or start a business, the imputed interest rules will not apply provided (1) the total outstanding loan balance owed to you by the borrower at all times during the year does not exceed $100,000, and (2) the borrower's net investment income *(15.10)* is $1,000 or less.

If the borrower's net investment income for the year exceeds $1,000, the imputed interest rules apply, but the imputed interest is limited to his or her net investment income. If on any day during the year the outstanding loan balance owed to you by the borrower exceeds $100,000, interest will be imputed for that day under the regular rules. If a principal purpose of a loan is the avoidance of federal taxes, imputed interest is not limited to the borrower's net investment income.

Filing Instruction

Tax Return Statement Requirements

A lender reporting imputed interest income or a borrower claiming an interest deduction must attach statements to their income tax returns reporting the interest, how it was calculated, and the names of the parties and their tax identification numbers.

> **EXAMPLES**
>
> 1. At the beginning of 2002, you make a $75,000 interest-free loan to your son, payable on demand, which he uses for a down payment on a home. This is the only outstanding loan between you and your son. Your son's net investment income for 2002 is $650. Since the loan does not exceed $100,000, and your son's net investment income does not exceed $1,000, the imputed interest rules do not apply; you do not have to report the "foregone interest" as interest income.
>
>   For gift tax purposes, the foregone interest is a taxable gift. Using the IRS blended annual rate for 2002 of 2.78%, the foregone interest of $2,085 ($75,000 × 2.78%) is a taxable gift, but the gift does not have to be reported if the annual gift tax exclusion of $11,000 per donee applies; *see 33.1*.
>
> 2. Same facts as in Example 1 above except that your son's net investment income is $1,500. Since net investment income exceeds $1,000, the imputed interest income rules apply, but the imputed interest is limited to the $1,500 of net investment income. Thus, although the foregone interest using the blended annual rate is $2,085, you report only $1,500 of imputed interest income.

Exceptions for compensation-related loans. For compensation-related and corporate-shareholder loans, the imputed interest rules do not apply to any day on which the total amount of outstanding loans between the parties is $10,000 or less, provided the principal purpose of the loan is not tax avoidance. Certain low-interest loans given to employees by employers to buy a new residence in a new job location are exempt from the imputed interest requirements.

Loans to continuing care facilities. Senior citizens moving into a community with a continuing care facility are required to pay a fee to the facility. The fee may be treated as a "loan" subject to the imputed interest rules to the extent the fee is refundable and it exceeds specified limits. These rules are discussed in Chapter 34.

4.32 Minimum Interest on Seller-Financed Sales

The law requires minimum interest charges for seller-financed sales. If the minimum rate is not charged, the IRS imputes interest at the minimum applicable rate requiring both buyer and seller to treat part of the purchase price as interest even though it is not called interest in the sales contract. Generally, interest at the applicable federal rate (AFR) must be charged; see the chart at the end of this section for minimum required rates. For example, investment property is sold on the installment basis for $100,000 and the parties fail to charge adequate interest. Assume the IRS imputes interest of $5,000. For tax purposes, $95,000 is allocated to the sale of the property and the principal amount of the debt; the balance is imputed interest of $5,000, taxable to the seller and deductible by the buyer if allowed under the rules of Chapter 15.

Two statute classes. The minimum or imputed interest rules are covered by two Internal Revenue Code statutes: Sections 1274 and 483. Under both, the same minimum interest rates apply but the timing of interest reporting is different, as discussed below.

Section 483 applies to any payment due more than six months after the date of sale under a contract which calls for some or all payments more than one year after the date of sale. If the sales price cannot exceed $3,000, Section 483 does not apply. Transactions within Section 483 are sales or exchanges of: (1) principal residences; (2) any property if total payments, including interest and any other consideration to be received by the seller, cannot exceed $250,000; (3) farms if the total price is $1 million or less; and (4) sales of land between family members to the extent the aggregate sales price of all sales between the same parties in the same year is $500,000 or less.

If the selling price exceeds the respective $250,000, $1 million, or $500,000 amount listed in (2) through (4) above, the sale is subject to Section 1274 reporting rules provided some or all payments are due more than six months after the date of sale. Section 1274 also applies to all other transactions where neither the debt instrument nor the property being sold is publicly traded as long as some payments are deferred more than six months.

Timing of interest reporting. One important practical difference between the two statutes covering minimum interest involves the timing of the reporting and deducting of interest.

Caution

Buyer's Personal-Use Property

If adequate interest is not charged on an installment sale of personal-use property, such as a residence to be used by the buyer, imputed interest rules do not apply to the buyer. Thus, the buyer may not deduct the imputed interest. The buyer's deduction is limited to the payment of interest stated in the contract if a deduction is allowed under the home mortgage interest rules in Chapter 15.

Under Section 483, a seller and lender use their regular reporting method for imputed interest. For a cash-basis seller, interest is taxed when received; a cash-basis buyer deducts interest when paid if a deduction is allowable. However, if too much interest is allocated to a payment period, the excess interest is treated as prepaid interest, and the deduction is postponed to the year or years interest is earned. Section 483 also describes imputed interest as unstated interest.

Under Section 1274, the interest element is generally reported by both buyer and seller according to the OID accrual rules, even if they otherwise report on the cash basis. Where the seller financing is below an annual threshold ($3,012,500 for 2002 sales), the parties can elect the cash method to report the interest regardless of the OID and accrual rules if: (1) the seller-lender is on a cash-basis method and is not a dealer of the property sold and (2) the seller and buyer jointly elect to use the cash method. The cash-basis election binds any cash-basis successor of the buyer or seller. If the lender transfers his interest to an accrual-basis taxpayer, the election no longer applies; interest is thereafter taxed under the accrual-method rules. The OID rules also do not apply to a cash-basis buyer of personal-use property; here, the cash-basis debtor deducts only payments of interest required by the contract, assuming a deduction is allowed under the home mortgage rules discussed in Chapter 15.

Figuring applicable federal rate (AFR). There is no imputed interest if the sales contract provides for interest that is at least equal to the AFR. *See* the chart below for determining the AFR.

Assumptions of loans. The imputed interest rules of Sections 1274 and 483 do not generally apply to debt instruments assumed as part of a sale or exchange, or if the property is taken subject to the debt, provided that neither the terms of the debt instrument nor the nature of the transactions are changed.

Important: In planning deferred or installment sales, review Treasury regulations to the Internal Revenue Code Sections 483 and 1274 for further examples and details.

Minimum Interest Rate for Seller Financing	
Type—	*Description—*
Applicable federal rates	The IRS determines the AFR rates which are published at the beginning of each month in the Internal Revenue Bulletin. There are three AFR rates depending on the length of the contract: *Short-term AFR*—A term of three years or less. *Mid-term AFR*—A term of over three years but not over nine years. *Long-term AFR*—A term of over nine years. The imputed interest rules do not apply if the interest rate provided for in the sales contract is at least the lesser of (1) the lowest AFR in effect during the three-month period ending with the month in which a binding written sales contract is entered into, *or* (2) the lowest AFR in effect during the three-month period ending with the month of sale. If insufficient interest is charged, the total unstated interest is allocated to payments under an OID computation.
9% safe harbor rate	If seller financing in 2002 is $4,217,500 or less, the minimum required interest is the lower of 9% compounded semiannually and the applicable federal rate (AFR). The amount of seller financing is the stated principal amount under the contract. If the seller-financed amount exceeds $4,217,500, the minimum interest rate is 100% of the AFR. The threshold for the 9% safe harbor is indexed for inflation. The 9% safe harbor provides a benefit only if it is less than the AFR, but in recent years the AFR has been much lower than 9%. Thus, until prevailing interest rates increase, charging interest at the AFR will allow a lower rate than the 9% safe harbor. IRS regulations allow the parties to use an interest rate lower than the AFR if it is shown that the borrower could obtain a loan on an arm's-length basis at lower interest.
Seller-financed sale-leaseback transactions	Interest equal to 110% of AFR must be charged.
Sales of land between family members	To the extent that the sales price does not exceed $500,000 during a calendar year, the minimum required interest rate is 6%, compounded semiannually. To prevent multiple sales from being used to avoid the $500,000 limit, the $500,000 ceiling applies to all land sales between family members during the same year. To the extent that the $500,000 sales price limit is exceeded, the general 9% or 100% of AFR rules apply.

Chapter 5

Reporting Property Sales

Long-term capital gains are generally taxed at lower rates than those imposed on ordinary income. You receive the benefit of these low rates by preparing Schedule D, on which you report property sales and compute tax on long-term capital gains.

If in 2002 you sold property and will be receiving payments in a later year, you may report the sale as an installment sale on Form 6252 and spread the tax on your gain over the installment period; see 5.21.

Sales of business assets are reported on Form 4797. As discussed in *44.8*, most assets used in a business are considered Section 1231 assets, and capital gain or ordinary loss treatment may apply depending upon the result of a netting computation made on Form 4797 for all such assets sold during the year.

Special types of sale situations are detailed in other chapters.

See Chapter 29 for the exclusion of gain on the sale of a principal residence.

See Chapter 32 for figuring gain or loss on the sale of mutual-fund shares.

See Chapter 6 for tax-free exchanges of property.

See Chapter 30 for sales of stock dividends, stock rights, wash sales, short sales, and sales by traders in securities.

Figuring Capital Gains and Losses

5.1 Tax Pattern of Property Sales

1. Property is classified according to its nature and your purpose for holding it; *see 5.2*, the table on the next page, and holding period rules at *5.3* and *5.9–5.12*.

2. If you sell property at a gain, the applicable tax rate depends on the classification of the property (*see* the table on the next page) and, in the case of capital assets, the period you held the property before sale. Short-term capital gains are subject to regular income tax rates. Capital gain rates lower than the regular rates apply only to long-term capital gains. A capital gain is long term if you held the asset for more than one year; *see 5.3*.

    A capital gain rate is applied to long-term capital gains if the rate is less than the top regular income tax rate applied to your taxable income. If your top tax bracket for 2002 is 15%, the capital gain tax rate applied to gains realized from the sale of long-term capital assets held for more than a year is generally 10% or 8%; the 8% rate applies if the asset was held over five years; *see 5.3*. If your top regular income tax bracket for 2002 is 27% or more, the capital gains rate is 20% for gains realized on sales of property held for more than a year and a 25% tax rate applies to recaptured Section 1250 gain on certain sales of depreciable real estate; *see 5.3*. If your top bracket exceeds 15%, a 28% rate will apply to sales of collectibles; *see 5.3*.

    Sales of capital assets must generally be reported on Schedule D of Form 1040, and the lower capital gain rates are applied in Part IV of Schedule D, where you compute your tax liability taking into account the favorable capital gain rates. If you have either 28% gain or unrecaptured Section 1250 gain, use the worksheet on page D-9 of the Schedule D instructions to compute your tax liability. Filing Schedule D may not be necessary if your only capital gains are from a mutual fund or REIT; *see 32.5*.

3. Loss deductions are allowed on the sale of investment and business property but not personal assets; *see* the table on the next page. Capital loss deductions in excess of capital gains are limited to $3,000 annually, $1,500 if married filing separately; *see 5.4* and *5.5* for details on the capital loss limitations.

5.2 How Property Sales Are Classified and Taxed

The tax treatment of gains and losses is not the same for all types of property sales. Tax reporting generally depends on your purpose in holding the property, as shown in the table on the next page.

When capital gain or loss treatment does not apply. Certain sales do not qualify for capital gain or loss treatment. Business inventory and property held for sale to customers are not capital assets. Depreciable business and rental property are not capital assets, but you may still realize capital gain after following a netting computation for Section 1231 assets discussed at *44.8*.

Although assets held for *personal* use, such as a car or home, are technically capital assets, you may not deduct a capital loss on their sale.

Certain other assets held for investment or personal use are excluded by law from the capital asset category. These include copyrights, literary or musical compositions, letters, memoranda, or similar property that: (1) you created by your personal efforts or (2) you acquired as a gift from the person who created the property or for whom the property was prepared or produced. Also excluded are letters, memoranda, or similar property prepared or produced for you by someone else. Finally, U.S. government publications obtained from the government for free or for less than the normal sales price do not qualify as capital assets.

Stock is generally treated as a capital asset, but losses on *Section 1244 stock* of qualifying small businesses may be claimed as ordinary losses on Form 4797, rather than on Schedule D as capital losses subject to the $3,000 deduction limit ($1,500 if married filing separately); *see 30.20*.

Traders in securities may elect to report their sales as ordinary income or loss rather than as capital gain or loss; *see 30.23*.

Small business stock deferral or exclusion. As discussed in *5.7*, taxable gains from the sale of publicly traded securities may be postponed if you roll over the proceeds to stock or a partnership interest in an SSBIC (specialized small business investment company). Furthermore, gains from the sale of qualifying small business stock may be deferred by making a tax-free rollover to other small business stock.

Caution

Loss on Personal-Use Assets
You may not deduct a capital loss on the sale of property held for personal use, such as a car or vacation home. The loss is not deductible.

Losses on the sale of property held for investment, such as stock or mutual-fund shares, are fully deductible against capital gains but any excess loss is subject to the $3,000 limit discussed at *5.4*.

Filing Instruction

Organize Sales by Holding Period
The way you report sales of property in 2002 depends on the holding periods of the sold property, as explained in *5.3*.

Filing Tip

Holding Periods
The time you own an asset determines short-term or long-term treatment. The short-term holding period is a year or less, the long-term period more than one year; *see 5.9–5.12*.

Capital or Ordinary Gains and Losses From Sales and Exchanges of Property

If you sell—	Your gain is—	Your loss is—	Reported on—
Stocks, mutual funds, bonds, land, art, gems, stamps, and coins held for investment are capital assets.	*Capital gain.* Holding period determines short-term or long-term gain treatment; *see 5.3.* Security traders may report ordinary income and loss under a mark-to-market election; *see 30.24.*	*Capital loss.* Capital losses are deductible from capital gains with only $3,000 of any excess deductible from ordinary income, $1,500 if married filing separately; *see 5.4.*	Schedule D. However, if the only amounts you have to report on Schedule D are mutual-fund capital gain distributions, then you may report the distributions directly on Form 1040A or Form 1040; *see 32.5.* Form 4797 for gains and losses of a trader in securities who makes the mark-to-market election; *see 30.24.*
Business inventory held for sale to customers. Also, accounts or notes receivable acquired in the ordinary course of business or from the sale of inventory or property held for sale to customers, or acquired for services as an employee.	*Ordinary income.* Such property is excluded by law from the definition of capital assets.	*Ordinary loss.* Ordinary loss is not subject to the $3,000 deduction limit imposed on capital losses. However, passive loss restrictions, discussed in Chapter 10, may defer the time when certain ordinary losses are deductible.	Schedule C if self-employed; Schedule F if a farmer; Form 1065 for a business operated as a partnership; Form 1120 or 1120-S for an incorporated business.
Depreciable residential rental property or trucks, autos, computers, machinery, fixtures, or equipment used in your business.	*Capital gain or ordinary income.* Section 1231, as explained in *44.8,* determines whether gain is taxable as ordinary income or capital gain. Where an asset such as an auto or residence is used partly for personal purposes and partly for business or rental purposes, the asset is treated as two separate assets for purposes of figuring gain or loss; *see 44.9.*	*Ordinary loss* if there is a net Section 1231 loss; *see 44.8.* However, if you are considered to be an investor in a passive activity, *see 10.12* and *10.13.*	Form 4797 for Section 1231 transactions.
Personal residence, car, jewelry, furniture, art objects, and coin or stamp collection held for personal use.	*Capital gain.* See *5.3* for the holding period rules that determine short-term or long-term gain treatment. Where an asset such as an auto or residence is used partly for personal purposes and partly for business or rental purposes, the asset is treated as two separate assets for purposes of figuring gain or loss; *see 44.9.* Tax on all or part of a profit from a sale of a principal residence may be avoided; *see* Chapter 29.	*Not deductible.* Losses on assets held for personal use are not deductible although profits are taxable.	Schedule D

Gains on the sale of qualifying small business stock issued after August 10, 1993, and held for more than five years qualify for a 50% exclusion; *see 5.7.*

Like-kind exchanges of business or investment property. Exchanges of *like-kind* business or investment property are subject to special rules that allow gain to be deferred, generally until you sell the property received in the exchange; *see 6.1.* When property received in a tax-free exchange is held until death, the unrecognized gain escapes income tax forever because the basis of property in the hands of an heir is generally the fair market value of the property at the date of death; *see 5.17.* A loss on a like-kind exchange is not deductible.

5.3 Capital Gains Rates and Holding Periods

Sales of capital assets during 2002 should be separated into short-term and long-term categories. Assets held for one year or less are in the short-term category and assets held for more than one year are in the long-term category. Follow the line-by-line computation on Schedule D (Form 1040) to report your sales and obtain the benefit of the lower rates on qualifying long-term gains.

A sample Schedule D, shown at *5.8,* illustrates the reporting of capital asset sales and the computation of tax liability using the favorable long-term capital gain rates. Mutual-fund and REIT investors may be able to apply the favorable rates in a worksheet included in the Form 1040 or Form 1040A instructions, without having to file Schedule D; *see 32.5.*

Held for a year or less. Gains and losses realized on sales of capital assets held for a year or less are short term and reported in Part I of Schedule D. Short-term gains and losses are netted in this part. A net gain is subject to regular tax rates. A net short-term loss offsets a net long-term gain, if any, from Part II of Schedule D. A net short-term loss in excess of net long-term gain is deductible up to the $3,000 capital loss limit; *see 5.4.*

Held for more than a year. Gains and losses on sales of capital assets held for more than a year are long term and reported in Part II of Schedule D. In this part of Schedule D, you net long-term gains and losses. A net long-term loss offsets a net short-term gain, if any, from Part I of Schedule D. If you have a net long-term gain and also a net short-term loss from Part I of Schedule D, the short-term loss offsets the net long-term gain. If the result is a net short-term loss, it is deductible up to the $3,000 capital loss limit; *see 5.4.* If you have a net long-term gain in excess of net short-term capital loss (if any), the excess is called *net capital gain* and it is this amount to which the favorable capital gain rates apply.

If your regular tax bracket is 15%, the rate is 8% for long-term capital gain from the sale of property that you held for more than five years. The rate is 10% for long-term gain from sales of assets held for more than one year but not over five years. The Schedule D instructions have a worksheet for figuring qualified five-year gain eligible for the 8% rate; this amount is then entered on Part IV of Schedule D where the capital gain rates are applied. However, the 8% and 10% rates do not apply to gains on collectible sales, unrecaptured Section 1250 gains, and gains on small business stock eligible for the 50% gain exclusion; these exceptions are discussed below.

If your regular tax bracket exceeds 15%, a 20% capital gain rate applies unless the exceptions for collectibles gains, unrecaptured Section 1250 gains, or small business stock gains apply, as discussed below. For assets acquired after 2000 and held for more than five years, the 20% rate will be reduced to 18%. Thus, the 18% rate will not be available until 2006 at the earliest. The 18% rate is also available for assets acquired before 2001 for which you made a "deemed sale election" on your 2001 return. The assets subject to the election were deemed sold for fair market value and immediately reacquired on January 1, 2001, or January 2 if publicly held securities. Your basis in the reacquired property is the fair market value reported on the deemed sale. The January 1 or 2, 2001, deemed reacquisition date begins your new holding period. If the assets are held for over five years, the 18% rate will apply on a sale in 2006 or later. If your top bracket exceeds 15% and you own appreciated property bought over five years ago, consider a gift of the property (*see 33.1* for the $11,000 annual gift tax exclusion) to a child age 14 or older (*see 24.2*), or other relative in the 15% bracket. Your donee picks up your holding period, and he or she can immediately sell the asset and pay tax at only 8%, instead of the 20% tax you would owe on a sale of the stock.

Gain from sales of collectibles. If your regular top rate bracket exceeds 28%, you may not use the 20% rate for long-term gains on the sale of collectibles such as art, antiques, precious metals, gems, stamps, and coins. The gains are listed in column (g) of Part II of Schedule D and taxed at 28% in the worksheet on page D-9 of the Schedule D instructions. If your regular top bracket

 Law Alert

Capital Gain Rates

The Economic Growth and Tax Relief Act of 2001 lowered ordinary income tax rates (*see* Chapter 22) but did not lower capital gain rates to maintain the differential between capital gain and ordinary income rates. There is no change to the 20% capital gain rate, the 25% rate for unrecaptured Section 1250 gain, or the 28% rate for collectibles gain.

The 10% capital gain rate for 15% bracket taxpayers is reduced to 8% for gains on assets held over five years. This change was enacted in 1997 but not effective until 2001. The 8% rate, like the 10% rate, does not apply to sales of collectibles, unrecaptured Section 1250 gains, or gains on qualified small business stock.

is 15%, you pay that rate on the gains. If your regular top bracket is 27%, the 27% rate generally applies, but if you also have gains eligible for the 20% rate, the worksheet computation may require a 28% rate for all or part of the collectibles gains.

Unrecaptured Section 1250 gain on sale of real estate. Long-term gain attributable to depreciation is not eligible for the 8%, 10%, or 20% rate. Generally, the gain attributable to depreciation, other than depreciation on older buildings that is recaptured as ordinary income *(44.2)*, is considered "unrecaptured Section 1250 gain." Such gain is subject to a 25% tax rate if your regular top bracket exceeds 15%, or a 15% rate if that is your regular top bracket. If you have long-term carryover losses or long-term losses on the sale of collectibles or small business stock eligible for the 50% gain exclusion, the losses reduce unrecaptured Section 1250 gain. The worksheet on page D-7 of the Schedule D instructions is used to figure the amount of unrecaptured Section 1250 gain, which is then entered on the worksheet on page D-9 of the instructions to compute total tax liability.

Capital gain distributions from mutual funds. Your fund will report long-term capital gain distributions on Form 1099-DIV. *See* Chapter 32 for details on how to report the distributions.

Capital gain from Schedule K-1. Net capital gain or loss from a pass-through entity such as a partnership, S corporation, estate, or trust is reported to you on a Schedule K-1. Report net short-term gain or loss in Part I of Schedule D and net long-term gain or loss in Part II of Schedule D.

Gain from sale of small business stock subject to 50% gain exclusion. If you claim the 50% exclusion on the sale of small business stock *(see 5.7)*, the remaining long-term gain is not eligible for the 10% or 20% rate. The gains are listed in column (g) of Part II of Schedule D and taxed at 28% in Part IV of Schedule D if your regular top rate bracket exceeds 28%. If your regular top bracket is 15%, you pay that rate on the gains. If your regular top bracket is 27%, the 27% rate generally applies, but if you also have gains eligible for the 20% rate, the Part IV computation may require a 28% rate for all or part of the small business stock gains.

Schedule D tax computation section. In Part IV of Schedule D, you figure your tax liability for 2002, taking into account the applicable 8%, 10%, or 20% capital gain rates.

If you elect to treat part or all of your net capital gain as investment income in order to increase your itemized deduction for investment interest on Form 4952 *(see 15.10)*, the elected amount is not eligible for preferential capital gain rates. When making the tax computation in Part IV of Schedule D, the net capital gain that you include on Form 4952 must be subtracted from the net capital gain figured in Parts II and III of Schedule D; the subtraction is made on Lines 22 and 23 of Schedule D.

If you have 28% rate gains or unrecaptured Section 1250 gain, you must use the worksheet on page D-9 of the Schedule D instructions to compute tax liability, which is then entered in Part IV of Schedule D.

Filing Tip

Keep Records of Loss Carryovers
Prior year capital losses that are not deductible may be claimed this year or in later years when you have capital gains to offset.

5.4 Capital Losses and Carryovers

Capital losses are fully deductible against capital gains on Schedule D, and if losses exceed gains, you may deduct the excess from up to $3,000 of other income on Form 1040. Net losses over $3,000 are carried over to future years. The $3,000 limit is reduced to $1,500 for married persons filing separately. On a joint return, the $3,000 limit applies to the combined losses of both spouses; *see 5.5*. In preparing your 2002 Schedule D, remember to include any capital loss carryovers from your 2001 return. Short-term carryover losses are entered on Line 6 of Part I and long-term carryover losses are entered on Line 14, Part II.

Death of taxpayer cuts off carryover. If an individual dies and on his or her final income tax return net capital losses, including prior year carryovers, exceed the $3,000 or $1,500 limit, the excess may not be deducted by the individual's estate. If the deceased individual was married, his or her unused individual losses may not be carried over by the surviving spouse; *see 5.5*.

Carryover if you have "negative" taxable income. A special computation may increase your carryover deduction where you have "negative" taxable income. If without considering personal exemptions you have a "negative taxable income," a net capital loss may not provide a tax benefit because other deductions have reduced taxable income to zero. In this case, you may be allowed a capital loss carryover for all or part of your net capital loss.

To determine the amount of the carryover, follow the steps of the worksheet in the Schedule D instructions. You first will figure how much of your net loss is treated as "used up" in the current year. The balance of the loss, if any, is carried over to the next year.

5.5   Capital Losses of Married Couples

On a joint return, the capital asset transactions of both spouses are combined and reported on one Schedule D. A carryover loss of one spouse may offset capital gains of the other spouse on a jointly filed Schedule D. Where you and your spouse separately incur net capital losses, $3,000 is the maximum capital loss deduction that may be claimed for the combined losses on your joint return. This limitation may not be avoided by filing separate returns. If you file separately, the deduction limit for each return is $1,500. Neither of you may deduct any of the other's losses on a separate return.

> **EXAMPLE**
>
> In 2002, you individually incurred net long-term capital losses of $5,000 and your spouse incurred net long-term losses of $4,000. If you file separate returns, the maximum amount deductible from ordinary income on each return is $1,500. The balance must be carried forward to 2003.
>
> If you had net losses below the $1,500 limit, you could not claim any part of your spouse's losses on your separate return.

Death of a spouse. The IRS holds that if a capital loss is incurred by a spouse on his or her own property and that spouse dies, the surviving spouse may not claim any unused loss carryover on a separate return.

> **EXAMPLE**
>
> In 1999, Alex Smith realized a substantial net long-term capital loss on separately owned property, which was reported on a 1999 joint return filed with his wife, Anne. Part of the excess loss (over the $3,000 limit) was carried over to the couple's 2000 joint return, and in 2001, before the carryover loss was used up, Alex died. Anne could claim the unused carryover, up to the $3,000 limit, on a joint return filed for 2001, the year of Alex's death. However, any remaining loss carryover to 2002 or later years is lost. Although the loss was originally reported on a joint return, Anne may claim only her allocable share of the loss on her individual returns for years after 2001, the year of Alex's death. However, since the loss property was owned solely by Alex, no part of the loss is allocable to Anne.

5.6   Losses May Be Disallowed on Sales to Related Persons

A loss on a sale to certain related taxpayers may not be deductible, even though you make the sale at an arm's-length price, the sale is involuntary (for example, a member of your family forecloses a mortgage on your property), or you sell through a public stock exchange and related persons buy the equivalent property; *see* Examples 1 and 2 on the following page.

Related parties. Losses are not allowed on sales between you and your brothers or sisters (whether by the whole or half blood), parents, grandparents, children, or grandchildren. Furthermore, no loss may be claimed on a sale to your spouse; the tax-free exchange rules discussed at *6.7* apply.

A loss is disallowed where the sale is made to your sister-in-law, as nominee of your brother. This sale is deemed to be between you and your brother. But you may deduct the loss on sales to your spouse's relative (for example, your brother-in-law or spouse's step-parent) even if you and your spouse file a joint return.

The Tax Court has allowed a loss on a direct sale to a son-in-law. In a private ruling, the IRS allowed a loss on a sale of a business to a son-in-law where it was shown that his wife (the seller's daughter) did not own an interest in the company. Losses have been disallowed upon withdrawal from a joint venture and from a partnership conducted by members of a family. Family members have argued that losses should be allowed where the sales were motivated by family hostility. The Tax Court ruled that family hostility may not be considered; losses between proscribed family members are disallowed in all cases.

Losses are barred on sales between an individual and a controlled partnership or controlled corporation (where that individual owns more than 50% in value of the outstanding stock or capital interests). In calculating the stock owned, not only must the stock held in your own name be

Filing Tip

Carryovers From Joint or Separate Returns

If you or your spouse has a capital loss carryover from a year in which separate returns were filed, and you are now filing a joint return, the carryovers from the separate returns may be combined on the joint return. If you previously filed jointly and are now filing separately, any loss carryover from the joint return may be claimed only on the separate return of the spouse who originally incurred the loss; *see 5.5*.

taken into account, but also that owned by your family. You also add (1) the proportionate share of any stock held by a corporation, estate, trust, or partnership in which you have an interest as a shareholder, beneficiary, or partner; and (2) any other stock owned individually by your partner.

Losses may also be disallowed in sales between controlled companies, a trust and its creator, a trust and a beneficiary, a partnership and a corporation controlled by the same person (more than 50% ownership), or a tax-exempt organization and its founder. An estate and a beneficiary of that estate are also treated as related parties, except where a sale is in satisfaction of a pecuniary bequest. Check with your tax counselor whenever you plan to sell property at a loss to a buyer who may fit one of these descriptions.

Related buyer's resale at profit. Sometimes, the disallowed loss may be saved. When you sell to a related party who resells the property at a profit, he or she gets the benefit of your disallowed loss. Your purchaser's gain up to the amount of your disallowed loss is not taxed; *see* Example 4 below.

EXAMPLES

1. You sell 100 shares of A Co. stock to your brother for $1,000. They cost you $5,000. You may not deduct your $4,000 loss.
2. The stock investments of a mother and son were managed by the same investment counselor. But neither the son nor mother had any right or control over the other's securities. The counselor followed separate and independent policies for each. Without the son's or his mother's prior approval, the counselor carried out the following transactions: (1) on the same day, he sold at a loss the son's stock in four companies and bought the same stock for the mother's account; and (2) he sold at a loss the son's stock in a copper company, and 28 days later bought the same stock for his mother. The losses of the first sale were disallowed, but not the losses of the copper stock sale because of the time break of 28 days. However, the court did not say how much of a minimum time break is needed to remove a sale-purchase transaction from the rule disallowing losses between related parties.
3. You own 30% of the stock of a company. A trust in which you have a one-half beneficial interest owns 30%. Your partner owns 10% of the stock of the same company. You are deemed the owner of 55% of the stock of that company (30%, plus one-half of 30%, plus 10%) and may not deduct a loss on the sale of property to that company since your deemed ownership exceeds 50%.
4. Smith bought securities in 1990 that cost $10,000. In 1993, he sold them to his sister for $8,000. The $2,000 loss was not deductible by Smith. His sister's basis for the securities is $8,000. In 2002, she sells them for $9,000. The $1,000 gain is not taxed because it is washed out by part of the brother's disallowed loss. If she sold the securities for $11,000, then only $1,000 of the $3,000 gain would be taxed.

5.7 Deferring or Excluding Gain on Small Business Stock Investment

To encourage investments in certain "small" businesses, the tax law provides special tax benefits.

Rollover from small business stock to small business stock. Gain on the sale of qualifying small business stock held for more than six months may be rolled over tax free to other small business stock. The rollover must be made within 60 days of the sale. To qualify as a small business, the gross assets of the corporation must be no more than $50 million when the stock is issued. An active business requirement must also be met. If the reinvestment in a qualifying small business is for less than the sale proceeds, your gain is taxed to the extent of the difference. Your basis in the small business stock acquired during the 60-day period is reduced by the amount of the deferred gain.

To elect deferral, follow the instructions to Schedule D.

Exclusion of 50% of gain on small business stock (Section 1202 exclusion). You only have to pay tax on 50% of a gain from the sale of qualified small business stock issued after August 10, 1993, *provided* you hold the stock for more than five years before the sale. If you qualify for the exclusion, the 50% of the gain that is taxable is subject to the 28% capital gain rate (unless your top regular tax bracket is 15%) on Schedule D, not the 20% or 10% rate; *see 5.3* and Schedule D instructions.

Planning Reminder

50% Exclusion
You generally may claim a 50% exclusion on a profitable sale of qualifying small business stock issued after August 10, 1993, provided you held the stock for more than five years before the sale. The balance of the gain is subject to the 28% capital gain rate unless your top regular tax bracket is 15%; *see 5.3*. A qualifying small business is one eligible for rollover treatment; 42% of the excluded gain must be added back to income as a preference item for purposes of the alternative minimum tax (Chapter 23).

SCHEDULE D (Form 1040)	Capital Gains and Losses	OMB No. 1545-0074

SCHEDULE D
(Form 1040)

Department of the Treasury
Internal Revenue Service   (99)

Capital Gains and Losses

► **Attach to Form 1040.**   ► **See Instructions for Schedule D (Form 1040).**

► **Use Schedule D-1 to list additional transactions for lines 1 and 8.**

OMB No. 1545-0074

20**02**

Attachment
Sequence No. **12**

Name(s) shown on Form 1040 | Your social security number

Part I   Short-Term Capital Gains and Losses—Assets Held One Year or Less

(a) Description of property (Example: 100 sh. XYZ Co.)	(b) Date acquired (Mo., day, yr.)	(c) Date sold (Mo., day, yr.)	(d) Sales price (see page D-5 of the instructions)	(e) Cost or other basis (see page D-5 of the instructions)	(f) Gain or (loss) Subtract (e) from (d)	
1 200 Shares Buma Rubber	7-23-2002	10-7-2002	600	400	200	
100 Shares Ajax Auto	3-13-2002	3-20-2002	2,400	3,000	(600)	
Dan Debtor	WORTHLESS LOAN		Statement Attached	400	(400)	
200 Shares XYZ Mutual Fund: "AVGB"	Various	9-24-2002	6,000	5,240	760	

2 Enter your short-term totals, if any, from Schedule D-1, line 2	**2**			
3 Total short-term sales price amounts. Add lines 1 and 2 in column (d)	**3**	9,000		
4 Short-term gain from Form 6252 and short-term gain or (loss) from Forms 4684, 6781, and 8824			**4**	
5 Net short-term gain or (loss) from partnerships, S corporations, estates, and trusts from Schedule(s) K-1			**5**	
6 Short-term capital loss carryover. Enter the amount, if any, from line 8 of your 2001 Capital Loss Carryover Worksheet			**6** ( )	
7 Net short-term capital gain or (loss). Combine lines 1 through 6 in column (f).			**7**	(40)

Part II   Long-Term Capital Gains and Losses—Assets Held More Than One Year

(a) Description of property (Example: 100 sh. XYZ Co.)	(b) Date acquired (Mo., day, yr.)	(c) Date sold (Mo., day, yr.)	(d) Sales price (see page D-5 of the instructions)	(e) Cost or other basis (see page D-5 of the instructions)	(f) Gain or (loss) Subtract (e) from (d)	(g) 28% rate gain or (loss) * (see instr. below)
8 100 Shares Acme Steel	10- 1- 1991	12-11-2002	11,000	6,000	5,000	
200 Shares Zero Computer	7- 10 -1997	8-6-2002	5,000	2,000	3,000	
Bond, Tech Company	8-10-1998	WORTHLESS		5,000	(5,000)	

9 Enter your long-term totals, if any, from Schedule D-1, line 9	**9**			
10 Total long-term sales price amounts. Add lines 8 and 9 in column (d)	**10**	16,000		
11 Gain from Form 4797, Part I; long-term gain from Forms 2439 and 6252; and long-term gain or (loss) from Forms 4684, 6781, and 8824	**11**			
12 Net long-term gain or (loss) from partnerships, S corporations, estates, and trusts from Schedule(s) K-1.	**12**			
13 Capital gain distributions. See page D-1 of the instructions	**13**	1,050		
14 Long-term capital loss carryover. Enter in both columns (f) and (g) the amount, if any, from line 13 of your 2001 Capital Loss Carryover Worksheet	**14** (950)	(950)		
15 Combine lines 8 through 14 in column (g)	**15**	(950)		
16 Net long-term capital gain or (loss). Combine lines 8 through 14 in column (f) **Next:** Go to Part III on the back.	**16**	3,100		

***28% rate gain or loss** includes all "collectibles gains and losses" (as defined on page D-6 of the instructions) and up to 50% of the eligible gain on qualified small business stock (see page D-4 of the instructions).

For Paperwork Reduction Act Notice, see Form 1040 instructions.   Cat. No. 11338H   Schedule D (Form 1040) 2002

Part III — Taxable Gain or Deductible Loss

17 Combine lines 7 and 16 and enter the result. If a loss, go to line 18. If a gain, enter the gain on Form 1040, line 13, and complete Form 1040 through line 41 . . . . **17** | **3,060**

> **Next:** • If both lines 16 and 17 are gains **and** Form 1040, line 41, is more than zero, complete Part IV below.
> • Otherwise, skip the rest of Schedule D and complete Form 1040.

18 If line 17 is a loss, enter here and on Form 1040, line 13, the **smaller** of **(a)** that loss or **(b)** ($3,000) (or, if married filing separately, ($1,500)). Then complete Form 1040 through line 39 **18**

> **Next:** • If the loss on line 17 is more than the loss on line 18 **or** if Form 1040, line 39, is less than zero, skip **Part IV** below and complete the **Capital Loss Carryover Worksheet** on page D-6 of the instructions before completing the rest of Form 1040.
> • Otherwise, skip **Part IV** below and complete the rest of Form 1040.

Part IV — Tax Computation Using Maximum Capital Gains Rates

19 Enter your unrecaptured section 1250 gain, if any, from line 17 of the worksheet on page D-7 of the instructions **19**

> **If line 15 or line 19 is more than zero, complete the worksheet on page D-9 of the instructions to figure the amount to enter on lines 22, 29, and 40 below, and skip all other lines below. Otherwise, go to line 20.**

20 Enter your taxable income from Form 1040, line 41 . . . . . . **20** | **75,000**
21 Enter the **smaller** of line 16 or line 17 of Schedule D . . . . **21** | **3,060**
22 If you are deducting investment interest expense on Form 4952, enter the amount from Form 4952, line 4e. Otherwise, enter -0- **22** | **- 0 -**
23 Subtract line 22 from line 21. If zero or less, enter -0- . . . . . **23** | **3,060**
24 Subtract line 23 from line 20. If zero or less, enter -0- . . . . . **24** | **71,940**
25 Figure the tax on the amount on line 24. Use the Tax Table or Tax Rate Schedules, whichever applies **25** | **13,216**
26 Enter the **smaller** of:
> • The amount on line 20 **or**
> • $46,700 if married filing jointly or qualifying widow(er); $27,950 if single; $37,450 if head of household; or $23,350 if married filing separately **26** | **46,700**

> **If line 26 is greater than line 24, go to line 27. Otherwise, skip lines 27 through 33 and go to line 34.**

27 Enter the amount from line 24 . . . . **27**
28 Subtract line 27 from line 26. If zero or less, enter -0- and go to line 34 **28**
29 Enter your qualified 5-year gain, if any, from line 7 of the worksheet on page D-8 . . **29**
30 Enter the **smaller** of line 28 or line 29 . . . **30**
31 Multiply line 30 by 8% (.08) **31**
32 Subtract line 30 from line 28 . . . . **32**
33 Multiply line 32 by 10% (.10) **33**

> **If the amounts on lines 23 and 28 are the same, skip lines 34 through 37 and go to line 38.**

34 Enter the **smaller** of line 20 or line 23 . . . . . . **34** | **3,060**
35 Enter the amount from line 28 (if line 28 is blank, enter -0-) . . . **35** | **- 0 -**
36 Subtract line 35 from line 34 . . . . **36** | **3,060**
37 Multiply line 36 by 20% (.20) . . . . **37** | **612**
38 Add lines 25, 31, 33, and 37 . . . . **38** | **13,828**
39 Figure the tax on the amount on line 20. Use the Tax Table or Tax Rate Schedules, whichever applies **39** | **14,053**
40 **Tax on all taxable income (including capital gains).** Enter the **smaller** of line 38 or line 39 here and on Form 1040, line 42 . . . . . . **40** | **13,828**

The amount of gain from any one issuer that is eligible for the 50% exclusion is limited to the greater of (1) 10 times your basis in the qualified stock that you disposed of during the year, or (2) $10 million ($5 million if married filing separately) minus any gain on stock from the same issuer that you excluded in prior years.

Rollover from publicly traded securities to SSBIC. You may be able to defer taxable gain on the sale of publicly traded securities provided the sale proceeds are rolled over within 60 days into common stock or a partnership interest in a "specialized small business investment company," or SSBIC. Subject to an annual deferrable limit (*see* below), the entire gain is deferrable if the cost of your SSBIC stock or partnership interest is at least equal to the sale proceeds. If the SSBIC investment is less than the sale proceeds, your gain is taxed to the extent of the difference.

The annual deferrable limit is $50,000, or $25,000 if you are married filing separately. There is a lifetime limit of $500,000, or $250,000 if married filing separately.

To elect deferral, you must report the sale on Schedule D and attach an explanation of your SSBIC investment; follow the Schedule D instructions. The deferred gain reduces the basis of your SSBIC stock or partnership interest.

An SSBIC is a small business (partnership or corporation) licensed by the Small Business Administration to invest in small businesses which are owned by socially or economically disadvantaged individuals.

Rollover of gain from sale of empowerment zone assets. You may be able to defer capital gain on the sale of qualified empowerment zone assets that you acquired after December 21, 2000, and held for more than one year. You must purchase replacement assets in the same empowerment zone during the 60-day period beginning on the date of the sale. *See* IRS Publications 550 and 954 for details.

5.8 Sample Entries of Capital Asset Sales on Schedule D

You report many different types of transactions on Schedule D of Form 1040: sales of securities, mutual-fund shares, worthless personal loans, sales of stock rights and warrants, sales of land held for investment, and sales of personal residences where part of the gain does not qualify for the home sale exclusion *(29.1)*. Although capital gain distributions from mutual funds and REITs are generally reported as long-term capital gains on Line 13 of Schedule D, investors who receive such distributions but have no other capital gains or losses to report may generally report the distributions directly on Form 1040 or 1040A without having to file Schedule D; *see 32.5* for details.

Different types of Schedule D entries are illustrated in the sample Schedule on pages 105 and 106. The entries correspond to the transactions below. For each transaction, assume that broker's commissions and state and local transfer taxes, if any, are added to the cost of the stock in column (e).

As shown on the sample Schedule D, the result of these transactions is a net short-term capital loss of $40 and a net long-term capital gain of $3,100. Combining them gives a net capital gain of $3,060 (see Line 17). In showing how tax liability is computed in Part IV of Schedule D, we have assumed that the taxpayer is married filing jointly and has taxable income (Line 41 of Form 1040) of $75,000. Under this set of facts, the 20% rate applies to the $3,060 net capital gain, and the total tax liability of $13,828 that is shown on Line 40 of the sample Schedule D is $225 lower than it would be if the gain were subject to ordinary income rates.

The following transactions are entered on the sample Schedule D on pages 105 and 106:

1. *Sale of stock (short-term gain)*—You bought 200 shares of Buma Rubber stock on July 23, 2002, for $400. On October 7, 2002, you sell the 200 shares for $600.

2. *Sale of stock received as a gift (short-term loss)*—Your father gave you a gift of 100 shares of Ajax Auto stock on March 13, 2002, which he had bought on February 15, 1990, for $4,000. The value of the stock at the time of the gift was $3,000. You sell the stock on March 20, 2002, for $2,400. Since the value of the stock at the time of the gift was less than your father's basis, your basis for loss purposes is the $3,000 date-of-gift value *(5.17)* and the holding period begins on the day after the date of the gift *(5.12)*.

3. *Worthless personal loan (short-term loss)*—You loaned $400 to your friend, Dan Debtor, on May 1, 2000. He was adjudged bankrupt on March 15, 2002. A worthless personal debt is deducted as a short-term capital loss; *see 5.33*. The IRS requires that you explain the deduction in a statement attached to your return. The statement should show: (1) the nature of the debt; (2) the name of the debtor and his or her relationship, if any, to you; (3) when the debt was due; (4) how you tried to collect it; and (5) how you determined it was worthless.

Caution

Selling Price Reported to IRS
If you sold stocks, bonds or other investment property through a broker, the sale is reported to the IRS on Form 1099-B. You are sent Copy B of Form 1099-B or a substitute statement. On your statement, the broker must indicate whether gross proceeds or gross proceeds minus commissions and option premiums were reported to the IRS. If the gross proceeds were reported, enter that amount as the sales price in column (d) of Schedule D and add any commissions or option premiums to cost basis in column (e). If only the net proceeds were reported, enter that amount as the sales price in column (d) of Schedule D and do not include commissions or option premiums in column (e).

4. *Sale of mutual-fund shares (short-term gain)*—You bought 160 shares of the XYZ Mutual Fund on February 5, 2002, for $4,000. On August 6, you bought another 240 shares for $6,480. You sell 200 of the shares on September 24, 2002, for $6,000. You decide to use the average basis method (single category) to figure the basis of the sold shares. Your average basis is $26.20 per share, the total cost basis of $10,480 divided by 400 shares. Thus, your basis for the 200 sold shares is $5,240 (200 × $26.20). In column (a) of Schedule D, enter "AVGB" to indicate that you are using an average basis. *See* Chapter 32 for further details on basis of mutual-fund shares.

5. *Sale of stock (long-term gain)*—You bought 100 shares of Acme Steel stock on October 1, 1991, for $6,000. On December 11, 2002, you sell the 100 shares for $11,000.

6. *Sale of stock (long term)*—You bought 200 shares of Zero Computer Co. stock for $2,000 on July 10, 1997. On August 6, 2002, you sell them for $5,000.

7. *Worthless bond*—On August 10, 1998, you bought a $5,000 bond of Tech Co. at par. The bond became completely worthless during 2002; *see 5.32*.

8. *Capital gain distributions*—You received capital gain distributions of $1,050 in 2002 from mutual funds.

9. *Long-term capital loss carryover*—You had a long-term capital loss carryover of $950 from your 2001 return. Note that the carryover would be first applied against long-term gains subject to the 28% rate *(see 5.3)*, if there were any.

Holding Period for Capital Assets

5.9 Counting the Months in Your Holding Period

The period of time you own a capital asset before its sale or exchange determines whether capital gain or loss is short term or long term.

These are the rules for counting the holding period:
1. A holding period is figured in months and fractions of months.
2. The beginning date of a holding month is generally the day after the asset was acquired. The same numerical date of each following month starts a new holding month regardless of the number of days in the preceding month.
3. The last day of the holding period is the day on which the asset is sold.

As a rule of thumb, use the numerical date on which you acquired the asset as the numerical date ending a holding month in each following month. However, if you acquire an asset on the last day of a month, a holding month ends on the last day of a following calendar month, regardless of the number of days in each month.

EXAMPLES
1. On September 24, 2002, you buy stock. The holding months begin on September 25, October 25, November 25, and December 25, and end on October 24, November 24, December 24, etc. A sale on or after September 25, 2003, would result in long-term gain or loss.
2. You buy stock on November 30. A holding month ends on December 31, January 31, February 28 (or 29 in a leap year), etc.

5.10 Holding Period for Securities

Rules for counting your holding period for various securities transactions are as follows:

Stock sold on a public exchange. The holding period starts on the day after your purchase order is executed (trading date). The day your sale order is executed (trading date) is the last day of the holding period, even if delivery and payment are not made until several days after the actual sale (settlement date).

Planning Reminder

Long-Term Holding Period of More Than a Year

To obtain the benefit of the 20% or 10% (if in the 15% bracket) capital gains rate, you must hold an asset more than a year before selling it.

EXAMPLES
1. On June 3, you sell a stock at a profit. Your holding period ends on June 3, although proceeds are not received until June 6.
2. You sell stock at a gain on a public exchange on December 31, 2002. The gain must be reported in 2002 even though the proceeds are received in 2003. The installment sale rule does not apply; *see 5.21.*

Stock subscriptions. If you are bound by your subscription but the corporation is not, the holding period begins the day after the date on which the stock is issued. If both you and the company are bound, the date the subscription is accepted by the corporation is the date of acquisition, and your holding period begins the day after.

Tax-free stock rights. When you exercise rights to acquire corporate stock from the issuing corporation, your holding period for the stock begins on the day of exercise, not on the day after. You are deemed to exercise stock rights when you assent to the terms of the rights in the manner requested or authorized by the corporation. An option to acquire stock is not a stock right.

Stock sold from different lots. If you purchased shares of the same stock on different dates and cannot determine which shares you are selling, the shares purchased at the earliest time are considered the stock sold first; this is called the FIFO (first-in, first-out) method; *see 30.2.*

> **EXAMPLE**
>
> You purchased 100 shares of ABC stock on May 3, 1995, 100 shares of ABC stock on May 1, 1997, and 300 shares of ABC stock on September 2, 1998. In 2002, you sell 250 shares of ABC stock, and are unable to determine when those particular shares were bought. Using the "first-in, first-out" method, 100 shares are from May 3, 1995, 100 shares from May 1, 1997, and 50 shares are from September 2, 1998. *See also 30.2.*

Commodities. If you acquired a commodity futures contract, the holding period of a commodity accepted in satisfaction of the contract includes your holding period of the contract, unless you are a dealer in commodities.

Employee stock options. When an employee exercises a stock option, the holding period of the acquired stock begins on the day after the option is exercised. If an employee option plan allows the exercise of an option by giving notes, the terms of the plan should be reviewed to determine when ownership rights to the stock are transferred. The terms may affect the start of the holding period for the stock.

Wash sales. After a wash sale, the holding period of the new stock includes the holding period of the old stock for which a loss has been disallowed; *see 30.6.*

Other references. For the holding period of stock dividends, *see 30.3*; for short sales, *see 30.5*; and for convertible securities, *see 30.7.*

5.11 Holding Period for Real Estate

The holding period starts the day after the date of acquisition, which is the earlier of: (1) the date title passes to you or (2) the date you take possession and you assume the burdens and privileges of ownership. In disputes involving the starting and closing dates of a holding period, you may refer to the state law that applies to your sale or purchase agreement. State law determines when title to property passes.

If you convert a residence to rental property and later sell the home, the holding period includes the time you held the home for personal purposes.

Year-end sale. The date of sale is the last day of your holding period even if you do not receive the sale proceeds until the following year. For example, you sell land at a gain on December 31, 2002, receiving payment in January 2003. The holding period ends on December 31, although the sale is reported in 2003 when the proceeds are received. Note that the December 31 gain transaction can be reported in 2002 by making an election to "elect out" of installment reporting; *see 5.23.* A sale at a loss is reported in 2002.

5.12 Holding Period for Gifts, Inheritances, and Other Property

Gift property. If, in figuring a gain or loss, your basis for the property under *5.17* is the same as the donor's basis, you add the donor's holding period to the period you held the property. If you sell the property at a loss using as your basis the fair market value at the date of the gift *(5.17)*, your holding period begins on the day after the date of the gift.

Inherited property. The law gives an automatic holding period of more than one year for inherited property. Follow the Schedule D instructions for reporting the sale of inherited property.

Planning Reminder

Year-End Sales
Tax reporting for year-end sales of real estate is different from that for publicly traded securities. Gain on a sale of realty at the end of 2002 may be deferred under the installment sale rules *(5.22)* if payments will be received in 2003 or later years. Gain on a sale of publicly traded securities at the end of 2002 must be reported on your 2002 return although you receive payment in 2003.

Filing Tip

Selling Inherited Property
When you sell property that you inherited, report the sale as long-term gain or loss on Schedule D even if you actually held the property for less than one year. The law automatically treats inherited property as if it were held for more than one year.

Where property is purchased by the executor or trustee and distributed to you, your holding period begins the day after the date on which the property was purchased.

Partnership property. When you receive property as a distribution in kind from your partnership, the period your partnership held the property is added to your holding period. But there is no adding on of holding periods if the partnership property distributed was inventory and was sold by you within five years of distribution.

Involuntary conversions. When you have an involuntary conversion and elect to defer tax on gain, the holding period for the qualified replacement property generally includes the period you held the converted property. A new holding period begins for new property if you do not make an election to defer tax.

Figuring Your Profit or Loss

Planning Reminder

Records for Rental Property Improvements
Keep records of permanent improvements and legal fees for rental property. These increase your basis and lower any potential gain when you sell the property.

5.13 Calculating Gain or Loss

In most cases, you know if you have realized an *economic* profit or loss on the sale or exchange of property. You know your cost and selling price. The difference between the two is your profit or loss. The computation of gain or loss for tax purposes is similarly figured, except that the basis adjustment rules may require you to increase or decrease your cost or selling price and the amount-realized rules may require you to increase the selling price. As a result, your gain or loss for tax purposes may differ from your initial calculation.

Figuring Gain or Loss on Schedule D

1. Amount realized or total selling price *(5.14)*. $_____
2. Cost or other unadjusted basis *(5.16)*. $_____
3. *Plus:* Improvements; certain legal fees *(5.20)*. $_____
4. *Minus:* Depreciation, casualty losses *(5.20)*. $_____
5. Adjusted basis: 2 *plus* 3 *minus* 4 *(5.20)*. $_____
6. Add selling expenses to 5. This is the total cost shown on Schedule D. $_____ $_____
7. Gain or loss: Subtract 6 from 1. $_____

EXAMPLE

You sell rental property to a buyer who pays you cash of $50,000 and assumes your $35,000 mortgage. You bought the property for $55,000 and made $12,000 of permanent improvements. You deducted depreciation of $7,250. Selling expenses were $2,000. Your gain on the sale is $23,250, figured as follows:

1. Amount realized *(5.14)*	
Cash	$50,000
Mortgage assumed by buyer	35,000
	$85,000
2. Original cost	55,000
3. *Plus* improvements	12,000
	$67,000
4. *Minus* depreciation	7,250
5. Adjusted basis	59,750
6. *Plus* selling expenses*	2,000
7. Total cost: Combined result of Lines 2–6	61,750
8. Gain: Subtract Line 7 from Line 1	$23,250

---

*Selling expenses on Schedule D. When reporting a sale on Schedule D, IRS instructions require you to include *selling expenses* (Step 6) in the column for *cost*, rather than as a reduction to the sales price. The only exception is where a broker has reported *net* sale proceeds (gross proceeds *less* selling expenses) on Form 1099-B; you would then report the net amount as the sales price. Where a broker has reported the *gross* sales price on Form 1099-B, the IRS wants you to treat sales commissions as an addition to cost (rather than a reduction to selling price) so that it can compare the gross amount shown on Form 1099-B with the sales price reported on your return.

Using the facts in the previous Example, you report the gross selling price of $85,000 in column (d) of Schedule D. In column (e), enter the adjusted basis of $59,750 *plus* the selling expenses of $2,000 for a total of $61,750. The final result, a gain of $23,250 ($85,000 – $61,750), is the same as if the selling price were reduced by the selling expenses.

5.14 Amount Realized Is the Total Selling Price

Amount realized is the tax term for the total selling price. It includes cash, the fair market value of additional property received, and any of your liabilities that the buyer agrees to pay. The buyer's note is included in the selling price at fair market value. This is generally the discounted amount that a bank or other party will pay for the note.

Sale of mortgaged property. The selling price includes the amount of the unpaid mortgage. This is true whether or not you are personally liable on the debt, and whether or not the buyer assumes the mortgage or merely takes the property subject to the mortgage. The full amount of the unpaid mortgage is included, even where the value of the property is less than the unpaid mortgage. *See also 31.9* for computing amount realized on foreclosure sales.

If, at the time of the sale, the buyer pays off the existing mortgage or your other liabilities, you include the payment as part of the sales proceeds.

Caution

Mortgaged Property
When you sell mortgaged property, you must include the unpaid balance of the mortgage as part of the sales price received, in addition to any cash.

> **EXAMPLES**
>
> 1. You sell property subject to a mortgage of $60,000. The seller pays you cash of $30,000 and takes the property subject to the mortgage. The sales price or "amount realized" is $90,000.
>
> 2. A partnership receives a nonrecourse mortgage of $1,851,500 from a bank to build an apartment project. Several years later, the partnership sells the project for the buyer's agreement to assume the unpaid mortgage. At the time, the value of the project is $1,400,000 and the partnership basis in the project is $1,455,740. The partnership figures a loss of $55,740, the difference between basis and the value of the project. The IRS figures a gain of $395,760, the difference between the unpaid mortgage and basis. The partnership claims the selling price is limited to the lower fair market value and is supported by an appeals court. The Supreme Court reverses, supporting the IRS position. That the value of property is less than the amount of the mortgage has no effect on the rule requiring the unpaid mortgage to be part of the selling price. A mortgagor realizes value to the extent that his or her obligation to repay is relieved by a third party's assumption of the mortgage debt.

5.15 Finding Your Cost

In figuring gain or loss, you need to know the "unadjusted basis" of the property sold. This term refers to the original cost of your property if you purchased it. The general rules for determining your unadjusted basis are in *5.16*. Basis for property received by gift or inheritance is in *5.17*; rules for surviving joint tenants are in *5.18*. Keep in mind that you have to adjust this figure for improvements to the property, depreciation, or losses; *see 5.20*.

5.16 Unadjusted Basis of Your Property

To determine your tax cost for property, first find in the following section the unadjusted basis of the property, and then increase or decrease that basis as explained at *5.20*.

Property you bought. Unadjusted basis is your cash cost plus the value of any property you gave to the seller. If you assumed a mortgage or bought property subject to a mortgage, the amount of the mortgage is part of your unadjusted basis.

Purchase expenses are included in your cost, such as commissions, title insurance, recording fees, survey costs, and transfer taxes.

When you buy real estate, you usually reimburse the seller for property taxes he or she paid that cover the period after you took title. If you bought the property before 1954, you add such payments to basis. If you bought the property after 1953, taxes paid are not added to basis because they are immediately deductible in the year paid; *see 16.6*. However, if at the closing you also paid property taxes attributable to the time the seller held the property, you add such taxes to basis.

Filing Tip

Basis of Mutual-Fund Shares
To figure gain or loss on the sale of mutual-fund shares where purchases are made at various times, you may use an averaging method to determine the cost basis of the shares sold; *see 32.10*.

> **EXAMPLE**
> You bought a building for $120,000 in cash and a purchase money mortgage of $60,000. The unadjusted basis of the building is $180,000.

Property obtained for services. If you paid for the property by providing services, the value of the property, which is taxable compensation, is also your adjusted basis.

Property received in taxable exchange. Technically, your unadjusted basis for the new property is the fair market value of the surrendered property at the time of exchange. In practice, however, the basis usually is equal to the fair market value of the property received. *See* below for tax-free exchanges.

> **EXAMPLE**
>
> You acquire real estate for $35,000. When the property has a fair market value of $40,000, you exchange it for machinery also worth $40,000. You have a gain of $5,000 and the basis of the machinery is $40,000.

Property received in a tax-free exchange. The computation of basis is made on Form 8824. If the exchange is completely tax free *(6.1)*, your basis for the new property will be your basis for the property you gave up in the exchange, plus any additional cash and exchange expenses you paid. If the exchange is partly nontaxable and partly taxable because you received "boot" *(6.3)*, your basis for the new property will be your basis for the property given up in the exchange, decreased by any cash received and by any liabilities on the property you gave up, and increased by any cash and exchange expenses you paid, liabilities on the property you received, and gain taxed to you on the exchange. Gain is taxed to the extent you receive "boot," in the form of cash or a transfer of liabilities that exceeds the liabilities assumed in the exchange; *see 6.3* for a discussion on taxable boot. *The Example at 6.3 illustrates the basis computation.*

> **EXAMPLES**
>
> 1. You exchange investment real estate, which cost you $20,000, for other investment real estate. Both properties have a fair market value of $35,000 and neither property is mortgaged. You pay no tax on the exchange. The unadjusted basis of the new property received in the exchange is $20,000.
>
> 2. Same facts as in Example 1, but you receive real estate worth $30,000 and cash of $5,000. On this transaction, you realize gain of $15,000 (amount realized of $35,000 less your basis of $20,000), but only $5,000 of the gain is taxable, equal to the cash "boot" received. Your basis for the new property is $20,000, figured this way:
>
> | | |
> |---|---|
> | Basis of old property | $20,000 |
> | *Less:* Cash received | 5,000 |
> | | 15,000 |
> | *Plus:* Gain recognized | 5,000 |
> | Basis of new property | $20,000 |

Property received from a spouse or former spouse. As explained at *6.7*, tax-free exchange rules apply to property transfers after July 18, 1984, to a spouse, or to a former spouse where the transfer is incident to a divorce. The spouse receiving the property takes a basis equal to that of the transferor. Certain adjustments may be required where a transfer of mortgaged property is made in trust.

If you received property before July 19, 1984, under a prenuptial agreement in exchange for your release of your dower and marital rights, your basis is the fair market value at the time you received it.

New residence purchased under tax deferral rule of prior law. If you sold your old principal residence and bought a qualifying replacement under the prior law deferral rules, your basis for the new house is what you paid for it, less any gain that was not taxed on the sale of the old residence.

Property received as a trust beneficiary. Generally, you take the same basis the trust had for the property. But if the distribution is made to settle a claim you had against the trust, your basis for the property is the amount of the settled claim.

If you received a distribution in kind for your share of trust income before June 2, 1984, the basis of the distribution is generally the value of the property to the extent allocated to distributable net income. For distributions in kind after June 1, 1984, in taxable years ending after June 1, 1984, your basis is the basis of the property in the hands of the trust. If the trust elects to treat the distribution as a taxable sale, your basis is generally fair market value.

Property acquired with involuntary conversion proceeds. If you acquire replacement property with insurance proceeds from destroyed property, or a government payment for condemned property, basis is the cost of the new property decreased by deferred gain; *see 18.23* for figuring the deferred gain. If the replacement property consists of more than one piece of property, basis is allocated to each piece in proportion to its respective cost.

Planning Reminder

Carryover Basis From Spouse or Ex-Spouse

If you receive a gift of property from your spouse or you receive property from a former spouse in a divorce settlement, your basis for the property is generally the same as the spouse's basis; *see 6.7.*

EXAMPLE

A building with an adjusted basis of $100,000 is destroyed by fire. The owner receives an insurance award of $200,000, realizing a gain of $100,000. He buys a building as a replacement for $150,000. Of the $100,000 gain, $50,000 is taxable, while the remaining $50,000 is deferred. Taxable gain is limited to the portion of the insurance award not used to buy replacement property ($200,000 − $150,000). The basis of the new building is $100,000:

Cost of the new building	$150,000
Less: deferred gain	50,000
Basis	$100,000

5.17 Basis of Property You Inherited or Received as a Gift

Special basis rules apply to property you received as a gift or that you inherited. Gifts from a spouse are subject to the rules discussed in *6.7*. If you are a surviving joint tenant who received full title to property upon the death of the other joint tenant, *see 5.18*.

Basis of Property Received as Gift

If the fair market value of the property *equalled or exceeded* the donor's adjusted basis *(5.20)* at the time you received the gift, your basis for figuring gain or loss when you sell it is the donor's adjusted basis plus all or part of any gift tax paid; *see* the gift tax rule below.

If on the date of the gift the fair market value was *less* than the donor's adjusted basis, your basis for purposes of figuring gain is the donor's adjusted basis, and your basis for figuring loss is the fair market value on the date of the gift.

EXAMPLE

Assume that in 1997 you received a gift of stock from your father that you sold in 2002. His adjusted basis was $1,000.

The basis you use to determine gain or loss depends on whether the fair market value of the stock on the date of the gift equalled or exceeded your father's $1,000 adjusted basis. If it did, your basis is your father's $1,000 basis and you will realize a gain if your selling price exceeds $1,000, as on Line 1 below, or a loss if the selling price is below $1,000, as on Line 4.

If the value of the stock on the date of the gift was less than $1,000 (father's basis) then you have: a gain if you sell for more than $1,000, as on Line 5; a loss if you sell for less than the date-of-gift value, as on Line 2; or neither gain nor loss if you sell for more than the date-of-gift value but no more than $1,000 (father's basis), as on Line 3.

If value of the gift at receipt was—	*And you sold it for—*	*Your basis is—*	*Your gain is—*	*Your loss is—*
1. $3,000	$2,000	$1,000	$1,000	none
2. 700	500	700	none	$200
3. 300	500	*	none	none
4. 1,500	500	1,000	none	500
5. 500	1,200	1,000	200	none

*On Line 3 of the Example, where you sell for more than the date-of-gift value but for no more than the donor's basis, there is neither gain nor loss. To see if you have a gain, you use the donor's $1,000 basis as your basis, but on a sale for $500, you have a loss ($500) and not a gain. To see if you have a loss, you use the $300 date-of-gift value of the stock as your basis, but on a sale for $500, you have a gain ($200) and not a loss. Thus, you have neither gain nor loss under the basis rules, which require you to use the donor's basis for determining if you have a gain and the date-of-gift value for determining if you have a loss.

Did the donor pay gift tax? If the donor paid a gift tax *(33.1)* on the gift to you, your basis for the property is increased under these rules:

1. For property received after December 31, 1976, the basis is increased for the gift tax paid by an amount that bears the same ratio to the amount of tax paid as the net appreciation in the value of the gift bears to the amount of the gift after taking into account the $10,000 annual gift tax exclusion *(33.1)*. The increase may not exceed the tax paid. Net appreciation in the value of

Caution

Basis for Gift

The basis of gift property you receive generally depends on the donor's basis. Make sure you get this information from the donor.

Filing Tip

No Gain or Loss

When you sell property received as a gift, it is possible that you may realize neither gain nor loss. *See* Line 3 of the Example on the left for an illustration of how this can happen.

any gift is the amount by which the fair market value of the gift exceeds the donor's adjusted basis immediately before the gift. *See* Example 2 below.

2. For property received after September 1, 1958, but before 1977, basis is increased by the gift tax paid on the property but not above the fair market value of the property at the time of the gift.

3. For property received before September 2, 1958, the gift tax paid increases the basis. But this increase may not be more than the excess of the fair market value of the property at the time of the gift over the basis of the property in the donor's hands. Ask the donor or his or her advisor for these amounts.

EXAMPLES

1. In 1975, your father gave you rental property with a fair market value of $78,000. The basis of the property in his hands was $60,000. He paid a gift tax of $15,000 on the gift. The basis of the property in your hands is $75,000 ($60,000 + $15,000).

2. In 2001, your father gave you rental property with a fair market value of $178,000. His basis in the property was $160,000. He paid a gift tax of $44,560 on a taxable gift of $168,000, after claiming the $10,000 annual exclusion. The basis of the property in your hands is your father's basis increased by the gift tax attributable to the appreciation. Gift tax attributable to the appreciation is:

$$\frac{\text{Appreciation}}{\text{Gift } minus \text{ annual exclusion}} \times \text{Gift tax paid}$$

$$\frac{\$18,000}{\$168,000} \times \$44,560 = \$4,774$$

Your basis for figuring gain or loss or depreciation is $164,774 ($4,774 + $160,000 father's basis).

Gift you received before 1921. Your basis is the fair market value of the property at the time of the gift.

Depreciation on property received as a gift. If the property is depreciable (*see* Chapter 42), your basis for computing depreciation deductions is the donor's adjusted basis (*5.20*), plus all or part of the gift tax paid by the donors as previously discussed.

When you sell the property, you must adjust basis (*5.20*) for depreciation claimed. If accelerated depreciation is claimed and you sell at a gain, you are subject to the ordinary income recapture rules discussed at *44.1*.

Basis of Inherited Property

Your basis for inherited property is generally the fair market value of the property on the date of the decedent's death, regardless of when you acquire the property. If the decedent died after October 21, 1942, and the executor elected to use an *alternate valuation date* after the death, your basis is the alternate value at that date.

If you owned the property jointly with the deceased, *see 5.18*.

If you inherit appreciated property that you (or your spouse) gave to the deceased person within one year of his or her death, your basis is the decedent's basis immediately before death, not its fair market value.

If the inherited property is subject to a mortgage, your basis is the value of the property, and not its equity at the date of death. If the property is subject to a lease under which no income is to be received for years, the basis is the value of the property—not the equity.

You might be given the right to buy the deceased person's property under his or her will. This is not the same as inheriting that property. Your basis is what you pay—not what the property is worth on the date of the deceased's death.

If property was inherited from an individual who died after 1976 and before November 7, 1978, and the executor elected to apply a carryover basis to all estate property, your basis is figured with reference to the decedent's basis. The executor must inform you of the basis of such property.

Community property. Upon the death of a spouse in a community property state, one-half of the fair market value of the community property is generally included in the deceased spouse's estate for estate tax purposes. The surviving spouse's basis for his or her half of the property is 50% of the total fair market value. For the other half, the heirs of the deceased spouse also have a basis equal to 50% of the fair market value.

 Filing Tip

Advantage of Leaving Appreciated Property to an Heir

Since your basis for inherited property is the value at the decedent's death or alternate valuation date, income tax is completely avoided on the appreciation in value that occurred while the decedent owned the property.

5.18 Joint Tenancy Basis Rules for Surviving Tenants

If you are a surviving joint tenant, your basis for the property depends on how much of the value was includible in the deceased tenant's gross estate, and this depends on whether the joint tenant was your spouse or someone other than your spouse.

Qualified joint interest rule for survivor of spouse who died after 1981. A "qualified joint interest" rule applies to a joint tenancy with right of survivorship where the spouses are the only joint tenants, and to a tenancy by the entirety between a husband and wife. Where the surviving spouse is a U.S. citizen, the general rule for deaths occurring *after 1981* is as follows: One-half of the fair market value of the property is includible in the decedent's gross estate. This is true regardless of how much each spouse contributed to the purchase price. Fair market value is fixed at the date of death, or six months later if an estate tax return is filed and the optional alternate valuation date is elected.

The surviving spouse's basis equals 50% of the date-of-death fair market value (the amount included in the decedent's gross estate), plus one-half of the original cost basis for the property; *see* Example 1 below. If no estate tax return was due because the value of the estate was below the filing threshold, the surviving spouse's basis is one-half of the fair market value of the property at the date of death (alternate valuation is not available) plus one-half of the original cost basis. If depreciation deductions for the property were claimed before the date of death, the surviving spouse must reduce basis by his or her share (under local law) of the depreciation; *see* Example 2 below.

If the surviving spouse is *not* a U.S. citizen on the due date of the estate tax return, the basis rule is generally the same as the rule discussed below for unmarried joint tenants.

 IRS Alert

Spousal Joint Tenancies Created Before 1977

If spouses jointly own property and one spouse dies, the surviving spouse generally receives a stepped-up basis for 50% of the date-of-death value. The IRS at one time took the position that the 50% stepped-up basis rule applied to pre-1997 spousal joint tenancies. However, after the Tax Court and two federal appeals courts allowed a surviving spouse a 100% stepped-up basis if the spousal joint tenancy was created before 1977 (*see* Example 3 in the left column), the IRS decided to follow the Tax Court decision and will no longer litigate the issue.

EXAMPLES

1. John and Jennifer Jones jointly own a house that cost them $50,000 in 1979. John paid $45,000 of the purchase price and Jennifer $5,000. In 2002, John dies when the house is worth $200,000. One-half, or $100,000, is included in his estate although he contributed 90% of the purchase price. For income tax purposes, Jennifer's basis for the house is $125,000.

One-half of cost basis	$25,000
Inherited portion	100,000
Jennifer's basis	$125,000

2. Same facts as in Example 1 except that the home was rental property for which $20,000 of depreciation deductions had been allowed before John's death. Under local law, Jennifer had a right to 50% of the income from the property and, thus, a right to 50% of the depreciation. Her basis for the property is $115,000: $125,000 as shown in Example 1, reduced by $10,000, her share of the depreciation.

3. The Gallensteins purchased farm property in 1955 as joint tenants; Mr. Gallenstein provided all the funds. When he died in 1987, Mrs. Gallenstein claimed that 100% of the property was includible in her husband's gross estate and she had a stepped-up basis for that full amount. The IRS argued that under the rules for estates of spouses dying after 1981, she received a stepped-up basis for only 50% of the date-of-death value. The federal appeals court for the Sixth Circuit (Kentucky, Michigan, Ohio, and Tennessee) agreed with Mrs. Gallenstein. The appeals court held that pre-1977 spousal joint tenancies were not affected when the law was changed to provide a 50% estate tax inclusion and 50% stepped-up basis for spousal deaths after 1981. For pre-1977 spousal joint tenancies, the prior law rule continues to apply: 100% of the date-of-death value of jointly held property is included in the estate of the first spouse to die unless it is shown that the survivor contributed towards the purchase. In this case, where Mrs. Gallenstein's deceased husband had paid the entire purchase price, her basis was 100% of the value of the property and she realized no taxable gain when she sold the property at a price equal to that stepped-up basis.

   The Tax Court and the Fourth Circuit Appeals Court (Maryland, North Carolina, South Carolina, Virginia, and West Virginia) agreed with the Sixth Circuit's approach of allowing a 100% stepped-up basis for a pre-1977 spousal joint interest where the deceased spouse had paid the entire purchase price. In October 2001, the IRS acquiesced to the Tax Court decision and will no longer litigate the issue.

If the statute of limitations has not expired, a surviving spouse who reported gain on a sale of property using the 50% basis rule should consult with his or her tax adviser about filing a refund claim based upon the 100% basis rule.

Planning Reminder

Joint Property Held With Non-Spouse

If you own property with someone other than your spouse, then at the other owner's death your basis for the property equals your original contribution to the purchase plus the portion of the property's value that was includible in the gross estate of the deceased owner.

Unmarried joint tenants. If you are a surviving joint tenant who owned property with someone other than your spouse, your basis for the entire property is your basis for your share before the joint owner died plus the fair market value of the decedent's share at death (or on the alternate valuation date if the estate uses the alternate date). Even if the estate is too small to require the filing of an estate tax return, you may still include the decedent's share of the date-of-death value in your basis. However, if no estate tax return is required, you may not use the alternate valuation date basis.

EXAMPLE

You and your sister bought a home in 1950 for $20,000. She paid $12,000, and you paid $8,000. Title to the house was held by both of you as joint tenants. In 2002, when she died, the house was worth $150,000. Since she paid 60% of the cost of the house, 60% of the value at her death, $90,000, is included in her estate tax return (or would be included if an estate tax return was due). Your basis for the house is now $98,000—the $8,000 you originally paid plus the $90,000 fair market value of your sister's 60% share at her death.

Exception for pre-1954 deaths. Where property was held in joint tenancy and one of the tenants died before January 1, 1954, no part of the interest of the surviving tenant is treated, for purposes of determining the basis of the property, as property transmitted at death. The survivor's basis is the original cost of the property.

Survivor of spouse who died before 1982. The basis rule for a surviving spouse who held property jointly (or as tenancy by the entirety) with a spouse who died before 1982 is generally the same as the above rule for unmarried joint tenants. However, special rules applied to qualified joint interests and eligible joint interests are discussed below.

EXAMPLE

A husband and wife owned rental property as tenants by the entirety that they purchased for $30,000. The husband furnished two-thirds of the purchase price ($20,000) and the wife furnished one-third ($10,000). Depreciation deductions taken before the husband's death were $12,000. On the date of his death in 1979, the property had a fair market value of $60,000. Under the law of the state in which the property is located, as tenants by the entirety, each had a half interest in the property. The wife's basis in the property at the date of her husband's death is $44,000, computed as follows:

Interest acquired with her own funds	$10,000
Interest acquired from husband ($2/3$ of $60,000)	40,000
	$50,000
Less: Depreciation of $1/2$ interest not acquired by reason of death ($1/2$ of $12,000)	6,000
Wife's basis at date of husband's death	$44,000

If she had not contributed any part of the purchase price, her basis at the date of her husband's death would be $54,000 ($60,000 fair market value less $6,000 depreciation).

Qualified joint interest and eligible joint interest where spouse died before 1982. Where, after 1976, a spouse dying before 1982 elected to treat realty as a "qualified joint interest" subject to gift tax, such joint property was treated as owned 50–50 by each spouse, and 50% of the value was included in the decedent's estate. Thus, for income tax purposes, the survivor's basis for the inherited 50% half of the property is the estate tax value; the basis for the other half is determined under the gift rules detailed in *5.17*. Personal property is treated as a "qualified joint interest" only if it was created or deemed to have been created after 1976 by a husband and wife and was subject to gift tax.

Where death occurred before 1982 and a surviving spouse materially participated in the operation of a farm or other business, an estate may elect to treat the farm or business property as an "eligible joint interest," which means that part of the investment in the property may be attributed to the surviving spouse's services and that part is not included in the deceased spouse's estate. Where such an election was made, the survivor's basis for income tax purposes includes the estate tax value of property included in the decedent's estate.

5.19 Allocating Cost Among Several Assets

Allocation of basis is generally required in these cases: when the property includes land and building; the land is to be divided into lots; securities or mutual-fund shares are purchased at different times; stock splits; and in the purchase of a business.

Purchase of land and building. To figure depreciation on the building, part of the purchase price must be allocated to the building. The allocation is made according to the fair market values of the building and land. The amount allocated to land is not depreciated.

Purchase of land to be divided into lots. The purchase price of the tract is allocated to each lot, so that the gain or loss from the sale of each lot may be reported in the year of its sale. Allocation is not made ratably, that is, with an equal share to each lot or parcel. It is based on the relative value of each piece of property. Comparable sales, competent appraisals, or assessed values may be used as guides.

Securities. *See 30.2* for details on methods of identifying securities bought at different dates. *See 30.3* for allocating basis of stock dividends and stock splits and *30.4* for allocating the basis of stock rights.

Mutual-fund shares. *See 32.10* for determining the basis of mutual-fund shares where purchases were made at different times.

Purchase price of a business. *See 44.9* for allocation rule.

5.20 How To Find Adjusted Basis

After determining the *unadjusted* cost basis for property under the rules at *5.16–5.19*, you may have to increase it or decrease it to find your *adjusted basis*, which is the amount used to figure your gain or loss on a sale, as shown at *5.13*.

1. **Additions to basis.** You add to unadjusted basis the cost of these items:

- *All permanent improvements and additions to the property and other capital costs.* Increase basis for capital improvements such as adding a room or a fence, putting in new plumbing or wiring, and paving a driveway. Also include capital costs such as the cost of extending utility service lines, assessments for local improvements such as streets, sidewalks, or water connections, and repairing your property after a casualty (for example, repair costs after a fire or storm).
- *Legal fees,* including fees incurred for defending or perfecting title, or for obtaining a reduction of an assessment levied against property to pay for local benefits.
- *Sale of unharvested land.* If you sell land with unharvested crops, add the cost of producing the crops to the basis of the property sold.

2. **Decreases to basis.** You reduce cost basis for these items:

- *Return of capital,* such as dividends on stock paid out of capital or out of a depletion reserve when the company has no available earnings or surplus; *see 4.11*.
- *Losses from casualties,* including insurance awards and payments in settlement of damages to your property.

> **EXAMPLE**
> Your vacation home, which cost $75,000, is damaged by fire. You deducted the uninsured loss of $10,000 and spent $11,000 to repair the property. Several years later, you sell the house for $90,000. To figure your profit, increase the original cost of the house by the $11,000 of repairs and then reduce basis by the $10,000 casualty loss to get an adjusted basis of $76,000 ($75,000 + $11,000 – $10,000). Your gain on the sale is $14,000 ($90,000 – $76,000).

- *Depletion allowances; see 9.15.*
- *Depreciation, first-year expensing deduction, ACRS deductions, amortization, and obsolescence on property used in business or for the production of income.* In some years, you may have taken more or less depreciation than was allowable.

  If you claim less than what was allowable, you must deduct from basis the allowable amount rather than what was actually claimed. You may file an amended return to claim the full allowable depreciation for a year. If the amended return deadline has passed, you may still get a deduction for the unclaimed depreciation by filing for an accounting method change under IRS Revenue Procedure 99-49. A deduction is generally claimed over a four-year period, but if the adjustment is less than $25,000, a one-year adjustment is allowed; *see* Revenue Procedure 99-49 for details.

 *Court Decision*

Improvements Covered by Note
In an unusual case, the owner of office condominiums financed substantial improvements to the units by giving promissory notes to a contracting company that he controlled. Before paying off the notes he sold the units. He included the cost of the improvements in basis to figure his gain on the sale, but the IRS, with the approval of a federal district court, held that this was improper. The court held that as a cash-basis taxpayer, he could not include the face amount of the notes in the basis of the condominiums until the notes were paid.

If you took more depreciation than was allowable, you may have to make the following adjustments: If you have deducted more than what was allowable and you received a tax benefit from the deduction, you deduct from basis the full amount of the depreciation. But if the excess depreciation did not give you a tax benefit, because income was eliminated by other deductions, the excess is not deducted from basis.

- **Amortized bond premium;** *see 4.17.*
- **Cancelled debt excluded from income.** If you did not pay tax on certain cancellations of debt because of bankruptcy or insolvency, or on qualifying farm debt or business real property, you reduce basis of your property for the amount forgiven under the rules at *11.8.*
- **Investment credit.** Where the full investment credit was claimed in 1983 or later years, basis is reduced by one-half the credit.

Reporting an Installment Sale

Law Alert

Installment Method Restored for Accrual-Basis Taxpayers

A law was enacted at the end of 1999 to prohibit accrual-basis taxpayers from using the installment method to report property sale gains. The law, applicable to sales after December 16, 1999, included exceptions for sales of farm property and certain residential lots and timeshares. Small business groups complained that the law made it more expensive for accrual-basis business owners to sell their businesses.

In response, on December 28, 2000, the Installment Tax Correction Act of 2000 (ITCA) restored availability of the installment sale method to accrual-method taxpayers by retroactively repealing the 1999 law. If pursuant to the 1999 law the entire proceeds of a sale after December 16, 1999, were reported by an accrual-method taxpayer on a return filed by April 16, 2001, an amended return may be filed to claim installment treatment for the sale. The amended return must be filed within the statute-of-limitations period (generally three years) for the year of the sale and for any other affected year. Complete Form 6252 for each year and attach it to the amended return.

5.21 Tax Advantage of Installment Sales

If you sell property at a *gain* in 2002 and you will receive one or more payments in a later year or years, you may use the installment method to defer tax unless the property is publicly traded securities or you are a dealer of the property sold. If you report the sale as an installment sale on Form 6252, your profit is taxed as installments are received. You may elect not to use the installment method if you want to report the entire profit in the year of sale; *see* Example 1 below and *5.23.*

Losses may not be deferred under the installment method.

How the installment method works. For each year you receive installment payments, report your gain on Form 6252. Installment income from the sale of a capital asset is then transferred to Schedule D. If your gain in the year of sale is long-term capital gain, gain in later years is also long term; short-term treatment in the year of sale applies also to later years. Interest payments you receive on the deferred sale installments are reported with your other interest income on Schedule B of Form 1040, not on Form 6252.

Installment income from the sale of business or rental property is figured on Form 6252 and then entered on Form 4797. If you make an installment sale of depreciable property, any *depreciation recapture (44.1)* is reported as income in the year of disposition. The recaptured amount is first figured on Form 4797 and then entered on Form 6252. On Form 6252, recaptured income is added to basis of the property for purposes of figuring the gross profit ratio for the balance of gain to be reported, if any, over the installment period; *see also 44.6.*

Installment sales of business or rental property for over $150,000 may be subject to a special tax if deferred payments exceed $5 million; *see 5.31.*

EXAMPLES
1. In 2002, you sell real estate for $100,000 that you bought in 1985 for $44,000. Selling expenses were $6,000. You are to receive $20,000 in 2002, 2003, and 2004, and $40,000 in 2005, plus interest of 7% compounded semiannually. Your gross profit is $50,000 ($100,000 contract price less $44,000 cost and $6,000 selling expenses). For installment sale purposes, your gross profit percentage, which is the percentage of each payment that you must report, is 50% ($50,000 profit ÷ $100,000 contract price). When the buyer makes the installment note payments, you report the following:

In	You report Payment of:	Income of:
2002	$20,000	$10,000
2003	20,000	10,000
2004	20,000	10,000
2005	40,000	20,000
Total	$100,000	$50,000

In 2002, you file Form 6252 to figure your gross profit and gross profit percentage. You report only $10,000 as profit on Schedule D (or Form 4797, if applicable). If you do not want to use the installment method, you make an election by reporting the entire gain of $50,000 on Schedule D or Form 4797.

> The buyer's interest payments are separately reported as interest income on Form 1040.

2. On December 16, 2002, you sell a building for $150,000, realizing a profit of $25,000. You take a note payable in January 2003. You report the gain in 2003. Receiving a lump-sum payment in a taxable year after the year of sale is considered an installment sale.

Year-end sales of publicly traded stock or securities. You have no choice about when to report the gain from a sale of publicly traded stock or securities made at the end of 2002. Any gain must be reported in 2002, even if the proceeds are not received until early 2003. The sale is not considered an installment sale.

Farm property. A farmer may use the installment method to report gain from the sale of property that does not have to be inventoried under his method of accounting. This is true even though such property is held for regular sale.

Dealer sales. Generally, dealers must report gain in the year of sale for personal property regularly sold on an installment plan or real estate held for resale to customers. However, the installment method may be used by dealers of certain time shares (generally time shares of up to six weeks per year) and residential lots, but only if an election is made to pay interest on the tax deferred by using the installment method. For further details, *see* the instructions to Schedule C of Form 1040.

5.22 Figuring the Taxable Part of Installment Payments

On the installment method, a portion of each payment other than interest represents part of your gain and is taxable. This taxable gain amount is based on the gross profit percentage or ratio, which is figured by dividing gross profit by the selling price or the contract price. The contract price is the same as the selling price unless an adjustment is made for an existing mortgage assumed or "taken subject to" by the buyer. The term *contract price* is used in the computation to describe only payments that the seller receives or is considered to have received. Thus, it does not include the buyer's assumption of an existing mortgage; *see* below for the mortgage adjustment to contract price. By following the line-by-line instructions to Form 6252, you get the gross profit percentage. Selling price, gross profit, and contract price are explained in the following paragraphs.

Interest equal to the *lesser* of 100% of the applicable federal rate and 9% compounded semiannually must generally be charged on a deferred payment sale. Otherwise, the IRS treats part of the sale price as interest; *see 4.32.*

EXAMPLE

On December 9, 2002, you sell real estate for $100,000. The property had an adjusted basis of $56,000. Selling expenses are $4,000. You are to receive installment payments of $25,000 in 2002, 2003, 2004, and 2005, plus interest at 7%, compounded semiannually. The gross profit percentage of 40% is figured as follows:

Selling price (contract price)	$100,000
Less: Adjusted basis and selling expenses	60,000
Gross profit	$ 40,000

$$\frac{\text{Gross profit}}{\text{Contract price}} = \frac{\$40,000}{\$100,000} = 40\% \text{ (gross profit percentage)}$$

In 2002, you report a profit of $10,000 (40% of $25,000) on Form 6252. Interest received is separately reported as income on your Form 1040. Similarly, in each of the following three years, a profit of $10,000 is reported so that by the end of four years, the entire $40,000 profit will have been reported.

Selling price. Include cash, fair market value of property received from the buyer, the buyer's notes (at face value), and any outstanding mortgage on the property that the buyer assumes or takes subject to. If, under the contract of sale, the buyer pays off an existing mortgage or assumes liability for any other liens on the property, such as taxes you owe, or pays the sales commissions, such payments are also included in the selling price.

Caution

Year-End Sales of Securities
You cannot defer to 2003 reporting of gain on a 2002 year-end sale of publicly traded securities, even if you do not receive payment until early January 2003.

Caution

Foreclosures
If your property is foreclosed, the amount of the mortgage is treated as sales proceeds even if you do not receive anything on the sale.

Interest, including minimum interest imputed under the rules in *4.32*, is not included in the selling price.

Notes of a third party given to you by the buyer are valued at fair market value.

Gross profit and gross profit percentage. Gross profit is the selling price less what the IRS calls installment sale basis, which is the total of adjusted basis of the property *(5.20)*, selling expenses, such as brokers' commissions and legal fees, and recaptured depreciation income, if any *(44.1)*.

Divide the gross profit by the contract price to get the gross profit percentage. Each year, you multiply this percentage by your payments to determine the taxable amount under the installment method.

Contract price where the buyer takes subject to or assumes an existing mortgage. To figure the gross profit percentage first reduce the selling price by the amount of your existing mortgages that the buyer assumes or takes the property subject to. The reduced amount is the *contract price*. You then divide your gross profit by the contract price to get the gross profit percentage.

If the mortgage exceeds your installment sale basis (total of adjusted basis of the property, selling expenses, and depreciation recapture), you are required to report the excess as a payment received in the year of sale and also increase the *contract price* by that excess amount. Where the mortgage equals or exceeds your installment sale basis, the gross profit percentage will be 100%; *see* Example 3 below.

In a wraparound mortgage transaction, the buyer does not assume the seller's mortgage or take the property subject to it, but instead makes payments that cover the seller's outstanding mortgage liability. At one time, the IRS treated a wraparound mortgage transaction as an assumption of a mortgage by the buyer and required a reduction of the selling price by the mortgage to compute the contract price. The Tax Court rejected the IRS position, and the IRS acquiesced in the decision. Currently, the IRS does not require a reduction of selling price for a wraparound mortgage in the Form 6252 instructions or in Publication 537; *see* Example 4 below.

> ### EXAMPLES
>
> 1. You sell a building for $300,000. The building was secured by an existing mortgage of $50,000 that you pay off at the sale closing from the buyer's initial payment. The contract price is $300,000.
>
> 2. Same facts as in Example 1, but the buyer assumes the mortgage of $50,000. The contract price is $250,000 ($300,000 – $50,000).
>
> 3. You sell a building for $90,000. The buyer will pay you $10,000 annually for three years and assume an existing mortgage of $60,000. The adjusted basis of the property is $45,000. Selling expenses are $5,000. The total installment sale basis is $50,000 ($45,000 plus $5,000). The mortgage exceeds this basis by $10,000 ($60,000 – $50,000). This $10,000 excess is included in the contract price and treated as a payment made in the year of sale. The contract price is $40,000:
>
> | | |
> |---|---:|
> | Selling price | $90,000 |
> | *Less:* Mortgage | 60,000 |
> | | $30,000 |
> | *Add:* Excess of mortgage ($60,000) over installment sale basis ($50,000) | 10,000 |
> | Contract price | $40,000 |
> | Selling price | $90,000 |
> | *Less:* Installment sale basis | 50,000 |
> | Gross Profit | $40,000 |
> | Gross profit percentage ($40,000 gross profit ÷ $40,000 contract price) | 100% |
>
> 4. Abel sells real property worth $2 million, encumbered by a mortgage of $900,000. Installment sale basis (adjusted basis plus selling costs) is $700,000. The buyer pays $200,000 cash and gives an interest-bearing wraparound mortgage note for $1.8 million. Abel remains obligated to pay off the $900,000 mortgage. The gross profit ratio is 65% ($1,300,000 gross profit ÷ $2,000,000 contract price). In the year of sale, Abel reports the $200,000 cash of which 65% of $200,000, or $130,000, is taxable income.

Change of selling price. If the selling price is changed during the period payments are outstanding, the gross profit percentage is refigured on the new selling price. The adjusted profit ratio is then applied to payments received after the adjustment.

Caution

Recapture of Depreciation or First-Year Expensing Deduction

The entire recaptured amount, discussed in *44.1–44.3*, is reported in the year of sale on Form 4797, even though you report the sale on the installment basis. An installment sale does not defer the reporting of the recaptured deduction. You also add the recaptured amount to the basis of the sold asset on Line 12 of Form 6252 to compute the amount of the remaining gain to be reported on each installment. *See* the instructions to Form 6252.

EXAMPLE

Jones sold real estate in 1999 for $100,000. His basis, including selling expenses, was $40,000, so his gross profit was $60,000. The buyer agreed to pay, starting in 2000, five annual installments of $20,000 plus 10% interest. As the gross profit percentage was 60% ($60,000 ÷ $100,000), Jones reported profit of $12,000 (60% of $20,000) on the installments received in 2000 and 2001.

In 2002, the parties renegotiated the sales price, reducing it from $100,000 to $85,000, and reducing payments for 2002, 2003, and 2004 to $15,000. Jones's original profit of $60,000 is reduced to $45,000 ($85,000 revised sales price less $40,000 basis). Of the $45,000 profit, $12,000 was reported in 2000 and an additional $12,000 in 2001. To get the revised profit percentage, Jones must divide the $21,000 of profit not yet received by the remaining sales price of $45,000 ($85,000 *less* $40,000 installments in 2000 and 2001). The revised profit percentage is 46.67% ($21,000 ÷ $45,000). In 2002, 2003, and 2004, Jones reports profit of $7,000 on each $15,000 installment (46.67% of $15,000).

Payments received. Payments include cash, the fair market value of property, and payments on the buyer's notes. Payments do not include receipt of the buyer's notes or other evidence of indebtedness, unless payable on demand or readily tradable. "Readily tradable" means registered bonds, bonds with coupons attached, debentures, and other evidences of indebtedness of the buyer that are readily tradable in an established securities market. This rule is directed mainly at corporate acquisitions. A third-party guarantee (including a standby letter of credit) is not treated as a payment received on an installment obligation.

If the buyer has assumed or taken property subject to a mortgage that exceeds your installment sale basis (adjusted basis plus selling expenses plus depreciation recapture, if any), you include as a payment in the year of the sale the excess of the mortgage over the installment basis; *see* the Johnson Example below.

EXAMPLE

Johnson sells a building for $160,000, subject to a mortgage of $60,000. Installments plus interest are to be paid over five years. His adjusted basis in the building was $30,000 and his selling expenses were $10,000, so his installment sale basis is $40,000 and his gross profit is $120,000 ($160,000 – $40,000). The contract price is also $120,000, the selling price of $160,000 less $40,000, the part of the mortgage that did not exceed the installment sale basis.

The $20,000 difference between the $60,000 mortgage and the installment sale basis of $40,000 is part of the contract price and is also treated as a payment received in the year of sale. Since the mortgage exceeds Johnson's installment sale basis, he is treated as having recovered his entire basis in the year of sale, and all installment payments will be taxable, as his gross profit ratio is 100%: gross profit of $120,000 ÷ contract price of $120,000. In the year of sale, Johnson must report as taxable gain 100% of the installment payment received, plus the $20,000 difference between the mortgage and his installment sale basis.

Pledging installment obligation as security. If, as security for a loan, you pledge an installment obligation from a sale of property of more than $150,000 (excluding farm or personal-use property), the net loan proceeds must be treated as a payment on the installment obligation. The net loan proceeds are treated as received on the later of the date the loan is secured and the date you receive the loan proceeds. These pledging rules do not apply if the debt refinances a debt that was outstanding on December 17, 1987, and secured by the installment obligation until the refinancing. If the refinancing exceeds the loan principal owed immediately before the refinancing, the excess is treated as a payment on the installment obligation. *See* the Form 6252 instructions.

5.23 Electing Not To Report on the Installment Method

If any sale proceeds are to be received after the year of sale, you must file Form 6252 and use the installment method unless you "elect out" by making a timely election to report the entire gain in the year of sale. If you want to report the entire gain in the year of sale, include it on Schedule D or Form 4797 by the due date for filing your return (plus extensions) for the year of sale. Do not use Form 6252. After the due date (plus extensions), a change from the installment method to full reporting in the year of sale may be made only with IRS consent. However, if your original return was filed on time, the IRS gives an automatic consent for you to make the election on an amended return filed no later than six months after the due date of your return, *excluding* extensions. Write

Caution

Extension of Pledge Rule

If a loan arrangement gives you the right to repay the debt by transferring an installment obligation, you are treated as if you had directly pledged the obligation as security for the debt. As a result, the loan proceeds are treated as a payment on the installment obligation, which will increase installment income for the year of the "deemed pledge."

Filing Tip

"Electing Out" of Installment Reporting

When you have losses to offset your gain in the year of sale, installment sale reporting may not be advantageous. In such a case, you may want to report the full gain in the year of sale so the gain may be offset by the losses. However, there is a risk. If the losses are later disallowed by an IRS audit, you may not be given a second chance to use the installment method to spread the gain over the payment period. The IRS *may* not allow you to revoke your "election out" on the grounds that to do so would result in tax avoidance.

"Filed pursuant to the section 301.9100-2" at the top of the amended return, and file it at the same address you used for your original return. If this automatic consent extension is not available, the IRS will give consent only in rare cases where it finds "good cause." The IRS may give consent if your tax preparer erroneously reported on the installment method and you promptly ask IRS permission to change to reporting of the entire gain. A change in the tax law is not considered "good cause" by the IRS.

Switching from full reporting to installment method. If you do report the entire gain in the year of sale, you may change to the installment method on an amended return only with the consent of the IRS. In a private ruling, the IRS refused to allow a seller to use the installment method after inadvertently including the entire gain from the sale on his return. Although reporting of the entire gain was a mistake, this was treated as an election not to use the installment method. The IRS refused permission to revoke the election on the grounds that a second chance to apply the installment method would be tax avoidance. However, in other private rulings, permission to revoke was granted where the seller's accountant erroneously reported the entire gain.

In one case, a seller "elected out" in a year in which he planned to deduct a net operating loss carryforward from an installment sale gain. In a later year, the IRS substantially reduced the loss. The seller then asked the IRS to allow him to revoke the "election out" so he could use the installment method. The IRS refused in a private ruling, claiming that the seller asked for the revocation to avoid tax. The installment sale would defer gain to a later year, which is a tax avoidance purpose.

5.24 Restriction on Installment Sales to Relatives

The installment sale method is not allowed where you sell depreciable property to a controlled business, or to a trust in which you or your spouse is a beneficiary. All payments to be received over the installment period are considered received in the year of sale.

Further, if you sell property to a relative on the installment basis, and the relative later resells the property, you could lose the benefit of installment reporting. If the family member's resale is within two years of the original sale, the original seller is taxed on that sale under the two-year rule discussed below.

> ### EXAMPLE
>
> In 2002, Jones sells land to his son for $250,000, realizing a profit of $100,000. The son agrees to pay in five annual installments of $50,000 starting in 2003. Later in 2002, the son sells the land to a third party for $260,000. Jones Sr. reports his profit of $100,000 in 2002, even though he received no payment that year. Payments other than interest received by Jones Sr. after 2002 are tax free because he reported the entire profit in 2002.

Two-year rule for property other than marketable securities. If you make an installment sale to a related party of property other than marketable securities, you are taxed on a second sale by the related party only if it occurs within two years of the initial installment sale and before all payments from the first installment sale are made. Related parties include a spouse, child, grandchild, parent, grandparent, brother or sister, controlled corporation (50% or more direct or indirect ownership), any S corporation in which you own stock or partnership in which you are a partner, a trust in which you are a beneficiary, or a grantor trust of which you are treated as the owner. You are treated as owning stock held by your spouse, brothers, sisters, children, grandchildren, parents, and grandparents.

You must report as additional installment sale income: (1) the proceeds from the related party's sale or the contract price from the initial installment sale, whichever is less, *minus* (2) installment payments received from the related party as of the end of the year. The computation is made in Part III of Form 6252.

The two-year period is extended during any period in which the buyer's risk is lessened by a put on the property, an option by another person to acquire the property, or a short sale or other transaction lessening the risk of loss.

Marketable securities. The two-year cutoff does not apply to the sale of marketable securities. For such marketable securities, you can be taxed on any related party's sale occurring before you receive all the payments under the initial installment sale.

Marketable securities are:

1. Securities listed on the New York Stock Exchange, the American Stock Exchange, or any city or regional exchange in which quotations appear on a daily basis, including foreign securities listed on a recognized foreign, national, or regional exchange;

Caution

Installment Sale to Relative

If you sell property on the installment basis to a relative who later resells the property, you could lose the benefit of installment reporting.

2. Securities regularly traded in the national or regional over-the-counter market, for which published quotations are available;

3. Securities locally traded for which quotations can readily be obtained from established brokerage firms;

4. Units in a common trust fund; and

5. Mutual-fund shares for which redemption prices are published.

Exceptions to two-year rule. There are exceptions to this related-party rule. Second dispositions resulting from an involuntary conversion of the property will not be subject to the related-party rule so long as the first disposition occurred before the threat or imminence of conversion. Similarly, transfers after the death of the person making the first disposition or the death of the person acquiring the property in the first disposition are not treated as second dispositions. Also, a sale or exchange of stock to the issuing corporation is not treated as a first disposition. Finally, you may avoid tax on a related party's second sale by satisfying the IRS that neither the initial nor the second sale was made for tax avoidance purposes.

Sales of depreciable property to related party. Installment reporting is not allowed for sales of depreciable property made to a controlled corporation or partnership (50% control by seller) and between such controlled corporations and partnerships. In figuring control of a corporation, you are considered to own stock held by your spouse, children, grandchildren, brothers or sisters, parents, and grandparents. Installment reporting is also disallowed on a sale to a trust in which you or a spouse is a beneficiary unless your interest is considered a remote contingent interest whose actuarial value is 5% or less of the trust property's value. On these related-party sales, the entire gain is reported in the year of sale, unless the seller convinces the IRS that the transfer was not motivated by tax avoidance purposes.

On a sale of depreciable property to a related party, if the amounts of payments are contingent (for example, payments are tied to profits), the seller must make a special calculation. He or she must treat as received in the year of sale all noncontingent payments plus the fair market value of the contingent payments if such value may be reasonably ascertained. If the fair market value of the contingent payments may not be reasonably calculated, the seller recovers basis ratably. The purchaser's basis for the acquired property includes only amounts that the seller has included in income under the basis recovery rule. Thus, the purchaser's basis is increased annually as the seller recovers basis.

5.25 Contingent Payment Sales

Where the final selling price or payment period of an installment sale is not fixed at the end of the taxable year of sale, you are considered to have transacted a "contingent payment sale." Special rules apply where a maximum selling price may be figured under the terms of the agreement or there is no fixed price but there is a fixed payment period, or there is neither a fixed price nor a fixed payment period.

Stated maximum selling price. Under IRS regulations, a stated maximum selling price may be determined by assuming that all of the contingencies contemplated under the agreement are met. When the maximum amount is later reduced, the gross profit ratio is recomputed.

> ### EXAMPLE
>
> Smith sells stock in Acme Co. for a down payment of $100,000 plus an amount equal to 5% of the net profits of Acme for the next nine years. The contract provides that the maximum amount payable, including the $100,000 down payment but exclusive of interest, is $2,000,000. Smith's basis for the stock is $200,000; $2,000,000 is the selling price and contract price. Gross profit is $1,800,000. The gross profit ratio is 90% ($1,800,000 ÷ $2,000,000). Thus, $90,000 of the first payment is reportable as gain and $10,000 as a recovery of basis.

Fixed period. When a stated maximum selling price is not determinable but the maximum payment period is fixed, basis—including selling expenses—is allocated equally to the taxable years in which payment may be received under the agreement. If, in any year, no payment is received or the amount of payment received is less than the basis allocated to that taxable year, no loss is allowed unless the taxable year is the final payment year or the agreement has become worthless. When no loss is allowed in a year, the basis allocated to the taxable year is carried forward to the next succeeding taxable year.

Caution

IRS Notice of Related Party Transfer

Where you transfer property to a related party, the IRS has two years from the date you notify it that there has been a second disposition to assess a deficiency with respect to your transfer.

Caution

Contingent Sales

An example of a contingent sale in which the selling price cannot be determined by the end of the year of the sale is a sale of your business where the selling price includes a percentage of future profits. You and your tax advisor should consult the technical rules in IRS regulation 15A.453-1(c) for details on reporting such sales.

Brown sells property for 10% of the property's gross rents over a five-year period. Brown's basis is $5,000,000. The sales price is indefinite and the maximum selling price is not fixed under the terms of the contract; basis is recovered ratably over the five-year period.

Year	Payment	Basis recovered	Gain
First	$ 1,300,000	$ 1,000,000	$ 300,000
Second	1,500,000	1,000,000	500,000
Third	1,400,000	1,000,000	400,000
Fourth	1,800,000	1,000,000	800,000
Fifth	2,100,000	1,000,000	1,100,000

No stated maximum selling price or fixed period. If the agreement fails to specify a maximum selling price and payment period, the IRS may view the agreement as a rent or royalty income agreement. However, if the arrangement qualifies as a sale, basis (including selling expenses) is recovered in equal annual increments over a 15-year period commencing with the date of sale. If in any taxable year no payment is received or the amount of payment received (exclusive of interest) is less than basis allocated to the year, no loss is allowed unless the agreement has become worthless. Excess basis not recovered in one year is reallocated in level amounts over the balance of the 15-year term. Any basis not recovered at the end of the 15th year is carried forward to the next succeeding year, and to the extent unrecovered, carried forward from year to year until basis has been recovered or the agreement is determined to be worthless. The rule requiring initial level allocation of basis over 15 years may not apply if you prove to the IRS that a 15-year general rule will substantially and inappropriately defer recovery of basis.

In some cases, basis recovery under an income forecast type of method may also be allowed.

Foreign currency. An installment sale with payments to be made in foreign currency or tangible payment units (such as bushels of wheat) is a contingent payment sale, but basis is allocated as if payment were fixed in U.S. dollars.

EXAMPLE

In 2001, Jones sells property for 10,000 English pounds. In 2002, 2,500 pounds are payable. In 2003, the balance of 7,500 pounds is payable. Basis in the property is $2,000. In 2002, 25% of the basis, or $500 (25% of $2,000), is allocated to the first payment. In 2003, $1,500 (75% of $2,000) is allocated to the second payment.

5.26 Using Escrow and Other Security Arrangements

You sell property and the sales proceeds are placed in escrow pending the possible occurrence of an event such as the approval of title or your performance of certain contractual conditions. The IRS may argue that installment reporting is not allowed unless there are escrow restrictions preventing immediate payment.

If the terms of the escrow involve no genuine conditions that prevent you from demanding immediate payment, there will be immediate tax. Substitution of an escrow account for unpaid notes or deeds of trust disqualifies installment reporting.

Filing Tip

Installment Reporting on Escrow Allowable

If an escrow arrangement imposes a substantial restriction, the IRS may allow installment reporting. An example of a substantial restriction: Payment of the escrow is tied to the condition that the seller refrain from entering a competing business for a period of five years. If, at any time during the escrow period, he or she engages in a competing business, all rights to the amount then held in escrow would be forfeited.

EXAMPLES

1. Anderson sold stock and mining property for almost $5 million. He agreed to place $500,000 in escrow to protect the buyer against his possible breaches of warranty and to provide security for certain liabilities. The escrow agreement called for Anderson to direct the investments of the escrow fund and receive income from the fund in excess of $500,000.

    The IRS claimed that in the year of sale Anderson was taxable on the $500,000 held in escrow on the ground that Anderson's control of the fund rendered the fund taxable immediately. Anderson argued he was only taxable as the funds were released to him, and the Tax Court agreed. The fund was not under his unqualified control. He might never get the fund if the liabilities materialized. Although Anderson had a free hand with investment of the money, he still lacked ultimate ownership.

2. Rhodes sold a tract to a buyer who was willing to pay at once the entire purchase price of $157,000. But Rhodes wanted to report the sale on the installment basis over a period of years. The buyer refused to execute a purchase money mortgage on the property to allow the installment sale election (required under prior law) because he wanted clear and unencumbered title to the tract. As a solution, Rhodes asked the buyer to turn over the purchase price to a bank, as escrow agent, which would pay the sum over a five-year period.

The escrow arrangement failed to support an installment sale. Rhodes was fully taxable on the entire price in the year of the sale. The buyer's payment was unconditional and irrevocable. The escrow arrangement involved no genuine conditions that could defeat Rhodes's right to payment, as the buyer could not revoke, alter, or end the arrangement.

3. In January, an investor sold real estate for $100,000. He received $10,000 as a down payment and six notes, each for $15,000, secured by a deed of trust on the property. The notes, together with interest, were due annually over the next six years. In July, the buyer deposited the remainder of the purchase price with an escrow agent and got the seller to cancel the deed of trust.

The agreement provides that the escrow agent will pay off the buyer's notes as they fall due. The buyer remains liable for the installment payments. The escrow deposit is irrevocable, and the payment schedule may not be accelerated by any party under any circumstances. According to the IRS, the sale, which initially qualified as an installment sale, is disqualified by the escrow account.

5.27 Minimum Interest on Deferred Payment Sales

The tax law requires a minimum amount of interest to be charged on deferred payment sales. The rules for imputing interest on sales are discussed at *4.32*. Imputed interest is included in the taxable income of the seller. Imputed interest is deductible by the buyer if the property is business or investment property, but not if it is used substantially all the time for personal purposes.

5.28 Dispositions of Installment Notes

A sale, a gift, an exchange or other transfer or cancellation of mortgage notes or other obligations received in an installment sale has tax consequences. If you sell or exchange the notes or if you accept less than face value in satisfaction of the obligation, gain or loss results to the extent of the difference between the basis of the notes and the amount realized. For example, if in satisfaction of an installment note, the buyer gives you other property worth less than the face value of the note, you have gain (or loss) to the extent your amount realized exceeds (or is less than) your *basis* in the installment note. The basis of an installment note or obligation is the face value of the note less the income that would be reported if the obligation were paid in full; *see* Example 2 below.

Gain or loss is long term if the original sale was entitled to long-term capital gain treatment. This is true even if the notes were held short term. If the original sale resulted in short-term gain or ordinary income, the sale of the notes gives short-term gain or ordinary income, regardless of the holding period of the notes.

Suppose you make an installment sale of your real estate, taking back a land contract. Later a mortgage is substituted for the unpaid balance of the land contract. The IRS has ruled that the substitution is not the same as a disposition of the unpaid installment obligations. There is no tax on the substitution.

 Caution

Charging Minimum Interest
If you do not charge a minimum interest rate, the IRS may do so. This would require you and the buyer to treat part of the purchase price as interest.

 Filing Tip

Installment Notes in Marital Transfer
A transfer of installment obligations to your spouse or a transfer to a former spouse that is incident to a divorce is treated as a tax-free exchange under the rules discussed in *6.7* unless the transfer is in trust.

EXAMPLES

1. You sell a lot for $20,000 that cost you $10,000. In the year of the sale, you received $5,000 in cash and the purchaser's notes for the remainder of the selling price, or $15,000. A year later, before the buyer makes a payment on the notes, you sell them for $13,000 cash:

Selling price of property	$20,000
Cost of property	10,000
Total profit	$10,000

Profit percentage, or proportion of each payment returnable as income, is 50% ($10,000 total profit ÷ $20,000 contract price)

Unpaid balance of notes	$15,000
Amount of income reportable if notes were paid in full (50% of $15,000)	7,500
Adjusted basis of the notes	$7,500

Your profit on the sale is $5,500 ($13,000 – $7,500). It is capital gain if the sale of the lot was taxable as capital gain.

2. You sell a lot on the installment basis for $200,000 that cost you $120,000. In the year of sale, you received $20,000 in cash and the buyer's note for $180,000. Your gross profit percentage is 40% ($80,000 total profit ÷ $200,000 contract price).

Two years later, the buyer is facing financial difficulties and is unable to make payments on the $180,000 note. In satisfaction of the installment note, the buyer agrees to give you two other parcels of real estate, each worth $50,000. By accepting less than the $180,000 face value of the note in satisfaction of the obligation, you realize an $8,000 capital loss; the difference between the amount you realize and your basis in the installment obligation is figured as follows:

Amount realized	$100,000
($50,000 for each parcel)	
Face value of note	180,000
Less: Amount of income reportable if note was paid in full given 40% profit percentage (40% of $180,000 = $72,000)	72,000
Basis in installment note	$108,000

The difference between the $100,000 amount realized and $108,000 basis gives you an $8,000 loss. Assuming your profit on the original sale was long-term capital gain, the loss would be deducted as a long-term capital loss.

Gift of installment obligation. If the installment obligations are disposed of other than by sale or exchange, such as when you make a gift of the installment obligations to someone else, gain or loss is the difference between the basis of the obligations and their fair market value at the time of the disposition. If an installment obligation is *cancelled* or otherwise becomes unenforceable, the same rule for determining gain or loss applies. However, no gain or loss is recognized on a gift to a spouse; see 6.7.

A gift of installment obligations to a person other than a spouse or to a charitable organization is treated as a taxable disposition. Gain or loss is the difference between the basis of the obligations and their fair market value at the time of the gift. If the notes are donated to a qualified charity, you may claim a contribution deduction for the fair market value of the obligations at the time of the gift.

Transfer at death. A transfer of installment obligations at the death of the holder of the obligation is not taxed as a disposition. As the notes are paid, the estate or beneficiaries report income in the same proportion as the decedent would have, had he or she lived. A transfer of installment obligations to a revocable trust is also not taxed. However, the estate is subject to tax if the obligation is cancelled, becomes unenforceable, or is transferred to the buyer because of the death of the obligation holder.

5.29 Repossession of Personal Property Sold on Installment

When a buyer defaults and you repossess personal property, either by a voluntary surrender or a foreclosure, you may realize gain or loss. The method of calculating gain or loss is similar to the method used for disposition of installment notes; see 5.28. Gain or loss is the difference between the fair market value of the repossessed property and your basis for the installment obligations satisfied by the repossession. This rule is followed whether or not title has been kept by you or transferred to the buyer. The amount realized is reduced by costs incurred during the repossession. The basis of the obligation is face value less unreported profit.

If the property repossessed is bid in at a lawful public auction or judicial sale, the fair market value of the property is presumed to be the purchase or bid price, in the absence of proof to the contrary.

Gain or loss in the repossession is reported in the year of the repossession.

EXAMPLE

In December 2001, you sell furniture for $1,500—$300 down and $100 a month plus 6% interest beginning January 2002. You reported the installment sale on your 2002 tax return. The buyer defaulted after making three monthly payments. You foreclosed and repossessed the property; the fair market value was $1,400. The legal costs of foreclosure were $100. The gain on the repossession in 2002 is computed as follows:

Fair market value of property repossessed		$ 1,400
Basis of the buyer's notes at time of repossession:		
Selling price	$ 1,500	
Less: Payments made	600	
Face value of notes at repossession	$ 900	
Less: Unrealized profit (assume gross profit percentage of $33^{1}/_{3} \times \$900$)	$ 300	
		600
Gain on repossession		$ 800
Less: Repossession costs		100
Taxable gain on repossession		$ 700

Repossession gain or loss keeps the same character as the gain or loss realized on the original sale. If the sale originally resulted in a capital gain, the repossession gain is also a capital gain.

Your basis in the repossessed property is its fair market value at the time of repossession.

Real property. Repossessions of real property are at *31.12.*

5.30 Boot in Like-Kind Exchange Payable in Installments

An exchange of like-kind property is tax free unless boot is received. "Boot" may be cash or notes. If you transfer property subject to a mortgage and the amount of the mortgage you give up exceeds the mortgage you assume on the property received, that excess is boot; *see 6.3.* Boot is taxable, and if payable in installments, the following rules apply. Contract price is reduced by the fair market value of like-kind property received. Gross profit is reduced by gain not recognized. "Payment" does not include like-kind property.

The same treatment applies to certain tax-free reorganizations that are not treated as dividends, to exchanges of certain insurance policies, exchanges of the stock of the same corporation, and exchanges of United States obligations.

 Planning Reminder

Taxable Boot Received in Exchange

If you make an exchange of like-kind property and also receive cash or other property that is payable in one or more future years, you may report the gain using the installment method.

EXAMPLE

In 2002, property with an installment sale basis (basis plus selling expenses) of $400,000 is exchanged for like-kind property worth $200,000, plus installment obligations of $800,000, of which $100,000 is payable in 2003, plus interest. The balance of $700,000 plus interest will be paid in 2004. The contract price is $800,000 ($1 million selling price less $200,000 like-kind property received). The gross profit is $600,000 ($1 million less $400,000 installment sale basis). The gross profit ratio is 75% (gross profit of $600,000 ÷ contract price of $800,000). Like-kind property is not treated as a payment received in the year of sale, so no gain is reported in 2002. In 2003, gain of $75,000 will have to be reported (75% gross profit ratio × $100,000 payment), and in 2004 there will be a gain of $525,000 (75% of $700,000 payment).

5.31 "Interest" Tax on Sales Over $150,000 Plus $5 Million Debt

If deferred payments from installment sales of over $150,000 exceed $5 million, an interest charge is imposed on the tax-deferred amount. The special tax applies to sales of business or rental personal property as well as real estate for over $150,000.

Farm property and personal-use property, such as a residence, are exempt from the tax.

How to report interest tax. The interest charge is an additional tax. The method of computing the interest tax is complicated; the rules are in Internal Revenue Code Section 453A. In general, you compute the ratio of the face amount of outstanding installment obligations in excess of $5 million to the face amount of all outstanding installment obligations. This ratio is multiplied by the year-end unrecognized gain on the obligation, the top tax rate (38.6% for 2002), and also by the IRS interest rate for the last month of the year.

The interest tax is reported on Line 61 of Form 1040, the line for total tax. The tax is considered personal interest, and is not deductible; *see* Chapter 15.

Pledge rule for property sales over $150,000. If as security for a debt you pledge an installment obligation received on a sale of property exceeding $150,000 (other than farm property or personal-use property), the net proceeds of the secured debt are treated as a payment on the installment obligations, as discussed at *5.22*.

Dealer sale of time shares and residential lots. The above interest tax and pledging rules do not apply to installment obligations from the sale of certain time-share rights (generally time shares of up to six weeks per year) or residential lots. However, under a separate rule, the seller must pay interest on tax deferred under the installment method; *see* the instructions to Schedule C of Form 1040 for reporting the interest charge as an additional tax.

Worthless Securities and Bad Debt Deductions

5.32 Worthless Securities

You may deduct as a capital loss on Schedule D for 2002 the cost basis of securities that have become worthless in 2002. Capital loss treatment applies unless ordinary loss treatment is available for worthless Section 1244 stock; *see 30.20*.

A loss of worthless securities is deductible only in the year the securities become completely worthless. The loss may not be deducted in any other year. You may not claim a loss for partially worthless stock. However, if there is a market for it, sell the stock and deduct the capital loss on Schedule D.

Because it is sometimes difficult to determine the year in which a security becomes completely worthless, the law allows you to file a refund claim within seven years from the due date of the return for the proper year (the year the security actually became completely worthless), or if later, within two years from the date you paid the tax for that year.

To support a deduction for 2002, you must show:

1. The stock had some value in 2001. That is, you must be ready to show that the stock did not become worthless in a year prior to 2002. If you learn that the stock did become worthless in a prior year, file an amended return for that year; *see* the Filing Tip on refunds on the left.
2. The stock became totally worthless in 2002. You must be able to present facts fixing the time of loss during this year. For example, the company went bankrupt, stopped doing business, and is insolvent. Despite evidence of worthlessness, such as insolvency, the stock may be considered to have some value if the company continues to do business, or there are plans to reorganize the company. No deduction may be claimed for a partially worthless corporate bond.

If you are making payments on a negotiable note you used to buy the stock that became worthless and you are on the cash-basis method, your payments are deductible losses in the years the payments are made, rather than in the year the stock became worthless.

If the security is a bond, note, certificate, or other evidence of a debt incurred by a corporation, the loss is deducted as a capital loss, provided the obligation is in registered form or has attached interest coupons. A loss on a worthless corporate obligation is always deemed to have been sustained on the last day of the year, regardless of when the company failed during the year.

If the obligation is not issued with interest coupons or in registered form, or if it is issued by an individual, the loss is treated as a bad debt. If you received the obligation in a business transaction, the loss is fully deductible. You may also make a claim for a partially worthless business bad debt. If it is a nonbusiness debt, the loss is a capital loss and no claim may be made for partial worthlessness; *see 5.33*.

When to deduct worthless stock. If at the end of 2002 a company is in financial trouble but you are not sure whether its condition is hopeless, it is advisable to claim the deduction for 2002 to protect your claim. This advice was given by a court: "The taxpayer is at times in a very difficult position in determining in what year to claim a loss. The only safe practice, we think, is to claim a loss for the earliest year when it may possibly be allowed and to renew the claim in subsequent years if there is a reasonable chance of its being applicable for those years."

If you claim the deduction for 2002 and it turns out that complete worthlessness did not occur until a later year, claim the deduction for the proper year and then file an amended return for 2002 to eliminate the deduction.

Long-term or short-term loss. A sale is presumed to have occurred at the end of the year, regardless of when worthlessness actually occurred during the year.

 Filing Tip

Refund Deadline for Worthless Stock

You have seven years from the due date of your return to claim a refund based on a deduction of a bad debt or worthless security.

For example, if you have held securities that you learn became worthless in 1995, you still have until April 15, 2003, to file for a refund of 1995 taxes by claiming a deduction for the worthless securities on an amended return (Form 1040X) for 1995.

EXAMPLE
You bought 100 shares of Z Co. stock on July 1, 1999. On March 18, 2002, the stock is considered wholly worthless. The loss is deemed to have been incurred on December 31, 2002. The loss is deducted as a long-term capital loss; the holding period is from July 2, 1999, to December 31, 2002.

Ordinary loss on Small Business Investment Company (SBIC) stock. On Form 4797, investors may take ordinary loss deductions for losses on the worthlessness or sale of SBIC stock. The loss may also be treated as a business loss for net operating loss purposes. However, a loss realized on a short sale of SBIC stock is deductible as a capital loss. A Small Business Investment Company is a company authorized to provide small businesses with equity capital. Do not confuse investments in these companies with investments in small business stock (Section 1244 stock) discussed at Chapter 30.

S corporation stock. If an S corporation's stock becomes worthless during the taxable year, the basis in the stock is adjusted for the stockholder's share of corporate items of income, loss, and deductions before a deduction for worthlessness is claimed.

Bank deposit loss. If you lose funds in a bank that becomes insolvent, you may claim the loss as a nonbusiness bad debt *(5.33)*, a casualty loss *(18.4)*, or in some cases, an investment expense *(19.24)*.

5.33 Tax Consequences of Bad Debts

When you lend money or sell on credit and your debtor does not repay, you may deduct your loss. The type of deduction depends on whether the debt was incurred in a business or personal transaction. This distinction is important because business bad debts receive favored tax treatment.

Business bad debt. A business bad debt is fully deductible from gross income on Schedule C if you are self-employed, or on Schedule F if your business is farming. In addition, you may deduct partially worthless business debts; *see 40.6* for details.

Nonbusiness bad debt. A nonbusiness bad debt is deducted as a short-term capital loss on Schedule D. This is a limited deduction. In 2002, you deduct it from capital gains, if any, and $3,000 of other income. Any excess is deductible as a capital loss carryover in 2003 and later years; *see 5.4*. You may not deduct partially worthless nonbusiness bad debts. The debt must be totally worthless.

Examples of nonbusiness bad debts:

- You enter into a deal for profit that is not connected with your business; for example, debts arising from investments are nonbusiness bad debts.
- You make a personal loan to a family member or friend with a reasonable hope of recovery and are not in the business of making loans.
- You are assigned a debt that arose in the assignor's business. The fact that he or she could have deducted it as a business bad debt does not make it your business debt. A business debt must arise in your business.
- You pay liens filed against your property by mechanics or suppliers who have not been paid by your builder or contractor. Your payment is considered a deductible bad debt when there is no possibility of recovering reimbursement from the contractor and a judgment obtained against him or her is uncollectible.
- You lose a deposit on a house when the contractor becomes insolvent.
- You loan money to a corporation in which you are a shareholder, and your primary motivation is to protect your investment rather than your job; *see 5.35*.
- You had an uninsured savings account in a savings association that went into default; *see 18.5*.
- You are held secondarily liable on a mortgage debt assumed but not paid by a buyer of your home. Your payment to the bank or other holder of the mortgage is deductible as a bad debt if you cannot collect it from the buyer of the home.

5.34 Four Rules To Prove a Bad Debt Deduction

To determine whether you have a bad debt deduction in 2002, read the four rules explained below. Pay close attention to the fourth rule, which requires proof that the debt became worthless in the year the deduction is claimed. Your belief that your debt is bad, or the mere refusal of the debtor to pay, is not sufficient evidence. There must be an event, such as the debtor's bankruptcy, to fix the debt as worthless.

Planning Reminder

Selling Before the Security Becomes Worthless
To claim a deduction for worthless stock or bonds, you must be able to prove that the stock became completely worthless in the year for which you are claiming the deduction. Sometimes you can avoid the problem of proving worthlessness by selling while there is still a market for the security. For example, a company is on the verge of bankruptcy, but in 2003 there is some doubt about the complete worthlessness of its securities. You might sell the securities for whatever you can get for them and claim the loss on the sale. However, if the security became worthless in a prior year, say in 2002, a sale for a nominal sum in 2003 will not give you a deduction in 2003.

Caution

Accounts and Notes Receivable
You may claim a bad debt deduction for accounts and notes receivable on unpaid goods or services only if you have included the amount due as gross income. Thus, if a client or customer fails to pay a bill for services rendered, you do not have a deductible bad debt where you have not reported the amount as income; *see 40.6*.

Filing Instruction

Nonbusiness Bad Debt

If a nonbusiness bad debt became totally worthless in 2002, claim it as a short-term capital loss in Part I of Schedule D. Attach a statement describing the loan, your relationship to the debtor, how you tried to collect it, and why you decided it was worthless.

Planning Reminder

Debt Worthless Before Due

You do not have to wait until the debt is due in order to deduct a bad debt. Claim the deduction for the year that you can prove worthlessness occurred.

Rule 1. You must have a valid debt. You have no loss if your right to repayment is not fixed or depends upon some event that may not happen. Thus, advances to a corporation already insolvent are not valid debts. Nor are advances that are to be repaid only if the corporation has a profit. Voluntary payment of another's debt is also nondeductible. If usurious interest was charged on a worthless debt, and under state law the debt was void or voidable, the debt is not deductible as a bad debt. However, where the lender was in the business of lending money, a court allowed him to deduct the unpaid amounts as business losses.

If advances are made to a company that has lost outside borrowing sources and is thinly capitalized, with heavy debt-to-equity ratio, this indicates that the advances are actually capital contributions and not loans.

Rule 2. A debtor-creditor relationship must exist at the time the debt arose. You have a loss if there was a promise to repay at the time the debt was created and you had the right to enforce it. If the advance was a gift and you did not expect to be repaid, you may not take a deduction. Loans to members of your family, to a controlled corporation, or to a trust may be treated as gifts or contributions to capital.

Rule 3. The funds providing the loan or credit were previously reported as income or part of your capital. If you are on the cash basis, you may not deduct unpaid salary, rent, or fees. On the cash basis, you do not include these items in income until you are paid.

Rule 4. You must show that the debt became worthless during 2002. To prove the debt became worthless in 2002, you must show:

First, that the debt had some value at the end of the previous year (2001), and that there was a reasonable hope and expectation of recovering something on the debt. Your personal belief unsupported by other facts is not enough.

Second, that an identifiable event occurred in 2002—such as a bankruptcy proceeding—that caused you to conclude the debt was worthless. In the case of a business debt that has become partially worthless, you need evidence that the debt has declined in value. Additionally, reasonable collection steps must have been undertaken. That you cancel a debt does not make it worthless. You must still show that the debt was worthless when you cancelled it. You do not have to go to court to try to collect the debt if you can show that a court judgment would be uncollectible.

Third, that there is no reasonable hope the debt may have some value in a later year. You are not required to prove that there is no possibility of ever receiving some payment on your debt.

Effect of statute of limitations. A debt is not deductible merely because a statute of limitations has run against the debt. Although the debtor has a legal defense against your demand for payment, he or she may still recognize the obligation to pay. A debt is deductible only in the year it becomes worthless. This event—for example, the debtor's insolvency—may have occurred even before the statute became effective. What if your debtor recognized his or her moral obligation to pay in spite of the expiration of the statute of limitations, but dies before paying? Your claim would be defeated if the executor raises the statute of limitations. You have a bad debt deduction in the year you made the claim against the estate.

Guarantor or endorsement losses as bad debts. If you guarantee a loan and must pay it off after the principal debtor defaults, your payment is deductible as a business bad debt if you had a business reason for the guarantee. For example, to protect a business relationship with a major client, you guarantee the client's loan. Your payment on the guarantee qualifies as a business bad debt. If, as a result of your payment, you have a legal right to recover the amount from the client (right of subrogation or similar right), you may not claim a bad debt deduction unless that right is partially or totally worthless.

A loss on a guarantee may be a nonbusiness bad debt if you made the guarantee to protect an investment, such as where you are a main shareholder of a corporation and guarantee a bank loan to the company. No deduction is allowed if you guaranteed the loan as a favor to a relative or friend. *Bank deposit losses are discussed at 18.5.*

5.35 Loans by Stockholders

It is a common practice for stockholders to make loans to their corporations or to guarantee loans made to the company by banks or other lenders. If the corporation fails and the stockholder is not repaid or has to make good on the guarantee, the stockholder is generally left with a nonbusiness bad debt (nonbusiness bad debts are deductible only as a short-term capital loss on Schedule D; *see 5.33*) unless he or she can prove that a business loan was made. To prove a business loan, the stockholder usually has to show that he or she wanted to protect his or her job with the company. The only other situation in which a business bad debt may be claimed is where the stockholder is in the business of making loans and the loan was made in that capacity; or he or she is in the business of promoting corporations for a fee or for profits on their sale.

Self-employed individuals deduct business bad debts on Schedule C; *see 40.6*. Employee-stockholders who loan money to their corporations to keep their jobs may claim bad debt deductions for unpaid amounts only as miscellaneous itemized deductions subject to the 2% floor; *see 19.1*.

 *Court Decision*

Loan To Protect Job
A Supreme Court test requires a shareholder-employee claiming a business bad debt deduction to show that the primary and dominant motive of the loan was to protect his or her job, rather than investment in the company; *see* the Examples at *5.35*.

EXAMPLES

1. To determine an executive's motive for making a loan, the Supreme Court reviewed his salary, outside income, investment in the company, and the size of his loan. His pay was $12,000 ($7,000 after tax); his outside income was $30,000. He had a $38,900 investment in the company and loaned it $165,000. On the basis of these figures, the Court concluded he could not have advanced $165,000 to protect an after-tax salary of $7,000. He was protecting his investment, not his job, and only a nonbusiness bad debt (short-term capital loss) could be claimed.

2. Litwin founded several energy start-up companies after he retired in 1974 from the Litwin Corporation. In 1980, he founded AFS, to which he made loans of $150,000 and guaranteed another $350,000 of loans. AFS went bankrupt in 1984.

   A federal appeals court followed the Supreme Court's approach (Example 1) to determine that Litwin had an employment-related motive for the loans. His primary reason for setting up the company was to stay employed and remain "useful" to society. Given his background and advanced age, his best chance for ongoing employment was to start his own company. The majority of his time and energy was spent on AFS, even after he sold his controlling interest in the corporation and had only limited opportunities to capitalize on his remaining investment. True, Litwin deferred his salary for three years, but evidence showed that he intended to draw a salary in the future. Most importantly, Litwin took a sizeable risk when he personally guaranteed loans that exceeded his investment in AFS. The court noted that a taxpayer is probably not attempting to protect an investment in a company when guaranteed loans far exceed the value of the investment.

Loan to key employees. A loan by a stockholder to key employees was held to be a business bad debt in the following case.

EXAMPLE

Carter, the president and majority owner of two corporations, loaned money to two key employees to buy stock in the corporations. He wanted to guarantee the employees' future participation in the company. Both corporations went bankrupt, and the employees defaulted on the loans. Carter deducted both loans as business bad debts, contending he was protecting his job.

The IRS argued he had a nonbusiness bad debt; he was merely protecting his investment as a stockholder. The Tax Court disagreed. He made the loans to encourage the future of a business that would provide him salary income rather than dividends or appreciation on his stock.

5.36 Family Bad Debts

The IRS views loans to relatives, especially to children and parents, as gifts, so that it is rather difficult to deduct family bad debts.

To overcome the presumption of a gift when you advance money to a relative, take the same steps you would in making a business loan. Take a note, set a definite payment date, and require interest and collateral. If the relative fails to pay, make an attempt to collect. Failure to enforce collection of a family debt is viewed by the courts as evidence of a gift, despite the taking of notes and the receipt of interest.

Husband's default on child support—a basis for wife's deductible bad debt? A wife who supports her children when her husband defaults on court-ordered support payments may consider claiming her expenses as a nonbusiness bad debt deduction, arguing that her position is similar to a guarantor who pays a creditor when the principal debtor defaults. The IRS does not agree with the grounds of such a claim and will disallow the deduction; its position is supported by the Tax Court.

The federal appeals court for the Ninth Circuit left open the possibility that such a claim may have merit if a wife can show: (1) what she spent on the children; and (2) that her husband's obligation to support was worthless in the year the deduction is claimed.

The Tax Court has subsequently reiterated its position that defaulted child support payments are not a basis for a bad debt deduction. Following these Tax Court decisions, the IRS also announced its continuing opposition to the Ninth Circuit's suggestion that a deduction may be possible. The IRS holds that since the support obligation of the defaulting spouse is imposed directly by the divorce court, the other parent who pays support to make up for the arrearage has no "basis" to support a bad debt deduction.

Periodically, legislation has been proposed to allow a bad debt deduction for unpaid child support, but none of the proposals have been enacted into law.

Caution

Formalize Loan With Relative

To protect against a possible IRS claim that your loan was a gift and not a loan, put the loan in writing with repayment terms as if the debtor were a third party.

Chapter 6

Tax-Free Exchanges of Property

You may exchange property without incurring a tax in the year of exchange if you meet the rules detailed in this chapter. Gain may be taxed upon a later disposition of the property because the basis of the property received in the exchange is usually the same as the basis of the property surrendered in the exchange. Thus, if you exchange property with a tax basis of $10,000 for property worth $50,000, the basis of the property received in exchange is fixed at $10,000, even though its fair market value is $50,000. The gain of $40,000 ($50,000 – $10,000), which is not taxed, is technically called "unrecognized gain." If you later sell the property for $50,000, you will realize a taxable gain of $40,000 ($50,000 – $10,000).

Where property received in a tax-free exchange is held until death, the unrecognized gain escapes income tax forever because basis of the property in the hands of an heir is generally the value of the property at the date of death. If the exchange involves the transfer of boot, such as cash or other property, gain on the exchange is taxable to the extent of the value of boot.

You may not exchange U.S. real estate for foreign real estate tax-free.

Tax-free exchanges between related parties may become taxable if either party disposes of the exchanged property within a two-year period.

Filing Instruction

Depreciation of Property Received in Exchange

If you make a like-kind exchange of depreciable MACRS property *(42.4)* for other MACRS property, your basis for the new property is the same as the basis of the traded property. You depreciate that basis over the remaining recovery period, and using the same rate and convention *(42.5)* as for the traded property.

If you also paid cash as part of the exchange, you have an additional basis attributable to that investment that is depreciable as new MACRS property subject to a new recovery period.

Caution

Exchanging Depreciable Realty Subject to Depreciation Recapture

Recapture provisions supersede tax-free exchange rules. Thus, if you exchange a depreciable building placed in service before 1987, depreciation recapture may apply, so check the consequences of any "recapture" element. For example, if you exchange the building for land, the recaptured amount is fully taxable as ordinary income; *see 44.2*.

6.1 Trades of Like-Kind Property

You may not have to pay tax on gain realized on the "like-kind" exchange of business or investment property. By making a qualifying exchange, you can defer the gain. For tax-free treatment, you must trade property held for business use or investment for like-kind business or investment property. If the properties are not simultaneously exchanged, the time limits discussed in *6.4* must be satisfied. Gain is *completely* tax free only if you do not receive any "boot"; as discussed in *6.3*, gain is taxed to the extent of boot received. Where gain on a qualifying exchange is deferred and not immediately taxed, it may be taxable in a later year when you sell the property because your basis for the new property is generally the same as the basis for the property you traded; basis is discussed at *5.16 – 5.20*.

If you make a qualifying like-kind exchange with certain related parties, tax-free treatment may be lost unless both of you keep the exchanged properties for at least two years; *see 6.6*.

The term *like-kind* refers to the nature or character of the property, that is, whether real estate is traded for real estate. It does not refer to grade or quality, that is, whether the properties traded are new or used, improved or unimproved. In the case of real estate, land may be traded for a building, farm land for city lots, or a leasehold interest of 30 years or more for an outright ownership in realty. Trades of personal property are discussed at *6.2*.

> **EXAMPLES**
> 1. Jones, a real estate investor, purchased Parcel A for investment in 1986 for $5,000. In 1998, he exchanged it for another parcel, Parcel B, which had a fair market value of $50,000. The gain of $45,000 was not taxed in 1998.
> 2. Same facts as above, except that in 2002 Jones sells Parcel B for $50,000. His taxable gain is $45,000. The "tax-free" exchange rules have the effect of deferring tax on appreciation until the property received in the exchange is sold.
> 3. Same facts as in 1 above, but the value of Parcel B was $3,000 in 1998. Jones could not deduct the loss in 1998. The basis of the parcel is $5,000, the same as the basis of Parcel A. If Jones sells Parcel B in 2002 for $3,000, he may deduct a loss of $2,000.

Losses. If a loss is incurred on a like-kind exchange, the loss is not deductible, whether you receive only like-kind property or "unlike" property together with like-kind property. However, a deductible loss may be incurred if you give up unlike property as part of the exchange; the loss equals any excess of the adjusted basis of the unlike property over its fair market value.

Reporting an exchange. You must file Form 8824 to report an exchange of like-kind property. If you figure a recognized gain or loss on Form 8824, you also must report the exchange on Schedule D (investment property) or Form 4797 (business property).

See 6.6 for reporting an exchange with a related party.

Property not within the tax-free trade rules:

Property used for personal purposes (but exchanges of principal residences may qualify as tax free under different rules; *see* Chapter 29)
Foreign real estate
Property held for sale
Inventory or stock-in-trade
Securities
Notes
Partnership interest; *see* below

See also 31.3 for tax-free exchanges of realty and *6.12* for tax-free exchanges of insurance policies.

Exchange of partnership interests. Exchanges of partnership interests in different partnerships are not within the tax-free exchange rules. Under IRS regulations, tax-free exchange treatment is denied regardless of whether the interests are in the same or different partnerships.

If you made an election to exclude a partnership interest from the application of partnership rules, your interest is treated as interest in each partnership asset, not as an interest in the partnership.

Real estate or personal property in foreign countries. You may not make a tax-free exchange of U.S. real estate for foreign real estate. However, in the case of an involuntary conversion *(18.22)*, a tax-free reinvestment may be made in foreign real estate.

Similarly, you may not make tax-free exchanges of personal property used predominantly in the U.S. for personal property used predominantly outside the U.S.

6.2 Personal Property Held for Business or Investment

An exchange of depreciable tangible personal property held for productive business or investment use may qualify for tax-free treatment if it meets either the general like-kind test at *6.1* or a more specific "like-class" test created by IRS regulations. The assumption of liabilities is treated as "boot"; *see 6.3*. Where each party assumes a liability of the other party, the respective liabilities are offset against each other to figure boot, if any.

Under the like-class test, there are two types of "like" classes: (1) General Asset Classes and (2) Product Classes. The like-class test is satisfied if the exchanged properties are both within the same General Asset Class or the same Product Class. A specific asset may be classified within only one class. Thus, if an asset is within an Asset Class, it is not within a Product Class. The Asset Class or Product Class is determined as of the date of the exchange. This limitation may disqualify an exchange when exchanged assets do not fit within the same Asset Class and are not allowed to qualify within the Product Class; *see* the Brown Example below.

General Asset Classes. There are 13 classes of depreciable tangible business property. Here are some of the asset classifications: office furniture, fixtures, and equipment (class 00.11); information systems: computers and peripheral equipment (class 00.12); data handling equipment, except computers (class 00.13); airplanes and helicopters, except for airplanes used to carry passengers or freight (class 00.21); automobiles and taxis (class 00.22); light trucks (class 00.241); heavy trucks (class 00.242); and over-the-road tractor units (class 00.26). For example, trades of trucks in class 00.241 would be of like class.

Product Classes. Under a coding system of the Standard Industrial Classification (SIC) Manual, tangible depreciable assets are assigned a four-digit product-class number. For example, a grader is exchanged for a scraper. Neither item is within a General Asset Class, but both are in the same Product Class, SIC Code 3533. They are, therefore, of a like class.

Planning Reminder

The "Like-Class" Test
To qualify for tax-free treatment, depreciable tangible property held for productive business or investment use does not need to satisfy the "like-kind" test. The exchanged properties only need to be like in "class." This test is satisfied if the exchanged properties are both within the same General Asset Class or the same Product Class; *see 6.2*. The Asset Class or Product Class is determined at the time of transfer.

> ### EXAMPLES
>
> 1. Baker exchanges a personal computer used in his business for a printer. Both assets are productively used in business and are in the same General Asset Class of 00.12; the exchange meets the like-class test.
>
> 2. Brown exchanges an airplane (asset class 00.21) used in her business for a heavy truck (asset class 00.242). The exchanged properties are not of a like class. Furthermore, since each property is within a specific General Asset Class, the Product Class test may not be applied to qualify the exchange. Brown must report any gain realized on the exchange because the properties also do not meet the general like-kind test.

Intangible personal property and goodwill. Exchanges of intangible personal property (such as a patent or copyright) or nondepreciable personal property must meet the general like-kind test to qualify for tax-free treatment; the like-class tests do not apply. However, regulations close the door for qualifying exchanges of goodwill in an exchange of going businesses. According to the regulations, goodwill or going concern value of one business can never be of a like kind to goodwill or going concern value of another business.

Exchanges of multiple properties. Generally, exchanges of assets are considered on a one-to-one basis. Regulations provide an exception for exchanges of multiple properties, such as an exchange of businesses. Transferred assets are separated into exchange groups. An exchange group consists of all properties transferred and received in the exchange that are of a like kind or like class. All properties within the same General Asset Class or same Product Class are in the same exchange group. For example, automobiles and computers are exchanged for other automobiles and computers; two exchange groups are set up—one for the automobiles and the other for the computers. If the aggregate fair market values of the properties transferred and received in each exchange group are not equal, the regulations provide calculations for setting up a residual group for purposes of calculating taxable gain, if any.

All liabilities of which a taxpayer is relieved in the exchange are offset against all liabilities assumed by the taxpayer in the exchange, regardless of whether the liabilities are recourse, nonrecourse, or are secured by the specific property transferred or received. If excess liabilities are assumed by the taxpayer as part of the exchange, regulations provide rules for allocating the excess among the properties.

Caution

Deducting a Loss

You may deduct a loss incurred on an exchange if it is attributable to unlike property *transferred* in the exchange. The loss is recognized to the extent that the basis of the unlike property (other than cash) transferred exceeds its fair market value. However, a loss is not recognized if the unlike property is *received* together with the like-kind property in the exchange. Such a loss is *not* deductible.

6.3 Receipt of Cash and Other Property—"Boot"

If, in addition to like-kind *(6.1)* property, you receive cash or other property (unlike kind), gain is taxable up to the amount of the cash and the fair market value of any *unlike* property received. The additional cash or unlike property is called "boot." If a loss was incurred on the exchange, the receipt of boot does not permit you to deduct the loss unless it is attributable to *unlike*-kind property you gave up in the exchange.

If you transfer mortgaged property, the amount of the mortgage is part of your boot. If both you and the other party transfer and receive mortgaged property, the party giving up the larger debt treats the excess as taxable boot. The party giving up the smaller debt does not have boot; *see also 31.3.* If you pay cash to the other party, add this to the mortgage you receive in figuring which party has given up the larger debt.

Form 8824. The computation of boot, gain (or loss), and basis of the property received is made on Form 8824.

EXAMPLE

Jones owns an apartment house with a fair market value of $220,000, subject to an $80,000 mortgage. His adjusted basis is $100,000. Jones exchanges his building for Smith's apartment building, which has a value of $250,000, subject to a $150,000 mortgage. Jones also receives $40,000 in cash. Smith's adjusted basis for the building he trades is $175,000. Smith and Jones each pay $5,000 in exchange expenses.

The sample Forms 8824 for Jones and Smith on the next page show how they report the exchange. On Line 15, they show the boot received; their taxable gain is limited to this boot. For Jones, boot is the $40,000 in cash received. The $80,000 in liabilities transferred to Smith is not included because it does not exceed the $150,000 of liabilities Jones assumed.

For Smith, the Line 15 boot is $30,000:

Mortgage transferred	$150,000
Less: Mortgage assumed	(80,000)
Less: Cash paid	(40,000)
Boot received by Smith	$30,000

On Line 18, Jones and Smith increase their basis for the buildings they traded by exchange expenses and the net amounts paid to the other party. For Jones, the Line 18 total of $175,000 includes:

Adjusted basis of building traded		$100,000
Plus: Exchange expenses		5,000
Plus: Net mortgage assumed:		
Mortgage assumed	$150,000	
Less: Mortgage transferred	80,000	70,000
	70,000	$175,000

For Smith, the Line 18 total of $180,000 includes:

Adjusted basis of building traded		$175,000
Plus: Exchange expenses		5,000
Plus: Net amount paid:		
Mortgage assumed	$80,000	
Plus: Cash paid	40,000	
Less: Mortgage transferred	(150,000)	0
	(30,000)	$180,000

The liabilities Smith assumed and the cash he paid are not included on Line 18 because their total does not exceed the $150,000 of liabilities he transferred to Jones.

Line 25 shows the basis of the buildings Jones and Smith received in the exchange.

6.4 Time Limits for Deferred Exchanges

Assume you own property that has appreciated in value. You want to sell it and reinvest the proceeds in other property, but you would like to avoid having to pay tax on the appreciation. You can avoid the tax if you are able to arrange an exchange for like-kind *(6.1)* property.

Sample Form 8824 for Jones (see the Example on the preceding page)

Part III	**Realized Gain or (Loss), Recognized Gain, and Basis of Like-Kind Property Received**		

Caution: *If you transferred **and** received **(a)** more than one group of like-kind properties or **(b)** cash or other (not like-kind) property, see **Reporting of multi-asset exchanges** in the instructions.*

Note: *Complete lines 12 through 14 **only** if you gave up property that was not like-kind. Otherwise, go to line 15.*

12	Fair market value (FMV) of other property given up	12	
13	Adjusted basis of other property given up	13	
14	Gain or (loss) recognized on other property given up. Subtract line 13 from line 12. Report the gain or (loss) in the same manner as if the exchange had been a sale	14	
15	Cash received, FMV of other property received, plus net liabilities assumed by other party, reduced (but not below zero) by any exchange expenses you incurred (see instructions)	15	**40,000**
16	FMV of like-kind property you received	16	**250,000**
17	Add lines 15 and 16	17	**290,000**
18	Adjusted basis of like-kind property you gave up, net amounts paid to other party, plus any exchange expenses **not** used on line 15 (see instructions)	18	**175,000**
19	**Realized gain or (loss).** Subtract line 18 from line 17	19	**115,000**
20	Enter the smaller of line 15 or line 19, but not less than zero	20	**40,000**
21	Ordinary income under recapture rules. Enter here and on Form 4797, line 16 (see instructions)	21	**- 0 -**
22	Subtract line 21 from line 20. If zero or less, enter -0-. If more than zero, enter here and on Schedule D or Form 4797, unless the installment method applies (see instructions)	22	**40,000**
23	**Recognized gain.** Add lines 21 and 22	23	**40,000**
24	Deferred gain or (loss). Subtract line 23 from line 19. If a related party exchange, see instructions	24	**75,000**
25	**Basis of like-kind property received.** Subtract line 15 from the sum of lines 18 and 23	25	**175,000**

For Paperwork Reduction Act Notice, see page 4.   Cat. No. 12311A   Form **8824** (2002)

Sample Form 8824 for Smith (see the Example on the preceding page)

Part III	**Realized Gain or (Loss), Recognized Gain, and Basis of Like-Kind Property Received**		

Caution: *If you transferred **and** received **(a)** more than one group of like-kind properties or **(b)** cash or other (not like-kind) property, see **Reporting of multi-asset exchanges** in the instructions.*

Note: *Complete lines 12 through 14 **only** if you gave up property that was not like-kind. Otherwise, go to line 15.*

12	Fair market value (FMV) of other property given up	12	
13	Adjusted basis of other property given up	13	
14	Gain or (loss) recognized on other property given up. Subtract line 13 from line 12. Report the gain or (loss) in the same manner as if the exchange had been a sale	14	
15	Cash received, FMV of other property received, plus net liabilities assumed by other party, reduced (but not below zero) by any exchange expenses you incurred (see instructions)	15	**30,000**
16	FMV of like-kind property you received	16	**220,000**
17	Add lines 15 and 16	17	**250,000**
18	Adjusted basis of like-kind property you gave up, net amounts paid to other party, plus any exchange expenses **not** used on line 15 (see instructions)	18	**180,000**
19	**Realized gain or (loss).** Subtract line 18 from line 17	19	**70,000**
20	Enter the smaller of line 15 or line 19, but not less than zero	20	**30,000**
21	Ordinary income under recapture rules. Enter here and on Form 4797, line 16 (see instructions)	21	**- 0 -**
22	Subtract line 21 from line 20. If zero or less, enter -0-. If more than zero, enter here and on Schedule D or Form 4797, unless the installment method applies (see instructions)	22	**30,000**
23	**Recognized gain.** Add lines 21 and 22	23	**30,000**
24	Deferred gain or (loss). Subtract line 23 from line 19. If a related party exchange, see instructions	24	**40,000**
25	**Basis of like-kind property received.** Subtract line 15 from the sum of lines 18 and 23	25	**180,000**

For Paperwork Reduction Act Notice, see page 4.   Cat. No. 12311A   Form **8824** (2002)

Caution

Strict Time Limits

No extensions of time are allowed if the 45-day or 180-day statutory deadlines for a deferred exchange cannot be met. If extra time is needed for finding suitable replacement property, it is advisable to delay the date of your property transfer because the transfer date starts the 45-day identification period.

The problem is that it may be difficult to find a buyer who has property you want in exchange, and the time for closing the exchange is restricted. If IRS tests are met, intermediaries and security arrangements may be used without running afoul of constructive receipt rules that could trigger an immediate tax.

Deferred exchange distinguished from a reverse exchange. A *deferred* exchange is one in which you first transfer investment or business property and then later receive like-kind investment or business property *(6.1)*. If before you receive the replacement property you actually or constructively receive money or unlike property as full payment for the property you have transferred, the transaction will be treated as a sale rather than a deferred exchange. In that case, you must recognize gain (or loss) on the transaction even if you later receive like-kind replacement property. In determining whether you have received money or unlike property, you may take advantage of certain safe harbor security arrangements that allow you to ensure that the replacement property will be provided to you without jeopardizing like-kind exchange treatment; *see* below for the safe harbor security tests.

A *reverse* exchange is one in which you acquire replacement property before you transfer the relinquished property. The like-kind exchange rules generally do not apply to reverse exchanges. However, the IRS has provided safe harbor rules that allow like-kind exchange treatment to be obtained if either the replacement property or the relinquished property is held in a *qualified exchange accommodation arrangement (QEAA)*; *see 6.5* for the QEAA tests.

Time limits for completing deferred exchanges. You generally have up to 180 days to complete an exchange, but the period may be shorter. Specifically, property will not be treated as like-kind property if received (1) more than 180 days after the date you transferred the property you are relinquishing or (2) after the due date of your return (including extensions) for the year in which you made the transfer, whichever is earlier. Furthermore, the property to be received must be identified within 45 days after the date on which you transferred property.

If the transaction involves more than one property, the 45-day identification period and the 180-day exchange period are determined by the earliest date on which any property is transferred. When the identification or exchange period ends on a Saturday, Sunday, or legal holiday, the deadline is not advanced to the next business day (as it is when the deadline for filing a tax return is on a weekend or holiday).

How to identify replacement property. You must identify replacement property in a written document signed by you and either hand delivered, mailed, telecopied, or otherwise sent before the end of the 45-day identification period to a person involved in the exchange other than yourself or a related party. The identification may also be made in a written agreement. The property must be unambiguously described by a legal description or street address.

You may identify more than one property as replacement property. However, the maximum number of replacement properties that you may identify without regard to the fair market value is three properties. You may identify any number of properties provided the aggregate fair market value at the end of the 45-day identification period does not exceed 200% of the aggregate fair market value of all the relinquished properties as of the date you transferred them. If, as of the end of the identification period, you have identified more than the allowable number of properties, you are generally treated as if no replacement property has been identified.

Receipt of security. In a deferred exchange, you want financial security for the buyer's performance and compensation for delay in receiving property. To avoid immediate tax, you must not make a security arrangement that gives you an unrestricted right to funds before the deal is closed.

EXAMPLE

You and Jones agree to enter a deferred exchange under the following terms and conditions. On May 17, 2002, you transfer to Jones real estate that has been held for investment; it is unencumbered and has a fair market value of $100,000. On or before July 1, 2002 (the end of the 45-day identification period), you must identify like-kind replacement property. On or before November 13, 2002 (the end of the 180-day exchange period), Jones is required to buy the property and transfer it to you. At any time after May 17, 2002, and before Jones has purchased the replacement property, you have the right, upon notice, to demand that he pay you $100,000 instead of acquiring and transferring the replacement property. However, you identify replacement property, and Jones purchases and transfers it to you. According to the regulations, you have an unrestricted right to demand the payment of

$100,000 as of May 17, 2002. You are therefore in constructive receipt of $100,000 on that date. Thus, the transaction is treated as a taxable sale, and the transfer of the real property does not qualify as a tax-free exchange. You are treated as if you received the $100,000 for the sale of your property and then purchased replacement property.

Safe harbor tests for deferred exchange security arrangements. If one of the following safe harbors applies to your security arrangement, you are not taxed as if a sale were made and like-kind exchange treatment may be obtained.

The first two "safe harbors" cover transfers dealing directly with the buyer. The third allows the use of professional intermediaries who, for a fee, arrange the details of the deferred exchange. The fourth allows you to earn interest on an escrow account. The safe harbors generally prohibit you from receiving money or other non-like-kind property before replacement property is received. The terms of the agreement govern whether your right to receive the funds is limited as required by the safe harbor rules; possible state law complications are disregarded.

1. The transferee may give you a mortgage, deed of trust, or other security interest in property (other than cash or a cash equivalent), or a third-party guarantee. A standby letter of credit may be given if you are not allowed to draw on such standby letter except upon a default of the transferee's obligation to transfer like-kind replacement property.
2. The transferee may put cash or a cash equivalent in a qualified escrow account or a qualified trust. The escrow holder or trustee must not be related to you. Your rights to receive, pledge, borrow, or otherwise obtain the cash must be limited. For example, you may obtain the cash after all of the replacement property to which you are entitled is received. After you identify replacement property, you may obtain the cash after the later of (1) the end of the identification period and (2) the occurrence of a contingency beyond your control that you have specified in writing. You may receive the funds after the end of the identification period if within that period you do not identify replacement property. In other cases, there can be no right to the funds until the exchange period ends.
3. You may use a *qualified intermediary* if your right to receive money or other property is limited (as discussed in safe harbor rule 2, above). A qualified intermediary is an unrelated party who, for a fee, acts to facilitate a deferred exchange by entering into an agreement with you for the exchange of properties pursuant to which the intermediary acquires your property from you, acquires the replacement property, and transfers the replacement property to you. The acquisitions may be on the intermediary's own behalf or as the agent of any party to the transaction.

   The transfer of property that is facilitated by the use of a qualified intermediary may occur through a "direct deed" of legal title by the current owner of the property to you. The transferee of your property does *not* have to receive title to the property you want and then transfer it to you.

   There are restrictions on who may act as an intermediary. You may not employ any person as an intermediary who is your employee or is related to you or has generally acted as your professional adviser, such as an attorney, accountant, investment broker, real estate agent, or banker, in a two-year period preceding the exchange. Related parties include family members and controlled businesses or trusts (*see 5.6*), except that for purposes of control, a 10% interest is sufficient under the intermediary rule. The performance of routine financial, escrow, trust, or title insurance services by a financial institution or title company within the two-year period is not taken into account. State laws that may be interpreted as fixing an agency relationship between the transferor and transferee or fixing the transferor's right to security funds are ignored.

   In a simultaneous exchange, the intermediary is not considered the transferor's agent.
4. You are permitted to receive interest or a "growth factor" on escrowed funds if your right to receive the amount is limited as discussed under safe harbor rule 2.

Payment of acquisition and closing costs. The use of funds from a security account to pay specific acquisition and closing costs such as commissions, prorated taxes, and recording and transfer fees will not result in constructive receipt of the remaining funds.

6.5 Qualified Exchange Accommodation Arrangements (QEAAs) for Reverse Exchanges

The like-kind exchange rules (*6.1*) generally do not apply to a so-called reverse exchange in which you acquire replacement property *before* you transfer relinquished property. However, if you use a qualified exchange accommodation arrangement (QEAA), the transfer may qualify as a like-kind exchange.

 *Filing Instruction*

Filing Form 8824
The IRS requires related parties who exchange property to file Form 8824 for the year of the exchange and also for the two years following the exchange. If either party disposes of the property received in the original exchange in any of these years, the deferred gain must be reported in the year of disposition as if the property had been sold.

The two-year period is suspended for a holder of exchanged property who has substantially diminished his or her risk of loss, such as by use of a put or short sale.

Under a QEAA, either the replacement property or the relinquished property is transferred to an exchange accommodation titleholder (EAT) who is treated as the beneficial owner of the property for federal income tax purposes. If the property is held in a QEAA, the IRS will accept the qualification of property as either replacement property or relinquished property, and the treatment of an EAT as the beneficial owner of the property for federal income tax purposes.

The IRS has set numerous technical requirements for QEAAs. Property is held in a QEAA only if you have a written agreement with the EAT, the time limits for identifying and transferring the property are met, and the qualified indicia of ownership of property are transferred to the EAT.

The EAT must meet all the following requirements: (1) Hold qualified indicia of ownership (*see* below) at all times from the date of acquisition of the property until the property is transferred within the 180-day period (*see* below); (2) be someone other than you, your agent, or a person related to you or your agent; (3) be subject to federal income tax. If the EAT is treated as a partnership or S corporation, more than 90% of its interests or stock must be owned by partners or shareholders who are subject to federal income tax.

The IRS defines qualified indicia of ownership as either legal title to the property, other indicia of ownership of the property that are treated as beneficial ownership of the property under principles of commercial law (for example, a contract for deed), or interests in an entity that is disregarded as an entity separate from its owner for federal income tax purposes (for example, a single member limited liability company) and that holds either legal title to the property or other indicia of ownership.

There are time limits for identifying and transferring property under a QEAA. No later than 45 days after the transfer of qualified indicia of ownership of the replacement property to the EAT, you must identify the relinquished property in a manner consistent with the principles for deferred exchanges discussed at 6.4. If qualified indicia of ownership in replacement property have been transferred to the EAT, then no later than 180 days after that transfer, the replacement property must be transferred to you either directly or indirectly through a qualified intermediary, defined earlier in 6.4. If the EAT receives qualified indicia of ownership in the relinquished property, then no later than 180 days after that transfer, the relinquished property must be transferred to a person other than you, your agent at the time of the transaction, or a person who is related to you or your agent.

Note: For further details on the IRS's guidelines for QEAAs, *see* Revenue Procedure 2000-37.

6.6   Exchanges Between Related Parties

Tax-free treatment of like-kind exchanges between related persons may be lost if either party disposes of property received in the exchange within two years after the date of the last transfer that was part of the exchange. Any gain not recognized on the original exchange is taxable as of the date of the later disposition of the original like-kind property by either party within the two-year period. If a loss was not recognized, the loss becomes deductible if allowed under the rules in 5.6.

Indirect dispositions of the property within the two-year period, such as transfer of stock of a corporation or interests in a partnership that owns the property, may also be treated as taxable dispositions.

Related parties. Related persons falling within the two-year rule include your children, grandchildren, parent, brother, or sister, controlled corporations or partnerships (more than 50% ownership), and a trust in which you are a beneficiary. A transfer to a spouse is not subject to the two-year rule unless he or she is a nonresident alien.

Plan to avoid two-year rule. If you set up a prearranged plan under which you first transfer property to an unrelated party who within two years makes an exchange with a party related to you, the related party will not qualify for tax-free treatment on that exchange.

Exceptions. No tax will be incurred on a disposition made because of death; in an involuntary conversion provided the original exchange occurred before the threat of the conversion; or if you can prove that neither the exchange nor the later disposition was for a tax avoidance purpose.

6.7   Property Transfers Between Spouses and Ex-Spouses

Under Section 1041, all transfers of property between spouses are treated as tax-free exchanges, *other* than transfers to a nonresident alien spouse, certain trust transfers of mortgaged property, and transfers of U.S. Savings Bonds; these exceptions are discussed below. Section 1041 applies to transfers during marriage as well as to property settlements incident to a divorce. In a Section 1041 transfer, there is no taxable gain or deductible loss to the transferor spouse. The transferee-spouse takes the transferor's basis in the property, and so appreciation in value will be taxed to the recipient on a later sale.

Planning Reminder

Recipient Spouse Bears Tax Consequences of Transferred Property

Under the tax-free exchange rules, there is no taxable gain or deductible loss on the transfer of property, even if cash is received for the property or the other spouse (or former spouse) assumes liabilities or gives up marital rights as part of a property settlement. The spouse who receives property may incur tax on a later sale because his or her basis in the property is the same as the transferor-spouse's basis; *see* the Examples in 6.7. Because the transferee bears the tax consequences of a later sale, he or she should consider the potential tax on the appreciation in negotiating a marital settlement. In a marital settlement, the transferee spouse can lessen the tax burden by negotiating for assets that have little or no unrealized appreciation.

A transfer is "incident to a divorce" if it occurs either within one year after the date the marriage ceases or, if later, is related to the cessation of the marriage, such as a transfer authorized by a divorce decree. Under temporary regulations, any transfer pursuant to a divorce or separation agreement occurring within six years of the end of the marriage is considered "incident to a divorce." Later transfers qualify only if a transfer within the six-year period was hampered by legal or business disputes such as a fight over the property value.

EXAMPLES

1. In a property settlement accompanying a divorce, a husband plans to transfer to his wife stock worth $250,000 that cost him $50,000. In deciding whether to agree to the transfer, the wife should be aware that her basis for the stock will be $50,000; if she sells the stock, she will have to pay tax on the $200,000 gain. This tax cost should be accounted for in arriving at the settlement.

2. Basis of the property in the hands of the transferee-spouse is not increased even if cash is paid as part of the transfer. For example, a husband received a house originally owned by the wife as part of a marital settlement. Her basis for the house was $32,200. He paid her $18,000 cash as part of the settlement and when he later sold the house for $64,000, he argued that his basis for purposes of computing profit was $50,200—the wife's $32,200 basis plus his $18,000 cash payment. The IRS refused to consider the cash payment as part of basis, and the Tax Court agreed that the carryover basis rule applies.

Nonresident alien. The tax-free exchange rule does not apply to transfers to a nonresident alien spouse or former spouse.

Transfers of U.S. Savings Bonds. The IRS has ruled that the tax-free exchange rules do not apply to transfers of U.S. Savings Bonds. For example, if a husband has deferred the reporting of interest on E or EE bonds and transfers the bonds to his ex-wife as part of a divorce settlement, the deferred interest is taxed to him on the transfer. The wife's basis for the bonds is the husband's basis plus the income he realizes on the transfer. When she redeems the bonds, she will be taxed on the interest accrued from the date of the transfer to the redemption date.

Payment for release of community property interest in retirement pay. The Tax Court allowed tax-free treatment for a payment made to a wife for releasing her community property claim to her husband's military retirement pay. The IRS had argued that the tax-free exchange rules discussed in this section did not apply to the release of rights to retirement pay that would otherwise be subject to ordinary income tax. The Tax Court disagreed, holding that the tax-free exchange rule applies whether the transfer is for relinquishment of marital rights, cash, or other property.

Transfers in trust. The tax-free exchange rules generally apply to transfers in trust for the benefit of a spouse or a former spouse if incident to a divorce. However, gain cannot be avoided on a trust transfer of heavily mortgaged property. If the trust property is mortgaged, the transferor spouse must report a taxable gain to the extent that the liabilities assumed by the transferee spouse plus the liabilities to which the property is subject (even if not assumed) exceed the transferor's adjusted basis for the property. If the transferor realizes a taxable gain under this rule, the transferee's basis for the property is increased by the gain.

Sole proprietorship sale to spouse. Tax-free exchange rules may apply to a sale of business property by a sole proprietor to a spouse. The buyer spouse assumes a carryover basis even if fair market value is paid. The transferor is not required to recapture previously claimed depreciation deductions or investment credits. However, the transferee is subject to the recapture rules on premature dispositions or if the property ceases to be used for business purposes.

Agreements existing on July 18, 1984. The tax-free exchange rules generally apply to transfers made after July 18, 1984. Transfers made under agreements in effect before July 19, 1984, are subject to the tax-free rule only if both spouses make an election to have the tax-free rule apply. The election must be made on a signed statement attached to the first tax return filed by the transferor-spouse for the year in which the first transfer occurs. The transferor must also attach the statement to returns for later years in which a transfer is made under the election.

Divorce-related redemptions of stock in closely held corporation. When a married couple own all (or most) of the stock in a closely held corporation, the corporation may redeem the stock of one of the spouses as part of an overall divorce settlement. Does the transferring spouse avoid tax on the redemption under the Section 1041 tax-free exchange rules?

Court Decision

Interest on Marital Property Settlements

Parties may agree to pay interest on property transfers relating to divorce settlements when payments are to be made over time. The actual property transfer is generally a tax-free exchange. According to the Tax Court, the interest is separate and apart from the property transferred. The deductibility of the interest paid depends on the nature of the property transferred. Interest allocated to residential property, for instance, is deductible as residential mortgage interest; interest allocated to investment property is deductible as investment interest subject to the net investment income limit. *See* Chapter 15.

IRS Alert

Divorce Transfer of Nonqualified Options or Nonqualified Deferred Compensation

According to the IRS, if a vested interest in nonqualified stock options or nonqualified deferred compensation is transferred to a former spouse as part of a property settlement, the transferor-spouse does not have to report any income under the Section 1041 rules at 6.7. When the transferee-spouse later exercises the options or receives the deferred compensation, he or she will be taxed on the option spread (2.17) or the deferred compensation as if he or she was the employee.

Under an exception, if the parties to the divorce specifically provided in an agreement or court order before November 9, 2002, that the transferor will be taxed on the income attributable to the transferred interest, the IRS will recognize that provision. Section 1041 will not apply and the transferor rather than the transferee will be taxed.

If the redemption of one of the spouses' stock is treated as a transfer to a third party *on behalf of* the other spouse, Section 1041 applies and the transferor-spouse would escape tax on the redemption. However, there has been much confusion and litigation as to the standards for determining whether a redemption is "on behalf of" the non-transferor spouse, and whether different tests should apply for determining the tax treatment of each spouse. Court decisions have generally supported tax-free treatment for a spouse whose stock is redeemed under the terms of the couple's divorce or separation instrument, or where the other (non-transferring) spouse requests or consents to the redemption. However, the courts are divided on the issue of whether the non-transferor spouse, who is left in control of the corporation, has realized a constructive dividend as a result of the redemption. *See* Example 2 for the disputed positions taken by Tax Court judges in the *Read* case.

In response to the inconsistent standards used by the courts, the IRS has proposed an amendment to its regulations to provide a specific rule for determining which spouse will be taxed on the redemption. The proposed regulation would allow tax-free exchange treatment under Section 1041 to the transferor spouse (whose stock was redeemed) only if under applicable law the redemption is treated as resulting in a constructive dividend to the non-transferor spouse. If constructive dividend treatment does not apply to the non-transferor spouse, the form of the redemption transaction should be followed and the transferor-spouse taxed on the redemption. The IRS proposal adopts the position of some of the dissenting judges in the *Read* case; *see* Example 2 below. The spouses are allowed to provide in a divorce or separation agreement executed after August 2, 2001, that constructive dividend treatment to the non-transferor spouse is intended, and the IRS will accept that designation provided the spouses' tax returns reflect such treatment. Apart from such post–August 2, 2001, agreements, the proposed regulations apply only to redemptions that are pursuant to agreements entered into after the rules are adopted as final regulations. These had not yet been published when this book went to press. *See* the *Supplement* for further developments.

Planning Reminder

Transfers to Third Parties

If you transfer property to a third party on behalf of your spouse or former spouse where the transfer is required by a divorce or separation instrument, or if you have your spouse's or former spouse's written request or consent for the transfer, the transfer is tax free to you under Section 1041. The transfer is treated as if made to your spouse or former spouse, who then retransfers the property to the third party. A written request or consent must specifically state that the tax-free exchange rules of Code Section 1041 are intended, and you must receive it before filing the tax return for the year of the transfer. As discussed in the Examples on this page, a divorce-related stock redemption may qualify for Section 1041 treatment as a transfer "on behalf of" the other spouse.

EXAMPLES

1. A federal district court and the Ninth Circuit Court of Appeals held that, under Section 1041, a wife was not taxable on the redemption of her stock by the couple's closely held corporation where the redemption was pursuant to their divorce agreement and incorporated into the divorce decree. The Ninth Circuit viewed the transfer as if the husband had received the stock directly from the wife and then transferred it to the company.

   After the Ninth Circuit held that the redemption was not taxable to the wife, the IRS argued in a separate case against the nonredeeming husband that he received a taxable constructive dividend. However, the Tax Court disagreed, holding that there was no dividend to the husband because under state law he was merely a guarantor; he was not primarily and unconditionally obligated to buy the stock. The IRS did not appeal the Tax Court decision.

   In this unusual situation, the IRS is in the position of being unable to collect tax on the redemption proceeds from either the transferor or transferee spouse.

2. After William and Carol Read divorced, William, pursuant to their divorce decree, elected to have their controlled corporation purchase all of Carol's stock. A Tax Court majority held that her transfer was on behalf of William and qualified for Section 1041 nonrecognition treatment.

   The Tax Court majority also held that William realized a constructive dividend on the corporation's redemption of Carol's stock. However, the majority relied on a concession by William and did not specify a legal standard for determining whether he should be taxed. Concurring judges suggested that constructive dividend treatment for William followed automatically from the holding that Carol's stock transfer was on his behalf and thus within Section 1041. There were four dissenting opinions, all of which held that under traditional law for constructive dividends, there is no constructive dividend unless William had a "primary and unconditional obligation" to buy the shares, an obligation the corporation satisfied by making the redemption. Most of the dissenters argued that William did not have such an obligation and should not be taxed. They further argued that if William was not obligated to buy the shares, Section 1041 does not apply and thus Carol realized capital gain on the redemption of her shares. Other dissenting judges held that a spouse can never avoid taxable gain under Section 1041 on a redemption incident to divorce.

3. The Eleventh Circuit Court of Appeals allowed tax-free treatment to a redemption of a wife's stock, following the Tax Court majority in *Read* (Example 2). The redemption was on behalf of her ex-husband. The redemption was required by their divorce decree and it left him in control of 98% of the corporation's stock. He had guaranteed the corporation's 10-year promissory note to her, and the terms of the note specifically said that the guarantee was in his interests.

Furthermore, although the corporation's note did not provide for interest, interest income was not imputed to the wife. Imputed interest does not apply where the underlying transfer is not taxable under Section 1041.

6.8 Tax-Free Exchanges of Stock

Gain on the exchange of common stock for other common stock (or preferred for other preferred of the same company) is not taxable. Similarly, loss realized on such an exchange is not deductible. The exchange may take place between the stockholder and the company or between two stockholders.

An exchange of preferred stock for common, or common for preferred, in the same company is generally not tax free, unless the exchange is part of a tax-free recapitalization. In such exchanges, the company should inform you of the tax consequences.

Convertible securities. Conversion of securities under a conversion privilege is tax free under the rules discussed at *30.7*.

6.9 Joint Ownership Interests

The change to a tenancy in common from a joint tenancy is tax free. You may convert a joint tenancy in corporate stock to a tenancy in common without income-tax consequences. The transfer is tax free even though survivorship rights are eliminated. Similarly, a partition and issuance of separate certificates in the names of each joint tenant is also tax free.

A joint tenancy and a tenancy in common differ in this respect. On the death of a joint tenant, ownership passes to the surviving joint tenant or tenants. But on the death of a tenant holding property in common, ownership passes to his or her heirs, not to the other tenant or tenants with whom the property was held.

A tenancy by the entirety is a form of joint ownership recognized in some states and can be only between a husband and wife.

Dividing properties held in common. A division of properties held as tenants in common may qualify as tax-free exchanges.

For example, three men owned three pieces of real estate as tenants in common. Each man wanted to be the sole owner of one of the pieces of property. They disentangled themselves by exchanging interests in a three-way exchange. No money or property other than the three pieces of real estate changed hands, and none of the men assumed the others' liability. The transactions qualified as tax-free exchanges and no gain or loss was recognized.

Receipt of boot. Exchanges of jointly owned property are tax free as long as no "boot," such as cash or other property, passes between the parties; *see 6.3*.

6.10 Setting up Closely Held Corporations

Tax-free exchange rules facilitate the organization of a corporation. When you transfer property to a corporation that you control solely in exchange for corporate stock, no gain or loss is recognized on the transfer. For control, you alone or together with other transferors (such as partners, where a partnership is being incorporated) must own at least 80% of the combined voting power of the corporation and 80% of all other classes of stock immediately after the transfer to the corporation. If you receive securities in addition to stock, the securities are treated as taxable "boot." The corporation takes your basis in the property, and your basis in the stock received in the exchange is the same as your basis in the property. Gain not recognized on the organization of the corporation may be taxed when you sell your stock, or the corporation disposes of the property.

 Caution

Consider Taxable Transfer
Before making a property transfer to a closely held corporation, consult an accountant or an attorney on the tax consequences. There may be instances when you have potential losses or you desire the corporation to take a stepped-up basis that would make tax-free treatment undesirable.

> **EXAMPLE**
>
> You transfer a building worth $100,000, which cost you $20,000, to your newly organized corporation in exchange for all of its outstanding stock. You realize an $80,000 gain ($100,000 – $20,000) that is not recognized. Your basis in the stock is $20,000; the corporation's basis in the building is $20,000. The following year, you sell all your stock to a third party for $100,000. The $80,000 gain is now recognized.

Transfer of liabilities. When assets subject to liabilities are transferred to the corporation, the liability assumed by the corporation is not treated as taxable "boot," but your stock basis is reduced by the amount of liability. The transfer of liabilities may be taxable when the transfer is part of a tax avoidance scheme, or the liabilities exceed the basis of the property transferred to the corporation.

6.11 Exchanges of Coins and Bullion

An exchange of "gold for gold" coins or "silver for silver" coins may qualify as a tax-free exchange of like-kind investment property. An exchange is tax free if both coins represent the same type of underlying investment. An exchange of bullion-type coins for bullion-type coins is a tax-free like-kind exchange. For example, the exchange of Mexican pesos for Austrian coronas has been held to be a tax-free exchange as both are bullion-type coins.

However, an exchange of silver bullion for gold bullion is not tax free. Silver and gold bullion represent different types of property. Silver is an industrial commodity, whereas gold is primarily an investment in itself. Similarly, an exchange of U.S. gold collector's coins for South African Krugerrands is taxable. Krugerrands are bullion-type coins whose value is determined solely by metal content, whereas the U.S. gold coins are numismatic coins whose value depends on age, condition, number minted, and artistic merit, as well as metal content. Although both coins appear to be similar in gold content, each represents a different type of investment.

6.12 Tax-Free Exchanges of Insurance Policies

These exchanges of insurance policies are considered tax free:

- Life insurance policy for another life insurance policy, endowment policy, or an annuity contract.
- Endowment policy for another endowment policy that provides for regular payments beginning no later than the date payments would have started under the old policy, or in exchange for an annuity contract.
- Annuity contract for another annuity contract with identical annuitants.

These exchanges are not tax free:

- Endowment policy for a life insurance policy, or for another endowment policy that provides for payments beginning at a date later than payments would have started under the old policy.
- Annuity contract for a life insurance or endowment policy.
- Transfers of life insurance contracts where the insured is not the same person in both contracts. The IRS held that a company could not make a tax-free exchange of a key executive policy where the company could change insured executives as they leave or join the firm.

 *Planning Reminder*

Financially Troubled Insurer

If your annuity contract or insurance policy is with an insurance company that is in a rehabilitation, conservatorship, insolvency, or a similar state proceeding, you may surrender the policy and make a tax-free reinvestment of the proceeds in a new policy with a different insurance company. The transfer must be completed within 60 days. If a government agency does not allow you to withdraw your entire balance from the troubled insurance company, you must assign all rights to any future distributions to the issuer of the new contract or policy. *See* IRS Revenue Procedure 92-44.

Chapter 7

Retirement and Annuity Income

Retirement planning may be the final frontier for achieving substantial tax shelter benefits. For employees, coverage in a qualified employer retirement plan is a valuable fringe benefit, as employer contributions are tax free within specified limits. Certain salary-reduction plans allow you to make elective deferrals of salary that are not subject to income tax. An advantage of all qualified retirement plans is that earnings accumulate tax free until withdrawal.

Along with tax savings opportunities come technical restrictions and pitfalls. For example, retirement plan distributions eligible for rollover are subject to a mandatory 20% withholding tax if you receive the distribution rather than asking your employer to make a direct trustee-to-trustee transfer of the distribution to an IRA or another qualified employer plan.

This chapter discusses tax treatment of annuities and employer plan distributions, including how to avoid tax penalties, such as for distributions before age 59 $\frac{1}{2}$. IRAs are discussed in Chapter 8. Retirement plans for self-employed individuals are discussed further in Chapter 41.

A tax credit is available to low-to-moderate income taxpayers who make traditional or Roth IRA contributions, electives deferrals to a 401(k) or other employer plan, and voluntary after-tax contributions to a qualified plan. The credit is discussed in Chapter 22.

Distributions From Qualified Retirement Plans

401(k), 403(b), and Government Tax-Deferred Savings Plans

Reporting Commercial Annuities

Employee Annuities

Also refer to:

Key to Tax-Favored Retirement Plans

Type—	General Tax Considerations—	Tax Treatment of Distributions—
Company qualified plan	A company qualified pension or profit-sharing plan offers these benefits: (1) You do not realize current income on your employer's contributions to the plan on your behalf. (2) Income earned on funds contributed to your account compounds tax free. (3) Your employer may allow you to make voluntary contributions. Although these contributions may not be deducted, income earned on the voluntary contributions is not taxed until withdrawn.	If you were born before 1936 and receive a lump sum, tax on employer contributions and plan earnings may be reduced by a special averaging rule; *see 7.4.* If you receive a lump-sum distribution including company securities, unrealized appreciation on those securities is not taxed until you finally sell the stock; *see 7.10.* Distributions before age 59 ½ are generally subject to penalties, but there are exceptions; *see 7.15.* Rather than pay an immediate tax, you may elect to roll over a lump-sum payment to an IRA account; *see 7.7.* If you collect your retirement benefits as an annuity over a period of years, *see 7.25.*
Plans for self-employed	You may set up a self-employed retirement plan called a Keogh plan if you earn self-employment income through your performance of personal services. You may deduct contributions up to limits discussed in Chapter 41; income earned on assets held by the plan is not taxed. You must include employees in your Keogh under rules explained in Chapter 41. Other retirement plan options, such as a SEP or SIMPLE plan, are also discussed in Chapter 41.	You may not withdraw Keogh plan funds until age 59 ½ unless you are disabled or meet other exceptions at 7.15. Qualified distributions to self-employed persons or to beneficiaries at death may qualify for favored lump-sum treatment under the rules discussed in 7.2. Distributions from a SEP are subject to traditional IRA rules; *see 8.8.* Distributions from a SIMPLE-IRA also are subject to traditional IRA rules, but a 25% penalty (instead of 10%) applies to pre-age 59 ½ distributions in the first two years; *see 8.18.*
IRA and Roth IRA	Anyone who has earned income may contribute to a traditional IRA, but the contribution is deductible only if certain requirements are met. Your status as a participant in an employer retirement plan and your income determine whether you may claim a deduction up to the $3,000 limit ($3,500 if age 50 or older), a partial deduction, or no deduction at all. *See* Chapter 8 for these deduction limitations. Income earned on IRA accounts is not taxed until the funds are withdrawn. This tax-free buildup of earnings also applies where you make nondeductible contributions to a Roth IRA under the rules in Chapter 8.	Traditional IRA distributions are fully taxable unless you have previously made nondeductible contributions; *see 8.9.* A taxable withdrawal before age 59 ½ is subject to a 10% penalty, but there are exceptions if you are disabled, have substantial medical expenses, pay medical premiums while unemployed, or receive payments in a series of substantially equal installments; *see 8.12* for details on these and other exceptions. Starting at age 70 ½, you must receive minimum annual distributions to avoid a 50% penalty; *see 8.13.* Distributions from a Roth IRA of contributions are tax free. Distributions of earnings are taxable unless you are over age 59 ½ and have held the account for at least five years; *see 8.23.*
SEP	A simplified employee pension plan set up by your employer allows the employer to contribute to an IRA more than you can under regular IRA rules; *see 8.15.* You do not have to include in your 2002 income any employer contributions to your account. Elective deferrals of salary may be made to qualifying plans set up before 1997; *see 8.16.*	Withdrawals from a SEP are taxable under the rules explained above for IRAs.
Deferred salary or 401(k) plans	If your company has a profit-sharing or stock bonus plan, the tax law allows the company to add a cash or deferred pay plan that can operate in one of two ways: (1) Your employer contributes an amount for your benefit to your trust account. You are not taxed on your employer's contribution. (2) You agree to take a salary reduction or to forego a salary increase. The reduction is placed in a trust account for your benefit. The reduction is treated as your employer's contribution. See 7.18. Income earned on the trust account accumulates tax free until it is withdrawn.	Withdrawals are penalized unless you have reached age 59 ½, become disabled, or meet other exceptions listed at 7.15. If you were born before 1936 and receive a qualifying lump sum, tax on the lump sum may be computed according to the rules in 7.2.

Distributions From Qualified Retirement Plans

7.1 Retirement Distributions on Form 1099-R

On Form 1099-R, payments from pensions, annuities, IRAs, Roth IRAs, SIMPLE IRAs, insurance contracts, profit-sharing, and other employer plans are reported to you and the IRS. Social Security benefits are reported on Form SSA-1099; *see* Chapter 34 for the special rules to apply in determining the taxable portion of Social Security benefits.

Here is a guide to the information reported on Form 1099-R. A sample form is on the next page.

Box 1. The total amount received from the payer is shown here without taking any withholdings into account. If you file Form 1040, report the Box 1 total on Line 15a if the payment is from an IRA, or on Line 16a if from a pension or an annuity. However, if the amount is a qualifying lump-sum distribution for which you are claiming averaging, use Form 4972; *see 7.4.*

If you file Form 1040A, report the Box 1 total on Line 11a if from an IRA or on Line 12a if from a pension or an annuity.

If you are receiving the distribution as a beneficiary of an employee who died before August 21, 1996, you may be entitled to a $5,000 death benefit exclusion; *see 7.27.*

If an exchange of insurance contracts was made, the value of the contract will be shown in Box 1, but if the exchange qualified as tax free, a zero taxable amount will be shown in Box 2a and Code 6 will be entered in Box 7.

Boxes 2a and 2b. The taxable portion of distributions from employer plans and insurance contracts may be shown in Box 2a. The taxable portion does not include your after-tax contributions to an employer plan or insurance premium payments.

If the payer cannot figure the taxable portion, the first box in 2b should be checked; Box 2a should be blank. You will then have to figure the taxable amount yourself. A payment from a pension or an annuity is only partially taxed if you contributed to the cost and you did not recover your entire cost investment before 2002. *See 7.22* (commercial annuity) or *7.25* (employee annuity) for details on computing the taxable portion if you have an unrecovered investment.

The payer of a traditional IRA distribution will probably not compute the taxable portion, and in this case, the total distribution from Box 1 will be entered as the taxable portion in Box 2a. This amount is fully taxable unless you have made nondeductible contributions, in which case Form 8606 is used to figure the taxable portion of the distribution; *see 8.9.* Form 8606 is also used to figure the taxable part, if any, of a Roth IRA distribution; *see 8.23.*

If the payment is from an employer plan and the "total distribution" box has been checked in 2b, *see 7.2* for possible rollover and special averaging options. The taxable amount in Box 2a should not include net unrealized appreciation (NUA; *see 7.10*) in any employer securities included in the lump sum or the value of an annuity contract included in the distribution.

Box 3. If the payment is a lump-sum distribution, you were born before 1936, and you participated in the plan before 1974, the amount shown here may be treated as capital gain; *see 7.5.*

Box 4. Any federal income tax withheld is shown here. Do not forget to include it on Line 62 of Form 1040 or Line 39 of Form 1040A. If Box 4 shows any withholdings, attach Copy B of Form 1099-R to your return.

Box 5. If you made after-tax contributions to your employer's plan, or paid premiums for a commercial annuity or insurance contract, your contribution is shown here, less any such contributions previously distributed. IRA or SEP contributions (*see* Chapter 8) are not shown here.

Box 6. If you received a qualifying lump-sum distribution that includes securities of your employer's company, the total net unrealized appreciation (NUA) is shown here. Unless you elect to pay tax on it currently (*7.10*), this amount is not taxed until you sell the securities. If you did not receive a qualifying lump sum, the amount shown here is the net unrealized appreciation attributable to your after-tax employee contributions, which are also not taxed until you sell the securities; *see 7.10.*

Box 7. In Box 7, the payer will indicate if the distribution is from a traditional IRA, SEP, or SIMPLE and enter codes that are used by the IRS to check whether you have reported the distribution correctly, including the penalty for distributions before age 59 ½.

If you are under age 59 ½ and the payer knows that you qualify for an exception to the 10% early distribution penalty (*7.15*), such as the exception for separation of service after age 55 for an employer-plan distribution, Code 2 will be entered in Box 7. Code 3 will be used if the disability

 *Filing Instruction*

Conversion of Traditional IRA to Roth IRA
If in 2002 you converted a traditional IRA to a Roth IRA, the conversion amount is included in Box 1 and in Box 2a of Form 1099-R as a taxable distribution. The entire conversion amount is generally taxable on your 2002 return; *see 8.21.*

exception applies. Code 4 is the exception for distributions paid to beneficiaries. If Code 1 is entered, this indicates that you were under age 59 ½ at the time of the distribution and as far as the payer knows, no penalty exception applies. However, although Code 1 is entered, you may not be subject to a penalty. For example, you may qualify for the medical expense exception *(7.15)* or you may have made a tax-free rollover instead of having your employer make a direct rollover under the rules at *7.7.*

If the employer did make a direct rollover, Code G will be entered if the direct rollover was to an IRA and Code H if to another employer's qualified plan or tax-sheltered annuity.

If you are at least age 59¹/₂, Code 7 should be entered.

If you are the beneficiary of a deceased employee, Code 4 should be entered. The 10% early distribution penalty does not apply.

If you contribute to a 401(k) plan and are a highly compensated employee, your employer may have to make a corrective distribution to you of contributions (and allocable income) that exceed allowable nondiscrimination ceilings. In this case, the employer will enter Code 8 if the corrective distribution is taxable in 2002, Code P if taxable in 2001, or Code D if taxable in 2000.

If you receive a lump-sum distribution that qualifies for special averaging, Code A will be entered; *see 7.4* for averaging rules.

Box 8. If the value of an annuity contract was included as part of a lump sum you received, the value of the contract is shown here. It is not taxable when you receive it and should not be included in Boxes 1 and 2a. For purposes of computing averaging on Form 4972, this amount is added to the ordinary income portion of the distribution; *see 7.4.*

Box 9. If several beneficiaries are receiving payment from an employer plan total distribution, the amount shown in Box 9a is your share of the distribution.

Boxes 10–15. The payer may make entries in these boxes to show state or local income tax withholdings.

Filing Tip

Lump-Sum Distribution

If you are paid a distribution that qualifies for lump-sum averaging, Code A will be entered in Box 7 of Form 1099-R. *See 7.4* for averaging rules.

☐ VOID   ☐ CORRECTED

PAYER'S name, street address, city, state, and ZIP code	1 Gross distribution	OMB No. 1545-0119	Distributions From Pensions, Annuities, Retirement or Profit-Sharing Plans, IRAs, Insurance Contracts, etc.
StarShine Systems, Inc. Retirement Plan **1220 Silver Lake Drive** **City, State 1X001**	$ **182,438**	**2002**	
	2a Taxable amount $ **182,438**	Form **1099-R**	

	2b Taxable amount not determined ☐	Total distribution ☒	Copy 1 For State, City, or Local Tax Department

PAYER'S Federal identification number	RECIPIENT'S identification number	3 Capital gain (included in box 2a)	4 Federal income tax withheld	
X0-1101X01	**010-XX-10XX**	$ **8,620**	$ **36,488**	

RECIPIENT'S name **Andrew Kellogg**		5 Employee contributions or insurance premiums $	6 Net unrealized appreciation in employer's securities $	

Street address (including apt. no.) **44 Hampton Lane**		7 Distribution code **7A**	IRA/ SEP/ SIMPLE ☐	8 Other $ %	

City, state, and ZIP code **City, State 1X011**		9a Your percentage of total distribution %	9b Total employee contributions $	

Account number (optional)		10 State tax withheld $ $	11 State/Payer's state no.	12 State distribution $ $
		13 Local tax withheld $ $	14 Name of locality	15 Local distribution $ $

Form **1099-R**   Department of the Treasury - Internal Revenue Service

7.2 Lump-Sum Distributions

If you are entitled to a lump-sum distribution from a company retirement plan or self-employed Keogh plan, you may avoid current tax by asking your employer to make a direct rollover of your account to an IRA or another qualified employer plan. If the distribution is made to you, 20% will be withheld, but it is still possible to make a tax-free rollover within 60 days; *see 7.7* for rollover details.

If you receive a lump sum and do *not* make a rollover, the taxable part of the distribution (shown in Box 2a of Form 1099-R) must be reported as ordinary pension income on your return unless you were born before 1936 and qualify for special averaging as discussed below. Your after-tax contributions and any net unrealized appreciation (NUA, *7.10*) in employer securities that are included in the lump sum are recovered tax free; they are not part of the taxable distribution.

A taxable distribution before age $59\frac{1}{2}$ is subject to a 10% penalty in addition to regular income tax, unless you qualify for an exception; *see 7.15*.

Lump-sum distribution defined. A lump-sum distribution is the payment within a single taxable year of a plan participant's entire balance from an employer's qualified plan. If the employer has more than one qualified plan of the same kind (profit-sharing, pension, stock bonus), you must receive the balance from all of them within the same year. A series of payments may qualify as a lump-sum distribution provided you receive them within the same tax year. The account balance does not include deductible voluntary contributions you made after 1981 and before 1987; these are not eligible for lump-sum distribution treatment.

Requirements for 10-year averaging or capital gain election. If you were born before 1936 and receive a qualified lump-sum distribution (defined above), you generally may elect to figure your tax on the distribution using the 10-year averaging method. If you participated in the plan before 1974, you may elect to apply a 20% rate to the pre-1974 part of the lump-sum distribution if 20% is lower than the averaging rate.

However, averaging and capital gain treatment are not allowed for a lump-sum distribution if any of the following are true: (1) you rolled over any part of the lump-sum distribution to an IRA or an employer qualified plan, (2) you received the distribution during the first five years that you participated in the plan, (3) you previously received a distribution from the same plan and you rolled it over tax free to an IRA or another qualified employer plan, (4) you elected 10-year or five-year averaging or capital gain treatment for any other lump-sum distribution after 1986, (5) after 2001 you rolled over to the same plan a distribution from a 403(b) plan *(7.20)* or a governmental 457 plan *(7.21)*.

See 7.4 and *7.5* for details on electing averaging and the 20% capital gain rate.

If you are the beneficiary of a deceased plan participant, the participant's age, not yours, determines your right to claim averaging, and the five-year participation rule does not apply; *see 7.6*.

Spousal consent to lump-sum distribution. If you are married, you may have to obtain your spouse's consent to elect a lump-sum distribution; *see 7.11*.

Withholding tax. An employer must withhold a 20% tax from a lump-sum distribution that is paid to you and not rolled over directly by the employer; *see 7.7* for further details.

Beneficiaries. A surviving spouse who receives a lump-sum distribution upon the death of an employee may avoid tax by making a tax-free rollover to his or her own IRA. Beneficiaries other than surviving spouses may not make a tax-free rollover; *see 7.7*.

If the deceased employee was born before 1936, any beneficiary (not just a surviving spouse) may elect special averaging or capital gain treatment for a lump-sum distribution of the account; *see 7.6*.

Court ordered lump-sum distribution to a spouse or former spouse. A distribution received by a spouse or former spouse of an employee under a qualified domestic relations order (QDRO) may be eligible for tax-free rollover or, in some cases, special averaging treatment; *see 7.12*.

7.3 Lump-Sum Options If You Were Born Before 1936

You may avoid current tax on a lump-sum distribution by having your employer make a direct rollover *(7.8)* of the distribution to an IRA or qualified plan of another employer. The IRS allows the plan of a new employer to accept a direct rollover from your old employer even though you are not yet able to contribute to the new plan because of a minimum length of service or age requirement.

Caution

Prior Rollover Bars Averaging
You may not claim averaging for a lump-sum distribution if you previously received a distribution from the same plan that was rolled over tax free *(7.7)* to an IRA or to another qualified employer plan.

Once in a Lifetime Election

You are allowed to elect averaging only once as a plan participant after 1986. If before 1987 you elected 10-year averaging and were under age 59$^1/_2$, you may elect averaging for a current distribution. However, if you were over age 59$^1/_2$ when you made the pre-1987 election, you are barred from electing averaging again.

If you were born before 1936, have not previously elected averaging, and elect averaging for a distribution received in 2002, you will not be able to claim averaging again if you join another company and receive a lump-sum distribution from the new employer.

Even if you are barred from electing averaging for a lump sum from your own plan, you can make the election as a beneficiary of a deceased plan participant born before 1936.

Caution

Averaging Not Allowed for Those Born After 1935

If you were born after 1935, a lump-sum distribution from your plan is not eligible for averaging.

If you receive the distribution, a 20% tax will be withheld. If you later decide to make a rollover, you have 60 days from the time of receiving the distribution to do so; *see 7.8*. However, to avoid tax on the entire distribution, you will have to include in the rollover an amount equal to the withheld tax. Withholding is discussed further at *7.8* and *26.11*. Ordinary income tax rates apply to the amount not rolled over, unless you are eligible for averaging or the 20% capital gain method.

Consider options in advance if you expect to receive a lump sum eligible for averaging. Plan ahead if you expect to receive a lump-sum distribution eligible for averaging *(7.2)*. You must decide whether to pay tax currently using the averaging method (and possibly the 20% capital gain method for pre-1974 participation), or to defer tax by making a tax-free rollover *(7.7)*. If you receive more than one lump sum during the year, you must make the same choice for all of them; you may not roll over one lump sum and claim averaging for another.

Keep in mind the time constraints for making a rollover. If you do not request a direct rollover from the payer plan to an IRA or another employer plan, you have only 60 days from the day you receive the distribution to complete a personal rollover; *see 7.8*.

If you are changing jobs, a direct rollover or personal rollover may be made to a traditional IRA or a qualified plan of your new employer. However, if the distribution is rolled over to a traditional IRA, you lose the right to claim averaging for those assets unless the IRA is a "conduit IRA" that serves as a holding account until a later rollover may be made to another employer's plan. As long as the distribution and earnings on the distribution are the only assets in the conduit IRA, a rollover may be made from that account to a new employer's plan, from which a lump-sum distribution eligible for averaging may later be received; *see* the Planning Reminder on page 154. Distributions from a traditional IRA are taxable as ordinary income.

If you plan to continue working and expect to receive another lump sum in the future, you may not claim averaging for the current lump sum and also for the later distribution. Averaging may be claimed only once as a plan participant after 1986.

An IRA rollover cannot be revoked to claim averaging. If you make a rollover to an IRA, you cannot change your mind and cancel the IRA account in order to apply special averaging. The rollover election is irrevocable, according to an IRS regulation that has been upheld by the Tax Court. If an IRA rollover account is revoked, the entire distribution is taxable as ordinary income, and a 10% penalty may be imposed if the recipient is under age 59$^1/_2$ *(7.15)*.

Disqualification of retirement plan. If you receive a lump-sum distribution from a plan that loses its exempt status, the IRS may argue that the distribution does not qualify for lump-sum treatment. Under the IRS position, you may not roll over the distribution to an IRA or elect special averaging. The Tax Court previously took the position that if the plan qualified when contributions were made, an allocable portion of the distribution was a qualified lump sum. However, the majority of appeals courts that reviewed Tax Court decisions on this issue supported the IRS position. In response, the Tax Court reversed its position and adopted the harsher IRS approach: no part of the distribution qualifies for rollover or averaging if the plan loses its exempt status.

7.4 Averaging on Form 4972

If you were born before 1936 and the other averaging tests at *7.2* are satisfied, you may elect on Form 4972 to compute the tax on a lump-sum distribution received during 2002 using a 10-year averaging method based on 1986 tax rates for single persons. A five-year averaging method was allowed for lump-sum distributions received before 2000 by plan participants over age 59$^1/_2$, but this option is no longer available.

If you were born after 1935, you may not elect averaging for a lump-sum distribution of your account balance. However, you may elect averaging as the beneficiary of a deceased plan participant who was born before 1936; *see 7.6*.

Averaging on 2002 returns. If you qualify for averaging *(7.2)*, follow IRS instructions to Form 4972 for applying the 10-year averaging method. If you received more than one qualified lump sum, you may elect averaging for one of the distributions only if you elect averaging for all.

The amount eligible for averaging is the taxable portion of the distribution shown in Box 2a of Form 1099-R. You may also elect to add to the Box 2a amount any net unrealized appreciation in employer securities (shown in Box 6) included in the lump sum. If you are receiving the distribution as a beneficiary of a plan participant who died before August 21, 1996, follow the instructions to Form 4972 for claiming a death benefit exclusion that reduces the Box 2a taxable portion.

Form **4972**	**Tax on Lump-Sum Distributions** (From Qualified Plans of Participants Born Before 1936) ▶ **Attach to Form 1040 or Form 1041.**	OMB No. 1545-0193 **20**02
Department of the Treasury Internal Revenue Service		Attachment Sequence No. **28**

Name of recipient of distribution	Identifying number
Andrew Kellogg	**010 - XX - 10XX**

Part I Complete this part to see if you can use Form 4972

			Yes	No
1	Was this a distribution of a plan participant's entire balance (excluding deductible voluntary employee contributions and certain forfeited amounts) from all of an employer's qualified plans of one kind (pension, profit-sharing, or stock bonus)? If "No," **do not** use this form	1	X	
2	Did you roll over any part of the distribution? If "Yes," **do not** use this form	2		X
3	Was this distribution paid to you as a beneficiary of a plan participant who was born before 1936? . . .	3		X
4	Were you **(a)** a plan participant who received this distribution, **(b)** born before 1936, **and (c)** a participant in the plan for at least 5 years before the year of the distribution?	4	X	
	If you answered "No" to both questions 3 **and** 4, **do not** use this form.			
5a	Did you use Form 4972 after 1986 for a previous distribution from your own plan? If "Yes," **do not** use this form for a 2002 distribution from your own plan	5a		X
b	If you are receiving this distribution as a beneficiary of a plan participant who died, did you use Form 4972 for a previous distribution received for that participant after 1986? If "Yes," **do not** use the form for this distribution	5b		

Part II Complete this part to choose the 20% capital gain election (see instructions)

6	Capital gain part from Form 1099-R, box 3	6	8,620
7	Multiply line 6 by 20% (.20) . . . . ▶	7	1,724
	If you also choose to use Part III, go to line 8. Otherwise, include the amount from line 7 in the total on Form 1040, line 42, or Form 1041, Schedule G, line 1b, whichever applies.		

Part III Complete this part to choose the 10-year tax option (see instructions)

8	Ordinary income from Form 1099-R, box 2a minus box 3. If you did not complete Part II, enter the taxable amount from Form 1099-R, box 2a.	8	173,818
9	Death benefit exclusion for a beneficiary of a plan participant who died before August 21, 1996	9	- 0-
10	Total taxable amount. Subtract line 9 from line 8	10	173,818
11	Current actuarial value of annuity from Form 1099-R, box 8. If none, enter -0-	11	- 0-
12	Adjusted total taxable amount. Add lines 10 and 11. If this amount is $70,000 or more, **skip** lines 13 through 16, enter this amount on line 17, and go to line 18	12	173,818
13	Multiply line 12 by 50% (.50), but **do not** enter more than $10,000 . [13]		
14	Subtract $20,000 from line 12. If line 12 is $20,000 or less, enter -0- . . . . . [14]		
15	Multiply line 14 by 20% (.20) . [15]		
16	Minimum distribution allowance. Subtract line 15 from line 13	16	
17	Subtract line 16 from line 12	17	173,818
18	Federal estate tax attributable to lump-sum distribution	18	- 0-
19	Subtract line 18 from line 17. If line 11 is zero, **skip** lines 20 through 22 and go to line 23 . .	19	173,818
20	Divide line 11 by line 12 and enter the result as a decimal (rounded to at least three places). . . . . [20] .		
21	Multiply line 16 by the decimal on line 20 . . . . . [21]		
22	Subtract line 21 from line 11 . . . . . [22]		
23	Multiply line 19 by 10% (.10).	23	17,382
24	Tax on amount on line 23. Use the Tax Rate Schedule in the instructions	24	3,012
25	Multiply line 24 by ten (10). If line 11 is zero, **skip** lines 26 through 28, enter this amount on line 29, and go to line 30	25	30,120
26	Multiply line 22 by 10% (.10) . . . . [26]		
27	Tax on amount on line 26. Use the Tax Rate Schedule in the instructions . . . . . [27]		
28	Multiply line 27 by ten (10)	28	
29	Subtract line 28 from line 25. (Multiple recipients, see instructions.) . . . . ▶	29	30,120
30	**Tax on lump-sum distribution.** Add lines 7 and 29. Also include this amount in the total on Form 1040, line 42, or Form 1041, Schedule G, line 1b, whichever applies . . . . . . ▶	30	31,844

For Paperwork Reduction Act Notice, see instructions.   Cat. No. 13187U   Form **4972** (2002)

If the distribution includes capital gain (Box 3 of Form 1099-R) and you want to apply the special 20% capital gain rate *(7.5)*, you should subtract the capital gain in Box 3 from the taxable amount in Box 2a and apply averaging to the balance of ordinary income.

The tax computed on Form 4972 is reported on Form 1040, Line 42, as an additional tax. It is completely separate from the tax computed on your other income reported on Form 1040.

See the following Example and the Sample Form 4972 on the preceding page.

EXAMPLE

Andrew Kellogg was born before 1936. In 2002, he retired from StarShine Systems, Inc., and received a lump-sum distribution of $182,438, before withholdings. The Form 1099-R provided by the company (*see* page 148) shows in Box 3 a capital gain portion of $8,620, attributable to pre-1974 participation.

On Form 4972, Andrew applies the special 20% rate to the capital gain portion for a tax of $1,724. He then figures the tax on the $173,818 ordinary income part of the distribution under the 10-year averaging method. As shown on the sample Form 4972 on page 151, Andrew's total tax on the distribution is $31,844, the sum of the $30,120 tax under 10-year averaging and the $1,724 tax on the capital gain portion. In Andrew's case, the special 20% capital gains rate is advantageous because it results in a lower tax than if the capital gain were treated as ordinary income subject to the averaging computation. The tax would be $32,360 if the special capital gain rate was not elected.

Community property. Only the spouse who has earned the lump sum may use averaging. Community property laws are disregarded for this purpose. If a couple files separate returns and one spouse elects averaging, the other spouse is not taxed on the amount subject to the computation.

EXAMPLE

A husband in a community property state receives a lump-sum distribution of which the ordinary income portion is $10,000. He and his wife file separate returns. If averaging is not elected, $5,000, or one-half, is taxable on the husband's return and the other $5,000 on his wife's return. However, if he elects the averaging method, only he reports the $10,000 on Form 4972.

 Filing Tip

Pre-1974 Capital Gain Portion of Distribution

If you were born before 1936 and a portion of your lump-sum distribution is attributable to plan participation before 1974 *(7.5)*, you may treat it as ordinary income eligible for averaging, or you may elect to treat it as capital gain taxable at a flat 20% rate; choose the method on Form 4972 that gives the lower overall tax.

7.5 Capital Gain Treatment for Pre-1974 Participation

The portion of a qualifying lump-sum distribution attributable to pre-1974 participation is eligible for a 20% capital gain rate if you were born before 1936 and the other tests at *7.2* are met.

On Form 1099-R, the company paying the lump-sum distribution shows the capital gain portion in Box 3. The ordinary income portion is Box 2a (taxable amount) *minus* Box 3. If you elect to treat the pre-1974 portion as capital gain subject to a flat rate of 20% on Form 4972, the tax on the balance of the distribution may be figured under the averaging method *(7.4)*. The 20% rate for the capital gain portion is fixed by law, and applies regardless of the tax rate imposed on your other capital gains. Alternatively, you may elect to treat the capital gain portion as ordinary income eligible for averaging. You may not elect to report any portion of the pre-1974 portion of the lump-sum distribution as long-term capital gain on Schedule D.

Under the one-time election rule, if you elect to apply the averaging and/or 20% capital gain rule for a 2002 distribution, you may not elect averaging or capital gain treatment for any later distribution.

Capital gain treatment not allowed for individuals born after 1935. If you were born after 1935, you may *not* treat any portion of a lump-sum distribution as capital gain. You may not apply the flat 20% rate to the pre-1974 portion of the lump-sum distribution on Form 4972, or include any part of it as capital gain on your 2002 Schedule D.

7.6 Lump-Sum Payments Received by Beneficiary

A beneficiary of a deceased employee or self-employed plan participant may elect 10-year averaging on Form 4972 for a qualifying lump-sum distribution *(7.2)* because of the participant's death, provided the participant was born before 1936. The age of the beneficiary is irrelevant. A beneficiary may elect averaging even though the deceased employee was in the plan for less than five years. If the participant was born before 1936 and had participated in the plan before 1974, a 20% capital gain election may be made for that portion of the distribution *(7.5)*, and the averaging method applied to the balance.

Form 4972 is used to compute tax under the averaging method or to make the 20% capital gain election *(7.5)*. Follow the Form 4972 instructions to claim the up-to-$5,000 death benefit exclusion *(7.27)* where the plan participant died before August 21, 1996. Any federal estate tax attributable to the distribution reduces the taxable amount on Form 4972. Any election that you make as a beneficiary does not affect your right to elect lump-sum treatment for a distribution from your own plan.

A lump sum paid because of an employee's death may qualify for capital gain and averaging treatment, although the employee received annuity payments before death.

An election may be made on Form 4972 only once as the beneficiary of a particular plan participant. A beneficiary who receives more than one lump-sum distribution for the same participant in the same year must treat them all the same way. Averaging must be elected for all of the distributions on a single Form 4972 or for none of them.

Payment received by a second beneficiary (after the death of the first beneficiary) is not entitled to lump-sum treatment or the death benefit exclusion.

Beneficiaries of plan participants born after 1935. A beneficiary may *not* claim averaging or capital gain treatment for a lump-sum distribution if the plan participant was born after 1935.

Distribution to trust or estate. If a qualifying lump sum is paid to a trust or an estate, the employee, or, if deceased, his or her personal representative, may elect averaging.

EXAMPLE

Gunnison's father was covered by a company benefit plan. The father died, as did Gunnison's mother, before benefits were fully paid out. Gunnison received a substantial lump sum. He argued that he collected on account of his father's death. The IRS disagreed.

The Tax Court and an appeals court sided with the IRS. Gunnison was entitled to the payment following his mother's death, not his father's death. For special lump-sum treatment, the payout must arise solely on account of the death of the covered employee.

7.7   Tax-Free Rollovers From Qualified Plans

A rollover allows you to make a tax-free transfer of a distribution from a qualified employer retirement plan to another qualified plan or to a traditional IRA. If a rollover is made to a traditional IRA, later distributions are subject to the IRA rules *(8.8)* and will not qualify for special averaging *(7.4)*. Starting in 2002, a tax-free rollover from a qualified plan may also be made to a 403(b) plan *(7.20)* or governmental 457 plan *(7.21)* that accepts rollovers.

Eligible rollover distributions. Almost all taxable distributions received from a qualified corporate or self-employed pension, profit-sharing, stock bonus, or annuity plan are eligible for tax-free rollover. The major exceptions are substantially equal periodic payments over your lifetime or over a period of at least 10 years, hardship distributions, and minimum distributions *(7.13)* required after age $70^1/_2$; *see* below for other ineligible distributions.

Starting in 2002, after-tax contributions may be rolled over to a traditional IRA. A trustee-to-trustee transfer of after-tax contributions may also be made to a qualified defined contribution plan that agrees to separately account for the after-tax amount.

Caution: If the distribution is for part of your account balance and you roll it over, a later lump-sum distribution from the plan will not qualify for averaging; *see 7.4.*

Rollover options. If you want to make a tax-free rollover of an eligible rollover distribution, you should instruct your employer to directly roll over the funds to a traditional IRA you designate or to the plan of your new employer. You could also choose to have the distribution paid to you, and within 60 days you could make a tax-free rollover yourself. *However, to avoid the 20% mandatory withholding tax, you must elect to have the plan make a direct rollover. If an eligible rollover distribution is paid to you, the 20% withholding tax applies. Before a distribution is made, your employer must provide you with written notice concerning the rollover options and the withholding tax rules.* See 7.8 *for further details on the direct rollover and personal rollover alternatives.*

Rollover from employer plan to IRA after age $70^1/_2$. Starting with the year you reach age $70^1/_2$, you may no longer make contributions to a traditional IRA. However, if you are over age $70^1/_2$ and you receive an eligible rollover distribution from your employer's plan, you may instruct your employer to make a direct rollover of the distribution to a traditional IRA, as discussed in *7.8*. If you receive the distribution from the employer, a 20% tax will be withheld. You may then make a tax-free rollover within 60 days of the distribution; *see 7.8* for the discussion of "personal rollovers." In the year of the rollover, you must receive a minimum distribution from the IRA; *see 8.13*.

Filing Tip

Lump Sums to Multiple Beneficiaries

A lump-sum distribution to two or more beneficiaries may qualify for averaging and capital gain treatment, so long as the plan participant was born before 1936. Each beneficiary may separately elect the averaging method for the ordinary income portion, even though other beneficiaries do not so elect. Follow the Form 4972 instructions for multiple recipients.

Caution

Direct Rollover to Roth IRA Not Allowed

You may *not* roll over an employer plan distribution to a Roth IRA. You may make a tax-free rollover to a traditional IRA and then make a taxable conversion to a Roth IRA if you qualify under the rules at *8.21*.

Also disallowed is a rollover from an employer plan to a SIMPLE IRA *(8.17)*.

Beneficiaries. The only beneficiary who may make a tax-free rollover is a surviving spouse, as discussed in *7.8*.

Distributions that may not be rolled over. Any lump-sum or partial distribution from your account is eligible for rollover *except for the following:*

- Hardship distributions from a 401(k) plan or 403(b) plan *(7.19)*.
- Payments that are part of a series of substantially equal payments made at least annually over a period of 10 years or more or over your life or life expectancy (or the joint lives or joint life and last survivor expectancies of you and your designated beneficiary).
- Minimum required distributions after attaining age $70\frac{1}{2}$ or retiring *(7.13)*.
- Corrective distributions of excess 401(k) plan contributions and deferrals.
- Dividends on employer stock.
- Life insurance coverage costs.
- Loans that are deemed to be taxable distributions because they exceed the limits discussed in *7.16*.

For all of the above taxable distributions that are *ineligible* for rollover, you may elect to completely avoid withholding on Form W-4P.

7.8 Direct Rollover or Personal Rollover

If you receive an eligible rollover distribution *(7.7)* from a qualified plan, you may choose a direct rollover, or if you actually receive the distribution you may make a personal rollover. To avoid withholding, choose a direct rollover. You must receive a written explanation of your rollover rights from your employer before an eligible rollover distribution is made.

Direct Rollover to Traditional IRA or Another Employer Plan

If you choose to have your employer make a direct rollover of an eligible rollover distribution to a traditional IRA or another eligible employer plan *(7.7)*, you avoid tax on the payment and no tax will be withheld. If you are changing jobs and want a direct rollover to the plan of the new employer, make sure that the plan accepts rollovers; if it does not, choose a direct rollover to a traditional IRA.

When you select the direct rollover option, your employer may transfer the funds directly by check or wire to the new plan, or you may be given a check payable to the new plan that you deliver.

In choosing a direct rollover to a traditional IRA, the terms of the payer-employer's plan will determine whether you may divide the distribution among several IRAs or whether you will be restricted to one IRA. For example, you may want to split up your distribution into several traditional IRAs, but the employer may force you to select only one. After the direct rollover is made, you may then diversify your holdings by making tax-free trustee-to-trustee transfers to other traditional IRAs.

You may elect to make a direct rollover of part of your distribution and to receive the balance. The portion paid to you will be subject to 20% withholding and is not eligible for special averaging. The IRS allows plan administrators to bar a partial direct rollover if the rollover amount is less than $200.

A direct rollover will be reported by the payer plan to the IRS and to you on Form 1099-R, although the transfer is not taxable. The direct rollover will be reported in Box 1 of Form 1099-R, but zero will be entered as the taxable amount in Box 2a. In Box 7, Code G should be entered if the direct rollover was to a traditional IRA and Code H if to another qualified employer plan or to a tax-sheltered annuity.

Personal Rollover After Receiving a Distribution

If you do not tell your employer to make a direct rollover of an eligible rollover distribution, and you instead receive the distribution yourself, you will receive only 80% of the taxable portion (generally the entire distribution unless you made after-tax contributions); 20% will be withheld. Withholding does not apply to the portion of the distribution consisting of net unrealized appreciation from employer securities that is tax-free under the rules at *7.10*.

Although you receive only 80% of the taxable eligible rollover distribution, the full amount before withholding will be reported as the gross distribution in Box 1 of Form 1099-R. To avoid tax you must roll over the full amount within 60 days to a traditional IRA or another eligible employer plan. However, to roll over 100% of the distribution you will have to use other funds to replace the 20% withheld. If you roll over only the 80% received, the 20% balance will be taxable; *see* the John

Planning Reminder

IRA Conduit Between Employer Plans

If you roll over an employer plan distribution to a traditional IRA, the IRA may be used as a conduit to another company plan. If you join a company with a plan that accepts rollovers, the funds in the conduit IRA may be transferred to the new plan. A qualifying lump-sum distribution from the new employer plan may be eligible for special averaging if you were born before 1936 and the rolled-over distribution was *not* from a 403(b) plan or governmental 457 plan; *see 7.2*. The conduit IRA must consist of only the assets (or proceeds from the sale of such assets) distributed from the first qualified plan and income earned on the account. You may not contribute to the account set up as a conduit. If you want to make IRA contributions, set up another IRA.

Anderson Example below. For the taxable part that is not rolled over, you may not use special averaging or capital gain treatment even if you meet the age test in *7.4*. In addition, if the distribution was made to you before you reached age $59^{1}/_{2}$, the taxable amount will be subject to a 10% penalty unless you are disabled, separating from service after reaching age 55, or have substantial medical expenses; *see 7.15* for a full list of exceptions.

If a distribution includes your voluntary after-tax contributions to the qualified plan, they are tax free to you when you receive them. However, starting in 2002, after-tax contributions may be rolled over; *see* "eligible rollover distributions" in *7.7*.

A rollover *may* include salary deferral contributions that were excludable from income when made, such as qualifying deferrals to a 401(k) plan. The rollover may also include accumulated deductible employee contributions (and allocable income) made after 1981 and before 1987. Your employer's retirement plan may invest in a limited amount of life insurance which is then distributed to you as part of a lump-sum retirement distribution. You may be able to roll over the life insurance contract to the qualified plan of your new employer but not to a traditional IRA. The law bars investment of IRA funds in life insurance contracts.

You may not claim a deduction for your rollover.

Planning Reminder

Pre-Age-59$^{1}/_{2}$ Distributions

If you are under age $59^{1}/_{2}$ and do not roll over an eligible distribution, you will generally be subject to a 10% penalty in addition to regular income tax. However, penalty exceptions apply if you separate from service and are age 55 or older, you are disabled, or you pay substantial medical expenses; *see 7.15* for a full list of penalty exceptions.

EXAMPLE

In January 2003, John Anderson retires. He is due a lump-sum distribution of $100,000 from a qualified plan of his company. If he instructs his employer to make a direct rollover of the amount to a traditional IRA or eligible employer plan, there is no tax withholding, and the $100,000 is transferred tax free.

Now assume that John decides not to choose a direct rollover because he is planning to use the funds to invest in a business. The plan will pay him $80,000 and withhold a tax of $20,000 that John will apply to his tax liability when he files his 2003 return. But, say, a month later John changes his mind about the investment and now wants to roll over his benefits to a traditional IRA. He must make the rollover within 30 days because 30 days of the 60-day rollover period have already passed. Furthermore, to avoid tax on the entire distribution, he must deposit $100,000 in the traditional IRA, even though $20,000 tax has been withheld. If he does not have the $20,000, he must borrow the $20,000 and deposit it in the IRA. If he rolls over only $80,000, he must report $20,000 as a taxable distribution on his 2003 return and if John is under age $59^{1}/_{2}$, the 10% penalty for early withdrawals would apply; based on these facts, John does not qualify for a penalty exception *(7.15)*.

Reporting a personal rollover on your return. When you receive a distribution that could have been rolled over, the payer will report on Form 1099-R the full taxable amount before withholding, although 20% has been withheld. However, if you make a rollover yourself within the 60-day period, the rollover reduces the taxable amount on your tax return. For example, if in 2002 you were entitled to a $100,000 lump-sum distribution and received $80,000 after mandatory 20% withholding and then you rolled over the full $100,000 into an IRA, report $100,000 on Line 16a of Form 1040 or Line 12a of Form 1040A, but enter zero as the taxable amount on Line 16b or Line 12b and write "Rollover" next to the line. If you roll over only part of the distribution, the amount of the lump sum *not* rolled over is entered as the taxable amount. Remember to include the 20% withholding on the line for federal income tax withheld.

Figuring the 60-day period for personal rollovers. A rollover must be completed by the 60th day following the day on which you receive the distribution.

The IRS has strictly applied the 60-day requirement for personal rollovers even where failure to meet the deadline is not the taxpayer's fault, such as where errors are made by the financial institution handling the rollover. However, for distributions after 2001, the IRS has discretion to waive the 60-day deadline on equitable grounds where events beyond your reasonable control prevented you from meeting the deadline. According to a Congressional committee report, health reasons, natural disasters, errors made by financial institutions, or postal errors should be qualifying reasons.

Extension of 60-day rollover period for frozen deposits. If you receive a qualifying distribution from a retirement plan and deposit the funds in a financial institution that becomes bankrupt or insolvent, you may be prevented from withdrawing the funds in time to complete a rollover within 60 days. If this happens, the 60-day period is extended while your account is "frozen." The 60-day rollover period does not include days on which your account is frozen. Further, you have a minimum of 10 days after the release of the funds to complete the rollover.

Caution

IRA Rollover Election Is Irrevocable

A rollover from an employer plan to a traditional IRA is irrevocable, according to the IRS. At the time of the rollover, you must elect in writing to irrevocably treat the contribution as a rollover. If a qualifying lump-sum distribution is made to you and you roll it over, you may not later change your mind in order to claim averaging even though you were born before 1936 and the other tests for averaging are met *(7.4)*. Before making a rollover, figure what the current tax would be on the lump-sum distribution under the special averaging method. Compare it with an estimate of the regular tax that will be payable on a later distribution of the rolled-over account from the IRA.

Other points to consider in deciding whether to roll over a lump sum are discussed at *7.2 and 7.3*.

Multiple rollover accounts allowed. You may wish to diversify a distribution in different investments. There is no limit on the number of rollover accounts you may have. A lump-sum distribution may be rolled over to several traditional IRAs.

Rollover by Surviving Spouse

A surviving spouse is the only beneficiary who may make a tax-free rollover. If you are your deceased spouse's beneficiary, you may roll over your interest in his or her qualified plan account. You may choose to have the plan make a direct rollover to your own traditional IRA. The advantage of choosing the direct rollover is to avoid a 20% withholding. If the distribution is paid to you, 20% will be withheld. You may make a rollover within 60 days, but to completely avoid tax, you must include in the rollover the withheld amount, as illustrated in the John Anderson Example on page 155. If you receive the distribution but do not make the rollover, you will be taxed on the distribution, but if your spouse was born before 1936, you may be able to use special averaging *(7.4)* to compute the tax. As a surviving spouse, you are *not* subject to the 10% penalty for premature distributions *(7.15)* even if you are under age $59^{1}/_{2}$.

Distributions made before 2002 could be rolled over by a surviving spouse only to a traditional IRA. Distributions after 2001 may also be rolled over by a surviving spouse to his or her employer's qualified plan, 403(a) qualified annuity, 403(b) tax-sheltered annuity, or governmental section 457 plan. However, if the surviving spouse was born before 1936 and wants to preserve the option of electing averaging *(7.4)* or capital gain treatment (for pre-1974 participation, *see 7.5*) for a later distribution from his or her employer's qualified plan, the surviving spouse should *not* roll over the deceased spouse's account to *that* plan. If the rollover is made to the surviving spouse's qualified plan, a lump-sum distribution from the plan will not be eligible for averaging or capital gains treatment.

Rollover of distribution received under a divorce or support proceeding. In a qualified domestic relations order (QDRO) meeting special tax law tests, a state court may give you the right to receive all or part of your spouse's or former spouse's retirement benefits. You can choose to have the payment made to you or you can instruct the plan to make a direct rollover to a traditional IRA or to your employer's qualified plan if it accepts rollovers. Alternatively, if the distribution is paid to you, 20% withholding will apply. You may complete a rollover within 60 days under the rules for personal rollovers discussed earlier. If you do not make the rollover, the distribution you receive is taxable, but you may be able to elect special averaging if averaging would have been allowed had it been received by your spouse or former spouse; *see 7.12*. If only part of the distribution is rolled over, the balance is taxed as ordinary income in the year of receipt. In figuring your tax, you are allowed a prorated share of your former spouse's cost investment, if any. You may not elect averaging or capital gain treatment for the portion not rolled over. You are *not* subject to the 10% penalty for premature distributions even if under age $59^{1}/_{2}$.

Nonspouse beneficiaries. If you are a beneficiary other than a spouse, you cannot choose to have the plan make a direct rollover and you cannot make a rollover yourself if payment is made to you. Distributions must begin under the payment rules for beneficiaries discussed at *7.14*, unless special averaging is available for a lump-sum distribution of the account; *see 7.6*.

Court Decision

Stock Purchased With Cash Withdrawal Cannot Be Rolled Over

A taxpayer withdrew cash from his Keogh accounts and used most of the net distribution (after withholdings) to buy stock, which was then transferred to an IRA within 60 days of the withdrawal. He treated the entire distribution as a tax-free rollover but the IRS and Tax Court held it was taxable. The transfer of stock to the IRA was not a tax-free rollover; only the cash distribution itself could be rolled over. A negligence penalty was also imposed.

A direct rollover from the Keogh accounts to an IRA would have been tax free; the stock could then have been purchased through the new IRA.

7.9 Rollover of Proceeds From Sale of Property

A lump-sum distribution from a qualified plan may include property, such as non-employer stock; *see 7.10* for employer securities. If you plan to roll over the distribution, you may find that a bank or other plan trustee does not want to take the property. You cannot get tax-free rollover treatment by keeping the property and rolling over cash to the new plan. If you sell the property, you may roll over the sale proceeds to a traditional IRA as long as the sale and rollover occur within 60 days of receipt of the distribution. If you roll over all of the proceeds, you do not recognize a gain or loss from the sale; the proceeds are treated as part of the distribution. If you make a partial rollover of sale proceeds, you must report as capital gain the portion of the gain that is allocable to the retained sale proceeds.

If you receive cash and property, and you sell the property but only make a partial rollover, you must designate how much of the rolled-over cash is from the employer distribution and how much from the sale proceeds. The designation must be made by the time for filing your return (plus any extensions) and is irrevocable. If you do not make a timely designation, the IRS will allocate the rollover between cash and sales proceeds on a ratable basis; the allocation will determine tax on the retained amount.

If you made after-tax contributions to the plan, you may not roll over the portion of the distribution equal to your contributions.

7.10 Distribution of Employer Stock or Other Securities

If you are entitled to a distribution from an employer plan that includes employer stock (or other employer securities), you may be able to take advantage of a special exclusion rule. If you withdraw the stock from the plan in a taxable distribution instead of rolling it over to a traditional IRA or another employer plan, tax on the "net unrealized appreciation," or NUA, may be deferred until you sell the stock. The amount of deferrable NUA generally depends on whether or not the distribution is a lump-sum distribution.

Lump-sum distribution. If you receive appreciated stock or securities as part of a lump-sum distribution, net unrealized appreciation (increase in value since purchase of securities) is not subject to tax at the time of distribution unless you elect to treat it as taxable.

For purposes of the NUA exclusion, a lump-sum distribution is the payment within a single year of the plan participant's entire balance from all of the employer's qualified plans of the same kind (all of the employer's profit-sharing plans, or all pension or stock bonus plans). Further, the distribution must be paid to: (1) a participant after reaching age $59\frac{1}{2}$, (2) an employee-participant who separates from service (by retiring, resigning, changing employers, or being fired), (3) a self-employed participant who becomes totally and permanently disabled, or (4) a beneficiary of a deceased plan participant.

Assuming the election to treat the NUA as current income is not made, you are taxed only on the original cost of the stock when contributed to the plan. Tax on the appreciation is delayed until the shares are later sold by you at a price exceeding cost basis.

The NUA in employer's securities is shown in Box 6 of the Form 1099-R received from the payer. It is *not* included in the taxable amount in Box 2a.

If, when distributed, the shares are valued at below the cost contribution to the plan, the fair market value of the shares is subject to tax. If you contributed to the purchase of the shares and their value is less than your contribution, you do not realize a loss deduction on the distribution. You realize a loss only when the stock is sold or becomes worthless *(5.32)* at a later date. If a plan distributes worthless stock, you may deduct your contributions to the stock as a miscellaneous itemized deduction subject to the 2% of adjusted gross income floor.

Election to waive tax-free treatment. You may elect to include the NUA in employer stock or securities as income. You might consider making this election when you want to accelerate income to the current year by taking into account the entire lump-sum distribution. If you were born before 1936 and are claiming averaging or capital gain treatment on Form 4972 *(7.4)*, follow the form instructions for adding the unrealized appreciation to the taxable distribution. If you are not filing Form 4972, the election to include the unrealized appreciation as ordinary income is made by reporting it on Line 16b (taxable pensions and annuities) of Form 1040 or Line 12b of Form 1040A.

EXAMPLES

1. *Shares valued below your cost contribution.* You contributed $500 and your employer contributed $300 to buy 10 shares of company stock having at the time a fair market value of $80 per share. When you retire, the fair market value of the stock is $40 per share, or a total of $400. You do not realize income on the distribution, and you do not have a deductible loss for the difference between your cost contribution and the lower fair market value. Your contribution to the stock is its basis. This is $50 per share. If you sell the stock for $40 per share, you have a capital loss of $10 per share. However, if you sell the stock for $60 per share, you have gain of $10 per share.

2. *Appreciated shares.* You receive 10 shares of company stock that was purchased entirely with the employer's funds. Your employer's cost was $50 a share. At the time of a lump-sum distribution, the shares are valued at $80 a share. Your employer's contribution of $50 a share, or $500, is included as part of your taxable distribution. The appreciation of $300 is not included, assuming you do not elect to be taxed currently on the appreciation. The cost basis of the shares in your hands is $500 (the amount currently taxable to you). The holding period of the stock starts from the date of distribution. However, if you sell the shares for any amount exceeding $500 and up to $800, your profit is long-term capital gain regardless of how long you held the shares. If you sell

for more than $800, the gain exceeding the original unrealized appreciation of $300 is subject to long-term capital gain treatment only if the sale is long term from the date of distribution. Thus, if within a month of the distribution you sold the shares for $900, $300 would be long-term gain; $100 would be short-term gain.

Distribution not a lump sum. If you receive appreciated employer securities in a distribution that does not meet the lump-sum tests above, you report as ordinary income the amount of the employer's contribution to the purchase of the shares and the appreciation allocated to the employer's cost contribution. You do not report the amount of appreciation allocated to your own after-tax contribution to the purchase. In other words, tax is deferred only on the NUA attributable to your after-tax employee contributions. Net unrealized appreciation is shown in Box 6 of Form 1099-R. Cost contributions must be supplied by the company distributing the stock.

EXAMPLE

A qualified plan distributes 10 shares of company stock with an average cost of $100, of which the employee contributed $60 and the employer, $40. At the date of distribution, the stock had a fair market value of $180. The portion of the unrealized appreciation attributable to the employee's contribution is $48 (60% of $80); the employer's is $32 (40% of $80). The employee reports $72 as income: the employer's cost of $40 and the employer's share of appreciation, which is $32. For purposes of determining gain or loss on a later sale, the employee's basis for each share is $132, which includes the employee contribution of $60 and the $72 reported as taxable income.

7.11 Survivor Annuity for Spouse

If you have been married for at least a year as of the annuity starting date, the law generally requires that payments to you of vested benefits be in a specific annuity form to protect your surviving spouse. All defined benefit and money purchase pension plans must provide benefits in the form of a *qualified joint and survivor annuity (QJSA)* unless you, with the written consent of your spouse, elect a different form of benefit. A qualified joint and survivor annuity must also be provided by profit-sharing or stock bonus plans if you elect a life annuity payout or the plan does not provide that your nonforfeitable benefit is payable in full upon your death to your surviving spouse, or to another beneficiary if the spouse consents or there is no surviving spouse.

Under a QJSA, you receive an annuity for your life and your surviving spouse receives an annuity for his or her life that is no less than 50% of the amount payable during your joint lives. You may waive the QJSA only with your spouse's consent. Without the consent, you may not take a lump-sum distribution or a single life annuity ending when you die. A single life annuity pays higher monthly benefits during your lifetime than the qualified joint and survivor annuity. If benefits begin under a QJSA and you divorce the spouse to whom you were married as of the annuity starting date, that former spouse will be entitled to the QJSA survivor benefits if you die unless there is a contrary provision in a QDRO *(7.12)*.

The law also requires that a *qualified pre-retirement survivor annuity (QPSA)* be paid to your surviving spouse if you die before the date vested benefits first become payable or if you die after the earliest payment date but before retiring. The QPSA is automatic unless you, with your spouse's consent, agree to a different benefit.

Your plan should provide you with a written explanation of these annuity rules within a reasonable period before the annuity starting date, as well as the rules for electing to waive the joint and survivor annuity benefit and the pre-retirement survivor annuity.

Plan may provide exception for marriages of less than one year. The terms of a plan may provide that a QJSA or QPSA will not be provided to a spouse of the plan participant if the couple has been married for less than one year as of the participant's annuity starting date (QJSA) or, if earlier, the date of the participant's death (QPSA).

Cash out of annuity. If the present value of the QJSA is $5,000 or less, your employer may "cash out" your interest without your consent or your spouse's consent by making a lump-sum distribution of the present value of the annuity before the annuity starting date. After the annuity starting date, you and your spouse must consent to a cash-out. Written consent is required for a cash-out if the present value of the annuity exceeds $5,000. Similar cash-out rules apply to a QPSA.

Planning Reminder

Spouse Must Consent in Writing to Your Waiver

Your spouse must consent in writing to your waiver of a required annuity and the selection of a different type of distribution. A spouse's consent must be witnessed by a plan representative or notary public. An election to waive the qualified joint and survivor annuity may be made during the 90-day period ending on the annuity starting date. An election to waive the qualified pre-retirement survivor annuity may be made any time after the first day of the plan year in which you reach age 35. A waiver is revocable during the time permitted to make the election.

7.12 Court Distributions to Former Spouse Under a QDRO

As a part of a divorce-related property settlement, or to cover alimony or support obligations, a state domestic relations court can require that all or part of a plan participant's retirement benefits be paid to a spouse, former spouse, child, or other dependent. Administrators of pension, profit-sharing, or stock bonus plans are required to honor a qualified domestic relations order (QDRO) that meets specific tax law tests. For example, the QDRO generally may not alter the amount or form of benefits provided by the plan, but it may authorize payments after the participant reaches the earliest retirement age, even if he or she continues working. A QDRO may provide that the recipient spouse is entitled to all, some, or none of the spousal survivor benefits payable under the plan.

QDRO distributions to spouse or former spouse. If you are the spouse or former spouse of an employee and you receive a distribution pursuant to a QDRO, the distribution is generally taxable to you. However, you may make a tax-free rollover to a traditional IRA or to an eligible employer plan, as discussed at *7.7*. If your spouse or former spouse (the plan participant) was born *before* 1936, a distribution to you of your entire share of the benefits may be eligible for special averaging, provided the distribution, if received by your spouse (or former spouse), would satisfy the lump-sum distribution tests at *7.2*. If the distribution qualifies, you may use Form 4972 to claim 10-year averaging, and possibly the 20% capital gain election; *see 7.4*. If your spouse (or former spouse) was born after 1935, you may *not* elect averaging or 20% capital gain treatment for the distribution. Transfers from a governmental or church plan pursuant to a qualifying domestic relations order are also eligible for special averaging or rollover treatment.

To create a valid QDRO, the court order must contain specific language. The recipient spouse (or former spouse) must be assigned rights to the plan participant's retirement benefits plan, and must be referred to as an "alternate payee" in the court decree. The decree must identify the retirement plan and indicate the amount and number of payments subject to the QDRO. Both spouses must be identified by name and address.

If the above information is not clearly provided in the decree, QDRO treatment may be denied and the plan participant taxed on the retirement plan distributions, rather than the spouse who actually receives payments.

Distributions to a child or other dependent. Payments from a QDRO are taxed to the plan participant, not to the dependent who actually receives them, where the recipient is not a spouse or former spouse.

7.13 When Retirement Benefits Must Begin

The longer you can defer taking retirement distributions from your company plan or self-employed Keogh plan, the greater will be the tax-free buildup of your retirement fund. To cut off this tax deferral, the law requires minimum distributions to begin no later than a specified date in order to avoid an IRS penalty.

If you are not a more-than-5% owner, the required beginning date is generally the later of these dates: (1) April 1 following the year in which you reach age $70\frac{1}{2}$, *or* (2) April 1 following the year in which you retire. For example, if you are not a more-than-5% owner, reach age $70\frac{1}{2}$ in 2003, and do not retire until 2004, the first required minimum distribution from the plan does not have to be made to you until April 1, 2005, the year after the year of retirement. If you own a business interest of more than 5%, your required beginning date is April 1 of the year following the year in which you reach age $70\frac{1}{2}$, even if you are still working.

However, an IRS regulation permits a plan to require all employees, and not just more-than-5% owners, to begin required minimum distributions no later than April 1 of the year after the year in which age $70\frac{1}{2}$ is attained. Plans are allowed to offer in-service distributions at an earlier specified age, such as after attaining age $59\frac{1}{2}$ in a profit-sharing plan, or at normal retirement age in a pension plan.

Caution

Drafting a QDRO
Drafting a QDRO involves technical details that legal counsel must carefully review. To ease the drafting burdens and reduce litigation over the effect of QDRO provisions, Congress passed a law requiring the IRS to provide sample language for inclusion in a QDRO that meets tax law requirements. The IRS sample language and a discussion of QDRO requirements is in IRS Notice 97-11.

Caution

Effect of Waiting Until April Deadline
You have until April 1 of the year after the year in which you reach age $70\frac{1}{2}$, or if later, until April 1 of the year following the year of retirement, to take your first required minimum distribution from your employer's plan; *see 7.13*. However, if no distribution is taken during the year in which you reach age $70\frac{1}{2}$ or your retirement year (whichever is later), you will have to take two distributions during the following year. For example, if you retire and reach age $70\frac{1}{2}$ in 2003, and delay receipt of your first distribution until between January 1 and April 1, 2004, you must also receive a distribution for 2004 by December 31, 2004. This could substantially increase your 2004 taxable income, and possibly subject more of your Social Security benefits to tax (*see* Chapter 34).

How Much Must You Receive After the Required Beginning Date?

The required beginning date rules apply to distributions from all qualified corporate and self-employed Keogh plans, qualified annuity plans, and Section 457 plans of tax-exempt organizations. The rules also apply to distributions from tax-sheltered annuities *(7.20)* but only for benefits accrued after 1986; there is no mandatory beginning date for tax-sheltered annuity benefits accrued before 1987.

In 2002, the IRS finalized regulations that provide a simplified method for calculating required minimum distributions from defined contribution plans such as 401(k) plans and profit-sharing plans. The final regulations build upon the proposed regulations issued in 2001 and generally provide lower required minimum distributions than those required under the cumbersome 1987 regulations that applied previously.

Under the final IRS rules, required minimum distributions for most plan participants are based on a uniform lifetime table. The table, shown at *8.13*, provides a distribution period based on the assumption that the participant has a beneficiary exactly 10 years younger than he or she is. For example, for a 71-year-old participant, the uniform lifetime table provides a distribution period of 26.5 years, the joint life expectancy of a 71-year-old and a 61-year-old. Each year, the distribution period from the table is divided into the prior year's account balance to determine the required minimum distribution. The table is used for all participants, regardless of who is actually named as beneficiary, with one exception: the participant's sole beneficiary is his or her spouse who is more than 10 years younger than the participant. In that case, the actual joint life expectancy of the participant and the spouse is used, resulting in a longer distribution period and thus a smaller required minimum distribution.

You do not have to calculate your required minimum distribution. Your plan administrator will do so. The administrator had the option of basing the required minimum distributions for 2002 on the new regulations. The regulations must be followed in determining the required minimum distributions for years after 2002.

IRS Alert

New Required Minimum Distribution Rules

As discussed at *7.13*, final IRS regulations simplifying the calculation of required minimum distributions that must be received by plan participants after the required beginning date.

7.14 Payouts to Beneficiaries

As the beneficiary of an employee's qualified plan account, your distribution options depend on the terms of the plan. You may prefer the option of receiving payments over your life expectancy but the plan may require that you receive a lump-sum distribution or allow installment payments over only a limited number of years.

Although the new IRS final regulations *(see 7.13)* generally allow beneficiaries to use a life expectancy distribution method, the IRS rules represent the longest permissible payment period. Employer plans are allowed to require a shorter period and most do.

If you receive a lump-sum distribution, you generally may claim special averaging if the plan participant was born before 1936; *see 7.6.*

If you are a surviving spouse and receive a lump-sum distribution, you may make a tax-free rollover to another plan *(7.7)* whether or not special averaging is allowed for the distribution. Nonspouse beneficiaries may not make a tax-free rollover.

If the plan does give you the option of taking distributions over your life expectancy as allowed by the IRS rules, and you are the employee's surviving spouse, you may be able to delay the commencement of distributions for several years. If your spouse died before the year in which he or she attained age $70\frac{1}{2}$, and you are the sole designated beneficiary of the account as of September 30 of the year following the year of death, you do not have to begin receiving distributions until the end of the year in which your spouse would have attained age $70\frac{1}{2}$. This is an exception to the general rule that requires distributions under the life expectancy method to begin by the end of the year following the year in which the employee died.

7.15 Penalty for Distributions Before Age $59\frac{1}{2}$

A 10% penalty generally applies to taxable distributions made to you before you reach age $59\frac{1}{2}$ from a qualified corporate or Keogh plan, qualified annuity plan, and tax-sheltered annuity plan, but there are several exceptions. For example, the penalty does not apply to distributions made to you after separation from service if the separation occurs during or after the year in which you reach age 55. A full list of exceptions is shown below.

If no exception applies, the penalty is 10% of the taxable distribution. If you make a tax-free rollover *(7.7)*, the distribution is not taxable and not subject to the penalty. If a partial rollover is made, the part not rolled over is taxable and subject to the penalty.

A similar 10% penalty applies to IRA distributions before age $59\frac{1}{2}$; *see 8.12* for IRA penalty rules. The penalty is 25% if a distribution before age $59\frac{1}{2}$ is made from a SIMPLE IRA in the first two years of plan participation; *see 8.18*. The penalty for pre–age $59\frac{1}{2}$ distributions from deferred annuities is at *7.22*. The penalty generally does *not* apply to Section 457 plans of tax-exempt employers or state or local governments. However, if after 2001 a rollover is made to a governmental Section 457 plan from a qualified plan, 403(b) annuity, or IRA, a later distribution from the Section 457 plan is subject to the penalty to the extent of the rollover.

Exceptions to the penalty. The following distributions are exempt from the 10% penalty, even if made to you before age $59\frac{1}{2}$. If your employer knows that an exception applies, a code for the exception will be entered in Box 7 of Form 1099-R on which the distribution is reported.

- Distributions that you roll over tax free under the "direct rollover" or "personal rollover" rules in *7.8*.

- Distributions made on account of your total disability.

- Distributions after separation from service if you are age 55 or over in the year you retire or leave the company.

- Distributions to the extent that you pay deductible medical expenses exceeding 7.5% of adjusted gross income (whether or not an itemized deduction for medical expenses is claimed).

- Distributions received after separation from service that are part of a series of substantially equal payments (at least annually) over your life expectancy, or over the joint life expectancy of yourself and your designated beneficiary. If you claim the exception and begin to receive such a series of payments but then before age $59\frac{1}{2}$ you receive a lump sum or change the distribution method and you are not totally disabled, a recapture penalty tax will apply. The recapture tax applies the 10% penalty to all amounts received before age $59\frac{1}{2}$, as if the exception had never been allowed, plus interest for that period. However, in private rulings, the IRS has allowed the annual distribution amount to be reduced without penalty after the account is divided in a divorce settlement. The recapture tax also applies to payments received before age $59\frac{1}{2}$ if substantially equal payments are not received for at least five years.

- Involuntary distributions that result from an IRS levy on your plan account.

- Distributions paid to an alternate payee pursuant to a qualified domestic relations court order (QDRO).

- Distributions made pursuant to a designation under the 1982 Tax Act (TEFRA).

- Distributions to an employee who separated from service by March 1, 1986, provided that accrued benefits were in pay status as of that date under a written election specifying the payout schedule.

Hardship distributions for college or home-buying costs. The 10% penalty applies to a hardship distribution that you receive before age $59\frac{1}{2}$ from a 401(k) plan *(7.19)* or 403(b) tax-sheltered annuity plan *(7.20)* where it is used to pay tuition costs or to buy a principal residence. Such hardship distributions do not qualify for a penalty exception, although a penalty exception generally applies for IRA distributions used for such purposes *(see 8.12* for limitations).

Corrective distributions from 401(k) plans. If you are considered a highly compensated employee and excess elective deferrals or excess contributions are made on your behalf, a distribution of the excess to you is not subject to the penalty.

Beneficiaries exempt from the penalty. If you are the beneficiary of a deceased plan participant, you are not subject to the 10% penalty, regardless of your age or the participant's age.

Filing Form 5329 for exceptions. If your employer correctly entered a penalty exception code in Box 7 of Form 1099-R, you do not have to file Form 5329 to claim the exception. You also do not have to file Form 5329 if you made a tax-free rollover of the entire taxable distribution. You must file Form 5329 if you qualify for an exception, other than the rollover exception, that is not indicated in Box 7 of Form 1099-R.

7.16 Restrictions on Loans From Company Plans

Within limits, you may receive a loan from a qualified company plan, annuity plan, 403(b) plan, or government plan without triggering tax consequences. The maximum loan you can receive without tax is the lesser of 50% of your vested account balance or $50,000, but the $50,000 limit is subject

Caution

Penalty Exception for Substantially Equal Payments

The substantially equal payments exception to the 10% early distribution penalty is generally revoked if qualifying payments are not received for at least five years. For example, you separate from service when you are age 57 and you begin to receive a series of qualifying substantially equal payments. When you are age 61, you stop the payments or modify the payment schedule so that it no longer qualifies. Unless the IRS permits an exception, the 10% penalty applies to the payments received before age $59\frac{1}{2}$ because the five-year test was not met.

Filing Instruction

Reporting the Early Distribution Penalty

If you received a distribution before age $59\frac{1}{2}$, do not qualify for a penalty exception, and Code 1 is shown in Box 7 of your Form 1099-R, multiply the taxable distribution by 10% and enter that amount as the penalty on Line 58 of Form 1040; write "no" next to Line 58 to indicate that Form 5329 does not have to be filed. If you are subject to the penalty and Code 1 is not entered in Box 7 of Form 1099-R, you must file Form 5329.

You may also have to file Form 5329 to claim a penalty exception. However, filing the form is not required if you qualify for the rollover exception or you qualify for another exception that is correctly coded in Box 7 of Form 1099-R.

to reductions where there are other loans outstanding; *see* below. Loans must be repayable within five years, unless they are used for buying your principal residence. Loans that do not meet these guidelines are treated as taxable distributions from the plan. If the plan treats a loan as a taxable distribution, you should receive a Form 1099-R with Code L marked in Box 7.

These rules generally apply only to employees. For a self-employed person, a retirement plan loan is a prohibited transaction that usually results in penalties; *see 41.9.*

If your vested accrued benefit is $20,000 or less, you are not taxed if the loan, when added to other outstanding loans from all plans of the employer, is $10,000 or less. However, as a practical matter, your maximum loan may not exceed 50% of your vested account balance because of a Labor Department rule that allows only up to 50% of the vested balance to be used as loan security. Loans in excess of the 50% cap are allowed only if additional collateral is provided.

If your vested accrued benefit exceeds $20,000, then the maximum tax-free loan depends on whether you borrowed from any employer plan within the one-year period ending on the day before the date of the new loan. If you did not borrow within the year, you are not taxed on a loan that does not exceed the lesser of $50,000 or 50% of the vested benefit.

If there were loans within the one-year period, the $50,000 limit must be further reduced. The loan, when added to the outstanding loan balance, may not exceed $50,000 less the excess of (1) the highest outstanding loan balance during the one-year period (ending the day before the new loan) over (2) the outstanding balance on the date of the new loan. This reduced $50,000 limit applies where it is less than 50% of the vested benefit; if 50% of the vested benefit was the smaller amount, that would be the maximum tax-free loan.

Planning Reminder

Borrowing From Your Company Retirement Account

You generally may obtain a tax-free loan from your employer's retirement plan up to the lesser of 50% of your vested account balance or $50,000. *See 7.16* for lower tax-free loan limits where you have other outstanding loans, and for repayment requirements.

> **EXAMPLE**
>
> Your vested plan benefit is $200,000. Assume that in December 2002 you borrow $30,000 from the plan. On November 1, 2003, when the outstanding balance on the first loan is $20,000, you want to take another loan without incurring tax.
>
> You may borrow an additional $20,000 without incurring tax: The $50,000 limit is first reduced by the outstanding loan balance of $20,000—leaving $30,000. The reduced $30,000 limit is in turn reduced by $10,000, the excess of $30,000 (the highest loan balance within one year of the new loan) over $20,000 (the loan balance as of November 1).

Repayment period. Generally, loans within the previously discussed limits must be repayable within five years to avoid being treated as a taxable distribution. However, if you use the loan to purchase a principal residence for yourself, the repayment period may be longer than five years; any reasonable period is allowed. This exception does not apply if the plan loan is used to improve your existing principal residence, to buy a second home, or to finance the purchase of a home or home improvements for other family members; such loans are subject to the five-year repayment rule.

Level loan amortization required. To avoid tax consequences on a plan loan, you must be required to repay using a level amortization schedule, with payments at least quarterly. According to Congressional committee reports, you may accelerate repayment, and the employer may use a variable interest rate and require full repayment if you leave the company.

Giving a demand note does not satisfy the repayment requirements. The IRS and Tax Court held the entire amount of an employee's loan to be a taxable distribution since his demand loan did not require level amortization of principal and interest with at least quarterly payments. It did not matter that the employee had paid interest quarterly and actually repaid the loan within five years.

If required installments are not made, the entire loan balance must be treated as a "deemed distribution" from the plan under IRS proposed regulations. However, the IRS allows the plan administrator to permit a grace period of up to one calendar quarter. If the missed installment is not paid by the end of the grace period, there is at that time a deemed distribution in the amount of the outstanding loan balance.

Caution

Unpaid Loan Taxable If You Leave Job

If you leave your company before your loan is paid off, the company will reduce your vested account balance by the outstanding debt. For example, if your vested account balance is $100,000, and the outstanding loan is $20,000, your account balance is reduced to $80,000. If you elect to receive the balance, rather than choosing a direct rollover, $20,000 will be withheld (20% of the full $100,000) and you will receive only $60,000; *see 7.8.* However, the full $100,000 is treated as a taxable distribution. If you do not roll over *(7.8)* the entire $100,000 within 60 days, you will be taxed on the portion not rolled over, and possibly be subject to a 10% penalty if you were under age 59½ at the time of the distribution *(see 7.15).*

Under IRS regulations, loan repayments may be suspended for up to one year if the borrower takes a leave of absence during which he or she is paid less than the installments due. However, the installments after the leave must at least equal the original required amount and the loan must be repaid by the end of the allowable repayment period (five years if not used to buy a principal residence). For example, when his vested account balance is $80,000, Joe Smith takes out a $40,000 non–principal residence loan on July 1, 2002, to be repaid with interest in level monthly installments of $825 over five years. He makes nine payments and then takes a year of unpaid leave. When he returns to work he can either increase his monthly payment to make up for the missed payments or resume paying $825 a month and on June 30, 2007, repay the entire balance owed in a lump sum.

Spousal consent generally required to get a loan. All plans subject to the joint and survivor rules in *7.11* must require spousal consent in order to use your account balance as security for the loan in case you default. Check with your plan administrator for consent requirements.

Interest deduction limitations. If you want to borrow from your account to buy a first or second residence and you are not a "key" employee *(3.3)*, you can generally obtain a full interest deduction by using the residence as collateral for the loan; *see 15.2*. Your account balance may not be used to secure the loan. Key employees are not allowed any interest deduction for plan loans.

If you use a plan loan for investment purposes and are not a key employee, and the loan is not secured by your elective deferrals (or allocable income) to a 401(k) plan or tax-sheltered annuity, the loan account interest is deductible up to investment income; *see 15.10*. Interest on loans used for personal purposes is not deductible, unless your residence is the security for the loan.

401(k), 403(b), and Government Tax-Deferred Savings Plans

7.17 Tax Benefits of 401(k) Plans

If your company has a profit-sharing or stock bonus plan, it has the opportunity of giving you additional tax-sheltered pay. The tax law allows the company to add a cash or deferred pay plan, called a 401(k) plan.

Your company may offer to contribute to a 401(k) plan trust account on your behalf if you forego a salary increase, but in most plans, contributions take the form of salary-reduction deferrals. Under a salary-reduction agreement, you elect to contribute a specified percentage of your wages to the 401(k) plan instead of receiving it as regular salary. In addition, your company may match a portion of your contribution. A salary-reduction deferral is treated as a contribution by your employer that is not taxable to you if the annual contribution limits are not exceeded.

Salary-reduction deferrals. Making elective salary deferrals allows you to defer tax on salary and get a tax-free buildup of earnings within your 401(k) plan account until withdrawals are made.

An annual limit applies to salary-reduction deferrals. For 2002, the limit was $11,000, or $12,000 for plan participants age 50 or older if the plan permitted the additional contributions. For 2003, these limits will increase to $12,000 and $14,000, respectively. *See 7.18* for further details, including the higher limits that will apply for years after 2003. The maximum deferral is lower for employees of "small" employers who adopt a SIMPLE 401(k); *see* below.

Elective deferrals within the annual limit are *pre-tax* contributions, so they are not subject to income tax withholding. However, the contributions are subject to Social Security and Medicare withholdings.

Your employer may not require you to make elective deferrals in order to obtain any other benefits, apart from matching contributions. For example, benefits provided under health plans or other compensation plans may not be conditioned on your making salary deferrals to a 401(k) plan.

Distributions. Withdrawals from a 401(k) plan before age $59^1/_2$ are restricted, as explained at *7.19*. For those born before 1936, a lump-sum distribution may be eligible for averaging under the rules in *7.4*. Mandatory 20% withholding applies to a lump sum as well as other distributions that are eligible for averaging; exceptions are at *7.7*.

Nondiscrimination rules. The law imposes strict contribution percentage tests to prevent discrimination in favor of employees who are highly compensated. If these tests are violated, the employer is subject to penalties and the plan could be disqualified unless the excess contributions (plus allocable income) are distributed back to the highly compensated employees within specified time limits.

SIMPLE 401(k). Nondiscrimination tests are eased for employers who adopt a 401(k) plan with SIMPLE contribution provisions. A SIMPLE 401(k) may be set up only by employers who in the preceding year had no more than 100 employees with compensation of at least $5,000. An employer who contributes to a SIMPLE 401(k) must report on a calendar-year basis and may not maintain another qualified plan for employees eligible to participate in the SIMPLE plan.

If the SIMPLE contribution requirements are met, the plan is considered to meet 401(k) nondiscrimination requirements. Employee elective deferrals may not exceed an annual limitation, which was $7,000 for 2002 and which will increase by $1,000 annually until it reaches $10,000 for 2005, with the $10,000 limit subject to cost-of-living increases in later years. The plan may also allow additional contributions by participants who are age 50 or older by the end of the year. The limit on the additional contribution was $500 for 2002 and will increase by $500 annually through 2006 after which cost-of-living adjustments will apply.

Planning Reminder

Automatic 401(k) Plan Coverage
The IRS has given approval to 401(k) plans in which newly hired employees who do not elect to opt out are enrolled automatically, with a specified percentage of their pay contributed to the plan. Even though the employees do not make affirmative elections to contribute, such plans are qualified provided that the employees are given advance notice of their right either to receive cash or have the designated amount contributed by the employer to the plan.

Law Alert

Elective Deferral Limits Will Continue To Increase
The elective deferral limit for 401(k) plans, 403(b) tax-sheltered annuities *(7.20)*, Section 457 plans *(7.21)*, and salary-reduction SEPs *(8.16)* is $11,000 for 2002, $12,000 for 2003, $13,000 for 2004, $14,000 for 2005, and $15,000 for 2006. For SIMPLE plans, the limit is $7,000 for 2002, $8,000 for 2003, $9,000 for 2004, and $10,000 for 2005.

For plan participants age 50 or older, these limits are further increased if the employer elects to allow such additional contributions. For plans other than SIMPLE plans, the additional amount is $1,000 for 2002, $2,000 for 2003, $3,000 for 2004, $4,000 for 2005, and $5,000 for 2006. For SIMPLE plans, the additional amount is half as much ($500 for 2002, $1,000 for 2003, etc.).

The employer must either match the employee deferral, up to 3% of compensation, or contribute 2% of compensation for all eligible employees, whether or not they make elective deferrals. All contributions are nonforfeitable. No other type of contribution is allowed. In figuring the 3% or 2% employer contribution, compensation is subject to an annual compensation ceiling; for 2002 it is $200,000.

Partnership plans. Partnership plans that allow partners to vary annual contributions are treated as 401(k) plans by the IRS. Thus, elective deferrals are subject to the annual limit *(7.18)* and the special 401(k) plan nondiscrimination rules apply.

7.18 Limit on Salary-Reduction Deferrals

Employer plans must limit elective deferrals to the annual tax-free ceiling; otherwise, the plan could be disqualified. The 401(k) plan salary-reduction limit, which was $11,000 for 2002, increases to $12,000 for 2003 and then by $1,000 annually through 2006. The $15,000 limit for 2006 will be subject to cost-of-living increases in later years. The same limits apply to 403(b) tax-sheltered annuity plans *(7.20)* and simplified employee pension plans established before 1997 *(8.16)*. If you participate in more than one such plan, the limit applies to the total salary reductions for all the plans. Certain highly compensated employees may be unable to take advantage of the maximum annual tax-free ceiling because of restrictions imposed by nondiscrimination tests.

A plan may allow additional deferrals to be made by participants who are age 50 or older by the end of the year. The limit on the additional contribution, $1,000 for 2002, will increase by $1,000 annually until it reaches $5,000 in 2006, after which cost-of-living adjustments will apply. If the plan permits the additional contribution, participants age 50 or older (by the end of the year) can exceed the otherwise applicable plan-provided limit or the regular annual deferral limit.

To avoid the strict nondiscrimination tests for employee elective deferrals and employer matching contributions, an employer may make contributions to a SIMPLE 401(k); *see 7.17.*

An employer may make matching or other contributions, provided the total contribution for the year, including the employee's pre-tax salary deferral and any employee after-tax contributions, does not exceed the annual limit for defined contribution plans, which for 2002 was the *lesser* of 100% of compensation or $40,000.

Correcting excess deferrals. A single plan must apply the annual limit on salary deferrals in order to maintain qualified status. However, if you participate in more than one plan, and the total salary deferrals for the year exceed the annual limit, the IRS requires you to report the excess as wages on Line 7 of Form 1040. Furthermore, by April 15 of the year following the year of the excess, you should allocate the excess among the plans and withdraw it, plus income allocable to the excess. If you do, the corrective distribution is not taxable; the distribution of the excess income is taxable in the year it is distributed. If an excess deferral allocated to a 401(k) plan or 403(b) tax-sheltered annuity is not withdrawn by the April 15 deadline, it will be taxed again when distributed from the plan. If an excess deferral to a salary-reduction SEP set up before 1997 *(see 8.16)* is *not* withdrawn by the April 15 deadline, it is treated as a regular IRA contribution that could be subject to the penalty for excess IRA contributions *(see 8.7)*. Excess deferrals (and earnings) distributed by the April 15 deadline are not subject to the 10% penalty for premature distributions *(7.15)* even if you are under age $59^1/_2$.

7.19 Withdrawals From 401(k) Plans Restricted

By law, you may not withdraw funds attributable to elective salary-reduction contributions to a 401(k) plan unless (1) you no longer work for the employer maintaining the plan; (2) you have reached age $59^1/_2$; (3) you have become totally disabled; (4) you can show financial hardship; (5) you are the beneficiary of a deceased employee; or (6) the plan is terminated and no successor defined contribution plan (other than an employee stock ownership plan) is maintained by the employer.

Under IRS rules, it is difficult to qualify for hardship withdrawals; *see* below. If you do qualify, the withdrawal is taxable, and if you are under age $59^1/_2$, it is subject to the 10% early distribution penalty unless you are disabled or meet the medical expense exception to the penalty *(7.15)*.

The hardship provision and age $59^1/_2$ withdrawal allowance do not apply to certain "pre-ERISA" money purchase pension plans (in existence June 27, 1974).

Withdrawals before age $59^1/_2$. Withdrawals for medical disability, financial hardship, or separation from service are subject to the 10% penalty for premature withdrawals unless you meet one of the exceptions listed at *7.15*.

Loans. If you are allowed to borrow from the plan, the loan restrictions at *7.16* apply.

Caution

Reduced Deferral Limit for Highly Compensated Employees

To avoid discrimination problems an employer may set a lower limit for elective salary deferrals by highly compensated employees than the ceiling generally allowed ($11,000 for 2002).

If, after contributions are made, the plan fails to meet the nondiscrimination tests, the excess contributions will either be returned to the highly compensated employees or kept in the plan but recharacterized as after-tax contributions. In either case, the excess contribution is taxable. Form 1099-R will indicate the excess contribution.

Employers may avoid the nondiscrimination tests by meeting the SIMPLE plan contribution rules; *see 7.17*.

Qualifying for hardship withdrawals. IRS regulations restrict hardship withdrawals of pre-tax salary deferrals. If you qualify under the following restrictive rules you may withdraw your elective deferrals. Income allocable to elective deferrals may be withdrawn as part of a hardship distribution only in limited circumstances. If the plan so provides, income may be withdrawn if it was credited to your account by a cut-off date that is no *later* than the end of the last plan year ending before July 1, 1989.

The IRS requires you to show an immediate and heavy financial need that cannot be met with other resources.

Financial need includes the following expenses (this list may be expanded by the IRS in rulings):

- Purchase of a principal residence for yourself (but not mortgage payments);
- Tuition, related fees and room and board for the next 12 months of post-secondary education for yourself, your spouse, children, or other dependents;
- Medical expenses previously incurred for yourself, your spouse, or dependents or expenses incurred to obtain medical care for such persons;
- Preventing your eviction or mortgage foreclosure; and
- Paying funeral expenses for a family member.

Even if you can show financial need, you may not make a hardship withdrawal if you have other resources to pay the expenses. You do not have to provide your employer with a detailed financial statement, but you must state to your employer that you cannot pay the expenses with: compensation, insurance, or reimbursements; liquidation of your assets without causing yourself hardship by virtue of the liquidation; stopping your contributions, including salary deferrals, to the plan; other distributions or nontaxable loans from plans of any employer; or borrowing from a commercial lender. Your spouse's assets, as well as those of your minor children, are considered to be yours unless you show that they are not available to you. For example, property held in trust for a child or under the Uniform Transfers (or Gifts) to Minors Act is not treated as your property.

Under a special rule, you are considered to lack other resources if you have taken all available distributions from all plans of the employer, including nontaxable loans, and you suspend making any contributions to any of the employer's qualified and nonqualified deferred compensation plans for at least 6 months after receipt of the hardship distribution. Furthermore, all of the employer's plans must provide that for the year after the year of the hardship distribution, elective contributions must be limited to the excess of the annual salary deferral limitation over the elective contributions made for the year of the hardship distribution.

7.20 Annuities for Employees of Tax-Exempts and Schools (403(b) Plans)

If you are employed by a state or local government public school, or by a tax-exempt religious, charitable, scientific, or educational organization, or are on the civilian staff or faculty of the Uniformed Services University of the Health Sciences (Department of Defense), you may be able to arrange for the purchase of a nonforfeitable tax-sheltered annuity. Tax-sheltered annuities may also be purchased by self-employed ministers and by non-tax-exempt employers of ordained or licensed ministers or chaplains. Another name for a tax-sheltered annuity is a 403(b) plan. A 403(b) plan may invest funds for employees in mutual-fund shares as well as in annuity contracts.

The purchase of the annuity or mutual-fund shares is generally made through pre-tax salary-reduction contributions. Your plan may allow you to make after-tax contributions, and the employer may make non-elective contributions.

Note: As the following contribution rules for tax-sheltered annuities have been stated in general terms, we suggest that you also consult your employer or the issuer of the contract. IRS Publication 571 has detailed examples.

Limit on tax-free contributions. Tax-free salary reductions are limited to the annual ceiling for elective deferrals, which for 2002 is generally $11,000. The plan may permit additional deferrals for participants who are age 50 or older; *see 7.18* for the deferral limits.

If, in addition to a tax-sheltered annuity, you make salary deferrals to a 401(k) plan, SIMPLE plan, or simplified employee pension plan, the annual salary-reduction limit applies to the total deferrals; *see 7.18.* If you defer more than the annual limit, the excess is taxable. Further, if a salary-reduction deferral in excess of the annual limit is made and the excess is not distributed to you by April 15 of the following year, the excess will be taxed twice—not only in the year of deferral but again in the year it is actually distributed. To avoid the double tax, any excess deferral plus the income attributable to such excess should be distributed no later than April 15 of the year following the year in which the excess deferral is made; *see 7.18.*

 Law Alert

No Rollover of Hardship Distribution

A hardship distribution from a 401(k) plan is not eligible for rollover *(7.7)* to an IRA or an eligible employer plan. Your employer will not apply 20% withholding to the distribution, as mandatory withholding applies only to rollover-eligible distributions *(7.7).*

 Law Alert

403(b) Plan Contributions

The exclusion allowance, which before 2002 limited employer contributions to 403(b) plans, has been repealed.

Planning Reminder

Switching Annuity Investments

To change tax-sheltered annuity investments, you may direct the issuer of your current annuity contract to make a direct transfer of your account to a different issuer. The transfer is tax free, provided that distributions with respect to salary-reduction contributions are allowed under both contracts only when the employee reaches age 59$^1/_2$, separates from service, becomes disabled, suffers financial hardship, or dies.

The annual salary-reduction ceiling is generally increased by $3,000 for employees of educational organizations, hospitals, churches, home health service agencies, and health and welfare service agencies who have completed 15 years of service. However, the extra $3,000 annual deferral may not be claimed indefinitely. There is a lifetime limit of $15,000 on the amount of extra deferrals allowed. Furthermore, the extra deferrals may not be claimed after lifetime elective deferrals to the plan exceed $5,000 multiplied by your years of service. Publication 571 has a worksheet for figuring the extra deferral.

Salary-reduction contributions are treated as employer contributions. The salary reduction plus any non-elective contributions made by the employer for the year are tax free only if they do not exceed the annual limit on employer contributions to a defined contribution plan, which for 2002 is the lesser of 100% of compensation or $40,000.

Distributions from tax-sheltered annuities. Distributions attributable to salary-reduction contributions to a 403(b) tax-sheltered annuity are allowed only when an employee reaches age 59$^1/_2$, has experienced a severance from employment, becomes disabled, suffers financial hardship, or dies. The hardship distribution rules are the same as for 401(k) plans; *see 7.19*. Annuity payments are taxed under the general rules for employees, discussed at *7.25*. Payments are fully taxable if the only contributions to the plan were salary-reduction contributions excluded from income (pre-tax contributions) under the annual limits discussed earlier in this section.

Non-annuity distributions from a tax-sheltered annuity do not qualify for special averaging *(7.4)*, but a tax-free rollover of a distribution may be made to another tax-sheltered annuity or traditional IRA unless the distribution is not eligible for rollover under the rules at *7.7*. Starting in 2002, an eligible rollover distribution *(7.7)* from a 403(b) plan may also be rolled over to a qualified plan or governmental Section 527 plan. However, if a rollover from a 403(b) plan to a qualified plan is made, a subsequent lump-sum distribution from the qualified plan will not be eligible for special averaging *(7.4)* or capital gain treatment *(7.5)* even if you were born before 1936 and those provisions would otherwise be available. If you do not choose to have the payer of the distribution make a direct rollover, mandatory 20% withholding will be applied. You may then personally make a rollover within 60 days, but you would have to include the withheld amount in the rolled-over amount to avoid tax on the entire distribution. *See 7.8* for further rollover and withholding details.

Benefits accruing after 1986 are subject to the required beginning date rules discussed at *7.13* and a penalty may be imposed for failure to take minimum required distributions. Benefits accrued before 1987 are not subject to the required minimum distribution rules until the year you reach age 75.

7.21 Government and Exempt Organization Deferred Pay Plans

Federal government employees may make tax-free salary-reduction contributions to the Federal Thrift Savings Fund. Employees of state and local governments and of tax-exempt organizations may be able to make tax-free salary-reduction contributions to a Section 457 deferred compensation plan.

Federal employees. Federal employees may elect to defer up to 10% of their basic pay to the Federal Thrift Savings Fund, but no more than the limit on elective deferrals. The deferral limit starting in 2002 is the same as for 401(k) plans; *see 7.18*. Deferrals are not taxed until distributed from the plan. The deferred amount is counted as wages for purposes of computing Social Security taxes and benefits.

 Law Alert

Higher Contribution Limits

For years after 2001, the 2001 Tax Act increases the deferrable limit for Section 457 plans to the amount allowed in a 401(k) or 403(b) plan *(7.18)* and increases the compensation percentage from 33$^1/_3$% to 100%.

Distributions from the Thrift Savings Fund are generally fully taxable. However, lump-sum distributions are eligible for special averaging under the rules discussed in *7.4*, or tax-free rollover treatment; *see 7.7*. If you separate from service before the year in which you reach age 55, you are subject to the 10% penalty for premature distributions unless you are disabled or qualify for the medical exception discussed at *7.15*.

Section 457 plans. State and local governments and tax-exempt organizations other than churches may set up Section 457 deferred compensation plans. For years after 2001, employees may annually defer compensation up to the 401(k) elective deferrable limit, which for 2002 was $11,000, with the limit increasing in $1,000 increments until it reaches $15,000 in 2006; *see 7.18*. Employees in state and local government 457 plans who are 50 or older may be permitted by the plan to make additional contributions; *see 7.18*. A limited "catch-up" provision may allow employees in the last three years before reaching normal retirement age to defer larger amounts. The "catch-up" rule allows up to double the regular limit to be deferred, provided that the full deferrable limit has not been used in prior years. For state and local government plan participants, the deferral limit under the three-year rule will never be less than the regular deferral limit for the year plus the additional contribution limit for participants age 50 or older.

For years before 2002, deferred compensation (and allocable income) was not taxed until paid or otherwise made available. For years after 2001, the "made available" rule continues to apply to employees of non-governmental organizations, but amounts deferred under governmental 457 plans are taxed only when paid.

Distributions to employees or beneficiaries generally may not be made before the year the employee turns age $70^1/_2$, has a severance from employment, or faces an "unforeseeable" emergency, assuming the plan allows payment in cases of emergency. Under IRS regulations, an unforeseeable emergency generally means severe financial hardship resulting from a sudden illness or accident of the employee or a dependent, or loss of property due to a casualty. If the employee can obtain funds by ceasing deferrals to the plan or by liquidating assets without causing himself or herself severe financial hardship, payment from the plan is not allowed. The regulations specifically prohibit payments from the plan to purchase a home or pay for a child's college tuition.

After 2001, eligible rollover distributions *(7.7)* from a governmental 457 plan (but not a non-governmental plan) may be rolled over tax free to a traditional IRA, another 457 plan, a qualified plan, or 403(b) plan. Rollovers of eligible distributions may also be made to governmental 457 plans. If a rollover from a governmental 457 plan is made to a qualified plan, special averaging *(7.4)* and capital gain treatment *(7.5)* will *not* be allowed for a lump-sum distribution from the qualified plan even if such treatment would otherwise be available.

See 7.13 for required distribution starting dates after age $70^1/_2$ and minimum payout rules.

Note: Check with your employer for other details on Section 457 contributions and distribution rules.

Caution

Unforeseen Emergency Distributions

If you can show severe financial hardship arising from a sudden illness or accident, or loss of property due to events beyond your control, and you are unable to obtain funds elsewhere, you may make a withdrawal from your employer's Section 457 plan. However, the need to buy a home or pay college expenses does not qualify as an unforeseeable emergency.

Reporting Commercial Annuities

7.22 Figuring the Taxable Part of Your Annuity

Tax treatment of a distribution depends on whether you receive it before or after the annuity starting date, and on the amount of your investment. A cash withdrawal before age $59^1/_2$ from an annuity contract is generally subject to a 10% penalty, but there are exceptions; the penalty is discussed at the end of this section. If your annuity is from an employer plan and it started after July 1, 1986, *see 7.25*.

The *annuity starting date* is either the first day of the first period for which you receive a payment or the date on which the obligation under the contract becomes fixed, whichever is later. If your monthly payments start on August 1, 2003, for the period starting July 1, 2003, July 1, 2003, is your annuity starting date.

Payments before the annuity starting date. If your commercial annuity contract was purchased *after* August 13, 1982, withdrawals before the annuity starting date are taxable to the extent that the cash value of the contract, immediately before the distribution, exceeds your investment in the contract. This rule also applies to withdrawals that are attributed to investments made after August 13, 1982, where the contract was purchased before August 14, 1982. Loans under the contract or pledges are treated as cash withdrawals. Withdrawals from contracts bought by a qualified retirement plan are discussed at *7.25*.

If the contract was purchased before August 14, 1982, withdrawals *before* the annuity starting date are taxable only if they exceed your investment. Loans are tax free and are not treated as withdrawals subject to this rule. Where additional investments were made after August 13, 1982, cash withdrawals are first considered to be tax-free distributions of the investment before August 14, 1982. If the withdrawal exceeds this investment, the balance is fully taxable to the extent of earnings on the contract, with any excess withdrawals treated as a tax-free recovery of the investment made after August 13, 1982.

Payments on or after the annuity starting date. If the withdrawal is a regular (not variable) annuity payment, that part of the annuity payment allocated to your cost investment is treated as a nontaxable return of the cost; the balance is taxable income earned on the investment. You may find the taxable part of your annuity payment by following the six steps listed below under "Taxable Portion of Annuity Payments." If you have a variable annuity, the computation of the tax-free portion is discussed following Step 6.

Filing Tip

Surrender of Contract

Payments on a complete surrender of the annuity contract or at maturity are taxable only to the extent they exceed your investment.

Payments on or after the annuity starting date that are not part of the annuity, such as dividends, are generally taxable, but there are exceptions. If the contract is a life insurance or endowment contract, withdrawals of earnings are tax free to the extent of your investment, unless the contract is a modified endowment contract.

Taxable Portion of Commercial Annuity Payments

If the payer of the contract does not provide the taxable amount in Box 2a of Form 1099-R, you can compute the taxable amount of your commercial annuity using the following steps.

Step 1: Figure your investment in the annuity contract. If you have no investment in the contract, annuity income is fully taxable; therefore, ignore Steps 2 through 6.

Planning Reminder

Lifetime Exclusion Limit

For an annuity starting after 1996, payments become taxable once they exceed your investment minus the value of any refund feature.

If your annuity is—	Your cost is—
Single premium annuity contract	The single premium paid.
Deferred annuity contract	The total premiums paid.
A gift	Your donor's cost.
An employee annuity	The total of your after-tax contributions to the plan plus your employer's contributions that you were required to report as income; see 7.25.
With a refund feature	The value of the refund feature.

From cost, you subtract the following items:

- Any premiums refunded, and rebates or dividends received on or before the annuity starting date.
- Additional premiums for double indemnity or disability benefits.
- Amounts received under the contract before the annuity starting date to the extent these amounts were not taxed; *see* above.
- Value of a refund feature; *see* below.

Value of refund feature. Your investment in the contract is reduced by the value, if any, of the refund feature.

Your annuity has a refund feature when these three requirements are present: (1) the refund under the contract depends, even in part, on the life expectancy of at least one person; (2) the contract provides for payments to a beneficiary or the annuitant's estate after the annuitant's death; and (3) the payments to the estate or beneficiary are a refund of the amount paid for the annuity.

The value of the refund feature is figured by using a life expectancy multiple that may be found in Treasury Table III or Table VII, depending on the date of your investment; the tables are in IRS Publication 939.

Where an employer paid part of the cost, the refund is figured on only the part paid by the employee.

The refund feature is considered to be zero if (1) for a joint and survivor annuity, both annuitants are age 74 or younger, the payments are guaranteed for less than $2^1/_2$ years, and the survivor's annuity is at least 50% of the first annuitant's (retiree's) annuity or (2) for a single-life annuity without survivor benefits, the payments are guaranteed for less than $2^1/_2$ years and you are age 57 or younger if using the new (unisex) annuity tables, age 42 or younger if male and using the old annuity tables, or age 47 or younger if female and using the old annuity tables.

Also subtract from cost any tax-free recovery of your investment received *before* the annuity starting date, as previously discussed.

Planning Reminder

Life Expectancy Tables

The life expectancy tables for figuring your expected return are in IRS Publication 939.

Step 2: Find your expected return. This is the total of all the payments you are to receive. If the payments are to be made to you for life, your expected return is figured by multiplying the amount of the annual payment by your life expectancy as of the nearest birthday to the annuity starting date. The annuity starting date is the first day of the first period for which an annuity payment is received. For example, on January 1 you complete payment under an annuity contract providing for monthly payments starting on July 1 for the period beginning June 1. The annuity starting date is June 1. Use that date in computing your investment in the contract under Step 1 and your expected return.

If payments are for life, you find your life expectancy in IRS tables included in IRS Publication 939. The table for single life annuities is shown on page 171. When using the table, your age is the age at the birthday nearest the annuity starting date. If you have a joint and survivor annuity and after your death the same payments are to be made to a second annuitant, the expected return is based on your joint life expectancy. Use Treasury Table II in IRS Publication 939 to get joint life expectancy if the entire investment was before July 1, 1986. Use Treasury Table VI if any investment was made after June 30, 1986. If your joint and survivor annuity provides for a different payment amount to the survivor, you must separately compute the expected return for each annuitant; this method is explained in Publication 939. Adjustments to the life expectancy multiple are required when your annuity is payable quarterly, semiannually, or annually. The required adjustment is discussed in *7.23*.

If the payments are for a fixed number of years or for life, whichever is shorter, find your expected return by multiplying your annual payments by a life expectancy multiple found in Treasury Table IV if your entire investment was before July 1, 1986, or Table VIII if any investment was made after June 30, 1986.

If payments are for a fixed number of years (as in an endowment contract) without regard to your life expectancy, find your expected return by multiplying your annual payment by the number of years.

Note: See 7.23 for more information on the life expectancy tables.

Step 3: Divide the investment in the contract (Step 1) by the expected return (Step 2). This will give you the tax-free percentage of your yearly annuity payments. The tax-free percentage remains the same for the remaining years of the annuity, even if payments increase due to a cost-of-living adjustment. A different computation of the tax-free percentage applies to variable annuities; *see* below.

If your annuity started before 1987, and you live longer than your projected life expectancy (shown in the IRS table), you may continue to apply the same tax-free percentage to each payment you receive. Thus, you may exclude from income more than you paid. However, if your annuity starting date is after 1986, your lifetime exclusion may not exceed your net cost, generally your unrecovered investment as of the annuity starting date, without reduction for any refund feature. Once you have recovered your net cost, further payments are fully taxable.

If your annuity starting date is after July 1, 1986, and you die before recovering your net cost, a deduction is allowed on your final tax return for the unrecovered cost. If a refund of the investment is made under the contract to a beneficiary, the beneficiary is allowed the deduction. The deduction is claimed as a miscellaneous itemized deduction that is *not* subject to the 2% adjusted gross income floor; *see* Chapter 19.

Step 4: Find your total annuity payments for the year. For example, you received 10 monthly payments of $100 as your annuity began in March. Your total payments are $1,000, the monthly payment multiplied by 10.

Step 5: Nontaxable portion—multiply the percentage in Step 3 by the total in Step 4. The result is the nontaxable portion (or excludable amount) of your annuity payments.

Step 6: Taxable portion—subtract the amount in Step 5 from the amount in Step 4. This is the part of your annuity for the year that is subject to tax.

Note: An example of figuring the taxable and nontaxable portions for a single life annuity is in *7.23*.

Variable annuities. If you have a variable annuity that pays different benefits depending on cost-of-living indexes, profits earned by the annuity fund, or similar fluctuating standards, the tax-free portion of each payment is computed by dividing your investment in the contract (Step 1 above) by the total number of payments you expect to receive. If the annuity is for a definite period, the total number of payments equals the number of payments to be made each year multiplied by the number of years you will receive payments. If the annuity is for life, you divide the amount you invested in the contract by a multiple obtained from the appropriate life expectancy table; *see* Step 2. The result is the tax-free amount of annual annuity income.

If you receive a payment that is *less* than the nontaxable amount, you may elect when you receive the next payment to recalculate the nontaxable portion. The amount by which the prior nontaxable portion exceeded the payment you received is divided by the number of payments you expect as of the time of the next payment. The result is added to the previously calculated nontaxable portion, and the sum is the amount of each future payment to be excluded from tax. A statement must be attached to your return explaining the recomputation.

> **EXAMPLES**
>
> 1. Andrew Taylor's total investment of $12,000 for a variable annuity was made after June 30, 1986. The annuity starting date is January 1, 2002. The annuity is paid starting July 2, 2002, in varying annual installments for life. Andrew's age (nearest birthday) at the January 1 starting date is 65. He uses a life expectancy multiple of 20.0, the amount shown in Table V on page 171 for a person age 65. The amount of each payment excluded from tax is:
>
> | | |
> |---|---:|
> | Investment in the contract | $12,000 |
> | Multiple (from Table V) | 20.0 |
> | Amount of each payment excluded from tax ($12,000 ÷ 20) | $600 |
>
>   If the first payment is $920, then 320 ($920 – $600) will be included in Andrew's 2002 income.
>
> 2. Assume that, after receiving the 2002 payment of $920 in Example 1, Andrew receives $500 in 2003 and $1,200 in 2004. None of the 2003 payment is taxed, as $600 is excludable from each annual payment. Andrew may also elect to recompute his annual exclusion starting with the 2003 payment. The exclusion is recomputed as follows:
>
> | | |
> |---|---:|
> | Amount excludable in 2003 | $600 |
> | Amount received in 2003 | 500 |
> | Difference | $100 |
> | Multiple as of 1/1/2004 (*see* Table V on page 171 for age 67) | 18.4 |
> | Amount added to previously determined annual exclusion ($100 ÷ 18.4) | $5.43 |
> | Revised annual exclusion for 2004 and later years ($600 + $5.43) | $605.43 |
> | Amount taxable in 2004 ($1,200 – $605.43) | $594.57 |

Penalty on Premature Withdrawals From Deferred Annuities

As discussed above, withdrawals before the annuity starting date may be taxable or tax free, depending on whether investments were made after August 13, 1982.

Withdrawals before age $59\frac{1}{2}$ are also generally subject to a penalty of 10% of the amount includable in income; *see* the Filing Tip on the left. A withdrawal from an annuity contract is penalized unless:

1. You have reached age $59\frac{1}{2}$ or have become totally disabled.
2. The distribution is part of a series of substantially equal payments, made at least annually over your life expectancy or over the joint life expectancies of you and a beneficiary. If you can avoid the penalty under this exception and you change to a nonqualifying distribution method within five years or before age $59\frac{1}{2}$, such as where you receive a lump sum, a recapture tax will apply to the payments received before age $59\frac{1}{2}$.
3. The payment is received by a beneficiary or estate after the policyholder's death.
4. Payment is from a qualified retirement plan, tax-sheltered annuity, or IRA; in this case the penalty rules of *7.15* (qualified plans) or *8.8* (IRAs) apply.
5. Payment is allocable to investments made before August 14, 1982.
6. Payment is from an annuity contract under a qualified personal injury settlement.
7. Payment is from a single-premium annuity where the starting date is no more than one year from the date of purchase.
8. Payment is from an annuity purchased by an employer upon the termination of a qualified retirement plan and held until you separated from service.

7.23 Life Expectancy Tables

IRS unisex actuarial tables must be used if you made *any* investment in a commercial annuity contract after June 30, 1986. Generally, life expectancies are longer under the unisex tables than under the prior male-female tables. The unisex life expectancy table for single life annuities is IRS Table V from Publication 939, shown on page 171. The unisex table for ordinary joint life and last survivor annuities is Table VI, in IRS Publication 939.

If your *entire* investment was before July 1, 1986, you use the older male/female tables. The tables, IRS Tables I through IV, are in Publication 939. Table I, shown on page 171, is for single life expectancies. Table II, for ordinary joint life and last survivor annuities, is in Publication 939.

You may make an irrevocable election to use the unisex tables for all payments received under the contract, even if you did not make an investment after June 30, 1986.

 Filing Tip

Form 5329

If no exception to the early withdrawal penalty applies, you compute the 10% penalty in Part I of Form 5329. The penalty is 5% instead of 10% if as of March 1, 1986, you were receiving payments under a specific schedule pursuant to your written election. Attach an explanation to Form 5329 if you are applying the 5% rate.

TABLE I *(see 7.23)* Investments Before July 1, 1986

Ages			Ages			Ages		
Male	Female	Multiples	Male	Female	Multiples	Male	Female	Multiples
6	11	65.0	41	46	33.0	76	81	9.1
7	12	64.1	42	47	32.1	77	82	8.7
8	13	63.2	43	48	31.2	78	83	8.3
9	14	62.3	44	49	30.4	79	84	7.8
10	15	61.4	45	50	29.6	80	85	7.5
11	16	60.4	46	51	28.7	81	86	7.1
12	17	59.5	47	52	27.9	82	87	6.7
13	18	58.6	48	53	27.1	83	88	6.3
14	19	57.7	49	54	26.3	84	89	6.0
15	20	56.7	50	55	25.5	85	90	5.7
16	21	55.8	51	56	24.7	86	91	5.4
17	22	54.9	52	57	24.0	87	92	5.1
18	23	53.9	53	58	23.2	88	93	4.8
19	24	53.0	54	59	22.4	89	94	4.5
20	25	52.1	55	60	21.7	90	95	4.2
21	26	51.1	56	61	21.0	91	96	4.0
22	27	50.2	57	62	20.3	92	97	3.7
23	28	49.3	58	63	19.6	93	98	3.5
24	29	48.3	59	64	18.9	94	99	3.3
25	30	47.4	60	65	18.2	95	100	3.1
26	31	46.5	61	66	17.5	96	101	2.9
27	32	45.6	62	67	16.9	97	102	2.7
28	33	44.6	63	68	16.2	98	103	2.5
29	34	43.7	64	69	15.6	99	104	2.3
30	35	42.8	65	70	15.0	100	105	2.1
31	36	41.9	66	71	14.4	101	106	1.9
32	37	41.0	67	72	13.8	102	107	1.7
33	38	40.0	68	73	13.2	103	108	1.5
34	39	39.1	69	74	12.6	104	109	1.3
35	40	38.2	70	75	12.1	105	110	1.2
36	41	37.3	71	76	11.6	106	111	1.0
37	42	36.5	72	77	11.0	107	112	0.8
38	43	35.6	73	78	10.5	108	113	0.7
39	44	34.7	74	79	10.1	109	114	0.6
40	45	33.8	75	80	9.6	110	115	0.5
						111	116	0.0

TABLE V *(see 7.23)* Investments After June 30, 1986

Age	Multiple	Age	Multiple	Age	Multiple
5	76.6	42	40.6	79	10.0
6	75.6	43	39.6	80	9.5
7	74.7	44	38.7	81	8.9
8	73.7	45	37.7	82	8.4
9	72.7	46	36.8	83	7.9
10	71.7	47	35.9	84	7.4
11	70.7	48	34.9	85	6.9
12	69.7	49	34.0	86	6.5
13	68.8	50	33.1	87	6.1
14	67.8	51	32.2	88	5.7
15	66.8	52	31.3	89	5.3
16	65.8	53	30.4	90	5.0
17	64.8	54	29.5	91	4.7
18	63.9	55	28.6	92	4.4
19	62.9	56	27.7	93	4.1
20	61.9	57	26.8	94	3.9
21	60.9	58	25.9	95	3.7
22	59.9	59	25.0	96	3.4
23	59.0	60	24.2	97	3.2
24	58.0	61	23.3	98	3.0
25	57.0	62	22.5	99	2.8
26	56.0	63	21.6	100	2.7
27	55.1	64	20.8	101	2.5
28	54.1	65	20.0	102	2.3
29	53.1	66	19.2	103	2.1
30	52.2	67	18.4	104	1.9
31	51.2	68	17.6	105	1.8
32	50.2	69	16.8	106	1.6
33	49.3	70	16.0	107	1.4
34	48.3	71	15.3	108	1.3
35	47.3	72	14.6	109	1.1
36	46.4	73	13.9	110	1.0
37	45.4	74	13.2	111	0.9
38	44.4	75	12.5	112	0.8
39	43.5	76	11.9	113	0.7
40	42.5	77	11.2	114	0.6
41	41.5	78	10.6	115	0.5

Multiple Adjustment Table

If the number of whole months from the annuity starting date to the first payment date is—	0–1	2	3	4	5	6	7	8	9	10	11	12
And payments under the contract are to be made:												
Annually	+0.5	+0.4	+0.3	+0.2	+0.1	0.0	0.0	–0.1	–0.2	–0.3	–0.4	–0.5
Semiannually	+0.2	+0.1	0.0	0.0	–0.1	–0.2						
Quarterly	+0.1	0.0	–0.1									

If you invested in the contract both before July 1, 1986, and after June 30, 1986, and you are the first person to receive annuity payments under the contract, you may make a special election to use the prior tables for the pre–July 1986 investment and the unisex tables for the post–June 1986 investment. *See* IRS Publication 939 for further information. Treasury Regulation 1.72-6(d) has examples showing how to figure the post–June 1986 and pre–July 1986 investments.

Birthday nearest annuity starting date. In looking up single life or joint life expectancy in the applicable table, use your age (and the age of a joint annuitant) at the birthday nearest to the annuity starting date. The number in the table next to this age is the life expectancy multiple used to figure the tax-free and taxable portions of a monthly annuity; *see* the following Examples.

Adjustments for nonmonthly payments. An adjustment is required when your annuity payments are received quarterly, semiannually, or annually; *see* Example 3 below.

EXAMPLES

1. Bill Jones was 66 years old on April 14, 2002. On May 1, 2002, he received his first monthly annuity check of $1,000. This covered his annuity payment for April. Bill's annuity starting date was April 1, 2002, and his entire investment was before July 1, 1986.

   Looking at Table I on page 171 under "Male" at age 66 (age on birthday nearest April starting date), Bill finds the multiple 14.4. (He does not have to adjust that multiple because the payments are monthly.) Bill multiplies the 14.4 by $12,000 ($1,000 a month for a year) to find his expected return of $172,800. Assume there is no refund feature and Bill's net cost (*see* Step 3 in *7.22* above) is $129,600. He divides his expected return into the net cost and gets his exclusion percentage of 75%. Until Bill recovers his net cost, he receives tax free 75% of his annuity payments and is taxable on 25%. In 2002, Bill receives $8,000 ($1,000 in May through December) and reports $2,000 as the taxable amount:

Amount received	$8,000
Amount excludable (75%)	6,000
Taxable portion	$2,000

   For 2003, Bill will receive annuity payments for the full year. The amount received will be $12,000; amount excludable, $9,000; and taxable portion, $3,000. The excludable and taxable portions will remain the same in later years until Bill has excluded his net cost of $129,600. After that, the annuity payments will be fully taxable.

2. Same facts as in Example 1 except there was an investment after June 30, 1986, and Table V is used. Looking at Table V under age 66, Bill finds the multiple 19.2. The same multiple applies to males and females. Multiplying the 19.2 by $12,000 gives an expected return of $230,400. Using a net cost of $129,600, the exclusion percentage is 56.25% ($129,600 ÷ $230,400). For 2002, Bill reports annuity income as follows:

Amount received	$8,000
Amount excludable (56.25%)	4,500
Taxable portion	$3,500

   For 2003, $12,000 is received. The amount excludable will be $6,750, and the taxable portion, $5,250. The same treatment will apply in later years until Bill has excluded his net cost of $129,600. Thereafter, all payments will be fully taxable.

3. You receive quarterly annuity payments. Your first payment comes on January 15, covering the first quarter of the year. Since the period between the starting date of January 1 and the payment date of January 15 is less than one month, you adjust the life expectancy multiple according to the table at the bottom of page 171, by adding 0.1. If the life expectancy multiple from the IRS table was 14.4, the adjusted multiple is 14.5.

7.24 When You Convert Your Endowment Policy

When an endowment policy matures, you may elect to receive a lump sum, an annuity, an interest option, or a paid-up life insurance policy. If you elect—

A lump sum. You report the difference between your cost (premium payments less dividends) and what you receive.

An annuity before the policy matures or within 60 days after maturity. You report income in the years you receive your annuity. *See 7.22* for how to report annuity income. Use as your investment in the annuity contract the cost of the endowment policy less premiums paid for other benefits such as double indemnity or disability income. If you elect the annuity option more than 60 days after maturity, you report income on the matured policy as if you received the lump sum; *see* above rule. The lump sum is treated as the cost investment in the annuity contract.

An interest option before the policy matures. You report only the interest as it is received, provided you do not have the right to withdraw the policy proceeds. If you have the right to withdraw the proceeds, you are treated as in constructive receipt; the difference between your cost and what you receive would be taxed as if you had received a lump sum.

Paid-up insurance. You report the difference between the present value of the paid-up life insurance policy and the premium paid for the endowment policy. In figuring the value of the insurance policy, you do not use its cash surrender value, but the amount you would have to pay for a similar policy with the company at the date of exchange. Your insurance company can give you this figure. The difference is taxed at ordinary income tax rates.

Tax-free exchange rules apply to the policy exchanges listed at *6.12.*

Sales of endowment, annuity, or life insurance policies are taxable as ordinary income, not as capital gains.

The proceeds of a veteran's endowment policy paid before the veteran's death are not taxable.

Employee Annuities

7.25 Reporting Employee Annuities

Tax treatment of employee annuity payments from a qualified employee plan, qualified employee annuity, or tax-sheltered annuity *(7.20)* depends on the amount of your contributions and your annuity starting date. These rules are discussed in *7.25–7.28.* If payments are from a nonqualified employee plan, you must use the rules at *7.22* for commercial annuities.

Fully taxable payments if you have no investment in the plan. If you did not contribute to the cost of a pension or employee annuity, and you did not report as income your employer's contributions, you are fully taxed on payments after the annuity starting date. On your 2002 return, you report fully taxable payments on Line 16b of Form 1040 or Line 12b of Form 1040A.

An employee is taxed on the full value of a nonforfeitable annuity contract that the employer buys him or her if the employer does not have a qualified pension plan. Tax is imposed in the year the policy is purchased. A qualified plan is one approved by the IRS for special tax benefits.

Disability pension before minimum retirement age. Disability payments received before you reach the minimum retirement age (at which you would be entitled to a regular retirement annuity) are fully taxable as wages. After minimum retirement age, payments are treated as an annuity; *see 7.26.*

Partially taxable payments if you have an investment in the plan. If you and your employer both contributed to the cost of your annuity, the part of each payment allocable to your investment is tax free and the balance is taxable. You generally must use the simplified method to figure the tax-free portion allocable to your investment; *see 7.26* for details.

Cost and cost adjustments are explained in *7.27.*

7.26 Simplified Rule for Calculating Taxable Employee Annuity

If you have an investment in the plan and your annuity starting date is *after November 18, 1996,* you must use the simplified method explained below to figure the tax-free portion of your annuity payments from a qualified employer plan, qualified employee annuity, or 403(b) tax-sheltered annuity. The only exception is for an annuitant who is age 75 or older at the time payments begin and has payments guaranteed for at least five years; he or she must use the six-step method discussed at *7.22* for commercial annuities rather than the simplified rule.

A beneficiary receiving a survivor annuity may use the simplified method.

 Filing Tip

Form 1099-R
On Form 1099-R, the payer of a pension or annuity may tell you how much is taxable. If not, you may make the tax-free calculation (1) using the "simplified" method explained at *7.26* or (2) for a fee, ask the IRS to calculate the taxable amount.

If you have reported annuity payments using the prior law simplified method for annuities starting after July 1, 1986, and before November 19, 1996, continue using that method for figuring the tax-free part of your annual payments; *see* Table I below.

Figuring taxable and tax-free payments under the simplified method. Under the simplified method, a level tax-free portion is determined for each monthly payment with the following steps:

 *Filing Instruction*

Simplified Method Mandatory
If your annuity starting date is after November 18, 1996, you must use the simplified rule at *7.26* unless you are age 75 and have payments guaranteed for five or more years.

Step 1. Figure your investment in the contract as of the annuity starting date. Include premiums you paid and any after-tax contributions you made to the employer's pension plan; *see 7.27*. Beneficiaries may increase the investment by any allowable death benefit exclusion, up to $5,000, but only if the employee died before August 21, 1996.

Step 2. Divide the investment from Step 1 by the number of expected monthly payments shown in Table I or Table II below, using your age on the annuity starting date. The result is the tax-free recovery portion of each monthly payment. However, multiply this amount by three (3 months) to get the tax-free portion if payments are made quarterly rather than monthly. The tax-free portion remains the same if a spouse or other beneficiary receives payments under a joint and survivor annuity after the employee's death.

Use either Table I or Table II, described below. Table II is used for annuities based on more than one life if the annuity starting date is after December 31, 1997.

Table I: Use this table if the annuity starting date was after July 1, 1986, and before January 1, 1998, whether the annuity is based on your life only or is a joint and survivor annuity.

Also use Table I if the annuity starting date was after December 31, 1997, and the annuity is based on your life only.

Table II: Use this table if the annuity starting date is after December 31, 1997, and benefits are based on the life of *more than* one annuitant. For example, use this table if you started to receive payments in 2002 under a joint and survivor annuity. If there is more than one survivor annuitant, the primary annuitant's age plus the youngest survivor annuitant's age is the combined age used for Table II. If there is no primary annuitant and the annuity is payable to several survivor annuitants, the ages of the oldest and youngest are combined. Disregard a survivor annuitant whose entitlement to payment is contingent on something other than the primary annuitant's death.

Table I

Age of primary annuitant at starting date	Number of expected monthly payments	
	Annuity starting date before November 19, 1996	*Annuity starting date after November 18, 1996*
55 and under	300	360
56–60	260	310
61–65	240	260
66–70	170	210
71 and over	120	160

Table II

Combined ages of annuitants at starting date	Number of expected monthly payments
110 and under	410
111–120	360
121–130	310
131–140	260
141 and over	210

Step 3. Multiply the Step 2 result by the number of monthly payments received during the year; this is the total tax-free payment for the current year. However, if any part of your cost was previously recovered tax free in years after 1986, the tax-free amount is limited to the excess of your investment from Step 1 over the prior year recoveries.

Step 4. Subtract the Step 3 tax-free payment from the total pension received this year; this is the taxable pension you must report on Form 1040 or Form 1040A. If the payer of the annuity shows a higher taxable amount on Form 1099-R, use the amount figured here.

EXAMPLE

Fred Smith, age 57, retires and beginning August 1, 2002, he receives payments under a joint and 50% survivor annuity with his wife Betty, also age 57. Fred receives an annuity of $1,500 per month and Betty will receive a survivor annuity of $750 per month after Fred's death. Fred's investment in the plan was $29,000. To figure the tax-free portion of each payment, Fred divides his $29,000 investment by 360, the number of expected monthly payments shown in Table II for two annuitants with a combined age of 114 years. The result, or $80.56, is the tax-free portion of each $1,500 payment. The balance of each payment , or $1,419.44 ($1,500 – $80.56), is taxable. On his 2002 return, Fred reports $7,097.20 (5 payments × $1,419.44) as taxable annuity payments.

If Fred dies before the receipt of 360 payments, Betty will also exclude $80.56 from each of her payments of $750 until a total of 360 payments (hers and Fred's) have been recovered. After 360 payments are received, all subsequent payments will be fully taxable. If Betty dies before the 360th payment, a deduction for the unrecovered investment is allowed on her final income tax return; the deduction is a miscellaneous itemized deduction *not* subject to the 2% AGI floor.

7.27 Employee's Cost in Annuity

For purposes of figuring the tax-free recovery of your investment under the general rules of *7.22* or the simplified rule of *7.26*, include the following items paid as of the annuity starting date as your cost in an employee annuity:

- Premiums paid by you or by after-tax withholdings from your pay.
- Payments made by your employer and reported as additional pay.

If you are a beneficiary of a deceased employee who died before August 21, 1996, you may be able to claim a death benefit exclusion of up to $5,000 to reduce the tax on payments received on behalf of the employee. You may be entitled to all or part of the up-to-$5,000 exclusion. If the employee had more than one beneficiary, the total exclusion for that employee is $5,000, and it must be divided among you and the other beneficiaries in proportion to the benefits received.

If you are receiving a survivor annuity, the allowable exclusion is added to the employee's cost investment in the annuity to figure the tax-free and taxable portion of the payments under the simplified method *(7.26)* or general method *(7.22)*. If you are the survivor under a joint and survivor annuity, you may *not* claim the death benefit exclusion if the deceased had received any payment under the joint and survivor contract after reaching minimum retirement age.

7.28 Withdrawals Before Annuity Starting Date

You generally may not make tax-free withdrawals from your employer's qualified retirement plan, qualified employee annuity plan, or 403(b) plan before the annuity starting date, even if your withdrawals are less than your investment. On a withdrawal before the annuity starting date, you must pay tax on a portion of the withdrawal unless the exceptions below apply. The portion of the withdrawal allocable to your investment is recovered tax free; the portion allocable to employer contributions and income earned on the contract is taxed. To compute the tax-free recovery, multiply the withdrawal by this fraction:

$$\frac{\text{Your total investment}}{\text{Your vested account balance or accrued benefit}}$$

Your investment and vested benefit are determined as of the date of distribution.

Filing Instruction

Separate Death Benefit Payment

If as a beneficiary you receive a one-time death benefit payment that is *not* made from a qualified employer retirement plan, report the payment as "Other income" on Form 1040. Report the excess of the payment over the allowable death benefit exclusion if the employee died before August 21, 1996.

Caution

Favorable Recovery Rules

Both of the favorable cost recovery rules discussed in *7.28* under "Exceptions" are complicated and you should consult your plan administrator to determine if the exceptions apply and how to make the required calculations.

Exceptions. More favorable investment recovery rules are allowed in the following cases:

1. *Employer plans in effect on May 5, 1986.* If on May 5, 1986, your employer's plan allowed distributions of employee contributions before separation from service, the above pro-rata recovery rule applies only to the extent that the withdrawal exceeds the total investment in the contract on December 31, 1986.

    For example, assume that as of December 31, 1986, you had an account balance of $9,750, which included $4,000 of your own contributions. If the plan on May 5, 1986, allowed pre-retirement distributions of employee contributions, you may receive withdrawals up to your $4,000 investment without incurring tax.

2. *Separate accounts for employee contributions.* A defined contribution plan (such as a profit-sharing plan) is allowed to account for employee contributions (and earnings on the contributions) separately from employer contributions. If separate accounting is maintained, withdrawals of employee contributions from the separate account may be made tax free. A defined benefit pension plan may also maintain employee contributions (and earnings) in a separate account to which actual earnings and losses are allocated.

7.29 Civil Service Retirement

As discussed at *7.26,* the simplified method must be used to compute the tax-free and taxable portions of each withdrawal if your annuity starting date is after November 18, 1996.

If you leave federal government service before retirement or transfer to a job not under the federal retirement system and you are not entitled to an immediate annuity, you may receive a refund of your contributions (plus any interest). If the refund exceeds your contributions, the excess is taxable.

Retirees with a life-threatening illness may be able to elect a reduced annuity in order to receive a lump-sum credit for their total contributions to the plan; *see* IRS Publication 721 for figuring the taxable portion of the lump sum if the election was made.

Cost of civil service annuity. For purposes of figuring the tax-free portion of each annuity payment your *cost* equals the withholdings from your federal government pay that were contributed to the Civil Service retirement fund. Also, if you repaid to the retirement fund amounts that you previously had withdrawn, or paid into the fund to receive full credit for certain uncovered service, the entire amount you paid, including that designated as interest, is part of your cost. You may not claim an interest deduction for any amount designated as interest.

The annuity statement you received when your annuity was approved shows your "total contributions" to the retirement fund (your cost) and the "monthly rate" of your annuity benefit. The monthly rate is the rate before adjustment for health benefits coverage and life insurance, if any.

A future increase in your civil service pension or your survivor's benefit is not treated as annuity income but is reported in full as miscellaneous income and is not reduced by the exclusion ratio. However, an increase effective on or before a survivor's civil service annuity commences must be taken into account in computing the expected return or in determining the aggregate amount receivable under the annuity.

If you made voluntary contributions to the retirement fund that you use to fund an additional monthly benefit, you report the portion of your annuity attributable to the voluntary contributions as a separate annuity, taxable under the rules at *7.26.* If you made voluntary contributions, an information return which you receive each year will state the portion of your monthly payments attributable to your voluntary contributions. If instead of increasing your monthly benefit you receive a refund of your voluntary contributions plus accrued interest, the interest is taxable in the year you receive it.

Planning Reminder

Accrued Leave

A lump-sum payment for accrued annual leave received upon retirement is not part of your annuity. It is treated as a salary payment and is taxable as ordinary income.

7.30 Retired Military Personnel Allowed Annuity Election

If, when you retire from the military, your pay is reduced to provide an annuity for your spouse or certain child beneficiaries, you do not report that part of your retirement pay used to fund the annuity.

For example, you are eligible to receive retirement pay of $500 a month. You elect to receive $400 a month to obtain an annuity of $200 a month for your spouse on your death. You report $400 a month for tax purposes during your lifetime, rather than the $500. On your death, your spouse generally will report the full $200 a month received as income.

Veteran's benefit deposits. If you elected to receive veteran's benefits instead of some or all of your retirement pay, you may have been required to deposit with the U.S. Treasury an amount equal to the reduction for the annuity. If so, you do not report retirement pay until it equals the amount deposited.

Beneficiaries. If all of the retired person's consideration for the contract (previously taxed reductions) has not been offset against retirement income at the time of death, the beneficiary excludes all payments under the contract until the exclusions equal the remaining consideration for the contract not previously excluded by the deceased. As soon as this amount is excluded, the beneficiary reports all later payments as income.

Chapter 8

IRAs

There are several types of IRAs: Traditional IRAs, Roth IRAs, SIMPLE IRAs, and SEPs. You may personally set up a traditional or Roth IRA with your bank or broker. SIMPLE IRAs *(8.18)* and SEPs *(8.15)* are available only if your employer offers such plans.

The contribution limit for both traditional and Roth IRAs is $3,000 for 2002–2004, and will increase to $5,000 by 2008. The limits are increased still further for individuals who are age 50 or older; *see 8.2* and *8.20*.

Traditional IRA contributions may be fully deductible, partly deductible or not deductible at all, depending on whether you (and your spouse) have retirement coverage where you work and if so, whether your income subjects you to the deduction phase-out rules; *see 8.4*.

Distribution rules for traditional IRAs and Roth IRAs are discussed in this chapter. Traditional IRA distributions are generally fully taxable and if made before age $59\frac{1}{2}$, subject to a penalty; *see 8.12* for penalty exceptions. Minimum distributions from a traditional IRA must begin after you reach age $70\frac{1}{2}$; *see 8.13*.

Roth IRAs are an alternative to traditional IRAs. Although contributions are not deductible, the major tax advantage of the Roth IRA is that tax-free withdrawals of earnings may be made after a five-year waiting period if you are over age $59\frac{1}{2}$; *see 8.23*. Tax-free withdrawals of contributions may be made at any time. A traditional IRA may also be converted to a Roth IRA. If necessary, a Roth IRA may be recharacterized back to a traditional IRA, and subsequently reconverted to a Roth IRA. *See 8.20* for annual contributions, *8.21* for conversions, and *8.22* for recharacterizations and reconversions.

Low-to-moderate-income taxpayers may be able to claim a tax credit on Form 8880 for 2002 contributions to a traditional IRA, Roth IRA, SIMPLE IRA, or salary-reduction SEP, as well as deferrals to other employer-sponsored retirement plans. The credit is discussed in Chapter 22.

Starting and Contributing to a Traditional IRA

8.1 Starting a Traditional IRA

You may set up a traditional (non-Roth) IRA by making annual contributions *(see 8.2)* that may be deductible *(see 8.4* for deduction rules) or nondeductible *(see 8.6)*, or by rolling over a distribution received from a qualified employer plan or from another IRA. On a rollover, you can avoid immediate tax when you receive a lump-sum payment upon retirement, changing jobs, or disability; *see 7.8.* If your employer allows it, you may contribute to a traditional IRA (or Roth IRA; *see 8.19)* by direct deposit through a payroll deduction plan. IRA accounts provide tax-free accumulation of earnings until withdrawals are made.

Roth IRAs. Annual contributions to a Roth IRA and conversions of traditional IRAs to Roth IRAs are discussed at *8.19–8.21.*

Restrictions on traditional IRAs. You may not freely withdraw IRA funds until the year you reach age $59^1/_2$ or become disabled. If you take money out before that time, you are subject to a penalty; *see 8.8.* Pledging the account as collateral is treated as a taxable distribution from the account; *see 8.12.* In the year you reach age $70^1/_2$, you may no longer make traditional IRA contributions, and you must start to withdraw *(8.13)* from the account. All IRA withdrawals are fully taxable except for amounts allocable to nondeductible contributions; *see 8.8* and *8.9.* Special averaging for lump-sum distributions does not apply. Excess contributions *(8.7)* are penalized.

If your IRA loses value because of poor investments, you may not deduct the loss. A loss is allowed only if you make nondeductible contributions that you have not recovered when the account is depleted; *see 8.9.*

Types of traditional IRAs. You may set up an IRA as:

1. *An individual retirement account* with a bank, savings and loan association, federally insured credit union, or other qualified person as trustee or custodian. An individual retirement account is technically a trust or custodial account. Your contribution may be invested in vehicles such as certificates of deposit, mutual funds, and certain limited partnerships.
2. *An individual retirement annuity* by purchasing an annuity contract (including a joint and survivor contract for the benefit of you and your spouse) issued by an insurance company; no trustee or custodian is required. The contract, endorsed to meet the terms of an IRA, is all that is required. Contracts issued after November 6, 1978, must provide for flexible premiums up to the annual contribution limit, so that if your compensation changes, your payment may also change. As borrowing or pledging of the contract is not allowed under an IRA, the contracts will not contain loan provisions. Endowment contracts issued after November 6, 1978, that provide life insurance protection may not be used as individual retirement annuities.

You may set up one type of IRA one year and choose another form the next year. You also may split your contribution between two or more investment vehicles. For example, you are eligible to contribute $3,000 for 2002 if under age 50. You may choose to put $1,500 into an investment retirement annuity and $1,500 into an individual retirement account with a bank, mutual fund, or brokerage firm.

You do not have to file any forms with your tax return when you set up or make contributions to a deductible IRA. Form 8606 must be attached to Form 1040 or Form 1040A if you make nondeductible IRA contributions; *see 8.6.* The trustee or issuer of your IRA will report your contribution to the IRS on Form 5498, and you should receive a copy.

Self-Directed IRA. If you wish to take a more active role in managing your IRA investments, you may set up a "self-directed" IRA using an IRS model form. The model trust (Form 5305) and the model custodial account agreement (Form 5305-A) meet the requirements of an exempt individual retirement account and so do not require a ruling or determination letter approving the exemption of the account and the deductibility of contributions made to the account. If you use this method, you still have to find a bank or other institution or trustee to handle your account or investment. Investments in a self-directed IRA are subject to restrictions; *see* the Caution on this page.

SIMPLE IRA. If you work for a company with 100 or fewer workers, your employer may set up a SIMPLE IRA to which you may make salary-reduction contributions; *see 8.17.*

 Filing Tip

IRA Fees and Brokerage Commissions

Fees paid to set up or manage an IRA, and annual account maintenance fees, are not considered IRA contributions provided they are separately billed. They are investment expenses that may be deducted as a miscellaneous itemized deduction subject to the 2% adjusted gross income floor; *see 19.1.* However, broker's commissions that are paid when you make investments for your IRA are not separately deductible, according to the IRS. They are considered IRA contributions subject to the $3,000 contribution limit.

 Caution

Restrictions on Collectibles Investments

If you have a self-directed traditional IRA and you invest in collectibles, such as art works, gems, stamps, antiques, rugs, metals, guns, or certain coins, you will have to pay a tax on your investment. The investment is treated as a taxable distribution to you in the year you make it. Coins are treated as collectibles, except for state-issued coins or certain U.S. minted gold, silver, and platinum coins. There is also an exception for gold, silver, platinum, or palladium bullion held by the IRA trustee, provided the fineness of the metal meets commodity market standards. If bullion is stored with a company other than the IRA trustee, the investment is subject to the deemed distribution rule for collectibles.

Law Alert

Increased Contribution Limits
The maximum contribution limit for traditional and Roth IRAs, which was $2,000 in 2001, increases to $3,000 for 2002–2004, $4,000 for 2005–2007, and $5,000 for 2008, after which the $5,000 limit will be adjusted for inflation. Individuals age 50 and over can contribute an additional $500 for 2002–2005 and an additional $1,000 for 2006 and later years.

Contributions after the end of the taxable year. You have until April 15, 2003 (the regular filing due date for your 2002 return) to make deductible or nondeductible IRA contributions for 2002. You must make your contribution by April 15, 2003, even if you get an extension to file your return. If you are short of cash, you may borrow the funds to make the contribution without jeopardizing the deduction. If an IRA deduction entitles you to a refund, you can file your return early, claim the IRA deduction, and if you receive the refund in time, apply it towards an IRA contribution before the due date.

8.2 Traditional IRA Contributions Must Be Based on Earnings

You may make contributions to a traditional IRA for 2002 of up to $3,000, $3,500 if you are age 50 or older in 2002, provided you have wage, salary, or net self-employment earnings and that you have not reached age $70\frac{1}{2}$ by the end of the year. If your earned income is less than $3,000 ($3,500 if age 50 or older), the contribution limit is 100% of your pay or net earned income if self-employed. Contributions for 2002 may be made up to the filing deadline of April 15, 2003, for 2002 returns; this is the deadline even if you obtain a filing extension for your 2002 return.

If you are married filing jointly, you may each contribute up to $3,000 (or $3,500 if age 50 or older) to an IRA for 2002, as long as your combined compensation covers the contributions; *see 8.3*.

Contributions up to these limits are *fully deductible* on your 2002 return if *neither you nor your spouse* is an active participant in an employer or self-employed retirement plan. Deductions for active plan participants are phased out for single persons with 2002 modified adjusted gross income over $34,000. The phase-out threshold on a joint return is generally $54,000 for 2002, but a more favorable $150,000 phase-out threshold applies to a jointly filing spouse who is not a plan participant; *see 8.3* and *8.4*.

Contribution limit increased by $500 if age 50 or older. If you are age 50 or older by the end of 2002, an additional contribution of up to $500 may be made for 2002, increasing your contribution limit to the lesser of $3,500 or your taxable compensation. If you are an active participant in an employer retirement plan, the $3,500 limit is subject to the phaseout rule at *8.4*.

Taxable compensation. Traditional IRA contributions, whether deductible or nondeductible, must be based on taxable compensation received for rendering personal services, such as salary, wages, commissions, tips, fees, bonuses, jury fees, or net earnings from self-employment (less Keogh plan contributions on behalf of the self-employed). An IRA contribution (deductible or nondeductible) may not be based upon:

1. Investment income such as interest, dividends, or profits from sales of property;
2. Deferred compensation, pensions, or annuities; or
3. Income earned abroad for which the foreign earned income exclusion is claimed.

Caution

Broker's Restriction on IRA Transfers
Before you invest in an IRA, carefully review the terms of the agreement for restrictions. One investor who put his IRA in a brokerage account was not allowed by the trustee to transfer from one account to another. Furthermore, the trustee reserved some of the IRA funds to cover broker fees and other transfer costs. The investor asked the IRS if these restrictions violated the tax law. The IRS, in a private letter ruling, said there was no violation. An IRA is a contractual agreement between the IRA trustee and the participant. Although the tax laws do not place limitations on direct IRA-to-IRA transfers, the trustees of a particular account may restrict such transfers.

> **EXAMPLE**
>
> A trader whose sole income was derived from stock dividends and gains in buying and selling stocks contributed to an IRA. The IRS disallowed the deduction on the grounds that his income was not earned income.

If you live in a community property state, the fact that one-half of your spouse's income is considered your income does not entitle you to make contributions to an IRA. The contributions must be based on pay earned through your services.

Only cash contributions are deductible; contributions paid by check are considered cash for this purpose.

Working for spouse. If you work for your spouse, you may make an IRA contribution provided you actually perform services and receive an actual payment of wages. A wife who worked as a receptionist and assistant to her husband, a veterinarian, failed to meet the second test. Her husband did not pay her a salary. Instead, he deposited all income from his business into a joint bank account held with his wife. In addition, no federal income tax was withheld from her wages. In a ruling, the IRS held that the wife could not set up her own IRA, even though she performed services; she failed to receive actual payment. Depositing business income into a joint account is neither actual nor constructive payment of the wife's salary. Furthermore, any deduction claimed for the wife's wages was disallowed.

Self-employed may make IRA contributions. IRA contributions may be based on net self-employment earnings *(45.1)*, after taking into account deductible Keogh or SEP retirement plan contributions *(41.5)* and the deduction for one-half of self-employment tax liability *(45.3)*. If you have a net loss for the year, you may not make an IRA contribution unless you also have wages.

If you have more than one self-employed activity, you must aggregate profits and losses from all of your self-employed businesses to determine if you have net income on which to base an IRA contribution. For example, if one self-employed business produces a net profit of $15,000 but another a net loss of $20,000, you may not make an IRA contribution based on the net profit of $15,000 since you have an overall loss. This netting rule does not apply to salary or wage income. If you are an employee who also has an unprofitable business, you may make an IRA contribution based on your salary.

If you have a self-employed retirement plan from your business, you are considered an active participant in a retirement plan for purposes of the adjusted gross income phase-out rules discussed at *8.4.*

Taxable alimony treated as compensation. A divorced spouse with little or no earnings may treat taxable alimony as compensation, giving a basis for deductible IRA contributions. If you are divorced, you generally may make an IRA contribution for 2002 equal to 100% of taxable alimony up to the $3,000 limit ($3,500 if age 50 or older). However, if you are an active participant in an employer plan and your adjusted gross income exceeds the $34,000 threshold for unmarried individuals, *see 8.4* for the phaseout of the deduction limit. Taxable alimony is alimony paid under a decree of divorce or legal separation, or a written agreement incident to such a decree; *see* Chapter 37. It does not include alimony payments made under a written agreement that is not incident to such a decree.

No contributions to traditional IRA allowed for those age 70$^1/_2$. Even if you still have earnings, you may not make contributions to a traditional IRA for the year in which you reach age 70$^1/_2$, or any later year. For example, if you were born in the last six months of 1931 or the first six months of 1932, you will reach age 70$^1/_2$ in 2002 and may not make any traditional IRA contributions for 2002 or later years.

If you have a nonworking spouse under age 70$^1/_2$, you may contribute to his or her IRA, even though no contribution may be made to your own traditional IRA because you have reached age 70$^1/_2$; *see 8.3.*

8.3 Contributions to a Traditional IRA If You Are Married

If both you and your spouse earned compensation in 2002 of at least $3,000 and are under age 70$^1/_2$ at the end of the year, each of you may make a contribution of up to $3,000 to a traditional IRA for 2002 by April 15, 2003. Under the spousal IRA rule, the $3,000 per spouse contribution limit applies even if only one of you works, provided you file jointly and your combined compensation is at least $6,000. An additional contribution of up to $500 can be made for a spouse who is age 50 or older so long as there is compensation to cover it.

Contributions for 2002 are fully deductible up to the $3,000 limit ($3,500, if applicable) if neither you nor your spouse was covered by an employer retirement plan during the year. If either of you was an active plan participant, you are both considered active participants, and a deduction may be limited or disallowed depending on your modified adjusted gross income (MAGI). However, if you file jointly and only one of you was an active plan participant, a more favorable MAGI phase-out rule applies to the nonparticipant spouse, so that the spouse without coverage may be able to claim a deduction even if the participant spouse may not. The deduction phase-out rules are discussed below.

Spousal IRA contribution on joint return for nonworking or low-earning spouse. On a joint return for 2002, the contribution limit is $3,000 for each spouse as long as the combined compensation of both spouses is at least $6,000. If both spouses were age 50 or older in 2002, the limit for each is raised to $3,500, so long as the combined compensation of both spouses is at least $7,000. This spousal IRA rule allows a spouse with minimal earnings to "borrow" compensation from his or her spouse in order to reach the maximum contribution limit. In figuring their combined compensation for purposes of the "borrowing" rule, the higher earning spouse's compensation is reduced by his or her deductible IRA contribution and by any regular contributions made by the higher earning spouse to a Roth IRA for the year.

 Filing Tip

Self-Employed Earnings

If you have a net profit from a sideline business and make a deductible contribution to a Keogh plan or SEP (*see* Chapter 41), the deductible contribution reduces modified adjusted gross income for IRA deduction purposes (and for Roth IRA contribution purposes; *see 8.19*).

 *Planning Reminder*

Roth IRA Contributions after Age 70 $^1/_2$

Contributions to a traditional IRA may not be made after age 70$^1/_2$, but contributions to a Roth IRA may be made even if you are over age 70$^1/_2$, provided you have compensation *(8.2)* to support the contribution and your income is within the limit allowed under the Roth IRA contribution rules; *see 8.20.*

Filing Tip

Deduction on Joint Return

If you and your spouse have combined earnings of at least $6,000 and modified adjusted gross income of $54,000 or less, each of you may claim an IRA deduction for contributions of up to $3,000 on your 2002 joint return.

Planning Reminder

Phase-Out Rule for Nonparticipant Spouses

If you are not covered by an employer retirement plan but your spouse is, and you file a joint return for 2002, your individual deduction limit is not subject to the phase-out rule unless modified adjusted gross income (MAGI) on the joint return is between $150,000 and $160,000. Your spouse, who is covered by an employer plan, is subject to the deduction phaseout for 2002 if modified adjusted gross income on the joint return is between $54,000 and $64,000.

EXAMPLE

Rhonda and Elliot Richards file a joint return for 2002. Both are under age 50 in 2002. Rhonda had salary income of $42,000 in 2002. Elliot was a full-time student and had no compensation. Rhonda may contribute up to $3,000 to a traditional IRA for 2002. Even though Elliot did not work, he also may contribute up to $3,000 to a traditional IRA. Since Rhonda's earnings exceeded $6,000, $3,000 of the earnings may be credited to Elliot for contribution purposes.

If Rhonda and Elliot's modified adjusted gross income (MAGI; *see 8.4*) for 2002 does not exceed $54,000, contributions up to the $3,000 limit are fully deductible. If MAGI on their joint return exceeded $54,000 and if Rhonda were an active participant in her employer's retirement plan during 2002, her deduction would be phased out over a MAGI range of $54,000–$64,000. Elliot would be allowed a full $3,000 deduction so long as the joint return MAGI was less than $150,000. *See* the phase-out rule below.

Deduction phase-out rule for spouses filing jointly for 2002. If either you or your spouse was an active participant in an employer retirement plan during 2002, the phase-out rule may limit or completely disallow an IRA deduction. However, even if one or both of you were active participants in an employer plan, the phase-out rule does not apply and you may each deduct contributions up to the $3,000 limit ($3,500 if age 50 or older) if your 2002 joint return modified adjusted gross income (MAGI; *see 8.4*) is $54,000 or less.

If both of you were active plan participants for 2002, the deduction limit is phased out if your joint return MAGI is between $54,000 and $64,000. No deduction is allowed for either of you if joint return MAGI is $64,000 or more.

If you were not an active plan participant in 2002 but your spouse was, a different phase-out rule applies to each of you. Your spouse, as an active plan participant, is subject to the deduction phaseout if MAGI on the joint return is between $54,000 and $64,000; no deduction is allowed if MAGI is $64,000 or more. However, as the nonparticipant spouse, your deduction limit is not subject to phaseout unless MAGI on the joint return is over $150,000. Your deduction is phased out if joint MAGI is between $150,000 and $160,000, and no deduction is allowed if MAGI is $160,000 or more.

See 8.4 for an example of how the reduced deduction limit is figured if MAGI is within the above phase-out ranges.

Deduction phase-out rule for married persons filing separately for 2002. If you are married, live together at any time during 2002, file separately, and either of you is an active participant in an employer plan, the other spouse is also considered an active participant. Both of you are subject to the $0 to $10,000 MAGI deduction phaseout; *see 8.4*.

If you live apart for all of 2002, you each figure IRA deductions as if single. Thus, the more favorable deduction phase-out range of $34,000 to $44,000 applies if you are covered by an employer retirement plan; *see 8.4*. If you are not covered, you may claim a full deduction on your separate return.

Contributions for spouses under age $70\frac{1}{2}$. If in 2002 you were age $70\frac{1}{2}$ or over and had taxable compensation, you may contribute to a spousal IRA for 2002 if your spouse is nonworking and is under age $70\frac{1}{2}$ at the end of the year. The entire contribution must be allocated to the nonworking spouse. No contribution may be made to your own traditional IRA for the year in which you reach age $70\frac{1}{2}$, or any later year. However, you may contribute to a Roth IRA even if you are over age $70\frac{1}{2}$, provided your compensation is within the Roth IRA limits; *see 8.20*.

8.4 IRA Deduction Restrictions for Active Participants in Employer Plan

If you are covered by an employer retirement plan, including a self-employed plan, you may be unable to make deductible IRA contributions to a traditional IRA. When you have coverage, your right to claim a full deduction, a limited deduction, or no deduction at all depends on your modified adjusted gross income (MAGI). If you are married, and your spouse has employer plan coverage for 2002, you are also considered to have coverage in most cases. However, if you file jointly and do not individually have employer plan coverage, a special MAGI phase-out rule may allow you to deduct IRA contributions even if a deduction for your spouse is limited or barred.

If you are unmarried and do not have employer plan coverage, or if you are married and neither of you has coverage, an IRA deduction of up to $3,000 ($3,500 if age 50 or older) for 2002 is allowed as long as you have compensation of $3,000 ($3,500 if age 50 or older) or more. The deduction phase-out rules do not apply, regardless of your income.

Generally, you are considered to be "covered" by a retirement plan if you are an active participant in the plan for any part of the plan year ending within your taxable year; *see* the Sara Wartes Example below. If you are an employee, your Form W-2 for 2002 should indicate whether you are covered for the year; if you are, the "Retirement plan" box within Box 13 of Form W-2 should be checked. Active participation in a self-employed Keogh plan or SEP (Chapter 41) is treated as employer plan coverage for purposes of the IRA deduction phase-out rules. Active participation is explained further at *8.5*.

EXAMPLE

Sara Wartes, a college teacher, quit her job in 1988 and withdrew all of the contributions she had made to her employee pension plan. The Tax Court held that Sara could not claim an IRA deduction in that year. Sara was an active participant in the college plan during 1988 and under the phase-out rules based upon adjusted gross income, no IRA deduction was allowed. The court noted that the active participation test is not made at the end of the year. Participation in a company plan at any time during the year triggers the deduction phase-out rules. This is true even where a person has forfeitable benefits.

You are not an active plan participant but your spouse is. Even if you were not an active participant in an employer retirement plan at any time in 2002, your IRA deduction limit for 2002 may be phased out because of your spouse's coverage. However, if you file jointly, your own deduction is not limited unless modified adjusted gross income (MAGI) on the joint return exceeds $150,000 (this amount does not change annually). For your spouse who has employer plan coverage, the rule is different: the phase-out threshold for his or her 2002 deduction is joint MAGI of $54,000.

The deduction is phased out over the next $10,000 of MAGI exceeding the phase-out threshold. Thus, you as a nonparticipant are not allowed any deduction if MAGI on your joint return is $160,000 or more. A deduction for your spouse as an active participant is completely phased out if joint return MAGI for 2002 is $64,000 or more.

Stricter phase-out rules apply to married persons filing separately if they live together at any time during the year. If you lived with your spouse at any time during 2002 and either of you was an active plan participant in 2002, you are both subject to the $0 – $10,000 MAGI phase-out range on separate returns. Neither of you may claim an IRA deduction if the MAGI on your separate return is $10,000 or more.

If you are married filing separately and you lived apart for all of 2002, your spouse's plan participation does not affect your IRA deduction. Take into account only your own participation, if any, and if you are an active participant, your IRA deduction under the phase-out rules is figured as if you were single. If you are not an active participant, you may claim the full $3,000 deduction limit for 2002 ($3,500 if age 50 or older).

Modified adjusted gross income (MAGI) determines your deduction limit if you or your spouse is an active plan participant. If either you or your spouse is an active plan participant, you still may be allowed a full or limited deduction, but this will depend on whether your 2002 modified adjusted gross income (MAGI) is within the phase-out range that applies to you as shown below.

MAGI is generally equal to the total income shown on your return *minus* adjustments to income other than for IRA deductions. However, if you are claiming a deduction for student loan interest *(38.6)*, or qualified college tuition and fees *(38.13)*, the deduction must be *added back* to adjusted gross income to get MAGI. If you are claiming an exclusion for employer-provided adoption assistance *(3.5)* or an exclusion for interest on U.S. EE Savings Bonds used for tuition *(38.4)*, you must add back that excluded amount to adjusted gross income to get MAGI. If you worked abroad and are claiming the foreign earned income exclusion *(36.1)*, or a foreign housing exclusion or deduction *(36.4)*, these amounts also must be added back to adjusted gross income to get MAGI.

Figuring Your 2002 IRA Deduction Under the Phase-Out Rules

If you are an active plan participant for 2002, or you file a joint return for 2002 and your spouse was an active participant, the full $3,000 (or $3,500 if age 50 or older) deduction limit is available to you only if your modified adjusted gross income (MAGI) is below a phase-out threshold shown below. The de-

Planning Reminder

Roth IRA vs. Deductible IRA

Even if you qualify for a full IRA deduction, you may want to consider making a nondeductible contribution to a Roth IRA *(8.20)*. For example, you may be willing to give up the current tax deduction in order to create a Roth IRA from which distributions will be completely tax free after age 59¹/₂ and a five-year waiting period has passed. If you choose to make a deductible contribution to a traditional IRA, distributions from the traditional IRA will be taxable. You may also prefer the Roth-IRA advantage of not having to take minimum distributions starting at age 70¹/₂, as is required with traditional IRAs.

duction limit is phased out over the first $10,000 of MAGI exceeding the threshold, so that if MAGI exceeds the phase-out threshold by $10,000 or more, no deduction is allowed. The phase-out threshold is $0 if you are married filing separately, you lived together at any time in 2002, and either of you was an active plan participant.

Phase-out threshold for 2002 returns. On 2002 returns, the $3,000 (or $3,500 if age 50 or older) deduction limit is subject to phaseout if modified adjusted gross income exceeds:

- $34,000 if you are single or head of household;
- $34,000 if you are married filing separately, you lived apart from your spouse for all of 2002, and you were an active plan participant during 2002. If you lived apart the entire year and you were *not* an active participant, you qualify for the full deduction limit; the phase-out rule is inapplicable to you even if your spouse was an active plan participant.
- $54,000 if you are married filing jointly and both you and your spouse were active plan participants during 2002, or you are a qualifying widow or widower;
- $54,000 if you are married filing jointly and you are an active plan participant during 2002 but your spouse was not. You use the $54,000 threshold; your spouse uses the $150,000 threshold;
- $150,000 if you are married filing jointly and you were not an active plan participant at any time during 2002 but your spouse was. You use the $150,000 threshold; your spouse uses the $54,000 threshold; and
- $0 if you are married filing separately, you lived with your spouse at any time in 2002, and *either* you or your spouse was an active plan participant during 2002. You and your spouse are both subject to the "0" threshold on 2002 returns so long as you lived together at any time in 2002 and *either* of you was an active plan participant during the year.

The phase-out applies to the first $9,999 of MAGI exceeding the $34,000, $54,000, $150,000, or zero phase-out threshold. If your MAGI exceeds the threshold by $10,000 or more, you are not allowed any IRA deduction.

Phase-out Range for Deduction Limit on 2002 Returns

If your phase-out threshold (see *above*) is—	Deduction limit is phased out if MAGI is—	No deduction if MAGI is—
$34,000	Between $34,000 and $44,000	$44,000 or more
$54,000	Between $54,000 and $64,000	$64,000 or more
$150,000	Between $150,000 and $160,000	$160,000 or more
$0	$0–$9,999	$10,000 or more

Law Alert

Income Phase-Out Limits After 2002

The $34,000 and $54,000 MAGI phase-out deduction thresholds for 2002 will both increase for 2003 by $6,000, to $40,000 and $60,000, respectively. The phase-out thresholds will increase by $5,000 annually until the phase-out range reaches $50,000–$60,000 in 2005 for single persons and $80,000–$100,000 in 2007 for married persons filing jointly.

Figure your excess MAGI and compute the deduction limit under the phase-out rule. If your MAGI is within the $10,000 phase-out range, figure your excess MAGI by subtracting the phase-out threshold from your MAGI. If the excess MAGI is $10,000 or more, you are not allowed any IRA deduction; the entire deduction is phased out.

If the excess MAGI is less than $10,000, you are allowed a portion of the deduction limit. If you are under age 50 in 2002, the deduction limit generally equals $3,000 minus 30% of the MAGI in excess of the phase-out threshold. If age 50 or older in 2002, the deduction limit is generally $3,500 minus 35% of the MAGI in excess of the phase-out threshold. A result that is not a multiple of $10 is rounded up to the next highest multiple of $10. If the rounded up amount is less than $200, it is increased to $200. You can figure the limit in your case by applying the following four steps. The Examples below illustrate the computation.

1. Enter excess of your MAGI over your phase-out threshold _____
2. Multiply Step 1 by 30%, or by 35% if you were age 50 or older at the end of 2002 _____
3. Subtract Step 2 from $3,000, or from $3,500 if you were age 50 or older at end of 2002 _____
4. If Step 3 is not a multiple of $10, round it up to the next highest multiple of $10. If the result is under $200, increase it to $200. This is your deductible limit. _____

Nondeductible contributions. Any contributions exceeding the amount allowed under the above rules may be treated as nondeductible IRA contributions. *See 8.6* for further details. Alternatively, the excess may be contributed to a Roth IRA if allowed under the rules at *8.20*.

Figuring your IRA deduction if you receive Social Security benefits. If you or your spouse *(8.3)* is an active participant in an employer plan and either of you receives Social Security benefits, you need to make an extra computation before you can figure whether an IRA deduction is allowed. Follow the rules discussed at *34.3* to determine if part of your Social Security benefits would be subject to tax, assuming no IRA deduction were claimed. If none of your benefits would be taxable, you follow the regular rules above for determining IRA deductions. If part of your Social Security benefits would be taxable, MAGI for IRA purposes is increased by the taxable benefits. The allowable IRA deduction is then taken into account to determine the actual amount of taxable Social Security. IRS Publication 590 has worksheets for making these computations.

EXAMPLES

1. Rob Porter is single and under age 50 at the end of 2002. He is an active participant in an employer retirement plan. His salary for 2002 is $32,000 and his MAGI for 2002 is $35,343. His MAGI exceeds the $34,000 phase-out floor for single persons by $1,343. Rob figures a deduction limit for 2002 of $2,600 as follows:

   1. Excess of MAGI over phase-out threshold
      for single persons ($35,343 – $34,000) $1,343.00
   2. 30% of Step 1   402.90
   3. $3,000 minus Step 2 $2,597.10
   4. Round Step 3 to the next highest multiple of $10.
   This is Rob's deductible limit.   2,600.00

2. Ted and Lynn Baker are both under age 50 at the end of 2002 and they file a 2002 joint return. They report wages of $26,000 for Ted and $28,000 for Lynn. Their modified adjusted gross income (MAGI) is $57,025. Ted and Lynn are both active participants in employer retirement plans in 2002 and so they are both subject to the $54,000 phase-out threshold. The deduction limit for each of them is $2,100, figured as follows:

   1. Excess of MAGI over phase-out threshold for
      married couples filing jointly ($57,025 – $54,000) $3,025.00
   2. 30% of Step 1   907.50
   3. $3,000 minus Step 2 $2,092.50
   4. Round Step 3 to the next highest multiple of $10.
   This is the deductible limit for Ted and also for Lynn.
   On their joint return, they can each deduct IRA contributions of up to $2,100, for a total maximum deduction
   of $4,200. $2,100.00

3. Assume the same facts as in Example 2 except that only Lynn was an active participant in an employer plan. Ted and Lynn must figure their deduction limitations separately using different phase-out thresholds.

   For Lynn, the same $2,100 deduction limit applies as in Example 2. The $54,000 phase-out threshold applies, her excess MAGI is $ 3,025 ($57,025 MAGI on joint return – $54,000 threshold), and her deduction limit as shown in Example 2 is $2,100.

   For Ted, the special $150,000 threshold for nonparticipant spouses applies. Since joint return MAGI is well below the $150,000 threshold, he is not affected by the phase-out rules and may deduct IRA contributions up to the $3,000 ceiling for 2002.

8.5 Active Participation in Employer Plan

Active participants in an employer retirement plan are subject to the phase-out rules for deducting contributions discussed at *8.4*. When a married couple files jointly and only one of the spouses was an active plan participant for the taxable year, a more favorable phase-out range applies to the nonparticipant spouse than to the spouse who was an active participant; *see 8.4* for details.

An employer retirement plan means:

1. A qualified pension, profit-sharing, or stock bonus plan, including a qualified self-employed Keogh plan, SIMPLE IRA, or simplified employee pension (SEP) plan;
2. A qualified annuity plan;

Active Participant Status

You are treated as an active participant in a 401(k) plan, profit-sharing plan, stock bonus plan, or money-purchase pension plan if contributions are made or allocated to your account for the plan year that ends within your tax year. Under this rule, you may be considered an active participant for a year during which no contributions by you or your employer are made to your account; *see* the Examples on this page.

3. A tax-sheltered annuity; and

4. A plan established for its employees by the United States, by a state or political subdivision, or by any agency or instrumentality of the United States or a state or political subdivision, but not eligible state Section 457 plans.

Form W-2. If your employer checks the "Retirement plan" box within Box 13 of your 2002 Form W-2, this indicates that you were an active participant in your employer's retirement plan during the year. If you want to make a contribution before you receive your Form W-2, check the following guidelines and consult your plan administrator for your status.

Type of plan. Under any type of plan, if you are considered an active participant for any part of the plan year ending with or within your taxable year, you are treated as an active participant for the entire taxable year. Because of this plan year rule, you may be treated as an active participant even if you worked for the employer only part of the year. Under IRS guidelines, it is possible to be treated as an active participant in the year of retirement and even in the year after retirement if your employer maintains a fiscal year plan.

The plan year rule works differently for defined benefit pension plans than for defined contribution plans such as profit-sharing plans, 401(k) plans, money purchase pension plans, and stock bonus plans. These rules are discussed below.

If you are married, and either you or your spouse is treated as an active participant for 2002, *see* 8.3 for the effect on the other spouse.

Defined benefit pension plans. You are treated as an active participant in a defined benefit pension plan if, for the plan year ending with or within your taxable year, you are eligible to participate in the plan. Under this rule, as long as you are eligible, you are treated as an active participant, even if you decline participation in the plan or you fail to make a mandatory contribution specified in the plan. Furthermore, you are treated as an active participant even if your rights to benefits are not vested.

Defined contribution plan. For a defined contribution plan, you are generally considered an active participant if "with respect to" the plan year ending with or within your taxable year (1) you make elective deferrals to the plan; (2) your employer contributes to your account; or (3) forfeitures are allocated to your account. If any of these events occur, you are treated as an active participant for that taxable year, even if you do not have a vested right to receive benefits from your account.

> **EXAMPLES**
> 1. Pat O'Neil joins a company in 2002 that has a 401(k) plan (a type of defined contribution plan) with a plan year starting July 1 and ending the following June 30. He is not eligible to participate in the plan year ending June 30, 2002. After he becomes eligible to participate in the second half of 2002, he elects to defer 6% of his 2002 salary to the 401(k) plan for the plan year ending June 30, 2003. Although he makes elective deferrals to the plan during 2002, he is *not* considered an active participant for 2002 because his contributions were made for the plan year ending in 2003. He *will* be considered an active participant in 2003, even if he decides not to defer any part of his 2003 salary for the plan year ending June 30, 2004.
> 2. Clarise Jones's employer has a defined benefit pension plan with a plan year starting July 1 and ending the following June 30. She is not excluded from participating. If she retired during September 2002, she is considered an active participant for 2002 because she was eligible to participate during the plan year ending during 2002. She will also be considered an active participant for 2003. Although she will retire before the end of the plan year starting July 1, 2002, and ending June 30, 2003, she will still be eligible to participate during part of that plan year (July 1, 2002, until retirement in September 2002), and since the 2002–2003 plan year ends within her 2003 tax year, she will be considered an active participant for 2003.

8.6 Nondeductible Contributions to Traditional IRAs

If you are not allowed to deduct any IRA contributions for 2002 because of the phase-out rule *(8.4)*, you may make *nondeductible* contributions of up to $3,000 ($3,500 if age 50 or over at the end of 2002) where you have compensation of at least that much. If the deduction limit is reduced under the phase-out rules of *8.4*, you may make a nondeductible contribution to the extent the maximum contribution limit of $3,000 (or $3,500) exceeds the deductible limit figured under *8.4*.

However, if you are not barred from making Roth IRA contributions *(see 8.20)* because of your income level, the Roth IRA has advantages over the nondeductible traditional IRA. Although both types of plans allow earnings to accumulate tax free until withdrawal, the Roth IRA has advantages at withdrawal. After a five-year period, completely tax-free withdrawals of earnings as well as contributions may be made from a Roth IRA if you are age $59^1/_2$ or older, you are disabled, or you withdraw no more than $10,000 for first-time home-buyer expenses. Even within the first five-year period, contributions may be withdrawn tax free from a Roth IRA. On the other hand, withdrawals from a nondeductible traditional IRA are partially taxed if any deductible contributions to any traditional IRA were previously made. Even if only nondeductible contributions had been made, earnings from traditional IRAs are taxed at withdrawal. Furthermore, contributions after age $70^1/_2$ may be made only to a Roth IRA, and mandatory required minimum distributions are not required from a Roth IRA, as they are from a traditional IRA. *See 8.19–8.24* for Roth IRA details.

Form 8606. You must file Form 8606 to report nondeductible contributions to a traditional IRA unless you withdraw the contribution as discussed below. You must list on Form 8606 the value of all of your IRAs as of the end of the year, including amounts based on deductible contributions. If you are married and you and your spouse both make nondeductible contributions, you must each file a separate Form 8606. A $50 penalty may be imposed for not filing Form 8606 unless there is reasonable cause. Furthermore, if you overstate the amount of designated nondeductible contributions made for any taxable year, you are subject to a $100 penalty for each such overstatement unless you can demonstrate that the overstatement was due to reasonable cause. You may file an amended return for a taxable year and change the designation of IRA contributions from deductible to nondeductible or nondeductible to deductible.

If you make contributions to a traditional IRA during the year, you may not know whether you will be allowed to claim a deduction under the phase-out rules in *8.4.* You can make your contribution without knowing whether it is deductible or not and figure your deduction when you file your return. Any nondeductible amount would be reported on Form 8606. However, if you do not want to make nondeductible contributions, you may wait until after the end of the year when you can determine your MAGI and active participant status; you have until the April filing due date (without extensions) to make a deductible contribution; for 2002 returns, the filing due date is April 15, 2003.

Withdrawing nondeductible contributions. If you make an IRA contribution for 2002 and later realize it is not deductible, you may make a tax-free withdrawal of the contribution by the filing due date (plus extensions), instead of designating the contribution as nondeductible on Form 8606. To do this, you must also withdraw the earnings allocable to the withdrawn contribution and include the earnings as income on your 2002 return. You might want to make the withdrawal if you incorrectly determined that a contribution would be deductible and you do not want to leave nondeductible contributions in your account. However, making the withdrawal could subject you to bank penalties for premature withdrawals, or other withdrawal penalties imposed by the IRA trustee. Furthermore, if you are under age $59^1/_2$, the 10% premature withdrawal penalty applies to the withdrawn earnings unless one of the exceptions at *8.12* is available.

8.7 Penalty for Excess Contributions to Traditional IRAs

If you contribute more than the allowable amount to a traditional IRA, whether deductible or nondeductible, the excess contribution may be subject to a penalty tax of 6%. The penalty tax is cumulative. That is, unless you correct the excess, you will be subject to another penalty on the excess contribution in the following year. The penalty tax is not deductible. The penalty is figured in Part III of Form 5329, which must be attached to Form 1040.

The 6% penalty may be avoided by withdrawing the excess contribution by the due date for your return, including extensions, plus any income earned on it. The withdrawn excess contribution is not taxable provided no deduction was allowed for it. The withdrawn earnings must be reported as income on your return for the year in which the excess contribution was made. The earnings should be reported to you as a taxable distribution on Form 1099-R. If you are under age $59^1/_2$ (and not disabled) when you receive the income, the 10% premature withdrawal penalty applies to the income. Similar rules apply to withdrawals of excess employer contributions to a simplified employee pension plan *(8.15)* made by the due date for your return.

If an excess contribution for 2002 is *not* withdrawn by the due date for your 2002 return, but you filed by the due date, the IRS allows the withdrawal to be made no later than six months after the original due date (without extensions), provided the related earnings are reported on an amended return that explains the withdrawal; *see* the Form 5329 instructions for details. If the withdrawal is

Planning Reminder

Roth IRA Alternative
A Roth IRA is a nondeductible IRA that offers significant tax and retirement planning advantages. Contributions up to the annual limit *(see 8.20)* may be made if modified adjusted gross income is below $95,000 if you are single and $150,000 if married filing jointly. In general, after the five-year period beginning with the first taxable year for which a Roth IRA contribution was made, tax-free withdrawals may be made if you are age $59^1/_2$ or older, you are disabled or you have qualifying first-time home-buyer expenses. Existing IRAs may be rolled over to Roth IRAs if your modified adjusted gross income is $100,000 or less; *see 8.21* for further details.

Planning Reminder

Form 8606 for Traditional IRA Distributions
Keep a copy of each Form 8606 filed showing nondeductible contributions and keep a separate record of deductible contributions. When you make withdrawals from a traditional IRA, the portion of each withdrawal allocable to nondeductible contributions is not taxed. You may not completely avoid tax even if you withdraw an amount equal to your nondeductible contributions. The tax-free portion of the withdrawal is figured on Form 8606. The rules for figuring tax on withdrawals are at *8.9*.

not made, the 6% penalty will apply to your 2002 return but it may be avoided for 2003 by withdrawing the excess by the end of 2003. Instead of withdrawing the excess contribution during 2003, you may also avoid a penalty for 2003 by reducing your allowable 2003 IRA contribution by the 2002 excess. *See* IRS Publication 590 and Form 5329 for details.

If you deducted an excess contribution in an earlier year for which total contributions were $2,000 or less, you may make a tax-free withdrawal of the excess by filing an amended return to correct the excess deduction. However, the 6% penalty tax applies for each year that the excess was still in the account at the end of the year.

See IRS Publication 590 for further information on correcting excess contributions made in a prior year.

Roth IRAs. A similar 6% penalty applies on Form 5329 to excess contributions to a Roth IRA; *see* Form 5329 and IRS Publication 590 for further details.

Taking Money Out of a Traditional IRA

8.8 Taxable Distributions From Traditional IRAs

If all of your IRA contributions were deductible, any traditional IRA distribution you receive that you do not roll over or redeposit within 60 days *(8.10)* will be taxable. Not only are distributions taxable, but the timing and amount of IRA payments is subject to these restrictions:

- Distributions in 2002 before age $59^1/_2$ are subject to a 10% tax penalty, unless you are totally disabled, meet exceptions for paying medical costs, receive annual payments under an annuity-type schedule or you qualify for another exception. The penalty and the exceptions are discussed at *8.12*.
- After you reach age $70^1/_2$, you must start to receive annual distributions under a life-expectancy calculation. The required starting date is the April 1 of the year after the year in which you reach age $70^1/_2$. For example, if you reach age $70^1/_2$ during 2002 you must start taking IRA distributions by April 1, 2003. Failure to take the minimum required annual distribution can result in penalties. These rules are discussed in *8.13*.

How to report IRA distributions on your 2002 return. All IRA distributions are reported to you and to the IRS on Form 1099-R; *see* the guide to Form 1099-R on pages 147–148. Form 1099-R must be attached to your return only if federal tax has been withheld. You can avoid withholding by instructing the payer not to withhold using Form W-4P (or a substitute form); *see 26.11*.

If you have never made nondeductible contributions, your IRA withdrawals are fully taxable and should be reported on Line 15b of Form 1040 or Line 11b of Form 1040A. If you have made deductible and nondeductible contributions, complete Form 8606 to figure the nontaxable and taxable portions as discussed in *8.9*. Then you report the total IRA withdrawal on Line 15a of Form 1040 or Line 11a of Form 1040A and enter only the taxable portion on Line 15b or Line 11b, respectively.

If you have an individual retirement annuity, your investment in the contract is treated as zero so all payments are fully taxable. Distributions from an endowment policy due to death are taxed as ordinary income to the extent allocable to retirement savings; to the extent allocable to life insurance, they are considered insurance proceeds.

Proceeds from U.S. retirement bonds (which were issued by the Treasury before May 1982) are taxable in the year the bonds are redeemed. However, you must report the full proceeds in the year you reach age $70^1/_2$ even if you do not redeem the bonds.

Loan treated as distribution. If you borrow from your IRA account or use it as security for a loan, you generally are considered to have received your entire interest. Borrowing will subject the account or the fair market value of the contract to tax at ordinary income rates as of the first day of the taxable year of the borrowing. Your IRA account loses its tax-exempt status. If you use the account or part of it as security for a loan, the portion that is pledged is treated as a distribution. However, under the rollover rules, a short-term loan may be made by withdrawing IRA funds and redepositing them in an IRA within 60 days, subject to the once-a-year rollover rule at *8.10*.

IRS seizure of IRA treated as distribution. The Tax Court has held that an IRS levy of an IRA to cover back taxes is a taxable distribution to the account owner, even though the funds are transferred directly from the account to the IRS and not actually received by the owner. Where the owner is under age $59^1/_2$, the 10% penalty for early withdrawals *(8.12)* does *not* apply to involuntary distributions attributable to an IRS levy.

8.9 Partially Tax-Free Traditional IRA Distributions Allocable to Nondeductible Contributions

If you ever made a nondeductible contribution to a traditional IRA, you must file Form 8606 to report a 2002 distribution from any of your traditional IRAs, even if the distribution is from an IRA to which only nondeductible contributions were made. All of your IRAs are treated as one contract. If you receive distributions from more than one IRA in the same year, they are combined for reporting purposes on Form 8606. When you withdraw an amount from any IRA during a taxable year and you previously made both deductible and nondeductible IRA contributions, the part of your withdrawal that is allocable to your nondeductible contributions is tax-free; any balance is taxable. You may not claim that you are withdrawing only your tax-free contributions, even if your withdrawal is less than your nondeductible contributions. If you withdraw amounts from your nondeductible account, you will incur tax. You make the computations on Form 8606. The six steps below reflect the IRS method used on Form 8606 to figure the nontaxable and taxable portions of the IRA distributions.

The rule requiring you to combine nondeductible and deductible IRAs when making IRA withdrawals does not apply to withdrawals from a Roth IRA. A Roth IRA is treated separately. After a five-year period, withdrawals after age $59^1/_2$ from a Roth IRA are completely tax-free; *see 8.23.*

A bank or other payer of a distribution from a traditional IRA will not indicate on Form 1099-R whether any part of a distribution is a tax-free return of basis allocable to nondeductible contributions. It is up to you to keep records that show the nondeductible contributions you have made. IRS instructions require you to keep copies of all Forms 8606 on which nondeductible contributions have been designated, as well as copies of (1) your tax returns for years you made nondeductible contributions to traditional IRAs; (2) Forms 5498 showing all IRA contributions and showing the value of your IRAs for each year you received a distribution; and (3) Form 1099-R and Form W-2P showing IRA distributions. According to the IRS, you should keep such records until you have withdrawn all IRA funds.

Figuring the taxable portion of a traditional IRA distribution. If you received a distribution from a traditional IRA in 2002 and have ever made nondeductible contributions to any of your traditional IRAs, follow Steps 1–6 to determine the tax-free and taxable portions of the 2002 distribution. These steps assume that you did not convert a traditional IRA to a Roth IRA during 2002. If you did convert a traditional IRA to a Roth IRA, follow the instructions to Form 8606.

Step 1.   Total IRA withdrawals during 2002.

Step 2.   Total nondeductible contributions to all IRAs made by the end of 2002. Tax-free withdrawals of nondeductible contributions in prior years reduce the total. If you made any contributions to traditional IRAs for 2002 (including a contribution made between January 1 and April 15, 2003) that may be partly nondeductible because your modified adjusted gross income is within the deduction phase-out range shown in *8.4* for active plan participants, you should include the contributions in the Step 2 total.

Step 3.   Add Step 1 to the value of all your IRAs (include SIMPLE IRAs and SEP IRAs) as of the end of 2002. If you received an IRA distribution within the last 60 days of 2002 that was rolled over to another IRA within the 60-day rollover period *(8.10) but* not until 2003, add the 2003 rollover to the year-end balance.

Step 4.   Divide Step 2 by Step 3. This is the tax-free percentage of your IRA withdrawal.

Step 5.   Multiply the Step 4 percentage by Step 1. This amount is tax free.

Step 6.   Subtract Step 5 from Step 1. This amount is fully taxable.

Court Decision

Penalty on Garnished IRA
The Tax Court held that an IRA owner received a taxable distribution when a bank enforced a court's garnishment award for past-due child support by transferring his IRA to his ex-wife. The Tax Court found that the distribution to the owner's former wife was a discharge of indebtedness to her and was constructively received by him. Whether the transfer of funds was voluntary or in settlement of a legal obligation was held to be of no consequence. The 10% tax penalty for distributions before age $59^1/_2$ also applied.

EXAMPLE

In 2002, Nick James withdraws $5,000 from his traditional IRA, having made deductible IRA contributions of $8,000 and nondeductible contributions of $6,000 as follows:

Year	Deductible	Nondeductible
1991	$2,000	0
1992	2,000	0
1993	2,000	0
1994	1,000	$1,000
1995	1,000	1,000
1996	0	2,000
1997	0	2,000
	$8,000	$6,000

Assume that at the end of 2002, Nick's total IRA account balance, including earnings, is $17,500, and that this is his first IRA withdrawal. On Form 8606 for 2002, Nick figures that $1,350 of the $5,000 IRA withdrawal is tax free and $3,650 is taxable.

Step 1.	IRA withdrawal	$5,000
Step 2.	Nondeductible contributions	6,000
Step 3.	IRA balance at end of the year ($17,500) *plus* Step 1	22,500
Step 4.	Tax-free percentage: $6,000 ÷ $22,500	27%
Step 5.	Tax-free withdrawal: 27% × $5,000	1,350
Step 6.	Taxable withdrawal: $5,000 – $1,350	$3,650

The total $5,000 withdrawal should be reported on Line 15a of Form 1040 or on Line 11a of Form 1040A, and the taxable $3,650 portion should be entered on Line 15b (Form 1040) or on Line 11b (Form 1040A).

Deductible IRA loss based on unrecovered nondeductible contributions. According to the IRS, a loss may be allowed if all IRA funds have been distributed and you have not recovered your basis in nondeductible contributions.

EXAMPLE

Paula Brown makes nondeductible IRA contributions of $10,000 from 1994–1998. In 2002, she withdraws $6,000. The year-end balance is $8,000. The tax-free portion of the withdrawal is $4,286 ($10,000 nondeductible contributions ÷ $14,000 total of withdrawal plus year-end balance × $6,000 withdrawal).

After the withdrawal, her account balance is $8,000; her basis is $5,714 ($10,000 – $4,286). If because of poor investments the value of the IRA fell to $3,000 by the end of 2002 and she withdrew the entire $3,000 balance, she could claim a $2,714 loss ($5,714 basis – $3,000 distribution), but only as a miscellaneous itemized deduction subject to the 2% floor *(19.1)* on Schedule A of Form 1040.

8.10 Tax-Free Rollovers and Direct Transfers to Traditional IRAs

There are two types of tax-free rollovers that you can make to a traditional IRA. You may roll over funds to a traditional IRA from a qualified company or self-employed retirement plan, 403(b) plan, or governmental 457 plan; *see 7.8*. You may also use a rollover to switch funds from one traditional IRA to another, although another option, a direct transfer, may be a more advantageous way of changing IRA investments.

Direct transfer from one IRA to another. A *direct transfer* is made by instructing the trustee of a traditional IRA to transfer all or part of your account to another IRA trustee. Direct transfers are tax free because you do not receive the funds. The tax law does not require a waiting period between direct transfers, whereas rollovers are subject to a once-a-year limitation, as discussed below.

For example, assume you have a traditional IRA at Bank "A" and decide to switch your account to Mutual Fund "ABC." The mutual fund will provide you with transfer request forms that you complete and return to the fund, which will then forward the forms to the bank to complete the direct transfer. The transfer from the bank to the mutual fund is tax free. Because the IRA funds were not paid to you, the transfer is not considered a rollover subject to the once-a-year rollover limitation. This means that if within one year you become unhappy with the performance of Mutual Fund "ABC," you may make another tax-free direct transfer of your IRA to Fund "XYZ" or to Bank "B."

Rollover within 60 days. If you withdraw funds from a traditional IRA, you have 60 days to make a tax-free rollover to another traditional IRA. The amount you receive from your old IRA must be transferred to the new plan by the 60th day after the day you received it. Amounts not rolled over within the 60-day period must be treated as a taxable distribution for the year you received the distribution (not the year in which the 60-day period expired, if that is later).

The IRS may waive the 60-day rollover deadline on equitable grounds if you receive a distribution after 2002 and the rollover cannot be completed on time because of events beyond your reasonable control, such as illness, natural disaster, or a financial institution's error. An extension to the 60-day deadline is also allowed if your distribution is "frozen" and cannot be withdrawn from an insolvent or bankrupt financial institution; *see* below.

Planning Reminder

Deducting Loss

A loss on an IRA investment is deductible only if your basis in nondeductible contributions has not been received after the entire account has been distributed.

Planning Reminder

60-Day Loan From IRA

You can take advantage of the rollover rule to borrow funds from your IRA if you need a short-term loan to pay your taxes or other expenses. As long as you redeposit the amount in an IRA within 60 days you are not taxed on the withdrawal; the redeposit is considered a tax-free rollover. You may roll over the funds to a different IRA from the one from which the withdrawal was made. A second withdrawal from the same IRA within one year would be taxable as discussed below.

Once you complete a rollover between traditional IRAs, you must wait one year before you can roll over the same funds; *see* below.

The once-a-year rollover rule applies separately to each of your IRAs. A tax-free rollover may occur only once in a one-year period starting on the date you receive the first distribution. If within that one-year period you receive a distribution from the previously rolled over IRA, the distribution is taxable and if you are under age $59^1/_2$, could be subject to the 10% penalty for premature distributions; *see 8.12*. However, this rule applies separately to each of your traditional IRAs. For example, you have one traditional IRA invested in a bank and another invested in a mutual fund. Within the same one-year period, you may roll over the bank IRA to a different traditional IRA and you may also roll over the mutual-fund IRA to a different traditional IRA. However, neither of the new IRAs may be rolled over again within the one-year period starting on the date that you received the distribution from the original traditional IRA.

There is an exception to the one-year waiting period between rollovers if the second distribution is made from an insolvent financial institution by the FDIC (Federal Deposit Insurance Corporation) acting as receiver. The exception applies only if the receiver makes the distribution to you because it is unable to find a buyer for the insolvent institution.

Note: A *direct transfer* may be used as discussed above if you want to invest in another IRA within the one-year period.

Deposits in insolvent financial institutions. The 60-day limit for completing a rollover is extended if the funds are "frozen" and may not be withdrawn from a bankrupt or insolvent financial institution. The 60-day period is extended while the account is frozen and you have a minimum of 10 days after the release of the funds to complete the rollover.

If a government agency takes control of an insolvent bank, you might receive an "involuntary" distribution of your IRA account from the agency. According to the IRS and Tax Court, such a payment is subject to the regular IRA distribution rules. For example, a couple received payment for their $11,000 IRA balance from the Maryland Deposit Insurance Fund after the bank in which the funds were invested became insolvent. The Tax Court held that the payment was taxable, even though the distribution was from a state insurance fund and not from the bank itself. Furthermore, since they were under age $59^1/_2$, the 10% penalty for early distributions *(8.12)* was imposed, even though the distribution was involuntary. The tax and penalty could have been avoided by making a rollover of the distribution within 60 days, but this was not done.

8.11 Transfer of Traditional IRA to Spouse at Divorce or Death

If you receive your former spouse's IRA pursuant to a divorce decree or written instrument incident to the decree, the transfer is not taxable to either of you. From the date of transfer the account is treated as your IRA. If you are legally separated, a transfer of your spouse's IRA to you is tax free if made under a decree of separate maintenance or written instrument incident to the decree. The transferred account is then treated as your IRA.

How to make a divorce-related transfer. If you are required to transfer IRA assets to your spouse or former spouse by a decree of divorce or separate maintenance, or a written instrument incident to such a decree, use one of these transfer methods to avoid being taxed on the transfer: (1) change the name on the IRA from your name to the name of your spouse or former spouse, or (2) direct your IRA trustee to transfer the IRA assets directly to the trustee of a new or existing IRA in the name of your spouse or former spouse.

If you simply withdraw money from your IRA and pay it to your spouse, you will be treated as having received a taxable distribution from your IRA. If you are under age $59^1/_2$, you will be subject to the 10% early distribution penalty as well as regular tax on the withdrawal.

QDRO transfer of employer plan benefits to your IRA. If you receive your share of your spouse's or former spouse's benefits from an employer plan under a qualified domestic relations order (QDRO), the distribution is taxable to you unless you roll it over to a traditional IRA or another eligible retirement plan *(7.8)*. Special averaging may be available; *see 7.12*. If you roll over only part of a qualifying QDRO distribution, you figure the tax on the retained portion by taking into account a prorated share of your former spouse's cost investment.

Surviving spouse. If you inherit your spouse's IRA when he or she dies, you may elect to treat the IRA as your own, or you may receive distributions from the account as a beneficiary. *See 8.14* for a discussion of these options.

 Filing Tip

Reporting a Rollover on Your 2002 Return

If you rolled over a qualifying distribution from an employer plan to an IRA *(7.8)*, report the total distribution on Line 16a of Form 1040 or Line 12a of Form 1040A. Enter zero as the taxable amount on Line 16b or Line 12b if the entire amount was rolled over. If only part of the distribution was rolled over, enter the portion not rolled over on Line 16b or Line 12b. Write "Rollover" next to the line.

If you rolled over funds from one IRA to another, the total distribution should be reported on Line 15a of Form 1040 or Line 11a of Form 1040A. If the entire distribution was rolled over, enter zero as the taxable amount on Line 15b or Line 11b. Otherwise, enter the amount not rolled over on Line 15b or Line 11b. Write "Rollover" next to the line.

If you made a tax-free direct transfer from one IRA to another, you do not have to report it on your return.

8.12 Penalty for Traditional IRA Withdrawals Before Age 59¹/₂

You have to pay a 10% penalty if you receive a distribution from a traditional IRA before you are age 59¹/₂, *unless* (1) you make a qualifying rollover to another IRA *(8.10)*, (2) you are totally disabled, (3) you pay medical expenses exceeding 7.5% of adjusted gross income, (4) you receive unemployment compensation for at least 12 consecutive weeks and pay medical insurance premiums, (5) you pay qualified higher education expenses, (6) the distribution is $10,000 or less and used for qualified first-time home-buyer expenses, (7) the distribution is one of a series of payments being made under one of several annuity-type methods, (8) you are a beneficiary receiving IRA distributions following the death of the owner, or (9) the distribution was due to an IRS levy on your IRA.

The penalty is 10% of the taxable IRA distribution. For example, if before age 59¹/₂ you withdraw $3,000 from your traditional IRA, you must include the $3,000 as part of your taxable income and, in addition, pay a $300 penalty tax. If part of a premature distribution is tax free because it is allocable to nondeductible contributions *(see 8.9)* or rolled over to another IRA *(8.10)*, the 10% penalty applies only to the taxable portion of the distribution.

If you are subject to the 10% early distribution penalty but not to the penalties discussed at *8.7* and *8.13*, the penalty is entered directly on Form 1040, Line 58.

If you do not owe the penalty because you qualify for an exception, you may have to file Form 5329 with Form 1040, depending on whether the payer of the distribution correctly marked the exception in Box 7 of Form 1099-R. If you qualify for the annuity-method exception and the payer correctly indicated that exception by marking Code 2 in Box 7, you do not have to file Form 5329. Similarly, if you are the beneficiary of a deceased IRA owner and the payer has correctly noted that with Code 4 in Box 7, you do not have to file Form 5329 to claim the exception.

If you qualify for the disability exception *(see* below), it is unlikely that the payer will know of that fact and thus Code 3 (for the disability exception) will probably not be marked in Box 7 of Form 1099-R. In that case, you must file Form 5329 to claim the exception. You also must file Form 5329 if the annuity method or beneficiary exception applies but it is not coded in Box 7 of Form 1099-R.

If you rolled over your entire distribution within 60 days to another IRA *(8.10)*, the penalty does not apply and Form 5329 does not have to be filed.

Spousal beneficiaries. Beneficiaries are exempt from the pre–age 59¹/₂ penalty. If you inherit an IRA from your deceased spouse and elect to treat it as your *own* IRA as discussed at *8.14*, you are not eligible for the beneficiary exception; distributions from the account before you reach age 59¹/₂ will be subject to the penalty unless another exception applies. The beneficiary exception applies if the account is maintained in the name of your deceased spouse and you are receiving the distribution as a spousal beneficiary under the rules at *8.14*.

Disability exception. To qualify for the disability exception, you must be able to show that you have a physical or mental condition that can be expected to last indefinitely or result in death and that prevents you from engaging in "substantial gainful activity" similar to the type of work you were doing before the condition arose.

In one case, a 53-year-old stockbroker claimed that his IRA withdrawal of over $200,000 should be exempt from the 10% penalty because he suffered from mental depression. However, the Tax Court upheld the IRS imposition of the penalty because he continued to work as a stockbroker.

Medical expense exception. If you withdraw IRA funds in a year in which you pay substantial medical costs, part of the distribution may avoid the pre–age 59¹/₂ penalty. If your unreimbursed medical expenses in the year of the distribution exceed 7.5% of your adjusted gross income, the distribution, to the extent of the excess, is not subject to the penalty. The medical costs must be eligible for the itemized medical deduction *(see* Chapter 17), but the IRA penalty exception applies whether you itemize or claim the standard deduction.

Unemployed person's medical insurance exceptions. If you are unemployed and received unemployment benefits under Federal or state law for at least 12 consecutive weeks, you may make penalty-free IRA withdrawals to the extent of medical insurance premiums paid during the year for you, your spouse, and your dependents. The withdrawals may be made in the year the 12-week unemployment test is met, or in the following year. However, the penalty exception does not apply to distributions made more than 60 days after you return to the work force.

Self-employed persons who are ineligible by law for unemployment benefits may be treated as meeting the 12-week test, and thus eligible for the exception, under regulations to be issued by the IRS.

Planning Reminder

Medical Expense Penalty Exceptions

Two medical-related exceptions apply to the pre–age 59¹/₂ penalty. If in the year of the IRA distribution you pay deductible medical expenses that exceed 7.5% of your adjusted gross income, the penalty does not apply to distributions that exceed the 7.5% threshold.

The other exception applies to IRA owners who receive unemployment benefits for at least 12 consecutive weeks. If medical insurance premiums are paid in the year of the IRA distribution, the penalty does not apply to the extent of the premiums.

Higher education expenses exception. A penalty exception is allowed for IRA distributions that do not exceed higher education expenses, including graduate school costs, for you, your spouse, your or your spouse's children, or your or your spouse's grandchildren that you paid during the year of the IRA distribution. Eligible expenses include tuition, room and board for a person who is at least a half-time student, fees, books, supplies, and equipment.

First-time home-buyer expense exception. A penalty exception is allowed for up to $10,000 of qualifying "first-time" home-buyer expenses. The penalty does not apply to IRA distributions that are used within 120 days to buy, construct, or reconstruct a principal residence for you, your spouse, child, grandchild, or ancestor of you or your spouse. A qualifying first-time home-buyer is someone who did not have a present ownership interest in a principal residence in the two-year period before the acquisition of the new home. The exception applies only for $10,000 of home-buyer expenses. This is a lifetime cap per IRA owner and not an annual limit.

IRS levy. The 10% penalty does not apply to an "involuntary" distribution due to an IRS levy on your IRA.

Annuity Schedule Payments Avoid 10% Penalty

You may avoid the penalty if you are willing to receive annual distributions under one of the annuity-type methods discussed in this section. Before arranging an annuity-type schedule, consider these points: all of the payments will be taxable (unless allocable to nondeductible contributions, as discussed in *8.9*), and if you do not continue the payments for a minimum number of years, the IRS will impose the 10% penalty for all taxable payments received before age $59^1/_2$, plus interest charges.

The payments must continue for five years, or until you reach age $59^1/_2$, whichever period is *longer*. Thus, if you are in your 40s, you would have to continue the scheduled payments until you are age $59^1/_2$. If you are in your mid-50s, the minimum payout period is not as serious a burden, as you only need to continue the scheduled payments for a five-year period, starting with the date of the first distribution, provided that the period ends after you reach age $59^1/_2$. During this minimum period, the arranged annuity-type schedule may not be changed unless you become disabled. For example, taking a lump-sum distribution of your account balance before the end of the minimum payout period would trigger the retroactive penalty, plus interest charges. Increasing the payments by a cost-of-living adjustment will also trigger the penalty. After the minimum payout period, you can discontinue the payments or change the method without penalty.

The minimum payout period rules do not apply to totally disabled individuals or to beneficiaries of deceased IRA owners.

If you would like to take advantage of this penalty exception, you may apply one of the following three payout methods that have been approved by the IRS in private rulings:

1. *Life expectancy method.* This is the easiest method to figure but provides smaller annual payments than the other methods. Figure the annual withdrawal by dividing your account balance by your life expectancy or by the joint life and last survivor expectancy of you and your beneficiary.

For example, you are age 50 in 2003 and have an IRA of $100,000 at the beginning of the year. You may take a penalty-free payment of $2,924 in 2002 ($100,000 account balance ÷ 34.2 life expectancy). You may use the Beneficiary's Life Expectancy Table at *8.14*. The annual penalty-free amount will generally increase in later years, with the exact amount depending on your account balance and whether you recalculate your life expectancy under the table each year (based on your age) or you simply reduce your life expectancy by one for each year that has elapsed since the year that you received the first payment.

If instead of using your single life expectancy you used the joint life and last survivor expectancy of you and your beneficiary, the annual penalty-free amount would be smaller given the longer joint life expectancy. For example, if your beneficiary was age 45, your joint life and last survivor life expectancy would be 43.2 years (using ages 50 and 45), and the penalty-free withdrawal $2,315 ($100,000 account balance ÷ 43.2). *See* below for a sample section of the IRS joint life and last survivor life expectancy table. The full IRS table showing joint life and last survivor life expectancy is in IRS Publication 590 and can also be obtained from your IRA trustee.

If before 2002 you began receiving a series of payments using the life expectancy method, you may switch to the new life expectancy tables issued by the IRS as part of the final required minimum distribution regulations. The new single life table is shown at *8.14* and the new joint life and last survivor expectancy table is shown in part below and in full in IRS Publication 590.

Caution

Professional Advice Required
For Methods 2 and 3, you should get the assistance of a tax professional and an actuary to help plan a series of payments that will qualify for the penalty exception.

2. ***Amortization method.*** Under this method, you amortize your IRA account balance like a mortgage, using the same life expectancy as under Method 1 (your single life expectancy or the joint life and last survivor expectancy of you and your beneficiary) and a long-term interest rate that is reasonable when the payments commence. In private rulings, the IRS approved the use of interest rates based on federal rates, such as the applicable federal rate used for figuring minimum interest on seller-financed sales *(4.32)*, or the rate of interest under Pension Benefit Guaranty Corporation regulations.

Under the amortization method, the annual penalty-free withdrawal will be larger than under Method 1. For example, using an interest rate of 8% (assuming that is a reasonable rate), a 50-year-old with a $100,000 account balance may withdraw $8,679 without penalty in the first year, as opposed to $2,924 under Method 1. The payment in future years will depend on how life expectancy is adjusted.

3. ***Annuity factor method.*** This method is similar to the amortization method but it allows you to use insurance mortality tables (such as the UP-1984 Mortality Table) that project shorter life expectancy tables than the IRS life expectancy tables used under Methods 1 and 2. If an interest rate of 8% and the UP-1984 mortality table were used for a 50-year-old with a $100,000 account balance, the penalty-free withdrawal in the first year would be $9,002, as opposed to $2,924 under Method 1 or $8,679 under Method 2.

Joint Life and Last Survivor Life Expectancy
(see "Life expectancy method" on page 193)

Ages	30	31	32	33	34	35	36	37	38	39	40	41	42	43	44	45	46	47	48	49	50	51	52	53	54	55	56	57	58	59
30	60.2	59.7	59.2	58.8	58.4	58.0	57.6	57.3	57.0	56.7	56.4	56.1	55.9	55.7	55.5	55.3	55.1	55.0	54.8	54.7	54.6	54.5	54.4	54.3	54.2	54.1	54.0	54.0	53.9	53.8
31	59.7	59.2	58.7	58.2	57.8	57.4	57.0	56.6	56.3	56.0	55.7	55.4	55.2	54.9	54.7	54.5	54.3	54.1	54.0	53.8	53.7	53.6	53.5	53.4	53.3	53.2	53.1	53.0	53.0	52.9
32	59.2	58.7	58.2	57.7	57.2	56.8	56.4	56.0	55.6	55.3	55.0	54.7	54.4	54.2	53.9	53.7	53.5	53.3	53.2	53.0	52.9	52.7	52.6	52.5	52.4	52.3	52.2	52.1	52.1	52.0
33	58.8	58.2	57.7	57.2	56.7	56.2	55.8	55.4	55.0	54.7	54.3	54.0	53.7	53.4	53.2	52.9	52.7	52.5	52.3	52.2	52.0	51.9	51.7	51.6	51.5	51.4	51.3	51.2	51.2	51.1
34	58.4	57.8	57.2	56.7	56.2	55.7	55.3	54.8	54.4	54.0	53.7	53.3	53.0	52.7	52.4	52.2	52.0	51.7	51.5	51.4	51.2	51.0	50.9	50.8	50.6	50.5	50.4	50.3	50.3	50.2
35	58.0	57.4	56.8	56.2	55.7	55.2	54.7	54.3	53.8	53.4	53.0	52.7	52.3	52.0	51.7	51.5	51.2	51.0	50.8	50.6	50.4	50.2	50.0	49.9	49.8	49.7	49.5	49.4	49.4	49.3
36	57.6	57.0	56.4	55.8	55.3	54.7	54.2	53.7	53.3	52.8	52.4	52.0	51.7	51.3	51.0	50.7	50.5	50.2	50.0	49.8	49.6	49.4	49.2	49.1	48.9	48.8	48.7	48.6	48.5	48.4
37	57.3	56.6	56.0	55.4	54.8	54.3	53.7	53.2	52.7	52.3	51.8	51.4	51.1	50.7	50.4	50.0	49.8	49.5	49.2	49.0	48.8	48.6	48.4	48.2	48.1	47.9	47.8	47.7	47.6	47.5
38	57.0	56.3	55.6	55.0	54.4	53.8	53.3	52.7	52.2	51.7	51.3	50.9	50.4	50.1	49.7	49.4	49.1	48.8	48.5	48.2	48.0	47.8	47.6	47.4	47.2	47.1	47.0	46.8	46.7	46.6
39	56.7	56.0	55.3	54.7	54.0	53.4	52.8	52.3	51.7	51.2	50.8	50.3	49.9	49.5	49.1	48.7	48.4	48.1	47.8	47.5	47.3	47.0	46.8	46.6	46.4	46.3	46.1	46.0	45.8	45.7
40	56.4	55.7	55.0	54.3	53.7	53.0	52.4	51.8	51.3	50.8	50.2	49.8	49.3	48.9	48.5	48.1	47.7	47.4	47.1	46.8	46.5	46.3	46.0	45.8	45.6	45.5	45.3	45.1	45.0	44.9
41	56.1	55.4	54.7	54.0	53.3	52.7	52.0	51.4	50.9	50.3	49.8	49.3	48.8	48.3	47.9	47.5	47.1	46.7	46.4	46.1	45.8	45.5	45.3	45.1	44.8	44.7	44.5	44.3	44.2	44.0
42	55.9	55.2	54.4	53.7	53.0	52.3	51.7	51.1	50.4	49.9	49.3	48.8	48.3	47.8	47.3	46.9	46.5	46.1	45.8	45.4	45.1	44.8	44.6	44.3	44.1	43.9	43.7	43.5	43.3	43.2
43	55.7	54.9	54.2	53.4	52.7	52.0	51.3	50.7	50.1	49.5	48.9	48.3	47.8	47.3	46.8	46.3	45.9	45.5	45.1	44.8	44.4	44.1	43.8	43.6	43.3	43.1	42.9	42.7	42.5	42.4
44	55.5	54.7	53.9	53.2	52.4	51.7	51.0	50.4	49.7	49.1	48.5	47.9	47.3	46.8	46.3	45.8	45.4	44.9	44.5	44.2	43.8	43.5	43.2	42.9	42.6	42.4	42.1	41.9	41.7	41.5
45	55.3	54.5	53.7	52.9	52.2	51.5	50.7	50.0	49.4	48.7	48.1	47.5	46.9	46.3	45.8	45.3	44.8	44.4	44.0	43.6	43.2	42.8	42.5	42.2	41.9	41.6	41.4	41.2	40.9	40.7
46	55.1	54.3	53.5	52.7	52.0	51.2	50.5	49.8	49.1	48.4	47.7	47.1	46.5	45.9	45.4	44.8	44.3	43.9	43.4	43.0	42.6	42.2	41.8	41.5	41.2	40.9	40.7	40.4	40.2	40.0
47	55.0	54.1	53.3	52.5	51.7	51.0	50.2	49.5	48.8	48.1	47.4	46.7	46.1	45.5	44.9	44.4	43.9	43.4	42.9	42.4	42.0	41.6	41.2	40.9	40.5	40.2	40.0	39.7	39.4	39.2
48	54.8	54.0	53.2	52.3	51.5	50.8	50.0	49.2	48.5	47.8	47.1	46.4	45.8	45.1	44.5	44.0	43.4	42.9	42.4	41.9	41.5	41.0	40.6	40.3	39.9	39.6	39.3	39.0	38.7	38.5
49	54.7	53.8	53.0	52.2	51.4	50.6	49.8	49.0	48.2	47.5	46.8	46.1	45.4	44.8	44.2	43.6	43.0	42.4	41.9	41.4	40.9	40.5	40.1	39.7	39.3	38.9	38.6	38.3	38.0	37.8
50	54.6	53.7	52.9	52.0	51.2	50.4	49.6	48.8	48.0	47.3	46.5	45.8	45.1	44.4	43.8	43.2	42.6	42.0	41.5	40.9	40.4	40.0	39.5	39.1	38.7	38.3	38.0	37.6	37.3	37.1
51	54.5	53.6	52.7	51.9	51.0	50.2	49.4	48.6	47.8	47.0	46.3	45.5	44.8	44.1	43.5	42.8	42.2	41.6	41.0	40.5	40.0	39.5	39.0	38.5	38.1	37.7	37.4	37.0	36.7	36.4
52	54.4	53.5	52.6	51.7	50.9	50.0	49.2	48.4	47.6	46.8	46.0	45.3	44.6	43.8	43.2	42.5	41.8	41.2	40.6	40.1	39.5	39.0	38.5	38.0	37.6	37.2	36.8	36.4	36.0	35.7
53	54.3	53.4	52.5	51.6	50.8	49.9	49.1	48.2	47.4	46.6	45.8	45.1	44.3	43.6	42.9	42.2	41.5	40.9	40.3	39.7	39.1	38.5	38.0	37.5	37.1	36.6	36.2	35.8	35.4	35.1
54	54.2	53.3	52.4	51.5	50.6	49.8	48.9	48.1	47.2	46.4	45.6	44.8	44.1	43.3	42.6	41.9	41.2	40.5	39.9	39.3	38.7	38.1	37.6	37.1	36.6	36.1	35.7	35.2	34.8	34.5
55	54.1	53.2	52.3	51.4	50.5	49.7	48.8	47.9	47.1	46.3	45.5	44.7	43.9	43.1	42.4	41.6	40.9	40.2	39.6	38.9	38.3	37.7	37.2	36.6	36.1	35.6	35.1	34.7	34.3	33.9
56	54.0	53.1	52.2	51.3	50.4	49.5	48.7	47.8	47.0	46.1	45.3	44.5	43.7	42.9	42.1	41.4	40.7	40.0	39.3	38.6	38.0	37.4	36.8	36.2	35.7	35.1	34.7	34.2	33.7	33.3
57	54.0	53.0	52.1	51.2	50.3	49.4	48.6	47.7	46.8	46.0	45.1	44.3	43.5	42.7	41.9	41.2	40.4	39.7	39.0	38.3	37.6	37.0	36.4	35.8	35.2	34.7	34.2	33.7	33.2	32.8
58	53.9	53.0	52.1	51.2	50.3	49.4	48.5	47.6	46.7	45.8	45.0	44.2	43.3	42.5	41.7	40.9	40.2	39.4	38.7	38.0	37.3	36.7	36.0	35.4	34.8	34.3	33.7	33.2	32.8	32.3
59	53.8	52.9	52.0	51.1	50.2	49.3	48.4	47.5	46.6	45.7	44.9	44.0	43.2	42.4	41.5	40.7	40.0	39.2	38.5	37.8	37.1	36.4	35.7	35.1	34.5	33.9	33.3	32.8	32.3	31.8

8.13 Mandatory Distributions From a Traditional IRA After Age 70 $^1/_2$

By April 1 of the year following the year in which you reach age 70$^1/_2$, you have to start receiving annual IRA distributions under a schedule that meets tax law tests. If you do not receive the minimum amount required by the tax law, a penalty tax of 50% applies to the difference between the minimum amount you should have received and the amount you did receive. The penalty is reported on Form 5329, which must be attached to Form 1040. The minimum distribution rules apply to account owners of traditional IRAs, as discussed in this section, and to beneficiaries of traditional IRAs, as discussed in *8.14*. Roth IRA owners *(8.19)* are not subject to minimum distribution requirements, but beneficiaries of Roth IRAs are *(8.24)*.

EXAMPLE

During 2003, Chris Calano reaches age 70$^1/_2$ and receives $3,000 from his traditional IRA. The required minimum distribution was $3,817. He must pay a penalty tax of $409 (50% of $817), unless it is waived by the IRS.

When must your first required minimum distribution be received? Your required beginning date is April 1 of the year following the year in which you reach age 70$^1/_2$. For example, if you reached age 70$^1/_2$ during 2002, you may receive a minimum distribution for 2002 during 2002 or you may delay it until 2003 so long as it is received no later than April 1, 2003. You will also have to receive a minimum distribution for 2003 by December 31, 2003. Thus, if you do not take your first distribution during 2002, and wait until between January 1 and April 1, 2003, you will have to take two distributions in 2003, one by April 1 and another by December 31. This could increase your 2003 taxable income substantially. Distributions for later years must be taken by December 31 of each year.

If you reach age 70$^1/_2$ during 2003, your first distribution must be no later than April 1, 2004. If you have an individual retirement annuity, your insurance company should gear your payments to meet minimum distribution requirements.

New IRS Rules Simplify and Generally Reduce Required Minimum Distributions From Traditional IRAs, SEP IRAs, and SIMPLE IRAs

Your IRA trustee may help you figure how much you must withdraw from your traditional IRA for 2002 to avoid an IRS penalty. If that does not happen and you must figure the required minimum distribution yourself, you can use the final IRS regulations released in April 2002. The final regulations may be used to figure your required minimum distributions for 2002 and must be used for 2003 and later years. If you have been receiving required minimum distributions from your IRAs under the prior IRS rules, you may switch to the new rules for figuring the required minimum distribution for 2002 that you must receive by December 31, 2002. SEP IRAs and SIMPLE IRAs are treated as traditional IRAs for purposes of the required minimum distribution rules. You may figure the required minimum distribution for 2002 using either the 2001 proposed regulations or the prior proposed regulations from 1987, but electing to apply the final regulations is generally advantageous. The following discussion is based on the final regulations.

For years after 2002, you will not have to figure your required minimum distribution yourself, as discussed in the next paragraph.

Reporting requirement for IRA trustees and custodians begins in 2003. By January 31, 2003, your IRA trustee or custodian must either tell you what your required minimum distribution for 2003 is, or remind you that a minimum distribution is required and offer to compute the amount for you upon your request.

IRA trustees and custodians report to the IRS (and to you) on Forms 5498 the value of your IRAs as of the end of the year and any contributions made for the year. On Form 5498 for 2003, which will be filed in 2004, IRA trustees and custodians must indicate whether a minimum distribution from your account is required for 2004, but the amount does not have to be shown. This will put the IRS on notice that you are due a required minimum distribution.

For the moment, these reporting rules apply only to IRA owners and not to inherited IRAs, but reporting may be extended to beneficiaries at a later date.

 IRS Alert

New IRS Rules for Figuring Required Minimum Distributions

IRS final regulations issued in April 2002 simplify the calculation of required minimum distributions and reduce for many IRA owners the minimum amount that must be withdrawn from traditional IRAs. The new rules may be used by IRA owners to figure the required minimum distribution for 2002, and must be used starting in 2003. The final regulations follow the approach of proposed regulations issued in January 2001, but new life expectancy tables were released with the final regulations. The new tables reflect slightly longer life expectancy periods that allow a small reduction in the required minimum distributions.

Importance of reviewing your beneficiary designations. As discussed below, the amount of required minimum distributions during your lifetime under the final regulations is not affected by the identity of your beneficiary (or beneficiaries) unless your sole beneficiary is your spouse who is more than 10 years younger than you are. However, after your death, your beneficiary designations assume importance not only for determining who will receive the funds but also for purposes of determining the maximum period of years over which distributions can be spread. You should review your beneficiary designations and if you have not done so, name a successor (contingent) beneficiary for each of your IRAs should your primary beneficiary predecease you. The maximum distribution period after your death will depend on the determination of the designated beneficiary as of September 30 of the year following the year of your death. For example, if the designated beneficary for the account is an individual, the maximum distribution period will be his or her life expectancy. However, if your estate was named as the beneficiary, the estate would not be a designated beneficiary and the heir who inherits the account through the estate could not extend distributions over his or her life expectancy. Depending on whether your death was before or after your required beginning date, the heir would have to withdraw the entire account within five years or over your remaining life expectancy figured as of the year of death. *See 8.14* for details on determining the designated beneficiary and the payout rules for inherited IRAs.

Figuring Your Required Minimum Distributions

Most IRA owners use the uniform table. Under the new IRS rules, required minimum distributions are figured the same way by all IRA owners except for those whose sole beneficiary is a spouse more than 10 years younger.

A uniform life expectancy table provides a distribution period based only on the IRA owner's age. The Uniform Lifetime Table shown on page 198 assumes that every account holder has a beneficiary exactly 10 years younger than he or she is, regardless of who is named as beneficiary, or even if no beneficiary has been designated when required minimum distributions begin.

There is only one exception to use of the uniform table. You do not use the uniform table if your spouse is the sole beneficiary of your IRA for the entire year, and he or she is more than 10 years younger than you are. In this case, your required minimum distribution is based on the actual joint life expectancy of you and your spouse, giving you a longer distribution period than that provided by the uniform table, which assumes a 10-year age differential between IRA owner and beneficiary.

See Step 2 below for applying the uniform life expectancy table or the joint life and last survivor expectancy table if the exception for more-than-10-years-younger spousal beneficiaries applies.

Steps for figuring your required minimum distribution. For each of your traditional IRAs, figure the required minimum distribution you must receive using the following steps. Keep in mind that once you have separately determined the required minimum distribution for each IRA, the IRS allows you to withdraw the total required minimum distribution for the year from any of the accounts in any combination you choose.

Step 1: Find the account balance of your IRA as of the previous December 31. If you reach age 70$^1/_2$ during 2002, the account balance to be used for figuring your first required minimum distribution is the account balance for December 31, 2001, even if the actual distribution for 2002 is not made until the first quarter of 2003 (January 1–April 1). For purposes of figuring your required minimum distribution for 2003, use the 2002 year-end balance, even if you took the first-year distribution in the first quarter of 2003.

Step 2: Divide the account balance (Step 1) by the applicable life expectancy. As discussed above, your life expectancy under the new IRS rules is taken from the uniform life expectancy table unless your sole beneficiary is your spouse who is more than 10 years younger than you are. The Uniform Lifetime Table, shown on page 198, provides a joint life expectancy for you and a "deemed" beneficiary who is exactly 10 years younger than you are. Your beneficiary's actual age does not matter. The life expectancy period from the uniform table applies even if you have not named a beneficiary as of your required beginning date (April 1 of the year after the year you reach age 70$^1/_2$). Furthermore, you continue to use the uniform table even if you change your beneficiary or beneficiaries after starting to receive minimum required distributions, unless the change results in the naming of your spouse as sole beneficiary for the entire year and you qualify to use the joint life and last survivor expectancy table because your spouse is more than 10 years younger than you are.

Your "deemed" life expectancy from the uniform table is the number of years listed next to your age on your birthday in the year for which you are making the computation. For example, if you are figuring your required minimum distribution for 2002, and you are age 71 on your birthday in 2002, your life expectancy from the table, based on age 71, is 26.5 years. For 2003, your life expectancy from the table, using age 72, will be 25.6 years.

Exception for younger spouses. If the sole beneficiary of your IRA is your spouse and he or she is more than 10 years younger than you are, do not use the uniform table. Use the actual joint life expectancy of you and your spouse, which will allow you to spread out distributions over an even longer period. This rule applies only if your spouse meets the age test and is the sole beneficiary of your entire interest in the IRA at all times during the calendar year for which the required minimum distribution is being figured. If your spouse is named beneficiary during the year or he or she is one of several beneficiaries on the account, the uniform table must be used for that year. Your spouse would not meet the sole beneficiary test. However, if you are married on January 1 of a year and during the year you divorce or your spouse dies, you are considered married for the entire year and may use the spousal exception to figure that year's required minimum distribution using the joint life table.

If the exception for spousal beneficiaries applies, find your joint life expectancy from the IRS table corresponding to both of your ages on your birthdays for the year of the computation. For example, if you are age 71 on your birthday in 2002 and your spouse on his or her birthday is age 58, use a joint life expectancy of 28.6 years to figure your required minimum distribution for 2002. This is more than the 26.5-year distribution period provided by the uniform table for a 71-year-old. *See* page 199 for a sample section of the joint life and last survivor expectancy table from IRS Publication 590.

Step 3: If you have more than one IRA, total the required minimum distributions for all the accounts. After figuring the required minimum distribution for each of your IRAs under Step 2, total the amounts. This is the minimum you must receive for the year; you are, of course, free to withdraw more than that. Although you must calculate the minimum required distribution separately for each account, you do not have to make withdrawals from each of them. The total minimum required distribution from all accounts may be taken from any one account, or more than one account if you prefer. For example, if you have five bank IRAs, you may take the entire required distribution from the bank where you have the largest balance, or from any other combination of banks. *See* Example 3 below. The entire distribution is taxable unless part is allocable to nondeductible IRA contributions, as explained in *8.9.*

EXAMPLES

1. John Smith reached age 70½ in 2001 and used the uniform table in the 2001 proposed regulations to take his first required minimum distribution. His primary IRA beneficiary is his wife, Jane. On their birthdays in 2002, John is age 72 and Jane is 70. The balance in John's IRA at the end of 2001 was $300,000.

   To figure the required minimum distribution for 2002 under final IRS regulations, John looks in the Uniform Lifetime Table (page 198) next to his age to find a life expectancy of 25.6 years. Although Jane is 70, the uniform table provides a deemed joint life expectancy of 25.6 years on the assumption that John's beneficiary is 62, 10 years younger than he is. John's required minimum distribution for 2002 under the new rules, which he must receive by December 31, 2002, is $11,719 ($300,000 ÷ 25.6). By electing to use the new uniform table provided under the final regulations, John can slightly reduce his required minimum distribution for 2002. Under the table used with the 2001 proposed regulations, John's deemed life expectancy would be 24.4 years and his required minimum distribution would be $12,295. The difference is only $576, but by reducing the required distribution, John's tax liability for 2002 is also reduced. Use of the final regulations is optional for 2002 but mandatory for 2003 and later years.

2. Joe Blake reached age 70½ in March 2002. A minimum distribution for 2002 must be received from his traditional IRA by April 1, 2003. As of December 31, 2001, Joe's IRA balance was $200,000. The 2001 year-end balance is used in the computation even if the distribution for 2002 is made in the first quarter of 2003 (by the April 1 deadline). Joe's beneficiary is his wife, who is age 63 on her birthday in 2002. On his 2002 birthday, Joe is age 71. Here is how Joe figures his required minimum distribution for 2002 under the final IRS regulations:

Step 1. Account balance of $200,000.

Step 2. Based on Joe's age of 71, the life expectancy from the uniform table is 26.5 years. The table assumes that Joe has a beneficiary who is age 61 (10 years younger than he is). The fact that his wife is age 63 does not matter.

Step 3. Divide Step 1 by Step 2.

$200,000 ÷ 26.5 = $7,547. Joe must receive the $7,547 by April 1, 2003.

The second minimum distribution, due by December 31, 2003, is based upon the 2002 year-end account balance, even if the distribution for 2002 was not made until early 2003 (by April 1).

3. Cynthia Lowell has two IRAs. She reached age 70$\frac{1}{2}$ on January 15, 2002, and thus must receive her first distribution by April 1, 2003. The beneficiary of IRA-1 is her brother, who is age 61 on his birthday in 2002; the account balance of IRA-1 as of December 31, 2001, was $100,000. The beneficiary of IRA-2 is her husband, who was age 74 on his birthday in 2002; the account balance of IRA-2 at the end of 2001 was $10,000.

To figure her required minimum distribution for 2002, Cynthia uses the IRS's uniform table. The ages of her beneficiaries do not affect the computation.

IRA-1: Under the new IRS rules, the first minimum required distribution is $3,774. This is the account balance of $100,000 divided by 26.5, the life expectancy from the uniform table for a person age 71 (Cynthia's age on her birthday in 2002).

IRA-2: Under the new IRS rules, the first minimum required distribution is $377, the account balance of $10,000 divided by 26.5, the life expectancy from the uniform table, using age 71.

The total required distribution of $4,151 from both IRAs must be received by April 1, 2003. Cynthia may withdraw the money from either one or both of the IRAs.

Uniform Lifetime Table*

IRA Owner's Age	Distribution Period	IRA Owner's Age	Distribution Period
70	27.4	93	9.6
71	26.5	94	9.1
72	25.6	95	8.6
73	24.7	96	8.1
74	23.8	97	7.6
75	22.9	98	7.1
76	22.0	99	6.7
77	21.2	100	6.3
78	20.3	101	5.9
79	19.5	102	5.5
80	18.7	103	5.2
81	17.9	104	4.9
82	17.1	105	4.5
83	16.3	106	4.2
84	15.5	107	3.9
85	14.8	108	3.7
86	14.1	109	3.4
87	13.4	110	3.1
88	12.7	111	2.9
89	12.0	112	2.6
90	11.4	113	2.4
91	10.8	114	2.1
92	10.2	115 and over	1.9

*Use this table unless your spouse is your sole IRA beneficiary who is more than 10 years younger than you are. In this case, use the IRS's joint life and last survivor expectancy table with the actual ages of both spouses (see the sample table on the next page), which will provide a longer life expectancy distribution period than the above table provides.

Joint Life and Last Survivor Expectancy Table
(for use by owners whose spouses are more than 10 years younger)*

Age	70	71	72	73	74	75	76	77	78	79	80	81	82	83	84	85	86	87	88	89	90
35	48.7	48.7	48.7	48.6	48.6	48.6	48.6	48.6	48.6	48.6	48.5	48.5	48.5	48.5	48.5	48.5	48.5	48.5	48.5	48.5	48.5
36	47.8	47.7	47.7	47.7	47.7	47.7	47.6	47.6	47.6	47.6	47.6	47.6	47.6	47.6	47.6	47.5	47.5	47.5	47.5	47.5	47.5
37	46.8	46.8	46.8	46.7	46.7	46.7	46.7	46.7	46.6	46.6	46.6	46.6	46.6	46.6	46.6	46.6	46.6	46.6	46.6	46.6	46.6
38	45.9	45.9	45.8	45.8	45.8	45.7	45.7	45.7	45.7	45.7	45.7	45.7	45.6	45.6	45.6	45.6	45.6	45.6	45.6	45.6	45.6
39	44.9	44.9	44.9	44.8	44.8	44.8	44.8	44.8	44.7	44.7	44.7	44.7	44.7	44.7	44.7	44.7	44.6	44.6	44.6	44.6	44.6
40	44.0	44.0	43.9	43.9	43.9	43.8	43.8	43.8	43.8	43.8	43.7	43.7	43.7	43.7	43.7	43.7	43.7	43.7	43.7	43.7	43.7
41	43.1	43.0	43.0	43.0	42.9	42.9	42.9	42.9	42.8	42.8	42.8	42.8	42.8	42.8	42.7	42.7	42.7	42.7	42.7	42.7	42.7
42	42.2	42.1	42.1	42.0	42.0	42.0	41.9	41.9	41.9	41.9	41.8	41.8	41.8	41.8	41.8	41.8	41.8	41.8	41.8	41.7	41.7
43	41.3	41.2	41.1	41.1	41.1	41.0	41.0	41.0	40.9	40.9	40.9	40.9	40.9	40.9	40.8	40.8	40.8	40.8	40.8	40.8	40.8
44	40.3	40.3	40.2	40.2	40.1	40.1	40.1	40.0	40.0	40.0	40.0	39.9	39.9	39.9	39.9	39.9	39.9	39.9	39.9	39.8	39.8
45	39.4	39.4	39.3	39.3	39.2	39.2	39.1	39.1	39.1	39.1	39.0	39.0	39.0	39.0	39.0	38.9	38.9	38.9	38.9	38.9	38.9
46	38.6	38.5	38.4	38.4	38.3	38.3	38.2	38.2	38.2	38.1	38.1	38.1	38.1	38.0	38.0	38.0	38.0	38.0	38.0	38.0	38.0
47	37.7	37.6	37.5	37.5	37.4	37.4	37.3	37.3	37.2	37.2	37.2	37.2	37.1	37.1	37.1	37.1	37.1	37.0	37.0	37.0	37.0
48	36.8	36.7	36.6	36.6	36.5	36.5	36.4	36.4	36.3	36.3	36.3	36.2	36.2	36.2	36.2	36.2	36.1	36.1	36.1	36.1	36.1
49	35.9	35.9	35.8	35.7	35.6	35.6	35.5	35.5	35.4	35.4	35.4	35.3	35.3	35.3	35.3	35.2	35.2	35.2	35.2	35.2	35.2
50	35.1	35.0	34.9	34.8	34.8	34.7	34.6	34.6	34.5	34.5	34.5	34.4	34.4	34.4	34.3	34.3	34.3	34.3	34.3	34.3	34.2
51	34.3	34.2	34.1	34.0	33.9	33.8	33.8	33.7	33.6	33.6	33.6	33.5	33.5	33.5	33.4	33.4	33.4	33.4	33.4	33.3	33.3
52	33.4	33.3	33.2	33.1	33.0	33.0	32.9	32.8	32.8	32.7	32.7	32.6	32.6	32.6	32.5	32.5	32.5	32.5	32.5	32.4	32.4
53	32.6	32.5	32.4	32.3	32.2	32.1	32.0	32.0	31.9	31.8	31.8	31.8	31.7	31.7	31.7	31.6	31.6	31.6	31.6	31.5	31.5
54	31.8	31.7	31.6	31.5	31.4	31.3	31.2	31.1	31.0	31.0	30.9	30.9	30.8	30.8	30.8	30.7	30.7	30.7	30.7	30.7	30.6
55	31.1	30.9	30.8	30.6	30.5	30.4	30.3	30.3	30.2	30.1	30.1	30.0	30.0	29.9	29.9	29.9	29.8	29.8	29.8	29.8	29.8
56	30.3	30.1	30.0	29.8	29.7	29.6	29.5	29.4	29.3	29.3	29.2	29.2	29.1	29.1	29.0	29.0	29.0	28.9	28.9	28.9	28.9
57	29.5	29.4	29.2	29.1	28.9	28.8	28.7	28.6	28.5	28.4	28.4	28.3	28.3	28.2	28.2	28.1	28.1	28.1	28.0	28.0	28.0
58	28.8	28.6	28.4	28.3	28.1	28.0	27.9	27.8	27.7	27.6	27.5	27.5	27.4	27.4	27.3	27.3	27.2	27.2	27.2	27.2	27.1
59	28.1	27.9	27.7	27.5	27.4	27.2	27.1	27.0	26.9	26.8	26.7	26.6	26.6	26.5	26.5	26.4	26.4	26.4	26.3	26.3	26.3
60		27.2	27.0	26.8	26.6	26.5	26.3	26.2	26.1	26.0	25.9	25.8	25.8	25.7	25.6	25.6	25.5	25.5	25.5	25.4	25.4
61			26.3	26.1	25.9	25.7	25.6	25.4	25.3	25.2	25.1	25.0	24.9	24.9	24.8	24.8	24.7	24.7	24.6	24.6	24.6
62				25.4	25.2	25.0	24.8	24.7	24.6	24.4	24.3	24.2	24.1	24.1	24.0	23.9	23.9	23.8	23.8	23.8	23.7
63					24.5	24.3	24.1	23.9	23.8	23.7	23.6	23.4	23.4	23.3	23.2	23.1	23.1	23.0	23.0	22.9	22.9
64						23.6	23.4	23.2	23.1	22.9	22.8	22.7	22.6	22.5	22.4	22.3	22.3	22.2	22.2	22.1	22.1
65							22.7	22.5	22.4	22.2	22.1	21.9	21.8	21.7	21.6	21.6	21.5	21.4	21.4	21.3	21.3
66								21.8	21.7	21.5	21.3	21.2	21.1	21.0	20.9	20.8	20.7	20.7	20.6	20.5	20.5
67									21.0	20.8	20.6	20.5	20.4	20.2	20.1	20.1	20.0	19.9	19.8	19.8	19.7
68										20.1	20.0	19.8	19.7	19.5	19.4	19.3	19.2	19.2	19.1	19.0	19.0
69											19.3	19.1	19.0	18.8	18.7	18.6	18.5	18.4	18.3	18.3	18.2
70												18.5	18.3	18.2	18.0	17.9	17.8	17.7	17.6	17.6	17.5
71													17.7	17.5	17.4	17.3	17.1	17.0	16.9	16.9	16.8
72														16.9	16.7	16.6	16.5	16.4	16.3	16.2	16.1
73															16.1	16.0	15.8	15.7	15.6	15.5	15.4
74																15.4	15.2	15.1	15.0	14.9	14.8
75																	14.6	14.5	14.4	14.3	14.2
76																		13.9	13.8	13.7	13.6
77																			13.2	13.1	13.0
78																				12.6	12.4
79																					11.9

*Use this table to figure your required minimum distribution only if your spouse is your sole beneficiary and is more than 10 years younger than you are; see 8.13. Find your age (as of your birthday for the year you are making the computation) on the horizontal line and your spousal beneficiary's age in the vertical column. For example, if you are age 74 and your spousal beneficiary is 63, the life expectancy factor is 23.3. If your age or your spouse's age is not shown here, refer to IRS Publication 590.

Caution

Estate as Beneficiary

If you have your estate as beneficiary of your IRA and you die before your required beginning date, the entire account must be withdrawn by the fifth year following the year of your death. If you die on or after the required beginning date, the account must be distributed over the balance of your single life expectancy, determined by your age in the year of death. *See* the table on page 203.

8.14 Inherited Traditional IRAs

Although inheritances are generally tax free *(11.4)*, distributions that you receive as a beneficiary of a traditional IRA are taxable. However, if the account owner made nondeductible contributions to the account, distributions allocable to those contributions on Form 8606 are tax free under the rules at *8.6*. Taxable distributions received as a beneficiary are *not* subject to the 10% penalty for distributions received before age $59^1/_2$ *(8.12)*.

You must receive required minimum distributions from the inherited account. If you are the "designated beneficiary" as determined under the final IRS regulations discussed below, distributions may be spread over your life expectancy. If the required minimum distribution for a year is not received, you are subject to a penalty tax of 50% on the difference between the required minimum amount and the amount actually received. You may, of course, accelerate payments and receive more than the required minimum distribution. A surviving spouse beneficiary may elect to treat the account as his or her own IRA or roll it over to his or her own IRA; this option is not available to nonspouse beneficiaries.

A beneficiary of a Roth IRA must also receive required minimum distributions but under different rules. Furthermore, the distributions are generally taxable only if the Roth IRA owner dies within the first five years after establishing the Roth IRA and account earnings are received by the beneficiary within the five-year period; *see 8.24*.

Final Regulations Clarify Distribution Rules for Traditional IRA Beneficiaries

The final IRS regulations released in April 2002 establish new distribution rules for beneficiaries of deceased IRA owners. The rules for beneficiaries are considerably more complicated than the new simplified calculations for IRA owners *(see 8.13)*, but for many beneficiaries they are more favorable than the prior rules, allowing them to extend the period over which distributions can be spread. This is not true in all cases, and for beneficiaries receiving distributions under the prior rules, the required minimum distributions may actually increase in 2003 when use of the final regulations is mandatory. Use of the final regulations is optional for purposes of figuring 2002 required distributions.

The final regulations made technical changes to the 2001 proposed regulations. Many of the changes involve the determination of the "designated" beneficiary, which in turn determines the *maximum period* over which required minimum distributions can be spread following the account holder's death. In general, required minimum distributions are payable over the single life expectancy of the designated beneficiary. The final regulations include a revised single life expectancy table, shown at the end of this section, which reflects slightly longer life expectancies than the old table.

Distribution period depends on identity of designated beneficiary as of September 30 of year following year of IRA owner's death. Any individual named by the IRA owner as a beneficiary can be a designated beneficiary, but for purposes of determining the maximum period over which required minimum distributions are payable, there can be only one "designated" beneficiary for each traditional IRA. Under the final IRS regulations, the determination of the designated beneficiary is not made until September 30 of the year following the year of the IRA owner's death. The 2001 proposed regulations had set the determination date as December 31 of the year following the year of the account owner's death, but this created a practical problem because that is also the date by which nonspouse beneficiaries must receive their first required minimum distribution. The final regulations change the determination date to September 30 of the year following the year of the owner's death. Moving up the determination date by three months provides more time to calculate and distribute the first required minimum distribution.

A designated beneficiary must be an individual named by the account owner or designated under the plan as of the date of death. A beneficiary named through an estate, either under the owner's will or by state law, cannot be a designated beneficiary for required minimum distribution purposes. An estate or a charity cannot be a designated beneficiary. Trust beneficiaries may qualify if certain tests are met, as discussed below.

The delay in determining the designated beneficiary does *not* mean that new beneficiaries can be added after the owner's death. However, after the account owner's death and prior to the September 30 determination date, a beneficiary named as of the date of death can be eliminated by means of the beneficiary's qualified disclaimer or distribution of the beneficiary's benefit. For example, a qualified written disclaimer made no later than nine months after the IRA owner's death (and before any benefits have been received) can be used by an older primary beneficiary to pass an

IRA to a younger contingent beneficiary. The disclaimer, made by the September 30 determination date, leaves the younger beneficiary as the designated beneficiary, thereby allowing required minimum distributions to be spread out over his or her longer life expectancy. An estate may *not* disclaim its interest in order to create a designated beneficiary. A beneficiary's interest can also be cashed out by the September 30 determination date, leaving the balance to other co-beneficiaries named by the owner. For example, if a charity and an individual are named as co-beneficiaries, and the charity's interest is cashed out by the September 30 determination date, the remaining beneficiary can use his or her life expectancy to figure required minimum distributions.

Splitting account among multiple beneficiaries. If as of the September 30 date there is more than one individual designated beneficiary and the account has *not* been split into separate accounts for each of them, the oldest beneficiary is considered to be the designated beneficiary. In that case, the oldest beneficiary's life expectancy (i.e., the shortest life expectancy) is the period over which all the beneficiaries must receive required minimum distributions.

The final regulations state that the account may be split into separate accounts by December 31 of the year following the year of the owner's death to allow each individual beneficiary to take distributions over his or her own life expectancy. Given the inconsistency between this December 31 deadline and the September 30 determination date, it is advisable to establish the separate accounts by the September 30 date to ensure separate life expectancies.

Individual and non-individual beneficiary for same account. If as of the September 30 determination date there is a *non-individual* beneficiary other than a qualifying trust, as well as one or more individual beneficiaries, the owner is treated as *not* having a designated beneficiary. If the owner's death was after his or her required beginning date (April 1 of the year after the year age $70^1/_2$ is reached), the regulations require minimum distributions to be made over the owner's remaining life expectancy. If the owner died before the required beginning date without a designated beneficiary, the entire account must be distributed by the end of the fifth year following the year of death. If the interest of the non-individual beneficiary is distributed from the plan and separate accounts are established for the individual beneficiaries by the September 30 deadline, the individual beneficiaries can base required minimum distributions on their own life expectancies.

Trust as beneficiary. If a trust is named the beneficiary of the account, the trust beneficiaries may be treated as designated beneficiaries if certain tests are met. The trust must be irrevocable or become irrevocable upon the account owner's death. Documentation of the trust beneficiaries must be provided to the IRA trustee or plan administrator. The deadline under the final regulations for providing the documentation is October 31 of the year following the year of the owner's death. If that date has already passed, the deadline is extended until October 31, 2003.

Beneficiary's death before September 30 determination date. If an individual named as a beneficiary by the account owner dies after the owner but before the September 30 date for determining the designated beneficiary, that individual continues to be treated as a designated beneficiary under the final regulations. This rule allows his or her life expectancy to be used by a successor beneficiary named by the original beneficiary or who inherits the account through the estate of the original beneficiary.

Owner's death on or after required beginning date. If an owner dies on or after the required beginning date (April 1 of the year after the year the owner reaches age $70^1/_2$), and there is a designated beneficiary, required minimum distributions are generally payable over his or her life expectancy. However, if on the date of death the designated beneficiary is older than the owner, the final regulations allow the beneficiary to receive required minimum distributions over the owner's remaining life expectancy rather than over the beneficiary's shorter life expectancy.

If the owner did not receive his or her required minimum distribution for the year of death, the beneficiary must receive that amount in the year of death or as soon as possible in the next year.

The first required beneficiary distribution must be received in the year following the year of the owner's death. The required distribution is the year-end account balance for the year of death divided by the designated beneficiary's life expectancy in the year following the year of death, taken from the Beneficiary's Single Life Expectancy Table, shown on page 203. For example, assume an IRA owner dies in 2002, after receiving the required minimum distribution for 2002. The designated beneficiary is his son, who is age 47 in 2003. The life expectancy table provides a life expectancy of 37 years for a 47-year-old. If the account balance at the end of 2002 was $100,000, the son must receive a required minimum distribution in 2003 of $2,703 ($100,000 ÷ 37). That is the minimum distribution required by the IRS rules; he can choose to withdraw more than that. The initial 37-year life expectancy is reduced by one year for each succeeding year when making the computation for the later years. The required minimum distribution for each subsequent year is figured by dividing the applicable life expectancy into the account balance at the end of the prior year.

Owner's death before required beginning date. If an owner dies before the required beginning date and there is an individual designated beneficiary, the period for receiving required minimum distributions is generally the life expectancy of the designated beneficiary. The life expectancy method is the "default" rule under the final regulations, but the plan may require application of the five-year rule, or the plan may allow the account owner or beneficiary to elect the five-year rule. Under the five-year rule, the entire account must be distributed by the end of the fifth year after the year of the owner's death. The five-year rule always applies if the owner dies before the required beginning date and there is no designated beneficiary.

Current beneficiaries receiving distributions under prior life expectancy method must redetermine life expectancy for 2003. For 2003, a beneficiary who has been receiving distributions over his or her own life expectancy or someone else's life expectancy will have to retroactively apply the final regulations and redetermine the designated beneficiary as of September 30 of the year following the year of the account owner's death. The remaining life expectancy of the redetermined designated beneficiary, if any, must be used to figure the required minimum distributions for 2003 and later years. In some cases, the redetermination process will not change the designated beneficiary and the refigured life expectancy will be longer than the life expectancy being used under the old rules. However, the "look back" to September 30 of the year following the year of the owner's death could result in a shortening of the applicable life expectancy and an increase in the required distributions. For example, if the owner's estate was the beneficiary as of the September 30 date, there would be no designated beneficiary and the IRA owner's remaining life expectancy would have to be used to figure the required distributions after 2002 even if a longer life expectancy had been used previously.

At the time this book went to press, the IRS had not provided examples of the computations required by the redetermination procedure. *See* the *Supplement* and IRS Publication 590.

Current beneficiaries may be able to switch from five-year rule to life expectancy method. If the IRA owner died before the required beginning date and a designated beneficiary named by the owner has been subject to the five-year rule, either by affirmative election or default, the final regulations allow the beneficiary to switch to the life expectancy method if the plan allows the switch and the five-year distribution period has not ended. Any distributions required for prior years under the life expectancy method that have not yet been taken must be received by the *earlier* of December 31, 2003, or the end of the five-year period (December 31 of the fifth year after the year of the owner's death). Thus, if the account owner died before 1997, the five-year period would have ended before 2002 so the switch cannot be made. If the owner died in 1997, the five-year period ends December 31, 2002. If the owner died in 1998, the deadline is December 31, 2003.

Surviving spouse's rollover or election to treat IRA as his or her own. A surviving spouse who is the sole beneficiary of an IRA with unlimited withdrawal rights may elect to treat the IRA as his or her own by retitling the IRA in his or her name. If the surviving spouse contributes to the IRA or does not receive a timely required minimum distribution under the beneficiary rules, the surviving spouse is deemed to have made the election. The final regulations confirm that to make the election, the surviving spouse must take the required minimum distribution for the year of the owner's death to the extent that it was not received by the owner.

Regardless of whether a surviving spouse is the IRA owner's sole beneficiary, the spouse can roll over a distribution from the IRA within 60 days to his or her own IRA, provided the rollover does not include a required minimum distribution that the deceased IRA owner did not receive for the year of death.

If the surviving spouse elects to treat the inherited IRA as his or her own or makes a spousal roll over, the surviving spouse is then subject to the same rules as any IRA owner. The surviving spouse should immediately name a new beneficiary for the IRA. The regular distribution rules apply, including the 10% penalty for taxable distributions received before age $59^1/_2$ *(8.8).* If the surviving spouse is under age $70^1/_2$, required minimum distributions may be delayed until April 1 of the year following the year in which he or she reaches age $70^1/_2$, at which time distributions will be based on the uniform table for owners *(8.13).*

IRS Alert

Current Beneficiary's Switch to New Rules

Beneficiaries who have been taking distributions under the prior life expectancy rules must redetermine the designated beneficiary and the applicable life expectancy for 2003.

Some beneficiaries who have been receiving distributions under the five-year rule may be able to switch to the life expectancy method.

Surviving spouse as sole beneficiary. If the election to treat an inherited IRA or spousal rollover is not made, a surviving spouse must receive required minimum distributions as a beneficiary. A surviving spouse who is under age $59^1/_2$ and needs the funds from the IRA may prefer this option because withdrawals, although taxable (unless allocable to nondeductible contributions made by the deceased spouse), are not subject to the 10% penalty for pre-$59^1/_2$ distributions (8.12).

If the surviving spouse is the sole designated beneficiary, required minimum distributions are based on his or her life expectancy from the Beneficiary's Single Life Expectancy Table. Each year, life expectancy is recalculated using the spouse's attained age during the year. A spousal beneficiary is the only beneficiary who may recalculate life expectancy. Others must reduce their life expectancy from the Single Life Table for the year after the year of the owner's death by one year in each succeeding year.

If a surviving spouse is the sole designated beneficiary and the deceased spouse died before the year in which age $70^1/_2$ would have been attained, the surviving spouse does not have to begin receiving required minimum distributions until the year that the deceased spouse would have reached age $70^1/_2$.

 *Planning Reminder*

Surviving Spouse Under Age $70^1/_2$
If you inherit your spouse's traditional IRA and you are under age $70^1/_2$, you may delay the start of required minimum distributions by treating the IRA as your own.

Beneficiary's Single Life Expectancy Table

Age	Life expectancy	Age	Life expectancy
0	82.4	56	28.7
1	81.6	57	27.9
2	80.6	58	27.0
3	79.7	59	26.1
4	78.7	60	25.2
5	77.7	61	24.4
6	76.7	62	23.5
7	75.8	63	22.7
8	74.8	64	21.8
9	73.8	65	21.0
10	72.8	66	20.2
11	71.8	67	19.4
12	70.8	68	18.6
13	69.9	69	17.8
14	68.9	70	17.0
15	67.9	71	16.3
16	66.9	72	15.5
17	66.0	73	14.8
18	65.0	74	14.1
19	64.0	75	13.4
20	63.0	76	12.7
21	62.1	77	12.1
22	61.1	78	11.4
23	60.1	79	10.8
24	59.1	80	10.2
25	58.2	81	9.7
26	57.2	82	9.1
27	56.2	83	8.6
28	55.3	84	8.1
29	54.3	85	7.6
30	53.3	86	7.1
31	52.4	87	6.7
32	51.4	88	6.3
33	50.4	89	5.9
34	49.4	90	5.5
35	48.5	91	5.2
36	47.5	92	4.9
37	46.5	93	4.6
38	45.6	94	4.3
39	44.6	95	4.1
40	43.6	96	3.8
41	42.7	97	3.6
42	41.7	98	3.4
43	40.7	99	3.1
44	39.8	100	2.9
45	38.8	101	2.7
46	37.9	102	2.5
47	37.0	103	2.3
48	36.0	104	2.1
49	35.1	105	1.9
50	34.2	106	1.7
51	33.3	107	1.5
52	32.3	108	1.4
53	31.4	109	1.2
54	30.5	110	1.1
55	29.6	111+	1.0

Simplified Employee Pension Plans (SEPs)

8.15 SEP Basics

Caution

Employees over Age 70¹/₂

An employee over age 70¹/₂ may still participate in an employer SEP plan. Minimum distributions from the plan must begin as discussed in *7.13*.

A simplified employee pension plan (SEP) set up by an employer allows the employer to contribute to an employee's IRA account more money than is allowed under regular IRA rules. For 2002, your employer generally could contribute and deduct up to 25% of your compensation or $40,000, whichever is less. Your employer's SEP contributions are excluded from your pay and are not included on Form W-2 unless they exceed the limit. If contributions exceed the limit, the excess is included in your gross income and a 6% penalty tax may be imposed unless the excess (plus allocable income) is withdrawn by the due date of the return, plus extensions; *see 8.7*. If you are under age 59¹/₂, the 10% early distribution penalty may apply to the withdrawal of income earned on the excess contributions; *see 8.12*.

Self-employed plans. Self-employed individuals may set up a SEP as an alternative to a Keogh plan; *see* Chapter 41.

Eligibility. A SEP must cover all employees who are at least age 21, earn over $450 (this amount may be adjusted after 2002 for inflation), and who have worked for the employer at any time during at least three of the past five years. Union employees covered by union agreements may generally be excluded.

SEP salary-reduction arrangements. If a qualifying small employer set up a salary-reduction SEP before 1997, employees may contribute a portion of their pay to the plan instead of receiving it in cash; *see 8.16*.

SEP distributions. Distributions from a SEP, including salary-reduction SEPs established before 1997, are subject to the regular distribution rules for traditional IRAs discussed at *8.8*.

8.16 Salary-Reduction SEP Set up Before 1997

Law Alert

Salary-Reduction SEP Contribution Limit Increase

The elective deferral limit for salary-reduction SEPs increases to $12,000 for 2003 and then by $1,000 per year until the limit reaches $15,000 for 2006. If the plan allows it, the deferral limit for participants age 50 or older is increased by $2,000 for 2003 and then by an additional $1,000 per year through 2006.

Qualifying small employers may offer employees the option of deferring a portion of their salary to an IRA. There are two types of salary-reduction IRAs, with different eligibility and contribution rules: (1) salary-reduction SEPs established before 1997 and (2) "SIMPLE" IRA accounts established after 1996.

After 1996, an employer may establish a SIMPLE plan but not a salary-reduction SEP. Rules for SIMPLE IRAs established after 1996 are at *8.17–8.18*. A salary-reduction SEP that was established before 1997 may continue to receive contributions under the prior law rules discussed below, and employees hired after 1996 may participate in the plan, subject to those rules.

Salary-reduction SEPs established before 1997. Salary reductions are allowed for a year only if the employer had no more than 25 employees eligible to participate in the SEP at any time during the prior taxable year. Furthermore, at least 50% of the eligible employees must elect the salary-reduction option, and the deferral percentage for highly compensated employees may not exceed 125% of the average contribution of regular employees.

If salary reductions are allowed, the maximum salary-reduction contribution for 2002 was $11,000 ($12,000 for participants age 50 or older if the plan permitted the extra deferral). Deferrals over $11,000 ($12,000 if extra deferral for participants age 50 or older was allowed) are taxable, and if not timely distributed to the employee, can be taxed again when distributed from the plan. *See* the Law Alert on this page for increases to the salary-reduction limit for years after 2002. These are the same limits as for 401(k) plans *(7.18)*.

If an employee contributes to both a SEP and a 401(k) plan, the annual limit applies to the total salary reductions from both plans. If an employee makes salary-reduction contributions to a SEP and also to a tax-sheltered annuity plan *(7.20)*, the annual limit generally applies to the total salary reductions to both plans. In some cases, employees with at least 15 years of service may be able to defer an additional $3,000 to the tax-sheltered annuity plan as discussed at *7.20*.

8.17 Who Is Eligible for a SIMPLE IRA?

A SIMPLE IRA is a salary-reduction retirement plan that qualifying small employers may offer their employees. For 2002, salary-reduction contributions of up to $7,000 ($7,500 for participants age 50 or older if the plan allows the increase) could be made by eligible employees and the limit is increasing after 2002; *see* the Law Alert on the right. Employers are required to make matching contributions or a flat contribution, as discussed in *8.18*. The SIMPLE IRA replaces the salary-reduction SEP, which after 1996 may be used only by an employer that had established the plan before 1997; *see 8.16*.

Qualifying employers. A SIMPLE IRA may be maintained only by an employer that (1) in the previous calendar year had no more than 100 employees who earned compensation of $5,000 or more and (2) does not maintain any other retirement plan (unless the other plan is for collective bargaining employees). A self-employed individual who meets these tests may set up a SIMPLE IRA, as discussed in Chapter 41.

In determining whether the 100-employee test is met for the prior year, all employees under the common control of the employer must be counted. For example, Joe Smith owned two businesses in 2002—a computer rental company with 80 employees and a computer repair company with 60 employees. If they all earned at least $5,000, they all count towards the 100 limit, so if Joe decides in 2003 to set up a retirement plan for his businesses, a different type of plan must be used. He may not establish a SIMPLE IRA for either business under the 100-employee limit.

If a SIMPLE IRA is established but the employer in a later year grows beyond the 100-employee limit, the employer generally has a two-year "grace period" during which contributions may continue to be made.

Eligible employees. In general, an employee must be allowed to contribute to a SIMPLE IRA for a year in which he or she is reasonably expected to earn $5,000 or more, provided at least $5,000 of compensation was received in *any two* prior years, whether or not consecutive. If the employer owns more than one business (under common control rules) and sets up a SIMPLE IRA for one of them, employees of the other business must also be allowed to participate if they meet the $5,000 compensation tests. Employees who are covered by a collective bargaining agreement may be excluded if retirement benefits were the subject of good-faith negotiations.

The employer may lower or eliminate the $5,000 compensation requirement in order to broaden participation in the plan. No other conditions on eligibility, such as age or hours of work, are permitted.

Deadline for setting up a SIMPLE IRA. An employer generally may establish a SIMPLE IRA effective on any date between January 1 and October 1 of a year. If the employer (or a predecessor employer) previously maintained a SIMPLE IRA, a new SIMPLE IRA may be effective only on January 1 of a year. A new employer that comes into existence after October 1 of a year may establish a SIMPLE IRA for that year if the plan is established as soon as administratively feasible after the start of the business.

The employer may use a model SIMPLE IRA approved by the IRS to set up a SIMPLE IRA. Form 5304-SIMPLE allows employees to select a financial institution to which the contributions will be made. With Form 5305-SIMPLE, the employer selects the financial institution to which contributions are initially deposited, but employees have the right to subsequently transfer their account balances without cost or penalty to another SIMPLE-IRA at a financial institution of their own choosing. Use of the IRS model forms is optional; other documents satisfying the statutory requirements for a SIMPLE IRA may be used.

SIMPLE IRA contributions and distributions. Contribution and distribution rules for SIMPLE IRAs are discussed in *8.18*.

Law Alert

Increase to SIMPLE IRA Contribution Limit
The limit on SIMPLE IRA salary-reduction contributions increases to $8,000 for 2003, $9,000 for 2004, and $10,000 for 2005. If the plan permits individuals age 50 or older to make additional contributions, the maximum additional amount is $1,000 for 2003, $1,500 for 2004, $2,000 for 2005, and $2,500 for 2006.

Planning Reminder

401(k) SIMPLE Plans
An employer with a 401(k) plan that reports on the calendar year may avoid the regular 401(k) nondiscrimination tests by following the contribution rules for SIMPLE IRAs; *see 7.17*.

8.18 SIMPLE IRA Contributions and Distributions

The only contributions that may be made to a SIMPLE IRA are elective salary-reduction contributions by employees and matching or non-elective contributions by employers. All contributions are fully vested and nonforfeitable when made.

Eligible employees *(see 8.17)* may elect each year to make salary-reduction contributions to the plan up to the annual elective deferral limit; *see 8.17.* Salary-reduction contributions are excluded from the employee's taxable pay on Form W-2 and not subject to federal tax withholding. They are subject to FICA withholding for Social Security and Medicare tax.

Eligible employees must be given notice by the employer of their right to elect salary-reduction contributions and at least 60 days to make the election. After the first year of eligibility, the election to defer for the upcoming year is made during the last 60 days (at minimum) of the prior calendar year. If the employer uses model IRS Form 5304-SIMPLE or 5305-SIMPLE, a notification document is included.

If an employee contributes to a SIMPLE IRA and also to a 401(k) plan of another employer for the same year, the annual limit on tax-free salary-reduction deferrals *(see 8.17)* applies. Deferrals over the annual limit are taxable and must be removed to avoid being taxed again when distributed from the plan; *see 7.18.*

Employer contributions. Each year, the employer must make either a matching contribution or a fixed "non-elective" contribution. If the employer chooses matching contributions, the employee's elective salary-reduction contribution generally must be matched, up to a limit of 3% of the employee's compensation. For up to two years in any five-year period, the 3% matching limit may be reduced to as low as 1% for each eligible employee.

Instead of making either the 3% or reduced limit matching contribution, the employer may make a "non-elective" contribution equal to 2% of each eligible employee's compensation. If this option is chosen, the 2% contribution must be made for eligible employees whether or not they elect to make salary-reduction contributions for the year. The 2% contribution is subject to an annual compensation limit, which for 2002 was $200,000. Thus, for 2002, the maximum 2% non-elective contribution was $4,000 (2% of $200,000) even if an employee earned more than $200,000. The 3% matching contribution is not subject to the annual compensation limit, but only to the annual salary-reduction limit *(8.17).*

The employer must notify eligible employees of the type of contribution it will be making for the upcoming year prior to the employees' 60-day election period for making elective salary-reduction contributions.

The employer must make the matching or non-elective contributions by the due date for filing the employer's tax return (plus extensions) for the year.

> **EXAMPLE**
>
> Martin's 2003 salary is $80,000. He elects to make an $8,000 salary-reduction contribution to his employer's SIMPLE IRA plan. If his employer elects the 3% matching rule, the matching contribution is limited to $2,400, 3% of Martin's compensation.
>
> If Martin's salary were $260,000, he could make the $8,000 salary-reduction contribution and the employer's matching contribution would also be $8,000; the 3% match (3% of $260,000 is $7,800) cannot exceed the $8,000 contribution made by Martin.

Distributions from a SIMPLE IRA. A distribution from a SIMPLE IRA is generally subject to the regular traditional IRA distribution rules; *see 8.8.* However, for the first two years, a higher penalty for distributions before age $59\frac{1}{2}$ *(see 8.12)* applies. The pre-$59\frac{1}{2}$ penalty is increased to 25% from 10%, assuming no penalty exception applies, if the distribution is received during the two-year period starting with the employee's initial participation in the plan. After the first two years, the regular 10% penalty applies.

In the initial two-year period, a tax-free rollover or direct trustee-to-trustee transfer *(see 8.10)* of a SIMPLE IRA may be made to another SIMPLE IRA. For a distribution made after 2001 and after two years of participation, a tax-free rollover or direct transfer may be made to a traditional IRA, qualified plan, 403(b) plan, or state or local government 457 plan, as well as to a SIMPLE IRA.

The mandatory distribution rules that apply to regular IRAs after age $70\frac{1}{2}$ also apply to SIMPLE IRAs *(see 8.13).*

Planning Reminder

Employer's Intended Contributions

The IRS model notification included with Form 5304-SIMPLE or 5305-SIMPLE requires the employer to tell employees how much the employer will be contributing for the upcoming year.

Caution

Increased Pre–Age 59$\frac{1}{2}$ Penalty

In the first two years of SIMPLE IRA participation, the penalty for distributions before age $59\frac{1}{2}$ is increased from 10% to 25%.

8.19 Roth IRA Advantages

As with traditional IRAs, earnings accumulate within a Roth IRA tax free until distributions are made. The key benefit of the Roth IRA is that tax-free withdrawals of contributions may be made at any time and earnings may be withdrawn tax free after a five-year holding period by an individual who is age $59^1/_2$ or older, is disabled, or who pays qualifying first-time home-buyer expenses.

Contributions after age $70^1/_2$ may be made to a Roth IRA, but not to a traditional IRA, and the minimum required distribution rules that apply to traditional IRAs after age $70^1/_2$ *(8.13)* do not apply to Roth IRAs. Thus, a Roth IRA can remain intact after age $70^1/_2$ and continue to grow tax free. The balance of the account not withdrawn during the owner's lifetime generally may be paid out to the beneficiaries tax free over their life expectancies, thereby providing a substantial tax-deferred buildup within the plan over an extended period *(8.24)*.

The opportunity to obtain such benefits makes the Roth IRA an attractive retirement planning and estate planning option. However, certain high-income taxpayers are not eligible to make Roth IRA contributions.

There are two ways in which you may establish a Roth IRA: (1) by making annual nondeductible contributions or (2) by converting a traditional IRA to a Roth IRA. Each alternative is subject to an income limitation. Individuals with modified adjusted gross income up to $100,000 may convert a traditional IRA to a Roth IRA by paying a current tax, as discussed in *8.21*. Nondeductible annual contributions may be made to a Roth IRA subject to an income limitation as discussed at *8.20*. Individuals who qualify for deductible IRA contributions as well as the Roth IRA should consider whether the tax value of deductible contributions outweighs the advantage of future tax-free distributions from the Roth IRA; distributions from traditional deductible IRAs are taxable.

Roth IRA contributions are discussed at *8.20* and distribution rules at *8.23*.

8.20 Annual Contributions to a Roth IRA

Nondeductible contributions may be made annually to a Roth IRA if you have compensation for personal services and your modified adjusted gross income (MAGI) is less than $95,000 if you are unmarried, or less than $150,000 if married filing jointly. The annual contribution limit is $3,000 for 2002–2004 with further increases in later years; *see* the Law Alert on the right. In addition, the $3,000 limit for 2002–2004 is increased to $3,500 for individuals who are age 50 or older before the end of the year; *see* the Law Alert on the right. Contributions up to the annual limit are allowed if you have taxable compensation of at least that much, subject to the phase-out rules. The contribution limit is phased out for unmarried taxpayers with MAGI between $95,000 and $110,000, and for joint filers with MAGI between $150,000 and $160,000. For a married person filing separately who lived with his or her spouse at any time during the year, the contribution limit is phased out for MAGI between $0 and $10,000. A married person filing separately who lived apart from his or her spouse for the entire year is treated as unmarried.

The Roth IRA rules do not replace the traditional IRA nondeductible contribution rules *(8.6)*. For an individual who is unable to contribute to a Roth IRA because the contribution limit is phased out, and is unable to make deductible IRA contributions because of the phase-out rules for active plan participants *(8.4)*, nondeductible contributions may still be made to a traditional IRA under the rules at *8.6*.

Spousal contribution on joint return for nonworking or low-earning spouse. If you are married filing jointly, you generally may contribute up to the annual limit (*see* above) for each spouse to a Roth IRA so long as the total compensation of both spouses is at least double the limit. This is the same spousal contribution rule as for traditional IRAs *(8.3)*; the lower-earning spouse is allowed to "borrow" compensation of the higher-earning spouse for contribution purposes. However, the Roth IRA contribution limit may be reduced because of the MAGI phase-out rules, as discussed in the next paragraph.

Caution

Roth IRA Contribution Deadline
The deadline for making Roth IRA contributions for 2002 is April 15, 2003, the regular due date for your 2002 return. This is the contribution deadline even if you obtain a filing extension for your 2002 return.

Law Alert

Increase to Roth IRA Contribution Limit
The 2001 Tax Act increases the maximum contribution limit for Roth IRAs to $3,000 for 2002–2004, $4,000 for 2005–2007, and $5,000 for 2008. After 2008, the $5,000 limit would be subject to inflation indexing. For individuals age 50 or older, the regular contribution limit is increased by $500 for 2002–2005 and by $1,000 for 2006 and later years.

MAGI phase-out of Roth IRA contribution limit. The maximum annual Roth IRA contribution limit (*see* above) is phased out if your modified adjusted gross income (MAGI) is between:

- $150,000 and $160,000, if you are married filing jointly;
- $95,000 and $110,000, if you are single, head of household, qualified widow(er), or married filing separately and you lived apart for the entire year;
- $0 and $10,000, if you are married filing separately and you lived with your spouse at any time during the year.

For purposes of the phase-out rule, MAGI is figured in the same way as under the traditional IRA deduction phase-out rules *(8.4)*, except that a taxable conversion *(8.21)* from a traditional IRA to a Roth IRA is disregarded and any deductible traditional IRA contribution is also disregarded. The MAGI phase-out rule applies to Roth IRA contributions regardless of whether you are covered by an employer retirement plan, unlike the deductible traditional IRA phase-out rules *(8.4)*, which apply only to active plan participants.

The MAGI formula reduces the contribution limit by an amount that bears the same ratio to the limit as your "excess MAGI" (MAGI over phase-out threshold) bears to the phase-out range (which is either $10,000 or $15,000, depending on your filing status as shown above). *See* the Example below for the way the phase-out limit is computed. If the phase-out formula results in a reduced contribution limit that is not a multiple of $10, round it up to the next highest $10. If the reduced limit is between $0 and $200, you are allowed a $200 contribution limit.

Contributing to Roth IRA and traditional IRA for the same year. If you contribute to both a traditional IRA and Roth IRA for the same year, total contributions for the year to all the accounts are limited to the annual limit, or your compensation if that is less. The annual limit is applied first to the traditional IRA contributions and then to the Roth IRA contributions. Thus, the maximum contribution limit for 2002 to a Roth IRA is the lesser of (1) $3,000, or $3,500 if age 50 or older, or (2) taxable compensation, minus deductible *(8.4)* or nondeductible *(8.6)* contributions to traditional IRAs.

However, if you are subject to the MAGI phaseout for Roth IRA contributions, as discussed above, the maximum Roth IRA contribution limit is the lesser of these two amounts: (1) the annual contribution limit (*see* above) or, if less, compensation, minus contributions for the year to traditional IRAs, or (2) the contribution limit figured under the MAGI phase-out rule.

Excess contributions. If Roth IRA contributions exceed the allowable limit, the excess contribution is subject to a 6% penalty tax unless you withdraw the excess, plus any earnings on the excess contribution, by the filing due date including extensions. The earnings must be reported as income for the year the contribution was made.

Contribution deadline. Contributions to a Roth IRA for a year may be made by the filing due date, without extensions. For 2002 contributions, the deadline is April 15, 2003.

EXAMPLE

In 2002, Mark is under age 50 and single. His 2002 salary is $90,000 and modified adjusted gross income (MAGI) is $98,000, $3,000 more than the $95,000 phase-out threshold for Roth IRA contributions. Under the MAGI phase-out rule, Mark's Roth IRA contribution limit for 2002 is reduced by $600, from $3,000 to $2,400. The $600 reduction equals the $3,000 limit multiplied by the phase-out percentage of 20% ($3,000 MAGI over the phase-out threshold ($98,000 – $95,000) ÷ $15,000 phase-out range for single persons).

If Mark was age 50 or over in 2002, the $3,500 contribution limit would be reduced by $700 to $2,800 (20% phase-out percentage × $3,500 limit = $700 reduction).

8.21 Converting a Traditional IRA to a Roth IRA

If your modified adjusted gross income (MAGI) is $100,000 or less, and you are not married filing separately, you may make a taxable conversion of a traditional IRA to a Roth IRA. A conversion may be made by directing the trustee of your traditional IRA to make a trustee-to-trustee transfer of your IRA to a new Roth IRA trustee, or by keeping the account with the same trustee but instructing the trustee to change the registration of the account from a traditional IRA to a Roth IRA. You may also make a conversion by receiving a distribution from your traditional IRA and rolling it over to a Roth IRA; the rollover must be completed within 60 days from the time you receive the distribution.

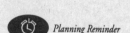

Planning Reminder

Contributions After Age 70½

That you are over 70½ years of age is no bar to setting up and contributing to a Roth IRA, provided you have taxable compensation on which to base an annual contribution and your income is below the $100,000 ceiling for converting a traditional IRA to a Roth IRA.

Caution

Consider the Tax Cost of a Conversion

If your modified adjusted gross income is $100,000 or less, you may roll over or convert a traditional IRA to a Roth IRA. If you do so, the rollover or conversion is taxable, unless the transferred amount is allocable to nondeductible contributions.

If you plan to convert a traditional IRA to a Roth IRA, figure the tax due on the conversion and then weigh (1) whether you have sufficient funds outside the plan to pay the tax and (2), where there is a substantial tax due on the conversion, whether you want to give up the future income that would be earned on the funds used to pay the tax.

You may also convert a SEP *(8.15)* to a Roth IRA. A SIMPLE IRA *(8.18)* may be converted to a Roth IRA if more than two years have passed since you began participation in the SIMPLE IRA.

$100,000 MAGI limit. The transfer to a Roth IRA is allowed only if your modified adjusted gross income (MAGI) for the year of the rollover or conversion is $100,000 or less. A married person filing separately who lives with his or her spouse at any time during the year may *not* convert a non-Roth IRA to a Roth IRA, regardless of income.

The amount of the rollover or conversion is not taken into account in determining if the $100,000 MAGI limit is exceeded. However, the transferred amount is included in income for regular tax purposes; *see* below.

If a conversion to a Roth IRA is made towards the end of the year by taking a withdrawal from a traditional IRA and then rolling it over to the Roth IRA within 60 days, the income for the year of the withdrawal, rather than the income for the year the rollover is completed, is used when determining if the $100,000 MAGI conversion ceiling is exceeded. The conversion contribution is considered made for the year in which the withdrawal from the traditional IRA is made.

For a taxpayer who is eligible to make deductible contributions to a traditional IRA, MAGI is not reduced by the deductible contribution when applying the $100,000 MAGI limit.

Married IRA owners. If you are married, a conversion to a Roth IRA is generally allowed only if you file a joint return. The $100,000 MAGI ceiling applies to the combined MAGI of both spouses on the joint return. If you file a separate return and lived with your spouse at any time during the year, a conversion to a Roth IRA is not allowed. If you lived apart from your spouse for the entire year, you may make a conversion to a Roth IRA if the MAGI reported on your separate return does not exceed the $100,000 MAGI ceiling.

Minimum required IRA distributions. If you are considering a rollover or conversion of a traditional IRA to a Roth IRA, and are age $70^1/_2$ or older, minimum required distributions from the traditional IRA before 2005 are counted by the IRS towards the $100,000 income ceiling for rollovers and conversions. For example, if your modified adjusted gross income (MAGI) for 2003 without considering your minimum required distribution is $92,000, and the required distribution for 2003 from your traditional IRA is $10,000, your MAGI for Roth IRA purposes is $102,000 according to the IRS and you are not eligible to make a conversion or rollover to a Roth IRA. Starting in the year 2005, minimum required distributions will be disregarded for purposes of the $100,000 MAGI test.

Required minimum distributions may not be converted. If you are age $70^1/_2$ or older, you may not convert to a Roth IRA amounts that represent required minimum distributions *(8.13)* from a traditional IRA. The required minimum distribution is not eligible for conversion and if you make a conversion to a Roth IRA before receiving your required minimum distribution for the year of conversion, an amount equal to the required minimum distribution is treated as a taxable distribution from the traditional IRA, followed by a regular annual contribution to a Roth IRA subject to the contribution limit *(8.20)*. Amounts over the annual limit would be an excess contribution subject to a 6% penalty tax unless the excess is withdrawn.

How a conversion is taxed. You must report the conversion of a traditional IRA to a Roth IRA on Form 8606 as a taxable distribution, except to the extent that the account was allocable to nondeductible contributions (under the rules at *8.6*). The conversion is taxable in the year it is made unless you "undo" the conversion with a timely recharacterization, as discussed in *8.22*. If you make a transfer by withdrawing funds from a traditional IRA towards the end of 2002 and in 2003 you complete a rollover to a Roth IRA within 60 days of the withdrawal, this is treated as a 2002 conversion that is taxable on your 2002 return, except for any part allocable to nondeductible traditional IRA contributions and any recharacterized *(8.22)* amount.

The increase in your regular adjusted gross income from the conversion could reduce the itemized deductions *(13.7)*, personal exemptions *(21.16)*, or rental losses *(10.2)* you may claim. The increase could also trigger tax on Social Security benefits *(34.3)* or subject more of the benefits to tax.

If properly and timely completed, a conversion from a traditional IRA to a Roth IRA is exempt from the 10% penalty on taxable distributions received before age $59^1/_2$ *(8.12)*.

8.22 Recharacterizations and Reconversions

If you convert a traditional IRA to a Roth IRA and it turns out that your modified adjusted gross income exceeds the $100,000 ceiling *(8.21)*, the conversion is considered a "failed" conversion that will result in tax penalties unless the converted amount is recharacterized. A conversion made by a married taxpayer who files a separate return is also considered a failed conversion; separate filers are ineligible for a conversion to a Roth IRA unless the spouses lived apart for the entire year *(8.21)*.

Recharacterization of Roth IRA to Traditional IRA and Vice Versa

The recharacterization rule is not limited to reversing a failed conversion to a Roth IRA. A regular Roth IRA contribution (up to the annual limit) may be recharacterized as a contribution to a traditional IRA if, for example, doing so would allow you to claim an IRA deduction under the rules discussed at 8.4. Similarly, if you contribute to a traditional IRA and decide that you would like to switch to a Roth IRA, you may recharacterize the contribution by transferring the contribution plus allocable income to a Roth IRA. A recharacterization generally must be made by the filing due date, but an extension may be allowed, as discussed in 8.22. If you recharacterize a traditional IRA contribution to a Roth IRA, the transfer is treated as if it were made to the Roth IRA on January 1 of the year in which the original traditional IRA contribution was made, regardless of when the recharacterization occurred. This may be an advantage for purposes of establishing the beginning of the five-year holding period for tax-free distributions of Roth IRA earnings; *see 8.23.*

Caution

Limits on Reconversions to Roth IRA

After converting a traditional IRA to a Roth IRA, you may undo the conversion by recharacterizing the account as a traditional IRA. If you want to reconvert to a Roth IRA, you must stay within the IRS guidelines. A reconversion may not be made until the year following the year of the original conversion. *See 8.22* for further details.

Without a recharacterization, a failed conversion is treated as a regular contribution to the Roth IRA, subject to the 6% excess contribution penalty unless the excess is withdrawn; *see 8.20.* In addition to regular tax on the distribution from the traditional IRA, you may be subject to the 10% penalty for distributions before age $59^{1}/_{2}$.

These penalties may be avoided by recharacterizing the contribution, in effect "undoing" the failed conversion. This is done by making a direct trustee-to-trustee transfer of the Roth IRA contribution, plus the allocable earnings, to a traditional IRA, or by transferring the Roth IRA to a traditional IRA within the same financial institution (same trustee). The effect of the recharacterization is to disregard the conversion to the Roth IRA and to treat the original transfer from the traditional IRA as having been originally contributed to the transferee IRA.

There are also other types of recharacterizations. You may want to recharacterize your Roth IRA if the value of the account has dropped substantially since the conversion. You may recharacterize the Roth IRA contribution as part of a plan to reconvert back to a Roth IRA when the taxable conversion value is lower; *see* the discussion of reconversions below. You also may recharacterize a regular Roth IRA contribution as a traditional IRA contribution, or a traditional IRA contribution as a regular Roth IRA contribution; *see* the Planning Reminder on this page.

To make an election to recharacterize, notify the trustee of the account being recharacterized and the transferee trustee (if different) of your intent to recharacterize, specifically identify the amounts subject to the election, and direct the transferor trustee to make the transfer.

IRS regulations generally require that a recharacterization election and the actual transfer be made on or before the due date, including extensions, for filing the tax return for the year of the conversion. However, the IRS allows timely filers an automatic extension of six months from the original filing due date, excluding extensions. Thus, the deadline for timely 2001 filers to recharacterize a 2001 conversion was October 15, 2002. To recharacterize a conversion made in 2002, you have until October 15, 2003, provided that you file your 2002 return by April 15, 2003, or you obtain a four-month extension by April 15, 2003, and then file by the extended due date. *See* the instructions to Form 8606 for how to report the conversion and the recharacterization. If you file a timely return and pay tax on the converted amount, and then recharacterize by the extended October 15 deadline, you must file an amended return. For example, by April 15, 2003, you file your 2002 return, which includes a taxable conversion made in 2002, and then by October 15, 2003, you recharacterize the converted amount back to a traditional IRA. You must file an amended 2002 return to report the recharacterization and claim a refund for the tax paid on the conversion. The amended return must be filed, within the regular amendment period, generally three years; *see 49.1.* On the amended return, write "Filed pursuant to Section 301.9100-2."

What if you miss the IRS recharacterization deadlines? A regulation gives the IRS authority to grant a further six-month extension if an "innocent" mistake was made and you act in good faith by promptly asking the IRS for the additional time after discovering the error (Reg. Sec. 301.9100-3). In several private rulings, the IRS has allowed the extra extension to taxpayers who missed the deadline and who requested recharacterization relief before the IRS discovered that they did not qualify for the conversion or that the attempted recharacterization had not been timely made. At the time of each request, the statute of limitations had not yet passed; if it had, the IRS would almost surely have denied the requests. Each of the taxpayers was given six months from the ruling date to recharacterize the Roth IRA back to a traditional IRA.

Reconverting to a Roth IRA after a recharacterization. As discussed above, a traditional IRA that has been converted to a Roth IRA may be transferred back to a traditional IRA in a recharacterization. That amount may subsequently be reconverted back to a Roth IRA. This recharacterization/reconversion rule may allow an IRA owner to lower the tax due on a conversion to a Roth IRA. For example, if you convert a traditional IRA to a Roth IRA and the value of the account drops as a result of a stock market decline, you may be able to reduce the taxable conversion amount value by recharacterizing the account as a traditional IRA and then reconverting to a Roth IRA at a time when the value of the account is lower. The amount that you must include in income from the conversion is based on the value of the account as of the date of the reconversion.

However, the IRS has imposed a waiting period before a reconversion may be made. You may not convert to a Roth IRA, recharacterize back to a traditional IRA, and reconvert the same funds to a Roth IRA in the same calendar year. If you converted a traditional IRA to a Roth IRA and also recharacterized that amount back to a traditional IRA during 2002, you may not reconvert those same funds to a Roth IRA until 2003. If the recharacterization was made in the last 30 days of 2002, you must wait until the 30th day following the date of the recharacterization before a valid reconversion may be made in early 2003.

The more-than-30-day waiting period also applies if in 2003 you recharacterize a conversion made in 2002; *see* the Joe Smith Example below. A reconversion after the 2003 recharacterization is treated as a new conversion in 2003, subject to the $100,000 MAGI ceiling and other conversion qualification rules discussed in *8.21*.

The effect of the waiting period is to make it impossible to take immediate advantage of a stock market decline that lowers the value of a Roth IRA. If you want to recharacterize back to a traditional IRA and then reconvert to a Roth IRA in order to lower the taxable conversion amount, you will have to wait a minimum of 30 days before reconverting. By that time, the value of the reconverted account may be as high, or higher, than it was at the time of the recharacterization.

If a reconversion is attempted before the end of the waiting period, the attempt will be treated as a "failed" conversion. A failed conversion is treated as a taxable distribution from the traditional IRA followed by a regular contribution to a Roth IRA. The pre–age $59\frac{1}{2}$ early distribution penalty could apply to the taxable distribution *(8.12)* and the deemed regular contribution to the Roth IRA would be subject to the 6% excess contribution penalty *(8.7)*. A failed conversion may be remedied by making a timely recharacterization to a traditional IRA.

EXAMPLE

Joe Smith converts a traditional IRA to a Roth IRA during 2002. In early 2003, he realizes that his modified adjusted gross income (MAGI) for 2002 exceeds the $100,000 ceiling, making him ineligible for a conversion. He recharacterizes the Roth IRA as a traditional IRA on January 15, 2003. Joe may not reconvert that amount to a Roth IRA until February 14, 2003. This is the first day after the 30-day period that began on January 15, 2003, the date of the recharacterization and ended on February 13, 2003.

If Joe attempts to reconvert before February 14, 2003, the transfer will be treated as a "failed" conversion. Unless the failed conversion amount is recharacterized back to a traditional IRA, it will be treated as a taxable distribution from the traditional IRA; the 10% penalty for pre–age $59\frac{1}{2}$ distributions could also apply. It will also be treated as a regular contribution to a Roth IRA and the amount over the annual limit *(8.20)* would be subject to the 6% excess contribution penalty tax. To avoid these tax consequences, Joe may recharacterize the failed conversion back to a traditional IRA and later reconvert it to a Roth IRA at any time on or after February 14, 2003. Assume that Joe reconverts to a Roth IRA on February 21, 2003. The transfer is considered a 2003 conversion that will be valid only if Joe's 2003 MAGI does not exceed the $100,000 ceiling. If Joe recharacterizes the February 21 conversion amount back to a traditional IRA during 2003, he must wait until 2004 before he may reconvert that amount again.

8.23 Distributions From a Roth IRA

A distribution from a Roth IRA is tax free if it is a *qualified* distribution, as discussed below. Even if a distribution is not a qualified distribution, it is tax free to the extent it does not exceed your regular Roth IRA contributions *(8.20)* and conversion contributions *(8.21)*. The part of a non-qualified distribution allocable to earnings is taxable, but distributions are considered to be from contributions first and then from earnings; *see* the ordering rule below for the allocation between contributions and earnings.

You may make a tax-free direct transfer from one Roth IRA to another. A tax-free rollover of a Roth IRA distribution may be made to another Roth IRA if you complete the rollover within 60 days.

You do not have to receive minimum required distributions from a Roth IRA after you reach age $70\frac{1}{2}$ as you would from a traditional IRA *(see 8.13)*. No Roth IRA distributions at all are required during your lifetime. After your death, your beneficiaries will be subject to a minimum distribution requirement; *see 8.24*.

Qualified Roth IRA distributions are tax free. Two tests must be met for a Roth IRA distribution to be "qualified," and thus completely tax free: (1) the distribution must be made after the end of the five-year period beginning with the first day of the first taxable year for which any Roth IRA contribution was made *and* (2) one of the following conditions must be met:

- you are age $59\frac{1}{2}$ or older when the distribution is made,
- you are disabled,
- you use the distribution to pay up to $10,000 of qualifying first-time home-buyer expenses as discussed below, *or*
- you are a beneficiary receiving distributions following the death of the account owner.

Filing Instruction

Form 8606

IRS Form 8606 must be filed to report Roth IRA distributions. It is also used to report a conversion to a Roth IRA. If you recharacterized part of the converted amount, you must report the non-recharacterized amount on Form 8606. The recharacterized portion is not reported on Form 8606, but an explanation must be attached to your return; follow the Form 8606 instructions.

Planning Reminder

Five-Year Holding Requirement

For a withdrawal of earnings from a Roth IRA to be tax free, the five-year holding period test must be met as well as one of the other conditions for a qualified distribution. Taxpayers who made a Roth IRA contribution for 1998, the first year for which Roth IRA contributions could be made, can receive a qualified distribution in 2003 if they are age $59^1/_2$ or older. The five-year holding period ended December 31, 2002.

IRS Alert

Loss on Liquidation of Roth IRA

Given recent stock market declines, you may have a loss on your Roth IRA investment. If you liquidate all of your Roth IRA accounts, and the total distribution is less than your contributions to all of the Roth IRAs, you may be able to claim the difference as a deductible loss. However, the deduction is allowed only as a miscellaneous itemized deduction subject to the 2%-of-adjusted-gross-income floor *(19.1)* on Schedule A.

Caution

Early Withdrawal From Conversion IRA

The 10% penalty *(8.12)* for pre–age $59^1/_2$ distributions may apply if within five years of making a conversion to a Roth IRA, a distribution from that Roth IRA is received. The penalty applies to the portion of the withdrawal allocable to the conversion amount that was taxable in the year of the conversion. This is so even if the withdrawal is tax free under the ordering rule for Roth IRA distributions.

Five-year holding period. Even if you are age $59^1/_2$ or older or meet one of the other tests for qualified distributions, you must also satisfy the five-year holding period test in order to make tax-free withdrawals of earnings from a Roth IRA. The five-year holding period begins with January 1 (assuming you are a calendar-year taxpayer) of the first year for which any Roth IRA contribution is made. You have only one five-year period regardless of the number of Roth IRAs you have. For example, if you made a regular Roth IRA contribution for 1998 at any time between January 1, 1998, and April 15, 1999, your five-year holding period begins January 1, 1998. If in a later year you convert *(8.21)* a traditional IRA to a Roth IRA, or make a regular Roth IRA contribution *(8.20)*, you do not begin a new five-year holding period for that Roth IRA. In this case, the five-year period for all your Roth IRAs begins January 1, 1998, and ends December 31, 2002.

If you receive a Roth IRA distribution after the end of your five-year holding period, and you also meet one of the other qualified distribution requirements such as being age $59^1/_2$ or older, the distribution is completely tax free. If you receive a distribution before satisfying both the five-year holding period requirement and one of the other qualified distribution requirements, and the withdrawal exceeds your contributions, the excess is taxable and possibly subject to the 10% penalty for pre–age $59^1/_2$ distributions *(see 8.12)*. Under the ordering rules discussed below, Roth IRA distributions are treated as being made first from contributions and then from earnings.

Ordering rules for distributions. Even if a distribution is not fully tax free as a qualified distribution, it is not taxable to the extent of your Roth IRA contributions. All of your Roth IRAs are treated as one account for purposes of determining if contributions or earnings have been withdrawn. If a distribution does not exceed total contributions to all of your Roth IRAs, it is not taxable.

Where you have made both regular annual contributions and conversion contributions to a Roth IRA, the regular contributions are considered to be withdrawn first. Then, conversion contributions are considered to be withdrawn in the order in which they were made. If part of a conversion contribution was not treated as a taxable distribution (because it was allocable to nondeductible contributions in the converted traditional IRA), the taxable part of the conversion is deemed withdrawn before the nontaxable part. Taking into account the taxable part of a conversion contribution before the nontaxable part (if any) of the conversion contribution may be important for purposes of determining whether the 10% early distribution penalty applies to the withdrawal of a conversion contribution within five years of the conversion *(see below)*.

Earnings on Roth IRA contributions are considered to be withdrawn last, after all contributions are taken into account. If the distribution is not a qualified distribution, the withdrawn earnings are subject to tax and if you are under age $59^1/_2$, to the 10% early distribution penalty *(see 8.12 for penalty exceptions)*.

Withdrawals within five years of conversion to Roth IRAs. The regular 10% early withdrawal penalty applies if withdrawals from a conversion Roth IRA are made by taxpayers under age $59^1/_2$ before January 1 of the fifth year after the year of the conversion. Unless a penalty exception is available, the 10% penalty applies to the extent that a withdrawal within the five-year period is allocable under the ordering rule *(see above)* to the taxable part of the conversion. Under the ordering rule for Roth IRA distributions, the entire withdrawal may be tax free because it does not exceed regular Roth IRA contributions, plus conversion contributions, but the 10% penalty still applies if a taxable conversion amount is deemed to be withdrawn before the end of the five-year period. The five-year period for purposes of this penalty rule is figured separately for each conversion contribution.

Distribution used for up to $10,000 of first-time home-buyer expenses. Tax-free treatment will apply to a Roth IRA distribution received after the first five-year period and used for up to $10,000 of qualifying "first-time" home-buyer expenses. The $10,000 limit is a lifetime cap per IRA owner, not an annual limitation. Expenses qualify if they are used within 120 days of the distribution to pay the acquisition costs of a principal residence for you, your spouse, your child, or your grandchild, or an ancestor of you or your spouse. The residence does not have to be the homeowner's "first" home. A qualifying first-time home-buyer is considered to be someone who did not have a present ownership interest in a principal residence in the two-year period before the acquisition of the new home. If the home-buyer is married, both spouses must satisfy the two-year test. Eligible acquisition costs include buying, constructing, or reconstructing the principal residence, including reasonable settlement, financing, and closing costs.

8.24 Distributions to Beneficiaries After the Death of a Roth IRA Owner

If you are the surviving spouse of the Roth IRA owner and you are the owner's sole Roth IRA beneficiary, you may elect to treat the inherited account as your own Roth IRA. If you treat the account as your own, you do not have to take distributions from the account at any time, since a Roth IRA owner is not subject to minimum distribution requirements. If you take some distributions from the account, you are not locked into a specific distribution schedule unless you agree to that schedule.

Surviving spouses who do not elect to treat an inherited Roth IRA as their own, and beneficiaries other than surviving spouses, must receive required minimum distributions. If there is an individual designated beneficiary under the final IRS regulations as of September 30 of the year following the year of the Roth IRA owner's death *(see 8.14)*, distributions are generally payable over the life expectancy of the designated beneficiary; *see* the Single Life Expectancy table at the end of *8.14*. Although it is unlikely, the plan document may require distributions under the five-year rule, which requires that the entire account be distributed by December 31 of the fifth year following the year of the owner's death. The plan may allow a choice between the life expectancy rule and the five-year rule.

If you are the surviving spouse and are sole beneficiary of the Roth IRA, you may delay the start of required minimum distributions until whichever is later: December 31 of the year the owner would have reached age $70^1/_2$, or December 31 of the year following the year of the owner's death. For a nonspouse beneficiary, required minimum distributions must begin by the end of the year following the year of the Roth IRA owner's death.

If there is no designated beneficiary under the IRS rules, such as where the Roth IRA owner's estate is the beneficiary, the account must be paid out under the five-year rule.

Five-year holding period for tax-free treatment. The same five-year holding period for receiving fully tax-free distributions that applied to the account owner *(8.23)* also applies to you as the beneficiary. The five-year holding period began on January 1 of the year for which the owner's first Roth IRA contribution was made. If you receive distributions before the end of the five-year holding period, the distributions will be tax free to the extent that they are a recovery of the owner's Roth IRA contributions and taxable to the extent they are earnings. If you are under age $59^1/_2$, the 10% early distribution penalty does *not* apply to a receipt of taxable earnings. Under the ordering rule for distributions discussed in *8.23*, contributions are deemed to be withdrawn before earnings. Distributions you receive after the end of the five-year holding period are completely tax free.

Caution

Final Regulations Require Required Minimum Distributions
Under the final IRS regulations, the 50% penalty for not receiving a required minimum distribution applies even if the distribution is tax-free.

Chapter 9

Income From Rents and Royalties

Use Schedule E of Form 1040 to report real estate rental income and expenses. You must also file Form 4562 to claim depreciation deductions for buildings you acquired in 2002.

Use Schedule C instead of Schedule E if you provide additional services for the convenience of the tenants, such as maid service. That is, Schedule C is used to report payments received for the use and occupancy of rooms or other areas in a hotel, motel, boarding house, apartment, tourist home, or trailer court where services are provided primarily for the occupant.

If you rent out an apartment or room in the same building in which you live, you report the rent income less expenses allocated to the rental property; *see 9.4.*

The law prevents most homeowners from deducting losses (expenses in excess of income) on the rental of a personal vacation home or personal residence if the owner or close relatives personally use the premises during the year. Tests based on days of personal and rental use determine whether you may deduct losses, as explained in *9.7.*

Rental losses may also be limited by the passive activity rules discussed in Chapter 10. Real estate professionals may avoid the passive restrictions on rental income. An investor who actively manages property may deduct rental losses of up to $25,000 under an exception to the passive activity loss restrictions.

Use Schedule E to report royalties, but if you are a self-employed author, artist, or inventor, report royalty income and expenses on Schedule C.

Business rentals of equipment, vehicles, or similar personal property are reported on Schedule C, not Schedule E.

Rental Income and Deductions

9.1 Reporting Rental Income and Expenses

On the cash basis, you report rent income on your tax return for the year in which you receive payment or in which you "constructively" receive it, such as where payment is credited to your bank account.

On the accrual basis, you report income on your tax return for the year in which you are entitled to receive payment, even if it is not actually paid. However, you do not report accrued income if the financial condition of the tenant makes collection doubtful. If you sue for payment, you do not report income until you win a collectible judgment.

Advance rentals. Advance rentals or bonuses are reported in the year received, whether you are on the cash or accrual basis.

Tenant's payment of landlord's expenses. The tenant's payment of your taxes, interest, insurance, mortgage amortization (even if you are not personally liable on the mortgage), repairs, or other expenses is considered additional rental income to you. If your tenant pays your utility bills or your emergency repairs and deducts the amount from the rent payment, you must include as rental income the full rental amount, not the actual net payment. However, you can claim an offsetting deduction for expenses, such as repairs, that would have been deductible had you paid them.

Tenant's payment to cancel lease. A tenant's payment for cancelling a lease or modifying its terms is considered rental income in the year you receive it regardless of your method of accounting. You may deduct expenses incurred because of the cancellation or modification and any unamortized balance of expenses paid in negotiating the lease.

Insurance. Insurance proceeds for loss of rental income because of fire or other casualty are rental income.

Improvements by tenants. You do not realize taxable income when your tenant improves the leased premises, provided the improvements are not substitute rent payments. Furthermore, when you take possession of the improvements at the time the lease ends, you do not realize income. However, you may not depreciate the value of the improvements as the basis to you is considered zero.

Property or services. If you receive property or services instead of money, include the fair market value of such property or services as rental income.

If you agree upon a specified price for services rendered, that price is generally treated as the fair market value.

Rental losses. Rental income may be offset by deductions claimed for depreciation, mortgage interest, and repair and maintenance costs. However, if these expenses exceed rental income, the resulting loss is subject to deduction limitations. If you do not qualify as a real estate professional *(10.3)*, you generally may not deduct rental losses from other income (such as salary, interest, and dividends). Rental losses may offset only other rental and passive activity income. However, if you perform some management role, you may deduct from other income *real estate* rental losses of up to $25,000, provided your adjusted gross income does not exceed $100,000 *(see 10.2)*. The passive activity restrictions have the positive effect of making rental income attractive. Consider purchasing rental property if you have passive tax losses that may be used to offset the rental income.

Passive loss restrictions, which also affect tax credits, are discussed in Chapter 10.

9.2 Checklist of Rental Deductions

The expenses in this section are deductible from rental income on Schedule E of Form 1040 in determining your profit.

Real estate taxes. However, special assessments for paving, sewer systems, or other local improvements are not deductible; they are added to the cost of the land. *See 16.6* through *16.9* for real estate tax deductions.

 Caution

Security Deposits
Distinguish advance rentals, which are income, from security deposits, which are not. Security deposits are amounts deposited with you solely as security for the tenant's performance of the terms of the lease, and as such are usually not taxed, particularly where local law treats security deposits as trust funds. If the tenant breaches the lease, you are entitled to apply the sum as rent, at which time you report it as income. If both you and your tenant agree that a security deposit is to be used as a final rent payment, it is advance rent. Include it in your income when you receive it.

Construction period interest and taxes. These expenses generally have to be capitalized and depreciated; *see 16.4*.

Depreciation of a rental building. You may start claiming depreciation in the month the building is ready for tenants. For example, you bought a house in May 2002 and spent June and July making repairs. The house is ready to rent in August and you advertise for tenants. You begin depreciation as of August, even if a tenant does not move in until September or some later month. The month the building is ready for tenants is the month that determines the first-year depreciation write-off under the mid-month convention. *See 9.5* for the monthly depreciation rates.

Depreciation for furniture and appliances. Furniture, carpeting, and appliances such as stoves and refrigerators used in residential rental property are considered five-year property for MACRS depreciation purposes.

Management expenses, such as a fee paid to a company for collecting the rent.

Maintenance expenses, such as heating, repairs, lighting, water, electricity, gas, telephone, coal, and other service costs; *see 9.3*.

Salaries and wages paid to superintendents, janitors, elevator operators, and service and maintenance personnel.

Traveling expenses to look after the properties. If you travel "away from home" to inspect or repair rental property, be prepared to show that this was the primary purpose of your trip, rather than vacationing or other personal purposes. Otherwise, the IRS may disallow deductions for round-trip travel costs.

Legal expenses for dispossessing tenants. But expenses of long-term leases are capital expenditures deductible over the term of the lease.

Interest on mortgages and other indebtedness. But expenses and fees for securing loans are nondeductible capital expenditures.

Commissions paid to collect rentals. But commissions paid to secure long-term rentals must be deducted over the life of the lease. Commissions paid to acquire the property are capitalized.

Premiums for fire, liability, and plate glass insurance. If payment is made in one year for insurance covering a period longer than one year, you amortize and deduct the premium over the life of the policy, even though you are on a cash basis.

Also deductible is a premium paid to secure a release from a mortgage in order to get a new loan.

Tax return preparation. You may deduct as a rental expense the part of a tax preparation fee allocable to Part 1 of Schedule E (income or loss from rentals or royalties). You may also deduct, as a rental expense, a fee paid to a tax consultant to resolve a tax underpayment related to your rental activities.

Charging below fair market rent. If you rent your property to a friend or relative for less than the fair rental value, you may deduct expenses and depreciation only to the extent of the rental income; *see 9.8*.

Co-tenants. One of two tenants-in-common may deduct only half of the maintenance expenses even if he or she pays the entire bill. A tenant-in-common who pays all of the expenses of the common property is entitled to reimbursement from the other co-tenant, so one-half of the bill is not his or her ordinary and necessary expense. Each co-tenant owns a separate property interest in the common property that produces separate income for each. Each tenant's deductible expense is that portion of the entire expense that each separate interest bears to the whole, and no more.

Costs of cancelling lease. A landlord may pay a tenant to cancel an unfavorable lease. The way the landlord treats the payment depends on the reason for the cancellation. If the purpose of the cancellation is to enable the landlord to construct a new building in place of the old, the cancellation payment is added to the basis of the new building. If the purpose is to sell the property, the payment is added to the cost of the property. If the landlord wants the premises for his or her own use, the payment is deducted over the remaining term of the old lease. If the landlord gets a new tenant to replace the old one, the cancellation payment is also generally deductible over the remaining term of the old lease.

Court Decision

Co-Tenant's Deduction for Real Estate Taxes

The Tax Court allowed a co-tenant to deduct more than her proportionate share of real estate taxes. According to the court, the deduction test for real estate taxes is whether the payment satisfies a personal liability or protects a beneficial interest in the property. In the case of co-tenants, nonpayment of taxes by the other co-tenants could result in the property being lost or foreclosed. To prevent this, a co-tenant who pays the tax is protecting his or her beneficial interest and, therefore, is entitled to deduct the payment of the full tax.

EXAMPLE

Handlery Hotels, Inc., had to pay its lessee $85,000 to terminate a lease on a building three years before the lease term expired. Handlery entered into a new 20-year lease on more favorable terms with another lessee. Handlery amortized the $85,000 cancellation payment over the three-year unexpired term of the old lease. The IRS claimed that the payment had to be amortized over the 20-year term of the new lease because it was part of the cost of obtaining the new lease. A federal district court agreed with the IRS, but an appeals court sided with Handlery. Since the unexpired lease term is the major factor in determining the amount of the cancellation payment, the cost of cancellation should be amortized over that unexpired term.

9.3 Distinguishing Between a Repair and an Improvement

Maintenance and repair expenses are not treated in the same way as expenses for improvements and replacements. Only maintenance and incidental repair costs are deductible against rental income. Improvements that add to the value or prolong the life of the property or adapt it to new uses are capital improvements. Capital improvements may not be deducted currently but may be depreciated under the rules at *42.13*. If you make improvements to property before renting it out, add the cost of the improvements to your basis in the property.

A repair keeps your property in good operating condition. For example, repairs include painting, fixing gutters or floors, fixing leaks, plastering, and replacing broken windows. However, putting a recreation room in an unfinished basement, paneling a den, putting up a fence, putting in new plumbing or wiring, putting on a new roof, and paving a driveway are all examples of capital improvements depreciable under *42.13*.

Repairs may not be separated from capital expenditures when both are part of an improvement program; *see* Example 2 below.

EXAMPLES

1. The cost of painting the outside of a building used for business purposes and the cost of papering and painting the inside are repair costs and may be deducted. The replacement of a roof or a change in the plumbing system is a capital expenditure that must be depreciated under MACRS; *see 42.13*.

2. Amanda Jones buys a dilapidated business building and has it renovated and repaired. The total cost comes to about $130,000, of which $17,800 is allocable to the repairs. The cost of the repairs is not deductible because the entire project is a capital expenditure. When a general improvement program is undertaken, you may not separate repairs from improvements. Both become an integral part of the overall betterment and are a capital investment, although a portion could be characterized as repairs when viewed independently.

 *Planning Reminder*

Repairs and Improvements
What if repairs and improvements are unconnected and not part of an overall improvement program? Assume you repair the floors of one story and improve another story by cutting new windows. You probably may deduct the cost of repairing the floors provided you have separate bills for the jobs. To safeguard the deduction, schedule the work at separate times so that the two jobs are not lumped together as an overall improvement program.

Normal maintenance or major improvement? Normal maintenance expenses were distinguished from major improvement costs in a case involving a major hotel where improvements and maintenance were generally done at the same time. The operators of the hotel capitalized the cost of the improvements but claimed expense deductions for the cost of painting and repapering rooms. The IRS disallowed the deductions, claiming they were part of the improvement program. The operators claimed that the papering and painting were normal and usual maintenance work required to keep the hotel in first-class condition. The Tax Court disagreed and sided with the IRS. However, on appeal, the appeals court allowed the deduction. The "rehabilitation doctrine" does not apply where it can be shown that repairs are part of a normal range of ongoing maintenance. Here, the painting and papering only served to maintain the first-class status of the hotel. The fact that the work was done under a general improvement plan did not defeat the deduction. Any commercial enterprise, such as a hotel, that annually spends large sums of money on replacements and repairs must do so under a detailed plan and budget.

How To Report Rentals of Residential and Vacation Homes

9.4 Reporting Rents From a Multi-Unit Residence

If you rent out an apartment or room in a multi-unit residence in which you also live, you report rent receipts and deduct expenses allocated to the rented part of the property on Schedule E of Form 1040. Expenses allocated to rental are deductible, whether or not you itemize deductions. You deduct interest and taxes on your personal share of the property as itemized deductions on Schedule A of Form 1040 if you itemize deductions.

If expenses exceed rental income on Schedule E, your loss deduction is subject to the passive loss rules discussed in Chapter 10. The loss, if it comes within the $25,000 allowance *(10.2)* or the exception for real estate professionals *(10.3)*, may be deducted from any type of income. If you cannot claim the allowance, the loss may be deducted only from passive activity income.

If your only passive activity losses are rental losses of $25,000 or less from actively managed rental real estate and your modified adjusted gross income is $100,000 or less, you do not have to use Form 8582 to deduct losses under the $25,000 allowance; *see 10.12.*

Court Decision

Rented Rooms That Are Not Separate Dwelling Units

A rental loss was denied to an owner of a two-story, four-bedroom house when he rented out two bedrooms to separate tenants after he lost his job. Although individual locks were placed on the doors of the rented bedrooms, the tenants and the owner shared access to the kitchen, bathroom, and other parts of the house. The Tax Court held that the rented rooms were not separate and distinct from the rest of the house that the owner used. The house was a single dwelling unit shared by the owner and tenants and under the personal-use rules at *9.7*, the owner could not claim a rental loss.

EXAMPLE

You buy a three-family house in March 2002. You occupy one floor as your personal residence and starting in June 2002 you rent out the other two floors. The house cost you $300,000 ($270,000 for the building and $30,000 for the land). Two-thirds of the basis of the building is subject to depreciation, or $180,000 (2/3 of $270,000). For a building placed in service in June, the depreciation rate is 1.970%, as shown in the table on the next page. This is how you deduct expenses for 2002:

	Total	Deduct itemized deductions	Deduct on Schedule E	Not deductible
Taxes	$6,000	$2,000	$4,000	
Interest	3,900	1,300	2,600	
Repairs	3,000		2,000	$1,000
Depreciation	3,546 (1.970% × $180,000)		3,546	
	$16,446	$3,300	$12,146	$1,000

The taxes and interest allocated to personal use are deductible on Schedule A if you itemize deductions. Repairs allocated to your apartment are nondeductible personal expenses.

If you or close relatives personally use the rented portion during the year and expenses exceed income, loss deductions may be barred under the rules in *9.7*.

9.5 Depreciation on Converting a Home to Rental Property

When you convert your residence to rental property, you may depreciate the building. You figure depreciation on the *lower* of:

- Fair market value of the building at the time you convert it to rental property; *or*
- Adjusted basis. This is your original cost for the building, exclusive of land, plus permanent improvements minus casualty or theft loss deductions claimed on prior tax returns.

You claim MACRS depreciation based on a $27\frac{1}{2}$-year recovery period. The specific rate for the year of conversion is the rate for the month in which the property is ready for tenants. For example, you move out of your home in May and make some minor repairs. You advertise the house for rent in June. Depreciation starts in June because that is when the home is ready for rental, even if you do not actually obtain a tenant until a later month. Under a mid-month convention, the house is treated as placed in service during the middle of the month. This means that one-half of a full month's depreciation is allowed for that month. In the table on the next page, the monthly depreciation rates for the year the property is placed in service and the next 16 years are shown. The table incorporates the mid-month convention.

EXAMPLE

In 1988, you bought a house for $125,000, of which $100,000 is allocated to the house; the $25,000 balance is allocated to the land. In June 2002, you move out of the house and rent it. At that time, the fair market value of the house exclusive of the land is $150,000. The depreciable basis of the house is the lower adjusted basis of $100,000. The depreciation rate for placing the house in service in June is 1.970%, as shown in the table below. Thus, your 2002 depreciation deduction is $1,970 ($100,000 × 1.970%). Your 2003 depreciation deduction is $3,636 ($100,000 × 3.636%).

Depreciating a rented cooperative apartment. If you rent out a co-op apartment, you may deduct your share of the total depreciation claimed by the cooperative corporation. The method for computing your share depends on whether you bought your co-op shares as part of the first offering. If you did, follow these steps: (1) Ask the co-op corporation officials for the total real estate depreciation deduction of the corporation, not counting depreciation for office space that cannot be lived in by tenant-shareholders. (2) Multiply Step 1 by the following fraction: number of your co-op shares divided by total shares outstanding. The result is your share of the co-op's depreciation, but you may not deduct more than your adjusted basis.

The computation is more complicated if you bought your co-op shares after the first offering. You must compute your depreciable basis as follows: Increase your cost for the co-op shares by your share of the co-op's total mortgage. Reduce this amount by your share of the value of the co-op's land and your share of the commercial space not available for occupancy by tenant-stockholders. Your "share" of the co-op's mortgage, land value, or commercial space is the co-op's total amount for such items multiplied by the fraction in Step 2 above, that is, the number of your shares divided by the total shares outstanding. After computing your depreciable basis, multiply that basis by the depreciation percentage for the month your apartment is ready for rental.

Basis to use when you sell a rented residence. For purposes of figuring gain, you use adjusted basis at the time of the conversion, plus subsequent capital improvements, and minus depreciation and casualty loss deductions. For purposes of figuring loss, you use the *lower* of adjusted basis and fair market value at the time of the conversion, plus subsequent improvements and minus depreciation and casualty losses. You may have neither gain nor loss to report; this would happen if you figure a loss when using the above basis rule for gains and you figure a gain when using the basis rule for losses.

Depreciation on a vacant residence. If you move from your house before it is sold, you generally may not deduct depreciation on the vacant residence while it is held for sale. The IRS will not allow the deduction, and, according to a Tax Court case, a deduction is possible only if you can show that you held the house expecting to make a profit on an increase in value over and above the value of the house when you moved from it. That is, you held the house for sale on the expectation of profiting on a future increase in value after abandoning the house as a residence.

 *Planning Reminder*

Obtain Appraisal

Have an appraiser estimate the fair market value of the house when it is rented. The appraisal will help support your basis for depreciation or a loss deduction on a sale if your return is examined.

Depreciation: Use the Row for the Month the Residence Is Ready for Rental in the First Rental Year

Month	1	2	3	4	5	6	7	8	9	10	11	12
Year												
1	3.485%	3.182%	2.879%	2.576%	2.273%	1.970%	1.667%	1.364%	1.061%	0.758%	0.455%	0.152%
2–9	3.636	3.636	3.636	3.636	3.636	3.636	3.636	3.636	3.636	3.636	3.636	3.636
10	3.637	3.637	3.637	3.637	3.637	3.637	3.636	3.636	3.636	3.636	3.636	3.636
11	3.636	3.636	3.636	3.636	3.636	3.636	3.637	3.637	3.637	3.637	3.637	3.637
12	3.637	3.637	3.637	3.637	3.637	3.637	3.636	3.636	3.636	3.636	3.636	3.636
13	3.636	3.636	3.636	3.636	3.636	3.636	3.637	3.637	3.637	3.637	3.637	3.637
14	3.637	3.637	3.637	3.637	3.637	3.637	3.636	3.636	3.636	3.636	3.636	3.636
15	3.636	3.636	3.636	3.636	3.636	3.636	3.637	3.637	3.637	3.637	3.637	3.637
16	3.637	3.637	3.637	3.637	3.637	3.637	3.636	3.636	3.636	3.636	3.636	3.636
17	3.636	3.636	3.636	3.636	3.636	3.636	3.637	3.637	3.637	3.637	3.637	3.637

9.6 Renting to a Relative

The tax law distinguishes between a rental of a unit used by a close relative as a principal residence and a rental of a unit that is not the relative's principal residence, such as a second home or vacation home. It is easier to deduct a rental loss on the principal residence rental.

On a fair market rental of a unit used by the close relative as a principal residence, your relative's use is *not* considered personal use by you that could bar a loss under the personal-use test in *9.7*. A relative's use of the unit as a second or vacation home *is* attributed to you in applying the personal-use test at *9.7*, even if you receive a fair market value rent.

Close relatives who come within these rules are: brothers and sisters, half-brothers and half-sisters, spouses, parents, grandparents, children, and grandchildren.

Fair market rental is the amount a person who is not related to you would be willing to pay. The most direct way to determine fair market rental is to ask a real estate agent in your neighborhood for comparative rentals.

9.7 Personal Use and Rental of a Residential Unit During the Year

The number of days of personal and rental use determines how you must report income and expenses of a residential unit in which you live part of a taxable year and rent or offer for rent for the days you do not live there.

Before reading the daily-use tests, list your days of use in 2002:
Fair market rental days:_____
Personal-use days:_____

Personal-use days may also include rental days to family members listed at *9.6* and use days under co-ownership agreements. *See 9.8* for details on personal-use days.

The daily-use tests apply to any "dwelling unit" you rent out that is also used as a residence during the year by yourself or other family members. A dwelling unit may be a house, apartment, condominium, cooperative, house trailer, mini motor home, boat, or similar property with basic living accommodations, including any appurtenant structure such as a garage. A dwelling unit does not include property used exclusively as a hotel, motel, inn, or similar establishment.

EXAMPLE

Barranti inherited a residence from her grandmother. The house was in a state of disrepair. A real estate agent estimated the fair market rental rate for the house to be between $700 and $750 per month. Barranti rented the house to her brother for $500 a month while he repaired the structure. After a year, he moved out and Barranti sold the house and claimed a rental loss and a loss on the sale. The Tax Court disallowed both losses. The below-market rental to Barranti's brother was treated as her own personal use of the house, preventing the rental loss deduction. The below-market rental was also treated as evidence that Barranti held the property for personal purposes and therefore she could not deduct the loss on the sale either.

Rental of less than 15 days during the taxable year. If you rent the unit for fewer than 15 days in the taxable year, you do not report the rental income and the only deductions allowed are those you would be allowed anyway as a homeowner. That is, if you itemize deductions on Schedule A, you deduct mortgage interest, real estate taxes, and casualty losses, if any. No other rental expenses such as depreciation and maintenance expenses are deductible. Interest is generally fully deductible if the home qualifies as a first or second home under the mortgage interest rules discussed in Chapter 15.

Rental of 15 days or more in the taxable year. A daily-use test determines whether your use of the unit during the taxable year is treated as residential use that requires you to limit your deductions to the rental income under the rules in *9.9*. You are considered to have used the unit as a residence if your personal-use days during the year (determined under *9.8*) exceeded 14 days, or, if greater, 10% of the days on which the unit was rented to others at a fair market rental price.

When the unit is treated as a residence, rental expenses are deductible on Schedule E only to the extent of rental income, following the rules in *9.9*. Expenses not deductible in the current year under this limitation may be carried forward and will be deductible up to rental income in the following year. The deduction limit is irrelevant if your rental income exceeds expenses. You report the rental income and claim the deductible expenses on Schedule E.

If your personal-use days do *not* exceed 14 days or 10% of the fair market rental days, whichever is more, your rental deductions are not limited by the personal-use test. However, a loss deduction is subject to the passive activity loss restrictions discussed at *10.1*.

EXAMPLES

1. In 2002, you rented out a condominium unit in Florida at a fair market rental for 260 days. If you used the unit personally for 27 or more days, the condominium is considered a residence subject to the deduction limitation rules at *9.9* because your personal use exceeds 26 days, 10% of the fair market rental days. If you used the unit for 26 days or less, you may treat the unit for the taxable year as rental property and you may deduct a loss, if any, subject to the passive activity rules at *10.1*.

   Where rental days exceed 140 days, as a rule of thumb, you can figure that for every 10 days of fair-rent use, you may use the unit personally for one day. Thus, if you rented a vacation unit for 11 months, you could personally use it for a month or so without jeopardizing a deduction of a rental loss (rental of 330 days would permit 33 days of personal use).

2. Assume the same unit as in Example 1 but you rented the unit for 130 days. If you used the unit personally for 14 days or less, you may treat the unit as a rental property. To treat it as a residence, your personal use would have to exceed 14 days, since 14 days is greater than 10% of the rental days.

9.8   Counting Personal-Use and Rental Days

In applying the personal-use test in *9.7*, personal-use days are:

- Days you used the residence for personal purposes other than days primarily spent making repairs or getting the property ready for tenants.
- Days on which the residence is used by your spouse, children, grandchildren, parents, brothers, sisters, or grandparents. However, if such a relative pays you a fair rental value to use the home as a principal residence, the relative's use is not considered personal use by you. If you rent a vacation home to such relatives, their use is considered personal use by you even if they pay a fair rental value amount; *see* Example 1 below.

   The same rules apply to days of use by a relative of a co-owner of the property.
- Days on which the residence is used by any person under a reciprocal arrangement that allows you to use some other dwelling during the year.
- Days on which you rent the residence to any person for less than fair market value.
- Days that a co-owner of the property uses the residence, unless the co-owner's use is under a shared-equity financing agreement discussed later in this section.

An owner is not considered to have personally used a home that is used by an employee if the value of such use is tax-free lodging required as a condition of employment; *see 3.11*.

Shared-equity financing agreements for co-owners. Use by a co-owner is not considered personal use by you if you have a shared-equity financing agreement under which: (1) the co-owner pays you a fair rent for using the home as his or her principal residence; and (2) you and your co-owner each have undivided interests for more than 50 years in the entire home and in any appurtenant land acquired with the residence.

Any use by a co-owner that does not meet these two tests is considered personal use by you if, for any part of the day, the home is used by a co-owner or a holder of any interest in the home (other than a security interest or an interest under a lease for fair rental) for personal purposes. For this purpose, any other ownership interest existing at the time you have an interest in the home is counted, even if there are no immediate rights to possession and enjoyment of the home under such other interest. For example, you have a life estate in the home and your friend owns the remainder interest. Use by either of you is personal use.

EXAMPLES

1. A son rented a condominium in Florida to his parents, who split their time between the Florida apartment and the home they owned in Illinois. Although the parents paid a fair amount for the Florida condo, the son's rental deductions were limited by the IRS and the Tax Court to interest and real estate taxes that did not exceed the rental income. The parents' rental days were attributed to the son under the 14 day/10% rental day limit since the home in Illinois, and not the Florida apartment, was their principal residence.

 Planning Reminder

Shared-Equity Financing Agreements

As an investor, you can help finance the purchase of a principal residence for a family member or other individual. The rental income you receive for your ownership share in the property may be offset by deductions for your share of the mortgage interest, taxes, and operating expenses you pay under the terms of the agreement, as well as depreciation deductions for your percentage share. Rental losses are subject to the passive loss restrictions in Chapter 10.

The other co-owner living in the house may claim itemized deductions for payment of his or her share of the mortgage interest and taxes.

2. You and your neighbor Joe are co-owners of a vacation condominium. You rent the unit out whenever possible; Joe uses the unit for two weeks every year. As Joe owns an interest in the unit, both of you are considered to have used the unit for personal purposes during those weeks.
3. You and your neighbor Tom are co-owners of a house under a shared-equity financing agreement. Tom lives in the house and pays you a fair rental price. Even though Tom has an interest in the house, the days he lives there are not counted as days of personal use by you because Tom rents the house as a main home under a shared-equity financing agreement.
4. You rent a beach house to Jane. Jane rents her house in the mountains to you. You each pay a fair rental price. You are using your house for personal purposes on the days that Jane uses it because your house is used by Jane under an arrangement that allows you to use her house.

Rental of principal residence prior to sale. You are not considered to have made any personal use of a principal residence that you rent or try to rent at a fair rental for (1) a consecutive period of 12 months or more *or* (2) a period of less than 12 months that ends with the sale or exchange of the residence. For example, you move out of your principal residence on May 31, 2002, offering it for rental as of June 1. You rent it from June 15 until mid-November, when you sell the house. Under the special rental period rule, your use of the house from January 1 until May 31, 2002, is *not* counted as personal use. This means that deductions for the rental period are not subject to the rental income limitation discussed in *9.9*.

Rental pool arrangements. In proposed regulations, the IRS holds that a rental pool is not a basis for counting fair rental days. However, the proposed regulations permit rental pool participants to elect to average the actual rental of their units. Unanimous consent is required to elect the averaging rule. If the election is made, the number of rental days for a unit is determined by multiplying the aggregate number of days that all units in the rental pool were rented at fair rental during the pool season by a fraction. The numerator of the fraction is the number of participation days of a particular unit; the denominator is the aggregate number of participation days of all the units.

The IRS may apply the rental pool rule to a rental guarantee option. The Tax Court supported the IRS position, but an appeals court did not, in the following Example.

Caution

Rental Pool Arrangements

Pool arrangements have been devised to avoid the loss restriction by attempting to increase the days the home is held for a fair rental value. They have not been successful. Courts have ruled that only days on which a home is actually rented count as fair rental days, not days of availability through the rental pool.

EXAMPLE

Razavi owned a condo in Florida and elected to take a rental guarantee option from the resort operator over a three-year period. The annual guaranteed rent was $21,000 plus 40% of rentals over $52,500. In 1987, the resort actually received gross rentals of $48,300 for the unit, but Razavi received $21,000 under the guarantee and claimed a rental loss deduction. The IRS disallowed the loss because it claimed that Razavi personally used the unit for 27 days, exceeding 10% of the 200 days the unit had actually been rented.

Razavi claimed that the 27 days were less than 10% of the 338 days covered by a rental guarantee. That is, the guarantee covered 365 days less 27 days of personal use. The Tax Court disagreed on the grounds that the guarantee was based on a rental period of between 142 days and 179 days and this was far below the 270 rental days needed to support his 27 personal-use days.

The Sixth Circuit allowed the loss. The $21,000 guarantee was a fair rental for the entire year based on rentals of comparable units. Although Razavi probably could have earned more than $21,000 with daily or weekly rentals, such short-term rentals also would have carried added risks and responsibilities that he was able to avoid by choosing the rent guarantee.

9.9 Allocating Expenses to Rental Days

When you rent out your home for part of the year at fair market value and also use it personally on some days during the taxable year, expenses are allocated between personal and rental use. By law, deductible expenses of renting are limited by this fraction:

$$\frac{\text{Days of fair market rental}}{\text{Total days of rental and personal use}}$$

The days a vacation home is held out for rent but not actually rented are not counted as rental days.

There is a conflict of opinion between the IRS and the courts over the issue of whether the above fractional formula applies also to interest and taxes. According to the IRS, it does. According to the courts, interest and taxes are allocated on a daily basis. Thus, if a house is rented for 61 days in the year, one-sixth of the deductible interest and taxes ($^{61}/_{365}$) is deducted first from the rental income. This rule allows a larger amount of other expenses to be deducted from rental income than is allowed under the IRS application of the formula; *see* Example 2 on the next page.

Claiming expenses if personal use bars a loss deduction. If your personal use of a residence exceeds the 14-day /10% test in *9.7*, the residence was rented for at least 15 days during the year, and the expenses allocated to rental use exceed rental income, the allocable rental expenses are deducted from rental income in a specific order:

1. The rental portion of the following expenses is fully deductible on Schedule E of Form 1040, even if the total exceeds rental income: deductible home mortgage interest *(15.1)*, real estate taxes, deductible casualty and theft losses (Chapter 18), and directly related rental expenses. Directly related rental expenses are rental expenses not related to the use or maintenance of the residence itself, such as office supplies, rental agency fees, advertising, and depreciation on office equipment used in the rental activity.

2. If there is any rental income remaining after the income is reduced by the expenses in Step 1, the balance is next offset by the rental portion of operating expenses for the residence itself, such as utilities, repairs, and insurance. Do not include depreciation on the rental part of the home in this group.

3. If any rental income remains after Step 2, depreciation on the rental portion of the residence may be deducted from the balance.

Step 1 expenses, as well as the expenses from Steps 2 and 3 that offset rental income, are deducted on the applicable lines of Schedule E. Operating expenses from Step 2 and depreciation from Step 3 that exceed the balance of rental income are carried forward to the next year as rental expenses for the same property. In the next year, the carried-over expenses are deductible only to the extent of rental income from the property for that year, even if your personal use of the residence does *not* exceed the 14-day/10% test in *9.7* for that year.

If you itemize deductions, you claim the *personal-use* portion of deductible mortgage interest, real estate taxes, and casualty and theft losses on Schedule A of Form 1040.

Interest expenses. If you personally use a rental vacation home for more than the greater of 14 days or 10% of the fair market rental days *(9.7)*, the residence may be treated as a qualifying second residence under the mortgage interest rules; *see 15.1.* The interest on a qualifying second home is generally fully deductible and is not subject to disallowance under the passive activity restrictions in Chapter 10. As shown above, the portion of the deductible mortgage interest allocable to the rental portion is deducted from rental income (along with taxes) before other expenses.

Filing Tip

Carryover of Disallowed Expenses
If your deductions for operating expenses and depreciation are limited by the personal-use rules, the disallowed amounts may be carried over to the following year.

EXAMPLES

1. You rent out your vacation home for 61 days in 2002, receiving rent of $2,000. You use the home yourself for 61 days. You may deduct expenses only up to the amount of this income because your personal use exceeds the 14-day/10% rental test. Your expenses are mortgage interest of $1,600, real estate taxes of $800, and maintenance and utility costs of $1,200. Depreciation (based on 100% rental use) is $1,500. Assume the vacation home is a qualifying second home *(15.1)*, so that all the interest is deductible under the mortgage interest rules. Under the IRS method, one-half of all the expenses (61 rental days divided by 122 total days of use), including the interest and taxes, are deducted in this order:

Rent income		$2,000
Less: Interest	$ 800	
Taxes	400	1,200
		$ 800
Less: Maintenance		600
		$ 200
Less: Depreciation		$ 200
		$ 200

Court Decision

Allocation of Taxes and Interest
The IRS position on allocating mortgage interest and real estate taxes to rental income is not as favorable as the position adopted by the Tax Court and several appeals courts; *see* Example 2 on the next page.

Under the Tax Court's method of allocating interest and taxes, one-sixth of the interest and taxes (61/365) would be deducted from rental income, rather than one-half as under the IRS method.

The balance of the depreciation is not deductible. It may be carried forward to the following year.

The balance of interest and taxes is deductible as itemized deductions provided you claim itemized deductions on Schedule A of Form 1040.

If the vacation home were not a qualifying second residence as discussed in *15.1,* the interest would not be deducted with taxes from the $2,000 of rental income, but would be treated as an operating expense and deducted along with the maintenance expenses.

2. The Boltons paid interest and property taxes totaling $3,475 on their vacation home. Maintenance expenses (not including depreciation) totaled $2,693. The Boltons stayed at the home 30 days and rented it for 91 days, receiving rents of $2,700. Because the personal use for 30 days exceeded the 14-day limit, the Boltons could deduct rental expenses only up to the gross rental income of $2,700, reduced by interest and taxes allocable to rental. In figuring the amount of interest and taxes deductible from rents, they divided the number of rental days, or 91, by 365, the number of days in the year. This gave them an allocation of 25%. After subtracting $869 for interest and taxes (25% of $3,475) from rental income, they deducted $1,831 ($2,700 – $869) of maintenance expenses from rental income.

The IRS argued that 75% of the Boltons' interest and tax payments had to be allocated to the rental income. The IRS used an allocation base of 121 days of personal and rental use. Thus, the IRS allocated 75% ($91/_{121}$) of the interest and taxes, or $2,606, to gross rental income of $2,700. This allocation allowed only $94 maintenance expenses to be deducted ($2,700 – $2,606).

The Tax Court sided with the Boltons and an appeals court (the Ninth Circuit) agreed. The IRS method of allocating interest and taxes to rental use is bizarre. Interest and taxes are expenses that accrue ratably over the year and are deductible even if a vacation home is not rented for a single day. Thus, the allocation to rental use should be based on a ratable portion of the annual expense by dividing the number of rental days by the number of days in a year.

The Tenth Circuit appeals court also supports the Tax Court allocation method.

Planning Reminder

Profit Motive

A profit motive is presumed if you can show a profit for at least three of the last five years you engaged in rental activities. The IRS, however, may *rebut* this presumption. For a way to fight this rebuttal, consult *40.10.*

9.10 Rentals Lacking Profit Motive

If you rent a residential unit for 15 days or more and a loss is not barred under the personal-use limitation in *9.7,* the IRS may attempt to disallow a loss by claiming that you had no profit motive in placing the unit up for rent. If the IRS makes such an argument, you must try to prove a profit motive, as discussed in *40.10.* Any loss disallowed on these grounds may not be carried over to a later year.

EXAMPLES

1. *(Loss allowed.)* In 1973, Clancy purchased a house and land in a coastal resort area of California. Prior to the purchase, Clancy was told by a renting agent that he could expect reasonable income and considerable appreciation from the property. Previously, he had sold similar property in the same development at a profit. After the purchase, Clancy spent $5,000 to prepare the house for rental, and gave a rental agency the exclusive right to offer the property for rent. The house was available for rent 95% of the time in 1973, and 100% of the time in 1974. However, rentals proved disappointing, totaling only $280 in 1973 and $1,244 in 1974, despite the active efforts of the agency to rent the property. However, the house did appreciate in value and was eventually sold at a profit of $14,000. In 1973 and 1974, Clancy deducted rental expenses of approximately $21,000, which the IRS disallowed. The IRS claimed that the house was not rental property used in a business. Furthermore, as Clancy knew that he could not make a profit from the rentals, he could not be considered to hold the property for the production of income.

The Tax Court agreed that the expenses were not deductible business expenses. But this did not mean they were not deductible as expenses of income production. Although the rental income from the property was minimal, Clancy acquired and held the property expecting to make a profit on a sale. He had previously sold similar property at a profit and was told to expect considerable rental income as well as appreciation from the new house. Where an owner holds property, as Clancy did here, because he or she believes that it may appreciate in value, such property is held for the production of income. Further evidence that Clancy held the property to make a profit: He rarely used it for personal purposes and an agent actively sought to rent it.

2. *(Loss allowed.)* Nelson bought a condominium, hired a rental agent, and even advertised in the *Wall Street Journal* and *Indianapolis Star*. He also listed the unit for sale. During 1974, he was unable to rent the apartment but deducted expenses and depreciation of over $6,100, which the IRS disallowed. The IRS argued that he did not buy the unit to make a profit but to shelter substantial income from tax. The Tax Court disagreed. Although his efforts to rent were not successful in 1974, he was successful in later years in renting the unit. He rarely visited the apartment other than to initially furnish it. When he went on vacation, he went abroad or to other vacation spots.

3. *(Loss disallowed.)* The Lindows purchased a condominium that they rented out during the prime winter rental season. However, over an eight-year period their expenses consistently exceeded rental income. The Tax Court agreed with the IRS that expenses in excess of rental income were not deductible. Substantial, repeated losses, even after the initial years of operation, indicated that the operation was not primarily profit-oriented. The rental return during the prime rental season could not return a profit. Even if the condominium were fully rented for the entire prime rental season, annual claimed expenses would exceed rent income. The couple also used the unit for several months and intended to live there on retirement. They did not consider putting the unit up for sale with an agent. Finally, that they had detailed records of income and expenses did not prove a business venture. Records, regardless of how detailed, are insufficient to permit the deduction of what are essentially personal expenses.

IRS may challenge losses claimed on temporary rental before sale. If you are unable to sell your home and must move, it may be advisable to put it up for rent. This way you may be able to deduct maintenance expenses and depreciation on the unit even if it remains vacant. However, the IRS has disallowed loss deductions for rentals preceding a sale on the ground that there was no "profit motive" for the rental under the rules discussed at *40.10*. Courts have allowed loss deductions in certain cases.

EXAMPLES

1. The IRS and Tax Court disallowed a loss deduction for rental expenses under the "profit-motive rules" *(40.10)* where a principal residence was rented for 10 months until it could be sold. According to the Tax Court, the temporary rental did not convert the residence to rental property. Since the sales effort was primary, there was no profit motive for the rental. Thus, no loss could be claimed; rental expenses were deductible only to the extent of rental income. The favorable side of the Tax Court position: Since the residence was not converted to rental property, the owners could under prior law rules defer tax on the gain from the sale by buying a new home. An appeals court reversed the Tax Court and allowed both tax deferral and a loss deduction. The rental loss was allowed since the old home was actually rented for a fair rental price. Furthermore, the owners had moved and could not return to the old home, which was rented almost continuously until sold.

2. In 1976, a couple bought a condo apartment in Pompano Beach, Florida. In 1983, they decided to move and listed the unit for either sale or rent with a local real estate broker. Sale of the unit was difficult because of the saturation of the Florida real estate market. Rental of the unit was also difficult because the condominium association's rules barred the rental of condominium units on a seasonal basis. The unit remained unrented until it was sold in 1986 for a substantial gain. In 1984, the couple deducted a $9,576 rental loss ($7,596 for maintenance expenses and $1,980 for depreciation). The IRS disallowed the deduction as not incurred in a bona fide rental activity. The Tax Court allowed the deduction. The couple made an honest and reasonable effort to rent the condominium. Lack of rental income was caused by a slack rental market and the condominium association rules prohibiting short-term rentals.

Royalty Income and Deductions

9.11 Reporting Royalty Income

Royalties are payment for use of patents or copyrights or for the use and exhaustion of mineral properties. Royalties are taxable as ordinary income and are reported on Schedule E (Form 1040). Depletion deductions relating to the royalties are also reported on Schedule E. If you own an operating oil, gas, or mineral interest, or are a self-employed writer, investor, or artist, you report royalty income, expenses, and depletion on Schedule C.

Examples of Royalty Income

License fees received for use, manufacture, or sale of a patented article.

Renting fees received from patents, copyrights, and depletable assets (such as oil wells).

Authors' royalties including advance royalties if not a loan.

Royalties for musical compositions, works of art, etc.

Proceeds of sale of part of your rights in an artistic composition or book, for example, sale of motion picture or television rights.

Royalties from oil, gas, or other similar interests; *see 9.16.* To have a royalty, you must retain an economic interest in the minerals deposited in the land you have leased to the producer. You usually have a royalty when payments are based on the amount of minerals produced. However, if you are paid regardless of the minerals produced, you have a sale that is taxed as capital gain if the proceeds exceed the basis of the transferred property interest. Bonuses and advance royalties that are paid to you before the production of minerals are taxable as royalty income and are entitled to an allowance for depletion. However, bonuses and advance royalties for gas and oil wells and geothermal deposits are not treated as gross income for purposes of calculating percentage depletion. If the lease is terminated without production and you received a bonus or advance royalty, you report as income previously claimed depletion deductions. You increase the basis of your property by the restored depletion deductions.

9.12 Production Costs of Books and Creative Properties

Freelance authors, artists, and photographers may deduct their costs of producing original works in the years that the expenses are paid or incurred. The uniform capitalization rules that generally apply to property that you produce *(see 40.3)* do not apply.

You qualify for current expense deductions if you are self-employed and you *personally create* literary manuscripts, musical or dance scores, paintings, pictures, sculptures, drawings, cartoons, graphic designs, original print editions, photographs, or photographic negatives or transparencies. However, the exception to the uniform capitalization rules does not apply to, and thus current deductions are not allowed for, expenses relating to motion picture films, videotapes, printing, photographic plates, or similar items.

If you conduct business as an owner-employee of a personal service corporation and you are a qualifying author, artist, or photographer, the corporation may claim current deductions related to your expenses in producing books or other eligible creative works. Substantially all of the corporation's stock must be owned by you and your relatives.

9.13 Deducting the Cost of Patents or Copyrights

If you create an artistic work or invention for which you get a government patent or copyright, you may depreciate your costs over the life of the patent or copyright. Basis for depreciation includes all expenses that you are required to capitalize in connection with creating the work, such as the cost of drawings, experimental models, stationery, and supplies; travel expenses to obtain material for a book; fees to counsel; government charges for patent or copyright; and litigation costs in protecting or perfecting title.

If you purchased the patent or artistic creation, depreciate your cost over the remaining life of the patent or copyright. If your cost for a patent is payable annually as a fixed percentage of the revenue derived from use of the patent, the depreciation deduction equals the royalty paid or incurred for that year. However, if a copyright or patent is acquired in connection with the acquisi-

Planning Reminder

Passive Income Exception

Certain working oil and gas interests are exempt from the passive activity loss restrictions; *see 10.10.*

Caution

Hobby Loss Restrictions

Authors and artists with expenses exceeding income may be barred by the IRS from claiming loss deductions; *see 40.10.*

tion of a business, the cost is amortizable over a 15-year period as a Section 197 intangible; *see 42.18*.

If you inherited the patent or rights to an artistic creation, your cost is the fair market value either at the time of death of the person from whom you inherited it *(5.17)* or the alternate valuation date if elected by the executor. You get this cost basis even if the decedent paid nothing for it. Figure your depreciation by dividing the fair market value by the number of years of remaining life.

If your patent or copyright becomes valueless, you may deduct your unrecovered cost or other basis in the year it became worthless.

9.14 Intangible Drilling Costs

Intangible drilling and development costs include wages, fuel, repairs, hauling, and supplies incident to and necessary for the preparation and drilling of wells for the production of oil or gas, and geothermal wells. For wells you are developing in the United States, you can elect to deduct the costs currently as business expenses or treat them as capital expenses subject to depreciation or depletion.

Electing current deductions. The election applies only to costs of drilling and developing items that do not have a salvage value. You must make this election by deducting the expenses on your income tax return for the first tax year in which you pay or incur the costs.

Tax-shelter investors may deduct prepayments of drilling expenses only if the well is "spudded" within 90 days after the close of the taxable year in which the prepayment is made. The prepayment must also have a business purpose, not be a deposit, and not materially distort income. The investor's deduction is limited to his or her cash investment in the tax shelter. For purposes of this limitation, an investor's cash investment includes loans that are not secured by his or her shelter interest or the shelter's assets and loans that are not arranged by the organizer or promoter. If the above tests are not met, a deduction may be claimed only as actual drilling services are provided.

Recapture of intangible drilling costs for oil, gas, geothermal, or mineral property. Upon the disposition of oil, gas, geothermal, or other mineral property placed in service after 1986, ordinary income treatment applies to previously claimed deductions for intangible drilling and development costs for oil, gas, and geothermal wells, and to mineral development and exploration costs. Depletion deductions, discussed in *9.15*, are also generally subject to this ordinary income treatment upon disposition of the property.

For oil, gas, or geothermal property placed in service before 1987, ordinary income treatment applies on the disposition of a working or operating interest to the extent that intangible drilling and development cost deductions exceeded what would have been allowed if the costs had been deducted through cost depletion. Recapture for geothermal property applies only to wells commenced after September 30, 1978.

AMT and intangible drilling costs. If you are an independent oil or gas producer or royalty owner, intangible drilling costs for oil and gas production are not treated as tax preference items for purposes of alternative minimum tax (AMT). However, the reduction in your AMT income from not treating intangible drilling costs as a tax preference is limited. The reduction may not exceed 40% of your AMT income, figured as if excess intangible drilling costs were still a tax preference item and without regard to any AMT net operating loss deduction; *see* the instructions to Form 6251.

9.15 Depletion Deduction

Properties subject to depletion deductions are mines, oil and gas wells, timber, and exhaustible natural deposits.

Two methods of computing depletion are: (1) cost depletion and (2) percentage depletion. If you are allowed to compute under either method, you must use the one that produces the *larger* deduction. In most cases, this will be percentage depletion. For timber, you must use cost depletion.

Cost depletion. The cost depletion of minerals is computed as follows: (1) divide the total number of units (such as tons or barrels) remaining in the deposit to be mined into the adjusted basis of the property; and (2) multiply the unit rate found in Step 1 by the number of units for which payment is received during the taxable year if you are on the cash basis, or by the number of units sold if you are on the accrual basis.

Adjusted basis is the original cost of the property, less depletion allowed, whether computed under the percentage or cost depletion method. It does not include nonmineral property such as mining equipment. Adjusted basis may not be less than zero.

 Caution

Drilling Expense Prepayments
Prepayments of drilling expenses are only deductible if the well is "spudded" within 90 days after the close of the taxable year in which the prepayment was made, and the deduction is limited to the original amount of the investment.

Timber depletion is based on the cost of timber (or other basis in the owner's hands) and does not include any part of the cost of land. Depletion takes place when standing timber is cut. Depletion must be computed by the cost method, not by the percentage method. However, instead of claiming the cost depletion method, you may elect to treat the cutting of timber as a sale subject to capital gain or loss treatment. For further details, *see* IRS Publication 535.

Percentage depletion. Percentage depletion is based on a certain percentage rate applied to annual gross income derived from the resource. In determining gross income for percentage depletion, do not include any lease bonuses, advance royalties, or any other amount payable without regard to production. A deduction for percentage depletion is allowed even if the basis of the property is already fully recovered by prior depletion deductions. The percentage to be applied depends upon the mineral involved; the range is from 5% up to 22%. For example, the maximum 22% depletion deduction applies to sulphur, uranium, and U.S. deposits of lead, zinc, nickel, mica, and asbestos. A 15% depletion percentage applies to U.S. deposits of gold, silver, copper, iron ore, and shale.

Taxable income limit. For properties other than oil and gas, the percentage depletion deduction *may not exceed* 50% of taxable income from the property computed without the depletion deduction. In computing the 50% limitation, a net operating loss deduction is not deducted from gross income. A 100% taxable income limit applies to oil and gas properties; *see 9.16.*

Oil and gas property. Percentage depletion for oil and gas wells was repealed as of January 1, 1975, except for the following exemptions: (1) small independent producers and royalty owners and (2) for gas well production. *See 9.16* for these oil and gas percentage depletion exemptions.

9.16 Oil and Gas Percentage Depletion

Small independent producers and royalty owners generally are allowed to deduct percentage depletion at a 15% rate for domestic oil and gas production. However, a higher rate may be allowed for qualifying "marginal" production, as discussed on the next page. The deduction is subject to a taxable income limit.

The 15% rate applies to a small producer exemption that equals the gross income from a maximum daily average of 1,000 barrels of oil or 6 million cubic feet of natural gas, or a combination of both. Gross income from the property does not include advance royalties or lease bonuses that are payable without regard to the actual production.

The depletable natural gas quantity depends on an election made annually by independent producers or royalty owners to apply part of their 1,000-barrel-per-day oil limitation to natural gas. The depletable quantity of natural gas is 6,000 cubic feet times the barrels of depletable oil for which an election has been made. The election is made on an original or amended return or on a claim for credit or refund. For example, if your average daily production is 1,200 barrels of oil and 6.2 million cubic feet of natural gas, your maximum depletable limit is 1,000 barrels of oil, which you may split between the oil and gas. You could claim depletion for 500 barrels of oil per day and for 3 million cubic feet of gas per day: 3 million cubic feet of gas is the equivalent of the remaining 500 barrels of oil limit (500 barrels × 6,000 cubic feet depletable gas quantity equals 3 million cubic feet of gas).

Transferees who received their interest in a "proven" oil or gas property after October 11, 1990, are allowed percentage depletion under the regular rules.

Transferees receiving "proven" properties after 1974 and before October 12, 1990, are not allowed percentage depletion unless the transfer was made because of the death of the prior owner, a tax-free transfer to a controlled corporation, a transfer between commonly controlled corporations, or changes in beneficiaries of a trust where the changes are due to births, adoptions, or deaths within a single family.

Ineligible retailers and refiners. The small producer exemption is not allowed to any producer who owns or controls a retail outlet for the sale of oil, natural gas, or petroleum products. It is also not allowed to a refiner who refines more than 50,000 barrels of oil on any one day of the taxable year; the limit is based on inputs of crude oil into the refinery process, rather than outputs. A taxpayer is not treated as a retailer where gross sales of oil and gas products are less than $5 million in any one year or if all sales of oil or natural gas products occur outside the United States, and none of the taxpayer's domestic production is exported. Bulk sales of oil or natural gas to industrial or utility customers are not to be treated as retail sales.

Figuring average daily domestic production. Average daily production is figured by dividing your aggregate production during the taxable year by the number of days in the taxable year. If you hold a partial interest in the production (including a partnership interest), production rate is found by multiplying total production of such property by your income percentage participation in such property.

The production over the entire year is averaged regardless of when production actually occurred. If average daily production for the year exceeds the 1,000-barrel or 6-million-cubic-feet limit, the exemption must be allocated among all the properties in which you have an interest.

Taxable income limits on percentage depletion. The percentage depletion deduction for a small producer or royalty owner may not exceed the *lesser* of (1) 100% of the net income from the property before the depletion allowance or (2) 65% of your net income from all sources computed without regard to the depletion deduction allowed under the small producer's exemption, any net operating loss carryback, and any capital loss carryback.

The above 100% limit is suspended for production from marginal production properties (*see* below) during taxable years starting after 1997 and before 2004.

Limitations where family members or related businesses own interests. The daily exemption rate is allocated among members of the same family in proportion to their respective production of oil. Similar allocation is required where business entities are under common control. This affects interests owned by you, your spouse, and minor children; by corporations, estates, and trusts in which 50% of the beneficial interest is owned by the same or related persons; and by a corporation that is a member of the same controlled group.

Higher depletion for marginal production. Depending on the "reference price" for crude oil (*see* below), independent producers and royalty owners may be allowed a higher depletion rate for *marginal production,* defined as oil or natural gas from "stripper well property" or property producing substantially all "heavy" oil. A stripper well property is one from which average daily production, divided by the number of all producing wells on the property, is 15 or fewer "barrel equivalents." A barrel equivalent is a barrel of oil or 6,000 cubic feet of natural gas.

The 15% rate is increased by 1% for each whole dollar that the "reference price" (the average annual wellhead price as estimated by the IRS) of domestic crude oil for the previous year was below $20 per barrel. However, since the reference price for 2001 exceeded $20 per barrel ($21.86), the basic 15% rate applies for marginal production in 2002.

 Law Alert

Percentage Depletion on Marginal Production

Since 1998, the taxable income limit on percentage depletion from marginal production of oil and natural gas has been suspended. The suspension had been scheduled to expire for tax years beginning after 2001, but it has been extended through tax years beginning before 2004.

Chapter 10

Loss Restrictions: Passive Activities and At-Risk Limits

The passive activity laws were intended to discourage tax-shelter investments, but their reach goes beyond tax shelters to cover all real estate investors and persons who invest in businesses as "silent partners" or who are not involved full time in the business. The passive activity rules prevent an investor from deducting what the law defines as a passive loss from salary, self-employment income, interest, dividends, sales of investment property, or retirement income. Such losses are deductible only from income from other passive activities. Losses disallowed by the passive activity rules are suspended and carried forward to later taxable years and become deductible only when passive income is realized or substantially all of the activity is sold.

Casualty and theft losses are not passive losses unless they are of the type usually occurring in a business, such as shoplifting theft losses.

On your tax return, passive income items and allowable deductible items are reported as regular income and deductions. For example, rental income and allowable deductions are reported on Schedule E. However, before you make these entries, you may have to prepare Form 8582, which identifies your passive income and losses and helps you to determine whether passive loss items are deductible.

At-risk rules generally limit losses for an activity to your cash investment and loans for which you are personally liable, as well as certain nonrecourse financing for real estate investments. *See 10.17.*

Passive Activity Restrictions

10.1 Rental Activities

Rental activities (real estate or personal property) are *automatically* treated as passive unless you qualify as a real estate professional *(10.3)* or the rentals are considered by law to be business activity as discussed below. If "automatic" passive activity treatment applies, you may not deduct a rental loss against nonpassive income such as salary or investment income unless you can take advantage of the up-to-$25,000 allowance that applies to rental real estate losses *(10.2)*. Even where rental income or loss is not automatically treated as passive because you qualify as a real estate professional or because the activity is excluded from the rental category and treated as a business (*see* the list below), income or loss will still be "passive" unless you materially participate *(10.6)* in the business activity.

What is a rental activity? Except for activities specifically excluded from the rental category (*see* the list of rentals treated as businesses below), rentals include all activities in which a customer pays for the use of tangible property (real estate or personal property). Such activities include rentals of apartments and commercial office space (whether long- or short-term); long-term rentals of office equipment, automobiles, and/or a vessel under a bareboat charter or a plane under a dry lease (no pilot or captain and no fuel); and net-leased property. A property is under a net lease if the deductions (other than rents and reimbursed amounts) are less than 15% of rental income or where the lessor is guaranteed a specific return or is guaranteed against loss of income.

Rentals treated as business activity. Although rental activities are generally treated as "passive," the following six activities are excluded from the category of rental activity and thus losses from the activities are not deductible under the $25,000 rental real estate loss allowance *(10.2)*. The fact that these activities are not treated as rentals does not mean that the passive activity rules are inapplicable. Income or loss from these activities will still be treated as passive income or loss if you fail to meet one of the business material participation tests at *10.6*.

1. **The average period of customer use of the property is seven days or less.** Short-term rentals of vacation units, autos, videocassettes, tuxedos, and hotel and motel rooms are *not* considered rental activities if the average period of customer use is seven days or less. You figure the average period of customer use for the year by dividing the aggregate number of days in all rental periods that end during the tax year by the number of rentals. Each period during which a customer has a continuous or recurring right to use the property is treated as a separate rental.

   A loss from a seven-day-or-less real estate rental activity is *not* eligible for the up-to-$25,000 loss allowance *(10.2)*. Since it is not treated as a real estate rental activity, it may not be included in the election to aggregate rental real estate activities under the real estate professional rules at *10.3*.

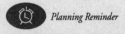 *Planning Reminder*

Vacation Home Rentals

If you rent out a vacation unit for an average rental period of seven days or less at a loss, the loss is treated as a business loss deductible from nonpassive income if you meet the material participation tests at *10.6*. If you do not materially participate, the loss is treated as a passive loss, deductible only from passive income. The loss does not qualify for the up-to-$25,000 rental loss allowance discussed in *10.2* because the property is not treated as rental property.

> **EXAMPLE**
>
> The Toups purchased a cottage in Callaway Gardens, a vacation resort south of Atlanta, Georgia. The unit was rented for short-term periods of seven days or less during the year to resort guests. The resort's operator was the sole managing and rental agent. Over a three-year period, they deducted net losses of $46,848. Under the seven-days-or-less rule, the activity was not a rental activity, but the IRS disallowed their losses as passive activity losses because they were passive investors who did not materially participate in the activity. The Toups argued that they materially participated, spending more than 300 hours each year preparing an annual budget and cash flow analysis and meeting with other owners to set rental fees and inspect the grounds.
>
> The Tax Court sided with the IRS. The losses were passive because the Toups did not materially participate in the resort operation. They had nothing to do with running the resort on a day-to-day basis. Their activity was merely that of investors.

2. **The average period of customer use of the property is more than seven days but is 30 days or less, and you provide significant personal services.** Personal services include only services performed by individuals and do not include (a) services necessary to permit the lawful use of the property; (b) construction or repair services that extend the useful life of the property for a period substantially longer than the average period of customer use; and (c) services that are provided with long-term rentals of high-grade commercial or

residential real property such as cleaning and maintenance of common areas, routine repairs, trash collection, elevator service, and security guards.

Note: For purposes of Exceptions 2 and 3, if more than one class of property is rented as part of the same activity, average period of customer use is figured separately for each class. The average period of customer use (as explained in Exception 2) is multiplied by the ratio of gross rental income from that class to the total rental income from the activity; *see* the Form 8582 instructions.

3. **Regardless of the average period of customer use, extraordinary personal services are provided so that rental is incidental.** This applies to institutions providing hospital patients room and board.

4. **Rental is incidental to a nonrental activity.** A rental of property is excluded from the rental activity category if the property is held mainly for investment or for use in a business. A rental is considered incidental to an investment activity if the principal purpose of holding the property is to realize gain from its appreciation and the gross rental income from the property for the year is less than 2% of the unadjusted basis or fair market value of the property, whichever is less.

A rental is incidental to a business activity if (1) you own an interest in the business during the year, (2) the rented property was predominately used in that business during the current year or during at least two of the immediately preceding five tax years, and (3) gross rental income from the property is less than 2% of the lower of the unadjusted basis of the property or its fair market value. Under test (2), a rental may qualify for the exception although it is not rented to the related business in the current year, so long as it was used in the business in two or more of the preceding five years.

> **EXAMPLE**
>
> Kyle Gail owns unimproved land with a fair market value of $400,000 and an unadjusted basis of $300,000. He holds it for the principal purpose of realizing gain from its appreciation. To help reduce the cost of holding the land, he leases it to a rancher for grazing purposes at an annual rental of $3,500. The gross rental income of $3,500 is less than 2% of the lower of the fair market value or the unadjusted basis of the land. The rental of the land is not a rental activity.

5. **Providing property to a partnership or S corporation that is not engaged in rentals.** If you own an interest in a partnership or S corporation and you contributed property to it as an owner, the contributed property is not considered a rental activity. For example, if as a partner you contribute property to a partnership, your distributive share of partnership income will not be considered as income from a rental activity. However, this exception will not apply if the partnership is engaged in a rental activity.

6. **The property is generally allowed for the non-exclusive use of customers during fixed business hours, such as operating a golf course.** The customers are treated as licensees, not lessees.

Grouping rental and nonrental business activities. Where you conduct rental as well as nonrental business activities, you may not group a rental activity with a nonrental activity, unless they form an appropriate economic unit and one of the activities is considered insubstantial in relation to the other. No guidelines are provided for determining what is "substantial" or "insubstantial."

Under an exception, a rental of property to a business may be grouped together with the business, although one activity is not insubstantial to the other, provided each business owner has the same proportionate ownership in the rental activity and the activities are an appropriate economic unit.

Real property rentals and personal property rentals. An activity involving the rental of realty and one involving the rental of personal property may not be treated as a single activity, unless the personal property is provided in connection with the real property or the realty is provided in connection with the personal property.

10.2 Rental Real Estate Loss Allowance of up to $25,000

If you are not a real estate professional *(10.3)* but you actively participate by performing some management role in a real estate rental venture, you may deduct up to $25,000 of a real estate rental loss against your regular, nonpassive income such as wages. The allowance is phased out if your modified adjusted gross income (MAGI) is between $100,000 and $150,000. You generally take the allowance into account on Schedule E but Form 8582 is sometimes required; *see 10.12.*

The allowance applies only to real estate rentals not excluded from the rental category by the rules at *10.1.* For example, short-term vacation home rentals averaging seven days or less do not qualify for the allowance. The allowance applies only to real estate rentals, not to any rentals of equipment or other personal property.

Planning Reminder

Rental of Personal Residence

Renting a personal residence is not treated as a passive rental activity if you personally use the home for more than the greater of (1) 14 days or (2) 10% of the days the home is rented for a fair market rental amount. On Schedule E, you may claim a full deduction for the rental portion of real estate taxes and mortgage interest, assuming the home is a principal residence or qualifying second home under the mortgage interest rules *(15.1)*.

See 9.9 for limitations on deductions of other rental expenses.

A trust may not qualify for the $25,000 allowance. Thus, you may not circumvent the $25,000 ceiling or multiply the number of $25,000 allowances by transferring rental real properties to one or more trusts. However, an estate may qualify for the allowance if the decedent actively participated in the operation. The estate is treated as an active participant for two years following the death of the owner.

Married filing separately. If you file separately and at any time during the taxable year live with your spouse, you may not claim the allowance. If you are married but live apart from your spouse for the entire year and file a separate return, the $25,000 allowance and the adjusted gross income phase-out range are reduced by 50%. Thus, the maximum allowance on your separate return is $12,500 and this amount is phased out by 50% of MAGI over $50,000. Therefore, if your MAGI exceeds $75,000, no allowance is allowed.

Active participation test must be met. To qualify for the allowance, you must meet an *active participation test.* Having an agent manage your property does not prevent you from meeting the test, but you must show that you or your spouse participates in management decisions, such as selecting tenants, setting rental terms, and reviewing expenses. The IRS may not recognize your activity as meeting the test if you merely ratify your manager's decisions. You (together with your spouse) must also have at least a 10% interest in the property. Limited partners are not considered active participants and do not qualify for the allowance.

If a decedent actively participated in property held by an estate, the estate is deemed to actively participate for the two years following the death of the taxpayer.

EXAMPLES

1. You live in New York and own a condominium in Florida that you rent through an agent. You set the rental terms and give final approval to any rental arrangement. You also have final approval over any repairs ordered by the agent. You are an active participant and may claim the $25,000 rental allowance.
2. A married couple who owned a time-share interest in an ocean-front condominium rented the condo during their allotted period to vacationers. They claimed a rental loss that the IRS held did not qualify for the up-to-$25,000 allowance. Since the average rental period for their unit was seven days or less, the rentals were excluded from the category of rental activity; *see 10.1.*

Figuring the $25,000 allowance. First match income and loss from all of your rental real estate activities in which you actively participate. A net loss from these activities is then applied to net passive income (if any) from other activities to determine the $25,000 allowance. Gains from pre-1987 installment sales are passive income if the sold property was from an activity that would have been considered passive had the passive activity rules been in effect before 1987. If you rent out a personal residence, rental income or loss may be exempt from the passive activity rules; *see* the Planning Reminder on page 232. The allowance may not be used against carryover losses from prior taxable years when you were not an active participant.

EXAMPLE

David Chung has a $90,000 salary, $15,000 income from a limited partnership, and a $26,000 loss from rental real estate in which he actively participated. The $26,000 loss is first reduced by the $15,000 of passive income. The remaining balance of the $11,000 rental loss is deducted from the salary income.

Phaseout of the $25,000 allowance. For purposes of the allowance phaseout, *modified adjusted gross income (MAGI)* is adjusted gross income shown on your return, but you should disregard:

- Any passive activity income or loss.
- Any loss allowed under *10.3* for real estate professionals.
- Taxable Social Security and railroad retirement payments (Chapter 34). For example, if your adjusted gross income on Form 1040 is $90,000, and that includes $5,000 of taxable Social Security benefits, your modified adjusted gross income is $85,000.
- Deductible IRA contributions (Chapter 8).
- The deduction on Form 1040 for one-half of self-employment tax liability (Chapter 45).

 Filing Tip

Rental Allowance Based on Income

The rental loss allowance is phased out when your modified adjusted gross income is over $100,000. For every dollar of income over $100,000, the loss allowance is reduced by 50 cents. When your modified adjusted gross income reaches $150,000, the allowance is completely phased out. An explanation of modified adjusted gross income and an example of how the phaseout works is under the heading "Phaseout of the $25,000 allowance" on this page.

If modified AGI is—	Loss allowance is—
Up to $100,000	$25,000
110,000	20,000
120,000	15,000
130,000	10,000
140,000	5,000
150,000 or more	0

- Deductible student loan interest (Chapter 38).
- Overall loss from a publicly traded partnership (*see* instructions to Form 8582).
- Excluded interest on U.S. Savings Bonds used for paying tuition in the year the bonds are redeemed. If you are allowed to exclude the interest from income for regular tax purposes (Chapter 38), the interest must still be included for purposes of the allowance phaseout.
- Employer-provided adoption assistance that is a tax-free fringe benefit (Chapter 3). The assistance must be included in MAGI for purposes of applying the allowance phase-out rule.

A rental loss that is carried over because it exceeds the allowance may be deductible in a later year if you continue to meet the active participation rule.

EXAMPLES

1. In 2002, Liz Blake had $120,000 in salary, $5,000 of partnership income from a limited partnership, and a $31,000 loss from a rental building in which she actively participates. She may deduct only $15,000 of the rental loss. The remaining $11,000 must be carried over to 2003. The $5,000 limited partnership income and the $31,000 rental loss are disregarded in figuring MAGI because they are passive. Her deduction and carryover are computed as follows:

Modified adjusted gross income	$120,000
Less: amount not subject to phaseout	$100,000
Amount subject to phaseout	$ 20,000
Phase-out percentage	50%
Portion of allowance phased out	$ 10,000
Maximum rental allowance offset	$ 25,000
Less: Amount phased out	$ 10,000
Deductible rental loss allowance offset in 2002	$ 15,000
Passive loss from rental real estate	$ 31,000
Less: Passive income from partnership	$ 5,000
Passive activity loss	$ 26,000
Less: Deductible rental loss allowance in 2002	$ 15,000
Carryover loss to 2003	$ 11,000

2. In 2003, Liz's modified adjusted gross income is below the phase-out range and she continues to actively participate in the rental building, which incurred a loss of $5,000. Under the allowance, she may deduct a rental loss of $16,000 (the current loss plus the carryover loss).

Real estate allowance for tax credits. On Form 8582-CR, a deduction equivalent of up to $25,000 may allow a credit that otherwise would be disallowed. You must meet the active participation test in the year the credit arose. The $25,000 allowance is generally subject to the regular MAGI phase-out rule.

To claim low-income housing and rehabilitation credits, you need not meet the active participation test. Furthermore, for rehabilitation credits and credits for low-income housing property placed in service before 1990, the phaseout for the $25,000 allowance starts at MAGI of $200,000 ($100,000 if married filing separately and living apart the entire year); thus, the deduction equivalent is completely disallowed when MAGI reaches $250,000. The phaseout is figured on Form 8582-CR. There is no MAGI phaseout for low-income housing property placed in service after 1989, unless you have a pass-through interest in a partnership or S corporation that you acquired before 1990.

The *deduction equivalent* of a credit is the amount which, if allowed as a deduction, would reduce your tax by an amount equal to the credit. For example, a tax credit of $1,000 for a taxpayer in the 27% bracket equals a deduction of $3,704 and would come within the $25,000 allowance provided you actively participated. In the 27% bracket, the equivalent of a $25,000 deduction is a tax credit of $6,750 ($25,000 × 27%). Thus, if you have a rehabilitation credit of $7,000 and you are in the 27% bracket, the $25,000 allowance may allow you to claim $6,750 of the credit, while the balance of the credit would be carried forward to the following year.

If in one year you have both losses and tax credits, the $25,000 allowance applies first to the losses, then to tax credits from rental real estate with active participation, then to tax credits for rehabilitation or low-income housing placed in service before 1990, and finally to tax credits for low-income housing placed in service after 1989.

The allowance and net operating losses. If losses are allowed by the $25,000 allowance but your nonpassive income and other income are less than the loss, the balance of the loss may be treated as a net operating loss and may be carried back and forward; *see 40.18* for further details.

Planning Reminder

Proving Management Activities

To take advantage of the $25,000 loan allowance, make sure you have proof of active management, such as approving leases and repairs.

10.3 Real Estate Professionals

Real estate rental activities are not automatically passive *(10.1)* for qualifying real estate professionals. If you meet a two-part personal services test (Test 1), any rental real estate activity in which you materially participate (Test 2) is *not* a passive activity. Income or loss from the rental real estate is reported as nonpassive on Schedule E (Form 1040).

Test 1: Qualifying as a real estate professional. You must meet both of the following two activity tests for the tax year:

1. More than 50% of your personal services in all of your businesses must be performed in real property businesses in which you materially participate *(10.6)*. For this purpose, a real property business means any real property development, redevelopment, construction, reconstruction, acquisition, conversion, rental operation, management, leasing, or brokerage trade or business. Real estate financing is not included. Personal services performed as an employee are *not* treated as performed in a real estate business unless you are considered a "more than 5% owner" in the employer. That is, you must own more than 5% of the outstanding stock or more than 5% of total combined voting powers of all stock issued by the corporation. In a noncorporate employer such as a partnership, you must own more than a 5% capital or profit interest.
2. More than 750 hours of your services are in real property businesses in which you materially participate *(10.6)*.

For purposes of determining hours of material participation under (1) and (2) above, each interest in rental real estate property is treated as a separate activity unless you elect to treat all of your interests as one rental activity as discussed below. If, under the rules in *10.1*, you group a rental real estate activity with a business activity, that rental activity is not treated as rental real estate for purposes of the real estate professional rules.

Attorneys who specialize in real estate practice while participating in a rental business may not treat the legal practice as material participation for purposes of qualifying as real estate professionals.

For a married couple filing jointly, both the "50% of services test" and the "750 hours test" must be met by one of the spouses individually, without regard to the other spouse's services, although participation by the taxpayer's spouse counts in determining whether a taxpayer materially participates in the real property businesses.

A closely held C corporation qualifies under the real estate professional rules if in a taxable year more than 50% of the gross receipts of the corporation are from a real property business in which the corporation materially participates under the rules at *10.15*.

Test 2: Rental real estate activity material participation. If you qualify as a real estate professional under Test 1 above, you must still show that you materially participate in your rental real estate activity(ies) to avoid passive activity treatment. If you have more than one rental real estate activity and elect to aggregate (*see* below), total participation in all of the activities is combined in applying the material participation tests in *10.6*. If an election to aggregate has not been made, material participation must be determined separately for each rental property.

Election to aggregate rental real estate activities. If in a prior year rental real estate activities were treated separately, you may elect to aggregate activities for any year you qualify as a real estate professional by attaching a statement to your original tax return for that year. The statement must contain a declaration that you are a qualifying real estate professional and are treating all of your rental real estate activities as a single activity under Internal Revenue Code Section 469(c)(7)(A). The election is binding for all future years in which you qualify as a real estate professional, even if there are intervening years in which you do not qualify. In the nonqualifying years, the election has no effect. You may not revoke the election in a later year unless there has been a material change in circumstances that you explain in a statement attached to your original return for the year of revocation. That the election no longer gives you a tax advantage is not a basis for a revocation.

 *Planning Reminder*

Tax Break for Real Estate Professionals

Proving professional status and material participation allows you to avoid passive loss limitations. You may improve your ability to meet the material participation tests in *10.6* by aggregating your rental real estate activities. However, you may not want to aggregate activities if you have passive losses from non–real estate activities and have rental income from an operation that, if treated as passive income, could be offset by the losses.

Also be aware that if you elect to group all of your rental real estate activities as one activity and later sell one of the rental properties, you will probably be unable to deduct suspended losses from that property because of the rule that requires "substantially all" of your interest in an activity (here, the combined activity) to be disposed of in order to deduct suspended losses; *see 10.13*.

EXAMPLE

Kosonen owned seven rental properties. In 1994, he worked on all his properties a total of 877 hours, which qualified him as a real estate professional. But he could not meet the material participation test for each of the individual properties. If he could aggregate the activities, the material participation test would be met for the combined activity, allowing him to deduct his net rental losses against nonpassive income.

On his 1994 return, he reported the losses from all the activities as an aggregate deduction and treated it as nonpassive. The IRS disallowed the deduction because he had not made a specific election to aggregate. Kosonen argued that by claiming on his return the total of his losses, he had put the IRS on notice that he was aggregating his rental activities.

The Tax Court disagreed. A specific election is required to put the IRS on notice that a taxpayer is a qualifying real estate professional making the election to aggregate rental activities. Reporting the net losses on his return as an aggregate active (nonpassive) loss was not enough because Kosonen could also have reported his net losses as active if he had materially participated in each of the seven activities and had not elected to aggregate.

If the election to aggregate is made and there is net income for the aggregated activity, the income may be offset by prior year suspended losses from any of the aggregated rental real estate activities regardless of which of the rental activities produced the income.

Rental loss allowance may apply to nonqualifying rental activity. A real estate professional may also be able to claim all or part of the $25,000 rental loss allowance *(10.2)*. For example, you are a real estate professional and meet the material participation test for one rental real estate activity but not for another and do not elect to aggregate. Losses from the nonqualifying activity qualify for the rental allowance. Furthermore, suspended prior year losses from the qualifying activity may also be deductible under the rental loss allowance, as illustrated in the following Example.

EXAMPLE

Jane Morton owns a rental building in Manhattan and a rental building in Newark. In 2002, she qualifies as a real estate professional. She does not elect to treat the two buildings as one activity. She materially participates in the operations of the Manhattan building, which has $100,000 of disallowed passive losses from prior years and a $20,000 loss for 2002. She does not materially participate in the operation of the Newark building, which has $40,000 of rental income for 2002. Jane also has $50,000 of income from other nonpassive sources.

The $20,000 loss from the Manhattan building is treated as nonpassive and offsets $20,000 of the $50,000 nonpassive income from other sources.

Jane can also use $40,000 of the $100,000 prior year suspended losses from the Manhattan building to offset the $40,000 of passive income from the Newark building in 2002. Of the $60,000 remaining suspended loss, $25,000 may be deducted under the rental loss allowance provided Jane's MAGI is under $100,000, the phase-out threshold for the allowance *(10.2)*.

The rental loss allowance is deducted from the $30,000 of remaining nonpassive income, leaving Jane with $5,000 of nonpassive income for 2002. The balance of suspended losses of $35,000 ($60,000 – $25,000 rental allowance) may be used in 2003 to offset income from the Newark building or passive income from other sources.

Interests in S corporations and partnerships. Your interest in rental real estate held by a partnership or an S corporation is treated as a single interest in rental real estate if the entity grouped its rental real estate as one rental activity. If not, each rental real estate activity of the entity is treated as a separate interest in rental real estate. However, you may elect to treat all interests in rental real estate, including the rental real estate interests held by an S corporation or partnership, as a single rental real estate activity.

If you hold a 50% or greater interest in the capital, income, gain, loss, deduction, or credit in a partnership or S corporation for the taxable year, each interest in rental real estate held by the entity is treated as a separate interest in rental real estate, regardless of the entity's grouping of activities. However, you may elect to treat all interests in rental real estate, including your share of the rental real estate interests held by the entities, as a single rental real estate activity.

Limited partners. Generally, a person who has a limited partnership interest in rental real estate must establish material participation by participating for more than 500 hours during the year or meeting Test 5 or Test 6 at *10.6*. This material participation rule also generally applies if an election is made to aggregate limited partnership interests in rental real estate with other rental real estate interests. However, these more stringent rules may be avoided if less than 10% of the gross rental income for the taxable year from all rental real estate activities is attributed to limited partnership interests. In such a case, you may make the election to aggregate all rental real estate activities and determine material participation under any of the seven tests at *10.6*.

Caution

Consistent Treatment Required

Once you treat activities separately or group them together as a single activity, the IRS generally requires you to continue the same treatment in later taxable years. You can regroup activities only if the original treatment was "clearly inappropriate" or has become clearly inappropriate because of a material change in circumstances.

10.4 Participation May Avoid Passive Loss Restrictions

To avoid passive activity treatment of income and loss from a business investment, you must show material participation in that activity. The word "activity" does not necessarily relate to one specific business. If you invest in several businesses, you may be able to treat all or some of those activities as one activity or treat each separately.

Determining aggregate or separate treatment for your activities is discussed at *10.5* and material participation tests are discussed at *10.6*.

For a rental activity, material participation tests apply only if you are trying to qualify for the passive activity exception for real estate professionals at *10.3*. For other rental real estate operators or investors, an "active" participation test that requires only certain management duties may allow you to deduct rental losses of up to $25,000; see *10.2*.

10.5 Classifying Business Activities as One or Several

If you are in more than one activity, determining aggregate or separate treatment is important for:

Deducting suspended losses when you dispose of an activity. If the activity is considered separate from the others, you may deduct a suspended loss incurred from that activity when you dispose of it. If it is not separate from the others, the suspended loss is deductible only if you dispose of substantially all of your investment; *see 10.13*.

Applying the material participation rules of *10.6*. If activities are separate and apart from each other, the material participation tests are applied to each activity separately. If the activities are aggregated as one activity, material participation in one activity applies to all.

Determining if you meet the 10% interest requirement for active participation under the rules discussed at *10.2*.

Earmarking a business activity. You may use any reasonable method under the facts and circumstances of your situation to determine if several business activities should be grouped together or treated separately. To be grouped together, the IRS says that the activities should be "an appropriate economic unit" for measuring gain or loss. For making this determination, the IRS sets these general guidelines: (1) similarities and differences in types of business; (2) the extent of common control; (3) geographic location; (4) the extent of common ownership; and (5) interdependencies among the activities. Interdependency is measured by the extent to which several business activities buy or sell among themselves, use the same products or services, have the same customers and employees, or use a single set of books and records.

The IRS will not require that all five factors be present for grouping for multiple activities.

Rental activities. Rental activities may not be grouped with business activities unless one of the exceptions discussed at *10.1* applies.

> **EXAMPLE**
>
> Lance Jones has a significant interest in a bakery and a movie theater at a shopping mall in Baltimore and in a bakery and a movie theater in Philadelphia. The IRS does not explain what constitutes a significant interest. In grouping his activities into appropriate economic units based on the relevant facts and circumstances, Jones could: (1) group the theaters and bakeries into a single activity; (2) place the two theaters into one group and the bakeries into a second group; (3) put his Baltimore businesses into one group and his Philadelphia businesses in another group; or (4) treat the two bakeries and two movie theaters as four separate activities.
>
> Once he chooses a grouping, he must consistently use that grouping for all future years unless a material change makes the grouping inappropriate. His decision is also subject to IRS review and, if questioned, he must show the factual basis for his grouping.

IRS may regroup activities. The IRS may regroup your activities if your grouping does not reflect one or more appropriate economic units and a primary purpose of the grouping is to circumvent the passive loss rules.

> **EXAMPLE**
>
> Five doctors operate separate medical practices and also invest in tax shelters that generate passive losses. They form a partnership to operate X-ray equipment. In exchange for the equipment contributed to the partnership, each doctor receives limited partnership inter-

ests. The partnership is managed by a general partner selected by the doctors. Partnership services are provided to the doctors in proportion to their interests in the partnership and service fees are set at a level to offset the income generated by the partnership against individual passive losses. Under these facts, the IRS will not allow the medical practices and the partnership to be treated as separate activities as this would circumvent the passive loss limitations by generating passive income from the partnership to offset the tax-shelter losses. The IRS will require each doctor to treat his or her medical practice and interests in the partnership as a single activity.

Partnerships and S corporations. A partnership or S corporation must group its activities under the facts and circumstances test. Once a partnership or S corporation determines its activities, the partners or shareholders are bound by that decision and may not regroup them. The partners and shareholders then apply the facts and circumstances test to combine the partnership or S corporation activities with, or separate them from, their other activities.

Special rule for certain limited partners and limited entrepreneurs. A limited entrepreneur is a person with an ownership interest who does not actively participate in management. A limited entrepreneur or limited partner in films, videotapes, farming, oil and gas, or the renting of depreciable property generally may combine each such activity only with another of such activities in the same type of business, and only if he or she is a limited entrepreneur or partner in both. Grouping of such activities with other activities in the same type of business in which he or she is not a limited partner or entrepreneur is allowed if the grouping is appropriate under the general facts and circumstances test.

10.6 Material Participation Tests for Business

The IRS has seven tests for determining material participation in a business. Some tests require only a minimum amount of work, such as 500 hours a year, and others only 100 hours. You need to meet only one of the seven tests to qualify as a material participant. If you do, then the income and loss from that business is treated as *nonpassive*.

The tests apply whether you do business as a sole proprietor or in an S corporation or partnership. Losses and credits passed through S corporations and partnerships are subject to passive activity rules.

If you are a limited partner, you are by law not a material participant unless you satisfy certain conditions discussed at *10.11*.

Your tax position towards the IRS participation rules will depend on whether the particular activity produces income or loss. If you have passive activity losses from other activities, you may prefer to have a profitable business activity treated as a passive activity in order to offset the income by the losses from passive activities. On the other hand, if the business activity operates at a loss and you do not have passive income from other sources, you may want to meet the material participation test for that business activity in order to claim current loss deductions. IRS strategy in reviewing your activities would be the opposite. If your return were under audit, an agent would attempt to prevent you from treating income from a business activity as passive. For example, the IRS, by applying Tests 5 and 6, can prevent a retired person from treating post-retirement income from a prior business or profession as passive income to offset passive losses from another activity. If you realize a loss in one passive activity, Test 4 may prevent you from generating passive income by merely reducing your participation in another activity.

Material participation results in nonpassive treatment. There are two key terms: material participation and significant participation. If you materially participate by meeting one of the seven IRS tests, your activity is not a passive activity. For example, under Test 1, work for more than 500 hours in an activity is considered material participation. Under Test 4, significant participation is work for more than 100 hours but less than 500 hours at an activity in which you do not otherwise materially participate. The IRS applies a significant participation rule to convert passive activity income into nonpassive income and to convert several significant participation activities into material participation if the total participation in those activities exceeds 500 hours; *see* Test 4.

Work by you or your spouse that counts as participation. Any work you do in a business in which you have an ownership interest is treated as "participation." If you are married, work by your spouse in the activity during the tax year is treated, for purposes of the following tests, as participation by you. This is true even if your spouse does not own an interest in the business or if you file separately. However, the following type of work is not treated as participation:

Planning Reminder

Proof of Material Participation

Material participation must be determined on an annual basis. Show proof of your participation by keeping an appointment book, calendar, or log of the days and time spent in the operation. If you want to treat contacts by phone as material activity, keep a log of phone calls showing the time and purpose of the calls.

Caution

Overcoming Investor Status

The IRS will not recognize time spent as an investor as "participation" unless you can show you are involved in daily operations or management of the activity. According to the IRS, this requires you to be at the business site on a regular basis. Even if you do appear daily, the IRS may ignore such evidence if there is an on-site manager or you have full-time business obligations at another site. Activity of an investor includes the studying and reviewing of financial reports for your own use that are considered unrelated to management decisions. If you invest in a business that is out of state or a distance from your home, you may also find it difficult to prove material participation.

1. Work that is not of a type customarily done by an owner of an activity, if one of the principal reasons for the performance of the work is to avoid the passive loss rules (*see* the Example below).
2. An investor's review of financial statements or analysis that is unrelated to day-to-day management or operation of the activity.

EXAMPLE

An attorney owns an interest in a professional football team for which he performs no services. He anticipates a net loss from the football activity and to qualify as a material participant, he hires his wife to work 15 hours a week as an office receptionist for the team. Although a spouse's participation in an activity generally qualifies as participation by both spouses, the receptionist work here does not qualify as participation because (1) it is not the type of work customarily done by an owner of a football team and (2) the attorney hired his spouse to avoid disallowance of a passive loss.

IRS Tests for Material Participation

If you meet one of the following tests for the year in question, you are considered to have materially participated in that activity, and therefore the activity is considered *nonpassive* for that year. Tests 5 and 6 prevent retired individuals from treating post-retirement income as passive income.

Test 1. You participate in the activity for more than 500 hours during the tax year.

Test 2. Your participation in the activity for the tax year constitutes substantially all of the participation in the activity of all individuals including non-owners for the year.

Test 3. You participate in the activity for more than 100 hours during the tax year, and your participation is at least as great as that of any other person including non-owners for that year.

EXAMPLE

Joan Brown and Pat Collins are partners in a moving van business that they conduct entirely on weekends. They both work for eight hours each weekend. Although neither partner participates for more than 500 hours (Test 1), they are both treated as material participants under Test 3 because they each participate for more than 100 hours and no one else participates more.

Test 4. You are active in several enterprises but each activity does not in itself qualify as material participation. However, if you spend more than 100 hours in each activity and the total hours of these more-than-100-hour activities exceeds 500, you are treated as a material participant in each of these activities. This test is referred to as the "significant participation" test.

EXAMPLES

1. Mike Smith is a full-time accountant with ownership interests in a restaurant and shoe store. He works 150 hours in the shoe store and 360 hours in the restaurant. Under the significant participation test (Test 4), Smith is considered a material participant in both activities, as the total hours of both exceed 500.
2. Carl Young invests in five businesses. In activity (a) he works 110 hours; in activity (b), 100 hours; in activity (c), 125 hours; in activity (d), 120 hours; and in activity (e), 140 hours. He does not qualify under the significant participation test (Test 4). Although his total hours in the five activities exceed 500, activity (b) is ignored in the total count because the hours did not exceed 100. The total of the four other activities is 495.
3. Assume that Young worked one hour more for activity (b). It and all of the other activities would be considered as meeting the significant material participation test. The total hours are 596. Assuming that activity (a) totaled 125 hours and activity (b) remained at 100 hours or less, he would meet the test for all of the activities except for activity (b), which did not exceed 100 hours. The total of the four qualified activities is 510 hours.

 Caution

Retired Farmers

Retired or disabled farmers are treated as materially participating in a farming activity if they materially participated for five of the eight years preceding their retirement or disability. A surviving spouse is also treated as materially participating in a farming activity if the real property used in the activity meets the estate tax rules for special valuation of farm property passed from a qualified decedent and the surviving spouse actively manages the farm.

Test 5. You materially participated in the activity for any five tax years during the 10 tax years preceding the tax year in question. The five tax years do not have to be consecutive. Use only Test 1 for determining material participation in years before 1987. Thus, if you are retired but meet the five-out-of-10-year participation test, you are currently considered a material participant, with the result that net income is treated as nonpassive, rather than passive. If you retired from a personal service profession, an even stricter rule applies; *see* Test 6.

Test 6. In a personal service activity, you materially participated for any three tax years preceding the tax year in question. The three years do not have to be consecutive. Use only Test 1 for determining material participation in years before 1987. Examples of personal services within this test are the professions of health, law, engineering, architecture, accounting, actuarial science, the performing arts, consulting, or any other trade or business in which capital is not a material income-producing factor.

Test 7. Under the facts and circumstances test, you participate in the activity on a regular, continuous, and substantial basis. *According to the IRS, you do not come within this test if you participate less than 100 hours in the activity.*

For limited partner rules, *see 10.11.* For participation rules for personal service and closely held corporations, *see 10.15.*

10.7 Tax Credits of Passive Activities Limited

You may generally not claim a tax credit from a passive activity unless you report and pay taxes on income from a passive activity. Furthermore, the tax allocated to that income must be at least as much as the credit. If the tax credit exceeds your tax liability on income allocable to passive activities, the excess credit is not allowed. Use Form 8582-CR to figure the allowable credit. Suspended credits are not allowed when property is disposed of. The credits may be used only when passive income is earned.

EXAMPLE

Ben Wall has a $1,000 credit from a passive activity. He does not report income from any passive activity. He may not claim the credit because no part of his tax is attributed to passive activity income. The credit is suspended until he has income from a passive activity and he incurs tax on that income. All or part of the credit may then be claimed to offset the tax. If he disposed of his interest before using a suspended credit, the credit may no longer be claimed but the election to reduce basis, discussed below, could be made.

Credits for real estate activities. As discussed at *10.2*, more favorable tax credit rules apply to real estate activities.

Basis adjustment for suspended credits. If the basis of property was reduced by tax credits, you may elect on Form 8582-CR to add back a suspended credit to the basis when your entire interest in an activity is disposed of. If the property is disposed of in a transaction that is not treated as a fully taxable disposition as discussed at *10.13*, then no basis adjustment is allowed.

EXAMPLE

Mark places in service rehabilitation credit property and claims an allowable credit of $50, which also reduces basis by $50. However, under the passive loss rule, he is prevented from claiming the credit. In a later year, he disposes of his entire interest in the activity, including the property whose basis was reduced. He may elect to increase basis of the property by the amount of the original basis adjustment.

Filing Tip

Portfolio Income Accounting
You cannot deduct passive losses from portfolio income. The tax law broadly defines "portfolio income" to include nonbusiness types of income including interest, dividends, and profits on the sale of investment property.

10.8 Determining Passive or Nonpassive Income and Loss

The purpose of the passive loss rules is to prevent you from deducting passive losses from nonpassive income. Passive losses are losses from business activities in which you do not materially participate *(10.6)* or losses from rental activities that are not deductible under the $25,000 allowance *(10.2)* or which do not qualify you as a real estate professional *(10.3)*. In some cases, as explained in *10.9*, passive income may be recharacterized as nonpassive income.

Where you do not materially participate in a business activity, passive income or loss is determined by matching income and expenses of that activity. Portfolio income *(see* below) earned by the activity or any pay that you earn is not included to determine passive income or loss.

Portfolio income. Portfolio income is nonpassive income and broadly defined as income that is not derived in the ordinary course of business of the activity. Portfolio income includes interest, dividends, annuities, and royalties from property held for investment. However, interest income on loans and investments made in the business of lending money or received on business accounts receivable is generally not treated as portfolio income; *see 10.9* for special recharacterization rules. Similarly, royalties derived from a business of licensing property are not portfolio income to the person who created the property or performed substantial services or incurred substantial costs.

Portfolio income also includes gains from the sale of properties that produce portfolio income or are held for investment.

Expenses allocable to portfolio income, including interest expenses, do not enter into the computation of passive income or loss.

Sale of property used in activity. Gain realized on the sale of property used in the activity is generally treated as passive activity income if at the time of disposition the activity was passive. Under this rule, if you transact an installment sale, the treatment of installment payments depends on your status at the time of the initial sale. If you were not a material participant in the year of sale, installment payments in a later year are treated as passive income, even if you become a material participant in the later year. However, an exception to the year-of-sale status rule applies to certain sales of property formerly used in a passive activity; *see 10.16*.

Installment payments from a pre-1987 installment sale are treated as passive income if the activity would have been considered passive had the passive activity rules been in effect before 1987.

Although gain on the sale of property is generally passive income if the activity is passive at the time of sale, there is an exception that could recharacterize the gain as nonpassive income if the property was formerly used in a nonpassive activity; *see 10.16* for details.

Compensation for personal services is not passive activity income. The term "compensation for personal services" includes only (1) earned income, including certain payments made by a partnership to a partner and representing compensation for the services of the partner; (2) amounts included in gross income involving the transfer of property in exchange for the performance of services; (3) amounts distributed under qualified plans; (4) amounts distributed under retirement, pension, and other arrangements for deferred compensation of services; and (5) Social Security benefits includible in gross income.

Passive activity gross income also does not include (1) income from patent, copyright, or literary, musical, or artistic compositions, if your personal efforts significantly contributed to the creation of the property; (2) income from a qualified low-income housing project; (3) income tax refunds; and (4) payments on a covenant not to compete.

Passive activity deductions. Deductible expenses that offset passive income of an activity must be related to the passive activity, such as real property taxes. The following are not considered passive activity deductions:

Casualty and theft losses if similar losses do not recur regularly in the activity.
Charitable deductions.
Miscellaneous itemized deductions subject to the 2% AGI floor.
State, local, and foreign income taxes.
Carryovers of net operating losses or capital losses.
Expenses clearly and directly allocable to portfolio income.
Loss on the sale of property producing portfolio income.
Loss on the sale of your entire interest in a passive activity to an unrelated party. The loss is allowed in full; *see 10.13*.

Interest deductions. Interest expenses attributable to passive activities are treated as passive activity deductions and are not subject to the investment interest limitations. For example, in 2002, if you have net passive loss of $100, $40 of which is of interest expense, the entire $100 is a passive loss. $40 of the loss is not subject to the investment interest limitation discussed in *15.10*. Similarly, income and loss from passive activities generally are not treated as investment income or loss in figuring the investment interest limitation.

If you rent out a vacation home that you personally use for more than the greater of 14 days or 10% of the fair market rental days *(9.7)*, you may treat the residence as a qualified second residence under the mortgage interest rules; *see 15.1*. Interest on such a qualifying second home is generally fully deductible, and the deductible interest *(15.1)* is not treated as a passive activity deduction. The rental portion of the interest is deducted on Schedule E of Form 1040 and the personal-use portion on Schedule A if itemized deductions are claimed; *see 9.9*.

Self-charged management fees or interest. For an individual with interests in several business entities, the payment of management fees by one of the entities to another is in effect a payment by the owner to himself. However, if the taxpayer materially participates in the entity providing the management services but not in the entity that pays the fees, the passive loss rules prevent the "self-charged" expense from offsetting the income from the payment. IRS proposed regulations allow a netting deduction *only* for self-charged interest but not for any other self-charged expense.

> **EXAMPLE**
>
> As an employee of his S corporation, Hillman provided real estate management services to rental real estate partnerships in which he had invested. On his personal return, he reported the management fees as passed-through S corporation income and deducted his allocable share of the fee payments by the partnership. The IRS disallowed the deduction: Since Hillman materially participated in the S corporation but not the partnerships, the fee payments by the partnerships were passive activity expenses that could not be deducted against the S corporation's nonpassive fee income. The fact that IRS regulations allow a deduction for self-charged interest does not mean that other self-charged passive expenses should also be deductible.
>
> The Tax Court agreed with Hillman that there is no difference between interest and other self-charged expenses. The legislative history indicates a Congressional intent to allow deductions for self-charged expenses because they do not result in a net accretion to the taxpayer's wealth.
>
> However, the Fourth Circuit, while sympathetic to Hillman's situation, reversed the Tax Court. Nothing in the tax law allows self-charged expenses to be deducted against nonpassive income. Although there is no reason why management fees should be distinguished from interest, the legislative history on self-charged expenses specifically mentioned only interest as an exception to the general statutory rule. The Congressional Committee reports that gave the IRS discretion to provide a deduction for other self-charged expenses did not limit that discretion. Unless the IRS changes its regulations, relief must come from Congress. The Fourth Circuit noted that while the denial of a deduction in this situation appears harsh, the deduction is not completely lost; the fee payments may be carried forward to later years as a passive expense.
>
> After the Fourth Circuit ruled against him, Hillman went back to the Tax Court and tried an alternative argument in an attempt to deduct the management fees paid by the partnerships. He argued that the fees were nonpassive deductions that could offset the nonpassive income from the S corporation because the payment of the fees, by itself, constituted a separate business distinguishable from the passive rental activities of the partnerships. The Tax Court disagreed. The management fees were incurred in connection with the rental activities and thus were passive deductions. The Tax Court again acknowledged the unfairness of denying a deduction for the "self-charged" fees. Hillman's plight is lamentable, but as the Fourth Circuit ruled, relief can only come from Congress if the IRS does not liberalize its regulation on self-charged expenses.

10.9 Passive Income Recharacterized as Nonpassive Income

There is an advantage in treating income as passive income when you have passive losses that may offset the income. However, the law may prevent you from treating certain income as passive income. The conversion of passive income to nonpassive income is technically called "recharacterization." This may occur when you do not materially participate in the business activity, but are sufficiently active for the IRS to consider your participation as significant. Recharacterization may also occur when you rent property to a business in which you materially participate, rent nondepreciable property, or sell development rental property.

Significant participation. The IRS compares income and losses from all of your activities in which you work more than 100 hours but less than 500 and that are not considered material participation under the law. If you show a net aggregate gain, part of your gain is treated as nonpassive income according to the computation illustrated in the following Example.

> **EXAMPLE**
>
> Carol Warren invests in three business activities—A, B, and C. She does not materially participate in any of the activities during 2002 but participates in Activity A for 105 hours, in Activity B for 160 hours, and in Activity C for 125 hours. Her net passive income or loss from the three activities is:
>
> | | A | B | C | Total |
> |---|---|---|---|---|
> | Passive activity gross income | $600 | $700 | $900 | $2,200 |
> | Passive activity deductions | (200) | (1,000) | (300) | (1,500) |
> | Net passive activity income | $400 | ($300) | $600 | $700 |

Caution

"Recharacterization" of Passive Income

As discussed at *10.16*, gain on the sale of property used in a passive activity may be recharacterized as nonpassive income if the property was formerly used in a nonpassive activity.

Carol's passive activity gross income from significant participation passive activities of $2,200 exceeds passive activity deductions of $1,500. A ratable portion of her gross income from significant participation activities with net passive income for the tax year (Activities A and C) is treated as gross income that is not from a passive activity. The ratable portion is figured by dividing:

1. The excess of her passive activity gross income from significant participation over passive activity deductions from such activities (here $700) by
2. The net passive income of only the significant participation passive activities having net passive income (here $1,000). The ratable portion is 70%.

Thus, $280 of gross income from Activity A ($400 × 70%) and $420 of gross income from Activity C ($600 × 70%) is treated as nonpassive gross income. This adjustment prevents $700 from being offset by passive losses from another activity.

Net interest income from passive equity-financed lending. Gross income from "equity-financed lending activity" is treated as nonpassive income to the extent of the lesser of the equity-financed interest income or net passive income. An activity is an "equity-financed lending activity" for a tax year if (1) the activity involves a trade or business of lending money and (2) the average outstanding balance of the liabilities incurred in the activity for the tax year does not exceed 80% of the average outstanding balance of the interest-bearing assets held in the activity.

Incidental rental of property by development activity. Where gains on the sale of rental property are attributable to recent development, passive income treatment may be lost if the sale comes within the following tests: (1) the rental started less than 12 months before the date of disposition; and (2) you materially participated or significantly participated in the performance of services enhancing the value of the property. The 12-month period starts at the completion of the development services that increased the property's value.

Self-rental rule: Renting to your business. If you rent a building to your business, the rental income, normally treated as passive income, may be recharacterized by the IRS as nonpassive income where you also have losses from other rentals. Recharacterization prevents you from deducting the rental losses against the net rental income. Although not specifically written into the law, the recharacterization rules are incorporated in IRS regulations. For the recharacterization rule to apply, you must "materially participate" in the business renting the property; *see* the following Example.

 Caution

Property Rented to Nonpassive Activity (Self-Rental Property)
You may not generate passive income by renting property to a business in which you materially participate. *See* "Self-rental rule: Renting to your business" on this page.

EXAMPLE

Krukowski, an attorney who operated two businesses through wholly owned C corporations, claimed that the IRS's recharacterization regulations were arbitrary and capricious. He rented personally owned buildings to the corporations, one of which ran a health club and the other the attorney's law firm. He reported net income of $175,149 from the rental to the law firm and a $69,100 net loss from the rental to the health club. He deducted the loss from the income and reported net rental income of $106,049. The IRS disallowed the loss offset by recharacterizing the rental income from the law firm as nonpassive income. Recharacterization could be applied under the regulations because the time spent by the attorney in the law firm was material participation. The attorney had to report rental income of $175,149; the health club rental loss was treated as a "suspended" passive loss.

Before the Tax Court, the attorney claimed that the recharacterization rule was arbitrary and contrary to the passive loss statute. The Court disagreed. The law authorizes the IRS to write regulations interpreting the law. Further, Congressional committee reports contemplate that the IRS would define nonpassive income in such a way as to prevent a taxpayer from offsetting active business income with passive business losses.

The Seventh Circuit Court of Appeals affirmed the Tax Court. The IRS was given authority by Congress to enact the self-rental rule as a way of eliminating tax shelters. Two other appeals courts, the First and Fifth Circuits, have also upheld the IRS regulation.

Rental of property with an insubstantial depreciable basis. This rule prevents you from generating passive rental income with vacant land or land on which a unit is constructed that has a value substantially less than the land. If less than 30% of the unadjusted basis *(5.16)* of rental property is depreciable, and you have net passive income from rentals (taking into account carried-over passive losses from prior years), the net passive income is treated as nonpassive income.

EXAMPLES

1. A limited partnership buys vacant land for $300,000, constructs improvements on the land at a cost of $100,000, and leases the entire property. After the rental period, the partnership sells the property for $600,000, realizing a gain. The unadjusted basis of the depreciable improvements of $100,000 is only 25% of the basis of the property of $400,000. The rent and the gain allocated to the improvements are treated as nonpassive income.

2. Shirley offset a passive rental loss from an investment in a limited partnership, LP, which was a substantial owner of a general partnership, GP, against rental income from an investment in a joint venture, JV. JV had leased to GP land on which GP constructed a shopping center. The IRS held that the rental income from JV was nonpassive rental income within the 30% test and could not be offset by the passive rental loss. The Tax Court agreed and also rejected Shirley's attempt to aggregate her investment activities in JV and LP as one activity. The operations of each group, JV, LP, and GP, were separate and not owned by the same person. She was not the direct owner of any of the units. Further, the aggregation rule does not apply to property falling within the 30% test.

Licensing of intangible property. Your share of royalty income in a partnership, S corporation, estate, or trust is treated as nonpassive income if you invested after the organization created the intangible property, performed substantial services, or incurred substantial costs in the development or marketing of it. *See* Publication 925 for further details.

10.10 Working Interests in Oil and Gas Wells

Working interests are generally not treated as passive activities. This is true whether you hold your interest directly or through an entity, provided your liability is not limited. As long as you have unlimited liability, you need not materially participate in the activity. A working interest is one burdened with the financial risk of developing and operating the property, such as a share in tort liability (for example, uninsured losses from a fire); some responsibility to share in additional costs; responsibility for authorizing expenses; receiving periodic reports about drilling, completion, and expected production; and the possession of voting rights and rights to continue operations if the present operator steps out.

Limited liability. If you hold a working interest through any of the following entities, the entity is considered to limit your liability and you are subject to the passive loss rules: (1) a limited partnership interest in a partnership in which you are not a general partner; (2) stock in a corporation; or (3) an interest in any entity other than a limited partnership or corporation that, under applicable state law, limits the liability of a holder of such interest for all obligations of the entity to a determinable fixed amount.

Working interests are considered on a well-by-well basis. Rights to overriding royalties or production payments, and contract rights to extract or share in oil and gas profits without liability for a share of production costs, are not working interests.

10.11 Partnership Rules

If you are a partner, your level of personal participation in partnership activity during the partnership year determines whether your share of income or loss is passive or nonpassive. Generally, limited partners are subject to passive activity treatment, but there are some exceptions. On Schedule K-1 of Form 1065, the partnership will identify each activity it conducts and specify the income, loss, deductions, and credits from each activity.

EXAMPLE

Don Bailey is a general partner of a fiscal year partnership that ends on March 31, 2002. During that fiscal year he was inactive. Since he did not materially participate, his share of partnership income or loss reported in 2002 is passive activity income or loss, even if he becomes active from April 1, 2002, to the end of 2002.

Planning Reminder

Limited Liability for Oil or Gas Well

A working interest in an oil or gas well is exempt from the passive activity restrictions if your liability is not limited. The following forms of loss protection are disregarded and, thus, are not treated as limiting your liability: protection against loss by an indemnification agreement; a stop-loss agreement; insurance; or any similar arrangement or combination of agreements.

Not treated as passive income are payments for services and certain guaranteed payments made in liquidation of a retiring or deceased partner's interest unless attributed to unrealized receivables and goodwill at a time the partner was passive.

Gain or loss on the disposition of a partnership interest may be attributed to different trade, investment, or rental activities of the partnership. The allocation is made according to a complicated formula included in IRS regulations.

Payments to a retired partner. Gain or loss is treated as passive only to the extent that it would be treated as such at the start of the liquidation of the partner's interest.

Limited partners. A limited partner is generally not considered to be a material participant in a partnership activity, and, thus, treats income or loss as passive, except in these cases:

1. The limited partner participates for more than 500 hours during the tax year; *see* Test 1 in *10.6.*
2. The limited partner materially participated in the partnership during prior years under either Test 5 or Test 6 at *10.6.*
3. The limited partner is also a general partner at all times during the partnership tax year that ends with or within the partner's taxable year and any of the material participation tests *(10.6)* are met.

To determine material participation in rental real estate activities under the special rules for real estate professionals, Test 1 or Test 5 of *10.6* must generally be met, but *see* the exception at *10.3.*

A limited partner is not considered to be an "active participant" and thus does not qualify for the $25,000 rental loss allowance discussed in *10.2.*

 Planning Reminder

Publicly Traded Partnerships (PTPs)
A PTP is a partnership whose interests are traded on established securities exchanges or are readily tradable in secondary markets. PTPs that are not treated as corporations for tax purposes are subject to special rules that allow losses to be used only to offset income from the same PTP. *See* the instructions to Form 8582.

10.12 Form 8582

The purpose of Form 8582 is to assemble in one place items of income and expenses from passive activities in order to determine the effect of the passive loss rules on these items. After this determination, income and allowable deductions are reported as regular income and deductions in appropriate schedules attached to your tax return. For example, net profits of a self-employed person who is not active in the business are reported on Schedule C, sales of capital assets of a passive activity are reported on Schedule D, your share of partnership income and allowable deductions is reported on Schedule E, and rental income and allowable deductions are reported on Schedule E.

Schedule D or Form 4797. Gains or losses from the sale of assets from a passive activity or from the sale of a partial interest that is less than "substantially all" of your entire interest in a passive activity are reported on Schedule D or on Form 4797 (sale of business property, *see* Chapter 44). The gain is also entered on Form 8582. Losses must first be entered on Form 8582 to see how much, if any, is allowable under the passive loss restrictions before an amount can be entered as a loss on Schedule D or Form 4797.

A disposition of an insubstantial part of your interest in the activity does not allow a deduction of suspended passive losses from prior years. When you dispose of your *entire* interest in a passive activity to a nonrelated party in a fully taxable transaction, your losses for the year plus prior year suspended losses from the activity are fully deductible. The same rule applies to a partial disposition only if you are disposing of *substantially all* of the activity and you have proof of the current year and prior year suspended losses allocable to the disposed-of portion. You net the gain or loss from the disposition with the net income or loss from current year operations and any prior year suspended passive losses. If the netting gives you an overall gain, you need to file Form 8582 only if you have other passive activities. If you have an overall loss after the netting, you do not file Form 8582.

Schedule E. If you have a net profit from rental property or other passive activity reported on Schedule E and you also have losses from other passive activities, the income reported on Schedule E is also entered on Form 8582. A net loss from rental activities generally must be entered on Form 8582 but Form 8582 is not needed if you qualify for the full $25,000 allowance *(10.2)* for rental real estate losses and meet these tests:

Your only passive activities are rental real estate activities and you have no suspended prior year passive losses from such activities;

You have no credits related to passive activities;

You actively participated in the rental real estate operations;

Your total losses from the rental real estate activities are $25,000 or less ($12,500 or less if married filing separately and you lived apart from your spouse all year);

Your modified adjusted gross income is $100,000 or less ($50,000 or less if married filing separately and you lived apart from your spouse all year); and

You do not own any interest in a rental real estate activity as a limited partner or beneficiary of a trust or estate.

If you have a loss from a passive interest in a partnership, trust, estate, or S corporation, you first determine on Form 8582 whether the loss is deductible on Schedule E.

Schedule F. A passive activity farm loss is entered on Form 8582 to determine the deductible loss. If only part of the loss is allowed, only that portion is claimed on Schedule F. A net profit from passive farm activities is also entered on Form 8582 to offset losses from other passive activities.

Other tax forms. Other forms tied to Form 8582 are Form 4797 (sale of business assets or equipment), Form 4835 (farm rental income), and Form 4952 (investment interest deductions). For further details see Form 8582; also *see* IRS Publication 925 for filled-in sample forms.

10.13 Suspended Losses Allowed on Disposition of Your Interest

Losses and credits that may not be claimed in one year because of the passive activity limitations are suspended and carried forward to later years. The carryover lasts indefinitely, until you have passive income against which to claim the losses and credits. No carryback is allowed. What if you have suspended losses and later materially participate in the business in which the loss was realized? The losses remain as passive losses but may offset nonpassive income of that activity.

> **EXAMPLE**
>
> In 2001, Nick Milo was not a material participant in a business activity and his share of losses was $10,000, which was suspended because he had no passive income. In 2002, he becomes a material participant in the business and his share of income is $1,000. The $1,000 is treated as nonpassive income, and he may apply $1,000 of the suspended loss to offset that income.

Allocation of suspended loss. If your suspended loss is incurred from several activities, you allocate the loss among the activities using the worksheets accompanying Form 8582. The loss is allocated among the activities in proportion to the total loss. If you have net income from significant participation activities (Test 4 at *10.6*), such activities may be treated as one single activity in making the allocation; *see* the instructions to Form 8582.

Disposition of a passive interest. A fully taxable sale of your interest to a nonrelated person will allow you to claim suspended deductions from the activity. Worthlessness of a security in a passive activity is treated as a disposition. An abandonment also releases suspended losses.

On a disposition, the suspended losses plus any current year income or loss from the activity are combined with the gain or loss from the disposition; *see* the Examples below and follow the instructions to Form 8582 for reporting the net gain or loss.

Partial disposition. You may for the taxable year in which there is a disposition of *substantially all* of an activity treat the part disposed of as a separate activity. You must show: (1) the amount of prior year suspended deductions and credits allocable to that part of the activity for the taxable year, and (2) the amount of gross income and any other deductions and credits allocable to that part of the activity for the taxable year.

> **EXAMPLES**
> 1. Jill Stein has a 5% interest in a limited partnership with an adjusted basis of $42,000. In 2002, she sells her interest in the partnership to an unrelated person for $50,000. For 2002, she has a current year loss from the partnership (shown on Schedule K-1) of $3,000. She also has $2,000 of suspended passive losses from prior years that have been carried forward to 2002. Jill's $8,000 gain from the sale of her interest is combined on Form 8582 with the current year loss and suspended losses giving her an overall gain of $3,000, figured as follows:
>
> | | |
> |---|---|
> | Sales price | $50,000 |
> | *Less:* Adjusted basis | $42,000 |
> | Gain | $8,000 |
> | *Less:* Current year loss | $3,000 |

Caution

Partial Disposition

To deduct suspended passive losses on a disposition of part of an activity, the part disposed of must constitute substantially all of the activity; *see 10.13.*

Caution

$3,000 Capital Loss Limit

Capital losses incurred on a disposition of a passive interest are also subject to the general $3,000 loss limitation ($1,500 if married filing separately) discussed at *5.4.*

Suspended losses	$2,000	$5,000
Overall gain		$3,000

If Jill has *other* passive activities, the $8,000 gain would be reported as current year income on Form 8582. The $3,000 current year loss and $2,000 suspended losses would also be entered on Form 8582.

    If this was Jill's *only* passive activity, she does not have to file Form 8582. The gain from the sale is reported on Schedule D and the current year and suspended losses are reported as nonpassive losses on Schedule E.

2. Assume that Jill's suspended losses from prior years were $10,000 instead of $2,000. She has an overall loss of $5,000 after combining the gain from the sale of $8,000, the current year loss of $3,000, and the suspended losses of $10,000.

    Since there is an overall loss after combining the gain and losses, Jill does not file Form 8582. The current year loss plus the suspended losses are reported as nonpassive losses on Schedule E and the gain from the disposition on Schedule D.

3. Assume in Example 1 that Jill sold her interest for $30,000 instead of $50,000. She would have a $12,000 loss on the sale ($42,000 adjusted basis less $30,000 sales price). Combining the loss with the current year loss of $3,000 and the $2,000 of suspended losses, she has an overall loss of $17,000.

    Since there is an overall loss, Jill does not file Form 8582. The current year loss plus the suspended losses are reported as nonpassive losses on Schedule E. The $12,000 loss on the sale is reported on Schedule D as a capital loss. Under the regular rules for capital losses, the loss will offset capital gains for 2002 and any excess will be deductible only up to $3,000 *(5.4)*. Assuming the $3,000 limit applies, Jill has a $9,000 capital loss carryover to 2002.

Gifts. When a passive activity interest is given away, you may not deduct suspended passive losses. The donee's basis in the property is increased by the suspended loss if he or she sells the property at a gain. If a loss is realized by the donee on a sale of the interest, the donee's basis may not exceed fair market value of the gift at the time of the donation.

Death. On the death of an investor in a passive interest, suspended losses are deductible on the decedent's final tax return, to the extent the suspended loss exceeds the amount by which the basis of the interest in the hands of the heir is increased.

EXAMPLE

An owner dies holding an interest in a passive activity with a suspended loss of $8,000. After the owner's death, the heir's stepped-up basis for the property (equal to fair market value) is $6,000 greater than the decedent's basis. On the decedent's final return, $2,000 of the loss is deductible ($8,000 – $6,000).

Installment sales. If the passive activity interest is sold at a profit on the installment basis, suspended losses are deducted over the installment period in the same ratio as the gain recognized each year bears to the gain remaining to be recognized as of the start of the year. For example, if you realize a gain of $10,000 and report $2,000 of gain each year for five years, in the year of sale you report 20% of your total gain under the installment method, and 20% of your suspended losses are also allowed. In the second year, you report $2,000 of the remaining $8,000 gain and 25% of the remaining losses ($2,000 ÷ $8,000) are allowed.

10.14 Suspended Tax Credits

If you have tax credits that were barred under the passive activity rules, they may be claimed only in future years when you have tax liability attributable to passive income. However, in the year you dispose of your interest, a special election may be available to decrease your gain by the amount of your suspended credit; *see* below.

Basis election for suspended credits. If you qualify for an investment credit (under transition rules) or a rehabilitation credit, you are required to reduce the basis of the property even if you are unable to claim the credit because of the passive activity rules. If this occurs and you later dispose of your entire interest in the passive activity, including the property whose basis was reduced, your gain will be increased by virtue of the basis reduction although you never benefitted from the credit. To prevent this, you may reduce the taxable gain by electing to increase the pre-transfer basis of the property by the amount of the unused credit.

Law Alert

Deemed Sale for 2001 Does Not Trigger Suspended Losses

If a deemed sale was made on a tax return for 2001 in order to qualify the asset as five-year gain property eligible for the 18% capital gains rate in 2006 or later *(5.3)*, the deemed sale and reacquisition is not considered a disposition of the entire interest in the activity that would allow a deduction of all suspended losses. Under a technical correction made by the Job Creation and Worker Assistance Act of 2002, the gain from the deemed sale is passive income that can be offset by passive activity deductions for 2001, including any suspended losses carried forward to 2001. Suspended losses in excess of the deemed gain remain suspended.

Filing Tip

Installment Sale of Your Interest

If you sell your passive activity interest at a profit and have suspended losses, you may deduct a percentage of the losses each year during the installment period; *see 10.13.*

EXAMPLE

Dan Brown places in service rehabilitated credit property qualifying for a $50 credit, but the credit is not allowed under the passive loss rules. However, his basis is still reduced by $50. In a later year, Brown makes a taxable disposition of his entire interest in the activity and in the rehabilitation property. Assuming that no part of the suspended $50 credit has been used, Brown may elect to increase his basis in the property by the unused $50 credit.

10.15 Personal Service and Closely Held Corporations

To prevent avoidance of the passive activity rules through use of corporations, the law imposes restrictions on income and loss offsets in closely held C corporations and personal service corporations.

Unless the material participation tests discussed in this section are met, the activities of a personal service corporation or a closely held corporation are considered passive activities, subject to the restrictions on loss deductions and tax credits. For purposes of these passive activity rules, a closely held C corporation is a corporation in which more than 50% in value of the stock is owned by five or fewer persons during the last half of the tax year.

A personal service corporation is a C corporation the principal activity of which is the performance of personal services by the employee-owners. Personal services are services in the fields of health, law, engineering, architecture, accounting, actuarial sciences, performing arts, or consulting. An employee-owner is any employee who on any day in the tax year owns any stock in the corporation. If an individual owns any stock in a corporation which in turn owns stock in another corporation, the individual is deemed to own a proportionate part of the stock in the other corporation. Further, more than 10% of the corporation's stock by value must be owned by owner-employees for the corporation to be a personal service corporation.

Material participation. A personal service corporation or closely held corporation is treated as materially participating in an activity during a tax year *only if* either:

1. One or more stockholders are treated as materially participating in the activity and they directly or indirectly hold in the aggregate more than 50% of the value of the corporation's outstanding shares; *or*
2. The corporation is a closely held corporation and in the 12-month period ending on the last day of the tax year, the corporation had at least one full-time manager, three full-time employees, none of whom own more than 5% of the stock, and business deductions exceeded 15% of gross income from the activity.

A stockholder is treated as materially participating or significantly participating in the activity of a corporation if he or she satisfies one of the seven tests in *10.6* for material participation. For purposes of applying the significant participation test (Test 4 at *10.6*), an activity of a personal service or closely held corporation will be treated as a significant participation activity for a tax year *only if*:

1. The corporation is not treated as materially participating in the activity for the tax year; and
2. One or more individuals, each of whom is treated as significantly participating in the activity directly or indirectly, hold in the aggregate more than 50% of the value of the outstanding stock of the corporation. Furthermore, in applying the seven participation tests, all activities of the corporation are treated as activities in which the individual holds an interest in determining whether the individual participates in an activity of the corporation; and the individual's participation in all activities other than activities of the corporation is disregarded in determining whether his or her participation in an activity of the corporation is treated as material participation under the significant participation test (Test 4 at *10.6*).

Closely held corporation's computation of passive loss. Even if a closely held corporation does not meet the material participation tests above, it still qualifies for a slight break from the passive loss restrictions. A closely held corporation may use passive activity deductions to offset not only passive activity gross income but also *net active income*. Generally, net active income is taxable income from business operations, disregarding passive activity income and expenses, and also disregarding portfolio income and expenses; *see 10.8*. Passive activity losses cannot offset portfolio income.

If a corporation stops being closely held, its passive losses and credits from prior years are not allowable against portfolio income but continue to be allowable only against passive income and net active income.

Tax liability on net active income may be offset by passive activity credits.

Filing Tip

Stockholder Activity

A stockholder may be treated as materially participating in his company's business; *see* the tests on this page.

10.16 Sales of Property and of Passive Activity Interests

Gain on the sale or disposition of property is generally passive or nonpassive, depending on whether your activity is passive or nonpassive in the year of sale or disposition. Thus, gain on the sale of property used in a rental activity is generally treated as passive income, as is the gain on property used in a nonrental business if you did not materially participate in the business in the year of sale. On the other hand, gain on the sale of property is generally nonpassive if the property was used in a business that you materially participated in during the year of sale. However, exceptions described below may change this treatment.

Where you transact an installment sale, treatment of gain in later years depends on your status in the year of sale. For example, if you were considered a material participant in a business, all gain is treated as nonpassive income, including gain for later installments. If you were in a rental activity or were not a material participant in a nonrental business, the gain is treated as passive income, unless the exceptions in this section apply. Current gain from a pre-1987 installment sale is passive income if the activity would have been passive, assuming the passive activity rules were in effect at the time of the sale.

Gain on substantially appreciated property formerly used in nonpassive activity. Even if an activity is passive in the year that you sell substantially appreciated property, gain on the sale is treated as nonpassive unless the property was used in a passive activity for either 20% of its holding period or the entire 24-month period ending on the date of the disposition. Property is substantially appreciated if fair market value exceeds 120% of its adjusted basis.

> ### EXAMPLE
>
> In 1991, Andy Jones buys a building for use in a business in which he materially participates until March 31, 2001. On April 1, 2002, he rents the building. On December 31, 2003, he sells the building. Gain from the sale is treated as nonpassive although the building was used in a passive rental activity in the year of the sale. The building was used in a passive rental activity for 21 months before disposition (April 1, 2002, through December 31, 2003). Thus, it was not used in a passive activity for the entire 24-month period ending on the date of the sale. Further, the 21-month period during which the building was used in a passive activity is less than 20% of Jones's holding period of 12 years.

Property used in more than one activity in a 12-month period preceding disposition. You are required to allocate the amount realized on the disposition and the adjusted basis of the property among the activities in which the property was used during a 12-month period preceding the disposition. For purposes of this rule, the term "activity" includes personal use and holding for investment. The allocation may be based on the period for which the property is used in each activity during the 12-month period. However, if during the 12-month period the value of the property does not exceed the lesser of $10,000 or 10% of the value of all property used in the activity at the time of disposition, gain may be allocated to the predominant use.

> ### EXAMPLE
>
> Joe Smith sells a personal computer for $8,000. During the 12-month period that ended on the date of the sale, 70% of Smith's use of the computer was in a passive activity. Immediately before the sale, the fair market value of all property used in the passive activity, including the personal computer, was $200,000. The computer was predominantly used in the passive activity during the 12-month period ending on the date of the sale. The value of the computer, $8,000, did not exceed the lesser of $10,000 or 10% of the $200,000 value of all property used in the activity immediately before the sale. Thus, the amount realized and the adjusted basis are allocated to the passive activity.

Disposition of partnership and S corporation interests. Gain or loss from the disposition of an interest in a partnership and S corporation is generally allocated among the entity's activities in proportion to the amount that the entity would have allocated to the partner or shareholder for each of its activities if the entity had sold its interest in the activities on an "applicable valuation date."

Gain is allocated only to appreciated activities. Loss is allocated only to depreciated activities. The entity may select either the beginning of its tax year in which the holder's disposition occurs or the date of the disposition as the applicable valuation date.

Claiming suspended loss on disposition of interest in passive activity. A fully taxable sale of your entire interest or of substantially all of your interest to a nonrelated person will allow you to claim suspended loss deductions from the activity. These rules are fully discussed in 10.13.

Dealer's sale of property similar to property sold in the ordinary course of business. IRS regulations set down complex tests that determine whether the result of the sale is treated as passive or nonpassive income or loss.

At-Risk Rules

Caution

At-Risk Rules Limit Loss Deductions

The purpose of at-risk rules is to keep you from deducting losses from investments in which you have little cash invested and no personal liability for debts.

10.17 At-Risk Limits

The at-risk rules prevent investors from claiming losses in excess of their actual tax investment by barring them from including nonrecourse liabilities as part of the tax basis for their interest. Almost all ventures are subject to the at-risk limits. Real estate placed in service after 1986 is subject to the at-risk rules as well, but most real estate nonrecourse financing can qualify for an exception; *see 10.18.*

> **EXAMPLE**
>
> Crystal Parker invests cash of $1,000 in a venture and signs a nonrecourse note for $8,000. In 2002, her share of the venture's loss is $1,200. The at-risk rules limit her deduction to $1,000, the amount of her cash investment; as she is not personally liable on the note, the amount of the liability is not included as part of her basis for loss purposes.

Losses disallowed under the at-risk rules are carried over to the following year; *see 10.21.*

Form 6198. If you have amounts that are not at risk, you must file Form 6198 to figure your deductible loss. A separate form must be filed for each activity. However, if you have an interest in a partnership or S corporation that has more than one investment in any of the following four categories, the IRS currently allows you to aggregate all of the partnership or S corporation activities within each category. For example, all partnership or S corporation films and videotapes may be treated as one activity in determining amounts at risk. The aggregation rules may be changed by the IRS; *see* the instructions to Form 6198.

1. Holding, producing, or distributing motion picture films or videotapes;
2. Exploring for or exploiting oil or gas properties;
3. Exploring for, or exploiting, geothermal deposits (for wells commenced on or after October 1, 1978); *and*
4. Farming. For this purpose, farming is defined as the cultivation of land and the raising or harvesting of any agricultural or horticultural commodity—including raising, shearing, breeding, caring for, or management of animals. Forestry and timber activities are not included, but orchards bearing fruits and nuts are within the definition of farming. Certain activities carried on within the physical boundaries of the farm may not necessarily be treated as farming.

In addition to the previous categories, the law treats as a single activity all leased depreciable business equipment (Section 1245 property) that is placed in service during any year by a partnership or S corporation.

Exempt from the at-risk rules are C corporations which meet active business tests and are not in the equipment leasing business or any business involving master sound recording, films, videotapes, or other artistic, literary, or musical property. For details on the active business tests, as well as a special at-risk exception for equipment leasing activities of closely held corporations, *see* IRS Publication 925.

The at-risk limitation applies only to tax losses produced by expense deductions that are not disallowed by reason of another provision of the law. For example, if a prepaid interest expense is deferred under the prepaid interest limitation *(15.14),* the interest will not be included in the loss subject to the risk limitation. When the interest accrues and becomes deductible, the expense may be considered within the at-risk provision. Similarly, if a deduction is deferred because of farming syndicate rules, that deduction will enter into the computation of the tax loss subject to the risk limitation only when it becomes deductible under the farming syndicate rules.

Filing Tip

Form 6198

If you have invested an amount for which you are not at risk, such as a nonrecourse loan, you generally must file Form 6198 to figure a deductible loss. However, nonrecouse financing for real estate that secures the loan is treated as an at-risk investment in most cases; *see 10.18.*

Effect of passive loss rules. Where a loss is also subject to the at-risk rules, you apply the at-risk rules first. If the loss is deductible under the at-risk rules, the passive activity rules then apply. On Form 6198 (at risk), you figure the deductible loss allowed as at risk and then carry the loss over to Form 8582 to determine the passive activity loss.

10.18 What Is At Risk?

The following amounts are considered at risk in determining your tax position in a business or investment:

Cash;
Adjusted basis of property that you contribute; and
Borrowed funds for which you are personally liable to pay.

At-risk basis is figured as of the end of the year. Any loss allowed for a year reduces the at-risk amount as of the start of the next year. Therefore, if a loss exceeds your at-risk investment, the excess loss will not be deductible in later years unless you increase your at-risk investment; *see* the Example below and *10.21*.

Personal liability alone does not assure that the borrowed funds are considered at risk. The lender must have no interest in the venture other than as creditor.

> **EXAMPLE**
>
> Julie Kahn, an investor, pays a promoter of a book purchase plan $45,000 for a limited partnership interest. The promoter is the general partner. Kahn pays $30,000 cash and gives a note for $15,000 on which she is personally liable. Her amount at risk is $30,000; the $15,000 personal liability note is not counted because it is owed to the general partner.

Special at-risk rule for real estate financing. For real property placed in service after 1986, you may treat nonrecourse financing from unrelated commercial lenders or from government agencies as amounts at risk if the financing is secured by the real estate. Loans from the seller or promoter do not qualify. Third-party nonrecourse debt from a related lender, other than the seller or promoter, may also be treated as at risk, providing the terms of the loan are commercially reasonable and on substantially the same terms as loans involving unrelated persons.

If you acquired an interest after 1986 in a partnership or S corporation, the above at-risk rules apply to your share of real estate losses, regardless of when the partnership or S corporation placed the property in service.

Pledges of other property. If you pledge personally owned real estate used outside the activity to secure a nonrecourse debt and invest the proceeds in an at-risk activity, the proceeds may be considered part of your at-risk investment. The proceeds included in basis are limited by the fair market value of the property used as collateral (determined as of the date the property is pledged as security) less any prior (or superior) claims to which the collateral is subject.

Partners. A partner is treated as at-risk to the extent that basis in the partnership is increased by the share of partnership income. That partnership income is then used to reduce the partnership's nonrecourse indebtedness will have no effect on a partner's amount at risk. If the partnership makes actual distributions of the income in the taxable year, the amount distributed reduces the partner's amount at risk. A buy-sell agreement, effective at a partner's death or retirement, is not considered for at-risk purposes.

Activities begun before 1976. A special rule determines the amount at risk as of the first day of the first tax year after 1975. Again, you start with the amounts considered at risk. Losses incurred and deducted in taxable years before 1976 first reduce the basis allocated to amounts considered not at risk, such as nonrecourse loans. If the losses exceed the amount not at risk, the excess reduces the at-risk investment. Distributions reduce at-risk amounts. *See* the instructions to Form 6198.

10.19 Amounts Not At Risk

The following may not be treated as part of basis for at-risk purposes in determining your tax position in a business or investment:

Liabilities for which you have no personal liability, except in the case of certain real estate financing; *see 10.18*.

Liabilities for which you have personal liability, but the lender also has a capital or profit-sharing interest in the venture.

Recourse liabilities convertible to a nonrecourse basis.

Money borrowed from a relative listed at 5.6 who has an interest in the venture, other than as a creditor, or from a partnership in which you own more than a 10% interest.

Funds borrowed from a person whose recourse is solely your interest in the activity or property used in the activity.

Amounts for which your economic loss is limited by a nonrecourse financing guarantee, stop-loss agreement, or other similar arrangement.

Investments protected by insurance or loss reimbursement agreement between you and another person. If you are personally liable on a mortgage but you separately obtain insurance to compensate you for any mortgage payments, you are at risk only to the extent of the uninsured portion of the personal liability. You may, however, include as at risk any amount of premium paid from your personal assets. Taking out casualty insurance or insurance protecting you against tort liability is not considered within the at-risk provisions, and such insurance does not affect your investment basis.

Caution

Lender Has Interest

Even if you are personally liable for a debt, you are not considered at risk if the lender has an interest in the activity other than as a creditor.

EXAMPLES

1. Some commercial feedlots in livestock feeding operations may reimburse investors against any loss sustained on sales of the livestock above a stated dollar amount per head. Under such "stop-loss" orders, an investor is at risk only to the extent of the portion of his or her capital against which he or she is not entitled to reimbursement. Where a limited partnership makes an agreement with a limited partner that, at the partner's election, his or her partnership interest will be bought at a stated minimum dollar amount (usually less than the investor's original capital contribution), the partner is considered at risk only to the extent of his or her investment exceeding the guaranteed repurchase price.

2. A TV film promoter sold half-hour TV series programs to individual investors. Each investor gave a cash down payment and a note for which he or she was personally liable for the balance. Each investor's note, which was identical in face amount, terms, and maturity date, was payable out of the distribution proceeds from the film. Each investor also bought from the promoter the right to the unpaid balance on another investor's note. The promoter arranged the distribution of the films as a unit and was to apportion the sales proceeds equally among the investors.

   The IRS held that each investor is not at risk on the investment evidenced by the note. Upon maturity, each may receive a payment from another investor equal to the one that he or she owes.

3. A gold mine investment offered tax write-offs of four times the cash invested. For $10,000 cash, an investor bought from a foreign mining company a seven-year mineral claim lease to a gold reserve. Under the lease, he could develop and extract all of the gold in the reserve. At the same time, he agreed to spend $40,000 to develop the lease before the end of the year. To fund this commitment, the investor authorized the promoter to sell an option for $30,000 to a third party who was to buy all the gold to be extracted. The $30,000 along with the $10,000 down payment was to be used to develop the reserve. The promoter advised the investor that he could claim a $40,000 deduction for certain development costs.

   The IRS ruled that $30,000 was not deductible because the amount was not "risk capital." The investor got $30,000 by selling an option that could be exercised only if gold were found. If no gold were found, he would be under no obligation to the option holder. The investor's risk position for the $30,000 was substantially the same as if he had borrowed from the option holder on a nonrecourse basis repayable only from his interest in the activity.

   The Tax Court struck down a similar plan on different grounds. Without deciding the question of what was at risk, the court held that the option was only a right of first refusal. Thus, $30,000 was taxable income to the investor in the year of the arranged sale.

4. David Krepp, an investor, purchases cattle from a rancher for $10,000 cash and a $30,000 note payable to the rancher. Krepp is personally liable on the note. In a separate agreement, the rancher agrees to care for the cattle for 6% of Krepp's net profits from the cattle activity. Krepp is considered at risk for $10,000; he may not increase the amount at risk by the $30,000 borrowed from the rancher.

Limited partner's potential cash call. Under the terms of a partnership agreement, limited partners may be required to make additional capital contributions under specified circumstances. Whether such a potential cash call increases the limited partner's at-risk amount has been a matter of dispute.

In one case, the IRS and Tax Court held that a limited partner was not at risk with respect to a partnership note where, under the terms of the partnership agreement, he could be required to make additional capital contributions if the general partners did not pay off the note at maturity. The possibility of such a potential cash call was too uncertain; the partnership might earn profits to pay off the note and even if there were losses, the general partners might not demand additional contributions from the limited partners.

However, a federal appeals court reversed, holding that the limited partner was at risk because his obligation was mandatory and "economic reality" insured that the general partners would insure their rights by requiring the additional capital contribution.

In another case, limited partners relied upon the earlier favorable federal appeals court decision to argue that they were at risk where they could be required by the general partners to make additional cash contributions, but only in order to cover liabilities or expenses that could not be paid out of partnership assets. So long as the partnership was solvent, the limited partners could "elect out" of the call provision. Because of this election, the Tax Court held that the limited partners' obligation was contingent, rather than unavoidable as in the earlier federal appeals court case. Thus, the cash call provision did not increase their at-risk amount.

10.20 At-Risk Investment in Several Activities

If you invest in several activities, each is generally treated separately when applying the at-risk limitation on Form 6198. You generally may not aggregate basis, gains, and losses from the activities for purposes of at-risk limitations. Thus, income from one activity may not be offset by losses from another; the income from one must be reported while the losses from the other may be nondeductible because of at-risk limitations.

However, you may aggregate activities that are part of a business you actively manage. Activities of a business carried on by a partnership or S corporation qualify if 65% or more of losses for the year are allocable to persons who actively participate in management.

The law allows partnerships and S corporations to treat as a single activity all depreciable equipment (Section 1245 property) that is leased or held for lease and placed in service in any tax year. Furthermore, you may aggregate all partnership or S corporation activities within the four categories of films and videotapes, oil and gas properties, geothermal properties, and farms; *see 10.17*.

10.21 Carryover of Disallowed Losses

A loss disallowed in a current year by the at-risk limitation may be carried over and deducted in the next taxable year, provided it does not fall within the at-risk limits or the passive loss limits in that year. The loss is subject to an unlimited carryover period until there is an at-risk basis to support the deduction. This may occur when additional contributions are made to the business or when the activity has income which has not been distributed.

Gain from the disposition of property used in an at-risk activity is treated as income from the activity. In general, the reporting of gain will allow a deduction for losses disallowed in previous years to be claimed in the year of disposition.

 Filing Tip

Carryover Losses
Losses disallowed by at-risk rules are carried over and may be deductible in a later year.

10.22 Recapture of Losses Where At Risk Is Less Than Zero

To prevent manipulation of at-risk basis after a loss is claimed, there is a special recapture rule. If the amount at risk in an activity is reduced to below zero because of a distribution or a change in the status of an indebtedness from recourse to nonrecourse, income may be realized to the extent of the negative at-risk amount. The taxable amount may not exceed the amount of losses previously deducted.

The recaptured amount is not treated as income from the activity for purposes of determining whether current or suspended losses are allowable.

The recaptured amount is treated as a deduction allowable to that activity in the following year. *See* IRS Publication 925 for further details.

Chapter 11

Other Income

Income items discussed in this chapter are reported on Line 10 or 21 of Form 1040 or on a Schedule E and then transferred to Line 17 of Form 1040.

- Taxable state tax refunds are reported on Line 10 of Form1040.

- Prizes, gambling winnings, and awards are reported on Line 21 of Form 1040.

- Your share of partnership, S corporation, trust, or estate income or loss is reported in Schedule E according to Schedule K-1 statements provided you by the entity.

- Income from farming is reported on Schedule F.

Further reporting details are discussed in this chapter.

Prizes; Lottery and Gambling Winnings

11.1 Prizes and Awards

Prizes and awards are taxable income except for an award or prize that meets *all* these four tests:

1. It is primarily in recognition of religious, charitable, scientific, educational, artistic, literary, or civic achievement.
2. You were selected without any action on your part.
3. You do not have to perform services.
4. You assign the prize or award to a government unit or tax-exempt charitable organization. You must make the assignment before you use or benefit from the award. You may not claim a charitable deduction for the assignment.

Prize taxed at fair market value. A prize of merchandise is taxable at fair market value. For example, where a prize of first-class steamship tickets was exchanged for tourist-class tickets for a winner's family, the taxable value of the prize was the price of the tourist tickets. What is the taxable fair market value of an automobile won as a prize? In one case, the Tax Court held that the taxable value was what the recipient could realize on an immediate resale of the car.

Employee achievement awards. The above restrictions on tax-free treatment do not apply to awards from employers for length of service or safety achievement. The rules for such employee awards are at *3.10* and *20.25*.

11.2 Lottery and Sweepstake Winnings

Sweepstake, lottery, and raffle winnings are taxable as "other income" on Line 21 of Form 1040. The cost of tickets is deductible only to the extent you report winnings, and only if you itemize deductions. The deduction is claimed on Schedule A as a miscellaneous deduction that is *not* subject to the 2% adjusted gross income (AGI) floor (Chapter 19). For example, if you buy state lottery tickets and win a 2002 drawing, you may deduct the cost of your losing tickets in 2002 up to the amount of your winnings.

When a minor wins a state lottery and the prize is held by his or her parents as custodians under the Uniform Transfers to Minors Act, the prize is taxed to the minor in the year the prize is won.

Installment payments. If winnings are payable in installments, you pay tax only as installments are received. If within 60 days of winning a prize you have an option to choose a discounted lump-sum payment instead of an annuity, and you elect the annuity, you are taxed as the annuity payments are received. Merely having the cash option does not make the present value of the annuity taxable in the year the prize is won. This law generally applies to prizes won after October 21, 1998. The law applies to casino jackpots as well as lottery or sweepstake winnings.

11.3 Gambling Winnings and Losses

Gambling winnings are taxable. Losses from gambling are deductible only up to the gains from gambling. You may not deduct a net gambling loss even though a particular state says gambling is legal. Nor does it matter that your business is gambling. You may not deduct the loss even if you are a professional gambler.

If you are not a professional gambler, gambling income is included on Form 1040 as "other income" on Line 21. Gambling losses (not exceeding the amount of the gains) are deductible as "miscellaneous deductions" on Schedule A. The losses are *not* subject to the 2% AGI floor (Chapter 19). According to the IRS, professional gamblers who bet only for their own account are not in a business and must deduct losses (up to gains) as itemized deductions. However, the Supreme Court has held that full-time gamblers may deduct losses as business expenses even if they place wagers only for themselves. According to the Supreme Court, in order to be considered engaged in a business, a gambler must prove that he or she gambles full time to earn a livelihood and not merely as a hobby.

To prove your losses in the event your return is questioned, you must retain evidence of loss.

Filing Tip

Winnings Paid in Installments
Gambling losses are deductible as miscellaneous deductions up to the amount of your gambling winnings. Lottery winnings paid in installments qualify as such gambling winnings. If you receive lottery winnings in 2002, for instance, you may deduct any gambling losses incurred in 2002 up to the amount of that installment. Lottery winnings paid in installments do not lose their characteristic as gambling winnings.

Court Decision

Assignment of Future Lottery Payments
Courts have agreed with the IRS that a lump sum received for assigning the rights to future state lottery payments is taxed as ordinary income, not capital gain. The right to receive annual lottery payments is not a capital asset.

EXAMPLES

1. To appear on *Wheel of Fortune*, Whitten traveled from Chicago to Los Angeles, spending $1,820 for transportation, meals, and lodging. When he won cash prizes of $14,850 plus an automobile, he tried to offset his winnings by the travel costs, claiming they were gambling losses on Schedule A not subject to the 2% AGI floor. The IRS and Tax Court disagreed; travel costs are not like wager or bet losses.

Court Decision

Gambler Not Taxed on Cancelled Gambling Debt

The federal appeals court for the Third Circuit (New Jersey, Pennsylvania, and Delaware) held that the settlement by an Atlantic City casino of a gambler's $3.4 million debt for $500,000 was not taxable. The debt was not enforceable under New Jersey law because the casino did not comply with state regulations on issuance of credit. Furthermore, the gambling chips were not "property" securing the debt; they had no economic value outside the casino.

2. Trump Casino in Atlantic City gave Libutti, a high roller at its gaming tables, over $2.5 million in "comps" during a three-year period in which he lost over $8 million. The comps included 10 expensive automobiles, jewelry, European vacations, and tickets to sporting events. Libutti reported the comps as income and then claimed a matching miscellaneous deduction for gambling losses not subject to the 2% floor. The IRS disallowed the deduction, claiming that the comps were not gambling income because they were perks given to stimulate his desire to gamble at Trump's, and not winnings from the success of his wagers.

   The Tax Court disagreed. Libutti would not have received the comps unless he gambled at high stakes in Trump's casino. Although the comps did not directly hinge on the success or failure of his wagers, the comps were sufficiently related to his gambling losses to allow the deduction.

11.4 Gifts and Inheritances

Gifts and inheritances you *receive* are not taxable. However, distributions taken from an inherited traditional IRA *(8.14)*, and distributions from inherited qualified plan accounts such as 401(k) and profit-sharing plan accounts, are taxable, except for amounts attributable to nondeductible contributions made by the deceased account owner.

Income earned from gift or inherited property after you receive it is taxable.

Describing a payment as a gift or inheritance will not necessarily shield it from tax if it is, in fact, a payment for your services. Treatment of gifts to employees is covered at *2.4*.

A sale of an expected inheritance from a living person is taxable as ordinary income.

Planning Reminder

Gifts You Make

You may have to file a gift tax return if your gifts to an individual within the year exceed $11,000; *see 33.1*.

EXAMPLES

1. An employee is promised by his employer that he will be remembered in his will if he continues to work for him. The employer dies but fails to mention the employee in his will. The employee sues the estate, which settles his claim. The settlement is taxable.
2. A nephew left his uncle a bequest of $200,000. In another clause of the will, the uncle was appointed executor, and the bequest of the $200,000 was described as being made in lieu of all commissions to which he would otherwise be entitled as executor. The bequest is considered tax-free income. It was not conditioned upon the uncle performing as executor. If the will had made the bequest contingent upon the uncle's acting as executor, the $200,000 would have been taxed.
3. An attorney performed services for a friend without expectation of pay. The friend died and in his will left the attorney a bequest in appreciation for his services. The payment was considered a tax-free bequest. The amount was not bargained for.
4. A lawyer agreed to handle a client's legal affairs without charge; she promised to leave him securities. Twenty years later, under her will, the lawyer inherited the securities. The IRS taxed the bequest as pay. Both he and the client expected that he would be paid for legal services. If the client meant to make a bequest from their agreement, she should have said so in her will.

State Tax Refunds and Other Recovered Deductions

11.5 Refunds of State and Local Income Tax Deductions

A refund of state or local income tax is not taxable if you did not previously claim the tax as an itemized deduction in a prior year. For example, if you claimed the standard deduction on your 2001 return and in 2002 you received a refund for state tax withheld from your 2001 wages, the refund is not taxable on your 2002 return.

If you did claim the refunded tax as an itemized deduction, the refund is taxable only to the extent that your itemized deductions exceeded the standard deduction you could have claimed in the prior year. If, in addition to the tax refund, you received recoveries of other itemized deductions, the same computation applies to determine the taxable portion of the total recovery; *see 11.6*.

The computation of the taxable refund is different if, in the year the refunded item was claimed, you were subject to the 3% reduction of itemized deductions. In this case, the IRS provides a special method explained in Publication 525.

EXAMPLE

On your 2001 return, you filed as a single taxpayer. You claimed itemized deductions of $4,800, of which $2,600 was for state and local taxes, $1,600 was for mortgage interest, and $600 was for charitable contributions. Your deductions exceeded by $250 the $4,550 standard deduction you could have claimed. The deductions were not subject to the 3% reduction discussed at *13.7*.

In 2002, you received from the state a $750 refund for 2001 state taxes. You must report $250 of the refund as income on your 2002 Form 1040. The taxable recovery is limited to the $250 difference between the claimed itemized deductions of $4,800 and the $4,550 standard deduction for 2001.

If you had a negative taxable income in 2001, the taxable recovery figured under the above rule is reduced by the negative amount. If you had a negative taxable income of $100 in 2001, only $150 of the refund would be taxable.

Allocating a refund recovery. If in 2002 you received a refund of state or local taxes and also a recovery of other deductions, and only part of the total recovery is taxable, you allocate the taxable amount of the recovery according to the ratio between the state tax refund and the other recovery. You do this by first dividing the state refund by the total of all itemized deductions recovered. The resulting percentage is then applied to the taxable recovery to find the amount to report as the tax refund on Line 10 of Form 1040; other taxable recoveries are reported on Line 21.

EXAMPLE

In 2002, you received a refund of state income taxes of $500 and a recovery of other itemized expenses of $2,000 deducted for 2001. You figure that only $1,500 of the recovery is taxable because your total 2001 itemized deductions were $1,500 more than the standard deduction you could have claimed. As a state tax refund is reported separately from other recoveries, you must find how much of the taxable recovery is attributed to the refund. By dividing the state tax refund by the amount of the total recovery, you find that 20% is attributed to the refund ($500/$2,500). Thus, 20% of the taxable recovery, or $300 (20% of $1,500), is reported as a state refund on Line 10, Form 1040, and the balance of $1,200 on Line 21, Form 1040. Also attach a statement showing that the allocation of recoveries required the reporting on Line 10, Form 1040, of an amount less than the actual state refund shown on Form 1099-G.

Refund of state tax paid in installments over two tax years. If you pay estimated state or local income taxes, your last tax installment may be in the year you receive a refund. In this case, you allocate the refund between the two years; *see* the following Example.

EXAMPLE

Your estimated state income tax for 2001 was $4,000, which you paid in four equal installments. You made your fourth payment in January 2002. No state income tax was withheld during 2001. In 2002, you received a state tax refund of $400 for 2001. You claimed itemized deductions on your 2001 and 2002 federal returns. You allocate the $400 refund between 2001 and 2002. As you paid 75% ($3,000 ÷ $4,000) of the estimated tax in 2001, 75% of the $400 refund, or $300, is allocated to 2001. On your 2002 return, you include $300 as income on Line 10, Form 1040. You also attach a statement explaining that the amount on Line 10 is less than the $400 refund shown on the Form 1099-G received from the state in 2002 because of the allocation required for the estimated tax installment made in January 2002.

When you figure your 2002 deduction for state income taxes, you reduce the $1,000 paid in January by $100. Your 2002 deduction for state income taxes will include the January net amount of $900 plus any estimated state income taxes paid in 2002 for 2002, any state income tax withheld during 2002, and any state income tax for 2001 that you paid when you filed your 2001 state return in 2002.

 Planning Reminder

Refund of State and Local Tax

A state and local tax refund received in 2002 is taxable only if you claimed the tax as an itemized deduction, and only to the extent that your itemized deductions in that year exceeded the standard deduction you could have claimed.

To help you figure the taxable portion of 2001 itemized deductions recovered in 2002, 2001 standard deduction amounts are shown on the next page.

Note: If the $300 refund allocated to 2001 in the previous Example was more than the excess of your 2001 itemized deductions over the 2001 standard deduction you could have claimed, you report only that excess as income on your 2002 return. If in 2001 you were subject to the 3% reduction to itemized deductions, *see* IRS Publication 525 for figuring the taxable portion of the refund. Also *see 11.6* for reducing the taxable amount if you had a negative taxable income, or if you recovered a bad debt or other non-itemized deduction.

Standard Deduction for 2001: Use This To Figure Whether Recovery of Itemized Deductions in 2002 Is Taxable

If you were—	2001 standard deduction was—
Married filing jointly	$7,600
Single	4,550
Head of household	6,650
Married filing separately	3,800
Qualifying widow or widower	7,600
Single age 65 or over	5,650
Single and blind	5,650
Single age 65 or over and also blind	6,750
Married filing jointly with:	
One spouse age 65 or over	8,500
Both spouses age 65 or over	9,400
One spouse blind under age 65	8,500
Both spouses blind under age 65	9,400
One spouse age 65 or over and also blind	10,300
One spouse age 65 or over and other spouse blind and under age 65	9,400
One spouse age 65 or over and also blind; other spouse blind and under age 65	10,300
Both spouses age 65 or over and also blind	11,200
Qualifying widow or widower age 65 or over	8,500
Qualifying widow or widower and blind	8,500
Qualifying widow or widower age 65 or over and also blind	9,400
Head of household age 65 or over	7,750
Head of household and blind	7,750
Head of household age 65 or over and also blind	8,850
Married filing separately age 65 or over*	4,700
Married filing separately and blind*	4,700
Married filing separately age 65 or over and also blind*	5,600

If on your 2001 return you claimed your spouse as an exemption (21.2), add $900 if he or she was either blind or age 65 or older; add $1,800 if he or she was both blind and age 65 or older.

11.6 Other Recovered Deductions

The income rule applied to refunds of state income tax in *11.5* applies also to the recovery of other items for which you claimed a tax deduction, such as a refund of adjustable rate mortgage interest *(15.1)*, reimbursement of a deducted medical expense *(17.4)*, a reimbursed casualty loss *(18.2)*, a return of donated property that was claimed as a charitable deduction *(14.1)*, and a payment of debt previously claimed as a bad debt *(5.33)*.

Filing Instruction

Negative Taxable Income

If your taxable income was a negative amount in the year in which the recovered item was deducted, you reduce the recovery includible in income by the negative amount. For example, if the taxable recovery would be $1,700 but you had a negative taxable income of $500 for the year the deduction was claimed, only $1,200 is taxable.

EXAMPLE

You filed a joint return for 2001 and claimed itemized deductions of $8,700, which exceeded your standard deduction of $7,600. You were not subject to the 3% reduction to itemized deductions. In 2002, you received the following recoveries for amounts deducted for 2001:

Medical expenses	$ 200
State income tax refund	400
Interest expense	325
Total	$ 925

The total recovery of $925 is taxable on your 2002 return. It is less than $1,100, the excess of your 2001 itemized deductions over the allowable standard deduction ($8,700 – 7,600). You report the state and local income tax refund of $400 on Line 10, Form 1040, and the balance of $525 on Line 21, Form 1040.

If the total recovery had been $2,500 instead of $925, $1,100 would be taxable (the excess of $8,700 over $7,600). The $1,400 balance would be tax free.

Tax credit in prior year. If you recover an item deducted in a prior year in which tax credits exceeded your tax, you refigure the prior year tax to determine if the recovery is taxable. Add the amount of the recovery to taxable income of the prior year and figure the tax on the increased taxable income. If your tax credit exceeds the recomputed tax, do not include the recovery in income. If the tax credit is less than the recomputed tax, include the recovery in income to the extent the recovery reduced your tax in the prior year. The recovery may reduce an available credit carryforward to a later year.

Alternative minimum tax in the prior year. If you were subject to the alternative minimum tax (AMT) in the year the recovered deduction was claimed, recompute your regular and AMT tax for the prior year based on the taxable income you reported plus the recovered amount. If inclusion of the recovery does not change your total tax, you do not include the recovery in income. If your total tax increases by any amount, you include the recovery in income to the extent the deduction reduced your tax in the prior year. The recovery may reduce a carryforward of a tax credit based on prior year AMT.

Recovery of previously deducted items used to figure carryover. A deductible expense may not reduce your tax because you have an overall loss. If in a later year the expense is repaid or the obligation giving rise to the expense is cancelled, the deduction of that expense will be treated as having produced a tax reduction if it increased a carryover that has not expired by the beginning of the taxable year in which the forgiveness occurs. For example, you are on the accrual basis and deducted but did not pay rent in 2001. The rent obligation is forgiven in 2002. The 2001 rent deduction is treated as having produced a reduction in tax, even if it resulted in no tax savings in 2001, if it figured in the calculation of a net operating loss that has not expired or been used by the beginning of 2002, the year of forgiveness. The same rule applies to other carryovers such as the investment credit carryover.

Damages and Debt Cancellation

11.7 How Legal Damages Are Taxed

Compensatory damages for physical injury or physical sickness are tax free, whether fixed by a court or in a negotiated settlement. Damages for *nonphysical* personal injuries, such as for discrimination, back pay, or injury to reputation, are taxable; a limited exception for certain emotional distress damages may be available as discussed below. Damages for lost profits, breach of contract, or interference with business operations are taxable. Interest added to an award is taxable, even if the award is tax-free damages for physical injury.

When damages compensate for the loss of property, you have taxable gain if the damages exceed adjusted basis of the property. A deductible loss will generally be allowed when the recovery is less than adjusted basis. The nature of the gain or loss takes on the same character (that is, capital gain or loss or ordinary income gain or loss) as the property lost.

Emotional distress. Damages for emotional distress are tax free if attributable to a physical injury or sickness. If emotional distress damages are unrelated to a physical injury or sickness, as in a discrimination action, the damages are taxable with one exception: Damages up to the amount of actual medical care expenses attributable to emotional distress are tax free. Apart from the medical expenses exception, damages for emotional distress are taxable when received for a personal injury

 *Planning Reminder*

Legal Fees

If the damages are tax free, you may not deduct your litigation costs. If your damages are fully taxed, you may deduct all of your litigation costs. If your damages are only partially taxed, then you deduct only that portion of your litigation costs attributed to the taxed damages.

However, legal fees related to your job or investments are deductible only as miscellaneous expenses subject to the 2% adjusted gross income floor; see 19.26.

If your attorney was paid a contingent fee from a taxable award, you generally must report the entire award as income and deduct the attorney's fee as a miscellaneous expense subject to the 2% floor; see 11.7.

other than a physical injury or sickness. This is true even where the emotional distress damages cover physical symptoms such as insomnia, headaches, and stomach disorders. The emotional distress by itself is not treated as a physical injury or sickness.

Punitive damages. Punitive damages are taxable, even if they relate to a physical injury or sickness. This law specifically applies to damages received after August 20, 1996. An exception in the law allows an exclusion from income for punitive damages awarded under an Alabama wrongful death statute; the punitive damages are the only damages that may be awarded under state law. A 1996 Supreme Court decision held that punitive damages were taxable even under the pre-1996 amendment to the law if under the state statute punitive damages did not provide compensation for injuries, but were intended to punish wrongdoing by the defendant who was sued.

Attorney's contingent fee paid from taxable award. If you receive taxable damages, such as back pay in an employment dispute, and a percentage goes directly to your attorney under a contingent fee agreement, can you exclude from your income the contingent fee payment, so that you are only taxed on the net amount you receive? The answer is no according to the IRS, Tax Court, and five appeals courts (the Third, Seventh, Ninth, Tenth, and Federal Circuits): you must include the entire award as income even though you were never entitled to the contingent fee portion. These courts hold that the contingent fee may not be excluded from income because of the assignment of income doctrine. The client has earned the entire award; the contingent fee is merely a cost of litigation. However, three appeals courts (Fifth, Sixth, and Eleventh) have allowed an exclusion for the contingent fee under specific state laws that give the attorney an interest in the client's cause of action. The Tax Court will allow the exclusion if the case before it is appealable to one of the Circuits that has allowed an exclusion.

If the contingent fee portion of an award is held to be taxable, it is generally impossible to offset the income by deducting the fee. The fee is deductible for regular tax purposes only as a miscellaneous itemized deduction subject to the 2%-of-adjusted-gross-income floor *(19.26)*, which may reduce or eliminate the deduction. Furthermore, taxpayers subject to the alternative minimum tax (AMT) are unable to deduct the fee at all. *See also 19.27.*

11.8 Cancellation of Debts You Owe

If a debt is cancelled or forgiven other than as a gift or a bequest the debtor generally must include the cancelled amount in gross income for tax purposes. Exclusions are allowed for discharges of farm or business real estate debt and debts of insolvent and bankrupt persons, as explained below.

Form 1099-C. You should receive Form 1099-C from a federal government agency, credit union, or bank that cancels or forgives a debt you owe of $600 or more. The IRS receives a copy of the form. Generally, the amount of cancelled debt shown in Box 2 of Form 1099-C must be reported as "other income" on Line 21 of Form 1040, unless one of the exclusions discussed below applies.

Discounted mortgage repayment. A prepayment of a home mortgage at a discount is taxable. The income is reported on Line 21, Form 1040. The tax treatment of a foreclosure sale or voluntary conveyance to a creditor is discussed at *31.9*.

> **EXAMPLE**
>
> A bank allows a homeowner to prepay a low-interest mortgage of $20,000 for $18,000. The discount of $2,000 is taxable as ordinary income.

Foreclosure sale. If a creditor forecloses on your property or you voluntarily convey property to avoid a foreclosure sale, you may realize ordinary cancellation-of-debt income as well as capital gain or loss; *see 31.9*.

Cancellation of student loans. A cancelled student loan is taxable income with this exception: If a loan by a government agency, by a government-funded loan program of an education organization, or by a qualified hospital organization is cancelled because you worked for a period of time in certain geographical areas in certain professions, such as practicing medicine in rural areas or teaching in inner-city schools, then the cancelled amount is not taxable.

Debts cancelled in bankruptcy. Debt cancelled in a bankruptcy case is not included in your gross income. Instead, certain losses, credits, and basis of property must be reduced by the amount excluded from income. These losses, credits, and basis of property are called "tax attributes." The amount of cancelled debt is used to reduce the tax attributes in the order listed below:

Law Alert

Holocaust Restitution Payments Tax Free
The 2001 Tax Act provides a broad exclusion from gross income for Holocaust restitution payments. Tax-free treatment applies to payments received after December 31, 1999, by persons persecuted by Nazi Germany or any Nazi-controlled or allied country, as well as to payments received by heirs or estates of such persecuted persons. Persecution on the basis of race, religion, physical or mental disability, or sexual orientation is covered.

Excludable restitution includes compensation for assets that were stolen or lost before, during, or after World War II and to life insurance issued by European insurers immediately before and during the war. Tax-free treatment also applies to interest earned on escrow accounts and funds established in settlement of Holocaust victim claims against European banks or corporations.

Planning Reminder

Loans Cancelled by Foundations
Student loans cancelled by educational organizations may be tax free if the loan was made under a program that encourages students to provide public service by working in occupations or areas with unmet needs. The services must be under the direction of a governmental unit or tax-exempt charity. Services to the lender organization do not qualify.

1. Net operating losses and carryovers—dollar for dollar of debt discharge;
2. Carryovers of the general business credit—$33^1/_3$ cents for each dollar of debt discharge;
3. AMT minimum tax credit as of the beginning of the year immediately after the taxable year of the discharge—$33^1/_3$ cents for each dollar of debt discharge;
4. Net capital losses and carryovers—dollar for dollar of debt discharge;
5. Basis of depreciable and nondepreciable assets—dollar for dollar of debt discharge (but not below the amount of your total undischarged liabilities);
6. Passive activity loss and credit carryovers—dollar for dollar of debt discharge for passive losses; $33^1/_3$ cents for each dollar of debt discharge in the case of passive credits; and
7. Foreign tax credit carryovers—$33^1/_3$ cents for each dollar of debt discharge.

After these reductions, any remaining balance of the debt discharge is disregarded. On Form 982, you may make a special election to first reduce the basis of any depreciable assets before reducing other tax attributes in the order above. Realty held for sale to customers may be treated as depreciable assets for purposes of the election. The election allows you to preserve your current deductions, such as a net operating loss carryover or capital loss carryover, for use in the following year. The election also will have the effect of reducing your depreciation deductions for years following the year of debt cancellation. If you later sell the depreciable property at a gain, the gain attributable to the basis reduction will be taxable as ordinary income under the depreciation recapture rules discussed at *44.1.*

Separate bankruptcy estate. If you are an individual debtor who files for bankruptcy under Chapter 7 or 11 of the Bankruptcy Code, a separate "estate" is created consisting of property that belonged to you before the filing date. This bankruptcy estate is a new taxable entity, completely separate from you as a taxpayer. The estate is represented by a trustee who manages the estate for the benefit of any creditors. The estate earns its own income and incurs expenses. The trustee reports the estate's income or loss on a separate return (Form 1041). The creation of a separate bankruptcy estate also gives you a "fresh start"; with certain exceptions, wages you earn and property you acquire after the bankruptcy case has begun belong to you and do not become part of the bankruptcy estate.

A separate estate is not created for an individual who files for bankruptcy under Chapter 12 or 13.

In a Chapter 7 or 11 case, the tax attribute reductions are made to the attributes in the bankruptcy estate. Reductions are not made to attributes of an individual debtor that come into existence after the bankruptcy case begins or that are treated as exempt property under bankruptcy rules. Basis reduction does apply to property transferred by the bankruptcy estate to the individual.

Debts discharged while you are insolvent. If your debt is cancelled outside of bankruptcy while you are insolvent, the cancellation does not result in taxable income to the extent of the insolvency. Insolvency means that liabilities exceed the fair market value of your assets immediately before the discharge of the debt. The IRS and Tax Court hold that in determining whether liabilities exceed the value of assets at the time of a debt discharge, a taxpayer must include assets that are shielded from creditors under state law. This is true even though for federal bankruptcy purposes creditor-exempt assets do not have to be counted in determining whether an individual seeking bankruptcy protection is insolvent.

If liabilities do exceed the value of assets, the discharged debt is not taxed to the extent of your insolvency and is applied to the reduction of tax attributes on Form 982 in the same manner as to a bankrupt individual. If the cancelled debt exceeds the insolvency, any remaining balance is treated as if it were a debt cancellation of a solvent person and, thus, it is taxable unless it is a qualifying farming debt or business real estate debt as discussed later in this section.

See the Example below for the IRS approach to figuring insolvency upon a debt cancellation.

EXAMPLE

In 1995, Jones borrowed $1,000,000 from Chester and signed a note payable for that amount. Jones was not personally liable on the note, which was secured by an office building valued at $1,000,000 that he bought from Baker with the proceeds of Chester's loan. In 2002, when the value of the building declined to $800,000, Chester agreed to reduce the principal of the loan to $825,000. At the time, Jones held other assets valued at $100,000 and owed another person $50,000.

To determine the extent of Jones's insolvency, the IRS compares the value of Jones's assets and liabilities immediately before the discharge. According to the IRS, his assets total $900,000: the building valued at $800,000 plus other assets of $100,000. His liabilities total $1,025,000: the other debt of $50,000 plus the liability on the note, which the IRS

Filing Tip

Bankrupt Persons
Special rules apply to debt cancellations under bankruptcy law. A debt cancelled in a bankruptcy case is not included in your income, but certain losses, credits, and basis of property must be reduced by the amount of excluded income.

considered to be $975,000, equal to the $800,000 value of the building and the discharged debt of $175,000. Jones is insolvent by $125,000 ($1,025,000 in liabilities less $900,000 in assets). As $175,000 was the amount of the discharged debt and Jones was insolvent to the extent of $125,000, only $50,000 is treated as taxable income.

Partnership debts. When a partnership's debt is discharged because of bankruptcy, insolvency, or if it is qualified farm debt or business real estate debt that is cancelled, the discharged amount is allocated among the partners. Bankruptcy or insolvency is tested not at the partnership level, but separately for each partner. Thus, a bankrupt or insolvent partner applies the allocated amount to reduce the specified tax attributes as previously discussed. A solvent partner may not take advantage of the rules applied to insolvent or bankrupt partners, even if the partnership is insolvent or bankrupt.

S corporation debts. The tax consequences of a debt discharge are determined at the corporate level. The Job Creation and Worker Assistance Act of 2002 overrode a 2001 Supreme Court decision that had allowed discharged debt of an insolvent S corporation to pass through to the shareholders as tax-exempt income. As a result of the pass-through, a stockholder could increase his or her basis in the S corporation, which in turn could allow a deduction for suspended losses. However, under the 2002 Act, a debt discharge after October 11, 2001, that is excludable from the S corporation's income because of insolvency or bankruptcy does not pass through to the shareholders and thus does not increase the shareholders' basis.

Purchase price adjustment for solvent debtors. If you buy property on credit and the seller reduces or cancels the debt arising out of the purchase, the reduction is generally treated as a purchase price adjustment (reducing your basis in the property). Since the reduction is not treated as a debt cancellation, you do not realize taxable income on the price adjustment. This favorable price adjustment rule applies only if you are solvent and not in bankruptcy, you have not transferred the property to a third party, and the seller has not transferred the debt to a third party, such as with the sale of your installment contract to a collection company.

Qualified farm debt. A solvent farmer may avoid tax from a discharge of indebtedness by an unrelated lender, including any federal, state, or local government agency, if the debt was incurred in operating a farm business. This relief is available only if 50% or more of your total gross receipts for the preceding three taxable years was derived from farming. The excluded amount first reduces tax attributes such as net operating loss carryovers and business tax credits, next reduces basis in all property other than farmland, and then reduces the basis in land used in the farming business. *See* IRS Publication 225 for details.

Business real estate debt. A solvent taxpayer may elect to avoid tax on a discharge of qualifying real property business debt. Such a discharge may occur where the fair market value of the property securing the debt has fallen in value. This relief applies to debt discharges after 1992. The debt must have been incurred or assumed in connection with business real property and must be secured by such property. A debt incurred or assumed after 1992 must be incurred or assumed to buy, construct, or substantially improve real property used in a business, or to refinance such acquisition debt (up to the refinanced amount). Debt incurred after 1992 to refinance a pre-1993 business real property debt (up to the refinanced amount) also qualifies. The debt must be secured by the property. Discharges of farm indebtedness do not qualify but may be tax free under the separate rules discussed earlier.

The maximum amount that can be excluded from income is the excess of the outstanding loan principal (immediately before the discharge) over the fair market value (immediately before the discharge) of the real property securing the debt, less any other outstanding qualifying real property business debts secured by the property. The excludable amount also may not exceed the taxpayer's adjusted basis for all depreciable real property held before the discharge. The excluded amount reduces basis in all depreciable real property.

Effect of basis reduction on later disposition of property. A reduction of basis is treated as a depreciation deduction so that a profitable sale of the property at a later date may be subject to the rules of recapture of depreciation; *see 44.1.*

Filing Instruction

Price Adjustments Not Taxed
If you bought property on credit and the seller cancels or reduces your purchase-related debt, this is a price adjustment, not a taxable cancellation of debt.

Partners, S Corporation Shareholders, and Trust and Estate Beneficiaries

11.9 Schedule K-1

Although partnerships, S corporations, trusts, and estates are different types of tax entities, they share a common tax-reporting characteristic. The entity itself generally does not pay income taxes. As a partner, shareholder, or beneficiary, you report your share of the entity's income or loss. The entity files a Schedule K-1 with the IRS that indicates your share of the income, deductions, and credits passed through from the entity. You will receive a copy of the Schedule K-1, which you should keep for your records; it does not have to be attached to your tax return.

11.10 How Partners Report Partnership Profit and Loss

A partnership files Form 1065, which informs the IRS of partnership profit or loss and each partner's share on Schedule K-1. The partnership pays no tax on partnership income; each partner reports his or her share of partnership net profit or loss and special deductions and credits, whether or not distributions are received from the partnership, as shown on Schedule K-1. Income that is not distributed or withdrawn increases the basis of a partner's partnership interest.

Your share reported to you on Schedule K-1 (Form 1065) is generally based on your proportionate capital interest in the partnership, unless the partnership agreement provides for another allocation.

Your partnership must give you a copy of Schedule K-1 (Form 1065), which lists your share of income, loss, deduction, and credit items, and where to report them on your return. For example, your share of income or loss from a business or real estate activity is reported on Schedule E and is subject to passive activity adjustments, if any. Interest and dividends are reported on Schedule B, royalties on Schedule E, and capital gains and losses on Schedule D. Your share of charitable donations is claimed on Schedule A if you itemize deductions. Tax preference items for alternative minimum tax purposes are also listed.

Health insurance premiums. A partnership that pays premiums for health insurance for partners has a choice. It may treat the premium as a reduction in distributions to the partners. Alternatively, it may deduct the premium as an expense and charge each partner's share as a guaranteed salary payment taxable to the partner. For 2002, the partner reports the guaranteed payment shown on Schedule K-1 as nonpassive income on Schedule E and may deduct 70% of the premium on Line 30, Form 1040, as an above-the-line deduction from gross income; *see 12.2.* Starting in 2003, the deduction increases to 100%.

Guaranteed salary and interest. A guaranteed salary that is fixed without regard to partnership income is taxable as ordinary wages and not as partnership earnings. If you receive a percentage of the partnership income with a stipulated minimum payment, the guaranteed payment is the amount by which the minimum guarantee exceeds your share of the partnership income before taking into account the minimum guarantee.

Interest on capital is reported as interest income.

Self-employment tax. As a partner, you pay self-employment tax on your net partnership income, including guaranteed salary and other guaranteed payments. The self-employment tax is explained in Chapter 45. Limited partners do not pay self-employment tax, unless guaranteed payments are received; *see 45.2.*

Special allocations. Partners may agree to special allocations of gain, income, loss, deductions, or credits disproportionate to their capital contributions. The allocation should have a substantial economic effect to avoid an IRS disallowance. The IRS will not issue an advance ruling on whether an allocation has a substantial economic effect. If the allocation is rejected, a partner's share is determined by his or her partnership interest.

To have substantial economic effect, a special allocation must be reflected by adjustments to the partners' capital accounts; liquidation proceeds must be distributed in accordance with the partners' capital accounts, and following a liquidating distribution, the partners must be liable to the partnership to restore any deficit in their capital.

Caution

IRS Matching Program for Schedules K-1

In 2002, IRS computers began matching information reported on Schedules K-1 by partnerships, S corporations, and trusts with the individual tax returns of partners, shareholders, and beneficiaries. By mid-year 2002, the IRS had sent out about 65,000 notices to taxpayers whose individual returns for 2000 did not match the K-1 information.

Filing Instruction

Partnership Elections

The partnership, not the individual partners, makes elections affecting the computation of partnership income such as the election to defer involuntary conversion gains, to amortize organization and start-up costs, and to choose depreciation methods, including first-year expensing. An election to claim a foreign tax credit is made by the partners.

If there is a change of partnership interests during the year, items are allocated to a partner for that part of the year he or she is a member of the partnership. Thus, a partner who acquires an interest late in the year is barred from deducting partnership expenses incurred prior to his entry into the partnership. If the partners agree to give an incoming partner a disproportionate share of partnership losses for the period after he or she becomes a member, the allocation must meet the substantial economic effect test to avoid IRS disallowance.

See IRS regulations to Code Section 704, IRS Publication 541, and Form 1065 instructions for further details.

Reporting transfers of interest to IRS. If you transfer a partnership interest that includes an interest in partnership receivables and appreciated inventory, you must report the disposition to the partnership within 30 days, or, if earlier, by January 15 of the calendar year after the year of the transfer. The partnership in turn files a report with the IRS on Form 8308. You must also attach a statement to your income tax return describing the transaction and allocating basis to the receivables and inventory items. The IRS wants to keep track of such dispositions because partners have to pay ordinary income tax on the portion of profit attributable to the receivables and inventory.

Within 30 days of your transfer, provide the partnership with a statement that includes the date of the exchange and identifies the transferee (include Social Security number if known). You can be penalized for failure to notify the partnership. You and your transferee should receive a copy of the Form 8308 that the partnership will send to the IRS along with its Form 1065.

Generally, the partnership must file a separate Form 8308 for each transfer but the IRS may allow a composite Form 8308 for the calendar year if there were at least 25 reportable transfers.

Recognition of gain by partner on distribution of contributed property. Under a restrictive law (Code Section 737), a partner who contributes appreciated property to a partnership may incur tax on the pre-contribution gain if within seven years *other* property is received from the partnership that is valued at more than the partner's basis in the partnership. Under another law (Code Section 704(c)(1)(B)), if appreciated property contributed by a partner is distributed to a *different* partner within seven years of the contribution, the contributing partner is taxed on the pre-contribution gain as if the property had been sold at fair market value on the date of distribution.

Caution

Partner May Be Taxed on Pre-Contribution Gain

The rules subjecting partners to tax on pre-contribution gain when they contribute property and the partnership makes a later distribution are complicated and hedged with restrictions. Consult a tax advisor before making transfers of appreciated property to, or taking distributions from, a partnership.

11.11 When a Partner Reports Income or Loss

You report your share of the partnership gain or loss for the partnership year that ends in your tax reporting year. If you and the partnership are on a calendar-year basis, you report your share of the 2002 partnership income on your 2002 income tax return. If the partnership is on a fiscal year ending March 31, for example, and you report on a calendar year, you report on your 2002 return your share of the partnership income for the whole fiscal year ending March 31, 2002—that is, partnership income for the fiscal year April 1, 2001, through March 31, 2002.

If a Section 444 election of a fiscal year is made on Form 8716, a special tax payment must be computed for each fiscal year and if the computed payment exceeds $500, it must be paid to the IRS. The tax payment is figured and reported on Form 8752. The tax does not apply to the first tax year of a partnership's existence but Form 8752 must still be filed. In later years, a refund of prior payments is available to the extent the prior payments exceed the payment required for the current fiscal year. For example, if the required payment was $12,000 for the fiscal year July 1, 2002–June 30, 2003, and the required payment for the fiscal year starting July 1, 2003, is $10,000, a $2,000 refund may be claimed on Form 8752. Refunds of prior year payments also are available if the fiscal-year election is terminated and a calendar year adopted or if the partnership liquidates.

See *IRS Publication 541 for further information on partnership reporting.*

11.12 Partnership Loss Limitations

Your share of partnership losses may not exceed the adjusted basis of your partnership interest. If the loss exceeds basis, the excess loss may not be deducted until you have partnership earnings to cover the loss or contribute capital to cover the loss. The basis of your partnership interest is generally the amount paid for the interest (either through contribution or purchase) less withdrawals plus accumulated taxed earnings that have not been withdrawn. You also have a basis in loans to the partnership for which you are personally liable.

A partner's basis is not increased by accrued but unpaid expenses such as interest costs and accounts payable unless the partnership uses the accrual accounting method. However, basis is increased by capitalized items allocable to future periods such as organization and construction period expenses.

Partners are subject to the "at-risk" loss limitation rules. These rules limit the amount of loss that may be deducted to the amount each partner personally has at stake in the partnership, such as contributions of property and loans for which the partner is personally liable. *See 10.17* for a discussion of the "at-risk" rules.

Furthermore, if the IRS determines that a tax-shelter partnership is not operated to make a profit, deductions may be disallowed even where there is an "at-risk" investment.

Finally, any loss not barred by these limitations may be disallowed under the passive activity rules discussed in Chapter 10.

11.13 Unified Tax Audits of Partnerships

Tax audits of both a partnership of more than 10 partners and its partners must be at the partnership level. To challenge the partnership treatment of an item, the IRS must generally audit the partnership, not the individual partner. To avoid a personal audit of a partnership item, a partner should report partnership items as shown on the partnership return or identify any inconsistent treatment on his or her return. Otherwise, the IRS may assess a deficiency without auditing the partnership.

For a partnership-level audit, the partnership names a "tax matters partner" (TMP) to receive notice of the audit. If one is not named, the IRS will treat as a TMP the general partner having the largest interest in partnership profits at the end of the taxable year involved in the audit. Notice of the audit must also be given to the other partners. All partners may participate in the partnership audit. If the IRS settles with some partners, it is not required to offer consistent settlement terms. However, the IRS is required to apply the tax law consistently.

Within 90 days after the IRS mails its final determination, the TMP may appeal to the Tax Court; individual partners have an additional 60 days to file a court petition if the TMP does not do so. An appeal may also be filed in a federal district court or the claims court if the petitioning partner first deposits with the IRS an amount equal to the tax that would be owed if the IRS determination were sustained. A Tax Court petition takes precedence over petitions filed in other courts. The first Tax Court petition filed is heard; if other partners have also filed petitions, their cases will be dismissed. If no Tax Court petitions are filed, the first petition filed in federal district court or the claims court takes precedence. Regardless of which petition takes precedence, all partners who hold an interest during the taxable year involved will be bound by the decision (unless the statute of limitations with respect to that partner has run out).

Exception for 10 or fewer partners. The unified audit rules do not apply if there are 10 or fewer partners. The exception applies if all the partners are individuals (but not nonresident aliens), estates of deceased partners, or C corporations. C corporations are allowed under this exception under a law effective for taxable years ending after August 5, 1997. A husband and wife (and their estates) are treated as one partner.

11.14 Stockholder Reporting of S Corporation Income and Loss

S corporations are subject to tax reporting rules similar to those applied to partnerships. However, shareholders who work for the corporation are treated as employees for payroll tax purposes. They do not pay self-employment tax on their salary income or other receipts from the corporation.

Your company must give you a copy of Schedule K-1 (Form 1120-S), which lists your share of income or loss, deductions, and credits that must be reported on your return. For example, your share of business income or loss is reported on Schedule E and is subject to passive activity adjustments, if any. Interest and dividends from other corporations are reported on Schedule B, capital gains and losses on Schedule D, Section 1231 gains or losses on Form 4797, and charitable donations on Schedule A. Tax preference items for alternative minimum tax purposes are also listed.

Health insurance premimums paid by an S corporation for more-than-2% stockholders are treated as wages, deductible on Form 1120-S by the corporation and reported to the stockholder on Form W-2. A more-than-2% shareholder who reports premiums as wages for 2002 may deduct 70% of the premium on Line 30 of Form 1040 as an adjustment to income.

Allocation to shareholders. The following items are allocated to and pass through to the shareholders based on the proportion of stock held in the corporation:

- Gains and losses from the sale and exchange of capital assets and Section 1231 property, as well as interest and dividends on corporate investments and losses. Investment interest expenses subject to the rules discussed at *15.10* also pass through.

Court Decision

Settlements Need Not Be Consistent

Neither the IRS nor the Department of Justice is required to offer consistent settlements to audited partners so long as they do not discriminate for arbitrary reasons. After a partner sued for a refund, the Court of Federal Claims refused to compel the government to settle his case on the same favorable terms offered to other partners.

Caution

Family S Corporations

The IRS has the authority to change the amounts of items passed through to stockholders to properly reflect the value of services rendered or capital contributed by family members of one or more S corporation shareholders. If you are a member of a family of an S corporation shareholder and perform services or furnish capital to the corporation without receiving reasonable compensation, the IRS may reallocate salary or interest income to you from the other shareholders to reflect the value of your services or capital. The term "family" includes only a spouse, parents, ancestors, children, and any trusts for the benefit of such relatives.

- Tax-exempt interest. Tax-exempt interest remains tax free in the hands of the stockholders but increases the basis of their stock. Dividends from other companies may qualify for the exclusion.

- First-year expense deduction (Section 179 deduction).

- Charitable contributions made by the corporation.

- Foreign income or loss.

- Foreign taxes paid by the corporation. Each stockholder elects whether to claim these as a credit or deduction.

- Tax preference items.

- Recovery of bad debts and prior taxes.

If your interest changed during the year, your pro rata share must reflect the time you held the stock.

The Tax Court and several federal appeals courts have held that an S corporation shareholder's basis is not increased by guaranteeing a loan to the corporation where there is no actual economic outlay. The Tax Court disagrees with the approach of another federal appeals court that allowed an increased basis where the lender looked to the guarantor-shareholder as the primary obligor on the guaranteed loan. *See also 11.8* for treatment of debt cancellations.

Passive activity rules limit loss deductions. Losses allocated to you may be disallowed under the passive activity rules discussed in Chapter 10.

Basis adjustments. Because of the nature of S corporation reporting, the basis of each shareholder's stock is subject to change. Basis is increased by the pass-through of income items and by loans to the S corporation for which the shareholder is personally liable, and basis is reduced by the pass-through of loss items and the receipt of certain distributions. Because income and loss items pass through to stockholders, an S corporation has no current earnings and profits. An income item will not increase basis, unless you actually report the amount on your tax return. The specific details and order of basis adjustments are listed in IRS Publication 589.

Planning Reminder

Basis Limits Loss Deductions

Deductible losses may not exceed your basis in S corporation stock and loans to the corporation. If losses exceed basis, the excess loss is carried over and becomes deductible when you invest or lend an equivalent amount of money to the corporation. This rule may allow for timing a loss deduction. In a year in which you want to deduct the loss, you may contribute capital to the corporation. If a carryover loss exists when an S election terminates, a limited loss deduction may be allowed.

EXAMPLES

1. A calendar-year corporation incurs a loss of $10,000. Smith and Jones each own 50% of the stock. On May 1, Smith sells all of his stock to Harris. For the year, Smith was a shareholder for 120 days, Jones for 365 days, and Harris for 245 days. The loss is allocated on a daily basis; the daily basis of the loss is $27.3973 ($10,000 divided by 365 days). The allocation is as follows:

   Smith: $1,644 ($27.3973 × 120 days × 50% interest)

   Jones: $5,000 ($27.3973 × 365 days × 50% interest)

   Harris: $3,356 ($27.3973 × 245 days × 50% interest)

2. Same facts as in Example 1, except that on May 1, Smith sells only 50% of his stock to Harris. The allocation for Smith accounts for his 50% interest for 120 days and his 25% interest for the remainder of the year.

   Smith: $3,322 ($27.3973 × 120 days × 50% plus $27.3973 × 245 days × 25%)

   Jones: $5,000 (as above)

   Harris: $1,678 ($27.3973 × 245 days × 25%)

Filing Instruction

Consistent Reporting by Beneficiaries

Beneficiaries of trusts and estates must report items consistently with the Schedule K-1 provided by the trust or estate. If an item is treated inconsistently and a statement identifying the inconsistency is not attached to the return, the IRS may make a summary assessment for additional tax without issuing a deficiency notice.

11.15 How Beneficiaries Report Estate or Trust Income

Trust or estate income is treated as if you had received the income directly from the original source instead of from the estate or trust. This means capital gain remains capital gain, ordinary income is fully taxed, and tax-exempt income remains tax free. Tax preference items of a trust or estate are apportioned between the estate or trust and beneficiaries, according to allocation of income.

You report your share of trust or estate income on Schedule B as shown on the Schedule K-1 (Form 1041) sent to you by the trustee. Dividends and interest from the trust are reported on Schedule B of Form 1040 and capital gains on Schedule D. Income or loss from real estate or business activities shown on Schedule K-1 is reported by you on Schedule E, subject to the passive activity restrictions discussed in Chapter 10.

Reporting rule for revocable grantor trusts. A grantor who sets up a revocable trust or keeps certain powers over trust income or corpus must report all of the trust income, deductions, and credits. This rule applies if a grantor retains a reversionary interest in the trust that is valued at more than 5% of the trust (valued at the time the trust is set up); *see 33.3*. If a grantor is also a trustee of a revocable trust and all the trust assets are in the United States, filing Form 1041 is not necessary. The grantor simply reports the trust income, deductions, and credits on Form 1040. *See* the Form 1041 instructions for reporting requirements.

11.16 Deductions for Income Subject to Estate Tax

If you receive income that was earned by but not paid to a decedent before death, such as wages, IRA and qualified plan distributions, lottery prize winnings, or installment sale proceeds, you are said to have "income in respect of a decedent," or IRD. You report the IRD on your return. If the decedent's estate paid estate tax that was attributable to the IRD you received, you may claim an itemized deduction for the estate tax paid on that income. No deduction is allowed for state death taxes. Ask the executor of the estate for data in computing the deduction.

> **EXAMPLE**
> When Jim Bennett's uncle died, he was owed a fee of $1,000. He also had not collected accrued bond interest of $500. Bennett, as the sole heir, will collect both items and pay income tax on them. These items are called "income in respect of a decedent." Assume that an estate tax of $390 was paid on the $1,500. Bennett collects the $1,000, which he reports on his income tax return. If he itemizes deductions, he may deduct $260, computed as follows:
>
> $$\frac{\$1,000}{\$1,500} \times \$390 = \$260$$
>
> When he collects the $500, he will deduct the balance, or $130 ($390 − $260).

IRD deduction claimed on Schedule A. The deduction is generally claimed on Line 27 of Schedule A as a miscellaneous itemized deduction that is not subject to the 2% AGI floor. However, if you receive long-term capital gain income, such as an installment payment on a sale transacted before a decedent's death, the estate tax attributed to the capital gain item is not claimed as a miscellaneous deduction. The deduction is treated as if it were an expense of sale and, thus, reduces the amount of gain.

11.17 Who Is a Farmer?

The term "farmer" includes all individuals, partnerships, syndicates, and corporations that cultivate, operate, or manage a farm for profit or gain, either as owners or tenants. Thus, partners in a partnership that operates a farm are considered farmers.

The term "farm" includes stock, dairy, poultry, fruit and truck farms, plantations, ranches, and all land used for farming operations. A fish farm where fish are specially fed and raised, and not just caught, is a farm. Animal breeding farms, such as mink, fox, and chinchilla farms, are also considered farms.

Farm loss deductions may also be restricted by the at-risk rules and passive activity rules described in Chapter 10.

If your farm losses exceed your other income, *see 40.18*.

Important: A guide to reporting farm income and loss may be obtained at your local Internal Revenue Service Center or from your County Farm Agent. It is called Farmer's Tax Guide (IRS Publication 225).

11.18 Forms Farmers File

Use Schedule F to report income from a farm you operate as an individual. The profit or loss computed on Schedule F is then included on Line 18 of Form 1040. Schedule F is also used as a basis for figuring self-employment tax on Schedule SE, which must also be filed with Form 1040. Sales of farm equipment and dairy or breeding livestock are reported on Form 4797.

Filing Instruction

Lump-Sum Distributions From Qualified Retirement Plans

When a beneficiary receiving a lump-sum distribution because of an employee's death reports the distribution using the special averaging method (Chapter 7), the taxable amount of the distribution must be reduced by the estate taxes attributable to the distribution. *See* the Form 4972 instructions when calculating the tax under averaging.

Farm Income or Loss

Caution

Gentleman Farming

To be treated as farmers, individuals must be engaged in farming for gain or profit. Farm losses of a part-time "gentleman" farmer may be disallowed on the grounds that the farm is not operated to make a profit but is a hobby. The hobby rules explained at 40.10 apply in determining the existence of a profit motive in farming operations. Favorable evidence of an intention to make a profit are: You do not use your farm for recreation. You have tried to cut losses by switching from unsuccessful products to other types of farming. Losses are decreasing. Losses were caused by unexpected events. You have a bookkeeping system. You consult experts. You devote personal attention to the farm.

If you operate through a partnership, the details of your farm operation are shown on Schedule F and Form 1065. Your share of the partnership net income or loss is included on Form 1040.

Individual farmers who are on a calendar-year basis (ending December 31) may pay their entire estimated tax for 2002 on Form 1040-ES by January 15, 2003, if at least two-thirds of gross income for 2001 or 2002 is from farming. A final return for 2002 is required by April 15, 2003. However, you may file your final return by March 3, 2003, instead of making an estimated tax payment for 2002 in January 2003.

11.19 Income Averaging for Farmers

A farmer may elect to average 2002 farm income over three years on Schedule J of Form 1040. On Schedule J, one-third of elected farm income is allocated to each of 1999, 2000, and 2001. The tax for 2002 equals the tax liability figured without elected farm income plus increases in tax liability for the three prior years by including allocated elected farm income.

Elected farm income is taxable income attributable to a farming business. Gain from the sale of property, other than land, regularly used by the farmer for a substantial period in a farming business is treated as attributable to a "farming business." A farming business is the trade or business of farming, including operating a nursery or sod farm, or the raising or harvesting of trees bearing fruit, nuts, or other crops, or ornamental trees.

The election to average farming income is irrevocable unless Treasury regulations allow an exception.

Income averaging is available for all tax years beginning after December 31, 1997.

Income averaging may not be elected by estates or trusts.

 Filing Tip

Negative Taxable Income in Prior Three Years

When figuring your tax under the averaging method on Schedule J, you may use negative taxable income for a base year (any of the three preceding years) for which deductions exceeded gross income. *See* the Schedule J instructions for details.

Claiming Deductions

In this part, you will learn how to reduce your tax liability by claiming deductions from gross income, and either the standard deduction or itemized deductions. Pay special attention to—

- Deductions you may claim directly from gross income in arriving at adjusted gross income. These are allowed even if you claim the standard deduction. *See* Chapter 12.

- The standard deduction. Although the standard deduction (*see* Chapter 13) may provide an automatic tax reduction, read the chapters on itemized deductions to see that you have not overlooked itemized deductions for charitable donations, interest expenses, state and local taxes, medical expenses, casualty and theft losses, miscellaneous expenses for job costs, and investment expenses.

- The 3% reduction of certain itemized deductions if your 2002 adjusted gross income, or AGI (Line 35 of Form 1040), exceeds $137,300 (or $68,650 if you are married and file separate returns). *See* Chapter 13.

- Personal exemptions. Each personal exemption claimed on your 2002 return—for yourself, your spouse, your children, and other dependents, is the equivalent of a $3,000 deduction. *See* Chapter 21 for exemption rules, including the phaseout of exemptions for certain high-income taxpayers.

- Other deductions that are discussed in the following chapters:

  Chapter 40   Business expenses
  Chapter 9   Rental expenses
  Chapter 43   Automobile expenses

Chapter 12

Deductions Allowed in Figuring Adjusted Gross Income

Adjusted gross income (AGI) is the amount used in figuring the 7.5% floor for medical expense deductions *(17.1)*, the 10% floor for personal casualty and theft losses *(18.11)*, the 2% floor for miscellaneous itemized deductions *(19.1)*, the charitable contribution percentage limitations *(14.17)*, and the 3% reduction of itemized deductions *(13.7)*.

If you follow the instructions and order of the tax return, you will arrive at adjusted gross income automatically. But if you are planning the tax consequences of a transaction in advance of preparing your return, *12.1* will explain how to figure adjusted gross income (AGI).

There is an advantage in being able to claim deductions directly from gross income in arriving at adjusted gross income, since such deductions are allowed even if you claim the standard deduction and do not itemize deductions on Schedule A of Form 1040. Another advantage of such deductions is that they also reduce state income tax for taxpayers residing in states that compute tax based on federal adjusted gross income. This chapter will explain the deductions that qualify for the direct deduction from gross income.

Expenses Deductible Directly From Gross Income

12.1 Figuring Adjusted Gross Income (AGI)

Adjusted gross income is the difference between gross income in Step 1 and the deductions listed in Step 2.

Step 1. Figure gross income. This is all income received by you from any source, such as wages, salary, tips, gross business income, income from sales and exchanges of property, interest and dividends, rents, royalties, annuities, pensions, etc. But gross income does not include such items as tax-free interest from state or local bonds *(4.24)*, tax-free parsonage allowance *(3.12)*, tax-free insurance proceeds (Chapter 33), gifts and inheritances *(11.4)*, Social Security benefits that are not subject to tax under the rules at *34.3*, tax-free scholarship grants *(38.1)*, tax-free board and lodging *(3.11)*, and other tax-free fringe benefits (Chapter 3).

Step 2. Deduct from your 2002 gross income only the following items:

Repayment of supplemental unemployment benefits required because of receipt of trade readjustment allowances *(2.9)*

Forfeiture-of-interest penalties because of premature withdrawals *(4.16)*

Capital loss deduction up to $3,000 *(5.4)*

IRA contributions *(8.4)*

Rent and royalty expenses *(9.2)*

50% of self-employed tax liability *(12.2)*

Health insurance deduction if self-employed *(12.2)*

Student loan interest *(38.6)*

Jury duty pay turned over to your employer *(12.2)*

Performing artist's qualifying expenses *(12.2)*

Reforestation expenses *(12.2)*

Moving expenses *(12.3)*

Medical savings account (Archer MSA) contributions *(17.17)*

Educator expenses *(12.2)*

Alimony payments *(37.1)*

Tuition and fees deduction *(38.13)*

Business expenses *(40.7)*

Net operating losses *(40.19)*

Keogh or SEP retirement plan contributions for yourself *(41.5)*

Hybrid vehicle deduction *(43.13)*

Step 3. The difference between Steps 1 and 2 is adjusted gross income.

12.2 Claiming Deductions From Gross Income

Many deductions taken directly from gross income in arriving at adjusted gross income are deducted on Form 1040 schedules devoted to a specific activity, such as business deductions claimed on Schedule C (Chapter 40), capital losses claimed on Schedule D (Chapter 5), and real estate rental expenses claimed on Schedule E (Chapter 9). Where an expense is not claimed on a specific schedule, it is deducted on Lines 23–34 of Form 1040. Deductions that are claimed directly from gross income on Form 1040 are referred to as "above-the-line" deductions, as they are allowed in figuring adjusted gross income and do not have to be claimed as itemized deductions.

Here is a list of the above-the-line deductions claimed on Lines 23–34 of Form 1040. Many of them are discussed in detail elsewhere in this book. Moving expenses are discussed in this chapter at *12.3–12.8*. The others are discussed below.

On Form 1040A, four deductions from gross income may be claimed: educator expenses on Line 16, traditional IRA deductions on Line 17, and student loan interest on Line 18, and tuition and fees on Line 19. To claim any other deduction from gross income you must file Form 1040.

Educator expenses—Line 23 of Form 1040; Line 16 of Form 1040A. Teachers, instructors, counselors, principals, or aides who work at private or public elementary or secondary schools (kindergarten through grade 12) for at least 900 hours during the school year generally may deduct up to $250 of out-of-pocket costs for books and classroom supplies. Eligible expenses include computer equipment, including related software and services, other equipment, and supplementary materials used in the classroom. For courses in health or physical education, supplies must be related to athletics to qualify.

If eligible expenses exceed the $250 limit, the excess may be deductible as a miscellaneous itemized expense.

The $250 deduction limit may have to be reduced or eliminated completely if certain tax-free amounts are received during the year. The deduction is reduced by tax-free interest on savings bonds used for tuition *(38.4)* and tax-free distributions from qualified tuition programs *(38.5)* and Coverdell education savings accounts *(38.12)*.

Unless the law is changed, the up-to-$250 deduction will be allowed for just two years — 2002 and 2003.

Traditional IRA deduction—Line 24 of Form 1040; Line 17 of Form 1040A. Enter your deductible IRA contribution here, including a contribution for your spouse if you file jointly. The deductible limits, including the phase-out rules for individuals covered by employer retirement plans, are explained at *8.3–8.4.*

Student loan interest deduction—Line 25 of Form 1040; Line 18 of Form 1040A. Within limits, you may deduct interest you pay on a qualified student loan. *See 38.6* for details.

Tuition and fees deduction—Line 26 of Form 1040; Line 19 of Form 1040A. Up to $3,000 of college tuition and fees may be deducted if MAGI does not exceed $65,000 for single and head of household filers and $130,000 for joint returns. *See 38.13* for details.

Medical savings account (Archer MSA) deduction—Line 27 of Form 1040. If you are self-employed or employed by a qualifying small business and have high-deductible health coverage, a deduction for contributions to an Archer MSA may be allowed. *See 17.17* for the deduction rules.

Moving expenses—Line 28 of Form 1040. Deductible moving expenses are discussed in this chapter at *12.3–12.8.*

50% of self-employment tax—Line 29 of Form 1040. After you figure your self-employment tax liability on Schedule SE, you deduct 50% of it here as an income tax deduction. *See 45.3–45.4* for the calculation of self-employment tax.

Self-employed health insurance deduction—Line 30 of Form 1040. If you were self-employed in 2002, you may claim 70% of health insurance premiums paid in 2002 for yourself, your spouse, and your dependents. The deduction is also allowed if you are a general partner in a partnership, a limited partner receiving guaranteed payments, or you received wages from an S corporation in which you were a more-than-2% shareholder.

If you have a qualified long-term care policy, the deductible portion of the premiums under the rules at *17.15* is included in the 70% deduction.

The 70% deduction may not exceed your net profit from the business under which the health premiums are paid, less deductions claimed on Line 29 (50% of self-employment tax) and Line 31 (Keogh, SEP, or SIMPLE retirement plan contributions).

Any balance of premiums not deductible under the special 70% rule may be claimed as an itemized medical expense subject to the 7.5% income floor *(17.4).*

Keogh plan contributions and self-employed SEP or SIMPLE deductions—Line 31 of Form 1040. *See* Chapter 41 for further details.

Penalty on early savings withdrawals—Line 32, *see 4.16.*

Hybrid car deduction—Line 34 of Form 1040. Individuals may deduct $2,000 of the cost of a hybrid (clean-fuel) vehicle used for nonbusiness purposes. Enter the deduction on Line 34 and write "Clean-Fuel" and the deducted amount on the dotted line next to Line 34. *See 43.13* for further details.

Alimony paid—Line 33a, *see* Chapter 37.

 Caution

Reduction of 70% Deduction
The 70% health insurance deduction may not be claimed for any month during 2002 that you were eligible to participate in an employer's subsidized health plan, including a plan of your spouse's employer. If the deduction would be barred for any month because of such eligibility and you have long-term care coverage that is not employer subsidized, you may claim the 70% deduction for the allowable portion of the long-term care premiums *(17.15).*

Jury duty pay turned over to employer—Line 34 of Form 1040. If you receive your regular pay while on jury duty and turn over your jury duty fees to your employer, report the fees as other income on Line 21, Form 1040 and claim an offsetting deduction on Line 34. Write "Jury pay" and the amount on the dotted line next to Line 34.

Expenses of performing artists—Line 34 of Form 1040. As a performing artist, you may deduct job expenses from gross income, whether or not itemized deductions are claimed, if you have:

1. Two or more employers in the performing arts during 2002 with at least $200 of earnings from at least two of them.
2. Expenses from acting or other services in the performing arts that exceed 10% of gross income from such work; and
3. Adjusted gross income (before deducting these expenses) that does not exceed $16,000.

If you are married, a joint return must be filed to claim the deduction, unless you lived apart from your spouse during the whole year. The $16,000 adjusted gross income limitation applies to your combined incomes. If both spouses are performing artists, the $16,000 adjusted income limit applies to the combined incomes, but each spouse must separately meet the two-employer test and 10% expense test for his or her job expenses to be deductible on the joint return.

You report the performing artist expenses on Form 2106 (or Form 2106-EZ where eligible) and enter the total as a "write-in amount" on Line 34 of Form 1040, instead of on Schedule A. Write "QPA" and the deducted amount on the dotted line next to Line 34. If you do not meet the tests, the expenses are deducted on Schedule A subject to the 2% AGI floor *(19.1)*.

State and local officials—Line 34. State and local officials paid on a fee basis may deduct from gross income unreimbursed business expenses. Next to Line 34 identify the expenses.

Repayment of supplemental unemployment benefits—Line 34. As explained at *2.9,* you may claim a deduction from gross income for the repayment or in some cases a tax credit. Claim the deduction on Line 34 and on the adjacent dotted line write the amount and label it "subpay TRA" (trade readjustment allowances).

Reforestation amortization—Line 34 of Form 1040. If you do not have to file Schedule C or F to report income from a timber activity, an amortization deduction for qualifying reforestation expenses may be claimed on Line 34 of Form 1040. Amortization is allowed over an 84-month period; *see* Code Section 194 for details. On Line 34, the amortization deduction should be labeled "RFST."

Costs of Moving to a New Job Location

12.3 What Moving Costs Are Deductible?

You may deduct unreimbursed expenses of moving your household goods and traveling to a new job location, provided you meet
- A 50-mile distance test *(12.4),* and
- A 39-week or 78-week work test for remaining in the new location *(12.5–12.6).* A deduction may be claimed even if the work test has not been met by the filing due date; *see 12.7.*

You claim the moving expense deduction as an adjustment to gross income on Form 1040, Line 28, whether you claim the standard deduction or itemized deductions.

If your expenses are reimbursed, you do not have to report the reimbursement, provided your employer reimburses you under an accountable plan; *see 20.31* and *12.8.*

If the tests are met, you may deduct on your 2002 return the following unreimbursed moving expenses incurred during 2002:

1. *Traveling costs of yourself and members of your household en route from your old to the new locality.* Here, you include the costs of transportation and lodging for yourself and household members while traveling to your new residence. Lodging before departure for one day after the old residence is unusable and lodging for the day of arrival at the new locality are included. If you use your own car, you may either deduct your actual costs of gas, oil, and repairs (but not depreciation) during the trip or take a deduction based on the rate of 13¢ a mile. Also add parking fees and tolls. Meal expenses are not a deductible moving expense.

Filing Tip

Family Move
It is not necessary for you and members of your household to travel together, or at the same time, to claim a deduction for the expenses incurred by each family member.

2. ***The actual cost of moving your personal effects and household goods.*** This includes the cost of packing, crating, and transporting furniture and household belongings, in-transit storage up to 30 consecutive days, insurance costs for the goods, and the cost of moving a pet or shipping an automobile to your new residence. You may also deduct expenses of moving your personal effects from a place other than your former home, but only up to the estimated cost of such a move from your former home. Also deduct the cost of connecting or disconnecting utilities when moving household appliances. The cost of connecting a telephone in your new home is not deductible.

In one case, a moving expense deduction was allowed for the cost of shipping a sailboat. The IRS had disallowed the deduction, claiming the sailboat was not a "personal effect." The Tax Court, however, allowed the deduction based on these facts: the couple were active sailors and frequently used the boat; they lived on the sailboat for two weeks immediately before they moved and also for nine weeks after they arrived in the new location; and they kept on board personal effects such as a refrigerator, kitchen utensils, and chairs. According to the court, the boat was so "intimately related" to their lifestyle that it should be considered a deductible personal effect.

Delay in moving to new job location. You may delay moving to the area of a new job location. A delay of up to one year does not jeopardize a deduction for moving expenses. Furthermore, if you move to the new job area within one year, your family may stay in the old residence for a longer period. Their later moving expenses will generally be deductible, even though incurred after one year. For example, the IRS allowed a moving expense deduction to a husband who immediately moved to a new job location, although his wife and children did not join him until 30 months after he began the new job. They delayed so that the children could complete their education. The IRS held that since part of the moving expenses were incurred within one year, the moving expenses incurred later were also deductible.

Nondeductible expenses. You may not deduct the cost of travel incurred for a maid, nurse, chauffeur, or similar domestic help (unless the person is also your dependent), expenses of refitting rugs and drapes, forfeited tuition, car tags or driver's license for the state you move to, losses on disposing of memberships in clubs, mortgage penalties, expenses for trips to sell your old house, or loss on the sale of the house. Furthermore, when your employer reimburses you for such costs, you realize taxable income equal to the amount of the reimbursement.

You may not deduct the cost of transporting furniture that you purchased en route from your old home.

You may not deduct the cost of pre-move house-hunting trips, temporary living expenses, or expenses of selling, purchasing, or leasing the old or new residence, such as attorneys' fees, real estate fees, or costs of settling an unexpired lease. Meal expenses while traveling to your new residence are not deductible.

12.4 The Distance Test

The distance between your new job location and your former home must be at least 50 miles more than the distance between your old job location and your former home. For this purpose, your home may be a house, apartment, trailer, or even a houseboat, but not a seasonal residence such as a summer cottage. If you had no previous job or you return to full-time work after a long period of unemployment or part-time work, the new job location must be at least 50 miles from your former home. Self-employed individuals are also subject to the mileage test.

The location of your new residence is not considered in applying the mileage test. However, if the distance between your new residence and the new job location is more than the distance between your old residence and new job location, your moving expenses may be disallowed unless you can show (1) you are required to live there as a condition of employment or (2) an actual decrease in commuting time or expense results.

If you worked for more than one employer, you find the shortest of the most commonly traveled routes from your old residence to your former principal place of employment.

Your job location is where you spend most of your working time. If you work at various locations, the job location is where you report to work. If you work for several employers on a short-term basis and get jobs through a union hall system, the union hall is considered your job location.

Moving overseas. A member of the Armed Forces may deduct the cost of moving his or her family to an overseas post.

If you take a new job overseas and qualify for the foreign earned income exclusion, moving expenses allocable to the excluded income are not deductible; *see 36.6.*

 Filing Tip

Meeting the Mileage Test
Use the following worksheet to see if your move satisfies the 50-mile test. Find the shortest of the most commonly traveled routes in measuring the distances.

Distance between	In miles
1. Old residence and new job location	_____
2. Old residence and old job location	_____
3. Difference (must be at least 50 miles)	_____

Alien moving to the U.S. The deduction is not limited to U.S. citizens and residents. An alien may deduct the cost of travel here to work at a full-time position.

> **EXAMPLES**
>
> 1. Your company's office is in the center of a metropolitan area. You live 18 miles from your office. You are transferred to a new office and buy a new house. To deduct moving costs, you must show that the location of the new office is at least 50 miles from your previous residence.
> 2. Your old job was four miles from your former residence and your new job is 55 miles from your former residence. You move to a house that is less than 50 miles from your old house. Nevertheless, you have met the 50-mile test since your new job is 51 miles further from your former home than your old job was.

12.5 The 39-Week Test for Employees

In addition to meeting the distance test *(12.4)*, you must work in the locality of the new job as a full-time employee for at least 39 weeks during the 12-month period immediately following your arrival at the new job location. You do not need to have a job prior to your arrival at the new location. Your family does not have to arrive with you. The 39 weeks of work need not be consecutive or with the same employer. You may change jobs provided you remain in the same general commuting area for 39 weeks. The 39-week test does not apply to employees who become disabled and lose their jobs, or who die.

If you are temporarily absent from work through no fault of your own, due to illness, strikes, shutouts, layoffs, or natural disasters, your temporary absence counts toward the 39-week requirement as full-time employment.

> **EXAMPLE**
>
> You accept a position with a company 600 miles from your former position. You move to the new location. After you have worked in the new position 14 weeks, you resign and take another job with a nearby company. You may add the 14 weeks of work with the first company to 25 weeks with the second company to meet the 39-week requirement.

Job transfers. The 39-week period is also waived if you are transferred from your new job for your employer's benefit. However, it must be shown that you could have satisfied the 39-week test except for the transfer.

What if *you* initiate the transfer? The IRS held in a ruling that the 39-week test is not waived if an employee initiates the transfer, even if the employer approves. An individual was not allowed to deduct the costs of moving across the country to take a government position when, within 39 weeks of taking the position, he applied for and took another government job in another area. The IRS disallowed the deduction, although the government reimbursed part of the employee's moving expenses to the new job post, thereby indicating that it considered the transfer to be in the government's interest. According to the IRS, the waiver of the 39-week test applies to transfers initiated by employers, not by employees.

Joint returns. On a joint return, either spouse may meet the time test. But the work time of one spouse may not be added to the time of the other spouse.

> **EXAMPLE**
>
> Smith moves from New York to a new job in Denver. After working full time for 30 weeks, he resigns from his job and cannot find another position during the rest of the 12-month period. He may not deduct his moving expenses. But assume that Mrs. Smith also finds a job in Denver at the same time as her husband and continues to work for at least 39 weeks. Since she has met the 39-week test, the moving expenses from New York to Denver paid by her husband are deductible, provided they file a joint return. However, if Mrs. Smith had worked for only nine weeks, her work period could not be added to her husband's to meet the 39-week test.

Planning Reminder

Loss of Job

If you lose your job for reasons other than your willful misconduct, the 39-week requirement is waived. Should you resign or lose your job for willful misconduct, a part-time job will not satisfy the 39-week test. The time test is not waived because you reach mandatory retirement age first where this retirement was anticipated.

Filing Tip

Job Status

For purposes of the 39-week test, full-time status is determined by the customary practices of your occupation in the area. If work is seasonal, off-season weeks count as work weeks if the off-season period is less than six months and you have an employment agreement covering the off-season.

12.6 The 78-Week Test for the Self-Employed and Partners

In addition to meeting the distance test *(12.4)*, you must work full time in the area of the new business for at least 78 weeks during the 24 months immediately following your arrival, of which at least 39 weeks occur in the first 12 months. The full-time work requirement may prevent semi-retired hobbyists, students, or others who work only a few hours a week in self-employed trades or occupations from claiming the deduction.

You are considered to have obtained employment at a new principal place of work when you have made substantial arrangements to begin such work.

The time test is waived if disability or death prevents compliance.

Change of employee or self-employed status. If you start work at a new location as an employee and then become self-employed before meeting the 39-week employee time test, you must meet the 78-week test. Time spent as an employee is counted along with the time spent self-employed in meeting the test.

If, during the first 12 months, you change from working as a self-employed person to working as an employee, you may qualify under the 39-week employee time test, provided you have 39 weeks of work as an *employee*. If you do not have 39 weeks as an employee in the first 12 months, you must meet the 78-week test.

Joint returns. Where you file a joint return, you deduct moving expenses if either you or your spouse can satisfy the time test based on individual work records.

12.7 Claiming Deductible Moving Expenses

Qualifying unreimbursed moving expenses *(12.3)* incurred during 2002 are deductible on your 2002 return whether you claim the standard deduction or itemize deductions. Report your expenses and nontaxable employer reimbursements on Form 3903. Qualifying unreimbursed moving expenses from Form 3903 are then deducted on Form 1040, Line 28, as an adjustment to gross income.

Claiming the deduction before meeting the time test. If the due date for filing your tax return arrives before you can satisfy the 39-week *(12.5)* or 78-week *(12.6)* work test, you may, nevertheless, deduct unreimbursed moving expenses. If you subsequently fail to complete the work requirement, you have to file an amended return or report income; *see* the Example below. If you file your return without taking the deduction, you may file an amended return after meeting the time test to claim the deduction.

> **EXAMPLE**
> You move to a new location on November 1, 2002. At the end of the year, you have worked in your new position only nine weeks. You deduct your moving expenses on your 2002 tax return even though you did not complete the 39- or 78-week period of work. But if, after you file the 2002 return, you move from the location before completing the applicable 39-week or 78-week work period, you must report as income the amount of moving expenses deducted in 2002 on the return for the year you move from the location. Alternatively, you may file an amended 2002 return on which you eliminate the deduction.

12.8 Reimbursements of Moving Expenses

If your employer reimburses you for deductible moving expenses *(12.3)* under an accountable plan, the reimbursement should not be reported as salary or wage income on Form W-2. The requirements for an accountable plan are similar to those discussed for business travel expenses at *20.31*.

Qualified moving expenses an employer pays to a third party, such as to a moving company, are not reported on Form W-2.

A reimbursement for expenses that do *not* qualify for a deduction, such as pre-move house-hunting costs, temporary living expenses, meal costs, or real estate expenses, is reported as compensation on your Form W-2.

On Form 3903, you report your deductible expenses in excess of nontaxable reimbursements, and enter the deductible amount on Form 1040, Line 28, as an adjustment to gross income.

If in 2002 you had deductible moving expenses that you claim on your 2002 return and you receive a reimbursement for the expenses in 2003, you report your employer's reimbursement as compensation in 2003. Alternatively, you may prefer to delay the deduction until 2003. You may deduct on your 2003 return the excess of your 2002 expenses over the nontaxable reimbursement received in 2003.

 Caution

Reimbursement for Loss on Sale of a Home

To encourage or facilitate an employee's move, an employer may reimburse the employee for a loss incurred on the sale of his or her home. The IRS taxes such reimbursements as pay.

Chapter 13

Claiming the Standard Deduction or Itemized Deductions

Claim the standard deduction only if it exceeds your allowable itemized deductions for mortgage interest, property taxes, medical costs, charitable donations, casualty losses, and miscellaneous deductions for job costs and investment expenses. Generally, a single person may claim a 2002 standard deduction of $4,700; a head of household, $6,900; a married couple filing jointly or a qualifying widow(er), $7,850; and a married person filing separately, $3,925. Larger standard deductions are allowed to those who are age 65 or over or blind, and lower standard deductions are allowed to dependents with only investment income.

Before deciding whether to itemize or claim the standard deduction, read Chapters 14 through 20 to see that you have not overlooked any itemized deductions. To itemize, you must file Form 1040 and report your deductions on Schedule A.

Key to Itemized Deductions and the Standard Deduction for 2002

Item—	Explanation—	Limitations and Examples—
Standard deduction	The standard deduction is fixed by law according to your filing status and age. The standard deduction in 2002 is: $7,850 if you are married filing jointly or a qualifying widow or widower. $4,700 if you are single. $6,900 if you are a head of household. $3,925 if you are married filing separately. If you are age 65 or over or blind, your standard deduction is substantially larger; *see 13.4.*	A married person filing separately may not use the standard deduction if his or her spouse itemizes deductions; *see 13.3.* The standard deduction may not be claimed by a nonresident or dual-status alien or on a return filed for a short taxable year caused by a change in accounting period. A lower standard deduction of $750 is allowed to dependents with only unearned income; *see 13.5.*
Itemized deductions	You should itemize deductions on Schedule A if your deductions exceed the standard deduction for your filing status. Itemized deductions include charitable contributions, interest expenses, local and state taxes, medical and dental costs, casualty and theft losses, job and investment expenses, and educational costs.	Individual itemized deductions are subject to limitations and some higher-income taxpayers are subject to a 3% reduction, as explained below. **EXAMPLE** You are single and may claim the standard deduction of $4,700 for 2002. However, your allowable itemized deductions are $5,000. You claim $5,000 on Schedule A of Form 1040.
3% reduction	If your 2002 adjusted gross income (AGI) exceeds $137,300, itemized deductions other than medical expenses, casualty and theft losses, gambling losses, and investment interest expenses are reduced by 3% of the excess AGI over $137,300. If you are married filing separately, the reduction applies if your AGI exceeds $68,650; *see 13.7.*	The total reduction may not exceed 80% of your deductions. **EXAMPLE** Your joint return adjusted gross income (AGI) for 2002 is $172,700. Your itemized deductions for mortgage interest, state income taxes, and charitable donations are $20,000. The AGI excess over $137,300 is $35,400. Therefore, itemized deductions are reduced by $1,062 (3% of $35,400). On Schedule A you may deduct $18,938 ($20,000 – $1,062).
Charitable contributions	You may deduct donations to religious, charitable, educational, and other philanthropic organizations that have been approved to receive deductible contributions; *see 14.1.*	The contribution deduction is generally limited to 50% of adjusted gross income *(14.17).* Lower ceilings apply to property donations and contributions to foundations. The deductible amount is included in the 3% reduction explained above.
Interest expenses	You may deduct interest on qualified home mortgages, points, home equity loans, and interest on loans to carry investments.	Interest on investment loans is deductible only to the extent of net investment income *(15.10).* Interest on personal and consumer loans is not deductible. Interest on home mortgages that do not meet the tests at *15.1* is not deductible. Deductions for home mortgage interest and points are included in the 3% reduction explained above.
Taxes	You may deduct payments of state, local, and foreign real property and income taxes, as well as state and local personal property taxes. You claim your deduction for real estate taxes on the tax return of the year in which you paid the taxes, unless you report on the accrual basis; *see 16.6.*	No dollar limitation. The deductible amount is included in the 3% reduction explained above.

Item—	Explanation—	Limitations and Examples—
Medical expenses	You may deduct payments of medical expenses for yourself, your spouse, and your dependents *(17.1)*. A checklist of deductible medical items is at *17.2*. With the exception of insulin, drugs are deductible *only* if they require a prescription by a physician.	Only expenses in excess of 7.5% of adjusted gross income are deductible.
Casualty and theft losses	You may deduct personal property losses caused by storms, fires, and other natural events and as the result of theft *(18.1)*.	Each individual casualty loss must exceed $100 and the total of all losses during the year must exceed 10% of adjusted gross income; *see 18.11*.
Job expenses	You may deduct unreimbursed costs of union dues, job educational courses, work clothes, entertainment, travel, and looking for a new job.	Included as miscellaneous expenses of which only the excess over 2% of adjusted gross income is deductible; *see 19.1*. The 2% floor does not apply to performing artists *(12.2)*, handicapped employees, or job-related moving expenses *(12.3)*. The deductible amount is included in the 3% reduction explained above.
Investment expenses and tax preparation costs	You may deduct investment expenses and other expenses of producing and collecting income, expenses of maintaining income-producing property, expenses of preparing your tax return or refund claims, and IRS audits.	Included as miscellaneous expenses of which only the excess over 2% of adjusted gross income is deductible; *see 19.1*. The deductible amount is included in the 3% reduction explained above.

13.1 Claiming the Standard Deduction

On your 2002 return, you are allowed a standard deduction, which is an "automatic" deduction you may claim regardless of your actual expenses. The standard deduction is not integrated into the tax rate schedules or tax tables. On your return, you deduct the standard deduction from adjusted gross income (AGI), assuming you do not claim itemized deductions on Schedule A of Form 1040; *see* the Example below.

The ***basic standard deduction*** is allowed if you are under age 65 and not blind. The amount is adjusted each year to reflect inflation. For 2002, the basic standard deduction is:

$7,850 if married filing jointly or a qualifying widow(er);

$6,900 if filing as a head of household;

$4,700 if single; *and*

$3,925 if married filing separately.

A married person filing separately must itemize deductions and may not claim any standard deduction if the other spouse itemizes on a separate return; *see 13.3*.

> **EXAMPLE**
>
> Ben Green is age 25 and single. In 2002, he has salary income of $36,050 and interest income of $1,000. He makes a tax deductible contribution of $2,000 to a traditional IRA; the deduction is allowed since he is not covered by a company retirement plan *(8.5)*. Green claims the standard $4,700 deduction because his itemized deductions are less than that.
>
> | | | |
> |---|---:|---:|
> | Gross income: | | |
> | Salary | $36,050 | |
> | Interest income | 1,000 | $37,050 |
> | Deduction from gross income: | | |
> | IRA *(8.3)* | | 2,000 |
> | Adjusted gross income | | $35,050 |
> | *Less:* Standard deduction | | 4,700 |
> | | | $30,350 |
> | *Less:* Exemption *(21.1)* | | 3,000 |
> | Taxable income | | $27,350 |

Age 65 or older or blind. For taxpayers age 65 or over, or taxpayers of any age who are blind, the basic standard deduction is increased by an additional amount; *see 13.4.*

Dependents. Individuals who may be claimed as dependents by other taxpayers are generally limited to a $750 standard deduction, unless they have earned income; *see 13.5.*

Dual-status alien. You are generally not entitled to any standard deduction if for part of the year you are a nonresident and part of the year a resident alien. However, a standard deduction may be claimed on a joint return if your spouse is a U.S. citizen or resident and you elect to be taxed on your worldwide income; *see 1.5.*

13.2 When To Itemize

Claim the standard deduction only if it exceeds your allowable itemized deductions for charitable donations, certain local taxes, interest, allowable casualty losses, miscellaneous expenses, and medical expenses. If your deductions exceed your standard deduction, you elect to itemize by claiming the deductions on Schedule A of Form 1040. However, if you are married filing separately and your spouse itemizes deductions, you also must itemize, even if the standard deduction exceeds your itemized deductions; *see 13.3.*

> **EXAMPLE**
>
> Ellen Bates is single and her 2002 adjusted gross income is $35,000. Her itemized deductions total $5,200. As the $4,700 standard deduction is less than her itemized deductions, she claims itemized deductions of $5,200 on Schedule A.

13.3 Husbands and Wives Filing Separate Returns

If you and your spouse file separate returns *(1.3)* for 2002, and neither of you is a qualifying head of household *(1.12)*, you must both claim itemized deductions or limit yourselves to a standard deduction of $3,925 each. You must both make the same election; when one of you itemizes the other is not entitled to any standard deduction. That is, if your spouse has itemized deductions exceeding $3,925 and elects to itemize, you must also itemize, even if your itemized deductions are less than $3,925.

On a separate return, each spouse may deduct only those itemized expenses for which he or she is liable and pays. This is true even if one spouse pays expenses for the other. For example, if a wife owns property, then the interest and taxes imposed on the property are her deductions, not her husband's. If he pays them, neither one may deduct them on separate returns. The husband may not because they were not his liability. The wife may not because she did not pay them. This is true also of casualty or theft losses.

No restrictions if divorced or legally separated. Following a divorce or legal separation under a decree of divorce or separate maintenance, you and your former spouse are free to compute your tax as you each see fit, without reference to the way the other files. Both of you are treated as single. If you have itemized deductions, you may elect to claim them, and your former spouse is not required to itemize. The standard deduction is not limited to $3,925. Head of household tax rates may be available under the rules at *1.12.*

Head of household possibility if you live apart from your spouse. If you are separated but do not have a decree of divorce or separate maintenance, both of you must either itemize or claim the standard deduction of $3,925 for 2002. However, if you are married and live apart from your spouse and meet the following conditions, you may file your 2002 return as a head of household *(1.12)* and may choose between a $6,900 standard deduction and itemizing deductions:

- Your spouse was not a member of your household during the last six months of 2002.
- You maintained as your home a household which was, for more than half of 2002, the main home for your child, adopted child, or stepchild. You also qualify if your home was the main home of a foster child for the entire year. You or your child are treated as living in the home during a temporary absence.
- You are entitled to claim the child as a dependent *(21.1)* or the child's other parent has the right to the exemption under the rules discussed at *21.11.*
- You provide over half the cost of supporting the household.

As a head of household, you may elect to itemize without regard to whether your spouse itemizes or not. If you elect not to itemize, your 2002 standard deduction as a head of household is $6,900 if you are under age 65 and not blind. If you are age 65 or over or blind, your standard deduction is increased by $1,150; *see 13.4.* The filing status of your spouse remains married filing separately. He or she must itemize deductions if you itemize. If you claim the $6,900 standard deduction for a head of household (or $8,050 if age 65 or older, or blind), he or she can itemize or claim the $3,925 standard deduction for married persons filing separately.

Filing Instruction

Changing an Election
If you filed your return using the standard deduction and want to change to itemized deductions, or you itemized and want to change to the standard deduction, you may do so within the three-year period allowed for amending your return. If you are married and filing separately, each of you must consent to and make the same change; you both must either itemize or claim the standard deduction.

13.4 Standard Deduction If 65 or Older or Blind

A larger standard deduction is provided for persons who are age 65 or over or who are blind. The larger deduction for blindness is allowed regardless of age.

Age and blindness are determined as of December 31, 2002. However, if your 65th birthday is January 1, 2003, you may claim the standard deduction for those age 65 or over on your 2002 return.

Your total standard deduction consists of two parts: (1) The basic standard deduction shown in *13.1* for your filing status plus (2) an extra standard deduction for being age 65 or older or blind. The amount of the extra deduction for 2002 is $1,150 if you are filing as single or head of household; and $900 if you are married, whether filing jointly or separately, or your filing status is qualifying widow(er). The chart below lists the total standard deduction, including the extra amount.

If you are married filing separately, you may claim the standard deduction only if your spouse also claims the standard deduction on his or her return; *see 13.3.*

Check applicable boxes

	65 or older	Blind
Yourself	☐	☐
Your spouse if you file a joint return	☐	☐
Your spouse if you file separately and can claim an exemption for your spouse *(21.2)*	☐	☐
Total checks____		

If you are—	Number of checks are—	Standard deduction for 2002 is—
Single	1	$5,850
	2	7,000
Married filing jointly *(1.4)* or qualifying widow or widower *(1.11)*	1	8,750
	2	9,650
	3	10,550
	4	11,450
Married filing separately *(13.3)*	1	4,825
	2	5,725
	3	6,625
	4	7,525
Head of household *(1.12)*	1	8,050
	2	9,200

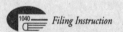
Filing Instruction

Total or Partial Blindness

An additional standard deduction is allowed to a person who is completely blind as of December 31, 2002. You also qualify if you are partially blind and attach a letter certified by your doctor stating that you cannot see better than 20/200 in your better eye with lenses or that your field of vision is 20 degrees or less. Keep a copy of this letter. If the certification states that your vision will never improve beyond these limits, you will not have to file a new certification in later years; you will only have to attach a statement referring to the earlier certification.

13.5 Standard Deduction for Dependents

The following restrictive rules apply to you only if you may be claimed as a dependent *(see 21.1)*. If you earn gross income of $3,000 or more in 2002, you may *not* be claimed as a dependent by anyone other than your parent, and you may be claimed by your parent only if you are under age 19 or a full-time student under age 24; *see 21.6.* If you are *not* a dependent because of the $3,000 income test, your standard deduction is shown in *13.1* or in *13.4.* If you *may* be claimed as a dependent, your standard deduction is figured under the rules below. You *may* elect to itemize deductions if these exceed the allowable standard deduction. If you are married and your spouse itemizes on a separate return, you *must* itemize; *see 13.3.*

Dependent under age 65 and not blind. If you can be claimed as another taxpayer's dependent for 2002, your standard deduction is the greater of $750 *or* earned income plus $250, but no more than the basic standard deduction shown in *13.1* for your filing status.

EXAMPLE

1. Susan, age 17, is claimed as a dependent by her parents. For 2002, she has earned income of $350 and interest income of $500. Her standard deduction is $750, the greater of $750 or $600, the total of her earned income ($350) and $250.
2. Assume that Susan's earned income is $2,000 rather than $350. Her standard deduction for 2002 is $2,250, the greater of $750 or $2,250, the total of her earned income ($2,000) and $250.

Dependents age 65 or older or blind. Your standard deduction is the total of these two steps:

Step 1. The greater of $750 *or* earned income plus $250; *plus*

Step 2. $900 if you are married or a qualifying widow or widower, or $1,150 if single or head of household. If you are age 65 or older *and* you are also blind, multiply the applicable figure, $900 or $1,150, by two.

The worksheets below incorporate these steps for computing your 2002 standard deduction.

Standard Deduction for Dependents in 2002 With Earned Income of $500 or Less

If your filing status is—	Standard deduction is—
Single or head of household	
Under age 65 and not blind	$ 750
Age 65 or older or blind	1,900
Age 65 or older and blind	3,050
Married, or qualifying widow(er)	
Under age 65 and not blind	$ 750
Age 65 or older or blind	1,650
Age 65 or older and blind	2,550

Standard Deduction for Dependents in 2002 Who Are Under Age 65 and Not Blind With Earned Income Exceeding $500

1. Enter your earned income *plus* $250.* $ _____
2. Enter:

   $4,700 if you are single,
   $6,900 if head of household,
   $7,850 if qualifying widow(er) or married filing jointly, or
   $3,925 if married filing separately.   _____

3. Enter the smaller of Lines 1 and 2. This is your standard deduction.   _____

Standard Deduction for Dependents in 2002 Who Are Age 65 or Older or Blind With Earned Income Exceeding $500

1. Enter your earned income *plus* $250.* $ _____
2. Enter:

   $4,700 if you are single,
   $6,900 if head of household,
   $7,850 if qualifying widow(er) or married filing jointly, or
   $3,925 if married filing separately.   _____

3. Enter the smaller of Lines 1 and 2.   _____
4. Enter:

   $1,150 if you are single or head of household and are either age 65 or older or blind.
   $900 if you are married filing jointly or separately, or a qualifying widow(er) and are either age 65 or older or blind.
   If both age 65 or older and blind, the $1,150 or $900 amounts are doubled to $2,300 and $1,800.   _____

5. Add Lines 3 and 4. This is your standard deduction.   _____

*Include pay for services and taxable scholarships (38.1). Include net earnings from self-employment and then subtract 50% of self-employment tax liability (45.3) when figuring earned income. However, if your gross income (earned and unearned) is $3,000 or more, you may be claimed as a dependent only by your parent, and only if you are under age 19 or a full-time student under age 24; see 21.6.

 Caution

Determine Dependency Status First

The reduced standard deduction rules apply to you if you *may* be claimed as a dependent on another tax return, such as by your parents. If you can be claimed as a dependent under the rules at *21.1*, it does not matter if you are actually claimed as a dependent.

 Filing Tip

Higher Standard Deduction for Dependents With Earned Income

For 2002, an individual who may be claimed as a dependent may add $250 to earned income in figuring the allowable standard deduction; *see* the worksheets on this page.

13.6 Prepaying or Postponing Itemized Expenses

Before the end of the year, check your records for payments of deductible itemized expenses. If you find that your payments up to that time are slightly less than the allowable standard deduction for that year, accelerating payment of an expense that you would otherwise pay in the following year could allow you to itemize. For example, at the end of 2002, you may make an additional charitable contribution, or pay a state or local tax bill not due until 2003, or extend by one year professional association dues or job-related subscriptions. You cannot deduct prepayments of interest, insurance premiums, or rent on investment property.

On the other hand, making the year-end payment might still not increase your deductions enough to itemize. In that case, you would get no tax benefit from the payment. By postponing the payment until the next year, you may make it easier to itemize on that year's return.

If your year-to-year payments of itemized expenses have consistently been below the standard deduction, a prepayment or postponement strategy may allow you to itemize in at least one of two consecutive years, enabling you to reduce your taxes over the two-year period without increasing your overall expenditures; *see* the following Example.

Planning Reminder

Prepaying Deductible Expenses May Allow You To Itemize

As the end of the year approaches, check your records for payments of deductible itemized expenses. If these payments are slightly less than the allowable standard deduction for the year, making a year-end payment of a deductible expense that you would otherwise pay in the following year could allow you to itemize.

13.7 3% Itemized Deduction Reduction

If your 2002 adjusted gross income (AGI) exceeds $137,300 ($68,650 if married filing separately) some of your itemized deductions are disallowed. First figure your itemized deductions under the regular rules; *see* Chapters 14 through 20 for details and limitations on specific types of expenses. Then reduce the total of otherwise allowable itemized deductions by the following, which are *not* subject to reduction:

- Medical and dental expenses
- Investment interest
- Casualty losses
- Theft losses
- Gambling losses

The balance of your itemized deductions are generally reduced by 3% of the excess of your AGI over the $137,300 (or $68,650) threshold. Use the worksheet on the next page to figure the reduction. The 3% reduction creates an added tax cost to earning additional income; *see 28.2.*

Worksheet for 3% Reduction

1. Enter your 2002 adjusted gross income. $_____
2. Enter $137,300 ($68,650 if married filing separately). _____
3. Subtract Line 2 from Line 1. _____
4. Multiply the amount on Line 3 by 3% (.03). _____
5. Enter total allowable itemized deductions from Schedule A before the 3% reduction. _____
6. Enter the amount included on Line 5 for allowable medical and dental expenses, investment interest, casualty or theft losses, and gambling losses. These deductions are *not* subject to the reduction. _____
7. Subtract Line 6 from Line 5.* _____
8. Multiply the amount on Line 7 by 80% (.80). _____
9. Enter the smaller of Line 4 or Line 8. This is the disallowed amount. _____
10. Subtract Line 9 from Line 5. This is the net amount of itemized deductions you may claim on Schedule A for 2002. $_____

If the amount on Line 7 is zero, the reduction does not apply.

 Caution

Itemized Deductions May Be Reduced

If your 2002 adjusted gross income exceeds $137,300, or $68,650 if married filing separately, some or all of your itemized deductions are subject to a reduction. In general, your total deduction is reduced by 3% of the excess of your adjusted gross income over the $137,300 or $68,650 floor.

EXAMPLE

Dan Sommer is single and his 2002 adjusted gross income on Form 1040 is $206,400. On Schedule A, Dan reports $31,000 of itemized expenses, after applying the 7.5% floor for itemized medical costs and the 2% floor for miscellaneous itemized deductions. Since his AGI exceeds $137,300, part of his itemized deduction will be disallowed.

Medical expense deduction (after 7.5% floor)	$ 700
State and local income taxes	13,000
Real estate taxes	2,341
Home mortgage interest	5,000
Charitable donation	9,000
Miscellaneous expenses (after 2% floor)	959
Total	$ 31,000

All of the deductions except medical expenses are subject to the 3% reduction.

Following the steps of the worksheet shown above, Dan figures that $2,073 of his deductions are disallowed, leaving a net deduction of $28,927:

1.	Adjusted gross income	$ 206,400
2.	*Less:* threshold	137,300
3.	Excess	69,100
4.	3% of Line 3	2,073
5.	Itemized deductions	31,000
6.	*Less:* medical deductions (not subject to the 3% reduction)	700
7.	Itemized deductions subject to the 3% reduction	30,300
8.	80% of Line 7	24,240
9.	Smaller of (4) or (8) is disallowed	2,073
10.	Net itemized deductions allowable on Schedule A (Line 5 *less* Line 9)	$28,927

The Sample Schedule A on the next page shows the reduced deduction on Line 28 ($31,000 – $2,073 disallowed = $28,927).

SCHEDULES A&B **(Form 1040)** Department of the Treasury Internal Revenue Service (99)	**Schedule A—Itemized Deductions** (Schedule B is on back) ► **Attach to Form 1040.** ► **See Instructions for Schedules A and B (Form 1040).**			OMB No. 1545-0074 **2002** Attachment Sequence No. **07**	

Name(s) shown on Form 1040 — **Dan Sommer**
Your social security number — **XX1 98 5637**

Medical and Dental Expenses		**Caution.** Do not include expenses reimbursed or paid by others.			
	1	Medical and dental expenses (see page A-2)	1	16,180	
	2	Enter amount from Form 1040, line 36	2	206,400	
	3	Multiply line 2 above by 7.5% (.075)	3	15,480	
	4	Subtract line 3 from line 1. If line 3 is more than line 1, enter -0-	4		700
Taxes You Paid (See page A-2.)	5	State and local income taxes	5	13,000	
	6	Real estate taxes (see page A-2)	6	2,341	
	7	Personal property taxes	7		
	8	Other taxes. List type and amount ► _____	8		
	9	Add lines 5 through 8	9		15,341
Interest You Paid (See page A-3.) **Note.** Personal interest is not deductible.	10	Home mortgage interest and points reported to you on Form 1098	10	5,000	
	11	Home mortgage interest not reported to you on Form 1098. If paid to the person from whom you bought the home, see page A-3 and show that person's name, identifying no., and address ► _____ _____	11		
	12	Points not reported to you on Form 1098. See page A-3 for special rules	12		
	13	Investment interest. Attach Form 4952 if required. (See page A-3.)	13		
	14	Add lines 10 through 13	14		5,000
Gifts to Charity If you made a gift and got a benefit for it, see page A-4.	15	Gifts by cash or check. If you made any gift of $250 or more, see page A-4	15	9,000	
	16	Other than by cash or check. If any gift of $250 or more, see page A-4. You **must** attach Form 8283 if over $500	16		
	17	Carryover from prior year	17		
	18	Add lines 15 through 17	18		9,000
Casualty and Theft Losses	19	Casualty or theft loss(es). Attach Form 4684. (See page A-5.)	19		
Job Expenses and Most Other Miscellaneous Deductions (See page A-5 for expenses to deduct here.)	20	Unreimbursed employee expenses—job travel, union dues, job education, etc. You **must** attach Form 2106 or 2106-EZ if required. (See page A-5.) ► _____ _____	20		
	21	Tax preparation fees	21	587	
	22	Other expenses—investment, safe deposit box, etc. List type and amount ► **Tax Court legal fees, $4,500**	22	4,500	
	23	Add lines 20 through 22	23	5,087	
	24	Enter amount from Form 1040, line 36	24	206,400	
	25	Multiply line 24 above by 2% (.02)	25	4,128	
	26	Subtract line 25 from line 23. If line 25 is more than line 23, enter -0-	26		959
Other Miscellaneous Deductions	27	Other—from list on page A-6. List type and amount ► _____	27		
Total Itemized Deductions	28	Is Form 1040, line 36, over $137,300 (over $68,650 if married filing separately)? ☐ **No.** Your deduction is not limited. Add the amounts in the far right column for lines 4 through 27. Also, enter this amount on Form 1040, line 38. ► ☒ **Yes.** Your deduction may be limited. See page A-6 for the amount to enter.	28		28,927

For Paperwork Reduction Act Notice, see Form 1040 instructions.   Cat. No. 11330X   Schedule A (Form 1040) 2002

Chapter 14

Charitable Contribution Deductions

By making deductible donations, you help your favorite philanthropy and at the same time receive a tax benefit. Donations to organizations qualified to receive deductible contributions give you a tax reduction if you itemize deductions. For example, if you are in the 27% tax bracket, a donation of $1,000 reduces your taxes by $270. By donating appreciated securities and real estate held long term, you can increase the amount of your tax savings by avoiding the tax that would have been owed if you had sold the property and donated the proceeds. If you do volunteer work for a qualified charity, you may deduct your unreimbursed expenses.

If you contributed at least $250 to a charity in 2002, you must get a written receipt from the organization to substantiate the donation. A cancelled check is not sufficient evidence for a cash donation of $250 or more; see 14.15.

Also be aware that if you claim deductions for property valued at more than $500, you must attach Form 8283 to Form 1040. If the value you claimed exceeds $5,000, you also may have to obtain a written appraisal.

There are deduction ceilings depending on the type of donation and the nature of the charity. The ceiling for cash donations made to public philanthropies is 50% of adjusted gross income, and for gifts of capital gain property, 30% of adjusted gross income. For other ceilings, see 14.17.

If your adjusted gross income for 2002 exceeds $137,300 ($68,650 if married filing separately), your charitable contribution deduction is subject to the 3% reduction of itemized deductions explained in 13.7.

Qualifying Charitable Donations

14.1 Deductible Contributions

Charitable contributions are deductible only as itemized deductions on Schedule A of Form 1040. The deduction is subject to the 3% reduction of total itemized deductions explained at *13.7* if your adjusted gross income exceeds $137,300 ($68,650 if married filing separately).

You may deduct donations to religious, charitable, educational, and other philanthropic organizations approved by the IRS to receive deductible contributions; *see* the listing later in this section. If you are unsure of the tax status of a philanthropy, ask the organization about its status, or check the IRS list of tax-exempt organizations (IRS Publication 78). Donations to the federal, state, and local government are also deductible.

Substantiating your donations. Keep a cancelled check or receipt from the charity as proof of donations under $250. For donations of $250 or more, you need to obtain a written acknowledgment that notes any benefits or goods that you received in exchange. *See 14.15* for details on the substantiation requirements.

Year-end donations. You deduct donations on the tax return filed for the year in which you paid them in cash or property. A contribution by check is deductible in the year you give the check, even if it is cashed in the following year. A check mailed and dated on the last day of 2002 is deductible in 2002. A postdated check with a 2003 date is not deductible until 2003. For checks of $250 or more, get a written receipt by the filing due date of your return (the cancelled check is not sufficient substantiation; *see 14.15*). A pledge or a note is not deductible until paid. Donations made through a credit card are deductible in the year the charge is made. Donations made through a pay-by-phone bank account are not deductible until the payment date shown on the bank statement.

Delivering securities. If you are planning to donate appreciated securities near the end of the year, make sure that you consider these delivery rules in timing the donation. If you unconditionally deliver or mail a properly endorsed stock certificate to the donee or its agent, the gift is considered completed on the date of delivery or mailing, provided it is received in the ordinary course of the mails. If you deliver the certificate to your bank or broker as your agent, or to the issuing corporation or its agent, your gift is not complete until the stock is transferred to the donee's name on the corporation's books. This transfer may take several weeks, so, if possible, make the delivery at least three weeks before the end of the year to assure a current deduction.

Debts. You may assign to a charity a debt payable to you. A deductible contribution may be claimed in the year your debtor pays the charity.

Limits on deduction. Depending on the nature of the organization and the donated property, a deduction ceiling of 50%, 30%, or 20% of adjusted gross income applies. In general, the deduction ceiling is 50% for cash contributions and 30% for contributions of appreciated property held long term. *See 14.17* for details on the deduction ceilings. Where donations in one year exceed the percentage limits, a five-year carryover of the excess may be allowed; *see 14.18*.

A deduction may also be limited under the 3% reduction rule discussed at *13.7*.

Organizations Qualifying for Deductible Donations

The following types of organizations may qualify to receive deductible contributions:

A domestic nonprofit organization, trust, community chest, fund, or foundation that is operated exclusively for one of the following purposes:

Religious. Payments for pew rents, assessments, and dues to churches and synagogues are deductible.
Charitable. In this class are organizations such as Boy Scouts, Girl Scouts, American Red Cross, Community Funds, Cancer Societies, CARE, Salvation Army, Y.M.C.A., and Y.W.C.A.
Scientific, literary, and educational. Included in this group are hospitals, research organizations, colleges, universities, and other schools that do not maintain racially discriminatory policies; and leagues or associations set up for education or to combat crime, improve public morals, and aid public welfare.
Prevention of cruelty to children or animals.
Fostering amateur sports competition. However, the organization's activities may not provide athletic facilities or equipment.

 Filing Tip

Donating Appreciated Securities

You get a tax deduction for the full market value when you donate appreciated securities traded on an established securities market that you have held more than one year. In addition, you also avoid paying capital gains tax on the securities' appreciation.

Domestic nonprofit veterans' organizations or auxiliary units.

A domestic fraternal group operating under the lodge system. The contributions must be used exclusively for religious, charitable, scientific, literary, or educational purposes; or for the prevention of cruelty to children or animals.

Nonprofit cemetery and burial companies, where the voluntary contribution benefits the whole cemetery, not only your plot.

Legal services corporations established under the Legal Services Corporation Act. Such corporations provide legal assistance to financially needy people in noncriminal proceedings.

The United States, a U.S. possession, a state, city, or town or Indian tribal government. The gift must be for public purposes. The gift may be directed to a government unit, or it may be to a government agency such as a state university, a fire department, a civil defense group, or a committee to raise funds to develop land into a public park. Donations may be made to the Social Security system (Federal Old Age and Survivors Insurance Trust Fund). Donations may be made to the federal government to help reduce the national debt; checks should be made payable to "Bureau of the Public Debt."

14.2 Nondeductible Contributions

The following types of contributions are not deductible:

1. Payments to political campaign committees or political action committees.

2. Payments to an organization that devotes a substantial part of its activities to lobbying, trying to influence legislation, or carrying on propaganda or whose lobbying activities exceed certain limits set by the law, causing the organization to lose its tax-exempt status. The IRS has disallowed contributions to a civic group opposing saloons, nightclubs, and gambling places, although the group also aided libraries, churches, and other public programs.

3. Donations to or on behalf of specific individuals, even if needy or worthy. Generally, scholarships for specific students, or gifts to organizations to benefit only certain groups. However, the IRS in private rulings has allowed deductions for scholarship funds that are limited to members of a particular religion, so long as that religion is open to all on a racially nondiscriminatory basis, and to scholarship funds open only to male students.

4. Gifts to organizations such as:
   Fraternal groups—except when they set up special organizations exclusively devoted to charitable, educational, or other approved purposes.
   Professional groups such as those organized by accountants, lawyers, and physicians—except when they are specially created for exclusive charitable, educational, or other philanthropic purposes. The IRS will disallow unrestricted gifts made to state bar associations, although such organizations may have some public purposes. Some courts have allowed deductions for donations to bar associations on the ground that their activities benefit the general public. However, an appeals court disallowed deductible donations to a bar association that rates candidates for judicial office.
   Clubs for social purposes—fraternities and sororities are generally in this class. Unless an organization is exclusively operated for a charitable, religious, or other approved purpose, you may not deduct your contribution, even though your funds are used for a charitable or religious purpose.

5. Donations to civic leagues, communist or communist-front organizations, chambers of commerce, business leagues, or labor unions.

6. Contributions to a hospital or school operated for profit.

7. Purchase price of church building bond. To claim a deduction, you must donate the bond to the church. The amount of the deduction is the fair market value of the bond when you make the donation. Interest on the bond is income each year, under the original issue discount rules discussed in *4.19*, where no interest will be paid until the bond matures.

8. Donations of blood to the Red Cross or other blood banks.

9. Contributions to foreign charitable organizations or directly to foreign governments. Thus, a contribution to the State of Israel was disallowed. Similarly, contributions to international charitable organizations are nondeductible; but *see 14.1*.

Donation of services. You may not deduct the value of volunteer work you perform for charities. But you can deduct unreimbursed expenses incurred during such work; *see 14.4*.

 Caution

Foreign Charities
You may deduct donations to domestic organizations that distribute funds to charities in foreign countries, as long as the U.S. organization controls the distribution of the funds overseas. An outright contribution to a foreign charitable organization is not deductible. Some exceptions to this ban are provided by international treaties. For example, if you have income from Canadian or Mexican sources, there is a limited exception for contributions to certain Canadian or Mexican organizations. For details, write IRS, Assistant Commissioner (International), Attention CP: IN: D: CS, 950 L'Enfant Plaza, S.W., Washington, D.C. 20024.

Free use of property. You may not deduct the rental value of property you allow a charity to use without charge. That is, if you allow a charity rent-free use of an office in your building, you may not deduct the fair rental value. You also have no deduction when you lend money to a charity without charging interest.

To raise money for a charity, supporters of the organization may donate rental time for their vacation home, to be auctioned off to the public. No deduction is allowed for donating the rental time; *see 14.10*.

Parents' support payments of children serving as Mormon missionaries. According to the Supreme Court, support payments made by parents directly to their children who serve as missionaries are not deductible because the church does not control the funds.

14.3 Contributions That Provide You With Benefits

A contribution to a qualifying organization *(14.1)* is generally deductible only to the extent that you intend to give more than the value of benefits you receive and actually do so.

If you contribute $75 or less and receive benefits, the organization may tell you the value of the benefits. If your contribution exceeds $75, the organization by law *must* give you a written statement that estimates the value of the benefits provided to you and instructs you to deduct only the portion of your contribution that *exceeds* the benefits. However, the disclosure statement does not have to be provided to you if you receive only token benefits, or if you receive from a religious organization only "intangible religious benefits."

EXAMPLES

1. You contribute $200 to a philanthropy and receive a book that you have seen on sale for prices ranging between $18 and $25. The charity estimates the value at $20. As the estimate is between the typical retail prices, it is acceptable to the IRS. Although the book sold at a price as high as $25, you may treat the $20 estimate as fair market value and claim a deduction of $180.

2. A charitable organization sponsors an art auction and provides a catalogue that lists the items being auctioned and estimates of fair market value. The catalogue lists the value of a vase at $100. At the auction, you bid and pay $500 for the vase. Because you were aware of the estimate before the auction and paid more for the vase, you may deduct $400.

Dues. Dues paid to a qualified tax-exempt organization are deductible to the extent they exceed the value of benefits from the organization, such as monthly journals, use of a library, or the right to attend luncheons and lectures. As discussed above, you generally must be provided with an estimate of any benefits you received if your donation exceeds $75.

If dues are paid to a social club with the understanding that a specified part goes to a qualifying charity *(14.1)*, you may claim a charitable deduction for dues earmarked for the charity. If the treasurer of your club is actually the agent of the charity, you take the deduction in the year you give him or her the money. If the treasurer is merely your agent, you may take the deduction only in the year the money is remitted to the charity.

Benefit tickets. Tickets to theater events, tours, concerts, and other entertainments are often sold by charitable organizations at prices higher than the regular admission charge. The difference between the regular admission and the higher amount you pay is deductible as a charitable contribution. If you decline to accept the ticket or return it to the charity for resale, your deduction is the price you paid.

The charity should explain to you how much is deductible. The charity must provide an explanation if you paid more than $75; *see* the discussion above.

If the ticket is at or below its normal cost, no deduction is allowed unless you decline the ticket or return it to the charity.

If tickets were purchased for a charity-sponsored series of events and the average cost of a single event is equal to or less than the cost of an individual performance, then a deduction for a returned ticket is based upon the time the ticket was held. Generally, you may deduct only your cost. However, if you have held the ticket for more than a year, you may deduct the price the charity will charge on resale of the ticket.

EXAMPLE

A couple claimed a full deduction for regular-price tickets to a high-school fund-raising event that they did not attend. They argued that they were entitled to the deduction because they received no benefit from their ticket purchase. The IRS disallowed the deduction and the Tax Court agreed, holding that a donor receives a benefit by merely having the right to attend the event. To claim a deduction for the price of the tickets the couple should have returned them to the charity.

Donation for the right to buy athletic stadium tickets. If you contribute to a public or nonprofit college or university and receive the right to buy preferential seating at the school's athletic complexes, you may deduct 80% of the contribution to the school. The 80% deduction also applies where your contribution gives you the right to buy seating in stadium skyboxes, suites, or special viewing areas. The cost of any tickets you buy is not deductible. The deduction is allowed only to the extent that you receive the right to buy tickets rather than the tickets themselves. For example, if in exchange for a substantial donation you receive a season ticket worth $200, your payment is reduced by $200 before applying the 80% deductible percentage.

Token Items and Membership Benefits That Do Not Reduce Your Deduction

Token items. Popular fund-raising campaigns, such as those for museums, zoos, and public TV, offer token items such as calendars, tote bags, tee shirts, and other items carrying the organization's logo. You are allowed a full deduction for your contribution if the item is considered to be of insubstantial value under IRS guidelines.

The charity must tell you how much of your contribution is deductible in the solicitation that offers the token item. If the items are insubstantial in value, the charity should tell you that your payment is fully deductible. For example, if in 2002 you contributed at least $39.50, and the offered items cost the charity no more than $7.90, the value of the benefits is ignored and a full 2002 deduction is allowed. A full deduction for 2002 is also allowed if the items were worth no more than 2% of the contribution, or $79, whichever is less. The $39.50, $7.90, and $79 amounts change annually for inflation.

Newsletters or program guides that are not of commercial quality are treated as token items having no fair market value or cost if their primary purpose is to inform members about the organization's activities, and they are not available to nonmembers by paid subscription or through newsstand sales.

Publications with articles written for compensation and advertising are treated as commercial-quality publications for which the organization must figure value to determine if a full deduction is allowed under the "insubstantial value" test. Professional journals, whether or not they have such articles and advertising, will generally be treated as commercial-quality publications that must be valued.

Membership benefits. If you contribute $75 or less for an annual membership in a qualified charity (see 14.1) you may deduct your entire payment under IRS guidelines provided either of the following is true:

1. You receive membership privileges that can be exercised frequently, such as free or discounted parking or admission, or discounts on gift shop or mail order merchandise, *or*
2. Your membership entitles you to admission to events that are open only to members and the organization's reasonably projected cost per person for each event excluding overhead (as of the time the membership package is offered) is no more than the annual limit for "low cost articles." For 2002, the "low cost article" limit is $7.90.

If you pay more than $75 for a membership package, the IRS allows you and the organization to disregard the benefits available under a $75-or-less package.

14.4 Unreimbursed Expenses of Volunteer Workers

If you work without pay for an organization listed at *14.1*, you may deduct as charitable contributions your unreimbursed expenses in providing the services. This includes commuting expenses to and from its place of operations, and meals and lodging on a trip away from home *(20.6)* for the organization.

 Caution

Bingo and Lotteries

You may not deduct the cost of raffle tickets, bingo games, or tickets for other types of lotteries organized by charities.

 Filing Tip

Estimated Value of Benefits

You may rely on a written estimate from the organization of the value of any benefits given to you unless it seems unreasonable. Although the value of benefits received generally reduces your deductible contribution, certain token items and membership benefits do not reduce the amount of your deduction.

 Filing Tip

Volunteer's Auto Allowance

If you use your car to do volunteer work for a charity, you may deduct a flat mileage allowance of 14¢ a mile.

To qualify for the deduction, the expenses must be incurred for a domestic organization that authorizes you to travel. You may not deduct the value of your donated services.

Keep records, such as cancelled checks, to substantiate the amount of your out-of-pocket expenses. To deduct an unreimbursed expense of $250 or more, such as for a plane ticket or a luncheon you hosted on behalf of the organization, IRS regulations require that for each such expense, a statement be obtained from the charitable organization that acknowledges the services you provide. The acknowledgment must describe the services, and state whether you were provided any goods or services by the charity. If so, an estimate of their value must be given unless the benefits are "intangible religious benefits." The acknowledgment must be obtained by the date you file your return, but if you file after the due date (or extended due date if you get an extension), the acknowledgment must be obtained by the due date of your return, including extensions. For 2002 returns, the due date is April 15, 2003, unless you get an extension.

Deductible expenses. If in 2002 you used your car in providing volunteer services for a charity, you may deduct either the actual operating costs of your car or a flat mileage rate of 14¢ a mile allowed by the IRS. Parking fees and tolls are deductible under both methods.

EXAMPLE

Jill Patton is a volunteer worker for a philanthropy. In the course of her volunteer work during 2002, she drove her car 1,000 miles. She may claim a contribution deduction of $140, plus tolls and parking.

Also deductible as charitable contributions are:
- Uniform costs required in serving the organization
- Cost of telephone calls, and cost of materials and supplies you furnished such as stamps or stationery
- Travel expenses, including meals and lodging on overnight trips away from home as an official delegate to a convention of a church, charitable, veteran, or other similar organization. If you are a member but not a delegate, you may not deduct travel costs, but you may deduct expenses paid for the benefit of your organization at the convention.
- All related expenses in hosting a fund-raiser are deductible, from the invitations to the food and drink.

The IRS does not allow a deduction for "babysitting" expenses of charity volunteer workers. Although incurred to make the volunteer work possible, babysitting costs are a nondeductible personal expense. Furthermore, the expense is not a dependent care cost; it is not related to a paying job.

Recreational purposes may bar travel expense deduction. To claim a charitable deduction for travel expenses of a research project for a charitable organization, you must show the trip had no significant element of personal pleasure, recreation, or vacation.

EXAMPLES

1. Al Jones sails from one Caribbean island to another and spends eight hours a day counting whales and other forms of marine life as part of a project sponsored by a charitable organization. According to the IRS, he may not claim a charitable deduction for the cost of the trip.

2. Sara Smith works on an archaeological excavation sponsored by a charitable organization for several hours each morning, with the rest of the day free for recreation and sightseeing. According to the IRS, she may not deduct the cost of the trip.

3. Myra Scott, a member of a chapter of a local charitable organization, travels to New York City and spends the entire day at the required regional meeting. According to the IRS, she may deduct her travel expenses as a charitable donation, even if she attends a theater in the evening.

 *Planning Reminder*

Foster Parent Expenses

If you receive payments from a state agency to reimburse you for the costs of caring for a foster child in your home, and you can show that your support costs exceed the reimbursements, the excess is deductible as a charitable contribution. Keep detailed records to substantiate your support payments.

14.5 Support of a Student in Your Home

A limited charitable deduction is allowed for support of an elementary or high-school student in your home under an educational program arranged by a charitable organization. If the student is not a relative or your dependent, you may deduct as a charitable contribution your support payments up to $50 for each month the student stays in your home. For this purpose, 15 days or more of a calendar month is considered a full month. You may not deduct any payments received from the charitable organization if any reimbursements are received for the student's maintenance. The only exception is that if you prepay a "one-time" expense such as a hospital bill or vacation for the child at the request of the child's parents or the sponsoring charity, and you are later reimbursed, you may deduct your unreimbursed expenses.

To support the deduction, be prepared to show a written agreement between you and the organization relating to the support arrangement. Keep records of amounts spent for such items as food, clothing, medical and dental care, tuition, books, and recreation in order to substantiate your deduction. No deduction is allowed for depreciation on your house.

Donations of Property

14.6 What Kind of Property Are You Donating?

Generally, a deduction for the fair market value of donated property may be claimed, but the tax law does not treat all donations of appreciated property in the same way. Whether the full amount of the fair market value of the property is deductible depends on the type of property donated, your holding period, the nature of the philanthropy, and the use to which the property is put by the philanthropy.

Save records to support the market value and cost of donated property. Get a receipt or letter from the charitable organization acknowledging and describing the gift. You *must* get a receipt for donations of property valued at $250 or more; *see 14.15*. Lack of substantiation may disqualify an otherwise valid deduction. Furthermore, if the total claimed value of your 2002 property donations exceeds $500, you must report the donation on Form 8283, which you attach to Schedule A, Form 1040. *See also 14.12* for when you need an appraisal of the value of the property.

Figuring value. When donating securities listed on a public exchange, fair market value is readily ascertainable from newspaper listings of stock prices. It is the average of the high and low sales price on the date of the donation.

To value other property, such as real estate or works of art, you will need the services of an experienced appraiser. Fees paid to an appraiser are not deductible as a charitable contribution, but rather as a miscellaneous itemized deduction *(19.25)* subject to the 2% adjusted gross income floor.

Fair market value deductible for intangible personal property (such as securities) and real estate held long term. Fair market value is deductible where you have held such property long term (longer than one year) and you give it to a publicly supported charity or to a private foundation that qualifies as a 50% limit organization, but you may not deduct more than 30% of adjusted gross income, as discussed at *14.17.* A five-year carryover for the excess is allowed; *see 14.18.* If the donation exceeds the 30% ceiling, you may consider a special election that allows you to apply the 50% ceiling; *see 14.19.*

A contribution of appreciated securities or real estate held long term has two tax advantages that reduce the real cost of making the contribution:

1. Your taxes are reduced by the deduction of the fair market value of the property. For example, you donate appreciated stock that is selling at $1,000. You are in the 27% tax bracket. The deduction for the donation reduces your taxes by $270.

2. You avoid the tax you would have paid on a sale of the stock. Assume that your cost for the stock was $400 and that your regular top bracket is 27%. On a sale at $1,000, you would pay tax of $120 (20% capital gain rate on $600 profit). By donating the stock, you save that $120 plus $270 from the $1,000 deduction, for a total tax savings of $390. Your "cost" for donating the $1,000 asset is $610 ($1,000 − $390).

The IRS ruled that you may not claim a deduction on donated stock if you retain the voting rights, even though the charity has the right to receive dividends and sell the stock. The right to vote is considered a substantial interest and is crucial in protecting a stockholder's investment.

If you are planning a year-end donation of securities, keep in mind that the gift is generally not considered complete until the properly endorsed securities are mailed or delivered to the charity or its agent; *see 14.1.*

Filing Instruction

Long-Term Holding Period
In this chapter, property held "long term" is property held more than one year by the donor.

Caution

Appraisal Fees
A fee paid for an appraisal of donated real estate or art is not deductible as a charitable contribution. It may be claimed only as a miscellaneous itemized deduction subject to the 2% floor *(see 19.25).*

Deduction limited to cost for appreciated property not held long term and ordinary income property. This is property that, if sold by you at its fair market value, would not result in long-term capital gain. The deduction for donations of this kind is restricted to your cost for the property. Examples include: stock and other capital assets held by you for one year or less, inventory items donated by business, farm crops, depreciable business property to the extent that depreciation recapture (Chapter 44) rules would apply on a sale, Section 306 stock (preferred stock received as a tax-free stock dividend, usually in a closely held corporation), and works of art, books, letters, and memoranda donated by the person who prepared or created them. *See 14.9* for art objects. For example, a former Congressman claimed a charitable deduction for the donation of his papers. His deduction was disallowed. His papers were ordinary income property, and since his cost basis in the papers was zero, he could claim no deduction.

EXAMPLE
Bob James holds stock that cost him $1,000. It is now worth $1,500. If he holds it for one year or less and donates it to a philanthropy, his deduction would be limited to $1,000. He would get no tax benefit for the appreciation of $500. On the other hand, if the stock were held over a year, he could claim a deduction for the full market value of the stock on its donation.

Tangible personal property held long term. Automobiles, works of art, jewelry, furniture, books, equipment, and fixtures (severed from realty) are examples of tangible personal property. When held over a year, deductions for donations of this type of asset may be subject to restrictions that will limit your deduction to cost basis. If the philanthropy to which you donate the property does not put it to a use that is related to its tax-exempt charitable function, the deduction must be reduced by the amount of long-term capital gain that would have been realized if the property had been sold at fair market value. If the charity sells your gift to obtain cash for its exempt purposes, your donation is treated as being put to a nonrelated use by the charity, and your deduction must be reduced by the long-term gain element; *see* the Example below.

If the donation of tangible personal property is to a 50% deduction limit organization such as a church or college, and you must reduce the deduction as a *nonrelated* gift, the reduced gift is then subject to the 50% annual deduction ceiling discussed at *14.17*. If the organization's use of the property is *related* to its tax-exempt charitable purposes, and it is a 50% limit organization, you may deduct the property's fair market value subject to the 30% of adjusted gross income deduction ceiling; *see 14.17*. Alternatively, you may elect to deduct up to 50% of adjusted gross income by reducing the deduction by the long-term gain; *see 14.19*.

EXAMPLE
You contribute a painting held several years to a college that displays it in a library where art students may study it. The college's use of the painting is related to its tax-exempt educational purposes and you may deduct fair market value. However, if the college sold the painting and used the proceeds for educational purposes, its use would be treated as nonrelated, and you would have to reduce your deduction by the long-term capital gain element. However, if on the date of the donation you could reasonably anticipate that the painting would not be sold (or put to another nonrelated use), you may deduct fair market value, even if it is in fact sold at a later date.

Donating mortgaged property. A donation of mortgaged property may be taxable. Before you give mortgaged property to a charity, have an attorney review the transaction. You may deduct the excess of fair market value over the amount of the outstanding mortgage. However, you may realize a taxable gain. The IRS and Tax Court treat the transferred mortgage debt as cash received in a part-gift, part-sale subject to the bargain-sale rules discussed at *14.8*. You will realize a taxable gain if the transferred mortgage exceeds the portion of basis allocated to the sale part of the transaction. This is true even if the charity does not assume the mortgage.

EXAMPLE
Bob Hill donates to a college land held over a year that is worth $250,000 and subject to a $100,000 mortgage. His basis is $150,000. Hill's charitable contribution deduction is $150,000 ($250,000 − $100,000). He also is considered to have made a bargain sale for $100,000

Caution

Tangible Personal Property
When you donate collectibles and artwork held long term, you get a full deduction for the fair market value of the property if the items are used in connection with the charity's main activity or tax-exempt purpose.

If the charity sells your property, your deduction is limited to your basis in the property (what you paid for it, rather than its appreciated value). Protect a deduction for fair market value by obtaining a letter from the charity stating that it intends to use your gift in connection with its tax-exempt purposes.

Caution

IRS Warning on Auto Donations
The IRS issued a warning to donors and promoters of automobile donation programs promising a charitable donation equal to the current blue book value regardless of the condition of a donated auto. The IRS warned of tax penalties. The charity would jeopardize its tax-exempt status, and the donor could face tax penalties and interest stemming from the disallowance of the charitable deduction.

Not all car donation programs were threatened, such as where a charity holds its own auction or uses the donated car for its tax-exempt purpose. To substantiate an auto donation deduction, keep photographs, service records, and written appraisals to prove the condition of the donated car.

(transferred mortgage debt) on which he realized $40,000 long-term capital gain. 40% of the transaction is treated as a bargain sale:

$$\frac{\$100,000 \text{ (amount of mortgage)}}{\$250,000 \text{ (fair market value)}} = 40\%$$

Basis allocated to sale: 40% of $150,000, or $60,000

Amount realized	$100,000
Allocated basis	60,000
Gain	$ 40,000

Donating capital gain property to private non-operating foundations. You generally may not deduct the full fair market value of gifts of capital gain property to private non-operating foundations that are subject to the 20% deduction ceiling for non–50% limit organizations discussed at *14.17*. (Capital gain property is property that, if sold by you at fair market value, would result in long-term capital gain.) The deduction must be reduced by the long-term gain that would have been realized if the property had been sold at fair market value. In other words, your deduction is limited to your cost basis.

An exception is available for certain contributions of stock to a private non-operating foundation; *see* below.

Stock donation to private non-operating foundation. A deduction for fair market value is allowed on a donation to a non-operating private foundation of appreciated publicly traded stock held long term. To qualify, there must be readily available market quotations on an established securities market for the stock on the date of the contribution. If you or family members donated more than 10% of a corporation's stock, the fair market value deduction is allowed only for the first 10%. Under the family aggregation rule, your contributions of stock in a particular publicly traded corporation are aggregated with those of your spouse, brothers, sisters, parents and grandparents, children, grandchildren, and great-grandchildren to all private non-operating foundations, whether the foundations are related or not. If the 10% limit is exceeded, the excess contributions are subject to the cost basis deduction limitation.

The IRS has ruled that for purposes of applying the 10% limit, you must take into account previous stock contributions that the private foundation sold before the new contributions were made. Once publicly traded stock is donated to a private foundation, it must be counted toward the 10% limit, even if it is later disposed of. Furthermore, the value of each contribution at the time it is made is the value taken into account for applying the 10% limitation; prior contributions are not revalued each time there is a new contribution.

U.S. Saving Bonds. You may not donate U.S. Saving Bonds, such as EE bonds, because you may not transfer them. They are nonnegotiable. You must first cash the bonds and then give the proceeds to the charity, or surrender the bonds and have new ones registered in the donee's name. When you do this, you have to report the accrued interest on your tax return. Of course, you will get a charitable deduction for the cash gift.

Gift of installment obligations. You may deduct your donation of installment notes to a qualified philanthropy. However, if you received them on your sale of property that you reported on the installment basis, you may realize gain or loss on the gift of the notes; *see 5.28*. The amount of the contribution is the fair market value of the obligation, not the face amount of the notes.

14.7 Property That Has Declined Below Cost

Unless the charity needs the property for its own use, you should not donate property whose value has declined below your cost. Your deduction is limited to the fair market value. You may not claim a deductible loss when you make a gift. When the property is held for investment or business purposes, you may get the loss deduction by first selling the property and then a charitable deduction by donating the cash proceeds of the sale.

EXAMPLE

Betty Dunn owns securities that cost $20,000 several years ago but have declined in value to $5,000. A donation of these securities gives a charitable contribution deduction of $5,000. If Betty sold the securities for $5,000, she could claim a long-term capital loss of $15,000. She could then donate the sales proceeds and claim a $5,000 charitable deduction for the cash contribution.

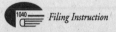 *Filing Instruction*

Donating Used Clothing or Furniture

If you donate used clothing, furniture, or household appliances, deduct their fair market value, which is usually much less than your original cost. For your records, get a statement from the donee organization acknowledging the gift and describing the property. Also keep a record of your original cost. If the claimed value of your donation exceeds $500, you must complete Form 8283; *see 14.12*. For each individual contribution with a claimed value of $250 or more, you must get a receipt as explained in *14.15*.

If the property is a personal asset such as clothing, appliances, furniture, or an automobile, you may not deduct a loss on the sale. It makes no difference whether you sell the property and donate the sales proceeds or donate the property. Your deductible donation is the value of the property.

14.8 Bargain Sales of Appreciated Property

A sale of appreciated property to a philanthropy for less than fair market value allows you to claim a charitable deduction while receiving proceeds from the sale. However, you must pay a tax on part of the gain attributed to the sale. That is, the transaction is broken down into two parts: the sale and the gift.

To compute gain on the sale, you allocate the adjusted basis of the property between the sale and the gift following these steps:

Step 1. Divide the sales proceeds by the fair market value of the property. If the property is mortgaged, include the outstanding debt as sale proceeds.

Step 2. Apply the Step 1 percentage to the adjusted basis of the property. This is the portion of basis allocated to the sale.

Step 3. Deduct the resulting basis of Step 2 from the sales proceeds to find the gain.

You may deduct the donated appreciation if full market value would be deductible on a straight donation (no sale) under the rules at *14.6*. Thus, the donated appreciation is deductible if the property is securities or real estate held long term or long-term tangible personal property related to the charity's exempt function; *see* Example 1 below. However, if a deduction for the property (assuming no sale) would be reduced to cost basis as discussed in *14.6*, your charitable deduction on the sale is also reduced; *see* Example 2 below. This reduction affects sales of capital gain property held short term; ordinary income property; tangible personal property not related to the charity's exempt function; depreciable personal property subject to recapture; and sales of capital gain property to private non-operating foundations.

EXAMPLES

1. Lana Briggs sells to a university for $12,000 stock over a year. The adjusted basis of the stock is $12,000, and the fair market value is $20,000. On the sale, she recouped her investment and donated the appreciation of $8,000, but, at the same time, she realized taxable gain of $4,800 computed as follows: The percentage of basis applied to the sale is 60% ($12,000 sale proceeds ÷ $20,000 fair market value). Thus, 60% of the $12,000 basis, or $7,200, is allocated to the sale. Gain on the sale equals the $12,000 sale proceeds less the $7,200 allocated basis, or $4,800.

2. Joel Marx sells to his church stock held short term for his basis of $4,000. The stock is worth $10,000. Using the allocation method in Example 1, 40% ($4,000 sale proceeds ÷ $10,000 fair market value) of his $4,000 basis, or $1,600, is allocated to the sale. Thus, he has a short-term capital gain of $2,400 ($4,000 sale proceeds − $1,600 allocated basis). Furthermore, his deductible charitable contribution is also $2,400, equal to the 60% of basis allocated to the gift (60% of $4,000 = $2,400).

Basis allocation applies even if a deduction is barred by the annual ceiling. The basis allocation rules for determining gain on a bargain sale apply even if the annual deduction ceilings *(14.17)* bar a deduction in the year of the donation and in the five-year carryover period.

EXAMPLE

The Hodgdons contributed real estate valued at $3.9 million but subject to mortgage debt of $2.6 million. The IRS treated the mortgage debt as sales proceeds and figured gain based on the difference between the debt and the portion of basis allocated to the sale element. The Hodgdons claimed that the basis allocation rule, which increased the amount of their gain, should not apply. Earlier in the year, they had made another donation that used up their charitable deduction ceiling for that year as well as for the following five-year carryover period. The Tax Court held that the basis allocation rule applied because a charitable deduction was "allowable," even if the contribution did not actually result in a deduction in the carryover period.

14.9 Art Objects

You may claim a charitable deduction for a painting or other art object donated to a charity. The amount of the deduction depends on (1) whether you are the artist; (2) if you are not the artist, how long you owned it; and (3) the type of organization receiving the gift.

If you owned the art work short term, your deduction is limited to cost, under the rules applying to donations of ordinary income property at *14.6.*

If you owned the art work long term (see 14.6), your deduction depends on the way the charity uses the property. If the charity uses it for its exempt purposes, you may deduct the fair market value. However, if the charity uses it for unrelated purposes, your deduction is reduced by 100% of the appreciation. A donation of art work to a general fund-raising agency would be reduced because the agency would have no direct use for it. It would have to sell the art work and use the cash for its exempt purposes.

Appraisals. Be prepared to support your deduction with detailed proof of cost, the date of acquisition, and how value was appraised. The appraisal fee is treated as a "miscellaneous" itemized deduction subject to the 2% adjusted gross income floor; *see 19.25. See also 14.12* for appraisal requirements.

The IRS has its own art advisory panel to assess whether the fair market value claimed for donated art works is reasonable.

Requesting advance valuation of art from the IRS. To avoid a later dispute, you may ask the IRS for an advance valuation of art that you have had appraised at $50,000 or more. A request for an IRS Statement of Value (SOV) may be submitted for income tax, gift tax, or estate tax purposes. The IRS has the discretion to value items appraised at less than $50,000 if the SOV request includes at least one item appraised at $50,000 or more, and the IRS determines that the valuation is in the best interest of efficient tax administration.

A request for an SOV must be submitted to the IRS before filing the tax return reporting the donation. The request must include a copy of an appraisal for the item of art and a $2,500 fee, which pays for an SOV for up to three items of art. There is an additional charge of $250 for each item of art over three. It takes the IRS between six and 12 months to issue an SOV.

If the IRS agrees with the value reported on the appraisal, the IRS will issue an SOV approving the appraisal. If the IRS disagrees, the IRS will issue an SOV indicating its own valuation and stating the reasons it disagrees with the appraised amount. Regardless of whether you agree with the IRS appraisal, the SOV must be attached to and filed with the return reporting the donation. If you file the return before the SOV is issued, a copy of your request for the SOV must be attached to your return and on receipt of the SOV, an amended return must be filed with the SOV attached. For further SOV details, *see* IRS Revenue Procedure 96-15.

 Caution

Donations of Personal Creative Works

If you are the artist, your deduction is limited to cost regardless of how long you held the art work or to what use the charity puts it. In the case of a painting, the deduction would be the lower of the cost for canvas and paints and the fair market value.

 *Filing Instruction*

Appraisal Required

If you claim a deduction for art of $20,000 or more, you must attach a copy of a signed qualifying appraisal to Form 8283 and file it with your return; *see 14.12* for further details.

EXAMPLES

1. You give your college a painting that you have owned for many years. Its cost was $100 but it is now worth $1,000. The school displays the painting in its library for study by students. This use is related to the school's educational purposes. Your donation is deductible at fair market value. If, however, the school proposed to sell the painting and use the proceeds for general education purposes, its use would not be considered related. Your deduction would be reduced by the $900 appreciation to $100. That the school sells the painting does not necessarily reduce the donation if you show that, when you made the gift, it was reasonable to anticipate that your gift would not be put to such unrelated use.

2. You donate to the Community Fund a collection of first edition books held for many years and worth $5,000. Your cost is $1,000. Since the charity is a general fund-raising organization, its use of your gift is not related. Your deduction would be $1,000 ($5,000 less $4,000).

3. You contribute to a charity antique furnishings you owned for years. The antiques cost you $500 and are now worth $5,000. The charity uses the furnishings in its office in the course of carrying on its functions. This is a related use. Your contribution deduction is $5,000.

Donating a partial interest in an art collection. You may deduct the value of a donated partial interest in an art collection, such as where you give a museum the right to exhibit the works for a specific period during the year. The deduction is allowed even if the museum does not take possession of the art works, provided it has the right to take possession.

Keeping a reversionary interest. The IRS may challenge a charitable deduction where you retain some control over the donated property. However, if the possibility of the property reverting back to you is considered to be remote, a deduction may be allowed. For example, a taxpayer who donated her art collection to a museum was allowed to claim a charitable deduction even though she retained the right to decide where and how the art would be displayed. Disputes concerning art displays would be settled by a mutually acceptable museum curator. If the museum breached a condition, it had a period of time to cure the violation. If the violation was not cured, the ownership would revert back to the donor. The IRS allowed the deduction; the retained rights were fiduciary in nature and the possibility of the art reverting to the donor was so remote as to be negligible.

14.10 Interests in Real Estate

No deduction is allowed for the rental value of property you allow a charity to use free of charge. This is the case even if the property is used directly in furtherance of the organization's charitable purpose.

If you donate an undivided fractional part of your entire interest, a deduction will be allowed for the fair market value of the proportionate interest donated.

A donation of an option is not deductible until the year the option to buy the property is exercised.

Remainder interest in a home or farm. You may claim a charitable deduction for a gift of the remainder value of a residence or farm donated to a charity, even though you reserve the use of the property for yourself and your spouse for a term of years or life. Remainder gifts generally must be made in trust. However, where a residence or farm is donated, the remainder interest must be conveyed outright, not in trust. A remainder interest in a vacation home or in a "hobby" farm is also deductible. There is no requirement that the home be your principal residence or that the farm be profitable.

Contribution of real property for conservation purposes. A deduction may be claimed for the contribution of certain partial interests in real property to government agencies or publicly supported charities for exclusively conservational purposes. Deductible contributions include: (1) your entire interest in real property other than retained rights to subsurface oil, gas, or other minerals; (2) a remainder interest; or (3) an easement, restrictive covenant, or similar property restriction granted in perpetuity. The contribution must be in perpetuity and further at least one of the following "conservation purposes"—preservation of land areas for outdoor recreation, education, or scenic enjoyment; preservation of historically important land areas or structures; or the protection of plant, fish, and wildlife habitats or similar natural ecosystems.

To obtain the deduction, there must be legally enforceable restrictions that prevent you from using your retained interest in the property in a way contrary to the intended conservation purpose. The donee organization must be prohibited from transferring the contributed interest except to other organizations that will hold the property for exclusively conservational purposes. If you retain an interest in subsurface oil, gas, or minerals, surface mining must generally be specifically prohibited. However, there is a limited exception where the mineral rights and surface interests have been separately owned since June 12, 1976. A deduction will be allowed if the probability of surface mining is so remote as to be considered negligible. The exception does not apply if you are related to the owner of the surface interest or if you received the mineral interest (directly or indirectly) from the surface owner.

> **EXAMPLE**
>
> To help a charity raise money, one owner allowed the charity to auction off a week's stay in his vacation home, and the highest bidder paid the charity a fair rental. The IRS ruled that not only was the owner's donation not deductible, but the one week stay by the bidder was considered personal use by the owner for purposes of figuring deductions for rental expenses. True, if the owner had directly rented the property to the bidder, the bidder's payment of a fair rental value would have been counted as a rental day and not a personal use day. However, the donation for charitable use is not a business rental, and the bidder's rental payment to the charity is not considered a payment to the owner.

 Caution

Donating Vacation Home Use Not Advisable

To raise funds, a charitable organization may ask contributors who own vacation homes to donate use of the property, which the charity then auctions off to the public. Be warned that if you offer your home in this way you will not only be denied a charitable deduction for your generosity, but you may jeopardize your deduction for rental expenses: A deduction is not allowed for giving a charity the free use of your property. *See* the Example at the end of *14.10*.

Furthermore, the bidder's use of the home pushed the owner over the personal-use ceiling, which in turn prevented him from deducting a rental loss. A rental loss may not be claimed if personal use of a home exceeds the greater of 14 days and 10% of the number of days the home is rented at fair rental value *(9.7)*. Here, the owner personally used the home for 14 days and rented the home for 80 days. The rental expenses exceeded rental income. If the bidder's use of the home was not considered his personal use, the owner could have deducted the loss because his personal use did not exceed the 14-day limit (which was more than 10% of the 80 rental days). However, by adding the bidder's seven days of use to the owner's 14 days, the resulting 21 days of personal use exceeded the 14-day ceiling.

14.11 Life Insurance

You may deduct the value of a life insurance policy if the charity is irrevocably named as beneficiary and you make both a legal assignment and a complete delivery of the policy. A deduction may be disallowed where you reserve the right to change the beneficiary.

The amount of your deduction generally depends on the type of policy donated. Your insurance company can furnish you with the information necessary to calculate your deduction. In addition, you may deduct premiums you pay after you assign the policy.

Deducting premium payments on donated policy. If you assign a life insurance policy to a charity and continue to pay the premiums, you generally may deduct the premiums. However, in states where charities do not have an "insurable interest" in the donor's life, the IRS may challenge income tax and gift tax deductions for the premium payments. The IRS took this position in a private ruling interpreting New York law. In response, New York amended its insurance code to allow individuals to buy a life insurance policy and immediately transfer it to a charity. The IRS then revoked the earlier ruling but it did not announce a change in its position. Thus, the IRS may challenge premium deductions of donors in other states where a charity's insurable interest is not clearly provided by state law.

 Caution

Split-Dollar Insurance Arrangements

No deduction is allowed for giving a charitable organization money with the understanding that it will be used to pay premiums on life insurance, annuities, or endowment contracts for your benefit or that of a beneficiary designated by you.

Sample—Form 8283

Form **8283** (Rev. October 1998) Department of the Treasury Internal Revenue Service	**Noncash Charitable Contributions** ▶ Attach to your tax return if you claimed a total deduction of over $500 for all contributed property. ▶ See separate instructions.	OMB No. 1545-0908 Attachment Sequence No. **55**

Name(s) shown on your income tax return: **David Diaz** — Identifying number **01X-X1-01X1**

Note: *Figure the amount of your contribution deduction before completing this form. See your tax return instructions.*

Section A—List in this section **only** items (or groups of similar items) for which you claimed a deduction of $5,000 or less. Also, list certain publicly traded securities even if the deduction is over $5,000 (see instructions).

Part I Information on Donated Property—If you need more space, attach a statement.

	(a) Name and address of the donee organization	(b) Description of donated property
A	Red Cross City, State 11XXX	Blankets and used clothing items
B	Community Food Center City, State 11X1X	Minivan - 1992
C		(8 cylinders / 100,000 miles)
D		
E		

Note: *If the amount you claimed as a deduction for an item is $500 or less, you do not have to complete columns (d), (e), and (f).*

	(c) Date of the contribution	(d) Date acquired by donor (mo., yr.)	(e) How acquired by donor	(f) Donor's cost or adjusted basis	(g) Fair market value	(h) Method used to determine the fair market value
A	7-23-2002				200	Thrift Shop Value
B	11-19-2002	4-6-1992	Purchase		2,500	Blue Book Value
C						
D						
E						

Caution

Charity Reports Transfer Within Two Years

If the charity sells or otherwise disposes of appraised property within two years after your gift, it must notify the IRS on Form 8282 and send you a copy. The IRS could compare the selling price received by the charity with the value you claimed on Form 8282. Reporting on Form 8282 is not required by the charity if in Part II, Section B of Form 8283 you indicated that the appraised value of the item was not more than $500. Similar items such as a collection of books by the same author, stereo components, or place settings of silverware may be treated as one item. Reporting is also not required for donated property that the organization uses or distributes without consideration, if this use furthers the organization's tax-exempt function or purpose.

14.12 Form 8283 and Written Appraisal Requirements

Attach Form 8283 to your Form 1040 for 2002 if the total deduction claimed for all of your donations of property exceeds $500. The IRS may disallow your deduction if you fail to attach Form 8283.

If you are claiming a deduction exceeding $5,000 for an item, or for a group of similar items (such as coins, stamps, books, paintings, or buildings), you need a written appraisal, which must be summarized in Section B, Part I of Form 8283. The appraiser must complete Part III in Section B of Form 8283. However, you do not need a written appraisal for publicly traded securities and nonpublicly traded stock of $10,000 or less. Keep the appraisal for your records unless you donate art valued at $20,000 or more. In that case, you must attach a complete copy of the appraisal to Form 8283. Furthermore, you may be asked by the IRS to submit a color photograph (8" × 10") or a slide of the art (4" × 5").

If you need an appraisal, get one from an unrelated professional no earlier than 60 days before your gift, and you must receive it by the due date (including extensions) of your return on which you claim the deduction.

For property donations exceeding $5,000, the donee organization must acknowledge the receipt of the property on Section B, Part IV of Form 8283.

Penalty for overvaluation. You may be penalized for a substantial overvaluation of donated property; *see 14.16.*

Appraisal fees. A fee paid to an appraiser is not considered a charitable deduction but is deductible as a "miscellaneous" expense subject to the 2% adjusted gross income floor; *see 19.25.*

14.13 Business Inventory

Self-employed business owners generally may not deduct more than cost for donations of inventory. If a charitable deduction is claimed, costs incurred in a year prior to the year of donation must be removed from opening inventory and excluded from the cost of goods sold when figuring business gross profit for the year of the contribution.

No contribution deduction is allowed for a gift of merchandise that was produced or acquired in the year donated. Instead, the cost is added to the cost of goods sold to figure gross profit for the year of the contribution. Business deductions are not subject to the percentage limitation applied to donations.

14.14 Donations Through Trusts

Outright gifts are not the only way to make deductible gifts to charities. You may transfer property to a charitable lead trust or a charitable remainder trust to provide funds for charity.

A charitable lead trust involves your transfer of property to a trust directed to pay income to a charity you name, for the term of the trust, and then to return the property to you or to someone else. A charitable remainder trust is one that provides income for you or another beneficiary for life, after which the property passes to a charity.

Trust arrangements require the services of an experienced attorney who will draft the trust in appropriate form and advise you of the tax consequences.

Deductions for gifts of income interests in trust. Current law is designed to prevent a donor from claiming an immediate deduction for the present value of trust income payable to a charity for a term of years. In limited situations, you may claim a deduction if either: (1) You give away all of your interests in the property to qualifying *(14.1)* organizations. For example, you put your property in trust, giving an income interest for 20 years to a church and the remainder to a college. A deduction is allowed for the value of the property. Or (2) you create a unitrust or annuity trust, and are taxed on the income. A unitrust for this purpose provides that a fixed percentage of trust assets is payable to the charitable income beneficiary each year. An annuity trust provides for payment of a guaranteed dollar amount to the charitable income beneficiary each year. A deduction is allowed for the present value of the unitrust or annuity trust interest.

Because income remains taxable to the grantor, alternative (2) will probably not be chosen, unless the income of the trust is from tax-exempt securities. If such a trust is created, a tax may be due if the donor dies before the trust ends or is no longer the taxable owner of trust income. The law provides for recapture of part of the tax deduction, even where the income was tax exempt.

Charitable remainder trusts. A charitable deduction is allowable for transfers of property to charitable remainder trusts only if the trust meets these requirements: The income payable for a noncharitable income beneficiary's life or a term of up to 20 years must be guaranteed under a unitrust

Life Income Plans

A philanthropy may offer a life income plan (pooled income fund) to which you transfer property or money in return for a guaranteed income for life. After your death, the philanthropy has full control over the property. If you enter such a plan, ask the philanthropy for the amount of the deduction that you may claim for the value of your gift.

or annuity trust. If a donor gives all of his or her interests in the property to the charities, the annuity or unitrust requirements need not be satisfied. The value of the charitable deduction allowable for a gift in trust is determined by IRS tables.

Reporting Charitable Contributions

14.15 Records Needed To Substantiate Your Contributions

The type of records you must keep to substantiate your donations generally depends on their amount and whether you are contributing cash or property. The requirements are stricter for contributions of $250 or more than for smaller contributions.

Contributions under $250. A cancelled check or a dated receipt is proof of a donation under $250. For a property donation, your receipt should contain a description of the property. You should keep records showing the fair market value of the property and your cost basis.

You need a receipt and explanation from the charity for contributions of $250 or more. A written receipt or acknowledgment is necessary to prove charitable contributions of $250 or more; *see* below. You may not rely on a cancelled check to document a cash contribution of $250 or more. The receipt requirement does not apply if the donation is less than $250, but if the contribution exceeds $75, you must be given a disclosure statement from the charity estimating the value of any benefits you received in return for the donation.

The IRS exempts from the receipt requirement grantors of a charitable lead trust, charitable remainder annuity trust, or charitable remainder unitrust. Since a specific charity does not have to be designated as beneficiary at the time the trust transfer is made, there may be no organization available to provide a receipt.

Content of receipt. A receipt for a donation of $250 or more may be a letter, e-mail, computer-generated form, or postcard. If you gave cash, the amount of the donation must be shown. If you gave property, the property must be described in the receipt or acknowledgment, but the charity does not have to value it.

 Caution

Contributions of $250 or More
A cancelled check is not sufficient proof of a donation of $250 or more. You must get a written acknowledgment or receipt from the charitable organization.

Proving Your Donations	
If you contribute—	You need—
$75 or less	A cancelled check or receipt from the charity
More than $75 but less than $250	A cancelled check or receipt from the charity. If you received benefits, the charity is required to give you a "disclosure" statement that estimates the value of any benefits you received, such as concert tickets or books. The statement will tell you to deduct only the excess of your contribution over the value of the benefits. If a required disclosure statement is not provided when contributions are solicited, it must be provided when you make a contribution exceeding $75. The disclosure statement is not required if the only benefits you receive are "token items" as discussed in *14.3*. Nor is it required where you contribute to a religious organization and the only benefits you receive are "intangible religious benefits." An example of an intangible religious benefit would be admission to religious ceremonies. A Congressional committee report also suggests that tuition for wholly religious education that does not lead to a recognized degree would qualify.
$250 or more	A receipt or acknowledgment from the charity. You may not rely on a cancelled check to document a cash contribution of $250 or more. A receipt is also required for a donation of property if you are claiming a deduction of $250 or more, but the charity does not have to value the property, just describe it. If you received any goods or services from the charity in exchange for the contribution, the receipt must estimate their value unless you receive only "token" items or "intangible religious benefits" as discussed in the preceding paragraph. The deadline for obtaining receipts is the date you file your return. If you file after the filing due date or extended due date, get the receipt by the due date or extended due date. Where the contribution is $250 or more, and both the receipt requirement and the disclosure requirement apply, the charity may satisfy both requirements with the same document. Keep the statement from the charity with your tax records; do not attach it to your tax return. If your total deduction for all property donations exceeds $500, you must report the contributions on Form 8283. If you are not allowed to deduct fair market value for a property donation under the rules at *14.6*, you must attach a statement to Form 8283 explaining the reduction for the appreciation. For property deductions exceeding $5,000, you need a written appraisal, as discussed in *14.12*.

Filing Tip

Right To Buy Athletic Stadium Tickets

The IRS considers 20% of the amount paid for the right to buy college or university athletic seating to be the fair market value of the right. You may deduct 80% *(see 14.3)*. When your payment is $312.50 or more, you are considered to have made a contribution of at least $250 ($250 = 80% of $312.50), requiring a written acknowledgment from the charity.

Planning Reminder

Advance Valuation of Art From IRS

To protect against the possibility of a valuation dispute that could lead to a penalty where you are claiming a deduction of at least $50,000 for a work of art, you may request a valuation from the IRS prior to the time you file. *See 14.9* for obtaining the IRS valuation.

Filing Tip

Cash Gifts

A donation of cash to a church, college, or publicly supported charity is deductible up to 50% of your adjusted gross income; *see* the list on page 303 of organizations to which contributions eligible for the 50% limit may be made.

The receipt must state whether or not you have received any goods or services from the charity in exchange for the contribution. If you have, the receipt must include a statement describing such benefits and estimating their value. However, "token" items and certain membership benefits, as described in *14.3*, do not have to be described or valued. There is also an exception if the contribution is to a religious organization and the *only* benefits received are "intangible" religious benefits, such as admission to religious ceremonies; these do not have to be described or valued, but the statement must indicate that they are the sole benefits provided.

Payments throughout the year. For purposes of the $250 receipt threshold, each payment is generally considered separate. Thus, for small donations made during the year, you do not have to obtain a receipt even if they total $250 or more.

If contributions are made by payroll deductions from your wages, the amount withheld from each paycheck is treated separately. A receipt is not required unless withholding on a single paycheck is at least $250. A pay stub or Form W-2 from the employer indicating the amount of a single withholding over $249 is considered a valid "receipt"; a pledge card or other document from the charity must state that you have not received benefits in exchange for the payroll deduction contribution.

Deadline for 2002 donation receipts. For a 2002 contribution, the deadline for obtaining a receipt is the date you file your 2002 return. If you file after the filing due date or extended due date, get the receipt by the due date or extended due date.

A charity must provide a disclosure statement if you contribute more than $75 and receive benefits. If you contribute more than $75 but less than $250 to a charity, you do not have to get a written receipt but the charity is required to give you a "disclosure" statement that estimates the value of any benefits you received, such as concert tickets or books. The statement will tell you to deduct only the excess of your contribution over the value of the benefits. If a required disclosure statement is not provided when contributions are solicited, it must be provided when you make a contribution exceeding $75.

14.16 Penalty for Substantial Overvaluation of Property

If the IRS disallows a portion of your claimed deduction for appreciated property on the grounds that you have overvalued it, you may be subject to a penalty as well as additional tax. The penalty applies only for substantial overvaluations that result in a tax underpayment exceeding $5,000. There are two levels of penalty, depending on the extent of overvaluation:

20% penalty. If the value claimed is 200% or more of the correct amount and results in a tax underpayment exceeding $5,000, the penalty is 20% of the resulting tax underpayment.

40% penalty. If the value claimed is 400% or more of the correct amount and results in a tax underpayment exceeding $5,000, the penalty is 40% of the resulting underpayment.

In determining whether the 200% or 400% overvaluation threshold is met, each property claimed on your return is considered separately. Thus, if on the same return you overvalue Property A by 180% and Property B by 250%, the penalty may be imposed only against Property B, even though on an aggregate basis the overvaluation for both properties is at least 200%.

If there is an overvaluation of at least 200% for more than one property, the resulting tax underpayments are combined to determine if the $5,000 underpayment threshold has been met. For example, Property C is overvalued by 300%, resulting in a $1,000 tax underpayment, and Property D is overvalued by 400%, for a tax underpayment of $4,500. As the total underpayment exceeds $5,000, both overvaluations are subject to the penalty.

Reliance on appraisal may avoid penalty. Even though you have an overvaluation subject to the penalty, you may avoid it under a reasonable cause exception if you relied on an appraisal, but only if the appraisal and the appraiser who prepared it were qualified under IRS regulations and, in addition, you made a good faith, independent investigation of the value of the property.

A professional appraiser who knowingly overvalues charitable deduction property is subject to a $1,000 penalty.

14.17 Ceiling on Charitable Contributions

Unless you make donations that are very substantial in relation to your adjusted gross income (Line 35, Form 1040), you do not have to be concerned with the deduction ceilings discussed in this section. For cash contributions, the deduction ceiling is generally 50% of adjusted gross income, but in some cases a 30% limit applies. For property donations, the deduction limit is generally 30% of adjusted gross income, although it sometimes is 50% or even 20%. As detailed below, the specific limit for each donation depends on whether it is made to a "50% limit organization" and whether it is capital gain property. Where you have made contributions subject to different ceilings, the ceilings are applied in a specific order and are subject to an overall ceiling of 50% of adjusted gross income. If your deduction is limited by any of the ceilings, a five-year carryover is allowed for the excess; see 14.18.

Even if none of your charitable contributions are subject to the ceilings, your overall charitable deduction is subject to the 3% reduction to itemized deductions if your 2002 adjusted gross income exceeds $137,300 ($68,650 if married filing separately); see 13.7.

Volunteer expenses. The deduction ceiling for unreimbursed expenses you incur doing volunteer work for a charity (14.4) is 50% of adjusted gross income if your services were for a 50% limit organization such as a church or college (see the list below), or 30% of adjusted gross income if the services were on behalf of an organization other than a 50% limit organization.

30% limit for contributions for the use of an organization. If a donation is treated as for the use of, rather than directly to, any organization, it is deductible under the 30% ceiling described below for contributions to organizations that are not 50% limit organizations.

This 30% ceiling applies to a charitable unitrust or annuity trust income interest that is deductible under the rules discussed at 14.14. A charitable remainder trust transfer is also subject to the 30% limit if the trust provides that after the death of the income beneficiary, the property is to be held in the trust for the benefit of the charity, rather than distributed to the charity.

Deductible expenses for supporting a student in your home (see 14.5) are considered to be for the use of a charitable organization and thus subject to the 30% ceiling for contributions to organizations that are *not* 50% limit organizations.

Contributions to 50% Limit Organizations

Organizations in the 50% limit category include churches, schools, publicly supported charities, and private foundations in the list below. Cash contributions to such organizations are deductible up to 50% of adjusted gross income and contributions of capital gain property held long term generally are deductible up to 30% of adjusted gross income.

The 50% deduction ceiling also applies to donations to the United States, Puerto Rico, a U.S. possession, a state, a political subdivision of a state or U.S. possession, or an Indian tribal government.

50% ceiling. Contributions of cash, ordinary income property, and capital gain property held short term are deductible up to 50% of adjusted gross income if made to the following types of charitable organizations:

- Churches, synagogues, mosques, and other religious organizations.
- Schools, colleges, and other educational organizations that normally have regular faculties and student bodies in attendance on site.
- Hospitals and medical research organizations associated with hospitals.
- Government-supported or publicly supported foundations for state and municipal universities and colleges.
- Religious, charitable, educational, scientific, or literary organizations that receive a substantial part of their financial support from the general public or a government unit. Libraries, museums, drama, opera, ballet and orchestral societies, community funds, the American Red Cross, the Heart Fund, and the United Way are in this category. Also included are organizations to prevent cruelty to children or animals, or to foster amateur sports (provided they do not provide athletic facilities or equipment).
- Private operating foundations.
- Private non-operating foundations that distribute their contributions annually to qualified charities within 2 ½ months after the end of their taxable year.
- Private non-operating foundations that pool donations and allow donors to designate the charities to receive their gifts, if the foundation pays out all income within 2 ½ months after the end of the tax year.
- Organizations that normally receive more than one-third of their support from the general public or governmental units.

Filing Instruction

Appreciated Securities and Real Estate

When you contribute appreciated securities or real estate that you have held for more than a year to a church, college, or other organization treated as a 50% limit organization, your deduction for the property donation is limited to 30% of your adjusted gross income unless you elect the 50% ceiling as discussed at 14.19.

Filing Instruction

Carryover for Excess Contributions

If you contribute cash and property in the same year, your deductions may be subject to different limits, such as 50% of adjusted gross income for the cash and 30% for the property. Follow the steps and Examples at the end of this section for applying the ceilings.

If your donation exceeds the limits, you may carry over the excess for five years.

30% ceiling for capital gain property held long term. The deduction ceiling is generally 30% (not 50%) of adjusted gross income where you donate to a 50% limit organization property that would have resulted in long-term capital gain had you sold it at fair market value.

The 30% ceiling applies where the fair market value of the property is deductible under the rules discussed in *14.6*. This includes donations of appreciated securities and real estate held long term. It also includes donations of appreciated tangible personal property (such as furniture or art) held long term where the organization's use of your gift is directly related to its tax-exempt charitable purposes.

However, you may elect to apply the 50% ceiling instead of the 30% ceiling to such property donations if you reduce the fair market value of the property by the appreciation; *see 14.19*.

If you donate tangible personal property held long term that is *not* used by the organization for its tax-exempt charitable purposes, so that your deduction must be reduced for the appreciation *(14.6)*, the reduced amount is deductible under the 50% ceiling.

Contributions to Non–50% Limit Organizations

If a contribution is made to a qualifying organization that is *not* in the above list of 50% limit organizations, a 30% or 20% deduction ceiling applies. Organizations in this category include veterans' organizations, fraternal societies, nonprofit cemeteries and private non-operating foundations that do not meet the payout requirements for 50% limit status.

The 30% limit applies to contributions of cash, ordinary income property, and capital gain property held short term. The 20% limit applies to contributions of capital gain property held long term (more than one year). However, the actual ceiling may be less than 30% or 20% of adjusted gross income where in the same year you have made contributions to 50% limit organizations. In that case, follow Steps 2 and 4 of the following section on applying the deduction ceilings.

Applying the Deduction Ceilings

The various deduction ceilings are applied in a specific order, with the total deduction for the year limited to 50% of adjusted gross income. Check above for the ceilings that apply to your donations and then apply the ceilings in the following order. *See 14.18* for carryover rules if a portion of your deduction is barred by the deduction ceilings.

1. 50% of adjusted gross income ceiling for contributions to 50% limit organizations.
2. 30% of adjusted gross income ceiling for contributions to organizations that are *not* 50% limit organizations, except for contributions of capital gain property subject to the 20% ceiling under Step 4 below.

    If any contributions to 50% limit organizations were made, including donations of capital gain property that are subject to the 30% ceiling under Step 3 below, this Step 2 ceiling is the lesser of (1) 30% of adjusted gross income or (2) 50% of adjusted gross income minus the contributions to the 50% limit organizations.
3. 30% of adjusted gross income ceiling for contributions of capital gain property to 50% limit organizations.

    If contributions qualifying for the 50% ceiling (Step 1) were made, your deduction for these 30% limit contributions is the lesser of (1) 30% of adjusted gross income or (2) 50% of adjusted gross income minus the contributions qualifying for the 50% ceiling.
4. 20% of adjusted gross income ceiling for contributions of capital gain property to organizations that are not 50% limit organizations.

    If contributions are deductible under any of the other ceilings (Steps 1–3), you may deduct contributions subject to the 20% ceiling only to the extent that there is any adjusted gross income remaining under the overall 50% adjusted gross limit.

Filing Instruction

Different Ceilings

If you made charitable contributions subject to several deduction ceilings, the deductions are applied against adjusted gross income in the specific order shown at the right.

EXAMPLES

1. Linda Jones in 2002 contributes to a church $22,000 in cash and land held long term valued at $35,000. Her adjusted gross income is $100,000, so the total deduction for the year may not exceed $50,000 under the 50% overall limit. Since the $22,000 cash contribution subject to the 50% ceiling is considered first, the deduction for the land (subject to the 30% ceiling under Step 3 above) is limited to $28,000, the difference between the $50,000 overall limit and the $22,000 cash gift. Jones may carry over the unused $7,000 donation attributable to the land.

2. Earl Smith in 2002 has an adjusted gross income of $100,000. He contributes land worth $40,000 to a college, deductible under the 30% ceiling of Step 3 above. He also contributes $30,000 in cash to a non-operating private foundation subject to the 30% ceiling discussed in Step 2 above. The 30% limitation for cash gifts to non-operating private foundations is applied before the 30% limitation applicable to gifts of capital gain property to public charities. The deduction for the cash gift is reduced to $10,000 (50% of $100,000 adjusted gross income, or $50,000, minus $40,000 gift to college). The deduction for the land is limited to $30,000 (30% of $100,000). Accordingly, Smith's charitable contribution deduction for 2002 is $40,000 ($10,000 + $30,000).

Smith is allowed to carry over *(14.18)* the amounts disallowed by the ceilings: $20,000 ($30,000 – $10,000) for the cash gift and $10,000 ($40,000 – $30,000) for the land.

14.18 Five-Year Carryover for Excess Donations

If you make donations that are not deductible because they exceed the 50%, 30%, or 20% of adjusted gross income ceilings discussed in *14.17*, you may carry the excess over the next five years. In each carryover year, the original percentage ceiling applies. For example, where contributions of appreciated long-term intangible personal property or real estate (or tangible personal property put to a related use by the charity) exceed the 30% ceiling for capital gain property *(14.17)*, the excess remains subject to the 30% ceiling in the carryover years.

In any carryover year, you must first figure your deduction for contributions in the current year under the applicable 50%, 30%, or 20% ceilings. For each category of property carried over, the carryover contributions are deductible only after the deduction for current year donations is figured. The total deduction in the carryover year, for both current year and carryover contributions, cannot exceed 50% of adjusted gross income for the carryover year.

EXAMPLE

In 2002, you contribute to a university stock held over a year with a fair market value of $19,000. The contribution is subject to the 30% ceiling for capital gain property *(14.17)*. You also have a $2,000 carryover from 2001 for a cash gift to your church subject to the 50% ceiling. Your 2002 adjusted gross income is $40,000. Under the 30% ceiling, the deduction for the contribution of stock is limited to $12,000 (30% of $40,000 adjusted gross income). Since the overall deduction limit is $20,000 (50% of $40,000 adjusted gross income), the $2,000 carryover from 2001 is fully deductible. The total deduction on your 2002 return is $14,000 ($12,000 plus $2,000 carryover). You carry over to 2003 the $7,000 balance from the gift of stock that was subject to the 30% ceiling.

14.19 Election To Reduce Property Gift Appreciation

Although the 30% ceiling generally applies to long-term intangible property (such as securities) and real estate contributed to 50% limit organizations *(see 14.17)*, you may elect the 50% ceiling, provided you reduce the fair market value of the property by 100% of the appreciation on all such donations during the year. The reduction also applies to donations of tangible personal property related in use to the organization's charitable function. In most cases, this election should be made only where the amount of appreciation is negligible. Where there is substantial appreciation, the increase in the deduction may not make up or exceed the required 100% reduction, which allows you to claim a deduction only for your cost basis in the property. If the election is made in a year in which there are carryovers of capital gain property subject to the 30% ceiling, the carryovers are subject to reduction; *see* IRS Publication 526.

The election of the 50% ceiling is made by attaching a statement to your original return or amended return filed by the original due date. Even where no formal electing statement is made, claiming a deduction without the appreciation in order to come within the 50% ceiling is treated as an election. A formal or "informal" election is not revocable unless a material mistake is shown. A revocation based on a reconsideration of tax consequences is not considered sufficient grounds.

 *Planning Reminder*

Project Your Income

When planning substantial donations that may exceed the annual ceiling, make a projection of your income for at least five years. Although the carryover period of five years will probably absorb most excess donations, it is possible that the excess may be so large that it will not be completely absorbed during the year of the contribution and the five-year carryover period. It is also possible that your income may drop in the future so that you cannot adequately take advantage of the excess.

Chapter 15

Itemized Deduction for Interest Expenses

On Schedule A of Form 1040, you may deduct three types of interest charges:

- Home mortgage interest
- Points
- Investment interest

These deductions are also subject to limitations:

- Home mortgage interest and points are subject to the 3% reduction of itemized deductions if your adjusted gross income (AGI) exceeds $137,300 ($68,650 for married persons filing separate returns).
- Investment interest is deductible only up to the amount of net investment income *(15.10)* but is not included in the 3% reduction computation. The 3% reduction rule is discussed at *13.7.*

Interest on personal loans (such as loans to buy autos and other personal items and credit card finance charges) is not deductible with the exception of qualifying student loan interest; *see* Chapter 38.

Interest on loans for business purposes is fully deductible on Schedule C. Interest on loans related to rental property is fully deductible from rental income on Schedule E. Whether interest is a business, investment, or a personal expense generally depends upon the use made of the money borrowed, not on the kind of property used to secure the loan. However, interest on a loan secured by a first or second home may be deductible as home equity mortgage interest regardless of the way you use the loan.

Interest on a loan used to finance an investment in a passive activity is subject to the limitations discussed in Chapter 10. However, if you rent out a second home that qualifies as a second residence, the portion of mortgage interest allocable to rental use is deductible as qualified mortgage interest and is not treated as a passive activity expense.

Home Mortgage Loans

15.1 Home Mortgage Interest

You generally may deduct on Schedule A (Form 1040) qualifying mortgage interest on up to two residences (*see* two-residence limit, below). However, if your 2002 adjusted gross income exceeds $137,300 ($68,650 if married filing separately), your mortgage interest deduction is subject to the 3% reduction of itemized deductions; *see 13.7.*

Mortgage loan obtained after October 13, 1987. Whether you can take a full mortgage interest deduction for a loan taken out after October 13, 1987, depends on the amount of the mortgage debt and how you use the proceeds. Loans used to buy, construct, or improve a first or second home are called *home acquisition loans*, and up to $1 million of such debt qualifies for a mortgage interest deduction, $500,000 if married filing separately. Loans used for any other purpose are called *home equity loans* by the tax law, and up to $100,000 of such debt qualifies for an interest deduction; the home equity limit is $50,000 for married persons filing separately.

Loan must be secured by residence. To deduct interest on a home acquisition or home equity loan, the loan must be secured by your main home or a second home. For the loan to be "secured," it must be recorded or satisfy similar requirements under state law. For example, if a relative gives you a loan to help you purchase a home, the relative must take the legal steps required to record the loan with local authorities; otherwise, you may not deduct interest on the loan. The IRS, in a private ruling, held that interest paid by a homeowners' association on a loan to rebuild the common area is not deductible by the individual homeowners where their residences are not pledged as collateral.

Home acquisition loans are further discussed at *15.2. Home equity loans* are discussed at *15.3.* If you *refinance your mortgage, see 15.7.*

Mortgage loan obtained before October 14, 1987. You may deduct all of the interest on a loan secured by a first or second home if the loan was obtained before October 14, 1987. Technically, such loans are considered home acquisition debt, but they are treated as "grandfathered debt," exempt from the $1 million loan limit ($500,000 for married persons filing separately).

However, the amount of your pre–October 14, 1987, loan reduces the $1 million (or $500,000) limit on home acquisition debt after October 13, 1987; *see 15.2.* It also reduces the fair market value limit for home equity debt; *see 15.3.* If you refinance your loan, *see 15.7.*

Two-residence limit for qualifying mortgage debt. The rules for deducting qualifying acquisition debt or home equity debt apply to loans secured by your principal residence and one other residence. A residence may be a condominium or cooperative unit, houseboat, mobile home, or house trailer that has sleeping, cooking, and toilet facilities. If you own more than two houses, you decide which residence will be considered your second residence. Interest debt secured by the second residence is deductible under the rules for acquisition debt *(15.2)* or home equity debt *(15.3).*

A residence that you rent out for any part of the year may be treated as a second residence only if you use it for personal nonrental purposes for more than the greater of 14 days or 10% of the rental days. In counting rental days, include days that the home is held out for rental or listed for resale. In counting days of personal use, use by close relatives generally qualifies as your personal use; *see 9.6.*

Interest on debt secured by a residence other than your principal or second home may still be deductible, if you use the proceeds for investment or business purposes; *see 15.12.*

Interest on mortgage credit certificates. Under special state and local programs, you may obtain a "mortgage credit certificate" to finance the purchase of a principal residence or to borrow funds for certain home improvements. Generally, a qualifying principal residence may not cost more than 90% of the average area purchase price, 110% in certain targeted areas. A tax credit for interest paid on the mortgage may be claimed. The credit is computed on Form 8396 and claimed on Line 52 of Form 1040. The credit equals the interest paid multiplied by the certificate rate set by the governmental authority, but the maximum annual credit is $2,000. If you claim the credit, your home mortgage interest deduction is reduced by the amount of the current year credit claimed on Form 8396.

 *Planning Reminder*

Home Acquisition Loan Limits
Interest is deductible on up to $1 million of home acquisition loans taken out after October 13, 1987 ($500,000 limit if married filing separately). Mortgage loans taken out before October 14, 1987, are not subject to the $1,000,000 (or $500,000) limit. However, outstanding loans from before October 14, 1987, reduce the $1 million (or $500,000) ceiling for post–October 13, 1987, loans.

 Planning Reminder

Mortgage Interest on a Third Home
Interest on debt secured by a residence *other than* your principal or second home may still be deductible, if you use the proceeds for investment or business purposes; *see 15.12.*

> **EXAMPLE**
>
> You pay $5,000 interest for a mortgage issued under a qualifying mortgage credit certificate. Under its terms, you are allowed a tax credit of $750. You may claim the balance of your mortgage interest, or $4,250 ($5,000 – $750), as an itemized deduction. If the allowable credit exceeds tax liability, a three-year carryover is allowed for the excess credit.

If you buy a home using a qualifying mortgage credit certificate and sell that home within nine years, you must recapture part of the tax credit on Form 8828.

15.2 Home Acquisition Loans

Under the mortgage interest rules, a qualifying "home acquisition loan" is a loan used to buy, build, or substantially improve your principal residence or second home, provided the debt is secured by that same residence.

Interest paid on such home acquisition loans is fully deductible if the total debt does not exceed $1,000,000, or $500,000 if you are married filing separately. The $1,000,000 (or $500,000) limit applies to acquisition loans taken out after October 13, 1987.

If your mortgages taken after October 13, 1987, exceed the $1,000,000 (or $500,000) limit, you must use IRS worksheets included in Publication 936 to figure the amount of your deductible interest. Furthermore, if you incurred substantial loans before October 14, 1987, and later purchase a new home, your deduction for the mortgage for the new home may be limited. The $1 million limit for acquisition debt after October 13, 1987, is reduced by the amount of outstanding pre–October 14, 1987, debt.

Although interest on a pre–October 14, 1987, debt is generally fully deductible regardless of the size of the loan, refinancing a pre–October 14, 1987, debt for more than the existing balance subjects the excess to the $1 million ceiling; *see 15.7.*

Generally, a debt qualifies as being incurred in buying, constructing, or improving a residence if you satisfy IRS tracing rules *(15.12)* that prove the use of the loan proceeds for such residential purposes. Even if you cannot prove under the tracing rules that a loan was used to buy a residence, a loan will be treated by the IRS as incurred for buying a home to the extent you can show acquisition expenses within 90 days before or 90 days after incurring the loan. Special construction loan and improvement loan rules are discussed in *15.4* and *15.5.*

Interest on a mortgage to buy or build a home other than your principal residence or qualifying second home is treated as nondeductible personal interest. If a nonqualifying home is rented out, the part of the mortgage interest that is allocable to the rental activity is treated as passive activity interest subject to the limitations discussed in Chapter 10; the interest allocable to your personal use is nondeductible personal interest.

A married couple filing jointly may designate as a second residence a home owned or used by either spouse.

If a married couple files separately, each spouse may generally deduct interest on debt secured by one residence. However, both spouses may agree in writing to allow one of them to deduct the interest on a principal residence plus a designated second residence.

Cooperatives. In the case of housing cooperatives, debt secured by stock as a tenant-stockholder is treated as secured by a residence. The cooperative should provide you with the proper amount of your deductible interest. If the stock cannot be used to secure the debt because of restrictions under local law or the cooperative agreement, the debt is still considered to be secured by the stock if the loan was used to buy the stock. For further details on allocation rules, *see* IRS Publication 936.

Line-of-credit mortgages. If you had a line-of-credit mortgage on your home on October 13, 1987, and you borrowed additional amounts on this line of credit after that date, the additional borrowed amounts are treated as a mortgage taken out after October 13, 1987. If the newly borrowed amounts are used to buy, build, or improve your first or second home, they are treated as home acquisition debt subject to the $1 million or $500,000 limit. If used for any other purpose, the amounts are subject to the home equity debt rules at *15.3.*

Mortgage interest paid after house destroyed. If your principal residence or second home *(15.1)* is destroyed and the land is sold within a reasonable period of time following the destruction, the IRS treats the property as a residence for purposes of deducting interest payments on the mortgage during the period between the destruction of the residence and the sale of the land. In one case, the IRS allowed the interest deduction where a sale of land took place 26 months after the destruction of a home by a tornado.

Court Decision

Family Financing of Residence

The Tax Court allowed a taxpayer to deduct mortgage interest payments on a loan that his brother obtained when the taxpayer's poor credit rating prevented him from obtaining a mortgage loan. The brother bought the house but allowed the taxpayer and his wife to live there on the condition that they make the mortgage payments directly to the bank.

The IRS disallowed the taxpayer's deduction for the mortgage interest on the grounds that he was not liable for the mortgage debt; his brother was. However, the Tax Court allowed the deduction, holding that the taxpayer was the equitable owner of the home and that he was legally obligated to his brother to pay off the mortgage.

If the destroyed residence is reconstructed and reoccupied within a reasonable period of time following the destruction, the property will continue to be treated as a residence during that period, and the interest payments on the mortgage on the property will be deductible. The IRS allowed an interest deduction where reconstruction began 18 months after, and was completed 34 months after, destruction of the home.

15.3 Home Equity Loans

For interest deduction purposes, qualifying home equity debt is the *lesser* of:

1. $100,000, or $50,000 if married filing separately, *or*
2. The fair market value of your principal residence and second home, reduced by the amount of acquisition debt *(15.2)* and by any "grandfathered" pre–October 14, 1987, mortgages *(15.1)*. According to the IRS, fair market value, acquisition debt, and grandfathered debt are determined on the date that the last debt was secured by the home.

The debt must be secured by your first or second home to qualify. If you have a second home as well as a principal residence, the above limitation under (1) and (2) applies to the total debt for both homes. Interest on a qualifying home equity loan is deductible regardless of the way you spend the proceeds, unless it is used to buy tax-exempt obligations *(15.11)*.

On loans exceeding the home equity debt limit, interest may be deductible if the proceeds are used for investment or business purposes. Otherwise, interest on the excess is nondeductible personal interest.

EXAMPLES

1. You bought your house for $200,000 subject to a mortgage of $150,000. When the mortgage principal is $120,000 and the fair market value of the house is $210,000, you take out a home equity loan. Interest on a home equity loan of up to $90,000 is fully deductible. Qualifying home equity debt may not exceed the difference between the fair market value of the house ($210,000) and the current acquisition debt ($120,000). If the value of the house exceeded $220,000, you could have borrowed up to the $100,000 limit as a qualifying home equity loan.
2. The fair market value of your house is $200,000 and the current mortgage is $160,000. You may deduct interest on a home equity loan of up to $40,000 ($200,000 – $160,000).

A loan may qualify partially as acquisition debt and partially as home equity debt where part of it is used to refinance an existing acquisition debt. The refinanced amount is still considered acquisition debt. Debt in excess of the refinanced amount is either home equity debt subject to the $100,000 ceiling or home acquisition debt subject to the $1 million ceiling, depending on the way the proceeds are used; *see 15.7*.

15.4 Home Construction Loans

Interest on a home construction loan may be fully deductible from the time construction begins for a period of up to 24 months while construction takes place. Within the 24-month period, the loan is considered acquisition debt subject to the $1 million ceiling *(15.2)*, provided that the home is a principal residence or second home when it is actually ready for occupancy. Furthermore, the loan proceeds must be directly traceable to home construction expenses, including the purchase of a lot, and the loan must be secured by the lot to be treated as acquisition debt. According to the IRS, if construction begins before a loan is incurred, the loan is treated as acquisition debt to the extent of construction expenses within the 24-month period *before* the loan. In determining when a loan is "incurred" for purposes of this 24-month rule, you can treat the date of a written loan application as the date the loan was "incurred," provided you receive the loan within 30 days after loan approval.

Interest incurred on the loan before construction begins is treated as nondeductible personal interest (*see* Example 1 on the next page). If construction lasts more than 24 months, interest after the 24-month period also is treated as nondeductible personal interest.

Interest on loans taken out within 90 days *after* construction is completed may qualify for a full deduction. The loan is treated as acquisition debt to the extent of construction expenses within the last 24 months before the residence was completed, plus expenses through the date of the loan (*see* Example 2 on the next page). For purposes of the 90-day rule, the loan proceeds generally are treated as received on the loan closing date. However, a debt may be considered "incurred" on the date a

Planning Reminder

Home Equity Loan To Pay Consumer Debts

Interest on consumer loans is not deductible, but you can use a home equity line-of-credit mortgage to pay off existing consumer debts and finance future consumer expenses. However, although interest on a home equity loan is fully deductible for regular tax purposes if within the $100,000 limit, the interest is not deductible for purposes of alternative minimum tax, unless the loan proceeds were used to improve your first or second home; *see 23.2*.

Filing Tip

Mortgage Fees Not Deductible

You may not deduct expenses incurred in obtaining a mortgage loan, such as loan assumption fees or costs of an appraisal or credit report.

written loan application is made, provided the loan proceeds are actually received within 30 days after loan approval. If a loan application is made within the 90-day period and it is rejected, and a new application with another lender is made within a reasonable time after the rejection, a loan from the second lender will be considered timely even if more than 90 days have passed since the end of construction.

EXAMPLES

1. On January 12, 2002, you borrow $100,000 to buy a residential lot. The loan is secured by the lot. You begin construction of a principal residence on January 1, 2003, and use $250,000 of your own funds for construction expenses. The residence is completed December 31, 2004.

   The interest paid in 2002 is nondeductible personal interest. It was paid before the 24-month qualifying construction period that started January 1, 2003, and ended December 31, 2004.

   Interest paid in 2003 and 2004 is fully deductible as the $100,000 loan is treated as acquisition debt for the 24-month construction period.

2. Same facts as in Example 1, but on March 17, 2005, you take out a $300,000 mortgage on the completed house to raise funds. You use $100,000 of the loan proceeds to pay off the $100,000 loan on the lot and keep the balance.

   All of the interest on the $300,000 loan is fully deductible because the loan qualifies as acquisition debt; $100,000 of the debt is treated as acquisition debt used for construction, since it was used to refinance the original 2002 debt to purchase the lot. The $200,000 balance is also treated as a construction loan under the 90-day rule. It was borrowed within 90 days after the residence was completed, and it reimbursed construction expenses of at least $200,000 incurred within 24 months before the completion date.

3. On January 12, 2002, you purchased a residential lot and began building a home on the lot using $45,000 of your personal funds. The home was completed on October 31, 2002. On November 24, 2002, you received a loan of $36,000 that was secured by the home. The debt may be treated as taken out to build the home as it was taken out no later than 90 days after the home was completed, and expenditures of at least $36,000 were made within the period of 24 months before the home was completed.

⚠ *Caution*

Mortgage Interest Reported on Form 1098

Banks and other lending institutions report mortgage interest payments of $600 or more to the IRS on Form 1098. You should receive a copy of Form 1098 or a similar statement by January 31, 2003, showing your mortgage payments in 2002. Deductible points *(15.8)* paid on the purchase of a principal home are included on Form 1098.

15.5 Home Improvement Loans

Loans used for substantial home improvements are treated as acquisition debt subject to the $1 million ceiling for loans after October 13, 1987; *see 15.2*. Include only the cost of home improvements that must be added to the basis of the property because they add to the value of the home or prolong useful life. Repair costs are not considered.

EXAMPLE

Your current acquisition mortgage is $100,000. You borrow $20,000 to build a new room. Your qualifying acquisition debt is now $120,000.

If substantial improvements to a home are begun but not completed before a loan is incurred, the loan will be treated as acquisition debt (assuming the debt is secured by the home) to the extent of improvement expenses made within 24 months before the loan. If the loan is incurred within 90 days after an improvement is completed, the loan is treated as acquisition debt (assuming the debt is secured by the home) to the extent of improvement expenses made within the period starting 24 months before completion of the improvement and ending on the date of the loan.

15.6 Mortgage Payment Rules

Payments to the bank or lending institution holding your mortgage may include interest, principal payments, taxes, and fire insurance premiums. Deduct only interest and tax payments. You may not deduct the payments of mortgage principal and insurance premiums.

In the year you sell your home, check your settlement papers for interest charged up to the date of sale; this amount is deductible.

Mortgage credit. If you qualify for the special tax credit for interest on qualified home mortgage certificates, you only deduct interest in excess of the allowable credit; *see 15.1.*

Jointly owned property. When mortgaged property is jointly owned, a joint owner who pays the entire interest charge may deduct the amount of the entire payment.

Prepayment penalty. A penalty for prepayment of a mortgage is deductible as interest.

Mortgage assistance payments. You may not deduct interest paid on your behalf under Section 235 of the National Housing Act.

Delinquency charges for late payment. According to the IRS, a late payment charge is deductible as mortgage interest if it was not for a specific service provided by the mortgage holder. In one case, the Tax Court agreed with the IRS that delinquency charges imposed by a bank were not interest where they were a flat percentage of the installment due, regardless of how late payment was. The late charges were primarily imposed by the bank to recoup costs related to collection efforts, such as telephone calls, letters, and supervisory reviews. They were also intended to discourage untimely payments by imposing a penalty.

Graduated payment mortgages. Monthly payments are initially smaller than under the standard mortgage on the same amount of principal, but payments increase each year over the first five- or 10-year period and continue at the increased monthly amount for the balance of the mortgage term. As a cash-basis taxpayer, you deduct the amount of interest actually paid even though, during the early years of the mortgage, payments are less than the interest owed on the loan. The unpaid interest is added to the loan principal, and future interest is figured on the increased unpaid mortgage loan balance. The bank, in a year-end statement, will identify the amount of interest actually paid. (An accrual-basis taxpayer may deduct the accrued interest each year.)

Reverse mortgage loan. Homeowners who own their homes outright may in certain states cash in on their equity by taking a "reverse mortgage loan." Typically, 80% of the value of the home is paid by a bank to a homeowner in a lump sum or in installments. Principal is due when the home is sold or when the homeowner dies; interest is added to the loan and is payable when the principal is paid. The IRS has ruled that an interest deduction may be claimed by a cash-basis home-owner only when the interest is paid, not when the interest is added to the outstanding loan balance.

Shared appreciation mortgage. Under a shared appreciation mortgage (SAM) for a personal residence, the lender agrees to charge a fixed rate of interest that is lower than the prevailing market rate. In return, the homeowner promises to pay a percentage of the appreciation on the property at a later date to make up the difference. The fixed-rate interest is deductible when paid and the percentage of appreciation is also treated as interest that you can deduct in the year of payment, subject to the limits discussed at *15.2*. For example, you agree to pay interest of 9% plus 40% of the appreciation in the value of the property within 10 years or earlier if you sell the home or pay off the mortgage. If, at the end of 10 years, the residence is not sold or the loan repaid, you may refinance at the prevailing rate the outstanding balance plus the interest based on the appreciation. If you refinance with the same lender, you may not claim an immediate deduction for the extra interest. The execution of a note is not considered payment. The amount covering the extra interest is deducted ratably over the period of the new loan. If you refinance with another lender and use the funds to pay off the old loan plus the extra interest, the extra interest is deductible in the year of payment, subject to the limits of *15.2*.

Redeemable ground rents. In a ground rent arrangement, you lease rather than buy the land on which your home is located. Ground rent is deductible as mortgage interest if: (1) the land you lease is for a term exceeding 15 years (including renewal periods) and is freely assignable; (2) you have a present or future right to end the lease and buy the entire interest; and (3) the lessor's interest in the land is primarily a security interest. Payments to end the lease and buy the lessor's interest are not deductible ground rents.

15.7 Interest on Refinanced Loans

When you refinance a mortgage on a first or second home *(15.1)* for the same amount as the remaining principal balance on the old loan, there is no change in the tax treatment of interest. In other words, if interest was fully deductible on the old loan, then it is fully deductible on the new loan.

If you refinance a home mortgage for more than the existing balance, the deductibility of interest on the excess amount depends upon how you use the funds and the amount of refinancing. If

 Filing Tip

Joint Liability on Mortgage
If you do not personally receive a Form 1098 but a person (other than your spouse with whom you file a joint return) who is also liable for and paid interest on the mortgage received a Form 1098, you deduct your share of the interest and attach a statement to your Schedule A showing the name and address of the person who received the form. If you are the payer of record on a mortgage on which there are other borrowers entitled to a deduction for the interest shown on the Form 1098 you received, provide them with information on their share of the deductible amount.

the excess amount is used to buy, build, or substantially improve your first or second home, then it is considered home acquisition debt; *see 15.2.* If the excess plus all other home acquisition loans does not exceed $1 million ($500,000 if married filing separately), the interest is fully deductible. If the excess is used for any other purpose, such as to pay off credit card debt or to finance a child's education, the excess is considered home equity debt; *see 15.3.* If the excess plus all other home equity loans does not exceed $100,000 ($50,000 if married filing separately), the interest is fully deductible. If the refinanced loan is partly home acquisition debt and partly home equity debt, the overall limit of $1.1 million applies ($1 million home acquisition debt and $100,000 home equity debt) or, if married filing separately, $550,000 ($500,000 home acquisition debt and $50,000 home equity debt).

Interest paid on loans in excess of home acquisition and home equity debt ceilings is generally treated as nondeductible personal interest unless the proceeds are used for business or investment purposes; *see 15.12.*

EXAMPLE

In 1997, Robert and Michelle Stein purchased a home for $250,000. They put $50,000 down and obtained a $200,000, 30-year mortgage secured by the home. In 2002, when their house is worth $300,000 and there is a $175,000 principal balance on the mortgage, they refinance to take advantage of lower interest rates. The refinanced mortgage is for $225,000, payable over 20 years. The Steins use $175,000 to pay off the old mortgage, $30,000 to purchase a car and to pay off credit card debt, and the remaining $20,000 to build a new deck on their home.

The interest on up to $175,000 of the debt incurred to pay off the old mortgage is fully deductible; the amount equals the outstanding balance before refinancing and also falls within the $1 million home acquisition debt ceiling. The $20,000 used to remodel the house is also treated as home acquisition debt. Interest on this amount is fully deductible; the amount falls within the $1 million ceiling when added to the $175,000.

The $30,000 used to buy a car and pay off credit cards is treated as home equity debt. Interest on this amount is fully deductible; the amount falls within the $100,000 ceiling.

Pre–October 14, 1987, loans. Refinanced pre–October 14, 1987, loans are not subject to the $1 million home acquisition and $100,000 home equity debt ceilings during the period of the original loan term. However, after the end of the original loan term, the ceilings apply to the refinanced amount as explained above. Furthermore, where a refinanced pre–October 14, 1987, debt exceeds the remaining principal balance, the excess is also subject to the $1 million home acquisition and $100,000 home equity debt ceilings.

Points Paid on Refinancing

The IRS does not allow a current deduction for points on a refinanced mortgage. According to the IRS, the points must be deducted ratably over the loan period, unless part of the new loan is used for home improvements. Thus, if you pay points of $2,400 when refinancing a 20-year loan on your principal residence, the IRS allows you to deduct only $10 a month, or $120 each full year.

A federal appeals court rejected the IRS allocation rule where points are paid on a long-term mortgage that replaces a short-term loan; *see* the Court Decision on this page.

If part of a refinancing is used for home improvements to a principal residence, the IRS allows a deduction for a portion of the points allocable to the home improvements.

EXAMPLE

In June 2002, Craig Smith refinances his home mortgage, which has a principal of $80,000 outstanding. The new loan is for $100,000, payable over 15 years starting in July 2002. He uses $80,000 to pay off the old $80,000 balance and the remaining $20,000 is used for home improvements. Assume that at the closing of the new loan, Smith pays points of $2,000 from his separate funds. In the year of payment he may deduct $400 allocable to the 20% of the loan used for home improvements. He may also deduct the ratable portion of the $1,600 balance of the points, which must be deducted over the period of the new loan. The ratable portion is $53 ($1,600 ÷ 180-month loan term × 6 months in 2002). Thus, Craig's total deduction for points in 2002 is $453 ($400 + $53).

Court Decision

Current Deduction for Points on Refinancing

Huntsman replaced a three-year loan used to purchase his principal residence with a 30-year mortgage. He deducted $4,400 of points paid on the new mortgage. The IRS and the Tax Court held that the points had to be deducted over the 30-year loan term.

The Federal Appeals Court for the Eighth Circuit disagreed and allowed a full deduction in the year the points were paid. The first loan was temporary and merely a step in obtaining permanent financing for the purchase of the principal residence.

The IRS has announced that in areas outside of the Eighth Circuit, it will continue to disallow full deductions in the year of payment for points paid on refinancings. The Eighth Circuit includes only these states: Minnesota, Iowa, North and South Dakota, Nebraska, Missouri, and Arkansas. In these states, the IRS will not challenge deductions for points on refinancing agreements similar to Huntsman's that replace short-term financing with long-term permanent financing.

In a later case, the Tax Court held that the *Huntsman* exception does not apply where a borrower refinances a long-term mortgage to take advantage of lower interest rates; the points must be deducted over the term of the new mortgage.

Mortgage ends early. If you are ratably deducting points on a refinanced loan and you refinance again, or the mortgage ends early because you prepay it or the lender forecloses, you can deduct the remaining points in the year the mortgage ends.

15.8 "Points"

Lenders sometimes charge "points" in addition to the stated interest rate. The points increase the lender's upfront fees, but in return borrowers generally are charged a lower interest rate over the loan term. Points are either treated as a type of prepaid interest *(15.14)* or as a nondeductible service fee, depending on what the charge covers. If the points qualify as interest, they are deductible over the term of the loan unless they are paid on the purchase or improvement of your principal residence, in which case they are deductible in the year they are paid, as discussed below. If you pay points on a loan to purchase or improve a second home, you must deduct the points ratably over the term of the loan.

Points are treated as interest if your payment is solely for your use of the money and is not for specific services performed by the lender that are separately charged. Whether a payment is called "points" or a "loan origination fee" does not affect its deductibility if it is actually a charge for the use of money. The purpose of the charge—that is, for the use of the money or the services rendered—will be controlling. For example, you may not deduct points that are fees for services, such as appraisal fees, preparation of a mortgage note or deed of trust, settlement fees, notary fees, abstract fees, commissions, and recording fees.

If you are *selling* property and you assume the buyer's liability for points, do not deduct the payment as interest but include it as a selling expense that reduces the amount realized on the sale.

Deduction for Points on Purchase or Improvement of Principal Residence

Points are generally treated as prepaid interest *(15.14)* that must be deducted over the period of the loan. However, there is an exception for points you pay on a loan to buy, build, or improve your principal residence. The points on such loans are deductible in the year paid if these tests are met: (1) the loan is secured by your principal residence; (2) the charging of points is an established business practice in the geographic area in which the loan is made; (3) the points charged do not exceed the points generally charged in the area; (4) the amount of points is computed as a percentage of the loan and specifically earmarked on the loan closing statement as "points," "loan origination fees," or "loan discount"; and (5) you pay the points directly to the lender; *see* "Points withheld from the principal," below.

Points paid by seller are deductible by buyer. The seller's payment is treated as an adjustment to the purchase price that the seller gives to you as the buyer and that you then turn over to the lender to pay off the points. You must reduce your cost basis for the home by the seller-paid points.

Points withheld from the principal. Points withheld from the principal of a loan used to buy your principal residence are treated as if you paid them directly to the lender if, at or before closing, you have made a down payment, escrow deposit, or earnest money payment that is at least equal to the amount of points withheld. These payments must have been from your own funds and not from funds that have been borrowed from the lender as part of the overall transaction.

If the loan is used to *improve* your principal residence, the points are not immediately deductible if withheld from the loan principal. You must pay the points with funds that have not been obtained from the lender to claim the full deduction in the year of payment. Otherwise, the deduction must be spread over the loan term.

Points on second home. If you pay points on a mortgage secured by a second home or a vacation home, the points are not fully deductible in the year of payment; you must claim the deduction ratably over the loan term.

Points paid on refinancing. The IRS does not allow a current deduction for points on a refinanced mortgage (*see 15.7* for further information).

Deduct balance of points if mortgage ends early. If you are deducting points over the term of the loan because a full first-year deduction is not allowed, you are allowed to deduct the balance in the year the mortgage ends, such as when you refinance or prepay the loan, or the lender forecloses. For example, if you refinanced your mortgage in 1997 and paid points, those points had to be amortized over the loan term *(15.7)*. If in 2002 you refinance again and pay points again, the balance of the points from the 1997 loan are deductible on your 2002 return, and the points on the new loan must be amortized over the loan term.

Caution

Service Fees Are Not Deductible Points

You may not deduct as points amounts that are for specific lender services. To be deductible, points on the purchase of a principal residence must be prepaid interest for the use of the loan money.

Filing Tip

Amortize Points Starting in Second Year

A married couple purchased a principal residence and paid points late in the year. For the year of the purchase, their standard deduction exceeded their itemized deductions. The IRS ruled that claiming the standard deduction for the year the points are paid would not entirely forfeit the deduction for points. The points may be amortized starting in the second year. Assuming that they itemize deductions starting in the second year, the allocable portion of the points may be deducted each year over the remaining loan term.

Caution

Points Reported to the IRS

Points you paid in 2002 on the purchase of your principal residence will be reported to the IRS by the lender on Form 1098 if they meet the five tests explained earlier. Seller-paid points are also included on Form 1098. Form 1098 is used by the IRS to check on the deduction you claim for points on Line 10 of Schedule A. Points paid on an improvement loan for your principal residence are deductible on Line 12 of Schedule A if they meet the tests; they are not shown on Form 1098.

15.9 Cooperative and Condominium Apartments

Cooperative apartments. If you are a tenant-stockholder of a cooperative apartment, you may deduct your portion of:

- Interest paid by the cooperative on its debts, provided you do not pay interest on more than two residences; *see 15.1.* This includes your pro rata share of the permanent financing expenses (points) of the cooperative on its mortgage covering the housing project.
- Taxes paid by the cooperative *(16.6).* However, if the cooperative does not own the land and building but merely leases them and is required to pay real estate taxes under the terms of the lease, you may not deduct your share of the tax payment.

In some localities, such as New York City, rent control rules allow tenants of a building converted to a cooperative to remain in their apartments even if they do not buy into the co-op. A holdover tenant may prevent some co-op purchasers from occupying an apartment. The IRS ruled that the fact that a holdover tenant stays in the apartment will not bar the owner from deducting his or her share of the co-op's interest and taxes.

Condominiums. If you own an apartment in a condominium, you have a direct ownership interest in the property and are treated, for tax purposes, just as any other property owner. You may deduct your payments of real estate taxes and mortgage interest. You may also deduct taxes and interest paid on the mortgage debt of the project allocable to your share of the property. The deduction of interest from condominium ownership is also subject to the two-residence limit discussed at *15.1.* If your condominium is used part of the time for rental purposes, you may deduct expenses of maintenance and repairs and claim depreciation deductions subject to the rules in *9.7.*

Investment Loans

15.10 Investment Interest Limitations

Interest paid on margin accounts and debts to buy or carry other investments is deductible up to the amount of net investment income on Schedule A. If you do not have investment income such as interest, you may not deduct investment interest. Investment interest in excess of net investment income may be carried forward and deducted from next year's net investment income.

You compute the deduction for investment interest on Form 4952, which must be attached to Form 1040. The deduction is *not* subject to the 3% reduction of itemized deductions if your adjusted gross income exceeds $137,300 ($68,650 if married filing separately); *see 13.7.*

What is investment interest? It is all interest paid or accrued on debts incurred or continued to buy or carry investment property such as interest on securities in a margin account. However, interest on loans to buy tax-exempt securities is not deductible; *see 15.11.*

Investment interest does not include any qualified residence interest *(15.1),* production period interest that is capitalized *(16.4),* or interest related to a passive activity *(10.8).*

Investment property includes property producing portfolio income (interest, dividends, or royalties not realized in the ordinary course of business) under the passive activity rules discussed in Chapter 10, and property in activities that are not treated as passive activities, even if you do not materially participate, such as working interests in oil and gas wells.

Passive activity interest is not investment interest. Interest expenses incurred in a passive activity such as rental real estate *(10.1),* or a limited partnership or S corporation in which you do not materially participate *(10.6),* are taken into account on Form 8582 when figuring net passive income or loss. This includes interest incurred on loans used to finance your investment in a passive activity. Do not treat passive activity interest as investment interest on Form 4952.

However, interest expenses allocable to *portfolio* income (non–business activity interest, dividends, or royalties) from a limited partnership or S corporation are investment interest and not passive interest. The investment interest will be listed separately on Schedule K-1 received from the partnership or corporation.

Computing the Deduction

Deductible investment interest is limited to net investment income. Net investment income is the excess of investment income over investment expenses. The key terms *investment income* and *investment expenses* are defined below.

 Caution

Interest on Loans To Buy Market Discount Bonds and Treasury Bills

Limits apply to the deduction for interest on loans used to buy or carry market discount bonds *(4.20)* and Treasury bills *(4.27)* acquired after July 18, 1984.

Investment income. Investment income is generally gross income from property held for investment, such as interest, dividends, annuities, and royalties. Income or expenses considered in figuring profit or loss of a passive activity *(10.8)* is not considered investment income or expenses. Property subject to a net lease is not treated as investment property, as it is within the passive activity rules.

If you have net capital gains (net long-term capital gains exceeding net short-term losses) from the sale of investment property such as stocks or mutual-fund shares, such gains are not treated as investment income unless you specifically elect to include them in investment income on Form 4952. If you make this election, you may not apply preferential capital gain rates *(5.3)* to the amount of the net capital gains treated as investment interest on Form 4952. If you make the election on Form 4952, the elected amount is subtracted from net capital gains when applying the capital gain tax rates on Part IV of Schedule D. *See* the IRS instructions to Form 4952.

Investment expenses. There are expenses, other than interest, directly connected with the production of investment income. However, for purposes of determining net investment income, only those investment expenses (other than interest) allowable after figuring the 2% floor for miscellaneous itemized deductions *(19.24)* are taken into account. The 2% floor will bar a deduction for some of the miscellaneous itemized deductions. For purposes of this net investment income computation, assume that miscellaneous itemized deductions other than investment expenses are disallowed first.

Net investment income. Reducing investment income by investment expenses gives you net investment income. Your deduction for investment interest expenses is limited to this amount; any excess interest expense for 2002 may be carried over to 2003, as discussed below.

Where to enter the deduction on your return. The deduction figured on Form 4952 is generally entered on Line 13 of Schedule A as investment interest. However, if the interest is attributable to royalties, you may have to enter the interest on Schedule E; follow the Form 4952 instructions. Furthermore, there is an additional complication if you have investment interest for an activity for which you are not "at risk" *(10.18)*. After figuring the investment interest deduction on Form 4952, you must enter the portion of the interest that is attributable to the at-risk activity on Form 6198. The amount carried over to Form 6198 is subtracted from the investment interest deduction claimed on Form 4952.

Carryover to 2003 and future years. Investment interest in excess of net investment income for 2002 may be carried forward to 2003 and is deductible in 2003 to the extent that when added to 2003 investment interest expenses it does not exceed net investment income. If not used in 2003, the carryforward extends indefinitely to 2004 and future years.

Caution

Electing To Treat Long-Term Gains as Investment Income
If you elect on Form 4952 to treat net capital gains as investment income in order to increase your 2002 investment interest deduction, that amount of gain is not taken into account when applying capital gain rates in Part IV of Schedule D.

EXAMPLE

For 2002, Larry Jones has $10,000 of investment income from interest and dividends. He has investment expenses, other than interest, of $3,200, after taking into account the 2% floor on miscellaneous itemized deductions. His investment interest expense from securities margin account loans is $8,000. Jones also has income of $2,000 from a passive partnership investment.

Jones's net investment income is $6,800: $10,000 of investment income less $3,200 of non-interest investment expenses. The passive activity income from the partnership is not included in investment income.

Jones's investment interest deduction for 2002 is limited to the $6,800 of net investment income. The $1,200 of investment interest in excess of net investment income ($8,000 – $6,800) is carried forward to 2003.

15.11 Debts To Carry Tax-Exempt Obligations

When you borrow money in order to buy or carry tax-exempt bonds, you may not deduct any interest paid on your loan. Application of this disallowance rule is clear where there is actual evidence that loan proceeds were used to buy tax-exempts or that tax-exempts were used as collateral. But sometimes the relationship between a loan and the purchase of tax-exempts is less obvious, as where you hold tax-exempts and borrow to carry other securities or investments. IRS guidelines explain when a direct relationship between the debt and an investment in tax-exempts will be inferred so that no interest deduction is allowed. The IRS will *not* infer a direct relationship between a debt and an investment in tax-exempts in these cases:

Caution

Tax-Exempt Income From Mutual Fund

You may not deduct interest on loans used to buy or carry tax-exempt securities. If you receive exempt-interest dividends from a mutual fund during the year, you may deduct interest on a loan used to buy or carry the mutual-fund shares only to the extent that the proceeds can be allocated to taxable dividends you also receive.

1. The investment in tax-exempts is not substantial. That is, it is not more than 2% of the adjusted basis of the investment portfolio and any assets held in an actively conducted business.

2. The debt is incurred for a personal purpose. For example, an investor may take out a home mortgage instead of selling his tax-exempts and using the proceeds to finance the home purchase. Interest on the mortgage is deductible under the rules at *15.1*.

3. The debt is incurred in connection with the active conduct of a business and does not exceed business needs. But if a person reasonably could have foreseen when the tax-exempts were purchased that he or she would have to borrow funds to meet ordinary and recurrent business needs, the interest expenses are not deductible.

The guidelines infer a direct relationship between the debt and an investment in tax-exempts in this type of case: An investor in tax-exempts has outstanding debts not directly related to personal expenses or to his or her business. The interest will be disallowed even if the debt appears to have been incurred to purchase other portfolio investments. Portfolio investments include transactions entered into for profit, including investments in real estate, that are not connected with the active conduct of a business; *see* the Example below.

> **EXAMPLE**
>
> An investor owning $360,000 in tax-exempt bonds purchased real estate in a joint venture, giving a purchase money mortgage and cash for the price. He deducted interest on the mortgage. The IRS disallowed the deduction, claiming the debt was incurred to carry tax-exempts. A court allowed the deduction. A mortgage is the customary manner of financing such a purchase. Furthermore, since the purchase was part of a joint venture, the other parties' desires in the manner of financing had to be considered.

15.12 Earmarking Use of Loan Proceeds

The IRS has set down complex record keeping and allocation rules for claiming interest deductions on loans used for business or investment purposes, or for passive activities. The rules deal primarily with the use of loan proceeds for more than one purpose and the commingling of loan proceeds in an account with unborrowed funds. The thrust of the rules is to base deductibility of interest on the *use* of the borrowed funds. The allocation rules do not affect mortgage interest deductions on loans secured by a qualifying first or second home; *see 15.1*.

Keep separate accounts for business, personal, and investment borrowing. For example, if you borrow for investment purposes, keep the proceeds of the loan in a separate account and use the proceeds only for investment purposes. Do not use the funds to pay for personal expenses; interest is not deductible on personal loans other than qualifying student loans (Chapter 38). Furthermore, do not deposit loan proceeds in an account funded with unborrowed money, unless you intend to use the proceeds within 30 days of the deposit. By following these directions, you can identify your use of the proceeds with a specific expenditure, such as for investment, personal, or business purposes, and the interest on the loan may be treated as incurred for that purpose. The 30-day rule is discussed below.

The IRS treats undisbursed loan proceeds deposited in an account as investment property, even though the account does not bear interest. When proceeds are disbursed from the account, the use of the proceeds determines how interest is treated; *see* Examples 1 and 2 on the following page.

30-day disbursement rule. If you deposit borrowed funds in an account with unborrowed funds, a special 30-day rule allows you to treat payments from the account as made from the loan proceeds. Where you make more than one disbursement from such an account, you may treat any expenses paid within 30 days before or after deposit of the loan proceeds as if made from the loan proceeds. Thus, you may allocate interest on the loan to that disbursement, even if earlier payments from the account have been made; *see* Example 3 on the next page. If you make the disbursement after 30 days, the IRS requires you to allocate interest on the loan to the first disbursement; *see* Example 4 on the following page. Furthermore, if an account includes only loan proceeds and interest earned on the proceeds, disbursements may be allocated first to the interest income and then to the loan proceeds.

Allocation period. Interest is allocated to an expenditure for the period *beginning* on the date the loan proceeds are used or treated as used and *ending* on the earlier of either the date the debt is repaid or the date it is reallocated.

Accrued interest is treated as a debt until it is paid, and any interest accruing on unpaid interest is allocated in the same manner as the unpaid interest is allocated. Compound interest accruing on such debt, other than compound interest accruing on interest that accrued before the beginning of the year, may be allocated between the original expenditure and any new expenditure from the same account on a straight-line basis. That is done by allocating an equal amount of such interest expense to each day during the taxable year. In addition, you may treat a year as *twelve 30-day months* for purposes of allocating interest on a straight-line basis.

Payments from a checking account. A disbursement from a checking account is treated as made at the time the check is written on the account, provided the check is delivered or mailed to the payee within a reasonable period after the writing of the check. You may treat checks written on the same day as written in any order. A check is presumed to be written on the date appearing on the check and to be delivered or mailed to the payee within a reasonable period thereafter. However, the presumption may not apply if the check does not clear within a reasonable period after the date appearing on the check.

Change in use of property. You must reallocate interest if you convert debt-financed property to a different use; for example, when you buy a business auto with an installment loan, interest paid on the auto is business interest, but if during the year you convert the auto to personal use, interest paid after the conversion is personal interest.

Order of repayment. If you used loan proceeds to repay several different kinds of debt, the debts being repaid are assumed to be repaid in the following order: (1) personal debt; (2) investment debt and passive activity debt other than active real estate debt; (3) debt from a real estate activity in which you actively participate; (4) former passive activity debt; and (5) business debt. *See* Example 5 below. Payments made on the same day may be treated as made in any order.

Keep Loans Separate

To safeguard your investment and business interest deductions, you must earmark and keep a record of your loans. You should avoid using loan proceeds to fund different types of expenditures.

EXAMPLES

1. On January 1, you borrow $10,000 and deposit the proceeds in a non–interest-bearing checking account. No other amounts are deposited in the account during the year and no part of the loan is repaid during the year. On April 1, you invest $2,000 of the proceeds in a real estate venture. On September 1, you use $4,000 to buy furniture.

   From January 1 through March 31, interest on the entire undisbursed $10,000 is treated as investment interest. From April 1 through August 31, interest on $2,000 of the debt is treated as passive activity interest and interest on $8,000 of the debt is treated as investment interest. From September 1 through December 31, interest on $4,000 of the debt is treated as personal interest; interest on $2,000 is treated as passive activity interest; and interest on $4,000 is treated as investment interest.

2. On September 1, you borrow money for business purposes and deposit it in a checking account. On October 15, you disburse the proceeds for business purposes. Interest incurred on the loan before the disbursement of the funds is treated as investment interest expense. Interest starting on October 15 is treated as business interest. However, you may elect to treat the starting date for business interest as of the first of the month in which the disbursement was made—that is, October 1—provided all other disbursements from the account during the same month are similarly treated.

3. On September 1, you borrow $5,000 to invest in stock and deposit the proceeds in your regular checking account. On September 10, you buy a TV and stereo for $2,500 and on September 11 invest $5,000 in stock, using funds from the account. As the stock investment was made within 30 days of depositing the loan proceeds in the account, interest on the entire loan is treated as incurred for investment purposes.

4. Same facts as in Example 3, but the TV and stereo were bought on October 1 and the stock on October 31. As the stock investment was not made within 30 days, the IRS requires you to treat the purchase of the TV and the stereo for $2,500 as the first purchase made with the loan proceeds of $5,000. Thus, the 50% of loan interest that is allocated to the stereo purchase is nondeductible.

5. On July 12, Smith borrows $100,000 and immediately deposits the proceeds in an account. He uses the proceeds as follows:

August 31	$40,000 for passive activity
October 5	$20,000 for rental activity
December 24	$40,000 for personal use

Using Borrowed Funds To Pay Interest

To get an interest deduction you must pay the interest; you may not claim a deduction by having the creditor add the interest to the debt. If you do not have funds to pay the interest, you may borrow money to pay the interest. The borrowed funds must be from a different creditor. The IRS disallows deductions where a debtor borrows from the same creditor to make interest payments on an earlier loan. The second loan is considered a device for getting an interest expense deduction without actually making payments. The Tax Court and several federal appeals courts have sided with the IRS.

On January 19 of the following year, Smith repays $90,000. Of the repayment, $40,000 is allocated as a repayment of the personal expenditure, $40,000 of the passive activity, and $10,000 of the rental activity. The outstanding $10,000 is treated as debt incurred in a rental activity.

Timing of Interest Deductions

15.13 Year To Claim an Interest Deduction

As a cash-basis taxpayer, you deduct interest in the year of payment except for prepayments of interest; *see 15.14*. Giving a promissory note is not considered payment. Increasing the amount of a loan by interest owed, as with insurance loans, is also not considered payment and will not support a deduction. If a person pays your interest obligation with the understanding you will repay him or her, you take the deduction in the year the interest is paid, not when you repay him or her. However, an accrual-basis taxpayer generally deducts interest in the year the interest accrues; *see 40.3*.

Here is how a cash-basis taxpayer treats interest in the following situations:

On a life insurance loan, where proceeds are used for a deductible (nonpersonal) purpose, you claim a deduction in the year in which the interest is paid. You may not claim a deduction when the insurance company adds the interest to your debt. You may not deduct your payment of interest on an insurance loan after you assign the policy.

On a margin account with a broker, interest is deductible in the year in which it is paid or your account is credited after the interest has been charged. But an interest charge to your account is not payment if you do not pay it in cash or the broker has not collected dividends, interest, or security sales proceeds that may be applied against the interest due. Note that the interest deduction on margin accounts is subject to investment interest limitations; *see 15.10*.

For partial payment of a loan used for a deductible (nonpersonal) purpose, interest is deductible in the year the payment is credited against interest due. When a loan has no provision for allocating payments between principal and income, the law presumes that a partial payment is applied first to interest and then to principal, unless you agree otherwise. Where the payment is in full settlement of the debt, the payment is applied first to principal, unless you agree otherwise. Where there is an involuntary payment, such as that following a foreclosure sale of collateral, sales proceeds are applied first to principal, unless you agree to the contrary. *See also 15.12* for the effect of payments on the allocation of debt proceeds.

Note renewed. You may not deduct interest by merely giving a new note. You claim a deduction in the year the renewed note is paid. The giving of a new note or increasing the amount due is not payment. The same is true when past due interest is deducted from the proceeds of a new loan; this is not a payment of the interest.

15.14 Prepaid Interest

If you prepay interest on a loan used for *investment* or *business* purposes you may not deduct interest allocable to any period falling in a later taxable year. The prepaid interest must be deducted over the period of the loan, whether you are a cash-basis or accrual-basis taxpayer.

Points paid on the purchase of a *principal residence* are generally fully deductible in the year paid; *see 15.8*. Points paid on refinancing generally are not deductible; *see 15.7*.

Treatment of interest included in a level payment schedule. Where payments of principal and interest are equal, a large amount of interest allocated to the payments made in early years of a loan will generally not be considered prepaid interest. However, if the loan calls for a variable interest rate, the IRS may treat interest payments as consisting partly of interest, computed under an average level effective rate, and partly of prepaid interest allocable to later years of the loan. An interest rate that varies with the "prime rate" does not necessarily indicate a prepaid interest element.

Planning Reminder

Business Investment Loans
If you prepay business or investment loan interest, you must spread the interest deduction over the period of the loan. In the year of payment, you may deduct only the interest allocable to that year.

When you borrow money for a deductible purpose and give a note to the lender, the amount of your loan proceeds may be less than the face value of the note. The difference between the proceeds and the face amount is interest discount. For loans that do not fall within the OID rules in *4.18*, such as loans of a year or less, interest is deductible in the year of payment if you are on the cash basis. If you use the accrual basis, the interest is deductible as it accrues.

EXAMPLE

In February 2001, you borrow $1,000 for an investment and receive $900 in return for your $1,000 note. You repay the full loan in January 2002. You are on the cash basis. You do not deduct the interest of $100 when the note is given. The $100 interest is treated as investment interest *(15.10)* when the loan is paid in 2002.

For loans that fall within OID rules, your lender should provide a statement showing the interest element and the tax treatment of the interest.

Chapter 16

Deductions for Taxes

If you itemize deductions on Schedule A, you may deduct your 2002 payments of state, local, and foreign income taxes and real property taxes, as well as state and local personal property taxes. State and local sales taxes are not deductible.

To increase your deduction for state and local taxes, consider making a year-end prepayment of estimated tax liability. You also may be able to increase withholdings from your pay to increase your deduction.

If you pay transfer taxes on the sale of securities or investment real estate, the taxes are not deductible. However, they increase your cost basis when figuring your profit or loss.

Taxes paid in operating a business are generally deductible, except for sales taxes, which are added to the cost of the property.

Taxes claimed as itemized deductions are subject to the 3% reduction of itemized deductions if your adjusted gross income exceeds $137,300, or $68,650 if married filing separately; *see 13.7*.

16.1 Deductible Taxes

If you itemize deductions for 2002 on Schedule A, you may deduct your 2002 payments of:

- State, local, and foreign income taxes
- State, local, and foreign real property taxes
- State and local personal property taxes

In figuring deductible state or local income taxes, include the amount of state or local income tax withheld from your 2002 pay, any state or local estimated tax you paid in 2002, and any part of a prior year refund that you credited to your 2002 state or local tax. Also, do not forget to include tax that you paid in 2002 when you filed your 2001 state and local tax returns.

Taxes incurred in your business are generally deductible on Schedule C; see 16.11.

If your 2002 adjusted gross income exceeds $137,300, or $68,650 if married filing separately, your deduction for taxes is subject to the 3% reduction computation explained at 13.7.

Claim the deduction for deductible taxes on the tax return for the year in which you paid the taxes, unless you report on the accrual basis; see 16.8.

 Filing Tip

State Tax Paid in 2002

In figuring your 2002 itemized deduction for state and local income taxes paid, remember to include tax that you paid in 2002 when you filed your 2001 state and local tax returns.

Checklist of Taxes

Type of tax—	Deductible as itemized deduction—
Admission	No
Alcoholic beverage	No
Assessments for local benefits	No
Automobile license fees not qualifying as personal property tax	No
Cigarette	No
Customs duties	No
Driver's license	No
Estate—federal or state	No*
Excise—federal or state, for example, on telephone service	No
Gasoline—federal	No
Gasoline and other motor fuel—state and local	No
Gift taxes—federal and state	No
Income—federal (including alternative minimum tax)	No
Income—state, local, or foreign	Yes
Inheritance tax	No
Mortgage tax	No
Personal property—state or local	Yes
Poll	No
Real estate (state, local, or foreign)	Yes
Regulatory license fees (dog licenses, parking meter fees, hunting and fishing licenses)	No
Sales and use tax on personal property	No
Social Security	No
Tolls	No
Transfer taxes on securities and real estate	No

* But *see 11.17* for miscellaneous itemized deduction for estate tax paid on "income in respect of a decedent."

16.2 Nondeductible Taxes

Sales taxes on personal property are not deductible as itemized deductions. Transfer taxes paid on the sale of securities or investment real estate are not separately deductible, but you may increase your cost basis by the transfer tax in figuring profit or loss on Schedule D.

Gasoline taxes. State and local taxes on gasoline used for personal purposes are not deductible. If you travel for business, the taxes are deductible as part of your gasoline expenses.

16.3 Deducting State Income Taxes

You may deduct on your 2002 return state and local income taxes withheld from your pay and estimated state and local taxes paid in 2002. Also deduct the balance of your 2001 state and local taxes you paid during 2002. If in 2003 you pay additional state income tax on your 2002 income, you deduct the payment on your 2003 tax return.

State income taxes may be claimed only as itemized deductions, even if attributed solely to business income. That is, state income taxes may not be deducted as business expenses from gross income.

To increase your itemized deductions on your 2002 return, consider prepaying state income taxes before the end of 2002. The prepayment is deductible provided the state tax authority accepts prepayments and state law recognizes them as tax payments. The IRS has ruled, however, that prepayments are not deductible if you do not reasonably believe that you owe additional state tax. Do not make prepayments if you may be subject to alternative minimum tax; *see* Chapter 23.

If you report on the accrual basis and you contest a tax liability, claim the deduction in the year of payment.

You may deduct on your federal return state and local income taxes allocable to interest income that is exempt from federal tax but not state and local income tax. However, state and local taxes that are allocated to other federal exempt income are not deductible. For example, state income tax allocated to a cost-of-living allowance exempt from federal income tax is not deductible as a state tax.

Mandatory employee contributions to the following state disability or unemployment insurance funds are deductible as state income taxes: California, New Jersey, or New York Nonoccupational Disability Benefit Fund, Rhode Island Temporary Disability Benefit Fund, and Washington State Supplemental Workmen's Compensation Fund.

However, employee contributions to a private or voluntary disability plan in California, New Jersey, or New York have been held by the IRS to be nondeductible.

Mandatory employee contributions to a state unemployment fund are deductible.

Note: A refund of state income taxes claimed as an itemized deduction may have to be reported as income; *see 11.5.*

16.4 When Taxes and Interest Are Capitalized

Uniform capitalization rules (Code Section 263A) may prevent you from deducting taxes and interest incurred on business and investment real estate during a construction or development period; *see 40.3.* According to a Tax Court decision, the development period for land started when a development plan was submitted to zoning authorities. The developer was required to capitalize real estate taxes on the raw land, even though no actual development had occurred.

Election to capitalize. Where property such as nonproductive and undeveloped land is not subject to the uniform capitalization rules of Code Section 263A, you may elect to capitalize taxes and interest instead of deducting them. You capitalize the expenses by adding these amounts to the basis of the property. Capitalization may be to your advantage if you do not need the immediate deduction because you have little or no income to offset, or because you do not have itemized deductions or expect a greater tax benefit by adding the taxes to the basis.

To make the election, attach to your return a statement of expenses you elect to capitalize; IRS permission is not required. The election must apply to all similar expenses for the same project. An election for unimproved and unproductive real property applies only for the year for which it is made.

16.5 Assessments

Assessments by homeowner's association not deductible as taxes. Assessments paid to a local homeowner's association for the purpose of maintaining the common areas of the residential project and for promoting the recreation, health, and safety of the residents are not deductible as real property taxes.

Assessments for government services. If property is used solely as your residence, you may not deduct charges for municipal water bills (even if described as a "tax"), sewer assessments, assessments for sanitation service, or title registration fees. A permit fee to build or improve a personal residence is added to the cost basis of the house.

Filing Tip

Refund Credited to State Estimated Tax

If you were entitled to a refund on your 2001 state tax return and you credited the overpayment towards your 2002 estimated state tax, do not forget to include the credited amount with other 2002 payments of state and local income tax on your 2002 Schedule A.

Assessments for local benefits are deductible if they cover maintenance or repairs of streets, sidewalks, or water or sewer systems, or interest costs on such maintenance. However, assessments for construction of streets, sidewalks, or other local improvements that tend to increase the value of your property are not deductible as real estate taxes. You add such assessments to your cost basis for the property.

If you are billed a single amount, you may deduct the portion allocable to assessments for maintenance or repairs. The burden is on you to support the allocation.

16.6 Deducting Real Estate Taxes

You may deduct payments of real estate tax on your property if you claim itemized deductions on Schedule A. The monthly mortgage payment to a bank or other mortgage holder generally includes amounts allocated to real estate taxes, which are paid to the taxing authority on their due date. Mortgage payments allocated to real estate taxes are deductible in the year you make the payments only if the mortgage holder actually pays the taxes to the tax authority by the end of that year. Typically, banks will furnish you with a year-end statement of disbursements to taxing authorities, indicating dates of payment.

16.7 Tenants' Payment of Taxes

You generally may not deduct a portion of your rent as property taxes. This is so even where state or local law identifies a portion of the rent as being tied to tax increases.

Tenants have been allowed a deduction for property taxes in the following areas: In Hawaii tenants with leases of 15 years or more may deduct the portion of the rent representing taxes. In California, tenants who have their names placed on the tax rolls and who pay the taxes directly to the taxing authority may claim a deduction.

In New York, liability for tax is placed directly on the tenant and the landlord is a collecting agent for paying over the tax to the taxing authorities; the landlord also remains liable for the tax. The IRS ruled that it will not permit tenants to deduct a portion of rent as a payment of taxes.

Filing Tip

Cooperative Apartments
Tenant-stockholders of a cooperative housing corporation may deduct their share of the real estate taxes paid by the corporation. However, no deduction is allowed if the corporation does not own the land and building but merely leases them and pays taxes under the lease agreement. *See also 15.9.*

EXAMPLE

A municipal rent control ordinance allowed landlords to charge real property tax increases to the tenants as a monthly "tax surcharge." The ordinance stated that the surcharge was not to be considered rent for purposes of computing cost-of-living rental increases. The IRS ruled that the tenant may not deduct the "tax surcharge" as a property tax. The tax is imposed on the landlord, not on the tenant. The city ordinance, which permitted the landlord to pass on the tax increases to a tenant, did not shift liability for the property taxes from the landlord to the tenant. For federal tax purposes, the surcharge is merely an additional rental payment by the tenant. Similarly, "rates tax" or "renters' tax" imposed on tenants was ruled to be nondeductible because the tax is imposed on the person using the property rather than the property itself.

16.8 Allocating Taxes When You Sell or Buy Realty

When property is sold, the buyer and seller apportion the real estate taxes imposed on the property during the "real property year." A "real property year" is the period that a real estate tax covers. This allocation is provided for you in a settlement statement at the time of closing. If you want to figure your own allocations, your local tax authority can give you the "real property year" of the taxes you plan to apportion. With this information, you then make the following allocation. If *you* are the:

Seller, you deduct that portion of the tax covering the beginning of the real property year through the day before the sale.

Buyer, you deduct the part of the tax covering the date of the sale through the end of the real property year.

EXAMPLE

The real property year in East County starts April 1 and ends March 31. On July 2, 2002, you sell realty located in East County to Jones. Assume the real estate tax for the real property year ending March 31, 2003, is $1,000. You deduct $252 ($^{92}/_{365}$ of $1,000, since there are 92 days in the period beginning April 1 and ending July 1, 2002). Jones deducts $748 ($^{273}/_{365}$ of $1,000, since there are 273 days in the period beginning July 2, 2002, and ending March 31, 2003).

Form 1099-S for Sale of Principal Residence

A sale of a principal residence generally does not have to be reported on Form 1099-S if the seller gives the real estate agent responsible for the closing written assurance that the home was the seller's principal residence and that the full gain on the sale is excludable from income (*see* Chapter 29).

Filing Instruction

Buyer's Share of Real Estate Tax

If you sold a house in 2002 and received Form 1099-S, check Box 5 for the amount of real estate tax that you paid in advance and that is allocable to the buyer. The buyer may deduct this amount. You subtract it from the amount you paid when claiming your 2002 itemized deduction for real estate taxes.

The allocation of taxes between the buyer and seller is mandatory whether or not your contract provides for an allocation. However, you do not allocate taxes of a real property year when property is sold before the real property year. This rule prevents the seller from deducting any part of the tax for that year, even though it became a personal liability or lien while he or she owned the property. The buyer gets the deduction because he or she owns the property for the entire real property year. You also do not allocate taxes when property is sold after the real property year. This rule prevents the buyer from deducting the tax for that year even though it becomes a personal liability or lien after he or she takes possession of the property. The seller gets the deduction because the tax covers the property year in which the seller owns the property. The allocation is limited to a tax covering a property year during which both the seller and the buyer own the property.

Form 1099-S. If Form 1099-S is filed by the mortgage lender or real estate broker responsible for the closing, Box 5 will show the buyer's share of the real estate tax paid in advance by the seller. For example, Smith sells her house in Green County, where the real estate tax is paid annually in advance. In the year of sale she paid $1,200 in real estate taxes. Assuming that the home is sold at the end of the ninth month of the real property tax year, the amount of the real estate tax allocable to the buyer is $300 ($100 per month × 3 months). This amount, which is shown as paid by the seller in advance on an HUD-1 (Uniform Settlement Statement) form provided at the closing, is reported as the buyer's share of the real estate tax in Box 5 of Form 1099-S.

When to deduct allocated taxes. After you have made the allocation based on the "real property year," you then must fix the year in which you deduct your share of the allocated tax. Here you consider your method of reporting your income—cash or accrual basis—and the date on which either you or the other party became liable for the tax or paid the tax. If neither you nor the other party is liable for the tax under local law, then the party who holds the property at the time the tax became a lien on the property is considered liable. Check the following rules to determine when you deduct the apportioned tax:

Seller on the cash basis—If the buyer is liable for the tax under local law, the seller may deduct his or her share of the allocated tax either in the year of the sale or a later year when the tax is actually paid. If the seller is liable for the tax under local law, and the tax is not payable until after the sale date, the seller may deduct the tax either in the year of sale or in the year he or she pays the tax.

Buyer on the cash basis—If the seller is liable for the tax under local law, the buyer may deduct the tax either in the year of sale or when the tax is actually paid. If the buyer is liable for the tax, he or she deducts the tax in the year the tax is paid.

Seller on the accrual basis—The seller accrues his or her share of the tax on the date of the sale, unless taxes have been accrued ratably over the years. If this is so, the last accrual is the sale date.

Buyer on the accrual basis—If the seller is liable for the tax, the buyer accrues his or her share of the tax on the date of the sale, unless taxes are accrued ratably. If taxes are accrued ratably, the accrual begins with the date of sale. If the buyer is liable for the tax, he or she deducts the tax in the return for the year the tax accrues unless an election is made to accrue ratably from the date of sale.

Seller's deduction in excess of the allocated amount is taxed. If, in the year before the sale, the seller deducts an amount for taxes in excess of the allocated amount, the excess must be reported as income in the year of the sale. This may happen when the seller is on the cash basis and pays the tax in the year before the sale.

EXAMPLE

A real property tax of $1,000 is due and payable on November 30 for the following calendar year. On November 30, 2001, Keith Jones, who uses the cash basis and reports on a calendar year, pays the 2002 tax. On June 30, 2002, he sells the real property. Under the apportionment rule, Jones is allowed to deduct only $493 ($\frac{180}{365}$ of $1,000, since there are 181 days in the period from January 1 to June 29, 2002) of the tax for the 2002 real property tax year. But Jones has already deducted the full amount in the 2001 return. Therefore, he reports as income that part of the tax deduction that he was not entitled to under the apportionment.

Buyer may not deduct payment of seller's back taxes. The back taxes paid are added to the cost of the newly purchased property. The amount realized by the seller is increased by the buyer's payment of back taxes.

Seller's payment upon buyer's failure to pay. If a buyer is obligated to pay taxes under a land contract but fails to pay, the owner who pays the tax may deduct the payment if the tax is assessed to him or her.

Buyer of foreclosed property. If you buy realty at a tax sale and you do not receive immediate title to the property under state law until after a redemption period, you may not be able to deduct payment of realty taxes for several years.

16.9 Who May Deduct Real Property Taxes

A person who pays a property tax must have an ownership interest in the property to deduct the payment. The following table summarizes who may deduct payments of real property taxes.

If the tax is paid by—	Then it is deductible by—
You, for your spouse	Neither, if your spouse has title to the property, and you each file a separate return. This is true even if the mortgage requires you to pay the taxes. The tax is deductible on a joint return.
You, as owner of a condominium	You deduct real estate tax paid on your separate unit. You also deduct your share of the tax paid on the common property.
Your cooperative apartment or corporation	You deduct your share of real estate tax paid on the property; *see 15.9.* But if the organization leases the land and building and pays the tax under the terms of the lease, you may not deduct your share.
A life tenant	A court allowed the deduction to a widow required to pay the taxes under a will for the privilege of occupying the house during her life.
A tenant	The tenant of a business lease may deduct the payment of tax as additional rent, not tax. The tenant of a personal residence may not deduct the payment as either a tax or rent expense, unless placed on the real estate assessment rolls so that the tax is assessed directly against him or her; *see 16.7.*
You, as a local benefit tax to maintain, repair, or meet interest costs arising from local benefits	You deduct only that part of the tax that you can show is for maintenance, repair, or interest. If you cannot make the allocation, no deduction is allowed. If the benefit increases the value of the property, you add the nondeductible assessment to the basis of the property.
You, where your property was foreclosed for failure to pay taxes	You may not deduct the taxes paid out of the proceeds of the foreclosure sale if your interest in the property ended with the foreclosure.
Tenant by the entirety or joint tenant	The tenant who is jointly and severally liable and who pays the tax. If real property is owned by husband and wife as tenants by the entirety or joint tenants, either spouse may deduct the taxes paid on a separate return or a joint return.
Tenant in common	When property is owned as a tenancy in common, under an IRS rule, a tenant may deduct only his or her share of the tax, even if the entire tax was paid. However, in one case the Tax Court allowed a deduction for the full amount where a co-tenant's payment protected her against the possibility of foreclosure in the event the other co-tenants failed to pay their share of the taxes; *see 9.2.*
A mortgagee	No deduction. If tax is paid before the foreclosure, it is added to the loan. If paid after the foreclosure, it is added to the cost of property.

16.10 Automobile License Fees

You may not deduct an auto license fee based on weight, model, year, or horsepower. But you may deduct a fee based on the value of the car as a state personal property tax if these three tests are met: (1) the fee is an *ad valorem* tax, based on a percentage of value of the property; (2) it is imposed on an annual basis, even though it is collected more or less frequently; and (3) it is imposed on personal property. This third test is met even though the tax is imposed on the exercise of a privilege of registering a car or for using a car on the road.

The majority of state motor vehicle registration fees are not *ad valorem* taxes and do not qualify for the deduction. Various states and localities impose *ad valorem* or personal property taxes on motor vehicles that may qualify for the deduction. If you pay fees or taxes on your auto in these states, we suggest you contact a state or local authority to verify the amount of tax qualifying: Arizona, California, Colorado, Connecticut, Georgia, Indiana, Iowa, Maine, Massachusetts, Minnesota, Mississippi, Montana, Nebraska, Nevada, New Hampshire, Oklahoma, Washington, and Wyoming.

16.11 Taxes Deductible as Business Expenses

That a tax is not deductible as an itemized deduction does not mean you may not deduct it elsewhere on your return. For example, you may generally deduct property taxes incurred as a cost of doing business on Schedule C. Here are some other examples:

If you pay excise taxes on merchandise you sell in your business, you deduct the tax as a business expense.

If you pay Social Security taxes (FICA) on your employees' wages, you deduct the tax as a business expense on Schedule C.

If you pay sales tax on business property, you add the tax to the cost of the property for depreciation purposes. If the tax is paid on nondepreciable property, the tax is included in the currently deductible cost.

If you pay sales tax on a deductible business meal, the tax is deductible as part of the meal costs, subject to the cost limit discussed at *20.24*.

50% self-employment tax deduction. One-half of the self-employment tax figured on Schedule SE is deductible from gross income on Line 29 of Form 1040, rather than on Schedule C; *see 45.3*.

Note: If you are not a material participant in the business, your Schedule C expenses are subject to passive activity limitations; *see* Chapter 10.

16.12 Foreign Taxes

You may deduct your payment of foreign real property taxes and income and excess profits taxes as itemized deductions. Where you pay foreign income or excess profits tax, you have an election of either claiming the tax as a deduction or a credit. Claiming the credit may provide a larger tax savings; *see 36.14*.

 Filing Tip

Value Portion of Auto License Fee

If an automobile license fee is based partly on value and partly on weight or other tests, the tax attributed to the value is deductible. For example, assume a registration fee based on 1% of value, plus 40¢ per hundred-weight. The part of the tax equal to 1% of value qualifies as an *ad valorem* tax and is deductible as a personal property tax on Schedule A.

Chapter 17

Medical and Dental Expense Deductions

Tax relief for the high cost of medical care is limited. Medical expenses are deductible only if you itemize and only if you have expenses exceeding 7.5% of your adjusted gross income. Expenses up to 7.5% of AGI are not deductible.

Carefully review the list of deductible expenses in this chapter so that you do not overlook any deductible expenses. Include payments of doctors' fees, health-care premiums, prescription medicines, travel costs for obtaining medical care, and eligible home improvements.

If you are married, both you and your spouse work, and one of you has substantial medical expenses, filing separate returns may result in a lower overall tax.

Deductible medical expenses are *not* subject to the 3% reduction of itemized deductions that applies on 2002 returns if adjusted gross income exceeds $137,300 ($68,650 if married filing separately).

Qualifying long-term care expenses may be treated as medical expenses subject to the 7.5% of AGI floor, including a specified deductible amount of premiums paid for a qualifying long-term care contract; *see 17.15.*

Deductible contributions to medical savings accounts (Archer MSAs) may be made by self-employed individuals and employees of certain small businesses; *see 17.17.*

A new law allows workers displaced from jobs by import competition to claim a refundable tax credit for health insurance premiums. The credit is claimed on Form 8885; *see 22.5.*

17.1 Medical Expenses Must Exceed 7.5% of AGI

The tax law provides only a limited opportunity to deduct medical costs for you, your spouse, and your dependents (17.7). A wide range of expenses, such as those listed on page 330, qualify as deductible medical expenses if you itemize expenses on Schedule A of Form 1040. However, you may not be able to claim the deduction because of a percentage floor. You may deduct only expenses exceeding 7.5% of your adjusted gross income (AGI). Adjusted gross income is explained at 12.1. For 2002, adjusted gross income is shown on Line 35 of Form 1040.

Married persons filing joint returns apply the 7.5% floor to their combined adjusted gross income.

On your 2002 return, you may deduct expenses paid in 2002 by cash or check (unless the check is postdated to 2003) for yourself, your spouse (17.6), or dependents (17.7). If you borrow to pay medical or dental expenses, you claim the deduction in the year you use the loan proceeds to pay the bill, not in the later year when you repay the loan. If you paid medical or dental expenses by credit card in 2002, the deduction is allowed in 2002, although you do not pay the charge bill until 2003.

EXAMPLES

1. Frank Ryan's adjusted gross income (AGI; see 12.1) is $20,000 for 2002. His unreimbursed medical expenses were $1,000 for doctor and dentist visits, $210 for prescribed drugs and medicines, and $625 for medical insurance premiums. If he itemizes deductions on Schedule A, he may deduct medical expenses of $335, figured this way:

Unreimbursed expenses	$1,000
Premiums	625
Drugs	210
Total	$1,835
Less: 7.5% of adjusted gross income (7.5% of $20,000)	1,500
Medical expense deduction	$335

2. Same as facts as in Example 1 except that Frank's AGI is $30,000, not $20,000. Here, Frank may not claim any medical deduction because his expenses of $1,835 do not exceed $2,250, 7.5% of his AGI.

17.2 Allowable Medical Care Costs

In determining whether you have paid deductible medical expenses exceeding the 7.5% AGI floor (17.1), include the cost of diagnosis, cure, mitigation, treatment, or prevention of disease or any treatment that affects a part or function of your body. Also include qualifying costs you paid for your spouse (17.6) and your dependents (17.7). *See* the checklist of deductible expenses on page 330.

Expenses that are *solely* for cosmetic reasons are not deductible. Also, expenses incurred to benefit your general health are not deductible even if recommended by a physician; see 17.3.

Medicine and drugs. To be deductible, medicines and drugs other than insulin must be obtainable solely through a prescription by a doctor. Insulin is deductible even though a prescription may not be required.

Marijuana is not deductible even if prescribed by a doctor in a state allowing the prescription.

You may not deduct the cost of over-the-counter medicines and drugs, such as aspirin and other cold remedies, even if you have a doctor's prescription.

Stop-smoking programs. The cost of smoking cessation programs is a deductible medical expense, as well as nicotine withdrawal drugs that require a physician's prescription. If you paid such costs before 2002 but did not claim the deduction, you may file an amended return (49.2) to claim a refund for a year that is not closed by the statute of limitations. Over-the-counter nicotine patches and gums are not deductible.

Exercise and weight-reduction programs. If you incur costs for such programs to improve your *general* health, the costs are not deductible even if your doctor has recommended them. However, if your doctor has recommended a program as treatment for a *specific* condition, such as heart disease or hypertension, the IRS allows a deduction for the cost.

In 2002, the IRS ruled that obesity is itself a disease. If a physician has made a diagnosis of obesity, the costs of joining a weight-loss program and additional fees for meetings are eligible medical expenses. However, reduced-calorie diet foods that are substitutes for foods normally consumed are not deductible even if they are part of the program; *see* "Special foods" below.

The IRS position applies retroactively. An amended return may be filed to claim obesity program fees paid in recent years not closed by the statute of limitations *(49.2)*.

Special foods. According to the IRS, the cost of special foods or beverages is not a deductible medical expense if the food or beverages substitute for those normally consumed.

Filing Tip

Childbirth Classes

A mother-to-be may deduct the cost of classes instructing her in Lamaze breathing and relaxation techniques, stages of labor, and delivery procedures. If her husband or other childbirth "coach" also attends the classes, the portion of the fee allocable to the coach is not deductible. Costs of classes on early pregnancy, fetal development, or caring for newborns also are not deductible.

> **EXAMPLE**
>
> To alleviate an ulcer, your doctor puts you on a special diet. According to the IRS, the cost of your food and beverages is not deductible. The special diet replaces the food you normally eat.

The Tax Court has set its own standard for deducting the extra cost of special foods as medical costs. The test is to show a medical need for taking the special food and the extra cost of the health food over ordinary food. Only the extra cost is deductible.

> **EXAMPLES**
>
> 1. Anna Von Kalb suffered from hypoglycemia and her physician prescribed a special high protein diet, which required her to consume twice as much protein as an average person and exclude all processed foods and carbohydrates. She spent $3,483 for food, and deducted 30%, or $1,045, as the extra cost of her high protein diet. The IRS disallowed the deduction, claiming that the protein supplements were a substitute for foods normally consumed. The Tax Court disagreed. The high protein food did not substitute for her usual diet but helped alleviate her hypoglycemia. Thus, she may deduct its additional expense.
>
> 2. The Bechers suffered from allergies and were advised by a physician to eat organically grown food to avoid the chemicals in commercial food. The Bechers claimed a medical expense deduction of $2,255, the extra cost of buying organic food.
>   The IRS disallowed the deduction and the Tax Court agreed. They did not present evidence that their allergies could be cured by limiting their diet to organic food. That the food was beneficial to their general health and was prescribed by a doctor is not sufficient for a deduction.

Caution

Deducting Costs of Health Improvement Programs

Exercise and weight-reduction programs are deductible as treatments for specific conditions, but not as ways to improve your general health, even if your doctor has recommended them; *see 17.2.*

17.3 Nondeductible Medical Expenses

The most common nondeductible medical expense is the cost of over-the-counter medicines and drugs, such as aspirin and other cold remedies. A deduction for over-the-counter medicines is disallowed even if you have a doctor's prescription. Expenses incurred to improve your general health, such as exercise programs not related to a specific condition, are not deductible. Also *see* the checklist on page 331.

Cosmetic surgery. A medical expense deduction is allowed for cosmetic surgery if it is necessary to improve a disfigurement related to a congenital abnormality, disfiguring disease, or an accidental injury.

You may not deduct the cost of cosmetic surgery or other procedures that do not have a medical purpose. Thus, face lifts, hair transplants, electrolysis, and liposuction intended to improve appearance are generally not deductible. However, in one case, the Tax Court allowed an exotic dancer to claim a depreciation deduction for breast implants essential for her business; *see 19.8.*

17.4 Reimbursements Reduce Deductible Expenses

Insurance or other reimbursements of your medical costs reduce your potential medical deduction. Reimbursements for loss of earnings or damages for personal injuries and mental suffering do not have to be taken into account. A reimbursement first reduces the medical expense for which it is paid. The excess is then applied to your other deductible medical costs.

Deductible Medical Expenses

Professional Services

Chiropodist
Chiropractor
Christian Science practitioner
Dermatologist
Dentist
Gynecologist
Neurologist
Obstetrician
Ophthalmologist
Optician
Optometrist
Orthopedist
Osteopath
Pediatrician
Physician
Physiotherapist
Plastic surgeon; but see 17.3.
Podiatrist
Practical or other nonprofessional nurse for medical services only, not for care of a healthy person or a child who is not ill. Costs for medical care of elderly person unable to get about or person subject to spells are deductible; see 17.12.
Psychiatrist
Psychoanalyst
Psychologist
Registered nurse
Surgeon
Unlicensed practitioner services are deductible if the type and quality of the services are not illegal.

Dental Services

Artificial teeth
Cleaning teeth
Dental X-rays
Extracting teeth
Filling teeth
Gum treatment
Oral surgery
Straightening teeth

Equipment and Supplies

Abdominal supports
Air conditioner where necessary for relief from an allergy or for relieving difficulty in breathing; see 17.13.
Ambulance hire
Arches

Artificial eyes, limbs
Autoette (auto device for handicapped person)
Back supports
Braces
Contact lenses and solutions
Cost of installing stair-seat elevator for person with heart condition; see 17.13.
Crutches
Elastic hosiery
Eyeglasses
Fluoridation unit in home
Hearing aids
Heating devices
Invalid chair
Iron lung
Orthopedic shoes—excess cost over cost of regular shoes
Oxygen or oxygen equipment to relieve breathing problems caused by a medical condition
Reclining chair if prescribed by doctor
Repair of special telephone equipment for the deaf
Sacroiliac belt
Special mattress and plywood bed boards for relief of arthritis or spine
Splints
Truss
Wheelchair
Wig advised by doctor as essential to mental health of person who lost all hair from disease

Medical Treatments

Abortion
Acupuncture
Blood transfusion
Childbirth delivery
Diathermy
Electric shock treatments
Hearing services
Hydrotherapy (water treatments)
Injections
Insulin treatments
Laser eye surgery or radial keratotomy to improve vision
Navajo healing ceremonies ("sings")
Nursing
Organ transplant
Prenatal and postnatal treatments
Psychotherapy

Sterilization
Radial keratotomy
Radium therapy
Ultraviolet ray treatments
Vasectomy
Whirlpool baths
X-ray treatments

Medicines and Drugs

Cost of prescriptions only; over-the-counter medicine is not deductible.

Laboratory Examinations and Tests

Blood tests
Cardiographs
Metabolism tests
Spinal fluid tests
Sputum tests
Stool examinations
Urine analyses
X-ray examinations

Hospital Services

Anesthetist
Hospital bills
Oxygen mask, tent
Use of operating room
Vaccines
X-ray technician

Premiums for Medical Care Policies

See 17.5 for the way to deduct:
Blue Cross and Blue Shield
Contact lens replacement insurance
Federal Voluntary Medicare (Part B) and Federal Medicare (Part A) by persons not covered by Social Security
Health insurance covering hospital, surgical, and other medical expenses
Membership in medical service cooperative

Miscellaneous

Alcoholic inpatient care costs
Birth control pills or other birth control items prescribed by your doctor
Braille books—excess cost of Braille works over cost of regular editions

Childbirth classes for expectant mother
Clarinet lessons advised by dentist for treatment of tooth defects
Convalescent home—for medical treatment only
Drug treatment center—inpatient care costs
Fees paid to health institute where the exercises, rubdowns, etc., taken there are prescribed by a physician as treatments necessary to alleviate a physical or mental defect or illness
Kidney donor's or possible kidney donor's expenses
Lead-based paint removal to prevent a child who has had lead poisoning from eating the paint. Repainting the scraped area is not deductible.
Legal fees for guardianship of mentally ill spouse where commitment was necessary for medical treatment
Lifetime care—advance payments made either monthly or as a lump sum under an agreement with a retirement home; see 17.11.
Long-term care costs for chronically ill; see 17.15.
Nurse's board and wages, including Social Security taxes paid on wages
Remedial reading for child suffering from dyslexia
School—payments to a special school for a mentally or physically impaired person if the main reason for using the school is its resources for relieving the disability; see 17.10.
"Seeing-eye" dog and its maintenance
Smoking cessation programs
Special school costs for physically and mentally handicapped children; see 17.10.
Telephone-teletype costs and television adapter for closed caption service for deaf person
Travel to obtain medical care; see 17.9.
Wages of guide for a blind person
Weight-loss program to treat obesity or other specific disease; see 17.2.

Nondeductible Medical Expenses

Antiseptic diaper service

Athletic club expenses

Babysitting fees to enable you to make doctor's visits

Boarding school fees paid for healthy child while parent is recuperating from illness

Bottled water bought to avoid drinking fluoridated city water

Cost of divorce recommended by a psychiatrist

Cost of hotel room suggested for sex therapy

Cost of moving away from airport noise by person suffering a nervous breakdown

Cost of trips prescribed by a doctor for a "change of environment" to boost an ailing person's morale

Dance lessons advised by a doctor as general physical and mental therapy

Divorced spouse's medical bills

Domestic help; but *see 17.12* if nursing duties are performed.

Ear piercing

Funeral, cremation, burial, cemetery plot, monument, or mausoleum

Health programs offered by resort hotels, health clubs, and gyms

Illegal operations and drugs

Marijuana, even if prescribed by a physician in a state permitting the prescription

Marriage counseling fees

Massages recommended by physician for general stress reduction

Maternity clothes

Premiums on policies guaranteeing you a specified amount of money each week in the event hospitalization

Scientology fees

Special food or beverage substitutes; but *see 17.2.*

Tattooing

Toothpaste

Transportation costs of a disabled person to and from work

Travel costs to favorable climate when you can live there permanently

Travel costs to look for a new place to live—on a doctor's advice

Tuition and travel expenses to send a problem child to a particular school for a beneficial change in environment; *see 17.10.*

Weight-loss program to improve general health; *see 17.2.*

How Your Medical Expense Deduction Is Reduced by the 7.5% Floor

Your medical expenses are

If your adjusted gross income is	$1,000	$1,500	$2,000	$2,500	$3,000	$3,500	$4,000	$4,500	$5,000	$5,500	$6,000	$6,500	$7,000	$7,500
							You may deduct							
$ 15,000	0	375	875	1,375	1,875	2,375	2,875	3,375	3,875	4,375	4,875	5,375	5,875	6,375
$ 20,000	0	0	500	1,000	1,500	2,000	2,500	3,000	3,500	4,000	4,500	5,000	5,500	6,000
$ 25,000	0	0	125	625	1,125	1,625	2,125	2,625	3,125	3,625	4,125	4,625	5,125	5,625
$ 30,000	0	0	0	250	750	1,250	1,750	2,250	2,750	3,250	3,750	4,250	4,750	5,250
$ 35,000	0	0	0	0	375	875	1,375	1,875	2,375	2,875	3,375	3,875	4,375	4,875
$ 40,000	0	0	0	0	0	500	1,000	1,500	2,000	2,500	3,000	3,500	4,000	4,500
$ 45,000	0	0	0	0	0	125	625	1,125	1,625	2,125	2,625	3,125	3,625	4,125
$ 50,000	0	0	0	0	0	0	250	750	1,250	1,750	2,250	2,750	3,250	3,750
$ 55,000	0	0	0	0	0	0	0	375	875	1,375	1,875	2,375	2,875	3,375
$ 60,000	0	0	0	0	0	0	0	0	500	1,000	1,500	2,000	2,500	3,000
$ 65,000	0	0	0	0	0	0	0	0	125	625	1,125	1,625	2,125	2,625
$ 70,000	0	0	0	0	0	0	0	0	0	250	750	1,250	1,750	2,250
$ 75,000	0	0	0	0	0	0	0	0	0	0	375	875	1,375	1,875
$ 80,000	0	0	0	0	0	0	0	0	0	0	0	500	1,000	1,500
$ 85,000	0	0	0	0	0	0	0	0	0	0	0	125	625	1,125
$ 90,000	0	0	0	0	0	0	0	0	0	0	0	0	250	750
$ 95,000	0	0	0	0	0	0	0	0	0	0	0	0	0	375
$ 100,000	0	0	0	0	0	0	0	0	0	0	0	0	0	0

EXAMPLE

Gail Hurz paid $800 in medical insurance premiums. She paid doctor and hospital bills totaling $700 and purchased prescription drugs costing $150. Group hospitalization insurance reimbursed $300 for doctors and hospital bills and $25 for medicines and drugs. Her adjusted gross income is $15,000. Her deduction is computed as follows:

Prescription drugs	$150
Medical care expenses	700
Premiums	800
Total	$1,650
Less reimbursement	325
	$1,325
Less: 7.5% of $15,000	1,125
Medical expense deduction	$200

Personal injury settlements or awards. Generally, a cash settlement recovered in a personal injury suit does not reduce your medical expense deduction. The settlement is not treated as reimbursement of your medical bills. But when part of the settlement is specifically earmarked by a court or by law for payment of hospital bills, the medical expense deduction is reduced.

If you receive a settlement for a personal injury that is partly allocable to future medical expenses, you reduce medical expenses for these injuries by the allocated amount until it is used up.

Fake claims. Medical reimbursements for fake injury claims are treated as taxable income; *see* the following Example.

EXAMPLE

Dodge, with the aid of a "friendly" doctor, arranged to be hospitalized for alleged back injuries and realized over $200,000 from HIP policies. The IRS charged that the insurance proceeds were taxable income. Dodge argued they were tax-free reimbursements of medical costs.

The Tax Court sided with the IRS. The tax-free rules cover the payment of legitimate medical costs. Here there were no legitimate medical costs of actual injuries. Dodge took out the policies in a scam arrangement with the doctor.

Reimbursements in excess of your medical expenses. If you paid the entire premium for health insurance, you are not taxed on payments from the plan even if they exceed your medical expenses for the year. If you and your employer each contributed to the policy, you generally have to include in income that part of the excess reimbursement that is attributable to employer premium contributions not included in your gross income.

However, you do not have to report any excess reimbursements that are tax-free payments for permanent disfigurement or loss of bodily functions, as discussed in *3.2*.

If your employer paid the total cost of the policy and the contributions were not taxed to you, you report as income all of your excess reimbursement, unless it covers payment for permanent injury or disfigurement *(3.2)*.

For the treatment of insurance reimbursements of long-term care costs, *see 17.15*.

EXAMPLES

1. Henry Knight pays premiums of $240 and $120 for two personal health insurance policies. His total medical expenses are $900. He receives $700 from one insurance company and $500 from the other. The excess reimbursement of $300 ($1,200 – $900) is not taxable because he paid the entire premium on the policy.

2. Lionel Guest's employer paid premiums of $1,800 for two employee health insurance policies covering medical expenses. Guest's medical expenses in one year are $900. He receives $1,200 from the two companies. The entire $300 excess is taxable because Guest's employer paid the total cost of the policy and the contributions were not taxed to him.

3. Kay Brown's employer paid a premium of $1,000 for a group health policy covering Brown, and Brown herself paid $300 for a personal health policy. Her medical expenses are $900. She receives reimbursements of $1,200, $700 under her employer's policy

Caution

Reimbursements Exceeding Expenses

If you have more than one policy and receive reimbursements that exceed your total medical expenses for the year, you must pay tax on all or part of the reimbursement where your employer paid premiums on the policies; *see* the Examples below.

and $500 under her own policy. Brown's reimbursements exceed expenses by $300, but the taxable portion attributed to her employer's premium contribution is $175, computed this way:

Reimbursement allocated to Brown's policy	
($500 ÷ $1,200) × $900	$375
Reimbursement allocated to employer's policy	
($700 ÷ $1,200) × $900	$525
Taxable excess allocated to employer's policy	
($700 − $525)	$175

4. Mike Green's employer paid $1,200 for a health insurance policy but contributed only $450 and deducted $750 from Green's wages. Green also paid $300 for a personal health insurance policy. His medical expenses are $900. He recovered $700 from the employer's policy and $500 from his personal policy. The excess attributable to the employer's policy is $175 (computed as in Example 3 above). However, the taxable portion is only $65.63. Both Green and his employer contributed to the cost of the employer's policy and a further allocation is necessary:

Green's contribution	$750
Employer's contribution	450
Total cost of policy	$1,200
Ratio of employer's contribution to annual cost of policy	
(450 ÷ 1,200, or 37.50%)	
Taxable portion: 37.50% of excess reimbursement of $175	$65.63

Reimbursement in a later year may be taxed. If you took a medical expense deduction in one year and are reimbursed for all or part of the expense in a later year, the reimbursement may be taxed in the year received. The reimbursement is generally taxable income to the extent the deduction reduced your tax in the prior year. For further details for figuring taxable income on a recovery of a prior deduction, *see 11.6*.

EXAMPLES
1. In 2001, Anna Gurchani had adjusted gross income of $12,000. She claimed itemized deductions that exceeded her allowable standard deduction by $1,000; on her Schedule A, Gurchani listed medical expenses of $2,300. She deducted $1,400, computed as follows:

Medical expenses	$2,300
Less: 7.5% of $12,000	900
Allowable deduction	$1,400

In 2002 she collects $300 from insurance, reimbursing part of her 2001 medical expenses. If she had collected that amount in 2001, her medical expense deduction would have been $1,100. The entire reimbursement of $300 is subject to tax in 2002. It is the amount by which the 2001 deduction of $1,400 exceeds the deduction of $1,100 that would have been allowed if the reimbursement had been received in 2001.

2. Same facts as in Example 1 above, but Anna did not deduct medical expenses in 2001 because she did not itemize deductions. The reimbursement in 2002 is not taxable.

17.5 Premiums of Medical Care Policies

You may deduct as medical expenses premiums paid for medical care policies covering yourself, your spouse (17.6), or dependents (17.7). There is no separate deduction for health insurance premiums. All qualifying premiums are treated as medical expenses subject to the overall 7.5% AGI floor. Included as deductible medical expenses are premiums you paid for health insurance that covers hospital, surgical, drug costs, and other medical expenses. Also deductible are premiums paid for contact lens replacement insurance and premiums on policies providing solely for indemnity for hospital and surgical expenses. Include premiums for Medicare Part B supplemental insurance. Payment for voluntary coverage under Medicare (Part A) is deductible by those over age 65 who are not covered by Social Security. Deductions may be claimed for membership payments in associations furnishing cooperative or free-choice medical services, group hospitalization, or clinical care policies, including HMOs (health maintenance organizations) and medical care premiums paid to colleges as part of a tuition bill, if the amount is separately stated in the bill.

Law Alert

Self-Employed Deduction

A 70% deduction for health insurance premiums you paid as a self-employed person in 2002 is generally allowed directly from gross income on Line 30 of Form 1040; *see 12.2*. Premiums not deductible under the 70% limitation are included with other premiums for purposes of figuring the itemized deduction for medical expenses.

The deduction for self-employed taxpayers' medical insurance premiums increases to 100% in 2003 and thereafter.

Filing Tip

Should Spouses File Separately?

If you are married and both you and your spouse have separate incomes, and one of you has substantial medical expenses, consider filing separate returns. This way the 7.5% floor will apply separately to your individual incomes, not to the higher joint income. To make sure which option to take—filing jointly or separately—you compute your tax on both types of returns and choose the one giving the lower overall tax; *see 1.2.*

Premiums paid before you reach age 65 for medical care insurance for protection after you reach age 65 are deductible in the year paid if they are payable on a level payment basis under the contract (1) for a period of 10 years or more or (2) until the year you reach age 65 (but in no case for a period of less than five years).

Premiums for qualifying long-term care policies are deductible subject to the limits explained in *17.15.*

Nondeductible premiums. You may *not* deduct premiums for a policy guaranteeing you a specified amount each week (not to exceed a specified number of weeks) in the event you are hospitalized. Also, no deduction may be claimed for premiums paid for a policy that compensates you for loss of earnings while ill or injured, or for loss of life, limb, or sight. If your policy covers both medical care and loss of income or loss of life, limb, or sight, no part of the premium is deductible unless (1) the contract or separate statement from the insurance company states what part of the premium is allocated to medical care and (2) the premium allocated to medical care is reasonable.

You may not deduct part of the car insurance premiums for medical insurance coverage for persons injured by or in your car where the premium covering you, your spouse *(17.6)*, or your dependents *(17.7)* is not stated separately from the premium covering medical care for others.

Self-employed deduction of 70%. If you were self-employed in 2002, you may claim a special deduction on Form 1040, Line 30, for 70% of health insurance premiums paid in 2002 for yourself, your spouse, and your dependents. The deduction is also allowed if you received wages from an S corporation in which you were more than a 2% shareholder, you were a general partner, or were a limited partner who received guaranteed payments.

The 70% deduction may not be claimed for any month during 2002 that you were eligible for coverage under an employer's subsidized health plan, including a plan of your spouse's employer. Also, the deduction may not exceed your net earnings from the business under which the health premiums are paid. *See 12.2* for further details on the 70% deduction.

Any balance of premiums not deductible under the 70% rule may be claimed as an itemized medical expense subject to the 7.5% income floor *(17.1).*

17.6 Expenses of Your Spouse

You may deduct as medical expenses your payments of medical bills for your spouse if you were married either at the time the expenses were incurred or at the time the bills were paid. That is, you may deduct your payment of your spouse's medical bills even though you are divorced or widowed, if, at the time the expenses were incurred, you were married. Furthermore, if your spouse incurred medical expenses before you married and you pay the bills after you marry, you may deduct the expense.

EXAMPLES

1. Your spouse has doctor bills covering an operation performed in 2001, before you were married. You married in 2002. You pay those bills in 2002. You may claim a 2002 medical expense deduction for your payment.
2. In October 2001, your spouse had dental work done. In February 2002, you are divorced; in April 2002, you pay your former spouse's dental bills. You may deduct the payment on your 2002 tax return.
3. In 2002, you pay medical expenses for your spouse who died in 2001. You remarry in 2002. On a 2002 joint return filed with your new spouse, you may deduct your payment of your deceased spouse's medical expenses.

Filing separately in community property states. If you and your spouse file separately and live in a community property state, any medical expenses paid out of community funds are treated as paid 50% by each of you. Medical expenses paid out of separate funds of one spouse can be deducted only by that spouse.

17.7 Expenses of Your Dependents

You may deduct your payment of medical bills for your children or other dependents, subject to the 7.5% floor at *17.1.* You may deduct the expenses of a person who was your dependent either at the time the medical services were provided or at the time you paid the expenses. In determining dependent status for medical expense purposes, you may disregard two of the regular tests listed at *21.1* for claiming an exemption for a dependent. You may deduct the medical costs of a person who qualifies as your dependent under the relationship test, the support test, and the citizen or resident test. The gross income test and the joint return test do not have to be met. *See* Examples 1–3 below.

A child may not deduct medical expenses paid with his or her parent's welfare payments; *see* Example 4 below.

EXAMPLES

1. You contribute more than half of your married son's support, including a payment of a medical expense of $800. Because he filed a joint return with his wife, you may not claim him as a dependent *(21.13)*. But you still may include your payment of the $800 medical expense with your other qualifying medical expenses since you contributed more than half of his support.

2. Your mother, a U.S. citizen, underwent an operation in November 2001. You paid for the operation in February 2002. You may deduct the cost of the operation in 2002 if you furnished more than one-half of your mother's support in either 2001 or 2002.

3. Same facts as Example 2, except your mother is a citizen and resident of Italy. You may not deduct the cost of the operation. She is not a U.S. citizen or a resident of the United States, Canada, or Mexico and thus does not qualify as a dependent for exemption purposes *(21.12)* or for medical deduction purposes.

4. A son is the legal guardian of his mother who is mentally incompetent. As guardian, he received his mother's state welfare and Social Security benefits, which he deposited in his personal bank account and used to pay part of his mother's medical expenses. On his tax return, he claimed a deduction for the total medical expenses paid on behalf of his mother. The court held that he could deduct only medical expenses in excess of the amounts received as welfare and Social Security payments. The benefits, to the extent used to pay medical expenses, represented the mother's payments in her own behalf.

Divorced and separated parents. You may be able to deduct your payment of your child's medical costs, even though your ex-spouse is entitled to claim the child as a dependent. For purposes of the medical deduction, the child is considered to be the dependent of *both* parents if (1) they are divorced or legally separated under a court agreement, separated under a written agreement, or married but living apart during the last six months of 2002; (2) the child was in the custody of one or both parents for more than half of 2002; and (3) more than half of the child's 2002 support was provided by both parents.

Adopted children. You may deduct medical expenses of an adopted child if you may claim the child as a dependent either when the medical services are rendered or when you pay the expenses. An adopted child may be claimed as a dependent when a court has approved the adoption. In the absence of a court decree, the child is your dependent if he or she was placed in your home by an authorized agency and was a member of your household the rest of the year; *see 21.3*. If he or she has not been placed in your custody by an authorized agency, you have to show that the child lived in your home for the entire year.

If you reimburse an adoption agency for medical expenses it paid under an agreement with you, you are considered to have paid the expenses. But reimbursement of expenses incurred and paid before adoption negotiations does not qualify them as your medical expenses and you may not deduct them.

You may not deduct medical expenses for services rendered to the natural mother of the child you adopt.

Multiple support agreements. If you may claim a person as your dependent under a multiple support agreement *(21.10)*, your unreimbursed payments of that person's medical expenses are deductible. Even if you may not claim the dependent exception for 2002 because the person has a gross income of $3,000 or more, you may still deduct your payment of medical expenses provided the other multiple support agreement tests are met.

 *Filing Instruction*

Multiple Support Agreement
If you may claim a person as your dependent under a multiple support agreement, include with your medical expenses only the amount you actually pay for the dependent's medical expenses. If you are reimbursed by others who signed the multiple support agreement, you must reduce your deduction by the amount of reimbursement.

EXAMPLE

Ingrid Fromm and her brother and sister share equally in the support of their mother. Part of their mother's support includes medical expenses. Should the three of them share in the payment of the bills or should only one of them pay the bills? The answer: Payment should be made by the person who may claim the mother as a dependent under a multiple support agreement. Only that person may deduct the payment. If Ingrid is going to claim her as an exemption, she should pay the bill. She may deduct the payment although she did not contribute more than half of her mother's support. If her brother and sister reimburse her for part of the bill, she may include only the unreimbursed portion in her medical expenses. Neither Ingrid's brother nor her sister may deduct this share. Thus, a deduction is lost for these amounts.

17.8 Decedent's Medical Expenses

If you pay the medical expenses of your deceased spouse or dependent *(17.7)*, you may claim the payment as a medical expense in the year you pay the expenses, whether that is before or after the person's death.

If the executor or administrator of the estate pays the decedent's medical expenses within one year after the date of death, an election may be made to treat the expenses as if the deceased had paid them in the year the medical services were provided. The executor or administrator may file an amended return for the year the services were provided and claim them as a medical deduction for that year, assuming the period for filing the amended return *(49.2)* has not passed.

If the election is made by the executor to claim the expenses as an income tax deduction, they may not be claimed as a deduction on the estate tax return. The executor must file a statement with the decedent's income tax return that the expenses have not been deducted on the estate tax return and the estate waives its right to deduct them for estate tax purposes.

If medical expenses are claimed as an income tax deduction, the portion of the expenses that are below the 7.5% floor, and, therefore, not deductible, may not be deducted on the estate tax return. Although the expenses were not actually deducted, the IRS considers them to be part of the overall income tax deduction.

Filing Tip

Deductible Travel Costs

The costs of trips to receive medical treatment are deductible as medical expenses subject to the 7.5% AGI floor. The costs of a trip to a conference to learn about medical treatment may be deductible if recommended by a doctor.

EXAMPLE

Oscar Reyes incurred medical expenses of $5,000 in 2001 and $3,000 in 2002. He died June 1, 2002, without having paid these expenses. He had already filed his 2001 return before the due date. In August 2002, his executor pays the $8,000 in medical expenses. The executor may file an amended return for 2001, claim a medical expense deduction for the $5,000, and get a refund for the increased deductions. The executor may claim the remaining $3,000 as a medical expense deduction on Reyes's final return for 2002.

17.9 Travel Costs May Be Medical Deductions

Travel costs to a doctor's office, hospital, or clinic where you, your spouse, or your dependents receive medical care are deductible medical expenses, subject to the 7.5% AGI floor.

The amount of the deduction is limited to the cost of transportation, such as the cost of operating a car, bus, taxi, or train fares, and the costs of hiring a car service or ambulance. Plane fares to another city are allowed by the IRS so long as obtaining medical care is the primary purpose of the trip; *see* below for lodging expense rule. If you used your automobile in 2002 to obtain medical care, you may deduct a flat rate of 13¢ a mile and, in addition, you may deduct parking fees and tolls. If, however, auto expenses exceed this standard mileage rate, you may deduct your actual out-of-pocket costs for gas, oil, repairs, tolls, and parking fees. Do not include depreciation, general maintenance, or car insurance. The cost, as well as the operating and repair costs, of a wheelchair, autoette, or special auto device for a handicapped person is deductible if not used mainly for commuting.

EXAMPLE

In 2002, you drove your car to a doctor's office for treatment 40 times. Each round trip was 25 miles. If you use the IRS's flat mileage rate, you include $130 (1,000 miles × 13¢) as medical expenses on your 2002 return. If you incurred tolls or parking fees during the trips, add these expenses to the mileage costs.

Medical conferences. Travel costs and admission fees to a medical conference are deductible medical expenses if an illness suffered by you, your spouse, or your dependents is the subject of the conference. For example, the IRS allowed a parent to deduct the registration fees and cost of traveling to a medical conference dealing with treatment options for a disease suffered by her dependent child. The child's doctor had recommended the conference. During the conference, most of the parent's time was spent attending sessions on her child's condition. Any recreational activities were secondary. If the parent had attended the conference because of her own condition the same deductions would have been allowed.

Lodging and meals while attending the conference were not deductible; these are allowed only if treatment is received at a licensed hospital or similar facility, as discussed below.

Lodging expenses. If you are receiving inpatient care at a hospital or similar facility, your expenses, including lodging and meals, are deductible. If you are not an inpatient, lodging expenses while away from home are deductible as medical expenses if the trip is primarily to receive treatment from a doctor in a licensed hospital, hospital-related outpatient facility, or a facility equivalent to a hospital. Meal expenses are not deductible unless they are paid as part of inpatient care.

Caution

Meal Costs of Medical Trip

While transportation to receive medical care is a deductible medical expense subject to the 7.5% AGI floor, meals while on a trip for medical treatment are not deductible. They simply replace the meals you normally would eat. However, if you are hospitalized, the cost of meals while an inpatient is a deductible expense.

EXAMPLE

Polyak spent the winter in Florida on the advice of her doctor to alleviate a chronic heart and lung condition. While in Florida, she stayed in a rented trailer that cost $1,426. She saw a physician for treatment of an infection and to renew medications. She deducted the trailer costs as a medical deduction, which the IRS and Tax Court disallowed. Although her Florida trip was primarily for mitigating her condition, she did not travel to receive medical care from a physician in a licensed hospital or related outpatient facility. The medical care was routine and incidental to her travel to Florida. Her deduction for transportation costs to Florida was not contested by the IRS, which conceded that the trip was primarily for and essential to her health.

The deduction for lodging while receiving treatment as an outpatient at a licensed hospital, clinic, or hospital-equivalent facility is limited to $50 per night per person. For example, the limit is $100 if a parent travels with a sick child. The IRS ruled that the $50 allowance could be claimed by a parent for a six-week hotel stay while her eight-year-old daughter was treated in a nearby hospital for serious injuries received in an automobile accident. The mother's presence was necessary so that she could sign release forms.

Deductible Transportation Costs

Examples of travel costs that have been allowed as medical deductions by rulings or court decisions are:

- Nurse's fare if nurse is required on trip
- Parent's fare if parent is needed to accompany child who requires medical care
- Parent's fare to visit his child at an institution where the visits are prescribed by a doctor
- Trip to visit specialist in another city
- Airplane fare to a distant city in which a patient used to live to have a checkup by a family doctor living there. That he could have received the same examination in the city in which he presently lived did not bar his deduction.
- Trip to escape a climate that is bad for a specific condition. For example, the cost of a trip from a northern state to Florida during the winter on the advice of a doctor to relieve a chronic heart condition is deductible. The cost of a trip made solely to improve a post-operative condition by a person recovering from a throat operation was ruled deductible.
- Travel to an Alcoholics Anonymous club meeting if membership in the group has been advised by a doctor
- Disabled veteran's commuting expenses where a doctor prescribed work and driving as therapy
- Wife's trip to provide nursing care for an ailing husband in a distant city. The trip was ordered by her husband's doctor as a necessity.
- Driving prescribed as therapy
- Travel costs of kidney transplant donor or prospective donor

Nondeductible Transportation Costs

- Trip for the general improvement of your health
- Traveling to areas of favorable climates during the year for general health reasons, rather than living permanently in a locality suitable for your health

- Meals while on a trip for outpatient medical treatment—even if cost of transportation is a valid medical cost. However, a court has allowed the deduction of the extra cost of specially prepared food.
- Trip to get "spiritual" rather than medical aid. For example, the cost of a trip to the Shrine of Our Lady of Lourdes is not deductible.
- Moving a family to a climate more suitable to an ill mother's condition. Only the mother's travel costs are deductible.
- Moving household furnishings to area advised by physician
- Operating an auto or special vehicle to go to work because of a disability
- Convalescence cruise advised by a doctor for a patient recovering from pneumonia
- Loss on sale of car bought for medical travel
- Medical seminar cruise taken by patient whose condition was reviewed by physicians taking the cruise

17.10 Schooling for the Mentally or Physically Disabled

You may deduct as medical expenses the costs of sending a mentally or physically disabled person to a special school or institution to overcome or alleviate his or her disability. Such costs may cover:

- Teaching of Braille or lip reading
- Training, caring for, supervising, and treating a mentally retarded person
- Cost of meals and lodgings, if boarding is required at the school
- Costs of regular education courses also taught at the school, provided they are incidental to the special courses and services furnished by the school

The fact that a particular school or camp is recommended for an emotionally disturbed child by a psychiatrist will not qualify the tuition as a deduction if the school or camp has no special program geared to the child's specific personal problem. However, you may deduct the costs of maintaining a mentally retarded person in a home specially selected to meet the standards set by a psychiatrist to aid in an adjustment from life in a mental hospital to community living.

Payment for future medical care expenses is deductible if immediate payment is required by contract.

EXAMPLES

1. An emotionally disturbed child was sent to a private school maintaining a staff of three psychologists. His father deducted the school fee of $6,270 as a medical expense. The IRS disallowed the amount, claiming that the child, who was neither mentally retarded nor handicapped, was sent to school primarily for an education. The Tax Court allowed the father to deduct $3,000 covering the psychological treatment.

2. A retarded boy had been excluded from several schools for the mentally handicapped because he needed close attention. The director of a military academy had extensive experience in training young boys. Although it was not the usual practice of the academy to enroll mentally handicapped children, the director accepted the boy on a day-to-day basis as a personal challenge. The Tax Court held that the cost of both tuition and transportation to bring the boy to and from the school were deductible medical expenses. The primary purpose of the training given the boy was not ordinary education but remedial training designed to overcome his handicap. But note that, in other cases, a deduction for tuition of a military school to which a child was sent in order to remove him from a tense family environment, and the cost of a blind boy's attendance at a regular private school that made a special effort to accommodate his Braille equipment, were disallowed.

17.11 Nursing Homes

A payment for medical services, meals, and lodging to a nursing home, convalescent home, home for the aged, or sanitarium is a deductible medical expense if you, your spouse, or dependent is confined for medical treatment.

If the main reason for admission is not to obtain medical care, but you can show the part of the cost covering actual medical and nursing care, that amount is deductible, but not the cost of meals and lodging.

In an unusual case, a court allowed a medical expense deduction for apartment rent of an aged parent.

Caution

Counseling at a Private School

The parent of a child with psychological problems may deduct only that part of a private school fee directly related to psychological aid given to the child.

Filing Tip

Meal Costs at a Nursing Home

If the patient entered a nursing home to receive medical care, a deduction may be taken for meals and lodging while there, in addition to medical care costs.

EXAMPLE

A doctor recommended to Ungar that his 90-year-old mother, convalescing from a brain hemorrhage, could receive better care at less expense in accommodations away from a hospital. A two-room apartment was rented, hospital equipment installed, and nurses engaged for seven months. The rent totaled $1,400. Ungar's sister, who worked in her husband's shoe store, nursed her mother for six weeks. Ungar paid the wages of a clerk who was hired to substitute for his sister in the store. Ungar deducted both the rent and wages as medical expenses. The IRS disallowed them; a Tax Court reversed the IRS's decision. The apartment rent was no less a medical expense than the cost of a hospital room. As for the clerk's wages, they too were deductible medical costs. The clerk was hired specifically to allow the daughter to nurse her mother, thereby avoiding the larger, though more direct, medical expense of hiring a nurse.

Establishing medical purpose. The following facts are helpful in establishing the full deductibility of payments to a nursing home, convalescent home, home for the aged, or sanitarium:

- The patient entered the institution on the direction or suggestion of a doctor.
- Attendance or treatment at the institution had a direct therapeutic effect on the condition suffered by the patient.
- The attendance at the institution was for a specific ailment rather than for a "general" health condition. Simply showing that the patient suffers from an ailment is not sufficient proof that he or she is in the home for treatment.

Payment for future lifetime care. Generally, no deduction is allowed for prepayment of medical expenses for services to be performed in a later taxable year. However, in the Examples below, the IRS allowed a deduction where there was a current obligation to pay.

EXAMPLES

1. A 78-year-old man entered into an agreement with a retirement home. For a lump-sum payment, the home agreed to provide lifetime care, including medical care, medicine, and hospitalization. The lifetime care fee was calculated without regard to fees received from other patients and was not insurance. The home allocated 30% of the lump-sum payment to medical expenses based on its prior experience. The IRS holds that this part of the payment is deductible in the year paid. It holds that the legal obligation to pay the medical expenses was incurred at the time the lump-sum payment was made, even though medical services would not be performed until a future time, if at all. Should any portion of the lump-sum payment be refunded, that part attributable to the deducted amount must be reported as income.

2. Parents contracted with an institution to care for their handicapped child after their death. The contract provided for payments as follows: 20% on signing, 10% within 12 months, 10% within 24 months, and the balance when the child enters. Payment of specified amounts at specified intervals was a condition imposed by the institution for its agreement to accept the child for lifetime care. Since the obligation to pay was incurred at the time payments were made, they are deductible as medical expenses, although the medical services were not to be performed until a future time, if at all.

3. A couple entered a retirement home that would provide them with accommodations, meals, and medical care for life. They paid a founder's fee of $40,000 and a monthly fee of $800. If they leave the home, they may get a refund of a portion of the founder's fee. Fifteen percent of the monthly fee and 10% of the founder's fee will be used for medical care and 5% of the founder's fee will be used for construction of a health facility. On the basis of these figures, the couple may deduct as medical costs 10% of the founder's fee and 15% of the monthly fee. However, the portion of the founder's fee for the possible health facility does not qualify as a medical expense. Finally, any refund of the founder's fee received in a later year may be income to the extent medical deductions were previously claimed for the fees.

 Caution

Nurse's Services
The cost of a nurse's services is a deductible medical expense, even if the nurse is not licensed or registered, so long as he or she provides the patient with medical services. If household services are also provided, only the portion of the nurse's pay attributable to the provision of medical services qualifies.

17.12 Nurses' Wages

The costs of a nurse attending an ill person are deductible. Costs include any Social Security or Medicare (FICA) tax paid by you. You may deduct the expenses of a nurse who is not registered or licensed so long as he or she provides you with medical services. Medical services include giving medications, changing dressings, and bathing and grooming the patient. If the nurse also performs domestic services, deduct only that part of the pay attributable to medical services for the patient.

The cost of an attendant's meals is included in your medical expenses. Divide total food costs among the household members to determine the attendant's share.

Costs eligible for tax credit. If, in order to work, you pay a nurse to look after a physically or mentally disabled dependent, you may be able to claim a credit for all or part of the nurse's wages as a dependent care expense. You may not, however, claim both a credit and a medical expense deduction. First, you claim the nurse's wages as a dependent care cost. If not all of the wages are allowed as care costs because of the expense limits (Chapter 25), the remaining balance is deductible as a medical expense.

The salary of a clerk hired specifically to relieve a wife from working in her husband's store in order to care for her ill mother was allowed as a medical expense; *see* the Ungar Example in *17.11*.

EXAMPLES

1. Dodge's wife was arthritic. He was advised by her doctor to have someone take care of her to prevent her from falling. He moved her to his daughter's home and paid the daughter to care for her mother. He deducted the payments to his daughter. The IRS disallowed the deduction, claiming that the daughter was not a trained nurse. The Tax Court allowed that part of the deduction specifically attributed to nursing aid. Whether a medical service has been rendered depends on the nature of the services rendered, not on the qualifications or title of the person who renders them. Here, the daughter's services, following the doctor's advice, qualify as medical care.

2. An attendant hired by a quadriplegic performs household duties, in addition to caring for his medical and personal needs. The quadriplegic pays him wages and also provides food and lodging. According to the IRS, a medical expense deduction is allowable only for that portion of the wages attributable to medical and personal care. The wages are apportioned on the basis of time spent performing nursing-type services and time spent performing household duties. The same allocation is used to determine the portion of the cost of the attendant's meals that is deductible as a medical expense. However, the attendant's lodging is not deductible as a medical expense, unless the quadriplegic shows additional expenditures directly attributable to lodging the attendant, such as paying increased rent for an apartment with another bedroom for the attendant.

17.13 Home Improvements as Medical Expenses

A disease or ailment may require the construction of special equipment or facilities in a home: A heart patient may need an elevator to carry him or her upstairs; a polio patient, a pool; and an asthmatic patient, an air cleaning system.

You may deduct the full cost of minor equipment installed for a medical reason if it does not increase the value of your property, as, for example, the cost of a detachable window air conditioner. Where equipment increases the value of your property, you may generally take a medical deduction only to the extent that the cost of the equipment exceeds the increase in the value of the property. This increased-value test does not apply to certain structural changes to a residence made by a handicapped person, as discussed at the end of this section. If the equipment does not increase the value of the property, its entire cost is deductible, even though it is permanently fixed to the property.

EXAMPLE

Mike Gerard's daughter suffered from cystic fibrosis. While there is no known cure for the disease, doctors attempt to prolong life by preventing pulmonary infection. One approach is to maintain a constant temperature and high humidity. A doctor recommended that Gerard install a central air-conditioning unit in his home for his daughter. It cost $1,300 and increased the value of his home by $800. The $500 balance was a deductible medical expense.

Prepaid home construction costs. Zipkin suffered from multiple chemical sensitivity syndrome and built a house with special filtering and ventilation systems. The cost of the special features exceeded the fair market value of the home by $645,000. She claimed a deduction for the full amount when the house was completed. The IRS disallowed the deduction for the construction costs incurred in the years before the home was completed. Zipkin successfully argued before a federal district court that the construction costs should be treated as prepaid medical expenses that

 Caution

Does Equipment Increase Value of Home?

When special equipment is installed in your home to alleviate a disease or ailment, you must determine if it increases the value of your home. You generally may claim a medical deduction only to the extent that the cost of the equipment exceeds the increase in value. However, if you install a ramp or railing, widen doorways or hallways, or add similar improvements to cope with a disability, these are usually treated by the IRS as not adding to the value of the home.

are deductible in the year medical benefits are received. The federal court allowed Zipkin to deduct the full amount in the year the home became habitable.

Deducting the cost of a swimming pool. If swimming is prescribed as physical therapy, the cost of constructing a home swimming pool may be partly deductible as a medical expense but only to the extent the cost exceeds the increase in value to the house. However, the IRS is likely to question any deduction because of the possibility that the pool may be used for recreation. If you can show that the pool is specially equipped to alleviate your condition and is not generally suited for recreation, the IRS will allow the deduction unless the expense is considered to be "lavish or extravagant." For example, the IRS allowed a deduction for a pool constructed by an osteoarthritis patient. His physician prescribed swimming several times a day as treatment. He built an indoor lap pool with specially designed stairs and a hydrotherapy device. Given these features, the IRS concluded that the pool was specially designed to provide medical treatment.

In one case the IRS tried to limit the cost of a luxury indoor pool built for therapeutic reasons to the least expensive construction. The Tax Court rejected the IRS position, holding that a medical expense is not to be limited to the cheapest form of treatment; on appeal, the IRS position was adopted.

If, instead of building a pool, you buy a home with a pool, can you deduct the part of the purchase price allocated to the pool? The Tax Court said no. The purchase price of the house includes the fair market value of the pool. Therefore, there is no extra cost above the increase in the home's value that would support a medical expense deduction.

The operating costs of an indoor pool were allowed by the Tax Court as a deduction to an emphysema sufferer.

A deduction is barred where the primary purpose of the improvement is for personal convenience rather than medical necessity.

EXAMPLES
1. Ken Cherry was advised by his doctor to swim to relieve his severe emphysema and bronchitis. He could not swim at local health spas; they did not open early enough or stay open late enough to allow him to swim before or after work. His home was too small for a pool. He bought a lot and built a new house with an indoor pool. He used the pool several times a day, and swimming improved his condition; if he did not swim, his symptoms returned. Cherry deducted pool operating costs of $4,000 for fuel, electricity, insurance, and repairs. The IRS disallowed the deductions, claiming that the pool was used for personal recreation. Besides, it did not have special medical equipment. The Tax Court allowed the deduction. Cherry built the pool to swim in order to exercise his lungs. That there was no special equipment is irrelevant; Cherry did not need special ramps, railings, a shallow floor, or whirlpool. Finally, his family rarely used the pool.
2. Doug Haines broke his leg in a skiing accident and underwent various forms of physical therapy, including swimming. To aid his recovery, his physician recommended that he install a swimming pool at his home. The Tax Court agreed with the IRS that the cost of the pool was not deductible. Although swimming was beneficial to his condition, he needed special therapy only for a limited period of time, and he could have gotten it at less cost at a nearby public pool. Finally, because of weather conditions, the pool could not be used for about half of the year.

Cost of maintaining and operating improvement. The expense of maintaining and operating equipment installed for medical reasons may be claimed as a medical expense, even if the cost of the equipment and its installation is not deductible under the rules in this section.

Handicapped persons. The increased-value test does not apply to a handicapped person who makes structural changes to a residence such as adding ramps, modifying doorways and stairways, installing railings and support bars, and altering cabinets, outlets, fixtures, and warning systems. Such improvements are treated for medical deduction purposes as not increasing the value of the home. Lifts, but not elevators, also are in this category. The full cost of such improvements is added to other deductible expenses and the total is deductible to the extent that it exceeds the 7.5% AGI floor.

17.14 Costs Deductible as Business Expenses

In some cases, expenses may be deductible as business expenses rather than as medical expenses. Claiming a business deduction is preferable because the deduction is not subject to the 7.5% adjusted gross income floor.

 Filing Tip

Disability-Related Job Costs
If you are disabled and incur costs to enable you to work, the payments may be treated as a deductible business expense rather than as a medical expense.

The cost of a checkup required by your employer is a miscellaneous job expense subject to the 2% of adjusted gross income floor *(19.3)*.

> **EXAMPLE**
>
> An airline pilot is required by his company to take a semi-annual physical exam at his own expense. If he fails to produce a resultant certificate of good health, he is subject to discharge. The cost of such checkups certifying physical fitness for a job is an ordinary and necessary business expense. If the doctor prescribes a treatment or further examinations to maintain the pilot's physical condition, the cost of these subsequent treatments or examinations may be deducted only as medical expenses, even though they are needed to maintain the physical standards required by the job. Thus, a professional singer who consults a throat specialist may not deduct the fee as a business expense. The fee is a medical expense subject to the 7.5% AGI floor.

The Tax Court allowed a licensed social worker working as a therapist to deduct psychoanalysis costs as an education expense.

Disabled persons. Some expenses incurred by a physically or mentally disabled person may be deductible as business expenses rather than as medical expenses. A business expense deduction may be allowed if the expense is necessary for you to satisfactorily perform your job and is not required or used, except incidentally, for personal purposes.

If you are self-employed, claim the deduction on Schedule C *(40.6)*.

If you are an employee, the expenses are listed on Form 2106 and if not reimbursed, entered on Schedule A; *see 19.4*. The expenses are a fully deductible miscellaneous itemized deduction; the 2% AGI floor does *not* apply.

> **EXAMPLES**
>
> 1. A professor is paralyzed from the waist down and confined to a wheelchair. When he attends out-of-town business meetings, he has his wife, a friend, or a colleague accompany him to help him with baggage, stairs, narrow doors, and to sit with him on airplanes when airlines will not allow wheelchair passengers without an attendant. While he does not pay them a salary, he does pay their travel costs. He may deduct these costs as business expenses. They are incurred solely because of his occupation.
> 2. An attorney uses prostheses due to bilateral amputation of his legs and takes medication several times a day for other ailments. On both personal and business trips, his wife or a neighbor accompanies him to help him travel and receive medication. He may deduct the out-of-town expenses paid for his neighbor only as a medical expense. The neighbor's services are not business expenses because assistance in personal activities is regularly provided. When his wife accompanies him, he may deduct her transportation costs as a medical expense; her food and lodging are nondeductible ordinary living expenses.

17.15 Long-Term Care Costs of Chronically ill

You may deduct as medical expenses (subject to the 7.5% adjusted gross income floor) your unreimbursed expenses for qualifying long-term care services that you require because you are "chronically ill" or because your spouse or dependent is chronically ill.

Qualifying long-term care services for a chronically ill individual. A chronically ill person is someone who has been certified by a licensed health-care practitioner within the preceding 12 months as being unable to perform for a period of at least 90 days at least two of the following activities without substantial assistance: eating, toileting, dressing, bathing, continence, or transferring. Also qualifying as chronically ill is someone who requires substantial supervision because of severe cognitive impairment, such as from Alzheimer's disease.

Qualifying long-term care services for a chronically ill individual are broadly defined as necessary diagnostic, preventive, therapeutic, curing, treating, mitigation, and rehabilitative services, and also maintenance or personal care services. The services must be provided under a plan of care prescribed by a licensed health-care practitioner, who may be a physician, a registered nurse, a licensed social worker, or other individual meeting Treasury requirements. Services provided by a spouse or relative are deductible only if that person is a licensed professional; services provided by a related corporation or partnership do not qualify.

 Filing Tip

Long-Term Care Insurance
Unreimbursed expenses for long-term care services to care for a chronically ill patient are deductible medical expenses subject to the 7.5% AGI floor. Depending on your age, all or part of premiums paid for a qualifying policy are includible in your medical expenses.

Deductible premium costs of long-term care policies. Depending on your age, all or part of your premium payments for a qualified long-term care policy may be included as deductible medical expenses, subject to the 7.5% adjusted gross income floor. To qualify, the policy must provide for long-term care services for the chronically ill (*see* above). The amount of the deductible premium depends on your age at the end of the year. For 2002, the maximum deductible premium amounts are: $240 if you are age 40 or younger at the end of 2002; $450 for those age 41 through 50; $900 for those age 51 through 60; $2,390 for those age 61 through 70; and $2,990 for those over age 70. These limits may be increased for 2003 by an inflation factor; *see* the *Supplement*.

If you are considering purchase of a long-term care insurance policy, make sure that it qualifies for the tax treatment explained in this section. A qualified contract must provide only for coverage of qualified long-term care services and be guaranteed renewable; it may not provide for a cash surrender value or money that can be assigned, pledged, or borrowed; it may not reimburse expenses covered by Medicare except where Medicare is a secondary payer or the contract makes *per diem* payments without regard to expenses.

Benefits paid by qualified long-term care policies. Benefits for an indemnity-type contract are tax free to the extent they pay or reimburse long-term care expenses. Benefits paid from a *per diem* type contract are tax free up to $210 a day in 2002. If *per diem* payments are received for the full year, the 2002 exclusion is $76,650. If *per diem* payments exceed $210, the excess over $210 is tax free to the extent of unreimbursed long-term care costs. Any balance of the excess is taxable. In 2003, the $210 limit may be adjusted for inflation.

EXAMPLE

In 2002, you receive *per diem* long-term care benefits of $225 under a qualifying long-term care policy. Your actual daily costs are above $225. No part of the benefit payments is taxable provided you have proof of actual costs.

17.16 Life Insurance Used To Pay Medical Costs of Terminally ill

A person who is terminally ill may be forced to cash in a life insurance policy to pay medical bills and other living expenses. Insurance companies have developed life insurance policies with accelerated death benefit clauses to help terminally ill patients meet the high cost of medical care. Where a policy lacks an accelerated payment clause, it is also possible to sell a life insurance policy to a viatical settlement company that specializes in buying policies from ill persons who require funds to pay expenses.

Accelerated death benefits and viatical settlement proceeds received by terminally ill individuals are *not taxed*.

Life insurance used by chronically ill. A chronically ill individual may sell a life insurance policy to a viatical settlement company to pay for long-term care costs. However, tax-free treatment is determined under the tax rules applied to long-term care policies in *17.15*. Thus, if the proceeds exceed the $210 *per diem* limit for 2002 and also exceed actual long-term care costs, the excess is taxable. Accelerated life insurance proceeds paid under a long-term care rider are also subject to the rules in *17.15*.

17.17 Archer MSAs

Archer MSAs (previously called Medical Savings Accounts) are designed to lower the costs of providing medical expense reimbursement plans for employees of certain small businesses and self-employed persons. To do this, a medical plan combines a high-deductible health insurance policy to cover catastrophic costs and a tax-sheltered savings account that you use to pay routine medical expenses that fall below the policy deductible. More specifically, an Archer MSA combines:

1. A high-deductible health insurance policy with deductibles fixed by law. For individual coverage, the deductible in 2002 must be between $1,650 and $2,500. For family coverage, the deductible in 2002 must be between $3,300 and $4,950. Annual out-of-pocket costs excluding premiums must be limited to $3,300 for individual coverage and $6,050 for family coverage. The policy deductible and out-of-pocket limits may be increased for 2003 by an inflation factor; *see* the *Supplement*.

Filing Instruction

Form 8853

If you received payments in 2002 from a qualified long-term care policy, you must figure the amount of taxable payments, if any, on Form 8853.

Planning Reminder

MSA Contribution Deadline

You have until April 15, 2003, to make a deductible contribution to an Archer MSA for 2002.

2. A medical savings account, or Archer MSA, to which annual contributions may be made based on the amount of the deductible set by the health insurance policy. For a person with individual coverage, the maximum contribution is 65% of the policy deductible. For someone with family coverage, the maximum contribution is 75% of the policy deductible. To contribute the maximum amount, you must have the policy for the entire year. If you obtained high-deductible health plan coverage during the year, one-twelfth of the limit may be contributed for each full month of coverage.

Income earned on Archer MSA funds accumulates tax free. An Archer MSA can be with an insurance company, bank, or other financial institution that has been approved by the IRS for this purpose. Archer MSA contributions are reported to the IRS on Form 5498-MSA.

Contributions by self-employed. Here are the tax consequences of making an Archer MSA contribution if you are self-employed:

1. You may deduct the health insurance premium element. For 2002, you may deduct 70% of the health insurance premium payments made in 2002 directly from gross income on Line 30 of Form 1040; *see 12.2* for restrictions. The balance of premiums not deductible on Line 30 may be treated as a medical expense deductible on Schedule A if your total medical expenses exceed 7.5% of your adjusted gross income. For 2003, 100% of the premiums will be deductible directly from income on Form 1040.

2. For 2002, you report your Archer MSA contribution on Form 8853 and deduct the contribution directly from gross income on Line 27 of Form 1040. The contribution may not exceed the net self-employment income from the business through which you have the high-deductible health insurance.

EXAMPLE

Jones, who is self-employed, pays $400 per month for family coverage in 2002 under a high-deductible health plan. If he has coverage for 10 months in 2002, he can contribute $3,000 to an Archer MSA for the year ($4,800 annual deductible ÷ 12 months × 10 months of coverage × 75% maximum contribution = $3,000). On Line 30 of Form 1040, Jones can deduct $2,800 (70% of $4,000 in premiums) and he can include the balance of the premiums as part of medical expenses subject to the 7.5% adjusted gross income floor on Schedule A.

He reports the $3,000 MSA contribution on Form 8853 and as long as his net earnings from self-employment are at least $3,000, he deducts the $3,000 contribution on Line 27 of Form 1040.

Contributions by or for employees of qualifying small businesses. Small business employers having an average of 50 or fewer employees in either of the two prior calendar years may choose to offer Archer MSA plans for their employees. The employer may fully finance the contracts or pay for the insurance element while allowing the employee to contribute to the Archer MSA account. If the employer finances the full costs of the plan, the payments are not taxed under the rules at *3.1.* If the employer contributes anything to an employee's Archer MSA, the employee is not allowed to make any Archer MSA contribution for that year; *see 3.1.* If no employer contributions to the Archer MSA are made and the employee contributes to the Archer MSA, the employee reports the contribution on Form 8853 and may deduct the contribution up to the allowable limit from gross income on Line 27 of Form 1040. Any health insurance premiums paid by the employee are combined with other medical expenses paid during the year with the total being deductible only to the extent it exceeds 7.5% of adjusted gross income.

Distributions from Archer MSA. You can take a distribution from your Archer MSA to pay for medical expenses that are not reimbursable under your high-deductible plan. A distribution is tax free if it is used for qualifying medical expenses of you, your spouse, or your dependents. Generally, these are costs that could be claimed as an itemized deduction if you paid them directly. Premiums for long-term care insurance, for health coverage while you are receiving unemployment benefits, or for continuing coverage (COBRA) from a former employer qualify; other insurance premiums do not. Tax may be imposed on a distribution used to pay medical expenses of someone who was not covered by a high-deductible plan when the expenses were incurred; *see* Form 8853 for details.

Archer MSA distributions are reported on Part III of Form 8853, which must be attached to Form 1040. A taxable distribution from Form 8853 is reported on Line 21 of Form 1040 as "other income." A taxable distribution is also subject to a 15% penalty unless you are age 65 or older, or disabled.

Chapter 18

Casualty and Theft Losses and Involuntary Conversions

All casualty and theft losses are claimed on Form 4684. The tax treatment of an unreimbursed casualty or theft loss depends on the purpose for which you held the damaged, destroyed, or stolen property. A loss of property held for:

• *Personal purposes* is subject to the sudden events test *(18.1)* and the deduction is reduced by $100 and an additional 10% of your adjusted gross income *(18.11)* on Form 4684.

The itemized deduction claimed for personal-use property is not subject to the 3% reduction computation; *see 13.7.*

• *Income-producing purposes,* such as negotiable securities, should be claimed on Form 4684 and then entered on Line 27 of Schedule A. The loss deduction is not subject to the 2% AGI floor *(19.1)* or the 3% reduction *(13.7)* that applies to a loss deduction for income-producing property.

• *Business or rental purposes* is claimed on Form 4684 and then as a loss on Form 4797. It is not subject to any floor or the sudden event test. Follow the instructions to Form 4684.

If you have realized a gain, you may defer tax by replacing or repairing the property; *see 18.18.*

Appraisal fees and other incidental costs, such as taking photos to establish the amount of the loss, are claimed as a miscellaneous itemized deduction on Line 22 of Schedule A, Form 1040.

Deductible Casualty Losses

18.1 Sudden Event Test for Casualty Losses

To be a deductible casualty loss, property must be damaged or destroyed as the result of a sudden, unexpected, or unusual event. A sudden event is one that is swift, not gradual or progressive. An unexpected event is one that is ordinarily unanticipated and unintended. An unusual event is one that is not a day-to-day occurrence and that is not typical of the activity in which you were engaged. Chance or a natural phenomenon must be present. Examples include earthquakes, hurricanes, tornadoes, floods, severe storms, landslides, and fires. Loss due to vandalism during riots or civil disorders also is treated as a casualty loss. Damage to your car from an accident is generally deductible; *see 18.7*. Courts have allowed deductions for other types of accidents; *see* Example 2 below. The requirement of suddenness is designed to bar deductions for damage caused by a natural action such as erosion, corrosion, and termite infestation occurring over a period of time.

The IRS and the courts have generally disallowed casualty deductions based on a loss in property value due to permanent buyer resistance rather than actual physical damage; *see* Examples 4 and 5 below.

EXAMPLES

1. A homeowner claimed a loss for water damage to wallpaper and plaster. The water entered through the window frame. The loss was disallowed. He gave no evidence that the damage came from a sudden or destructive force, such as a storm. The damage may have been caused by progressive deterioration.

2. Mr. White accidentally slammed the car door on his wife's hand. In pain, she shook her hand vigorously. A diamond flew out of her ring's setting, which was loosened by the impact. The diamond was never found. The IRS disallowed the deduction, contending that a casualty loss requires a cataclysmic event. The Tax Court disagreed. A deductible casualty loss occurs whenever an accidental force is exerted against property, and its owner is powerless to prevent the damage because of the suddenness. The IRS has accepted the decision.

3. A boat, which was in a poor state of repair, was equipped with a pump that automatically began operating when the water in the hull rose above a certain level. One day, the dockside power source failed, and the boat sank at its mooring within four hours. The IRS claimed that no deductible casualty occurred because the leakage was a chronic problem. The Tax Court allowed the deduction. The sinking was not a direct result of the boat's leaking hull, but of the failure of the on-board water pump.

4. A Brentwood couple, whose home was near the O.J. Simpson house, filed for a refund in federal district court to claim a $400,000 casualty loss deduction. The couple claimed that the double murder and the media frenzy surrounding the Simpson trial caused permanent buyer resistance in their neighborhood, lowering the value of their home by at least $400,000. The district court denied the refund. The couple relied on a 1986 case in which the Eleventh Circuit appeals court allowed Finkbohner a casualty loss deduction based on permanent buyer resistance when 12 nearby homes were razed by local authorities following severe floods and the lots were required to be kept as open space. However, the Brentwood couple's case was appealable to the Ninth Circuit, and the Ninth Circuit requires that a casualty loss be based on actual physical damage caused by a fire, storm, or other sudden unusual event and not merely buyer resistance. Therefore, the claim for a casualty loss deduction for the Brentwood home was denied.

   In a similar case, the Tax Court denied a casualty loss deduction to O.J. Simpson's next-door neighbors, who claimed they had suffered a permanent devaluation of their home's value due to the trial publicity. The Tax Court holds that actual physical damage is required for a deduction.

5. A 1983 avalanche caused $9,000 of physical damage to the Lunds' vacation home in Sundance, Utah, but they claimed a $221,000 deduction. They argued that there was a permanent loss in property value due to the avalanche risk in the area. Local authorities blocked road access during heavy snowfalls and some neighbors had decided not to rebuild destroyed homes. A federal district court agreed with the IRS that their loss could not exceed the actual physical damage. There may have been temporary buyer resistance following the avalanche, but not a permanent change in the area itself as there was in the Eleventh Circuit *Finkbohner* case mentioned above in Example 4.

Is drought damage deductible? The IRS does not generally allow deductions for drought damage. An agent may argue that the loss resulted from progressive deterioration, which does not fit the legal definition of a personal casualty loss. Courts have allowed deductions for severe drought where the damages occur in the same year as the drought.

If the damage becomes noticeable a year later, a court will view this as evidence of progressive deterioration that does not qualify as a deductible casualty. Where there are drought conditions, inspect your property for damage before the end of the year and claim a deduction for the damage in that year to negate an IRS argument that damage was caused by progressive deterioration.

Damage to surrounding property. Loss due to buyer resistance because of damage to surrounding property is generally not deductible. However, the Eleventh Circuit allowed a deduction. *See* Example 4 above.

Damage to trees. The destruction of trees by southern pine beetles over a period of 5 to 10 days was held by the IRS to be a casualty. One court decided similarly where the destruction occurred over a 30-day period. For figuring the casualty deduction for tree and shrub damage, *see 18.6*.

Deduction despite faulty construction. A plumber stepped on a pipe that was improperly installed. Resulting underground flooding caused damage of over $20,000. The IRS argued that this was caused by a construction fault and thus was not a casualty loss. The Tax Court disagreed. The plumber caused the damage. Improper construction was only an element in the causative chain.

Foreseeable events and preventable accidents. The IRS may disallow a deduction by claiming that the loss was foreseeable and therefore not a deductible casualty loss; *see* the following Examples.

Loss Prevention Measures

The cost of preventive measures, such as burglar alarms or smoke detectors, or the cost of boarding up property against a storm, is not deductible.

EXAMPLES

1. Heyn owned a hillside lot on which he contracted for the building of a home. A soil test showed a high proportion of fine-grain dense sandstone, which is unstable. His construction contract called for appropriate shoring up and support. But, because of the contractor's negligence, a landslide occurred. The IRS disallowed the loss on the ground that it was not a "casualty" because the danger was known before Heyn undertook the project and because of the negligence involved. The court disagreed. The contractor's negligence is not a factor in determining whether there was a casualty. For example, an automobile collision is considered a casualty, even if caused by negligent driving. Foreseeability is not a factor. A weather report may warn property owners to take protective steps against an approaching hurricane, but losses caused by the hurricane are deductible. The IRS has agreed to accept the decision.

2. Mrs. Kane placed her dirty ring in a glass of ammonia. Not knowing the contents of the glass, her husband emptied it into the sink and started the automatic garbage disposal, crushing the ring. The court allowed a full deduction for the loss, which it said resulted from a destructive force. That Mr. Kane was negligent has no bearing on whether the event was a casualty.

3. At Christmastime in 1982, Hananel left his 1974 Plymouth Valiant in Chicago in an area in which the city was towing away cars to make room for construction work. When he returned a week later, he found that his car was missing and reported it stolen. A month later, he learned that the city pound had towed the car away and then crushed it because its ownership could not be determined. He claimed a casualty loss for the car. The IRS disallowed the deduction, claiming that the towing and crushing were not an unforeseeable event, and thus did not qualify as a casualty.

    The Tax Court agreed that Hananel could have foreseen that leaving the car on the street subjected it to being towed. He was negligent. However, the penalty for this is a towing charge. He could not have foreseen its destruction. Therefore, the destruction occurred from an unusual and unexpected event, and he was allowed to claim a casualty loss deduction.

4. Destruction of a lawn through the careless use of weed killer was held by the Tax Court to be a casualty.

Loss From Termites

Termite damage is generally nondeductible since it often results from long periods of termite infestation. Proving a sudden action in the sense of fixing the approximate moment of the termite invasion is difficult. Some courts have allowed a deduction, but the IRS will bar deductions for termite damage under any conditions based on a study that found that serious termite damage results only after an infestation of three to eight years. Examples of other nondeductible casualty losses are at *18.9*.

18.2 When To Deduct a Casualty or Theft Loss

Generally, you deduct a casualty loss in the year the casualty occurs, regardless of when you repair or replace damaged or destroyed property. However, for a qualifying disaster area loss *(18.3)*, you have the option of claiming the loss on your return for the year immediately preceding the year in which the disaster occurred. If a casualty occurs in one year and you do not discover the damage until a later year, or you know damage has been inflicted, but you do not know the full extent of the loss because you expect reimbursement in a later year, here is what to do:

If you reasonably expect reimbursement in a later year. You should deduct in the year the casualty occurred only that part of your loss (after applying the personal property floors discussed in *18.11*) for which you do not expect reimbursement. For example, if you expect a full insurance recovery in 2003 for a 2002 loss, you would take no deduction on your 2002 return.

If you do not expect any reimbursement and deduct a loss in 2002, but you receive insurance or other reimbursement in 2003, the reimbursement is taxable in 2003 to the extent that the 2002 deduction gave you a tax benefit by reducing your 2002 taxable income; *see 11.6*. You may not amend your 2002 tax return.

> **EXAMPLE**
>
> In 1969, Hurricane Camille destroyed oceanfront real estate owned jointly by two brothers. The buildings were insured under two policies that included wind damage but not losses resulting from floods, tidal waves, or water. The insurers, claiming the tidal wave had caused the destruction, denied their claim. The brothers consulted an attorney about the possibility of suit against the insurance companies, but there seemed to be little likelihood of recovery, so the brothers deducted their shares of the casualty loss in 1969. However, in January 1970, the adjusters of both companies changed their decisions, reimbursing the brothers for more than two-thirds of their loss. One of the brothers filed an amended 1969 tax return, reducing the previously reported casualty loss.
>
> The IRS claimed that the insurance recovery was taxable in the year of receipt, 1970, to the extent that the prior deduction reduced 1969 income. The brother claimed that he made an error in claiming the deduction in 1969 because he had a reasonable prospect of reimbursement. Thus it was proper to reduce the deduction by the reimbursement on an amended return.
>
> The Tax Court disagreed. Tax liability is based on facts as they exist at the end of each year. A recovery in a later tax year does not prove that a reasonable prospect of recovery existed in the earlier year. Amendments to previously filed tax returns may be made only to correct mathematical errors or miscalculations, not to rearrange facts and readjust income for two years.

If your reimbursement is less than you expected. Assume you took no loss deduction in 2001 because you expected to recover your entire loss in 2002—but the insurance company refuses to pay your claim. When do you deduct your loss? You deduct your loss in the year you find that you have no reasonable prospect of recovery. For example, you sue the company in 2002, with a reasonable prospect of winning your claim. However, in 2003, a court rules against you. You deduct your loss in 2003, subject to the personal property floors in *18.11*.

If you, as lessee, are liable to the lessor for damage to property, you may deduct the loss in the year you pay the lessor.

If you do not discover the loss until a later year. In this case, IRS regulations do not specifically allow a deduction for the loss in the year it is discovered, but court decisions have. In one case, an unseasonable blizzard damaged a windbreak planted to protect a house, buildings, and livestock. The damage to the evergreens did not become apparent until the next year, when about half of the trees died and the others were of little value. The court held that the loss occurred in the later year. In another case, hurricane damage did not become apparent for two years. The Tax Court allowed the deduction in the later year. Where drought damage occurs, *see 18.1*.

If your loss is in a federal disaster area. If your property is damaged in an area eligible for federal disaster assistance, you have a choice of years for which the loss may be claimed; *see 18.3*.

If reimbursements exceed your adjusted basis for the property. Receiving reimbursements in excess of adjusted basis results in a gain that you must report on your return unless you acquire qualifying replacement property and elect to defer the gain; *see 18.18*.

⚠️ *Caution*

Deducting Loss in Proper Year
Read the rules on this page to insure that you deduct your casualty loss in the correct year.

If a loss deduction was claimed in a prior year, you must report the reimbursement as income to the extent the prior deduction reduced your taxable income in the year claimed; *see 11.6.*

18.3 Disaster Losses

If you suffer a loss from a disaster in an area declared by the President as warranting federal assistance, you may deduct the loss either on the return for the year of the loss or on the return of the prior tax year. *See 18.12* for figuring the deductible loss.

You may elect to claim the deduction on a tax return for the previous year any time on or before the *later* of (1) the due date (without extensions) of the return for the year of the disaster *or* (2) the due date considering any extension for filing the return for the prior tax year. For a 2002 disaster loss, you generally have until April 15, 2003, to amend a 2001 tax return to claim the 2002 loss for 2001. In the case of a 2003 disaster loss, you generally have until April 15, 2004, to amend a 2002 tax return to claim the 2003 loss for 2002.

Revoking your decision. After making your election of which year to claim the disaster loss, you have 90 days in which to revoke it. After the 90-day period, the election becomes irrevocable. However, where an early election is made, you have until the due date for filing your return for the year of the disaster to change your election. Your revocation of an election is not effective unless you repay any credit or refund resulting from the election within the revocation period. A revocation made before you receive a refund will not be effective unless you repay the refund within 30 days after you receive it.

Homeowners forced to relocate. If you were forced to relocate or demolish your home in a disaster area, you may be able to claim a loss even though the damage, such as from erosion, does not meet the sudden event test in *18.1.* For example, after a severe storm, there is danger to a group of homes from nearby mudslides. State officials order homeowners to evacuate and relocate their homes. Disaster loss treatment is allowed provided: (1) the President has determined that the area warrants federal disaster relief; (2) within 120 days of the President's order, you are ordered by the state or local government to demolish or relocate your residence; and (3) the home was rendered unsafe by the erosion or other disaster. The law applies to vacation homes and rental properties, as well as to principal residences.

If these tests are met, the loss in value to your home is treated as a disaster loss so that you may elect to deduct the loss either in the year the demolition or relocation order is made or in the prior taxable year.

Fiscal year. If you are on a fiscal year, an election may be made for disaster losses occurring after the close of a fiscal year on the return for that year. For example, if your fiscal year ends June 30, and you suffer a disaster loss at any time between July 1, 2002, and June 30, 2003, you may elect to deduct it on your return for the fiscal year ending June 30, 2002.

Disaster relief grants and loans. Cancellation of part of a disaster loan under the Disaster Relief Act is treated as a reimbursement that reduces your loss; *see 18.15.* Grants to disaster victims under the Disaster Relief Act are not taxable, but the grant is considered a reimbursement reducing your deductible loss.

IRS interest abatement. For declared disasters, the IRS will abate interest on taxes due for the period covered by an extension to file tax returns and pay taxes.

Insurance Proceeds for Damaged or Destroyed Residence

Destruction of principal residence and contents. Generally, you have a taxable gain if you receive insurance proceeds in excess of your adjusted basis for damaged or destroyed property *(18.18).* However, where your principal residence is destroyed, any gain from the receipt of insurance proceeds may generally be excluded from gross income under the $250,000 ($500,000 if married filing jointly) home sale exclusion; *see 29.1.* If the home sale exclusion is not available to you or if the gain exceeds your exclusion, the nonexcludable gain may be deferred under the involuntary conversion rules if you buy a replacement residence; *see 18.18.*

Where your principal residence is damaged or destroyed in a Presidentially declared disaster, favorable involuntary conversion rules eliminate tax on some of the gain and make it easier to defer the balance. These rules apply to renters as well as home owners.

1. You do not have to pay tax on gain from insurance proceeds received for "unscheduled" personal property in your principal residence (rented or owned). Personal property is unscheduled if it is not separately listed on a schedule or rider to the basic insurance policy.

Filing Tip

Accelerating a Tax Refund With Disaster Loss

Disaster loss rules give you a chance to deduct a loss earlier than under general rules. This may result in a tax refund for the prior year. You may make an election to claim the loss for the prior year in a signed statement attached to an amended return for that year if the original return has already been filed. List the date of the disaster and where the property was located (city, town, county, and state). To amend a filed return for the prior year, use Form 1040X. Consider making the election if the deduction on the return of the prior year gives a greater tax reduction than if claimed on the return for the year in which the loss occurred, or if you need the refund for the prior year tax and do not want to wait until you file your return for the year of the disaster to claim the loss.

Law Alert

Tax-Free Disaster Relief Payments

The Victims of Terrorism Tax Relief Act of 2001 provides a tax exemption for disaster relief payments from any source to reimburse or pay uninsured costs of repairing or rehabilitating a personal residence, or replacing its contents, as a result of a Presidentially declared disaster, terroristic or military actions, and catastrophic events designated by the Secretary of the Treasury. The exemption also applies to relief covering personal, family, living, or funeral expenses incurred as a result of the above types of "qualified disasters."

Planning Reminder

IRS Interest Abatement

If the IRS extends the due date to file tax returns and pay taxes for a person in an area declared to be a disaster area by the President, the IRS will abate interest on past-due taxes for the period covered by the extension.

2. Insurance proceeds received for the home itself or for *scheduled* property are treated as received for a single item of property. Gain on this combined insurance pool may be deferred by reinvesting in replacement property that is similar or related in service or use to either the damaged residence or its contents. If the cost of a new principal residence and/or contents equals or exceeds the combined insurance pool, you may elect to defer any gain attributable to the insurance recovery; *see 18.20* for making the election. The deferred gain reduces your basis in the replacement property. The period for purchasing replacement property ends four years after the end of the first tax year in which any part of your gain is realized. If the cost of the replacement property is less than the combined insurance pool, your gain is taxed to the extent of the unspent reimbursement.

EXAMPLE

You rent an apartment as your principal residence. Your apartment and its contents were completely destroyed by a hurricane in 2002; the county in which your apartment was located was declared a disaster area. You received insurance proceeds of $17,000 for unscheduled personal property in your apartment. The proceeds are not taxable.

Sale of land underlying destroyed principal residence or second home. If your principal residence is destroyed in a Presidentially declared disaster, and you decide to relocate elsewhere and sell the underlying land, the IRS treats the sale and the destruction as a single involuntary conversion. If you have a gain that is not excludable under the home sale exclusion rules (Chapter 29), the land sale proceeds are combined with your insurance recovery for purposes of figuring deferrable gain under the involuntary conversion replacement rules *(18.18)*. All of the gain resulting from the insurance recovery may be deferred if a new principal residence is purchased within the four-year replacement period and it costs at least as much as the combined insurance and sales proceeds. The replacement period ends four years after the close of the first year in which any part of your gain is realized.

The same gain deferral rule applies if a second residence such as a vacation home that qualifies for a mortgage interest deduction *(15.1)* is destroyed, but in that case the replacement period is two years *(18.21)* instead of four years.

Note: The IRS treats the sale of land and destruction of a residence as a single involuntary conversion even if the destruction was *not* in a Presidentially declared disaster area. In this case, a two-year (rather than four-year) replacement period applies.

18.4 Who May Deduct a Casualty or Theft Loss

The casualty and theft loss deduction may be claimed only by the owner of the property. For example, a husband filing a separate return may not deduct the loss of jewelry belonging to his wife; only she may deduct it on her separate return.

On jointly owned property, the loss is divided among the owners. If you and your spouse own the property jointly, you deduct the entire loss on a joint return. If you file separately, each owner deducts his or her share of the loss on each separate return.

If you have a legal life estate in the property, the loss is apportioned between yourself and those who will get the property after your death. The apportionment may be based on actuarial tables that consider your life expectancy.

You may claim a casualty loss for property lost or destroyed by your dependent if you own the property. You may not claim a loss deduction for destroyed property that belongs to your child who has reached majority, even though he or she is still your dependent.

Lessee. A person leasing property may be allowed to deduct payments to a lessor that compensate for a casualty loss. A tenant was allowed to deduct as a casualty loss payment of a judgment obtained by the landlord for fire damage to the rented premises that had to be returned in the same condition as at the start of the lease. However, the Tax Court does not allow a deduction for the cost of repairing a rented car, as the lessee has no basis in the car.

EXAMPLE

You buy or lease a lot on which to build a cottage. Along with your purchase or lease, you have the privilege of using a nearby lake. The lake is later destroyed by a storm and the value of your property drops. You may not deduct the loss. The lake is not your property. You only had a privilege to use it, and this is not an ownership right that supports a casualty loss deduction.

Caution

Damage to Nearby Property

The casualty must have caused damage to your property. Damage to a nearby area that lowered the value of your property does not give you a loss deduction.

18.5 Bank Deposit Losses

If a bank in which you deposit funds fails and your loss is not covered by insurance, generally you may claim your loss either as a bad debt deduction or casualty loss. Furthermore, if none of the deposits were federally insured, an investment loss may be claimed. A casualty loss deduction may not be claimed for lost deposits in foreign financial institutions that are not organized and supervised under federal or state law.

Bad debt. You may claim a bad debt deduction for a loss of a bank deposit in the year there is no reasonable prospect of recovery from the insolvent or bankrupt bank. You claim the loss as a short-term capital loss on Schedule D (Form 1040) unless the deposit was made in your business. A non-business bad debt deduction is deductible from capital gains. If you do not have capital gains or the bad debt loss exceeds capital gains, only $3,000 of the loss may offset other income. The remaining loss is carried over. A lost deposit of business funds is claimed as a business bad debt; *see 5.33.*

Casualty loss. You may elect to take a casualty loss deduction for the year in which the loss can be reasonably estimated. The loss is subject to the 10% AGI floor for casualty losses. Once the casualty loss election is made, it is irrevocable and will apply to all other losses on deposits in the same financial institution.

    The casualty loss election may allow you to claim the loss in an earlier year because you do not have to wait until the year there is no prospect of recovery as required in the case of bad debts. The casualty loss election may also be advisable if other casualty losses may absorb all or part of the 10% AGI floor. The casualty loss election is not allowed to stockholders of the bank with more than a 1% interest, officers of the bank, or relatives of shareholders or officers.

Investment loss. If *none* of your deposits were federally insured and you reasonably estimate that you will not recover the funds, up to $20,000 ($10,000 if married filing separately) may be claimed on Schedule A (Form 1040) as an investment loss subject to the 2% adjusted gross income floor for miscellaneous itemized deductions *(19.24).* The $20,000 limit (or $10,000) applies to total losses from any one financial institution, regardless of the number of accounts you have. A separate $20,000 deduction limit applies to each financial institution. The $20,000 (or $10,000) limit is reduced by any insurance proceeds authorized by *state* law that you reasonably expect to receive. If you claimed a bad debt deduction for a lost deposit in a prior year and you qualify for the investment loss, you may file an amended return to claim the investment loss if the statute of limitations has not passed.

Reasonable estimate of casualty or investment loss. Generally, the trustees of the troubled bank will provide depositors with an estimate of the expected recovery and loss. In the year of that determination, you may claim the estimated loss deduction. If you deduct an estimated loss that is less than you are entitled to, you may claim the additional loss in the year of the final determination as a bad debt. If you deduct more than the actual loss, the excess loss must be reported as income in the year of the final determination. Failure to claim the loss in the year in which the loss can first be reasonably estimated does not bar a deduction in a later year.

    For any particular year, only one election may be made for losses in the same bank. If you elect the up-to-$20,000 investment loss for losses in one bank and your loss exceeds the limit, the balance may not be claimed as a casualty deduction. Similarly, if you elect casualty loss treatment, the amount that is not deductible because of the $100 and 10% of adjusted gross income floors is not deductible under the $20,000 investment loss rule.

 Filing Tip

Lost Bank Deposit

If you have other miscellaneous deductions that exceed 2% of adjusted gross income, claiming investment loss treatment may be preferable to treating the loss as a casualty subject to the 10% floor or a bad debt subject to the $3,000 limit.

18.6 Damage to Trees and Shrubs

Not all damage to trees and shrubs qualifies as a casualty loss. The damage must be occasioned by a sudden event; *see 18.1.* Destruction of trees over a period of 5–10 days by southern pine beetles is deductible. One court allowed a deduction for similar destruction over a 30-day period. However, damage by Dutch Elm disease or lethal yellowing disease has been held to be gradual destruction not qualifying as a casualty loss. The Tax Court has allowed a deduction for the cost of removing infested trees, but denied a deduction for the loss of trees after a horse ate the bark.

    If shrubbery and trees on *personal-use property* are damaged by a sudden casualty, you figure the loss on the value of the entire property before and after the casualty. You treat the buildings, land, and shrubs as one complete unit; *see* Example 2 below.

    In fixing the loss on *business* or *income-producing property,* however, shrubs and trees are valued separately from the building; *see* Example 1 below.

EXAMPLES

1. Wayne Smith bought an office building for $90,000. The purchase price was allocated between the land ($18,000) and the building ($72,000). Smith planted trees and ornamental shrubs on the grounds surrounding the building at a cost of $1,200. When the basis of the building had been depreciated to $66,000, a hurricane caused extensive property damage. The fair market value of the land and building immediately before the hurricane was $18,000 and $80,000; immediately afterwards it was $18,000 and $52,000. The fair market value of the trees and shrubs immediately before the casualty was $2,000 and immediately afterwards, $400. Insurance of $15,000 is received to cover damage to the building. Deductible losses are figured separately for the building and the trees and shrubs. The deduction for the building is $13,000, computed as follows:

Value of building immediately before casualty	$80,000
Less: Value immediately after casualty	52,000
Loss in value	$28,000
Less: Insurance received	15,000
Deduction allowed	$13,000

The deduction for the trees and shrubs is $1,200:

Value immediately before casualty	$2,000
Less: Value of trees immediately after casualty	400
Loss in value	$1,600*

   *However, the deductible loss cannot exceed the adjusted basis of the property, $1,200.

2. Same facts as in Example 1, except that Smith purchases a personal residence instead of an office building. Smith's adjusted gross income is $25,000, and this is his only loss. No allocation of the purchase price is necessary for the land and house because the property is not depreciable. Likewise, no individual evaluation of the fair market values of the land, house, trees, and shrubs is necessary. The amount of the deduction for the land, house, trees, and shrubs is $12,000, computed as follows:

Value of property immediately before casualty		$100,000
Less: Value of property immediately after casualty		70,400
Loss in value		$29,600
Less: Insurance received	$15,000	
10% floor ($2,500) and $100 floors	2,600	17,600
Deduction allowed		$12,000

18.7 Deducting Damage to Your Car

Damage to your car in an accident may be a deductible casualty loss unless caused by your willful conduct, such as drunken driving.

You may not deduct legal fees and costs of a court action for damages or money paid for damages to another's property because of your negligence while driving for commuting or other personal purposes. But if at the time of the accident you were using your car on business, you may deduct as a business loss a payment of damages to the other party's car. For purposes of a business loss deduction, driving between two locations of the same business is considered business driving but driving between locations of two separate businesses is considered personal driving. Therefore, the payment of damages arising from an accident while driving between two separate businesses is not deductible as a business expense.

A court has allowed casualty deductions for damage resulting from a child pressing the starter button of a car and from flying stones while driving over a temporary road. In a private letter ruling, the IRS disallowed a loss for damage to a race car by an amateur racer on the ground that in races, crashes are not an unusual event and so do not constitute a casualty.

If the deduction is questioned, be prepared to show the amount, if any, of your insurance recovery. A deduction is allowed only for uninsured losses. Not only must the loss be proved, but also that it was not compensated by insurance.

Towing costs are not included as part of the casualty loss.

A parent may not claim a casualty loss deduction for damage to a car registered in a child's name, although the parent provided funds for the purchase of the car.

Expenses of personal injuries arising from a car accident are not a deductible casualty loss.

Filing Tip

Auto Damage

Unreimbursed accident damage may be a deductible casualty loss.

Court Decision

Failure To Winterize Car

The Tax Court held that the loss of an engine because of a failure to use antifreeze is not deductible as a casualty loss since the damage is not the result of a destructive force or accident but of personal neglect.

Automobile used partly for business. When you use an automobile partly for personal use and partly for business, your loss is computed as though two separate pieces of property were damaged—one business and the other personal. The $100 and 10% floors reduce only the loss on the part used for personal purposes.

18.8 Theft Losses

The taking of property must be illegal under state law to support a theft loss deduction. That property is missing is not sufficient evidence to sustain a theft deduction. It may have been lost or misplaced. So if all you can prove is that an article is missing or lost, your deduction may be disallowed. Sometimes, of course, the facts surrounding the disappearance of an article indicate that it is reasonable to assume that a theft took place. A deduction has been allowed for the theft of trees.

You deduct a theft loss in the year you discover the property was stolen. If you have a reasonable chance of being reimbursed for your loss, you may not take a deduction until the year in which you learn there is no reasonable prospect of recovery.

A legal fee paid to recover stolen property has been held to be deductible as part of the theft loss. To figure the amount of a theft loss deduction, *see 18.12.*

Fraud by building contractors. A deduction was allowed when a building contractor ran away with a payment he received to build a residence. The would-be homeowner was allowed a theft loss deduction for the difference between the money he advanced to the contractor and the value of the partially completed house. In another case, a theft deduction was allowed for payments to subcontractors. The main contractor had fraudulently claimed that he had paid them before he went bankrupt.

Embezzlement losses are deductible as theft losses in the year the theft is discovered. However, if you report on a cash basis, you may not take a deduction for the embezzlement of income you have not reported. For example, an agent embezzled royalties of $46,000 due an author. The author's theft deduction was disallowed. The author had not previously reported the royalties as income; therefore, she could not get the deduction.

Fraudulent sales offers. Worthless stock purchases made on the representation of false and fraudulent sales offers are deductible as theft losses in the year there is no reasonable prospect of recovery. However, the illegal sale of unregistered stock does not support a theft loss deduction. In addition, buying stock from a bad tip and losing money is not deductible.

Kidnapping ransom. Payment of ransom to a kidnapper is generally a deductible theft loss. However, the expense of trying to find an abducted child is not a theft loss.

Fortune tellers. The Tax Court allowed a theft loss deduction in New York, where fortune telling is by law a theft-related offense. The law assumes that telling fortunes or promising to control occult forces is a form of fraud. An exception is made for fortune telling at shows for the purpose of entertaining or amusement. That a person voluntarily asks for advice does not bar the deduction. According to the court, a gullible person who gives money to fortune tellers in the belief that he or she will be helped is still defrauded or swindled. Theft is a broad term and includes theft by swindling, false pretenses, and any other form of guile. In this case, the taxpayer, who was suffering from depression, had become attached to two fortune tellers whom he claimed took him for over $19,000.

Riot losses. Losses caused by fire, theft, and vandalism occurring during riots and civil disorders are deductible. To support your claim of a riot loss, keep evidence of the damage suffered and the cost of repairs. Photographs taken prior to repairs or replacement, lists of damaged or missing property, and police reports would help to establish and uphold your loss deduction.

Foreign government confiscations. The IRS and courts have disallowed casualty deductions for confiscations of personal property by foreign governments. This includes deposits in foreign banks; the loss is limited to a short-term capital loss.

Swindled by friend. A theft loss deduction was allowed to a widow who gave her old beau over $2 million to acquire stock for her in his bank. He used the money to pay his personal debts. The IRS barred the theft loss, arguing that the widow failed to prove fraud. A district court disagreed and allowed the deduction. Under Oklahoma state law, a person who makes a promise in return for cash has committed larceny by fraud if he never intended to return the funds or make good on the promise. Here, that the widow gave him the money voluntarily does not bar a theft loss deduction. She parted with the funds based upon his false claim that he would invest the money for her when he had no intention of doing so, but planned all along to pay off his debts with the funds.

 *Planning Reminder*

Proving a Theft

Get statements from witnesses who saw the theft or police records documenting a break-in to your house or car. A newspaper account of the crime might also help.

When you suspect a theft, make a report to the police. Even though your reporting does not prove that a theft was committed, it may be inferred from your failure to report that you were not sure that your property was stolen. But a theft loss was allowed where the loss of a ring was not reported to the police or an attempt made to demand its return from the suspect, a domestic employee. The owner feared being charged with false arrest.

 *Filing Instruction*

If Stolen Property Is Recovered

If you claim a theft loss and in a later year the property is returned to you, you must refigure your loss deduction. If the refigured deduction is lower than the amount you claimed, the difference must be reported as income in the year of the recovery. To recalculate the loss, follow the steps in *18.12* for figuring deductible losses, but in Step 1, compute the loss in fair market value from the time the property was stolen until you recovered it. The lower of this loss in value, if any, or your adjusted basis for the property is then reduced by insurance reimbursements and the personal-use floors *(18.11)* to get the recalculated loss.

18.9 Nondeductible Losses

Certain losses, though "casualties" for you, may not be deducted if they are not due to theft, fire, or from some other sudden natural phenomenon. The following have been held to be nondeductible losses:

- Termite damage; *see 18.1*
- Carpet beetle damage
- Dry rot damage
- Damages for personal injuries or property damage to others caused by your negligence
- Legal expenses in defending a suit for your negligent operation of your personal automobile
- Legal expenses to recover personal property wrongfully seized by the police
- Expenses of moving to and rental of temporary quarters
- Loss of personal property while in storage or in transit
- Loss of passenger's luggage put aboard a ship. The passenger missed the boat and the luggage could not be traced.
- Accidental loss of a ring from your finger
- Injuries resulting from tripping over a wire
- Loss by husband of joint property taken by his wife when she left him
- Loss of a valuable dog (or family pet) that strayed and was not found
- Steady weakening of a building due to normal wind and weather conditions
- Damage to a crop caused by plant diseases, insects, or fungi
- Damage to property from drought in an area where a dry spell is normal and usual
- Damage to property caused by excavations on adjoining property
- Damage from rust or corroding of understructure of house
- Moth damage
- Dry well
- Losses occasioned by water pockets, erosion, inundation at still water levels, and other natural phenomena (there was no sudden destruction.)
- Death of a saddle horse after eating a silk hat
- A watch or spectacles dropped on the ground
- Sudden drop in the value of securities
- Loss of contingent interest in property due to the unexpected death of a child
- Improper police seizure of private liquor stock
- Chinaware broken by a family pet
- Temporary fluctuation of property value
- Damage to property from local government construction project
- Fire purposely set by owner
- Engine damage due to failure to use antifreeze

Note: Some of the above items may be allowed as business expenses.

Key To Proving a Casualty Loss

To prove—	You need this information—
That a casualty actually occurred	With a well-known casualty, like regional floods, you will have no difficulty proving the casualty occurred, but you must prove it affected your property. Photographs of the area, before and after, and newspaper stories placing the damage in your neighborhood are helpful. If only your property is damaged, there may be a newspaper item on it. Some papers list all the fire alarms answered the previous day. Police, fire, and other municipal departments may have reports on the casualty.
The cost of repairing the property	Cost of repairs is allowed as a measure of loss of repairing the value if it is not excessive and the repair merely restored your property to its condition immediately before the casualty. Save cancelled checks, bills, receipts, and vouchers for expenses of clearing debris and restoring the property to its condition before the casualty.
The value immediately before and after the casualty	Appraisals by a competent expert are important. Get them in writing—in the form of an affidavit, deposition, estimate, appraisal, etc. The expert—an appraiser, engineer, or architect—should be qualified to judge local values. Any records of offers to buy your property, either before or after the casualty, are helpful. Automobile "blue books" may be used as guides in fixing the value of a car. But an amount offered for your car as a trade-in on a new car is not usually an acceptable measure of value.

Key To Proving a Casualty Loss	
To prove—	*You need this information—*
Cost or other basis of your property—the deductible loss cannot be more than that	A deed, contract, bill of sale, or other document probably shows your original cost. Bills, receipts, and cancelled checks probably show the cost of improvements. One court refused to allow a deduction because an owner failed to prove the original cost of a destroyed house and its value before the fire. In another case, estimates were allowed where a fire destroyed records of cost. A court held that the homeowner could not be expected to prove cost by documents lost in the fire that destroyed her property. She made inventories after the fire and again at a later date. Her reliance on memory to establish cost, even though inflated, was no bar to the deduction. The court estimated the market value based on her inventories. If you acquired the property by gift or inheritance, you must establish an adjusted basis in the property from records of the donor or the executor of the estate; *see 5.17* and *5.18.*

18.10 Proving a Casualty Loss

If your return is audited, you will have to prove that the casualty occurred and the amount of the loss. The time to collect your evidence is as soon after the casualty as possible. The Key To Proving a Casualty Loss, above, indicates the information that you will need when computing your loss under the steps explained in *18.12.*

18.11 Floors for Personal-Use Property Losses

Casualty and theft losses to personal-use property are subject to "floors" that will reduce, and in some cases eliminate, your deduction. For each casualty or theft, a $100 reduction applies after the loss is computed under the steps at *18.12.* In addition, personal casualty and theft losses (after the $100 reduction) are deductible only to the extent they exceed 10% of your adjusted gross income.

The $100 floor. The $100 floor reduces casualty and theft losses of property used for personal purposes; *see* Step 5 in *18.12.* The $100 floor does not apply to losses of business property or property held for the production of income such as securities. If property used both in business and personal activities is damaged, the $100 offset applies only to the loss allocated to personal use.

For each casualty or theft during the year, a separate $100 reduction applies. For example, if you are involved in five different casualties during the year, there will be a $100 offset applied to each of the five losses. But when two or more items of property are destroyed in one event, only one $100 offset is applied to the total loss. For example, a storm damages your residence and also your car parked in the driveway. You figure the loss on the residence and car separately, but only one $100 offset applies to the total loss.

The $100 floor is applied after taking into account insurance proceeds received and insurance you expect to receive in a later year.

The $100 floor applies separately to the loss of each individual whose property has been damaged by a single casualty, even where the damaged property is owned by two or more individuals. The only exception is for a married couple filing jointly who apply only one $100 floor to their losses from a single casualty.

 Filing Tip

$100 Floor for Married Couples

Where a husband and wife file a joint return, only one $100 floor applies to a casualty loss suffered by either spouse, whether the property is owned jointly or separately. If separate returns are filed, each spouse must reduce his or her half of the loss on jointly owned property by $100. If the property is owned by one spouse, only that spouse can claim a casualty loss on a separate return.

EXAMPLES
1. Two sisters own and occupy a house that is damaged in a storm. Each sister applies the $100 floor to figure her separate deduction.
2. Your house is partially damaged by a fire that also damages the personal property of a houseguest. You are subject to one $100 floor and the houseguest is subject to a separate $100 floor.

10% AGI floor. The 10% adjusted gross income (AGI) floor applies to the total of all casualty and theft losses occurring during the taxable year to personal-use property. You must deduct 10% of your AGI from the total loss to determine your deduction. The Example below illustrates the application of the $100 floor to each separate casualty event and the 10% AGI floor to the total losses.

Sample—Form 4684; see Example 1 at top of page 358

Form **4684**	**Casualties and Thefts**	OMB No. 1545-0177
Department of the Treasury Internal Revenue Service	▶ See separate instructions. ▶ Attach to your tax return. ▶ Use a separate Form 4684 for each casualty or theft.	20**02** Attachment Sequence No. **26**

Name(s) shown on tax return	Identifying number

SECTION A—Personal Use Property (Use this section to report casualties and thefts of property **not** used in a trade or business or for income-producing purposes.)

1 Description of properties (show type, location, and date acquired for each):

Property **A** **Residence 2-8-1989**

Property **B** **Furniture 3-15-1990**

Property **C** _____

Property **D** _____

Properties (Use a separate column for each property lost or damaged from the same casualty or theft.)

		A	B	C	D
2	Cost or other basis of each property	76,000	5,000		
3	Insurance or other reimbursement (whether or not you filed a claim) (see instructions) **Note:** *If line 2 is more than line 3, skip line 4.*	2,000	500		
4	Gain from casualty or theft. If line 3 is **more** than line 2, enter the difference here and skip lines 5 through 9 for that column. See instructions if line 3 includes insurance or other reimbursement you did not claim, or you received payment for your loss in a later tax year				
5	Fair market value **before** casualty or theft	167,500	2,000		
6	Fair market value **after** casualty or theft	162,500	- 0 -		
7	Subtract line 6 from line 5	5,000	2,000		
8	Enter the **smaller** of line 2 or line 7	5,000	2,000		
9	Subtract line 3 from line 8. If zero or less, enter -0-	3,000	1,500		

10	Casualty or theft loss. Add the amounts on line 9 in columns A through D	10	4,500
11	Enter the **smaller** of line 10 or $100	11	100
12	Subtract line 11 from line 10 **Caution:** *Use only one Form 4684 for lines 13 through 18.*	12	4,400
13	Add the amounts on line 12 of all Forms 4684	13	4,400
14	Add the amounts from line 4 of all Forms 4684	14	- 0 -
15	• If line 14 is **more** than line 13, enter the difference here and on Schedule D. **Do not** complete the rest of this section (see instructions). • If line 14 is **less** than line 13, enter -0- here and go to line 16. • If line 14 is **equal** to line 13, enter -0- here. **Do not** complete the rest of this section.	15	
16	If line 14 is **less** than line 13, enter the difference	16	4,400
17	Enter 10% of your adjusted gross income from Form 1040, line 36. Estates and trusts, see instructions.	17	2,800
18	Subtract line 17 from line 16. If zero or less, enter -0-. Also enter the result on Schedule A (Form 1040), line 19. Estates and trusts, enter the result on the "Other deductions" line of your tax return	18	1,600

For Paperwork Reduction Act Notice, see page 4 of the instructions.   Cat. No. 12997O   Form **4684** (2002)

EXAMPLE

In January 2002, you have an uninsured jewelry theft loss of $1,000, and in July 2002 uninsured damage of $3,000 to your personal car. Your adjusted gross income is $25,000. Your deduction is $1,300 figured as follows:

Theft loss	$1,000	
Less	100	$ 900
Car damage	3,000	
Less	100	2,900
Total loss		3,800
Less 10% of $25,000		2,500
Deductible loss		$1,300

18.12 Figuring Your Loss on Form 4684

Form 4684 is used to report casualties or thefts of personal-use property, business property, or income-producing property. The deductible loss is usually the difference between the fair market value of the property before and after the casualty or theft *less* (1) reimbursements received for the loss and (2) $100 if the property was used for personal purposes. However, the loss may not exceed your adjusted basis *(5.20)* for the property, which for many items will be your cost. If your adjusted basis is less than the loss in value, your deduction is limited to basis, less reimbursements and the $100 floor for personal-use assets. After figuring all allowable casualty and theft losses for personal-use property, the total is deductible only to the extent it exceeds the 10% adjusted gross income floor *(18.11)*. Use the following five-step method for figuring the deductible amount.

Steps for calculating your deductible loss. The following five steps reflect the procedure on Form 4684 for computing a casualty or theft loss. If your loss is to business inventory, you do not have to use Form 4684, but may take the loss into account when figuring the cost of goods sold; *see* "Inventory losses" later in this section.

To figure your deductible loss, follow these five steps:

Step 1. Compute the loss in fair market value of the property. This is the difference between the fair market value immediately before and immediately after the casualty. You do *not* have to compute the loss in fair market value for business or income-producing property (such as a rental property) that has been *completely* destroyed or stolen; go to Step 2.

You will need written appraisals to support your claim for loss of value. You may not claim sentimental or aesthetic values or a fluctuation in property values caused by a casualty; you must deal with cost or market values of what has been lost. If the value of your property has been lowered because of damage to a nearby area, you do not have a deductible loss since your own property has not been damaged. No deduction may be claimed for estimated decline in value based on buyer resistance in an area subject to landslides.

For household items, the Tax Court has allowed losses based on cost less depreciation, rather than on the decrease in fair market value.

Step 2. Compute your adjusted basis for the property. This is usually the cost of the property plus the cost of improvements, less previous casualty loss deductions and depreciation if the property is used in business or for income-producing purposes. Unadjusted basis of property acquired other than by purchase is explained at *5.16.* Adjusted basis is explained at *5.20.*

Step 3. Take the lower amount of Step 1 or 2. For business or income-producing property that was stolen or completely destroyed, reduce adjusted basis from Step 2 by any salvage value.

Step 4. Reduce the loss in Step 3 by the insurance proceeds or other compensation for the loss; *see 18.15.* This is your deductible loss for business or income-producing property. If the property was used for personal purposes, apply the reductions in Step 5.

Step 5. If the property was used for personal purposes, the loss from Step 4 must be reduced by $100 and you may only deduct the balance to the extent it exceeds 10% of your adjusted gross income. If you have more than one personal casualty or theft, reduce the total combined loss by 10% of adjusted gross income; only the excess is deductible; *see 18.11.*

Filing Instruction

Reporting on Form 4684

If you are claiming a loss for personal-use property, use Section A on page 1 of Form 4684. If you suffered more than one casualty or theft during the year, use a separate Form 4684 for each one. The total deductible casualty or theft loss from Section A of Form 4684 is then entered on Line 19, Schedule A of Form 1040.

Filing Tip

Business or Income-Producing Property

If you are claiming a loss for property used in your business or income-producing activity, use Section B on page 2 of Form 4684 (not shown here). Losses from income-producing property are entered on Line 27 of Schedule A as "other miscellaneous deductions" and are not subject to the 2% adjusted gross income floor.

Caution

Incidental Expenses

Expenses that are incidental to a casualty or theft, such as medical treatment for personal injury, temporary housing, fuel, moving, or rentals for temporary living quarters, are not deductible as casualty losses.

EXAMPLES

1. Your home, which cost $76,000 in 1989, was damaged by a fire. The value of the house before the disaster was $167,500, but afterwards $162,500. The furniture cost $5,000 in 1990. Its value before the fire was set at $2,000. It was totally destroyed. The insurance company reimbursed you $2,000 for your house damage and $500 for your furnishings. This was the only casualty for the year. Your adjusted gross income is $28,000. You figure your loss for the furniture separately from the loss on the house but apply only one $100 reduction *(18.11)* because the damage was from a single casualty. *See* the sample Form 4684 on page 356 for how this loss is reported.

   1. Decrease in home's fair market value:

Value of house before fire	$167,500
Value of house after fire	162,500
Decrease in value	$ 5,000
2. Adjusted basis:	$ 76,000
3. Loss sustained (lower of 1 or 2)	$5,000
Less: Insurance	2,000
Loss on house	$3,000
4. Loss on furnishings (decreased value)*	$2,000
Less: Insurance	500
Loss on furnishings	$1,500
5. Total loss ($3,000 and $1,500)	$4,500
Less: $100 floor	100
Casualty loss (subject to 10% floor)	$4,400
6. 10% AGI floor (10% of $28,000 AGI)	$2,800
7. Casualty loss ($4,400 – $2,800)	$1,600

*The loss for the furnishings on Line 4 is $2,000, the decrease in fair market value, as this is lower than the $5,000 basis.

2. Depreciable business property with a fair market value of $1,500 and an adjusted basis of $2,000 is totally destroyed. Because property used in your business was totally destroyed (*see* Step 3 on page 357), your loss is measured by your adjusted basis of $2,000, which is larger than the $1,500 loss in fair market value. Salvage value, if any, reduces your deduction, but you disregard the $100 floor applied to casualty losses on personal property. If the property was used for personal purposes, the loss would have been limited to the $1,500 loss in market value less $100, leaving a loss of $1,400 subject to the 10% adjusted gross income floor.

Filing Tip

Appraisals for Disaster Relief

The IRS may accept an appraisal that is used to obtain federal loans or loan guarantees following a Presidentially declared disaster as proof of the amount of a casualty loss.

Business losses. Losses from business property are generally netted against gains from casualties or thefts on Form 4684 and the net gain or loss is entered on Form 4797. Follow the instructions to Form 4684 .

Inventory losses. A casualty or theft loss of inventory is automatically reflected on Schedule C in the cost of goods sold, which includes the lost items as part of your opening inventory. Any insurance or other reimbursement received for the loss must be included as sales income.

You may separately claim the inventory loss as a casualty or theft loss on Form 4684 instead of automatically claiming it as part of the cost of goods sold. If you do this, you must eliminate the items from inventory by lowering either opening inventory or purchases when figuring the cost of goods sold.

Cost less depreciation method for household items. The Tax Court has allowed casualty loss deductions based on cost less depreciation, rather than on the difference in fair market value immediately before and after the casualty. *See* the following Example.

EXAMPLE

Basing a deduction on the difference between the value of furnishings immediately before and immediately after a casualty may limit your deduction to the going price for second-hand furnishings. A homeowner whose furniture was destroyed by fire claimed that the fair market value immediately before the fire should be original cost less depreciation. He based his figures on an inventory prepared by certified public adjusters describing each item, its cost and age. The deduction figured this way came to approximately $27,500 ($55,000 cost, less $13,000 depreciation, a $14,400 insurance recovery, and the $100 floor).

The IRS estimated that the furniture was worth $15,304 before the fire and limited the deduction to $804 after accounting for the insurance and the $100 floor. The Tax Court disagreed. The householder's method of valuing his furniture is consistent with methods used by insurance adjusters who have an interest in keeping values low. He is not limited to the amount his property would bring if "hawked off by a secondhand dealer or at a forced sale." However, in another case, the court refused to allow the cost less depreciation formula where the homeowner's inventory list was based on memory.

18.13 Personal and Business Use of Property

For property held partly for personal use and partly for business or income-producing purposes, a casualty or theft loss deduction is computed as if two separate pieces of property were damaged, destroyed, or stolen. Follow the steps in *18.12* for figuring the allowable loss, but apply the $100 and 10% of adjusted gross income floors only to the personal part of the loss.

EXAMPLE

A building with two apartments, one used by the owner as his home and the other rented to a tenant, is damaged by a fire. The fair market value of the building before the fire was $169,000 and after the fire, $136,000. Its cost basis was $120,000. Depreciation taken before the fire was $14,000. The insurance company paid $20,000. The owner has adjusted gross income of $40,000. This is his only loss this year. He has a business casualty loss of $6,500 and a deductible personal casualty loss of $2,400 figured as follows:

	Business	Personal
1. Decrease in value of building:		
Value before fire ($169,000)	$84,500	$84,500
Value after fire ($136,000)	(68,000)	(68,000)
Decrease in value	$16,500	$16,500
2. Adjusted basis of building:	$60,000	$60,000
Less: Depreciation	(14,000)	
Adjusted basis	$46,000	$60,000
3. Loss sustained (lower of 1 and 2)	$16,500	$16,500
Less: Insurance (total $20,000)	($10,000)	($10,000)
4. Loss	$6,500	$6,500
Less: $100 floor and 10% of adjusted gross income	—	(4,100)
Deductible casualty loss	$6,500	$2,400

 Filing Tip

Help During Disasters and Emergencies

If you have damaged or lost property in a location declared by the President as a major disaster area, you may find additional assistance from the IRS at the Taxpayer Help section of their website: www.irs.gov.

18.14 Repairs May Be a "Measure of Loss"

The cost of repairs may be treated as evidence of the loss of value (Step 1 in *18.12*), if the amount is not excessive and the repairs do nothing more than restore the property to its condition before the casualty. An estimate for repairs will not suffice; only actual repairs may be used as a measure of loss. However, where you measure your loss by comparing appraisals of value for before and after the casualty, repairs may be considered in arriving at a post-casualty value even though no actual repairs are made.

Deduction not limited to repairs. A casualty loss deduction is not limited to repair expenses where the decline in market value is greater, according to a federal appeals court; *see* the following Example.

 Planning Reminder

Keep Records of Deductible Losses

If your property is damaged, you must reduce the basis of the damaged property by the casualty loss deduction and compensation received for the loss; *see 5.20.* When you later sell the property, gain or loss is the difference between the selling price and the reduced basis.

EXAMPLE

Connor claimed that the market value of his house dropped $93,000 after it was damaged by fire. His $52,000 cash outlay in repairing the house was reimbursed by insurance. He claimed a casualty loss of approximately $40,000, the uncompensated drop in market value. The IRS barred the deduction. The house was restored to pre-casualty condition. The cost of the repairs is a realistic measure of the loss, and, as the expense was fully compensated by insurance, Connor suffered no loss. A federal appeals court disagreed. The house dropped $70,000 in market value, of which $20,000 was uncompensated by insurance. The deduction is measured by the uncompensated difference in value before and after the casualty. It is not limited to the cost of repairs, even where the repair expense is less than the difference in fair market values. Had the repairs cost more than this difference, the IRS would not have allowed a larger deduction.

Caution

Failure To Make an Insurance Claim

If you are insured for your full loss and do not file a claim because you do not want to risk cancellation of liability coverage, you may not claim a deduction. If you do not file an insurance claim but your loss exceeds the coverage, the noncovered loss may be deductible. For example, if you have a $2,500 deductible on your personal automobile insurance policy, a loss of up to $2,500 would be reduced by the $100 floor and the balance would be deductible only to the extent the 10% of adjusted gross income floor *(18.12)* was exceeded.

18.15 Insurance Reimbursements

You reduce the amount of your loss *(18.12)* by insurance proceeds, voluntary payments received from your employer for damage to your property, and cash or property received from the Red Cross. Also reduce your loss by reimbursements you expect to receive in a later year; *see 18.2*. However, cash gifts from friends and relatives to help defray the cost of repairs do not reduce the loss where there are no conditions on the use of the gift. Also, gifts of food, clothing, medical supplies, and other forms of subsistence do not reduce the loss deduction nor are they taxable income.

Cancellation of part of a disaster loan under the Disaster Relief Act is treated as a partial reimbursement of the loss and reduces the amount of the loss. Payments from an urban renewal agency to acquire your damaged property under the Federal Relocation Act of 1970 are considered reimbursements reducing the loss.

Insurance payments for the cost of added living expenses because of damage to a home do not reduce a casualty loss. The payments are treated as separate and apart from payments for property damage. Payments for excess living costs are generally not taxable; *see 18.16*.

Passive activity property loss reimbursements. A reimbursement of a casualty or theft loss deduction is not considered passive activity income if the original loss was not treated as a passive deduction; *see 10.1*. The reimbursement may be taxed under the rule discussed at *11.6*.

Realizing a gain from insurance. If you receive insurance proceeds in excess of your adjusted basis for the property, you generally realize a gain, which you may be able to defer by buying replacement property; *see 18.18*.

18.16 Excess Living Costs Paid by Insurance Are Not Taxable

Your insurance contract may reimburse you for excess living costs when a casualty or a threat of casualty forces you to vacate your house. The payment is tax free if these tests are met:

1. Your principal residence is damaged or destroyed by fire, storm, or other casualty or you are denied use of it by a governmental order because of the occurrence or threat of the casualty.

2. You are paid under an insurance contract for living expenses resulting from the loss of occupancy or use of the residence.

Whether you have a taxable or tax-free reimbursement is figured at the end of the period you were unable to use your residence. Thus, if the dislocation covers more than one taxable year, the taxable income, if any, will be reported in the taxable year in which the dislocation ended.

The tax-free amount includes only excess living costs paid by the insurance company. The excess is the difference between (1) the actual living expenses incurred during the time you could not use or occupy your house and (2) the normal living expenses that you would have incurred for yourself and members of your household during the period. Living expenses during the period may include the cost of renting suitable housing and extraordinary expenses for transportation, food, utilities, and miscellaneous services. The expenses must be incurred for items and services (such as laundry) needed to maintain your standard of living that you enjoyed before the loss and must be covered by the policy.

Where a lump-sum settlement does not identify the amount covering living expenses, an allocation is required to determine the tax-free portion. In the case of uncontested claims, the tax-free portion is that part of the settlement that bears the same ratio to total recovery as increased living expense bears to total loss and expense. If your claim is contested, you must show the amount reasonably allocable to increased living expenses consistent with the terms of the insurance contract, but not in excess of coverage limitations specified in the contract.

The exclusion from income does not cover insurance reimbursements for loss of rental income or for loss of or damage to real or personal property; such reimbursements for property damage reduce your casualty loss; *see 18.15*.

If your home is used for both residential and business purposes, the exclusion does not apply to insurance proceeds and expenses attributable to the nonresidential portion of the house. There is no exclusion for insurance recovered for expenses resulting from governmental condemnation or order unrelated to a casualty or threat of casualty.

The insurance reimbursement may cover part of your normal living expenses as well as the excess expenses due to the casualty. The part covering normal expenses is income; it does not reduce your casualty loss.

EXAMPLES

1. On March 1, your home was damaged by fire. While it was being repaired, you and your spouse lived at a motel and ate meals at restaurants. Costs are $1,200 at the motel, $1,000 for meals, and $75 for laundry services. You make the required March payment of $790 on your home mortgage. Your customary $40 commuting expense is $20 less for the month because the motel is closer to your work. Your usual commuting expense is therefore treated as not being incurred to the extent of the $20 decrease. Furthermore, you do not incur your customary $700 food expense for meals at home, $75 for utilities, and $60 for laundry at home. Your insurance company pays you $1,700 for expenses. The tax-free exclusion for insurance payments is limited to $1,420, computed in the third column below. You must report as income $280 ($1,700 – $1,420).

	Expenses from casualty	Expenses not incurred	Increase (Decrease)
Housing	$1,200		$1,200
Utilities		$75	(75)
Meals	1,000	700	300
Transportation		20	(20)
Laundry	75	60	15
Total	$2,275	$855	$1,420

2. Same facts as in Example 1 except that you rented the residence for $400 per month and the risk of loss was to the landlord. You did not pay the March rent. The excludable amount is $1,020 ($1,420 less $400 normal rent not incurred). You would have to report as income the excess of the insurance received over the $1,020 exclusion.

18.17 Do Your Casualty Losses Exceed Your Income?

If your 2002 casualty or theft losses exceed your income, you pay no tax in 2002. You may also carry the excess loss back to 1999 and file a refund claim for that year. Any remaining loss may be carried back to 2000 and 2001 and carried forward to 2003 through 2022, or you may just carry your loss forward 20 years until it is used up. The excess casualty loss is carried back or forward as a net operating loss. *See 40.18* for net operating loss rules.

Note: The $100 and 10% of adjusted gross income floors for personal casualty losses apply only in the year of loss; you do not again reduce your loss in the carryback or carryover years.

Taxable Gain From Involuntary Conversions

18.18 Defer Gain by Replacing Property

If your property is destroyed, damaged, stolen, or taken by a government authority, this is considered to be an *involuntary conversion* for tax purposes. If upon an involuntary conversion you receive insurance or other compensation that exceeds the adjusted basis of the property, you realize a gain that is taxable unless you may defer tax under the rules in *18.19–18.23* or, in the case of a principal residence, avoid tax under the rules in Chapter 29.

You may elect to postpone tax on the full gain provided you invest the proceeds in replacement property the cost of which is equal to or exceeds the net proceeds from the conversion. Reinvestment requirements are discussed at *18.21–18.23.* The replacement period for personal-use property is two years; for business and investment property it is two or three years depending on the type of involuntary conversion; for a residence and its contents involuntarily converted due to a Presidentially declared disaster *(see 18.3)* it is four years; *see 18.21* for replacement periods.

Your basis in the replacement property is its replacement cost, minus any postponed gain. If you find that you cannot buy a replacement by the end of the period, ask the IRS for an extension of time *(see 18.21).*

Buying a replacement from a related party generally qualifies only if your gains from involuntary conversions are $100,000 or less *(see 18.22).*

 Filing Tip

Involuntary Conversion of Personal Residence

Gain on the conversion may escape tax under the rules discussed in Chapter 29. If not, tax may be deferred under the involuntary conversion replacement rules.

18.19 Involuntary Conversions Qualifying for Tax Deferral

For purposes of an election to defer tax on gains, "involuntary conversion" is more broadly defined than "casualty loss." You have an involuntary conversion when your property is:

Damaged or destroyed by some outside force.

Stolen, seized, requisitioned, or condemned by a governmental authority. If you voluntarily sell land made useless to you by the condemnation of your adjacent land, the sale may also qualify as a conversion. Condemnation of property as unfit for human habitation does not qualify. Condemnation, as used by the tax law, refers to the taking of private property for public use, not to the condemnation of property for noncompliance with housing and health regulations. Similarly, a tax sale to pay delinquent taxes is not an involuntary conversion.

Sold under a threat of seizure, condemnation, or requisition. The threat must be made by an authority qualified to take property for public use. A sale following a threat of condemnation made by a government employee is a conversion if you reasonably believe he or she speaks with authority and could and would carry out the threat to have your property condemned. If you learn of the plan of an imminent condemnation from a newspaper or other news media, the IRS requires you to confirm the report from a government official before you act on the news.

Farmers. Farmers also have involuntary conversions when:

Land is sold within an irrigation project to meet the acreage limitations of the federal reclamation laws; Cattle are destroyed by disease or sold because of disease; *or*
Draft, breeding, or dairy livestock is sold because of drought. The election to treat the sale as a conversion is limited to livestock sold over the number that would have been sold but for the drought. In some cases, livestock may be replaced with other farm property where there has been soil or other environmental contamination.

Should you elect to postpone gain? An election gives an immediate advantage: tax on gain is postponed and the funds that would have been spent to pay the tax may be used for other investments.

However, as a condition of deferring tax, the basis of the replacement property is generally fixed at the same adjusted basis as the converted property. If your reinvestment exceeds the insurance proceeds, the excess increases the basis of the replacement property. As long as the value of the replacement property does not decline, tax on the original gain is finally incurred when the property is sold.

Special rules for federally declared disaster areas are discussed at *18.3.*

> **EXAMPLE**
> Assume a rental building is destroyed by fire and a proper replacement is made. Assume that gain on the receipt of the insurance proceeds is taxable as capital gain. An election is generally not advisable if you have capital losses to offset the gain. However, even if you have no capital losses, you may still decide not to make the election and pay tax in order to fix, for purposes of depreciation, the basis of the new property at its purchase price, if the future depreciation deductions will offset income taxable at a higher rate than the current tax. If there is little or no difference between the two rates so that a net after-tax benefit from the depreciation would not arise, an election might be made solely to postpone the payment of tax.

18.20 How To Elect To Defer Tax

To defer tax on your gain, do not report the gain as income for the year it is realized. Attach to your return a statement giving details of the transaction, including computation of the gain and your intention to buy a replacement if you have not yet done so. *See 18.21* for replacement periods and IRS notification requirements.

If your property is condemned and you are given similar property, no election is necessary. Postponement of tax on the gain is required. For example, the city condemns a store building and gives you another store building the value of which exceeds the cost basis of the old one; gain is not taxed.

Partnerships. The election to defer gain must be made at the partnership level. Individual partners may not make separate elections unless the partnership has terminated, with all partnership affairs wound up. Dissolution under state law is not a termination for tax purposes.

18.21 Time Period for Buying Replacement Property

To defer tax, you generally must buy property similar or related in use *(18.22)* to the converted property within a fixed time period. The replacement period is either two, three, or four years:

1. A two-year replacement period applies for destroyed, damaged, or stolen property, whether used for business, investment, or personal purposes, but there is a four-year period for principal residences in Presidentially declared disaster areas *(18.3)*. A two-year period also applies to a condemned residence. The two-year period for damaged, destroyed, and stolen property *starts* on the date the property was destroyed, damaged, or stolen, and *ends* two years after the end of the year in which any part of your gain is realized.

2. A three-year replacement period applies for condemned business or investment real estate, excluding inventory. However, the two-year and not the three-year period applies if the condemned business or investment real estate is replaced by your acquiring control of a corporation that owns the replacement property.

3. A four-year replacement period applies for a principal residence damaged in a Presidentially declared disaster; *see 18.3*. The four-year replacement period *starts* on the date the residence is involuntarily converted and *ends* four years after the end of the first taxable year in which any part of the gain is realized.

Replacing condemned property. For condemnations, the two-year or three-year (investment or non-inventory business real estate) replacement period starts on the earlier of (1) the date you receive notification of the condemnation threat or (2) the date you dispose of the condemned property. The period ends two or three years after the end of the year in which gain on the condemnation is realized. You may make a replacement after a threat of condemnation. If you buy property before the actual threat, it will not qualify as a replacement even though you still own it at the time of the actual condemnation.

> **EXAMPLES**
>
> 1. On January 10, 2002, a parcel of investment real estate is condemned; the parcel cost $15,000. On February 28, 2002, you received a check for $23,500 from the state. You may defer the tax on the gain of $8,500 if you invest at least $23,500 in other real estate not later than December 31, 2005, the end of the three-year replacement period.
>
> 2. Business property was contaminated by dangerous chemicals, and after the Environmental Protection Agency ordered businesses and residents to relocate, the property was sold to the local government under a threat of condemnation. The owner was paid the full pre-contamination fair market value for the property. The owner wanted to defer gain under the three-year replacement rule for condemnations. However, the IRS said that part of the gain was deferrable under the two-year rule and part under the three-year rule. There were two conversions: (1) the contamination, subject to the two-year replacement rule; and (2) the later condemnation, subject to the three-year rule.
>
>   To determine the amount eligible for deferral for each period, an allocation must be made between the proceeds allocable to the destruction of the property and the proceeds allocable to the condemnation.
>
>   According to the IRS, the burden for making the allocation between the two conversions rests with the owner. The government's payments are allocable to the condemnation and, therefore, eligible for the three-year replacement rule, only to the extent of the post-contamination value. Practically speaking, it may be advisable to make the replacement within the two-year period, as it may be difficult to show the contaminated land had any value after the contamination.

Advance payment of award. Gain is realized in the year compensation for the converted property exceeds the basis of the converted property. An advance payment of an award that exceeds the adjusted basis of the property starts the running of the replacement period.

An award is treated as received in the year that it is made available to you without restrictions, even if you contest the amount.

Replacement by an estate. A person whose property was involuntarily converted may die before he or she makes a replacement. According to the IRS, his or her estate may not reinvest the proceeds within the allowed time and postpone tax on the gain. The Tax Court rejects the IRS position and has allowed tax deferral where the replacement was made by the deceased owner's estate. However, the Tax Court agreed with the IRS that a surviving spouse's investment in land did not

 Caution

Nullifying Deferral Election on Amended Return

If you elect to defer tax on a gain, intending to buy replacement property, but you fail to make a replacement within the time limit, you must file an amended return for the year of the gain and pay the tax that you had elected to defer. You also must file an amended return and report the gain not eligible for deferral if you invest in property that does not qualify as a replacement, or which costs less than the amount realized from the involuntary conversion.

However, if you elect to defer and make a timely qualifying replacement, you may not change your mind and pay tax on the gain in order to obtain a higher basis *(18.19)* for the replacement property. The Tax Court has agreed with the IRS that the election to defer is irrevocable once a qualified replacement is made within the time limits. Similarly, once you report to the IRS *(18.21)* that a qualified replacement has been made, you may not substitute other replacement property, even if the replacement period has not yet expired.

Extension of Time To Replace

Within the time limits, you must buy replacement property rather than merely contracting to do so. If you cannot replace property within the time required, ask your local District Director for additional time. Apply for an extension before the end of the period. If you apply for an extension within a reasonable time after the statutory period has run out, you must have a reasonable cause for the delay in asking for the extension.

defer tax on gain realized by her deceased husband on an involuntary conversion of his land. She had received his property as survivor of joint tenancy and could not, in making the investment, be considered as acting for his estate.

Giving IRS notice of replacement. If you have not bought replacement property by the time you file your return for the year of the involuntary conversion but you intend to do so, attach a statement to your return describing the conversion and the computation of gain, and state that you intend to make a timely replacement. Then, on the return for the year of replacement, attach a statement giving the details of your replacement property. This notice starts the running of the period of limitations for any tax on the gain. Failure to give notice keeps the period open. Similarly, a failure to give notice of an intention not to replace also keeps the period open. When you do not buy replacement property after making an election to postpone tax on the gain, file an amended return for the year in which gain was realized and pay the tax (if any) on the gain.

Assume you have a gain from an involuntary conversion and do not expect to reinvest the proceeds. You report the gain and pay the tax. In a later year, but within the prescribed time limits, you buy similar property. You may make an election to defer tax on the gain and file a claim for tax refund.

18.22 Types of Qualifying Replacement Property

Although exact duplication is not required, the replacement generally must be *similar* or *related in use* to the property that was involuntarily converted in order to defer tax. Where *real property* held for productive use in a business or for investment is converted through a *condemnation* or threat of condemnation, the replacement test is more liberal.[1] A replacement merely has to be of a *like kind* to the converted property.

Under the *like-kind* test, the replacement of condemned real estate with other real estate qualifies. Improved real property may be replaced by unimproved real property; *see 6.1.* Foreign and U.S. real property are considered to be of like kind for purposes of this test.

Under the *related-use* test, the replacement of unimproved land for improved land does not qualify. Under the related-use test, a replacement generally must be closely related in function to the destroyed property. For example, a condemned personal residence must be replaced with another personal residence. The replacement of a house rented to a tenant with a house used as a personal residence does not qualify for tax deferral; the new house is not being used for the same purpose as the condemned one. This functional test, however, is not strictly applied to conversions of rental property. Here, the role of the owner toward the properties, rather than the functional use of the buildings, is reviewed. If an owner held both properties as investments and offered similar services and took similar business risks in both, the replacement may qualify.

You may own several parcels of property, one of which is condemned. You may want to use the condemnation award to make improvements on the other land such as drainage and grading. The IRS generally will not accept the improvements as a qualified replacement. However, an appeals court has rejected the IRS approach in one case.

If it is not feasible to reinvest the proceeds from the conversion of livestock because of soil contamination or other environmental contamination, then other property (including real property) used for farming purposes is treated as similar or related and qualifies as replacement property.

Deferral may be barred when buying a replacement from a relative. The gain deferral rules do not apply if you buy a replacement from a close relative or a related business organization unless the total gain you realized for the year on all involuntary conversions on which there are realized gains is $100,000 or less. In determining whether gains exceed $100,000, gains are not offset by losses. This rule applies to involuntary conversions occurring after June 8, 1997. Affected related parties are the same as defined for loss transactions discussed at 5.6.

Buying controlling interest in a corporation. The replacement test may be satisfied by purchasing a controlling interest (80%) in a corporation owning property that is similar or related in service to the converted property.

Business and investment property in a disaster area. The similar or related-use tests do not have to be met when replacing business or investment property damaged or destroyed in a Presidentially declared disaster area. You may make a qualified replacement by buying any tangible property held for business use.

18.23 Cost of Replacement Property Determines Postponed Gain

To fully defer tax on the replacement of involuntarily converted property *(18.19)*, the cost of the replacement property must be equal to or exceed the net proceeds from the conversion. If replacement cost is no more than the adjusted basis of the converted property, you report the entire gain. If replacement cost is less than the amount realized on the conversion but more than the basis of the converted property, the difference between the amount realized and the cost of the replacement is reported as gain; you may elect to postpone tax on the balance of the gain. *See* Examples 1–3 below.

Condemnation award. The award received from a state authority may be reduced by expenses of getting the award such as legal, engineering, and appraisal fees. The treatment of special assessments and severance damages received when part of your property is condemned is explained at *18.24*. Payments made directly by the authority to your mortgagee may not be deducted from the gross award.

Do not include as part of the award interest paid on the award for delay in its payment; you report the interest as interest income. The IRS may treat as interest part of an award paid late, even though the award does not make any allocation for interest.

Relocation payments are not considered part of the condemnation award and are not treated as taxable income to the extent that they are spent for purposes of relocation; they increase basis of the newly acquired property.

Distinguish between insurance proceeds compensating you for loss of profits because of business interruption and those compensating you for the loss of property. Business interruption proceeds are fully taxed as ordinary income and may not be treated as proceeds of an involuntary conversion.

A single standard fire insurance policy may cover several assets. Assume a fire occurs, and in a settlement the proceeds are allocated to each destroyed item according to its fair market value before the fire. In comparing the allocated proceeds to the tax basis of each item, you find that on some items, you have realized a gain; that is, the proceeds exceed basis. On the other items, you have a loss; the proceeds are less than basis. According to the IRS, you may elect to defer tax on the gain items by buying replacement property. You do not treat the proceeds paid under the single policy as a unit, but as separate payments made for each covered item.

 Caution

Buying Replacement From Relative

Buying a replacement from a relative or related business organization will not defer gain unless total gains from involuntary conversions for the year are $100,000 or less.

EXAMPLES

1. The cost basis of your four-family apartment house is $175,000. It is condemned to make way for a thruway. After expenses, the net award from the state is $200,000. Your gain is $25,000. If you buy a similar apartment house for $175,000 or less, you report the entire $25,000 gain.

2. Same facts as in Example 1, except that you buy an apartment house for $185,000. Of the gain of $25,000, you report $15,000 as taxable gain ($200,000 – $185,000). You may elect to postpone the tax on the balance of the gain, or $10,000.

3. Same facts as in Example 1, but you buy an apartment house for $200,000. You may elect to postpone tax on the entire gain because you have invested all of the award in replacement property.

18.24 Special Assessments and Severance Damages

When only part of a property parcel is *condemned* for a public improvement, the condemning authority may:

1. Levy a special assessment against the remaining property, claiming that it is benefitted by the improvement. The authority usually deducts the assessment from the condemnation award.
2. Grant an award for severance damages if the condemnation of part of your property causes a loss in value or damage to the remaining property that you keep.

Special assessments reduce the amount of the gross condemnation award. If they exceed the award, the excess is added to the basis of the property. An assessment levied after the award is made may not be deducted from the award.

EXAMPLE

Two acres of a 10-acre tract are condemned for a new highway. The adjusted basis of the land is $30,000, or $3,000 per acre. The condemnation award is $10,000; the special assessment against the remaining eight acres is $2,500. The net gain on the condemnation is $1,500:

Condemnation award		$10,000
Less:		
Basis of two condemned acres	$6,000	
Special assessment	2,500	8,500
Net gain		$1,500

When both the condemnation award and severance damages are received, the condemnation is treated as two separate involuntary conversions: (1) A conversion of the condemned land. Here, the condemnation award is applied against the basis of the condemned land to determine gain or loss on its conversion; and (2) a conversion of part of the remaining land in the sense that its utility has been reduced by condemnation, for which severance damages are paid.

Net severance damages reduce the basis of the retained property. Net severance damages are the total severance damages, reduced by expenses in obtaining the damages and by any special assessment withheld from the condemnation award. If the damages exceed basis, gain is realized. Tax may be deferred on the gain through the purchase of replacement property under the "similar or related in use test" at *18.22*, such as adjacent land or restoration of the property to its original condition.

Allocating the proceeds between the condemnation award and severance damages will either reduce the gain or increase the loss realized on the condemned land. The IRS will allow such a division only when the condemnation authority specifically identifies part of the award as severance damage in the contract or in an itemized statement or closing sheet. The Tax Court, however, has allowed an allocation in the absence of earmarking where the state considered severance damages, and the value of the condemned land was small in comparison to the damages suffered by the remaining property. To avoid a dispute with the IRS, make sure the authority makes this breakdown. Without such identification, the IRS will treat the entire proceeds as consideration for the condemned property.

18.25 Reporting Gains From Casualties

If an involuntary conversion was the result of a *theft* or *casualty*, you have to prepare Form 4684. To report net gains, Form 4684 will direct you to Form 1040, Schedule D, or Form 4797, depending on the type of property involved. Generally, use of Form 4797 reflects the netting requirements for involuntary conversions of business, rental, or royalty property under Section 1231; *see 44.8*.

If the conversion occurred because of a *condemnation,* you use Form 4797 for business or investment property and Schedule D for personal-use property.

Filing Instruction

Business and Income-Producing Property

Follow the instructions to Form 4684 for reporting gains or losses from casualties and thefts of property used in a business or held for the production of income.

Chapter 19

Deducting Job Costs and Other Miscellaneous Expenses

Deductible miscellaneous expenses cover a wide and varied range of items, such as employee travel and entertainment expenses, work clothes expenses, union and employee professional dues, investment expenses, legal expenses, tax preparation expenses, and educational expenses. They also share a common limitation: the 2% adjusted gross income (AGI) floor. If your expenses do not exceed this floor, you may not deduct them. If the expenses exceed the floor, only the excess is deductible on Schedule A, as explained in *19.1*. Some job-related deductions, such as moving expenses and impairment-related work expenses, are not subject to the 2% AGI floor.

In addition to the 2% AGI floor, employees who incur unreimbursed meal and entertainment costs face this further restriction: Only 50% of meal and entertainment costs are deductible.

Miscellaneous deductions, except for gambling losses, are subject to the 3% reduction to itemized deductions *(13.7)* if your adjusted gross income exceeds $137,300 ($68,650 if you are married and file separate returns).

Miscellaneous Expenses on Schedule A

19.1 2% AGI Floor Reduces Miscellaneous Deductions

A floor of 2% of adjusted gross income (AGI) applies to the total of most miscellaneous deductions that are claimed on Schedule A of Form 1040. AGI is the amount on Line 35 of Form 1040. The purpose of the floor is to reduce or eliminate such deductions. Only expenses above the floor are deductible.

If your 2002 AGI exceeds $137,300, or $68,650 if married filing separately, deductible miscellaneous expenses (after applying the 2% AGI floor) are then subject to a further reduction under the 3% reduction computation discussed at *13.7*.

Miscellaneous expenses subject to the 2% AGI floor include:

- Unreimbursed travel, meals, and entertainment expenses of employees on trips away from home, *20.1* and *20.31*
- Taxable reimbursements of job expenses or taxable expense allowances under non-accountable plans, *20.34*
- Unreimbursed local transportation costs of visiting clients or customers, *19.8*
- Union dues, *19.5*
- Professional and business association dues, *19.5*
- Work clothes expenses, *19.6*
- Cost of looking for a new job, *19.7*
- Job agency fees, *19.7*
- Tax advice and preparation fees, *19.25*
- Appraisal fees related to casualty losses and charitable property contributions, *19.25*
- Investment expenses, such as IRA custodial fees, safe-deposit rentals, and fees to investment counselors, *19.24*
- Employee home office expenses, *19.13*
- Legal fees, *19.26*
- Education costs, *19.15*
- Business bad debt on a loan made to your employer to protect your job, *5.35*

Miscellaneous expenses not subject to the 2% AGI floor include:

- Casualty and theft losses from income-producing property
- Impairment-related work expenses for disabled employees, *19.4*
- Gambling losses up to gambling income, *11.3*
- Estate tax attributable to income in respect of a decedent, *11.17*
- The deduction for repayment of amounts held under a claim of right, *2.9*
- Amortizable bond premium on bonds purchased before October 23, 1986, *4.17*
- Unrecovered investments in pension on deceased retiree's final return, *7.22*
- Jury duty fees turned over to employer, *12.2*

Caution

2% AGI Floor

Most miscellaneous deductions are subject to a floor of 2% of your adjusted gross income (AGI), which may limit or bar a deduction. Your AGI is the amount on Line 35 of Form 1040.

EXAMPLES

1. You pay union dues of $380, work clothes costs of $400, and $150 for the preparation of your tax return. Your adjusted gross income (AGI) is $35,000. Your miscellaneous deduction on Schedule A after applying the 2% floor is $230:

Union dues	$380
Work clothes	400
Tax preparation	150
	$930
Less: 2% of $35,000	700
Deductible amount	$230

2. Your adjusted gross income (AGI) is $90,000. You pay the following deductible miscellaneous expenses:

Professional dues	$100
Investment counsel fee	300
Safe-deposit box	50
Tax preparation fee	500
Unreimbursed travel expenses	800
	$1,750

   Since the 2% floor of $1,800 (2% × $90,000) exceeds your miscellaneous expenses, none of the expenses are deductible.

19.2 Effect of 2% AGI Floor on Deductions

The table below shows the effect of the 2% AGI floor on miscellaneous deductible expenses. A higher bracket taxpayer may also be subject to the 3% reduction to itemized deductions discussed at *13.7*.

If your adjusted gross income (AGI) is—	Only miscellaneous expenses exceeding this amount are deductible—
$10,000	$200
20,000	400
30,000	600
40,000	800
50,000	1,000
60,000	1,200
70,000	1,400
80,000	1,600
90,000	1,800
100,000	2,000
200,000	4,000

19.3 Checklist of Job Expenses Subject to the 2% AGI Floor

The following expenses that are job related—ranging from professional dues and subscriptions to employment agency fees—are subject to the 2% AGI floor and so you may be unable to deduct them; *see 19.2*. Generally, you must file Form 2106 to claim job-related expenses that were not reimbursed by your employer. You enter your expenses and any reimbursements on Form 2106, and the allowable amount is then transferred to Line 20 of Schedule A (unreimbursed employee expenses), where it is subject to the 2% AGI floor along with other miscellaneous deductions; *see 19.1*. If you are using the standard mileage rate *(43.1)* for 2001 vehicle expenses, and you were not reimbursed by your employer for any job expenses, you may file Form 2106-EZ to report your auto and other job expenses.

You may enter your unreimbursed expenses directly on Line 20 of Schedule A without having to complete Form 2106 or Form 2106-EZ if you are not claiming any job-related travel, local transportation, meal, or entertainment expenses and you received no employer reimbursement at all for any of your other job costs (such as education expenses, union dues, or uniforms).

 *Filing Instruction*

Form 2106 or 2106-EZ
You generally must report your job-related expenses, and any employer reimbursements, on Form 2106. Form 2106-EZ is a shorter form that you may use if none of your job expenses are reimbursed and you deduct car expenses, if any, using the IRS flat mileage allowance.

Agency fees for job, *19.7*
Airfares, *20.5*
Auto club membership, *43.2*
Auto expenses, *19.4, 43.1*
Books used on the job, *19.5*
Bond costs, *19.24*
Business bad debt for loan to employer, *5.33* and *5.35*
Car insurance premiums, *43.2*
Cleaning costs, *19.6*
Commerce association dues, *19.5*
Commuting costs, *20.2*
Computers, *19.10*
Convention trips, *20.12* and *20.14*
Correspondence course, *19.16*
Depreciation, *42.1*
Dues, *19.5*
Educational expenses, *19.15–19.23*
Employment agency fees, *19.7*
Entertainment expenses, *20.15–20.29*
Equipment, *19.10–19.12*
Foreign travel costs, *20.11* and *20.14*

Furniture, *19.13*
Garage rent, *43.2*
Gasoline, *43.2*
Gasoline taxes, *43.2*
Gifts, *20.25*
Home office expenses, *19.13*
Hotel costs, *20.5*
Job-hunting costs, *19.7*
Labor union dues, *19.5*
Laundry, *19.6*
Legal expenses, *19.26*
Local transportation and travel away from home, *20.1*
Lodging, *20.5*
Magazines, *19.5*
Malpractice liability premiums, *40.6*
Meals, *20.3* and *20.4*
Medical examinations, *17.2*
Membership dues and fees, *19.5*
Motel charges, *20.5*
Moving expenses, *12.7*
Parking fees, *43.2*

Passport fees for business travel, *20.11*
Pay turned over to employer, *2.9*
Periodicals, *19.5*
Protective clothing, *19.6*
Rail fares, *20.5*
Reimbursed expenses, *20.30–20.34*
Safety helmets, *19.6*
Safety shoes, *19.6*
Secretarial convention, *20.12*
Subscriptions, *19.5*
Taxi fares, *20.5*
Telephone calls, *19.14*
Toll charges, *43.2*
Tools, *19.12*
Trade association dues, *19.5*
Tuition, *19.15–19.23*
Typewriter, *19.11*
Uniforms, *19.6*
Union dues, *19.5*
Work clothes, *19.6*

19.4 Job Expenses Not Subject to the 2% AGI Floor

Impairment-related work expenses. Unreimbursed impairment-related work expenses are reported on Form 2106 (or Form 2106-EZ where eligible) and then the unreimbursed portion is entered on Line 27 of Schedule A as a miscellaneous itemized deduction that is *not* subject to the 2% AGI floor. You have to show:

1. You are physically or mentally disabled. The physical or mental disability must result in a functional limitation of employment that substantially limits one or more major life activities. Generally, showing blindness or deafness will meet this test, but other disabilities that impair your ability to walk, speak, breathe, or perform manual tasks also may qualify if they limit the ability to work.

2. You incur the expenses in order to work. The expenses must be ordinary and necessary to allow you to work. Attendant care services at a place of employment that are necessary for you to work are also deductible.

Expenses of performing artists. As a performing artist, you may deduct job expenses from gross income, whether or not itemized deductions are claimed, *see 12.2*.

You report the performing artist expenses on Form 2106 (or Form 2106-EZ where eligible) and enter the total as a "write-in amount" on Line 34 of Form 1040, instead of on Schedule A. Write "QPA" next to Line 34. If you do not meet the tests, the expenses are deducted on Schedule A subject to the 2% AGI floor.

Expenses of teachers, instructors, counselors, principals, or aides. As a teacher, instructor, counselor, principal, or aide who works at least 900 hours during the school year, you can deduct up to $250 of out-of-pocket costs for books and classroom supplies directly from gross income on Form 1040, Line 23, or Form 1040A, on Line 16; *see 12.2*. Expenses over the $250 limit are deducted on Schedule A subject to the 2% floor.

The up-to-$250 deduction can only be claimed to the extent that qualified expenses exceed tax-free education savings bond interest, tax-free payments from qualified tuition programs, or tax-free withdrawals from Coverdell education savings accounts.

Moving expenses. Moving expenses to a new job location are not subject to the 2% AGI floor; *see 12.3*.

19.5 Dues and Subscriptions

You may deduct as miscellaneous itemized deductions, subject to the 2% AGI floor on Schedule A, dues paid to a:

- Professional society if you are a salaried lawyer, accountant, teacher, physician, or other professional
- Trade association if it is conducted for the purpose of furthering the business interests of its members
- Stock exchange if you are a securities dealer
- Community "booster" club conducted to attract tourists and settlers to the locality where the members do business
- Chamber of Commerce if it is conducted to advance the business interests of its members

Union costs. Union members may deduct as "miscellaneous" itemized deductions union dues and initiation fees. Similarly, non-union employees may deduct monthly service charges to a union. An assessment paid for unemployment benefits is deductible if payment is required as a condition of remaining in the union and holding a union job. Voluntary payments to a union unemployment benefit or strike fund are not deductible.

No deduction is allowed for mandatory contributions to a union pension fund applied toward the purchase of a retirement annuity; the contributions are treated as the cost of the annuity. Furthermore, to the extent that an assessment covers sick, accident, or death benefits payable to you or your family, it is not deductible. Similarly, an assessment for a construction fund to build union recreation centers was disallowed by the Tax Court, even though the payment was required for keeping the job.

Campaign costs for running for union office are not deductible.

Planning Reminder

Exceptions to the 2% Floor

Qualifying educator expenses, impairment-related expenses, and job expenses of performing artists are not subject to the 2% AGI floor.

Filing Tip

Life Insurance Agents and Food Deliverers

Statutory employees, such as full-time life insurance salespersons, may deduct expenses on Schedule C and so avoid the 2% AGI floor; *see 40.6* for further details.

Subscriptions. Subject to the 2% AGI floor, you may claim as miscellaneous itemized deductions unreimbursed payments for job-related subscriptions to professional journals and trade magazines.

19.6 Uniforms and Work Clothes

The cost of uniforms and other apparel, including their cleaning, laundering, and repair, is deductible *only* if the clothes are:

1. Required to keep your job; *and*
2. Not suitable for wear when not working.

The deduction is subject to the 2% AGI floor.

Special work clothes. Courts have held that the cost of special work clothes that protect you from injury is deductible even if you are not required to wear them to keep your job. However, you may not deduct the cost of special clothing, such as aprons and overalls, that protect your regular street clothing. Nor may you deduct the cost of ordinary clothes used as work clothes on the grounds that: (1) they get harder use than customary garments receive; (2) they are soiled after a day's work and cannot be worn socially; or (3) they were purchased for your convenience to save wear and tear on your better clothes. For example, a sanitation inspector, a machinist's helper, a carpenter, and a telephone repairman were not allowed to deduct the cost of their work clothes.

Employer allowance. An allowance paid by your employer for work clothes or a uniform is not reported as income, unless you do not substantiate the expenses to your employer. If you do substantiate the expenses, those exceeding the reimbursement are reported on Form 2106, and the deduction is subject to the 2% AGI floor; *see 20.30*.

High-fashion work clothes. That your job requires you to wear expensive clothing is not a basis for deducting the cost of the clothes if the clothing is suitable for wear off the job.

Deductions allowed. Deductions for costs of uniforms and work clothes have been allowed to:

Airline pilot
Bakery salesperson—for a uniform with a company label
Baseball player
Bus driver
Cement finisher for gloves, overshoes, and rubber boots
Civilian faculty members of a military school
Commercial fisherman for protective clothing, such as oil cloths, gloves, and boots
Dairy worker for rubber boots, white shirts, trousers, and cap worn only while inside the dairy
Entertainer for theatrical clothing used solely for performances
Exotic dancer for breast implants used as a "stage prop" essential to her business; *see* Example 8 in *19.9*

Factory foreman for white coat bearing the word "foreman" and the name of the company
Factory worker for safety shoes
Firefighter
Hospital attendant for work clothes; he came in contact with patients having contagious diseases
Jockey
Letter carrier
Meat cutter for special white shoes
Musician for formal wear
Paint machine operator for high top shoes and long leather gloves
Plumber for special shoes and gloves
Police officer
Railroad conductor
Railroad firefighter for boots, leather gloves, raincoat, caps, and work gloves

---

EXAMPLES

1. A painter may not deduct the cost of work clothing consisting of a white cap, a white shirt, white bib overalls, and standard work shoes. The clothing is not distinctive in character as a uniform would be. That his union requires him to wear such clothing does not make it a deductible expense.

2. A tennis pro who taught at private clubs was not allowed to deduct the cost of tennis outfits or shoes required for his job. He did not wear them outside of work and argued that he replaced the shoes every few weeks to reduce the chances of injury. However, the Tax Court upheld the IRS's disallowance of his deductions because the clothes and shoes are suitable for everyday wear; warm-up suits and tennis clothes are fashionable and frequently worn as casual wear. Furthermore, there was no evidence that his tennis shoes reduced chances of injury.

 Filing Tip

Uniform Required
Your claim of a work clothes deduction is helped if your employer requires you to wear a uniform. Uniform costs of reservists and service persons, in excess of any uniform allowance, are deductible if you are prohibited from wearing the uniform off duty.

 Filing Tip

Cleaning and Laundering
If you are allowed to deduct the cost of work clothes and uniforms, you also may deduct the cost of cleaning and laundering them. Also, courts have allowed the cost of cleaning and laundering to be deducted in situations where:

- The clothes could only be worn one day at a time because they became too dirty.
- Dirty clothes were a hazard; they became baggy and might have gotten caught in machinery.
- Clothes were worn only at work and a place for changing clothes was provided by the employer.
- A meat cutter had to wear clean work clothes at all times.

19.7 Expenses of Looking for a New Job

Subject to the 2% AGI floor, you may deduct expenses of looking for a new job in the *same line of work*, whether or not a new job is found. If you are unemployed when seeking a new job, and the period of unemployment has been substantial, the IRS may disallow the deduction.

EXAMPLE

The IRS disallowed the driving expenses of an unemployed secretary on the ground that she was not currently employed. The Tax Court disagreed and held that for purposes of deducting job-hunting expenses, she could still be considered in the business of being a secretary. She had worked as an administrative secretary with Toyota in San Francisco. The firm relocated, resulting in a 100-mile-per-day commute. She quit her job at the end of January 1984. From February to November 1984, she drove her Cadillac El Dorado over 4,600 miles looking for a new job. The Tax Court allowed her a depreciation deduction of $2,880 and $981 for car operating costs.

First Job

You may not deduct the expenses of seeking your first job.

Expenses of seeking your *first job* are not deductible, even if a job is obtained. Also, expenses of looking for a job in a different line of work are not deductible, even if you get the job.

The IRS may also dispute the deduction of search expenses of a previously employed professional who forms a partnership.

EXAMPLE

A CPA working for a firm decided to go out on his own. After a period of investigation, he formed a partnership with another CPA. The IRS disallowed his deduction of search expenses, claiming his expenses were incurred in a new business. As an employee he was in a different business from that of a self-employed practitioner. Thus, the expenses should be capitalized as a cost of setting up or organizing the partnership. The Tax Court disagreed, allowing the deduction. The travel expenses were incurred to seek work as a CPA, whether as a self-employed or employed CPA.

Employment Agency Fee

If your new employer pays the fee under an agreement with an agency, you may disregard the payment for tax purposes. However, if you pay the fee and deduct it as a job search expense and in a later year you are reimbursed by your employer, you must report the reimbursement as taxable income to the extent you received a tax benefit from the earlier deduction; *see 11.6.*

A company interested in your services may invite you to a job interview and agree to pay all of the trip expenses to its office, even if you are not hired. The company payment is tax free up to your actual expenses.

Travel expenses. If you travel to find a new job in the same line of work, such as an interview in a distant city, you may deduct travel expenses, including meals and lodging. If, during the trip, you also do personal visiting, you may deduct the transportation expenses to and from the area if the trip was primarily related to your job search. Time spent on personal activity is compared with time spent looking for a job to determine the primary purpose of the trip. If the transportation expenses to and from the destination are not deductible because the trip was primarily personal, you may still deduct the expenses of seeking a new job while you are away.

Are you between jobs? If you are between jobs and you continue to see and entertain your former customers, the IRS holds that you may not deduct the cost of entertainment and other business expenses during this period on the ground that you are not in business and earning income. However, the Tax Court in the following case allowed the deduction.

EXAMPLE

Haft was a successful jewelry salesman earning as much as $60,000 a year. In the fall of one year, he left his employer and started to look for a new connection. During the following year, he continued to maintain contacts with his former customers by entertaining buyers and their representatives. He deducted the expenses of entertaining and other business costs. The IRS disallowed the deduction, claiming he was not in business. The Tax Court disagreed. His lack of business income was temporary and resulted from a period of transition that lasted a reasonable time.

19.8 Local Transportation Costs

Unreimbursed local transportation costs to see your employer's clients or customers, such as taxi, bus, or train fares, are miscellaneous itemized deductions subject to the 2% AGI floor. Transportation from your regular job to a second job on the same day is also deductible. You may not deduct the cost of commuting from home to a regular job or second job, but commuting to a temporary work location *(20.2)* is deductible.

If you use your own car for job-related travel, you may deduct unreimbursed out-of-pocket costs for gasoline, tolls, and parking. The IRS mileage allowance *(43.1)* is available for the occasional business use of your personal car if you elected the allowance for the first year you used the car for business purposes; *see* the instructions to Form 2106 or Form 2106-EZ.

19.9 Unusual Job Expenses

The following are not typical deductible expenses. However, deductions in the following cases have been allowed.

EXAMPLES

1. *Shoeshine expense of a pilot.* Company rules required a commercial airline pilot to look neat, keep his hair cut, and wear conservative black shoes, properly shined. The pilot deducted as a business expense $100 for his haircuts and $25 for his shoe shines. The IRS disallowed the deductions, but the Tax Court allowed the cost of the shoe shines. The shoes were of a military type which he wore only with his pilot's uniform. The cost of keeping up a uniform is deductible. The haircuts were merely nondeductible personal expenses.

2. *Depreciation on furnishings bought by executive for his company office.* Following a quarrel with an interior decorator, a sales manager bought his own office furniture when his firm moved to new quarters. Rather than complain or ask for reimbursement, he footed the bill and deducted depreciation. The IRS disallowed the deduction, claiming the expense was that of his company. The Tax Court allowed the deduction. The manager's action was unusual, but prudent. He did not want to cause difficulties, and at the same time had to maintain his image as a successful manager. His expenses for furniture were appropriate and helpful.

3. *Salesman's cost of operating a private plane.* Sherman flew his own plane to visit clients in six southern states and deducted $18,000 as operating costs of the plane. The IRS disallowed the deduction, claiming there was no business reason for the plane. He could have taken commercial flights or used a company car to reach his clients. Furthermore, his company did not reimburse him for the private airplane costs, although it would cover costs of his car and commercial air travel. Finally, the amount of airplane expenses was unreasonable compared to his salary of $25,000. Sherman convinced the Tax Court that use of a private airplane was the only reasonable way he could cover his six-state sales area. He showed that most of his clients were not near commercial airports. Although the airplane costs were large in relation to his salary, they were still reasonable and, therefore, deductible.

4. *Executive's purchase of blazers for sales force.* Jetty, the president of an oil equipment manufacturing firm, thought that he could generate goodwill for the company if employees who attended industrial trade shows wore a blazer and vest set in the company colors. He personally paid and deducted $6,725 for 27 blazers and vests. The IRS disallowed the deduction on the grounds that it was a company expense and that Jetty should have sought reimbursement from the company.

   The Tax Court allowed the deduction. Paying for the clothes was a legitimate business expense for Jetty since he depended on bonuses for a large portion of his pay, and, as company president, he had responsibility for seeing to it that there were profits to share in. Furthermore, the outlay was not the type of expense covered by the company's manual on expense reimbursements.

5. *Repayment of layoff benefits to restore pension credit.* When he was laid off, an employee received a lump-sum payment from his company based on his salary and years of service. When he was rehired a year later, he repaid the lump sum in order to restore his pension credits and other benefit rights. The IRS ruled that he may deduct the repayment as a condition of being rehired; the repayment was required to restore employee benefits.

6. *Teaching supplies.* The IRS does not allow teachers a deduction for school supplies. Some courts have been lenient and have allowed teachers to deduct out-of-pocket expenses. In one case, however, a teacher could not convince a court that his deduction for the cost of paper, pens, glue, and other supplies was a business expense. He could not support his claim that the school did not supply enough equipment.

7. *Politician's expenses.* Elected officials may incur out-of-pocket expenses in excess of the allowances received from the government. They may deduct as miscellaneous deductions their payment of office expenses such as salaries, office rent, and supplies. Part-time officials may claim the deduction. The expenses are deductible even if they exceed the official's income.

8. *Depreciation for exotic dancer's breast implants.* Hess, an exotic dancer, enlarged her breasts to the abnormal size of 56N and claimed a $2,088 depreciation deduction for their cost. The IRS disallowed the deduction, claiming that cosmetic surgery is a personal expense. The Tax Court disagreed. Hess's expenses were incurred solely in furtherance of her business and not for her own personal benefit. The breast implants were not of the kind that women usually get to enhance their appearance. Rather, Hess enlarged her breasts to a "freakish" size to substantially increase her annual income, which she did. The court also compared the implants to special work clothes *(19.6)*, required for a job and not for personal wear. As an exotic dancer, Hess's large breasts are like a "costume" needed to keep her job. Although she could not remove them daily, she would have, if possible, because they caused her serious medical problems.

Computers, Phones, and Home Office Costs of Employees

19.10 Computers and Cellular Phones

Court Decision

Tax Court Allows Computer Deduction

The Tax Court allowed a first-year expensing deduction to a working couple who used the same home computer given these facts: The husband, a professor, used it to store historical data; the wife, a state transportation planner, used it to do extensive number crunching. What apparently won the decision for the couple was evidence that (1) the husband did not have access to a computer at the university, and (2) the state office in which the wife worked did not have funds to buy a computer. The court held that the use of the computer was necessary for them to properly do their jobs, and as the purchase of a computer spared their employers from having to provide them with computers, the purchase was for the employers' convenience.

In a later case, a telemarketing sales manager was allowed a first-year expensing deduction for a home computer and printer used to prepare reports. The key to winning the deduction was her supervisor's testimony that as a mid-level manager, she could not enter the office after regular hours to use a company computer, and that she was able to keep up with the volume of sales reports she was required to submit by using her home computer and accessing information via modem.

Computers (and peripherals) and cellular phones are treated as "listed property" subject to deduction restrictions: To get a first-year expensing deduction *(42.3)* or to claim any type of depreciation, the computer or cellular phone must be used for the convenience of your employer, which means your use of the equipment satisfies a substantial business need of your employer. The equipment must also be required as a condition of your job, which means that you cannot properly do your job without it. The IRS strictly interprets these requirements.

Computer. A letter from your employer stating that a computer is needed for your position does not by itself satisfy the deduction tests. Even where your employer encourages use of a personal computer that is used for basic job requirements, the IRS requires proof that you need your own computer to do your job because your employer does not provide one, or because the computer supplied by your employer is not adequate for your job. In the following Examples, the IRS disallowed depreciation writeoffs.

EXAMPLES

1. An electric company offered to help pay for its engineers' personal computers where this would improve productivity. Qualifying engineers received extra pay and had to buy a computer meeting company specifications, take approved computer courses, and agree to restrictions on resale of the computer. An engineer bought a computer and used it 95% of the time for writing business memos and reports, and studying business flow charts. He did not use the computer for entertainment.

   The IRS held that although the engineer's computer was work related and benefitted his employer, buying a computer was not required for his job; it was not "inextricably related" to proper job performance. Further, his participation in the employer's computer program was optional, not mandatory.

2. A professor of nursing, trying to keep her temporary position, bought a personal computer, needing a word processor for independent research papers and to document her qualifications for research grants. The research and external grant support were implied university requirements for faculty appointments. She did not have access to university word-processing equipment during regular work hours; and because of her classroom responsibilities, her research and grant development work had to be done on her own time. To help her pursue outside grants, the university bought her a "modem" that allowed a phone hook-up with its computer at night. Her computer was used 100% for research and grant work.

   As in Example 1, the IRS held that use of the computer was not "inextricably related" to proper job performance and did not qualify for a depreciation writeoff. Furthermore, there was no evidence that employees who did not use computers were professionally disadvantaged.

3. The IRS held that an insurance agent could not deduct depreciation for a laptop computer he used to help develop insurance plans for clients. The insurance company encouraged its agents to buy the computer because office computers were not generally accessible. According to the IRS, it is not enough that the agent's productivity increased or that he used the computer solely for business. Purchasing the computer was optional, not a mandatory job requirement. Employees who did not purchase computers were not professionally disadvantaged.

4. The IRS barred a third-grade teacher from deducting the cost of a Macintosh computer because it was not required for her job. She bought the computer using an interest-free loan from the school after the school decided that report cards and student evaluations would have to be prepared on a Macintosh instead of being written. The Tax Court and an appeals court sided with the IRS. It may have been convenient for the teacher to use a home computer but it was not required. Other teachers were able to timely complete their duties using school computers.

Cellular phones. The IRS has not released specific guidelines or rulings covering deduction requirements for cellular phones. In general, the "convenience of the employer" and "job condition" tests apply.

Claiming a deduction. If you can meet the "convenience of the employer" and "job condition" tests for a computer or cellular phone purchased in 2002, and you have records to prove that the unit is used more than 50% of the time for your job, you may write off the cost up to the $24,000 limit in 2002 for first-year expensing *(42.3)* or accelerated five-year MACRS depreciation rates *(42.5)* may be used. If business use of the unit is 50% or less, you may not use first-year expensing or regular MACRS but you may claim straight-line depreciation.

First-year expensing or depreciation is claimed on Form 4562 and then entered on Form 2106 or Form 2106-EZ along with other job-related costs. The deduction from Form 2106 or Form 2106-EZ is subject to the 2% AGI floor for miscellaneous deductions on Schedule A; *see 19.1.* If business use in a later year is 50% or less, *see* Example 2 at *42.10* for recapture rules.

You need to keep records documenting your percentage of business use for a computer or cellular phone.

19.11 Calculators, Copiers, Fax Machines, and Typewriters

The listed property requirements applied to computers and cellular phones *(19.9)* do not apply to calculators, copiers, fax machines, adding machines, and typewriters. This means that the restrictive convenience of the employer and job condition rules do not apply. However, to depreciate the cost of such equipment, you should be ready to prove that you need the equipment for your job, and keep a record of the time it is used for business. To claim first-year expensing *(42.3)*, rather than regular depreciation, you must use the equipment *more* than 50% of the time for business.

19.12 Small Tools

If you furnished your own small tools used on your job, you may deduct their cost if they are not expected to last beyond a year. The deduction is subject to the 2% AGI floor. The cost of tools with a useful life of more than a year must be recovered through depreciation or first-year expensing; *see 42.3.* Be prepared to substantiate your deduction with receipts showing the cost and type of tools purchased, and the business necessity for them.

19.13 Employee Home Office Deductions

The tax law has been drafted to prevent employees from deducting the expenses of an office at a home. The tests for deducting home office expenses are discussed at *40.12.* Even if an employee should meet one of the tests, such as doing administrative work at home, the employee must also show that the home office was required for the "convenience of his or her employer" in order to claim the deduction.

EXAMPLE

Charlie, a teacher, has a small office at school where he can grade papers and tests, work on lesson plans, and meet with parents and students. The school does not require him to work

Caution

Deducting Cellular Phone Costs
Cellular phone equipment must be used for the convenience of the employer and be a condition of your employment for you to be able to claim a depreciation deduction for the cost.

Filing Instruction

Office for Sideline Business
If you are an employee and also have a sideline business for which you use a home office, the office expenses are deductible if the office is used regularly and exclusively as your principal place of business or a meeting place with clients, customers, or patients. If the tests are met, you claim your home office expenses as a self-employed person on Form 8829, which you attach to Schedule C. The deduction may not exceed your income from the sideline business. *See* Chapter 40 for a sample Form 8829 and other deduction details.

Caution

Deducting Telephone Costs

To support your deduction, keep a record of business calls made at home or anywhere outside your employer's office.

at home, but he prefers to use the office he has set up in his home, and does not use the office the school provides. Although Charlie's home office is used for the administrative duties of teaching, Charlie may not deduct his home office expenses because he does not meet the convenience of the employer test. His employer provides him with an office at school and does not require him to work at home.

19.14 Telephone Costs

For business calls made outside of your employer's office or at home, keep a record or diary of business calls to support your deduction. To avoid the problem of allocating the costs of a single phone for both business and personal use, consider a separate phone for business use only.

Deduction barred for basic charge of first phone line. You may not claim as a deductible home office expense any part of the standard monthly charge for the first telephone line into your home. This disallowance rule only applies to the first telephone line. If you have more than one telephone line and use additional lines in a home office, costs for these lines remain deductible, subject to the restrictions at *19.13*. The restriction does not affect deductibility of long-distance calls, phone rentals, or optional services such as call waiting, call forwarding, three-way calling, or extra directory listings.

Deductible Education Costs

19.15 Types of Deductible Education Costs

If you improve your job or professional skills by attending continuing education or refresher classes, advanced academic courses, or vocational training, you may be able to deduct your expenses. As a self-employed business owner or professional, allowable expenses are deductible on Schedule C. However, as an employee, the tax benefit of an educational expense deduction is limited because the expenses are miscellaneous itemized deductions, which, together with any other miscellaneous expenses, are deductible on Schedule A only to the extent that the total exceeds 2% of your adjusted gross income; *see 19.1*.

Caution

Qualifying for New Business

Courses that qualify you for a new business or profession are not deductible even if you have no intention of entering that business or profession.

To deduct education costs, you must show that the following conditions are met:

1. You are employed or self-employed;
2. You already meet the minimum requirements of your job, business, or profession;
3. The course maintains or improves your job or professional skills, or you are required by your employer or by law to take the course to keep your present salary or position; *and*
4. The course does *not* lead to qualification for a new profession or business. The cost of courses preparing you for a new profession is not deductible, even if you take them to improve your skills or to meet your employer's requirements. This rule prevents the deduction of law school costs; *see 19.17*. Furthermore, the cost of a bar review course or CPA review course is not deductible because it leads to a new profession as an attorney or CPA. If courses lead to qualification for a new business or profession, no deduction is allowed even if you keep your current position.

If your courses meet the above requirements you may deduct the following education costs on Schedule C if self-employed or on Schedule A subject to the 2% AGI floor if the courses are related to your job:

1. Tuition, textbooks, fees, equipment, and other aids required by the courses.
2. Local transportation costs as discussed at *19.22*.
3. Travel to and from a school away from home, and lodging and 50% of meals while at school away from home; *see 19.22*. The IRS will not disallow traveling expenses to attend a school away from home or in a foreign country merely because you could have taken the course in a local school. But it may disallow your board and lodging and expenses at the school if your stay lasts longer than a year.

Further details of the deduction requirements are explained at 19.16.

Nondeductible courses. The cost of courses preparing you for a new profession or for meeting the minimum requirements for your job is not deductible, even if you take them to improve your skills or to meet your employer's requirements *(see 19.16)*. For a working person without a college degree, no deduction is allowed for the cost of obtaining a bachelor's degree, or an associate's degree that could lead to a bachelor's degree.

EXAMPLE

Edward, a self-employed golf instructor without an undergraduate degree, earned an associate's degree in business from the Golf Academy of the South. The IRS and Tax Court disallowed his deduction for tuition and fees. It does not matter that the courses may have improved his skills as a golf instructor. No deduction was allowed because completing the associate's program was a first step in acquiring a basic undergraduate degree that would qualify Edward for a variety of trades or businesses other than that of a golf instructor.

19.16 Work-Related Tests for Education Costs

You must meet an employment test to deduct educational expenses. Educational costs are not deductible if you are unemployed or inactive in a business or profession. The cost of "brush-up" courses taken in anticipation of resuming work is also not deductible. However, in one case, a court allowed an unemployed teacher to deduct the cost of tuition, fees, and books where the IRS conceded that the teacher, although unemployed, remained in the teaching profession while attending college classes.

You are not considered unemployed when you take courses during a vacation or temporary leave of absence; *see 19.21.*

Course must not meet minimum standards. You may not deduct the cost of courses taken to meet the minimum requirements of your job. The minimum requirements of a position are based on a review of your employer's standards, the laws and regulations of the state you live in, and the standards of your profession or business. That you are presently employed does not in itself prove that you have met the minimum standards for your job.

If minimum standards change after you enter a job or profession, courses you take to meet the new standards are deductible.

The minimum standards for teachers are discussed at *19.19.*

Course must maintain or improve job skills. To be deductible, the education must maintain or improve your current job skills. That you are established in your position and that persons in similar positions usually pursue such education indicates that the courses are taken to maintain and improve job skills. However, the IRS may not allow a deduction for a general education course that is a prerequisite for a job-related course.

If the courses lead to a change of position or promotion within the same occupation, a deduction for their cost will usually be allowed if your new duties involve the same general type of work. If, as a consequence of taking a job-related course, you receive a substantial advancement and the IRS questions the deduction of the course costs, be prepared to prove that you took the course primarily to maintain or improve skills of your existing job. However, if the course leads to qualification for a new profession, the IRS will disallow a deduction even if the course also improves current job skills.

Courses must not lead to qualification for a new profession. If a course improves your current job skills but leads to qualification for a new profession, the course is not deductible. For example, a deduction is not allowed for the cost of law school or medical school courses since they prepare you for a new profession. This is true even if you do not intend to practice medicine or law; *see 19.17* and *19.18.* The IRS with Tax Court approval has also held that a deduction is not allowed for the cost of college courses that are part of a degree program, such as a bachelor of arts or science degree; *see 19.15.*

If you are practicing your profession, the cost of courses leading to a specialty within that profession is deductible.

EXAMPLE

A practicing dentist returned to school full time to study orthodontics while continuing his practice on a part-time basis. When he finished his training, he limited his work to orth-

 Filing Tip

Are MBA Courses Deductible?

The cost of MBA courses is deductible if the courses enhance the skills required in your current position, are not a minimum job requirement, and do not qualify you for a new business. The IRS may question in a specific case whether there has been a change of business, particularly where taking the courses leads to a promotion. For a deduction, the courses must be related to your existing job responsibilities. The Tax Court has allowed deductions for MBA expenses where individuals with some managerial or administrative experience took the courses to improve job skills.

If your employer requires a master's degree as a minimum entrance requirement for your position, the cost of the courses is not deductible.

In one case, a college graduate who took a summer job before starting MBA courses was not allowed a deduction because he had not yet established himself in a business or employment; the summer position was just a temporary stage between schooling.

If your employer reimburses you for MBA courses that qualify for a deduction, the reimbursement is a tax-free working condition fringe benefit; *see 3.6.*

odontics. The IRS ruled he could deduct the cost of his studies. His post-graduate schooling improved his professional skills as a dentist. It did not qualify him for a new profession.

Further education required by employer or law. If, to retain your present job or rate of pay, your employer requires you to obtain further education, you may deduct the cost of the courses. The fact that you also qualified for a raise in pay or a substantial advancement in your position after completing the courses should not bar the deduction.

The employer's requirement must be for a bona fide business reason, not merely to benefit you. Only the minimum courses necessary for the retention of your job or rate of pay are considered by the IRS as taken to meet your employer's requirement. You must show any courses beyond your employer's minimum requirements were taken to maintain or improve your job skills.

19.17 Law School Costs

The IRS does not allow deductions for law school courses, because they qualify you for a new profession. Courts support the IRS position. A deduction is not allowed even if you do not intend to practice law. For example, teachers who took law school courses have been disallowed deductions although they intended to continue teaching.

Bar review courses. The costs of bar review courses and the bar exam are not deductible, even where you are seeking admission to the bar of a second state. However, fees paid to state bar admission authorities have been held to be amortizable over an attorney's life expectancy.

Additional legal education. An attorney may deduct the cost of a master's degree program (LL.M.). You must practice as an attorney before the expenses of further legal education are deductible.

> **EXAMPLE**
>
> The Tax Court allowed a lawyer to deduct educational expenses to obtain an LL.M. degree where he worked for a law firm as a beginning lawyer during the summer between graduating from law school and starting work on the LL.M. degree. He was admitted to the state bar before he graduated from law school, and the work he did during the summer was normally assigned to beginning lawyers rather than to law students.
>
> In another case, the IRS and Tax Court did not allow a deduction to a law school graduate who took LL.M. courses before passing the state bar or working as an attorney.

19.18 Courses Taken by Doctors and Nurses

The IRS allows general practitioners to deduct the cost of short refresher courses, even though the courses relate to specialized fields. These courses maintain or improve skills and do not qualify the doctor for a new profession.

A practicing psychiatrist may deduct the cost of attending an accredited psychoanalytic institute to qualify to practice psychoanalysis. A social worker has also been allowed a deduction for the cost of learning psychoanalysis. In one case, the Tax Court allowed a psychiatrist to deduct the cost of personal therapy sessions conducted through telephone conversations and tape cassettes. The court was convinced that the therapy improved his job skills by eliminating psychological blind spots that prevented him from understanding his patients' problems.

A licensed practical nurse may not deduct the costs of a college program that qualifies him or her as a "physician's assistant," which is a new business. Physicians' assistants and practical nurses are subject to different registration and certification requirements under state law, and, more importantly, the physician's assistant may perform duties, such as physical examinations and minor surgery, which go beyond practical nursing duties.

19.19 Courses Taken by Teachers

You must meet the minimum level of education for your present position as set down by law or regulations before you may deduct the cost of courses. The educational requirements are those that existed when you were hired. If your employer set no tests fixing a minimum educational level, you meet the minimum requirements when you become a member of the faculty. Whether you are a faculty member depends on the custom of your employer. You are ordinarily considered a faculty member if: (1) you have tenure, or your service is counted toward tenure; (2) the institution is contributing toward a retirement plan based on your employment (other than Social Security or a similar program); or (3) you have a vote in faculty affairs.

Caution

Law School Costs

Law school costs are not deductible, because a law degree qualifies you for a new profession; *see 19.17*. Costs of obtaining a Master of Laws degree (LL.M.), however, are deductible if you have practiced as an attorney before incurring the expense.

Employed teacher taking courses for teaching certificate. That you are already employed as a teacher, with all the responsibilities of a teacher, may not establish that you have met the minimum educational requirements. A school system that requires a bachelor's degree before granting a permanent teaching certificate may grant temporary or provisional certificates after a person has completed a number of college credits. Renewal of the provisional certificate may be conditioned on the teacher's continuing education for a bachelor's degree. In this case, the IRS will disallow a deduction for the educational costs. The minimum requirements are not met until the teacher has the degree.

19.20 Professor's Research Expenses

Research costs incurred by a college professor are deductible under this condition: He or she is appointed to lecture and teach with the understanding that research in the field will be carried on with the goal of incorporating the findings in teaching and writing. If this test is met, the IRS is satisfied that the research is an express requirement of the teaching position and that research expenses are deductible job expenses.

Deductible research costs include traveling expenses and costs of preparing a manuscript. If income is later realized from the research in the form of lecture or royalty fees, the previously deducted research costs may not again be deducted in determining the income realized from the research.

Expenses of a research project undertaken for a scholarly publication are not deductible if the research is not linked to an income-producing activity or job requirement.

19.21 Leave of Absence To Take Courses

If you are a teacher, the IRS will allow a deduction for full-time graduate courses you take during a leave of absence if these conditions are met: (1) the absence must not be for more than one year and (2) upon completion of the education courses, the same type of employment must be resumed, although you may take a job with a new employer. You may also have to show that you had more than a vague intention to go back to your employment—for example, that you were actually negotiating for a new teaching position and that, in fact, you did obtain a position soon after finishing the graduate courses.

19.22 Local Transportation and Travel Away From Home To Take Courses

If your courses meet the requirements at *19.15* and *19.16*, costs of local transportation and travel away from home are deductible.

Local transportation expenses. If your courses qualify for a deduction under *19.16*, you may deduct transportation costs of going from your job directly to school. Transportation costs include the actual costs of bus, subway, cab, or other fares, as well as the costs of using your car. According to the IRS, the return trip from school to home is also deductible if you are regularly employed and going to school on a *temporary* basis. You can also deduct the round-trip cost of transportation between your home and school if the classes are temporary and you are regularly employed. According to the IRS, you are going to school on a temporary basis if your courses are realistically expected to last for one year or less and actually do last no more than one year. This is the same one-year test for determining whether you can deduct the cost of commuting to a "temporary" work location *(20.2)* or living costs while away from home on a "temporary" assignment *(20.9)*. The IRS position is illustrated in the following Examples.

Planning Reminder

Teacher's Job Change
Elementary and secondary school teachers may deduct the cost of courses taken to make any of the following job changes: (1) elementary to secondary school classroom teacher; (2) classroom teacher in one subject (such as mathematics) to classroom teacher in another subject (such as English or history); (3) classroom teacher to guidance counselor; or (4) classroom teacher to principal.

The IRS held that a "discussion leader" in a college adult education program could not deduct the costs of a master's degree program that led to certification as a high school guidance counselor because this was a new business. The Tax Court disagreed, holding that the responsibilities of discussion leader are similar to the responsibilities of a school counselor. The court distinguished an earlier decision in which a classroom paraprofessional assistant was not allowed to deduct education costs that qualified her as a classroom teacher. The court considered this as a change in professions. A paraprofessional does not have the same control and responsibilities for classroom work as a classroom teacher.

EXAMPLES
1. You regularly work in Camden, New Jersey, and every night for three weeks you drive from home to attend a refresher course. The course is considered temporary. You may deduct the round-trip transportation costs between home and school. The deduction is allowed regardless of how far you travel.
   If you went directly from your job to the school, you may deduct transportation from work to school, and from school to home.
2. On six consecutive Saturdays, which are nonworkdays for you, you drive from home to attend a qualifying course. This is considered a temporary course. You are allowed a deduction for round-trip transportation between home and school, even though you are traveling on a nonworkday.

> 3. You regularly work in Camden, New Jersey, and after work you drive from home to take classes twice a week for 15 months. The IRS does not consider the course to be temporary. You may deduct the cost of going directly from work to school, but the costs of going between home and school are nondeductible.

Using your car. If you use your own car for transportation to school, you may deduct your actual expenses or use the standard mileage rate to figure the deductible amount. The standard mileage rate for 2002 is $36\frac{1}{2}$ cents per mile. Regardless of the method you use, you may deduct parking fees and tolls.

Travel and living expenses away from home. "Away from home" as explained at *20.6* has a special tax meaning. You are not away from home unless you are away overnight. If you are away from home to attend a qualifying course, you may deduct the cost of travel to and from the site of the course, plus lodging and 50% of meals while you are there.

Expenses of sightseeing, social visiting, and entertaining while taking the courses are not deductible. If personal reasons are your main purpose in going to the vicinity of the school, such as to take a vacation, you may deduct only the cost of the courses and your living expenses while attending school. You may not deduct the rest of your travel costs.

To determine the purpose of your trip, an IRS agent will pay close attention to the amount of time devoted to personal activities relative to the time devoted to the courses.

Is travel itself a form of education? A teacher generally may not deduct the cost of an "educational" trip to another state or country as a job expense. Although a trip may have educational value in that the teacher learns about people, culture, or places related to the courses that he or she teaches, the IRS position is that a specific statute, Code Section 274(m)(2), bars a deduction for travel that is a form of education. There may be exceptions where specific research can only be accomplished at a particular location, but a trip for "general" educational purposes does not qualify according to the IRS.

The Tax Court took a different view of the statute in a decision that opens the door to a deduction for teachers who travel overseas to take highly organized courses with regular lectures, a structured syllabus, tours to historically and culturally relevant sites, and extensive reading assignments. The Court allowed a California high-school English teacher and department chair to deduct $5,334 for her airfare, lodging, meals, and tuition for an 18-day trip to Greece in 1995. She was also allowed to deduct $7,705 for a two-week trip to Southeast Asia in 1996. In Greece, she took a course on Greek myths and legends and on the Asian trip, a course on Buddhist and Hindu traditions. Her school required neither course. For the Tax Court, the key to the deduction was the organized nature of the courses, which were sponsored by the Berkeley extension program, taught by university professors, and qualified for undergraduate credit, although the teacher was not taking the courses for credit. The regular lectures, tours, and readings were focused educational activities, not the type of mere educational travel that Congress intended to make nondeductible. After holding that a deduction was not barred by Section 272(m)(2), the Court still had to find that the courses had the primary purpose of maintaining or improving the teacher's skills, but it had little difficulty in doing so. The courses improved her teaching skills and helped her to develop curriculum. The Asian courses also helped her relate better to the predominantly Asian student population in her school. She spent most of her time attending courses and related programs and had minimal free time.

19.23 How To Deduct Education Costs on Your Return

The way you deduct educational expenses on your return depends on your occupational status. If you are:

An employee. If you have education costs that are deductible under *19.16* but that have not been reimbursed by your employer, you generally report the expenses on Form 2106 or Form 2106-EZ. However, you do not need Form 2106 or Form 2106-EZ and may report your educational expenses directly on Schedule A as unreimbursed employee expenses if: (1) you are not claiming job expenses for travel, transportation, meals, or entertainment; and (2) you received no reimbursements for education expenses or any other job-related costs. If your expenses were partially reimbursed, you must use Form 2106; Form 2106-EZ may not be used. On Schedule A, the 2% of adjusted gross income (AGI) floor applies.

As discussed at *19.4*, deductions for impairment-related work expenses are *not* subject to the 2% floor on Schedule A. Expenses of performing artists are not claimed as itemized deductions but are figured on Form 2106 (or 2106-EZ) and deducted directly from gross income on Line 34 of Form 1040.

Filing Tip

Deducting Employee Educational Costs

Unreimbursed education costs, such as for travel, tuition, books, fees, and meals, are deductible only if you claim itemized deductions. You generally must report your expenses on Form 2106 or in some cases Form 2106-EZ *(see 19.3)* before entering the deductible amount on Line 20 of Schedule A, where they and other miscellaneous itemized deductions are subject to the 2% AGI floor.

Employer reimbursements, including advances of deductible expenses, are not reported as income on your Form W-2 if you substantiate the expenses to your employer and return amounts in excess of the substantiated expenses. If these substantiation tests are not met, the expenses are reported as income on your Form W-2, and you must claim them on Form 2106 (or Schedule A if Form 2106 is not needed) as if they were unreimbursed. If your employer pays the tuition directly to the educational institution, you are not required to report the payment in any way on your return.

Teacher on sabbatical. Where a school system has a policy of paying teachers full salary during sabbatical leaves, a teacher on sabbatical may be required to pay a fixed percentage of salary into a fund to pay substitute teachers. A teacher reports the full amount of the salary paid during the sabbatical but may claim payments to the fund as miscellaneous itemized deductions subject to the 2% AGI floor.

A self-employed business owner or professional. If your education costs qualify under *19.16*, you deduct all of your education costs on Schedule C. You also attach a statement to your return explaining your deduction and the relationship of the education to your position.

A veteran receiving educational benefits from the VA. Educational assistance from the Department of Veterans Affairs (VA) is tax free, whether it covers educational or living expenses. The portion of the payment covering educational costs reduces your deductible educational expenses. If you use only part of the VA payment for qualifying courses, reduce your deduction by the part of the VA reimbursement covering the qualifying courses. The portion of the reimbursement, if any, that covers living expenses does not affect your deduction.

Investment, Legal, and Tax Advice Expenses

19.24 Checklist of Deductible Investment Expenses

The following investment expenses are deductible as miscellaneous expenses on Schedule A subject to the 2% adjusted gross income (AGI) floor. In addition, the 3% reduction for total itemized deductions applies if your adjusted gross income exceeds $137,300, or $68,650 if married filing separately; *see 13.7*.

- Accounting fees for keeping records of investment income.
- Bank deposit loss if not federally insured; *see 18.5*.
- Casualty or theft losses of income-producing property such as stock certificates, but not rental or royalty property; the deduction is figured on Form 4684 and entered on Schedule A.
- Fees for collecting interest and dividends. Also deductible are fees paid to a bank that acts as dividend agent in an automatic dividend reinvestment plan of a publicly owned corporation. Costs of collecting tax-exempt interest are not deductible; expenses deducted on an estate tax return are also not deductible. Fees paid to a broker to acquire securities are not deductible but are added to the cost of the securities. Commissions and fees paid by an investor on the sale of securities reduce the selling price; a dealer, however, may deduct selling commissions as business expenses.
- Fees to set up or administer an IRA. The fees must be billed and paid separately from the regular IRA contribution.
- Guardian fees or fees of committee for a ward or minor incurred in producing or collecting income belonging to the ward or minor or in managing income-producing property of the ward or minor.
- Investment management or investment planner's fees. However, fees allocated to advice dealing with tax-exempt obligations are not deductible.
- Investment fees from non–publicly offered mutual fund, shown in Box 5 of Form 1099-DIV.
- Legal costs; *see 19.26*.
- Premiums and expenses on indemnity bonds for the replacement of missing securities. If part of the expenses are refunded in the year the expenses are paid, only the excess expense is deductible. A refund in a later year is taxable income to the extent the expenses were deducted and reduced your tax; *see 11.6*.
- Proxy fight expenses where the dispute involves legitimate corporate policy issues, not a frivolous desire to gain membership on the board.
- Safe-deposit box rental fee or home safe to hold your securities, unless used to hold personal effects or tax-exempt securities.
- Salary of a secretary, bookkeeper, or other employee hired to keep track of your investment income.
- Subscriptions to investment services.

 *Planning Reminder*

Travel to Check Investments
Travel costs of a trip away from home *(20.6)* to look after investments, or to confer with your attorney, accountant, trustee, or investment counsel about the production of income, may be deducted as miscellaneous itemized deductions subject to the 2% of adjusted gross income floor. If you have investment property in a resort area, keep proof that the trip was taken primarily to check your investment property, not to vacation.

Caution

Investment Seminars

You may not deduct the cost of an investment or financial planning seminar or similar meeting.

Computer used to manage investments. Subject to the 2% floor, depreciation may be claimed; *see 42.10.*

Managing investment property. Expenses incurred in managing property held for income are deductible, even if the property does not currently produce income. Similarly, expenses incurred to avoid further losses or to reduce anticipated losses on such property are deductible.

Rental or royalty expenses. Expenses of earning royalty or rental income are deducted directly from the income, rather than as itemized deductions subject to the 2% AGI floor.

EXAMPLE

You pay deductible investment management fees of $1,500 a tax preparation fee of $500, and a safe-deposit box fee of $40. Your other miscellaneous expense deductions subject to the 2% floor are $500 for unreimbursed job expenses. Your adjusted gross income is $80,000. Your deduction after applying the 2% AGI floor is $940, figured as follows:

Investment management fees	$1,500
Tax preparation fee	500
Safe-deposit box fee	40
Other miscellaneous expenses	500
	$2,540
Less: 2% of $80,000	1,600
Total deductible	$ 940

Nondeductible travel costs. Investors may not deduct the costs of these types of trips:

- Trips to investigate prospective rental property.

- Trips to attend a convention, seminar, or similar meeting that deals with investment, financial planning, or the production or collection of income. Convention costs are deductible only in the case of a business activity; *see 20.12.*

- Trips to attend stockholder meetings. However, in a private letter ruling, one stockholder was allowed a deduction. He owned substantial stockholdings that had lost value because his corporation had been issuing stock to the public at prices below book value. He went to the annual shareholders' meeting to present a resolution requesting management to stop the practice; the resolution passed. Under such circumstances, the IRS held that the trip was directly related to his stockholdings and allowed him the deduction. The IRS distinguished his case from a ruling that bars most stockholders from deducting the cost of travel to an annual meeting. Here the stockholder's purpose in getting the resolution passed was more closely related to his investment activities than if he had attended the meeting, as most stockholders do, to pick up data for future investment moves.

Hobby expenses. For the limitations on deducting hobby expenses, *see 40.10.*

Home office of an investor. An investor may not deduct the costs of an office at home unless investing constitutes a business. For example, you get no deduction for use of a home office in your residence where you manage your investments and read financial periodicals and reports. These activities are not considered a business.

EXAMPLE

In his home office, Moller spent 40 hours a week managing four stock portfolios worth over $13 million. However, an appeals court held he could not deduct home office expenses despite the time spent there managing his investment. To deduct home office expenses, Moller had to show he was a trader. A trader is in a business; an investor is not. A trader buys and sells frequently to catch daily market swings. An investor buys securities for capital appreciation and income without regard to daily market developments. Here, Moller was an investor. He was primarily interested in the long-term growth potential of stock. He did not earn his income from the short-term stock turnovers. He had no significant trading profits.

Filing Tip

Tax Advice and Tax Return Preparation

You may deduct legal fees paid in 2002 for preparing your tax return or refund claim, or for representing you in a trial, examination, or hearing involving any tax; *see 19.25.* Legal fees incurred in defending against a tax imposed by a foreign country are also deductible. However, legal fees incurred in reducing an assessment on property to pay for local benefits are not deductible; the fees are capital expenses which are added to basis.

19.25 Costs of Tax Return Preparation and Audits

You may deduct your payment of fees charged for the services listed below, subject to the 2% AGI floor and the 3% reduction if AGI exceeds $137,300 ($68,650 if married filing separately); *see 13.7.*

- Preparing your tax return or refund claim involving any tax;

- Preparing and obtaining a private IRS ruling, including IRS filing fees; *and*
- Representing you before any examination, trial, or other type of hearing involving any tax.

Tax preparation fees include the cost of tax publications and tax preparation software programs. Any fee paid to electronically file your return is also included. The term "any tax" covers not only income taxes but also gift, property, estate, or any other tax, whether the taxing authority be federal, state, or municipal.

Tax practitioner's fees. Deductible fees for services of tax practitioners are claimed on Schedule A as miscellaneous itemized deductions on the tax return for the year in which the fee was paid. For example, if in March 2002 you paid an accountant to prepare your 2001 return, the fee is deductible on your 2002 return.

You deduct fees related to preparing Schedule C or F (and related business Schedules) on the Schedule C or F, thereby avoiding the 2% AGI floor on Schedule A. In one case, the Tax Court allowed a Schedule C deduction for a $55 tax preparation fee claimed by a self-employed lumberjack, although nonbusiness income was also reported on his return. Any allocation to the nonbusiness income would have been minimal. The Court noted that the IRS's position in disallowing the deduction reflected misguided zeal and was not only petty but impractical.

If you report rental or royalty income or loss on Schedule E, you deduct the allocated tax preparation fee on Schedule E.

An accountant's fee for arranging the purchase of real estate was deductible where the purchase was part of a plan to cut taxes; *see* the Collins Example below.

Personal checking account fees. These are nondeductible, even though the checks are used for tax records. Similarly, the per-check fee on an interest-bearing NOW account is nondeductible. However, fees charged on a bank money-market account may be deductible if check writing is severely limited and writing excess checks forfeits the status of the account as a money-market account.

Appraisal fees. Appraisals for determining a casualty loss or charitable donation are miscellaneous expenses.

> **EXAMPLES**
>
> 1. Stockholders of a closely held corporation negotiated with a publicly held company for a tax-free exchange of their stock. An accounting firm asked the IRS for a ruling to determine whether the exchange would be taxable or tax free. The accounting fee was $8,602. Of this, $7,602 was for the ruling and $1,000 was for fixing the basis of the new stock. The stockholders deducted the full fee, which the IRS disallowed because the fee was not charged for the preparation of a tax return nor for representation at a contest of a tax liability.
>   The Tax Court disagreed in part. The fee paid for the ruling was deductible; it was connected with determining the extent of the stockholders' liability, if any, in the proposed exchange. But a deduction could not be allowed for the $1,000 charged to determine the basis of the new stock. This was computed for the stockholders' information, not for determining tax liability. The disallowed fee could be added to the cost basis of the stock.
>
> 2. Collins paid an accountant $4,511 for tax advice to reduce his tax on a sweepstakes winning. He was advised to buy an apartment house under a contract obligation to make a large prepayment of interest (which was deductible under prior law). The accountant helped prepare contracts, escrow agreements, and other documents to implement the plan. Collins's deduction of his accountant's fee was disallowed. The IRS held that the fee was a capital expense in acquiring the property. The Tax Court disagreed. The accountant was hired to minimize Collins's income tax through the purchase of the building and the terms of the purchase. Therefore, his fee was deductible.

19.26 Deducting Legal Costs

A legal expense is generally deductible if the dispute or issue arose in the course of your business or employment or involves income-producing property. Legal expenses for personal lawsuits are not deductible unless you recover taxable damages. Legal fees incurred in obtaining an award of tax-free damages, such as for physical injuries *(11.7)*, are not deductible.

 Caution

Credit Card Fees Not Deductible
Companies authorized by the IRS to process credit card payments of taxes charge a convenience fee. The fee is not deductible as a tax preparation expense. Expenses for figuring tax liability are deductible but this is a fee to enable the payment of one's liability after it has been determined.

 Filing Tip

Deducting the Cost of This Book
The purchase of *Your Income Tax* in 2002 may be claimed as a miscellaneous expense deduction on your 2002 return. The cost, when included with other miscellaneous expenses, is subject to the 2% AGI floor. If you purchase the book in 2003, include the cost with your other miscellaneous expenses on your 2003 return.

 *Planning Reminder*

Allocate Fees for Tax Advice
There have been disputes over the deductibility of fees charged for general tax advice unconnected to the preparation of a return or a tax controversy. A deduction for fees charged for general tax advice not within these areas may be disallowed, unless the fee can be related to the production of business or investment income or the management of income-producing property. *See* the Examples in *19.25*.

If you are self-employed, your deduction for legal fees arising from a business-related dispute is claimed on Schedule C. Legal expenses related to your job as an employee or to investment activities are claimed as miscellaneous itemized deductions subject to the 2% AGI floor. The IRS may disallow the deduction on the ground that the legal dispute does not directly arise from the business or income activity. Thus, for example, the cost of contesting the suspension of a driver's license for drunken driving is not deductible despite a business need for the license; the suspension arose out of a personal rather than a business-related activity. A deduction may also be disallowed where the dispute involves title to property.

The legal costs of defending against disbarment are deductible.

For the deductibility of legal fees in organizing a new business, *see 40.11.*

Employment suits. The following Examples illustrate when legal costs for job-related matters may be deductible.

> ### EXAMPLES
>
> 1. An Army officer was allowed to deduct the cost of successfully contesting a court martial based on charges of misrepresentations in official statements and reports. He would have lost his position had he been convicted.
>
> 2. Tellier, a securities dealer, was convicted of mail fraud and securities fraud. He was allowed to deduct legal fees as business expenses related to his securities business. That he was found guilty of the criminal charge does not affect the deductibility of the expense. The deduction of legal expenses is not disallowed on public policy grounds since a defendant has a constitutional right to an attorney.
>
> 3. In an alimony action, Gilmore was successful in preventing his wife from securing stock and taking control of corporations from which he earned practically all his income. He was not allowed to deduct his legal costs. The dispute did not arise from an income-producing activity; the fact that an adverse determination of the dispute might affect his income did not make the legal expenses deductible.
>
> 4. A doctor who attempted to bribe a judge to suspend his sentence for tax evasion was convicted of the bribe attempt and lost his license to practice medicine. He could not deduct his defense costs. His practice of medicine did not give rise to his need for an attorney. The fact that the conviction affected his ability to earn income was merely a consequence of personal litigation.
>
> 5. Siket, a police officer, was not allowed to deduct expenses of successfully defending a criminal charge of assault while off duty. The origin of the claim was personal, even though a conviction might have been detrimental to his position as a police officer. The arrest did not occur within the performance of his duties; he was off duty and in a different municipality at the time of the arrest.
>
> 6. A resort company instructed its staff to stop serving drinks to intoxicated patrons and to encourage the patrons to either take a taxi home or to stay on the premises at a reduced rate. One of the company's executives attempted to deduct legal defense fees when he was charged with criminal sexual assault, arguing that the assault allegation arose from his business duty to procure a room for three intoxicated guests. The IRS and the Tax Court denied the deduction on the grounds that the allegation arose from the executive's second visit to the guests' room, not from the time he placed them in the room. Even if the alleged assault had occurred during the first visit, the executive personally violated company policy by not stopping the guests from drinking when they were already drunk.

Will contests and wrongful death actions. Legal costs of a will contest are generally not deductible because an inheritance is not taxable income. Similarly, legal fees incurred to collect a wrongful death award (which is tax-free income) are not deductible.

> ### EXAMPLE
>
> Parker, an heir who was left out of his grandmother's estate, sued to recover his inheritance. In a settlement, he received his share of his grandmother's property plus income earned on that property. The allocable portion of legal fees attributed to the income, which was taxable, was deductible; the balance of the fees was not deductible.

Planning Reminder

Lawyer's Bill Should Be Itemized
Your lawyer should bill you separately or itemize fees for services connected with deductible items (collection of taxable alimony or separate maintenance payments; or preparation of tax returns, tax audits, and tax litigation) and nondeductible capital items (expenses incurred in purchase of property or dispute over title).

Title issues or disputes. Legal costs related to the acquisition of property or to the determination of title to property, whether such property is business or personal, are nondeductible capital expenditures. They are added to the basis of the property. For example, litigation costs to fix the value of shares of dissident shareholders are not deductible because they are related to the purchase of the stock and are part of the cost of acquisition.

Legal fees incurred to acquire title to stock are also nondeductible.

Where a dispute over property does not involve title, such as in a recovery of income-producing securities loaned as collateral, the Tax Court holds that legal fees are deductible.

Personal injury actions. Where you recover taxable damages, you may deduct the legal fees. If the damages are not taxable, legal fees are not deductible; *see 11.7.*

Legal expenses incurred in marital actions. *See 37.8.*

Collecting Social Security. If you hire an attorney to press a claim for disputed benefits, such as disability benefits, you may deduct the legal fees only to the extent that your benefits are taxable under the rules of *34.3.* For example, if 50% of your Social Security benefits are taxable, 50% of your legal fees are treated as miscellaneous expenses subject to the 2% AGI floor.

Estate tax planning fee. All or part of an attorney's fee for estate tax planning services may be deductible. Estate tax planning usually involves tax and non-tax matters. To the extent that the services do not cover tax advice or income-producing property, the fee is not deductible. A bill allocating a fee between deductible and nondeductible services may help support a deduction claimed for the deductible portion of the fee.

Recovery of attorneys' fees from government. *See* Chapter 47.

19.27 Contingent Fees Paid Out of Taxable Awards

The courts and the IRS dispute the tax treatment of contingent fees paid out of taxable damage awards. The Fifth, Sixth, and Eleventh Circuit appeals courts have allowed the fees to be excluded from the litigant's income under specific state laws that give the attorney an interest in the client's cause of action. However, the Third, Fourth, Seventh, Ninth, Tenth, and Federal Circuits agree with the IRS that a client must report as taxable income a contingent fee paid directly to the attorney. The fact that the client was never entitled to the funds under the terms of the contingent fee arrangement is irrelevant.

The paid contingent fee, although deductible as a miscellaneous itemized deduction, may be limited or eliminated for regular tax purposes by the 2%-of-adjusted-gross-income floor *(19.1)*. Further, the net deduction may also be reduced by the overall 3% reduction to itemized deductions *(13.7)* imposed on higher-income taxpayers. Finally, if the alternative minimum tax (AMT) applies, the fee is not deductible at all *(23.2)*.

The Tax Court treatment of the contingent fee depends on the Circuit to which a taxpayer would appeal an adverse decision. If the case is appealable to a Circuit that would not allow an exclusion, a majority of Tax Court judges apply the assignment-of-income doctrine, requiring the client to include the contingent fee portion of the award in taxable income. That is, the entire damage award is treated as "earned" by the client, with the contingent attorney fees considered merely a cost of litigation that is subject to the limitations on deductions; *see* the Example below.

If the case is appealable to the Sixth, Fifth, or Eleventh Circuit (the last of which is bound by Fifth Circuit precedents from before October 1, 1982), the Tax Court will follow the holdings of these courts, which allow contingent fees to be excluded from income.

EXAMPLE

40% of Kenseth's $229,501 taxable age-discrimination settlement, or $91,800, was turned over to a law firm as a contingent fee. He argued that the contingent fee portion should be excluded from his gross income. If it were not excluded, he would be taxed on income he never received because the limitations on itemized deductions would prevent him from offsetting the income. The 2% AGI floor and 3% overall limitation on itemized deductions reduced his regular tax deduction for the fee to $81,800, and that reduced deduction was not allowed at all for alternative minimum tax (AMT) purposes, resulting in AMT liability of $17,198.

The Tax Court majority agreed with the IRS that Kenseth was taxable on the entire $229,501. It is up to Congress to deal with the inequitable consequences of the itemized deduction income floors and the AMT deduction disallowance rule.

The Seventh Circuit Court of Appeals affirmed the Tax Court decision.

Chapter 20

Travel and Entertainment Expense Deductions

Unreimbursed employee travel expenses are deductible but are subject to the 2% of adjusted gross income (AGI) floor on Schedule A. If you are self-employed, the 2% floor does not apply to travel expenses claimed on Schedule C. The types of deductible travel expenses are highlighted in the key to deductible travel and transportation expenses at the beginning of this chapter. Generally, you must be away from home to deduct travel expenses on business trips. On one-day business trips within the general area of your employment, only transportation costs may be deducted; meals may not.

To support your travel expense deductions, keep records that comply with IRS rules as explained at *20.26*. To avoid the 2% AGI floor, consider an "accountable" reimbursement arrangement of your travel expenses with your employer; *see 20.31*.

You report unreimbursed employee transportation and travel expenses on Form 2106 or on short form 2106-EZ if you are not reimbursed by your company and you do not claim depreciation on a car used for business.

Unreimbursed expenses from Form 2106 or 2106-EZ are entered on Schedule A, where they are subject to the 2% AGI floor.

An expense allowance for travel costs is not reported as income on Form W-2 if you substantiated the expenses to your employer and returned any unsubstantiated portion of the allowance; *see 20.31* for details.

If you are self-employed, you deduct travel costs on Schedule C. The 2% AGI floor does not apply, but only 50% of meal and entertainment expenses are deductible.

Commuting and Meal Expenses

20.1 Deduction Guide for Travel and Transportation Expenses

The following chart summarizes the rules for deducting local business transportation costs and travel expenses while "away from home" on business trips; *see 20.6* for when you are away from home. Generally, commuting expenses from your home to your place of business are not deductible; *see 20.2*. However, you may be able to claim a deduction for daily transportation expenses incurred in commuting to a temporary job location; *see* the chart below and *20.2*.

See *20.28* for how to report deductible expenses if you are self-employed, and *20.29* if you are an employee.

Key to Deductible Travel and Transportation Expenses

Your Travel Status—	Tax Rule—
Trips to see customers and clients	You may deduct your transportation expenses but not the cost of personal meals on one-day business trips within the general area of your tax home. On out-of-town business trips "away from home," lodging and meals are deductible as well as transportation costs.
Two job locations for one employer in the same area **EXAMPLE:** Your employer has two business locations in the city in which you live. You work about half of the time in each place—at one location in the morning and at the other in the afternoon.	You deduct transportation expenses from one location to the other. However, if, for personal reasons, such as the choice of a place for eating lunch, you do not go directly from one location to the other, you may deduct your transportation expenses only to the extent that they do not exceed the cost of going directly from the first location to the second. But say your employer has several locations in the same city, but you do not move from one location to another in the same day. You spend the entire day at one place. You may not deduct transportation expenses between your home and the various locations, even if you report to a different location each day.
Two different jobs in the same area **EXAMPLE:** You work for two different employers in the city in which you live. Most of the time you work a full work shift at your principal place of employment. Then you work a part-time shift for your second employer some distance away.	You may deduct the transportation expenses from one job to another within the same working day. But you may not claim the deduction if you return home after the first job and then, after supper, go to your second job.
Permanent job in an area other than where you have your residence **EXAMPLE:** You live with your family in Chicago, but work in Milwaukee. During the week, you stay in a hotel in Milwaukee and eat meals in a restaurant. You return to your family in Chicago every weekend.	Milwaukee is your "home" for tax purposes; *see 20.6*. Thus, your expenses for traveling to Milwaukee and your meals and lodging there are personal, nondeductible expenses.
Temporary assignment in an area other than where you have your residence **EXAMPLE:** You live in Kansas City, where you work. You have been assigned to duty in Omaha for 60 days. Occasionally, you return to Kansas City on your days off, but most of the time you stay in Omaha.	You may deduct the necessary expenses for traveling from Kansas City to Omaha and returning to Kansas City after your temporary assignment is completed. You may also deduct expenses for meals and lodging (even for your days off) while you are in Omaha. As discussed at *20.9*, deductions are not allowed on temporary assignments that are *expected* to last more than one year.
Weekend trip home from temporary assignment **EXAMPLE:** Same facts as in the Example above except that you return home to Kansas City during the weekend.	You are not "away from home" while you are in Kansas City on your days off and your meals and lodging while you are there are not deductible. However, you may deduct your traveling expenses (including meals and lodging, if any) from Omaha to Kansas City and back if they are no more than the amount it would have cost you for your meals and lodging if you had stayed in Omaha. If they are more, your deduction is limited to the amount you would have spent in Omaha. If you retain your room in Omaha while in Kansas City, your expenses of returning to Kansas City on days off are deductible only to the extent of the amount you would have spent for your meals had you stayed in Omaha.

Key to Deductible Travel and Transportation Expenses

Your Travel Status—	Tax Rule—
Temporary job location away from home where there are no living accommodations EXAMPLE: You live and work in Chicago. You have been assigned for three months to a construction job located 20 miles outside Nashville. There are no living facilities near the job site and you have to stay at a hotel in Nashville.	Under these circumstances, your necessary expenses in getting to and from your temporary job are business expenses and not commuting expenses. If you were employed at the site for an indefinite period *(20.9)*, then the costs of commuting would be nondeductible, regardless of the distance; *see 20.2.*
Taxi trips between customers' locations	The cab fares are deductible; *see 20.2.*
Seasonal jobs in different areas EXAMPLE: You live in Cincinnati, where you work for eight months each year. You earn the greater share of your annual income from that job. For the remaining four months of the year, you work in Miami. When in Miami, you eat and sleep in a hotel. You have been working on both of these jobs for several years and expect to continue to do so.	You have two recurring seasonal places of employment. Cincinnati is your principal place of employment. You may deduct the costs of your traveling expenses while away from Cincinnati working at your minor place of employment in Miami, including meals and lodging in Miami.
Trailer home moved to different job sites EXAMPLE: You are a construction welder. You live in a trailer that you move from city to city, where you work on construction projects. You have no other established home.	You may not deduct your expenses for meals and lodging. Each place where you locate becomes your principal place of business and, therefore, you are not "away from home."
Travel to school after work to take job-related courses	You may deduct travel costs if you meet the rules discussed at *19.22.*
Finding a new job in the same line of work EXAMPLE: You live in New York. You travel to Chicago for an interview for a new position.	You may deduct the cost of the trip and living expenses in Chicago; *see 19.7.*
Convention trip	You may deduct costs of travel to a business convention under the rules in *20.12.* If you are a delegate to a charitable or veterans' convention, you may claim a charitable deduction for the travel costs; *see 14.4.*
Trip to out-of-town college for educational courses	You deduct the cost of the trip if you meet the rules at *19.22.*
Trip for health reasons	You may deduct the cost of the trip as a medical expense if you meet the rules at *17.9.*

20.2 Commuting Expenses

The cost of travel between your home and place of work is generally not deductible, even if the work location is in a remote area not serviced by public transportation. Nor can you justify the deduction by showing you need a car for faster trips to work or for emergency trips. Travel from a union hall to an assigned job is also considered commuting. If you join a car pool, you may not deduct expenses of gasoline, repairs, or other costs of driving you and your passengers to work.

According to the IRS, if you install a telephone in your car and make calls to clients or business associates while driving to your office, you are still commuting and your expenses are not deductible. Similarly, the deduction is not allowed if you drive passengers to work and discuss business.

Deductible commuting expenses. The IRS allows these exceptions to its blanket ban on commuting expense deductions.

If you are on a business trip out of town, you may deduct taxi fares or other transportation costs from your hotel to the first business call of the day and all other transportation costs between business calls.

If you use your car to carry tools to work, you may deduct transportation costs where you can prove that they were incurred in addition to the ordinary, nondeductible commuting expenses. The deduction will be allowed even if you would use a car in any event to commute; *see* the Examples below.

EXAMPLES

1. Jones commuted to and from work by public transportation before he had to carry tools. Public transportation cost $2 per day to commute to and from work. When he had to use the car to carry the tools, the cost of driving was $3 a day and $5 a day to rent a trailer to carry the tools. Jones may deduct only the cost of renting the trailer. The IRS does not allow a deduction for the additional $1 a day cost of operating the car. It is not considered related to the carrying of the tools. It is treated as part of the cost of commuting, which is not deductible.

2. Same facts as above, but Jones does not rent a trailer. He uses the car trunk to store his tools. He may not claim a deduction because he incurs no additional cost for carrying the tools.

3. Smith uses his car regardless of the need to transport tools. He rents a trailer for $5 a day to carry tools. He may deduct $5 a day under the "additional-cost" rule.

Commuting to a temporary place of work. Whether you can deduct commuting expenses to a temporary place of work may depend on the location of the temporary assignment and whether you have a regular place of business or a home office that is your principal place of business. According to the IRS, if you have a *regular* place of work outside of your home, or you have a home office that is your principal place of business, you may deduct the cost of commuting between your home and a temporary (*see* below) work location, regardless of where the temporary location is. If you do not have a regular place of work but normally work at several locations in the metropolitan area where you live, you may deduct the costs of commuting to a temporary location that is outside that metropolitan area, but not to a temporary location within the metropolitan area.

If you do not have a regular place of work and all of your jobs are outside the metropolitan area where you live, none of your commuting costs are deductible under the IRS rule. In one case, a commuting cost deduction was denied to an iron worker who lived in Yuba City, California, and who obtained temporary work assignments at a union hall in Sacramento, 40 miles from her home. All of the temporary jobs were in or near Sacramento. The Tax Court agreed with the IRS that none of her commuting costs to the temporary locations were deductible because she did not work in the Yuba City area where she lived. Since all of her assignments were in other cities, her decision to live in Yuba City was for personal, not business, reasons.

What is a temporary place of work? A temporary work location is one at which your employment is realistically expected to last, and actually does last, for one year or less. If at first you realistically expect an assignment to last for no more than one year but that expectation changes, the IRS will generally treat the employment as temporary until the date that it became realistic to expect that the work would exceed one year.

Accountants, architects, engineers, and other professionals often have to travel to job sites of their clients. If such work at the site is temporary and they can show they also have a regular work office, they may deduct commuting expenses from their homes to their work sites.

 *Court Decision*

Self-Employed Person's Office at Home
If you are self-employed and your regular office is outside your home, you may not deduct the cost of commuting to the office or from that office to your home even if you work at home at a second job. However, in several cases, the Tax Court allowed self-employed persons whose home office was their principal place of business *(40.12)* to deduct travel costs beginning with the first business call of the day. The IRS now agrees with this approach.

 Caution

IRS Definition of "Temporary"
The IRS considers a work location temporary if the period of employment is realistically expected to last, and actually does last, one year or less. If you take an assignment expected to last more than a year but it actually lasts less than a year, your assignment is *not* considered temporary and commuting costs are not deductible.

EXAMPLE

The IRS ruled that a professional who spent 25–27% of his time at his employer's field office satisfied the regular place of business test. His remaining time was spent at client locations. These were considered temporary because he went to each client location only once every two years for two to three weeks at a time. He was allowed to deduct his unreimbursed costs of driving between his home and the client locations.

20.3 Overnight-Sleep Test Limits Deduction of Meal Costs

The overnight-sleep rule prevents the deduction of meal costs on one-day business trips. To be deductible, meal costs must be incurred while "away from home" and this test requires that they be on a business trip that lasts longer than a regular working day (but not necessarily 24 hours) and requires time off to sleep (not just to eat or rest) before returning home. Taking a nap in a parked car off the road does not meet the overnight-sleep test.

EXAMPLES

1. A New Yorker flies to Washington, D.C., which is about 250 miles away, to see a client. He arrives at noon, eats lunch, and then visits the client. He flies back to New York. He may deduct the cost of the plane fare, but not the cost of the lunch. He was not away overnight nor was he required to take time out to sleep before returning home.
2. Same facts as above except he sleeps overnight in a Washington hotel. He eats breakfast there, and then sees another client and returns home to New York in the afternoon. He may deduct not only the cost of the plane fare but also the cost of the meals while on the trip and the cost of the hotel, since he was away overnight.
3. A trucker's run is from Seattle to Portland and back. He leaves at about 2:00 A.M. and returns to Seattle the same day, getting in at about 6:00 P.M. While in Portland, he is released from duty for about four hours layover time to get necessary sleep before returning to Seattle. He may deduct the cost of meals because he is released at a layover location to obtain necessary sleep. Official release from duty, however, is not a prerequisite for satisfying the sleep or rest test.

Several courts held that the IRS rule was unreasonable and outdated in the world of supersonic travel, and they would have allowed the New Yorker on the one-day trip to Washington, D.C., to deduct the cost of his lunch. The Supreme Court disagreed and upheld the IRS rule as a fair administrative approach.

Meal costs during overtime. Such costs are not deductible if you are not away from your place of business. Thus, for example, a resident physician could not deduct the cost of meals and sleeping quarters at the hospital during overnight or weekend duty.

20.4 IRS Meal Allowance

If you find it difficult to keep records of meal costs while away from home *(20.3)* on business trips, you may prefer to claim an IRS meal allowance. In government tables, the allowance is referred to as the "M&IE" rate (meals and incidental expenses). The allowance covers, in addition to meals and tips for food servers, incidental expenses, such as laundry and tips for luggage handlers. Self-employed individuals may claim the allowance as well as employees who are not reimbursed for meals under an "accountable" plan; *see 20.31*. However, the meal allowance may not be used if your employer is your brother, sister, spouse, parent, child, grandparent, or grandchild, or if you own more than 10% of the employer's outstanding stock.

Meal allowance on 2002 tax returns. For travel within the continental U.S. (referred to as CONUS locations), the daily meal allowance (M&IE) for 2002 is usually $30 per day, but higher rates apply in certain high-cost areas designated by the government. The high-cost areas are generally major metropolitan cities or resort areas. The basic and high-cost area meal rates are determined by the federal government's General Services Administration (GSA) and the IRS allows taxpayers to use the applicable rates in figuring their meal allowance deduction.

The easiest way to obtain a listing of the CONUS M&IE rates is to go online to the General Services Administration (GSA) website at www.policyworks.gov/perdiem. The M&IE rates are included in the CONUS *per diem* table released by the GSA in October of each year to coincide with the federal government's fiscal year (October 1–September 30). Thus, the rates released in October 2001 apply to business trips from October 1, 2001, through September 30, 2002. The

Filing Tip

Reimbursement Plans
If your employer has an "accountable" reimbursement plan *(20.31)*, and you are reimbursed for meals up to the allowable meal allowance rate, the reimbursement will not be reported as income on your Form W-2.

rates released in October 2002 apply to business trips from October 1, 2002, through September 30, 2003. By checking the GSA website toward the end of 2002, you can get the M&IE rates for the first nine months as well as the rates that took effect on October 1, 2002, for the last three months of the year. In computing your meal allowance (M&IE) deduction for 2002 business trips, you can apply the rates that were in effect for the first nine months of the year to business trips in the last three months. You may use the first set of rates for the first nine months and the updated rates for the last three months. For trips within the last three months, you must consistently use either the rates in effect for the first nine months or the revised rates that took effect on October 1; you cannot switch between the sets of rates on a trip-by-trip basis.

The IRS provides the CONUS rates in Publication 1542, but in order to obtain the rates for all of 2002, you will need two editions of the publication. That is because the version released at the end of 2002 or in early 2003 will show the rates that took effect on October 1, 2002 (good for trips through September 30, 2003). Those rates cannot be used for the first nine months of 2002. For that, you will need to request the February 2002 edition of Publication 1542, which includes the CONUS rates for October1 2001–September 30 2002.

If you travel to more than one city on the same day, use the meal allowance for the area where you stay overnight.

Different rates apply for travel in Alaska, Hawaii, Puerto Rico, and U.S. possessions, as well as for travel to foreign countries. These rates (OCONUS) can be obtained by using links from the GSA website at www.policyworks.gov/perdiem.

You must keep a record of the time, place, and business purpose of the trips. As long as you have this proof, you may claim the allowance even if your actual costs are less than the allowance.

Transportation industry workers. Employees or self-employed persons in the *transportation industry* may elect to claim a meal allowance of $38 per day for all 2002 travel within the continental U.S. instead of applying the CONUS rates on a trip-by-trip basis. Also, an allowance of $42 per day may be elected for all travel outside the continental U.S.

Claiming the allowance. The allowance is prorated for the first and last day of a trip. You may claim 75% of the allowance for the days you depart and return. Alternatively, you may claim 100% of the allowance if you are away for a regular "9-to-5" business day.

If you are an employee and claim a deduction based on the allowance, you must reduce the deduction by 50% on Form 2106 or Form 2106-EZ. Furthermore, if you are an employee, the balance, when added to your other miscellaneous deductions, is subject to the 2% AGI floor on Schedule A. If you are self-employed, the deduction for meals is claimed on Schedule C, where it is subject only to the 50% reduction; *see 40.6.* Interstate truck drivers, pilots, railroad operators, and other transportation industry employees subject to Department of Transportation hours of service limits are allowed to deduct 65% for meals (instead of 50%) consumed in 2002 subject to those limits.

Deducting Travel Expenses Away From Home

20.5 Business Trip Deductions

The following expenses of a business trip *away from home (20.6)* are deductible if not reimbursed by your employer:

- Plane, railroad, taxi, and other transportation fares between your home and your business destination
- Hotel and other lodging expenses. You need receipts or similar evidence for lodging expenses; there is no IRS standard lodging allowance as there is for meals *(20.4).*
- Meal costs. You may claim your actual meal costs if you maintain records, or you may use the standard meal allowance discussed in *20.4.* Only 50% of the cost of the meal is deductible.
- Tips, telephone, and telegraph costs
- Laundry and cleaning expenses
- Baggage charges (including insurance)
- Cab fares or other costs of transportation to and from the airport or station and your hotel. Also deductible are cab fares or other transportation costs, beginning with your first business call of the day, of getting from one customer to another, or from one place of business to another.
- Travel costs to find a new job are deductible; *see 19.7.*
- Entertainment expenses incurred while traveling away from home are deductible under the rules at *20.6.*

Cruise ship. If you travel by cruise ship on a business trip, your deductible cruise costs are limited to twice the highest federal *per diem* rate for travel in the United States on that date multiplied by the number of days in transit.

EXAMPLE

You sail to Europe on business. While you are away, the highest *per diem* federal rate is $254 and the trip lasts five days. The maximum deduction for the cost of the trip is $2,540 (2 × $254 × 5). The double *per diem* rule applies without regard to the 50% limit on meal costs if meals are not separately stated in your bill. If a separate amount for meals or entertainment is included, such amount must be reduced by 50%.

The double *per diem* rule does not apply to cruise ship convention costs that are deductible up to $2,000 a year if all the ports of call are in the U.S. or U.S. possessions and if the ship is registered in the United States; *see 20.14.*

Important: Record-keeping requirements. See the section beginning at *20.26* for record-keeping rules to support a deduction for unreimbursed travel expenses or to avoid being taxed on employer reimbursements.

20.6 When Are You Away From Home?

You have to meet the "away from home" test to deduct the cost of meals (only 50% deductible) and lodging while traveling. You have to satisfy the overnight-sleep rule at *20.3* to be "away from home."

EXAMPLES

1. Your residence is in a suburb within commuting distance of New York City where you work full time. Your personal home and tax home are the same, that is, within the metropolitan area of New York City. You are away from home when you leave this area, say for Philadelphia. Meals and lodging are deductible only if you meet the overnight-sleep test; *see 20.3.*

2. Your residence is in New York City, but you work in Baltimore. Your tax home is Baltimore; you may not deduct living expenses there. But you may deduct travel expenses on a temporary assignment to New York City even while living at your home there.

3. A construction worker works for a utility company on construction sites in a 12-state area. Assignments are sent from his employer's regional office; he is not required to report to the office. The IRS ruled that his residence, which is in a city in the 12-state area, is his tax home.

Law Alert

Tax Home Defined

For travel expense purposes, your home is your place of business, employment, or post of duty, regardless of where you maintain your family residence. This tax home includes the entire city or general area of your business premises or place of employment. The area of your residence may be your tax home if your job requires you to work at widely scattered locations, you have no fixed place of work, and your residence is in a location economically suited to your work.

Are you constantly on the road? If you move from job to job and do not work within any particular locality, an IRS agent may disallow your travel deductions on the grounds that your tax home is wherever you work; thus, you are never "away from home." You are considered a transient worker.

If your deduction is questioned because you have no regular or main place of business, you may be able to show that your tax home is the area of your residence. If you meet the following three tests, the IRS will treat your residence as your tax home: (1) you do some work in the vicinity of your residence, house, apartment, or room and live there while performing services in the area; (2) you have mortgage expenses or pay rent for the residence while away on the road; and (3) the residence is in an area where you were raised or lived for a long time, or a member of your immediate family such as your parent or child lives in the residence, or you frequently return there.

According to the IRS, if you meet only two of these three tests, it will decide on a case-by-case basis if your residence is your tax home. If you meet less than two of the tests, the IRS will not allow a deduction; each of your work locations is treated as your tax home.

If you live in a trailer at each job assignment and have no other home, each job location is your principal place of business and you are not "away from home."

Permanent duty station of service members. The Supreme Court held that a member of the Armed Forces is not away from home when he or she is at a permanent duty station. This is true even if the service member has to maintain a separate home for family members who are not permitted to live at the duty station.

20.7 Fixing a Tax Home If You Work in Different Locations

If you regularly work in two or more separate areas, your tax home is the area of your principal place of business or employment. You are away from home when you are away from the area of your principal place of business or employment. Therefore, you may deduct your transportation costs to and from your minor place of business and your living costs there.

Professional sports players, coaches, and managers. When the only business of such persons is the professional sport, their home is the "club town." But if they are in another business in addition to their professional playing, how much time is spent and how much is earned at each place determines whether their club's hometown or the place of their off-season business is their tax home. If it is the club's hometown, they deduct travel and living expenses while away from that town—including the time they are where the second business is. (If the second place is where their families also live, they may not deduct the families' expenses there.) If the town where the other business is located is the tax home, then expenses in the club's hometown may be deducted.

Airline pilots. It is important for airline pilots who fly in and out of various locations to determine a tax home for income and deduction purposes. Generally, the IRS considers an airline pilot's tax home to be the airport at which the pilot is regularly based. For example, in one case the IRS barred a pilot from claiming the foreign earned income exclusion (36.1) because his tax home was deemed to be his base in New York, rather than in London, where he and his wife actually lived.

EXAMPLES

1. Sherman lived in Worcester, Mass., where he managed a factory. He opened his own sales agency in New York. He continued to manage the factory and spent considerable time in Worcester. The larger part of his income came from the New York business. However, he was allowed to treat New York as his minor place of business and to deduct his travel expenses to New York and his living expenses there because he spent most of his time in Worcester and his income there was substantial.

2. Benson, a consulting engineer, maintained a combination residence-business office in a home he owned in New York. He also taught four days a week at a Technological Institute in West Virginia under a temporary nine-month appointment. He spent three-day weekends, holidays, and part of the summer at his New York address. At the Institute, he rented a room in the student union building. The IRS disallowed transportation expenses between New York and West Virginia and meals and lodging there as not incurred while away from home. The Tax Court disagreed. A taxpayer may have more than one occupation in more than one city. When his occupations require him to spend a substantial amount of time in each place, he may deduct his travel expenses, including meals and lodging, at the place away from his permanent residence. That Benson's teaching salary happened to exceed his income from his private practice does not change the result.

20.8 Tax Home of Married Couple Working in Different Cities

When a husband and wife work and live in different cities during the week, one of them may seek to deduct travel expenses away from home. Such deductions have generally been disallowed, but courts have allowed some exceptions. Although for common law purposes the domicile of the husband may be the domicile of the wife, for tax purposes when each spouse works in a different city, each may have a separate tax home.

EXAMPLES

1. Robert worked in Wilmington, Delaware; his wife, Margaret, worked in New York City. During the weekend, she traveled to Wilmington and deducted, as travel expenses away from home, her living costs in New York and weekend travel expenses to Wilmington. She argued that because she and her husband filed a joint return, they were a single taxable unit, and the tax home of this unit was Wilmington where her husband lived. The deduction was disallowed. That a couple can file a joint return does not give them deductions that are not otherwise available to them as individuals. Margaret's tax home was New York, where she worked. Therefore, her expenses there are not deductible. And, as the weekend trips to Wilmington had no relationship to her job, they, too, were not deductible.

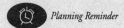
Planning Reminder

Determining Your Principal Place of Business

If you have more than one regular place of business, your tax home is your principal place of business. Your principal place of business or employment is determined by comparing: (1) the time ordinarily spent working in each area; (2) the degree of your business activity in each area; (3) the amount of your income from each area; (4) the taxpayer's permanent residence; and (5) whether employment at one location is temporary or indefinite.

No single factor is determinative. The relative importance of each factor will vary depending on the facts of a particular case. For example, where there are no substantial differences between incomes earned in two places of employment, your tax home is probably the area in which you spend more of your time. Where there are substantial income differences, your tax home is probably the area in which you earn more of your income.

2. Hundt and his wife lived in Arlington, Va., but he wrote and directed films in various parts of the country. He wrote screenplays either at his Arlington home or on location, but most of his business came from New York City, where he lived in hotels. One year, he spent 175 days in New York City on business and rented an apartment for $1,200 because it was cheaper than a hotel. He deducted half the annual rent for the New York apartment, the costs of traveling between Arlington and New York, and the cost of meals in New York. The IRS disallowed the expenses, finding New York to be his tax home. The Tax Court disagreed. Arlington was Hundt's tax home because (1) part of his income came from his creative writing in Arlington; and (2) his travel to other parts of the country was temporary. The fact that most of his income came from New York did not make New York his tax home.

 *Planning Reminder*

Federal Crime Investigations

Federal employees such as FBI agents and prosecutors who are certified by the Attorney General as traveling on behalf of the federal government in a temporary duty status to investigate, prosecute, or provide support services for the investigation or prosecution of a federal crime are not subject to the one-year limitation on deductibility of expenses while away from home on temporary assignments.

20.9 Deducting Living Costs on Temporary Assignment

A business trip or job assignment away from home *(20.6)* at a single location may last a few days, weeks, or months. If your assignment is considered *temporary,* you may deduct travel costs (*see* below) while there because your tax home has not changed. An assignment is considered temporary by the IRS if you realistically expect it to last for one year or less and it actually does last no more than one year. If an assignment is realistically expected to last more than a year it is considered *indefinite,* and you cannot deduct your living costs at the area of the assignment because that location becomes your tax home. This is true even if the assignment actually lasts only a year or less. That is, you can be away for a year or less and still be barred from claiming a deduction if at the time you started the assignment you realistically expected it to last for more than a year. Likewise, employment that is initially temporary may become indefinite due to changed circumstances; *see* the Examples below.

EXAMPLES

1. You are on a job assignment away from home in a single location that is expected to last (and it does in fact last) for one year or less. The IRS will treat the employment as temporary, unless facts and circumstances indicate otherwise. Expenses are deductible.
2. You are sent on a job assignment away from home at a *single* location. You expected that the job would last 18 months. However, due to financial difficulties you were transferred home after 11 months. Even though your assignment actually lasted for less than one year the IRS treats the employment as indefinite because you realistically expected it to last more than one year. Thus, your travel and living expenses while away from home are not deductible.
3. You are sent on a job assignment away from home at a *single* location. You expected that the job would last only nine months. However, due to changed circumstances occurring after eight months, you were asked to remain on the assignment for six more months. The IRS treats the assignment as temporary for eight months, and indefinite for the remaining time you are away from home. Thus; travel and living expenses you paid or incurred during the first eight months are deductible; expenses paid or incurred thereafter are not.

 Caution

Taking Your Family With You

If you take your family with you to a temporary job site, an IRS agent may argue that this is evidence that you considered the assignment to be indefinite. In the Michaels Example on this page, however, such a move was not considered detrimental to a deduction of living expenses at the job location.

Deductible travel costs on temporary trip. While on a temporary job assignment expected to last a year or less, you may deduct the cost of meals and lodging there, even for your days off. If you return home, say for weekends, your living expenses at home are not deductible. You may deduct travel expenses, meals, and lodging en route between your home and your job assignment provided they do not exceed your living expenses had you stayed at the temporary job location. If you keep a hotel room at the temporary location while you return home, you may deduct your round-trip expenses for the trip home only up to the amount you would have spent for meals had you stayed at the temporary workplace.

EXAMPLE

Michaels, a cost analyst for Boeing, lived in Seattle. He traveled for Boeing, but was generally not away from home for more than five weeks. Michaels agreed to go to Los Angeles for a year to service Boeing's suppliers in that area. He rented his Seattle house and brought his family with him to Los Angeles. Ten months later, Boeing opened a permanent office in Los Angeles and asked Michaels to remain there permanently. Michaels argued that his expenses for food and lodging during the 10-month period were deductible as "away from home" expenses. The IRS contended that the Los Angeles assignment was for an indefinite period.

The Tax Court sided with Michaels. He was told that the stay was for a year only. He leased his Seattle house to a tenant for one year, planning to return to it. He regarded his work in Los Angeles as temporary until Boeing changed its plans. The one-year period justified his taking the family but did not alter the temporary nature of the assignment.

Separate assignments over a period over a year. Where over a period of years you work on several separate assignments for one client, the IRS may attempt to treat the separate assignments as amounting to a permanent assignment and disallow living costs away from home, as in Mitchell's situation, below.

EXAMPLE

Mitchell, a publishing consultant who lived and worked out of his home in Illinois, advised a publisher of a magazine with offices in California. Over a five-year period, from 1991 to 1995, he worked on short job assignments that averaged 130 days a year for the magazine. Some assignments arose because of unforeseen events, such as the abrupt firing of a novice editor, the hiring of a new editor, and the editor's later absence because of cancer and her death. In 1994 and 1995, when working in California, he rented an apartment because it was cheaper than a hotel. He claimed lodging and meal expenses in California that the IRS disallowed on the grounds that his employment in California was not temporary; it lasted more than one year.

The Tax Court disagrees. Just because an independent contractor returns to the same general location in more than one year does not mean that he is employed there on an indefinite basis. Mitchell's work followed an on again, off again pattern. Each job assignment that lasted less than a year ended with no expectation of future employment. Throughout the five-year period, his consultancy services were required by unexpected events.

No regular job where you live. That you do not have regular employment where you live may prevent a deduction of living costs at a temporary job in another city. The IRS may disallow the deduction on the grounds that the expenses are not incurred while you are away from home; the temporary job site is the tax home.

Deducting Expenses of a Business-Vacation Trip

20.10 Business-Vacation Trips Within the United States

On a business trip to a resort area, you may also spend time vacationing. If the *primary purpose* of the trip is to transact business and the area is within the United States (50 states and the District of Columbia) you may deduct all of the costs of your transportation to and from the area, lodging, and 50% of meal expenses, even if you do spend time vacationing. If the main purpose of the trip is personal, you may not deduct any part of your travel costs to and from the area. The amount of time spent on business as opposed to sightseeing or personal visits is the most important issue in determining your primary purpose. Regardless of the primary purpose of your trip, you are allowed to deduct expenses related to the business you transacted while in the area.

No deductions will be allowed if you attend a convention or seminar where you are given videotapes to view at your own convenience and no other business-related activities or lectures occur during the convention. The trip is considered a vacation.

If your trip is primarily for business, and while at the business destination you extend your stay for a few days for nonbusiness reasons, such as to visit relatives, you deduct travel expenses to and from the business destination.

EXAMPLE

You work in Atlanta and make a business trip to New Orleans. You stay in New Orleans for six days and your total costs, including round-trip transportation to and from New Orleans, meals, and lodging, is $600, which you may deduct subject to the 50% limit for meals. If, on your way home, you spend three days in Mobile visiting relatives and incur an additional $200 in travel costs, your deduction is limited to the $600 (less 50% of meals) you would have spent had you gone home directly from New Orleans.

Reimbursement for weekend travel. If your employer extends your business trip over a weekend to take advantage of discount airfares that require a Saturday night stayover, you may deduct the cost of meals, lodging, and other incidental expenses incurred for the additional night. The reason for

Caution

Primary Business Purpose
If your return is examined, proving the business purpose of your trip depends on presenting evidence to convince an examining agent that the trip, despite your vacationing, was planned primarily to transact business. Keep a log or diary to substantiate business activities.

the stayover has a business purpose: to cut travel costs. If your employer pays for the expenses directly or if you are reimbursed under an accountable plan *(20.31)*, the payment is not taxable to you.

20.11 Business-Vacation Trips Outside the United States

On a business trip abroad, you may deduct your travel expenses (50% of meals), even though you take time out to vacation, provided you can prove: (1) the primary purpose of the trip was business and (2) you did not have control over the assignment of the trip.

Fixing the date of the trip does not mean that you had control over the assignment. IRS regulations assume that when you travel for your company under a reimbursement or allowance arrangement, you do not control the trip arrangements, provided also that you are not: (1) a managing executive of the company; (2) related to your employer *(see 20.4)*; or (3) have more than a 10% stock interest in the company. You are considered a managing executive if you are authorized without effective veto procedures to decide on the necessity of the trip. You are related to your employer if the employer is your spouse, parent, child, brother, sister, grandparent, or grandchild.

Rule for managing executives and self-employed persons. If you are a managing executive, self-employed, related to your employer, or have a more-than-10% stock interest, your deduction for transportation costs to and from your business destination may be limited. However, a full deduction for transportation costs is allowed if:

1. The trip outside the United States took a week or less, not counting the day you left the U.S. but counting the day you returned,

2. If the trip abroad lasted more than a week, you spent less than 25% of your time, counting the days your trip began and ended, on vacation or other personal activities, *or*

3. In planning the trip you did not place a major emphasis on taking a vacation.

If the vacationing and other personal activities took up 25% or more of your time on a trip lasting more than one week, and you cannot prove that the vacation was a minor consideration in planning the trip, you must allocate travel expenses between the time spent on business and that spent on personal affairs. The part allocated to business is deductible; the balance is not. To allocate, count the number of days spent on the trip outside the United States, including the day you leave the U.S. and the day you return. Then divide this total into the number of days on which you had business activities; include days of travel to and from a business destination.

If you vacation at, near, or beyond the city in which you do business, the expense subject to allocation is the cost of travel from the place of departure to the business destination and back. For example, you travel from New York to London on business and then vacation in Paris before returning to New York. The expense subject to allocation is the cost of traveling from New York to London and back; *see* Example 2 below. However, if from London you vacationed in Dublin before returning to New York, you would allocate the round-trip fare between New York and Dublin and also deduct the difference between that round-trip fare and the fare between New York and London; *see* Example 3 below.

Caution

Vacation Areas

If the IRS determines that you were primarily on vacation, it will disallow all travel costs except for costs directly related to your business in the area such as registration fees at a foreign business convention; *see 20.14*.

EXAMPLES

1. You fly from New York to Paris to attend a business meeting for one day. You spend the next two days sightseeing and then fly back to New York. The entire trip, including two days for travel en route, took five days. The plane fare is deductible. The trip did not exceed one week.

2. You fly from Chicago to New York, where you spend six days on business. You then fly to London, where you conduct business for two days. You then fly to Paris for a five-day vacation after which you fly back to Chicago. You would not have made the trip except for the business that you had to transact in London. The nine days of travel outside the United States away from home, including two days for travel en route, exceeded a week, and the five days devoted to vacationing were not less than 25% of the total travel time outside the U.S. The two days spent traveling between Chicago and New York, and the six days spent in New York, are not counted in determining whether the travel outside the United States exceeded a week and whether the time devoted to personal activities was less than 25%.

   Assume you are unable to prove either that you did not have substantial control over the arrangements of the trip or that an opportunity for taking a personal vacation was not a major consideration in your decision to take the trip. Thus, $5/9$ (five nonbusiness days out of nine days outside the U.S.) of the plane fare from New York to London and from London to New York is not deductible. You may deduct $^4/_9$ of the New-York-to-London round-trip fare, plus lodging, 50% of meals, and other allowable travel costs while in London. No deduction is allowed for any part of the costs of the trip from London to Paris.

3. Same facts as in Example 2, except that the vacation is in Dublin, which is closer to the U.S. than London. The allocation is based on the round-trip fare between New York and Dublin. Thus, $^4/_9$ of the New York to Dublin fare is deductible and $^5/_9$ is not deductible. Further, the IRS allows a deduction for the excess of the New-York-to-London fare over the New-York-to-Dublin fare.

Weekends, holidays, and business standby days. If you have business meetings scheduled before and after a weekend or holiday, the days in between the meetings are treated as days spent on business for purposes of the 25% business test just discussed. This is true although you spend the days for sightseeing or other personal travel. A similar rule applies if you have business meetings on Friday and the next scheduled meeting is the following Tuesday; Saturday through Monday are treated as business days. If your trip is extended over a weekend to take advantage of reduced airfares, the additional expense of meals, lodging, and other incidental expenses is deductible; *see 20.10.*

20.12 Deducting Expenses of Business Conventions

Conventions and seminars at resort areas usually combine business with pleasure. Therefore, the IRS scrutinizes deductions claimed for attending a business convention where opportunities exist for vacationing. Especially questioned are trips where you are accompanied by your spouse and other members of your family. Foreign conventions are discussed at *20.14*.

Generally, you may not deduct expenses of attending investment conventions and seminars; *see 19.24*. You also may not deduct the costs of business conventions or seminars where you merely receive a videotape of business lectures to be viewed at your convenience and no other business-related activities occur during the event.

In claiming a deduction for convention expenses, be prepared to show that the convention was connected with your business. Cases and IRS rulings have upheld deductions for doctors, lawyers, and dentists attending professional conventions. One case allowed a deduction to a legal secretary for her costs at a secretaries' convention. If you are a delegate to a business convention, make sure you prove you attended to serve primarily your own business interests, not those of the association. However, it is not necessary for you to show that the convention dealt specifically with your job. It is sufficient that attendance at the convention may advance or benefit your position. If you fail to prove business purpose, the IRS will allocate your expenses between the time spent on your business and the time spent as a delegate. You then deduct only the expenses attributed to your business activities.

EXAMPLES

1. An attorney with a general law practice was interested in international law and relations. He was appointed a delegate to represent the American branch of the International Law Association at a convention in Paris. The attorney deducted the cost of the trip and convention as business expenses which the IRS and a court disallowed. He failed to prove that attending the conference on international law helped his general practice. He did not get any business referrals as a result of his attendance at the convention. Nor did he prove the chance of getting any potential business from the conference.

2. An insurance agent doing business in Texas attended his company's convention in New York. One morning of the six-day convention was devoted to a business meeting and luncheon; the rest of the time was spent in sightseeing and entertainment. The company paid for the cost of the trip. The IRS added the reimbursement to the agent's pay and would not let him deduct the amount. The convention in New York served no business purpose. It was merely a method of entertaining company personnel. If there was any valid business to be transacted, the company could have called a meeting in Texas, the area of his home office.

3. A plywood company could not deduct the costs of entertaining 116 customers and employees at a New Orleans hotel during a Superbowl weekend. The company did not reserve conference rooms or make any other arrangements for organized business meetings. The IRS and two federal courts held that although business discussions may have occurred on a random basis, these were secondary to entertainment.

 Filing Tip

Weekend Expenses

If your business trip is extended over a weekend to take advantage of reduced airfares, the additional cost of meals, lodging, and other incidental expenses is deductible.

 Caution

Substantiate Convention Business

Keep a copy of the convention program and a record of the business sessions you attend. If the convention provides a sign-in book, sign it. In addition, keep a record of all of your business expenses as explained in *20.26*.

What expenses are deductible? If the convention trip is primarily for business, you may deduct travel costs both to and from the convention, food costs, tips, display expenses (such as sample room costs), and hotel bills. If you entertain business clients or customers, you may deduct these amounts too.

Food and beverage costs are subject to the 50% cost limitation rule as explained in *20.24*.

> **EXAMPLE**
>
> You attend a business convention held in a coastal resort city primarily for business reasons. During the convention period, you do some local sightseeing, social entertaining, and visiting—all unrelated to your business. You may deduct your traveling expenses to and from the resort, your living expenses at the resort, and other expenses such as business entertaining, sample displays, etc. But you may not deduct the cost of sightseeing, personal entertaining, and social visiting.

Keep records of your payments identifying expenses directly connected with your business dealings at the convention and those that are part of your personal activity, such as sightseeing, social visiting, and entertaining. Recreation costs are not deductible even though a part of your overall convention costs.

Fraternal organizations. You may not deduct expenses at conventions held by fraternal organizations, such as the American Legion, Shriners, etc., even though incidental business was carried on. However, delegates to fraternal conventions may in some instances deduct expenses as charitable contributions; *see 14.4.*

20.13 Travel Expenses of a Spouse or Dependents

Travel costs of a spouse, dependent, or any other individual who is not a business associate and who accompanies you on a business trip are not deductible unless that person is also your employee and has a bona fide business reason for taking the trip that would justify claiming a deduction if the person took the trip on his or her own.

Even though the travel costs of a non-employee spouse or other person are not deductible, you may deduct the cost of such person's participation in the entertainment of business clients at conventions or business trips if the trip or entertainment meets the tests at *20.21*. Generally, you may deduct the cost of goodwill entertaining of associates immediately before or after convention business meetings. A convention meeting qualifies as a bona fide business meeting.

> **EXAMPLES**
>
> 1. You and your spouse travel by car to a convention. You pay $120 a day for a double room. A single room would have cost $100 a day. Your spouse's presence at the convention was for social reasons. You may deduct the total cost of operating your car to and from the convention city. You may deduct $100 a day for your room. If you traveled by plane or railroad, you would deduct only your own fare.
>
> 2. Connie worked with her husband operating a home improvement contracting business. With him, she attended trade shows and conventions, where they ran a display booth. There, she talked about their company's services and solicited new business. The IRS disallowed the company's deduction of her travel expenses as having no business purpose. The Tax Court disagreed. Both Connie and her husband were officers and employees of the company. They attended the conferences together. As the IRS allowed her husband's expenses, it should have also allowed expenses attributed to her participation, especially as they were incurred together as employees.

20.14 Restrictions on Foreign Conventions and Cruises

You may not deduct expenses at a foreign convention outside the North American area unless you satisfy the rules at *20.11* and also can show the convention is directly related to your business and it was as reasonable for the meeting to be held outside the North American area as within it.

Apart from the United States, the North American area includes Mexico, Canada, Puerto Rico, U.S. Virgin Islands, American Samoa, Northern Mariana Islands, Guam, Marshall Islands, Micronesia, Palau and U.S. island possessions.

Conventions may also be held in eligible Caribbean countries that agree to exchange certain data with the U.S. and do not discriminate against conventions held in the United States. Barbados, Bermuda, Costa Rica, Dominica, Dominican Republic, Grenada, Guyana, Honduras, Jamaica,

 Filing Tip

How Much To Deduct for Spouse
If your spouse accompanied you on a business trip, your bills will probably show costs for both of you. These usually are less than twice the cost for a single person. To find what you may deduct where your spouse's presence is for personal and not qualifying business reasons, do not divide the bill in half. Figure what accommodations and transportation would have cost you alone and deduct that. The excess over the single person's costs is not deductible.

Saint Lucia, and Trinidad and Tobago have qualified and are considered to be within the North American area.

Check with the convention operator about whether the country in which your convention is being held has qualified.

Limited cruise ship deduction. Up to $2,000 a year is allowed for attending cruise ship conventions if all the ports of call are in the U.S. or U.S. possessions and if the ship is registered in the United States. A deduction is allowed only if you attach to your return statements signed by you and by an officer of the convention sponsor that detail the daily schedule of business activities, the number of hours you attended these activities, and the total days of the trip. Do not confuse the $2,000 limitation with the *per diem* limitation for cruise ship costs discussed at *20.5*. The *per diem* limitation does not apply to cruises that meet the tests for the up-to-$2,000 deduction.

Meals and Entertainment Expenses for Clients, Customers, or Employees

20.15 50% Deduction Limit

To be deductible at all, dining and entertainment costs for clients, customers, or employees must meet one of the restrictive tests at *20.16*. Even if the expenses qualify under one of the tests, only 50% of unreimbursed expenses are generally deductible and this 50% balance is reduced by the 2% AGI floor if you are an employee. Furthermore, all entertainment costs, including meals, must be backed up with records. If you do not keep adequate records, your deductions will be disallowed. The 50% deduction limit and exceptions to the limit are discussed at *20.24*.

20.16 The Restrictive Tests for Meals and Entertainment

Meal and entertainment costs are deductible, subject to the 50% limit *(20.24)*, if they are ordinary and necessary to your business, and also are either:

1. Directly related to the active conduct of your business *(20.17)*, *or*

2. Directly preceding or following a substantial and bona fide business discussion on a subject associated with the active conduct of your business. This test applies to dining and entertainment in which you seek new business or to goodwill entertainment to encourage the continuation of an existing business relationship. Under this test, you may entertain business associates in nonbusiness settings such as restaurants, theaters, sports arenas, and nightclubs, provided the entertainment directly precedes or follows the business discussion. Business associates are: established or prospective customers, clients, suppliers, employees, agents, partners, or professional advisers, whether established or prospective; *see 20.18*.

Ordinary and necessary expenses are those considered helpful and common practice in your business or profession; they do not have to be indispensable to your business.

20.17 Directly Related Dining and Entertainment

The directly related test limits the deduction of dining and entertainment costs at restaurants, nightclubs, on yachts, at sporting events, on hunting trips, and during social events.

The directly related test for dining and entertainment costs may be met in one of three ways: (1) under the generally related test; (2) as expenses incurred in a clear business setting; or (3) as expenses incurred for services performed. If dining or entertainment fails to meet the directly related tests, it may qualify under the rules discussed in *20.18*, which require the holding of a business discussion before or after the entertainment.

Generally related test. Under this test, you must show a business motive for the dining or entertainment and business activity during the entertainment. You must show that you had more than a general expectation of getting future income or other specific business benefit (other than goodwill). Although you do not have to prove that income or other business benefit actually resulted from the expense, such evidence will help support your claim. What type of business activity will an IRS agent look for? The agent will seek proof that a business meeting, negotiation, or discussion took place during the period of dining or entertainment. It is not necessary that more time be devoted to business than to entertainment. What if you did not talk business? You must prove that you would have done so except for reasons beyond your control.

 *Planning Reminder*

Scheduling Entertainment and Business Discussions

A business discussion generally must take place the same day as the dining or entertainment. If not, and your deduction is questioned, you must give an acceptable reason for the interval between the discussion and the dining or entertainment. IRS regulations recognize that a day may separate a business meeting and the entertainment of an out-of-town customer. He or she may come to your office to discuss business one day and you provide entertainment the next day, or you provide the entertainment on the first day and discuss business the day after.

The IRS does not estimate how long a business discussion should last. But it does warn that a meeting must involve a discussion or negotiation to obtain income or business benefits. It does not require that more time be devoted to the meeting than to the entertainment.

Caution

Hunting or Fishing Trips

The IRS presumes that entertainment during a hunting or fishing trip or on a yacht is not conducive to business discussion or activity. You must prove otherwise.

Clear business setting test. Expenses incurred in a clear business setting meet the directly related test provided also that you had no significant motive for incurring the expenses other than to further your business. Entertainment of people with whom you have no personal or social relationship is usually considered to have occurred in a clear business setting. For example, entertainment of business representatives and civic leaders at the opening of a new hotel or theatrical production to obtain business publicity rather than goodwill is considered to be entertainment in a clear business setting. Also, entertainment that involves a price rebate is considered to have occurred in a clear business setting, as, for example, when a hotel owner provides occasional free dinners at the hotel for a customer who patronizes the hotel.

The cost of a hospitality room displaying company products at a convention is also a directly related expense.

Entertainment occurring under the following circumstances or in the following places is generally *not* considered as directly related:

- You are not present during the entertainment.
- The distractions are substantial, as at nightclubs, sporting events, or during a social gathering such as a cocktail party.
- You meet with a group that includes persons other than business associates at cocktail lounges, country clubs, golf and athletic clubs, or at vacation resorts.

Services performed test. An expense is directly related if it was directly or indirectly made for the benefit of an individual (other than an employee) either as taxable compensation for services he or she rendered or as a taxable prize or award. The amount of the expense must be reported on an information Form 1099 (unless the amount is less than $600).

> **EXAMPLE**
>
> A manufacturer provides a vacation trip for retailers whose sales of his products exceed quotas. The value of the vacation is a taxable prize to the retailers. The vacation cost is a directly related entertainment expense for the manufacturer.

20.18 Goodwill Entertainment

Goodwill entertaining may qualify as deductible entertainment. Dining and entertainment costs may be deductible if a substantial and *bona fide* business discussion directly preceded or followed the dining or entertainment.

An officially scheduled meeting at a convention is generally considered a bona fide business discussion.

> **EXAMPLES**
>
> 1. During the day, you negotiate with a group of business associates. In the evening, you entertain the group and their spouses at a theater and nightclub. The cost of the entertainment is deductible, even though arranged to promote goodwill.
>
> 2. In the evening after a business meeting at a convention, you entertain associates or prospective customers and their spouses. You may deduct the entertainment costs.

Filing Tip

Allocating Payment Covering Lodging and Meals

A hotel may include meals in a room charge. In such cases, the room charge must be allocated between the meals/entertainment and lodging. The amount allocated to meals and entertainment is subject to the 50% cost limitation. If you receive a *per diem* allowance from your employer covering both lodging and meals under an accountable reimbursement plan, you may have to allocate part of the reimbursement to meals in order to deduct expenses in excess of the reimbursement; see 20.31.

20.19 Home Entertaining

The cost of entertaining business customers or clients at home is deductible provided a business discussion occurs before, during, or after the meal. When you claim such a deduction, be ready to prove that your motive for dining with them was business rather than social. Have a record of the entertainment costs, names of the guests, and their business affiliations.

20.20 Your Personal Share of Entertainment Costs

If the entertaining occurred while on a business trip away from home, you deduct your own meal costs as travel expenses away from home (20.6). If the entertaining occurred within the locality of your regular place of business, whether you will be allowed a deduction for your share will depend on the agent examining your return. The IRS said in a ruling that an agent will not disallow your deduction of your own part of the meal cost unless he or she finds that you are claiming a substantial amount that includes personal living expenses. In such a case, which generally is limited to situations where personal meals are regularly claimed as part of an "abusive" pattern, the agent will follow the stricter Tax Court rule (sometimes referred to as the "Sutter" rule) and allow only that part of the meal cost that exceeds what you would usually spend on yourself when alone.

20.21 Entertainment Costs of Spouses

A deduction is allowed for the spouses' share of the entertainment costs if they were present during entertainment that qualified as directly related entertainment under the general rule discussed in *20.17*. For goodwill entertainment, the cost of entertainment of the spouses is deductible if your share and the business associate's share of the entertainment is deductible. The IRS recognizes that when an out-of-town customer is accompanied by his or her spouse, it may be impracticable to entertain the customer without the spouse. Under such circumstances, the cost of the spouse's entertainment is deductible if the customer's entertainment costs are also deductible. Furthermore, if your spouse joined the party because the customer's spouse was present, the expenses of your spouse are also deductible.

20.22 Entertainment Facilities and Club Dues

You may not deduct the expenses of maintaining and operating facilities used to entertain clients and customers. By law, entertainment facilities are not considered business assets. Examples of entertainment facilities are yachts, hunting lodges, fishing camps, swimming pools, tennis courts, automobiles, airplanes, apartments, hotel suites, or homes in a vacation area. A season box seat or pass at a sporting event or theater is *not* considered an entertainment facility; *see* the special rule at *20.24* for skybox rentals.

The disallowance rule applies to operating expenses such as rent, utilities, and security, and also to depreciation, but not to such expenses as interest, taxes, and casualty losses that are deductible without having to show business purpose.

Exceptions. A deduction may be allowed for expenses such as the cost of food and drinks incurred at an entertainment facility, if they meet the rules discussed in *20.16* through *20.21*.

The Tax Court and the Eighth Circuit Court of Appeals held that if a company plane is used by employees for personal purposes and the value of the personal use (figured under IRS rules) is included in their taxable pay on Form W-2, the employer may deduct the full operating costs of the plane. The employer's deduction may exceed the taxable value included in the employees' income. The IRS has agreed to follow the appeals court decision.

Club dues. You may not deduct dues for country clubs, golf and athletic clubs, airline clubs, hotel clubs, business luncheon clubs, and other clubs organized for business, pleasure, recreation, or other social purposes. However, IRS regulations generally allow a deduction for dues paid to (1) civic or public service organizations such as Kiwanis, Lions, and Rotary clubs; (2) professional organizations such as medical or bar associations; and (3) chambers of commerce, trade associations, business leagues, real estate boards, and boards of trade. The deduction for dues is allowed provided that the organization in (1)–(3) does not have a principal purpose of providing entertainment for members or their guests.

20.23 Restrictive Test Exception for Reimbursements

As an employer, you can deduct expense allowances or other reimbursements of employee expenses that you treat as compensation and from which you withhold federal tax. You are not subject to the 50% deduction limit for meals and entertainment; the employee is, when claiming the meals on Form 2106.

A similar rule applies to meal allowances or reimbursements that you give to an independent contractor and that you report as compensation on Form 1099-MISC where the contractor does not adequately account for the expenses.

The restrictive tests of *20.16* do not apply to such reimbursements. They are deductible if they are "ordinary and necessary" business expenses, and you have records to back up the deduction.

20.24 50% Cost Limitation on Meals and Entertainment

You generally may not deduct the full amount of your deductible expenses for business meals and entertainment expenses, such as tickets to sports events. Unless one of the exceptions below applies, only 50% of the otherwise allowable amount for food, beverages, and entertainment is deductible.

Taxes and tips are considered part of the cost subject to the 50% limit. If your employer reimburses your expenses, the 50% limit applies to the employer.

The 50% limit applies to both employees and the self-employed. It applies to the IRS meal allowance deduction; *see 20.4*. For employee expenses the limit is taken into account on Form 2106 or 2106-EZ (if you are not reimbursed by your employer and do not claim depreciation for a business car), and on Schedule C for self-employment expenses.

 Law Alert

Transportation Industry Workers
Individuals subject to Department of Transportation limitations on hours of service, such as interstate truck drivers, may claim a higher deductible percentage of food and beverage costs when working away from home. The deductible amount is 65% in 2002 and 2003, and increases to 70% in 2004 and 2005, 75% in 2006 and 2007, and 80% for 2008 and later years.

EXAMPLES

1. You pay meal and entertainment costs of $5,000. Only $2,500 ($5,000 × 50%) is considered deductible.
2. Same facts as above, but your employer reimburses your costs after you account for the expenses. The employer's deduction is limited to $2,500. You have no deduction.

The deductible amount for a ticket treated as an entertainment expense is restricted to the face value of the ticket. Amounts in excess of face value paid to ticket agencies or scalpers are not deductible. The deductible cost of tickets is also subject to the 50% limitation.

EXAMPLE

You buy from a ticket broker five tickets to entertain clients. The face value of the tickets is $250. You paid $300 for them. The deductible amount is $125 (50% × $250).

Exceptions to 50% cost limitation. In the following cases, you may claim a full deduction for meals and entertainment; the 50% limitation does not apply:

1. As an employer, you pay for an employee's meals and entertainment that are treated as taxable compensation to the employee and as wages for purposes of withholding of income tax.
2. You reimburse an independent contractor for meal and entertainment expenses he or she incurs on your behalf and the contractor does not adequately account for the expenses. You deduct the reimbursements as compensation if they are ordinary and necessary business expenses.
3. As an employer, you incur expenses for recreational, social, or similar activities (including facilities) primarily for the benefit of employees who are not highly compensated employees. For example, the expenses of food, beverages, and entertainment for a company-wide summer party are not subject to the 50% limit.
4. Expenses for meals and entertainment, including the use of facilities made available to the general public, such as a free concert, for advertising or goodwill purposes. For example, the IRS allowed a real-estate broker to fully deduct the cost of free dinners it provided to potential investors who attended its sales presentations. The 50% deduction limitation for meals does not apply to promotional activities that are made available to the general public. The IRS relied on the following example in a 1986 Congressional committee report for purposes of allowing a 100% deduction: A wine merchant provides customers with wine and food to demonstrate the suitability of the wine with certain types of meals. The committee report indicated that the cost of the wine, food, and other costs associated with the wine-tasting function would be fully deductible.
5. Expenses for meals and entertainment sold to the public in your business, such as meal expenses if you run a restaurant, or the cost of providing entertainment if you run a nightclub. These expenses are fully deductible.
6. Food or beverage provided to your employees as a tax-free *de minimis* fringe benefit *(3.9)*. This would include expenses of a cafeteria on your premises for employees where meal charges cover the direct operating cost of the cafeteria. The *de minimis* benefit exception allows a full deduction for all meals provided to employees on employer premises if more than half of the employees who are provided meals are furnished them for the employer's convenience (substantial noncompensatory business purpose). If the more-than-half test is met, the meals are tax free to all the employees; *see 3.11*.
7. The price of tickets to charitable sports events (including amounts in excess of face value) provided the ticket package includes admission to the event. To qualify, a charitable sports event must: (1) be organized for the primary purpose of benefitting a tax-exempt organization; (2) contribute 100% of its net proceeds to such organization; and (3) use volunteers for substantially all work performed in carrying out the event. According to Congressional committee reports, a golf tournament that donates all its proceeds to charity is eligible to qualify under this exception, even if it offers prize money to the golfers who participate or uses paid concessionaires or security personnel. However, tickets to a college football game or similar scholastic events generally do not qualify because they do not satisfy the requirement that substantially all work be performed by volunteers.

Filing Tip

Meals Provided to Employees

An employer who provides meals to employees on employer premises is allowed a full deduction for all the meals provided that more than half of the employees who are provided meals are furnished them for substantial noncompensatory business reasons.

Skybox rental costs. A skybox is a private luxury seating area at a sports arena. Skybox seats are generally rented for the season or for a series of games such as the World Series. The deductible amount for a rental covering more than one game or performance may not exceed the sum of the face values of non-luxury box seat tickets for the number of seats in the box. The allowable amount is also subject to the 50% cost limitation. Separately stated charges for food or beverages at the skybox are deductible as entertainment expenses and are subject to the 50% cost rule. For example, assume that for two games, you paid $1,480 for a skybox containing 10 seats—$740 per game. The cost of 10 non-luxury box seat tickets for each game was $200, or $400 total. You may deduct 50% of the $400 non-luxury face value, or $200. If you had rented the skybox for one game, you could deduct $370 (50% of $740) for that skybox because the special limitation applies only where the rental is for more than one game or other performance.

20.25 Business Gift Deductions Are Limited

Deductions for gifts to business customers and clients are restricted. Your deduction for gifts is limited to $25 a person. You and your spouse are treated as one person in figuring this limitation even if you do not file a joint return and even if you have separate business connections with the recipient. The $25 limitation also applies to partnerships; thus a gift by the partnership to one person may not exceed $25, regardless of the number of partners.

In figuring the $25 limitation to each business associate, do not include the following items:

1. A gift of a specialty advertising item that costs $4 or less on which your name is clearly and permanently imprinted. This exception saves you the trouble of having to keep records of such items as pens, desk sets, plastic bags, and cases on which you have your name imprinted for business promotion.
2. Signs, displays, racks, or other promotional material that is used on business premises by the person to whom you gave the material.
3. Incidental costs of wrapping, insuring, mailing, or delivering the gift. However, the cost of an ornamental basket or container must be included if it has a substantial value in relation to the goods it contains.

If you made a gift to the spouse of a business associate, it is considered as made to the associate. If the spouse has an independent bona fide business connection with you, the gift is not considered as made to the associate unless it is intended for the associate's eventual use.

If you made a gift to a corporation or other business group intended for the personal use of an employee, stockholder, or other owner of the corporation, the gift generally is considered as made to that individual.

Theater or sporting event tickets given to business associates are entertainment, not gift, expenses if you accompany them. If you do not accompany them, you may elect to treat the tickets either as gifts, which are subject to the $25 limitation, or as entertainment expenses subject to the entertainment expense rules, such as the requirement to show a business conference before or after the entertainment and the 50% cost limitation.

Packaged food or drink given to a business associate is a gift if it is to be consumed at a later time.

Gifts not coming within the $25 limit are: (1) scholarships that are tax free under the rules in Chapter 38; (2) prizes and awards that are tax free under the rules in *11.1*; and (3) awards to employees, discussed below.

Awards to employees. There is an exception to the $25 gift deduction limitation for achievement awards of tangible personal property given to your employees in recognition of length of service or safety achievement. Special deduction limits apply to such achievement awards provided they are given as part of a presentation under circumstances indicating that they are not a form of disguised compensation. For example, awards will not qualify if given at the time of annual salary adjustments, or as a substitute for a prior program of cash bonuses, or if awards discriminate on behalf of highly compensated employees.

The amount of your deduction depends on whether the achievement award is considered a qualified plan award. You may deduct up to $1,600 for all qualified plan awards (safety and length of service) given to the same employee during the taxable year. If the award is not a qualified plan award, the annual deduction ceiling for each employee is $400. The $1,600 overall limit applies if the same employee receives some qualified plan awards and some non-qualified awards during the same year.

To be a qualified plan award, the award for length of service or safety achievement must be given under an established written plan or program that does not discriminate in favor of highly compensated employees. The average cost of all awards under the plan for the year (to all employees)

Caution

Employee Bonuses
Employee bonuses should not be labeled as gifts. An IRS agent examining your records may, with this description, limit the deduction to $25 unless you can prove the excess over $25 was compensation. By describing the payment as a gift, you are inviting an IRS disallowance of the excess over $25. This was the experience of an attorney who gave his secretary $200 at Christmas. The IRS disallowed $175 of his deduction. The Tax Court refused to reverse the IRS. The attorney could not prove that the payment was for services.

must not exceed $400. In determining this $400 average cost, awards of nominal value are not to be taken into account. In case of a partnership, the deduction limitation applies to the partnership as well as to each partner.

Safety and length of service. A length of service award does not qualify as an employee achievement award if it is given during the employee's first five years. Furthermore, only one length of service award every five years is considered an employee achievement award.

Safety awards granted to managers, administrators, clerical employees, or professional employees are not considered employee achievement awards. Furthermore, if during the year more than 10% of other employees (not counting managers, administrators, clerical employees, or professional employees) previously received safety awards, none of the later awards are subject to the employee achievement award rules.

Employee's tax. The employer's deductible amount for an employee achievement award is tax free to the employee; *see 3.10.* For example, you give a qualified plan award costing $1,800 to an employee. You may deduct only $1,600. The employee is not taxed on the award up to $1,600; the $200 balance is taxable.

Documenting Your T&E Expenses and Reporting Your Expenses

20.26 Record-Keeping Requirements

Your testimony—even if accepted by an IRS agent or a judge as truthful—is not sufficient to support a deduction of travel and entertainment expenses. By law, your personal claim must be supported by other evidence such as records or witnesses. The most direct and acceptable way is to have records that meet IRS rules discussed below. Failure to have adequate records will generally result in an examination of your return and in a disallowance of your travel and entertainment expense deductions. Only in unusual circumstances will evidence other than records provide all of the required details of proof.

If your expenses are reimbursed by your company, you must keep records to support the reimbursement arrangement with your company; *see 20.30.*

20.27 Substantiating Deductions for Travel and Entertainment

To satisfy the IRS requirements and to substantiate your expense deductions in the event of an audit, you need two types of records:

1. A diary, account book, or similar record to list the time, place, and business purpose of your travel and entertainment expenses; and
2. Receipts, itemized paid bills, or similar statements for lodging regardless of the amount, and for other expenses of $75 or more. But note these exceptions:

- A receipt for transportation expenses of $75 or more is required only when it is readily obtainable. For example, for air travel a receipt or a boarding pass is usually provided.
- A cancelled check by itself is not an acceptable voucher. If you cannot produce a bill or voucher, you may have to present other evidence such as a statement in writing from witnesses to prove business purpose of the expense.

A receipted bill or voucher must show (1) the amount of the expense; (2) the date the expense was incurred; (3) where the expense was incurred; and (4) the nature of the expense.

A hotel bill must show the name, location, date, and separate amounts for charges such as lodgings, meals, and telephone calls. A receipt for lodging is not needed if its cost is covered by a *per diem* allowance; *see 20.32.* The IRS will not allow a credit card statement to substitute for a lodging receipt. The IRS wants detailed receipts to catch personal items such as personal phone calls or the purchase of gifts.

A restaurant bill must show the restaurant's name and location, the date and amount of the expense, and, when a charge is made for items other than meals or beverages, a description of the charge.

Diary entries. Your diary does not have to duplicate data recorded on a receipt, provided that a notation in the diary is connected to the receipt. You are also not required to record amounts your company pays directly for any ticket or fare. Credit card charges should be recorded.

Planning Reminder

Credit Cards

Credit card charge statements for traveling and entertainment expenses meet the IRS tests, provided the business purpose of the expense is also shown. Credit card statements provide space for inserting the names of people entertained, their business relationship, the business purpose of the expense, and the portion of the expense to be allocated to business and personal purposes. These statements generally meet the IRS requirements of accounting to your employer for reimbursed expenses *(20.31)*, provided a responsible company official reviews them. The IRS will not accept a credit card statement as substantiation of a lodging expense.

Your records for entertainment costs must also show (1) the names of those you entertained; (2) the business purpose served by the entertainment; (3) the business relationship between you and your guests; and (4) the place of entertainment. Inattention to these details of substantiation can cost you the deduction. For example, an executive's company treasurer verified that the executive was required to incur entertainment expenses beyond reimbursed amounts. He also kept a cash diary in which he made contemporaneous notes of the amounts he spent. But he failed to note place, purpose, and business relationship. Consequently, there was no record that tied the expenses to his employment and the deduction was disallowed.

Excuses for Inadequate Records

Substantial compliance. If you have made a "good faith" effort to comply with the IRS rules, you will not be penalized if your records do not satisfy every requirement. For example, you would not automatically be denied a deduction merely because you did not keep a receipt.

Accidental destruction of records. If receipts or records are lost through circumstances beyond your control, you may substantiate deductions by reasonable reconstruction of your expenditures.

Exceptional circumstances. If, by reason of the "inherent nature of the situation," you are unable to keep adequate records, you may substantially comply by presenting the next best evidence. A supporting memorandum from your files and a statement from the persons entertained may be an adequate substitute. IRS regulations do not explain the meaning of "inherent nature of the situation."

Planning Reminder

How Long To Keep Records
You should keep your diary and supporting records for at least three years after the due date for the return that the records support. However, you may not have to keep these records if the information from them is submitted to your company under the rules applied to reimbursed expenses and allowances described at *20.30*.

EXAMPLES

1. Bryan's 1966 records were lost by a moving company. He claimed a T&E deduction of $15,301.87. The IRS estimated his T&E and other business expenses as $8,669 on the basis of his 1971 expense records. The Tax Court affirmed the IRS's approach. True, Bryan's loss of records made his burden of proof difficult, but he had to provide a reasonable reconstruction of his records to support his claimed deduction. His testimony of what he incurred in 1966 was not sufficient. A more accurate method was the IRS's use of his 1971 records and receipts.

2. Jackson claimed the IRS lost his records. He left his records with the IRS when he was audited, and the records were never returned. The Tax Court held that to be a good excuse for not producing his records and allowed a deduction on the basis of reconstructed records. Evidence that the IRS lost them: The IRS discovered Jackson's worksheet a year after the audit interview.

3. Murray claimed he lost his records when he was evicted from his apartment for failure to pay rent for a month. The Tax Court accepted his excuse on proof that he had kept records before they were lost. The eviction was beyond his control. However, if the records had been lost during a voluntary move, the loss would not have been excused, as in Example 1.

20.28 Reporting T&E Expenses If You Are Self-Employed

You must keep travel and entertainment (T&E) records following the rules in *20.27*. You may claim the meal allowance at *20.4* on overnight business trips. The reimbursement rules discussed in *20.30* do not apply to you.

In preparing your tax return, you report your expenses on the appropriate lines of Schedule C or Schedule C-EZ (if you qualify). You do not use Form 2106. An advantage of reporting on Schedule C (or C-EZ) is that your travel and entertainment expenses (T&E) are not subject to the 2% adjusted gross income (AGI) floor. Only 50% of meals and entertainment costs are deductible; *see 20.24* for exceptions.

20.29 Employee Reporting of Unreimbursed T&E Expenses

If you are paid a salary with the understanding that you will pay your own expenses and you pay all of your travel and entertainment (T&E) expenses *without* reimbursement, you report all of your salary or commission income as shown on Form W-2. You report your expenses on Form 2106 or Form 2106-EZ (if other tests are met). Meals and entertainment are only 50% deductible. You must also keep records as required by *20.27* to support your deduction. The deductible amount from Form 2106 or Form 2106-EZ is entered on Schedule A as a miscellaneous expense subject to the 2% AGI floor. Therefore, if your total miscellaneous expenses, including the unreimbursed T&E costs, do not exceed 2% of adjusted gross income, none of the miscellaneous expenses will be deductible.

If your employer has a reimbursement plan but the rules for accountable plans are *not* met, reimbursements are treated as part of your taxable pay; *see 20.34.*

Employer Reimbursement Plans

20.30 Tax Treatment of Reimbursements

Compliance rules are imposed on employees and employers for reporting reimbursed travel and entertainment expenses in order to prevent reimbursement arrangements from being used to avoid the 2% of adjusted gross income (AGI) floor for employee miscellaneous expenses. Plans that allow reimbursements that *do not* comply with the IRS rules are called *non-accountable plans.* All reimbursements under a nonaccountable plan are reported as salary or wage income on Form W-2. You then deduct your expenses as miscellaneous deductions subject to the 2% AGI floor; *see 20.34.*

If a plan meets the IRS rules, the plan is called an *accountable plan* and reimbursements made by the plan are not reported on Form W-2 as taxable wages. You also do not have to deduct expenses, assuming the reimbursement equals your expenses. In other words, there is a bookkeeping "wash" in which the full amount of expenses offsets the reimbursement without being reduced by the 2% AGI floor, and in the case of meal and entertainment costs, by the 50% reduction. Even though the employer may only deduct 50% of qualifying meal and entertainment expenses, you are not taxed on any part of a reimbursement of such costs if the accountable plan rules are met.

To qualify a plan as accountable, your employer must see to it that you submit adequate proof of your expenditures, and that you return any excess advances; *see 20.31.* To reduce record-keeping for actual costs, the company may reimburse you according to certain fixed *per diem* allowance rates; *see 20.32.* Your company must also determine how much of the advance or reimbursement, if any, is to be reported on your Form W-2.

Court Decision

Ask for Reimbursement

If you are entitled to reimbursement from your employer, make sure you ask for reimbursement. Failure to be reimbursed may prevent you from deducting your out-of-pocket expenses. A supervisor whose responsibility was to maintain good relations with his district and store managers entertained them and their families and also distributed gifts among them. His cost was $2,500, for which he could have been reimbursed by his company, but he made no claim. Consequently, the Tax Court disallowed the cost as a deduction on his return. The expense was the company's; any goodwill he created benefitted it. But because he failed to seek reimbursement, he was not allowed to convert company expenses into his own.

> **EXAMPLE**
>
> Your adjusted gross income is $85,000, and you incur T&E expenses of $1,600 that are reimbursed by your company. If the reimbursement arrangement does not meet the IRS rules, the $1,600 reimbursement is reported as wage income on your Form W-2. You may report the expenses on Form 2106 and after reducing meal and entertainment costs by 50%, enter the balance as a deduction on Schedule A as a miscellaneous expense subject to the 2% AGI floor. However, if these are your only miscellaneous expenses, you will not get the benefit of a deduction because they do not exceed 2% of $86,600 ($85,000 + $1,600), or $1,732. The $1,600 is fully taxable although spent for T&E.
>
> If your reimbursement arrangement qualified as an accountable plan, and you made an adequate reporting to your employer, the $1,600 would not be reported as income on your Form W-2, and you would not have to be concerned with the 2% floor for miscellaneous itemized deductions. There is a bookkeeping "wash." In other words, you receive a full deduction by substantiating the expenses to your employer.

Filing Tip

Failure To Timely Return Excess

If you fail to return excess payments within a reasonable time but you meet all of the other tests applied to an accountable plan, such as providing proof of the expenses, only the retained excess is taxed to you as if paid outside of an accountable plan.

Reimbursements of club dues or spousal travel costs. If you are reimbursed for nondeductible club dues *(20.22)* or nondeductible travel costs of a spouse or other person *(20.13)*, the reimbursement may be treated by your employer as taxable wages. If it is, you are not allowed an offsetting deduction. If the reimbursement is not treated as taxable wages by your employer, and you substantiate a business purpose for the club dues or for a travel companion's presence, the reimbursement is considered to be a tax-free working condition fringe benefit *(3.8).*

> **EXAMPLE**
>
> A company pays for the country club dues of an executive. It reimbursed dues of $20,000, and the executive used the club for business purposes 40% of the time. If the company does not treat the reimbursement as taxable wages but as a fringe benefit, $8,000 of the reimbursement is tax free to the executive; the $12,000 allocated to personal use is taxable.

20.31 What Is an Accountable Plan?

A reimbursement or allowance arrangement is an accountable plan if it requires you to:

- Adequately account to your employer for your expenses; *and*
- Return to your employer any excess reimbursement or allowance that you do not show was spent for ordinary and necessary business expenses.

If these terms are met and your expenses are fully reimbursed, you do not report the expenses or the reimbursement on your return. If the reimbursement is less than your payment of expenses, you use Form 2106 and Schedule A to claim a deduction for the unreimbursed expenses. The unreimbursed expenses are subject to the 2% AGI floor on Schedule A.

What is an adequate accounting? You adequately account to your employer by submitting bills and an account book, diary, or similar record in which you entered each expense at or near the time you had it. You must account to your employer for all amounts received as advances, reimbursements, or allowances, including amounts charged on a company credit card. Your records and supporting information must meet the rules discussed in *20.27*. You must also pay back reimbursements or allowances that exceed the expenses that you adequately accounted for, or the nonreturned excess will be taxable under the rules at *20.34* for non-accountable plans.

The accounting requirements are eased if you are reimbursed under a *per diem* arrangement covering meals, lodging, and incidental expenses *(20.32)* or you receive a flat mileage allowance *(20.33)*.

Time limits for receiving advances, substantiating expenses, and returning excess payments. The general rule is that these events must occur within a reasonable time. Under an IRS "safe harbor," the following payments are considered to be within a reasonable time:

- Advance payments—if given to you within 30 days before you reasonably anticipate to pay or incur expenses;
- Substantiation of expenses—if provided to your employer within 60 days after the expense is paid or incurred; and
- Return of excess—if done within 120 days after you pay or incur expense.

An employer may set up a "periodic statement method" to meet IRS rules. Here, an employer gives each employee periodic statements (at least quarterly) that list the amounts paid in excess of expenses substantiated by the employee and request substantiation of the additional amounts paid, or a return of the excess, within 120 days of the date of the statement. Substantiation or return within the 120-day period satisfies the reasonable time test.

Allocating reimbursements to meals and entertainment. Only 50% of meals and entertainment expenses are deductible. Therefore, if you adequately account for your expenses, and receive a flat reimbursement that is partly for meals and entertainment, and partly for other expenses, you must allocate part of the reimbursement to meals and entertainment if the employer has not provided an item-by-item breakdown. You must make this allocation if you want to deduct expenses exceeding reimbursements because on Form 2106, you must separately list meals and entertainment costs and reimbursements for meals and entertainment. The allocation is based on the percentage that your meal costs bear to the total T&E expenses.

> **EXAMPLE**
> You receive an allowance of $1,000 for travel expenses and have total expenses of $1,500, including $300 for meals. The percentage of your meals to total expenses is 20% (300 ÷ 1,500). On Form 2106, you show 20% of the allowance, or $200, as the allocable reimbursement for meals. The unreimbursed $100 balance for meals ($300 – $200) must be reduced to $50 by the 50% reduction for meals. You may deduct $400 of the $1,200 in expenses that were not for meals; 80% of the $1,000 travel allowance is allocated to such costs. The total deductible amount of $450 ($50 for meals and $400 for other expenses) is transferred from Form 2106 to Schedule A, where it is deductible as a miscellaneous itemized expense subject to the 2% AGI floor.

Caution

Excess *Per Diem* Allowances
If a *per diem* allowance exceeds the federal travel rate or the IRS high-low rate, the excess will be reported as income on your Form W-2, unless you return the excess; *see* Example 3 on the following page. The excess reportable on Form W-2 is also subject to income tax and FICA tax withholding.

20.32 *Per Diem* Travel Allowance Under Accountable Plans

Instead of providing a straight reimbursement for substantiated out-of-pocket travel expenses, an employer may use a *per diem* allowance to cover meals, lodging, and incidental expenses of employees on business trips away from home. Incidental expenses covered by a *per diem* arrangement may include tips, laundry, and cleaning fees, or similar expenses, but, under IRS rules, may not include cab fares, telephone, or telegram costs.

Planning Reminder

Importance of Adequate Accounting

If you adequately report expenses to your employer and return excess reimbursements, you are treated as being reimbursed under an accountable plan and generally do not have to report any reimbursement on your return; *see 20.31.*

If you are not related to the employer, you do not have to give your employer proof of your actual expenses if you receive a *per diem* allowance or reimbursement that is equal to or less than the federal travel rate for the particular area. You do have to account for the time, place, and business purpose of your travel. If you do not provide such an accounting for some travel days, you must be required to return the *per diem* allowance received for such days in order for the employer's plan to qualify.

For allowances covering lodging plus meals and incidental expenses for travel *within* the continental U.S., an employer may use an IRS high-low rate. The rate for the first nine months of 2002 was $125 per day for most areas or $204 per day for "high-cost" areas. The high-cost localities qualifying for the $204 rate in the first nine months of 2002 are shown in Revenue Procedure 2001-47. Employers can continue to use these rates for the rest of 2002, even if the rates or high-low localities change as of October 1, 2002. The IRS will issue a revenue procedure that includes any changes to the high-low rates effective October 1, 2002; *see* the *Supplement.* The revised edition of Publication 1542 will also have the changes.

Tables published by the government show the federal travel rate for areas within the continental U.S. (called CONUS locations) and for areas outside the continental U.S., including Hawaii and Alaska (called OCONUS locations). As discussed in *20.4*, new CONUS tables are released every October, effective for the government's October 1–September 30 fiscal year. The best way to obtain the CONUS *per diem* rates is from the General Services Administration website at www.policyworks.gov/perdiem. The OCONUS rates can also be accessed from the same website.

Employees related to the employer. The IRS *per diem* rules that allow you to avoid accounting for actual expenses do not apply if you work for a brother, sister, spouse, parent, child, grandparent, or grandchild. They also do not apply if you are an employee-stockholder who owns more than 10% of the company's stock.

Reporting a *per diem* allowance. If the allowance does not exceed the federal travel rate or IRS high-low rate, the reimbursement is not reported on Form W-2. If your expenses do not exceed the reimbursement, you do not have to report the expenses or the reimbursement on your tax return; *see* Example 1 below. If your expenses exceed the allowance, you may deduct the excess by reporting the expenses and reimbursement on Form 2106. The net amount from Form 2106, after applying the 50% reduction for meals, is claimed on Schedule A as a miscellaneous expense subject to the 2% AGI floor; *see* Example 2 below.

EXAMPLES

1. You take a three-day business trip to a locality at a time when the federal travel rate for the area is $106 per day. You account for the date, place, and business purpose of the trip. Your employer reimburses you $106 a day for lodging, meals, and incidental expenses, for a total of $318. Your actual expenses do not exceed this amount. Your employer does not report the reimbursement on your Form W-2. You do not have to report the reimbursement or deduct any expenses on your return.

2. Same facts as in Example 1, except that the reimbursement is less than your actual expenses of $450, for which you have records. On Form 2106, you report the $318 reimbursement and your $450 of expenses and also must allocate part of the allowance to meals to apply the 50% limit. The instructions to Form 2106 have a worksheet for making the allocation. The net amount from Form 2106 is deductible on Schedule A as a miscellaneous expense subject to the 2% AGI limit.

3. Same facts as in Example 1, except that you receive a *per diem* allowance of $114 per day—$8 per day more than the federal travel rate. If you do not return the excess of $24 ($8 × 3 days) within a reasonable time *(20.31)*, your employer must report the $24 as income in Box 1 of your Form W-2. The amount up to the federal travel rate, or $318, will be reported in Box 12 of Form W-2 with Code L, but not included as income.

Meal allowance only. If your employer gives you a *per diem* allowance covering only meals and incidental expenses, it is not taxable to you if you are not related to the employer and the allowance does not exceed the IRS meal allowance rates discussed at *20.4*.

For meals *outside* the continental U.S., the meal allowance rates in *20.4* do not apply. The allowable meal allowance rates are listed in the government's OCONUS tables.

20.33 Automobile Mileage Allowance

If in 2002 your employer paid you a fixed mileage allowance of up to 36.5 cents per mile, the amount of your automobile expenses is treated as substantiated, provided you show the time, place, and business purpose of your travel. If the allowance is in the form of an advance, it must be given within a reasonable period before the anticipated travel and you must also be required to return within a reasonable period *(20.31)* any portion of the allowance that covers mileage that you have not substantiated.

If these tests are met, the allowance will not be reported as income on Form W-2, and you will not have to report the allowance or expenses on your return; *see* Example 1 below. If you do not prove to your employer the time, place, and purpose of your travel, the entire reimbursement is treated as paid from a non-accountable plan and will be reported as income on Form W-2.

Your employer may reimburse you for parking fees and tolls in addition to the mileage allowance.

Caution

Allowance Exceeding IRS Rate
If you were given mileage allowance for 2002 in excess of 36.5 cents per mile, the excess will be included as wages on your Form W-2; *see* Example 2 on this page. If your allowance was less than 36.5 cents per mile, you may deduct the difference as a miscellaneous itemized deduction subject to the 2% AGI floor; *see* Example 3.

EXAMPLES
1. You drove 12,000 miles for business in 2002, and you account to your employer for the time, place, and business purpose of each trip. Your employer reimbursed you at the IRS rate of 36.5 cents per mile. None of the reimbursements will be reported as income on your Form W-2, and you do not have to report the reimbursements or any expenses on your return if your expenses do not exceed 36.5 cents per mile.
2. Same facts as in Example 1, except that you were reimbursed at 37 cents per mile. The amount using the IRS rate, or $4,380 (36.5¢ × 12,000 miles), is $60 less than the reimbursement of $4,440 (37¢ × 12,000). The $60 excess over the IRS rate will be reported as wages on your Form W-2.
   If you had records substantiating expenses over 36.5 cents per mile, you could claim them on Form 2106. The excess of your expenses over the IRS rate is shown on Form 2106, and that excess is claimed on Schedule A as a miscellaneous itemized deduction subject to the 2% AGI floor.
3. Same facts as in Example 1, except that you were reimbursed only 20 cents per mile. The reimbursements will not be reported as income on your Form W-2. You may deduct expenses up to the IRS rate by reporting the expense reimbursements on Form 2106. The amount of $4,380 using the IRS rate is $1,980 more than the reimbursement of $2,400 (20¢ × 12,000). The $1,980 excess of the IRS allowance over your reimbursements is shown on Form 2106 and then may be claimed as a miscellaneous itemized deduction on Schedule A subject to the 2% AGI floor.
   If you had records showing actual expenses of more than $4,380, you would claim those expenses on Form 2106 and not use the IRS fixed mileage allowance rate to figure your deduction.

Fixed and variable rate allowance (FAVR). In lieu of setting the allowance at the IRS standard mileage rate (36.5 cents per mile in 2002), an employer may use a fixed or variable rate allowance, called a FAVR, that gives employees a cents-per-mile rate to cover gas and other operating costs, plus a flat amount to cover fixed costs such as depreciation, insurance, and registration. A FAVR allowance must reflect local driving costs and allows employers to set reimbursements at a rate that more closely approximates employee expenses. If your employer sets up a qualifying FAVR under IRS guidelines, you will be required to provide records substantiating your mileage and certain car ownership information. Expenses up to the FAVR limits are deemed substantiated and will not be reported as wages on your Form W-2.

20.34 Reimbursements Under Non-Accountable Plans

A non-accountable plan is one that either does not require you to adequately account for your expenses or allows you to keep any excess reimbursement or allowances over the expenses for which you did adequately account.

Your employer reports allowances or reimbursements for a non-accountable plan as part of your salary income in Box 1 of your Form W-2. The allowance or reimbursement is also subject to income tax and FICA tax (Social Security) withholding. To claim deductions, you must use Form 2106 and itemize your deductions on Schedule A. Your expenses are subject to the 2% AGI floor and thus you may be unable to offset the taxable reimbursement (allowance) included on your Form W-2.

Chapter 21

Personal Exemptions

Each personal exemption you claim on your 2002 return is the equivalent of a $3,000 deduction. Exemptions for children, parents, and other dependents are allowed if the tests in this chapter are met.

If you have a high adjusted gross income, you may lose the benefit of your deduction under the phase-out rule discussed in *21.16*.

Number of Exemptions	Deduction Allowed
1	$ 3,000
2	6,000
3	9,000
4	12,000
5	15,000
6	18,000
7	21,000
8	24,000
9	27,000
10	30,000

21.1 How Many Exemptions May You Claim?

On your 2002 return, you may claim a $3,000 exemption for each of the following, provided you are not subject to the phaseout of exemptions for high income taxpayers *(see 21.16)*:

- **Yourself.** You claim an exemption for yourself unless you are the dependent of another taxpayer. If someone else can claim you as a dependent for 2002, you may not claim a personal exemption for yourself on your own return; this is true even if the other person does not actually claim you as a dependent. This rule prevents your child or other dependent from claiming an exemption on his or her return if you may claim an exemption for the child or other dependent.

- **Your spouse.** You claim your spouse as an exemption when you file a joint return. If you file a separate return, you claim your spouse as an exemption if he or she has no income and is not a dependent of another person; *see 21.2*.

- **Children, parents, and other dependents.** An individual qualifies as your dependent for 2002 if all of the following tests are met:

  1. The person you claim as your dependent is your relative *(21.3)* or is a member of your household *(21.4)*.

  2. Your dependent must have gross income for 2002 of under $3,000 *unless* he or she is your child who at the end of 2002 was under age 19 or was a full-time student under age 24; *see 21.5–21.6*.

  3. You contributed over half of the dependent's support *(21.7)* for 2002 or more than 10% of his or her support under the multiple support test at *21.10*.

  4. Your dependent is a U.S. citizen or national, or a resident of the United States, Canada, or Mexico; *see 21.12*.

  5. If your dependent is married, he or she does *not* file a joint return unless the exception at *21.13* is met.

Tests for Claiming Dependents

TEST 1. RELATIONSHIP OR MEMBER OF HOUSEHOLD TEST

The person must be either:

Your relative—child, stepchild, adopted child, grandchild, great-grandchild, son- or daughter-in-law, father- or mother-in-law, brother- or sister-in-law, parent, brother, sister, grandparent, step-parent, stepbrother or sister, half-brother or sister, and, if related by blood, an uncle, aunt, niece, or nephew. These relatives do not have to live with you. However, a foster child qualifies only if he or she is a member of your household for the entire year, apart from temporary absences; *see 21.3*.

Or—any person, whether related or not, who is a member of your household for the entire year, except for temporary absences. The exemption is not allowed if the person was your spouse at any time during the year, or if your relationship with such person is in violation of state law; *see 21.4*.

TEST 2. GROSS INCOME TEST

Your child—If at the end of 2002 your child was under age 19, or was a full-time student under age 24 *(21.6)*, his or her income does not matter. You can claim the child as your dependent if Tests 3, 4, and 5 are met. However, a child who was age 19–23 and not a full-time student at the end of the year, *or* who was age 24 or older, may be claimed as your dependent only if his or her gross income was less than $3,000 in 2002.

Other relatives or household members—must have gross income of less than $3,000 in 2002.

TEST 3. SUPPORT TEST

You either contribute more than half the dependent's support, or contribute more than 10% and together with others contribute more than half; *see 21.7* and *21.10*.

Total the dollar amount of support spent on a dependent by you, by others, and by the dependent. If your contribution is:
- *More than 50% of the total spent*—you claim the exemption.
- *More than 10% of the total spent and together with what you and the other contributors gave is more than 50% of the total spent*—you or one of the others who also contributed more than 10% may claim the exemption. You and the others must decide who is to claim the exemption. If you take it, you must attach to your return a Form 2120, "Multiple Support Declaration," signed by each person who contributed more than 10%.
- *Less than 50%, either alone or with the contribution of others*—neither you nor the other contributors may claim the exemption for the dependent.

Special support rules apply to divorced or separated parents; *see 21.11*.

TEST 4. CITIZENSHIP OR RESIDENT TEST

Your dependent is a United States citizen or national, or a resident of the United States, Canada, or Mexico; *see 21.12*.

TEST 5. JOINT RETURN TEST

Your married dependent does not file a joint return with his or her spouse; *see 21.13* for an exception.

Social Security numbers checked by IRS. The IRS verifies the Social Security numbers for both spouses on a joint return and for all claimed dependents; *see 21.14* and *21.15*.

21.2 Your Spouse as an Exemption

Your spouse is not your dependent for tax purposes. An exemption for a spouse is based on the marital relationship, not support. On a joint return, each spouse receives an exemption as a taxpayer. The name and Social Security number of each spouse listed on a joint return will be matched by the IRS against computer records of the Social Security Administration. If there is a mismatch, the exemption for that spouse will be disallowed; *see 21.14.*

On a separate return, you may claim your spouse as an exemption if he or she has no gross income and is not the dependent of another taxpayer. You may not claim an exemption for your spouse who has income, *unless you file a joint return that includes that income.* For example, if a wife files a separate return, her husband may not claim her as an exemption, even if she filed the return merely for a refund of taxes withheld on her wages.

If your spouse is a nonresident alien, has no income from U.S. sources, and is not a dependent of another person, you may claim an exemption for your spouse on a separate return.

If divorced or legally separated during the year. You may not claim your former spouse as an exemption if you are divorced or legally separated under a *final* decree of divorce or separate maintenance, even if you provided his or her entire support. However, an interlocutory (not final) decree does not bar you from claiming your spouse as an exemption.

EXAMPLE

An interlocutory (not final) decree of divorce is entered in 2002, and a final decree in 2003. For 2002, the couple may file a joint return on which exemptions for both are claimed. A marriage is not dissolved until a final decree is entered, which in this case is in 2003.

Your spouse died during the year. If you did not remarry and your deceased spouse had gross income, you may claim an exemption for your spouse only if you file a joint return that includes his or her income. You may claim the exemption on a separate return only if your spouse had no gross income and was not a dependent of another taxpayer.

EXAMPLE

Sylvia Smith dies on June 27. Her husband, Steve Smith, may file a joint return and claim Sylvia as an exemption. They were married as of the date of Sylvia's death. The joint return includes all of Steve's income for the year, but only that part of Sylvia's income earned up to June 27; *see 1.10.*

If you remarry before the end of the year in which your spouse died, you may not claim an exemption for your deceased spouse. If you file a joint return with your new spouse, you may be claimed as an exemption on that return. If you had *no* income for the year, you may be claimed as an exemption on both your deceased spouse's separate return and on a separate return filed by your new spouse, provided no one else may claim you as a dependent.

21.3 Test 1. Relationship Test

If the other tests are met (Tests 2–5 in *21.1*), you may claim an exemption for a dependent relative listed in this section, even if he or she is an adult, healthy, and capable of self-support. A relative listed below does not have to live with you. An unrelated person or distantly related person not listed below may still qualify as your dependent if he or she lives with you; *see 21.4.*

Your children. If your child was born at the end of 2002, you may claim a full $3,000 exemption for that child.

A stillborn child may not be claimed as an exemption. The exemption is allowed for a child who was born alive even if the infant lived for only a moment.

Stepchildren. Your stepchild is considered your child.

Adopted children. A *legally adopted* child is treated as your child. A child is considered legally adopted when a court decree is entered. In states allowing interlocutory (not final) adoption decrees, you may claim the exemption in the year the interlocutory decree is entered.

Caution

Spouses' Social Security Numbers and Names

Make sure that the names used when you and your spouse file your joint return match the names you have provided to the Social Security Administration. If there is a mismatch between a name and Social Security number, the IRS will disallow the exemption and then send you a notice that allows you to explain the discrepancy and restore the deduction; *see 21.14.*

Filing Instruction

You Must Report I.D. Numbers for Dependents

You must obtain and report on your return the Social Security number of each dependent claimed. Nonresident and resident aliens not eligible for Social Security numbers must have an individual taxpayer identification number; *see 21.15.*

If a court decree has not been entered, a child may be your dependent provided he or she was placed with you for adoption by an authorized adoption agency and was a member of your household for the rest of the year. If the child has not been placed with you for adoption by an agency, you may claim the child as a dependent *only* if he or she was a member of your household for the entire tax year; *see 21.4.*

Foster child. A foster child is considered to be your child if he or she is a member of your household for the entire year except for temporary absences.

Parents, grandparents, and other qualifying relatives. The following individuals also meet the relationship test: your parent, grandparent, great-grandparent, step-parent, grandchild, great-grandchild, brother, sister, half-brother, half-sister, stepbrother, stepsister, son- or daughter-in-law, father- or mother-in-law, and brother- or sister-in-law. If related by blood, aunts, uncles, nieces, and nephews also qualify.

Stepchild's husband or wife or child. Your stepchild's spouse does not meet the relationship test. Nor may you claim an exemption for a step-grandchild if you file a separate return. They are not on the list of relatives qualifying. But you may claim them as exemptions on a joint return. On a joint return, it is not necessary that the close relationship exist between the dependent and the spouse who furnishes the chief support. It is sufficient that the relationship exists with either spouse.

> **EXAMPLE**
>
> You contribute more than half of the support of the sister of your wife's mother (your wife's aunt). If you and your wife file a joint return, her aunt is allowed as an exemption on your joint return. But your wife's aunt's husband is not related by blood to you or your wife. You cannot claim an exemption for him, even on a joint return, unless he is a member of your household under the rules in *21.4.*

In-laws. Brother-in-law, sister-in-law, father-in-law, mother-in-law, son-in-law, and daughter-in-law are relatives by marriage. You may claim them as exemptions if you meet the other tests in this chapter.

You may claim an exemption for an in-law who was related to you by marriage and whom you continue to support after divorce or the death of your spouse.

> **EXAMPLE**
>
> Allen has contributed all the support of his father-in-law since he was married. Allen's wife died in 2001. Allen continued sole support of his wife's father in 2002. Allen may claim him as an exemption in 2002.

Death during the year. If a relative died during 2002 but was supported by you while alive, and you meet the other tests listed in this chapter, you may claim an exemption.

> **EXAMPLE**
>
> On January 21, 2002, your father died. Until that date, you contributed all of his support. You may claim him as an exemption for 2002. The full deduction is taken. Exemptions are not prorated.

21.4 Unrelated or Distantly Related Dependents Living With You

A friend or a relative not listed in *21.3*—such as a cousin who lives with you—can be your dependent. You may claim an unrelated or distantly related person as a dependent if the other dependent tests are met *and:*

1. The person is a member of your household; *and*
2. Your home is his or her principal home for the entire year, except for absences when attending school, vacationing, or being confined to a hospital. You may not claim a friend as an exemption when you live in his or her house even though you provide support. You are living in his or her household—not your own. Also, you cannot claim an exemption for a friend who lives in your home and renders you services in return for your care.

Filing Tip

Nephew, Niece, Uncle, and Aunt

Nephews, nieces, uncles, and aunts must be your blood relatives to qualify under the relationship test. For example, the brother or sister of your father or mother qualifies as your relative; their spouses do not. You may not claim your spouse's nephews, nieces, uncles, or aunts as your dependents unless you file a joint return.

EXAMPLES

1. Carol Barnes supports her cousin Phyllis, who lives in Carol's house all year. Carol can claim Phyllis as a dependent member of her household if Phyllis meets the citizenship test *(21.12)* and has gross income under $3,000 in 2002 *(21.5)*.
2. Roger Johnson provides a home for an orphan for seven months. He cannot claim the child as a dependent; the child did not live in his home for the entire year. However, if the child had been placed in his home for adoption by an authorized adoption agency, he or she could be claimed as Johnson's dependent although not a member of his household for the entire year; *see* the adopted children rule at *21.3*.
3. Mike Pilla supports a cousin, Janet, who lives in a house owned by him. Mike lives elsewhere and may not claim his cousin as a dependent because they do not live in the same home.

Your spouse or former spouse. Under the tax law, one spouse is not considered a dependent of the other; *see 21.2.* If you are divorced or legally separated during the year, your former spouse cannot qualify as your dependent even if he or she is a member of your household for the whole year.

Exemption for unmarried mate. An exemption for an unmarried mate depends on local law. Where the relationship violates local law, no exemption may be claimed; *see* the Example below.

EXAMPLE

Ensminger lived in North Carolina with a woman whom he supported. When he claimed an exemption for her, the IRS disallowed the exemption, claiming that under North Carolina law it is a misdemeanor for an unmarried man and woman to live together. When the Tax Court supported the IRS position, Ensminger appealed, arguing that the North Carolina law was an unconstitutional invasion of his right to privacy. The appeals court held that constitutionality was not an issue for the IRS and Tax Court to decide. The states are responsible for regulating domestic affairs. Federal tax law merely follows the direction of state law. If Ensminger lived in a state that did not hold his relationship illegal, he could claim the exemption.

In a similar case, a dependency exemption was allowed where the court ruled cohabitation did not violate Missouri law.

21.5 Test 2. Gross Income Limit for Dependents

A gross income limit applies to:

- Dependents who are not your children—such as parents, in-laws, sisters, brothers, uncles, aunts, and members of your household; *and*
- Your children who at the end of the year are age 19 or over and not full-time students, or children who are full-time students age 24 or older at the end of the year; *see 21.6.*

For 2002, the gross income test requires your dependent to have a gross income of less than $3,000. If a dependent has gross income in 2002 of $3,000 or more, he or she may not be claimed as an exemption, even if all of the support is provided by you. The only exception is for your children who are under age 19 or who are full-time students under age 24; *see 21.6.*

Gross income here means taxable income items includible in the dependent's tax return. It does not include nontaxable items such as gifts and tax-exempt bond interest. Gross income for a service-type business is gross receipts without deductions of expenses and for a manufacturing or merchandising business is total sales less cost of goods sold. A partner's share of partnership gross income, not the share of net income, is treated as gross income.

Social Security benefits are treated as gross income only to the extent they are taxable under the rules discussed at *34.3.*

 Filing Tip

Disabled Student

For purposes of the gross income test for dependents, gross income does not include income earned by a totally and permanently disabled individual at a school operated by a government agency or tax-exempt organization, if the school provides special instruction for alleviating the disability and the income is incidental to medical care received.

EXAMPLES

1. Larry Jones gives $4,000 a year for his father's support. The father owns a two-family house. He lives in one apartment and rents out the other for $300 a month, giving him a gross annual income of $3,600. After deducting interest and taxes, his net income is $2,400. Larry may not claim his father as a dependent as his 2002 gross income is not under $3,000.

2. Lisa Burr's son, age 21 and not a full-time student *(21.6)* in 2002, received $10,000 in damages for personal injuries suffered in an accident. His only other income was bank interest of $450. Since the damages are excluded from gross income *(11.7)*, the gross income test is satisfied. However, if Lisa's son used part of the damages to support himself, she may claim him as a dependent for 2002 only if her support contributions were larger; *see* the checklist of support items in *21.7*.

3. Kent Dolin's widowed father used $5,000 of his Social Security benefits and $1,200 in bank interest to support himself *(21.7)* in 2002. Under *34.3*, the benefits are not subject to tax and therefore not treated as gross income. His gross income of $1,200 is below the $3,000 limit. If Kent contributed more than $6,200 to his father's support, he meets the support test *(21.7)* and may claim his father as a dependent.

21.6 Children Under Age 19 or Full-Time Students Under Age 24

The tax law provides you with a break for dependent children. There is no gross income limit *(21.5)* for—

1. Your children who are under age 24 as of the end of the year if they are full-time students; *and*
2. Your children under age 19 as of the end of the year, whether or not they are students.

Such children may earn *any* amount and still be claimed as your dependents, provided you meet the support test *(21.7)* and the other exemption tests discussed in this chapter.

This rule applies to your child, stepchild, and adopted child. It also applies to a foster child who, for the entire year, is a member of your household. It does not apply to a grandchild, a son- or daughter-in-law, or a brother or sister who is a full-time student; they must have gross income of less than $3,000 in 2002 to qualify as your dependents.

Qualifying as a full-time student. A full-time student is one who attends school full time during at least five calendar months in the tax year. For example: attendance from February through some part of June—or from February through May and then at least one month from September through December—qualifies. The five months do not have to run consecutively. Attendance at a vocational, trade, or technical school for the five-month period qualifies, but not correspondence schools or on-the-job training courses.

 Caution

Students Age 24 or Older
The favorable rule that disregards income of full-time students applies only to students who are under age 24 as of the end of the year. If your child was age 24 or older at the end of 2002 and had gross income of $3,000 or more, you may not claim him or her as a dependent.

EXAMPLES

1. Benita Rosa's unmarried daughter, who is age 22, attended college full time until she graduated in June 2002. The gross income test does not apply to her earnings in 2002 because she was a full-time student for at least five months during the year. However, Benita must meet the support test *(21.7)* to claim her daughter as her dependent.

2. Peter Block's son John, who is age 19, worked during the first half of the year and then started college in September. Peter may not claim John as a dependent if John earned $3,000 or more. Although John is a full-time student as of the end of the year, he did not attend school for at least five months during the year.

Night school. Your child who attends night school is considered a full-time student *only if* he or she is enrolled for the number of hours or classes that is considered full-time attendance at a similar daytime school.

21.7 Test 3. 50% Support Test

If your dependent has no financial means and you are the only person contributing to his or her support during the year, you can skip the following discussion on support. You meet the support test. You contribute 100% of the dependent's support. If, however, the dependent or other persons or organizations contribute to his or her support, you have to determine whether your contribution exceeds 50% of the dependent's total support.

Meeting the support test. Follow these steps to figure support: (1) Total the value of the support contributed by you, by the dependent, and by others for the dependent. Use the checklists later in this section for determining what to include in total support and what to exclude. (2) Determine your share of the total. If your share is more than 50% of the dependent's total support, you meet the support test. It does not matter how many months or days you provided the support; only the total cost of the support is considered. You may not take the exemption if the dependent contributed 50% or more of his or her own support or 50% or more was contributed by others, including government sources. If the dependent or someone else did not contribute 50% or more of the support, and you contributed more than 10% of the total support, you may be able to claim the exemption under a multiple support agreement; *see 21.10.*

Divorced or separated parents contributing to support of their children should follow the special support rules at *21.11.*

Checklist of Support Items

- Food and lodging; *see 21.8*
- Clothing
- Medical and dental expenses, including premiums paid for health insurance policies and supplementary Medicare
- Education expenses such as tuition, books, and supplies. If your child receives a student loan and is the primary obligor, the loan proceeds are considered his or her own support contribution. This is true even if you are a guarantor of the loan. Scholarships received by full-time students are not treated as support; *see* the following checklist of nonsupport items.
- Cars and transportation expenses. Include the cost of a car bought for a dependent as support. If you buy a car but register it in your own name, the cost of the car is *not* support provided by you, but any out-of-pocket expenses you have for operating the car are part of your support contribution.
- Recreation and entertainment. A computer or TV set bought for your child or other dependent is support. Also include costs of summer camp, singing and dancing lessons, and musical instruments, as well as wedding expenses.

Personal savings and tax-exempt income may be support. In figuring a person's total support, include his or her tax-exempt income and personal savings if actually used for support items such as food, lodging, or clothing. Also include support items that are financed by loans. Income that is invested and not actually spent for support is not included in the earner's total support.

Social Security. Social Security benefits paid to children of deceased workers that are used for their support are treated as the children's contribution to their own support. Follow this rule even though benefits are paid to you as the child's parent or custodian. If the Social Security benefits used for a child's support are more than half of the child's total support, no one may claim the child as a dependent.

Where husband and wife are paid Social Security benefits in one check made out in their joint names, 50% is considered to be used by each spouse unless shown otherwise.

Government benefits. In figuring whether you have provided more than 50% of the dependent's support, you have to consider certain government benefits as support provided by a third party. For example, welfare, food stamps, or housing payments based on need are state support payments if they are used for support items. G.I. Bill education assistance is support provided by the government.

Foster care payments by a child placement agency to parents are support provided by the agency and not by the parents. The value of board, lodging, and education provided to a child in a state juvenile home is treated as support provided by the state.

When a person joins the Armed Forces, the value of board, lodging, and clothing he or she receives is treated as the government's support contribution. However, if *you* are in the Armed Forces, dependency allotments withheld from your pay and used to support your dependents are included in *your* support contributions for them. Also included in your support contribution is a military quarters allowance covering a dependent.

Caution

Support of Children Earning Income

Although there is no gross income test for your children who are under age 19 or who are full-time students under age 24, you must still meet the support test in this section to claim them as your dependents. If your child has income, be prepared to show either that the income was not used for his or her support, or that your support contributions were larger. Use the checklists in this section for determining what must be treated as "support."

Planning Reminder

Savings and Investments as Support

Income that is invested is not treated as support. However, personal savings are treated as support if they are used for food, clothing, lodging, or other support items.

Checklist of Items Not Counted as Support

- Federal, state, and local income taxes and Social Security taxes paid by the dependent from his or her own income
- Funeral expenses
- Life insurance premiums
- Medicare Part A (basic Medicare) and Part B (Supplementary Medicare benefits). In one case the IRS argued that Medicaid benefits were includible in total support but the Tax Court disagreed, holding that Medicaid is similar to excludable Medicare benefits.
- Medical insurance benefits received by the dependent
- Scholarships received by your child, stepchild, or legally adopted child who is a full-time student for at least five calendar months during the year. Scholarship aid is counted as support contributed by the child if he or she is not a full-time student for at least five months. Naval R.O.T.C. payments and payments made under the War Orphans Educational Assistance Act are scholarships that are not counted as support. State aid to a disabled child for education or training, including room and board, is a scholarship.

Planning Reminder

Dependents in the Armed Forces

If your dependent joins the military, the value of food, lodging, clothing, and educational assistance provided by the government constitutes government support.

EXAMPLES

1. Anna Chung's son invests half of his earnings from a part-time job and spends the other half on recreation. The invested earnings are not treated as support. If Anna's support payments exceed the amount her son spent for recreation, and no one else contributes to his support, Anna meets the support test.

2. Eric Hill receives Social Security benefits of $6,000 and also $300 in bank interest. He spends $4,400 on food, clothes, transportation, and recreation. The $4,400 spent is his contribution to his own support. Eric's rent, utilities, medical expenses, and other necessities are paid by his son, Mike. If Mike's payments exceed $4,400, and no one else contributes to Eric's support, Mike may claim Eric as a dependent.

21.8 Lodging and Food as Support

You count as support the *fair rental value* of a room, apartment, or house in which the dependent lives. In your estimate, you include a reasonable allowance for the rental value of furnishings and appliances, and for heat and other utilities. You do *not* add payments of rent, taxes, interest, depreciation, paint, insurance, and utilities. These are presumed to be accounted for in the fair rental estimate. The fair rental value of lodging you furnish a dependent is the amount you could reasonably expect to receive from a stranger for the lodging.

Planning Reminder

Lump-Sum Payment to Care Facilities

A lump-sum contribution covering a relative's stay in a long-term care facility is prorated over the relative's life expectancy to determine your current support contribution.

Does dependent live in his or her own home? If a qualifying relative listed at *21.3* lives in his or her own home, treat the total fair rental value as his or her own contribution to support. However, if you help maintain the home by giving cash, or you directly pay such expenses as the mortgage, real estate taxes, fire insurance premiums, and repairs, you reduce the total fair rental value of the home by the amount you contributed when figuring his or her own support contributions; *see* Example 1 below.

If you lived with your dependent rent-free in his or her home, the fair rental value of lodging furnished to you must be offset against the amounts you spent for your dependent in determining the net amount of your contribution to the dependent's support.

Food and other similar household expenses. If the dependent lives with you, you divide your total food expenses equally among all the members of your household, unless you have records showing the exact amount spent on the dependent; *see* the Examples in *21.9*. If he or she does not live with you, you count the actual amount of food expenses spent by or for that dependent.

Do you pay for a relative's care in a health facility? If you pay part of a relative's expenses for care in a state-supported hospital or nursing home, your payment is a support contribution. If you make a lump-sum contribution covering a relative's stay in an old-age home or other care facility, you prorate your payment over the relative's life expectancy to determine the current support contribution; *see* Example 2 on the following page.

EXAMPLES

1. You contribute $7,000 as support to your father who lives in his own home, which has a fair rental value of $8,000 a year. He uses $4,600 of the money you give him to pay real estate taxes and $2,400 for food. He spends $3,000 of his Social Security for recreation and invests the rest. He has no gross income *(21.5)* and receives no other support. Your father's contribution to his own support is $6,400:

Fair rental value of house	
($8,000 *less* $4,600 you gave for taxes)	3,400
Social Security spent	3,000
Father's contribution to his own support	$6,400

You may claim your father as a dependent because your contribution of $7,000 exceeds half of his total support of $13,400 (your $7,000 contribution and his $6,400 contribution).

2. A son secures his father's placement in a religious home for a lump-sum payment of $89,600. The payment was determined on the basis of $11,200 a year over the father's life expectancy of eight years. If the father dies within eight years, no refund is due. The son counts $11,200 as an annual contribution to his father's support. If this is more than half of his father's yearly support costs, the son may claim the exemption. If the father fails to reach his life expectancy, the son may not deduct any unused part of the $89,600 as a charitable deduction.

21.9 Examples of Allocating Support

The Examples in this section illustrate how you should allocate various support items when your contributions benefit more than one person or when your dependent provides part of his or her own support.

Earmarking support to one dependent. If you are contributing funds to a household consisting of several persons and the amount you contribute does not exceed 50% of the total household support, you may be able to claim an exemption for at least one dependent by earmarking your support to his or her use. Your earmarked contributions must exceed 50% of this dependent's support costs. Mark your checks for the benefit of the dependent, or provide the dependents with a written statement of your support arrangement at the time you start your payments. The IRS says its agents will generally accept such evidence of your arrangement. If you do not designate for whom you are providing support, your contribution is allocated equally among all members of a household (*see* Example 3 on the following page).

Filing Tip

Households with Several Dependents

If your contribution does not exceed 50% of total household support, earmark contributions to at least one of the dependents. This will allow you to claim at least one exemption. Without proper records, however, the IRS treats your contributions as made to the entire household.

EXAMPLES

1. Your father lives in your home with you, your spouse, and your three children. He receives Social Security benefits of $9,800, which are not subject to tax *(34.3)* and half of which ($4,900) he spends for his own clothing, travel, and recreation. You spend $6,600 for food during the year. You also paid his dental bill of $500. You estimate the annual fair rental value of the room furnished him as $3,600. Your father's total support is:

Social Security used for support	$4,900
Share of food costs ($\frac{1}{6}$ of $6,600)	1,100
Dental bill paid by you	500
Rental value of room	3,600
	$10,100

You can claim him as a dependent. You contributed more than half his total support, or $5,200 ($3,600 for lodging, $500 for dental, and $1,100 for food).

2. Your parents live with you, your spouse, and your two children in a house you rent. The annual fair rental value of their room is $3,000. Your father receives a tax-free government pension of $5,200, all of which he spent equally for your mother and himself for clothing and recreation. Your parents' only other income was $3,000 of tax-exempt interest. They did not make any other contributions towards their own support. Your total expense in providing food for the household is $6,000. You pay heat and utility bills of

$1,200. You paid your mother's medical expenses of $600. Your father's total support from all sources is $5,100 and your mother's is $5,700, figured as follows:

	Father	Mother
Fair rental value of room	$1,500	$1,500
Pension used for their support	2,600	2,600
Share of food costs ($1/6$ of $6,000)	1,000	1,000
Medical expenses for mother		600
	$5,100	$5,700

In figuring your parents' total support, you do not include the cost of heat and utilities, because these are presumed to be included in the fair rental value of the room ($3,000). The support you furnish your father, $2,500 (lodging, $1,500; food, $1,000), is not over half of his total support of $5,100. The support you furnish your mother, $3,100 (lodging, $1,500; food, $1,000; medical, $600), is over half of her total support of $5,700. You can claim your mother as a dependent but not your father. Since she did not have taxable income, the gross income test *(21.5)* is satisfied.

3. A husband who lives apart from his family without a divorce or legal separation sends his wife $3,240 to meet household expenses. A son and daughter live with her. The wife contributes from her own funds $6,480; an uncle sends her $1,080. The total amount going to meet household expenses from all sources is $10,800. On a separate return, the husband may not claim any exemptions for his children; his contributions are less than 50% of their total support. As he has not earmarked who is to get his contributions, his payments are allocated equally among the three members of the household. Each is considered to have received $1,080 from him. His contribution of $1,080 is less than half of the total support of $3,600 allocated to each child.

Contributed by:	Allocated to:			
	Wife	Son	Daughter	Total
Wife	$2,160	$2,160	$2,160	$6,480
Husband	1,080	1,080	1,080	3,240
Uncle	360	360	360	1,080
Total	$3,600	$3,600	$3,600	$10,800

4. Same facts as in Example 3 except that the husband notes on his monthly checks of $270 that $180 is for his son and $90 for his daughter. He may claim his son as an exemption on a separate return; he has contributed more than half of the son's support. As total household costs of $10,800 are allocated equally among the three household members, the wife's contribution is reallocated to make up for the difference created by the husband's increased support to the son. Here, the wife is considered to have contributed $3,240 to her own support.

Contributed by:	Allocated to:			
	Wife	Son	Daughter	Total
Wife	$3,240	$1,080	$2,160	$6,480
Husband		2,160	1,080	3,240
Uncle	360	360	360	1,080
Total	$3,600	$3,600	$3,600	$10,800

5. Assume that in Example 4 the mother contributed only $6,240 and her son contributed $240. There would be no change in tax consequences; however, the allocation of support contributions would differ. The son's contribution is added to the total household costs, which are allocated equally among the family members to find how much applies to each person's support. However, in determining support contributions, the son is treated as contributing $240 to his own support.

Contributed by:	Allocated to:			
	Wife	Son	Daughter	Total
Wife	$3,240	$ 840	$2,160	$6,240
Son		240		240
Husband		2,160	1,080	3,240
Uncle	360	360	360	1,080
Total	$3,600	$3,600	$3,600	$10,800

21.10 Multiple Support Agreements

Are you and others sharing the support of one person, but with no one individual providing more than 50% *(21.7)* of his or her total support? You may claim the dependent as an exemption if:

1. You gave more than 10% of the support;
2. The amount contributed by you and others to the dependent's support equals more than half the support;
3. Each contributor could have claimed the exemption—except that he or she gave less than half the support; *and*
4. Each contributor who gave more than 10% agrees to let you take the exemption. Each signs a Form 2120, "Multiple Support Agreement." You then attach the forms to your return.

Filing Instruction

Multiple Support Agreement

If you contribute more than 10% of a person's support and all other more-than-10% contributors agree to let you claim the exemption, each of them should sign a consent on separate Forms 2120 that you attach to your return.

EXAMPLES

1. You and your two brothers contribute $2,000 each toward the support of your mother. She contributes $1,000 of her own to support herself. Your two sisters contribute $500 each. Thus, the total support comes to $8,000. Of this, each brother gave 25% ($2,000 ÷ $8,000), for a total of 75%. Each sister gave $6\frac{1}{4}$% ($500 ÷ $8,000). You or one of your brothers may claim the exemption. Since each of you contributed more than 10% and the total of your contributions is more than half of your mother's support, you may decide among yourselves which of the three of you will claim the exemption. If you claim the exemption, your brothers must sign Forms 2120, which you attach to your return. If one of your brothers claims the exemption, you sign a Form 2120, which is attached to the return of the brother who claims the exemption. Since neither of your sisters furnished more than 10%, neither can claim the exemption; they need not sign Forms 2120.

2. Your mother's support totals $10,000; you contribute $3,000; your brother, $2,000; your father, $1,600; and your mother from her savings contributes $3,400. Assume your father does not file a tax return claiming your mother as an exemption. You and your brother cannot use your father's contribution to meet the more than 50% test required by Rule 2 above. Your father may not join in a multiple support agreement because your mother is not his dependent for tax purposes, although an exemption may be claimed for a wife on the basis of the marital relationship; *see 21.2.*

21.11 Special Support Test for Divorced or Separated Parents

A special rule favoring the "custodial parent" applies where divorced or separated parents together provide more than half of their child's total support and one or both of them have custody of the child for more than half the year. The "custodial parent" is the parent who had custody of the child for the greater portion of the year; *see* the custody rules below. Under the special rule, the custodial parent is treated as meeting the support test *(21.7)* for the child even if the noncustodial parent actually paid most of the child's support. Although the custodial parent is considered to have met the support test, and, thus, is generally able to claim an exemption for the child, the parents may arrange for the noncustodial parent to claim an exemption for a child in a divorce decree or separation agreement, or the custodial parent may waive his or her right to the exemption in favor of the noncustodial parent.

You must answer yes to the following three tests for the special parental-support rule to apply; otherwise, the general support rules discussed at 21.7 or 21.10 apply for determining who may claim the child as a dependent.

Are you either divorced or legally separated? For the special rules of this section to apply for 2002, you must be divorced or legally separated under a decree of divorce or separate mainte- nance, or separated under a written agreement, or live apart at all times during the last six months of 2002. According to the IRS, the "live apart" rule *does not* apply to unmarried couples who live apart for the last six months of the year. Congress did not intend for the special support test to apply to parents who were never married to each other.

Did either you or the other parent provide over 50% of the child's support? Nei- ther parent may claim the exemption unless the parents together gave more than 50% of the child's support for 2002. If you remarried, support contributions made during 2002 by your new spouse for the child are treated as your own contributions.

These special rules for parents do *not* apply if several people contributing more than 10% of the sup- port enter into a multiple support agreement *(21.10)* authorizing one of them to claim the exemption.

Was the child either in your custody or the custody of both you and the other parent for more than half the year? If the child was not in the custody of either or both parents for more than half of 2002, the exemption is claimed by the person who contributed more than 50% of the child's support *(see 21.7)*, or, if there is no such person, by the person designated in a multiple support agreement under the rules at *21.10*.

Custodial parent. If the previously discussed three tests are met and you had custody (defined below) for a greater portion of the year than the other parent, you are treated as meeting the sup- port test regardless of your actual support contribution. Thus, you may claim the exemption unless barred under the other exemption tests. However, you may allow the noncustodial parent to claim the exemption by waiving your right to it. The noncustodial parent may also be able to claim it under the terms of a divorce decree or separation agreement.

Custody is determined by the terms of a decree of divorce or separate maintenance or a written separation agreement. If a decree or agreement does not determine custody, the parent with physi- cal custody for most of the year is the custodial parent. This physical custody rule also applies if parents have joint custody under a decree or agreement, or if the issue of custody is the subject of legal proceedings as of the end of the year.

If you were divorced or separated during 2002, and before that time you had joint custody of the child, the parent who has custody for the greater period of time after the separation is consid- ered the custodial parent.

Custodial parent's waiver on Form 8332 allows noncustodial parent to claim ex- emption for child. As the custodial parent, you may waive the exemption by signing a written declaration on Form 8332. When you use the form for the first time, you indicate whether you are waiving the exemption for that year only or for future years as well. The noncustodial parent attaches the Form 8332 to his or her return and claims the exemption for the child. If the exemption has been waived for future years as well, a copy of the Form 8332 must be attached to the noncustodial parent's returns for the later years. A statement similar to Form 8332 may be used instead of the form.

Noncustodial parent granted exemption under divorce agreement after 1984. If you are the noncustodial parent and have been given the unconditional right to the exemption by a divorce decree or separation agreement that went into effect after 1984, you may attach to your return *either* Form 8332 or copies of the following pages from the decree or agreement: the page of the agreement that unconditionally states that you can claim the child as your dependent and that the other parent will not claim the child for specified tax years or for all future tax years; the cover page, on which you should write the custodial parent's Social Security number; and the signature page showing the other parent's signature and the date of the agreement.

Warning: Check the terms of the divorce decree to see that the custodial spouse has agreed to the waiver.

EXAMPLE

A 1993 Colorado divorce decree gave Miller's ex-wife physical custody of their two children but allowed him to claim the children as personal exemptions. Miller did this on his 1993 and 1994 returns, attaching portions of the divorce decree to support his deductions. How- ever, the Tax Court agreed with the IRS that the attachment of the divorce decree to the

Filing Instruction

Waiving Child's Exemption
The custodial parent may waive the exemption for a child for one or more years by signing a Form 8332. The other parent must then attach the form to his or her return for the first year of the waiver and a copy of the form for all future years the exemption is waived.

Filing Tip

Which Parent Should Claim Exemption?
Generally, if the noncustodial parent is in a higher tax bracket than the custodial parent, and both agree to maximize the tax savings from the exemption, the custodial parent should waive the exemption for the child in favor of the noncustodial parent. However, if a high- income noncustodial parent would be subject to the exemption phaseout *(21.16)*, it would be advisable for the lower-earning custodial par- ent to claim the exemption.

return was not a waiver of her exemption rights; the decree did not have her signature or specify the years of the waiver. Her attorney had signed the decree as a procedural step in the divorce, but this did not signify her agreement to the waiver. The state court may have intended Miller to have the exemptions, but the federal tax law spells out the circumstances under which a noncustodial parent may claim the exemptions, and Miller did not satisfy these requirements.

Noncustodial parent's exemption under pre-1985 divorce decree or agreement. If a pre-1985 decree or agreement gives you, as noncustodial parent, the right to the exemption, you must provide at least $600 for the support of the child in 2002 to be entitled to the exemption for the child. The exemption must be specifically allocated to you in a decree of divorce or separate maintenance or a written agreement executed before January 1, 1985.

21.12 Test 4. The Dependent Must Meet a Citizen or Resident Test

To claim a 2002 exemption for a dependent, the dependent must have at some time during 2002 qualified as a:

- Citizen or resident of the United States;
- United States national (one who owes permanent allegiance to the U.S.; principally, a person born in American Samoa who has not become a naturalized American citizen); *or*
- Resident of Canada or Mexico.

Child born abroad. A child born in a foreign country, one of whose parents is a nonresident alien and whose other parent is a U.S. citizen, qualifies as a U.S. citizen and thus as a dependent if the other tests are met.

If you are a U.S. citizen living abroad, you may claim as a dependent a legally adopted child who is not a U.S. citizen or resident if for the entire year your home was the child's principal residence and he or she is a member of your household.

21.13 Test 5. The Dependent Does Not File a Joint Return

You may not claim an exemption for a dependent who files a joint return with another. For example, if you meet the other four tests entitling you to an exemption for your married daughter as your dependent, but she files a joint return with her husband, you may not claim her as your dependent on your tax return.

Exception. Even if your dependent files a joint return, you may claim the exemption where the income of each spouse is under the income limit required for filing a return and the couple files a joint return merely to obtain a refund of withheld taxes. Under these circumstances, their return is considered a refund claim, and a dependency exemption may be claimed.

21.14 Spouses' Names and Social Security Numbers on Joint Return

The IRS checks the Social Security number (SSN) of each spouse on a joint return. If the SSN and name on the return do not match IRS/Social Security Administration records, the IRS will disallow the exemption for that spouse.

The most common reason for a mismatch is when, after marriage, one spouse takes the other spouse's last name, or a hyphenated name is used. An updated Social Security card should be obtained using Form SS-5, available from the Social Security Administration website at www.ssa.gov, or calling 1-800-772-1213.

If a new name is used on the return but Social Security Administration records have not been updated, the IRS will disallow that spouse's exemption unless the new name is shown on an enclosed Form W-2 or the name change is explained and documented, such as by enclosing a copy of a new driver's license or marriage certificate.

If a spouse's exemption is disallowed, the IRS will mail the taxpayers an explanatory notice. By contacting the IRS and verifying a name change, the exemption can be restored.

Caution

Should Married Dependents File Separately?

When a married dependent files a joint return, the parent cannot claim an exemption. The loss of the exemption may cost a parent more than the joint return saves the couple. In such a case, it may be advisable for the couple to file separate returns so that the parent may benefit from the larger tax saving.

If the couple decides to revoke their election to file jointly and then file separately in order to preserve the exemption for a parent, they must do so before the filing date for the return. Once a joint return is filed, the couple may not, after the filing deadline, file separate returns for the same year.

21.15 Reporting Social Security Numbers of Dependents

On your 2002 return, you must list the Social Security number (SSN) of each dependent you claim. Include the SSNs of parents or other adults you claim as dependents, as well as those of children.

An SSN may be obtained from the Social Security Administration for U.S. citizens and aliens who have been lawfully admitted for permanent residence or employment. If a dependent is a resident alien or nonresident alien ineligible to obtain an SSN, an individual taxpayer identification number (ITIN) must be obtained from the IRS by filing Form W-7.

If you are in the process of legally adopting a U.S. citizen or resident child who has been placed in your home by an authorized placement agency, and you cannot obtain a Social Security number for the child in time to file your tax return, you may use Form W-7A to apply to the IRS for a temporary adoption taxpayer identification number (ATIN).

If you fail to include a correct SSN or ITIN for a dependent claimed on your return, the IRS may disallow the exemption, although it may contact you and give you an opportunity to provide the number. If an exemption is disallowed, the IRS may assess the extra tax using a summary assessment procedure if you fail to request abatement of the assessment within 60 days of receiving notice; this procedure does not require issuance of a deficiency notice, so there is no appeal to the Tax Court.

To obtain a Social Security number for a dependent child, file Form SS-5 with your local Social Security Administration office. Parents of newborn children may request a number when filling out hospital birth-registration records.

Religious beliefs. Religious beliefs against applying for and using SSN numbers for their children do not excuse taxpayers from the obligation to provide them. That's what the Tax Court told the Millers, who had refused to use SSN numbers for claiming their two children as exemptions. They argued that SSNs are universal numerical identifiers equal to the "mark of the Beast," as described in the New Testament. However, they were willing to use Individual Taxpayer Identification Numbers (ITINs).

The Court held that the IRS properly refused to issue ITINs in this case because ITINs are issued only to taxpayers who are ineligible to receive SSNs, which are issued by the Social Security Administration. The couple had argued that the requirement to use SSNs "substantially burdened" their First Amendment right to free exercise of religion, which entitled them to relief under the religious Freedom Restoration Act of 1993. The Court held that it did not have to decide the "burden" issue because the IRS was able to show that the SSN requirement furthers a compelling governmental interest and is the least restrictive means of achieving this interest. Here, the Government has a compelling interest in effectively tracking claimed dependency exemptions and administering the tax system in a uniform and mandatory way. Moreover, the requirement to supply SSNs for dependent children has significantly reduced the improper claiming of dependents. Allowing the use of ITINs would be a less effective means of detecting fraud than requiring SSNs. If an individual entitled to an SSN was issued an ITIN, an SSN could later be obtained, allowing duplicate exemption claims to be made.

Planning Reminder

Filing for SSN or ITIN

If you are planning to claim an exemption for a dependent who as of the end of 2002 does not have the required Social Security number or individual taxpayer identification number, either you or that person should file Form SS-5 with the Social Security Administration or Form W-7 with the IRS (for an ITIN) as soon as possible in 2003 so the number may be obtained before the April 15, 2003, filing deadline.

21.16 Phaseout of Personal Exemptions for Higher Income Taxpayers

You will lose part or all of the $3,000 deduction for each 2002 personal exemption if your adjusted gross income (AGI) exceeds the threshold amount for your filing status. *Adjusted gross income* is explained at *12.1*. On your 2002 Form 1040, adjusted gross income is shown on Line 35.

If your 2002 status is—	Phaseout applies if AGI exceeds*—	Exemptions completely phased out if AGI exceeds—
Married filing jointly or qualified widow(er)	$206,000	$328,500
Head of household	171,650	294,150
Single	137,300	259,800
Married filing separately	103,000	164,250

These thresholds are adjusted annually for inflation.

Caution

Phaseout of Exemptions

On a 2002 return, you are not allowed to claim any deduction for personal exemptions if your adjusted gross income exceeds $259,800 if you are single, $328,500 if you are married filing jointly, $294,150 if you file as head of household, and $164,250 if you are married filing separately.

How the phaseout increases your marginal tax rate. The phaseout *increases* the effective marginal rate on earnings within the $122,500 phase-out range ($61,250 for married filing separately); *see* the Example below. The marginal rate increases with the number of exemptions.

Exemption Reduction Worksheet

1. Multiply $3,000 by the number of exemptions claimed on Form 1040, Line 6d.   1_____
2. Enter adjusted gross income (Line 35, Form 1040).   2_____
3. Enter phase-out threshold for your filing status:

Joint return:	$206,000
Single:	$137,300
Head of household:	$171,650
Married filing separately:	$103,000

                                                           3_____
4. Subtract Line 3 from Line 2.*   4_____
5. Divide Line 4 by $2,500 ($1,250 if married filing separately). Round up to next higher whole number if result is not a whole number (for example, round .005 to 1).   5_____
6. Multiply Line 5 by 2% and enter the number as a decimal.   6_____
7. Multiply Line 1 by Line 6. This amount is disallowed.   7_____
8. Subtract Line 7 from Line 1. **This is the amount that you deduct for exemptions on Line 40, Form 1040.**   8_____

*If Line 4 is zero or less, your exemptions are not reduced. Enter the amount from Line 1 on Form 1040, Line 40. If Line 4 is over $122,500 ($61,250 if married filing separately), you may not claim any deductions for exemptions. If Line 4 is more than zero but no more than $122,500 ($61,250 if married filing separately), proceed to Line 5.

EXAMPLE

Howard and Jessica are married. For 2002, they filed a joint return and claimed four exemptions. They reported adjusted gross income of $209,800 on Line 35 of Form 1040. Their exemptions are reduced by $480 to $11,520, figured as follows:

1. $3,000 × 4	$12,000
2. Adjusted gross income	$209,800
3. Phaseout threshold for joint return	206,000
4. AGI in excess of threshold	3,800
5. $3,800 (Line 4) ÷ 2,500 (1.52 rounded up to 2)	2
6. 2 (Line 5) × 2%	.04 (4%)
7. $12,000 (Line 1) × 4% (Line 6) is disallowed	480
8. Exemption deduction allowed (Line 1 less Line 7)	$11,520

Earning $3,800 over the phase-out threshold has cost Howard and Jessica a $480 deduction, which in their top 35% bracket (for 2002) is worth $168 (35% × $480). This $168 tax cost is in addition to the $1,330 regular tax on the excess earnings (35% × 3,800). The total tax liability attributed to the $3,800 earnings, or $1,498 ($1,330 + $168), represents an effective marginal tax rate of 39.42%:

$$\frac{\$1,498}{\$3,800} = 39.42\%$$

Law Alert

After 2005 Phaseout Reduced

Under the 2001 Tax Act, the phaseout of exemptions is to be gradually eliminated between 2006 and 2010.

PART 4

Personal Tax Computations

In this part, you will learn how to:

- **Figure your regular tax.** After claiming the standard deduction or itemized deductions *(13.1)* and deducting your allowable personal exemptions *(21.1)*, you figure your regular tax either by looking up the tax in the tax tables or by figuring the tax using the tax rate schedules; *see* Chapter 22.

- **Apply the alternative minimum tax.** If you have reduced your taxable income by certain deductions and tax benefits, you may be subject to the alternative minimum tax (AMT); for further details, *see* Chapter 23.

- **Figure estimated tax payments.** If you have investment and self-employment income, you generally have to pay quarterly estimated tax; *see* 27.1.

- **Compute the "kiddie tax."** If your child under age 14 has investment income exceeding $1,500, you must compute tax on that income as if it were your own. "Kiddie tax" rules are discussed in Chapter 24.

Chapter 22

Figuring Your Regular Income Tax Liability

There are two types of income tax rates: (1) regular rates, which apply to all taxpayers, and (2) alternative minimum tax (AMT) rates, which apply only if certain tax benefits, when added back to your income, result in an AMT tax that exceeds your regular tax.

Most taxpayers do not have to compute the regular tax. They find the tax for their income and filing status in IRS tax tables if their taxable income is less than $100,000. Tax rate schedules must be used to figure your regular income tax if taxable income is $100,000 or more. The tables and rate schedules are printed in Part 8 of this book.

The tax tables and tax rate schedules for 2002 reflect the 2001 Tax Act reductions to the tax rates, including the new 10% bracket.

Computation of the alternative minimum tax is more complicated and requires the preparation of Form 6251. AMT is discussed in Chapter 23.

22.1 Taxable Income

Your income tax liability is based on your taxable income. If your taxable income is less than $100,000, you must use the IRS tables to look up your tax; *see 22.2*. If your taxable income is $100,000 or more, you use the tax rate schedules to compute the tax; *see 22.3*. However, if you have net capital gains, you use the tax computation worksheet on Schedule D to figure your tax; *see 22.4*. Tax is figured on Form 8615 if the "kiddie tax" computation *(24.4)* must be made.

Taxable income is your adjusted gross income *(12.1)* minus the following: (1) your standard deduction or itemized deductions, whichever you claim (*see* Chapter 13), and (2) deductions for personal exemptions allowed under the rules discussed in Chapter 21. On Form 1040 for 2002, taxable income is entered on Line 41.

On Form 1040A and Form 1040EZ, the computation of taxable income generally takes fewer steps because only limited types of income and deductions may be reported. Itemized deductions may not be claimed. Personal exemptions for dependents may be claimed on Form 1040A but not on Form 1040EZ. *See* the table on page 7 for the types of income and deductions that may not be reported on these forms.

On Form 1040A for 2002, taxable income is entered on Line 27; on Form 1040EZ, it is on Line 6.

22.2 Using the Tax Tables

If you file Form 1040EZ or Form 1040A, you use the tax tables in Part 8 of this book to look up your regular income tax liability. If you file Form 1040, you also use the tax tables if your taxable income is *less* than $100,000; if your taxable income is $100,000 or more, you use the tax rate schedules shown in Part 8.

If you use the tax tables, you do not have to compute your tax mathematically. To use the tables you first figure your taxable income *(see 22.1)*, then turn to your income bracket and look for the tax liability listed in the column for your filing status. Filing status (single, married filing jointly, head of household, married filing separately, and qualifying widow(er)) is discussed in Chapter 1.

You may *not* use the tax tables and *must* use the schedules if you file for a short period (less than 12 months) due to a change of accounting period.

Estates and trusts may not use the tax tables.

Filing Instruction

Taxable Income Under $100,000

If you do not have net capital gains on Schedule D *(see 22.4)*, and are not using Form 8615 to compute the "kiddie tax" for a child under age 14 *(24.4)*, the IRS requires you to use the tax tables to determine the regular tax on your taxable income if it is less than $100,000. The tables are used even though in some cases the tax computed under the tax rate schedules is slightly lower.

EXAMPLES

1. You are single and have an adjusted gross income of $26,595 for 2002. You claim one personal exemption and the standard deduction.

Adjusted gross income		$26,595
Less: Standard deduction	$4,700	
Exemption	3,000	7,700
Taxable income		$18,895

   Your tax liability from the tax table is $2,531. The tax is shown in the column for single persons with taxable income of at least $18,850 but less than $18,900.

2. You are married filing jointly and have 2002 adjusted gross income of $36,400, itemized deductions of $7,900, and three exemptions.

Adjusted gross income		$36,400
Less: Itemized deductions	$7,900	
Exemptions (3 × $3,000)	9,000	16,900
Taxable income		$19,500

   Your tax liability from the tax table is $2,329.

22.3 Tax Rate Schedules

For 2002, there are six tax brackets: 10%, 15%, 27%, 30%, 35%, and 38.6%. *See* the tax rate schedules in Part 8 of this book. You compute your 2002 regular income tax using the tax rate schedules if your taxable income is $100,000 or more *or* you file for a short period due to a change of accounting period. *See 22.4* if you have net capital gains.

1. You file as a head of household with taxable income of $103,000 for 2002. You use Schedule Z to figure your tax.

Tax on first $96,700 (from Schedule Z)	$21,115.00
Tax on excess $6,300 at 30%	1,890.00
Total tax	$23,005.00

2. You are married and file a joint return with taxable income of $130,000 for 2002. You use Schedule Y-1 to figure your tax.

Tax on first $112,850 (from Schedule Y-1)	$24,265.50
Tax on excess $17,150 at 30%	5,145.00
Total tax	$29,410.50

22.4 Tax Calculation If You Have Long-Term Capital Gains

If a portion of your taxable income (see 22.1) consists of net capital gains (net long-term capital gains in excess of net short-term capital losses), you generally may take advantage of a favorable capital gains tax rate of 8% or 10% (if your regular top bracket is 15%) or 20% (if your regular top bracket exceeds 15%). Long-term gains on the sale of collectibles and the taxable part of gains on qualifying small business stock (5.7) are generally subject to a maximum rate of 27% (15% if that is your regular top bracket). You apply the capital gains rates and compute your regular income tax liability for the year by completing Schedule D (Form 1040) and attaching it to Form 1040. Part IV of Schedule D will lead you through the full calculations; see 5.3 and 5.7.

You generally do not have to compute your liability on Part IV of Schedule D if the only amounts you must report on Schedule D are capital gain distributions reported on Form 1099-DIV from mutual funds and real estate investment trusts (REITs). If the requirements discussed in Chapter 32 (see the "Key to Reporting Mutual-Fund Distributions") are met, your capital gain distributions may be entered on Line 13 of Form 1040 and the Capital Gain Tax Worksheet included in the Form 1040 instructions may be used to apply the capital gain rates and compute your regular income tax liability for 2002. If you file Form 1040A, the distribution is entered on Line 10 of Form 1040A and you apply the capital gain rates and figure your regular income tax liability on the worksheet printed in the instructions to Form 1040A.

22.5 Tax Credits

After applying the tax tables or rate schedules to get your regular tax liability, you may be able to reduce that liability as well as AMT liability (Chapter 23) by claiming tax credits. A new credit for retirement contributions is discussed below. The child credit, the dependent care credit, earned income credit, and adoption credit are discussed in Chapter 25. The education tax credits are discussed in Chapter 38. The credit for the elderly is discussed in Chapter 34 and the foreign tax credit in Chapter 36. The business tax credits are discussed in Chapter 40. Other tax credits that may reduce your liability are the mortgage interest credit (15.1) and the credit for prior year AMT (23.6).

If you worked for more than one employer in 2002 and Social Security taxes of more than $5,263.80 were withheld from your wages, the excess may be claimed as a credit in the "Payments" section of Form 1040; see 26.10.

Displaced worker's credit for health-care premiums (Form 8885). Certain workers who have lost their jobs due to foreign trade competition may claim a refundable tax credit for 65% of health-care premiums for continuing coverage (COBRA) or insurance in state-run programs. Premiums for individual health insurance policies qualify only if the taxpayer was covered under the plan for the 30-day period preceding the loss of employment. Certain retirees age 55 or older who are receiving benefits from the Pension Benefit Guaranty Corporation also qualify for the credit. Technical guidelines determine eligibility for the credit; see the instructions to Form 8885 for details. Starting in 2003, the credit will be paid to eligible taxpayers on an advance basis by the government.

District of Columbia first-time homebuyer credit (Form 8859). If you bought a home in the District of Columbia in 2002 and neither you nor your spouse owned a home in the District during the one-year period preceding your purchase, you may be entitled to a tax credit of up to $5,000 ($2,500 if married filing separately). On Form 8859, the credit is phased out for modified adjusted gross income between $70,000 and $90,000 if you are single or between $110,000 and $130,000 if married filing jointly.

Credit for qualified retirement savings contributions (saver's credit, Form 8880).
You may be eligible for the saver's tax credit if you made retirement plan contributions for 2002. To qualify, your adjusted gross income cannot exceed $50,000 if you are married filing jointly, $37,500 if you are a head of household, or $25,000 if you are single, married filing separately, or a qualified widow(er). Furthermore, you are ineligible if you were born after January 1, 1985, are claimed as a dependent on another taxpayer's 2002 return, or were a full-time student during five or more months in 2002.

Depending on your 2002 adjusted gross income, a credit percentage of 50%, 20%, or 10% applies, as shown in the following chart. Adjusted gross income is incresed by any exclusion for foreign earned income or income from Puerto rico or American Samoa, or foriegn housing exclusion or deduction.

Credit Rate	Adjusted Gross Income		
	Married, Joint	Head of Household	Others
50%	up to $30,000	up to $22,500	up to $15,000
20%	$30,001 – 32,500	$22,501 - $24,375	$15,001 – 16,250
10%	$32,501 – 50,000	$24,376 - $37,500	$16,251 – 25,000

The percentage applies to up to $2,000 of retirement contributions, $4,000 on a joint return. Eligible contributions include: (1) traditional IRA or Roth IRA contributions, (2) salary-reduction contributions to a 401(k) plan (including a SIMPLE 401(k), 403(b) plan, SIMPLE IRA, governmental Section 457 plan, or salary-reduction SEP, or (3) voluntary after-tax contributions to a qualified plan or 403(b) plan. However, the contributions must be reduced by taxable IRA or employer-plan distributions received from January 1, 2000, through April 15, 2003 (or later return due date if an extension is obtained), as well as all Roth IRA distributions received during the same period.

The credit is not refundable. It is limited to your tax liability (regular tax plus AMT, if any), reduced by certain other nonrefundable credits such as the dependent care credit or the Hope or Lifetime Learning credit.

Although the intent of the law was apparently to allow lower-income savers a maximum credit of $1,000, or $2,000 to married joint filers, it is impossible for anyone to obtain a $1,000 or $2,000 credit, given the way the credit is structured and the nonrefundable feature. Taxpayers eligible for the 50% credit bracket (adjusted gross income up to $15,000, $22,500, or $30,000, depending on filing status) will not have a high enough tax liability to absorb a $1,000 or $2,000 (joint return) credit.

Follow the instructions to Form 8880 to compute your allowable credit.

Chapter 23

Alternative Minimum Tax (AMT)

The purpose of AMT is to increase your tax if certain tax benefits result in a regular income tax that is lower than the tax that would apply if the benefits were added back to taxable income. You may owe AMT if you claimed:

- Itemized deductions, such as taxes, interest on home equity loans used for nonresidential purposes, medical expenses, and miscellaneous job and investment expenses.

- Certain tax-exempt interest, accelerated depreciation, and incentive stock option benefits.

- A substantial number of exemptions for dependents.

There are no specific tests to determine whether or not you are liable for AMT. You must first figure your regular income tax and then see whether tax benefit items must be added back to taxable income to figure alternative minimum taxable income, on which the AMT is figured. If after claiming the AMT exemption and applying the AMT rates of 26% and 28% the tentative alternative minimum tax exceeds your regular income tax, the excess is your AMT liability, which is added to the regular tax on your return.

AMT liability is figured on Form 6251 and is attached to Form 1040. If you file Form 1040A and report tax-exempt interest from private activity bonds subject to AMT, AMT liability, if any, is figured on a worksheet and the AMT is entered on the line for total tax on Form 1040A.

Key to AMT Rules

Item—	AMT Rule—
Tax rate	A 26% rate applies to AMT taxable income of $175,000 or less (after the AMT exemption), $87,500 or less if married filing separately. A 28% rate applies to AMT income exceeding the $175,000 or $87,500 threshold.
AMT taxable income	Regular taxable income without personal exemptions, increased or decreased by adjustments and increased by preferences.
AMT exemption	$49,000 if married filing a joint return (or a qualifying widow(er)); $35,750 if single or head of household; *or* $24,500 if married filing a separate return. Under a phase-out rule, these exemption amounts are reduced by 25¢ for each $1 that AMT taxable income (AMTI) exceeds $150,000 for joint filers or a qualifying widow(er), $112,500 if you file as a single person or head of household, and $75,000 for a married person filing separately. The exemption is completely phased out at $346,000 on a joint return and $255,500 on a single or head of household return. On a married person's separate return, the exemption is eliminated if AMT taxable income is $173,000 or more. Further, a married person filing separately must increase AMTI by 25% of AMTI exceeding $173,000.
AMT adjustments	Itemized deductions for taxes, certain interest, and most miscellaneous deductions are not allowed. Personal exemptions and the standard deduction are not allowed. MACRS depreciation is figured under the alternative MACRS system for real estate using 40-year straight-line recovery, and, for personal property, the 150% declining balance method. Incentive stock options; *see 23.2.* Mining exploration and development costs are allowable costs amortized over 10 years. For long-term contracts entered into after February 28, 1986, income is figured under the percentage-of-completion method. Pollution control facilities amortization is figured under alternate MACRS. Alternative tax net operating loss is allowed with adjustments. Circulation expenditures must be amortized ratably over three years. Research and experimental expenditures must be amortized ratably over 10 years. Passive activity losses are recomputed; certain tax-shelter farm losses may not be allowed.
AMT preference items	Tax-exempt interest from private activity bonds issued after August 7, 1986, *except* for qualifying 501(c)(3) bonds. Accelerated depreciation on real property and leased personal property placed in service before 1987—excess depreciation or amortization taken over straight-line deduction. If you sell qualified small business stock that qualifies for the 50% exclusion *(5.7)*, 42% of the excluded amount is an AMT preference item.
Adjusted gross income	In making AMT computations involving adjusted gross income limitations, use adjusted gross income as computed for regular tax purposes.
Partnership AMT	If you are a partner, include for AMT your distributive share of the partnership's adjustments and tax preference items. These are reported on Schedule K-1 (Form 1065). The partnership itself does not pay alternative minimum tax.
Trust or estate AMT	If you are a beneficiary of an estate or trust, consider for AMT your share of distributable net alternative minimum taxable income shown on Schedule K-1 (Form 1041). The estate or trust must pay tax on any remaining alternative minimum taxable income.
S corporation stockholder	If you are a shareholder, consider for AMT your share of the adjustments and tax preference items reported on Schedule K-1 (Form 1120-S).
Children subject to "kiddie tax"	Children under age 14 who are subject to the "kiddie tax" *(24.3)* may have to compute AMT liability on Form 6251. The 2002 AMT exemption for a child subject to the "kiddie tax" equals the child's earned income plus $5,500, but no more than the regular AMT $35,750 exemption for single persons.

23.1 Computing Alternative Minimum Tax on Form 6251

You use Form 6251 to compute AMT liability, if any. The checklist below gives an indication as to when you may have to use Form 6251. The checklist items are discussed at *23.2–23.5.*

If you check any of the items on the list, you should complete Form 6251 to determine if you are liable for AMT. These items are AMT adjustments and preferences and generally are added back to regular taxable income to calculate alternative minimum taxable income (AMTI).

AMTI is reduced by the allowable AMT exemption. Subject to the phase-out rule discussed in the "Key to AMT Rules" on the preceding page, the exemption is $35,750 if single or head of household, $49,000 if married filing jointly or qualifying widow(er), or $24,500 if married filing separately.

After reducing AMTI by the allowable exemption, a 26% AMT rate generally applies to the first $175,000 of AMT income ($87,500 if married filing separately), and a 28% rate applies to any balance of the AMT income. However, if you had net capital gains that qualify for reduced capital gains rates *(5.3)*, you apply the same capital gains rate for AMT purposes as for regular income tax purposes.

The resulting tax, less any AMT foreign tax credit, is the tentative AMT, which applies only to the extent it *exceeds* your regular income tax. For this purpose, regular income tax is the tax on your taxable income, without taking into account personal credits (such as the child tax credit or education credits), *minus* any special averaging tax on a lump-sum distribution or any regular foreign tax credit. The excess of tentative AMT over this regular tax, if any, is the AMT liability that you must report as an additional tax on Line 43 of Form 1040.

Follow the line-by-line instructions to Form 6251 to figure your AMT liability, if any.

Items subject to AMT: Check: ✓

1. Personal exemptions ❑
2. Standard deduction ❑
3. Itemized deductions for taxes, miscellaneous expenses, and medical expenses ❑
4. Interest on home equity debt used for nonresidential purposes ❑
5. Accelerated depreciation in excess of straight line ❑
6. Income from the exercise of incentive stock options ❑
7. Tax-exempt interest from private activity bonds ❑
8. Intangible drilling costs ❑
9. Depletion ❑
10. Circulation expenses ❑
11. Mining exploration and development costs ❑
12. Research and experimental costs ❑
13. Pollution control facility amortization ❑
14. Tax-shelter farm income or loss ❑
15. Passive income or loss ❑
16. Certain installment sale income ❑
17. Income from long-term contracts computed under percentage-of-income method ❑
18. Net operating loss deduction ❑
19. Foreign tax credit ❑
20. Investment expenses ❑
21. Gain on small business stock qualifying for 50% exclusion ❑

 Law Alert

2001 Tax Act Will Expose More Taxpayers to AMT

Even before the 2001 Tax Act, it was projected that over 12 million taxpayers would become subject to the AMT over the coming decade. The new tax law will increase the number by millions more. Since AMT is paid to the extent it exceeds regular income tax liability, and the 2001 Tax Act phases in income tax reductions without reducing AMT, apart from the minor AMT exemption increase, millions of taxpayers will not benefit from the 2001 Tax Act changes and will become subject to the AMT over the next 10 years unless Congress enacts AMT relief.

 Law Alert

Increase to AMT Exemption Is Temporary

The only AMT relief provided by the 2001 Tax Act is a small increase in the AMT exemption that lasts for four years. For the years 2001 through 2004 only, the AMT exemption increases to $49,000 from $45,000 for married couples filing jointly and qualifying widow(er)s. For single filers and heads of household, the exemption increases to $35,750 from $33,750. For married persons filing separately, the increase is to $24,500 from $22,500. Without further legislation, the exemption will fall back to the prior $45,000, $33,750, or $22,500 amount starting in 2005.

EXAMPLE

You are married filing jointly and for 2002 you have adjusted gross income of $135,000. You claim five personal exemptions. The starting point for figuring AMT on Form 6251 is the amount shown on Line 39 of Form 1040. This is $89,954, your AGI of $135,000 minus $45,046 of itemized deductions. Your personal exemptions are ignored for AMT purposes. The itemized deductions include $34,000 for state and local taxes and interest of $6,500 on a home equity mortgage loan used for nonresidential purposes (23.2). These deductions are adjustments for AMT purposes. You also have an MACRS depreciation adjustment of $1,000. Before figuring AMT on Form 6251, you complete Form 1040 and compute tax liability of $14,039 on taxable income of $74,954 ($135,000 AGI – $45,046 itemized deductions – $15,000 for five exemptions). You prepare Form 6251 (see below) and figure tentative minimum tax of $21,438. You must pay as AMT $7,399, the excess of the tentative minimum tax over the regular tax ($21,438–$14,039). You must pay the $7,399 in addition to your regular income tax. Enter the AMT on Line 43 of Form 1040.

Sample Form 6251

Form 6251

Department of the Treasury
Internal Revenue Service (99)

Alternative Minimum Tax—Individuals

▶ See separate instructions.

▶ Attach to Form 1040 or Form 1040NR.

OMB No. 1545-0227

2002

Attachment Sequence No. **32**

Name(s) shown on Form 1040

Your social security number

Part I — Alternative Minimum Taxable Income (See instructions for how to complete each line.)

1	If filing Schedule A (Form 1040), enter the amount from Form 1040, line 39, and go to line 2. Otherwise, enter the amount from Form 1040, line 36, and go to line 7. (If zero or less, enter as a negative amount.) **1**	**89,954**
2	Medical and dental. Enter the **smaller** of Schedule A (Form 1040), line 4, **or** 2½% of Form 1040, line 36 . **2**	
3	Taxes from Schedule A (Form 1040), line 9 . . . . **3**	**34,000**
4	Certain interest on a home mortgage **not** used to buy, build, or improve your home **4**	**6,500**
5	Miscellaneous deductions from Schedule A (Form 1040), line 26 . . . . **5**	
6	If Form 1040, line 36, is over $137,300 (over $68,650 if married filing separately), enter the amount from line 9 of the worksheet for Schedule A (Form 1040), line 28 . . . . **6** ( )	
7	Tax refund from Form 1040, line 10 or line 21 . . . . **7** ( )	
8	Investment interest expense (difference between regular tax and AMT) **8**	
9	Depletion (difference between regular tax and AMT) **9**	
10	Net operating loss deduction from Form 1040, line 21. Enter as a positive amount **10**	
11	Interest from specified private activity bonds exempt from the regular tax **11**	
12	Qualified small business stock (42% of gain excluded under section 1202) **12**	
13	Exercise of incentive stock options (excess of AMT income over regular tax income) **13**	
14	Estates and trusts (amount from Schedule K-1 (Form 1041), line 9) **14**	
15	Electing large partnerships (amount from Schedule K-1 (Form 1065-B), box 6) **15**	
16	Disposition of property (difference between AMT and regular tax gain or loss) **16**	
17	Depreciation on assets placed in service after 1986 (difference between regular tax and AMT) . . **17**	**1,000**
18	Passive activities (difference between AMT and regular tax income or loss) **18**	
19	Loss limitations (difference between AMT and regular tax income or loss) **19**	
20	Circulation costs (difference between regular tax and AMT) **20**	
21	Long-term contracts (difference between AMT and regular tax income) **21**	
22	Mining costs (difference between regular tax and AMT) **22**	
23	Research and experimental costs (difference between regular tax and AMT) **23**	
24	Income from certain installment sales before January 1, 1987 . . . . **24** ( )	
25	Intangible drilling costs preference **25**	
26	Other adjustments, including income-based related adjustments **26**	
27	Alternative tax net operating loss deduction . . . . **27** ( )	
28	**Alternative minimum taxable income.** Combine lines 1 through 27. (If married filing separately and line 28 is more than $173,000, see page 7 of the instructions) **28**	**131,454**

Part II — Alternative Minimum Tax

29 Exemption. (If this form is for a child under age 14, see page 7 of the instructions.)

IF your filing status is . . .	AND line 28 is not over . . .	THEN enter on line 29 . . .
Single or head of household	$112,500	$35,750
Married filing jointly or qualifying widow(er) . .	150,000	49,000
Married filing separately	75,000	24,500

If line 28 is **over** the amount shown above for your filing status, see page 7 of the instructions.

	29	**49,000**
30	Subtract line 29 from line 28. If zero or less, enter -0- here and on lines 33 and 35 and stop here . . **30**	**82,454**
31	• If you reported capital gain distributions directly on Form 1040, line 13, **or** you had a gain on both lines 16 and 17 of Schedule D (Form 1040) (as refigured for the AMT, if necessary), complete Part III on the back and enter the amount from line 57 here. **31**	**21,438**
	• **All others:** If line 30 is $175,000 or less ($87,500 or less if married filing separately), multiply line 30 by 26% (.26). Otherwise, multiply line 30 by 28% (.28) and subtract $3,500 ($1,750 if married filing separately) from the result.	
32	Alternative minimum tax foreign tax credit (see page 7 of the instructions) **32**	
33	Tentative minimum tax. Subtract line 32 from line 31 . . . . **33**	**21,438**
34	Tax from Form 1040, line 42 (minus any tax from Form 4972 and any foreign tax credit from Form 1040, line 45) **34**	**14,039**
35	**Alternative minimum tax.** Subtract line 34 from line 33. If zero or less, enter -0-. Enter here and on Form 1040, line 43 . . . . **35**	**7,399**

For Paperwork Reduction Act Notice, see page 8 of the instructions.   Cat. No. 13600G   Form **6251** (2002)

23.2 Adjustments for AMT

The starting point for figuring AMT is your adjusted gross income from Form 1040. This amount will generally be increased by adjustments on Form 6251.

Standard deduction or itemized deductions. If you claimed the standard deduction for regular tax purposes, the deduction is disregarded when figuring AMT liability; *see* the Filing Instruction on this page.

If you claimed itemized deductions for state and local taxes or miscellaneous deductions subject to the 2% AGI floor, you must add back all of such deductions to your regular taxable income (prior to personal exemptions) in order to figure alternative minimum taxable income.

If medical expenses in excess of the 7.5% AGI floor are deducted for regular tax purposes, you must add back to income on Form 6251 the smaller of the allowable medical deduction from Schedule A or 2.5% of adjusted gross income. The effect of this adjustment is to allow medical expenses as an AMT deduction only to the extent that they exceed 10% of AGI.

Taxes directly deductible from gross income for business or rental purposes remain deductible for AMT purposes.

If claimed for regular income tax purposes, the following itemized deductions are also allowed for AMT; they are not added back to regular taxable income when figuring alternative minimum taxable income (AMTI).

- Charitable contributions
- Casualty and theft losses exceeding 10% of AGI
- Wagering losses
- Claim of right deduction; *see 2.9.*
- Estate-tax deductions for income in respect of a decedent
- Impairment-related work expenses
- Home mortgage interest is allowed for AMT purposes with this exception: interest on home equity debt, taken out after June 30, 1982, where the loan was not used to buy, build, or substantially improve your first or second home (*see* below).
- Investment interest to the extent of net investment income

The 3% reduction for itemized deductions at *13.7* does not apply for AMT purposes.

Mortgage interest. Less interest may be deductible for AMT purposes than for regular tax purposes. No AMT adjustment is required for home mortgage interest paid on a debt incurred to buy, construct, or substantially rehabilitate your principal residence or qualifying second residence. The residence may be a house, apartment, cooperative apartment, condominium, or mobile home not used on a transient basis.

Interest on a mortgage taken out after June 30, 1982 is not deductible for AMT purposes if the proceeds are used for any purpose other than to buy, build, or substantially improve your principal or second residence. Furthermore, in the case of a mortgage refinanced after June 30, 1982, interest is deductible for AMT purposes only to the extent the new debt does not exceed the amount of the old debt immediately before the refinancing. Interest on the excess is not deductible for AMT purposes.

Interest on a mortgage debt incurred before July 1, 1982, for any purpose qualifies for an AMT deduction if the mortgage was secured by your principal residence or any other home used by you or a family member at the time the mortgage was taken out.

If an interest deduction is claimed on Schedule A for debt that does not qualify under these AMT rules, that interest is added back as an adjustment on Form 6251.

State and local taxes. State and local taxes deducted on Schedule A must be added back to taxable income in figuring AMT. If you received in 2002 a refund of state taxes deducted in a prior year, you enter the refund on Form 6251 as a negative adjustment that reduces taxable income in arriving at AMT taxable income.

MACRS depreciation. Depreciation allowed for AMT may differ from that allowed for regular tax purposes. However, there is no adjustment for property placed in service after September 10, 2001, that qualifies for the special depreciation allowance (*see 42.20*). For tangible personal property (such as cars or furniture) placed in service after 1986 and before 1999, the AMT depreciation rate is the 150% declining balance method over the alternative depreciation system recovery periods (ADS; *see 42.9*). For tangible personal property placed in service after 1998 other than property qualifying after

Filing Instruction

Standard Deduction and Exemptions Disallowed for AMT

If you claimed the standard deduction instead of itemizing deductions on Form 1040, you may not claim the standard deduction as an AMT deduction. Exemptions for yourself and your dependents are also not allowed for AMT purposes. The standard deduction and personal exemptions are disallowed by using adjusted gross income as the starting point for figuring AMT on Form 6251.

Court Decision

10 Children Subject Parents to AMT

A married couple found themselves paying AMT tax when their regular tax deduction of 12 personal exemptions for themselves and their 10 children was disregarded for AMT purposes. In the Tax Court, they argued that AMT was not intended to apply to taxpayers merely because they had large families. The Tax Court disagreed. Congress specifically wrote the law considering the effect of personal exemptions on AMT tax liability. The Tenth Circuit appeals court, although more sympathetic to the couple, agreed with the Tax Court that their situation fit within the AMT rules.

September 10, 2001, for the special depreciation allowance *(42.20)*, the 150% declining balance rate applies over the general depreciation system (GDS) recovery periods of three, five, seven, or 10 years *(42.4)*. Real property acquired after 1986 is depreciated for AMT over a 40-year period using the straight-line method. Depreciation deductions for films, videotapes, and sound recordings under the unit-of-production method or other method not based on a term of years are not adjusted under AMT.

If, for regular tax purposes, you use the regular 200% declining balance method to depreciate business equipment with a recovery period of three, five, seven, or 10 years, the difference between the regular depreciation and the 150% rate for AMT is an adjustment unless the property qualifies for the special depreciation allowance *(42.20)*. For real estate, the adjustment is the difference between the straight-line depreciation claimed for regular tax purposes using the recovery period discussed at *42.13* and the straight-line recovery over the AMT 40-year recovery period.

The adjustment for MACRS may result in providing more depreciation for AMT purposes where the AMT depreciation computation towards the latter part of the useful life of the property provides larger deductions than the regular MACRS deduction.

EXAMPLE

In one taxable year when AMT applies, Jones has two assets acquired after 1986. The regular MACRS depreciation for Asset A is $500 and for Asset B, $400. When applying the AMT rules, the depreciation for Asset A is $400 and for Asset B, $450. AMT taxable income is increased by $50. The adjustment accounts for post-1987 MACRS property held in the current year.

Asset A		
Regular depreciation	$500	
AMT depreciation	400	$100
Asset B		
Regular depreciation	$400	
AMT depreciation	450	(50)
Net adjustment to AMT		
Taxable income		$50

Property placed in service before 1987, unless it qualifies under the MACRS transitional rules, is subject to prior law tax preference rules. Prior law creates tax preference items when the ACRS deduction exceeds regular straight-line depreciation; *see 23.3*. A tax preference item always increases AMT taxable income.

Basis adjustment affects AMT gain or loss. When post-1986 depreciable assets are sold, gain for AMT purposes is figured on the basis of the property as adjusted by depreciation claimed for AMT purposes. This gain or loss will be different from the gain or loss figured for regular tax purposes where regular MACRS depreciation was used. (This AMT basis rule does not apply to property placed in service before 1987 except for transitional property within the post-1986 rules).

Similarly, recalculations of basis and gain are made for prior AMT adjustments taken for circulation expenditures, research and experimental expenditures, pollution control facilities, and mining exploration and development costs.

Incentive stock option (ISO). For regular tax purposes, you are not taxed when you exercise an incentive stock option (ISO); *see 2.17*. However, the exercise of an ISO can result in a substantial AMT liability. You generally must increase AMT income by including on Line 13 of Form 6251 the excess, if any, of:

1. The fair market value of the stock acquired through exercise of the option (determined without regard to any lapse restriction) when your rights in the acquired stock first become transferable or when these rights are no longer subject to a substantial risk of forfeiture, over

2. The amount you paid for the stock, including any amount you paid for the ISO used to acquire the stock.

If your rights in the acquired ISO stock are not transferable and are subject to a substantial risk of forfeiture, you do *not* have to report any adjustment for AMT. However, you may elect to include in AMT income for that year the excess of the stock's fair market value (determined without regard to any lapse restriction) over the exercise price upon the transfer to you of the stock acquired through exercise of the option. The election must be made no later than 30 days after the date of transfer; *see* the discussion of the Section 83(b) election at *2.18*.

 Caution

Selling ISO Stock to Avoid AMT Adjustment

If you exercise an incentive stock option and your rights in the acquired stock are transferable and not subject to a substantial risk of forfeiture, you have to treat as an AMT adjustment the excess of the fair-market value of the stock when the option was exercised over the option price. Unless you sell the stock by the end of that same year, you must report an AMT adjustment based on the value of the stock when the option was exercised, *even if* the value later declines substantially. You avoid the AMT adjustment if you sell the stock in the same year the option was exercised.

Note: If you acquire stock by exercising an ISO and you dispose of that stock in the *same* year, the tax treatment under the regular tax and the AMT is the same. No AMT adjustment is required.

If you report an AMT adjustment for stock acquired through the exercise of an ISO, increase the AMT basis of the stock by the amount of the adjustment. Since the AMT basis in stock acquired through an ISO is likely to differ from your regular tax basis, keep records for both AMT and regular tax purposes in order to figure your adjusted gain or loss in the year you sell the stock.

Mining exploration and development costs. The deduction allowed for regular tax purposes for mining exploration and development costs is amortized ratably over a 10-year period for AMT purposes.

If a mine is abandoned as worthless, all mining exploration and development costs that have not been written off are deductible in the year of abandonment.

Long-term contracts. The use of the completed contract method of accounting or certain other methods of accounting for long-term contracts is generally not allowable. For AMT, the percentage of completion method must be used. However, there is an exception for home construction contracts.

Amortization of certified pollution control facilities. For purposes of the alternative minimum tax, the amortization deduction for a certified pollution control facility placed in service after 1986 is determined under alternative MACRS; *see 42.9.*

Research and experimental expenditures. Costs are amortized over 10 years if incurred in a business in which you are not a material participant.

Passive tax-shelter farm losses. Generally, no AMT loss is deductible for any tax-shelter farm activity. A tax-shelter farm activity is any farming syndicate or any farming activity in which you do not materially participate. You may be treated as a material participant if a member of your family materially participates or you meet certain retirement or disability tests discussed at *10.6.*

Gains and losses reported for regular tax purposes from tax-shelter farm activities must be refigured by taking into account any AMT adjustments and preferences. However, a refigured loss is not allowed for AMT purposes except to the extent that you are insolvent at the end of the year. This means that you deduct the loss to the extent of your insolvency. Insolvency is the excess of liabilities over fair market value of assets. Any AMT-disallowed loss is carried forward to later years in which there is gain from that same activity, or until you dispose of the activity.

Passive losses from nonfarming activities. These are adjusted for preference or adjustment items not allowed for AMT purposes. For example, an adjustment for MACRS depreciation is made directly against the passive loss and is not treated as a separate AMT adjustment item. The loss allowed for AMT purposes is increased by the amount by which you are insolvent at the end of the year. *See* the instructions to Form 6251, which suggest that the AMT adjustment of passive losses be figured on a separate Form 8582 that you do not file.

23.3 Tax Preference Items

The following are tax preference items that increase the amount of 2002 AMT taxable income.

Tax-exempt interest on nonessential private activity bonds. For AMT purposes, you must include as a tax preference item the tax-exempt interest on qualified private activity bonds issued after August 7, 1986, except for qualified 501(c)(3) bonds used to benefit tax-exempt groups. Generally, private activity bonds issued after August 7, 1986, are subject to AMT, but for certain bonds meeting specific tests, the AMT rule applies to bonds issued on or after September 1, 1986. Interest paid on buying or carrying such bonds is deductible for AMT purposes.

> **EXAMPLE**
>
> You received $5,000 interest income from a private activity bond issued in 1992. You also had $100 of investment expense related to this bond. You enter $4,900 on Form 6251.

Exclusion on qualifying small business stock. If you sell small business stock qualifying for the 50% exclusion *(5.7),* 42% of the excluded amount, or 21% of the total gain (21% = 42% of 50% exclusion), is treated as an AMT preference item.

Planning Reminder

Incentive Stock Options

Your AMT basis in stock acquired through the exercise of an ISO is increased by the amount of the required AMT adjustment. Keep basis records for both AMT and regular tax purposes, since in the year the stock is sold, the gain reportable for AMT purposes should reflect the basis adjustment.

Caution

Passive Activity Losses

The law for AMT distinguishes between farm and nonfarm activities. Generally, no tax sheltered farm loss is deductible for AMT unless you are insolvent at the end of the year or the entire interest is disposed of.

Accelerated depreciation of property acquired before 1987. For real property placed in service before 1987, the difference between the depreciation that would have been allowable if the straight-line method had been used and accelerated depreciation claimed on real property during the taxable year is a tax preference item. The excess is computed separately for each asset depreciated through an accelerated method. For example, if you use ACRS 15-year, 18-year, or 19-year accelerated rates for regular tax purposes, figure the deduction for each such property under the straight-line method and report the excess of your regular tax deduction over the straight-line amount as a preference item.

For personal property leased to others before 1987, the preference item is the excess of the regular tax deduction over the depreciation that would have been allowed under the straight-line method, without regard to salvage value. The excess is computed separately for each asset. For 10-year property, a 15-year recovery period is used.

Note: See 23.2 for the MACRS adjustment rules for post-1986 assets.

Oil and gas preference items. Independent oil and gas producers and royalty owners do not have to compute preference items for excess percentage depletion deductions. Excess intangible drilling costs (IDC) are generally not treated as a preference item unless they exceed 40% of AMT income; *see* the instructions to Form 6251.

23.4 Net Operating Losses

A net operating loss (NOL) claimed for regular tax purposes must be recomputed for AMT after all other AMT adjustments and preference items are taken into account. The alternative tax net operating loss deduction allowed for AMT purposes is generally the amount of the regular net operating loss except that in figuring the nonbusiness deduction adjustment *(40.19)* only AMT itemized deductions are taken into account. Thus, for AMT purposes, state and local taxes and certain interest that are not allowable AMT deductions do not reduce nonbusiness income in figuring the alternative tax net operating loss deduction.

Under the Job Creation and Worker Assistance Act of 2002, an NOL for 2001 or 2002 that is carried back to prior years, or an NOL carryforward to 2001 or 2002, offsets 100% of AMTI. Prior law limited the alternative tax net operating loss deduction to 90% of AMTI (before taking into account the NOL). *See* the instructions to Line 27 of Form 6251 for further details on computing the alternative tax net operating loss deduction.

23.5 AMT Foreign Tax Credit

A revised foreign tax credit based on the foreign tax source AMT income may be claimed on Line 32 of Form 6251 as a reduction to tentative AMT. The AMT foreign tax credit may not offset more than 90% of AMT tax determined without regard to the foreign tax credit and alternative tax net operating loss deduction. Any foreign tax credit not allowed by the limit may be carried back and forward; *see* the instructions to Form 6251 for further details. The foreign tax credit is the only tax credit allowed in computing AMT.

23.6 AMT Tax Credit From Regular Tax

You may be able to reduce your regular 2002 tax by a tax credit based on prior year AMT taxes. The credit, which is computed on Form 8801, may be applied against your 2002 regular tax after deducting personal and general business credits. However, the tax credit is allowed only if your regular 2002 tax liability exceeds 2002 tentative alternative minimum tax liability computed on Form 6251. Follow the instructions to Form 8801.

23.7 Avoiding AMT

If you are within the range of the AMT tax, review periodically your income and expenses to determine whether to make certain tax elections, accelerate income, and/or defer the payment of expenses.

There are elections, such as the election of alternative straight-line MACRS depreciation, that may avoid AMT adjustments. However, such elections will increase your regular tax. Similarly, adjustment treatment for mining exploration and development costs, circulation expenses, and research expenses can be avoided by elections to amortize; *see 23.2*.

The following steps may also avoid or soften the impact of the AMT tax:

- Defer deductible expense items to a later year in which your income will be subject to regular tax rates exceeding your AMT tax rate (either 26% or 28% depending on your AMT income). Consider deferring payment of home mortgage interest and medical expenses. You will get a larger tax benefit from the deductions in the later year. In the case of unimproved real estate, consider an election to capitalize taxes and carry charges. Also, do not elect first-year expensing of business equipment.

- Defer if possible the exercise of an incentive stock option to a later year when you are not subject to AMT. The bargain element of an incentive stock option is an adjustment item subject to AMT. This is the difference between the option price and the fair market price of the stock on the date of exercise. If you exercise the option and it is subject to AMT as discussed in *23.2*, you may find yourself with an unexpected liability and short of liquid funds to meet your tax liability. To limit the adjustment item, you may stagger the exercise of options over more than one year.

Accelerating income. If you find that you will be subject to AMT in a current year, you may want to subject additional income in that year to the 26% or 28% AMT tax rate. In such a case, consider accelerating the receipt of income to that year. If you are in business, you might ask for earlier payments from customers or clients. If you control a small corporation, you might prepay salary or pay larger bonuses. But here be careful not to run afoul of reasonable compensation rules. You might also consider paying dividends.

 *Planning Reminder*

Accelerating Income

If you decide to accelerate income to a year in which you are subject to AMT, and you hold tax-deferred savings certificates with a maturity of one year or less, you might consider an early redemption to the current year. But here weigh the penalty cost of an early forfeiture. Similarly, you might make an early sale of U.S. Treasury bills to the current year.

Chapter 24

Computing the "Kiddie Tax" for Children Under Age 14

For 2002, investment income over $1,500 earned by a child under age 14 is taxed at the child's parent's tax rate. The child's parent or legal representative generally makes this tax computation, which is nicknamed the "kiddie tax."

The kiddie tax applies only to investment income, such as interest, dividends, rents, royalties, and profits on the sale of property. Income from wages and self-employment is not subject to the kiddie tax.

As the child's parent, you generally must use Form 8615 to report the income of a child under age 14. On Form 8615, the kiddie tax rules are applied and the tax is reported on the child's personal income tax return; *see 24.4.* The Form 8615 computation has no effect on the treatment of items on your own return or on your tax computation. You may instead elect on Form 8814 to report the child's investment income on your own return, provided the child received only interest and dividend income. If you elect on Form 8814 to report the child's investment income on your own return, your adjusted gross income will increase and this could adversely affect your right to claim various deductions; *see 24.5.*

If you are married but file separately, the parent with the larger amount of taxable income is responsible for the kiddie tax computation. If parents are divorced, separated, unmarried, or living apart for the last six months of the year, the parent who has custody of the child for the greater part of 2002 computes the tax. If a child cannot get tax information directly from a parent, the legal representative of the child may ask the IRS for the necessary information.

24.1 Filing Your Child's Return

To discourage substantial income splitting of investment income between parents and minor children, the tax law has complicated income reporting for parents and children by—

1. Imposing a "kiddie tax" that taxes a child's investment income over an annual floor ($1,500 for 2002) at the parent's tax bracket if the child is under 14 years of age at the end of the taxable year; *see 24.3.*
2. Barring a dependent child from claiming a personal exemption on his or her own tax return.
3. Limiting the standard deduction for a dependent child who has only investment income. For 2002 the deduction is $750; *see 13.5.*

Does your child have to file? For a child who can be claimed as a dependent, the income filing threshold is generally $750. If your dependent child has gross income (earned and investment income) of $750 or less for 2002, he or she is not subject to tax and does not have to file a tax return.

A 2002 return must be filed for a dependent child with investment income exceeding $250 and gross income of more than $750. If a dependent child has salary or other earned income but no investment income, a return does not have to be filed unless such earned income exceeds $4,700 in 2002. If your child's only income is from interest and dividends, you may be able to make an election to report the income on your own return; *see 24.5.*

Although a dependent child may not claim a personal exemption on his or her 2002 tax return, the child is allowed to claim at least a $750 standard deduction. A dependent child with earned income over $750 may claim a standard deduction up to those earnings plus an additional $250, but no more than the basic standard deduction, which is generally $4,700; *see 13.1.*

How to file a 2002 return for your child. If your child was under age 14 as of January 1, 2003, and had investment income of $1,500 or less, follow the regular filing rules and use Form 1040EZ, 1040A, or Form 1040 to report the child's income and deductions. The "kiddie tax" computation does not apply, so all of the child's income will be taxed at his or her own tax rate. If your child is unable to sign his or her tax return, you must do so; *see 1.13.*

If your child's investment income exceeded $1,500, the kiddie tax computation applies; *see 24.3.* Form 8615 must be filed to compute the kiddie tax unless your child's only income is interest and dividends and you elect to report your child's investment earnings on your own return as discussed at *24.5.* On Form 8615 you must provide your tax identification number and taxable income. Form 8615 is attached to the child's tax return; *see 24.4.*

If your child was age 14 or older as of January 1, 2003, your child should file Form 1040EZ, 1040A, or 1040, depending on the type of income and deductions he or she has. The special kiddie tax rules do not apply.

Child's AMT liability. A child who has substantial tax-exempt interest, tax preferences, or tax adjustments subject to the alternative minimum tax must compute tentative AMT liability on Form 6251; *see Chapter 23.*

24.2 Children Not Subject to the "Kiddie Tax"

For 2002 returns, the "kiddie tax" computation does *not* apply to—

- A child who was 14 years old or over on January 1, 2003.
- A child who on January 1, 2003, was under age 14 and who had 2002 gross investment income of $1,500 or less. The kiddie tax computation applies only to investment income exceeding $1,500. Furthermore, children who itemize deductions may in some cases exempt more than $1,500 from the computation; *see 24.3.*
- A child under age 14 if neither parent was alive at the end of 2002.

Filing Instruction

Child 14 or Over
The "kiddie tax" does not apply to a child who was 14 years old or older on January 1, 2003.

EXAMPLES

1. At the end of 2002, your son, whom you claim as your dependent, is age 14. He has interest income of $1,400 and salary income of $950 from his part-time job. His standard deduction is $1,200, the greater of earned income plus $250 *(see 13.5)* or $750. No personal exemption may be claimed. Assuming he has no itemized deductions, taxable income is $1,150 ($2,350 gross income – $1,200 standard deduction). The kiddie tax computation based on your top rate does not apply because your son is at least age 14 at the end of the year.

> 2. In 2002, your five-year-old daughter has interest income of $850. Taxable income of
> $100 is subject to tax at her own tax rate.
>
> | | |
> |---|---|
> | Interest income | $850 |
> | *Less:* standard deduction | 750 |
> | Taxable income | $100 |
>
> The kiddie tax computation does not apply because investment income does not exceed $1,500.

24.3 Children Under Age 14 Subject to the "Kiddie Tax"

The "kiddie tax" is a tax on a child's investment income at the parent's tax rate where the child's rate is lower. It applies for 2002 returns to a child who—

- Was under age 14 on January 1, 2003;
- Had either parent alive at the end of 2002; *and*
- Had investment income for 2002 exceeding $1,500. For a child who has itemized deductions of more than $750 that are directly connected to the production of investment income, the $1,500 exemption is increased, as explained below.

Figuring kiddie tax on child's or parent's return. The kiddie tax computation is generally made on Form 8615, which must be attached to your child's return. Sample Forms 8615 are at the end of this chapter. However, if the only income of your child who is under age 14 is interest and dividends and other tests are met, you may elect on Form 8814 to include your child's investment income on your own tax return, instead of computing the kiddie tax on Form 8615; *see 24.5.*

Kiddie tax on Form 8615 applies to investment income exceeding $1,500 floor. If your child files his or her own return, the "kiddie tax" computation on Form 8615 applies to the child's *net investment income*. For purposes of this rule, *net investment income* equals gross investment income minus $1,500 if your child does not itemize deductions on Schedule A. Thus, if your child does not itemize, the first $1,500 of investment income is exempt from the special computation. Investment income exceeding $1,500 is considered net investment income subject to the special computation; *see* Example 3 on the following page.

Gross investment income includes all taxable income that is not compensation for personal services. Include interest income, unless it is tax-exempt interest, dividends, capital gains, royalties, rents, and taxable pension payments. Payments from a trust are also included to the extent of distributable net income. Income in custodial accounts is treated as the child's income and is subject to the kiddie tax computation. Capital losses first offset capital gains, and any excess loss offsets up to $3,000 of other investment income.

Investment earnings on all of your child's property must be considered, even if the property was a gift from you or someone else, or if the property was produced from your child's wages, such as a bank account into which the wages were deposited. The wages themselves, or self-employment earnings, are not considered.

If your child does itemize deductions, and has more than $750 of deductions that are directly connected to the production of investment income, the $1,500 floor is increased. The floor is $750 plus the directly connected deductions. If the directly connected deductions are $750 or less, the regular $1,500 kiddie tax exemption applies, as in Example 4 on the following page. Directly connected itemized deductions are expenses paid to produce or collect income or to manage, conserve, or maintain income-producing property. Only the part of the total expenses exceeding the 2% AGI floor may be deducted. These expenses include custodian fees and service charges, service fees to collect interest and dividends, and investment counsel fees. If, after you subtract the itemized deductions, your child's net investment income exceeds his or her taxable income, you apply the tax to the lower taxable income, rather than to the net investment income.

EXAMPLES

(In all the following Examples, assume the child is your dependent for 2002 and under age 14 on January 1, 2003.)

1. The child has interest income of $480 and no other income for 2002. The child has no income tax liability and does not have to file a return.

Interest income	$480
Less: standard deduction	480
	0

Filing Tip

Investment Income Exceeding $1,500

You do not have to concern yourself with the kiddie tax computation if your child under age 14 had investment income of $1,500 or less for 2002. If investment income exceeded $1,500, the excess is subject to your top marginal tax rate, rather than your child's tax rate, under the computation on Form 8615.

Filing Tip

Floor Increase

If your child itemizes deductions and has more than $750 of deductions connected to the production of investment income, the $1,500 floor is increased to $750 plus the directly connected deductions.

2. The child has interest and dividend income of $950 and no other income for 2002. A standard deduction of $750 may be claimed. The balance of $200 is taxed at the child's regular tax bracket. Form 8615 does not have to be filed and the kiddie tax computation does not apply since investment income does not exceed $1,500.

3. For 2002, the child has dividend income of $1,850. After taking into account a standard deduction of $750, taxable income is $1,100, of which $350 is subject to the kiddie tax computation based on the parent's top tax bracket on Form 8615.

   Figuring taxable income:

Dividend income	$1,850
Less: standard deduction	750
	$1,100

Income subject to tax at parent's rate:	
Investment income	$1,850
Less: $1,500	1,500
	$350

   An example of the actual Form 8615 computation is at *24.4.* As an alternative to computing kiddie tax on $350 on Form 8615, the parent may elect to report the child's dividend income on his or her own return; *see 24.5.*

4. The child has $300 of wages and $1,750 of dividends and mutual-fund capital gain distributions for 2002. On Schedule A, the child claims itemized deductions of $400 related to investment income after the 2% AGI floor. The child also has $400 of other itemized deductions. Itemized deductions of $800 are claimed; they exceed the $750 standard deduction.

   Figuring taxable income:

Gross income	$2,050
Less: itemized deductions	800
Taxable income	$1,250

Income subject to tax at parent's rate:	
Investment income	$1,750
Less: greater of (1) $1,500 or (2) the sum of $750 and directly related expenses of $400	1,500
Net investment income subject to tax at parent's rate on Form 8615 *(24.4); see 24.5* for parent's alternative election	$250

24.4 Computing "Kiddie Tax" on Child's Return

If your child is subject to the "kiddie tax" under *24.3*, the tax is computed on Form 8615, which is attached to his or her return, unless you make the parent's election at *24.5*. Before your child's Form 8615 can be completed, your own taxable income must be determined. The amount to be entered on Form 8615 as the parent's taxable income depends on the parent's marital and filing status.

If the parents file a *joint return*, their joint taxable income is entered on Form 8615, along with the net investment income *(24.3)* of all their children under age 14. If the parents file *separate returns*, the larger of the parents' separate taxable incomes is used on the child's Form 8615.

Where parents are legally separated or divorced and custody of the child is shared, Form 8615 should be completed using the taxable income of the parent who has custody for the greater part of the year. If parents are married but living apart, and the custodial parent qualifies as unmarried under Test 1 at *1.12*, that parent's taxable income is used on Form 8615. If the custodial parent is not considered unmarried, the income of the parent with the larger taxable income is used. If the custodial parent has remarried and files a joint return with a new spouse, their joint return taxable income is used on the child's Form 8615. If the parents were never married but they live together with the child, the income of the parent with the larger taxable income is used; if the parents live apart, the income of the parent with custody for most of the year is used on Form 8615.

More than one child subject to kiddie tax. You file a separate Form 8615 for each child and on each form net investment income of all the children subject to the tax is included. The computed tax is allocated to each of your children, according to his or her share of their combined net investment income. This computation is incorporated in the steps of Form 8615 and by following the order of the form, you will make the proper allocation.

Planning Reminder

Prepare Your Return First
Before your child can complete Form 8615, or you prepare it for the child, your own taxable income must be determined.

As parents, the kiddie tax computation on Form 8615 does not affect your tax liability or the way you compute any limitation on deductions or credits. For example, the addition of the child's net investment income to your taxable income on Form 8615 does *not* affect the adjusted gross income floors for purposes of figuring your deduction for IRA contributions, medical expenses, or miscellaneous expenses.

> **EXAMPLE**
>
> For 2002, Bill and Betty Brown each file Form 1040A. Bill, age 12, has dividend income of $2,200; Betty, age 10, has $1,600. They each claim a standard deduction of $750. Neither may claim a personal exemption because they are claimed as dependents by their parents, Tom and Lilli Brown. Bill's taxable income after claiming the standard deduction is $1,450. Betty's is $850.
>
> Tom and Lilli Brown do not make the election *(24.5)* to report Bill's and Betty's dividends on their joint return. Forms 8615 are prepared and attached to the children's Forms 1040A, because each child is under age 14 and has more than $1,500 of investment income.
>
> Tom and Lilli report taxable income of $52,000 on their 2002 joint return. They use the IRS tax tables to look up their tax (the tables are in Part 8 at the back of this book). The tax on $52,000 is $7,843. The special computation on Form 8615 does not increase their joint return tax; it determines only the amount of Bill's and Betty's tax.
>
> As shown at the end of this chapter on sample Forms 8615, Bill's 2002 tax is $265 and Betty's 2002 tax is $103. If the special computation did not apply, Bill's 2002 tax would be $146 and Betty's tax would be $86. Thus, as a result of the special computation, the total tax bill for the children is increased by $136 ($368 – $232).

Planning Reminder

Estimating Tax on Form 8615
If you are unable to file your 2002 return by April 15, 2003, but your child's return is filed by the April 15 deadline, the child's Form 8615 may be based on an estimate of your tax liability. When you have the completed income information, file an amended return.

Estimating the kiddie tax in case of filing delay. If you are unable to file your return by April 15, 2003, the child's tax on Form 8615 may be based on an estimate. You may make a reasonable estimate of your taxable income on Form 8615 or may estimate the net investment income of children under age 14 if that information is not yet available. When you have the complete income details, file an amended return.

A reasonable estimate may be based on your 2001 taxable income and the 2001 investment income of the child. If a refund is due, the IRS will pay interest from April 15, 2003, or, if the return was filed late, from the filing date. If additional tax is due on the amended return, interest will be charged from April 15, but no penalty will be imposed.

24.5 Parent's Election To Report Child's Dividends and Interest

Instead of filing a separate return for your child *(24.4)* whose income is subject to the "kiddie tax," you may elect on Form 8814 to compute the kiddie tax on your return if all of the following tests are met:

- The child's income is only from interest and dividends (including mutual-fund capital gain distributions and Alaska Permanent Fund dividends);
- The total interest and dividends are over $750 but less than $7,500;
- Estimated tax payments were not made in the child's name and Social Security number for 2002, and there was no overpayment from the child's 2001 return applied to his or her 2002 estimated tax; *and*
- The child was not subject to 2002 backup withholding.

By making this election, and following the steps of Form 8814, you include in your income the child's interest and dividends to the extent they exceed $1,500. You also figure an additional tax equal to the smaller of $75 or 10% of your child's income over $750.

If parents are divorced, separated, unmarried, or living apart for the last six months of the year, the parent whose taxable income would be taken into account on Form 8615 *(24.4)* is the parent who may elect to report the income on his or her own return.

In figuring whether you owe alternative minimum tax (AMT), you must include as a tax preference item interest income your child receives from specified private activity bonds; *see 23.3* and Form 6251 instructions.

Should you make the election? The only advantage in making the election is to skip the paperwork involved in preparing a return in the child's name or returns in your children's names. This could save you money in the form of reduced tax preparation costs. However, including the child's income as your own increases your AGI, which may create these disadvantages:

- Subject you to the exemption phaseout *(21.16)* and 3% reduction computation *(13.7)* for itemized deductions.
- Make it more difficult to deduct job expenses and other miscellaneous itemized deductions, which are subject to a 2% AGI floor *(19.1)*, and medical deductions, subject to a 7.5% AGI floor *(17.1)*.
- Limit a deduction for IRA contributions under the phase-out rules *(8.4)*.
- Limit your ability to claim the special $25,000 rental loss allowance under the passive activity rules *(10.2)*.
- Increase local and state tax liability.

Finally, if you elect to report the child's income on your own return, you may not claim any deductions that your child would have been able to claim on his or her return such as investment expenses or a penalty on premature withdrawals from a savings account. On the other hand, reporting your child's interest or dividends increases your net investment income, which may allow you to claim a larger deduction for investment interest; *see 15.10*. Also, your ceiling for charitable donations may be increased. If you plan to report your child's income on your 2003 return, provide for the tax in your estimated tax payments or withholdings during 2003.

Caution

Reporting Child's Income on Your Return

Including the child's income on your return could be disadvantageous by making it more difficult for you to claim certain deductions and raising your state and local taxes.

EXAMPLE

Woodrow, age 10, received $2,000 of interest income in 2002. He has no other income and is not subject to backup withholding. No estimated tax payments were made in his name. His parents elect on Form 8814 to include his interest income on their 2002 tax return instead of filing a return for him. They include $500 of the interest ($2,000 – $1,500 floor) on Line 21 (other income) of their Form 1040. They also add $75 to their tax on Line 42 of Form 1040 and indicate that the amount is from Form 8814.

Sample Form 8814

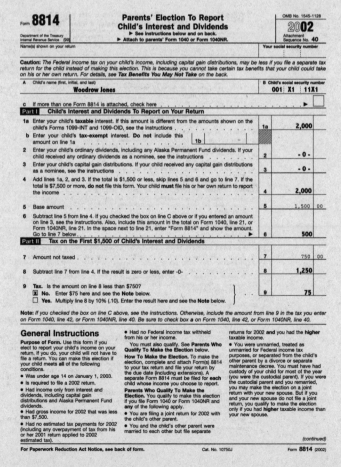

24.5 • Parent's Election To Report Child's Dividends and Interest

Form 8615 Worksheets—

The revised Form 8615 for 2001 was not available when this book went to press. The following worksheets illustrate the "kiddie tax" calculation. See the Supplement for possible changes to Form 8615.

Form 8615

Department of the Treasury
Internal Revenue Service (99)

Tax for Children Under Age 14 With Investment Income of More Than $1,500
► Attach only to the child's Form 1040, Form 1040A, or Form 1040NR.
► See separate instructions.

OMB No. 1545-0998
2002
Attachment Sequence No. **33**

Child's name shown on return: **Betty Brown**
Child's social security number: **X10 | 00 - 1111**

Before you begin: If the child, the parent, or any of the parent's other children under age 14 received capital gains (including capital gain distributions) or farm income, see **Pub. 929**, Tax Rules for Children and Dependents. It explains how to figure the child's tax using the **Capital Gain Tax Worksheet** in the Form 1040 or Form 1040A instructions, or **Schedule D or J** (Form 1040).

A Parent's name (first, initial, and last). Caution: See instructions before completing. **Tom Brown**

B Parent's social security number: **XXX | 11 - 0X11**

C Parent's filing status (check one):
☐ Single   ☒ Married filing jointly   ☐ Married filing separately   ☐ Head of household   ☐ Qualifying widow(er)

Part I   Child's Net Investment Income

1	Enter the child's investment income (see instructions)	1	1,600
2	If the child **did not** itemize deductions on **Schedule A** (Form 1040 or Form 1040NR), enter $1,500. Otherwise, see instructions	2	1,500
3	Subtract line 2 from line 1. If zero or less, **stop;** do not complete the rest of this form but do attach it to the child's return	3	100
4	Enter the child's **taxable income** from Form 1040, line 41; Form 1040A, line 27; or Form 1040NR, line 39	4	850
5	Enter the **smaller** of line 3 or line 4	5	100

Part II   Tentative Tax Based on the Tax Rate of the Parent

6	Enter the parent's **taxable income** from Form 1040, line 41; Form 1040A, line 27; Form 1040EZ, line 6; TeleFile Tax Record, line K; Form 1040NR, line 39; or Form 1040NR-EZ, line 14. If zero or less, enter -0-	6	52,000
7	Enter the total, if any, from Forms 8615, line 5, of **all other** children of the parent named above. **Do not** include the amount from line 5 above	7	700
8	Add lines 5, 6, and 7	8	52,800
9	Enter the tax on the amount on line 8 based on the **parent's** filing status above (see instructions). If the Capital Gain Tax Worksheet or Schedule D or J (Form 1040) is used, check here ► ☐	9	8,059
10	Enter the parent's tax from Form 1040, line 42; Form 1040A, line 28, minus any alternative minimum tax; Form 1040EZ, line 10; TeleFile Tax Record, line K; Form 1040NR, line 40; or Form 1040NR-EZ, line 15. **Do not** include any tax from **Form 4972 or 8814.** If the Capital Gain Tax Worksheet or Schedule D or J (Form 1040) was used to figure the tax, check here ► ☐	10	7,843
11	Subtract line 10 from line 9 and enter the result. If line 7 is blank, also enter this amount on line 13 and go to **Part III**	11	216
12a	Add lines 5 and 7 ... [12a] 800		
b	Divide line 5 by line 12a. Enter the result as a decimal (rounded to at least three places)	12b	× . 125
13	Multiply line 11 by line 12b	13	27

Part III   Child's Tax—If lines 4 and 5 above are the same, enter -0- on line 15 and go to line 16.

14	Subtract line 5 from line 4 ... [14] 750		
15	Enter the tax on the amount on line 14 based on the **child's** filing status (see instructions). If the Capital Gain Tax Worksheet or Schedule D or J (Form 1040) is used to figure the tax, check here ► ☐	15	76
16	Add lines 13 and 15	16	103
17	Enter the tax on the amount on line 4 based on the **child's** filing status (see instructions). If the Capital Gain Tax Worksheet or Schedule D or J (Form 1040) is used to figure the tax, check here ► ☐	17	86
18	Enter the **larger** of line 16 or line 17 here and on the **child's** Form 1040, line 42; Form 1040A, line 28; or Form 1040NR, line 40	18	103

For Paperwork Reduction Act Notice, see the instructions.   Cat. No. 64113U   Form **8615** (2002)

Form 8615

Department of the Treasury
Internal Revenue Service (99)

Tax for Children Under Age 14 With Investment Income of More Than $1,500
► Attach only to the child's Form 1040, Form 1040A, or Form 1040NR.
► See separate instructions.

OMB No. 1545-0998
2002
Attachment Sequence No. **33**

Child's name shown on return: **Bill Brown**
Child's social security number: **0XX | 11 - 111X**

Before you begin: If the child, the parent, or any of the parent's other children under age 14 received capital gains (including capital gain distributions) or farm income, see **Pub. 929**, Tax Rules for Children and Dependents. It explains how to figure the child's tax using the **Capital Gain Tax Worksheet** in the Form 1040 or Form 1040A instructions, or **Schedule D or J** (Form 1040).

A Parent's name (first, initial, and last). Caution: See instructions before completing. **Tom Brown**

B Parent's social security number: **XXX | 11 - 0X11**

C Parent's filing status (check one):
☐ Single   ☒ Married filing jointly   ☐ Married filing separately   ☐ Head of household   ☐ Qualifying widow(er)

Part I   Child's Net Investment Income

1	Enter the child's investment income (see instructions)	1	2,200
2	If the child **did not** itemize deductions on **Schedule A** (Form 1040 or Form 1040NR), enter $1,500. Otherwise, see instructions	2	1,500
3	Subtract line 2 from line 1. If zero or less, **stop;** do not complete the rest of this form but **do** attach it to the child's return	3	700
4	Enter the child's **taxable income** from Form 1040, line 41; Form 1040A, line 27; or Form 1040NR, line 39	4	1,450
5	Enter the **smaller** of line 3 or line 4	5	700

Part II   Tentative Tax Based on the Tax Rate of the Parent

6	Enter the parent's **taxable income** from Form 1040, line 41; Form 1040A, line 27; Form 1040EZ, line 6; TeleFile Tax Record, line K; Form 1040NR, line 39; or Form 1040NR-EZ, line 14. If zero or less, enter -0-	6	52,000
7	Enter the total, if any, from Forms 8615, line 5, of **all other** children of the parent named above. **Do not** include the amount from line 5 above	7	100
8	Add lines 5, 6, and 7	8	52,800
9	Enter the tax on the amount on line 8 based on the **parent's** filing status above (see instructions). If the Capital Gain Tax Worksheet or Schedule D or J (Form 1040) is used, check here ► ☐	9	8,059
10	Enter the parent's tax from Form 1040, line 42; Form 1040A, line 28, minus any alternative minimum tax; Form 1040EZ, line 10; TeleFile Tax Record, line K; Form 1040NR, line 40; or Form 1040NR-EZ, line 15. **Do not** include any tax from **Form 4972 or 8814.** If the Capital Gain Tax Worksheet or Schedule D or J (Form 1040) was used to figure the tax, check here ► ☐	10	7,843
11	Subtract line 10 from line 9 and enter the result. If line 7 is blank, also enter this amount on line 13 and go to **Part III**	11	216
12a	Add lines 5 and 7 ... [12a] 800		
b	Divide line 5 by line 12a. Enter the result as a decimal (rounded to at least three places)	12b	× . 875
13	Multiply line 11 by line 12b	13	189

Part III   Child's Tax—If lines 4 and 5 above are the same, enter -0- on line 15 and go to line 16.

14	Subtract line 5 from line 4 ... [14] 750		
15	Enter the tax on the amount on line 14 based on the **child's** filing status (see instructions). If the Capital Gain Tax Worksheet or Schedule D or J (Form 1040) is used to figure the tax, check here ► ☐	15	76
16	Add lines 13 and 15	16	265
17	Enter the tax on the amount on line 4 based on the **child's** filing status (see instructions). If the Capital Gain Tax Worksheet or Schedule D or J (Form 1040) is used to figure the tax, check here ► ☐	17	146
18	Enter the **larger** of line 16 or line 17 here and on the **child's** Form 1040, line 42; Form 1040A, line 28; or Form 1040NR, line 40	18	265

For Paperwork Reduction Act Notice, see the instructions.   Cat. No. 64113U   Form **8615** (2002)

446

Chapter 25

Child Tax Credit and Dependent Care, Earned Income (EIC), and Adoption Credits

The following family tax credits are discussed in this chapter: child tax credit, dependent care credit, earned income credit (EIC), and the adoption credit. Education tax credits are discussed in Chapter 38.

The child tax credit is $600 for each qualifying dependent child under age 17. To claim the credit, you must follow the steps of the "Child Tax Credit Worksheet." There is a phaseout of the credit, as explained in *25.2*. If the credit exceeds your tax liability, you may be entitled to a refundable credit called the "additional child credit" on Form 8812.

The dependent care credit is for working people who pay care costs that allow them the freedom to work. Depending on your income, the credit is 20% to 30% of up to $2,400 of care expenses for one dependent and up to $4,800 of expenses for two or more dependents. If your adjusted gross income exceeds $28,000, the maximum credit is $480 for one dependent and $960 for two or more dependents.

The earned income credit (EIC) is provided to low-income workers who support children, and a limited credit is allowed to certain workers without qualifying children; *see 25.12*.

On a 2002 return, an adoption credit of up to $10,000 may be claimed for costs of adopting a child under the age of 18 or a disabled person incapable of self-care.

Child Tax Credit

25.1 Child Tax Credit for Children Under Age 17

For 2002, you generally may claim a tax credit of $600 for each qualifying child who is under age 17 at the end of 2002. To figure the exact amount of your credit, however, you must complete the "Child Tax Credit Worksheet" in the IRS instructions to determine if your credit is limited. The credit may be limited under a phase-out rule based on modified adjusted gross income (*see* below) and the credit may not exceed your tax liability. However, if the credit does exceed tax liability, part or all of the excess may be refundable as an additional credit on Form 8812 if you have earned income over $10,350 or you have three or more children; *see 25.2.*

Qualifying child. The credit may be claimed for a child under age 17 at the end of 2002 whom you claim as a dependent. A "child" includes your child, stepchild, grandchild, or great-grandchild or descendant of any of these. A brother, sister, stepbrother, stepsister, or their descendant, also qualifies if cared for as your own child. An adopted child qualifies if placed with you by an authorized agency for legal adoption, even if the adoption is not final by the end of 2002. A foster child placed with you by an authorized agency and who is cared for as your own child qualifies if he or she lived with you for all of 2002, or was born in 2002 and lived with you the rest of the year, or lived with you in 2002 but died during the year.

Phaseout of credit. The credit is limited or eliminated if your adjusted gross income is above a threshold amount for your filing status. In applying the phaseout, AGI is increased by any foreign earned income exclusion, foreign housing exclusion or deduction, or possession exclusion for American Samoa residents. The phase-out threshold for each filing status is as follows.

Filing Status	*Phaseout Applies if MAGI exceeds*
Married filing jointly	$110,000
Head of household	75,000
Single	75,000
Qualifying widow(er)	75,000
Married filing separately	55,000

Changing your withholding. If you can claim the child tax credit, you may have too much tax withheld from your wages during the year. If so, you can claim more withholding allowances. File the new Form W-4 with your employer so that less income tax will be withheld.

25.2 Figuring the Child Tax Credit

You use the Child Tax Credit Worksheet in the IRS instruction booklet or in Publication 972 to figure the credit. You do not attach the worksheet to your return.

The credit is $600 times the number of your qualifying children. On the worksheet, the credit is reduced by $50 for each $1,000 (or fraction of $1,000) that your AGI exceeds the phase-out threshold *(25.1)* for your filing status. The worksheet computation also limits the credit (after any AGI phaseout) to your tax liability, reduced by certain personal tax credits.

Refundable portion of credit. If the full amount of the credit cannot be claimed on the Child Tax Credit Worksheet because of the tax liability limitation, you may be able to obtain a refund for the balance on Form 8812, Additional Tax Credit. The credit is refundable for 2002 to the extent of 10% of your taxable earned income in excess of $10,350. If your earned income is *not* over $10,350, a refundable credit may still be available if you have three or more qualifying children and you paid Social Security taxes that exceed your earned income credit *(25.12)*, if any. Follow the instructions to Form 8812.

Law Alert

Scheduled Increases to Child Tax Credit

The child tax credit of $600 per child for 2001–2004 will further increase to $700 for 2005–2008, to $800 for 2009, and to $1,000 for 2010 and later years.

EXAMPLES

1. In 2002, Carl and Abby have two dependent daughters under age 17. They have AGI of $34,000. They file a joint return. Their child tax credit is $1,200 ($600 × 2). Their AGI is less than the phase-out threshold for their filing status ($110,000). They claim the full credit of $1,200, assuming it is not limited to tax liability on the Child Tax Credit Worksheet.

2. Jane is single and has two dependent children under 17. Jane's AGI for 2002 is $77,500. She files her tax return as head of household. Because her AGI exceeds $75,000 (the phase-out amount for her filing status), the full credit of $1,200 ($600 × 2) is reduced on the Child Tax Credit Worksheet. For each $1,000 of excess AGI, or fraction of $1,000, $50 of the credit is phased out. The excess income of $2,500 is rounded up to $3,000 and multiplied by 5%, resulting in a credit reduction of $150 ($3,000 × 5%). Jane may claim a child tax credit of $1,050 ($1,200 − $150) so long as tax liability on the worksheet is at least that much.

Dependent Care Credit

25.3 Qualifying for Child and Dependent Care Credit

Did you hire someone to care for your children or other dependents while you work? If so, you may qualify for a tax credit for the expenses. You may claim the credit even if you work part time. The credit is generally available to the extent you have earnings from employment. Your employer may have a plan qualifying for tax-free child care and, if you are covered, you may be unable to claim a tax credit; *see 25.7*.

Where to claim the credit. The credit is claimed on Form 2441 if you file Form 1040, or on Form 1040A, Schedule 2. The size of the credit depends on the amount of care expenses and income. Depending on your income, the credit is 20% to 30% of up to $2,400 of care expenses for one dependent and up to $4,800 of expenses for two or more dependents. If your adjusted gross income exceeds $28,000, the maximum credit is $480 for one dependent and $960 for two or more dependents. *See* the chart in *25.4*.

Credit requirements. To qualify for the credit, you must:

1. Incur the care expenses in order to earn income. In the case of a married couple, this requires both spouses to work either at full- or part-time positions. An exception to the earned income rule is made for a spouse who is a full-time student or incapacitated *(25.5)*. Qualifying care expenses are discussed at *25.7*. Limits on the amount of qualifying costs are discussed at *25.4*.
2. Pay over 50% of the household maintenance costs for a qualifying dependent; *see 25.6*. You must report the dependent's name and Social Security number on Form 2441 or Schedule 2 of Form 1040A.
3. File jointly if you are married, unless you are separated under the rules discussed at *25.8*.
4. Hire someone *other than* your child who is under age 19 at the end of the year, your spouse, or a person you can claim as a dependent; *see 25.7*.
5. Have qualifying expenses in excess of tax-free reimbursements received from your employer; *see 25.7*.
6. Report on your tax return the name, address, and taxpayer identification number (Social Security number for individuals) of the child-care provider; *see* below.

Identifying care provider on your return. You must list the name, address, and taxpayer identification number of the person you paid to care for your dependent on Form 2441 if you file Form 1040, or on Form 1040A, Schedule 2. You do not need the taxpayer identification number if a tax-exempt charity provides the dependent care services. Failure to list the correct name, address, and number may result in a disallowance of the credit. To avoid this possibility, ask the provider to fill out Form W-10 or get the identifying information from a Social Security card, driver's license, or business letterhead or invoice. If a household employee has filled out Form W-4 for you, this may act as a backup record.

Withholding tax for a housekeeper. Where you employ help to care for your dependent in your home, you may be liable for FICA (Social Security) and FUTA (unemployment) taxes; *see 25.9*.

 Caution

Nonrefundable Credit
The dependent care credit is limited to your tax liability. In other words, if the credit amount exceeds the tax that you owe, you will not be given a refund of the difference.

25.4 Limits on the Dependent Care Credit

The credit is a percentage of expenses paid for the care of a dependent to allow you to work and earn income. Qualifying expenses are discussed at 25.7. The credit percentage depends on your income. The 2001 Tax Act increases the maximum credit, but not until 2003; see the adjacent Law Alert.

Limit on expenses. In figuring the credit, you may only take into account qualifying expenses (25.7) up to a limit of $2,400 for one dependent, or $4,800 for two or more dependents. The $2,400 or $4,800 limit applies even if your actual expenses are much greater. Further, the $2,400 or $4,800 limit must be reduced by tax-free benefits received from an employer's dependent care plan. Finally, if your earned income is less than the $2,400 or $4,800 limit, your credit is figured on the lower income amount.

Take into account only payments in 2002 for 2002 services. Your credit for 2002 must be based on payments made in 2002 for care services provided in 2002. If you paid for 2001 services in 2002, you may be able to claim an additional credit on your 2002 return, but only in limited circumstances, as discussed at the end of this section. If in 2002 you prepay for 2003 services, you must allocate your payment. Only payments for 2002 services should be counted toward the $2,400 or $4,800 limit when figuring your 2002 credit.

Credit percentage. Depending on your income, a credit percentage of 20% to 30% applies to your expenses up to the $2,400 (one dependent) or $4,800 (two or more dependents) limit. The maximum credit is 30% for families with adjusted gross income of $10,000 or less. For adjusted gross income over $10,000, the 30% credit is reduced by 1% for each $2,000 of adjusted gross income or fraction of $2,000 over $10,000, but not below 20%. The 20% credit applies to adjusted gross incomes exceeding $28,000.

The dependent care credit is nonrefundable; it is limited to your regular income tax liability; follow the IRS instructions.

Law Alert

Dependent Care Credit Liberalized Starting in 2003

Starting in 2003, the amount of expenses qualifying for the credit will increase from $2,400 to $3,000 for one dependent and from $4,800 to $6,000 for two or more dependents. The maximum credit percentage will increase from 30% to 35%. The 35% maximum credit percentage will apply to taxpayers with adjusted gross income (AGI) of $15,000 or less, and the percentage will phase down to 20% for taxpayers with AGI over $43,000.

Filing Tip

Employer Reimbursements Reduce Credit

Expenses qualifying for the dependent care credit are reduced by any tax-free reimbursements under a qualified employer dependent care program. That is, the reimbursements reduce the $2,400 expense limit for one dependent, or the $4,800 expense limit for two or more qualifying dependents; see 25.7. Your employer will report reimbursements in Box 10 of your Form W-2. You figure the tax-free portion of the reimbursement, and any reduction to the credit expense base, on Form 2441 if you file Form 1040 or on Schedule 2 if you file Form 1040A.

Allowable Credit			
	Your maximum credit		
Adjusted gross income	Credit percentage	One dependent	Two or more dependents
$10,000 or less	30%	$720	$1,440
10,001–12,000	29	696	1,392
12,001–14,000	28	672	1,344
14,001–16,000	27	648	1,296
16,001–18,000	26	624	1,248
18,001–20,000	25	600	1,200
20,001–22,000	24	576	1,152
22,001–24,000	23	552	1,104
24,001–26,000	22	528	1,056
26,001–28,000	21	504	1,008
28,001 and over	20	480	960

EXAMPLES

1. You pay $6,000 to a neighbor to care for your two children while you work. Your adjusted gross income is $31,000. The minimum credit percentage of 20% is applied to the maximum expense limit of $4,800, giving you a credit of $960.

2. Same as above, except you receive a tax-free reimbursement of $2,500 from your employer's plan. The reimbursement reduces the $4,800 expense limit to $2,300 ($4,800 – $2,500); see 25.7. Your credit is $460 (20% of $2,300). If the tax-free reimbursement were $4,800 or more (it cannot exceed $5,000), no credit would be allowed.

Additional credit for 2002 payment of 2001 dependent care expenses. Payments made in 2002 for 2001 services may be eligible for an additional credit but only if you did not use up the $2,400 or $4,800 expense limit when claiming your 2001 credit.

For example, the cost of day-care services for your child in 2001 was $3,000, half of which you paid in 2001 and half in early 2002. On your 2001 return, a credit was based on the $1,500 of expenses paid in 2001. Since you used only $1,500 of the $2,400 expense limit in 2001, the $900 of "unused" expenses is carried over to 2002. On your 2002 Form 2441 or Schedule 2 of Form 1040A, you multiply $900 by a credit percentage based on your 2001 adjusted gross income. Assuming your 2001 adjusted gross income was $30,000, the credit percentage is 20%. Thus, your additional 2002 credit is $180 (20% of $900). The $180 credit is claimed on Line 9 of Form 2441 or Schedule 2 (Form 1040A), and is in addition to the regular credit for 2002 care services. You must attach a statement explaining the carryover to 2002 and the computation of the additional credit.

25.5 Earned Income Test for Dependent Care Credit

To claim the credit, you must earn wage, salary, or self-employment income figured without regard to community property laws. Expenses for dependent care incurred while looking for a job may be included. However, you must have earnings during the year to claim the credit.

Earned income rule for married couples. Generally, both spouses must work at least part time, unless one is incapable of self-care or is a full-time student. If either you or your spouse earns less than the maximum $2,400 or $4,800 credit base (25.4), the base is limited to the smaller income.

EXAMPLE

John and Mary are married. In 2002, John earns $4,000. Mary earns $23,500. They incur care costs of $5,000 for their two children, ages 5 and 7. Their adjusted gross income including interest earnings is $27,742; their credit percentage is 21%. The maximum $4,800 credit base (for two or more dependents) is limited to John's lower income of $4,000. They may claim a credit of $840 ($4,000 × 21%) for 2002.

Spouses who are students or disabled. An incapacitated spouse or a spouse who is a full-time student is considered to have earned income of $200 a month for 2002 if expenses are incurred for one dependent, or $400 a month for two or more dependents. In 2003, the deemed earnings amount increases to $250 (one dependent) or $500 (two or more dependents) per month.

A full-time student is one who attends school full time during each of five calendar months during the year.

EXAMPLE

Same facts as in the Example above, except John was a full-time student for nine months and earned no income for the year. The credit base is limited to $3,600 ($400 × 9).

25.6 Household and Dependent Tests for Dependent Care Credit

To claim the credit you must maintain as your principal home a household for at least one of the following qualifying persons who lives with you:

1. A child *under the age of 13* whom you may claim as your dependent. If you are divorced or separated, and you had custody of the child for a longer time during the year than the other parent, you may be able to claim the credit even if the other parent is entitled to claim the child as a dependent; *see 25.8.*
2. Your spouse, if physically or mentally incapable of caring for him or herself.
3. A person, regardless of age, who is physically or mentally incapable of caring for himself or herself. For example, he or she needs help to dress or to take care of personal hygiene or nutritional needs, or requires constant attention to avoid hurting him- or herself or others. Relatives who qualify, if disabled, are listed at *21.3*. A nonrelative may also qualify if he or she is a member of your household for the entire year, except for temporary absences. Generally, the qualifying person must be your dependent, but if he or she has gross income of $3,000 or more for 2002, so that you may not claim an exemption (*21.5*) for that person, you may still claim a credit for his or her care costs.

 Filing Tip

No Credit if Neither Spouse Works

If both husband and wife are full-time students and neither works, they may not claim the credit for dependent care costs. While one student-spouse is considered to have earned income for 2002 of $200 (or $400) each month, the other spouse's earned income is zero. Care costs eligible for the credit are limited to the lesser amount of earned income, which in this case is zero.

> **EXAMPLE**
>
> You live with your mother, who is physically incapable of caring for herself. You hire a practical nurse to care for her in the home while you are at work. Payments to the nurse qualify as care costs. However, if you placed her in a nursing home, the cost of the nursing home would not qualify as a dependent care cost; but *see 17.11* for a possible medical expense deduction.

Filing Tip

Day-Care Center or Nursery School

The amount you pay to a day-care center or nursery school for a dependent child under age 13 is eligible for the credit, even if it covers such incidental benefits as lunch. However, tuition for a child in first grade or higher is not taken into account. If the dependent is not your child, costs for care outside the home qualify only if the dependent regularly spends at least eight hours per day in your home. Up to $2,400 a year of outside-the-home care expenses may be taken into account in figuring the credit for one dependent, and up to $4,800 for two or more.

If your child becomes age 13 during the year. Take into account expenses incurred for his or her care prior to the 13th birthday. However, you do not prorate the $2,400 limitation. For example, if your child becomes age 13 on May 1 and you incurred $2,400 in care expenses between January 1 and April 30, the entire $2,400 qualifies for the credit.

You must pay more than half of household costs. You are considered to have maintained a household if you (or you and your spouse) provided more than half the maintenance costs in 2002. You also qualify if you paid more than half the costs during a lesser period in which you had care cost expenses. Rent, mortgage interest, property tax and insurance, utility bills, upkeep, repairs, and groceries are considered maintenance costs. Do not count costs of clothing, education, medical expenses, vacations, life insurance, mortgage principal, and capital improvements, such as replacing a boiler.

In determining costs of maintaining a household for a care period of less than a year, the annual household costs are prorated over the number of calendar months within the period care costs were incurred. A period of less than a calendar month is treated as a calendar month.

Household of two or more families. If two or more families share living quarters, each family is treated as a separate household.

> **EXAMPLES**
>
> 1. The annual cost of maintaining a household is $6,600, and the period during which child-care costs qualified for the deduction is from June 20 to December 31. To meet the household test, you must furnish more than $1,925 in maintaining the household from June 1 to December 31. The allocation covers seven months (June 1 to December 31).
>
>   Cost of maintaining home: $7/_{12}$ of $6,600 = $3,850
>   Amount you must pay: 50% of $3,850 = $1,925
>
> 2. Two women, each with children, share a house. If each pays more than one-half of the household costs for her own family, each is treated as maintaining her separate household for purposes of the credit.

25.7 Expenses Qualifying for the Dependent Care Credit

If you do not receive tax-free dependent care benefits from an employer's plan, you may take into account up to $2,400 of the following types of expenses paid in 2002 when figuring the credit for one dependent, or up to $4,800 for two or more dependents. If you receive employer-financed dependent care, tax-free reimbursements reduce the $2,400 or $4,800 base.

1. Costs of caring for your child under age 13, incapacitated spouse, or incapacitated dependent in your home. If you pay FICA or FUTA taxes on your housekeeper's wages *(25.9)*, you may include your share of the tax (employer) as part of the wages when entering your qualifying expenses. Also include your housekeeper's share of FICA tax if you pay it. Note that these taxes may more than offset your allowable credit.

   The manner of care need not be the least expensive alternative. For example, where a grandparent resides with you and may provide adequate care for your child to enable you to work, the cost of hiring someone to care for the child is still eligible for the credit.

2. Ordinary domestic services in your home, such as laundry, cleaning, and cooking (but not payments to a gardener or chauffeur) that are partly for the care of the qualifying person. Expenses for the dependent's food, clothing, or entertainment do not qualify. Food costs for a housekeeper who eats in your home may be added to qualifying expenses. Extra expenses for a housekeeper's lodging (extra rent or utilities) also qualify.

3. Outside-the-home care costs for a child under age 13, as in a day-care center, day camp, nursery school, or in the home of a babysitter. Outside-the-home care costs also qualify if incurred for a handicapped dependent, regardless of age, provided he or she regularly spends at least eight hours per day in your home. However, the cost of schooling in the first grade or higher does not qualify for the credit. Costs for sleep-away camp also do not qualify for the credit.

The cost of driving a dependent to or from a day-care center or similar transportation does not qualify for a child-care credit. However, the Tax Court allowed a child-care credit for supervised bus transportation; the transportation was part of the actual child care.

Payments to relatives. No credit may be claimed for payments made to relatives for whom a dependency exemption is allowable (21.3). Thus, if you pay your mother to care for your child and you cannot claim your mother as a dependent, such payments qualify for the credit. The same rule applies for payments to unrelated persons who live with you and qualify as your dependents; see 21.4.

No credit may be claimed for payments to your child who is under 19 years of age at the close of the tax year, whether or not you may claim the child as a dependent.

Allocating expenses when employed less than an entire year. When an expense covers a period, part of which you were gainfully employed or in active search of gainful employment and part of which you were not employed or seeking employment, you must allocate expenses on a daily basis.

EXAMPLE

You are employed for only two months and 10 days. Monthly care expenses are $300. Eligible care expenses amount to $700 ($300 × 2 months, plus $1/_3$ of $300).

Employer-financed dependent care reduces credit base. Tax-free reimbursements under an employer's dependent care program reduce the $2,400 or $4,800 credit base. For example, if you have one child and you receive a $1,500 reimbursement of child-care costs from your company's plan, the amount eligible for the tax credit is reduced to $900 ($2,400 − $1,500). A reimbursement of $2,400 or more would bar any credit. The $4,800 credit expense limit for two or more dependents is similarly reduced. On your Form W-2, your employer will report the amount of tax-free reimbursement; see 3.4.

If your employer's plan allows you to fund a reimbursement account with salary-reduction contributions that are excluded from taxable pay (3.14), reimbursements from the account are considered employer-financed payments that reduce the $2,400 or $4,800 credit base. In deciding whether to make salary-reduction contributions, you should determine whether the tax-free reduction will provide a larger tax savings than that provided by the credit. You may find that the salary reduction provides the larger tax savings, taking into consideration not only the decrease in federal income tax, but also the Social Security tax and state and local taxes avoided by using the salary reduction. Further, by lowering your adjusted gross income, a salary reduction may enable you to claim a larger IRA deduction if you are subject to the deduction phase-out rule (8.4), or a larger deduction for miscellaneous itemized deductions subject to the 2% floor (19.1).

Allocation if expenses cover noncare services. If a portion of expenses is for other than dependent care or household services, only the portion allocable to dependent care or household services qualifies. No allocation is required if the non–dependent care services are minimal.

 Filing Tip

Care Costs Qualifying as Medical Expenses

Care costs, such as a nurse's wages, may also qualify as medical expenses, but you may not claim both the dependent care credit and the medical expense deduction. If you use the expenses to figure the credit and your care costs exceed the amount allowed as dependent care costs, the excess, to the extent it qualifies as a medical expense, may be added to other deductible medical costs.

EXAMPLES

1. A person accepts a full-time position and sends his 12-year-old child to boarding school. The expenses paid to the school must be allocated. The part representing care of the child qualifies; the part representing tuition does not.

2. A full-time housekeeper is hired to care for two children, ages 9 and 12. The housekeeper also drives the mother to and from work each day. The driving takes no longer than 30 minutes. No allocation is required because the non–dependent care services of chauffeuring are minimal.

3. You pay $6,000 for care of your child in your home. The expenses also qualify as medical expenses. Assume your adjusted gross income is $17,000. Your dependent care costs are limited to $2,400 and you may claim a credit of $624 ($2,400 × 26%). The

balance of $3,600 is deductible as medical expenses if you itemize deductions on Schedule A. If you had no other medical costs, your medical deduction would be $2,325 after deducting the 7.5% limitation on medical costs ($3,600 – $1,275, or 7.5% of $17,000).

25.8 Dependent Care Credit Rules for Separated Couples

A married person generally must file a joint return to claim the dependent care credit (25.3), but if you are living apart from your spouse you may claim the credit on a separate return if you meet the following tests:

1. You maintain as your home a household that a qualifying person (25.6) lives in for more than half the year;
2. You furnish over half the cost of maintaining the household for the entire year; *and*
3. Your spouse was not a member of the household during the *last six months* of the year.

If you satisfy these tests, you are treated as unmarried and may claim the credit on a separate return. You do not have to take your spouse's income into account or show that he or she is employed in order to claim a credit.

Your child may be a qualifying person for purposes of the credit even if you cannot claim the child as your dependent. This favorable rule applies if: you are legally divorced or separated, separated under a written agreement, or you lived apart from your spouse during the last six months of 2002; you or you and the other parent had custody of the child for more than half the year and provided more than half of the child's support; and you are the *custodial parent* (have custody longer than the other parent). If these tests are met, you may claim the credit for care of a dependent child who is under age 13 or physically or mentally incapable of caring for himself or herself even though you waive the dependency exemption on Form 8332 or are unable to claim the exemption under a pre-1985 divorce or separation agreement. The noncustodial parent may not claim the credit even if he or she is allowed the exemption.

Employment Taxes for Household Employees ("Nanny Tax")

Planning Reminder

FICA Threshold for Each Household Worker

If you employ more than one household worker, a babysitter and a gardener for instance, the $1,300 FICA threshold applies separately to each worker. For example, if in 2002 one worker earns $950 and the other earns $1,099, you do not have to pay Social Security or Medicare taxes for either worker.

Caution

Undocumented Workers

Household employees who work for you on a regular basis must verify their U.S. citizenship or their eligibility to work in the U.S. on Form I-9 from the Immigration and Naturalization Service. It is unlawful to knowingly hire an individual who is not legally entitled to work in the U.S.

25.9 Paying and Withholding Taxes for Household Employees

If you employ someone to care for your children or disabled dependents in your home, clean your residence, cook, or provide other personal services in or around your home, you may be obligated to pay and withhold Social Security and Medicare taxes (FICA) and also pay federal unemployment taxes (FUTA). FICA or FUTA taxes do not apply if the household worker is the employee of an agency that assigns the position, sets the fee, and requires reports from the worker.

The reporting requirements for FICA are at *25.10*, and the FUTA requirements at *25.11*.

Income taxes. Income tax withholding is not required for a household employee, but if the employee requests it and you agree, you pay the withheld tax under one of the reporting options discussed in *25.10*. Withholdings are based on a Form W-4 (Withholding Allowance Certificate) filed by the employee.

An employee who qualifies for the earned income credit may receive advance payments by giving you Form W-5; see *25.15*.

25.10 Social Security and Medicare Taxes (FICA) for Household Employees

You generally must withhold Social Security and Medicare taxes (FICA) from the pay of a household employee and also pay an equal amount yourself, unless the wages are below an annual threshold, which for 2002 was $1,300. Wages paid to your spouse, child under age 21, or parent for household services are generally exempt from this tax, as discussed at the end of this section. Also exempt are wages of any amount paid to a household employee who is under the age of 18 at any time during the year, so long as he or she does not work full time as a household worker. For example, if you hire a student under age 18 as a babysitter, Social Security and Medicare taxes do not apply regardless of the amount of wages you pay. However, if wages of $1,300 or more are paid in 2002 to a person under 18 years of age who works full time as a household employee, Social Security and Medicare taxes apply.

Once payments to non-exempt employees equal or exceed $1,300, the entire amount, including the first $1,300, is subject to FICA taxes.

The $1,300 threshold may be increased for 2003 by an inflation adjustment.

Tax rates. As an employer, you pay FICA at the rate of 7.65% of wages: 6.2% for Social Security and 1.45% for Medicare. For example, you pay a housekeeper $250 a week ($13,000 for the year). You must pay $994.50 in FICA and either withhold the same amount from the housekeeper's wages or pay the housekeeper's share yourself. In the unlikely case that wages exceed the wage limit for Social Security taxes (for example, $84,900 in 2002), there is an extra Medicare tax of 2.9%: 1.45% tax owed by you as the employer and 1.45% owed by the housekeeper. There is no wage limit on the additional 2.9% Medicare tax. You and the employee are each liable for the combined FICA rate of 7.65% (6.2% Social Security plus 1.45% Medicare) where 2002 wages are $84,900 or less. If wages exceed $84,900, the 7.65% rate applies to the first $84,900 and the 1.45% rate applies to the excess.

If you do not withhold the employee's share of FICA taxes, you are liable for the full amount. If you pay the employee's share of FICA taxes instead of deducting it from wages, you must treat your payment as additional wages when you report the employee's wages on Form W-2, but the payment is not considered wages for Social Security, Medicare, or FUTA tax purposes.

How to report and pay federal employment taxes. You compute 2002 FICA tax (Social Security and Medicare) on wages paid to household employees on Schedule H, which you attach to your 2002 Form 1040; Schedule H may not be used by Form 1040A filers.

You must include your employer identification number (EIN) on Schedule H. An EIN is a nine-digit number, separate from your Social Security number, that is obtained from the IRS by filing Form SS-4. If you previously obtained an EIN when paying taxes for other employees, use that number on Schedule H.

Form W-2. File a 2002 Form W-2 for each household employee to whom you paid Social Security and Medicare wages, or wages from which you withheld federal income tax. Give copies B, C, and 2 of Form W-2 to your household employee by January 31, 2003, and give copy A to the Social Security Administration by February 28, 2003.

Estimated Tax. In planning whether to make estimated tax installments during 2003 *(27.1)*, you should include an estimate of employment taxes for household employees as part of your estimate of 2003 income tax liability. Failure to consider the employment taxes could trigger an estimated tax penalty for 2003.

Reporting rules for self-employed persons who have regular business employees. Self-employed persons who have employees other than household employees may follow one of these two options:

1. Report FICA and FUTA taxes and any income tax withholding for household employees annually on Schedule H, and report FICA taxes and any income tax withholding for other employees quarterly on Form 941 and FUTA taxes annually on Form 940 (or 940-EZ); *or*

2. Report FICA taxes and any income tax withholding for *all* employees (household employees and other employees) quarterly on Form 941 and report FUTA taxes annually for all employees on Form 940 or Form 940-EZ.

Employers of household employees must also give copies of Form W-2 (Wage and Tax Statement) to each employee and to the Social Security Administration, as discussed above.

Reporting rules for an estate. If a person who hired household help dies during the year and the estate continues to employ the employee for domestic work, the estate includes the wages paid both by the decedent and the estate to determine whether taxes are due under the $1,300 test. Thus, if in 2002 a person before dying paid $500 to a domestic worker and her estate continued to employ the domestic worker and paid wages of $1,000, the estate is required to pay FICA taxes on wages of $1,500.

 Caution

Estimated Tax Penalty

As a household employer, you are subject to an estimated tax penalty *(see 27.1)* if your federal income tax withholdings or estimated tax payments *(see 27.1)* are insufficient to cover your household employment tax (Social Security, Medicare, and federal unemployment) liability.

Payments to your parent, child, or spouse. FICA tax does not apply to wages paid to your spouse for domestic services in your home. A similar exception applies to wages paid to your son or daughter under age 21, but note the rule that bars you from basing a dependent care credit on payments made to a child under age 19 *(25.7)*. Further, FICA generally does not apply to wages paid to your father or mother for domestic work in your home unless (1) you are divorced or widowed, or your spouse is disabled; and (2) you have a child living at home who is under age 18 or is disabled.

25.11 Federal Unemployment Taxes (FUTA) for Household Employees

As an employer, you are also liable for FUTA (federal unemployment taxes) if you pay cash wages of $1,000 or more for household services during any calendar quarter, or if you did so in any quarter in the preceding year. You do not pay FUTA on wages paid to your spouse, your parents, or your children under age 21. Your employee is not liable for FUTA.

The FUTA rate for 2002 is 6.2% on the first $7,000 of cash wages. However, there is a credit for payments to a state unemployment fund that reduces FUTA liability.

For wages paid to a household employee in 2002, you will generally report FUTA on Schedule H, which you attach to your Form 1040. If you have regular business employees, *see 25.10* for reporting options.

Earned Income Credit (EIC)

25.12 Qualifying Tests for EIC

The earned income credit (EIC) may be claimed not only by workers with qualifying children who meet the tests below, but also, in limited cases, by childless workers. For 2002, the EIC can be as much as $2,506 if you have one qualifying child, $4,140 if you have more than one qualifying child, and $376 if you do not have a qualifying child. There is a phaseout of the credit; *see 25.13*. You look up the credit amount in IRS tables included in the tax form instructions. The EIC is "refundable"; you will receive a refund from the IRS if the credit exceeds your tax liability.

Claiming the EIC for 2002 With Qualifying Children

You may claim the EIC on a 2002 return if you:

- Have earned income, such as wages and self-employment earnings, and also adjusted gross income of under $29,201 ($30,201 if married filing jointly) if you have one qualifying child or under $33,178 ($34,178 if married filing jointly) if you have two or more qualifying children. However, the credit begins to phase out at much lower income levels; *see 25.13* for the credit phase-out rules.
- Have a qualifying child who lived with you in your main home in the U.S. for more than six months in 2002; *see* below.
- File a joint return if married. If you lived apart from your spouse for the last half of the year, you may be able to claim the credit as a head of household.
- File Schedule EIC with your Form 1040 or Form 1040A. On Schedule EIC, you identify and provide information about a qualifying child. Your child's Social Security number must be entered on Schedule EIC.
- Are not a qualifying child of another person.
- Include on your return your Social Security number and, if married, that of your spouse.

A qualifying child. A qualifying child is your son, daughter, adopted child, grandchild, stepchild, or descendents of any of these who at the end of 2002 is under age 19 or under age 24 and a full-time student (enrolled full time during any five months), or any age if permanently and totally disabled. The qualifying person must live with you for over half the year. Your brother, sister, stepbrother or stepsister, or their descendents, who meet the age 19 or 24 test and live with you more than half the year also qualify if cared for as your own child. A foster child who lives with you for more than half the year qualifies only if the child was placed with you by an authorized placement agency and is cared for as your own child.

 Caution

Denial of Future Credits for Recklessness or Fraud
A taxpayer who negligently or fraudulently claims the EIC is prohibited from claiming future credits over a period of several years. The credit is disallowed for two years from the tax year for which it is determined that the EIC claim was claimed recklessly or in disregard of the rules. The period increases to 10 years from the most recent tax year for which it is found that the EIC was claimed fraudulently.

Household requirement. The qualifying child or foster child must have lived with you in your main home in the U.S. for more than six months. Temporary absences for school, vacation, medical care, or detention in a juvenile facility count as time lived at home.

A person in the U.S. Armed Forces who is stationed outside the U.S. on extended active duty is treated as maintaining a main residence within the U.S.

If you are married, you must file a joint return with your spouse to claim the credit. However, if your spouse did not live in your household for the last six months of the year, and you maintained a home for a child who lived with you for more than half of the year, you may claim the credit as a head of household; *see 1.12.*

Permanently and totally disabled. A person is permanently and totally disabled if: (1) he or she cannot engage in any substantial gainful activity because of a physical or mental condition and (2) a physician determines that the condition has lasted or is expected to last for at least a year or lead to death.

Qualifying child of two or more people. Beginning in 2002, new "tie-breaking" rules will determine who can take the EIC if a child meets the conditions to be a qualifying child of more than one person. These rules do not apply if the other person is your spouse and you are married filing a joint return.

If both parents are eligible to claim the credit for the same qualifying child and they do not file a joint return, the parent with whom the child resided for the longer period during the year may claim the child. If the child lived with each parent for the same amount of time, the child will be treated as the qualifying child of the parent who had the highest AGI for 2002.

If a parent and one or more nonparents are otherwise entitled to claim the child as a qualifying child, only the parent may claim the credit for the child. If none of the persons otherwise entitled to treat the child as a qualifying child are the child's parent, the child will be treated as the qualifying child of the person who had the highest AGI for 2002.

Married child. If your child was married at the end of 2002, he or she is your qualifying child only if you claim the child as a dependent on Form 1040 or Form 1040A, Line 6, or you waive the exemption in favor of the child's other parent, or the other parent may claim the exemption under a pre-1985 agreement.

If *you* are a qualifying child of another person, you may not claim the EIC even if you have a qualifying child and would otherwise qualify for the credit.

Nonresident aliens. An individual who is a nonresident alien for any part of the year is not eligible for the credit unless he or she is married and an election is made by the couple to have all of their worldwide income subject to U.S. tax.

Claiming the Credit for 2002 Without Qualifying Children

If you do not have a qualifying child, you may claim the EIC on a 2002 return if you:

- Have earned income, such as wages and self-employment earnings and also adjusted gross income under $11,060 ($12,060 if married filing jointly). However, *see 25.13* for the credit phase-out rule.
- Have your main home in the U.S. for more than six months in 2002.
- Are at least 25 but under age 65 at the end of 2002. If filing a joint return, either you or your spouse must satisfy this age test.
- File a joint return if married, unless you lived apart for the last six months and qualify to file as a head of household.
- Are not a dependent of another taxpayer.
- Are not a qualifying child of another taxpayer.
- Include your Social Security number on your return, and, if married, that of your spouse.

The rules discussed earlier for Armed Forces personnel and nonresident aliens with qualifying children also apply to individuals without children.

25.13 Income Tests for EIC

For purposes of the credit, earned income includes wages, salary, tips, commissions, jury duty pay, union strike benefits, certain disability pensions, U.S. military basic quarters and subsistence allowances, and self-employment earnings. Nontaxable employee compensation, such as salary deferrals, or excludable dependent care benefits, is not considered when computing the credit for 2002 and later years.

 Law Alert

New Definition of Earned Income for EIC Purposes
Starting in 2002, earned income does *not* include nontaxable employee compensation such as salary deferrals and reductions, excludable dependent care benefits, excludable education assistance, and excludable combat pay.

Law Alert

Increased Credit Phase-out Range for Married Persons Filing Jointly

Starting in 2002, married persons filing jointly have a slightly higher credit phase-out limit to ameliorate the "marriage penalty." The beginning and end of the phase-out range for joint filers is increased by $1,000 in 2002, 2003, and 2004. The increase will be $2,000 in 2005, 2006, and 2007; and $3,000 for tax years after 2007. The $3,000 increase may be adjusted for inflation after 2008.

Disqualifying income. For 2002, an individual is not eligible for the earned income credit if he or she has "disqualified income" exceeding $2,550. Disqualified income includes interest (taxable and tax-exempt), dividends, net rent and royalty income, net capital gain income, and net passive income that is not self-employment income.

Credit phases out with income. Starting in 2002, there are two different phase-out ranges, one for married couples filing jointly and another for taxpayers filing as single or head of household.

If you have only one qualifying child *(25.12)*, the 2002 credit begins to phase out in the EIC Table *(25.14)* if either earned income or adjusted gross income is at least $13,550 if filing as single or head of household or $14,550 if filing jointly. No credit is allowed if either earned income or AGI is $29,201 or more if filing as single or head of household or $30,201 or more filing jointly.

If you have two or more qualifying children, the credit begins to phase out if either earned income or adjusted gross income is at least $13,550 if filing as single or head of household or $14,550 if filing jointly. The credit is completely phased out if either earned income or AGI is $33,178 or more if filing as single or head of household, or $34,178 or more if filing jointly.

If you do not have any qualifying children, the phaseout of the credit begins when either earned income or AGI is at least $6,150 ($7,150 if married filing jointly), and the credit is completely phased out if either amount is $11,060 or more ($12,060 or more if married filing jointly).

Self-employed. If you were self-employed in 2002, your earned income for credit purposes is the net earnings shown on Schedule SE, *less* the income tax deduction for 50% of self-employment tax claimed on Line 27 of Form 1040. If your net earnings were less than $400, the net amount is your earned income for purposes of the credit. If you had a net loss, the loss is subtracted from any wages or other employee earned income. If you are a statutory employee, the income reported on Schedule C qualifies for the credit.

Foreign earned income. If you work abroad and claim the foreign income exclusion, you may *not* take the credit.

25.14 Look up EIC in Government Tables

After completing a worksheet in the IRS instructions that determines whether your earned income credit (EIC) is based on your earned income or adjusted gross income *(25.13)*, you then look up the amount of your credit in the EIC Table, which is shown in Part 8 of this book.

> **EXAMPLE**
>
> Jane is divorced. Her only income in 2002 is wages of $21,143. She supports her eight-year-old daughter, who lives with her for the entire year.
>
> To find her credit, Jane turns to the 2002 EIC Table. In the table, the credit shown for her income bracket is $1,291.

 Law Alert

Recertification Required if EIC Denied

If the IRS denies an EIC by issuing a deficiency notice, the credit may not be claimed in a future tax year unless you show on Form 8862 that you are eligible to take the credit. If the IRS recertifies eligibility, Form 8862 does not have to be filed again in subsequent tax years unless the IRS again denies the EIC in a deficiency proceeding.

25.15 Advance Payment of Earned Income Credit

If you believe you are entitled to an earned income credit, you may file a certificate, Form W-5, with your employer to have a portion of the credit added to your paycheck throughout the year. To get advanced earned income payments you must have a qualifying child *(25.12)*.

If you receive any advance payments, you must report them on Form 1040 or Form 1040A; your employer will include the amount in Box 9 of your Form W-2. If you receive advance payments in excess of the credit you are entitled to, the excess is treated as a tax you owe when you file your return. If the credit you are entitled to exceeds the advance payments, the excess credit reduces any other tax you owe. If the credit exceeds your liability, the difference is refunded to you.

Adoption Credit

25.16 Qualifying for the Adoption Credit

A tax credit of up to $10,000 may be available on your 2002 return for the qualifying costs of adopting a child under age 18, or a person who is physically and mentally incapable of self-care. The credit is phased out ratably for those with adjusted gross income (after certain adjustments) between $150,000 and $190,000.

The credit is claimed on Form 8839. If you paid qualifying adoption costs in 2002 but the adoption was not final at the end of the year, the credit may *not* be claimed on your 2002 return; *see* 25.17 for the credit timing rules.

Employer plans. As discussed at *3.5*, an exclusion from income is also available to employees if adoption expenses are paid through a qualifying employer program, subject to rules similar to that of the credit. If you receive employer adoption benefits that are less than your qualifying adoption expenses, you may be able to claim the credit.

25.17 Claiming the Adoption Credit on Form 8839

The adoption credit is claimed on Form 8839, which you attach to your Form 1040 or 1040A. On Form 8839, you provide the child's name, age, and taxpayer identification number (generally a Social Security number). On Form 8839 for 2002, you take into account the $10,000-per-child limitation and reduce the maximum allowable credit if your modified adjusted gross income is over $150,000 and under $190,000. No credit is allowed if modified adjusted gross income for 2002 is $190,000 or more. The $10,000 limit on qualifying expenses is not an annual limit but an overall limit that applies to each effort to adopt an eligible child, even if expenses are incurred over several years. If a 2002 credit is based on pre-2002 expenses, the prior law limit of $5,000 ($6,000 for special needs adoptions) applies; *see* the transition rule below.

If you are married, you generally must file a joint return to take the adoption credit or exclusion. You may take the credit or exclusion on a separate return if you are legally separated under a decree of divorce or separate maintenance, or if you lived apart from your spouse for the last six months of the tax year and (1) your home is the eligible child's home for more than half the year and (2) you pay more than half the cost of keeping up your home for the year.

Qualifying Expenses. Qualifying adoption expenses are reasonable and necessary adoption fees, court costs, attorney fees, and other expenses directly related to, and whose principal purpose is for, the legal adoption of an eligible child *(25.16)*. You may not claim a credit for the costs of a surrogate parenting arrangement or for adopting your spouse's child.

When to claim the adoption credit for a child who is a U.S. citizen or resident. If you pay qualifying expenses in any year before the year the adoption becomes final, the credit may be claimed in the year after the year of the payment, whether or not the adoption is final in that year. If you pay qualifying expenses in the year the adoption becomes final, the credit for those expenses is claimed in that year. If qualifying expenses are paid in any year after the year in which the adoption becomes final, the credit is claimed in the year of payment.

Transition rule: pre-2002 expenses remain subject to prior law $5,000/$6,000 limit. Prior to 2002, the maximum amount of qualifying adoption expenses that could be taken into account when computing the credit was $5,000, or $6,000 in the case of a special needs adoption. If you paid qualifying expenses in 2001 and the adoption was not final at the end of 2001, a credit for the 2001 expenses is allowed on your 2002 return under the regular credit timing rule. The 2002 credit for the 2001 expenses is subject to the $5,000 or $6,000 limit in effect for 2001, rather than the $10,000 limit applicable to expenses paid after 2001.

Foreign child. If you adopt a child who is not a U.S. citizen or resident at the time the adoption effort begins, a credit may not be claimed until the year the adoption becomes final. If adoption expenses are paid after the tax year in which the adoption became finalized, a credit for such expenses is allowed for the tax year of payment.

Special needs adoption finalized after 2002. An adoption is considered a "special needs" adoption if the child is a U.S. citizen or resident when the adoption process begins, and a state (or District of Columbia) determines that the child cannot or should not be returned to his or her parents and that because of special factors, assistance is required to place the child with adoptive parents.

If a special needs adoption is finalized after 2002, a special rule allows qualifying expenses to be grossed up to $10,000 in the year the adoption is finalized where the aggregate of qualifying expenses for that year and all prior years is under $10,000. Thus, if a special needs adoption is initiated in 2002 and finalized in 2003 and actual qualifying expenses for both years are $8,000, a $10,000 credit may be claimed for 2003. Total expenses are deemed to be $10,000, so the credit for 2003 includes not only the $8,000 of actual expenses, but also an additional $2,000, the excess of $10,000 over the actual expenses. This special rule applies only to finalized special needs adoptions.

 Law Alert

Credit Limit and Phase-out Threshold Subject to Inflation Adjustment in 2003
Starting in 2003, the $10,000 credit limit and $150,000 phase-out threshold may be increased by an inflation adjustment.

 Filing Tip

Unused Credit Carryforward
The amount of your allowable adoption credit for a year cannot be more than your tax liability for that year; follow the Form 8839 instructions. If your credit is more than this limit, you can carry forward any unused credit for the next five years, or until used, whichever comes first.

Chapter 26

Tax Withholdings

Withholding taxes gives the Government part of your income before you have a chance to use it. Withholding tax is imposed on salary and wage income, tip income, certain gambling winnings, pensions, and retirement distributions, but you may avoid withholding on retirement payments; *see 26.11*. Withholding is also imposed on interest and dividends if you do not give your taxpayer identification number to a payer of interest or dividend income.

You may increase or decrease withholdings on your wages by submitting a new Form W-4 to your employer. Withholdings may be reduced by claiming allowances based on tax deductions and credits.

Make sure that tax withholdings meet or help you meet the estimated tax rules that require withholdings plus estimated tax payments to equal 90% of your current year liability or the required percentage of the prior year's liability; *see* Chapter 27.

A 20% withholding rate applies to eligible rollover distributions from an employer retirement plan. You may avoid the withholding by instructing your employer to directly transfer the funds to an IRA or the plan of your new employer; *see 26.11*.

26.1 Withholdings Should Cover Estimated Tax

In fixing the rate of withholding on your wages, pay attention to the tests for determining whether sufficient income taxes have been withheld from your pay. A penalty will apply if your wage withholdings plus estimated tax payments (including prior year overpayments credited to current estimated tax) do not equal the lesser of 90% of your current tax liability or the required percentage of the prior year's tax; *see 27.1.*

Taxes are withheld from payments made to you for services that you perform as an employee; *see 26.2* for exceptions. By filing Form W-4, you claim exemptions for yourself, your spouse, and dependents. The number of exemptions claimed will either decrease or increase the amount of withholding. You also may claim withholding allowances for itemized deductions and credits such as the child tax credit, child and dependent care credit, education tax credits, adoption credit, credit for the elderly and totally disabled, the foreign tax credit, credit for home mortgages, the general business credit, and earned income credit (if you have not filed for an advance payment of the credit on Form W-5).

26.2 When Income Taxes Are Withheld on Wages

The amount of income tax withheld for your wage bracket depends on your marital status and the number of exemptions you claim. Exemptions for withholding correspond to the exemptions allowed on your tax return; *see 21.1.* You file a withholding certificate, Form W-4, with your employer, indicating your status and exemptions. Without the certificate, your employer must withhold tax as if you are a single person with no exemptions.

Cash payments or the cash value of benefits paid to an employee by an employer are subject to withholding, unless the payments are specifically excluded.

Income Taxes Are Withheld on:

- Payments to employees as salaries, wages, fees, commissions, pensions, retirement pay, vacation allowances, dismissal pay, etc. (whether paid in cash or goods). If regular wage withholding rates are not used on separately paid bonuses, commissions, and overtime pay, an employer may withhold at a flat rate of 27%. See 26.11 for withholding on pensions and annuities.
- Sick pay paid by your employer. If a third party pays you sick pay on a plan funded by your employer, you may request withholding by filing Form W-4S.
- Taxable group insurance coverage over $50,000.
- Reimbursements of expenses that do not meet qualifying rules of accountable plans discussed at *20.31.* Also, reimbursements from accountable plans that exceed federal rates if the employee does not return the reimbursement or show that it is substantiated by proof of expenses.
- Pay to members of the U.S. Armed Forces.
- Prize awarded to a salesperson in a contest run by his or her employer.
- Retroactive pay and overtime under the Fair Labor Standards Act.
- Taxable supplemental unemployment compensation benefits.

Income Taxes Are Not Withheld on:

- Payments to household workers. However, although income tax withholding is not required, the worker and the employer may make a voluntary withholding agreement; *see 25.9.*
- Payments to agricultural workers, college domestics, ministers of the gospel (except chaplains in the Armed Forces), casual workers, nonresident aliens, public officials who receive fees directly from the public, notaries, jurors, witnesses, precinct workers, etc.; but *see* voluntary withholding agreements, *26.3.*
- Pay for newspaper home delivery by children under age 18.
- Advances for traveling expenses if the employee substantiates expenses to the employer and if the employee returns any unsubstantiated amount; *see 20.31.*
- Value of tax-free board and lodging furnished by an employer.
- Fringe benefits not subject to tax.
- Substantiated reimbursements for deductible moving expenses or medical care benefits under a self-insured medical reimbursement plan.
- Death benefit payments to beneficiary of employee; wages due but unpaid at employee's death and paid to estate or beneficiary.
- Pay for U.S. citizen working abroad or in U.S. possessions to the extent that the pay is tax free; *see* Chapter 36 for rules.
- Earnings of self-employed persons; they may pay estimated tax installments throughout the year.

 *Filing Instruction*

Adjust Withholdings

If you do not expect withholdings to meet your final tax liability, ask your employer to withhold a greater amount of tax; *see 26.3.* On the other hand, if the withholding rate applied to your wages results in overwithholding, you may claim extra withholding allowances to reduce withholding during the year; *see 26.5* and *26.6.*

Form W-2. By January 31, 2003, your employer must give you duplicate copies of your 2002 Form W-2, which is a record of your pay and the withheld income and Social Security taxes. If you leave your job during the year, you may ask your employer for a Form W-2 by making a written request within 30 days of leaving the job.

26.3 Increasing Withholding

For withholding tax purposes, you do not have to claim all your exemptions. This will increase the amount withheld and help reduce the final tax payment on filing your tax return. It may also relieve you of having to make quarterly estimated tax payments, provided the withholdings are sufficient to meet your estimated tax liability; *see 27.1.* A waiver of exemptions for withholding taxes does not prevent you from claiming the "waived" exemptions on your final tax return. The waiver is merely a bookkeeping aid to your company's payroll department. If you find that even a waiver of exemptions does not cover all of the tax you want withheld, you may ask your employer on Form W-4 to withhold additional amounts from each paycheck.

26.4 Avoiding Withholding

If you had no income tax liability in 2002 and expect none for 2003, you may be exempt from income tax withholdings on your 2003 wages. If eligible, students working for the summer, retired persons, and other part-time workers do not have to wait for a refund of withheld taxes they do not owe. The exemption applies only to income tax withholding, not to withholdings for Social Security and Medicare *(26.10)*. However, if you can be claimed as a dependent on another person's tax return, you may not claim this special exemption if you expect total income (wages plus investments) to be more than $750 *(13.5)* and investment income to be more than $250. If the $750 and $250 amounts are increased due to an inflation factor, the higher amounts will be on the 2003 version of Form W-4.

If you cannot be claimed as a dependent by another person, you can claim the exemption from withholding if your total income is no more than the sum of your personal exemption and the standard deduction for your filing status.

To claim an exemption for 2003, you must file a withholding exemption certificate, Form W-4, with your employer. The form may be obtained from an IRS district office or from your employer. If you will file a joint return for 2003, do not claim an exemption on Form W-4 if the joint return will show a tax. An exemption claimed during 2003 will expire February 15, 2004.

26.5 Withholding Allowances

Too much income tax may be withheld from your pay if you have tax reduction items. The overpayment will be refunded when you file your return, but you lose the use of your money during the year. By filing Form W-4 with your employer, you may avoid this and reduce withholding taxes by claiming additional withholding allowances based on the following: (1) estimated itemized deductions; (2) IRA contribution deductions; (3) alimony deductions; (4) net losses from Schedule C, D, E, or F of Form 1040; and (5) tax credits such as the child tax credit, education credits, dependent care credit, credit for the elderly, earned income credit (if you did not request advance payment on Form W-5), and general business credit.

Working couples filing jointly should figure withholding allowances on their combined wage income, deductions, adjustments, and credits, but can divide the total number of allowances between them in any way they wish. On separate returns, the allowances must be figured separately.

If you work for only one employer and are unmarried, you may claim an additional withholding allowance. If you are married, you may claim the additional allowance if you work for only one employer and your spouse does not work, or your wages from a second job or your spouse's wages are $1,000 or less. This special allowance is only for withholding purposes. You may not claim it on your tax return.

If you work for two or more employers at the same time, you figure your withholding allowances based on the total income, and then split the allowances between the two jobs in any way you wish. Do not claim the same allowances with more than one employer at the same time.

File a new Form W-4 each year for withholding allowances based on itemized deductions and credits. Furthermore, you may have to file a new form to increase your withholding if withholding allowances you had been claiming are no longer allowed; *see 26.6.*

Planning Reminder

When To Change Withholdings

Adjust withholding if there will be a significant change in the tax you owe for 2003. Credits such as the child tax credit, Hope scholarship credit, and lifetime learning credit may reduce your 2003 tax. By decreasing your withholding now, you can get the benefit of the lower taxes throughout the year. On the other hand, a withholding increase may be advisable if previously claimed deductions or credits will not be available to you, or if you expect an increase in nonwage income such as capital gains. Check the instructions to Forms W-4 and 1040-ES for 2003 to help you adjust your withholdings.

Planning Reminder

Part-Year Employees May Avoid Overwithholding

Starting a new job in the middle of a year presents a withholding problem. The amount of tax withheld from your paycheck is figured by taking your weekly pay and multiplying this by a 52-week pay period. For example, if as a recent graduate you start a job on July 1 and your weekly pay is $1,000 for 26 weeks (July 1–December 31), your withholding will be based on an annual income of $52,000 ($1,000 × 52 weeks) and not the $26,000 you will actually earn that year. This will result in overwithholding. To alleviate this problem, you may ask your employer to calculate withholdings on what is known as the "part year" method if your work days during the year are expected to be 245 or fewer. This formula calculates withholding based on actual earnings rather than expected earnings over a full year of employment. As an alternative, you may elect to claim extra exemptions on Form W-4, which has the same effect of reducing the amount withheld each week from your paycheck.

A civil penalty of $500 may be imposed if, for purposes of claiming tax withholding allowances, you overstate your itemized deductions and credits or understate your wages without a reasonable basis. There is also a criminal penalty of up to $1,000 plus a jail sentence for willfully supplying false information.

26.6 When To File a New Form W-4

You should file a new Form W-4 any time the number of your exemptions or withholding allowances increases or decreases, such as when a child is born or adopted, you marry, you get a divorce, or your deductible expenses change.

Your employer may make the new Form W-4 effective with the next payment of wages. However, an employer may postpone the new withholding rate until the start of the first payroll period ending on or after the 30th day from the day you submit the revised form.

You must file a new Form W-4 within 10 days if the number of allowances previously claimed by you decreases because: you divorce or legally separate; you stop supporting a dependent; or a dependent for whom you claimed a withholding allowance will receive more than the exemption amount for the year ($3,000 in 2002), but this income restriction does not apply to your child who is under 19 years of age or a student under age 24 as of the end of the year.

The death of a spouse or a dependent in a current year does not affect your withholding until the next year but requires the filing of a new certificate, if possible, by the first business day in December, or within 10 days if the death is in December. However, a widow or widower entitled to joint return rates in the next two years as a qualifying widow or widower with a dependent child *(1.11)* need not file a new withholding certificate.

When you file on or before December 1, your employer must reduce your withholding as of January 1 of the next year.

26.7 Voluntary Withholding on Certain Government Payments

You can choose to have income tax withheld from Social Security benefits (and equivalent tier 1 Railroad Retirement benefits), unemployment compensation, crop damage payments, and Commodity Credit Corporation loans. The withholding request is made on Form W-4V. Electing to have tax withheld may eliminate the need to make estimated tax installments; *see 27.2*.

For unemployment compensation you may choose a withholding rate of 10%. For the other government payments, you may select a withholding rate of 7%, 10%, 15%, or 27%.

26.8 When Tips Are Subject to Withholding

Tips are subject to income tax and FICA (Social Security and Medicare) withholdings. If you receive cash tips amounting to $20 or more in a month, you must report the total amount of tips received during the month to your employer on Form 4070 (or a similar written report). Include cash tips paid to you in your own behalf. If you "split" or share tips with others, you include in your report only your share. You do not include tips received in the form of merchandise or your share of service charges turned over to you by your employer. Make the report on or before the 10th day after the end of the month in which the tips are received. (If the 10th day is a Saturday, Sunday, or legal holiday, you must submit the report by the next business day.) For example, tips amounting to $20 or more that are received during January 2003 are reported by February 10, 2003. Your employer may require more frequent reporting.

You are considered to have income from tips when you receive the tips, even if they are not reported to the employer.

Your employer withholds the Social Security, Medicare, and income tax due on the tips from your wages or from funds you give him or her for withholding purposes. If the taxes due cannot be collected on the tips, either from your wages or from voluntary contributions, by the 10th day after the end of the month in which tips are reported, you have to pay the tax when you file your income tax return.

Where wages are insufficient to meet all of the withholding liability, the wages are applied first to Social Security and Medicare tax.

Penalty for failure to report tips. Failure to report tip income of $20 or more received during the month to your employer may subject you to a penalty of 50% of the Social Security and Medicare tax due on the unreported tips, unless your failure was due to reasonable cause rather than to willful neglect.

Law Alert

Voluntary Withholding from Government Payments

The highest voluntary withholding rate is reduced from 27% in 2003 to 26% for 2004–05 and 25% in 2006 and later years.

Filing Instruction

Tip Reporting

If you have not reported tips of $20 or more in any month, or tips are allocated to you under the special tip allocation rules, you must compute Social Security and Medicare tax on that amount on Form 4137 and enter it as a tax due on Line 57 of Form 1040; attach Form 4137 to Form 1040. The unreported tips must be included as wages on Line 7 of Form 1040.

Tips of less than $20 per month are taxable but not subject to withholding.

Tip allocation reporting by large restaurants. To help the IRS audit the reporting of tip income, restaurants employing at least 10 people must make a special report of income and allocate tips based on gross receipts. For purposes of the allocation, the law assumes tip income of at least 8%. If you voluntarily report tips equal to your allocable share of 8% of the restaurant's gross receipts, no allocation will be made to you. However, if the total tips reported by all employees is less than 8% of gross receipts and you do not report your share of the 8%, your employer must make an allocation based on the difference between the amount you reported and your share of the 8% amount. The allocated amount is shown on Form W-2. However, taxes are not withheld on the allocated amount. Taxes are withheld only on amounts actually reported by employees. An employer or majority of employees may ask the IRS to apply a tip percentage of less than 8%, but no lower than 2%.

Reporting allocated tips. Your employer will show allocated tips in Box 8 of your Form W-2. However, this amount will not be included in Box 1 wages and you must add it to income yourself by reporting it on Line 7 of Form 1040. You also must compute Social Security and Medicare tax on the allocated tips on Form 4137 and enter the tax from Form 4137 on Line 57 of Form 1040. You may not use Form 1040A or Form 1040EZ.

Filing Instruction

Uncollected Social Security and Medicare Taxes

If your employer is unable to collect enough money from your wages during the year to cover the Social Security or Medicare tax on the tips you reported, the uncollected amount is shown on your Form W-2 in Box 12 with Code A next to it for Social Security or Code B for Medicare. You must report the uncollected amount on Line 61 of Form 1040 (total tax) as an additional tax due; write "UT" and show the amount next to Line 61.

26.9 Withholding on Gambling Winnings

Gambling winnings are generally reported by the payer to the IRS and to the winner on Form W-2G if the amount paid is $600 or more and at least 300 times the amount of the wager; the payer has the option of taking into account the wager in applying the $600 test. Different reporting rules apply to winnings from keno, bingo, and slot machines. Keno winnings are reported on Form W-2G if they are $1,500 or more, *reduced* by the wager. Winnings from bingo or slot machines of $1,200 or more, *not* reduced by the wager, are reported on Form W-2G.

Your winnings from gambling are subject to withholding if your winnings exceed:

1. $5,000 from lotteries, sweepstakes, and wagering pools (whether or not state-conducted), including church raffles, *pari-mutuel* betting pools and on- and off-track racing pools; or
2. $5,000 from other wagering transactions, if the proceeds are at least 300 times as large as the amount wagered, such as from wagers on horse races, dog races, or jai alai.

The withholding rate is 27% for 2002 and 2003. It will fall to 26% in 2004.

If your winnings exceed the $5,000 threshold, withholding applies to your gross winnings less your wagers, and not just the amounts over $5,000. Any withholdings will be shown on Form W-2G.

The IRS requires you to tell the payers of gambling winnings if you are also receiving winnings from identical wagers; winnings from identical wagers must be added together to determine if withholding is required.

If you have agreed to share your winnings with another person, give the payer a Form 5754. The payer will then prepare separate Forms W-2G for each of you.

Caution

Backup Gambling Withholding

Winnings from bingo, keno, and slot machines are not subject to income tax withholding. However, if you do not provide a taxpayer identification number, the payer will withhold tax at the 30% backup withholding rate *(26.12).*

26.10 FICA Withholdings

FICA withholdings are employee contributions for Social Security and Medicare coverage. Your employer is liable for the tax if he or she fails to make proper withholdings. The amount withheld is figured on your wages and is not affected by your marital status, number of exemptions, or the fact that you may be over age 65 and are collecting Social Security. On Form W-2, Social Security withholdings are shown in Box 4 and Medicare withholdings in Box 6.

Subject to FICA tax are your regular salary, commissions, bonuses, vacation pay, cash tips, group-term insurance coverage over $50,000, the first six months of sick pay, and contributions to cash or deferred (401(k)) pay plans or salary-reduction contributions to a simplified employee pension (SEP), SIMPLE IRA, or tax-sheltered annuity. Not subject to tax are the value of tax-free meals and lodgings, as discussed in *3.11,* and reimbursements for substantiated travel or entertainment expenses or for moving expenses.

Excess Social Security and Railroad Retirement withholding. If you have worked for more than one employer during 2002, attach all Copies B of Form W-2 to your return. Check to see that the total withheld in 2002 by your employers does not exceed your liability for Social Security taxes. The maximum 2003 liability for Social Security is $5,263.80, 6.2% on the first $84,900 of salary income. If too much was withheld, claim the excess as a payment on Line 65 of your 2002 Form 1040. On Form 1040A, the excess is added to your total tax payments; you cannot claim the excess on Form 1040-EZ.

Medicare tax is withheld at a rate of 1.45% on *all* salary and wage income.

Employees covered by the Railroad Retirement Tax Act (RRTA) receive Form W-2, which lists total wages paid and withholdings of income and Railroad Retirement taxes. Follow tax form instructions for claiming a credit for excess Railroad Retirement withholding.

If any one employer withheld too much Social Security or Railroad Retirement tax, you cannot claim the excess on your income tax return. You must ask that employer for a refund of the excess.

Wages you pay to your spouse or child. Wages you pay to your spouse for working in your business are subject to FICA tax and income tax withholding. Wages you pay to your child for working in your business are subject to income tax withholding but exempt from FICA if the child is under age 18. Wages you pay to your child under age 21 or to your spouse for domestic work or child care in your own home are exempt from FICA.

Student employees exempt from FICA. A statutory exemption from FICA taxes covers students who work for schools, colleges, and universities. The exemption benefits students whose work is incidental to their studies, as opposed to "career" employees who take courses while working for a school.

IRS guidelines provide a safe harbor for students enrolled at least half-time (half of whatever is considered full time) in undergraduate, graduate, or professional programs. Generally, such students will not be subject to FICA taxes regardless of the number of hours they work for their school, college, or university, or an affiliated organization, or the amount of compensation received. Additionally, students who are in the last marking period of their chosen course of study and enrolled in the number of credit hours needed to complete the requirements for certification will also qualify for the exemption even though they are enrolled with less than half-time status. However, the safe harbor does not apply to services performed while the student is not enrolled during school breaks of more than five weeks. Employment that continues over school breaks of five weeks or less while the student is not enrolled in classes will qualify for the exception so long as the student was enrolled on at least a half-time basis on the last day before the break and is eligible to enroll for the next academic period.

Although the exception generally applies to graduate and professional students, it does not apply to post-doctoral students and fellows, medical residents, and medical interns, who are treated as career employees. However, although the safe harbor exemption does not apply, an exemption may still be available for a particular career employee based on all the facts and circumstances.

26.11 Withholding on Retirement Distributions

Retirement distributions are subject to withholding taxes, but you may avoid withholdings. The method of avoiding withholding varies with the type of payment.

Periodic payments. If you receive periodic payments, such as an annuity, withholding is required unless you elect to avoid withholding on Form W-4P, or on a substitute form furnished by the payer. If you are a U.S. citizen or resident alien, withholding may not be avoided on pensions or other distributions paid outside the U.S. or U.S. possessions. Payment must be to your home address within the U.S. (or in a U.S. possession) to avoid withholding.

Unless you tell the payer otherwise, wage withholding tables are used to figure withholdings on periodic payments as if you were married and claiming three withholding exemptions. Withholding allowances may be claimed on Form W-4P for estimated itemized deductions, alimony payments, student loan interest, and deductible IRA contributions.

You may also request that the payer withhold a specific amount of additional tax for each payment.

Planning Reminder

Wages Paid to Household Employees

See 25.10 for FICA withholding on wages paid to household employees.

Caution

Employer Plan Distributions

Your employer must withhold 20% from a distribution paid to you if the distribution was eligible for tax-free rollover; *see 7.8.*

Planning Reminder

Rollover From Employer Plan
20% withholding does not apply to a distribution eligible for rollover *(7.8)* if you have the employer make a direct rollover to a qualified plan or IRA.

Nonperiodic payments from IRAs and commercial annuities. Nonperiodic payments are subject to withholding at a flat 10% rate unless you elect to avoid withholding on Form W-4P (or substitute form). IRA distributions that are payable upon demand are considered nonperiodic and, thus, subject to the 10% withholding rule.

Nonperiodic payments from qualified employer plans. Employers must withhold 20% from nonperiodic payments, such as lump-sum distributions that are eligible for tax-free rollover but which are paid directly to you. To avoid withholding you must direct your employer to make a direct rollover *(7.8)* of the funds to an IRA or to a defined contribution plan of your new employer. If you do not instruct your employer to make the direct transfer and elect to personally receive the distribution, 20% will be withheld before payment is made to you.

See 7.8 for a further explanation and an Example showing the effects of the withholding rule where you receive the distribution and then decide to make a rollover yourself.

26.12 Backup Withholding

Backup withholding is designed to pressure taxpayers to report interest and dividend income. You may be subject to backup withholding if you do not give your taxpayer identification number to parties paying you interest or dividend income, you give an incorrect number, or you ignore IRS notices stating that you have underreported interest or dividends. Your taxpayer identification number generally is your Social Security number or your employer identification number. The backup withholding rate is 30% for 2002 and 2003.

Backup withholding will apply to fees of $600 or more (Form 1099-MISC) for work you do as an independent contractor, payments from brokers (Form 1099-B), royalty payments (Form 1099-MISC), and certain gambling winnings *(see 26.9)* if you do not give the payer your taxpayer identification number.

Civil and criminal penalties can be imposed if you provide false information to avoid backup withholding.

Chapter 27

Estimated Tax Payments

Income taxes are collected on a pay-as-you-go basis through withholding on wages and pensions, as well as quarterly estimated tax payments on other income. Where all or most of your income is from wages, pensions, and annuities, you will generally not have to pay estimated tax, because your estimated tax liability has been satisfied by withholding. But do not assume you are not required to pay simply because taxes have been withheld from your wages. Always check your estimated tax liability. Withholding may not cover your tax; the withholding tax rate may be below your actual tax rate when considering other income such as interest, dividends, business income, and capital gains.

Your estimated tax must also include liability for self-employment tax, alternative minimum tax (AMT), and FICA withholding tax for household employees.

You have to make quarterly estimated tax payments during 2003 if your estimated tax liability, after accounting for withholding taxes, is $1,000 or more and the withholding taxes will not be at least 90% of your 2003 tax liability or 100% of your 2002 tax liability if your 2002 adjusted gross income (AGI) is $150,000 or less ($75,000 or less if you are married filing separately in 2003). If your 2002 AGI exceeds this $150,000 (or $75,000) threshold, the percentage test for 2002 tax liability is 110%.

Failure to pay a required estimated tax installment will subject you to a penalty based on the prevailing IRS interest rate applied to tax deficiences.

Estimated tax payments may be made with vouchers included with Form 1040-ES or by charging payments on certain credit cards. Residents of Puerto Rico during the entire taxable year also use Form 1040-ES. Nonresident aliens should use Form 1040-ES (NR).

27.1 Do You Owe an Estimated Tax Penalty for 2002?

When you have computed the exact amount of your 2002 tax liability on your 2002 return, you can determine if you are subject to an estimated tax penalty. If you owe less than $1,000 on your 2002 return after taking into account withheld taxes, you are not subject to a penalty. If the tax owed after withholdings is $1,000 or more, you can now determine whether your 2002 withholdings plus estimated tax installments were at least 90% (66$^2/_3$% for farmers and fishermen) of your 2002 total tax (regular tax plus alternative minimum tax and penalty taxes) *minus* certain tax credits. If you met the 90% test, you are not subject to an estimated tax penalty for 2002.

Even if the 90% test was not met, you may still generally avoid an estimated tax penalty if your withholdings and estimated tax installments for 2002 were at least 100% of the total tax on your 2001 return. This exception requires that the 2001 return covered all 12 months. However, if your 2001 adjusted gross income exceeded $150,000 ($75,000 if you are married filing separately for 2002), your withholdings plus estimated tax installments for 2002 had to be at least 112% of your 2001 total tax (not 100%) to qualify for this prior year liability exception.

To completely avoid a penalty for 2002 under either the 90% current year exception or the 100%/112% prior year exception, you must have paid at least 25% of the amount required under the applicable exception by each of the four payment dates. The penalty is figured separately for each payment period; *see* below.

Even if you owe $1,000 or more (after withholdings) on your 2002 return and you do not qualify for either the 90% current year exception or 100%/112% prior year exception, you are not subject to an estimated tax penalty for 2002 if you did not have to file a 2001 return or your 2001 total tax was zero. This exception applies only if you were a U.S. citizen or resident for all of 2001 and your 2001 tax year included 12 full months.

If you underestimated your 2002 liability because of an unexpected increase in income during 2002, or if you did not earn income evenly throughout 2002, such as where you operated a seasonal business, you may be able to lower or eliminate the penalty by using the *annualized income installment method.* Under this exception, you may avoid a penalty for an estimated tax installment by figuring the installment that would be due if the income (and deductions) earned before the date for the installment were *annualized.* Form 2210 and IRS Publication 505 have worksheets for applying the annualized income exception. The computation is complicated and its use may be discouraged by the complexity, despite the potential benefits.

Penalties are figured separately for each payment period. Separate penalty determinations must be made for each of the four 2002 estimated tax payment periods, as of the applicable installment dates: April 15, June 17, and September 16 in 2002, and January 15, 2003). This means that if, after taking into account withholdings from your pay, you underpaid an installment, you may owe a penalty for that period even though you overpaid later installments to make up the difference. The penalty for each period, which is based on prevailing interest rates, runs from the installment due date until the amount is paid or until the regular filing date for the final tax return, whichever is earlier.

Withholding payments are treated as if they were payments of estimated tax. In applying them, the total withholdings of the year are divided equally between each installment period unless you elect on Form 2210 to apply them to the periods in which they were actually withheld.

Figure the 2002 penalty for yourself on Form 2210 or let the IRS do it. You can use Form 2210 to determine any 2002 penalty, but the IRS encourages taxpayers to let the IRS compute any penalty. The IRS will figure the amount of any penalty and bill you for the amount if you do not complete Form 2210.

There is no penalty and you do not have to file Form 2210 if the tax liability shown on your 2002 return is less than $1,000, after taking into account withholdings. There also is no penalty if you had no tax liability for 2001, you were a U.S. citizen or resident for all of 2001, and your 2001 taxable year included 12 full months.

You *must* attach Form 2210 to your 2002 return if: (1) you use the annualized income exception; (2) you do not allocate wage withholdings in four equal amounts; (3) your required estimated tax payment for 2002 is based on the applicable percentage (100% or 112%) of the 2001 tax and a joint return is filed for either 2001 or 2002 but not both; or (4) you claim a penalty waiver; *see* below for waiver rules.

Planning Reminder

Credit Card Payments

You may charge estimated tax payments using a Visa, MasterCard, American Express, or Discover Card. *See* the Form 1040-ES instructions. If you charge estimated tax payments, you do not have to file Form 1040-ES vouchers.

If you *underpaid* for any payment period, the amount of the underpayment reduces the payment made in the following period. That is, an underpayment of one period is carried over to succeeding periods on Form 2210. If you underpay for a period, any payment you make after that installment date will be applied first to the earlier underpayment. Thus, even if you make the required payment for a period, you could still be subject to a penalty for that period because your payment is applied to a prior underpayment.

If you *overpaid* for any period, the excess carries over to the next period. The excess cannot be used to make up for an underpayment of the prior period. However, these rules apply only to installment payments made with Form 1040-ES vouchers or by credit card. They do not apply to withholdings, which are allocated equally over the year so that withholdings late in the year can reduce an underpayment for an earlier payment period.

Waiver of penalty for hardship, retirement, or disability. The IRS may waive the penalty if you can show you failed to pay the estimated tax because of casualty, disaster, or other unusual circumstances.

The IRS may also waive a penalty for a 2002 underpayment if in 2002 or 2001 you retired after reaching age 62 or became disabled, and you failed to make a payment due to reasonable cause and not due to willful neglect. To apply for the waiver, attach an explanation on Form 2210 that documents the circumstances supporting your waiver request.

27.2 Planning Estimated Tax Payments for 2003

In planning your payments for 2003, you do not want to pay more than is necessary to avoid a penalty. If you expect your 2003 income and deductions to be about the same as in 2002, apply 2003 tax rates (which will be in the *Supplement* and in the 2003 instructions to Form 1040-ES) to your 2002 taxable income and base your 2003 withholdings and quarterly estimated tax installments on 90% of that tax. If you were subject to self-employment tax or alternative minimum tax in 2002, add 90% of such taxes to your 2003 estimate.

Safe harbor for 2003 based on 2002 tax. If you are uncertain of the amount of your 2003 income and deductions, you can play it safe and avoid a possible penalty in 2003 by having withholdings and quarterly estimated tax installments equal to your 2002 tax liability if your 2002 adjusted gross income is $150,000 or less ($75,000 or less if married filing separately for 2003), provided you filed a 2002 return covering a full 12 months. If your 2002 AGI exceeds the $150,000 (or $75,000) threshold, your payments for 2003 must be at least 110% of your 2002 tax.

If an accurate estimate for 2003 is possible, it is generally advantageous to base your estimated payments on the 90% test rather than the 100%/110% prior year test, as using this prior year test will probably result in an overestimation of your liability unless the 2003 tax turns out to be substantially larger than the 2002 tax.

You may use the worksheet and the tax rate schedule included in the 2003 Form 1040-ES to figure your estimated tax liability and the required annual payment to avoid a penalty under either the 90% current year or prior year liability tests just discussed.

Reduce your 2003 estimated tax liability by expected withholdings from wages, pensions, and annuities. If after withholdings your estimated tax is $1,000 or more, you must make estimated tax payments unless the withholdings will cover at least 90% of your estimated 2003 liability or 100%/110% of your 2002 liability. If withholdings will not cover the amount required under the 90% or 100%/110% tests, you may pay the balance of the estimated tax with Form 1040-ES vouchers, by credit card, or by direct debit from your checking or savings account if you electronically file your 2002 return. The first installment is due April 15, 2003.

Crediting 2002 refund to 2003 estimated tax. If you are due a refund when you file your 2002 return, it may be credited to your 2003 estimated tax. You may also split up the amount due you. You may take part of the overpayment as a refund. The other part may be credited to your estimate of 2003 taxes. The IRS will credit the refund to the April installment of 2003 estimated tax unless you attach a statement to your return instructing the IRS to apply the refund to later installments.

Check your arithmetic before you apply an overpayment as a credit on your next year's estimate. If you apply too much, the amount credited may not be used to offset any additional tax due that the IRS determines you owe. For example, your 2002 return shows a $500 refund due, and you apply it towards your 2003 estimated tax. However, the IRS determines that you overpaid $200, not $500. You will be billed for the additional $300 tax, plus interest due; you may not offset the extra tax with the credited amount.

Planning Reminder

Annualized Income Method
If your income typically fluctuates throughout the year, or if your income unexpectedly changes during the year, you may base installment payments on the annualized income method. This method allows you to avoid a penalty for installment periods during which less income is earned by reducing the required estimated tax payment for such periods. To figure your installment payments, use the Annualized Estimated Tax Worksheet in IRS Publication 505. If you base installment payments on the annualized method, you must file Form 2210 with your return to determine if you are subject to an estimated tax penalty.

Farmers or fishermen. In figuring the required annual payment to avoid a penalty for 2003, a farmer or fisherman has to pay only $66^2/_3\%$ of the 2003 estimated liability, rather than 90%. A penalty may also be avoided by paying 100% of the 2002 tax, provided a tax return covering a 12-month period was filed for 2002; the 110% test for higher-income taxpayers does not apply to a farmer or fisherman. To qualify as a farmer or fisherman under these rules, at least two-thirds of gross income for 2002 or 2003 must be from farming or fishing.

27.3 Dates for Paying Estimated Tax Installments for 2003

The four installment dates for 2003 estimated tax are: April 15, 2003; June 16, 2003; September 15, 2003; and January 15, 2004. Later installments may be used to amend earlier ones; *see 27.1.* You do not have to file the January 15, 2004, voucher if you file your 2003 tax return and pay the balance of tax due by February 2, 2004.

If you use a fiscal year. A fiscal year is any year other than the calendar year. If you file using a fiscal year, your first estimated installment is due on or before the 15th day of the fourth month of your fiscal year. The second and third installments are due on or before the 15th day of the sixth and ninth months of your fiscal year with the final installment due by the 15th day of the first month of your next fiscal year.

Farmers and fishermen. Farmers only have to make one installment payment, generally by January 15 of the following year. The payment for 2003 must be made by January 15, 2004, or farmers may file their 2003 returns by March 1, 2004, instead of making an estimated tax payment. To qualify under these rules, a farmer must receive two-thirds of his or her 2002 or 2003 gross income from farming.

Fishermen who expect to receive at least two-thirds of their gross income from fishing pay estimated taxes as farmers do.

27.4 Estimates by Husband and Wife

A married couple may pay joint or separate estimated taxes. The nature of the estimated tax does not control the kind of final return you file.

Where a joint estimated tax is paid but separate tax returns are filed, you and your spouse can decide on how to divide the estimated payments between you. Either one of you can claim the whole amount, or you can agree to divide it in any proportion. If you cannot agree, the IRS will allocate the estimated taxes proportionally according to the percentage of total tax each spouse owes.

If separate estimated taxes are paid, overpayment by one spouse is not applied against an underpayment by the other when separate final returns are filed.

A joint estimated tax may be made by a husband and wife only if they are both citizens or residents of the United States. Both must have the same taxable year. A joint estimate may not be made by a couple who are divorced or legally separated under a decree. If a joint estimate is made and the spouses are divorced or legally separated later in that year, they may divide the joint payments between them under the above rule for spouses who file separately.

Responsibility for paying estimated tax rests upon each spouse individually. Each must pay if individually required by the rules.

If a joint estimated tax is made and one spouse dies, the estate does not continue to make installment payments. The surviving spouse is required to pay the remaining installments unless he or she amends. Amounts paid on the joint estimate may be divided as agreed upon by the spouse and the estate of the deceased. If they do not agree, the IRS will apportion the payments according to the percentage of the total tax owed by each spouse.

27.5 Adjusting Your Payments During the Year

If, during the year, your income, expenses, or exemptions change, refigure your estimated tax liability and adjust your payment schedule as shown in the following Examples. Increasing an installment payment cannot make up for an underpayment in a prior period; *see* Example 2. However, withholdings from pay, pensions, and IRA withdrawals can be allocated equally over all four periods and, thus, withholding increased at the end of the year may be applied to earlier periods.

If taxes paid in the previous installments total more than your revised estimate, you cannot obtain a refund at that time. You must wait until you file your final return showing that a refund is due.

Planning Reminder

Withholdings Cover Prior Underpayment

You have a choice in allocating withholdings from pay or other income that is subject to withholding: (1) You may treat your entire year's withholdings as having been withheld in equal amounts for each of the four payment periods or (2) you may allocate to each payment period the actual withholdings paid for that period. Also, if toward the end of the year you find that you have underestimated for an earlier period, ask your employer to withhold an extra amount that may be allocated equally over the four periods. This way, you may eliminate the underestimate for the earlier periods.

EXAMPLES

1. Smith, who is self-employed, figures that to avoid a penalty for 2003 under the estimated tax rules discussed above, he must make estimated tax installments of $6,000. By April 15, he pays an installment of $1,500. In June, he amends his estimate, showing a tax of $3,000 instead of $6,000. He refigures the installment schedule by dividing $3,000 by 4, which gives a payment rate of $750 for each period. As he paid $1,500 in April, the $750 overpayment covers his June obligation. By September 15, he pays $750; by January 15, 2004, he pays $750.

2. In September 2003, Jones finds that his estimated 2003 tax liability should be $25,000 rather than his original estimate of $20,000. He paid $5,000 as his April and June installments ($10,000 total). Under the amended schedule, he should have paid $6,250 per period ($25,000 ÷ 4); $6,250 by April 15 and $6,250 by June 16. Thus, there is a $2,500 underpayment ($12,500 − 10,000) for the first two periods.

   To cover the underpayment of $2,500, which carries over to the third payment period (June 1 through August 31), Jones's installment by September 15 must be at least $8,750 ($6,250 + $2,500). If less than $8,750 is paid, there will be an underpayment for the third payment period, as payments in that period are applied first to the carried-over underpayment of $2,500. If at least $8,750 is paid by September 15, there is no third period underpayment to be carried over, so the required installment for the fourth period (September 1 through December 31), due by January 15, 2004, will be $6,250. Unless an exception *(27.1)* applies, the underpayments for the first two periods will be subject to a penalty.

PART 5

Personal Tax Savings Plans

The chapters in this part will alert you to special tax-saving opportunities and tell you how to take advantage of tax-saving ideas and planning strategies.

Chapter 28

Tax Planning

Tax planning is a year-round activity. By planning income and deduction strategies, you may be able to reduce your tax. You may realize capital gain income subject to lower capital gain rates, defer certain income to a later year in which you expect to pay a lower tax, and accelerate deductions to a higher tax year. Tax-free investments are available and, within limits, income splitting with family members may be possible.

This chapter illustrates basic tax-planning strategies. In subsequent chapters, tax-savings plans for homeowners, families, investors, and executives are discussed.

28.1 When To Defer Income and Accelerate Deductions

When you expect to pay less tax in a future year than in a current year, consider deferring income and accelerating deductions. There are two strategies: (1) to postpone receipt of income to a year of lower tax rates and/or (2) to claim deductions for losses and expenses in the year you are subject to the higher tax rates. Under Economic Growth and Tax Relief Reconciliation Act of 2001, there are six tax rates. For 2002 and 2003, the rates are 10%, 15%, 27%, 30%, 35%, and 38.6%. Between 2004 and 2006, the rates over 15% will drop further as shown below.

Calendar Year	27% Rate Reduced To:	30% Rate Reduced To:	35% Rate Reduced To:	38.6% Rate Reduced To:
2004–2005	26%	29%	34%	37.6%
2006 and later	25%	28%	33%	35%

In planning to defer income and accelerate deductions, watch these tax-rule limitations.

Postponing income. You may not defer salary income by not cashing a paycheck or not taking salary that you have earned and that you can receive without restrictions. Under certain conditions, you may contract with your employer to defer the taxable receipt of current compensation to future years. To defer pay to a future period you must take some risk. You cannot have any control over your deferred pay account. If you are not confident of your employer's ability to pay in the future, you should not defer pay.

Accelerating deductions. In accelerating deductions, there are these limitations: You may not deduct prepaid interest and rent. Prepaid interest must be deducted over the period of the loan. Rentals must also be deducted over the rental period. However, you can generally deduct prepayments of state income tax and accelerate your payments of charitable contributions. Annual subscriptions to professional journals and business magazines can be renewed before the end of the year. If the subscription is for more than a year, you may deduct only the first-year prepayment. The cost of the later subscription must be deducted in the later year. Contributions, purchases, and business expenses charged to credit card accounts are deductible in the year of charge, even though you do not pay your charge account bill until the next year. You can also realize losses by selling business or investment property that has lost value in the year you want to incur the loss.

Making an extra donation at the end of the year also may provide an added deduction that may lower your tax. You may deduct a charitable gift made by check on the last day of the year, even if the check is not cashed until the new year begins. Charitable donations may be timed to give you the largest possible tax savings. If, toward the end of the year, you find that you need an extra deduction, you may make a deductible donation in late December. Doing so would be especially beneficial if you know that your tax bracket will be lower the following year; *see* Chapter 14 for further planning details.

Also *see* Chapter 13 for claiming the standard deduction and itemizing deductions in alternate years, and Chapter 23 for planning steps when you may be subject to alternative minimum tax.

Deferring interest income to next year. Buying six-month certificates after June 30 can defer interest reporting to the next year. As a general rule, you have to report interest credited to your savings account for 2002, even if the account is a passbook account and you did not present the passbook to have the amount entered. Similarly, interest coupons due and payable in 2002 are taxable on your 2002 return, regardless of when they were presented for collection. For example, a coupon due in December 2002, but presented for payment in 2003, is taxable in 2002. However, there are opportunities to defer interest in the following ways:

1. Buy a savings certificate after June 30 with a maturity of one year or less. Interest is taxable in the next year when the certificate matures, provided that interest is specifically deferred until the following year by the terms of the certificate.

2. Buy Treasury bills that come due next year. 26-week bills bought after June 30 will mature in the next year.

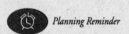
Planning Reminder

Deferring Business Income
If you are self-employed and are on the cash basis, you can defer income by delaying your billing at the end of the year or extending the time of collection. If you own a closely held corporation, you can time the payment of dividends and bonuses.

3. Buy Series EE bonds. These bonds may be cashed for their purchase price, plus an increase in their value over stated periods of time. The increase in redemption value is taxed as interest. You may defer the interest income until the year you cash the bond or the year the bond finally matures, whichever is earlier. Income deferral is also available for investments in U.S. "I-bonds"; *see 30.22.*

Timing sales of property. A sale is generally taxable in the year title to the property passes to the buyer. Since you can control the year title passes, you can usually defer income realized on the sale to the year in which you will pay less tax. Year-end sales of securities are discussed at *30.1.*

28.2 Earning Over the Thresholds for the Exemption Phase-out and Itemized Deduction Reduction

In figuring the tax cost of earning additional income, consider the phaseout of personal exemptions *(21.16)* or the 3% reduction to itemized deductions *(13.7).* When extra income, such as from a bonus, a freelance assignment, or a year-end sale of stock, pushes you over the *threshold* for the exemption phaseout or the 3% reduction, or if you already are over the threshold, your taxable income is increased not only by the earnings but also by the amounts disallowed by the phaseout or the 3% reduction. *See 21.16* for an example of how the effective tax rate on earnings is increased by the exemption phaseout.

For the 3% itemized deduction reduction on 2002 returns, the adjusted gross income (AGI) threshold is $137,300, except for married persons filing separately, who are subject to a $68,650 threshold. For the exemption phaseout, the AGI threshold is $137,300 for single persons, $171,650 for heads of household, $206,000 for married persons filing jointly and qualifying widow(er)s, and $103,000 for married persons filing separately.

You can estimate the amount of the increase in the effective rate on the additional income due to the exemption phaseout or 3% itemized deduction reduction by this equation:

$$\text{Increase in effective rate} = \frac{\text{Top bracket} \times \text{disallowed amount}}{\text{Excess income over threshold}}$$

Objective—	*Explanation—*
Realizing long-term capital gains	Long-term capital gains are taxed at rates lower than regular income taxes. *See* Chapter 5 for basic capital gain rules and Chapters 30 and 31 for discussions of special investment situations.
Earning tax-free income	You can earn tax-free income by— 1. Investing in tax-exempt securities. However, before you invest, determine whether the tax-free return will exceed the after-tax return of taxed income; *see 30.18*. 2. Taking a position in a company that pays tax-free fringe benefits, such as health and life insurance protection. For a complete discussion of tax-free fringe benefits, *see* Chapter 3. 3. Seeking tax-free education benefits with scholarship arrangements and educational IRAs; *see* Chapter 38. 4. Taking a position overseas to earn up to $80,000 tax free in 2003; *see* Chapter 36. 5. Investing in Roth IRAs; *see* Chapter 8.
Deferring income	You can defer income to years when you will pay less tax through— 1. Deferred pay plans, which are discussed in Chapter 2. 2. Qualified retirement plans such as 401(k) plans (*see* Chapter 7), Keogh plans (Chapter 41), and traditional IRA and Roth IRA plans (Chapter 8). 3. The year-end planning techniques explained in *28.1*. 4. Transacting installment sales when you sell property; *see 5.21*. 5. Investing in U.S. Savings EE bonds or I-bonds; *see 4.28 and 4.29, 30.21,* and *30.22*.
Income splitting tax benefits	Through income splitting you divide your income among several persons or taxpaying entities that will pay an aggregate tax lower than the tax that you would pay if you reported all of the income. Although the tax law limits income-splitting opportunities, certain business and family income planning through the use of trusts and custodian accounts can provide tax savings; *see* Chapters 24 and 33.
Tax-free exchanges	You can defer tax on appreciated property by transacting tax-free exchanges as discussed at *6.1* and *31.3*.
Buying a personal residence rather than renting	Homeowners are favored by the tax law. 1. Rather than paying rent, buy a home, condominium, or cooperative apartment. You may deduct interest and taxes. When you sell your home, you may avoid tax on gains of up to $250,000 if single and up to $500,000 if married filing jointly; *see* Chapter 29. 2. Homeowners can borrow on their home equity and deduct interest expenses; *see 15.3*.
Taking advantage of special personal tax breaks	The tax law provides several breaks for education expenses; *see* Chapter 38, which discusses scholarships, grants, tuition plans, bond tuition plans, education credits, Coverdell Education Savings Accounts, and student loan interest deduction. *See* Chapter 25 for personal tax credits such as the child tax credit, dependent care credit, and adoption credit.

Chapter 29

Tax Savings for Residence Sales

You may avoid tax on gain on the sale of a principal residence if you owned and used it for at least two years during the five-year period ending on the date of sale. If you are single, you may avoid tax on up to $250,000 of gain, $500,000 if you are married and file jointly.

If you used the residence for less than two years, you may avoid tax if you sold because of a change of job location or poor health; *see 29.4*.

You may not deduct a loss on the sale of a personal residence. Losses on the sale of property devoted to personal use are non-deductible. However, *see 29.9* and *29.10*, which explain under what conditions you may claim a loss deduction on the sale of a residence.

If you rent out a residential property and you or family members also use the residence during the year, rental expenses are subject to the special restrictions discussed at *9.7*.

$250,000/$500,000 Exclusion

Filing Instruction

Reporting Home Sale Gain

If the entire gain on the sale of your principal residence is excludable from income under the rules discussed in *29.1–29.7*, you do not have to report the sale at all on your return. If part of the gain is taxable, or you decide not to claim the exclusion for eligible gain, report the sale on Schedule D of Form 1040. Report the entire gain on Schedule D and on a separate line enter the excludable portion as a loss. Label the excludable amount as "Section 121 exclusion."

Planning Reminder

Form 1099-S

The settlement agent responsible for closing the sale of your principal residence must report the sale to the IRS on Form 1099-S if the sales price exceeded $250,000, or $500,000 if you are married filing jointly. If the price was $250,000/ $500,000 or less and you provide a written, signed certification that the full amount of your gain qualifies for the exclusion, the settlement agent may rely on the certification and not file the Form 1099-S or may choose to file the form anyway. IRS Revenue Procedure 98-20 has a sample certification form.

29.1 Avoiding Tax on Sale of Principal Residence

You may exclude from income up to $250,000 of gain realized on a sale or exchange of a residence in 2002, if you owned and occupied it as a principal residence for an aggregate of at least two years in the five-year period ending on the date of sale; *see 29.2.* If you are married filing jointly, you may be able to exclude up to $500,000 of gain; *see 29.3.*

Frequency of exclusion. If you meet the ownership and use tests for a principal residence, you may claim the exclusion when you sell it although you previously claimed the exclusion for another residence, provided that the sales are more than two years apart. If you claim the exclusion on a sale and within two years of the first sale you sell another principal residence, an exclusion may not be claimed on the second sale even if you meet the ownership and use tests for that residence. There is an exception if the second sale was due to a change in employment, health reasons, or unforeseen circumstances. In that case, a prorated exclusion is allowed; *see* the Reduced Exclusion Worksheet on page 483. Sales before May 7, 1997, are not taken into account in determining the number of sales within a two-year period.

Principal residence. A principal residence is not restricted to one-family houses but includes a mobile home, trailer, houseboat, and condominium apartment used as a principal residence. An investment in a retirement community does not qualify as a principal residence unless you receive equity in the property. In the case of a tenant-stockholder of a cooperative housing corporation, the residence ownership requirement applies to the ownership of the stock and the use requirement applies to the house or apartment that the stockholder occupies. If you sold stock in a cooperative housing corporation during the five-year period ending on the date of sale, you must have:

1. Owned stock for at least two years, *and*
2. Used the house or apartment that the stock entitles you to occupy as your principal residence for at least two years.

Business or rental use. If part of your home was rented out or used for business, *see 29.2* and *29.7.*

Home destroyed or condemned. If your home is destroyed or condemned, any gain realized on the conversion may qualify for the exclusion. Any part of the gain that may not be excluded (because it exceeds the limit) may be postponed under the rules explained in *18.18.*

Sale of remainder interest. You may choose to exclude gain from the sale of a remainder interest in your home. If you do, you may not choose to exclude gain from your sale of any other interest in the home that you sell separately. Also, you may not exclude gain from the sale of a remainder interest to a related party. Related parties include your brothers and sisters, half-brothers and half-sisters, spouse, ancestors (parents, grandparents, etc.), and lineal descendents (children, grandchildren, etc.). Related parties also include certain corporations, partnerships, trusts, and exempt organizations.

Expatriates. You may not claim the exclusion if Section 877(a)(1) of the Internal Revenue Code applies to you. That section applies to U.S. citizens who have renounced their citizenship (and long-term residents who have ended their residency) if one of their principal purposes was to avoid U.S. taxes.

Prior law election. The prior rollover rules applied to the sale of a principal residence made on or after August 5, 1997, under a contract binding on August 5, 1997. A similar rule applies to a sale transacted under a binding contract in effect as of August 5, 1997, where a replacement residence was acquired before August 6, 1997. *See* IRS Publication 523 for the effect of the prior rules on your current or future tax reporting.

The exclusion is not mandatory. You do not have to apply the exclusion to a particular qualifying sale. For example, you are unable to sell a residence when you acquire a new residence. When you finally are able to find a buyer for the first home, you also decide to sell the second residence. Assume both sales may qualify for the exclusion, but the potential gain on the first house will be less than the potential gain on the sale of the second home. You will not want to apply the exclusion to the sale of the first home if doing so will prevent you from applying the exclusion to the second sale because of the rule allowing an exclusion for only one sale every two years.

Federal subsidy recapture. If after 1990 your home was financed with the proceeds of a tax-exempt bond or a qualified mortgage credit certificate *(15.1)* and you sell or dispose of the home within nine years of the financing, you may have to recapture the federal subsidy received. Use Form 8828 to figure the amount of the recapture tax, which is reported on Line 61 of Form 1040 as a separate tax.

29.2 Meeting the Ownership and Use Tests

To qualify for the up-to-$250,000 exclusion, you must have owned and occupied a home as your principal residence for at least two years during the five-year period ending on the date of sale. The periods of ownership and use do not have to be continuous. The ownership and use tests may be met in different two-year periods, provided both tests are met during the five-year period ending on the date of sale. You qualify if you can show that you owned the home and lived in it as your principal residence for 24 full months or for 730 days (365 × 2) during the five-year period ending on the date of sale.

If you are married and file a joint return, you may claim an exclusion of up to $500,000 if one of you meets the ownership test and both of you meet the use test; *see 29.3.*

In counting the period of ownership and use of a residence that you bought as a replacement residence under the prior law rollover rules, you may include the ownership and use of all the prior residences bought under the rollover rules.

Even if the ownership and use tests are met, the exclusion is not allowed for a sale if within the two-year period ending on the date of sale, you sold another principal residence for which you claimed the exclusion. However, a reduced exclusion may be available under the rules at *29.4.*

Short Absences

Short temporary absences for vacations count as time you used the residence. This is true even if you rent out your residence during the vacation period.

EXAMPLES

1. From 1995 through August 2002, Janet lived with her parents in a house that her parents owned. In September 2002, she bought this house from her parents. She continued to live there until December 15, 2002, when she sold it at a gain. Although Janet lived in the home for more than two years, she did not own it for at least two years. She may not exclude any part of her gain on the sale, unless she sold because of a change in health or place of employment; *see 29.4.*

2. John bought and moved into a house in January 2000. He lived in it as his principal residence continuously until October 1, 2001, when he went abroad for a one-year sabbatical leave. On October 1, 2002, he sold the house. He does not meet the two-year use test. Because his leave was not a short, temporary absence, he may not include the period of leave in his period of use in order to meet the two-year use test. He may avoid tax on gain if he sold because of a changed job location or poor health; *see 29.4.*

3. Since 1991, Jonah lived in an apartment building that was changed to a condominium. He bought the apartment on December 1, 1998. In 2000, he became ill and on April 14 of that year he moved to his son's home. On July 10, 2002, while still living there, he sold the apartment.

    He may exclude gain on the sale because he met the ownership and use tests. The five-year period is from July 11, 1997, to July 10, 2002, the date of the sale of the apartment. He owned the apartment from December 1, 1998, to July 10, 2002 (over two years). He lived in the apartment from July 11, 1997 (the beginning of the five-year period) to April 14, 2000, a period of use of over two years.

4. On May 30, 1996, Amy moved into a home she bought and she lived in it until May 31, 1998, when she moved and put it up for rent. The house was rented from June 1, 1998, to March 31, 2000. Amy moved back into the house on April 1, 2000, and lived there until she sold it on January 31, 2002. During the five-year period ending on the date of the sale (February 1, 1997–January 31, 2002), Amy owned and lived in the house for more than the two-year period (24 months) required for the exclusion.

Five-year period—	Home use (months)—	Rental use (months)—
2/1/97–5/31/98	16	
6/1/98–3/31/00		22
4/1/00–1/31/02	22	
Total	38	22

    Amy may exclude gain up to $250,000 on the January 31, 2002, sale.

Multiple Use of a Residence

If in the year of sale part of the residence was used for business or rental to tenants, you apportion the sales price and basis of the house between the rental portion and the residential portion. You may claim the exclusion for both the residential and business (or rental) parts if you met the ownership and use tests for the entire residence. *See* the Examples at *29.7.*

5. In 1992, Carol bought a house and lived in it until January 31, 1999, when she moved and put it up for rent. The house was rented from February 1, 1999, until May 31, 2002. Carol moves back into the house on June 1, 2002, and lives there until she sells it on September 30, 2002. During the five-year period ending on the date of the sale (October 1, 1997 – September 30, 2002), Carol lived in the house for less than two years.

Five-year period—	Home use (months)—	Rental use (months)—
10/1/97–1/31/99	16	
2/1/99–5/31/02		40
6/1/02–9/30/02	4	
Total	20	40

Carol may not exclude any of the gain on the sale, unless she sold the house for health or employment reasons; *see 29.4.*

Incapacitated homeowner. A homeowner who becomes physically or mentally incapable of self-care is deemed to use a residence as a principal residence during the time in which the individual owns the residence and resides in a licensed care facility. For this rule to apply, the homeowner must have owned and used the residence as a principal residence for an aggregate period of at least one year during the five years preceding the sale.

If you meet this disability exception, you still have to meet the two-out-of-five-year ownership test to claim the exclusion.

Previous home destroyed or condemned. For the ownership and use tests, you may add time you owned and lived in a previous home that was destroyed or condemned if any part of the basis of the current home sold depended on the basis of the destroyed or condemned home.

29.3 Home Sales by Married Persons

Where a married couple owned and lived in their principal residence for at least two years during the five-year period ending on the date of sale, they may claim an exclusion of up to $500,000 of gain on a joint return.

Under the law, the up-to-$500,000 exclusion may be claimed on a joint return provided that during the five-year period ending on the date of sale: (1) *either* spouse owned the residence for at least two years, (2) *both* spouses lived in the house as their principal residence for at least two years, and (3) *neither* spouse is ineligible to claim the exclusion because an exclusion was previously claimed on a sale of a principal residence within the two-year period ending on the date of this sale. If Tests 1 and 3 are met but only one of you meets Test 2, your exclusion limit on a joint return is $250,000.

Filing Instruction

Exclusion for Married Couple

For a recently married couple, the exclusion limit is $250,000, not $500,000, where only one of the spouses has satisfied the ownership and use tests before a sale. Gain in excess of the $250,000 exclusion is reported on Schedule D; *see* the Filing Instruction on page 480.

EXAMPLES

1. You and your wife owned and occupied your principal residence for 10 years. In December 2002, you sell the house for a gain of $450,000. The gain is not taxable if you file jointly as the up-to-$500,000 exclusion applies.

2. As a widower, you used and owned your principal residence from June 1998 through the end of 2001. In January 2002, you remarried and you and your wife lived in the house for nine months. In October 2002, you sold the house and realized a gain of $350,000. You may claim an exclusion of $250,000 on your joint return; the balance of $100,000 is taxable. You meet the exclusion tests, but your wife does not. Thus, the exclusion is limited to $250,000.

Death of spouse before sale. If your spouse died before the date of sale, you are considered to have owned and used the property during any period of time when your spouse owned and used it as a principal home. This rule can enable you to satisfy the two-out-of-five-year ownership and use tests.

However, since the year of your spouse's death is the last year for which you may file a joint return, the sale must be completed by the end of that year to qualify for the up-to-$500,000 exclusion limit. If your spouse died late in the year and you do not complete a sale of the home until the following year, your exclusion limit is $250,000.

Divorce. If a residence is transferred to a taxpayer incident to divorce, the time during which the taxpayer's spouse or former spouse owned the residence is added to the taxpayer's period of ownership. A taxpayer who owns a residence is deemed to use the residence while the taxpayer's spouse or former spouse uses the residence under the terms of a divorce or separation.

Separate residences. Where a husband and wife own and live in separate residences, each spouse is entitled to a separate exclusion limit of $250,000 on the sale of his or her residence. If both residences are sold in the same year and each spouse met the ownership and use test for his or her separate residence, two exclusions may be claimed (up to $250,000 each), either on a joint return or on separate returns.

29.4 Reduced Maximum Exclusion

You may claim a prorated exclusion if you are forced to sell your principal residence because of a change in your place of employment or health or unforeseen circumstances, and you have not met the two-out-five-year ownership and use tests, or the sale is within two years of a previous home sale for which you claimed an exclusion. IRS regulations defining "unforeseen circumstances" where expected in the latter part of 2002 but had not yet been released when this book went to press. The *Supplement* will have an update.

If the reduced exclusion rules apply, the exclusion is generally prorated for the time spent in the residence over the two-year period. The IRS allocates the exclusion on a daily basis. You count the number of days of use and divide the sum by 730 days (365 × 2). Use the worksheet below to figure the reduced exclusion.

> **EXAMPLE**
>
> You bought and moved into your residence on April 1, 2001. In 2002, you move to a new job location in another state and sell your house at a gain of $50,000 on March 31, 2002. Since you owned and used your home for 365 days, your exclusion limit is reduced by 50%. You are single. Your reduced exclusion is $125,000 (50% of $250,000) and the gain of $50,000 is totally covered by the exclusion and is not taxable.

Worksheet for Reduced Exclusion

		(a) You	(b)* Your spouse
1.	Maximum exclusion.	$250,000	$250,000
2a.	Enter the number of days you used the home during the five-year period ending on the date of sale.	_____	_____
2b.	Enter the number of days you owned the home during the five-year period ending on the date of sale.**	_____	_____
2c.	Enter the smaller of Line 2a and Line 2b.	_____	_____
3.	Have you (or your spouse, if filing jointly) excluded gain from the sale of another home after May 6, 1997, and within the two-year period ending on the date of this sale? If no, skip Line 3 and enter the number of days from Line 2c on Line 4. If yes, enter the number of days between the date of sale of the other home and the date of sale of this home.	_____	_____
4.	Enter the smaller of Line 2c or Line 3.	_____	_____
5.	Divide the amount on Line 4 by 730 days. Enter the result as a decimal.	_____	_____
6.	Multiply the amount on Line 1 by the decimal amount on Line 5.	_____	_____
7.	Add the amounts in columns (a) and (b) of Line 6. This is your reduced exclusion.	_____	_____

* Use (b) only if you are married and filing a joint return.

** If married filing jointly and one spouse owned the property longer than the other spouse, both spouses are treated as owning the property for the longer period.

IRS Alert

Homeowners Affected by September 11 Attacks Can Claim Reduced Exclusion

In advance of the expected regulations defining unforeseen circumstances, the IRS has announced in Notice 2002-60 that the reduced exclusion rules apply if homeowners failed to meet the two-out-of-five-year ownership and use requirements because of the September 11 terrorist attacks.

You are eligible if your principal residence was damaged as a result of the attacks or if your spouse, a co-owner of the home, or a person living with you in the home was killed, became eligible for unemployment compensation, or had a change in employment or self-employment that resulted in an inability to pay basic reasonable living expenses for the household.

If you sold your home in 2001 and qualify for the reduced exclusion, you may file an amended return to claim the exclusion and receive a tax refund.

Filing Tip

Jointly Owned Home

If you and your spouse sell your jointly owned home and file a joint return, you figure your gain or loss as one taxpayer. If you file separate returns, each of you must figure your own gain or loss according to your ownership interest in the home. Your ownership interest is determined by state law.

If you and a joint owner other than your spouse sell your jointly owned home, each of you must figure your own gain or loss according to your ownership interest in the home.

Filing Tip

Form 1099-S

If you received Form 1099-S, Box 2 should show the total amount you received for your home. However, Box 2 does not include the fair market value of any property other than cash or notes, or any services you received or will receive. For these, Box 4 will be checked. If you can exclude the entire gain from a sale in 2002, the person responsible for closing the sale generally will not have to report it on Form 1099-S.

Caution

Repairs

These maintain your home in good condition but do not add to its value or prolong its life. You do not add their cost to the basis of your property. Examples of repairs include repainting your house inside or outside, fixing gutters or floors, repairing leaks or plastering, and replacing broken window panes. *See 9.3* when repairs tied to an improvement project may be capital improvements.

29.5 Figuring Gain or Loss

To figure the gain or loss on the sale of your principal residence, you must determine the *selling price*, the *amount realized*, and the *adjusted basis*. Worksheet 2 on page 489 may be used to figure gain or loss on the sale of a principal residence.

Gain or loss. The difference between the amount realized and adjusted basis is your gain or loss. If the amount realized exceeds the adjusted basis, the difference is a gain that may be excluded under the rules at *29.1*. If amount realized is less than adjusted basis, the difference is a loss. A loss on the sale of your main home may not be deducted, *see 29.8*.

Foreclosure or repossession. If your home was foreclosed on or repossessed, you have a sale. *See* Chapter 31.

Selling price. This is the total amount received for your home. It includes money, all notes, mortgages, or other debts assumed by the buyer as part of the sale, and the fair market value of any other property or any services received. The selling price does not include receipts for personal property sold with your home. Personal property is property that is not a permanent part of the home, such as furniture, draperies, and lawn equipment.

If your employer pays you for a loss on the sale or for your selling expenses, do not include the payment as part of the selling price. Include the payment as wages on Line 7 of Form 1040. (Your employer includes the payment with the rest of your wages in Box 1 of your Form W-2.)

If you grant an option to buy your home and the option is exercised, add the amount received for the option to the selling price of your home. If the option is not exercised, you report the amount as ordinary income in the year the option expires. Report the amount on Line 21 of Form 1040.

Amount realized. This is the selling price minus selling expenses. Selling expenses include commissions, advertising fees, legal fees, and loan charges paid by the seller, such as loan placement fees or "points."

Adjusted basis. This is the cost basis of your home increased by the cost of improvements and decreased by deducted casualty losses, if any, as explained in *29.6*. Cost basis is generally what you paid for the residence. If you obtained possession through other means, such as a gift or inheritance, *see 5.17*.

Seller-paid points. If the person who sold you your residence paid points on your loan, you may have to reduce your basis in the home by the amount of the points. If you bought your residence after 1990 but before April 4, 1994, you reduce basis by the points only if you chose to deduct them as home mortgage interest in the year paid. If you bought the residence after April 3, 1994, you reduce basis by the points, even if you did not deduct the points.

Settlement fees or closing costs. When buying your home, you may have to pay settlement fees or closing costs in addition to the contract price of the property. You may include in basis fees and closing costs that are for buying the home. You may not include in your basis the fees and costs of getting a mortgage loan. Settlement fees also do not include amounts placed in escrow for the future payment of items such as taxes and insurance.

Examples of the settlement fees or closing costs that you may include in the basis of your property are: (1) abstract fees (sometimes called abstract of title fees), (2) charges for installing utility services, (3) legal fees (including fees for the title search and preparing the sales contract and deed), (4) recording fees, (5) survey fees, (6) transfer taxes, (7) owner's title insurance, and (8) any amounts the seller owes that you agree to pay, such as certain real estate taxes, back interest, recording or mortgage fees, charges for improvements or repairs, and sales commissions.

Examples of settlement fees and closing costs *not* included in your basis are: (1) fire insurance premiums, (2) rent for occupancy of the home before closing, (3) charges for utilities or other services relating to occupancy of the home before closing, (4) any fee or cost that you deducted as a moving expense before 1994, (5) charges connected with getting a mortgage loan, such as mortgage insurance premiums (including VA funding fees), loan assumption fees, cost of a credit report, and fee for an appraisal required by a lender, and (6) fees for refinancing a mortgage.

Construction. If you contracted to have your residence built on land you own, your basis is the cost of the land plus the cost of building the home, including the cost of labor and materials, payments to a contractor, architect's fees, building permit charges, utility meter and connection charges, and legal fees directly connected with building the home.

Cooperative apartment. Your basis in the apartment is usually the cost of your stock in the co-op housing corporation, which may include your share of a mortgage on the apartment building.

29.6 Figuring Adjusted Basis

Adjusted basis in your home is cost basis *(29.5)* adjusted for items discussed below. Worksheet 1 on page 489 may be used to figure adjusted basis.

Cost basis is *increased* by improvements with a useful life of more than one year, special assessments for local improvements, and amounts spent after a casualty to restore damaged property.

Decreases to cost basis include: gain you postponed from the sale of a previous home before May 7, 1997, deductible casualty losses not covered by insurance, insurance payments you received or expect to receive for casualty losses, payments you received for granting an easement or right-of-way, depreciation allowed or allowable if you used your home for business or rental purposes, residential energy credit (generally allowed from 1977 through 1987) claimed for the cost of energy improvements added to the basis of your home, adoption credit you claimed for improvements added to the basis of your home, nontaxable payments from an adoption assistance program of your employer that you used for improvements added to the basis of your home, first-time homebuyers credit (allowed to certain first-time buyers of a home in the District of Columbia), and energy conservation subsidy excluded from your gross income because you received it (directly or indirectly) from a public utility after 1992 to buy or install any energy conservation measure. An energy conservation measure is an installation or modification that is primarily designed either to reduce consumption of electricity or natural gas or to improve the management of energy demand for a home.

Improvements. Improvements add to the value of your home, prolong its useful life, or adapt it to new uses. You add the cost of improvements to the basis of your property.

Examples of improvements include: bedroom, bathroom, deck, garage, porch, and patio additions, landscaping, paving driveway, walkway, fencing, retaining wall, sprinkler system, swimming pool, storm windows and doors, new roof, wiring upgrades, satellite dish, security system, heating system, central air conditioning, furnace, duct work, central humidifier, filtration system, septic system, water heater, soft water system, built-in appliances, kitchen modernization, flooring, wall-to-wall carpeting, attic, walls, and pipes.

Adjusted basis does not include the cost of any improvements that are no longer part of the home.

> **EXAMPLE**
> You installed wall-to-wall carpeting in your home 15 years ago. In 2002, you replace that carpeting with new wall-to-wall carpeting. The cost of the old carpeting is no longer part of adjusted basis.

Record-keeping. You should keep records to prove adjusted basis. Ordinarily, you must keep records for three years after the due date for filing your return for the tax year in which you sold your home. But you should keep home records as long as they are needed for tax purposes. These include: (1) proof of the home's purchase price and purchase expenses, (2) receipts and other records for all improvements, additions, and other items that affect the home's adjusted basis, (3) any worksheets you used to figure the adjusted basis of the home you sold, the gain or loss on the sale, the exclusion, and the taxable gain, and (4) any Form 2119 that you filed to postpone gain from the sale of a previous home before May 7, 1997.

29.7 Personal and Business Use of a Home

You may have used part of your property as your home and part for business or to produce income. If you sell the entire property and part of it was used for business or rental purposes during the year of sale, consider the transaction as the sale of two properties. You exclude gain on the part used as your home, assuming you meet the two-out-of-five-year ownership and use tests for that part; *see* Example 1 below. An exclusion may also be claimed for the business or rental part if you owned and lived in that part of the home for at least two years in the five-year period ending on the date of sale.

Planning Reminder

Gains Postponed Under Prior Law Rules

Gain on a previous home sale that you postponed under the prior law rollover rules reduces the basis of your current home if your current home was a qualifying replacement residence for the previous home. Postponed gains on several earlier sales may have to be taken into account under the basis reduction rule. The basis reduction will increase the gain on the sale of your current home.

EXAMPLES

1. You owned a four-unit apartment house for 10 years. For that entire period, you lived in one unit and rented out three units. You sold the apartment house in July of 2002. Your records show:

Cost	$80,000
Capital improvements	20,000
Depreciation (on 3 rented units only)	40,000
Selling price	120,000
Selling expenses	8,000

One-fourth of the apartment building was your home; you figure your excluded gain as follows:

	Personal ($1/4$)	Rental ($3/4$)
Selling price	$30,000	$90,000
Minus: Selling expenses	2,000	6,000
Amount realized	$28,000	$84,000
Basis (cost *plus* improvements)	$25,000	$75,000
Minus: Depreciation	–0–	40,000
Adjusted basis	$25,000	$35,000
Gain (amount realized *minus* adjusted basis)	$3,000	$49,000
Taxable gain		$49,000
Gain excluded	$3,000	

The rental portion gain of $49,000 is reported on Form 4797.

2. In 1995, Abel bought a house. He used $3/4$ of the house as his principal residence and $1/4$ for business purposes. On October 29, 2001, Abel retired and started using all of the house as his principal residence. On November 1, 2002, he sells the house at a gain.

   During the five-year period ending on the date of sale, Abel met the two-year use test only for $3/4$ of the house. Only gain from that part of the house qualifies for the exclusion, unless the sale is due to a change in health (or place of employment); *see 29.4*.

Depreciation after May 6, 1997. You may not exclude that part of your gain that is equal to any depreciation allowed or allowable for the business or rental use of your home after May 6, 1997. If you were entitled to take depreciation deductions because you used your home for business purposes or as rental property, you may not exclude the part of your gain equal to any depreciation allowed or allowable as a deduction for periods after May 6, 1997. If you can show by adequate records that the depreciation deduction allowed was less than the amount allowable, the gain up to the allowed depreciation deduction is the amount ineligible for the exclusion.

EXAMPLE

John sold his home in 2002, realizing a $30,000 gain. He meets the use and ownership tests to exclude the gain on the entire home, including a part of the home he used for business from July through December 2001. For those months of business use, he claimed $500 depreciation. He may exclude $29,500 ($30,000 – $500). He has a taxable gain of $500 equal to the depreciation deduction.

Selling Your Home at a Loss

29.8 No Loss Allowed on Personal Residence

A loss on the sale of your principal residence is not deductible. If part of your principal residence was used for business in the year of sale, treat the sale as if two pieces of property were sold. Report the business part on Form 4797. A loss is deductible only on the business part.

Second home or vacation home. If you sell at a loss a second home or vacation home (not your principal residence) that was used entirely for personal purposes, you report the loss transaction on Schedule D, even though the loss is not deductible. Instead of entering the loss amount in column (f) of Schedule D, write "Personal Loss." If in the year of sale part of the home was rented out or used for business, allocate the sale between the personal part and the rental or business part; report the personal part on Schedule D and the rental or business part on Form 4797.

29.9 Loss on Residence Converted to Rental Property

You are not allowed to deduct a loss on the sale of your personal residence. If you convert the house from personal use to rental use you may claim a loss on a sale if the value has declined below the basis fixed for the residence as rental property.

To figure basis for loss purposes, you first need to know the *lower* of (1) your adjusted basis for the house at the time of conversion or (2) the fair market value at the time of conversion. *Add* to the lower amount the cost of capital improvements made after the conversion, and *subtract* depreciation and casualty loss deductions claimed after the conversion. To deduct a loss, you have to be able to show that this basis exceeds the sales price. For example, if you paid $200,000 for your home and convert it to rental property when the value has declined to $150,000, your conversion date basis for the rental property is $150,000. If the property continues to decline in value, and you sell for $125,000 after having deducted $10,000 for depreciation, you may claim a loss of $15,000 ($140,000 – $125,000). Your loss deduction will not reflect the $50,000 loss occurring before the conversion.

> ### EXAMPLE
>
> In 1987, Adams bought a house in Fort Worth, Texas. He paid $124,000, put in capital improvements, and lived there until he was forced to put it on the market when he lost his job. In 1988, he listed the house with a broker for $145,000. After receiving no offers, he decided to lease the house through 1990. By October of 1989 Adams owed $4,551 in property taxes and was three months behind on his mortgage payments. Fearing foreclosure, he sold the house for $130,000.
>
> For purposes of figuring a loss, Adams assumed that the fair market value at the time of conversion was equal to the $145,000 list price. The adjusted basis of the house was $141,026. As this was less than the estimated fair market value of $145,000, he used the $141,026 adjusted basis to figure a loss of $11,026 ($130,000 – $141,026). The IRS claimed the fair market value at the time of conversion was equal to the actual sale price of $130,000. Since basis for the converted property is the lesser of fair market value ($130,000) or adjusted basis ($141,026), Adams had no loss on the sale.
>
> However, the Tax Court allowed a $5,000 loss by fixing the fair market value at the time of conversion at $135,000. It held that Adams sold at a lower price because of his weak financial position of which the buyer took advantage. The court figured the $135,000 as follows: $129,000 fair market value in 1987 (based on an appraisal report, which both parties agree was correct), plus $6,000 of appreciation attributable to the capital improvements made to the property after it was converted.

Profit-making purposes. Renting a residence is a changeover from personal to profit-making purposes. If the house is merely put up for rent or is rented for several months, the IRS may not recognize the house as rental property and may disallow the loss deduction. However, the Tax Court has approved a loss deduction where a house was rented on a 90-day lease with an option to buy. The court set down the following two tests for determining when a house is converted to rental property: (1) the rental charge returns a profit and (2) the lease prevents you from using or reoccupying the house during the lease period. Under the Tax Court approach, you have a conversion to rental property if you have a lease that gives possession of the house to the tenant during the lease period and if the rent, after deducting taxes, interest, insurance, repairs, depreciation, and other charges, returns you a profit.

Loss allowed on house bought for resale. A loss deduction is also allowed where you acquired the house as an investment with the intention of selling it at a profit, even though you occupied it incidentally as a residence prior to sale. For example, an owner bought a house with the intention of selling it. He lived in it for six years, but during that period it was for sale. He was allowed to deduct the loss on its sale by proving he lived in it to protect it from vandalism and to keep it in good condition so that it would attract possible buyers.

In another case, an architect and builder built a house and offered it for sale through an agent and advertisements. He had a home and no intention to occupy the new house. On a realtor's advice, he moved into the house to make it more saleable. Ten months later, he sold the house at a loss of $4,065 and promptly moved out. The loss was allowed on proof that his main purpose in building and occupying the house was to realize a profit by a sale; the residential use was incidental.

 Filing Tip

Loss Allowed

A loss may be claimed if you sell a house that has been converted from personal to rental use; *see 29.9.*

 Caution

Temporary Rental Before Sale

A rental loss may be barred on a temporary rental before sale. The IRS and Tax Court held that where a principal residence was rented for several months while being offered for sale, the rental did not convert the home to rental property. Deductions for rental expenses were limited to rental income; no loss could be claimed. A federal appeals court disagreed and allowed a rental loss deduction; also *see 9.7.*

Gain on rented residence. You have a gain on the sale of rental property if you sell for more than your adjusted basis at the time of conversion, plus subsequent capital improvements, and minus depreciation and casualty loss deductions. The sale is subject to the rules in Chapter 44 for depreciable property.

Stock in cooperative apartment. Normally, you get no deduction for a loss on the sale of your stock in a cooperative housing corporation. It makes no difference that you occasionally sublet your apartment. It is still not considered property used in a business. But you may get a loss deduction when there were non-stockholder tenants in the cooperative housing corporation when you bought your stock. Then, you get a partial capital loss deduction if you sell your stock or if it becomes worthless. To figure capital loss:

1. First find the difference between your cost and your selling price. This would ordinarily be your capital loss.
2. Then find the percentage of non-stockholding tenants (based on rental values) in the housing corporation when you bought your stock.
3. Apply this percentage to the loss you figured above. This is the capital loss you are allowed.

See 9.5 for when depreciation may be taken on the basis of the cooperative stock ownership.

Partially rented home. You may deduct a loss on a home sale if you rented part and occupied part for your own purposes. A loss on a sale is allowable on the rented portion, which is reported on Form 4797.

29.10 Loss on Residence Acquired by Gift or Inheritance

You may deduct a loss on the sale of a house received as an inheritance or gift if you personally did not use it and offered it for sale or rental immediately or within a few weeks after acquisition.

 *Planning Reminder*

Inherited Residence

If you inherit a residence in which you do not intend to live, it may be advisable to put it up for rent to allow for an ordinary loss deduction on a later sale. If you merely try to sell, and you finally do so at a loss, you are limited to a capital loss.

EXAMPLES

1. A couple owned a winter vacation home in Florida. When the husband died, his wife immediately put the house up for sale and never lived in it. It was sold at a loss. The IRS disallowed her capital loss deduction, claiming it was personal and nondeductible. The wife argued that her case was no different from the case of an heir inheriting and selling a home, since at the death of her husband her interest in the property was increased. The Tax Court agreed with her reasoning and allowed the capital loss deduction.
2. A widow inherited a house owned by her late husband and rented out by his estate. Shortly after getting title to the house, she sold it at a loss that she deducted as an ordinary loss. The IRS limited her to a capital loss deduction. The Tax Court agreed. She could not show any business activity. She did not negotiate the lease with the tenant who was in the house when she received title. She never arranged any maintenance or repairs for the building. Moreover, she sold the property shortly after receiving title, which indicates she viewed the house as investment, not rental, property.
3. An inherited residence was rented out by the owner to her brother for $500 a month when the fair market rental value was $700 to $750 per month. When she sold the residence at a loss, the IRS disallowed the loss, and the Tax Court agreed. The below-market rental was treated as evidence that she held the property for personal purposes, not as rental property or as investment property held for appreciation in value.

Worksheet 1. Adjusted Basis of Home Sold

1. Enter the cost basis of your old home. If you filed Form 2119 when you originally acquired your old home to postpone gain on the sale of a previous home, enter the adjusted basis of the new home from that Form 2119 . . . . _____
2. Seller-paid points, for home bought after 1990. (For *seller-paid points, see 15.8.*) Do not include any seller-paid points you previously subtracted to arrive at the amount entered on line 1, above . . _____
3. Subtract line 2 from line 1 . . . . _____
4. Settlement fees or closing costs. Do not include amounts previously deducted as moving expenses. If line 1 includes the adjusted basis of the new home from Form 2119, go to line 6.
   a. Abstract and recording fees . . . . _____
   b. Legal fees (including title search and preparing document) . . . . . . _____
   c. Surveys . . . . _____
   d. Title insurance . . . . _____
   e. Transfer or stamp taxes . . . . _____
   f. Amounts the seller owed that you agreed to pay (back taxes or interest, recording or mortgage fees, and sales commissions) . . . . _____
   g. Other . . . . _____
5. Add lines 4a through 4g . . . . _____
6. Cost of capital improvements. Do not include any capital improvements included on line 1 above _____
7. Special tax assessments paid on your old home for local improvements, such as streets and sidewalks _____
8. Other increases to basis . . . . _____
9. Add lines 3, 5, 6, 7, and 8 . . . . _____
10. Depreciation, related to the business use or rental of your old home, claimed (or allowable) . . . . _____
11. Residential energy credit (generally allowed from 1977 through 1987) and adoption credit claimed for any capital improvements included on line 6 and, if applicable, line 1 above. _____
12. Payments received for any easement or right-of-way granted . . . . . . _____
13. Other decreases to basis *(see 29.6)* . . . . _____
14. Add lines 10 through 13 . . . . _____
15. **ADJUSTED BASIS OF HOME SOLD.** Subtract line 14 from line 9. Enter here and on Worksheet 2, line 4 . . . . _____

Worksheet 2. Gain (or Loss), Exclusion, and Taxable Gain

Part 1–Gain (or Loss) on Sale
1. Selling price of home . . . . _____
2. Selling expenses . . . . _____
3. Subtract line 2 from line 1 . . . . _____
4. Adjusted basis of home sold. (From Worksheet 1, line 15.) . . . . . . _____
5. Subtract line 4 from line 3. This is the gain (or loss) on the sale. If this is a loss, stop here . . _____

Part 2–Exclusion and Taxable Gain
6. Enter any depreciation claimed on the property for periods after May 6, 1997. If none, enter zero _____
7. Subtract line 6 from line 5. (If the result is less than zero, enter zero.) . . . . _____
8. Maximum exclusion. *See 29.4.* . . . . _____
9. Enter the smaller of line 7 or line 8. This is your exclusion. If you are reporting the sale on the installment method, enter this amount on line 15 of Form 6252 . . . . _____
10. Subtract line 9 from line 5. This is your taxable gain. If the amount on line 6 of this worksheet is zero, report this taxable gain on Schedule D (Form 1040) on line 1 or 8 depending on how long you owned the residence. (Do not complete lines 11 and 12 of this worksheet.)
    If the amount on line 10 is zero, do not report the sale on your tax return.
    If the amount on line 6 is more than zero, complete lines 11 and 12 . . . . . _____
11. Enter the smaller of line 6 or line 10. Enter this amount on line 12 of the *Unrecaptured Section 1250 Gain Worksheet* in the instructions for Schedule D (Form 1040) . . . . . _____
12. Subtract line 11 from line 10. If the result is more than zero, report it on Schedule D on line 1 or 8 depending on how long you owned the residence. . . . . _____

Chapter 30

Tax Savings for Investors in Securities

You have the opportunity to control the taxable year in which to realize gains and losses. Gains and losses are realized when you sell, and if there are no market pressures, you can time sales to your advantage. To profit from the low 10% or 20% tax rate on long-term capital gains, pay attention to the more-than-one-year holding period for realizing long-term capital gains on the sale of securities. Realizing long-term capital gains will give you tax savings. However, do not overlook the fact that realizing substantial capital gains may subject you to the exemption phaseout and/or 3% reduction of itemized deductions. The 3% reduction increases the effective capital gain rate and, depending on the number of exemptions phased out, the effective rate will be still higher. Thus, it may be advisable to avoid realizing substantial capital gain income in a year you are subject to the exemption phaseout if that income can be deferred to a year in which you will have lower income and not be subject to the phaseout.

The $3,000 limitation ($1,500 if married filing separately) on deducting capital losses from other types of income is a substantial restriction. If you have capital losses exceeding the $3,000 (or $1,500) limit, it is advisable to realize capital gains income that can be offset by the losses.

Security Transactions

30.1 Planning Year-End Securities Transactions

First establish your current gain and loss position for the year. List gains and losses already realized from completed transactions. Then review the records of earlier years to find any carryover capital losses. Include nonbusiness bad debts as short-term capital losses. Then review your paper gains and losses and determine what losses might now be realized to offset realized gains or what gains might be realized to absorb your realized losses.

If you have already realized net capital losses exceeding $3,000 ($1,500 if married filing separately), you may want to realize capital gains that will be absorbed by the excess loss. Remember, only up to $3,000 (or $1,500) of capital losses exceeding net capital gain may be deducted from other income such as salary, interest, and dividends. Also, project your tax-bracket ranges in the current and next tax year. For example, assume that you are close to the threshold for the phaseout of exemptions and that realizing substantial gains will place you in the exemption phase-out range *(21.16)*. You may want to defer gain transactions to a year in which you will be in a lower bracket or not subject to the phaseout.

Planning for losses. Realizing losses may pose a problem if you believe the security is due to increase in value sometime in the near future. Although the wash-sale rule *(30.6)* prevents you from taking the loss if you buy 30 days before or after the sale, the following possibilities are open to you.

- If you believe the security will go up, but not immediately, you can sell now, realize your loss, wait 31 days, and then recover your position by repurchasing before the expected rise.
- You can hedge by repurchasing similar securities immediately after the sale provided they are not substantially identical. They can be in the same industry and of the same quality without being considered substantially identical. Check with your broker to see if you can use a loss and still maintain your position. Some brokerage firms maintain recommended "switch" lists and suggest a practice of "doubling up"—that is, buying the stock of the same company and then 31 days later selling the original shares. Doubling up has disadvantages: It requires additional funds for the purchase of the second lot, exposes you to additional risks should the stock price fall, and the new shares take a new holding period.

EXAMPLE

You own 100 shares of Steel Co. stock that cost you $10,000. In November 2002, the stock is selling at $6,000 ($60 a share × 100 shares). You would like to realize the $4,000 loss but, at the same time, you want to hold on to the investment. You buy 100 shares at a market price of $60 a share (total investment $6,000) and 31 days later sell your original 100 shares, realizing the loss of $4,000. You retain your investment in the new lot.

30.2 Earmarking Stock Lots

Keep a record of all your stock transactions, especially when you buy the stock of one company at varying prices. By keeping a record of each stock lot, you may control the amount of gain or loss on a sale of a part of your holdings. If you do not make an adequate identification, the IRS will treat the shares you bought first as the shares being sold under a first-in, first-out (FIFO) rule. You may *not* average the cost of stock loss; averaging is allowed only for mutual-fund shares *(32.10)*.

If your stock is held by your broker, the IRS considers that an adequate identification is made if you give instructions to your broker about which particular shares are to be sold, and you receive a written confirmation of your instructions from the broker or transfer agent within a reasonable time.

EXAMPLE

Over a three-year period, you bought the following shares of Acme Steel stock: In 1997, 100 shares at $77 per share; in 1998, 200 shares at $84 per share; and in 1999, 100 shares at $105 per share. When the stock is selling at $90, you plan to sell 100 shares. You may use the cost of your 1999 lot and get a $1,500 loss if, for example, you want to offset some gains or other income you have already earned this year. Or you may get capital gains of varying amounts by either selling the 1997 lot or part of the 1998 lot.

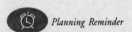
Planning Reminder

December 31 Deadline for 2002 Gains and Losses

If you want to realize gains on publicly traded securities, you have until December 31, 2002, to transact the sale. Gain is reported in 2002, although cash is not received until the settlement date in 2003. If you do not want to realize the gain in 2002, delay the trade date until 2003.

Losses are also realized as of the trade date; a loss on a sale made by December 31, 2002, is reported on your 2002 return.

You must clearly identify the lot you want to sell. Say you want a loss and sell the 1999 lot. Unless you identify it as the lot sold, the IRS will hold that you sold the 1997 lot under the "first-in, first-out" rule. This rule assumes that, when you have a number of identical items that you bought at different times, your sale of any of them is automatically the sale of the first you bought. So the cost of your first purchase is what you match against your selling price to find your gain or loss. Here is what to do to counteract the first-in, first-out rule: If you have stock certificates registered in your name, show that you delivered the 1999 stock certificates. If the broker is holding the stock, specifically identify the 1999 lot in your selling instructions and get a written confirmation. *See* the chart in *32.10* for averaging cost on the sale of mutual-fund shares.

How To Identify Securities

If your securities are—	Identify them by—
Registered in your own name	The number, your name, and any other identification that they bear.
In a margin account registered in a "street" name	A specified block or security bought on a designated day at a particular price. A mere intention to sell a particular share without informing the broker is without significance.
New certificates received for old in a recapitalization	Record the new certificate with the lowest number as being in exchange for the old certificate with the lowest number. Do this until all the new certificates are matched with all the old.
Shares exchanged for shares in a reorganization	Allocate each of the new certificates to each of the old in your records. Where the exchange involves several blocks of stock and there is no specific identification, the IRS says you must average your costs.
Shares received in a stock split	Match the new certificates with the old ones surrendered. Identification of your selling securities as the "highest cost" or "lowest cost" stock is insufficient. You have to match at the time of the split-up.
Stock dividends	The lot of stock on which you received the dividend. The new stock is part of the old lot. But if you receive one certificate for more than one lot, you may have to apply the first-in, first-out rule when you sell.
Acquired by exercise of nontaxed stock rights	The number, or other identification, of the lot you receive by exercising the rights. Each lot you so acquire is considered a separate lot received on the date of subscription.

30.3 Sale of Stock Dividends

A sale of stock originally received as a dividend is treated as any other sale of stock. The holding period of a *taxable* stock dividend *(4.8)* begins on the day after the date of distribution. The holding period of a *tax-free* stock dividend or stock received in a split *(4.6)* starts from the time you acquired the original stock.

EXAMPLE

You bought 100 shares of X Co. stock on December 3, 1997. On August 13, 2002, you receive 10 shares of X Co. stock as a tax-free stock dividend. On December 10, 2002, you sell the 10 shares at a profit. You report the sale as long-term capital gain because the holding period of the 10 shares goes back to your original purchase date of December 3, 1997, not August 13, 2002.

Basis of tax-free dividend in the same class of stock. Assume you receive a common stock dividend on common stock. You divide the original cost by the total number of old shares and new shares to find the new basis per share.

EXAMPLE

You bought 100 shares of common stock for $1,000, so that each share has a basis of $10. You receive 100 shares of common stock as a tax-free stock dividend. The basis of your 200 shares remains $1,000. The new cost basis of each share is now $5 ($1,000 ÷ 200 shares). You sell 50 shares for $560. Your profit is $310 ($560 – $250).

Basis of tax-free dividend in a different class of stock. Assume you receive preferred stock dividends on common stock. You divide the basis of the old shares over the two classes in the ratio of their values at the time the stock dividend was distributed.

EXAMPLE

You bought 100 shares of common stock for $1,000. You receive a tax-free dividend of 10 shares of preferred stock. On the date of distribution, the market value of the common stock is $9 a share and that of the preferred stock is $30. That makes the market value of your common stock $900 and your preferred stock $300. So you allocate 75% ($900 ÷ $1,200) of your $1,000 original cost, or $750, to your common stock and 25% ($300 ÷ $1,200) of your cost to the preferred stock.

Basis of taxable stock dividend. The basis of a taxable stock dividend is its fair market value at the time of the distribution. Its holding period begins on the date of distribution. The basis of the old stock remains unchanged.

EXAMPLE

You bought 1,000 shares of stock for $10,000. The company gives you a choice of a cash dividend or stock (one share for every hundred held). You elect the stock. On the date of the distribution, its market value was $15 a share. The basis of the new stock is $150 (10 × $15), the amount of the taxable dividend. The basis of the old stock remains $10,000.

The tax treatment of the receipt of stock as a dividend and in a split is discussed at *4.6*.

30.4 Stock Rights

The tax consequences of the receipt of stock rights are discussed at *4.6*. The following is an explanation of how to treat the sale, exercise, or expiration of nontaxable stock rights. The basis of taxable rights is their fair market value at the time of distribution.

Expiration of nontaxable distributed stock rights. When you allow nontaxable rights to expire, you do not have a deductible loss; you have no basis in the rights.

Sale of nontaxable distributed stock rights. If you sell stock rights distributed on your stock, you treat the sale as the sale of a capital asset. The holding period begins from the date you acquired the original stock on which the rights were distributed.

Purchased rights. If you buy stock rights, your holding period starts the day after the date of the purchase. Your basis for the rights is the price paid; this basis is used in computing your capital gain or loss on the sale.

If you allow purchased rights to expire without sale or exercise, you realize a capital loss. The rights are treated as having been sold on the day of expiration. When purchased rights become worthless during the year prior to the year they lapse, you have a capital loss that is treated as having occurred on the last day of the year in which they became worthless.

Figuring the basis of nontaxable stock rights. Whether rights received by you as a stockholder have a basis depends on their fair market value when distributed. If the market value of rights is less than 15% of the market value of your old stock, the basis of your rights is zero, unless you elect to allocate the basis between the rights and your original stock. You make the election on your tax return for the year the rights are received by attaching to your return a statement that you are electing to divide basis. Keep a copy of the election and the return.

If the market value of the rights is 15% or more of the market value of your old stock, you must divide the basis of the stock between the old stock and the rights, according to their respective values on the date of distribution.

No basis adjustment is required for stock rights that become worthless during the year of issue.

Planning Reminder

Basis of Public Utility Stock Received Under Dividend Reinvestment Plan

For several years before 1986, an exclusion was allowed for stock dividends received from public utility companies if the dividends were reinvested in stock. If you claimed the exclusion, the stock takes a zero basis. If you sell the stock, the entire sales proceeds of the stock are reported as long-term capital gain.

Planning Reminder

Exercise of Stock Rights

You realize no taxable income on the exercise of stock rights. Capital gain or loss on the new stock is recognized when you later sell the stock. The holding period of the new stock begins on the date you exercised the rights. Your basis for the new stock is the subscription price you paid plus your basis for the rights exercised.

EXAMPLE

You own 100 shares of M Co. that cost $10 a share. On September 15, there is a distribution of stock rights allowing for the purchase of one additional share of common for each 10 rights held at a price of $13 a share. The common stock is now worth $15 (ex-rights). The rights have a market value of 20¢ each. This is less than 15% of the market value of the stock. You can either: (1) choose not to spread the tax cost of the stock between the old stock and the rights or (2) elect to spread the tax cost as follows:

Cost of your old stock, 100 shares at $10, or $1,000.

Fair market value of old stock, 100 shares at $15, or $1,500.

Market value of 100 rights at 20¢, or $20.

Market value of both old stock and rights, or $1,520.

Apportionment of old stock:

$$\frac{1,500}{1,520} \times 1,000 = 986.84$$

Your new basis of old stock is $986.84 for 100 shares, or $9.87 a share. The tax cost of the rights is then calculated:

$$\frac{20}{1,520} \times 1,000 = \$13.16$$

The basis of the rights is $13.16 for 100 rights.

When you exercise your rights and 10 shares are bought, your basis for the new stock is $130 plus the cost of the rights of $13.16, or $143.16.

If the option of allocation is not exercised, the rights have a basis of zero and the basis of the new stock is $130. The basis of the old stock remains $1,000.

30.5 Short Sales

A short sale is a sale of stock that you do not own but borrow for purposes of the sale from a broker. The short sale is closed when you later buy stock or deliver stock you already own to replace the borrowed stock. One objective of a short sale is to profit from an anticipated drop in the market price of the stock; another objective may be to use the short sale as a hedge.

Tax rules applied to short sales are designed to prevent you from:

- Postponing gain to a later year when you sell short while holding an appreciated position in the same stock. This type of short sale is called "a sale against the box."
- Converting short-term gains to long-term gains.
- Converting long-term losses to short-term losses.

Generally, you report gain on a short sale in the year in which you close the short sale by delivery of replacement stock. However, this rule does not apply when you execute a short sale while holding an appreciated position in the same stock (short sale against the box) or substantially identical stock is acquired to close an appreciated short position. In such cases, the short sale or acquisition of substantially identical stock is treated as a constructive sale of an appreciated financial position and you must report the transaction in the year of the short sale, even though delivery of replacement stock is made in a later year; *see* Examples 2 and 3 below. However, there is this exception. The short sale is reported in the year of delivery of the replacement stock if you close the short sale before the end of the 30th day of the next year and continue to hold a similar position in the stock for at least 60 days after the closing of the short sale.

If the stock sold short becomes worthless before you close the short sale, you recognize taxable gain in the year the shares became worthless.

EXAMPLES

1. In February 2002, you expect the stock of Oil Co., which is currently selling at $110, to fall within several months. You sell short 500 shares for $55,000 (500 × $110). Two months later when the price falls to $90, you close the short sale (500 × $90 = $45,000). Your profit of $10,000 ($55,000 − $45,000) is treated as short-term capital gain.

2. In January 2002, you buy 100 shares of Steel Co. stock for $1,000 (100 × $10). In November 2002 when the stock is selling at $50, you execute a short sale of 100 shares (100 × $50 = $5,000). In February 2003, you deliver your shares to close the short sale. The tax law treats the short sale as a constructive sale of an appreciated financial position. You report the gain of $4,000 ($5,000 – $1,000) in 2002, the year of the short sale, not in 2003 when you close the sale. To shift tax reporting to 2003, you would have had to close the short sale by the 30th of January and obtain similar stock, which you would have had to hold for at least 60 days after the closing of the short sale. Also *see* Example 3 and *30.8* for further details on constructive sales.

3. A taxpayer who does not own any shares of XYZ stock directs his broker in January of Year 1 to sell short borrowed XYZ shares. On December 31 of Year 1, when the value of XYZ shares has decreased, the taxpayer directs the broker to close the short sale by purchasing XYZ shares in a "regular-way" sale, with actual delivery of the shares taking place at the beginning of Year 2. The IRS ruled that the short position is an appreciated financial position as of December 31, given the decrease in the stock price since the short sale. The purchase of replacement shares on December 31 is a constructive sale of the appreciated position. Gain is taxable in Year 1, not in Year 2 when the shares were delivered.

When analyzing short-sale transactions, ask yourself these questions:

1. When you sold short, did you or your spouse hold for one year or less securities substantially identical to the securities sold short? (Substantially identical securities are described at *30.6*.)

2. After the short sale, did you or your spouse acquire substantially identical securities on or before the date of the closing of the short sale?

If you answered "yes" to either or both of these questions, apply the following two rules:

Rule 1. Gain realized on the closing of the short sale is short term. The gain is short term regardless of the period of time you have held the securities as of the closing date of the short sale.

Rule 2. The beginning date of the holding period of substantially identical stock is suspended. The holding period of substantially identical securities owned or bought under the facts of question (1) or (2) does not begin until the date of the closing of the short sale (or the date of the sale, gift, or other disposition of the securities, whichever date occurs first). But note that this rule applies only to the number of securities that do not exceed the quantity sold short.

Losses. A loss on a short sale is not deductible until shares closing the short sale are delivered to the broker. You may not realize a short-term loss on the closing of a short sale if you held substantially identical securities long term (that is, for more than a year) on the date of the short sale. The loss is long term even if the securities used to close the sale were held for one year or less. This rule prevents you from creating short-term losses when you held the covering stock long term. Loss deductions on short sales may be disallowed under the wash-sale rules in *30.6*.

Expenses of short sales. Before you buy stock to close out a short sale, you pay the broker for dividends paid on stock you have sold short. If you itemize deductions, you may treat your payment as investment interest *(15.10)*, provided the short sale is held open at least 46 days, or more than a year in the case of extraordinary dividends. If the 46-day (or one-year) test is not met, the payment is generally not deductible and is added to basis; in counting the short-sale period, do not count any period during which you have an option to buy or are obligated to buy substantially identical securities, or are protected from the risk of loss from the short sale by a substantially similar position.

Under an exception to the 46-day test, if you receive compensation from the lender of the stock for the use of collateral and you report the compensation as ordinary income, your payment for dividends is deductible to the extent of the compensation; only the excess of your payment over the compensation is disallowed. This exception does not apply to payments with respect to extraordinary dividends.

An extraordinary dividend is generally a dividend that equals or exceeds the amount realized on the short sale by 10% for any common stock or by 5% for any preferred stock dividends. For purposes of this test, dividends on stock received within an 85-day period are aggregated; a one-year aggregation period applies if dividends exceed 20% of the adjusted basis in the stock.

Arbitrage transactions. Special holding period rules apply to short sales involved in identified arbitrage transactions in convertible securities and stock into which the securities are convertible. These rules can be found in Treasury regulations to Internal Revenue Code Section 1233.

Puts

The acquisition of a *put* (an option to sell) is treated as a short sale if you hold substantially identical securities short term at the time you buy the put. If you have held the underlying stock for one year or less at the time you buy the put, any gain on the exercise, sale, or expiration of the put is a short-term capital gain. The same is true if you buy the underlying stock after you buy the put but before its exercise, sale, or expiration. Your holding period for the underlying stock begins on the earliest of: (1) the date you dispose of the stock; (2) the date you exercise the put; (3) the date you sell the put; or (4) the date the put expires. However, the short-sale rules do not apply if on the same day you buy a put and stock that is identified as covered by the put. If you do not exercise the put that is identified with the stock, add its cost to the basis of the stock.

30.6 Wash Sales

The objective of the wash-sale rule is to disallow a loss deduction where you recover your market position in a security within a short period of time after the sale. Under the wash-sale rule, your loss deduction is barred if within 30 days of the sale you buy *substantially identical* stock or securities, or a "put" or "call" option on such securities. The wash-sale period is 61 days—running from 30 days before to 30 days after the date of sale. The end of a taxable year during this 61-day period does not affect the wash-sale rule. The loss is still denied. If you sell at a loss and your spouse buys substantially identical stock within this period, the loss is also barred.

The wash-sale rule does not apply to gains. It also does not apply to acquisitions by gift, inheritance, or tax-free exchange.

The wash-sale rule applies to investors and traders. It does not apply to dealers.

Loss on the sale of part of a stock lot bought less than 30 days ago. If you buy stock and then, within 30 days, sell some of those shares, a loss on the sale is deductible; the wash-sale disallowance rule does not apply.

> ### EXAMPLE
>
> You buy 200 shares of stock. Within 30 days, you sell 100 shares at a loss. The loss is not disallowed by the wash-sale rule. The wash-sale rule does not apply to a loss sustained in a bona fide sale made to reduce your market position. It does apply when you sustain a loss for tax purposes with the intent of recovering your position in the security within a short period. Thus if, after selling the 100 shares, you repurchase 100 shares of the same stock within 30 days after the sale, the loss is disallowed.

Oral sale-repurchase agreement. The wash-sale rule applies to an oral sale-repurchase agreement between business associates.

Defining "substantially identical." What is substantially identical stock or securities? Buying and selling General Motors stock is dealing in an identical security. Selling General Motors and buying Chrysler stock is not dealing in substantially identical securities.

Bonds of the same obligor are substantially identical if they carry the same rate of interest; that they have different issue dates and interest payment dates will not remove them from the wash-sale provisions. Different maturity dates will have no effect, unless the difference is economically significant. Where there is a long time span between the purchase date and the maturity date, a difference of several years between maturity dates may be considered insignificant. A difference of three years between maturity dates was held to be insignificant where the maturity dates of the bonds, measured from the time of purchase, were 45 and 48 years away. There was no significant difference where the maturity dates differed by less than one year, and the remaining life, measured from the time of purchase, was more than 15 years.

The wash-sale rules do not apply if you buy bonds of the same company with substantially different interest rates, buy bonds of a different company, or buy substantially identical bonds outside of the wash-sale period.

Warrants. A warrant falls within the wash-sale rule if it is an option to buy substantially identical stock. Consequently, a loss on the sale of common stocks of a corporation is disallowed when warrants for the common stock of the same corporation are bought within the period 30 days before or after the sale. But if the timing is reversed—that is, you sell warrants at a loss and simultaneously buy common stock of the same corporation—the wash-sale rules may or may not apply depending on whether the warrants are substantially identical to the purchased stock. This is determined by comparing the relative values of the stock and warrants. The wash-sale rule will apply only if the relative values and price changes are so similar that the warrants become fully convertible securities.

> ### EXAMPLES
>
> 1. You bought common stock of Appliance Co. for $10,000 in 1983. On June 26, 2002, you sold the stock for $8,000, incurring a $2,000 loss. A week later, you repurchased the same number of shares of Appliance stock for $9,000. Your loss of $2,000 on the sale is disallowed because of the wash-sale rule. The basis of the new lot becomes $11,000. The basis of the old shares ($10,000) is increased by $1,000, which is the excess of the purchase price of the new shares ($9,000) over the selling price of the old shares ($8,000).

Planning Reminder

Basis Adjusted for New Stock
Although the loss deduction is barred if the wash-sale rule applies, the economic loss is not forfeited for tax purposes. The loss might be realized at a later date when the repurchased stock is sold, because after the disallowance of the loss, the cost basis of the new lot is fixed as the basis of the old lot and adjusted (up or down) for the difference between the selling price of the old stock and purchase price of the new stock; *see* the Examples below.

2. Assume the same facts as in Example 1, except that you repurchase the stock for $7,000. The basis of the new lot is $9,000. The basis of the old shares ($10,000) is decreased by $1,000, which is the excess of the selling price of the old shares ($8,000) over the purchase price of the new shares ($7,000).

3. Assume that in February 2003 you sell the new lot of stock acquired in Example 1 above for $9,000 and do not run afoul of the wash-sale rule. On the sale, you realize a loss of $2,000 ($11,000 − $9,000).

Repurchasing fewer shares. If the number of shares of stock reacquired in a wash sale is less than the amount sold, only a proportionate part of the loss is disallowed.

EXAMPLE

You bought 100 shares of Stock A for $10,000. On December 9, 2002, you sell the lot for $8,000, incurring a loss of $2,000. On January 6, 2003, you repurchase 75 shares of Stock A for $6,000. Three-quarters ($^{75}/_{100}$) of your loss is disallowed, or $1,500 ($^{3}/_{4}$ of $2,000). You deduct the remaining loss of $500 on your return for 2002. The basis of the new shares is $7,500 ($6,000 cost *plus* $1,500 disallowed loss).

Holding period of new stock. After a wash sale, the holding period of the new stock includes the holding period of the old lots. If you sold more than one old lot in wash sales, you add the holding periods of all the old lots to the holding period of the new lot. You do this even if your holding periods overlapped as you purchased another lot before you sold the first. You do not count the periods between the sale and purchase when you have no stock.

Losses on short sales. Losses incurred on short sales are subject to the wash-sale rules. A loss on the closing of a short sale is denied if you sell the stock or enter into a second short sale within the period beginning 30 days before and ending 30 days after the closing of the short sale.

30.7 Convertible Stocks and Bonds

You realize no gain or loss when you convert a bond into stock, or preferred stock into common stock of the same corporation, provided the conversion privilege was allowed by the bond or preferred stock certificate.

Holding period. Stock acquired through the conversion of bonds or preferred stock takes the same holding period as the securities exchanged. However, where the new stock is acquired partly for cash and partly by tax-free exchange, each new share of stock has a split holding period. The portion of each new share allocable to the ownership of the converted bonds (or preferred stock) includes the holding period of the bonds (or preferred stock). The portion of the new stock allocable to the cash purchase takes a holding period beginning with the day after acquisition of the stock.

Basis. Securities acquired through the conversion of bonds or preferred stock into common take the same basis as the securities exchanged. Where there is a partial cash payment, the basis of the portion of the stock attributable to the cash is the amount of cash paid; *see* Examples 1 and 2 below.

If you paid a premium for a convertible bond, you may not amortize the amount of the premium that is attributable to the conversion feature.

EXAMPLES

1. On January 5, you paid $100 for a debenture of A Co. Your holding period for the debenture begins on January 6; *see 5.9*. The debenture provides that the holder may receive one share of A Co. common stock upon surrender of one debenture and the payment of $50. On October 19, you convert the debenture to stock on payment of $50. For tax purposes, you realize no gain or loss upon the conversion regardless of whether the fair market value of the stock is more or less than $150 on the date of the conversion. The basis and holding period for the stock is as follows: $100 basis for the portion attributed to the ownership of the debenture with the holding period beginning January 6; and $50 basis attributed to the cash payment with the holding period for this portion beginning October 20.

Planning Reminder

Tax Advantage of Wash-Sale Rule

Sometimes the wash-sale rule can work to your advantage. Assume that during December you are negotiating a sale of real estate that will bring you a large capital gain. You want to offset a part of that gain by selling certain securities at a loss. You are unsure just when the gain transaction will go through. It may be on the last day of the year, at which point it may be too late to sell the loss securities before the end of the same year.

You can do this: Sell the loss securities during the last week of December. If the profitable deal goes through before the end of the year, you need not do anything further. If it does not, buy back the loss securities early in January. The December sale will be a wash sale and the loss disallowed. When the profitable real estate sale occurs next year, you can sell the loss securities again. This time the loss will be allowed and will offset the gain.

2. Same facts as in the above Example, but you acquired the debenture on January 5 through the exercise of rights on that date. Since the holding period for the debenture includes the date of exercise of the rights, *see 30.4*, the portion of the stock allocable to the debenture takes a holding period beginning on January 6.

30.8 Constructive Sales of Appreciated Financial Positions

One aspect of a constructive sale of an appreciated financial position was discussed in *30.5*, dealing with short sales. The constructive sale rules apply not only to short sales of stock but also to other transactions such as an appreciated financial position in a partnership interest or certain debt obligations.

You have made a constructive sale of an appreciated financial position if you:

1. Enter into a short sale of the same or substantially identical property,
2. Enter into an offsetting notional principal contract relating to the same or substantially identical property,
3. Enter into a futures or forward contract to deliver the same or substantially identical property, *or*
4. Acquire the same or substantially identical property (if the appreciated financial position is a short sale, an offsetting notional principal contract, or a futures or forward contract).

You are also treated as having made a constructive sale of an appreciated financial position if a person related to you enters into any of the above transactions.

A contract for sale of any stock, debt instrument, or partnership interest that is not a marketable security is not a constructive sale if it settles within one year of the date you enter into it.

Tax treatment. If you are considered to have transacted a constructive sale, you report as taxable income gain on the financial position as if the position was sold at its fair market value on the date of the constructive sale. The property held by you receives a new holding period starting on the date of the constructive sale and its basis is the fair market value at that date. Thus, under the constructive sale rule you are also treated as immediately repurchasing the position as of the date of the constructive sale.

Closing a short sale to avoid a constructive sale. You may avoid the constructive sale rule if:

1. You close the transaction before the end of the 30th day after the end of your tax year,
2. You hold the appreciated financial position throughout the 60-day period beginning on the date you close the transaction,
3. Your risk of loss is not reduced at any time during that 60-day period by holding certain other positions.

If a closed transaction is reestablished in a substantially similar position during the 60-day period beginning on the date the first transaction was closed, this exception still applies if the reestablished position is closed before the end of the 30th day after the end of your tax year in which the first transaction was closed and, after that closing, tests (2) and (3) apply.

Caution

Constructive Sales of Appreciated Position

If you are subject to the constructive sale rules, you will have to report income as if you had made a sale although you still hold the position.

EXAMPLE

On October 2, 2002, you buy 100 shares of Oil Co. for $60 a share. On December 3, 2002, you sell short 100 shares of Oil Co. for $80 a share. On January 6, 2003, you buy for $75 a share 100 shares of Oil Co. to close the short sale. You hold the October lot for over 60 days after January 6, 2003. The December 2002 short sale is not treated as a constructive sale in 2002. You realized a loss of $5 per share when you closed the short position.

An appreciated financial position. You have an appreciated financial position interest in stock, a partnership interest, or a debt instrument (including a futures or forward contract, a short sale, or an option) if disposing of the interest would result in a gain.

An appreciated financial position does not include any position that is marked to market, including Section 1256 contracts. It also does not include any position in a debt instrument if:

1. The debt unconditionally entitles the holder to receive a specified principal amount,
2. The interest payments on the debt (or other similar amounts) are payable at a fixed rate or a variable rate described in Section 1.860G-1(a)(3) of the Regulations, *and*
3. The debt is not convertible, either directly or indirectly, into stock of the issuer (or any related person).

For the constructive sale rules, an interest in an actively traded trust is treated as stock unless substantially all of the value of the property held by the trust is debt that qualifies for the debt exception above.

A transaction treated as a constructive sale of an appreciated financial position is not treated as a constructive sale of any other appreciated financial position, as long as you continue to hold the original position. However, if you hold another appreciated financial position and dispose of the original position before closing the transaction that resulted in the constructive sale, you are treated as if, at the same time, you constructively sold the other appreciated financial position.

30.9 Straddle Losses

Tax accounting rules generally match losses against unrealized gains in offsetting straddle positions. Straddle rules apply to commodities and actively traded stock and to stock options used in straddle positions. Straddle positions include any stock that is part of a straddle in which at least one of the offsetting positions is: (1) an option tied to the stock or to substantially identical stock or securities; or (2) a position in substantially similar or related property other than stock. For example, there is a straddle of stock and substantially similar or related property if offsetting positions of stock and convertible debentures of the same corporation are held and price movements of the two positions are related.

Straddle rules apply also to stock of a corporation formed or used to take positions in personal property that offset positions taken by any shareholder. True *hedging* transactions are not subject to the straddle tax rules.

A call option is not treated as part of a straddle position if it is considered a qualified covered call option. A *qualified covered call option* is an option that a stockholder who is not a dealer grants on stock traded on a national securities exchange. Furthermore, the option must be granted more than 30 days before its expiration date and must not be "deep-in-the-money." A covered call option will not qualify if gain on the sale of the stock to be purchased by the option is reported in a year after the year in which the option is closed, and the stock is not held for 30 days or more after the date on which the option is closed. In such a case, the option is subject to the straddle loss deferral rules. The same loss deferment rule applies where the stock is sold at a loss, and gain on the related option held less than 30 days is reported in the next year.

Loss on a qualified covered call option with a strike price less than its applicable stock price is treated as long-term capital loss if loss realized on the sale of the stock would be long term. The holding period for stock subject to the option does not include any period during which the taxpayer is the grantor of the option.

A "deep-in-the-money" option is an option with a strike or exercise price that is below the lowest qualified benchmark. The technical rules for determining these values are not discussed in this book.

Tax rules for straddles. The following is an overview of the subject, and if you have transacted straddles, we suggest that you consult with an experienced tax practitioner.

Realized straddle losses are deductible at the close of a taxable year only if they exceed unrealized gains in an offsetting position. Thus, an investor may not deduct losses incurred in 2002 to the extent that he or she has an unrealized gain position in the open end of the straddle.

Straddle positions of related persons (such as a spouse or child) or controlled flow-through entities (such as a partnership or an S corporation) are considered in determining whether offsetting positions are held.

Realized losses that are not deductible at the end of the year are carried forward and become deductible when there is no unrealized appreciation in an offsetting position bought before the disposition of the loss position. This loss deferral rule may be avoided by identifying straddles before the close of the day of acquisition or at an earlier time that the IRS may set. Gain or loss in identified positions is generally netted; that is, a loss is recognized when the offsetting gain position has been closed.

You must disclose all straddle positions of unrealized gains at the close of a tax year or you may be subject to a negligence penalty unless failure to disclose is due to a reasonable cause.

The loss deferral rule does *not* apply to positions in a regulated futures contract or other Section 1256 contract subject to the marked-to-market system explained later in this section.

The loss deferral rule also does not apply to businesses that must hedge in order to protect their supplies of inventory or financial capital. Hedging transactions are subject to ordinary income or loss treatment. Hedging transactions entered into by syndicates do not qualify for the exception and are subject to the loss deferral rule if more than 35% of losses for a taxable year are allocable to

limited partners or entrepreneurs. Furthermore, hedging losses of limited partners or limited entrepreneurs are generally limited to their taxable income from the business to which the hedging transaction relates.

Conversion transactions. On certain so-called "conversion transactions," discussed at *30.10*, gain realized on the disposition of certain positions is treated as ordinary income instead of capital gain.

Marked-to-market rules for gain or loss on regulated futures contracts and other Section 1256 contracts. Gain or loss on regulated futures contracts is reported annually under the marked-to-market accounting system of regulated commodity exchanges. To settle margin requirements, regulated exchanges determine a party's account for futures contracts on a daily basis. Each regulated futures contract is treated as if sold at fair market value on the last day of the taxable year. Any capital gain or loss is arbitrarily allocated: 40% is short term and 60% is long term. Use Form 6781 to figure gains and losses on Section 1256 contracts that are open at the end of the year or that were closed out during the year. These amounts are then transferred from Form 6781 to Schedule D.

Under the law, a regulated futures contract is considered a Section 1256 contract. Other Section 1256 contracts subject to the marked-to-market rules are foreign currency contracts, dealer equity options, and non-equity options.

The marked-to-market rules do not apply to true hedging transactions executed in the normal course of business to reduce risks and that result in ordinary income or loss. Syndicates may generally not take advantage of this hedging exception if more than 35% of their losses during a taxable year are allocable to limited partners or entrepreneurs. Further, the ability of entrepreneurs or limited partners to deduct losses from hedging transactions is generally limited to taxable income from the business to which the hedging transaction relates.

Mixed straddle contracts. If you have a mixed straddle in which at least one but not all of the positions is a Section 1256 contract, the marked-to-market rules generally apply but you may elect to avoid this treatment and apply the regular straddle tax rules. The election, made on Form 6781, is irrevocable unless the IRS allows a revocation. Furthermore, the IRS allows an election to offset gains and losses from positions that are part of mixed straddles if you separately identify each mixed straddle or establish mixed straddle accounts for a class of activities for which gain and loss will be recognized and offset on a periodic basis.

Wash sales. Rules similar to wash-sale rules apply to losses arising from sales of shares that make up a straddle if within a 30-day period you acquire substantially identical shares; *see* IRS Publication 550 for further details.

Contract cancellations. Investors buying forward contracts for currency or securities may not realize ordinary loss by cancelling the unprofitable contract of the hedge transaction. Loss realized on a cancellation of the contract is treated as a capital loss.

Cash-and-carry transactions. You may not deduct carrying costs for any period during which the commodity or stock or option is part of a balanced position. The costs must be capitalized and added to basis. The rule does not apply to hedging straddles. Capitalized items are reduced by dividends on stock included in a straddle, market discounts, and acquisition discounts. These reductions, however, are limited to so much of the dividends and discounts as is included in income.

30.10 Capital Gain Restricted on Conversion Transactions

A "conversion transaction" is a transaction generally involving two or more positions taken with regard to the same or similar property. The investor is in the economic position of a lender who expects to receive income while undertaking no significant risks other than those of a lender. Where substantially all of your expected return is in the nature of interest on a loan from the following types of transactions, some or all of the income earned on the transaction is treated as ordinary income rather than capital gain:

- You acquire property and also agree to sell the property or substantially identical property for a determined price;
- You take offsetting positions on a straddle transaction; *or*
- You invest in a transaction marketed or sold as producing capital gain but your expected return is in the nature of interest on a loan.

Option dealers and commodity dealers are generally exempt from the new limitations.

Filing Instruction

Marked-to-Market Rules

Non-equity options and dealer equity options, which include options based on regulated stock indexes and interest rate futures, are taxed like regulated futures contracts. This means that they are reported annually under the marked-to-market accounting system. You treat all such options held at the end of the year as if they were disposed of at year-end for a price equal to fair market value. Any gain or loss is arbitrarily taxed as if it were 60% long term and 40% short term. It is advisable to ask your broker whether the specific options you hold come within this special rule.

You use Form 6781 to report 60/40% gains, which are then transferred to Schedule D.

Filing Tip

Reporting Conversion Transactions

You report conversion transactions on Form 6781. The ordinary income element is not reported as interest income, but as an ordinary gain on Form 4797.

Amount treated as ordinary income. In a conversion transaction, the amount of ordinary income is limited to an "applicable imputed income amount." This is generally the amount of interest that would have accrued on the net investment in the conversion transaction for the period ending on the date of disposition. To figure the interest element, 120% of the applicable federal rate, compounded semiannually, is used. The applicable rate is the federal short-term, mid-term, or long-term rate, depending on the term of the transaction. If the term is indefinite, the federal short-term rate is used. The federal rates are determined monthly and published in the Internal Revenue Bulletin.

> **EXAMPLE**
>
> On January 5, 2001, Jones buys stock for $100 and on the same day agrees to sell it to Brown for $115 on January 7, 2002. Assume the applicable federal interest rate is 5%. On January 7, 2002, Jones delivers the stock to Brown for $115. If the conversion transaction rule did not apply, Jones would recognize a capital gain of $15 ($115 sale price less $100 purchase price). However, under the conversion transaction rules, $12.36 of the gain is ordinary income ($12.36 is $100 times 6% compounded for two years; 6% is 120% of the 5% federal rate). The balance of the gain, or $2.64, is long-term capital gain ($15 *less* $12.36).
>
> Where a loan finances a conversion transaction and interest is capitalized (under a provision applied to straddles), the amount of ordinary income reported is reduced.
>
> If the conversion transaction involves a "built-in" loss, the loss is recognized without regard to the conversion rules. For example, if the loss is a capital loss, it remains a capital loss although the conversion rules apply to the transaction.

30.11   Puts and Calls and Index Options

You may buy options to buy and sell stock. On the stock exchange, these options are named *calls* and *puts*. A call gives you the right to require the seller of the option to sell you stock during the option period at a fixed price, called the exercise or strike price. A put gives you the right to require the seller of the option to buy stock you own at a fixed price during the option period. *See* the chart on the following page for an explanation of different option terms.

The option price depends on the value of the stock, the length of the option period, the volatility of the stock, and the demand and supply for options for the particular stock.

Puts may be treated as short sales. Be careful in using puts when you own stock covered by the put. If you have held the stock short term, the purchase of the put is a short sale. The exercise or expiration of the put will then be treated as the closing of the short sale. Short-sale rules, however, do not apply (1) when you hold stock long term, and (2) when you buy a put and the related stock on the same day and identify the stock with the put; *see 30.5.*

Buyers of options. If you buy an option, the tax treatment of your investment in the option depends on what you do with it.

1. If you sell it, you realize short-term or long-term capital gain or loss, depending upon how long you held the option.

2. If you allow the option to expire without exercise, you incur a short-term or long-term capital loss, depending on the holding period of the option. The expiration date is treated as the date the option is disposed of.

3. If you exercise a call and buy the stock, you add the cost of the call to the basis of the stock. If you exercise a put, the cost of the put reduces your amount realized when figuring gain or loss on the sale of the underlying stock.

Grantors of options. If you write an option through the exchange, you do not treat the premium received for writing the option as income at the time of receipt. You do not realize profit or loss until the option transaction is closed. This may occur when the option expires or is exercised or when you "buy in" on the exchange an option similar to the one you gave to end your obligation to deliver the stock. Here are the rules for these events:

1. If the option is not exercised, you report the premium as short-term capital gain in the year the option expires.

2. If the option is exercised, you add the premium to the sales proceeds of the stock to determine gain or loss on the sale of the stock. Gain or loss is short term or long term depending upon the holding period of the stock.

Planning Reminder

Speculate With Puts and Calls

Puts and calls allow you to speculate at the expense of a small investment—a call, for expected price rises, and a put, for expected price declines. They may also be used to protect paper profits or fix the amount of your losses on securities you own.

You do not have to exercise a put or call to realize your profit. You may sell the option to realize your profit. If you exercise a call, the cost of the call is added to the cost of the stock purchased. If you exercise a put, you reduce the selling price of stock sold by the cost of the put. If you do not exercise a call or put, you realize a capital loss.

3. If you "buy in" an equivalent option in a closing transaction, you realize profit or loss for the difference between the premium of the option you sold and the cost of the closing option. The profit or loss is treated as short-term capital gain or loss. However, a loss on a covered call that has a stated price below the stock price may be long-term capital loss if, at the time of the loss, long-term gain would be realized on the sale of the stock. Furthermore, the holding period of such stock is suspended during the period in which the option is open. Finally, year-end losses from covered call options are not deductible, unless the stock is held uncovered for more than 30 days following the date on which the option is closed.

Using a call as leverage. You expect a stock to appreciate in value but you do not have sufficient capital for a further investment. Instead of investing your limited amount of capital in an outright purchase, you might buy a call covering such stock. With a call, the same amount of capital allows you to speculate in many more shares than you could if you purchased stock outright. If the stock rises in value, your call also increases in value.

Key to Option Terms

Item—	Explanation—
Call option	An option contract that gives the holder the right to buy a specified number of shares of the underlying stock at the given exercise price on or before the option expiration date.
Put option	An option contract that gives the holder the right to sell a specified number of shares of the underlying stock at the given exercise price on or before the option expiration date.
Strike price/exercise price	The stated price per share for which the underlying stock may be bought (in the case of a call) or sold (in the case of a put) by the option holder upon exercise of the option contract.
At-the-money	An option is at-the-money if the exercise price of the option is equal to the market price of the underlying security.
In-the-money	A call option is in-the-money if the exercise price is less than the market price of the underlying security. A put option is in-the-money if the exercise price is greater than the market price of the underlying security.
Out-of-the-money	A call option is out-of-the-money if the exercise price is greater than the market price of the underlying security. A put option is out-of-the-money if the strike price is less than the market price of the underlying security.
Premium	The price of the option contract determined in the competitive marketplace, which the buyer of the option pays to the option writer.
Intrinsic value	The amount by which the option is in-the-money.
Time value (premium-intrinsic value)	The portion of the premium that is attributable to the amount of time remaining until the option's expiration date and to the fact that the underlying components that determine the value of the option may change during that time.
Secondary market	A market that provides for the purchase or sale of previously sold or bought options through closing transactions.
Expiration date	The expiration date is the last day on which an option may be exercised.
Writer	The seller of an option contract.

30.12 Exchange Option Trading

Option market exchanges such as the Chicago Board Options Exchange (CBOE) provide market conditions for trading in puts and call options. Financial sections of the daily newspapers provide data on the market prices and volume of the options.

Trading in options is highly speculative, attracting those who hope to make profits on minimum investments. At the same time, the market has provided investors and institutions holding large portfolios with an opportunity to earn income through the sale of options based on their holdings. Thus, it takes two to play the option game: (1) the owner of shares who sells an option on his or her stock and (2) the option buyer who generally speculates that, by buying an option for a smaller price than he or she would have to pay for the stock, a profit can be made if the price of the stock goes up. The odds generally favor the option seller.

If you are inexperienced in the use of options, read several technical explanations of the use of options before investing. Master the technical use of options such as straddles and hedges used by professional traders, as the outright purchase of straight calls is generally too speculative. Finally, do not overlook commission costs, which can cut into your profits or increase your losses.

Stock index options. Index options give you a chance to speculate on the general movement of stock prices. The success of the index option has tended to reduce interest in regular stock options given on individual stocks. On the other hand, index options are pegged to the price movement of the stocks that comprise the index option. Thus, with index options, you do not have to be concerned about the market fate of a particular stock. The stock group of the index option follows the general stock market movement. For example, assume that 100 stocks make up the index. The option contract represents an index multiplier of $100 times the index value of the group or basket of 100 stocks. Therefore, when a newspaper reports an index value of 170, which is also called the "strike price," the contract is worth $17,000. However, as the option is only a right to buy or sell this particular contract, you pay an option price that is only a percentage of the contract value. The particular option price is set by the market in an open auction.

Your role is to weigh how the market will fare within the option period. Should you anticipate lower interest rates within the option period, which can be from approximately a week up to three months, you might buy an index option, betting that the stock market will advance. For example, when the index is at 165, you buy an option for $1,200 with a strike price of 170. If the stock market advances during the option period, pushing the strike price to 177, you have won your bet. At 177, you might sell your option for $7,000, thereby making a $5,800 profit.

Do not let this example encourage you to enter the index option market precipitously. If you guess wrong, you have lost your money. In the example just cited, had the index not moved above 170, you would have lost $1,200. However, unlike other investments where the risk may be unlimited, options offer buyers a known risk in that the buyer cannot lose more than the premium paid for the option or, in other words, the price paid for the option.

If you are interested in playing the index option market, track the market for several months until you get used to the movement of the option. Plot hypothetical purchases and see how you would have fared. You might make a bundle—but, as at roulette, you might lose your shirt in a very short time.

Investment Opportunities

30.13 Reducing the Tax on Dividend Income

The tax on dividend income may be reduced by the following types of transactions:

- *Selling stock on which a dividend has been declared but not yet paid.* During the period a dividend is declared but not paid, the price of the stock includes the value of the dividend. If you plan to sell stock in this position and figure that the tax on the dividend reflected in the selling price will be less than the tax on the dividend received, transact the sale before the stock goes ex-dividend; *see 4.9.*
- *Investing in companies paying tax-free dividends.* Some companies pay tax-free dividends. A list of companies that do may be provided by your broker. When you receive a tax-free dividend, you do not report the dividend as income as long as the dividend does not exceed your stock basis. A tax-free dividend reduces the tax cost of your stock. Dividends in excess of basis produce capital gain; *see 4.11.*
- *Investing in companies paying stock dividends.* On receipt of a stock dividend, you generally do not have taxable income.

30.14 Treasury Bills and CDs

Short-term paper (maturity of one year or less) provides an opportunity for earning income on funds during periods of uncertainty in the stock and other investment markets. Funds that you do not wish to tie up long term and do not want to remain unproductive may be invested in Treasury bills, notes, or certificates of deposit. These investments offer safety and negotiability, earning current interest rates from the day of purchase to the day of redemption, either on maturity or sale.

Treasury bills. These are direct obligations of the U.S. Treasury issued to finance budgetary needs. Bills are offered for 4, 13, or 26-week maturities. Bills are sold at a discount at Treasury auctions held at the Federal Reserve Banks, which serve as agents for the Treasury. They are redeemed at face value. Your return on a Treasury bill is the difference between the discount price you pay for the bill and its face value, if you hold it to maturity, or the amount you receive for it on a sale before maturity. The selling price of a Treasury bill before maturity will vary with changes of current interest rates.

You may buy Treasury bills directly without charge from any Federal Reserve Bank, which gives you a receipt indicating that a book entry of your purchase has been recorded. Treasury bills may also be purchased directly from the government by submitting a paper tender, using an automated phone system (1-800-722-2678) or ordering through the *Treasury Direct* website at www.publicdebt.treas.gov. You also may buy or sell Treasury bills through your bank or stockbroker, who will charge you for handling the transaction.

Treasury bill yield. On the day of the auction, the Treasury will figure the average price bid by those who submitted acceptable competitive tenders. The difference between this average price and the full value of the Treasury bill is the *discount* at which the bill is sold. All noncompetitive tenders are filled at this price. The Treasury sends you a refund for the difference between the purchase price and the face value.

EXAMPLE

Assume the accepted average bid on three-month bills is $9,850. You gave the government $10,000. To reflect the actual purchase price of $9,850, the "discount" of $150 is refunded to you.

The equivalent annual yield on your Treasury bill is figured this way:

1. Find the yield on your investment by dividing discount by purchase price.
2. Convert this yield to the annual rate by multiplying the yield by 4.0110 (365 ÷ 91 days to maturity) if the term is 91 days and by 2.0055 (365 ÷ 182 days to maturity) if the term is 182 days. For example, on a 26-week (182 days) bill your discount is $165 (cost $9,835); the equivalent annual yield is:

$$\frac{\$165}{\$9,835} = .0168 \text{ and } .0168 \times 2.0055 = .0337, \text{ or } 3.37\% \text{ per year}$$

At maturity. Redemption is automatic at maturity, unless you notify the Treasury that you wish to roll over matured bills into new bills. The Treasury will electronically deposit the face amount of the bill into a savings or checking account you have previously designated. If you bought your bill through a bank, the bank will credit your account on the date the bill matures. To roll over your maturing bill, you follow the same procedures as in buying a new bill and use your matured bill as payment. If you purchase bills directly from the Treasury, a payment for the difference between the price of the new bills and the face value of your matured bills will be transferred electronically to your designated account.

Certificates of deposit. Certificates of deposit (CDs) are another form of short-term investment that offers a high degree of safety and negotiability.

Certificates of deposit represent money lent by investors to a bank for a specified short period of time, generally 30, 60, or 90 days, although certificates of deposit for six months to several years are also available.

Purchasing CDs. Certificates of deposit are generally purchased through your bank or broker. The rate of interest that banks will pay depends on supply and demand in the money market. The interest rate may vary with the size of your investment. For deposits of $100,000 or more, you may be able to get a jumbo CD at a higher rate than offered on smaller deposits.

Before investing, check with the bank for minimum investment requirements, charges, and restrictions on withdrawals, including penalties for withdrawals before maturity.

 Planning Reminder

Buying T-Bills
Most investors submit *noncompetitive tenders* (bids) for the Treasury bills they wish to buy. To submit a *competitive* tender, you must specify the price you are willing to pay for your bill, and you run the risk of bidding too low and not getting the bills you want. Noncompetitive tenders do not have to specify a price. They are filled at a price that is the average of the accepted competitive tenders for that specific auction. Check the Federal Reserve Bank in your area or the Treasury website at www.publicdebt.treas.gov for auction dates on Treasury bills. You may also buy or sell Treasury bills through your bank or your stockbroker, who will charge you for handling the transaction.

Planning Reminder

Cashing Treasury Bills Before Maturity
If you decide you need funds before the maturity date of your bill, you can sell it through a commercial bank, securities broker, or if it is held in a Treasury Direct account, through the government's Sell Direct program.

For bills sold before maturity, current interest rates will determine the amount you receive. The market value of Treasury bills is listed daily in the financial section of newspapers.

If you have an account with a broker, you may prefer to invest in CDs through your broker. Brokers offer CDs from various banks throughout the U.S. and can provide at times a higher current rate offered by a bank in an area that is not directly accessible to you.

Repurchase agreements (repos). This investment offered by banks and thrifts allows you to earn high interest rates by sharing in a portion of the bank's portfolio of government securities. The bank is required to repurchase your investment from you at your request. The minimum investment is $1,000; maturities vary, on average, three months. Repos are not FDIC or FSLIC insured, and there is no interest penalty for early repurchase, as long as you hold them for a minimum of a week or more. There may be a small service charge for early repurchase.

Commercial paper. Periodically during the year, many corporations requiring large sums of money to finance short-term customer receivables offer short-term promissory notes at high rates of interest. These notes are generally referred to as commercial paper. Although much of this paper is sold in units of $100,000 or more, commercial paper in denominations of $25,000 and even less is sometimes available.

Finance companies, automobile manufacturers, and large retail stores are types of businesses that typically issue commercial paper for periods ranging from one week to 270 days.

Investments in commercial paper may not be as liquid as other short-term paper and are subject to greater risks.

Tax-exempt notes are discussed at *30.18*.

30.15 Investing in Savings Institutions

Bank money-market accounts compete with money-market mutual funds. Bank money-market funds generally guarantee for one-week or one-month periods interest rates tied to the Treasury bill rate or the average money-market rate. Bank funds also offer this added attraction: They are federally insured. Bank money-market accounts require certain average monthly balances and if the account falls below the minimum, the interest rate is reduced.

Investments in money-market accounts allow you to take advantage of rising interest rates, but if market rates decline, so will your return. Investments in CDs allow you to lock into the highest available interest rate for a fixed period of time if you are concerned with a decline of rates during that period.

Withdrawals generally may be made from money-market accounts without penalty, subject to minimum account requirements. Premature withdrawals from CDs are penalized.

CD investments in savings institutions allow you to lock into high interest rates only for the short term, generally up to five years. If you are concerned that rates will substantially decline in the future, you may want to invest in a currently available investment that fixes a high rate over longer periods, such as bonds with long-term maturities. Corporate bond investments are discussed in *30.16*.

As indicated in *30.14*, stockbrokers may offer to their customers issues of CDs from various banks and may allow you to invest at a slightly higher rate than that offered by a local bank.

Investment options vary from bank to bank. Not all banks offer the maximum rates or compound interest in the same manner. Whether interest is compounded daily or annually will affect your rate of return. Each bank also has its own policy on procedures concerning maturity of certificates. Some banks automatically renew the CD for another term at the current rate unless notified to the contrary; some banks will not renew a matured CD without express authority from you. If you fail to act, you may find your funds switched to a day-of-deposit account on maturity. Banking institutions can also change their rules after you have opened an account.

30.16 Investing in Corporate Bonds

When you buy a corporate bond, you are lending money to the issuer of the bonds. You become a creditor of the issuing company. The corporation pledges to pay you interest on specified dates, generally twice a year, and to repay the principal on the date of maturity stated on the bond.

For investment purposes, a bond may be described according to the length of the period of maturity. Short-term bonds usually mature within one to five years, medium-term bonds in five to 20 years, and long-term bonds in 20 or more years.

Where the interest is paid out on a regular schedule, the bond is called a "current income" bond. An accrual or discount bond is a bond on which interest is accumulated and paid as part of the specified maturity value (the bond having been issued at a price lower than the specified maturity value).

 *Planning Reminder*

Deferring Interest Income

Defer interest income by buying a six-month tax-deferred certificate after June 30. Interest is taxable in the next year when the certificate matures if the terms of the certificate specifically defer the interest to maturity. If your bank offers you the choice of when to receive the interest, deferral is not allowed. You may also defer interest by buying Treasury bills that come due next year.

Figuring the yield of a bond. The investment value of bonds is generally expressed in rates of yield. There are four types of yield: the nominal or coupon yield; the actual yield; the current market yield; and the net yield to maturity.

The nominal or coupon yield is the fixed or contractual rate of interest stated on the bond. A bond paying 6% has a 6% nominal yield.

The actual yield is the rate of return based on the price at which the bond was purchased. If bought below par, the actual yield will exceed the nominal or coupon yield. If bought at a premium (above par), the actual yield will be less than the coupon or nominal yield. For example, if you paid $850 for a $1,000 bond paying 5% interest, the actual yield is 5.88% ($50 ÷ $850).

The current market yield is the rate of return on the bond if bought at the prevailing market price. It is figured in the same manner as actual yield.

Net yield to maturity represents the rate of return on the bond if it is held to maturity, plus appreciation allocated to a discount purchase or less reductions for any premium paid on a bond selling above par. If you buy a bond below par at a market discount, your annual return is proportionately increased by a part of the discount allocated to the number of years before maturity. If the discount was $50 on a bond with a five-year maturity, then your annual income return on the bond is increased by $10 ($50 ÷ 5). On the other hand, if you bought at a premium, the extra cost is a reduction against your income because you paid more than can be recovered at maturity. This cost is allocated over the remaining life of the bond. Thus, if you bought a five-year bond at $50 over par, your average annual return is reduced by $10 ($50 ÷ 5).

Call privileges may reduce the investment value of the bond. A call privilege gives the issuer a chance to redeem the obligation before maturity if interest rates have declined below the rate fixed by the obligation. A call privilege is a disadvantage to an investor; a favorable investment may be lost at a time the investor may not be able to replace it with another. To take some of the "sting" out of a call provision, the issuer may provide for the payment of a "premium" on the exercise of the call and a minimum period during which the bonds will not be called. The call premium is usually expressed as a percentage of the maturity value, for example, 105%. The amount of the premium varies with the length of the period in which the bond may be called. As the maturity date approaches, the call premium will decrease. Some bonds now carry a guarantee that they will not be called for a specified number of years, such as five or 10 years.

A call privilege generally will not be exercised if the going interest rate remains about the same as, or is higher than, the interest rate of the bond. If interest rates decline below the interest rate of the bond, the bond will probably be called because the issuer can obtain the borrowed money at lower cost elsewhere.

Interest on bearer bonds issued with coupons attached is paid when a bondholder clips the coupon and deposits it for payment. A registered bond carries the name of the owner, who receives his or her interest by mail from the issuing corporation.

Whether a bond is registered or in bearer form has no effect on its investment quality or yield. A coupon-type or bearer bond may be preferred by institutional investors because it can be transferred by hand without registration. However, this advantage must be weighed against the risks of loss through fire, theft, or casualty.

Issuing and trading bonds. New bond issues are generally placed through investment bankers who usually assist in the preparation of the issue. Often an issue may be sold directly by the issuing organization to an institutional investor. Many newly issued bonds are purchased directly from issuers or from their investment bankers by institutional investors before the bonds are offered to individual investors. Issuers prefer this type of placement as it involves less expense than a public offering. Normally, only the new issues (or part of new issues) that cannot be marketed this way are offered to private investors.

Bonds are also traded on the open market where individuals, as well as institutional buyers, may buy or sell them at competitive, market determined prices, through dealers or brokers.

Bond prices fluctuate in response to changes in interest rates and business conditions. In setting the daily price of a bond, the market weighs the current status, performance, and future prospects of the issuing corporation, as well as the interest rate and maturity period of the bond.

Calls under sinking fund redemption. A bond may be called in at par under the terms of a sinking fund arrangement. Not all bonds are called and those that are selected are picked by lot. Redemptions for sinking fund purposes account for only a small percentage of a single bond issue.

Planning Reminder

Weighing Long-Term Investment
To lock in interest rates, you may invest in a long-term bond. However, you may not want to tie up your capital long term. There is the possibility that a future increase in interest rates may reduce the value of your investment if you should need the principal before maturity.

Caution

Reporting Zero Coupon Bond Discount

Zero coupon bond discount is reported annually as interest over the life of the bond, even though interest is not received. This tax cost tends to make zero coupon bonds unattractive to investors, unless the bonds can be bought for IRA and other retirement plans that defer tax on income until distributions are made.

Zero coupon bonds also may be a means of financing a child's education. A parent buys the bond for the child. The child must report the income, and if the income is not subject to the parent's marginal tax bracket under the "kiddie tax" (Chapter 24), the income subject to tax may be minimal.

The value of zero coupon bonds fluctuates sharply with interest rate changes. This fact should be considered before investing in long-term zero coupon bonds. If you sell zero coupon bonds before the maturity term at a time when interest rates rise, you may lose part of your investment.

Planning Reminder

Electronic Deposit

Treasury notes and bonds are issued in book-entry form only; you do not receive a certificate. Under a direct deposit system, semiannual interest and principal at maturity is electronically deposited in a bank account that you designate.

But some issues may retain the right to use a blanket sinking fund under which they may redeem bonds paying interest at their highest rate.

Put privileges. A put privilege is the flipside of a call privilege. It permits the buyer to sell the bonds at par to the issuer after a stated number of years. This feature is valuable to investors in long-term bonds. If interest rates rise, investors are not locked into low yields.

Current interest rates affect the selling price of bonds so that you may gain or lose on your investment:

1. *If current interest rates increase over the interest rate of your bond, the market value of your bond will decline.* The decline in value has nothing to do with the credit rating of the issue. It simply means that other investors will buy only at terms that will give them the current higher return. If you bought a $1,000 bond paying a rate of 5% at par, and a few months later interest rates go to 6%, another investor will not pay $1,000 for the bond for a 5% return. To match the 6% return on a dollar, the market value of the bond will drop to a level that will return 6% on the money invested, based on its actual 5% return and the period remaining before maturity. Thus, during periods of rising interest rates, the price of bonds issued at lower rates in prior years declines. This can lead to substantial losses. Top-quality bonds are not immune from price declines; the highest credit rating will not protect the market value of a low-interest-paying bond. When this happens there also may be bond bargains, as prices on outstanding bonds decrease.

2. *If interest rates decline below the interest rate of your bond, the value of your bond will increase;* but at the same time, the company, if it has an exercisable call option, may redeem the bond to rid itself of the high interest cost and attempt to raise funds at current lower rates. Thus, an early redemption of the bond could upset your long-range investment plans in that particular issue.

Corporate zero coupon bond. A zero coupon bond is a deep discount obligation issued at considerably less than face value and redeemed at face at a set date. No annual interest is paid. A zero coupon bond allows an investor to lock in a return. He or she knows how much will be received at maturity and so avoids the problem of turning over investments at fluctuating short-term rates. However, zero coupon bonds may be subject to "call" provisions, as previously discussed; an early call would upset your projected return. Brokers have lists of zero coupon bonds; the prices vary with the credit rating of the companies, current market rates, maturity dates, and whether the bond is callable.

Floating rate or variable interest bonds. For investors unwilling to gamble on the future of interest rates, some bonds have been offered with floating interest rates. The rate is updated periodically, but there may be a floor and ceiling limiting the changes. The market price of the bond should remain near par since its interest rate moves with the market. Although this feature is a form of insurance for the investor, it may not be worth its added cost.

30.17 Treasury Bonds, Notes, and U.S. Agency Obligations

Federal government obligations are guaranteed by the federal government and are exempt from state and local taxes.

Treasury bonds and notes. Treasury bonds have maturity dates in excess of 10 years. The minimum denomination is $1,000. Interest is paid semiannually at a rate that varies with each issue. The Treasury Department has not offered a Treasury bond since it decided in October 2001 to suspend issuance of the 30-year bond.

Treasury notes are similar to Treasury bonds but have shorter maturity dates of from two to 10 years. Minimum investments range from $1,000 to $5,000, depending on the issue. Interest is paid semiannually and interest varies with each issue. Notes are purchased from commercial banks, securities firms, or directly from the U.S. Treasury or a Federal Reserve Bank.

Zero coupon Treasury bonds. Certain major brokerage houses have created zero coupon Treasury bonds by stripping the coupons from Treasury bonds and selling the bonds at deep discounts. They have been promoted under such names as TIGRS, LIONS, COUGARS, and CATS as investments suitable for IRAs, retirement plan trusts, and custodian accounts for minors. The U.S. Treasury itself offers its own version of the zero coupon bond under the name STRIPS. The government does not offer STRIPS directly to individual investors, but sells them to banks and brokers who then sell them to the public. Because STRIPS have the direct backing of the U.S. government, they are considered to be the safest zeros and generally yield up to one-tenth of one percent less than brokerage firm or bank created zero coupon bonds, such as TIGRS or CATS.

With all zero coupon Treasury obligations, an investor can select a particular maturity date suited to his or her needs, such as the year the investor will start taking IRA distributions or the year a child will start college. For tax reporting rules, *see 30.16* on corporate zero coupon bonds.

Other U.S. obligations, such as savings bonds, are discussed at *30.21* and Treasury bills at *30.14*.

Certain federal agencies, like the Tennessee Valley Authority, offer their own securities. The types of securities offered vary. Such securities must be purchased through brokers or commercial banks.

Federally chartered companies, such as the Government National Mortgage Association ("Ginnie Mae") and the Federal National Mortgage Association ("Fannie Mae"), authorize certain firms and institutions to issue securities based on insured mortgages. While interest on these securities is generally not exempt from state and local taxes, they offer the investor a higher yield than Treasury securities. Some of these obligations carry a U.S. government full faith and credit guarantee; some have only an implied guarantee; and some no backing from the federal government, but risk is generally considered to be negligible.

Ginnie Maes are offered in minimum denominations of $25,000. Monthly payments to security holders include not only interest, but also a return of principal. Rather than buying Ginnie Maes in the open market, you may consider investing in a mutual fund or trust that has a portfolio of such securities. Minimum investment units typically begin at $1,000.

30.18 Investing in Tax-Exempts

Interest on state and local obligations is not subject to federal income tax. It is also exempt from the tax of the state in which the obligations are issued. In comparing the interest return of a tax-exempt with that of a taxable bond, you figure the taxable return that is equivalent to the tax-free yield of the tax-exempt. This amount depends on your tax bracket. For example, a municipal bond of $5,000 yielding 4% is the equivalent of a taxable yield of 5.48% subject to the tax rate of 27%.

You can compare the value of tax-exempt interest to taxable interest for your tax bracket by using this formula:

$$\frac{\text{Tax-exempt interest rate}}{1 \text{ minus your tax bracket}}$$

Applying the tax rates scheduled for 2002 or 2003, the denominator of the above fraction is:

0.85 if your tax bracket is 15%
0.73 if your tax bracket is 27%
0.70 if your tax bracket is 30%
0.65 if your tax bracket is 35%
0.614 if your tax bracket is 38.6%

EXAMPLE

You are deciding between a tax-exempt bond and a taxable bond. You want to find which will give you more income after taxes. You have a choice between a tax-exempt bond paying 3% and a taxable bond paying 4.25%. Your tax bracket is 27%.

You find that the tax-exempt bond is a better buy in your tax bracket as it is the equivalent of a taxable bond paying 4.11%.

$$\text{Taxable Equivalent Rate (T)} = \frac{0.03}{0.73(1.00 - 0.27)}$$

$$T = .0411, \text{ or } 4.11\%$$

Ratings of tax-exempt bonds. As in the case of commercial bonds, tax-exempt issues are rated by services such as Standard & Poor's and Moody's. In rating a bond, the services will consider the size of the issuer, the amount of its outstanding debt, its past record in paying off prior debts, whether it has competent officials and a balanced budget, its tax assessment and collection record, and whether the community is dominated by a single industry that might be subject to economic change. Generally, an issuer with a good credit rating will offer lower interest rates than one plagued with revenue deficits or similar problems. A basic test is the sufficiency of tax yields or revenues even in times of economic stress.

 *Planning Reminder*

Municipal Bond Funds

Instead of purchasing tax-exempts directly, you may consider investing in municipal bond funds. The funds invest in various municipal bonds and, thus, offer the safety of diversity. The value of fund shares will fluctuate with the bond markets. Also, an investment in the fund may be as small as $1,000 compared with the typical $5,000 municipal bond. Check on fees and other restrictions in municipal bond funds.

General obligation bonds will normally be rated higher than revenue bonds because they have the support of the taxing power of the community. Revenue bonds (backed by the revenue of the issuer) may receive high ratings once a capacity to produce earnings is shown.

Purchase and trading of tax-exempts. Tax-exempt municipals are traded over the counter and are generally handled through a firm specializing in this field or having a department for municipals. Prices quoted represent a percentage of par. For example, a par value $5,000 bond quoted at 90 is selling for $4,500 (90% of $5,000); a par value $1,000 bond quoted at 90 is selling for $900 (90% of $1,000). It may not pay to buy tax-exempts unless you intend to hold them to maturity because the additional cost of selling a small order might be as much as a year's interest.

The bid and asked prices of tax-exempt bonds are generally not quoted in the daily newspapers, although some brokerage houses that specialize in them do print such prices. As in the general bond market, an offer of unusually high interest compared with the average bond rates may be an indication that the bonds are riskier than others.

The market for tax-exempts is not as large as the market for stock. This poses a risk if you ever need ready cash and are forced to sell a tax-exempt bond at a discount. If you are concerned with liquidity, restrict your investments to major general obligation bonds of state governments and revenue bonds of major authorities.

You may also invest in tax-free money-market mutual funds. These provide ready liquidity and protect the value of your principal by maintaining a $1 value per share. The tax-exempt yield is generally lower than from a municipal bond fund.

Tax-exempt notes. Although generally bought by banks and large corporations, short-term tax-exempt notes may be available to individuals. The majority of the notes are offered in face amounts of $25,000 and up, but sometimes in denominations of $5,000 and $10,000. They are issued by states and municipalities to tide them over until expected revenues are received or until longer-term money can be raised through an issue of long-term bonds. Where rising interest rates have made the cost of long-term issues high, a government authority may postpone a long-term offering and try to fill the gap with short-term notes. The interest rates on tax-exempt notes may be higher than on tax-exempt bonds if the authority is willing to pay the extra interest for the short term in the expectation that a future long-term offering may be placed at lower rates.

Interest on these short-term notes is exempt from federal tax. Many of the notes are from housing authorities and issued to pay construction costs on projects for which bonds will eventually be issued. Housing notes are guaranteed by the FHA and, because of their safety, their yields are lower than those of more speculative paper.

Tax law restrictions. Most municipal bonds that are issued before July 1, 1983, except for housing issues, are in the form of bearer bonds; the owners are not identified, and interest coupons are cashed as they come due. However, state and municipal bonds issued after June 30, 1983, with a maturity of more than one year, as well as obligations of the federal government and its agencies, are in registered form. Principal and interest are transferable only through an entry on the books of the issuer.

In buying state or local bonds, check the prospectus for the issue date and tax status of the bond. The tax law treats bonds issued after August 7, 1986, as follows:

1. "Public-purpose" bonds. These include bonds issued directly by state or local governments or their agencies to meet essential government functions, such as highway construction and school financing. These bonds are generally tax exempt.

2. "Qualified private activity" bonds. These include bonds issued to finance housing and student loans. There are limits on the amount of qualifying private activity bonds an authority may issue. Interest on qualifying bonds issued after August 7, 1986 (or after August 31, 1986, for certain bonds), is tax free for regular income tax purposes, but is a preference item to be added to taxable income if you are subject to alternative minimum tax (Chapter 23). Because of the AMT, a non-government-purpose bond may pay slightly more interest than public-purpose bonds. These may be a good investment if you are not subject to AMT or if your AMT liability is not substantial. Your broker can help you identify such bonds.

3. "Taxable" municipals. These are bonds issued for nonqualifying private purposes. They are subject to federal income tax, but may be exempt from state and local taxes in the states in which they are issued. Generally, bonds issued after August 15, 1986, are subject to this rule.

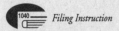
Filing Instruction

Interest Subject to AMT

Interest on qualified private activity bonds issued after August 7, 1986, is tax free for regular tax purposes but is a tax preference item for alternative minimum tax (AMT) purposes; *see* Chapter 23.

30.19 Investing in Unit Investment Trusts

A unit investment trust is a closed-end unmanaged portfolio of bonds marketed by investment houses. Yield is fixed for the life of the trust with interest payable semiannually or more frequently. As bonds in the portfolio mature, a unit holder receives a repayment of principal. Unit trusts provide investors with the possibility of locking into high yields for the long term. However, a trust has this disadvantage: If principal is needed before the end of the trust term, an investor may sacrifice substantial amounts of principal if interest rates rise or if the general investment market is shying away from long-term investments; even where the trust may offer a current return equal to market value, its price may be depressed because there may be few investors willing to take the risk of tying up their funds in long-term investments. Despite these drawbacks, the performance of unit trusts has been rated higher than that of similar mutual funds.

Unit trusts hold varying types of debt instruments. Tax-exempt municipal bond trusts, made up of tax-exempt obligations, are generally favored by investors in the top tax brackets. Taxable unit trusts hold investments such as corporate bonds, bank certificates of deposit, and Treasury obligations. Usually, units are offered in denominations of $1,000. An investor pays a front-end sales charge, but no management fee as there is no need for management once a unit trust is closed.

Maturities of the various trusts range as follows: The short-term, tax-exempt average is three years; intermediate, six to 12 years; and long-term, 18 to 30 years. An average for corporate intermediate is six years, with 25 years for long-term.

30.20 Ordinary Loss for Small Business Stock (Section 1244)

Shareholders of qualifying "small" corporations may claim within limits an ordinary loss, rather than a capital loss, on the sale or worthlessness of Section 1244 stock. An ordinary loss up to $50,000, or $100,000 on a joint return, may be claimed on Form 4797. On a joint return, the $100,000 limit applies even if only one spouse has a Section 1244 loss. Losses in excess of these limits are deductible as capital losses. Any gains on Section 1244 stock are reported as capital gain on Schedule D.

An ordinary loss may be claimed only by the original owner of the stock. If a partnership sells Section 1244 stock at a loss, an ordinary loss deduction may be claimed by individuals who were partners when the stock was issued. If a partnership distributes the Section 1244 stock to the partners, the partners may not claim an ordinary loss on their disposition of the stock.

If an S corporation sells Section 1244 stock at a loss, S corporation shareholders may not claim an ordinary loss deduction. The IRS with Tax Court approval limits shareholders' deductions to capital losses (which are deductible only against capital gains plus $3,000 ($1,500 if married filing separately); *see 5.4*).

To qualify as Section 1244 stock:

1. The corporation's equity may not exceed $1,000,000 at the time the stock is issued, including amounts received for the stock to be issued. Thus, if the corporation already has $600,000 equity from stock previously issued, it may not issue more than $400,000 worth of additional stock.

   If the $1,000,000 equity limit is exceeded, the corporation follows an IRS procedure for designating which shares qualify as Section 1244 stock.

   Preferred stock issued after July 18, 1984, may qualify for Section 1244 loss treatment, as well as common stock.
2. The stock must be issued for money or property (other than stock and securities).
3. The corporation for the five years preceding your loss must generally have derived more than half of its gross receipts from business operations and not from passive income such as rents, royalties, dividends, interest, annuities, or gains from the sales or exchanges of stock or securities. The five-year requirement is waived if the corporation's deductions (other than for dividends received or net operating losses) exceed gross income. If the corporation has not been in existence for the five years before your loss, then generally the period for which the corporation has been in existence is examined for the gross receipts test.

30.21 Savings Bonds

Savings bond purchases give you an opportunity to defer tax; *see 4.28*. EE bonds can be purchased for one-half the face value (ranging from $50 to a maximum of $10,000). I bonds purchased at face value provide an interest return that is keyed to inflation; *see 30.22*.

 *Planning Reminder*

Record-Keeping for Section 1244 Stock

You must keep records that distinguish between Section 1244 stock and other stock interests. Your records must show that the corporation qualified as a small business corporation when the stock was issued, you are the original holder of the Section 1244 stock, and it was issued for money or property. Stock issued for services does not qualify. In addition, the records should also show the amount paid for the stock, information relating to any property transferred for the stock, any tax-free stock dividends issued on the stock, and the corporation's gross receipts data for the most recent five-year period.

Failure to keep these records will be grounds for disallowing a loss that is claimed on Section 1244 stock.

EE bonds issued on or after May 1, 1997, earn interest at rates tied to Treasury securities immediately from the date of purchase through the next 30 years until the bond matures. Interest earned is 90% of the average market yield on five-year Treasury securities for the preceding six months. Interest is earned monthly, and compounded semiannually. Because the interest rates are dependent upon a variable market rate that changes every six months, there is no way to predict when a bond will reach its face value. In the unlikely event that a bond does not reach face value by the time it is 17 years old, the Treasury will make a one-time adjustment to increase the bond's value to face value at that time.

EE bonds issued on or after May 1, 1997, can be redeemed any time after six months from the date of issue, but bonds cashed in any time before five years are subject to a three-month interest penalty; *see* the Example below.

EXAMPLE

You purchased series EE bonds on May 1, 2001. If you cash them 24 months later, in May 2003, you get your original investment back plus 21 months of interest (instead of 24 months of interest) because of the three-month penalty for redemptions within the first five years of ownership.

EE bonds issued after April 30, 1995, but before May 1, 1997, earn interest at rates tied to Treasury Securities from the date of purchase through original maturity in 17 years. For the first five years they earn a rate (set each May 1 and November 1) that is equal to 85% of the average six-month Treasury bill rate for the preceding three-month period. From five years through 17 years, the rate is 85% of the average yield on five-year Treasury securities during the preceding six-month period.

EE bonds issued before May 1, 1995, earn a guaranteed minimum rate, and if held at least five years, a rate tied to five-year Treasury securities if that is greater than the minimum rate.

Deferring tax on savings bond interest. Unless you report the interest annually, Series E and EE bond interest is deferred *(4.29)* until the year you redeem the bond or it reaches final maturity. When you redeem the bond, the accumulated interest is taxable on your federal return but *not* taxable on your state and local income tax return. If in the year of redemption you use the proceeds to pay for higher education or vocational school costs, the accumulated interest may be tax free for federal tax purposes; *see* Chapter 38.

Interest accrual dates for Series E and Series EE savings bonds. Interest on Series E bonds accrues twice a year. The months of accrual depend on the issue date of the bond, as shown in the chart at the end of this chapter. When you cash a bond, you receive the value of the bond as of the last date that interest was added. If you cash a bond in between accrual months, you will not receive interest for the partial period. For example, if interest accrues in February and August, and you cash a bond in during July, you would earn interest only through February.

A similar twice-a-year accrual rule applies to certain Series EE bonds. *See* the chart at the end of this section.

Final maturity for savings bonds. Do not neglect the final maturity date for older bonds. After the final maturity date, no further interest will accrue. For example, E bonds issued in 1962 and in 1972 will reach final maturity in 2002. If you have bonds that are maturing and have deferred the reporting of interest, you may continue the deferral by exchanging the matured bonds for HH bonds. HH bonds are available in multiples of $500 and pay taxable interest semiannually. If the exchange is made, and you choose to continue the deferral, the interest on the E bonds will not be taxed until the HH bonds are cashed or reach maturity. HH bonds mature in 20 years. The exchange may be made within one year after the E bond reaches final maturity.

Caution

Timing Bond Redemptions
In the year you cash in a savings bond you could lose interest by cashing it in too soon. Interest accrues only twice a year on E bonds. Interest also accrues twice a year on EE bonds issued prior to March 1, 1993, bonds issued from May 1995 through April 1997, and bonds issued from March 1993 through April 1995 that are more than five years old. Bonds issued at different times have different accrual months. If you cash your bonds before the accrual month that applies to your bond, you will lose interest. For a list of interest accrual dates, *see* the chart at the end of this section.

Bond	Issue Date	Final Maturity
Series E	May 1941–November 1965	40 years after issue
	December 1965–June 1980	30 years after issue
Series EE	January 1980 or later	30 years after issue
Savings notes (Freedom Shares)	May 1967–October 1970	30 years after issue
H bonds	February 1957–December 1979	30 years after issue
HH bonds	January 1980 or later	20 years after issue

Accrual dates for Series HH bonds. Taxable interest on HH bonds obtained in exchange for savings bonds or savings notes accrues semiannually at a fixed rate. A fixed interest rate applies for the first 10 years you hold an HH bond and the rate is then reset. For HH bonds issued or entering an extended maturity period after February 1993, the rate is 4%. Interest on HH bonds issued before March 1, 1993, will retain their guaranteed minimum rate until they reach original maturity. Interest accrues on HH bonds until final maturity 20 years from the date of issue.

Accrual dates for Series H bonds. These bonds were available before 1980. They were bought at face value and pay semiannual interest that is taxable when received. If you own Series H bonds purchased through the exchange of Series E bonds, *see 4.28* for reporting interest. Final maturity for H bonds is 30 years from original issue.

30.22 I Bonds

Treasury "I bonds" provide a return that rises and falls with inflation. I bonds are issued at face value in amounts of $50, $75, $100, $200, $500, $1,000, $5,000, and $10,000. You may buy up to $30,000 of I bonds in any calendar year. I bonds may be purchased from most banks, credit unions, or savings institutions or online from the Treasury at www.publicdebt.treas.gov. They earn interest for 30 years. Interest is added to a bond monthly and paid when the bond is redeemed.

You forfeit three months of interest if an I bond is redeemed within the first five years. I bonds are not redeemable within the first six months.

Rates. Interest on an I bond is determined by two rates. One rate, set by the Treasury Department, remains constant for the life of the bond. The second rate is a variable inflation rate announced each May and November by the Treasury Department to reflect changes reported by the Bureau of Labor

 *Planning Reminder*

Treasury Inflation-Indexed Bonds
The Treasury also offers five-year, 10-year, and 30-year inflation-indexed bonds. They pay interest semiannually. The interest is subject to federal income tax when received, and the inflation adjustment to principal is also taxable in the year the adjustment is made. Do not confuse these issues with I bonds discussed on this page. Interest on I bonds fluctuates according to an inflation formula. You may defer reporting of interest earned on I bonds until the bond is redeemed or maturity is reached in 30 years.

Accrual Dates for Series E and EE Bonds

Issue Date—	Accrual Months—	Example—
June 1959– November 1965 E Bonds	Third month after issue month *and* ninth month after issue month. Bonds reach final maturity 40 years after issue.*	If you have a bond issued in September 1964, interest accrues every December (three months after the September issue month) and every June (nine months after the September issue month).
June 1969– November 1973 E Bonds	Fourth month after issue month *and* tenth month after issue month. Bonds reach final maturity 30 years after issue.*	If you have a bond issued in July 1973, interest accrues every November (four months after the July issue month) and every May (10 months after the July issue month).
December 1973– June 1980 E Bonds	Sixth month after issue month *and* original issue month. Bonds reach final maturity 30 years after issue.*	If you have a bond issued in May 1979, interest accrues every November (six months after the May issue month) and every May (month of original issue).
January 1980– February 1993 EE Bonds	Sixth month after issue month *and* original issue month. Bonds reach final maturity 30 years after issue.*	If you have a bond issued in June 1990, interest accrues every December (six months after the June issue month) and every June (month of original issue).
March 1993– April 1995 EE Bonds	Interest is credited on the first day of every month for the first five years, then semiannually, unless monthly increases are needed to guarantee a 4% return. Bonds reach final maturity 30 years after issue.*	
May 1995– April 1997 EE Bonds	Sixth month after issue month *and* original issue month. Bonds reach final maturity 30 years after issue.*	If you have a bond issued in August 1995, interest accrues every February (six months after the August issue month) and every August (month of original issue).
On or after May 1, 1997 EE Bonds	Interest is credited on the first day of the month. A three-month interest penalty is imposed if the bond is redeemed before five years. Bonds reach final maturity 30 years after issue.*	

Last interest accrual on final maturity date.

Statistics in the Consumer Price Index. If deflation sets in, a decline in the Consumer Price Index does not reduce the redemption value of the bond, even if the deflation rate exceeds the fixed rate.

Income tax reporting. Tax reporting for I bonds is similar to reporting on EE bonds, as explained in *30.21*. Investors may defer paying federal income taxes on I bond interest, which is automatically reinvested and added to the principal. Deferral applies to the fixed rate interest as well as the variable inflation rate interest. You may defer federal tax on the interest until you redeem the bond or the bond reaches maturity in thirty years. You may report the interest each year as it accrues instead of deferring the interest. I bond interest is exempt from state and local income taxes.

If an I bond is redeemed to pay for college tuition or other college fees, all or part of the interest may be excludable from income under the rules discussed in *38.4*.

Traders in Securities

30.23 Trader, Dealer, or Investor?

The tax law recognizes three types of individuals who may sell and buy securities. They are:

Investor. You are an investor if you buy and sell securities for long-term capital gains and to earn dividends and interest.

Trader. You may be a trader if you buy and sell securities to profit from daily market movements in the prices of securities and not from dividends, interest, or capital appreciation. Your buy and sell orders must be frequent and substantial. There are at present no clearcut tests to determine the amount of sales volume that qualifies a person as a trader. In fact, the term "trader" is not defined in the Internal Revenue Code or Treasury regulations. The IRS has not issued rulings for determining trader status.

Dealer. You are a dealer if you hold an inventory of securities to sell to others. Dealers report their profits and losses as business income and losses under special tax rules not discusses in this book.

Tax treatment of traders. The tax rules applied to traders are a hybrid of tax rules applied to investors and business persons, as discussed in the following paragraphs.

Reporting trader gains and losses. Unless a trader previously made a mark-to-market election, gains and losses are reported as capital gains and losses on Schedule D. As almost all or substantially all of a trader's sales are short-term, such gains are reported as short-term gains and losses as short-term losses. A net profit from Schedule D is *not* subject to self-employment tax *(45.1)*. Substantial losses subject to capital loss treatment are a tax disadvantage because capital losses in excess of capital gains are deductible only up to $3,000 of ordinary income in one tax year. True, carryover capital losses may offset capital gains in the next year, but your inability to deduct them immediately may subject you to paying a tax liability that might have been reduced or eliminated if the losses had been deductible for the year of the sale. If you are concerned about incurring substantial short-term capital losses that would be limited by capital loss treatment, you may consider a mark-to-market election *(see 30.24)*, which would allow you to treat your security gains and losses as ordinary income and loss.

Deducting trader expenses. Although a trader does not sell to customers but for his or her own account, a trader is considered to be in business. Expenses such as subscriptions and margin interest may be deducted as ordinary business losses on Schedule C of Form 1040. Home office expenses are deductible if the office is regularly and exclusively used as the principal place of conducting the trading business *(see 40.12)*; the deduction is computed on Form 8829 and entered on Schedule C.

An investor, on the other hand, may deduct margin interest only as an itemized deduction to the extent of net investment income *(15.10)*. Other investment expenses are allowed only as miscellaneous itemized deductions and only to the extent that, when added to other miscellaneous costs such as fees for tax preparation, they exceed 2% of adjusted gross income *(19.24)*. An investor's overall itemized deductions are also subject to the 3% reduction for higher-income taxpayers *(13.7)*. An investor may not deduct home office expenses since investment activities, no matter how extensive, are not considered a business; *see* the *Moller* decision discussed at *40.16*.

30.24 Mark-to-Market Election

A trader in securities may elect to have his gains and losses treated as ordinary gains and losses by making a mark-to-market election. As explained below, it is too late to make an election for 2002. In the absence of an election, gains and losses of a trader are treated as capital gains and losses on Schedule D.

Under the mark-to-market election, on Form 4797 you report as ordinary income or loss gains and losses on closed transactions plus unrealized gains and losses on securities owned at the end of your taxable year. Trader profits reported on Form 4797 are *not* subject to self-employment tax (*45.1*). Reported unrealized gain or loss on a security increases or reduces the basis of the security. For example, if you report an unrealized gain of $50 on stock with a cost of $100, you increase the basis of the stock to $150. If you later sell the stock for $90, you report a loss of $60 in the year of the sale. The requirement to report unrealized gains and losses at the end of the year and to adjust basis of shares is a change in accounting method that requires you to file Form 3115 with the IRS National Office and report required adjustments; *see* IRS Publication 550 and Revenue Procedure 99-17 for details.

Making the election is not proof that you are actually a trader in securities. If you are audited by the IRS, you must be able to prove that your activities are such that you are in the business of making money by buying and selling over short periods of time. As mentioned in *30.23*, there are no hard and fast rules that specify how many daily or short-term trades qualify you as a trader. Of course, extensive day trading would qualify.

You must make the election by the due date (without extensions) of the tax return for the year prior to the year for which the election is to be effective. Under this prior year tax return rule, it is too late to make an election for 2002, as this had to be done by April 15, 2002.

An election for 2003 must be made by April 15, 2003, on a statement attached to your original 2002 return. The statement should specify that effective for the taxable year starting January 1, 2003, you are electing to report gains and losses from your trading business under the mark-to-market rules of Section 475(f). However, in the case of a new taxpayer, a different rule applies. A new taxpayer is defined as a taxpayer for which no federal tax return was required to be filed for the taxable year immediately preceding the election year. A new taxpayer, such as a newly organized partnership, would make the election by placing a statement of election in its books and records no later than two months and 15 days after the first day of the election year. A copy of the statement also must be attached to the original tax return filed for the election year.

One of the conditions of the election is that you must clearly distinguish between securities held for investment and trading purposes. Holding investment securities in a separate account is advisable.

An election may not be changed in a later year except with IRS permission.

In light of the accounting requirements and the overall effect of reporting unrealized gains and losses, before making the election you should consult a professional experienced in the use of mark-to-market accounting.

See IRS Revenue Procedure 99-17 for details on making the mark-to-market election.

Chapter 31

Tax Savings for Investors in Real Estate

Real estate investors may take advantage of the following tax benefits:

- Sale of investment property may be taxed at capital gain rates.
- Depreciation can provide a source of temporary tax-free income; see 31.1.
- Rental income can be used to offset passive losses; see Chapter 10.
- Tax-free exchanges make it possible to defer tax on exchanges of real estate held for investment; see 31.3.

Losses on real estate transactions may be subject to the following disadvantages:

- Rental losses may not be deductible from other income such as salary, interest, and dividends unless you qualify as a real estate professional or for the special $25,000 rental loss allowance; see Chapter 10.
- Compromises of mortgage liability may subject you to tax; see 31.10.

Real Estate Investments

31.1   Investing in Real Estate Ventures

A real estate investment should provide a current income return and an appreciation in the value of the original investment. As an additional incentive, a real estate investment may in the early years of the investment return income subject to little or no tax. That may happen when depreciation and other expense deductions reduce taxable income without reducing the amount of cash available for distribution. This tax savings is temporary and limited by the terms and the amount of the mortgage debt on the property. Payments allocated to amortization of mortgage principal reduce the amount of cash available to investors without an offsetting tax deduction. Thus, the amount of tax-free return depends on the extent to which depreciation deductions exceed the amortization payments.

To provide a higher return of tax-free income, at least during the early years of its operations, a venture must obtain a constant payment mortgage that provides for the payment of fixed annual amounts that are allocated to continually decreasing amounts of interest and increasing amounts of amortization payments. Consequently, in the early years, a tax-free return of income is high while the amortization payments are low, but as the amortization payments increase, nontaxable income decreases. When this tax-free return has been substantially reduced, a partnership must refinance the mortgage to reduce the amortization payments and once again increase the tax-free return; *see* Examples 1 and 2 below.

The tax-free return is based on the assumption that the building does not actually depreciate at as fast a rate as the tax depreciation rate. If the building is depreciating physically at a faster rate, the so-called tax-free return on investment does not exist. Distributions to investors (over and above current income return) that are labeled tax-free distributions are, in fact, a return of the investor's own capital.

Caution

Management Fees
The promoter may be taking a real estate commission by having a commission paid to a company that he or she controls. A reliable promoter should disclose this fact and be willing to collect the commission only after the investors have recovered their capital. Also check the reasonableness of prepaid management fees and loan fees and whether or not the sale of property to the syndicate is from a corporation in which the syndicator has an interest. If there is such a sale, check its terms, price, interest rates, and whether there is any prepaid interest that may conceal a cash profit payout to the syndicator.

EXAMPLES

1. A limited partnership of 100 investors owns a building that returns an annual income of $100,000 after a deduction of operating expenses, but before a depreciation deduction of $80,000. Thus, taxable income is $20,000 ($100,000 – $80,000). Assuming that there is no mortgage on the building, all of the $100,000 is available for distribution. (Since the depreciation requires no cash outlay, it does not reduce the cash available for distribution.) Each investor receives $1,000. Taxable income being $20,000, only 20% ($20,000 ÷ $100,000) of the distribution is taxable. Thus, each investor reports as income only $200 of his or her $1,000 distribution; $800 is tax free.

2. Same facts as in Example 1, except that the building is mortgaged, and an annual amortization payment of $40,000 is being made. Consequently, only $60,000 is available for distribution, of which $20,000 is taxable. Each investor receives $600, of which $\frac{1}{3}$ ($20,000 ÷ $60,000), or $200, is taxed, and $400 is tax free. In other words, the $60,000 distribution is tax free to the extent that the depreciation deduction of $80,000 exceeds the amortization of $40,000—namely $40,000. If the amortization payment were increased to $50,000, only $30,000 of the distribution would be tax free ($80,000 – $50,000).

Reviewing an investment offering.   Consider the following pointers in reviewing an offering:

1. If the venture is constructing a development, discount projected income that may be eroded by increasing construction costs caused by inflation, material shortages, and labor disputes. Escalating costs not accounted for in long-term construction can jeopardize the project or income prospects. Adequate cash reserves should be available for emergencies.
2. Check the market conditions. Has there been overconstruction in the area? Is the area changing socially and economically?
3. Check the fees of managers. See that they are reasonable for your area. A promoter may conceal the amount of money he or she is drawing from the project.
4. Check the experience and reliability of the manager.

Real estate investment trusts (REITs).   The tax treatment of real estate investment trusts resembles that of open-end mutual funds. Distributions generally are taxed to the investors in the trust as dividend income. Distributed long-term capital gains are reported by the investors as long-term gains; also *see 4.4*. If the trust operates at a loss, the loss may not be passed on to the investors.

REMICs. A real estate mortgage investment company (REMIC) holds a fixed pool of mortgages. Investors are treated as holding a regular or residual interest. A REMIC is not a taxable entity for federal income tax purposes. It is generally treated as a partnership, with the residual interest holders as partners.

Investors with regular REMIC interests are treated as holding debt obligations. Interest income is reported on Form 1099-INT and original issue discount (OID) on Form 1099-OID.

The net income of the REMIC, after payments to regular interest holders, is passed through to the holders of residual interests. On Schedule E, residual holders report the income or loss reported to them by the REMIC on Schedule Q of Form 1066.

31.2 Sales of Subdivided Land—Dealer or Investor?

An investor faces a degree of uncertainty in determining the tax treatment of sales of subdivided realty. In some situations, investor status may be preferred, and in others, dealer status.

Capital gain on sale. Investor status allows capital gain treatment. Capital losses may offset the gains. For capital gain, an investor generally has to show that his or her activities were not those of a dealer but were steps taken in a liquidation of the investment. To convince an IRS agent or a court of investment activity, this type of evidence may present a favorable argument for capital gain treatment:

- The property was bought as an investment, to build a residence, or received as a gift or inheritance.
- No substantial improvements were added to the tract.
- The property was subdivided to liquidate the investment.
- Sales came through unsolicited offers. There was no advertising or agents.
- Sales were infrequent.
- There were no previous activities as a real estate dealer.
- The seller was in a business unrelated to real estate.
- The property was held for a long period of time.
- Sales proceeds were invested in other investment property.

Section 1237 capital gain opportunity. Section 1237 is a limited tax provision that provides a capital gain opportunity for subdivided lots only if arbitrary holding period rules and restrictions on substantial improvements are complied with. For example, the lots must generally be held at least five years before sale unless they were inherited. If the lots were previously held for sale to customers, or if other lots are so held in the year of sale, Section 1237 does not apply. Furthermore, substantial improvements must not have been made to the lots. According to the IRS, a disqualifying substantial improvement is one that increases the value of the property by more than 10%. The IRS considers buildings, hard surface roads, or utilities, such as sewers, water, gas, or electric lines, as substantial improvements.

Interest expense deductions. The distinction between an investor in land and a dealer is also important in the case of interest expenses. Dealer status is preferable here. Interest expenses incurred by an investor are subject to investment interest deduction limitations; *see* Chapter 15. On the other hand, interest expenses of a dealer in the course of business activities are fully deductible; *see* the Morley Example below.

Planning Reminder

Installment Sales

The distinction between an investor and dealer is significant if land is sold on the installment basis. Investor status is preferable if you want to elect the installment method. Dealers may not elect installment sale treatment; *see 5.21.*

> **EXAMPLE**
>
> Morley was interested in buying farm acreage to resell at a profit. Two and a half million dollars was set as the purchase price. To swing the deal, Morley borrowed $600,000. A short time later, his attempts to resell the property failed, and he allowed the property to be foreclosed. While he held the property he incurred interest costs of over $400,000, which he deducted. The IRS held the interest was not fully deductible. It claimed the interest was investment interest subject to investment interest restrictions. That is, the debt was incurred to purchase and carry investment property. The IRS position was based on the so-called "one-bite" rule, which holds that a taxpayer who engages in only one venture may not under any circumstances be held to be in a business as to that venture. Morley argued that he bought the property not as an investment property but as business property for immediate resale.
>
> The Tax Court sided with Morley, holding that he held the acreage as ordinary business property. The court rejected the "one-bite" rule. The fact that he had not previously sold business property did not mean that he could not prove that he held acreage for resale. Here, he intended promptly to resell it, and the facts supported his intention.

Passive activity. Income from sales of lots is not considered passive activity income. Thus, losses from sales of land may offset salary and other investment income. If you hold rental property and also sell land, make sure that your accounts distinguish between and separate each type of income. This way income and losses from land sales will not be commingled with rent income subject to the passive activity restrictions discussed in Chapter 10. Your activity in real property development counts towards qualifying you as a real estate professional who may deduct rental losses from nonpassive income if material participation tests are met; *see 10.3.*

31.3 Exchanging Real Estate Without Tax

You may trade real estate held for investment for other investment real estate and incur no immediate tax. The potential tax on the gain is postponed to the time you sell the new property for more than your basis. A tax-free exchange may also defer a potential tax due on gain from depreciation recapture and might be considered where the depreciable basis of a building has been substantially written off. Here, the building may be exchanged for other property that will give larger tax deductions.

Fully tax-free exchanges. To transact a fully tax-free exchange, you must satisfy these conditions:

- The property traded must be solely for property of a "like kind." The words *like kind* are liberally interpreted. They refer to the nature or character of the property, not its grade, quality, or use. Some examples of like-kind exchanges are: farm or ranch for city property; unimproved land for improved real estate; rental house for a store building; and fee in business property for 30-year or more leasehold in the same type of property; *see 6.1.* You may not make a tax-free exchange of U.S. real estate for real estate in foreign countries.
- The property exchanged must have been held for productive use in your business or for investment and traded for property to be held for productive use in business or investment. Therefore, trades of property used, or to be used, for personal purposes, such as exchanging a residence for rental property, cannot receive tax-free treatment. Special rules, however, apply when you trade your residence for another home; *see* Chapter 29.
- The trade must generally occur within a 180-day period, and property identification must occur within 45 days of the first transfer; *see 6.4* for further details of this test.

A real estate dealer cannot transact a tax-free exchange of property held for sale to customers. Also, an exchange is not tax free if the property received is held for immediate resale.

Tax-free exchanges between related parties are subject to tax if either party disposes of the exchanged property within a two-year period; *see 6.6.*

Disadvantage of tax-free exchange. Although the postponement of tax from a tax-free exchange is equivalent to an interest-free loan from the government equal to the amount you would have owed in taxes had you sold the property, this tax advantage is offset by a disadvantage in the case of an exchange of depreciable real estate. You must carry over the basis of the old property to the new property; *see* the following Example.

> **EXAMPLE**
>
> You have property with a basis of $25,000, now valued at $50,000, that you exchange for another property worth $50,000. Your basis for depreciation for the new property is $25,000.
>
> If—instead of making an exchange—you sell the old property and use the proceeds to buy similarly valued property, the tax basis for depreciation would be $50,000, giving you larger deductions than you would get in the exchange transaction. If increased depreciation deductions are desirable, then it may pay to sell the property and purchase new property. Tax may be spread by transacting an installment sale. Project the tax consequences of a sale and an exchange and choose the one giving the greater overall tax benefits. You may find it preferable to sell the property and purchase new property on which MACRS may be claimed.

Partially tax-free exchanges. Not all property exchanges are tax free. To be completely tax-free, the exchange must be solely an exchange of like-kind properties. If you receive "boot," such as cash or property that is not of like kind, gain is taxed up to the amount of the boot.

If you trade mortgaged property, the mortgage released is treated as boot; *see 6.3.* When there are mortgages on both properties, the mortgages are netted. The party giving up the larger mortgage and getting the smaller mortgage treats the excess as boot. *See* the Example below and also the Example in *6.3*, which illustrates how to report an exchange on Form 8824.

 *Planning Reminder*

Exchanging a Building for Land

A tax-free exchange may be advantageous in the case of land. Land is not depreciable, but it may be exchanged for a depreciable rental building. The exchange is tax free and depreciation may be claimed on the building. However, be aware of a possible tax trap if you exchange rental property for land and the building was subject to depreciation recapture: The recapture provisions override the tax-free exchange rules. The "recapture element" will be taxable as ordinary income.

If the amount of boot exceeds your actual gain, the entire gain is taxed; taxable boot cannot exceed the amount of your gain.

> **EXAMPLE**
> You own a small office building with a fair market value of $170,000, and an adjusted basis of $150,000. There is a $130,000 mortgage on the building. You exchange it for Low's building valued at $155,000, having a $120,000 mortgage, and for $5,000 in cash. You compute your gain in this way:
>
> *What you received*
> | | | |
> |---|---|---|
> | Present value of Low's property | | $155,000 |
> | Cash | | 5,000 |
> | Mortgage on building you traded | | 130,000 |
> | Total received | | $290,000 |
>
> *Less:*
> | | | |
> |---|---|---|
> | Adjusted basis of building traded | $150,000 | |
> | Mortgage assumed by you | 120,000 | 270,000 |
> | Actual gain on the exchange | | $20,000 |
>
> However, your actual gain of $20,000 is taxed only up to the amount of boot, $15,000.
>
> *Figuring boot*
> | | | |
> |---|---|---|
> | Cash received | | $5,000 |
> | Mortgage on building traded | $130,000 | |
> | Less: Mortgage assumed on Low's property | 120,000 | 10,000 |
> | Gain taxed to the extent of boot | | $15,000 |

31.4 Timing Your Real Property Sales

Generally, a taxable transaction occurs in the year in which title or possession to property passes to the buyer. By controlling the year title and possession pass, you may select the year in which to report profit or loss. For example, you intend to sell property this year, but you estimate that reporting the sale next year will incur less in taxes. You can postpone the transfer of title and possession to next year. Alternatively, you can transact an installment sale, giving title and possession this year but delaying the receipt of all or most of the sale proceeds until next year; see 5.21.

31.5 Cancellation of a Lease

Payments received by the tenant on the cancellation of a business lease held long term are treated as proceeds received in a Section 1231 transaction; see 44.8. Payments received by the tenant on cancellation of a lease on a personal residence or apartment are treated as proceeds of a capital asset transaction. Gain is long-term capital gain if the lease was held long term; losses are not deductible.

Payments received by a landlord from a tenant for cancelling a lease or modifying lease terms are reported as rental income when received; see 9.1.

Cancellation of a distributor's agreement is treated as a sale if you made a substantial capital investment in the distributorship. For example, you own facilities for storage, transporting, processing, or dealing with the physical product covered by the franchise. If you have an office mainly for clerical work, or where you handle just a small part of the goods covered by the franchise, the cancellation is not treated as a sale. Your gain or loss is ordinary income or loss. If the cancellation is treated as a sale, the sale is subject to Section 1231 treatment; see 44.8.

31.6 Sale of an Option

The tax treatment of the sale of an option depends on the tax classification of the property to which the option relates.

If the option is for the purchase of property that would be a capital asset in your hands, profit on the sale of the option is treated as capital gain. A loss is treated as a capital loss if the property subject to the option was investment property; if the property was personal property, the loss is not deductible. Whether the gain or loss is long term or short term depends on your holding period.

If the option is for a "Section 1231 asset" *(44.8)*, gain or loss on the sale of the option is combined with other Section 1231 asset transactions to determine if there is capital gain or ordinary loss.

If the option relates to an ordinary income asset in your hands, then gain or loss would be ordinary income or loss.

If you fail to exercise an option and allow it to lapse, the option is considered to have been sold on the expiration date. Gain or loss is computed according to the rules just discussed.

The party granting the option realizes ordinary income on its expiration, regardless of the nature of the underlying property. If the option is exercised, the option payment is added to the selling price of the property when figuring gain or loss.

31.7 Granting of an Easement

Granting an easement presents a practical problem of determining whether all or part of the basis of the property is allocable to the easement proceeds. This requires an opinion as to whether the easement affects the entire property or just a part of the property. There is no hard and fast rule to determine whether an easement affects all or part of the property. The issue is factual. For example, an easement for electric lines will generally affect only the area over which the lines are suspended and for which the right of way is granted. In such a case, an allocation may be required; *see* Example 1 below. If the entire property is affected, no allocation is required and the proceeds reduce the basis of the property. If only part of the property is affected, then the proceeds are applied to the cost allocated to the area affected by the easement. If the proceeds exceed the amount allocated to basis, a gain is realized. Capital gain treatment generally applies to grants of easements. The granting of a perpetual easement that requires you to give up all or substantially all of a beneficial use of the area affected by the easement is treated as a sale. The contribution to a government body of a scenic easement in perpetuity is a charitable contribution, not a sale.

Condemnation. If you realize a gain on a grant of an easement under a condemnation or threat of condemnation, you may defer tax by investing in replacement property; *see 18.18.*

Release of a restrictive covenant. A payment received for a release of a restrictive covenant is treated as a capital gain if the release involves property held for investment.

 *Planning Reminder*

Basis Allocation
In reviewing an easement, the IRS will generally try to find grounds for allocating part of a property owner's basis to easement proceeds, especially where the allocation will result in a taxable gain. In opposition, a property owner will generally argue that the easement affects the entire property or that it is impossible to make an allocation because of the nature of the easement or the particular nature of the property. If he or she can sustain an argument, the proceeds for granting the easement reduce the basis of the entire property; *see* Examples 1–3 on this page.

> **EXAMPLE**
>
> You sell several acres of land held for investment to a construction company subject to a covenant that restricts construction to residential dwellings. Later, the company wants to erect structures other than individual homes and pays you for the release of the restrictive covenant in the deed. You realize capital gain on receipt of the payment. The restrictive covenant is a property interest and a capital asset in your hands.

31.8 Special Tax Credits for Real Estate Investments

To encourage certain real estate investments, the tax law offers the following tax credits:

Low-income housing credit for buildings placed in service after 1986. Qualifying investors are allowed to claim a tax credit in annual installments over 10 years for qualifying newly constructed low-income housing and also to certain existing structures that are substantially rehabilitated. The amount of the credit depends on whether the building is new and whether federal subsidies are received. To claim the credit, you, as the building owner, must receive a certification from an authorized housing credit agency. The agency allocates a credit to you on Form 8609, which you use to claim the credit on Form 8586. You must attach to your return Form 8586, and, in some cases, also Form 8609 and Schedule A, Form 8609.

Rehabilitation credit for pre-1936 buildings or certified historic structures. On Form 3468, you may claim a 10% tax credit for rehabilitating pre-1936 buildings or a 20% credit for rehabilitating certified historic structures. For both types of rehabilitation credits, you must generally incur rehabilitation expenses of $5,000 or your adjusted basis in the building, whichever is greater.

Certified historic structure. A certified historic structure may be used for residential or non-residential purposes. The National Park Service must certify that a planned rehabilitation is in keeping with the building's historic status designation for the credit to be available.

In one case, a developer who rehabilitated a certified historic structure and donated a conservation easement to a historic society in the same year was required to base the credit computation on the rehabilitation expenses minus the charitable deduction claimed. If the donation had been made in a later year, a portion of the original credit claimed would be subject to recapture.

Pre-1936 buildings. The 10% credit for pre-1936 buildings applies only to nonresidential property. A substantial portion of the building's original structure must be retained after the rehabilitation. At least 75% of the external walls must be intact, with at least 50% kept as external walls. At least 75% of the existing internal structural framework must be kept in place.

Tax credit limitations. Tax credits for low-income housing and rehabilitating historic or pre-1936 buildings may be limited by passive activity restrictions on Form 8582-CR (Chapter 10) and by tax liability limits for the general business credit (Chapter 40).

For further details and credit conditions concerning the two types of rehabilitation credits, *see* Form 3468.

Court Decision

Rehabilitating Pre-1936 Building

In one case, the IRS and Tax Court interpreted the 75% external wall test for pre-1936 buildings as requiring that at least 75% of the existing external walls be retained in the same place, thereby denying the credit for a pre-1936 building that was relocated and then renovated. However, a federal appeals court disagreed, holding that there is no relocation restriction; the credit is allowed provided at least 75% of the external walls are retained as such after the renovation.

Foreclosures and Abandonments of Mortgaged Property

31.9 Foreclosures and Voluntary Conveyances to Creditors

If you are unable to meet payments on a debt secured by property, the creditor may foreclose on the property. A foreclosure sale or a voluntary conveyance of the property to the creditor is treated as a sale of the property. If you are personally liable on the debt, and if the value of the property is less than the cancelled debt, you also generally realize ordinary income on the debt cancellation.

Figuring gain or loss. Gain or loss is the difference between your adjusted basis in the property and the amount realized. Determining the amount realized depends on your liability for the debt:

If you are *not* personally liable on the debt, the amount realized includes the full amount of the cancelled debt, regardless of the value of the property.

If you are personally liable, the amount realized includes the portion of the cancelled debt that equals the fair market value of the property. If the fair market value of the property is less than the debt, the foreclosure or voluntary conveyance back to the creditor is treated as two separate transactions:

1. A sale of property. Gain or loss is the difference between adjusted basis and the amount realized, including the cancelled debt up to the fair market value of the property.

2. The receipt of ordinary income upon the cancellation of the debt for less than the face amount of the debt. You generally have cancellation of debt income equal to the excess of the cancelled debt over the fair market value of the property. However, this income may not be taxable, if you come within the exclusion rules discussed at *11.8*, such as being insolvent at the time of the foreclosure. *See also 31.10* for the exclusion on restructurings of business real property debt.

EXAMPLES

1. Jones could not meet the mortgage payments on a condominium that cost him $85,000. He had paid cash of $20,000 and taken a mortgage loan of $65,000 on which he was personally liable. When the remaining balance of the loan was $62,000, he defaulted, and the bank accepted his voluntary conveyance of the unit, cancelling the loan. Similar units at the time were selling for $60,000. On the transaction, Jones incurred a loss of $25,000: the difference between his adjusted basis of $85,000 and the fair market value of the unit of $60,000. The loss is not deductible because the unit was held for personal purposes. Jones also recognizes income on the cancellation of the loan because the amount of the debt exceeded the fair market value of the unit by $2,000. This amount is taxable, unless Jones can show he was insolvent at the time of the transfer to the bank; *see 11.8*.

2. Brown invested in a vacant lot. He put down cash of $10,000 and assumed a mortgage of $20,000. When he could not make payments on the mortgage, the bank foreclosed. The net proceeds from the foreclosure sale were $32,000. Brown received $12,000 and realized a capital gain of $2,000 (the difference between his adjusted basis of $30,000 and the amount realized of $32,000). There is no income from cancellation of indebtedness because the debt was less than the value of the property.

Foreclosure proceeds less than outstanding mortgage. Where a foreclosure sale does not cancel the mortgage debt, there is a conflict of opinion on how to compute the amount realized. Take this case:

In 1982, Aizawa bought rental property for $120,000, paying $30,000 down and giving the seller a $90,000 recourse mortgage note, payable in five years. The Aizawas made timely monthly interest payments but failed to pay off the principal at the end of the fifth year. In 1987, the sellers sued and got a judgment of $133,507 for the original principal due of $90,000, attorneys' fees of $25,000, and extra interest charges. Then, at a foreclosure sale, the sellers bought back the property for $72,700. The judgment and foreclosure sale left a deficiency judgment of $60,807.

The Aizawas deducted a $70,898 loss. They claimed the deficiency judgment of $60,807 should be deducted from the mortgage of $90,000, leaving an amount realized of $29,193. The difference between this amount and the $100,091 undepreciated basis of the property gave them a $70,898 loss. The IRS claimed that the amount realized was $90,000, the amount of the mortgage principal, so that the loss was only $10,091 ($100,091 less $90,000).

The Tax Court disagreed with both sides. The court held that the amount realized was the $72,700 proceeds from the foreclosure sale, so that a loss of $27,391 ($100,091 less $72,700) was incurred. The Aizawas' approach is wrong; they reduced the amount realized by the deficiency award they had not paid. The IRS approach is wrong; it included in the amount realized part of the mortgage debt that the Aizawas still owed.

The court recognized that its approach gave the Aizawas an additional loss of $17,300 ($90,000 less $72,700) based on a debt they might not repay. However, this advantage may be eliminated by later events. If they pay off the remaining debt, they may not deduct any additional loss. If they are discharged from paying the balance of the debt, they may be required to report income on the discharge if they are solvent.

Caution

Form 1099-A Notifies IRS

If your mortgaged property is foreclosed or repossessed, and the bank or other lender reacquires it, or if the lender knows that you have abandoned the property, you should receive from the lender Form 1099-A, which indicates foreclosure proceeds, the amount of your debt, and whether you were personally liable. The IRS may compare its copy of Form 1099-A with your return to check whether you have reported income from the foreclosure or abandonment.

If the lender also cancels your debt of $600 or more, you may instead receive Form 1099-C, on which the information about the foreclosure or repossession will be included.

Filing Tip

Reporting a Foreclosure or Voluntary Conveyance

You report a foreclosure sale or voluntary conveyance to a creditor on Schedule D if the property was held for personal or investment purposes.

Foreclosures and reconveyances of business assets are reported on Form 4797.

If income from cancellation of indebtness is realized and it is not excludable under the rules discussed at *11.8*, you report the taxable amount on Line 21, Form 1040.

31.10 Restructuring Mortgage Debt

Rather than foreclose on a mortgage, a lender (mortgagee) may be willing to restructure the mortgage debt by cancelling either all or part of the debt. As a borrower (mortgagor), do not overlook the tax consequences of the new debt arrangement. A debt cancellation or reduction is taxable unless it fits within specific exceptions, such as insolvency or bankruptcy. As discussed at *11.8*, there is no tax if the debt is restructured by the seller of the property or where a debt is reduced by a third-party lender and you are either insolvent, bankrupt, or are a qualifying farmer. These rules apply also to a restructuring of a nonrecourse debt on which you are not personally liable; *see* the Jones Example below, which shows the IRS approach to figuring insolvency upon a debt cancellation.

In the case of partnership property, tax consequences of the restructuring of a third-party loan are determined at the partner level. This means that if you are a partner and are solvent *(11.8)* you may not avoid tax on the transaction, even if the partnership is insolvent.

EXAMPLE

In 2001, Jones borrowed $1,000,000 from Chester and signed a note payable for $1,000,000. Jones was not personally liable on the note, which was secured by an office building valued at $1,000,000 that he bought from Baker with the proceeds of Chester's loan. In 2002, when the value of the building declined to $800,000, Chester agreed to reduce the principal of the loan to $825,000. At the time, Jones held other assets valued at $100,000 and owed another person $50,000. In 2002, Jones realized income of $175,000 on the reduction of the debt, but he can avoid tax to the extent he is insolvent.

To determine the extent of Jones's insolvency, the IRS compares Jones's assets and liabilities immediately before the discharge. According to the IRS, his assets total $900,000: the building valued at $800,000 plus other assets of $100,000. His liabilities total $1,025,000: the debt of $50,000 plus the liability on the note, which the IRS considers to be $975,000, equal to the $800,000 value of the building and the $175,000 discharged debt. The difference between the assets of $900,000 and liabilities of $1,025,000 is $125,000, the amount by which Jones is insolvent. As Jones is insolvent by $125,000, only $50,000 of the $175,000 discharged debt is treated as taxable income.

Restructuring debt on business real estate. A solvent taxpayer may avoid tax on a restructuring of qualifying business real estate debt *(11.8)* by electing to reduce the basis of depreciable real property by the amount of the tax-free debt discharge. The election to reduce basis is made on Form 982.

EXAMPLE

On July 1, 2002, Grant, who is solvent, owns a building worth $150,000 used in his business. It is subject to a first mortgage of $110,000 and a second mortgage of $90,000. Grant's basis in the building is $120,000. The second mortgagee agrees to reduce the second mortgage to $30,000. This results in debt discharge of $60,000 ($90,000 – $30,000). The $60,000 is considered debt discharge income. But Grant may elect to exclude $50,000. He reports the remaining $10,000 of discharged debt as taxable income. The exclusion limit is calculated as follows:

2nd mortgage before discharge		$90,000
Less: Fair market value of building	$150,000	
Less: First mortgage	110,000	40,000
Excludable amount		$50,000

On Form 982, Grant may elect to exclude $50,000 from tax because the basis of the building is sufficient to absorb a basis reduction of $50,000.

31.11 Abandonments

On an abandonment of business or investment property, you may claim an ordinary loss for the property's adjusted basis (when abandoned) on Form 4797. However, if the abandoned property is later foreclosed or repossessed, you may realize a gain or loss under the rules in *31.9* for foreclosures or voluntary conveyances to creditors. For example, if an abandonment loss for mortgaged property is claimed in 2001 but in 2002 the property is foreclosed upon by the lender, all or part of the cancelled debt will be treated as an amount realized by you on a sale in 2002. The amount realized depends on whether you were personally liable and the value of the property. If personally liable, you may also realize ordinary income from cancellation of the debt; *see 31.9*.

Abandoning a partnership interest. Where real estate values have sharply declined, partnerships may be holding realty subject to mortgage debt that exceeds the current value of the property. Some investors in such partnerships have claimed that they can abandon their partnership interests and claim abandonment losses. In one case, an investor in a partnership holding land in Houston, Texas, argued that he abandoned his partnership interest by making an abandonment declaration at a meeting of partners, and also declaring that he would make no further payments. He offered his interest to the others, who refused his offer. The IRS held that he failed to prove abandonment of his partnership interest or that the partnership abandoned the land. The Tax Court sided with the IRS, emphasizing his failure to show that the partnership abandoned the land. However, the appeals court for the Fifth Circuit reversed and allowed the abandonment loss. It held that the emphasis should be on the partner's actions, not the actions of the partnership. Although neither state law nor the IRS regulations described how a partnership interest is to be abandoned, the appeals court held that the partner's acts and declaration were sufficient to effect an abandonment of his partnership interest. The appeals court also held that the loss on the partnership interest could have been sustained on the basis of the worthlessness of his interest. The partnership was insolvent beyond hope of rehabilitation: (1) the partnership's only asset was land with a fair market value less than the mortgage debt; (2) the partnership had no source of income; and (3) the partners refused to contribute more funds to keep the partnership afloat.

In a subsequent case, the Tax Court held that a doctor had abandoned a movie production partnership interest when he refused to advance any more money or to participate in the venture because he disapproved of the content of the film being produced and feared it might jeopardize his position at a hospital operated by a religious organization. Also, the limited partners had voted to dissolve.

Planning Reminder

Foreclosure After Abandonment
If, after the year the abandoned loss is claimed, the partnership's mortgaged holdings are foreclosed upon or reconveyed to the lender, each partner's share of the cancelled debt may be treated as an amount realized on a sale, or as ordinary cancellation of debt income; *see 31.9*.

31.12 Seller's Repossession After Buyer's Default on Mortgage

When you, as a seller, repossess realty on the buyer's default of a debt that the realty secures, you may realize gain or loss. (If the realty was a personal residence, the loss is not deductible.) A debt is secured by real property whenever you have the right to take title or possession or both in the event the buyer defaults on his or her obligation under the contract.

Figuring gain on the repossession. Gain on the repossession is the excess of: (1) payments received on the original sales contract prior to and on the repossession, including payments made by the buyer for your benefit to another party, over (2) the amount of taxable gain previously reported prior to the repossession.

Gain computed under these two steps may not be fully taxable. Taxable gain is limited to the amount of original profit less gain on the sale already reported as income for periods prior to the repossession and less your repossession costs.

The limitation on gain does not apply if the selling price cannot be computed at the time of sale as, for example, where the selling price is stated as a percentage of the profits to be realized from the development of the property sold.

These repossession gain rules do not apply if you repurchase the property by paying the buyer a sum in addition to the discharge of the debt, unless the repurchase and payment was provided for in the original sale contract, or the buyer has defaulted on his or her obligation, or default is imminent.

In such cases, gain or loss on the repossession, and basis in the repossessed property, must be determined under the different rules for personal property; *see* IRS Publication 537 for details.

EXAMPLE

Assume you sell land for $25,000. You take a $5,000 down payment plus a $20,000 mortgage, secured by the property, from the buyer, with principal payable at the rate of $4,000 annually. The adjusted basis of the land was $20,000 and you elected to report the transaction on the installment basis. Your gross profit percentage is 20% ($5,000 profit divided by $25,000 selling price). In the year of sale, you include $1,000 in your income on the installment basis (20% of $5,000 down payment). The next year you reported profit of $800 (20% of $4,000 annual installment). In the third year, the buyer defaults, and you repossess the property. The amount of gain on repossession is computed as follows:

1. Compute gain:

Amount of money received ($5,000 *plus* $4,000)		$9,000
Less: Amount of gain taxed in prior years ($1,000 *plus* $800)		1,800
Gain		$7,200

2. Compute limit on taxable gain, assuming cost of repossession is $500:

Original profit		$5,000
Less:		
Gain reported as income	$1,800	
Cost of repossession	500	2,300
Taxable gain on repossession		$2,700

Caution

Character of Gain

The gain limitation rules discussed at *31.12* do not affect the character of the gain. Thus, if you repossess property as a dealer, the gain is subject to ordinary income rates. If you, as an investor, repossess a tract originally held long term whose gain was reported on the installment method, the gain is capital gain.

The basis of repossessed property. This is the adjusted basis of the debt (face value of the debt less the unreported profits) secured by the property, figured as of the date of repossession, increased by (1) the taxable gain on repossession *and* (2) the legal fees and other repossession costs you paid.

EXAMPLE

Same facts as in the previous Example. The basis of the repossessed property is computed as follows:

1. Face value of debt ($20,000 note *less* $4,000 payment)		$16,000
2. *Less:* Unreported profit (20% of the $16,000 still due on the note)		3,200
3. Adjusted basis at date of repossession		$12,800
4. *Plus:* Gain on repossession	$2,700	
Cost of repossession	500	3,200
5. Basis of repossessed property		$16,000

If you treated the debt as having become worthless or partially worthless before repossession, you are considered to receive, upon the repossession of the property securing the debt, an amount equal to the amount of the debt treated as worthless. You report as income the amount of any prior bad debt deduction and increase the basis of the debt by an amount equal to the amount reported as income.

If your debt is not fully discharged as a result of the repossession, the basis of the undischarged debt is zero. No loss may be claimed if the obligations subsequently become worthless. This rule applies to undischarged debts on the original obligation of the purchaser, a substituted obligation of the purchaser, a deficiency judgment entered in a court of law into which the purchaser's obligation was merged, and any other obligations arising from the transaction.

Personal residence. Special rules apply to repossessions and resales of a personal residence if: (1) under prior law, at least some of the gain on the original sale was not taxed because you made an election to avoid tax under the exclusion for those age 55 or older or you deferred gain on the purchase of a new residence, or you avoided tax on gain under the current law home sale exclusion discussed in Chapter 29; *and* (2) within a year after the repossession you resell the property.

The original sale and resale is treated as one transaction. You refigure the amount realized on the sale. You combine the selling price of the resale with the selling price of the original sale. From this total, you subtract selling expenses for both sales, the part of the original installment obligation that remains unpaid at the time of repossession, and repossession costs. The net is the amount realized on the combined sale-resale. Subtracting basis in the home from the amount realized gives the gain on the combined sale-resale before taking into account the exclusion or deferral rules. *See* Treasury Regulation Section 1.1038-2 for further details.

31.13 Foreclosure on Mortgages Other Than Purchase Money

If you, as a mortgagee (lender), bid in on a foreclosure sale to pay off a mortgage that is *not a purchase money mortgage*, your actual financial loss is the difference between the unpaid mortgage debt and the value of the property. For tax purposes, however, you may realize a capital gain or loss and a bad debt loss that are reportable *in the year of the foreclosure sale*.

Your bid is treated as consisting of two distinct transactions:

1. The repayment of your loan. To determine whether this results in a bad debt, the bid price is matched against the face amount of the mortgage.
2. A taxable exchange of your mortgage note for the foreclosed property, which may result in a capital gain or loss. This is determined by matching the bid price against the fair market value of the property.

EXAMPLES

1. *Mortgagee's bid less than market value.* You hold a $40,000 mortgage on property having a fair market value of $30,000. You bid on the property at the foreclosure sale at $28,000. The expenses of the sale are $2,000, reducing the bid price to $26,000. The mortgagor is insolvent, so you have a bad debt loss of $14,000 ($40,000 – $26,000). You also have a $4,000 capital gain (the fair market value of the property of $30,000 – $26,000).
2. *Mortgagee's bid equal to market value.* Suppose your bid was $32,000, and you had $2,000 in expenses. The difference between the net bid price of $30,000 and the mortgage of $40,000 is $10,000. As the mortgagor is insolvent, there is a bad debt loss of $10,000. Since the net bid price equals the fair market value, there is neither capital gain nor loss.
3. *Mortgagee's bid greater than market value.* Suppose your bid was $36,000 and you had $2,000 in expenses. Your bad debt deduction is $6,000—the difference between the mortgage debt of $40,000 and the net bid price of $34,000. You also had a capital loss of $4,000 (the difference between the net bid price of $34,000 and the fair market value of $30,000).

Where the bid price equals the mortgage debt plus unreported but accrued interest, you report the interest as income. But where the accrued interest has been reported, the unpaid amount is added to the collection expenses.

31.14 Foreclosure Sale to Third Party

When a third party buys the property in a foreclosure, the mortgagee receives the purchase price to apply against the mortgage debt. If it is less than the debt, the mortgagee may proceed against the mortgagor for the difference. Foreclosure expenses are treated as offsets against the foreclosure proceeds and increase the bad debt loss.

You deduct your loss as a bad debt. The law distinguishes between two types of bad debt deductions: business bad debts and nonbusiness bad debts. A business bad debt is fully deductible. A nonbusiness bad debt is a short-term capital loss that can be offset only against capital gains, plus a limited amount of ordinary income (5.33). In addition, you may deduct a partially worthless business bad debt, but you may not deduct a partially worthless nonbusiness bad debt. Remember this distinction if you are thinking of forgiving part of the mortgage debt as a settlement. If the debt is a nonbusiness bad debt, you will not be able to take a deduction until the entire debt proves to be worthless. But whether you are deducting a business or a nonbusiness bad debt, your deduction will be allowed only if you show the debt to be uncollectible—for example, because a deficiency judgment is worthless or because the mortgagor is declared bankrupt.

 Planning Reminder

Voluntary Conveyance

Instead of forcing you to foreclose, the mortgagor may voluntarily convey the property to you in consideration for your cancelling the mortgage debt. Your loss is the amount by which the mortgage debt plus accrued interest exceeds the fair market value of the property. If, however, the fair market value exceeds the mortgage debt plus accrued interest, the difference is taxable gain. The gain or loss is reportable in the year you receive the property. Your basis in the property is its fair market value when you receive it.

 Planning Reminder

Keep Records

Preserve evidence of the property's fair market value. At a later date, the IRS may claim that the property was worth more than your bid and may tax you for the difference. Furthermore, be prepared to prove the worthlessness of the debt in order to support the bad debt deduction.

EXAMPLE

You hold a $30,000 note and mortgage that are in default. You foreclose, and a third party buys the property for $20,000. Foreclosure expenses amount to $2,000. The deficiency is uncollectible. Your $12,000 loss is figured as follows:

Unpaid mortgage debt		$30,000
Foreclosure proceeds	$20,000	
Less: Expenses	2,000	
Net proceeds		18,000
Bad debt loss		$12,000

31.15 Transferring Mortgaged Realty

Mortgaging realty that has appreciated in value is one way of realizing cash on the appreciation without current tax consequences. The receipt of cash by mortgaging the property is not taxed; tax will generally be imposed only when the property is sold. However, there is a possible tax where the mortgage exceeds the adjusted basis of the property and the property is given away or transferred to a controlled corporation. Where the property is transferred to a controlled corporation, the excess is taxable gain. Further, if the IRS successfully charges that the transfer is part of a tax avoidance scheme, the taxable gain may be as high as the amount of the mortgage liability.

Gifts. The IRS holds that a gift of mortgaged property results in taxable income to the donor to the extent that the mortgage liability exceeds the donor's basis; *see 14.6.*

Chapter 32

Tax Pointers for Investors in Mutual Funds

Mutual-fund investments relieve you of the responsibility of making daily investment decisions for securities actively traded or affected by changing market conditions.

Mutual funds are either closed or open end. Open-end funds are more popular than closed-end funds. The value of and number of shares in the portfolio of an open-end fund change daily as investors purchase and redeem shares. A closed-end fund issues a fixed number of shares that trade like shares of publicly held corporations listed on the stock exchange. The daily price of its shares may be below or above the net value of its investment portfolio.

As a mutual-fund shareholder, you may receive several types of distributions, such as ordinary dividends, capital gain distributions, exempt-interest dividends, and return of capital distributions. The rules for reporting the different types of distributions are discussed in this chapter.

Different methods of identifying sold shares and determining the cost basis of those shares are also discussed. The choice of cost-basis methods will affect the computation of gain or loss on a sale of shares.

32.1 Investing in Stocks or Bonds Through Mutual Funds

A mutual fund is a professionally managed pool of individual investors' contributions invested in a variety of securities. Funds are designed and marketed to meet different investor objectives. Money-market mutual funds *(32.2)* allow investors to earn a return based on swings in the short-term money market. Income funds invest in either stocks paying high current dividends or bonds paying interest. Growth funds invest in securities that are expected to appreciate over the long term. Some aggressive growth funds invest in small, developing companies with short track records. Other growth funds invest primarily in established firms. International funds invest in stocks of companies outside the United States. Sector funds specialize in specific industries, such as utilities, gold, or high technology companies. Balanced funds try to promote long-term growth by maintaining a mix of investments in bonds and stocks. Index funds buy the stocks that constitute a broad-based index to replicate the index's performance.

Do some research to find a fund that matches your investment objectives. Check the fund's performance over a substantial period of from five to 10 years. Keep in mind that yields fluctuate and are not guaranteed. In funds other than money markets *(32.2)*, the value per share also fluctuates. Gain or loss may be realized when you redeem shares in growth or income mutual funds. Also consider the rate at which a fund turns over its assets. A fund with a high turnover rate will realize frequent capital gains and losses, increasing the likelihood that capital gain distributions will be short term rather than long term. Short-term capital gain distributions are taxed as ordinary income dividends. Long-term capital gain distributions are subject to the rules for long-term capital gains.

Compare sales charges and redemption fees, if any, before you buy. No-load funds do not have a sales charge. Financial sections of major newspapers list prices of mutual-fund offerings. A no-load fund has the same purchase price and redemption price for fund shares; different prices for purchases and redemptions indicate a sales charge. Funds available through a broker may have a charge for commissions.

32.2 Money-Market Mutual Funds

A money-market mutual-fund portfolio will generally include U.S. government obligations, CDs of major commercial banks, bankers acceptances, and commercial paper of prime-rated firms. Investors should check each fund's charges because they differ.

Yields, which change daily, are not guaranteed. Investments are not federally insured. Some state-chartered banks, however, offer money-market funds insured by a state insurance fund.

Gains and losses are generally not realized in money-market funds; shares are redeemed for exactly what you paid (usually $1 per share) plus accrued dividends if you reinvested your dividends instead of receiving them in cash. Some funds offer limited check-writing privileges.

Tax-free money-market funds. These funds invest in short-term notes of state and local governments issued in anticipation of tax receipts, bond sales, and other revenues, and in "project notes" issued by local entities and backed by the federal government. The dividends paid by these funds is exempt from federal income tax. The yields are lower than those of taxable funds, and are attractive only if they provide greater after-tax returns than similar taxable funds. These funds may offer check-writing privileges.

Investors in certain states may be able to invest in funds that pay dividends that are exempt from state and local, as well as federal, income tax.

A tax-free interest return may also be available through unit investment trusts holding tax-exempt state and municipal bonds. These trusts mature in a specified number of years or as called.

32.3 Timing Your Investment

You may buy a tax liability if you invest in a mutual fund that has already realized significant capital gains during the year. If you invest near the end of the year and the fund shortly thereafter makes a large year-end capital gain distribution, you will in effect have to pay tax on the return of your recently invested money.

On the "record date" for determining which shareholders receive the fund's dividends and capital gain distributions, the value of the fund's shares drops by the amount of the distributions. If you buy just before that, the higher cost for your shares will be offset by the distributions you receive, but you will have to pay tax on the distributions. On the other hand, because you paid the higher pre-distribution price, your higher basis will reduce any capital gain on a later sale, or increase any capital loss.

If you want to limit your current tax and forego the basis increase, postpone your investment until after the record date for distributions. By that time, the value per share that determines the price will have been reduced by the capital gain distribution. Before investing, you may be able to find out from the fund when distributions for the year are expected; investment publications showing the distribution dates for the previous year also may be consulted.

32.4 Reinvestment Plans

Funds allow you to reinvest dividends and capital gain distributions from the fund in new fund shares instead of receiving cash. You report such distributions as if you received them in cash. Form 1099-DIV sent to you by a fund reports the gross amount of taxable distributions that you must report on your return. *See* the chart on the next page for how to report them.

Keep track of reinvested distributions. If you reinvest your mutual-fund distributions instead of taking them in cash, keep a record of the distributions and of the shares purchased with the reinvestment. The reinvested distributions are considered your cost basis for the acquired shares. You need a record of reinvestments to figure your cost when you sell your shares; *see 32.9* for calculating gain on the sale of mutual-fund shares.

Reinvested distribution can trigger wash sale. If you redeem fund shares at a loss within 30 days before or after a dividend distribution is reinvested into your account, a "wash sale" results, and the portion of the loss allocable to the reinvestment is not deductible *(30.6)*. The allocable loss is disallowed even though the wash sale was inadvertently caused by the reinvestment. The disallowed loss is actually deferred, as it is added to the cost basis of the replacement shares and will affect the computation of gain or loss on a later sale.

32.5 Reporting Mutual-Fund Distributions

Mutual-fund distributions are reported to you and the IRS by the fund on Form 1099-DIV or substitute statement. Distributions that you reinvested to acquire additional shares are reported and taxed in the same way as distributions that are actually paid out to you.

The Form 1099-DIV from your fund may include several types of dividend and other distributions. Dividends that you reinvested instead of receiving in cash are included on Form 1099-DIV. A guide to the different distributions, and how you report them, is shown in the "Key to Reporting Mutual-Fund Distributions" on the next page.

32.6 Tax-Exempt Bond Funds

Dividend income from a tax-exempt bond fund is generally tax free, but capital gain distributions are taxable. Exempt-interest dividends are not shown by the fund on 1099-DIV, but are reported separately by the fund. You report tax-exempt interest on Line 8b of Form 1040 or of Form 1040A. The amount on Line 8b is not taxable, but if you receive Social Security benefits, the amount may affect the amount of taxable benefits; *see 34.3*.

Capital gain distributions are shown on Form 1099-DIV and must be reported on your return; *see* the "Key to Reporting Mutual-Fund Distributions" on the next page.

When you redeem your shares in a tax-exempt bond fund or exchange the fund shares for other shares in a different fund, you realize taxable capital gain or deductible loss.

If you received exempt-interest dividends on mutual-fund shares held for six months or less and sold those shares at a loss, the amount of your loss is reduced by the exempt-interest dividend. To reflect this adjustment, you increase the sales price reported on Line 1 in column (d) of Schedule D by the loss not allowed. Report the balance as a short-term capital loss.

Filing Instruction

Capital Gain Distributions
Your mutual fund will report capital gain distributions to you in Box 2a of Form 1099-DIV. Generally, these must be reported on Line 13 of Schedule D as long-term capital gains. However, if you do not need Schedule D to report other capital gains or losses, and certain other conditions are satisfied, you may enter your capital gain distributions directly on Line 13 of Form 1040 or Line 10 of Form 1040A and compute your tax on a worksheet in the IRS instructions. *See* the "Key to Reporting Mutual-Fund Distributions" on the next page.

Filing Instruction

Year-end Dividends
Mutual funds sometimes declare dividends at the end of a calendar year but do not pay them until January of the following year. If the dividend is declared in October, November, or December, and paid in the following January, the fund will report the distribution as taxable in the year it is declared.

EXAMPLE
In January 2002, you bought a mutual-fund share for $40. In February 2002, the mutual fund paid a $5 dividend from tax-exempt interest, which is not taxable to you. In March 2002, you sold the share for $34. If it were not for the tax-exempt dividend, your loss would be $6 ($40 – 34). However, you may deduct only $1, the part of the loss that exceeds the exempt-interest dividend ($6 – 5). On Schedule D in column (d), increase the sales price from $34 to $39 (the $5 nondeductible loss). You may deduct $1 as a short-term capital loss.

32.7 Fund Expenses

If you own shares in a *publicly offered* mutual fund, you do not pay tax on your share of the fund expenses. There should be no entry in Box 5 of your Form 1099-DIV. However, expenses of a *non-publicly offered* fund are included in Box 5 of Form 1099-DIV and must be reported as a taxable dividend, even though the amount has not actually been distributed to you. This amount is included as a fully taxable ordinary dividend in Box 1 of Form 1099-DIV. An offsetting deduction may be claimed on Schedule A as a miscellaneous itemized deduction, subject to the 2% adjusted gross income floor; *see 19.24.*

For purposes of figuring gain or loss when you redeem or exchange shares, load charges (sales fees) on the purchase of the shares may not be treated as part of your cost if you held the shares for 90 days or less and then reinvested the sales proceeds at a reduced load charge.

Key to Reporting Mutual-Fund Distributions

Type of Distribution	Shown by the Fund in	Where You Report
Ordinary dividends and short-term capital gain distributions.	Box 1, Form 1099-DIV	If *all* of your mutual-fund distributions from Forms 1099-DIV are ordinary dividends, you may report them on either Form 1040 or Form 1040A. If this total plus your other dividends from all sources is $400 or less, enter them on Line 9 of Form 1040 or Line 9 of Form 1040A. If more than $400, enter the amount on Line 5, Schedule B of Form 1040, or Line 5, Schedule 1 of Form 1040A. Short-term capital gain distributions must be reported as ordinary dividends. They may not be included on Schedule D as short-term capital gains, where they could be offset by short- or long-term capital losses. *Note:* If you also have nontaxable distributions from Form 1099-DIV, you may not use Form 1040A to report the ordinary dividends; your mutual-fund distributions must be reported on Form 1040; *see* below.
Capital gain distributions. (This represents your share of net long-term gains realized by a fund on sales made from its portfolio.)	Box 2a, Form1099-DIV	Schedule D of Form 1040. However, you do not have to file Schedule D if *all three* of the following apply: (1) the only amounts you have to report on Schedule D are capital gain distributions from Box 2a of Forms 1099-DIV or substitute statements; (2) none of the Forms 1099-DIV or substitute statements have an amount in Box 2b (28% rate gain), Box 2c (qualified five-year gain), Box 2d (unrecaptured Section 1250 gain), or Box 2e (Section 1202 gain); *and* (3) if you are itemizing deductions and filing Form 4952 (relating to investment interest expense deduction), the amount on Line 4e of that form is not more than zero. If all three of the above apply, you may enter your capital gain distributions on Line 13 of Form 1040. If the first two tests apply and you do not itemize, you may use Form 1040A and report the distributions on Line 10. Also, be sure you use the capital gain tax worksheet in the IRS instructions to figure your tax.
Return of capital distributions (nontaxable)	Box 3, 1099-DIV	A return of capital distribution is not taxable income. However, if your basis for your shares has been reduced to zero by return of capital gain distributions, report additional nontaxable distributions as either long-term or short-term capital gain on Schedule D of Form 1040, depending on how long you held the shares.
Exempt-interest dividends	A separate statement; not included on Form 1099-DIV. This will be sent to you within 60 days after the close of the fund's taxable year.	For informational purposes only, report along with other tax-exempt interest on Line 8b of Form 1040 or Form 1040A.
Undistributed capital gains	Undistributed gains shown on Form 2439, Box 1a Tax paid by fund shown on Form 2439, Box 2	Report the undistributed gains on Line 11 of Schedule D. To get a tax credit for the tax paid by the fund, enter the tax on Line 68 of Form 1040. Increase the basis of your mutual-fund shares by the excess of the undistributed gains included on Schedule D over the tax credit claimed on Line 68 of Form 1040.
Fund expenses from non-publicly offered funds	Box 5, Form 1099-DIV	If you itemize deductions on Form 1040, the expenses are deductible as miscellaneous expenses, subject to the 2% adjusted gross income floor *(19.1)*.
Foreign taxes	Box 6, Form 1099-DIV. Box 7 shows the country imposing the tax.	The foreign taxes may be claimed as a tax credit on Form 1116 or as an itemized deduction on Schedule A of Form 1040; *see 36.14.*

32.8 Tax Credits From Mutual Funds

Undistributed capital gains. Some mutual funds retain their long-term capital gains and pay capital gains tax on those amounts. Even though not actually received by you, you include as a capital gain distribution on your return the amount of the undistributed capital gain allocated to you by the fund. If the mutual fund paid a tax on the undistributed capital gain, you are entitled to a tax credit.

To claim the credit, check the Form 2439 sent to you by your fund, which lists your share of undistributed capital gain and the amount of tax paid on it by the fund. Enter your share of the tax the fund paid on this gain on Line 68 of Form 1040, and check the box for Form 2439. Attach Copy B of Form 2439 to your return to support your tax credit. Increase the basis of your stock by the excess of the undistributed capital gain over the amount of tax paid by the mutual fund, as reported on Form 2439.

Dividends from foreign investments. The dividends are taxable, but you may be able to claim a foreign tax credit (on Form 1116) or a deduction on Schedule A for your share of the fund's foreign taxes.

In Box 6 of Form 1099-DIV, the fund will report your share of the foreign taxes paid, and in Box 7, the name of the foreign country. The fund should give you instructions for claiming the foreign tax credit or deduction; also *see 36.14.*

32.9 Redemptions and Exchanges of Fund Shares

When you ask the fund to redeem all or part of your shares, you have transacted a sale subject to capital gain or loss rules explained in Chapter 5. Exchanges of shares of one fund for shares of another fund within the same fund "family" are treated as sales. If you owned the shares for more than one year, your gain or loss is long term; if you held them for a year or less, your gain or loss is short term. However, if you received a capital gain distribution before selling shares held six months or less at a loss, your loss must be reported as a long-term capital loss to the extent of the capital gain distribution attributable to the sold shares. Any excess loss is reported as a short-term capital loss. This restriction does not apply to dispositions under periodic redemption plans.

> **EXAMPLE**
> In June 2002, you bought mutual-fund shares for $1,000. In August, you received a capital gain distribution of $50, and you sold the shares for $850 in September. Instead of reporting a $150 short-term capital loss ($1,000 cost – $850 proceeds), you must report a long-term capital loss of $50, the amount of the capital gain distribution; the remaining $100 of the loss is a short-term capital loss.

Identifying the shares you sell. Determining which mutual-funds shares are being sold is necessary to figure your gain or loss and whether the gain or loss is short term or long term. *See 32.10* for the identification methods.

Holding period of fund shares. You determine your holding period by using the trade dates. The trade date is the date on which you contract to buy or redeem the mutual-fund shares. Do not confuse the trade date with the settlement date, which is the date by which the mutual-fund shares must be delivered and payment must be made. Most mutual funds will show the trade date on your purchase and redemption confirmation statements.

Your holding period starts on the day after the day you bought the shares. (The day you bought the shares is the trade date.) This same date of each succeeding month is the start of a new month regardless of the number of days in the month before. The day you dispose of the shares (trade date) is also part of your holding period.

32.10 Basis of Redeemed Shares

To figure gain or loss, you need to know the basis per share. Generally, your basis is the purchase price of the shares, including shares acquired by reinvesting distributions back into the fund, plus commission or load charges.

Load charges. Basis does not include load charges (sales fees) on the purchase of mutual-fund shares if you held the shares for 90 days or less and then exchanged them for shares in a different fund in the same family of funds at a reduced load charge.

 Caution

Wash-Sale Loss Disallowance
A loss on the redemption of fund shares is disallowed to the extent that within 30 days before or after the sale, you buy shares in the same fund. The wash-sale rule *(30.6)* is triggered even when the acquisition of new shares occurs automatically (within the 61-day period) under a dividend reinvestment plan.

 *Planning Reminder*

Keeping Track of Cost Basis
Keep confirmation statements for purchases of shares as well as a record of distributions that are automatically reinvested in your account. These will show the cost basis for your shares. Your basis is increased by amounts reported to you by the fund on Form 2439, representing the difference between your share of undistributed capital gains that you were required to report as income and your share of the tax paid by the fund on undistributed gains. Your basis is reduced by nontaxable dividends that are a return of your investment. Keep copies of Form 2439 and information returns showing nontaxable dividends.

Planning Reminder

Specific Identification Method

When you redeem part of your shares, the specific identification method of identifying the shares sold provides you the most flexibility. However, note the paperwork requirements for this method in Examples 1 and 2 on this page.

Planning Reminder

Shares Received as Gift

To determine your original basis of mutual-fund shares you acquired by gift, you must know the donor's adjusted basis, the date of the gift, the fair market value of the shares at the time of the gift, and whether any gift tax was paid on the shares. *See 5.17.*

EXAMPLE

You pay a $200 load charge on purchasing shares for $10,000 in Fund A. Within 90 days, you exchange the Fund A shares for Fund B shares. Because Fund A and Fund B are in the same family of funds, the $200 load charge that would otherwise be due on the purchase of the Fund B shares is waived. For purposes of figuring your gain or loss on the exchange of Fund A shares, your basis is $10,000, not $10,200. The disallowed $200 is added to the basis of the new Fund B shares, provided those shares are held more than 90 days. If the waived load charge on Fund B shares had been $100, basis for the original Fund A shares would be increased by $100, the excess of the original $200 load charge over the amount waived on the reinvestment.

Identifying the sold shares. If your shares in a mutual fund were acquired at different times, you need to know the basis of the particular shares you are selling in order to determine gain or loss. There are several methods of identifying which shares you are selling:

• *Specific Identification Method*—allows you to select exactly which shares are being sold, enabling you to determine your gain or loss and achieve a desired tax result (*see* Examples 1 and 2 below and the table on the next page). You may not use this method if you have used the averaging cost basis method on a prior sale from the same fund.

• *Average Cost Basis Method*—averages your cost for all shares in the fund (*see* Example 3 below). Once you elect to use average basis, you must continue to do so for all accounts in the same fund; *see* the table on the next page for averaging details.

• *First-in, first-out (FIFO) Method*—applies if you do not specifically identify the shares or elect the averaging method (*see* Examples 1 and 2 below).

See the chart on the next page for details on these identification methods.

EXAMPLES

1. In 1993, you bought 100 shares of a mutual fund for $10 a share. In 1996, you bought another 200 shares for $11 a share, and in 1997, another 500 shares for $15 a share. In 2002, you sell 130 shares at $20 a share, but do not specifically identify the shares being sold. Under the IRS FIFO method, you are treated as having first sold the original 100 shares from 1993, then 30 of the shares bought in 1996. Your basis for the sold shares is $1,330:

100 shares from 1993 costing $10 each	$1,000
30 shares from 1996 costing $11 each	330
	$1,330

    Your taxable gain is $1,270 ($2,600 sales price less $1,330 basis). Had you specifically designated shares from the most recent lot, which cost you more, you would have reduced the taxable gain. For example, if you had given the fund written instructions to sell 130 of the 500 shares that you bought in 1997 at $15 per share and the fund acknowledged in writing your instructions, your basis on the sale under the specific identification method would be $1,950 (130 × $15) instead of $1,330. Gain would be reduced from $1,270 to $650 ($2,600 sales price less $1,950 basis).

2. Hall sold by phone part of his holdings in two mutual funds acquired over a number of years without specifying the particular shares being sold. On his return, Hall claimed a net long-term capital loss of about $2,400 using a LIFO method (last-in, first-out). However, using the FIFO method, the IRS held that he had a long-term capital gain of $163,000. In the Tax Court, Hall argued that the specific identification rule applies only to stock certificates, not noncertificate shares left on deposit with a mutual fund. The court disagreed. Without specific identification, the IRS FIFO method is reasonable. If good records are kept, you can select the specific shares being sold at the time of sale. You cannot wait until you file your return to allot specific sales to gain a tax advantage.

    What if you give written instructions to a mutual fund that specific shares should be sold, but the fund does not acknowledge your specification in its written confirmation? Regulations require such a written confirmation within a reasonable time after the sale.

3. You bought 160 shares of the XYZ Mutual Fund on February 4, 1998, for $4,000. On August 5, 1998, you bought another 240 shares for $4,800. You obtained an additional 10 shares on December 15, 1998, when you reinvested a $300 dividend. On December 16, 1999, you obtained an additional 20 shares when you reinvested a $750 dividend. You sell 200 shares of the fund on September 23, 2002, for $8,000. Using the average basis method, your average basis is $22.91 per share.

Your total cost basis for all 430 shares is $9,850. Dividing $9,850 by 430 gives you an average basis per share of $22.91. Thus, your basis for the 200 sold shares is $4,582 (200 × $22.91 = $4,582).

Under the average-basis method, the shares you acquired first are the shares deemed to be sold for purposes of determining your capital gain holding period. Thus, you are deemed to have sold the 160 shares bought on February 4, 1998, and 40 of the 240 shares bought on August 5, 1998. The sold shares were held long term on the sale date of September 23, 2002. You have a $3,418 long-term capital gain on the sale: $8,000 proceeds less $4,582 basis figured under the average-basis method.

Key to Identifying Mutual-Fund Shares When You Sell

Method—	Tax Effect—
Specific identification of shares sold	If you sell some of your shares that have been left on deposit with an agent for the fund, and you identify the specific lot of shares being sold in your sell order, you can fix profit or loss on the sale, depending on the cost of the shares selected. *See* Example 1 on page 534. You should give the fund written instructions to sell shares that you bought on a particular date and at a particular price. Ask the fund for a written confirmation that acknowledges your instructions. The IRS requires that written confirmation of your instruction to sell particular shares be received within a reasonable time after the sale. The fund does not actually have to sell specific shares, just provide written confirmation that you instructed it to do so.
FIFO (First-in, first-out)	If you do not specifically identify the sold shares as just discussed, and you do not elect to average cost basis as discussed below, the IRS requires you to compute gain or loss as if shares were sold in the order that you acquired them. If the earliest acquired shares are treated as sold, taxable gain on a current sale will generally be higher than if the specific identification method was used, assuming that your least expensive shares were bought first; *see* Example 1 on page 534.
Averaging your basis	You may elect to average the cost of shares acquired at different times and prices. The election applies to mutual-fund shares held by an agent, usually a bank, in an account kept for the periodic acquisition or redemption of shares in the particular fund. You still need records of your total basis, but averaging avoids the difficult task of identifying the exact shares being sold. Many funds ease the record-keeping burden by providing to shareholders who have redeemed shares a statement showing their average cost basis under the single-category method. *See* Example 3 on page 534.

Under the averaging your basis method:

The single-category method is easier to apply than the double-category method, as explained below. To elect either averaging method, attach a note to your return specifying the chosen method. Once you have elected a method, you must continue to apply the same method for all sales or exchanges of shares in the same fund. However, you may use the specific identification method or the FIFO method, or the other averaging method for shares of other funds in the same "family" of funds. For example, if you own shares in the XYZ Co. growth fund and also in the XYZ Co. bond fund, you may use an averaging method for the bond fund shares and the specific identification method for the growth fund shares.

You can use the average cost basis for sales of shares in one mutual-fund family, and use the specific identification method for sales of shares of other fund families.

Single-category averaging. You figure the average cost per share by dividing your total basis for all shares in the account by the number of shares. For example, if you bought 100 shares of a fund in 1999 at $20 per share and another 100 shares in 2000 at $30 per share, your average basis per share is $25 ($5,000 total cost ÷ 200 shares). If you sell 50 shares in 2002 for $35 a share, your basis for the sold shares is $1,250 (50 × $25 average basis) and your gain on the sale is $500 ($1,750 sales proceeds less $1,250 basis). For holding period purposes, you are treated as having sold shares in the order you acquired them (first-in, first-out).

Double-category averaging. You have to separate your account shares into a long-term category for shares held more than one year and a short-term category for shares held one year or less. You figure the average cost per share in each category by dividing the total basis for all shares in that category by the number of shares in that category. You may specify to the agent handling share transactions the category from which you are selling. If you do not so specify, the long-term shares are deemed to have been sold first. If the number of shares sold exceeds the number in the long-term class, the excess shares are charged to the short-term class.

32.11 Comparison of Basis Methods

As discussed at *32.10*, your choice of basis method can have a significant effect on the computation of capital gains and losses when you sell a portion of your shares in a mutual fund. The following example compares the single averaging method to the specific identification and FIFO methods.

Transaction history. Assume that on February 7, 1992, you made an initial investment of $4,500 for 375 shares in ABC Mutual Fund at $12 per share. Under the dividend reinvestment plan, you reinvested a $400 dividend, received in December 1992, for an additional 40 shares at $10 per share. On June 10, 1993, you bought 350 shares at $15 per share. In December 1993 you reinvested your dividend, this time for 25 shares at $12 per share. On September 16, 1994, you bought 200 shares at $16 per share. You did not reinvest your dividends received in 1994–2003. On October 20, 2003, you ask ABC Mutual Fund to redeem 200 shares and you receive $20 per share. The table below illustrates your transactions.

Date	Action	Share Price	No. of Shares	Shares Owned
2/7/92	Invest $4,500	$12	375	375
12/18/92	Reinvest $400 dividend	$10	40	415
6/10/93	Invest $5,250	$15	350	765
12/14/93	Reinvest $300 dividend	$12	25	790
9/16/94	Invest $3,200	$16	200	990
10/20/2003	Redeem $4,000	$20	200	790

The following are three different ways to compute the basis of the shares redeemed on October 20, 2003.

Specific identification method. If you identify the shares you sold, you can use the adjusted basis of those shares to figure your gain or loss. You must specify the particular shares to be redeemed at the time of the sale, and must receive a written confirmation of your specification within a reasonable time. Depending on your situation, you may want to either maximize or minimize your gain or loss on the sale. Here, you will have a gain regardless of which shares are treated as being sold. Assuming you want to minimize your gain, then you would specify the 200 shares bought at $16 per share on September 16, 1994, as the shares sold. Since the shares were sold for $20 per share, the gain would be $4 per share, for a total of $800 of long-term capital gain ($4,000 – $3,200).

FIFO (first-in, first-out). If you do not identify which shares you sold or choose the averaging method, you must use the basis of the shares you acquired first as the basis of the shares sold. Therefore, the oldest shares still available, the February 7, 1992, shares, are considered sold first. Thus, the basis of the 200 shares sold would be $12 per share. Your long-term capital gain is $1,600 ($4,000 – $2,400).

Average cost. The ABC Mutual Fund may provide you with your average basis when you make the redemption. If it does not, you may compute the average basis for all shares owned at the time of disposition, regardless of how long you owned them, including shares acquired with reinvested dividends. The basis and gain is computed as follows: You total the number of shares owned prior to the sale, 990, and total your investment in these shares, which is $13,650. You divide $13,650 by 990, which gives an average cost of $13.79 per share and a total cost of $2,758 for the 200 shares. Your gain is $1,242 ($4,000 – $2,758). For holding period purposes, the shares sold are considered to be from the earliest lot in 1992, so your gain is long-term capital gain.

Result: The specific identification method gives you the lowest capital gain under this set of facts.

Caution

Get Written Confirmation for Specific Identification Method

If you want to take advantage of the specific identification method, make sure your broker sends you a written confirmation of your selling instructions. You should not rely on e-mail or oral affirmations.

The specific identification method allows you to designate specific shares as the shares sold, allowing you to minimize a gain on the sale or to select shares that, because of their basis, would give you a loss.

Chapter 33

Family Income Planning

Each additional dollar of ordinary income you receive, such as interest, dividends, and rent, is taxed in your highest bracket. If you can deflect income to a lower tax bracket of a child or other dependent relative, he or she will pay a smaller tax on the income than you would pay. However, the tax advantages of shifting income to children under age 14 are sharply reduced by the "kiddie tax"; *see* Chapter 24.

To split income, you must do more than make gifts of income. You must transfer the actual property from which the income is produced. For example, you do not avoid tax on interest by instructing your savings bank to credit interest to your children's account. Unless you actually transfer the complete ownership of the account to your child, the interest income is earned on money owned by you and must be reported by you. The same holds true with dividends, rents, and other forms of income. Unless you transfer the income-producing property, the income will be taxed to you.

You may not split earned income; income resulting from your services is taxed to you. You may not avoid this result by setting up trusts to receive your earned income.

Gift Planning

33.1 Gift Tax Basics

As family income planning generally requires the transfer of property, you must consider possible gift tax liability. For 2002 and 2003, the gift tax rates and credit are the same as those of the estate tax listed in Chapter 39.

Gift tax liability may be avoided by making gifts within an annual exclusion. For 2002, the annual per-donee exclusion is $11,000, or $22,000 if your spouse consents to "split" the gifts. The annual exclusion is allowed only for cash gifts or gifts of present interests in property; gifts of future interests do not qualify.

Gifts to a spouse who is a U.S. citizen are completely tax free because of the marital deduction. There also is an unlimited gift tax exclusion for paying someone else's tuition or medical expenses, if you directly pay the educational organization or care provider.

If you make an interest-free or low-interest loan to a family member, you may be subject to income tax and gift tax; *see 4.31*.

Filing a gift tax return for 2002. A gift tax return generally must be filed on Form 709 for a gift made during 2002 to an individual other than your spouse if it exceeds $11,000 or is a gift of a future interest (regardless of value). A return does not have to be filed for gifts qualifying for the tuition or medical expense exclusion.

Married couples who consent to split gifts of over $11,000 in 2002 to any one person must report the gifts to the IRS. No gift tax is due under the annual exclusion if the "split" gift is $22,000 or less. If your spouse consents to split gifts of up to $22,000 with you, you may be able to use a short form, Form 709-A, rather than Form 709 to report the gifts; *see* the form instructions.

Form 709 or Form 709-A generally must be filed by April 15th of the year following the year of the gift. If you get a filing extension for your income tax return, the extension also applies to the gift tax return. An additional extension may be granted by the IRS for gift tax returns filed on Form 709 if you show good cause; further extensions are not allowed for filing Form 709-A.

> **EXAMPLE**
>
> In July 2002 Randall Johnson makes a gift of publicly traded stock to his son, Philip, and his daughter, Ann. He gives each of them 1,000 shares of stock valued at $18,500 ($18.50 per share). His cost basis for the 2,000 shares was $24,000. On Form 709-A, Randall's wife, Claire, consents to split the gifts, thereby doubling the annual exclusion for gifts to each child. Neither Randall nor Claire made any other gifts during 2002. As a result of the gift splitting, no gift tax is due.
>
> If Randall's total gifts for the year to either Philip or Ann exceeded $22,000, the gifts could not be reported on Form 709-A; the longer Form 709 would have to be used.

Even where Form 709 must be filed, gift tax liability computed on the form may be offset by the credit. You and your spouse each have a $345,800 credit to offset taxable gifts made in 2002 and later years.

33.2 Custodial Accounts for Minors

A minor generally lacks the ability to manage property. You could create a formal trust, but this step may be costly. A practical alternative may be a custodial account under the Uniform Gifts to Minors Act (UGMA), or the Uniform Transfers to Minors Act (UTMA), which has replaced the UGMA in practically every state.

Custodial accounts set up in a bank, mutual fund, or brokerage firm can achieve income splitting; the tax consequences discussed below generally apply to such accounts. Trust accounts that are considered revocable under state law are ineffective in splitting income.

Although custodial accounts may be opened anywhere in the United States, the rules governing the accounts may vary from state to state. The differences between the laws of the states generally do not affect federal tax consequences.

There are limitations placed on the custodian. Proceeds from the sale of an investment or income from an investment may not be used to buy additional securities on margin. While a custodian should prudently seek reasonable income and capital preservation, he or she generally is not liable for losses unless they result from bad faith, intentional wrongdoing, or gross negligence.

 Law Alert

Annual Gift Tax Exclusion and Increased Credit

The annual gift tax exclusion, which had been $10,000 for many years, was increased by an inflation adjustment to $11,000 for 2002. Any adjustment for 2003 will be in the *Supplement*.

For 2002 and all later years, a $345,800 lifetime credit against gift tax is allowed, providing a lifetime exemption for $1 million of taxable gifts. If taxable gifts are made, the amount of the credit used to offset the gift tax in one year reduces the amount of credit that can be used against gift tax in a later year. The $1 million gift exemption will not increase after 2003 when the estate tax exemption is scheduled to increase from $1 million to $1.5 million *(39.5)*. The maximum gift tax rate will be reduced along with the maximum estate tax rate *(39.5)* from 2002 through 2009. Starting in 2010, the top gift tax rate will be the top prevailing income tax rate, scheduled to be 35% under the 2001 Tax Act.

Sample Form 709-A

Form **709-A** (Rev. November 2000) Department of the Treasury Internal Revenue Service	**United States Short Form Gift Tax Return** Calendar year 20.........	OMB No. 1545-0021

1 Donor's first name and middle initial **Randall M.**	2 Donor's last name **Johnson**	3 Donor's social security number **1X1 - 01 - X11X**

4 Address (number, street, and apartment number) **914 State Street**	5 Legal residence (domicile) **State XX**

6 City, state, and ZIP code **City, State 0X0X0**	7 Citizenship **USA**

8 Did you file any gift tax returns for prior periods? . . . . ☐ Yes ☒ No

If "Yes," state when and where earlier returns were filed ▶

9 Name of consenting spouse **Claire Johnson**	10 Consenting spouse's social security number **X1Z - 1X - 001X**

Note: *Do not use this form to report gifts of closely held stock, partnership interests, fractional interests in real estate, or gifts for which the value has been reduced to reflect a valuation discount. Instead, use Form 709.*

List of Gifts

(a) Donee's name and address and description of gift	(b) Donor's adjusted basis of gift	(c) Date of gift	(d) Value at date of gift
1. Philip S. Johnson, son 914 State Street, City, State 0X0X0 Gift of 1,000 shares of Central Net Corp. Common Stock (NASDAQ) at $18.50 per share on 7/16/2001 Cusip No. 001005684	$12,000	7/16/2001	$18,500
2. Ann C. Johnson, daughter 10 Lincoln Road, City, State 0X0X0 Gift of 1,000 shares of Central Net Corp. Common Stock (NASDAQ) at $18.50 per share on 7/16/2001 Cusip No. 001005684	$12,000	7/16/2001	$18,500

Consent — I consent to have the gifts made by my spouse to third parties during the calendar year considered as made one-half by each of us.

Consenting spouse's signature ▶ *Claire Johnson* Date ▶ **March 13, 2002**

Under penalties of perjury, I declare that I have examined this return, and to the best of my knowledge and belief, it is true, correct, and complete. Declaration of preparer (other than donor) is based on all information of which preparer has any knowledge.

Sign Here ▶ **Randell Johnson** **March 13, 2002**
Signature of donor Date

Paid Preparer's Use Only
Preparer's signature ▶ **Jonathan W. Carr** Date **3/13/2002** Check if self-employed ▶ ☐
Firm's name (or yours if self-employed), address, and ZIP code ▶ **200 Clove Road, Suite 600, City, State 0X0X0** Phone no. ▶ **(123) 456-7890**

For Disclosure, Privacy Act, and Paperwork Reduction Act Notice, see the instructions. Cat. No. 10171G Form **709-A** (Rev. 11-2000)

When the minor reaches majority age (depending on state law), property in the custodial account is turned over to him or her. No formal accounting is required. The child, now an adult, may sign a simple release freeing the custodian from any liability. But on reaching majority, the child may request a formal accounting if there are any doubts as to the propriety of the custodian's actions while acting as custodian. For this reason, and also for tax record-keeping purposes, a separate bank account should be opened in which proceeds from sales of investments and investment income are deposited pending reinvestment on behalf of the child. Such an account will furnish a convenient record of sales proceeds, investment income, and reinvestment of the same.

Income tax treatment of custodian account. Income from a custodian account is generally taxable to the child. However, taxable income from a custodial account in excess of the annual "kiddie" tax floor ($1,500 in 2002) is taxed at the parent's tax rate if the child is under age 14; computation of the "kiddie tax" is discussed in Chapter 24.

If a parent is the donor of the custodial property or the custodian of the account and income from the account is used to discharge the parent's legal obligation to support the child, the account income is taxed to the parent.

Gift tax treatment of custodial account. When setting up a custodial account, you may have to pay a gift tax. A transfer of cash or securities to a custodial account is a gift. But you are not subject to a gift tax if you properly plan the cash contributions or purchase of securities for your children's accounts. You may make gifts of up to $11,000 per person, which is shielded from gift tax by the annual exclusion. The exclusion applies each year to each person to whom you make a gift. If your spouse consents to join with you in the gift, you may give annually tax free up to $22,000 to each person.

If the custodial account is set up at the end of December, another tax-free transfer of $22,000 may be made in the first days of January of the following year. In this way, a total of $44,000 is shifted within the two-month period.

Even if gifts exceeding the $11,000 (or $22,000) exclusion are made, gift tax liability may be offset by the unified credit applied to gift and estate taxes.

Estate tax treatment of custodial account. The value of a custodial account will be taxed in your estate if you die while acting as custodian of an account before your child reaches his or her majority. However, you may avoid the problem by naming someone other than yourself as custodian. If you should decide to act as custodian, taking the risk that the account will be taxed in your estate, remember that no estate tax is incurred if the tax on your estate is offset by the estate tax credit; *see* Chapter 39.

If you act as custodian and decide to terminate the custodianship, care should be taken to formally close the account. Otherwise, if you die while retaining power over the account, the IRS may try to tax the account in your estate.

33.3 Trusts in Family Planning

You establish a trust by transferring legal title to property to a trustee who manages the property for one or more beneficiaries. As the one who sets up the trust, you are called the *grantor* or *settlor* of the trust. The trustee may be one or more individuals or an institution such as a bank or a trust company.

You can create a trust during your lifetime or by your will. A trust created during your lifetime is called an *inter vivos* trust; one established in your will is a testamentary trust. An *inter vivos* trust can be revocable or irrevocable. An irrevocable trust does not allow for changes of heart; it requires a complete surrender of property. By conveying property irrevocably to a trust, you may relieve yourself of tax on the income from the trust principal. Furthermore, the property in trust usually is not subject to estate tax, although it may be subject to gift tax. A trust should be made irrevocable only if you are certain you will not need the trust property in a financial emergency.

Trust income. Where a child is a trust beneficiary, the child reports distributable net trust income as taxable income. If the child is under the age of 14, distributable net income is subject to the "kiddie tax," discussed at *24.3*. Income that is accumulated for the benefit of a minor child is generally not taxable and, thus, not subject to the kiddie tax.

Grantor trusts. The grantor of a grantor trust is taxed on the income of the trust. A trust is treated as a grantor trust where the grantor has a reversionary interest (at the time of the transfer) of more than 5% of the value of the property transferred to the trust. Under an exception, a grantor

Planning Reminder

Custodial Securities Account

Purchase of securities through custodial accounts provides a practical method for making a gift of securities to a minor child, eliminating the need for a trust. The mechanics of opening a custodial account are simple. An adult opens a stock brokerage account for a minor child and registers the securities in the name of a custodian for the benefit of the child. The custodian may be a parent, a child's guardian, grandparent, brother, sister, uncle, or aunt. In some states, the custodian may be any adult or a bank or trust company. The custodian has the right to sell securities in the account and collect sales proceeds and investment income, and use them for the child's benefit or reinvestment. Tax treatment of custodial accounts is discussed on this page.

Planning Reminder

Revocable Trusts

In a revocable trust, you retain control over the property by reserving the right to revoke the trust. As such, it is considered an incomplete gift and offers no present income tax savings. Furthermore, the trust property will be included as part of your estate. But a revocable trust minimizes delay in passing property to beneficiaries if you die while the trust is in force. When you transfer property to a trust, the property is generally not subject to probate, administration expenses, delays attendant on distributions of estates, or claims of creditors. The interests of trust beneficiaries are generally more secure than those of heirs under a will because a will may be denied probate if found invalid.

is not treated as having a reversionary interest if that interest can take effect only upon the death before age 21 of a beneficiary who is a lineal descendant of the grantor. The beneficiary must have the entire present interest in the trust or trust portion for this exception to apply.

Given the highly compressed tax brackets for trust income, a grantor may intentionally retain an interest in the trust property so that he or she will be taxed under the grantor trust rules. By setting up such a "defective" grantor trust, trust income may be subject to lower tax at the grantor's tax bracket than under the trust rate schedule.

33.4 Gifts of Appreciated Property

Making a gift of appreciated property that will eventually be sold may reduce income tax. To shift the profit and the tax, the gift must be completed before the sale or before the donor has made a binding commitment to sell. By making a gift of interests in the property to several family members, it is possible to spread the profit and the tax among a number of taxpayers in the lowest tax bracket.

Warning: The IRS may claim that the gift was never completed if after sale the donor controls the sales proceeds or has the use of them.

Do not make a gift of property that has decreased in value if you want a deduction for the loss. Once you give the property away, the loss deduction is gone forever. Neither you nor your donee can ever take advantage of it. The better way is first to sell the property, get a loss deduction, and then make a gift of the proceeds.

33.5 Life Insurance Offers Tax Advantages

Insurance may provide a tax-free accumulation of cash. During the time you pay premiums, the value of your contract increases at compound interest rates. The increase is not subject to income tax. In addition, when your policy is paid at death to your beneficiaries, the proceeds are not subject to income tax; see 33.6.

Estate tax planning. To shelter life insurance proceeds from estate tax, you must not have ownership rights in the policy. If you have an existing policy, you must assign your ownership rights, such as the right to change beneficiaries, the right to surrender or cancel the policy, the right to assign it, and the right to borrow against it. An assignment must occur more than three years before death to exclude the proceeds from your estate.

Assigning group-term policies. Group insurance provided by an employer may be assigned. The IRS has agreed to follow a court decision holding that the power to convert a group policy into an individual policy when you leave the company will not subject the group-term insurance proceeds to estate tax. Since the conversion privilege is exercisable only by taking the economically disadvantageous step of quitting, this right is too remote to be considered a retained ownership right in the policy. If other incidents of ownership are transferred, such as the power to name beneficiaries and fix the type of benefit payable, the transfer will remove the policy from your estate.

The substitution of a new group carrier does not jeopardize assignments under a prior carrier.

When you plan to assign a policy, review your gift tax liability on such a transfer. In the case of an assignment of a group policy, the cost of the policy is determined by actuarially apportioning the employer's total premium payment among the covered employees. This is difficult for an individual employee to do, particularly where there are many employees, so the IRS generally allows employees to value the assigned policy using the same tax tables used to determine the amount of the employee's compensation where group coverage exceeds $50,000. See the table at 3.3. Key employees may not use the table to determine gift tax liability.

You may want to readjust your coverage to meet new family conditions. You can exchange your policies without tax; see 6.12.

Using a trust to purchase insurance. If you create a trust to carry a policy on your life by transferring income-producing property the income of which is used to pay the premiums, you are taxable on the trust income. Similarly, if your spouse creates the trust to carry the policy on your life, he or she is taxable on the trust income. This tax rule does not apply to the trust funding of life insurance covering the life of a third party other than your spouse. For example, a grandparent transfers income-producing property to a trust to pay the premiums on a policy on the life of his son. His grandchildren are named trust beneficiaries. The grandparent is not taxed on the income earned by the trust on the transferred property because the trust purchased insurance on his son's life, not his own.

 *Planning Reminder*

Transfers of Appreciated Property
Before making a gift of appreciated property, consider the fact that the appreciation on property passed by inheritance escapes income tax; the heir takes a basis equal to estate tax value, which is usually the fair market value at the date of death. Furthermore, appreciated property encumbered by a mortgage may result in income tax to the donor when a gift of the property is made; see 31.15.

Life Insurance

 *Court Decision*

Policy Owned by Beneficiary
If you are buying a new policy with yourself as the insured, and you want to keep the proceeds out of your gross estate, you must buy the policy in another's name, such as in your spouse's name, or have your beneficiary buy the policy. For example, a daughter applies for a $1 million policy on her father's life and is the policy owner under the terms of the policy. If the father pays the premiums, his payments are treated as gifts, but the proceeds paid at his death are not subject to estate tax because he never had ownership rights in the policy. In the past, the IRS contested this tax-free treatment, but now agrees to follow court decisions that allow it.

Insurance trust to receive proceeds. A trust may be used to receive insurance proceeds where there is concern that the beneficiary may be unable to manage a large insurance settlement. The trustee may be a bank or a person directed to invest the proceeds and pay income to beneficiaries according to standards provided in the trust. The trustee may be given the discretion to pay out more or less as circumstances warrant. He or she may be directed to terminate the trust when the beneficiaries reach a certain age, or when they demonstrate their ability to manage money. There may also be investment advantages in a trust. The trust investments may yield a higher rate of return than that of an insurance company under a settlement option.

Insurance proceeds are not subject to income tax whether paid directly to named beneficiaries or to a trust.

Single-premium policies. Single-premium policies have been touted as tax-sheltered investments. Companies offer competitive current returns and tax-free appreciation on your investment fund. The name of the policy is descriptive: You make a single-premium payment—$5,000, $10,000, $50,000, or more. Part of the premium goes for life insurance coverage and part towards an investment fund.

However, tax benefits of single-premium and other cash value policies have been cut back, as discussed below.

Universal life insurance plans. Universal life insurance offers tax-free buildup of interest income at current market rates and on death, tax-free receipt of insurance proceeds. A universal life insurance policy is made up of (1) life insurance protection and (2) a cash reserve on which interest income accumulates without tax.

The interest rate of universal life insurance is pegged to current bond market rates. Furthermore, a universal life policy lets you withdraw the cash reserve if you want to invest it elsewhere and to allocate how much of your premium payment is to cover insurance protection and how much is to go into the cash reserve.

The tax law sets limits on the amount of premiums that may be earmarked for the cash reserve. If these limits are violated, tax-free treatment for the proceeds may be lost. For these limits, check with the company issuing the policy.

A disadvantage of universal life insurance is that you must incur an upfront commission payment that may be 50% or more of the first premium. There may also be a fee for withdrawing the cash reserve.

See below for restrictions on withdrawals from cash value policies.

Tax on withdrawals from cash value modified endowment contracts. Contracts entered into after June 20, 1988, may be subject to tax penalties if they are considered "modified endowment contracts." Generally, a modified endowment contract is a contract that fails to satisfy a technical "seven-year-pay test." A contract fails the "seven-year-pay test" if the premiums paid during the first seven contract years exceed the sum of the net level premiums that would have been paid by that time had the contract provided for paid-up future benefits after the payment of seven level annual premiums.

Amounts received under modified endowment contracts that are not received as an annuity, such as dividends, cash withdrawals, loans, and amounts received upon a partial surrender of the contract, are taxable to the extent the cash surrender value of the contract exceeds the policyholder's investment. Withdrawals that are greater than the excess of cash surrender value over the investment are a tax-free return of capital. Assignments or pledges of a contract to cover burial or prearranged funeral expenses are not considered taxable distributions if the contractual death benefit is $25,000 or less.

To prevent marketing of multiple contracts as a means of avoiding these tax limitations, all modified endowment contracts issued by the same insurer or its affiliates to the same policyholder within the same calendar year are aggregated to determine the amount includible in income.

Penalty for early withdrawals from modified endowment contracts. A 10% premature withdrawal penalty applies to taxable distributions and loans unless the policyholder is over age 59 $\frac{1}{2}$, disabled, or the distribution is one of a series of substantially equal payments over life expectancy or over joint life expectancy with a beneficiary; for further details, *see 7.15.*

Caution

Universal Life Policy

A universal life policy allows a policyholder to apply premium payments to cash value instead of to death benefits. Death benefits may be tax free if the policies meet certain technical tests. These tests must be determined by the insurance company. Therefore, you must check with the company paying the proceeds as to whether the payments qualify as tax-free life insurance payments. Other names applied to universal life policies may be "flexible premium" and "adjustable life premium" policies.

Planning Reminder

Insurance Options

Before deciding on a universal insurance plan, consider whether the purchase of term insurance and an investment in money-market funds or long-term bonds may be a better alternative to a universal life plan.

33.6 How Life Insurance Proceeds Are Taxed to a Beneficiary

Life insurance proceeds received upon the death of the insured are generally tax free. However, insurance proceeds may be subject to estate tax so that the beneficiary actually receives a reduced amount; *see 39.2.*

Interest paid on proceeds left with the insurer is taxable except in this case: A surviving spouse who elects to receive installments rather than a lump sum does not pay tax on the first $1,000 of interest received each year if the decedent died before October 23, 1986.

Read the following checklist to find how your insurance receipts are taxed—

A lump-sum payment of the full face value of a life insurance policy: The proceeds are generally tax free. The tax-free exclusion also covers death benefit payments made under endowment contracts, workers' compensation insurance contracts, employers' group insurance plans, or accident and health insurance contracts. The exclusion does not apply to a policy combined with a nonrefund life annuity contract where a single premium equal to the face value of the insurance is paid.

Insurance proceeds may be taxable where the policy was transferred for valuable consideration. Exceptions to this rule are made for transfers among partners and corporations and their stockholders and officers.

Installment payments spread over your life under a policy that could have been paid in a lump sum: Part of each installment attributed to interest may be taxed. Divide the face amount of the policy by the number of years the installments are to be paid. The result is the amount that is received tax free each year.

If you are the surviving spouse of an insured who died before October 23, 1986, up to $1,000 of interest paid with the annual installment is also tax free. You are still treated as a spouse if separated from the insured at the date of his or her death, but not if divorced. (If you receive payments under a policy with a "family income rider," *see 33.7.*) The $1,000 interest exclusion is not allowed where the insured died after October 22, 1986.

> **EXAMPLE**
>
> Alice is the wife and beneficiary under her husband John's life insurance policy of $100,000. He died September 30, 1986. She elected to take installment payments for the rest of her life. Alice's life expectancy is 20 years. Thus, $5,000 ($100,000 ÷ 20) is the principal amount spread to each year. The first $6,000 received each year ($5,000 principal plus $1,000 of the spouse's special interest exclusion) is exempt from tax. If Alice lives more than 20 years, she may continue to treat up to $6,000 of annual payments as tax-free receipts.

If the policy guarantees payments to a secondary beneficiary if you should die before receiving a specified number of payments, the tax-free amount is reduced by the present value of the secondary beneficiary's interest in the policy. The insurance company can give you this figure.

Installment payments for a fixed number of years under a policy that could have been paid in a lump sum. Divide the full face amount of the policy by the number of years you are to receive the installments. The result is the amount that is received tax free each year.

> **EXAMPLE**
>
> Same facts as in the preceding Example, but Alice elects to take installment payments for 10 years. Then $10,000 ($100,000 ÷ 10) is the principal amount received tax free. So up to $11,000 per year may be received tax free by Alice, $10,000 of principal sum plus up to $1,000 of interest, under the surviving spouse's interest exclusion.

Installment payments when there is no lump-sum option in the policy: You must find the discounted value of the policy at the date of the insured's death and use that as the principal amount. The insurance company can give you that figure. After you find the discounted value, you divide it by the number of years you are to receive installments. The result is the amount that is tax free. The remainder is taxed.

Planning Reminder

Accelerated Death Benefits

A person who is terminally ill may withdraw without tax life insurance proceeds to pay medical bills and other living expenses. For policies lacking an accelerated benefits clause, it is possible to sell a life insurance policy without incurring tax to a viatical settlement company; *see 17.16.*

EXAMPLE

The insured died in 2002. Under an insurance policy, the surviving wife is entitled to $5,000 a year for life. Her life expectancy is 20 years. There is no lump sum stated in the policy. Say the discounted value of the wife's rights is $60,000. The principal amount spread to each year for the wife is $3,000 ($60,000 ÷ 20). Subtracting $3,000 from each annual $5,000 payment gives her taxable income of $2,000.

Payments to you along with other beneficiaries under the same policy, by lump-sum or varying installments. *See* the following Example for the way multiple beneficiaries may be taxed.

EXAMPLE

Under one life insurance policy of an insured man who died in 2002, a surviving wife, daughter, and nephew are all beneficiaries. The wife is entitled to a lump sum of $60,000. The daughter and nephew are each entitled to a lump sum of $35,000. Under the installment options, the wife chooses to receive $5,000 a year for the rest of her life. (She has a 20-year life expectancy.) The daughter and the nephew each choose a yearly payment of $5,000 for 10 years. This is how each yearly installment is taxed:

Wife: The principal amount spread to each year is $3,000. Subtracting $3,000 from the yearly $5,000 payment gives the wife taxable income of $2,000.

Daughter and Nephew: Both are taxed the same way. The principal amount spread to each of the 10 years is $3,500. Subtracting this $3,500 from the yearly $5,000 installment gives the daughter and the nephew taxable income of $1,500 each.

Interest only option. When proceeds are left on deposit under the "interest only" option, distributions of interest are fully taxed. A surviving spouse of an insured who died before October 23, 1986, may not exclude $1,000 interest under the "interest only" option. However, if the surviving spouse later elects to receive proceeds from the policy in installments, the interest exclusion applies from the time of the election.

33.7 A Policy With a Family Income Rider

Payments received under a family income rider are taxed under a special rule. A family income rider provides additional term insurance coverage for a fixed number of years from the date of the basic policy. Under the terms of a rider, if the insured dies at any time during the term period, the beneficiary receives monthly payments during the balance of the term period, and then at the end of the term period, receives the lump-sum proceeds of the basic policy. If the insured dies after the end of the term period, the beneficiary receives only the lump sum from the basic policy.

When the insured dies during the term period, part of each monthly payment received during the term period includes interest on the lump-sum proceeds of the basic policy (which is held by the company until the end of the term period). That interest is fully taxed. The balance of the monthly payment consists of an installment (principal plus interest) of the proceeds from the term insurance purchased under the family income rider. You may exclude from this balance: (1) a prorated portion of the present value of the lump sum under the basic policy and (2) an additional amount of up to $1,000 attributable to interest if you are a surviving spouse of an insured who died before October 23, 1986. The lump sum under the basic policy is tax free when you eventually receive it.

The rules here also apply to an integrated family income policy and to family maintenance policies, whether integrated or with an attached rider.

In figuring your taxable portions, ask the insurance company for its interest rate and the present value of term payments.

33.8 How Other Insurance Proceeds Are Taxed

Dividends paid by the insurance company as reduction of premiums (taken in cash, left as interest with the company, or used to accelerate the maturity of the policy) are not taxable. They serve to reduce the cost basis of your policy, thus increasing gain sometimes computed upon maturity of some policies. However, interest on such "dividends" is generally taxable, although the interest on GI insurance dividends left on deposit with the VA is tax free.

Matured endowment policies. You generally report as income the difference between the proceeds received and your investment; *see 7.24*. The payment on an endowment contract because of the insured's death is treated as the payment of tax-free life insurance proceeds provided the policy meets certain technical definitions not discussed in this book.

Sale of an endowment contract before maturity. Taxed as ordinary income; *see 7.24*.

Collection of proceeds on policy purchased by or assigned to you on the life of someone else. Where a policy is transferred for valuable consideration, only the amount paid and the premiums paid after the transfer are tax free when collected; the balance is taxed. There is no tax on life insurance proceeds paid under contracts that have been transferred to a partner or to a corporation in which the insured was a shareholder or officer.

 Caution

Surrender of Policy for Cash

If the cash received on the surrender of a policy exceeds the premiums paid less dividends received, the excess is taxed as ordinary income (not capital gain). If you take, instead, a paid-up policy, you may avoid tax; *see 6.12*. You get no deduction if there is a loss on the surrender of a policy.

Tax may be avoided by a terminally ill individual on the surrender of a policy under an accelerated death benefit clause or on a sale of the policy to a viatical settlement company; *see 17.16*.

Chapter 34

Special Rules for Senior Citizens

All of your Social Security benefits are tax free if your "provisional income," explained at *34.3*, is $25,000 or less if you are single, or $32,000 or less if you are married and file a joint return. No more than 50% of your benefits are subject to tax if you file a joint return and your provisional income is over $32,000 but no more than $44,000, or if you are single and your provisional income is over $25,000 but no more than $34,000. When provisional income exceeds $34,000 or $44,000 (depending on your filing status), more than 50%, but no more than 85%, of your benefits are subject to tax. If you are married and filing separately, and did not live apart for the whole year, you compute the amount of taxable benefits without considering the base amounts allowed on joint and single returns. If you are married filing separately and you lived apart the entire year, are a head of household, or are a qualifying widow(er), use the $25,000 and $34,000 base amounts for single persons.

If you continue to earn wages or self-employed income, you must pay FICA taxes or self-employment tax on that income regardless of your age. Do not confuse this rule with the Social Security benefit rule that allows full benefits for working after you reach age 65; *see 34.5*.

34.1 Senior Citizens Get Certain Filing Breaks

The following special tax rules favor senior citizens:

- *Higher filing thresholds.* If you are single and age 65 or older on or before January 1, 2003, you do not have to file a 2002 return unless your gross income is $8,850 or over. This is $1,150 more than for younger taxpayers. If you are married and you and your spouse are both age 65 or older, a joint return does not have to be filed unless your gross income is $15,650 or over, or $14,750 or over if only one of you is age 65 or older; *see* the chart on page 3 for further details.

- *Higher standard deduction.* If you are age 65 or older on or before January 1, 2003, you receive an additional standard deduction allowance if you do not itemize deductions. If you are single you get an additional $1,150 on your 2002 return, or $900 if you are married or a qualifying widow(er); *see 13.4.* Your 2002 standard deduction is $5,850 if you are single. If married filing jointly, it is $8,750 if one of you is age 65 or over, or $9,650 if both of you are; *see 13.4.*

- *Tax credit if age 65 or older.* This is a limited tax credit for taxpayers age 65 or older who receive little or no Social Security or Railroad Retirement benefits. The credit may also be available to persons under age 65 who are totally disabled; *see 34.7.* For example, if you are single, or married but only you are eligible, and receive more than $416 each month from Social Security, you may not claim the credit. If you are married and both you and your spouse are eligible for the credit and file a joint return, you may not claim the credit if you receive more than $625 each month from Social Security.

- *Social Security benefits may be exempt from tax.* The taxable portion of Social Security benefits may vary from year to year because it depends on an amount called "provisional income," which is explained at *34.3.* If you are married and file jointly, none of your net Social Security benefits are taxable in 2002 if your provisional income is not more than a base amount of $32,000. The base amount is $25,000 if your filing status is single, head of household, qualifying widow(er), or you are married filing separately and did not live with your spouse at any time during 2002. Married persons who file separately and live together at any time during the year are not allowed any base amount; *see 34.3* for computing taxable Social Security benefits.

34.2 Social Security Benefits Subject to Tax

If you received or repaid Social Security benefits in 2002, you should receive Form SSA-1099 by January 31, 2003. The form will show total benefits paid to you and any benefits you repaid to the government in 2002. Total benefits include monthly survivor and disability benefits, but not Supplemental Security Income (SSI), which is not taxable. Amounts withheld for Medicare premiums, workers' compensation offset, or attorneys' fees are itemized and included in Box 3, benefits paid in 2002. Keep Form SSA-1099 for your records; do not attach it to your return.

The *net benefit* shown in Box 5 of Form SSA-1099 (benefits paid less benefits repaid) is the benefit amount used to determine the taxable portion of your benefits (if any) under *34.3.*

Railroad Retirement benefits. The portion of your Tier 1 Railroad Retirement benefits that is equivalent to Social Security retirement benefits is subject to the computation at *34.3* for determining taxable benefits. If any part of your 2002 Tier 1 benefits is equivalent to Social Security benefits, you should receive Form RRB-1099 from the government by January 31, 2003. The *net* Social Security Equivalent Benefit shown on Form RRB-1099 is the amount used to determine taxable benefits under *34.3.* Other Tier 1 Railroad Retirement benefits, as well as Tier 2 benefits, are treated as pension income and not as Social Security benefits for tax purposes.

Benefits paid on behalf of child or incompetent. If a child is entitled to Social Security benefits, such as after the death of a parent, the benefit is considered to be the child's regardless of who actually receives the payment. Whether the child's benefit is subject to tax will depend on the amount of the child's income.

Workers' compensation. If you are receiving Social Security disability payments and workers' compensation for the same disability, your Social Security benefits may be reduced by the workers' compensation. For example, you are entitled to Social Security disability benefits of $5,000 a year. After receiving a $1,000 workers' compensation award, your disability benefits are reduced to $4,000. For purposes of the computation steps at *34.3*, you treat the full $5,000 as Social Security benefits.

Net benefits. The net benefit shown in Box 5 of Form SSA-1099 is the amount used to determine the taxable portion of your benefits. If Box 5 shows a negative amount (a figure in parentheses), none of your benefits are taxable. If the negative amount is related to Social Security benefits included in gross income in a prior year, you may be entitled to a deduction or a credit; *see* IRS

 Planning Reminder

Voluntary Withholding on Social Security Benefits in 2003

You can use your Social Security benefits to meet your estimated and final tax liability for 2003 by electing on Form W-4V to have tax withheld from benefits at a 7%, 10%, 15%, or 27% rate.

Publication 915 for further instructions on how to figure the deduction or credit when your repayments exceed your gross benefits.

Taxable Social Security benefits are not considered earnings and therefore may not be the basis of an IRA contribution *(8.2)*, earned income credit *(25.12)*, or foreign earned income exclusion *(36.2)*.

Nonresident aliens. Unless provided otherwise by tax treaty, 85% of a nonresident alien's Social Security benefits will be subject to the 30% withholding tax imposed on U.S. source income that is not connected with a U.S. trade or business. *See* IRS Publication 519 for further details.

34.3 Computing Taxable Social Security Benefits

You may use the worksheet in this section to determine the taxable portion of your Social Security benefits. The taxable portion of your benefits depends on your *provisional income* and your filing status. Part of your net Social Security benefits will be subject to tax if your *provisional income* exceeds a base amount of $25,000 or $32,000.

To figure *provisional income*, you will have to increase the total income shown on your return by certain tax-exempt amounts, and also by 50% of your net Social Security benefits, before subtracting adjustments to income other than the student loan interest deduction *(38.6)* and the tuition and fees deduction *(38.13)*. For example, *tax-exempt interest* reported on Line 8b of your return is included as part of provisional income for purposes of figuring the taxable part of your Social Security benefits, although this amount is not included when figuring your regular tax liability. On the worksheet below, provisional income is the amount computed for Line 7.

The *base amount* is $25,000 if your filing status is single, head of household, qualifying widow(er), or married filing separately and you lived apart from your spouse for all of 2002. The base amount is $32,000 if you are married filing jointly. You are not entitled to any base amount if you are married filing separately and you lived with your spouse at any time during 2002; *see* the Caution on this page.

Caution

Married Filing Separately

If you are married filing separately and during 2002 you lived with your spouse at any time, you must include in your taxable income the lesser of (1) 85% of your net Social Security benefits shown on Line 1 of the worksheet or (2) 85% of the provisional income shown on Line 7 of the worksheet.

Worksheet 1. **Figuring Your Taxable Benefits**

Before you start: Is your filing status *Married filing separately?*

   No. Go to line 1 below.

   Yes. Did you live apart from your spouse all year?

      No. Go to line 1 below.

      Yes. Do the following if you file:

            Form 1040: Enter "D" to the right of the word "benefits" on line 20a, then go to line 1 below.

            Form 1040A: Enter "D" to the right of the word "benefits" on line 14a, then go to line 1 below.

1. Enter the total amount from box 5 of ALL your Forms SSA-1099 and RRB-1099 .... **1.** _____

   Note: If line 1 is zero or less, stop here; none of your benefits are taxable. Otherwise, go on to line 2.

2. Enter one-half of line 1 .... **2.** _____

3. Enter the total of the amounts from:
   Form 1040: Lines 7, 8a, 8b, 9-14, 15b, 16b, 17-19, and 21
   Form 1040A: Lines 7, 8a, 8b, 9, 10, 11b, 12b, and 13 .... **3.** _____

4. *Form 1040A filers:* Enter the total of any exclusions for qualified U.S. savings bond interest (Form 8815, line 14) or for adoption benefits (Form 8839, line 26)
   Form 1040 filers: Enter the total of any exclusions/adjustments for:
     Qualified U.S. savings bond interest (Form 8815, line 14)
     Adoption benefits (Form 8839, line 26)
     Foreign earned income or housing (Form 2555, lines 43 and 48, or Form 2555-EZ, line 18), and
     Certain income of bona fide residents of American Samoa (Form 4563, line 15) or Puerto Rico .... **4.** _____

5. Add lines 2, 3, and 4 .... **5.** _____

6. *Form 1040A filers:* Enter the amounts from Form 1040A, lines 16 and 17. *Form 1040 filers:* Enter the amount from Form 1040, line 34, minus any amounts on Form 1040, lines 25 and 26 .... **6.** _____

7. Subtract line 6 from line 5 .... **7.** _____

8. Enter $25,000 ($32,000 if married filing jointly; $0 if married filing separately and you lived with your spouse at any time during 2002) .... **8.** _____

9. Subtract line 8 from line 7. If zero or less, enter -0- .... **9.** _____

   Note: If line 9 is zero or less, stop here; none of your benefits are taxable. (Do not enter any amounts on Form 1040, line 20a or 20b, or on Form 1040A, line 14a or line 14b. But if you are married filing separately and you lived apart from your spouse for all of 2002, enter -0- on Form 1040, line 20b, or on Form 1040A, line 14b.) Otherwise, go on to line 10.

10. Enter $9,000 ($12,000 if married filing jointly; $0 if married filing separately and you lived with your spouse at any time during 2002) .... **10.** _____

11. Subtract line 10 from line 9. If zero or less, enter -0-. .... **11.** _____

12. Enter the **smaller** of line 9 or line 10 .... **12.** _____

13. Enter one-half of line 12 .... **13.** _____

14. Enter the **smaller** of line 2 or line 13 .... **14.** _____

15. Multiply line 11 by 85% (.85). If line 11 is zero, enter -0- .... **15.** _____

16. Add lines 14 and 15 .... **16.** _____

17. Multiply line 1 by 85% (.85) .... **17.** _____

18. **Taxable benefits.** Enter the **smaller** of line 16 or line 17 .... **18.** _____

   Enter the amount from line 1 above on Form 1040, line 20a, or on Form 1040A, line 14a.
   Enter the amount from line 18 above on Form 1040, line 20b, or on Form 1040A, line 14b.

   Note: *If you received a lump-sum payment in this year that was for an earlier year, also complete Worksheet 2 or 3 and Worksheet 4 to see whether you can report a lower taxable benefit.*

EXAMPLES

1. Frank Adams, who is single, has 2002 earnings of $15,000 from a part-time job, $3,000 of interest income, and $2,000 of dividends. He also receives $8,000 of net Social Security benefits (Box 5 of Form SSA-1099). Completing the worksheet, Frank's provisional income on Line 7 is $24,000 ($15,000 + 3,000 + 2,000 + 50% of the $8,000 net Social Security benefits). Since $24,000 does not exceed the $25,000 base amount on Line 8 of the worksheet, none of Frank's Social Security benefits are taxable.

2. Sam and Fran Baker receive in 2002 net Social Security benefits (Box 5 of Form SSA-1099) of $15,000. Their taxable interest, dividends, and capital gains are $20,000, and tax-exempt interest is $10,000. They file a joint return. Their provisional income from Line 7 of the worksheet is $37,500 ($20,000 + 10,000 + 50% of the $15,000 net Social Security benefits). Since $37,500 exceeds the $32,000 base amount on Line 8 of the worksheet, part of their Social Security benefits will be taxed. On the sample worksheet shown below, Sam and Fran figure that $2,750 of their benefits are subject to tax:

Worksheet 1. Figuring Your Taxable Benefits

Before you start: Is your filing status *Married filing separately?*

No. Go to line 1 below.

Yes. Did you live apart from your spouse all year?

No. Go to line 1 below.

Yes. Do the following if you file:

Form 1040: Enter "D" to the right of the word "benefits" on line 20a, then go to line 1 below.

Form 1040A: Enter "D" to the right of the word "benefits" on line 14a, then go to line 1 below.

1. Enter the total amount from box 5 of ALL your Forms SSA-1099 and RRB-1099 .... **1. 15,000**

   Note: If line 1 is zero or less, stop here; none of your benefits are taxable. Otherwise, go on to line 2.

2. Enter one-half of line 1 .... **2. 7,500**

3. Enter the total of the amounts from:
   Form 1040: Lines 7, 8a, 8b, 9-14, 15b, 16b, 17-19, and 21
   Form 1040A: Lines 7, 8a, 8b, 9, 10, 11b, 12b, and 13 .... **3. 30,000**

4. Form 1040A filers: Enter the total of any exclusions for qualified U.S. savings bond interest (Form 8815, line 14) or for adoption benefits (Form 8839, line 26)
   Form 1040 filers: Enter the total of any exclusions/adjustments for:
   Qualified U.S. savings bond interest (Form 8815, line 14)
   Adoption benefits (Form 8839, line 26)
   Foreign earned income or housing (Form 2555, lines 43 and 48, or Form 2555-EZ, line 18), and
   Certain income of bona fide residents of American Samoa (Form 4563, line 15) or Puerto Rico .... **4. - 0 -**

5. Add lines 2, 3, and 4 .... **5. 37,500**

6. Form 1040A filers: Enter the amounts from Form 1040A, lines 16 and 17. Form 1040 filers: Enter the amount from Form 1040, line 34, minus any amounts on Form 1040, lines 25 and 26 .... **6. - 0 -**

7. Subtract line 6 from line 5 .... **7. 37,500**

8. Enter $25,000 ($32,000 if married filing jointly; $0 if married filing separately and you lived with your spouse at any time during 2002) **8. 32,000**

9. Subtract line 8 from line 7. If zero or less, enter -0- **9. 5,500**

   Note: If line 9 is zero or less, stop here; none of your benefits are taxable. (Do not enter any amounts on Form 1040, line 20a or 20b, or on Form 1040A, line 14a or line 14b. But if you are married filing separately and you lived apart from your spouse for all of 2002, enter -0- on Form 1040, line 20b, or on Form 1040A, line 14b.) Otherwise, go on to line 10.

10. Enter $9,000 ($12,000 if married filing jointly; $0 if married filing separately and you lived with your spouse at any time during 2002) **10. 12,000**

11. Subtract line 10 from line 9. If zero or less, enter -0- .... **11. - 0 -**

12. Enter the **smaller** of line 9 or line 10 .... **12. 5,500**

13. Enter one-half of line 12 .... **13. 2,750**

14. Enter the **smaller** of line 2 or line 13 .... **14. 2,750**

15. Multiply line 11 by 85% (.85). If line 11 is zero, enter -0- .... **15. - 0 -**

16. Add lines 14 and 15 .... **16. 2,750**

17. Multiply line 1 by 85% (.85) **17. 12,750**

18. Taxable benefits. Enter the **smaller** of line 16 or line 17 .... **18. 2,750**

   Enter the amount from line 1 above on Form 1040, line 20a, or on Form 1040A, line 14a.
   Enter the amount from line 18 above on Form 1040, line 20b, or on Form 1040A, line 14b.

   Note: If you received a lump-sum payment in this year that was for an earlier year, also complete Worksheet 2 or 3 and Worksheet 4 to see whether you can report a lower taxable benefit.

IRA contributions. Do *not* use the worksheet above if you are an active participant in an employer retirement plan and you plan to make deductible IRA contributions *(8.4)*. You must use the worksheets printed in IRS Publication 590. With the worksheets, you first determine the amount of Social Security benefits that would be subject to tax, assuming you did not claim any IRA deduction. That amount is then used to figure the allowable IRA deduction, taking into account any limitations under the phase-out rules *(8.4)*, and, finally, the allowable IRA deduction is used to compute the taxable portion of your Social Security benefits.

If you are not covered by an employer retirement plan, you may use the worksheet to figure the taxable portion of your Social Security benefits.

Planning Reminder

No Earnings Tests after Age 65

If you are 65 or over, you may earn as much as you can without forfeiting benefits. Benefit forfeitures for working while receiving benefits apply only to retirees under age 65.

Law Alert

Social Security Retirement Age

As of 2003, the retirement age for receiving full Social Security benefits begins to gradually increase from 65 to 67, as shown below.

Birth year—	Full Social Security retirement age—
Before 1938	65
1938	65 and 2 months
1939	65 and 4 months
1940	65 and 6 months
1941	65 and 8 months
1942	65 and 10 months
1943–1954	66
1955	66 and 2 months
1956	66 and 4 months
1957	66 and 6 months
1958	66 and 8 months
1959	66 and 10 months
1960 and after	67

34.4 Election for Lump-Sum Social Security Benefit Payment

If in 2002 you receive a lump-sum payment of benefits covering prior years, you have a choice as to how to determine the taxable portion of the benefits: (1) You may treat the entire payment as a 2002 benefit taxable under the rules in *34.3 or* (2) you may allocate the benefits between 2002 and the earlier years. Choose the method that provides the lowest required increase to income in the current year. For example, if you receive a 2002 lump-sum payment that includes benefits for 2001, you may find that an allocation of benefits is advantageous where your income over the two-year period has fluctuated and benefits allocated to 2001 would be subject to a lower taxable percentage than in 2002.

When you elect to allocate benefits to a prior year, you do not amend the return for that year. You compute the increase in income (if any) that would have resulted if the Social Security benefits had been received in that year. You then add that amount to the income of the current year.

See IRS Publication 915 for instructions and worksheets for making the allocation and figuring the amount to be reported on your return.

34.5 Retiring on Social Security Benefits

Retirement benefits are not paid automatically. You should file for Social Security retirement benefits three months before you want to start receiving benefits. The age for receiving full Social Security benefits, traditionally 65, is increasing for those born after 1937; *see* the Law Alert on this page. Reduced benefits may be elected if you are at least age 62. Even if you do not begin Social Security retirement benefits until after age 65, you should register with the Social Security Administration to ensure Medicare coverage.

If you are at least age 62 and elect reduced benefits, the reduction depends on the number of months between the start date and your full Social Security retirement age. For example, if you elect benefits at age 62 in 2003, the benefit reduction is about 23.33%.

If you delay benefits beyond full Social Security retirement age, your potential Social Security benefit increases for each year you delay retirement. The increase is 5% for those born in 1932, 5.5% for those born in 1933 or 1934, 6% for those born in 1935 or 1936, and 6.5% for those born in 1937 or 1938.

Benefits may be reduced because of earnings. Your benefits will be reduced during the time you are under the full retirement age, which is currently 65. Full retirement age starts to increase in 2003; *see* the Law Alert on retirement age on this page.

If you are under full retirement age and are receiving benefits, $1 of benefits will be deducted for each $2 earned above an annual limit. In 2002, the limit is $11,280 (the 2003 limit is listed in the *Supplement*). For the year you reach full retirement age, $1 of benefits is deducted for each $3 earned over a different limit, which for 2002 is $30,000. Only earnings before the month you reach full retirement age are counted. For the first year of retirement, a full benefit may be received for any month in which your earnings do not exceed $1/12$ of the annual limit, even if the yearly limit is exceeded. Starting with the month in which you reach full retirement age, you are entitled to full benefits with no limit on how much you may earn. You may receive any amount of income from sources other than work—for example, private pensions or investments—without affecting the amount of Social Security retirement benefits.

EXAMPLES

1. Jones retires and begins receiving Social Security benefits in January 2002 at age 62. He is entitled to receive $600 a month ($7,200 annually). He works and earns $21,200, which is $9,920 over the $11,280 limit. He loses $4,960 of benefits ($1 for every $2 over $11,280). However, since this is his first year of retirement, a full benefit would be paid for any month in which earnings were $940 ($1/12$ of $11,280) or less.

2. Smith, who began receiving benefits before 2002, is 64 at the beginning of 2002 and turns 65 in August 2002. He is entitled to monthly benefits of $600. He was fully employed during the year, earning $33,000 before August and $22,500 for the remainder of the year. The benefit reduction applied to his pre-August benefits is $1,000. He earned $3,000 over the $30,000 limit and only $1 for every $3 above that limit is applied as a benefit reduction. Starting in August, he begins to receive his full benefits regardless of the amount of his earnings.

So long as you continue to work, you pay Social Security taxes on your earnings, regardless of your age.

Request an estimate of benefits and copy of earnings record. You can get an estimate of retirement benefits by sending for Form SSA-7004. After mailing in a completed Form SSA-7004, you will receive a Personal Earnings and Benefit Estimate Statement, showing your earnings history, Social Security tax payments, and an estimate of your retirement, disability, and survivor's benefits.

Form SSA-7004 is available at your local Social Security office. You can also request the form from the Social Security Administration by calling 1-800-772-1213 or obtain it from the Social Security Administration website at www.ssa.gov.

34.6 How Tax on Social Security Reduces Your Earnings

There is an added tax cost of earning income if the earnings will subject your Social Security benefits to tax. Therefore, if your benefits are not currently exposed to tax, you have to figure *not only* the tax on the extra income *but also* the amount of Social Security benefits subjected to tax by those earnings. If the additional earnings will put you over the base amount *(34.3)*, then you will not only have to pay tax on the additional earnings but also on the Social Security benefits that will be subject to tax. As a result, the marginal tax rate on the extra income will be higher than the regular rate that would otherwise apply; *see* Example 2 below.

EXAMPLES

1. You are over age 65 and you and your spouse receive net Social Security benefits of $8,000. You file jointly. You have pension income of $25,000 and $3,000 in tax-exempt interest. Your provisional income *(34.3)* is $32,000. No part of your Social Security benefits is taxable because your provisional income of $32,000 does not exceed the $32,000 base amount for married persons filing jointly.

2. Same facts as in Example 1, except that you take a part-time job paying $8,000. This increases your provisional income to $40,000 and subjects $4,000 of Social Security benefits to tax.

Provisional income	$40,000
Less: Base amount	32,000
Excess	$8,000
50% of excess taxable *(34.3)*	$4,000

   The $8,000 of additional earnings increases your taxable income by $12,000, which is the $8,000 of earnings plus the $4,000 of Social Security benefits made taxable because of the increase in provisional income. Assuming a 15% tax rate, the tax on the $12,000 is $1,800 ($12,000 × 15%); the effective tax rate on the $8,000 earnings is 22.5% ($1,800 ÷ $8,000), rather than 15%. If you consider employment taxes, the effective tax rate is higher.

When earnings result in forfeiture of Social Security benefits. If you are under 65 years of age and receive Social Security benefits, it is possible under the current tax structure to earn extra income and yet have only a small gain or even lose money when considering the increased tax on the earnings and on Social Security benefits, and also the forfeiture of benefits when earnings exceed the annual retirement earnings test; *see 34.5*.

Therefore, before taking on work to earn extra income, you should compute the tax cost of the extra earnings and the loss of benefits. As a rule of thumb, you may figure the extra tax cost by multiplying the earnings by your top federal tax bracket and also by the FICA tax rate of 7.65% (Social Security and Medicare withholdings) and by your top rate for state or local taxes. But be aware that this composite rate ignores the effect of the increased tax from crossing the thresholds for taxing up to 50% or 85% of Social Security benefits. Therefore, in such cases, the tax cost will be greater than the estimated composite tax rate. For greater accuracy, figure your tax position as if you were preparing two tax returns: one that does not include the extra income and the other that does include the extra income. The tax difference is the extra income tax cost of earning the extra pay. Add to this cost the FICA tax on the extra earnings and any additional state or local taxes. Then figure the amount of benefits that will be forfeited. This will give you a net gain or in some cases a net loss. If you have a tax consultant, it may be advisable to ask the consultant to make the computations.

Tax Credit for the Elderly and Disabled

34.7 Claiming the Credit for the Elderly and Disabled

You may qualify for a tax credit for 2002 if you meet one of the following conditions:

- Your 65th birthday is on or before January 1, 2003; *or*
- You were under age 65 at the end of 2002, you retired before the end of 2002 because of permanent and total disability, and you received taxable disability income in 2002 from your former employer's disability plan. Disability income is taxable wages or payments in lieu of wages paid to you while you are absent from work because of permanent and total disability. Qualifying disability income does not include payments received after reaching mandatory retirement age.

However, even if you meet one of these tests, you will not be able to claim a credit if your Social Security benefits or adjusted gross income is too high; *see 34.9.*

Disabled. You are considered permanently and totally disabled if you are unable to engage in any substantial gainful activity by reason of any medically determinable physical or mental impairment that can be expected to result in death or that has lasted or can be expected to last for a continuous period of not less than 12 months.

For the first year you claim the credit, you need a physician's certification of your disability. For later years, new certifications are generally not required.

Nonresident aliens. You may not claim the credit if you are a nonresident alien at any time during 2002, unless you are married to a citizen or resident and you have elected to be treated as a resident; *see 1.5.*

Amount of credit. The amount of the credit is 15% times the base amount after reductions. The base amount for the credit is generally $7,500, $5,000, or $3,750, as shown in *34.8.* The base amount is reduced by nontaxable Social Security and other tax-free pensions, as well as by adjusted gross income exceeding specific limits as explained in *34.9.*

How to claim the credit. You claim the credit on Schedule R if you file Form 1040. If you file Form 1040A, claim the credit on Part 3. You may not claim the credit on Form 1040EZ.

The credit is not refundable. That is, it is allowed only up to your tax liability. Follow the tax form instructions.

Married couples. A married couple may claim the credit only if they file a joint return. However, if a husband and wife live apart at all times during the taxable year and file separately, the credit may be claimed on a separate return.

34.8 Base Amount for the Elderly or Disabled Credit

The law specifies an initial base amount for figuring the credit. This base amount is reduced by certain tax-free benefits and excess adjusted gross income; *see 34.9.* The credit is 15% of the base amount after reductions.

The initial base amount is:

- $5,000, if you are single, head of household, or are a qualifying widow(er).
- $5,000, if you file a joint return and only one spouse is eligible for the credit.
- $7,500, if you file a joint return and both spouses are eligible for the credit. The credit is figured solely on this base; a separate computation is not made for each spouse.
- $3,750, if you are married and file a separate return. The credit may be claimed on a separate return only if you and your spouse have lived apart at all times during the year.

Base amount if disabled. If you are under age 65 and permanently and totally disabled, the base amount for figuring the credit is the *lower* of your 2002 taxable disability income or the initial base amount for your filing status shown above. For example, if you are single, under age 65, permanently and totally disabled, and received taxable disability income of $4,800, you figure the credit on $4,800, which is less than the base of $5,000 for single persons.

Joint return and both spouses qualify for the credit. If one spouse is age 65 or over and one spouse is under age 65 and receives disability income, the initial base amount is the lesser of (1) $7,500 or (2) $5,000 *plus* the disability income of the spouse under age 65. If both spouses are under age 65 and disabled, the initial base amount is the total of their disability income, not exceeding $7,500.

 Law Alert

Lack of Inflation Adjustment Weakens Credit

Since 1983, the base amounts *(34.8)* and AGI phase-out thresholds *(34.9)* for figuring the credit have remained the same. Without increases for inflation, the number of taxpayers able to claim the credit has steadily dropped. Legislation has been proposed in Congress to raise the limits to what they would have been had they been indexed for inflation all along, but the change has not yet been enacted.

34.9 Reduction of the Credit Base Amount for the Elderly and Disabled

The $3,750, $5,000, or $7,500 credit base amount *(34.8)* is reduced by nontaxable pensions and Social Security, and also by "excess" adjusted gross income, figured as follows:

Nontaxable Social Security and pensions. The base amount is reduced by:

- Social Security and Railroad Retirement benefits that are *not taxable* under the rules in *34.3*; *and*
- Tax-free pension, annuity, or disability income paid under a law administered by the Veterans Administration or under other federal laws.

You do *not* reduce the base amount for: military disability pensions received for active service in the Armed Forces or in the Coast Guard and Geodetic Survey or Public Health Service; certain disability annuities paid under the Foreign Service Act of 1980; and workers' compensation benefits. However, if Social Security benefits are reduced by workers' compensation benefits, the amount of workers' compensation benefits is treated as Social Security benefits that reduce the base.

Excess adjusted gross income. You reduce the base amount by one-half of adjusted gross income (AGI) exceeding: $7,500 if you are single, head of household, or a qualified widow(er); $10,000 if you are married filing a joint return; or $5,000 if you are married, live apart from your spouse for the entire year, and file a separate return. Applying these income floors, the credit is no longer available to a single person when AGI reaches $17,500, $20,000 on a joint return where one spouse is eligible for the credit, $25,000 on a joint return where both spouses are eligible for the credit, and $12,500 where a married person files separately.

EXAMPLES

1. John Andrews is 58 years old and single. In 1998, he retired on permanent and total disability. In 2002, he receives a taxable disability pension of $9,400, nontaxable Social Security disability benefits of $2,500, and taxable interest of $100. Adjusted gross income (AGI) is $9,500 ($9,400 + $100). His credit is $225.

Initial base amount *(34.8)*	$5,000
Less: nontaxable Social Security disability	2,500
Less: 50% of AGI over $7,500	
(50% of ($9,500 *minus* $7,500))	1,000
Credit base amount	$1,500
Credit (15% of credit base amount)	$225

2. William White, age 53, retired in 1992 on permanent and total disability. In 2002, he received a taxable disability pension of $6,000 and nontaxable Social Security disability benefits of $3,000. He files a joint return with his wife, Helen, age 49, who had wages of $9,200 and a taxable disability pension of $1,000 from a job from which she retired on account of permanent and total disability. Their adjusted gross income (AGI) for 2002 is $16,200 ($6,000 + $9,200 + $1,000). They may claim a credit of $135.

Initial base amount	
(Taxable disability income; *see 34.8*)	$7,000
Less: Nontaxable Social Security	3,000
Less: 50% of AGI over $10,000	
(50% of ($16,200 – $10,000)	3,100
Credit base amount	$900
Credit (15% of credit base amount)	$135

 Caution

Low Social Security Benefits Required for Credit

The tax credit for the elderly or disabled is not available to an unmarried individual who receives $5,000 or more of nontaxable Social Security benefits or nontaxable federal pensions such as from the Veterans Administration. The $5,000 limit also applies if you are married filing jointly and only one spouse qualifies for the credit. The limit is $7,500 if you file a joint return and both spouses qualify for the credit.

Continuing Care Communities

34.10 Tax Effects of Moving to a Continuing Care Facility

Senior citizens who move into "continuing care" or "life-care" facilities pay large upfront entrance fees upon admittance, as well as monthly fees thereafter in return for a residence, meals, and lifetime health care, including long-term skilled nursing care, should that become necessary. The payments raise several tax issues discussed in this section and in *34.11*.

Portion of monthly fees deductible as medical expense. Part of the monthly fees to a life-care community are allocable to health care, which you may deduct as an itemized medical expense subject to the 7.5% floor; *see 17.1*. Continuing care facilities generally send a statement to the residents specifying the portion of their monthly service fees that went towards health care.

Caution

Charitable Contribution Deductions
Payments made to a tax-exempt organization that operates a life-care community are generally not deductible charitable contributions because you are receiving services in exchange. If you donate amounts over and above your regular monthly fees and do not receive any extra benefit as a result, you may deduct the excess payment as a charitable contribution; *see 14.3.*

What about the upfront payments required by life-care communities? Part may be allowable as a medical expense deduction if you can prove what part of the lump sum is allocable to future medical coverage. The IRS recognizes that a deduction may be based on a showing that the life-care facility historically allocates a specified percentage of the fee to future medical care. With such proof there is a current obligation to pay and the allocable medical expenses are deductible when the lump sum is paid. The IRS has allowed deductions in the situations described in the Examples at the end of *17.11.*

Separate sponsorship gift. In one case, an individual was allowed by the Tax Court and an appeals court to claim a charitable contribution deduction for a "sponsorship gift" paid to a life-care retirement facility where she and her husband were residents. The sponsorship gift was entirely separate from her entrance fee; it was not required for admission and did not entitle her to reduced monthly payments. She did not receive any extra benefit from her gift and was not entitled to a refund of any part of it.

34.11 Imputed Interest on Refundable Entrance Fees

You must pay a lump-sum entrance fee when you enter a continuing care community. Depending on the type of plan, a portion of the lump-sum fee may be refundable either to you if you move from the community or to your heirs upon your death. The payment of the fee may also reduce your monthly charges.

These features may result in an unexpected tax liability under the imputed interest rules. Part of the refundable entrance fee is considered a "loan" to the continuing care facility, so that imputed interest income may be charged to you under the rules in *4.31.* According to Congressional committee reports, these loan rules do *not* apply, and thus the imputed interest rules do not apply, to limited refund plans, under which the entrance fee is refundable on a declining pro rata basis over a relatively short number of years.

In applying the imputed interest rules, the tax law distinguishes between qualified and nonqualified continuing care facilities. The tax treatment of nonqualified facilities is currently in a state of limbo. The IRS has delayed ruling on the tax treatment of entrance fees to nonqualified facilities so that the imputed interest rules will not be applied until the IRS releases regulations requiring tax and explaining how to compute the amount of imputed interest. The tax treatment of qualified facilities is specifically covered by law and is explained in the following paragraphs. Generally, qualified care facilities provide long-term nursing care if and when a resident becomes incapacitated. A nonqualified facility provides only limited short-term care, which may be as short as 30 days.

Qualified continuing care facilities. The "loan" portion of an entrance fee of a qualified continuing care facility is not subject to imputed interest unless it exceeds an annual floor. For 2002, refundable loans of up to $148,800 are exempt from the imputed interest rules provided that (1) you or your spouse were at least age 65 during the year and (2) the care facility provides a separate living unit, meals, maintenance, routine medical care, and, if it later becomes necessary, future long-term nursing care for no substantial additional charge. Incoming residents must not initially require long-term nursing care, but such care must be provided when it becomes necessary. A traditional nursing home is not a qualified continuing care facility. The $148,800 exception is subject to increases for inflation.

Since only the refundable portion of the fee is treated as a loan, the larger the payment or refund percentage is, the greater the potential imputed interest liability is. For example, in 2002, you and your spouse paid $180,000 for a two-bedroom apartment. If your guaranteed refund percentage is 75%, the imputed interest rules would not apply in 2002 because the "loan," or $135,000 (75% of $180,000), is below the $148,800 floor. However, if the refund percentage is 85%, the loan is $153,000 (85% of $180,000), and the $4,200 excess over the $148,800 floor is subject to imputed interest.

If imputed interest applies, the care facility should give you a Form 1099 indicating the taxable amount.

Chapter 35

Members of the Armed Forces and Victims and Survivors of Terrorist Attacks

Special tax benefits are provided to Armed Forces personnel. A major tax-free benefit is the combat pay exclusion. Under this exclusion, members of the Armed Forces, including active duty reservists, may exclude from gross income all compensation for active service received for any month in which they served in a combat zone or were hospitalized as a result of any wound, injury, or disease incurred while serving in a combat zone. Commissioned officers are allowed an exclusion equal to the highest rate of basic pay at the top pay level for enlisted personnel, plus any hostile fire/imminent danger pay received for the month.

Other pay benefits may be tax free, and you may be able to get filing extensions and time extensions for home residence replacements. A list of tax-free benefits may be found at *35.2*. Filing extensions are discussed at *35.5*.

By Executive Order, Afghanistan, including its airspace, was designated a combat zone beginning September 19, 2001. Military personnel in Pakistan, Tajikistan, Jordan, Uzbekistan, and Kyrgyzstan are also treated as serving in the combat zone, as they directly support the Afghanistan operations.

The Victims of Terrorism Tax Relief Act of 2001 provides relief to victims of the September 11 attacks, the anthrax attacks, and the 1995 Oklahoma City bombing. The legislation provides income tax exemptions, exclusions for qualifying death benefits, and estate tax relief.

35.1 Taxable Armed Forces Pay and Benefits

Armed Forces personnel report as taxable pay the following items:

- Basic pay for active duty, attendance at a designated service school, back wages, drills, reserve training, and training duty
- Special pay for aviation career incentives, diving duty, foreign duty (for serving outside the 48 contiguous states and the District of Columbia), hazardous duty, medical and dental officers, nuclear-qualified officers, and special duty assignments
- Enlistment and reenlistment bonuses
- Payments for accrued leave, and personal money allowances paid to high-ranking officers
- Scholarships, such as the Armed Forces Health Professions Scholarship Program (AFHPSP) and similar programs, granted after August 16, 1986
- Student loan repayment from programs such as the General Educational Loan Repayment Program

State income tax withholding. A state that makes a withholding agreement with the Secretary of the Treasury may subject members of the Armed Forces regularly stationed within that state to its payroll withholding provisions. National Guard members and reservists are not considered to be members of the Armed Forces for purposes of this section.

Where and when to file. Mail your return to the Internal Revenue Service Center for the place you are stationed. For example, you are stationed in Arizona but have a permanent home address in Missouri; you send your return to the Service Center for Arizona. For filing extensions on entering the service, *see 35.7.*

35.2 Tax-Free Armed Forces Benefits

The following benefits are *not* subject to tax:

- Combat pay; *see 35.4*
- Living allowances for BAH (Basic Allowance for Housing). You may deduct mortgage interest and real estate taxes on your home even if you pay these expenses with BAH funds.
- BAS (Basic Allowance for Subsistence) living allowances
- Housing and cost-of-living allowances abroad, whether paid by the U.S. Government or by a foreign government
- VHA (Variable Housing Allowance)
- Family allowances for educational expenses for dependents, emergencies, evacuation to a place of safety, and separation
- Death allowances for burial services, death gratuity payments to eligible survivors (not more than $3,000), and travel of dependents to burial site
- Dislocation allowance, intended to partially reimburse expenses such as lease forfeitures, temporary living charges in hotels, and other expenses incurred in relocating a household
- Temporary lodging expense allowance intended to partially offset the added living expenses of temporary lodging within the United States for up to 10 days and up to 60 days abroad
- A moving-in housing allowance, intended to defray costs, such as for rental agent fees, home-security improvements, and supplemental heating equipment, associated with occupying leased space outside the United States
- Travel allowances for annual round trip for dependent students, leave between consecutive overseas tours, reassignment in a dependent-restricted status, and transportation for you or your dependents during ship overhaul or inactivation
- Defense counseling payments
- ROTC educational and subsistence allowances
- Survivor and retirement protection plan premium payments
- Uniform allowances paid to officers and uniforms furnished to enlisted personnel
- Medical or hospital treatment provided by the United States in government hospitals
- Pay forfeited on order of a court martial
- Education, training, or subsistence allowances paid under any law administered by the Department of Veterans Affairs (VA). However, deductible education costs must be reduced by the VA allowance.
- Adjustments in pay to compensate for losses resulting from inflated foreign currency
- Payments to former prisoners of war from the U.S. Government in compensation for inhumane treatment suffered at the hands of an enemy government
- Benefits under Servicemembers' Group Life Insurance
- Dividends on GI insurance. These are a tax-free return of premiums paid.
- Interest on dividends left on deposit with the Department of Veterans Affairs (VA). The IRS has revoked a prior ruling that subjected such interest to tax.

!!Caution

Community Property

If you are married and your domicile (permanent home to which you intend to return) is in one of the following states, your military pay is subject to community property laws of that state: Arizona, California, Idaho, Louisiana, Nevada, New Mexico, Texas, Washington, and Wisconsin. *See 1.6* for community property reporting rules.

Disability retirement pay. Your disability retirement pay may be tax free if you are a former member of the Armed Forces of any country, the Foreign Service, the Coast Guard, the National Oceanic and Atmospheric Administration, or the Public Health Service. Tax-free treatment of disability retirement pay is retroactive to the date of the application for benefits.

35.3 Deductions for Armed Forces Personnel

Members of the Armed Forces may deduct the items listed below as miscellaneous itemized deductions subject to the 2% adjusted gross income (AGI) floor; *see 19.1*:

- Board and lodging costs over those paid to you by the government while on temporary duty away from your home base
- Costs of rank insignia, collar devices, gold braids, etc., and the cost of altering rank insignia when promoted or demoted
- Contributions to a "Company" fund made according to Service regulations. But personal contributions made to stimulate interest and morale in a unit are not deductible.
- Court martial legal expenses in successfully defending against the charge of conduct unbecoming an officer
- Dues to professional societies. But you may not deduct dues for officers' and noncommissioned officers' clubs.
- Expense of obtaining increased retirement pay
- Out-of-pocket moving expenses for service-connected moves. The 50-mile test and the 39-week test generally required to deduct moving expenses do not have to be met; *see 12.3*.
- Subscriptions to professional journals
- Transportation, food, and lodging expenses while on official travel status. But you are taxed on mileage and *per diem* subsistence allowance.
- Uniforms. The cost and cleaning of uniforms are deductible if: (1) they must be worn on duty; (2) they cannot under military regulations be worn off duty; and (3) the cost exceeds any tax-free clothing allowance.

Filing Tip

Away From Home Base
If your ship or squadron is away from your "home" port or base, you may be able to deduct travel expenses while away. However, you are not considered "away from home" if you are at your *permanent* duty station or you are a naval officer assigned to permanent duty aboard a ship; *see also 20.6.*

35.4 Tax-Free Pay for Service in Combat Zone or Hazardous Duty Area

If your grade is below commissioned officer and you serve in a designated combat zone or hazardous duty area during any part of a month, *all* of your qualifying military pay (*see* below) for that month is excluded from your taxable income. You may also exclude military pay earned during any part of a month that you are hospitalized as a result of wounds, disease, or injury incurred in a combat zone or hazardous duty area. The exclusion for military pay while hospitalized does not apply to any month that begins more than two years after the end of combat activities in that combat zone or hazardous duty area. Your hospitalization does not have to be in the combat zone or hazardous duty area.

Officers. If you are a commissioned officer, you may exclude up to the highest rate of basic pay at the highest pay grade that enlisted personnel receive per month plus any hostile fire/imminent danger pay received for each month during any part of which you served in a combat zone or hazardous duty area.

If you are a commissioned warrant officer, you are considered an enlisted person.

What is included as tax-free pay? The following military pay qualifies for tax-free treatment: (1) active duty pay earned in any month you served in a combat zone or hazardous duty area; (2) a dislocation allowance if the move begins or ends in a month you served in a combat zone or hazardous duty area; (3) a reenlistment bonus if the voluntary extension or reenlistment occurs in a month you served in a combat zone or hazardous duty area; (4) pay for accrued leave earned in any month you served in a combat zone or hazardous duty area (the Department of Defense must determine that the unused leave was earned during that period); (5) pay received for duties as a member of the Armed Forces in clubs, messes, post and station theaters, and other nonappropriated fund activities. The pay must be earned in a month you served in a combat zone or hazardous duty area; and (6) awards for suggestions, inventions, or scientific achievements you are entitled to because of a submission you made in a month you served in a combat zone or hazardous duty area.

Service in the combat zone or hazardous duty area includes any periods you are absent from duty because of sickness, wounds, or leave. If, as a result of serving in a combat zone, you become a prisoner of war or missing in action, you are considered to be serving in the combat zone as long as you keep that status for military pay purposes.

Filing Tip

Who Qualifies for Exclusion?
Members of the U.S. Armed Forces qualifying for the exclusion include commissioned officers and enlisted personnel in all regular and reserve units under control of the Secretaries of Defense, Army, Navy, and Air Force, and the Coast Guard. Members of the U.S. Merchant Marines or the American Red Cross are not included.

Filing Tip

Reservist Insurance Payments Taxed
Insurance payments made to reservists by the Ready Reserve Mobilization Income Insurance Program (RRMIIP) are taxable as gross income. The payments are not excludable as combat pay because they are intended to replace lost civilian income. However, payments representing premium contributions to the fund are excluded from the reservist's income. The benefits received in excess of the contributed premiums are taxable.

Retirement pay and pensions do not qualify for the combat zone exclusion. According to a recent Fourth Circuit Court of Appeals decision, a Navy severance pay package was taxable although the recipient became entitled to the payment while on active duty in the Persian Gulf. The court differentiated the package, which was provided in order to entice the man to leave the service, from a reenlistment bonus provided as compensation for active service.

Combat zones and hazardous duty areas. A combat zone is any area the President of the United States designates by Executive Order as an area in which the U.S. Armed Forces are or have engaged in combat. An area becomes and ceases to be a combat zone on the dates designated by the President.

Afghanistan, including the airspace above, was designated a combat zone beginning September 19, 2001. Service in Jordan and Pakistan on or after September 19, 2001, and service in Kyrgyzstan and Uzbekistan on or after October 1, 2001, is considered to be in direct support of the Afghanistan operations and therefore treated as in the combat zone.

Effective March 24, 1999, the Balkan area was designated a combat zone including: the Federal Republic of Yugoslavia (Serbia/Montenegro), Albania, the Ionian Sea north of the 39th parallel, and the Adriatic Sea. Airspace above these areas is also part of the zone. As of November 21, 1995, a special law designated Bosnia and Herzegovina, Croatia, and Macedonia as a qualified hazardous duty area.

The following locations (including airspace) were designated as combat zones beginning January 17, 1991: the total land areas of Iraq, Kuwait, Saudi Arabia, Oman, Bahrain, Qatar, and the United Arab Emirates; the Persian Gulf; the Red Sea; the Gulf of Oman; the part of the Arabian Sea that is north of 10 degrees north latitude and west of 68 degrees east longitude; and the Gulf of Aden.

At the time this book went to press, the above designations were still in place. For any changes, *see* IRS Publication 3 and tax form instructions.

Qualifying service outside combat zone or hazardous duty area. Military service outside a combat zone or hazardous duty area is considered to be performed in a combat zone or hazardous duty area if: (1) the service is in direct support of military operations in the combat zone or hazardous duty area, and (2) the service qualifies you for special military pay for duty subject to hostile fire or imminent danger. Military pay received for this service will qualify for the pay exclusion if the other requirements are met. As mentioned above, service in Pakistan, Jordan, Tajikistan, Uzbekistan, and Kyrgyzstan meets these tests as supportive of the operations in Afghanistan.

Nonqualifying service. The following military service does not qualify as service in a combat zone or hazardous duty area: (1) presence in a combat zone while on leave from a duty station located outside the combat zone; (2) passage over or through a combat zone during a trip between two points that are outside a combat zone; and (3) presence in a combat zone solely for your personal convenience. Such service will not qualify you for the pay exclusion.

Hospitalized while serving in a combat zone or hazardous duty area. If you are hospitalized while serving in a combat zone or hazardous duty area for a wound, disease, or injury, it will be presumed to have been incurred while serving in the combat zone or hazardous duty area unless there is clear evidence to the contrary.

EXAMPLES

1. You are hospitalized for a specific disease after serving in a combat zone for three weeks, and the disease for which you are hospitalized has an incubation period of two to four weeks. The disease is presumed to have been incurred while you were serving in the combat zone. On the other hand, if the incubation period of the disease is one year, the disease would not have been incurred while you were serving in the combat zone.

2. You were hospitalized for a specific disease three weeks after you left the combat zone. The incubation period of the disease is from two to four weeks. The disease is considered to have been incurred while serving in the combat zone.

Form W-2. The wages shown in Box 1 of your Form W-2 should not include combat pay. Retirement pay is not combat pay.

35.5 Tax Deadlines Extended for Combat Zone or Hazardous Duty Area Service

You are allowed an extension of at least 180 days (*see* below) to take care of tax matters if you are a member of the Armed Forces who served in a combat zone or hazardous duty area. The extension applies to filing tax returns, paying taxes, filing a Tax Court petition, filing refund claims, and making an IRA contribution (*see* IRS Publication 3 for details). The time allowed for the IRS to begin an audit or take collection actions is also extended.

Support personnel. The deadline extension also applies if you are serving in a combat zone or hazardous duty area in support of the Armed Forces. This includes Red Cross personnel, accredited correspondents, and civilian personnel acting under the direction of the Armed Forces in support of those forces.

Members of the Armed Forces and civilian employees of the Defense Department who perform services outside the United States on or after March 24,1999, as part of Operation Allied Force qualify for the deadline extensions even if they serve outside the combat zone (Federal Republic of Yugoslavia, Albania, Adriatic Sea, Ionian Sea above the 39th parallel) so long as they are deployed away from their permanent duty station. Civilian employees of defense contractors who produce equipment for Operation Allied Force do not qualify for the deadline extensions unless they are serving in the combat zone in support of the U.S. Armed Forces.

Extension is a minimum of 180 days. Your deadline for taking actions with the IRS is extended for at least 180 days after the later of: (1) the last day you are in a combat zone or hazardous duty area (or the last day it qualifies as a combat zone or hazardous duty area), or (2) the last day of any continuous qualified hospitalization for injury from service in the combat zone or hazardous duty area. Hospitalization may be outside the United States, or up to five years of hospitalization in the United States.

Time in a missing status (missing in action or prisoner of war) counts as time in a combat zone or hazardous duty area.

In addition to the 180 days, a filing deadline is also extended by the number of days you had left to file with the IRS when you entered a combat zone or hazardous duty area. If you entered the combat zone or hazardous duty area before the time to file began, the deadline is extended by the entire filing time.

35.6 Tax Forgiveness for Combat Zone or Hazardous Duty Area Deaths

If a member of the Armed Forces is killed in a combat zone or hazardous duty area or dies from wounds or disease incurred while in these zones or areas, any income tax liability for the year of death or any earlier year including service in such zones or areas is waived. In addition, the service member's estate is entitled to a refund for income tax paid while serving there.

If a member of the Armed Forces was a resident of a community property state and his or her spouse reported half of the military pay on a separate return, the spouse may get a refund of taxes paid on his or her share of the combat zone or hazardous duty area pay.

Forgiveness benefits apply to an Armed Forces member serving outside the zone or area if service: (1) was in direct support of military operations there, and (2) qualified the member for special military pay for duty subject to hostile fire or imminent danger.

Missing status. The date of death for a member of the Armed Forces who was in a missing status (missing in action or prisoner of war) is the date his or her name is removed from missing status for military pay purposes. This is true even if death occurred earlier.

How tax forgiveness is claimed. If the individual died in a combat zone or in a terroristic or military action, you file as the individual's representative: (1) Form 1040 if a U.S. individual income tax return (Form 1040, 1040A, or 1040EZ) has not been filed for the tax year. Form W-2, Wage and Tax Statement, must accompany the return. (2) Form 1040X if a U.S. individual income tax return has been filed. A separate Form 1040X must be filed for each year in question.

IRS Alert

Combat Zone E-mail Address

The IRS has established an e-mail address, combatzone@irs.gov, for military personnel to ask questions about filing returns, paying taxes, and combat zone status. Responses to general questions will be communicated via e-mail. However, answers to questions that reference an individual's account information will be mailed to the last address of record; such information cannot be provided over the Internet.

Caution

Tax Forgiveness

Tax forgiveness does *not* apply to a U.S. civilian or military employee who dies as a result of an accident or a training exercise. Abatement also does not apply to terroristic action within the United States. However, abatement does apply if the individual dies in the U.S. from a wound or injury incurred in a terroristic or military action outside the United States.

Law Alert

Reduced Estate Tax Rate Schedule

Reduced estate tax rates apply to the estates of Armed Forces members (U.S. citizens or residents) who are killed in action while serving in a combat zone. The rates are in the instructions to Form 706. The tax determined using the rates is offset by generally applicable estate tax credits.

Check with your local IRS office for the address of the IRS office to which the return is filed.

An attachment should accompany any return or claim and should include a computation of the decedent's tax liability before any amount is forgiven and the amount that is to be forgiven.

The following documents must also accompany all returns and claims for refund: (1) Form 1310, Statement of Person Claiming Refund Due a Deceased Taxpayer; and (2) a certification from the Department of Defense. Department of State certification is required if the decedent was a civilian employee of an agency other than the Department of Defense.

Tax forgiveness for civilian or military personnel killed in terroristic or military action. Tax liability is waived for civilian or military U.S. government employees killed in terroristic or military actions outside the U.S., even if the President has not designated the area as a combat zone and it is not a hazardous duty area. Tax liability is waived for the period beginning with the taxable year before the year in which the injuries were incurred and ending with the year of death. Refund claims for prior years must generally be filed on Form 1040X by the later of three years from the time the original return was filed or two years from the time the tax was paid. However, if death occurred in a combat zone, the filing period is extended by the time served in the combat zone, plus the period of continuous hospitalization outside the U.S., plus an additional 180 days. The individual must also be a U.S. government employee both on the date of injury and date of death.

Determination of death for Vietnam MIAs. Under prior law, MIAs were generally presumed dead as of December 31, 1982. Under current law, the date of death of service members missing in action in Vietnam is the date determined by the Armed Forces. Thus, under current law, tax abatement may be available for years after 1982. Furthermore, the date of death, as determined by the Armed Forces, also applies for such rules as whether to file as a surviving spouse, and for postponing the due date for filing returns and paying taxes.

35.7 Extension To Pay Your Tax When Entering the Service

If you are unable to pay your tax when you enter the Armed Forces, you may get an extension until six months after your initial period of service ends. Get a form at the IRS office of your District Director or write a letter to the District Director or to the IRS office requesting payment (your spouse or parent may do it for you). An extension, without interest, may be given if your income dropped after entering the military *and* you actually apply for the extension.

The extension does not cover your spouse, who must file a separate return and pay the tax due. But you and your spouse may file a joint return before the postponement period expires even though your spouse filed a separate return for that particular year. No interest is charged on this postponement of your tax.

Automatic extension of time to file your return. If you are on duty outside the U.S. or Puerto Rico on April 15, 2003, you get an automatic two-month extension to file your 2002 return; *see* page 6.

Interest charged on back taxes. If you do not show hardship qualifying you for the above interest-free payment extension, the IRS may reduce its interest rate on the deficiency. The maximum interest rate the IRS may charge for taxes incurred prior to your entry into active service is 6%. This reduced rate applies only to the period of your active duty.

35.8 Tax Information for Reservists

Transportation costs to reservist meetings generally are not deductible. A possible exception is the cost of traveling from your regular job location to a meeting held on a regular workday or traveling from home to a meeting outside the metropolitan area where you live and normally work. The cost would be deductible, subject to the 2% adjusted gross income (AGI) floor for miscellaneous itemized deductions; *see 19.1.*

If you travel overnight away from your tax home *(20.6)* to a meeting or training camp, you may deduct expenses for transportation, lodging, and meals subject to the 50% reduction, but the deduction is subject to the 2% AGI floor for miscellaneous itemized deductions.

Filing Tip

Uniform Costs of Reservists

The cost and upkeep of uniforms is deductible only if you are prohibited from wearing them when off duty; *see 19.6.* A deduction allowed under this test must be reduced by any uniform allowance you receive, and the unreimbursed cost is subject to the 2% adjusted gross income (AGI) floor for miscellaneous itemized deductions.

Law Alert

Overnight Travel to National Guard and Reserve Meetings

Legislation has been proposed to allow National Guard and Reserve members to claim an above-the-line deduction from gross income for overnight travel costs, including meals and lodging, when attending Guard or Reserve meetings. The *Supplement* will report further developments.

If you are called for active duty away from your tax home, you may deduct travel expenses provided you keep your regular job while on active duty, return to it after you are released, and pay for those expenses at the military post. To the extent they exceed BAH (housing) and BAS (subsistence) allowances, the expenses are deductible only as a miscellaneous itemized deduction subject to the 2% AGI floor.

Deferring tax payments and reduction of IRS interest rate. If you owed a tax deficiency to the IRS before being called to active duty, the IRS may defer payment, without interest, if your ability to pay has been severely impaired by your call-up; *see 35.7.* If you are not allowed a deferment, the IRS will reduce its interest charge to 6% on the taxes you owed before your call-up.

35.9 Tax Relief for Victims and Survivors of Terrorist Attacks

The Victims of Terrorism Tax Relief Act of 2001, signed into law on January 23, 2002, provides income and estate tax relief to victims and survivors of the September 11 attacks, anthrax attacks occurring from September 11 through the end of 2001, and the 1995 Oklahoma City bombing. Specific information regarding the law and procedures for claiming the benefits can be found in IRS Publication 3920, Tax Relief for Victims of Terrorist Attacks.

Income tax waived for those killed. The income tax waiver for those killed in 2001 applies to tax year 2000 as well as 2001. Surviving spouses and executors have until April 15, 2004, to file an amended return for 2000. The waiver for 2001 is claimed on the 2001 income tax return filed for the decedent. Surviving spouses and executors of those killed in the Oklahoma City bombing have until January 22, 2003, to file amended returns for tax years 1994 and 1995.

The exemption applies to income tax (but not self-employment tax) for the year of death and at least one year prior. If the victim dies after the year of injury, three or more years may be covered, as the exemption period begins with the taxable year before the year in which the injury occurred. The minimum relief for all years is $10,000. If the decedent's total forgiven income tax liability for all eligible years is less than $10,000, the difference between $10,000 and the total forgiven tax liability for those years will be treated as a tax payment made by the decedent for the decedent's last tax year and refunded by the IRS to the estate. If both spouses died, the estate of each is eligible for the minimum $10,000 benefit; where only one spouse perished, only the decedent's part of the joint income tax liability is eligible for forgiveness.

Estate tax reduction. An alternative reduced rate table is provided in the Form 706 instructions for the estates of the terrorist attack victims. The estate tax is determined under the alternative reduced rate table and is offset by the regular unified credit and state death tax credit. The alternative table applies unless the executor specifically elects not to apply it.

Estates of the victims of the Oklahoma City bombing may refigure any estate tax due under the alternative table and claim a refund for the difference by January 23, 2003.

Tax-free payments to survivors. Certain types of relief payments can be excluded from income:

- September 11th Victim Compensation Fund of 2001
- Qualified disaster relief payments
- Payments from charitable organizations
- Disability payments from employers
- Death benefits from employers
- Cancelled debts
- Qualified payments to survivors of public safety officers
  See IRS Publication 3920 for further details.

Chapter 36

How To Treat Foreign Earned Income

There is a tax incentive for working abroad—in 2002 up to $80,000 of income earned abroad may escape U.S. income taxes and you may be entitled to an exclusion or deduction for certain housing costs. In measuring the economic value of this tax savings, consider the extra cost of living abroad. In some areas, the high cost of living and currency exchange rates will erode your tax savings.

The exclusion does not apply to investment income or to any other earned income that does not meet the exclusion tests.

To claim a foreign income exclusion you must satisfy a foreign residence or physical presence test (36.5).

Employees of the U.S. government may not claim an exclusion based on the government pay earned abroad.

36.1 Claiming the Foreign Earned Income Exclusion

In 2002 you may exclude up to $80,000 of foreign earned income. You must file a U.S. return if your gross income *exceeds* the filing threshold for your personal status, even though all or part of your foreign earned income may be tax free. The exclusion is not automatic; you must elect it. You elect the foreign earned income exclusion on Form 2555, which you attach to Form 1040. The housing cost exclusion *(36.4)* is also elected on Form 2555.

You may file simplified Form 2555-EZ if your 2002 foreign wages are $80,000 or less, you do not have self-employment income, and you do not claim the foreign housing exclusion, housing deduction, business, or moving expenses.

A separate exclusion is allowed for the value of meals and lodging received by employees living in qualified camps; *see 36.8.*

If you claim the foreign income exclusion of $80,000, you may not:
- Claim business deductions allocable to the excluded income;
- Make a deductible traditional IRA or Roth IRA contribution based on the excluded income; *or*
- Claim foreign taxes paid on excluded income as a credit or deduction.

In deciding whether to claim the exclusion, compare the overall tax (1) with the exclusion and (2) without the exclusion but with the full foreign tax credit and allocable deductions. Choose whichever gives you the lower tax; *see 36.3 and 36.6.*

Once you elect the exclusion, that election remains in effect for all future years unless you revoke it. If you revoke the election, you cannot elect the exclusion again during the next five years without IRS consent. A revocation is made in a statement attached to your return for the year you want it to take effect. The foreign earned income exclusion and the housing cost exclusion must be revoked separately.

Reinstating the exclusion. The IRS may consent to a reinstatement of the exclusion following a revocation under the following circumstances: you return for a period of time to the United States, you move to another foreign country with different tax rates, you change employers, or there has been substantial change in the tax law of the foreign country of residence or physical presence.

> **EXAMPLE**
>
> A U.S. citizen living abroad asked the IRS if the declaration of a tax holiday by a foreign country in 2000 was a substantial change of law. Prior to 1997, while working abroad he had claimed the foreign income exclusion. But in 1997 and 1998, he revoked the election and claimed a foreign tax credit for taxes paid on his foreign earnings. In 2000, he wanted to resume claiming the income exclusion due to the declaration of a tax holiday in the country in which he was employed. The IRS ruled that he can claim the exclusion. The declaration of a tax holiday is considered a substantial change of law because he went from being taxed to being exempt from tax.

36.2 What Is Foreign Earned Income?

Earned income includes salaries, wages, commissions, professional fees, and bonuses. Earned income also includes allowances from your employer for housing or other expenses, as well as the value of housing or a car provided by the employer. It may also include business profits, royalties, and rents, provided this income is tied to the performance of services. Earned income does not include pension or annuity income, payments for nonqualified employee trusts or nonqualified annuities, dividends, interest, capital gains, gambling winnings, alimony, or the value of tax-free meals or lodging under the rules at *3.11.* Foreign earned income does not include amounts earned in countries subject to U.S. government travel restrictions.

Foreign earned income eligible for the exclusion must be received no later than the taxable year after the year in which you perform the services. Pay is excludable in the year of receipt if you did not use the full exclusion in the year of the services.

U.S. government pay ineligible. If you are an employee of the U.S. government or its agencies, you may *not* exclude any part of your pay from your government employer. Courts have agreed with the IRS that U.S. government workers were U.S. employees even though they were paid from sources other than Congressionally appropriated funds. If you are not an employee of the U.S. government or any of its agencies, your pay is excludable even if paid by a government source. You are not an employee of the U.S. government if you work under a contract made between your employer and the government.

 Caution

Claiming Foreign Tax Credit Revokes Prior Election

If you have been claiming the exclusion and decide that it would be advantageous this year to forego the exclusion and instead claim the foreign tax credit for foreign earned income, be aware that claiming the credit is treated by the IRS as a revocation of the prior exclusion election. You may not claim an exclusion for the next five years unless the IRS allows you to re-elect the exclusion.

Claiming a foreign tax credit also may revoke a prior election to claim the housing cost exclusion. Depending on the foreign earned income in the year the credit is claimed, the credit may be considered a revocation of a prior earned income exclusion election and also a prior housing cost exclusion election, or as a revocation of only one of the elections.

A good faith error in calculating foreign earned income that leads to claiming a foreign credit will not be treated as a revocation of prior elections.

Under a special law, tax liability is waived for a civilian or military employee of the U.S. government killed in a military action overseas; *see 35.6.*

Profits from sole proprietorship or partnership. If your business consists solely of services (no capital investment), 100% of gross income is considered earned income. If services and capital are both income-producing factors, no more than 30% of your net profit may be considered earned income.

If you do not contribute any services to a business (for example, you are a "silent partner"), your share of the net profits is *not* earned income.

> **EXAMPLES**
> 1. A U.S. citizen resides in England. He invests in an English partnership that sells manufactured goods outside the U.S. He performs no services for the business. His share of net profits does not qualify as earned income.
> 2. Same facts as in Example 1, except he devotes his full time to the partnership business. Then up to 30% of his share of the net profits may qualify as earned income. Thus, if his share of profits is $50,000, earned income is $15,000 (30% of $50,000), assuming the value of his services is at least $15,000.
> 3. You and another person are consultants, operating as a partnership in Europe. Since capital is not an income-producing element, the entire gross income of the business is earned income.

The partnership agreement generally determines the tax status of partnership income in a U.S. partnership with a foreign branch. Thus, if the partnership agreement allocates foreign earnings to partners abroad, the allocation will be recognized unless it lacks substantial economic effect.

Fringe benefits. The value of fringe benefits, such as the right to use company property and facilities, is added to your compensation when figuring the amount of your earned income.

Royalties. Royalties from articles or books are earned income if you receive them for transferring all of your rights to your work, or you have contracted to write the articles or book for an amount in cash plus a royalty on sales.

Royalties from the leasing of oil and mineral lands and from patents are not earned income.

Reimbursement of employee expenses. Do not include reimbursement of expenses as earned income to the extent they equal expenses that you adequately accounted for to your employer; *see 20.31.* If your expenses exceed reimbursements, the excess is allocated according to the rules in *36.6.* If reimbursements exceed expenses, the excess is treated as earned income.

Straight commission salespersons or other employees who arrange with their employers, for withholding purposes, to consider a percentage of their commissions as attributable to their expenses treat such amounts as earned income.

Reimbursed moving expenses. Reimbursements of moving expenses are not reported as income if you adequately account to your employer for the expenses; *see 12.8.*

A reimbursement is taxable if received under a non-accountable plan or for moving expenses that are not deductible *(12.3)* or that you deducted in an earlier year. However, for purposes of claiming the earned income exclusion, the reimbursement may be considered to have been earned in a year other than the year of receipt. This is important because an exclusion is allowed only for the year income is earned. If the move is from the U.S. to a foreign country, the reimbursement is considered foreign earned income in the year of the move if you qualify under the foreign residence or physical presence test for at least 120 days during that tax year. Reimbursement of moving expenses from one foreign country to another is considered foreign earned income in the year of the move, if you qualify under the residency or physical presence test at the new location for at least 120 days during the tax year. If you do not meet one of these tests in the year of the move, the reimbursements are earned income that must be allocated between the year of the move and the following tax year.

A taxable reimbursement for a move back to the U.S. is considered income from U.S. sources if you continue to work for the same employer. If you move back to the U.S. and take a job with a new employer *or* if you retire and move back to the U.S. and your old employer reimburses your moving expenses under a prior written agreement or company policy, the reimbursement is con-

Caution

Rental Income

Rental income is generally not earned income. However, if you perform personal services, for example as an owner-manager of a hotel or rooming house in a foreign country, then up to 30% of your net rents may be earned income.

sidered to be for past services in the foreign country and qualifies as foreign earned income eligible for the exclusion. The reimbursement is considered earned in the year of the move if you qualified under the residency or physical presence test *(36.5)* for at least 120 days during the tax year. Otherwise, the reimbursement is allocated between the year of the move and the year preceding the move. *See* IRS Publication 54 for details.

36.3 Qualifying for the Foreign Earned Income Exclusion

You may elect the exclusion for foreign earned income only if your tax home is in a foreign country *and* you meet either the foreign residence test *or* the foreign physical presence test of 330 days. The tests are discussed at *36.5.* Tax home is discussed at *20.6–20.8.* If your tax home is in the U.S., you may not claim the exclusion but may claim the foreign tax credit and your living expenses while away from home if you meet the rules at *20.9* for temporary assignments that are expected to last, and actually do last, for one year or less. U.S. government employees may not claim either the earned income exclusion or housing exclusion based on government pay.

Exclusion prorated on a daily basis. If you qualify under the foreign residence or physical presence test for only part of 2002, the $80,000 exclusion limit is reduced on a daily basis.

EXAMPLES

1. You were a resident of France from February 20, 2000, until June 30, 2002. On July 1 you returned to the U.S. Since your period of foreign residency included all of 2001, thereby satisfying the foreign residence test, you may claim a prorated exclusion for 2002. As you were abroad for 181 of the 365 days in 2002, you exclude earnings up to $39,672, or $181/365$ of the $80,000 maximum exclusion. If you earned more than $39,672 from January through June 2002, the exclusion is limited to $39,672.

2. You worked in France from June 1, 2001, through September 30, 2002. Your only days outside France were a 15-day vacation to the U.S. in December 2001. You do not qualify for an exclusion under the foreign residence test because you were not abroad for a full taxable year; you were not abroad for either the full year of 2001 or 2002. However, you do qualify under the physical presence test; you were physically present abroad for at least 330 full days during a 12-month period. The 12-month period giving you the largest 2002 exclusion is the 12-month period starting October 21, 2001, and ending October 20, 2002. *See 36.5* for figuring the 12-month period. Since you were abroad for at least 330 full days during that 12-month period, you may claim an exclusion. In 2002, you were abroad for 293 days within the 12-month period (January 1 to October 20, 2002, is 293 days). Thus, you exclude earnings up to $293/365$ of the maximum exclusion. If your earnings in France for 2002 were $80,000, your exclusion is limited to $64,219 ($80,000 × $293/365$).

 Caution

Countries Subject to Travel Restrictions
You may not claim the foreign earned income exclusion, or the housing exclusion or deduction, if you work in a country subject to U.S. government travel restrictions. You are not treated as a bona fide resident of, or as present in, a country subject to the travel ban. Libya, Cuba, and Iraq are within this ban. Check Form 2555 for changes to this list.

If you are married and you and your spouse each have foreign earned income and meet the foreign residence or physical presence test, you may each claim a separate exclusion. If your permanent home is in a community property state, your earned income is not considered community property for purposes of the exclusion.

Foreign earnings from a prior year. Foreign income earned in a prior year but paid in 2001 does not qualify for the 2002 exclusion. However, if the income was attributable to foreign services performed in 2001, the pay is tax free in 2002 to the extent that you did not use the full 2001 exclusion of $78,000. Under another exception, payments received in 2002 for 2001 services are treated as 2002 income if the payment was within a normal payroll period of 16 days or less that included the last day of 2001. If the services were performed before 2001, no exclusion is available to shelter the pay.

Income for services performed in the U.S. does not qualify for the exclusion, even though it is paid to you while you are abroad.

Foreign tax credit. Foreign taxes paid on tax-free foreign earned income do not qualify for a credit or deduction. But if your foreign pay for 2002 exceeds $80,000, you may claim a foreign tax credit or deduction for the foreign taxes allocated to taxable income. The instructions to Forms 2555 and 1116 and IRS Publication 514 provide details for making the computation.

36.4 How To Treat Housing Costs

The housing costs of employees and self-employed persons are treated differently by the tax law. Employees get a housing exclusion; self-employed persons get a deduction from *taxable* foreign earned income. If you live in a special camp provided by your employer, all housing costs are excluded; *see 36.8*.

Exclusion for employer-financed housing costs. If you qualify for the exclusion for all of 2002 and your foreign wage or salary income plus the value of employer-financed housing costs in 2002 does not exceed $80,000, both parts of your pay package are tax free. Your housing costs are considered to be employer-financed as long as they are covered by salary, employer reimbursements, a housing allowance, or if they are paid directly by your employer. If wages plus employer-financed housing exceed $80,000, a special housing exclusion elected on Form 2555 will shelter part of your housing costs from tax. The housing exclusion is the difference between the employer's payment of reasonable housing expenses and a "base housing amount." The base housing amount is 16% of the salary for a U.S. government employee at the GS-14, Step 1 level as of the beginning of the year. If you qualify under the foreign residence or physical presence test for only part of 2002, your base amount is $29.70 for each qualifying day. If you qualify for the entire year, the base amount is $10,842; *see* Line 30 of Form 2555. Employer-financed housing payments exceeding this housing cost exclusion may also escape tax if your foreign salary is below the maximum foreign earned income exclusion. Your foreign earned income exclusion is limited to your foreign earned income minus your housing cost exclusion; *see* Example 1 below.

EXAMPLES

(Assume qualification for full-year exclusion)

1. In 2002, your salary for work abroad is $57,207 and your employer pays $14,492 for your housing. On Form 2555, you list $71,699 (salary *plus* housing) as your foreign earned income. Assume that the housing cost exclusion is $3,650 (housing costs of $14,492 exceeding a base housing amount of $10,842). Your earned income exclusion is $68,049: $71,699 earned income less $3,650 housing exclusion.

2. In 2002, you earn a salary of $60,108 abroad and your employer pays $14,492 for your housing. Assume the housing exclusion is $3,650 (housing costs of $14,492 exceeding a base housing amount of $10,842). All of your salary plus the full amount of the housing costs avoids tax: the housing cost exclusion of $3,650 and an earned income exclusion of $70,950 ($74,600 foreign earned income less $3,650 housing exclusion).

3. Same as Example 2 above, except that you earn $71,019. Foreign earned income is $85,511 ($71,019 *plus* $14,492), but the total amount of income not subject to tax is $83,650. The total tax-free amount is made up of the housing cost exclusion of $3,650 and the maximum foreign earned income exclusion of $80,000.

Reasonable housing expenses. Include rent, utilities other than telephone costs, insurance, parking, furniture rentals, and repairs for yourself, your spouse, and dependents living with you. The following expenses do not qualify: cost of purchasing a home, furniture, or accessories; home improvements; payments of mortgage principal; domestic labor; and depreciation on a home or on improvements to leased housing. Furthermore, interest and taxes that are otherwise deductible do not qualify for the exclusion.

You may include the costs of a separate household that you maintain outside the U.S. for your spouse and dependents because living conditions at your foreign home are adverse.

Self-employed persons. On Form 2555, self-employed individuals may claim a limited deduction for housing costs exceeding the base housing amount. You may claim this deduction only to the extent it offsets taxable foreign earned income. The deduction is claimed as an "adjustment to income" on Line 34 of Form 1040, even if you do not itemize deductions.

Where you may not deduct expenses because you do not have taxable foreign earned income, expenses may be carried forward one year and deducted in the next year to the extent of taxable foreign earned income.

If you are an employee and self-employed during the same year. Housing expenses above the base amount are partly excludable and partly deductible. For example, if half of your foreign earned income is from services as an employee, half of the excess housing expenses over the base amount are excludable. The remaining excess housing costs are deductible to the extent of taxable foreign earned income. Follow the instructions to Form 2555.

Countries ineligible for tax benefits. Housing expenses incurred in a country subject to a U.S. government travel restriction are not eligible for the tax benefits explained in this section. *See* Form 2555 instructions for a list of countries to which travel restrictions apply.

36.5 Meeting the Foreign Residence or Physical Presence Test

To qualify for the foreign earned income exclusion, you must be either a U.S. citizen (or U.S. resident entitled to tax treaty benefits) meeting the foreign residence test or a U.S. citizen or resident meeting the physical presence test in a foreign country. The following areas are not considered foreign countries: Puerto Rico, Virgin Islands, Guam, Commonwealth of the Northern Mariana Islands, American Samoa, or the Antarctic region.

Waiver of time test. If war or civil unrest prevented you from meeting the foreign residence or physical presence test, you may claim the exclusion for the period you actually were a resident or physically present abroad. Foreign locations and the time periods that qualify for the waiver of the residency and physical presence tests are listed in the instructions to Form 2555.

If, by the due date of your 2002 return (April 15, 2003), you have not yet satisfied the foreign residence or physical presence test, but you expect to meet either test after the filing date, you may either file on the due date and report your earnings or ask for a filing extension under the rules at *36.7*.

Foreign residence test. You must be a U.S. citizen who is a bona fide resident of a foreign country for an uninterrupted period that includes one full tax year; a full tax year is from January 1 through December 31 for individuals who file on a calendar-year basis. Business or vacation trips to the U.S. or another country will not disqualify you from satisfying the foreign residence test. If you are abroad more than one year but less than two, the entire period qualifies if it includes one full tax year.

EXAMPLE
You are a bona fide foreign resident from September 30, 2001, to March 25, 2003. The period includes your entire 2002 tax year. Therefore, up to $80,000 of your 2002 earnings is excludable. Your overseas earnings in 2001 and 2003 qualify for a proportionate part of the exclusion of $78,000 allowed for 2001 and $80,000 allowed for 2003.

To prove you are a foreign resident, you must show your intention to be a resident of the foreign country. Evidence tending to confirm your intention to stay in a foreign country includes: (1) your family accompanies you; (2) you buy a house or rent an apartment rather than a hotel room; (3) you participate in the foreign community activities; (4) you can speak the foreign language; (5) you have a permanent foreign address; (6) you join clubs there; or (7) you open charge accounts in stores in the foreign country.

You will not qualify if you take inconsistent positions toward your foreign residency. That is, you will *not* be treated as a bona fide resident of a foreign country if you have earned income from sources within that country, filed a statement with the authorities of that country that you are not a resident there, and have been held not subject to the income tax of that country. However, this rule does not prevent you from qualifying under the physical presence test.

If you cannot prove that you are a resident, check to determine if your stay qualifies under the physical presence test.

Physical presence test. To qualify under this test, you must show you were on foreign soil 330 days (about 11 months) during a 12-month period. Whether you were a resident or a transient is of no importance. You have to show you were physically present in a foreign country or countries for 330 full days during any 12-consecutive-month period. The 330 qualifying days do not have to be consecutive. The 12-month period may begin with any day. There is no requirement that it begin with your first full day abroad. It may begin before or after arrival in a foreign country and may end before or after departure from a foreign country. A *full* day is from midnight to midnight (24 consecutive hours). You must spend each of the 330 days on foreign soil. In departing from U.S. soil to go directly to the foreign country, or in returning directly to the U.S. from a foreign country, the time you spend on or over international waters does not count toward the 330-day total.

 Caution

Residence or Domicile?
Residence does not have the same meaning as *domicile*. Your domicile is a permanent place of abode; it is the place to which you eventually plan to return wherever you go. You may have a residence in a place other than your domicile. Thus, you may go, say, to Amsterdam, and take up residence there and still intend to return to your domicile in the U.S. But your leaving your domicile does not, by itself, establish a bona fide residence in a new place. You must intend to make a new place your residence.

EXAMPLES

1. On August 9, you fly from New York City to Paris. You arrive there at 10 a.m. August 10. Your first full qualifying day toward the 330-day period is August 11.
   You may count in your 330-day period:
   - Time spent traveling between foreign countries.
   - Time spent on a vacation in foreign countries. There is no requirement that the 330 days must be spent on a job.
   - Time spent in a foreign country while employed by the U.S. government counts towards the 330-day test, even though pay from the government does not qualify for the earned income exclusion.
   - Time in foreign countries, territorial waters, or travel in the air over a foreign country. However, you will lose qualifying days if any part of such travel is on or over international waters and takes 24 hours or more, or any part of such travel is within the U.S. or its possessions.
2. You depart from Naples, Italy, by ship on June 10 at 6:00 p.m. and arrive at Haifa, Israel, at 7:00 a.m. on June 14. The trip exceeded 24 hours and passed through international waters. Therefore, you lose as qualifying days June 10, 11, 12, 13, and 14. Assuming you remain in Haifa, Israel, the next qualifying day is June 15.

Choosing the 12-month period. You qualify under the physical presence test if you were on foreign soil 330 days during any period of 12 consecutive months. Since there may be several 12-month periods during which you meet the 330-day test, you should choose the 12-month period allowing you the largest possible exclusion if you qualify under the physical presence test for only part of 2002.

EXAMPLE

You worked in France from June 1, 2001, through September 30, 2002, and the next day you left the country. During this period, you left France only for a 15-day vacation to the U.S. during December 2001. You earned $82,000 for your work in France during 2002. Your maximum 2002 exclusion is figured as follows:

1. Start with your last full day, September 30, 2002, and count back 330 full days during which you were abroad. Not counting the vacation days, the 330th day is October 21, 2001. This is the first day of your 12-month period.

2. From October 21, 2001, count forward 12 months to October 20, 2002, which is the last day of your 12-month period.

3. Count the number of days in 2002 that fall within the 12-month period ending October 20, 2002. Here, the number of qualifying days is 293, from January 1 through October 20, 2002.

4. The maximum 2002 exclusion is $80,000 \times {}^{293}/_{365}$, or $64,219. You may exclude $64,219, the lesser of the maximum exclusion or your actual earnings of $82,000.

 Filing Tip

Overseas Moving Expenses
These expenses are generally treated as related to your foreign earnings. Thus, if you move to a foreign country and exclude your income, you may not deduct your moving expenses. If your earned income exceeds the exclusion limit, you allocate moving expenses between your tax-free and taxable earned income.

36.6 Claiming Deductions

You may not deduct expenses that are allocable to the foreign earned income and housing exclusions. If you elect the earned income exclusion, you deduct expenses as follows:

Personal or nonbusiness deductions, such as medical expenses, mortgage interest, and real estate taxes paid on a personal residence, are deductible if you itemize deductions. Business expenses that are attributable to earning excludable income are not deductible. Dependency exemptions are fully deductible; *see* Example 1 below.

If your foreign earnings exceed the exclusion ceiling, you allocate expenses between taxable and excludable income and deduct the amount allocated to taxable earned income; *see* Example 2 below.

EXAMPLES

1. You were a resident of Denmark and elect to exclude your wages of $70,000 from income. You also incurred unreimbursed travel expenses of $2,000. You may not deduct the travel expenses, since the amount is attributable to the earning of tax-free income.

2. You earn wages of $100,000 and satisfy the physical presence test. Your unreimbursed travel expenses for 2002 are $5,000, after reducing meals and entertainment by 50%. If you elect the $80,000 exclusion, 20% of the travel expenses, or $1,000, attributable to the taxable 20% of earnings, may be claimed as a miscellaneous itemized deduction on Schedule A (Form 1040) subject to the 2% AGI floor.

If your job expenses are reimbursed and the expenses are adequately accounted for to your employer *(20.30)*, the reimbursements are not reported as income on your Form W-2. If the reimbursement is less than expenses, the excess expenses are allocated as in Example 2 above.

You may have to allocate state income taxes paid on your income.

If either you or your spouse elects the earned income or housing exclusion, you may not claim an IRA deduction based on excluded income.

If you were reimbursed by your employer under a non-accountable plan, or if the reimbursement is for expenses that you deducted in an earlier year, the reimbursement is considered earned income in the year of receipt and is added to other earned income before taking the exclusion and making the allocation. *See 36.2* for allocating reimbursements between the year of the move and the following year for purposes of claiming the exclusion.

If, after working in a foreign country, your employer transfers you back to the U.S. or you move back to the U.S. to take a different job, your moving expenses are deductible under the general rules discussed in *12.3*. If your residence and principal place of work was outside the U.S. and you retire and move back to the U.S., your moving expenses are also deductible, except that you do not have to meet the 39-week test for employees or the 78-week test for the self-employed and partners.

Survivors of workers abroad returning to U.S. If you are the spouse or dependent of a worker who died while his or her principal place of work was outside the U.S., you may deduct your moving expenses back to the U.S. For the costs to be deductible, the move must begin within six months of the worker's death. The requirements for deducting moving expenses apply, except for the 39-week test for employees or the 78-week test for the self-employed and partners.

Compulsory home leave. Foreign service officers stationed abroad must periodically return to the U.S. to reorient themselves to American ways of life. Because the home leave is compulsory, foreign service officers may deduct their travel expenses; travel expenses of the officer's family are not deductible.

36.7 Exclusion Not Established When Your Return Is Due

When your 2002 return is due, you may not have been abroad long enough to qualify for the exclusion. If you expect to qualify under either the residence or physical presence test after the due date for your 2002 return, you may either (1) ask for an extension of time for filing your return on Form 2350 until after you qualify under either rule or (2) file your return on the due date, reporting the foreign income on the return, pay the full tax, and then file for a refund when you qualify.

If you will have tax to pay even after qualifying for the exclusion—for example, your earned income exceeds the exclusion—you may file for an extension to file but you will owe interest on the tax due. To avoid interest charges on the tax, you may take one of the following steps:

1. File a timely return and pay the total tax due without the application of the exclusion. When you do qualify, make sure you file a refund claim within the time limits discussed in Chapter 49; *or*
2. Pay the estimated tax liability when you apply for the extension to file on Form 2350. If the extension is granted, the payment is applied to the tax shown on your return when you file.

36.8 Tax-Free Meals and Lodging for Workers in Camps

If you must live in a camp provided by your employer, you may exclude from income the value of the lodging and meals furnished if the camp is (1) provided because you work in a remote area where satisfactory housing is not available; (2) located as near as is practical to the worksite; and (3) a common area not open to the public normally accommodating at least 10 employees.

You also may qualify for the earned income exclusion.

 Filing Tip

Extension of Time To File
If you are living and working abroad on April 15, 2003, you have an automatic extension to June 16, 2003. For an additional two months, file Form 4868 by June 16, 2003, and pay the estimated tax to limit interest and late payment penalties. For a longer extension, in anticipation of owing no tax on your foreign income, you may file Form 2350 either with the Internal Revenue Service, Philadelphia, Pennsylvania 19255, or with a local IRS representative. File Form 2350 before the due date for filing your 2002 return, which is June 16, 2003, if you are abroad and are on a calendar year. If you cannot get Form 2350, apply for the extension on your own stationery. State the facts you rely on to justify the extension and the earliest date you expect to be in a position to determine under which rule you will qualify. You will receive an official letter and copy granting the extension. Generally, you will be granted an extension for a period ending 30 days after the date you expect to qualify for the foreign earned income exclusion.

36.9 Virgin Islands, Samoa, Guam, and Northern Marianas

The Virgin Islands, Guam, American Samoa, and the Commonwealth of the Northern Mariana Islands have their own independent tax departments. Therefore, contact the particular tax authority for the proper treatment of your income and ask the IRS for the 2002 edition of Publication 570, *Tax Guide for Individuals With Income From U.S. Possessions.*

For tax information from Guam, write to Department of Revenue and Taxation, Government of Guam, P.O. Box 23607, GMF, Guam 96921. For information from the Commonwealth of the Northern Mariana Islands, write to the Division of Revenue and Taxation, Commonwealth of the Northern Mariana Islands, P.O. Box 5234, CHRB, Saipan, Northern Mariana Islands 96950. For information from American Samoa, write to the Tax Division, Government of American Samoa, Pago Pago, American Samoa 96799. Also *see* IRS Publication 570.

For information about tax liability in the Virgin Islands, write to Virgin Islands Bureau of Internal Revenue, 9601 Estate Thomas, Charlotte Amalie, St. Thomas, U.S. Virgin Islands 00802. Also *see* IRS Publication 570.

Possession exclusion. A possession exclusion applies to bona fide residents of American Samoa for the entire year. On Form 4563, such residents may exclude for U.S. tax purposes their income from sources in American Samoa, Guam, and the Commonwealth of the Northern Marianas and income effectively connected with a business in these possessions.

36.10 Earnings in Puerto Rico

If you are a U.S. citizen who is also a resident of Puerto Rico for the entire year, you generally report all of your income on your Puerto Rico tax return. Where you report income from U.S. sources on the Puerto Rico tax return, a credit against the Puerto Rico tax may be claimed for income taxes paid to the United States.

If you are not a resident of Puerto Rico, you report on a Puerto Rico return only income from Puerto Rican sources. Wages earned for services performed in Puerto Rico for the U.S. government or for private employers are treated as income from Puerto Rican sources.

U.S. tax returns. As a U.S. citizen, you must file a U.S. tax return reporting income from all sources. But if you are a bona fide resident of Puerto Rico for an entire tax year, you do not report on a U.S. tax return any income earned in Puerto Rico during your residence there, except amounts received for services performed in Puerto Rico as an employee of the U.S. government. Similar rules apply if you have been a bona fide resident of Puerto Rico for at least two years before changing your residence from Puerto Rico. On a U.S. tax return, you may not deduct expenses or claim tax credits allocable to the excludable income. Personal exemptions are fully deductible.

If you are not a bona fide resident of Puerto Rico for the entire tax year, or were not a bona fide resident for two years prior to the tax year, you report on your U.S. tax return all income you earned in Puerto Rico, as well as all income from other sources. If you are required to report income earned in Puerto Rico on your U.S. tax return, you may claim a credit for income tax paid to Puerto Rico. You figure the credit on Form 1116. *See* IRS Publication 570.

Planning Reminder

Information for Puerto Rico Filing

Information on Puerto Rico tax returns may be requested from the Department of the Treasury, Tax Assistance and Legislation Bureau, P.O. Box 50065, San Juan, Puerto Rico 00902-6265.

EXAMPLE

You and your spouse are bona fide residents of Puerto Rico during the entire year of 2002. You receive $25,000 in wages as an employee of the U.S. government working in Puerto Rico, a $100 dividend from a Puerto Rican corporation that does business in Puerto Rico, and a $500 dividend from a U.S. corporation that does business in the U.S. Your spouse earned $18,000 in wages from a Puerto Rican corporation for services performed in Puerto Rico. Your exempt and taxable income for U.S. federal tax purposes is as follows:

	Taxable	Exempt
Your wages	$25,000	
Your spouse's wages		$18,000
Puerto Rican corporation dividend		100
U.S. corporation dividend	500	
Totals	$25,500	$18,100

You file tax returns with both Puerto Rico and the U.S. You have gross income of $25,500 for U.S. tax purposes and $43,600 for Puerto Rican tax purposes. A tax credit may be claimed on the U.S. tax return for income taxes paid to Puerto Rico and on your Puerto Rico return for income taxes paid to the U.S on U.S. source income.

36.11 Tax Treaties With Foreign Countries

Tax treaties between the United States and foreign countries modify some of the rules discussed in this chapter. The purpose of the treaties is to avoid double taxation. Consult your tax advisor about the effect of these treaties on your income. IRS Publication 54 contains a list of tax treaties.

36.12 Exchange Rates and Blocked Currency

Income reported on your federal income tax return must be stated in U.S. dollars. Where you are paid in foreign currency, you report your pay in U.S. dollars on the basis of the exchange rates prevailing at the time the income is actually or constructively received. You use the rate that most closely reflects the value of the foreign currency—the official rate, the open market rate, or any other relevant rate. You may even be required to use the black market rate if that is the most accurate measure of the actual purchasing power of U.S. dollars in the foreign country. Be prepared to justify the rate you use.

Fulbright grants. If 70% or more of a Fulbright grant is paid in nonconvertible foreign currency, U.S. tax may be paid in the foreign currency. *See* IRS Publication 520 for details.

Blocked currency. A citizen or resident alien may be paid in a foreign currency that cannot be converted into American dollars and removed from the foreign country. If your income is in blocked currency, you may elect to defer the reporting of that income until: (1) the currency becomes convertible into dollars, (2) you actually convert it into dollars, or (3) you use it for personal expenses (for example, in the foreign country when you go there). Purchase of a business or investment in the foreign country is not the kind of use that is treated as a conversion. (4) You make a gift of it or leave it in your will. (5) You are a resident alien and you give up your U.S. residence.

If you use this method to defer the income, you may not deduct the expenses of earning it until you report it. You must continue to use this method after you choose it. You may only change with permission of the IRS.

You do not defer the reporting of capital losses incurred in a country having a blocked currency. There may be these disadvantages in deferring income:

- Many years' income may accumulate and all be taxed in one year.
- You have no control over the year in which the blocked income becomes taxable. You usually cannot control the events that cause the income to become unblocked.

You choose to defer income in blocked currency by filing a tentative tax return reporting your blocked taxable income and explaining that you are deferring the payment of income tax because your income is not in dollars or in property or currency that is readily convertible into dollars. You must attach to your tentative return a regular return, reporting any unblocked taxable income received during the year or taxable income that became unblocked during the year. When the currency finally becomes unblocked or convertible into a currency or property convertible to dollars, you pay tax on the earnings at the rate prevailing in the year the currency became unblocked or convertible. On the tentative return, note at the top: "Report of Deferrable Foreign Income, pursuant to Revenue Ruling 74-351." File separate returns for each country from which blocked currency is received. The election must be made by the due date for filing a return for the year in which an election is sought.

36.13 Information Returns on Foreign Currency

If you have a financial interest in, or signature or other authority over, a foreign bank account, a foreign securities account, or any other foreign financial account, you must report this fact on Form TDF 90-22.1 (Report of Foreign Bank and Financial Accounts) if the aggregate value of the accounts at any time during the year exceeds $10,000. The form does not have to be filed if the accounts were with a U.S. military banking facility operated by a U.S. financial institution. Taxpayers filing Form 1040 must also indicate on Schedule B whether they had an interest in a foreign account during the year. Form TDF 90-22.1 is not filed with your income tax return. The form must be filed by June 30 of the year following the year in which you had this financial interest. Foreign accounts for 2002 must be reported by June 30, 2003.

Treasury regulations impose reporting and record-keeping requirements for currency transfers to and from the U.S. Generally, transactions involving a physical transfer of funds or monetary instruments into or outside the U.S. must be reported if the amount involved exceeds $10,000 on any one occasion; *see* Form 4790.

 Filing Tip

Currency Gains and Losses
A special statute, Section 988, governs the treatment of gain or loss on currency transactions. An individual who disposes of foreign currency in a personal transaction is not subject to tax under Section 988 on gain resulting from fluctuating exchange rates if the gain on the transaction is $200 or less.

Financial institutions must file a Form 4789 for each deposit, withdrawal, exchange of currency, or any other currency transaction of more than $10,000.

36.14 Foreign Tax Credit

You may claim an itemized deduction for qualified foreign taxes or you may claim a foreign tax credit. You must file Form 1116 to compute your credit unless the *de minimis* exception discussed in the Filing Tip at the right applies. You may not claim a foreign tax credit or deduction for taxes paid on income not subject to U.S. tax. If all of your foreign earned income is excluded, none of the foreign taxes paid on such income may be taken as a credit or deduction on your U.S. return. If you exclude only part of your foreign pay, you determine which foreign taxes are attributable to excluded income and thus barred as foreign tax credits by applying the fractional computation provided in the instructions to Form 1116 and IRS Publication 514.

In one tax year, you may not elect to deduct some foreign taxes and claim others as a credit. One method must be applied to all taxes paid or accrued during the tax year. If you are a cash-basis taxpayer, you may claim a credit for accrued foreign taxes, but you must consistently follow this method once elected.

The credit is the amount of foreign taxes paid or accrued, not to exceed the effective U.S. tax on foreign income multiplied by a ratio of foreign taxable income over total taxable income.

Credit disallowed. The credit may *not* be claimed if:

- You are a nonresident alien. However, under certain circumstances, an alien who is a bona fide resident for an entire taxable year in Puerto Rico may claim the credit. Also, a nonresident alien engaged in a U.S. trade or business may claim a credit if he or she receives income *effectively connected* to that business.
- You are a citizen of a U.S. possession (except Puerto Rico) but not a U.S. citizen or resident.

No credit is allowed for taxes imposed by a country designated by the government as engaging in terroristic activities; *see* IRS Publication 514 for a list of these countries.

Taxes qualifying for the credit. The credit is allowed only for foreign income tax, excess profits taxes, and similar taxes in the nature of an income tax. It is not allowed for any taxes paid to foreign countries on sales, gross receipts, production, the privilege to do business, personal property, or export of capital. But it may apply to a:

- Tax similar to a U.S. tax on income.
- Tax paid by a domestic taxpayer in lieu of the tax upon income, which would otherwise be imposed by any foreign country or by any U.S. possession.
- Tax of a foreign country imposing income tax, where for reasons growing out of the administrative difficulties of determining net income or basis within that country, the tax is measured by gross income, sales, and number of units produced.
- Pension, unemployment, or disability funds of a foreign country; certain foreign social security taxes do not qualify.

Reporting foreign income on your return. You report the gross amount of your foreign income in terms of United States currency. You also attach a schedule showing how you figured the foreign income in United States currency.

> **EXAMPLE**
> You earn Canadian dividends of $100 (Canadian dollars), from which $15 of Canadian taxes were withheld. When the dividends were declared, a Canadian dollar could be exchanged for $.65 of United States currency. Therefore, the dividend of $100 (in Canadian dollars) is reported on your return as $65 ($100 × .65). The tax withheld that may be taken as a credit is $9.75 ($15 × .65).

36.15 Computing the Foreign Tax Credit

The foreign tax credit is based on the amount of foreign taxes you paid or accrued, subject to this overall limitation, which is figured on Form 1116:

$$\text{U.S. Tax} \times \frac{\text{Taxable income from all foreign sources}}{\text{Taxable income from all sources}}$$

 Filing Tip

De Minimis Foreign Tax Credits

An individual with $300 or less of creditable foreign taxes, $600 for married persons filing jointly, may elect to be exempt from the overall limitation shown at the beginning of *36.15*, provided that the only foreign source income is qualified passive income. If the election is made, a foreign tax credit may be claimed directly on Line 45 of Form 1040 without filing Form 1116.

Separate limitation categories. The above fractional limitation must be figured separately for specific categories of foreign income. These categories are (1) passive income (such as dividends, interest, rents, royalties, and gains on certain commodity transactions; (2) foreign interest income subject to withholding at a rate of 5% or more; (3) shipping and aircraft related income; (4) lump-sum retirement distributions from foreign sources subject to special averaging; (5) certain income derived in banking, insurance, or financing businesses. Taxable income for each category must be separately computed and the overall limitation fraction applied. A separate computation also must be made for all other foreign income not within these categories; this "other" income group is called "general limitation income." Follow the instructions to Form 1116 and see IRS Publication 514 for further details.

Recapture of foreign losses. If you sustain an "overall foreign loss" for any taxable year, a recapture provision treats part of foreign income realized in a later year as income from U.S. sources. By treating part of the later year's foreign income as U.S. income, the numerator of the fraction used to compute the overall limitation (*see* above) is reduced and this in turn reduces the maximum foreign tax credit that may be claimed in the later year. More specifically, the portion of foreign income in succeeding years that is treated as U.S. income equals the lower of (1) the amount of the loss or (2) 50% (or a larger percentage, as you may choose) of taxable income from foreign sources. An "overall foreign loss" means the amount by which the gross income for the taxable year from foreign sources for that year is exceeded by the sum of allocated deductions. For this purpose, the following deductions are not subject to recapture: operating loss deductions, any uncompensated foreign expropriation, and casualty loss. Special rules apply to dispositions of property if used predominantly outside the United States in a trade or business. *See* IRS Publication 514 for recapture details.

Taxable income. Income that is tax free under the foreign earned income exclusion is not taken into account when figuring taxable income. Foreign taxable income, for purposes of computing the ratio, is reduced by all expenses directly related to earning the income. Itemized deductions, such as medical expenses, that are not directly related to foreign sources are allocated to foreign income according to relative gross incomes from foreign and U.S. sources. You do not consider personal exemptions when figuring foreign or total taxable income.

The foreign tax credit may not exceed foreign taxes actually paid or accrued. Where a joint return is filed, the limitation is applied to the aggregate taxable income of both spouses.

A limited foreign tax credit may be applied against the alternative minimum tax; *see* Chapter 23.

Capital gains. In figuring the overall limitation, taxable income from foreign countries (the numerator) includes gain from the sale of capital assets only to the extent of foreign source capital gain net income, which is the lower of net capital gain from foreign sources or net capital gain from all sources. If you are entitled to a preferential capital gains rate, you must make an adjustment to account for the rate differential when figuring the credit. Gain on the sale of nondepreciable personal property sold outside the country of your residence may be treated as gain from U.S. sources, unless the gain is subject to a foreign income tax at a rate of 10% or more of the gain. *See* instructions to Form 1116.

36.16 Carryback and Carryover of Excess Foreign Tax Credit

Where the amount allowable as a credit under the overall basis is restricted, the excess may be carried back to the two preceding years and then carried forward to the five succeeding taxable years. The carryback or carryover will not be allowed in a year for which you have no income from foreign sources or the credit limitation already applies to taxes of that year. For further details, *see* IRS Publication 514.

Filing Tip

Choosing Credit or Deduction

If you qualify for a credit or deduction, you will generally receive a larger tax reduction by claiming a tax credit rather than a deduction. A deduction is only a partial offset against your tax, whereas a credit is deducted in full from your tax. Also, taking a deduction may bar you from carrying back an excess credit from a later year. However, a deduction may give you a larger tax saving if the foreign tax is levied at a high rate and the proportion of foreign income to U.S. income is small. Compute your tax under both methods and choose the one providing the larger tax reduction.

Chapter 37

Planning Alimony and Marital Settlements

Alimony payments that meet tax law tests in this chapter are deductible if you pay them, and taxable if you receive them. Payments are not deductible by the payer unless taxable to the recipient.

You claim a deduction for deductible alimony that you pay on Line 33a of Form 1040. You deduct the payments even if you claim the standard deduction rather than itemizing deductions. You must enter the Social Security number of your ex-spouse. Otherwise, your deduction may be disallowed and you may have to pay a $50 penalty. If you pay deductible alimony to more than one ex-spouse, enter the Social Security number of one of them and provide similar information for the others on a separate statement attached to your return.

If you receive taxable alimony, report the payments on Line 11 of Form 1040. You must give your ex-spouse your Social Security number and could be subject to a $50 penalty if you fail to do so.

37.1 Planning Alimony Agreements

Tax Rules for Alimony Payments

You can arrange beforehand the way in which the costs of a divorce are to be borne. You may specifically state in the decree or agreement that the alimony is neither taxable to the payee-spouse (under IRC Section 71) nor deductible by the payer-spouse (under IRC Section 215). Such a statement effectively disqualifies payments that otherwise would be taxable to the payee-spouse and deductible by the payer-spouse. A copy of the agreement that contains the statement must be attached to the tax return of the payee-spouse for each year the statement is applicable.

The first step in planning the after-tax consequences of alimony is convincing a couple that they may have a common financial interest; the second is projecting future tax consequences.

For example, assume that the husband is to make payments to the wife. If tax planning is approached from the viewpoint of each spouse separately, the tax deduction is an advantage for the husband; tax-free income is an advantage for the wife. However, both advantages cannot be achieved, and the couple must face the reality of the tax law, which allows the husband to deduct payments only if they are taxed as alimony to the wife. The husband and wife must compromise by setting amounts and tax consequences that balance their interests.

One approach is to view both spouses as a single economic tax unit. If this is done and the husband will be in a higher tax bracket during the payout period than the wife, an agreement should generally provide for taxable and deductible alimony. The tax savings provided by the deduction can conserve more of the husband's assets while providing funds required by the wife. The final amount of alimony to be paid depends on the spouses' tax brackets. Where tax brackets do not differ, there may be no advantage in making an agreement for taxable and deductible alimony when viewing the two parties as a unit.

If you agree that one spouse is to pay deductible alimony and the other spouse is to report the alimony as income, these rules must be met:

- The alimony must be paid under a decree of divorce or legal separation agreement or decree of support; *see 37.2.*

- The agreement must provide for cash payments; *see 37.3.* A noncash property settlement is not alimony. There is no minimum payout period for annual cash alimony payments of $15,000 or less. One payment of $15,000 can qualify as deductible and taxable alimony. There is also no minimum payout period for annual alimony payments exceeding $15,000. However, recapture of alimony deductions claimed in the first or second year may occur where annual payments of over $15,000 are scheduled and paid, but in the second or third year a reduced payment is made. To avoid recapture of deductions for payments over $15,000, carefully plan schedules of declining payments within the rules discussed at *37.7.*

- In providing for the support of children, a specific allocation to their support or the setting of certain contingencies disqualifies payments as deductible and alimony as taxable; *see 37.5.*

- Divorced and legally separated parties must not live in the same household when payments are made. If they live in the same household, alimony payments are not deductible or taxable. However, there are these exceptions: A spouse who makes payments while preparing to leave the common residence may deduct payments made within one month before the departure. Also, where you are separated under a written agreement, but not legally separated under a decree of divorce or separate maintenance, you may deduct alimony payments even if you both are members of the same household.

- The payer spouse's liability to pay alimony must end on the death of the payee spouse. The alimony agreement does not have to state expressly that payments end on death if liability ends under state law; *see 37.4.*

37.2 Decree or Agreement Required

Alimony, to be deductible and taxable, must be required by one of the following: (1) a decree of divorce or legal separation; (2) a written separation agreement; or (3) a decree of support. This rule applies to both pre-1985 and post-1984 decrees and agreements. Voluntary payments are not deductible or taxable.

 *Filing Instruction*

Reporting Alimony
If you paid alimony in 2002 meeting the deductible tests, claim your deduction on Line 33a of Form 1040, and enter the recipient's Social Security number. If you receive qualifying alimony payments, report them on Line 11 of Form 1040.

 *Planning Reminder*

Property Transfers
A property transfer to a former spouse that is incident to a divorce is generally treated as a tax-free exchange; *see 6.7* for details.

Divorced or legally separated. The obligation to pay alimony must be imposed by the decree of divorce or separate maintenance or a written agreement incident to the divorce or separation.

Alimony paid under a Mexican divorce decree qualifies. Payments under a Mexican or state decree declared invalid by another jurisdiction do not qualify according to the IRS. Two appeals courts have rejected the IRS position.

Support payments ordered by a court in a wife's home state qualify as alimony, even though not provided for by an *ex parte* divorce decree obtained by the husband in another state. Similarly, payments qualified when a state court increased support originally ordered before the husband obtained an uncontested Mexican divorce.

Payments made under a separation approved by a Roman Catholic ecclesiastical board do not qualify.

When a decree of divorce or separate maintenance fails to mention alimony, payments qualify as long as they are made under a written agreement considered "incident to" the decree.

Payments made under an agreement amended after a divorce or legal separation may also qualify, if the amendment is considered "incident" to the divorce or separation. For example, the IRS agrees that a written amendment changing the amount of alimony payments is incident to the divorce where the legal obligation to support under the original agreement survived the divorce. However, payments under an amended agreement did not qualify where the original agreement settled all rights between the husband and wife and made no provision for future support. The legal obligation to support the wife did not survive the divorce and could not be revived by the new agreement.

Annulments. Payments made under an annulment decree qualify as deductible (and taxable) alimony.

Separated from spouse. Where a husband and wife are separated and living apart, alimony is deductible by the payer-spouse and taxable to the payee-spouse provided it is paid under either a written separation agreement or decree of support.

A decree of support. Any court decree or order requiring support payments qualifies, including alimony *pendente lite* (temporary alimony while the action is pending) and an interlocutory (not final) divorce decree.

In certain community property states, payments under a decree of alimony *pendente lite* which do not exceed the wife's interest in community income are neither deductible by the husband nor taxable to the wife; payments exceeding the wife's interest are taxable to her and deductible by the husband.

37.3 Cash Payments Required

Only payments of cash, checks, and money orders payable on demand qualify as taxable and deductible alimony. Your cash payment to a third party for a spouse qualifies if made under the terms of a divorce decree or separation instrument. For example, you pay the rent, mortgage, tax, medical expenses, or tuition liabilities of your former spouse. The payments qualify if made under the terms of the divorce or separation instrument. If taxable as alimony, your former spouse may deduct your payment of real estate taxes, mortgage interest, or medical expenses if he or she claims itemized deductions. You may not deduct payments to maintain property owned by you but used by your spouse. For example, you pay the mortgage expenses, real estate taxes, and insurance premiums for a house that you own and in which your former spouse lives. You may not deduct those payments as alimony even if they are required by a decree or agreement.

Providing services or transferring or providing property does not qualify. For example, you may not deduct as alimony your note, the assignment of a third party note, or an annuity contract.

Premiums paid for term or whole life insurance on your life made under a divorce or separation instrument qualify as deductible alimony to the extent your former spouse owns the policy.

37.4 Payments Must Stop at Death

Liability for a payment must stop on the death of the payee-spouse. If not, none of the payments, whether made before or after the payee's death, qualify as taxable (to payee-spouse) or deductible (by payer-spouse) alimony.

 *Planning Reminder*

Payments to a Third Party

Cash payments to a third party may be deducted as alimony if they are under the terms of a divorce decree or separation instrument. You may also deduct as alimony payments made to a third party at the written request of the payee spouse. For example, your former wife asks you to make a cash donation to a charitable organization instead of paying alimony installments to her. Her request must be in writing and state that both she and you intend the payment to be treated as alimony. You must receive the written request before you file your return for the taxable year in which the payment was made. Your former wife may deduct the payment as a charitable contribution if she claims itemized deductions.

Key to Alimony and Marital Settlement Issues

Item—	Comments—
Alimony	The same rules determine whether alimony is deductible and taxable. For example, if a husband makes deductible alimony payments to his ex-wife, the payments are taxable to her. He may not deduct payments that are not taxable to her. If you are currently planning an alimony agreement, consider the tax consequences to both spouses. As current tax rates may be as high as 38.6% for one spouse and as low as 10% for the other, there may be a substantial tax savings to the couple, when considered as an economic unit, in negotiating an agreement that qualifies the payments as deductible alimony; *see 37.1.* **Note**: Prior tax rules that apply to pre-1985 agreements are not discussed in this chapter. If you have a problem involving a payment of alimony under a pre-1985 agreement, refer to a past issue of *Your Income Tax* or to IRS Publication 504.
Child support agreements	A payment fixed as payable for the support of your child may not qualify as deductible or taxable alimony; *see 37.5.*
Property settlements	Transfers of property between spouses that are incident to a divorce are treated as tax-free exchanges. There is no recognition of gain or loss. Future tax consequences should be considered by the spouse receiving appreciated property. When the property is sold, that spouse will be taxed on the appreciation. If this is so, that spouse may want to bargain for larger alimony payments or additional property to compensate for the projected future tax; *see 6.7.*
Alimony to nonresident alien	If you pay alimony payments to a nonresident alien, and you are a U.S. citizen or resident, you must withhold 30% (or a lower rate as set by treaty) on each payment for income tax purposes. *See* IRS Publications 504 and 515 for more information.
Exemptions for children	Exemptions for children of a divorced couple are governed by the rules explained at *21.11.* Further, where a spouse is in the income range requiring the phaseout or disallowance of personal exemptions *(21.16),* there may be no advantage in providing the exemption to that spouse. The exemption should be given to the spouse who may claim a full deduction for the exemption.
Annuity or endowment policy	Funds for payments of alimony may be provided through the purchase of an annuity or endowment policy. You may not deduct payments made under the policies assigned or purchased for your spouse. For example, to meet an alimony obligation of $500 a month, you buy your spouse a commercial annuity contract. The full $500 a month received by him or her is taxable. You may not deduct these payments.
Trust to pay alimony	To meet your alimony obligations, you may transfer income-producing property to a trust that is to pay the income to your spouse. You may not deduct payments made by the trust. You are not taxable on the income earned by the trust, even though it meets your alimony obligations. This tax treatment is the equivalent of receiving a tax deduction for paying alimony. If you receive alimony from a trust, ask the trustee how to report such income. Tax treatment may depend on whether the trust was created before 1985 or after 1984. If the trust was set up after 1984, as a beneficiary you generally report trust income under the general trust reporting rules in Chapter 11. These general trust rules may not apply to certain alimony trusts created before 1985 that were subject to the prior alimony rules. Distributions from such trusts may be treated as taxable alimony regardless of whether the distributions are from income or principal. In any event, the trustee should provide you with the necessary tax information.
Retirement plans	A state court can allocate your interest in a qualified retirement plan to a former spouse in a qualified domestic relations order. The benefits are taxed to your former spouse when they are paid to her or him. Benefits paid to another beneficiary, such as a child, are taxable to you; *see 7.12.*
Remarriage's effect on pre-1985 agreement	The tax deduction allowed for alimony payments made under a pre-1985 decree or agreement hinges on the obligation to support. Once the spouse receiving alimony remarries, the obligation to support generally ends under state law. In these states, any payment after remarriage is not considered alimony and is not deductible. For example, payments to a former wife made after remarriage are considered tax-free gifts if the former husband knows of the remarriage and that he is no longer obligated to pay. If she does not inform him of her remarriage, his payments are taxable to her but are not deductible by him.
Voluntary payments in excess of required alimony	Voluntary payments in excess of required alimony are not deductible or taxable as alimony. Amending the decrees retroactively to cover an increase does not qualify the increase as deductible and taxable alimony. The increase has to be approved by the court before the increased payments are made.

The divorce decree or separation agreement does not have to specifically state that payments end at death, if under state law the liability to pay ends on the death of the payee-spouse.

To the extent that one or more payments are to begin, increase in amount, or accelerate after the death of the payee-spouse, such payments may be treated as a substitute for the continuation of payments terminating on the death of the payee-spouse.

EXAMPLES

1. Under the terms of a divorce decree, Smith is obligated to make annual alimony payments of $30,000, terminating on the earlier of the end of six years or the death of Mrs. Smith. She also is to keep custody of their two minor children. The decree also provides that if on her death the children are still minors, Smith is to pay annually $10,000 to a trust each year. The trust income and corpus are to be used for the children until the youngest child reaches the age of majority. Under these facts, Smith's possible liability to make annual $10,000 payments to the trust is treated as a substitute for $10,000 of the $30,000 annual payments. $10,000 of each of the $30,000 annual payments does not qualify as alimony.

2. Same facts as in Example 1, but the alimony is to end on the earlier of the expiration of 15 years or the death of Mrs. Smith. Further, if Mrs. Smith dies before the end of the 15-year period, Smith will pay her estate the difference between the total amount that he would have paid had she survived and the amount actually paid. For example, if she dies at the end of the tenth year, he will pay her estate $150,000 ($450,000 – $300,000). Under these facts, his liability to make a lump-sum payment to the estate is a substitute for the full amount of each of the annual $30,000 payments. Accordingly, none of the annual $30,000 payments qualifies as alimony.

Attorneys' fees. Under the laws of many states, a court award of attorneys' fees remains enforceable after the death of the payee-spouse, thereby disqualifying a payer's alimony deduction for the payment and making it nontaxable to the payee-spouse. For example, a husband who was ordered by an Oklahoma court to pay his wife $154,000 for her attorneys' fees prior to the entry of a final divorce decree was unable to deduct his payment. The Tax Court and the Tenth Circuit Court of Appeals agreed with the IRS that under Oklahoma law, the husband's liability to pay the attorneys' fees would not have ended, as a hypothetical matter, had the wife died before the final decree was entered. The policy reason for the state law is to assure that attorneys get paid for their services, which will enable indigent clients to retain counsel in divorce actions.

In this situation, the payer can obtain a deduction if the attorneys' fees remain the liability of the payee-spouse and the court decree increases the amount of cash alimony to cover the fees, rather than having them paid separately. The cash alimony would be taxable to the payee-spouse. The payee-spouse's payment of the fees to the attorneys may be deductible, but only as a miscellaneous expense subject to the 2% of AGI floor.

37.5 Child Support Payments Are Not Alimony

A payment is fixed as payable for child support if the divorce or separation instrument specifically fixes an amount payable for support. That amount is not deductible or taxable as alimony.

Even if there is not a specific allocation to child support, a payment will be presumed by the IRS to be payable for child support if it is to be reduced on the happening of a contingency relating to the child, such as: the child reaches a specific age or income level, or the child leaves school, marries, leaves the parent's household, or begins to work.

EXAMPLE

On July 1, 2002, Thomas and Tina are divorced when their children, John (born July 15, 1987), and Jane (born September 23, 1989), are ages 14 and 12. Under the divorce decree, Thomas is to make monthly alimony payments of $2,000. The monthly payments are to be reduced to $1,500 on January 1, 2008, and to $1,000 on January 1, 2012. On January 1, 2008, the date of the first reduction, John will be 20 years, 5 months, and 17 days old. On January 1, 2012, the date of the second reduction, Jane will be 22 years, 3 months, and 9 days old. As

Caution

Alimony Reductions Tied to Child's Age

If a reduction in your payments is not specifically tied to your child's reaching majority age but the scheduled date for the reduction is within six months before or after your child reaches age 18 or 21 (or other age of majority under local law), the IRS holds that the reduction is tied to the child's age. The reduction amount will be treated as child support unless you can prove that the reduction is for some other purpose. The IRS makes the same presumption if you have more than one child and your alimony payments are to be reduced at least twice and each reduction is within one year of a different child's reaching a particular age between ages 18 and 24; *see* the Example on the right.

each reduction is to occur not more than one year before or after each child reaches the age of 21 years and four months, the IRS will presume that the reductions are associated with the happening of a contingency relating to the children. The two reductions total $1,000 per month and are treated as the amount fixed for the support of the children. Thus, $1,000 of the $2,000 monthly payment does not qualify as alimony. To avoid this result, Thomas must prove that the reductions were not related to the support of the children.

If both alimony and child support are specified and a payment is less than the total of the two amounts, then the payment is first allocated to child support.

Tax refund diversion for delinquent child support. The IRS can give your tax refund to a state that is paying support to your child if you fail to make support payments. The IRS will not notify you of the diversion until it is made to the state. However, the state agency must provide prior notice of the proposed offset and procedures for contesting it.

Minimum Payments and Recapture of Alimony

37.6 No Minimum Payment Period for Alimony

There is no minimum payment period, but a recapture rule applies where payments fall by more than $15,000 within the first three years; *see 37.7*.

37.7 3rd Year Recapture If Alimony Drops $15,000 or More

The recapture rules are designed to prevent the so-called "front loading" of property settlement payments disguised as alimony. However, the rules apply even where no property settlement was intended if you come within their terms. Here are the rules: Deductible payments made in the first year or second year may be recaptured (that is, reported as income) in the third year where payments within the first three years decline by more than $15,000. The three years are called "post-separation years." The first post-separation year is the first calendar year in which you pay alimony under a decree of divorce or separation agreement. The period does not begin with the year of the decree or agreement if no payments are made. Recapture does not apply to temporary support payments made before the final decree or agreement. The second and third post-separation years are the next two calendar years after the first post-separation year whether or not payments are made during those years.

Payments made in the second post-separation year are recaptured if the payments exceed the payments made in the third post-separation year by more than $15,000. Payments made in the first post-separation year are recaptured if they exceed the average payments made in the second post-separation year and the third post-separation year by more than $15,000. The Examples below illustrate how to make these computations.

When recapture does not apply. Recapture is not triggered if payments in both the first and second post-separation years do not exceed $15,000. Recapture also does not apply to:

- Payments made under a continuing liability to pay for at least three years a fixed part of your income from a business or property or from a job or self-employed business or profession, *or*

- Payments that end because of your death or the death of your former spouse or the remarriage of your former spouse at any time before the end of the third post-separation year.

The steps of recapture are:

Step 1. Recapture for the second-year payment is computed first. This is the excess, if any, of the second-year payment over the third-year payment, *minus* $15,000.

Step 2. Recapture for the first-year payment is computed next. There is recapture if the first-year payment exceeds by more than $15,000 the average payment made in the second and third years. In figuring the average payment, reduce the second-year payment by any recapture amount for the second year figured under Step 1.

 Filing Tip

Reporting Recapture on Your Return

The payer-spouse reports the recaptured amount as income in the third year and the payee-spouse claims a deduction for the same amount. The payer reports the recaptured amount on Form 1040, Line 11 (alimony received); cross out "received" and write "recapture" along with the payee-spouse's Social Security number.

The payee-spouse deducts the recaptured amount on Form 1040, Line 33a (alimony paid). He or she crosses out the word "paid" and writes "recapture," and also enters on that line the payer-spouse's Social Security number.

EXAMPLES

1. In 2000, Jones obtains a divorce and pays deductible alimony of $50,000. His wife reports $50,000 as income. In 2001 and 2002, he makes no payments. On his 2002 return, $35,000 of the first year 2000 deduction is recaptured ($50,000 – $15,000) and reported as income by Jones. His ex-spouse deducts $35,000.

2. In 2000, Smith makes his first alimony payment of $50,000; in 2001 he pays $20,000 and in 2002 he pays nothing. On his 2002 return, $32,500 is recaptured as follows:

Recapture of second-year payment:		
Payment in 2nd year		$20,000
Less: 3rd-year payment	$0	
Less: Allowance	15,000	15,000
Recapture for second year		$ 5,000
Recapture of first-year payment:		
Average calculation:		
Payment over the 2nd and 3rd years	$20,000	
Less: recapture in the 2nd year	$ 5,000	
	$15,000	
Average ($15,000 ÷ 2)	$ 7,500	
Payment in first year		$50,000
Less: Average	$ 7,500	
Less: Allowance	15,000	22,500
Recapture for first year		$27,500
Total recaptured in 2002:		
For second year		$ 5,000
For first year		$27,500
Total:		$32,500

37.8 Legal Fees of Marital Settlements

If you are receiving taxed alimony, you may deduct part of your legal fees. Ask your attorney to divide his or her fees into charges for arranging: (1) the divorce or separation and (2) details of the alimony payments.

You may be able to deduct the legal fees allocated to (2), but you may not deduct the fee attributed to the divorce or separation negotiation. The deduction is subject to the 2% adjusted gross income (AGI) floor on miscellaneous itemized deductions (*see* Chapter 19) and if you are subject to alternative minimum tax, the deduction is not allowed for AMT purposes (*see 23.2*). If the alimony is not taxed to you, you may not deduct any part of the fee. However, part of a fee allocated to a property settlement may be added to the basis of the property.

If you are paying deductible alimony, you may not deduct legal fees paid for arranging a divorce or for resisting your spouse's demands for alimony. Furthermore, you may not deduct legal fees incurred in resisting your spouse's claims to income-producing property the loss of which would affect your earnings. However, these rules do not bar you from deducting (subject to the 2% floor) that part of your legal fee that is identified as being paid for tax advice; *see 19.25.* The following types of proof may support a deduction:

- The fee is charged by a firm that limits its practice to state and federal matters and is engaged to advise on the consequences of a property settlement involving the transfer of property in exchange for other property and the release of the other spouse's marital rights in the property.

- The fee is charged by a firm engaged in general practice that assigns tax problems, such as the tax consequences of creating an alimony trust, to its special tax department. On the bill, an allocation is made for tax advice based on time, complexity of the case, and the amount of tax involved.

- An attorney handles the divorce for a fixed fee and also gives advice on the right to claim exemptions for the children following the divorce. The bill allocates part of the fee to the tax advice, based on time, and fees customarily charged in the locality for similar services.

 Caution

Spouse's Legal Fees

You may not deduct your payment of your spouse's legal fees as a miscellaneous itemized deduction, even if the fees are only for tax advice. Furthermore, as discussed at 37.4, a payment of your spouse's legal fees may not qualify as deductible alimony even if paid under court order because liability for the payment might survive the payee-spouse's death under state law.

Chapter 38

Educational Tax Benefits

The tax law provides several tax benefits for people attending school. If you can take advantage of them, you are in effect receiving a government subsidy that lowers the cost of education.

The following benefit provisions can provide substantial tax savings, but are hedged with restrictions that may bar or limit their availability: Hope and lifetime learning education tax credits, a student loan interest deduction, and a deferral of taxes on interest earned on contributions to state-sponsored college tuition programs and Coverdell ESAs. For 2002, a new deduction for higher education tuition and fees may be available if your income is too high to claim a Hope or lifetime learning credit; *see 38.13*.

Scholarships, Grants, Tuition Plans, and Student Loan Interest

38.1 Scholarships and Grants

Scholarships and fellowships of a degree candidate are tax free to the extent that the grants pay for tuition and course-related fees, books, supplies, and equipment that are required for courses. Amounts for room, board, and incidental expenses are taxable. If you are not a candidate for a degree (*see* the degree test below), your entire grant is taxable.

You must pay tax on grants or tuition reductions that pay for teaching or other services required as a condition of receiving the grant. This is true even if all degree candidates are required to perform the services. Thus, if you are a graduate student and receive a stipend for teaching, those payments are taxable, subject to withholding, and reported by the school on Form W-2. Similarly, no tax-free exclusion is allowed for federal grants where the recipient agrees to do future work with the federal government.

Degree test. Scholarships given to students attending a primary or secondary school, or to those pursuing a degree at a college or university, meet the degree test. Also qualifying are full-time or part-time scholarships for study at an educational institution that (1) provides an educational program acceptable for full-time credit towards a higher degree or offers a program of training to prepare students for gainful employment in a recognized occupation *and* (2) is authorized under federal or state law to provide such a program and is accredited by a nationally recognized accreditation agency.

38.2 Tuition Reductions for College Employees

Free or partially free tuition for *undergraduate* studies provided to a faculty member or school employee is generally not taxable. The tuition reduction may be for education at his or her own school or at a similar school. Tuition benefits may be taxable to highly compensated employees if the tuition plan discriminates in their favor. Tuition reductions that represent compensation for services are taxable.

Tax-free tuition benefits may also be provided to the employee's spouse, dependent child, a former employee who retired or left on disability, a widow or widower of an individual who died while employed by the school, or a widow or widower of a retired or disabled employee.

A child under the age of 25 qualifies for a tax-free tuition reduction if both parents have died and one of the parents qualified for tax-free tuition benefits. If the child is age 25 or over, tuition reductions are taxed even if both parents are deceased.

38.3 How Fulbright Awards Are Taxed

Fulbright awards for teaching, lecturing, or research are taxable unless you can claim the foreign earned income exclusion to avoid tax on the grant (Chapter 36). If you do not qualify for the exclusion, your overseas stay is temporary, and you intend to return to your regular teaching position in the United States, you may deduct the cost of your travel, meals, and lodgings overseas.

38.4 U.S. Savings Bond Tuition Plans

Consider the use of Series EE bonds *(30.21)* or I bonds *(30.22)* to fund part of a college savings program. You can defer the interest income until final maturity (30 years) or report the interest annually. The interest is not subject to state or local tax. For bonds purchased in your child's name, having your child report the interest annually may be advisable where it can be offset by the child's standard deduction or itemized deductions. To the extent interest is offset each year, it escapes tax; *see 4.29*.

Interest exclusion may be available if you redeem EE bonds issued after 1989 or I bonds. If you purchased EE bonds in your own name or jointly with your spouse after 1989 and have been deferring the reporting of interest income, you may be able to exclude accumulated interest from federal tax in the year you redeem the bonds if in that year you pay tuition and enrollment education fees or you contribute to a Coverdell ESA *(38.12)* or qualified tuition program *(38.5)*. The interest exclusion rule also applies to redemptions of I bonds. The exclusion, claimed on Form 8815, is subject to several limitations as discussed in the following paragraphs.

Who qualifies for the exclusion. You must be age 24 or over before the month in which the bonds are purchased, and the bonds must be issued solely in your name or in the joint names of you and your spouse. You may not claim the exclusion for bonds bought in your child's name or owned jointly with your child. In the year the bonds are redeemed you must pay tuition and enrollment fees or contribute to a Coverdell ESA or qualified tuition plan for yourself, your spouse, or your dependents. Thus, grandparents may not claim the exclusion if they buy savings bonds to

Caution

Graduate Teaching and Research Assistants

If you must teach, do research, or provide other services to obtain a tuition reduction for graduate studies, a tuition reduction from the school is tax free if it is in addition to regular pay for the services. If the tuition reduction is your compensation, it is taxable.

fund the college education of grandchildren unless the children are dependents of the grandparents in the year the bonds are cashed. Tuition and fees must be for a college, university, or vocational school that meets federal financial aid standards. Room and board are not eligible expenses. Married persons filing separately are *not* eligible for the exclusion.

Excludable amount and phase-out rule. The tax-free amount of EE or I bond interest is figured on Form 8815. The amount of the exclusion depends on the amount of educational expenses you pay and your modified adjusted gross income (MAGI) in the year of redemption. However, no exclusion is allowed to a married person who files separately, regardless of income or amount of expenses.

On Form 8815, educational expenses must be reduced by the amount of any nontaxable scholarship or fellowship grant, tax-free distributions from a qualified tuition plan *(see 38.5)*, educational expenses taken into account when figuring a Hope or lifetime learning credit *(see 38.7)*, and tax-free distributions from a Coverdell ESA *(see 38.12)*.

If after required reductions qualified expenses equal or exceed the redemption proceeds, 100% of the interest is potentially excludable, subject to the phaseout based on MAGI. If the redemption amount exceeds the amount of educational expenses (after any required reduction), the excludable amount is based on the ratio of expenses to the redemption amount and the phaseout computation.

A full interest exclusion is allowed for 2002 only to persons with MAGI below a phase-out threshold. For 2002, the MAGI phase-out ranges are $86,400 to $116,400 for married persons filing jointly and qualifying widow(er)s, and $57,600 to $72,600 for single persons and heads of household. For purposes of applying the phaseout, MAGI is generally your regular adjusted gross income plus the interest on the redeemed EE bonds, student loan interest *(38.6)* or tuition and fees *(38.13)* that you deduct, and foreign income items and employer-provided adoption assistance that you excluded from income. *See* the Form 8815 instructions.

EXAMPLE

In August 2002, you redeem a $10,000 EE bond that was issued in September 1991. You receive $9,304, including $5,000 principal and $4,304 interest. In 2002, your qualified higher education expenses total $12,500. After taking into account $5,000 of expenses used to figure a lifetime learning credit *(38.9)*, you show $7,500 of qualified higher education expenses on Form 8815. The excludable percentage of interest is 80.61% ($7,500 divided by $9,304). Thus, $3,469 (80.61% × $4,304) of the interest is potentially excludable from income, subject to the phase-out rules.

Assume that you are married filing jointly and have MAGI of $95,000. Following the phase-out steps on Form 8815, the exclusion is limited to $2,474.

38.5 Qualified Tuition Programs (Section 529 Plans)

State-sponsored qualified tuition programs (QTPs), also known as Section 529 plans, are designed to allow participants to take advantage of federal tax benefits, and some also offer state tax benefits. Each state has its own variation, so it is important to look at the details of the program in the state in which you live. Distributions from the plan can be used to pay the costs of college tuition and fees, books, supplies, and qualified room and board (for students enrolled at least half time). Starting in 2002, private colleges and universities may offer prepayment-type plans.

Types of plans. There are two basic types of state-sponsored college savings plans: (1) college tuition prepayment plans and (2) savings plans.

In a prepayment plan, a parent or other relative purchases tuition credits or certificates as a prepayment of a child's future college tuition. By prepaying tuition according to a set schedule, higher inflation-based tuition costs may be avoided where the child will not start college for many years.

Starting in 2002, private colleges and universities may establish a prepayment type of qualified tuition plan. Also beginning in 2002, a participant in a QTP can roll over the account balance into another QTP for the same beneficiary, tax free. This will, for example, allow participants to switch from a state-run QTP to a privately run QTP or a QTP in another state.

In a savings plan, deposits are made to a state-managed account for the benefit of a specified individual. Earnings build up tax free and are later distributed to pay the beneficiary's qualifying college costs. Plan eligibility is not tied to income of the contributor or beneficiary. The maximum plan amount varies with the state, but potentially can cover the full cost of college attendance.

For both types of plans, earnings are not taxed while the fund accumulates.

Law Alert

Private QTPs

Private colleges and universities may offer qualified tuition prepayment plans starting in 2002. Distributions from these private plans will be tax free starting in 2004 if used for qualified expenses.

Filing Tip

Qualified State Tuition Plans and Education Tax Credits

The student beneficiary of a qualified state tuition plan (or a taxpayer who claims the beneficiary as a dependent) can use withdrawals from the state tuition plan to pay for qualified tuition and related expenses that are eligible for the Hope and lifetime learning credits *(38.7)*.

Tax-free distributions starting in 2002. Beginning in 2002, withdrawals from state QTPs are not taxable if they do not exceed qualified higher education expenses. In prior years, the earnings portion of a distribution was taxable regardless of qualifying education costs.

To the extent distributions from a state QTP exceed qualified higher education expenses, or the beneficiary of the account does not attend college and a refund is made to the parent or other contributor, the earnings portion of the distribution or refund is taxable. A worksheet in IRS Publication 970 may be used to compute the taxable portion. In addition, a penalty equal to 10% of the taxable amount will be due under the same rule as for taxable Coverdell ESA distributions at *38.12.*

Withdrawals before 2004 from a qualified tuition plan of a private college or university are taxable to the extent they are allocable to earnings. A 10% penalty applies (before 2004) to the part of the taxable distribution which is *not* allocable to qualified higher education costs.

Qualified higher education expenses. Qualified higher education costs are tuition, fees, books, supplies, equipment, and reasonable room and board costs as determined by the educational institution. Also qualifying are expenses necessary for the enrollment or attendance of a special needs beneficiary.

Gift tax consequences. A contribution to a qualified state tuition program is treated as a completed gift of a present interest passed from the contributor to the beneficiary at the time of contribution. Annual contributions are eligible for the gift tax exclusion, which is currently $11,000 for a contribution from an individual (or $22,000 if from a married couple). If your contribution exceeds the regular annual exclusion, you may elect to treat up to $55,000 of the contribution ($110,000 for a married couple who elect gift splitting) as if it were made ratably over a five-year period. If the election is made, you have to report as a taxable gift on Form 709 only 20% of the total contribution (up to the $55,000 or $110,000 limit) in the year of contribution. In each of the next four years an additional 20% is reported. If the contribution exceeds the $55,000 (or $110,000) limit, the excess must be reported as a taxable gift on Form 709 in the year of the contribution.

38.6 Student Loan Interest Deduction

If you paid interest on a qualified student loan in 2002, you may be able to claim an above-the-line (directly from gross income) deduction of up to $2,500. Eligibility for the deduction is phased out if you have 2002 modified adjusted gross income (MAGI, *see* below) between $50,000 and $65,000, or between $100,000 and $130,000 if married filing a joint return. On a joint return, the deduction limit remains $2,500 even if you and your spouse each pay interest on a qualified student loan. If you are claimed as a dependent by another taxpayer, or you are married filing separately, you may not claim the deduction regardless of your income. The deduction is claimed on Line 25 of Form 1040 or Line 18 of Form 1040A. A worksheet in the form instructions may be used to figure your student loan interest deduction.

Qualified loans and expenses. A qualified student loan is one taken out to pay qualified higher education expenses for you, your spouse, or a person who was your dependent when you took out the loan. The expenses must be paid or incurred within a reasonable time before or after the loan was taken out, and the funds obtained must be used toward education furnished while the student is enrolled at least half-time in a program leading to a degree or other recognized educational credential at an eligible educational institution. Medical and graduate school programs are included. Eligible institutions are colleges, universities, vocational schools, and other post-secondary educational institutions eligible to participate in Department of Education student aid programs.

Qualified higher education expenses include tuition, fees, room and board, books, equipment, and other necessary expenses such as transportation. These costs must be reduced by:

1. Nontaxable employer-provided educational assistance benefits.
2. Nontaxable education IRA distributions.
3. U.S. Savings Bond interest excluded from income because it is used to pay higher education expenses.
4. Qualified tax-free scholarships.
5. Veterans' educational assistance benefits.
6. Tax-free gifts and inheritances received to pay education expenses.

 Law Alert

State QTP Distributions Tax Free in 2002

Distributions from a qualified state tuition program will be tax free beginning in 2002 if used for qualified higher education expenses. Distributions from private plans will not be tax free until 2004.

 *Law Alert*

60-Month Limitation Repealed

The 2001 Tax Act eliminated the 60-month limitation for student loan interest paid after 2001. Those prevented from deducting student loan interest before 2002 due to the 60-month limitation may deduct interest payments made on the same loan after 2001.

Loan origination fees and capitalized interest (unpaid interest that accrues and is added to the balance of the loan) can be counted as interest paid. In general, a payment, regardless of its label, is treated first as a payment of interest to the extent that accrued interest remains unpaid, second as a payment of any loan origination fees or capitalized interest, until such amounts are reduced to zero, and third as a payment of principal.

Repeal of prior law 60-month limit on deduction. For years before 2002, the deduction was allowed *only for the first 60 months* in which interest payments were required. The 60-month limitation has been repealed for interest paid after 2001. If you paid interest in 2002 on a qualified loan, the deduction is allowed even if interest on that same loan could not be deducted before 2002 because of the 60-month limitation.

EXAMPLE

You took out a qualified student loan in 1996. Beginning on October 1, 1996, you made a payment on the loan every month. As of the end of 2000, you had made 51 monthly interest payments. You could deduct the interest on your first nine payments for 2001. You could not deduct the interest on the next three payments because they were made after the 60-month period (October 1, 1996–September 30, 2001).

Beginning in January 2002, you can once again begin deducting the interest on your payments for the remaining life of the loan.

Dependents and married persons filing separately are ineligible. You may not claim a student loan interest deduction during any year in which someone claims you as a dependent. However, you may deduct interest payments made in a later year when you are no longer claimed as a dependent.

You may not claim a student loan interest deduction for any year in which you are married and file a separate tax return.

Other restrictions. A revolving line of credit is not a qualified loan unless you agree to use the funds solely to pay education costs.

You may not deduct interest paid on a loan from a relative as educational loan interest; *see 5.6*.

You may not claim a student loan interest deduction for any amount you may deduct under any other tax law provision, for example home mortgage interest. You also cannot use the deduction if you use part of the borrowed money for purposes other than education, for instance to make improvements to your house.

Phaseout. The interest deduction is reduced or eliminated if your modified adjusted gross income (MAGI) exceeds phase-out limits. The reduction applies to your deduction for 2002 if MAGI is more than $50,000, or more than $100,000 on a joint return. If MAGI is more than $65,000, or more than $130,000 on a joint return, you may not claim a deduction for 2002. MAGI is the same as the adjusted gross income shown on your return (disregarding student loan interest) unless you claim a deduction for higher education costs *(38.13)*, the exclusion for foreign earned income (Chapter 36), or certain other items of foreign income or expenses were excluded or deducted from your income. Such items generally must be added back to adjusted gross income.

If your MAGI is within the phase-out range, figure the reduction to the 2002 deduction by multiplying your deductible interest (up to the $2,500 limit) by a fraction, the numerator of which is your MAGI less $50,000, or $100,000 if married filing jointly, and the denominator of which is $15,000, or $30,000 if married filing jointly.

The student loan deduction worksheet in the Form 1040 or Form 1040A instructions can be used to figure the phase-out reduction and the amount of your deduction.

EXAMPLE

1. In 2002 you paid $900 interest on a qualified student loan. Your MAGI is $105,000 on a joint return. Your deduction is reduced by $150. You can deduct $750 ($900 – $150).

$$\$900 \times {}^{\$105,000 - \$100,000}/_{\$30,000} = \$150 \text{ reduction}$$

2. The same facts as in Example 1, except you paid $2,600 interest. The maximum deduction of $2,500 is reduced by $417. You can deduct $2,083 ($2,500 – $417).

$$\$2,500 \times {}^{\$105,000 - \$100,000}/_{\$30,000} = \$417 \text{ reduction}$$

Caution

Deduction Lost for Student Dependent's Loan

If your parent or someone else claims you as a dependent on his or her return, you may not deduct interest on your return for student loan interest you paid. Furthermore, the person who claims you as a dependent may not deduct the interest where you are the borrower legally obligated to repay the loan.

Law Alert

Deduction Eligibility Expanded

The 2001 Tax Act eases the eligibility requirements for the student loan interest deduction. Starting in 2002, the deduction is phased out for MAGI between $50,000 and $65,000, or between $100,000 and $130,000 if married filing a joint return.

Hope and Lifetime Learning Credits

Caution

Both Education Credits Not Allowed for the Same Student

You may not claim both the Hope credit and the lifetime learning credit for the same student's expenses for the same tax year. For example, if you pay more than $2,000 of qualified tuition expenses for your child, you may not claim the Hope credit for the first $2,000 of expenses and the lifetime learning credit for the balance.

Law Alert

Coordination of Savings Options Easier

Beginning in 2002, tax-free distributions from education IRAs and state QTPs can be received in the same year that an education credit is claimed, provided the distributions are not used to cover the same expenses for the same student.

38.7 Education Tax Credits

There are two tax credits for qualifying higher education expenses: The Hope credit and the lifetime learning credit. They are figured on Form 8863. Rules that apply to both credits are discussed in this section. The Hope credit is discussed further at *38.8* and the lifetime learning credit at *38.9*.

Who may claim a credit. If you pay qualifying higher education expenses for you, your spouse, or a person you claim as a dependent (*see* Chapter 21) on your return, and you are not subject to the credit phaseout because of the amount of your income, you may claim a credit on Form 8863. If married, you must file a joint return to claim either education credit. The credits reduce regular income tax and AMT liability for 2002 and 2003. The phaseout applies if your 2002 MAGI is between $41,000 and $51,000 if filing as single, head of household, or qualifying widow(er), or between $82,000 and $102,000 if married filing jointly. *See 38.10* for how the credit is reduced if MAGI is within the phase-out range.

If your child is claimed by you as your dependent, his or her payment of qualifying expenses is treated as your payment and you may claim the credit. If you do *not* claim an exemption for your child on your tax return, your child can claim a credit for qualified expenses that you paid.

What expenses qualify. Qualified tuition and related expenses are tuition and fees required for enrollment or attendance of an eligible student at an eligible educational institution (*see* below). Qualified expenses do *not* include room and board, insurance, medical expenses, transportation, or other personal or family living expenses. The cost of books, supplies, equipment, and student activity fees may be included *only* if it must be paid to the educational institution as a condition of enrollment. Hobby- or sport-related courses and noncredit courses do not qualify for the Hope credit unless they are part of the student's degree program *(38.8)*. Such courses qualify for the lifetime learning credit if they are part of a degree program or are taken to acquire or improve job skills.

Prepaid expenses. If in 2002 you pay qualified tuition and related expenses for an academic period that begins in the first three months of 2003, you can include the prepayment in figuring your 2002 credit. For example, if you pay $1,000 in December 2002 for qualified tuition for the winter 2003 semester that begins in January 2003, you can include that amount in figuring a 2002 credit.

Eligible students and eligible educational institutions. You, your spouse, or an eligible dependent may qualify as an eligible student if enrolled at an eligible educational institution for at least one academic period (semester, trimester, quarter) during the year. An eligible dependent is a person for whom you claim a dependency exemption on your tax return; *see* Chapter 21.

An eligible educational institution generally includes any accredited public, nonprofit, or proprietary *post-secondary* institution eligible to participate in the student aid programs administered by the Department of Education.

If you claim a deduction for higher education expenses on your tax return, for instance, for job-related courses, you may not claim a credit for those same expenses. Similarly, if you pay higher education expenses with a tax-free scholarship, Pell grant, or employer-provided educational assistance, you may not claim a credit for those amounts. You may, however, claim a credit for expenses paid from your (or your dependent's) earnings, loans, gifts, inheritances, and personal savings.

If you pay qualified expenses for more than one eligible student in the same year, you may choose to take credits on a per-student, per-year basis. Thus, you can claim the Hope credit for one child and the lifetime learning credit for another child in the same tax year.

Coordination with Coverdell ESAs or a qualified tuition program. Beginning in 2002, you may be able to claim a Hope credit and lifetime learning credit in the same year in which you receive a tax-free distribution from either a Coverdell ESA or a state qualified tuition program (QTP). The expenses taken into account as the basis of a Hope or lifetime learning credit reduce eligible expenses for purposes of figuring the tax-free part of an ESA or state QTP distribution.

Recapture of credit. If, in a later tax year, you receive a refund of an amount used to figure a higher education credit, you may have to repay all or part of the credit.

Phase-out of credits. Both credits are reduced under a phase-out formula if your modified adjusted gross income (MAGI) comes within the rules discussed in *38.10*.

38.8 Hope Credit

If you paid qualified tuition and related expenses in 2002 for an eligible student who at the beginning of 2002 had not yet completed the first or second year of college or other post-secondary institution, you generally may figure a Hope credit on Form 8863 of up to $1,500 for the qualified tuition and related expenses paid in 2002 for the student. However, the Hope credit may only be claimed twice for a particular student, so if you claimed the credit for a student in more than one prior year, you may not claim a 2002 credit for that student, even if the first two years of college had not been completed as of the start of 2002.

An eligible student must meet the following requirements: (1) be enrolled in one of the first two years of postsecondary education (generally, the freshman or sophomore years of college), (2) be enrolled in a program that leads to a degree, certificate, or other recognized educational credential, (3) be taking at least one-half of the normal full-time workload for his or her course of study for at least one academic period beginning during the calendar year, and (4) not have any felony conviction for possessing or distributing a controlled substance.

The amount of the Hope credit for 2002 is 100% of the first $1,000 plus 50% of the next $1,000 paid for *each* eligible student's qualified tuition and related expenses. This means that you can claim the full $1,500 for each eligible student for whom you pay at least $2,000 for qualified expenses. Your maximum Hope credit for 2002 is $1,500 times the number of eligible students. The $1,500 Hope credit limit may be indexed for inflation in 2003.

If a student completed the second year of post-secondary education before 2002, or if the Hope credit was claimed in two prior years, the lifetime learning credit, but not the Hope credit, may be claimed for that student's eligible 2002 expenses.

 Law Alert

Tax Liability Limitation on Education Credits
For 2002 and 2003, the Hope credit and the lifetime learning credit reduce regular income tax and AMT liability. The education credits may not provide a refund; if the amount of credit exceeds the tax you owe, the excess is not refunded to you.

EXAMPLE

Lucy and Ricky are married and file a joint tax return. For 2002, they claim their daughter Sophia as a dependent on their tax return and their modified adjusted gross income is $70,000. Sophia started her sophomore (second) year of studies at the local university in September 2002. Lucy and Ricky claimed a 2001 credit for their payment in 2001 of Sophia's freshman year expenses. In 2002 they paid tuition of $12,000 for Sophia. They can claim a $1,500 Hope credit for 2002, the maximum amount allowed.

38.9 Lifetime Learning Credit

For academic expenses paid during 2002, you may claim on Form 8863 a lifetime learning credit of up to $1,000 for the total qualified tuition and related expenses paid for yourself, your spouse, or your dependents enrolled in eligible educational institutions *(see 38.7)* during the year.

In contrast to the Hope credit, the lifetime learning credit does not have a degree requirement or a workload requirement. The credit may be claimed for one or more courses at an eligible educational institution that are either part of a post-secondary degree program or part of a nondegree program taken to acquire or improve job skills. The lifetime learning credit is not limited to students in the first two years of postsecondary education, as is the Hope credit, and it covers expenses for graduate-level degree work. There is also no limit on the number of years for which the lifetime learning credit can be claimed for each eligible student.

The lifetime learning credit is 20% of the first $5,000 paid for qualified tuition and related expenses for *all* eligible students in the family. Thus, the maximum lifetime learning credit you may claim for 2002 is $1,000 (20% of $5,000), subject to the income-based phaseout; *see 38.10*.

The $1,000 limit applies regardless of the number of eligible students for whom you pay education expenses. This aspect of the lifetime learning credit differs from the Hope credit, which may be claimed for each eligible student, up to $1,500 each *(see 38.8)*.

Beginning in 2003, the lifetime learning credit will be increased to 20% of the first $10,000 paid for qualified tuition and related expenses.

38.10 Income Phaseout of Education Credits

Both the Hope credit and the lifetime learning credit are phased out on Form 8863 for 2002 if your modified adjusted gross income is between $41,000 and $51,000 and you file as single, head of household, or qualifying widow(er), or between $82,000 and $102,000 on a joint return. For

2003, the MAGI phase-out ranges may be increased by an inflation adjustment. For most taxpayers, modified adjusted gross income is adjusted gross income (AGI) unless they have tax-free income earned abroad or from certain U.S. territories or possessions. If so, adjusted gross income is increased by such amounts.

Law Alert

Phaseout of Credits

2002 was the first year for which the phase-out thresholds were adjusted for inflation. The threshold was increased by $2,000 to $82,000 for joint filers and by $1,000 to $41,000 for others. You cannot claim any higher education credits for 2002 if your modified adjusted gross income exceeds $51,000 ($102,000 on a joint return). For 2003, these phase-out limits may again be indexed for inflation.

EXAMPLES

1. Ron and Jackie are married and file a joint tax return. Their MAGI for 2002 is $85,000. They pay $6,000 of qualifying expenses for their son, Leo, and $7,500 for their daughter, Ally. Both students are claimed as dependents on their parents' return. A Hope credit of $3,000, $1,500 for each child, is allowed prior to taking the phaseout into account. On Form 8863, they figure a $2,550 Hope credit after application of the phase-out rules. Their excess MAGI of $3,000 ($85,000 – $82,000 phase-out threshold) is 15% of the $20,000 phase-out range, so 15% of the tentative $3,000 credit is phased out and 85% is allowed.

2. John, unmarried, has a MAGI of $42,000. He pays $2,500 in qualified tuition and fees. He figures a lifetime learning credit of $500 (20% of qualified tuition and fees), before taking the phaseout into account. On Form 8863, he figures a $450 lifetime learning credit after application of the phase-out rules. John's excess MAGI of $1,000 ($42,000 – $41,000) is 10% of the $10,000 phase-out range, so he is allowed 90% of his tentative $500 credit and 10% is phased out.

Note: If you are not allowed a credit for your dependent child's expenses because of the MAGI phaseout, and your child has tax liability against which the credit may be claimed, you can forego claiming the child as a dependency exemption on your return, which would allow the credit to be claimed on the child's return. Consider which of the child's credit or your dependency exemption would provide the larger tax savings. If your income is high enough to require the phaseout of personal exemptions *(21.16)*, the value of the exemption may be minimal.

Coverdell Education Savings Accounts (Formerly Education IRAs)

38.11 Contributing to a Coverdell Education Savings Account (ESA)

A Coverdell Education Savings Account, or ESA, is a trust or custodial account set up specifically for the purpose of paying the qualified education expenses of the designated beneficiary of the account. A designated beneficiary must be a child under age 18 unless the beneficiary is a special needs beneficiary, as discussed below. Coverdell Education Savings Accounts were formerly known as Education IRAs.

Planning Reminder

New Contribution Limit and Deadline for Coverdell ESAs

The maximum contribution limit for Coverdell ESAs has increased to $2,000 from $500. The deadline for making annual contributions is also extended. Instead of having to contribute by December 31 each year, contributions can now be made as late as the original due date of your return (without extensions), this year April 15, 2003.

Contribution limit for 2002. For 2002, you may contribute up to $2,000 to a Coverdell ESA for a child under age 18. Contributions to a Coverdell ESA are not deductible. Any individual (including a child) can contribute to a child's Coverdell ESA if the individual's MAGI for 2002 is not more than $110,000 ($220,000 on a joint return). The $2,000 maximum contribution for each child is gradually reduced if the contributor's MAGI for 2002 is between $95,000 and $110,000 (between $190,000 and $220,000 in the case of a joint return). Total contributions for 2002 may not be more than $2,000 per designated beneficiary, regardless of the number of contributions or contributors. The final date on which you can make contributions to an ESA for any year is the due date of your return for that year (not including extensions).

A 6% excise tax applies to Coverdell ESA contributions that exceed $2,000 for 2002 for any beneficiary. The penalty is imposed on the beneficiary (Form 5329). The excise tax does not apply if the excess contributions (and any earnings) are withdrawn before the tax return due date including extensions.

Special needs beneficiary. Beginning in 2002, contributions to a Coverdell ESA for a special needs beneficiary may continue after the beneficiary reaches age 18. Also, the Coverdell ESA of a special needs beneficiary will no longer have to be emptied at age 30. The definition of "special needs" has not yet been established. Congress wants the IRS definition to include an individual who, because of a physical, mental, or emotional condition (including a learning disability), requires additional time to complete his or her education.

38.12   Distributions From Coverdell ESAs

A designated beneficiary of a Coverdell ESA is not taxed on withdrawals that do not exceed qualified education expenses. If the total withdrawals for a tax year exceed the qualified education expenses (*see* below), a portion of the withdrawals is taxable to the beneficiary. The taxable portion is the amount of the excess withdrawal allocable to earnings. IRS Publication 970 has a worksheet for making the computation.

Qualified education expenses. The 2001 Tax Act expanded the definition of qualified educational expenses for years 2002 and beyond. In addition to qualified higher education expenses (as defined at *38.5* for QTPs), qualified expenses for Coverdell ESA purposes include elementary and secondary education expenses, kindergarten through grade 12. The elementary or secondary school may be a public, private, or religious school. Eligible expenses for elementary and secondary school students include tuition, fees, academic tutoring, special services for special needs beneficiaries, books, supplies, computers and peripheral equipment, Internet access, and software. Software designed for sports or hobbies must be predominately educational in nature. Qualified expenses also include room and board, uniforms, transportation, and supplementary items and services including extended day programs required or provided by the school.

Coordination with education credits. Starting in 2002, if you claim a Hope credit or lifetime learning credit, you may also exclude a Coverdell ESA distribution from income in the same year provided the ESA distribution does not cover the same higher education expenses taken into account when figuring the credit.

Additional tax on taxable distributions. Generally, a taxable distribution is subject to a 10% additional tax. The 10% additional tax does not apply to distributions that are: (1) made to a beneficiary (or to the estate of the designated beneficiary) on or after the death of the designated beneficiary, (2) made because the designated beneficiary is disabled, (3) made because the designated beneficiary received a tax-free scholarship or educational assistance allowance that equals or exceeds the distribution, or (4) taxable only because the qualified ESA education expenses were reduced by expenses used in figuring a Hope or lifetime learning credit.

The 10% additional tax also does not apply to a distribution of an excess contribution (and allocable earnings) made before the tax return due date, including extensions.

Rollovers and other transfers. Withdrawn assets may be rolled over tax free from one Coverdell ESA to another for the benefit of the same beneficiary or a member of the beneficiary's family if the recipient is under age 30. The withdrawal is considered rolled over if it is paid to another Coverdell ESA within 60 days. Only one rollover per Coverdell ESA is allowed during the 12-month period ending on the date of the payment or withdrawal. For rollover purposes, members of the beneficiary's family include the beneficiary's spouse, child, grandchild, stepchild, brother, sister (and a sibling's son or daughter), half-sister, half-brother, stepbrother, stepsister, father, mother (and siblings of parents), grandfather, grandmother, stepfather, stepmother, in-laws, and the spouses of any of the above.

The designated beneficiary can be changed to a member of the beneficiary's family (included in the above list) with no tax consequences if the new beneficiary is under age 30. However, to be a qualified Coverdell ESA, the plan must require the account balance to be withdrawn no later than 30 days after the designated beneficiary reaches age 30, unless the beneficiary is a special needs beneficiary.

If the beneficiary dies before age 30, the account balance generally must be distributed to the beneficiary's estate within 30 days of the date of death. However, if the Coverdell ESA is transferred to a surviving spouse or other family member (defined above) who is under age 30, the account may be maintained until he or she reaches age 30.

 Filing Tip

Coordination with Education Credits

Starting in 2002, a Hope credit or lifetime learning credit may be claimed in the same year that a Coverdell ESA distribution is excluded from income as long as the distribution does not cover the same expenses for which a credit is claimed.

Deductible Higher Education Expenses

38.13   Deduction for Higher Education Expenses in 2002–2005

If your income does not exceed a specified ceiling, you may deduct up to $3,000 of qualifying higher education tuition and fees on your 2002 return. The deduction is claimed directly from gross income on Line 26 of Form 1040 (whether or not you itemize), or on Line 19 of Form 1040A.

You may *not* claim the deduction for expenses of a student for whom a Hope credit or lifetime learning credit is claimed. If you qualify for both, you must choose between the credit and the deduction. A credit generally provides a larger tax savings. If your income is too high to claim a credit or most of the credit is phased out because of your income (*38.10*), you may take advantage of the deduction.

Ineligible taxpayers. You may not claim the deduction if you are married filing separately. You are also ineligible if you may be claimed as a dependent on another taxpayer's return, whether or not you are actually so claimed.

Qualified higher education expenses. Expenses eligible for the deduction are the same as those qualifying for the Hope or lifetime learning credit. That is, the deduction is limited to tuition and enrollment fees paid to an eligible educational institution for yourself, your spouse or your dependents. The costs of student activity fees and course-related books qualify if they must be paid to the school. Eligible expenses paid in 2002 for an academic period starting in the first three months of 2003 are deductible for 2002. Eligible educational institutions include any college, university, vocational school, or other postsecondary institution eligible to participate in the financial aid programs of the Department of Education.

Deduction affected by excludable education benefits. Expenses eligible for the deduction are reduced by tax-free scholarships *(38.1)* and other tax-free educational assistance. If a Coverdell ESA distribution is tax free *(38.12)*, or you receive tax-free interest from an EE or I savings bond used for tuition *(38.4)*, the expenses used to figure the tax-free distribution or interest reduce the expenses eligible for the deduction. Expenses used to figure a tax-free distribution from a state QTP *(38.5)* reduce the deduction-eligible expenses only to the extent that the distribution is a return of earnings.

Income cut-off for deduction. The table below shows the amount of the deduction and the income cut-off. Note that there is no gradual phaseout for excess income. If your modified adjusted gross income (MAGI) exceeds the $65,000 or $130,000 ceiling, no deduction at all is allowed. For purposes of the deduction, MAGI is generally the same as the AGI shown on your return. AGI is increased by any exclusion for foreign earned income or income from Puerto Rico or American Samoa, or the foreign housing exclusion or deduction.

Termination after 2005. The deduction will last for only four years, from 2002 through 2005, unless Congress extends it.

Tax years	MAGI eligibility	Max. amount deductible
2002 and 2003	Not more than $65,000 (not married) or $130,000 (married filing jointly)	$3,000
	More than $65,000 (not married) or $130,000 (married filing jointly)	None
2004 and 2005	Not more than $65,000 (not married) or $130,000 (married filing jointly)	$4,000
	More than $65,000 but not more than $80,000 (not married) or more than $130,000 but not more than $160,000 (married filing jointly)	$2,000
	More than $80,000 (unmarried) or $160,000 (married filing jointly)	None

Chapter 39

Estate Taxes

The federal estate tax is a tax on the transfer of property at death. For estates of persons dying in 2002, the estate tax applies to taxable estates over $1 million, after taking into account allowable deductions, such as charitable bequests and property passing to a surviving spouse.

Under the Economic Growth and Tax Relief Reconciliation Act of 2001 (EGTRRA), the exclusion from federal estate tax will increase and the maximum estate tax rate will be reduced from 2002 through 2009 prior to the repeal of the estate tax in 2010. A modified carryover basis system will take effect for inherited assets when the estate tax is repealed. The top gift tax rate will also decline, but the gift tax will not be repealed. A $1 million lifetime exclusion from gift tax is allowed for taxable gifts after 2010; *see 33.1.*

Repeal of the estate tax will apply only for 2010 unless Congress extends the repeal provision of EGTRRA. Without a Congressional extension, the law in effect prior to the enactment of EGTRRA will be reinstated in 2011.

By following the guidelines in this chapter, you can estimate your potential estate. If your estate may be subject to tax, you may want to start thinking about property transfers that may reduce or avoid the estate tax. A brief review of estate tax plans is at *39.6,* and the gift tax is discussed in Chapter 33.

39.1 What Is the Estate Tax?

The estate you built up may not be entirely yours to give away. The federal government and, in most cases, at least one state government stand ready to claim their shares.

The federal estate tax is a tax on the act of transferring property at death. It is not a tax on the right of the beneficiary to receive the property; the estate and the estate alone pays the tax, although the property passing to individual beneficiaries may be diminished by the tax.

Understand what the word *estate* means in estate tax law so that you do not underestimate the value of your taxable estate. The estate includes not only your real estate (foreign and domestic), bank deposits, securities, and personal property such as art objects, but can also include insurance, your interest in trusts or jointly held property, and certain interests you have in other estates.

The general guide to federal estate taxation in this chapter will alert you to the potential extent of estate tax costs, and help you plan for estate tax savings that you may discuss with an experienced estate tax planning professional. Periodic re-evaluation of your estate plan is essential, expecially given the uncertainty as to whether the scheduled repeal of the estate tax for 2010 *(see 39.5)* will be made permanent.

39.2 Take Inventory

The first step in estate tax planning follows a simple business practice of taking inventory of everything you own. Listing your belongings takes thought, time, and a surprising amount of work. On your list you should include records of purchases, fire and theft insurance inventories, bankbooks, brokers' statements, etc. You should also include your cash, real estate (here and abroad), securities, mortgages, rights in property, trust accounts, personal effects, collections, and art works. Life insurance is includible if it is: (1) payable to your estate; (2) payable to others and you have kept "incidents of ownership" such as the right to change beneficiaries, surrender or assign the policy, or pledge it for a loan; or (3) you assign the policy and die within three years *(33.6)*.

If you own property jointly with your spouse, your estate includes only one-half its value.

If you had appraisals made of specially treasured items or collections, or property of substantial value, file such appraisals with your estate papers and then enter the value on your inventory.

Retirement benefits. The taxable estate generally includes benefits payable at your death from any of the following retirement plans: pension plan, profit-sharing plan, Keogh plan, individual retirement account, or annuity. However, the value of an annuity from an IRA or employer plan that is payable to a beneficiary other than your estate may qualify for a full or partial exclusion if IRA distributions began before 1985 or you separated from service before 1985; no exclusion is allowed to the extent of your own nondeductible contributions to the plan.

A full exclusion is allowed for IRA funds if you began taking distributions from the account before 1983 under a schedule that irrevocably set the form of benefits. If IRA distributions began in 1983 or 1984 and you irrevocably elected the form of benefits before July 18, 1984, a $100,000 exclusion is allowed.

If you began receiving distributions from an employer plan before 1983 under a schedule that irrevocably set the form of benefits, a full estate tax exclusion is allowed. If you separated from service in 1983 or 1984, a $100,000 exclusion is allowed if the form of benefits is not changed before death; this is true even if distributions did not begin until after 1984.

39.3 Finding the Value of Your Estate

When you have completed your inventory, assign to each asset what you consider to be its fair market value. This may be difficult to do for some assets. Resist the tendency to overvalue articles that arouse feelings of pride or sentiment and undervalue some articles of great intrinsic worth. For purposes of your initial estimate, it is better to err on the side of overvaluation. You can list ordinary personal effects at nominal value.

If you have a family business, your idea of its value and that of the IRS may vary greatly. Estate plans have been upset by the higher value placed on such a business by the IRS. You can protect your estate by anticipating and solving this problem with your business associates and counselors.

If your business is owned by a closely held corporation, and there is no ready or open market in which the stock can be valued, get some factual basis for a figure that will be reported on the estate tax return. One of the ways to do this is by arranging a buy-sell agreement with a potential purchaser. This agreement must fix the value of the stock. Generally, an agreement that binds both the estate and the purchaser and restricts lifetime sales of the stock will effectively fix the value of the stock for estate tax purposes. Another way would be to make a gift of some shares to a family member and have value established in gift tax proceedings.

 *Caution*

Trusts Includible in Estate

There are some assets that you might not ordinarily consider as part of your estate. Nevertheless, include in your inventory any trust arrangements created by you in which you have: (1) a life estate (the income or other use of property for life); (2) income that is to be used to pay your legal obligations (support of a child, for example); (3) the right to change the beneficiary or his or her interest (a power of appointment); (4) the right to revoke a trust transfer or gift; and (5) a reversionary interest (the possibility that the property can come back to you).

If a substantial part of your estate is real estate used in farming or a closely held business, your executor may be able to elect, with the consent of heirs having an interest in the property, to value the property on the basis of its farming or business use, rather than its highest and best use. The special use valuation, however, may not reduce the gross estate by more than $750,000, subject to adjustment for inflation. This savings may be recaptured from your heir if he or she stops using the property in farming or business within 10 years of your death.

39.4 How the Estate Tax Is Applied

A single unified rate schedule applies to a decedent's estate and all post-1976 lifetime gifts *over* the annual gift tax exclusion. Under the unified gift and estate tax rate, the overall tax on your property holdings is theoretically the same whether or not you make lifetime gifts. In actual cases, however, lifetime gifts may reduce the potential overall tax because of the annual gift tax exclusion *(33.1)*. After 2003, the credit for gift tax purposes will remain at $1 million while the credit for estate tax gradually increases as shown in *39.5*.

You may use IRS Form 706 to estimate what the estate tax would be on your estate. If you make no taxable gifts during your life, estimating estate tax on Form 706 is fairly easy. You start with the total market value of the property in the estate. This is called the *gross estate*. From the gross estate you subtract certain deductions. For example, administration expenses for the estate and charitable bequests are deductible. An unlimited marital deduction is allowed for bequests to a surviving spouse who is a U.S. citizen. The net amount after deductions is your taxable estate. A unified credit is subtracted from the tax calculated on the taxable estate; *see 39.5*. Other credits, including the state death tax credit, further reduce the federal estate tax on your estate. The state death tax credit will be phased out starting in 2002 and replaced by a deduction in 2005.

If you make taxable gifts after 1976, estimating your estate tax is more complicated. The estate tax and gift tax are cumulative. That is, the tax rate is applied to the sum of (1) your taxable estate at death, and (2) taxable lifetime gifts made after 1976 (other than gifts included in your estate). The tax you figure on both (1) and (2) is reduced by gift taxes payable on gifts made after 1976. The unified or applicable credit and other credits are then subtracted from the remaining amount. *See* the Form 706 instructions for details.

Generation-skipping transfers. Transfers that "skip" a generation, such as a gift to a grandchild, are subject to a special tax (computed on Schedule R of Form 706) if they exceed a lifetime exemption of $1 million per transferor, subject to inflation adjustments. Because of other exceptions and the complexity of these rules, you should consult an experienced tax practitioner if you are planning "skip" transfers.

39.5 Estate Tax Rates

Estates are entitled to a unified credit that generally shields from estate tax amounts up to the exclusion amount shown below. For estates that qualify for the special family-owned business deduction and that claim less than the maximum $675,000 deduction *(see* the Law Alert at the top left of this page), the exclusion amount may differ from the amount shown in the following table.

Individual dying in—	Exclusion amount—	Top estate tax rate—	Unified credit—
2001	$675,000	55%	$220,550
2002	$1 million	50%	$345,800
2003	$1 million	49%	$345,800
2004	$1.5 million	48%	$555,800
2005	$1.5 million	47%	$555,800
2006	$2 million	46%	$780,800
2007	$2 million	45%	$780,800
2008	$2 million	45%	$780,800
2009	$3.5 million	45%	$1,455,800
2010	Total repeal of estate tax		
2011	If Congress does not extend the repeal of the estate tax beyond 2010, then starting in 2011 the exclusion would be $1 million and the top estate tax rate would be 55%.		

Law Alert

Family-Owned Business

For estates of individuals dying before 2004, a special estate tax deduction may be allowed for a family business interest. Up to $675,000 of the adjusted value of the business may be deductible and the deduction, together with the exclusion amount, may shield up to $1.3 million of family business assets from estate tax.

The adjusted value of the family-owned business interests generally must exceed 50% of the decedent's adjusted gross estate. A business interest qualifies as family owned if it is at least 50% owned by the decedent's family, or if it is at least 70% owned by two families or 90% by three families and the decedent's family owns at least 30%. For five of the eight years preceding the date of death, the business interests had to be owned by the decedent or family members, and they must have materially participated in the business operations. The business interest must pass to family members or 10-year employees. Such qualified heirs are subject to a recapture tax if they do not meet a material participation test within 10 years of the date of death or if a disposition of the business interest is made to nonqualifying persons.

For details on this complicated deduction, *see* the instructions for Schedule T of Form 706. The 2001 Tax Act repeals the family-owned business interest deduction for estates of individuals dying after 2003.

Law Alert

Higher Exclusion and Lower Top Rate

The exclusion from federal estate tax increases to $1.5 million in 2004, $2 million in 2006, and $3.5 million in 2009, prior to the repeal of the estate tax in 2010.

In 2003, the top estate tax rate will fall to 49% (from 50%) and then drop an additional 1% each year until it reaches 45% in 2007. The top rate will remain at 45% in 2008 and 2009 leading up to repeal in 2010. Rates below the top rate will not be changed.

Unified Gift and Estate Tax Rates for Estates of Individuals Dying in 2002*				
If taxable amount is:				
Over—	But not over—	The tax is—	Plus%—	Of the amount over—
$0	$10,000	$0	18	$0
10,000	20,000	1,800	20	10,000
20,000	40,000	3,800	22	20,000
40,000	60,000	8,200	24	40,000
60,000	80,000	13,000	26	60,000
80,000	100,000	18,200	28	80,000
100,000	150,000	23,800	30	100,000
150,000	250,000	38,800	32	150,000
250,000	500,000	70,800	34	250,000
500,000	750,000	155,800	37	500,000
750,000	1,000,000	248,300	39	750,000
1,000,000	1,250,000	345,800	41	1,000,000
1,250,000	1,500,000	448,300	43	1,250,000
1,500,000	2,000,000	555,800	45	1,500,000
2,000,000	2,500,000	780,800	49	2,000,000
2,500,000	3,000,000	1,025,800	50	2,500,000

*See *the table showing the scheduled reduction in the top tax rate for 2003–2009.*

Law Alert

State Death Tax Credit Phasing Out

Most states impose a "pick up" estate tax based on the state death tax credit allowed for federal estate tax purposes. The federal credit for state death taxes is being phased out for estates of persons dying after 2001. The credit allowed under pre-2002 law is reduced by 25% in 2002, by 50% in 2003, and by 75% in 2004. In 2005, the credit is repealed and replaced with an estate tax deduction for death tax paid to any State or the District of Columbia.

Planning Reminder

Marital Deduction

To qualify for the marital deduction, the property must generally be given to the spouse outright or by other arrangements that are the legal equivalent of outright ownership. There is an exception for income interests in charitable remainder annuity or unitrusts and certain other qualified terminable interest property (QTIP) for which the executor makes an election.

39.6 Reducing or Eliminating a Potential Estate Tax

Here are general approaches to eliminating or reducing a potential estate tax: You can make direct lifetime gifts. Any appreciation on the property transferred will be removed from your estate. Furthermore, each gift, to the extent of the annual per donee exclusion ($11,000 in 2002), reduces your gross estate; see *33.1* and *33.2.* Life insurance can be assigned to avoid estate tax, provided the assignment takes place more than three years before death; see *33.6.* You can provide in your will for bequests that will qualify for the marital and charitable deductions.

The marital deduction. A married person may greatly reduce or eliminate estate tax by using the marital deduction. Property passing to a spouse is generally free from estate or gift tax because of an unlimited marital deduction.

Weigh carefully the tax consequences of leaving your spouse all of your property. For maximum tax savings, you may want to give your spouse only enough property to reduce your taxable estate to the exclusion floor *(see 39.5).* The unified credit amount will then eliminate tax on that amount at the time of your death. By leaving your spouse less than the maximum deductible amount, you may be able to reduce the estate tax at the time of his or her death.

Life insurance proceeds may qualify as marital deduction property. Name your spouse the unconditional beneficiary of the proceeds with unrestricted control over any unpaid proceeds. If your spouse is not given this control or general power of appointment, and there is no requirement that proceeds remaining on your spouse's death be payable to his or her estate, the insurance proceeds will not qualify for the marital deduction.

What should be done if you believe your spouse cannot manage property? You will not want to give complete and personal control. The law permits you to put the property in certain trust arrangements that are considered equivalent to complete ownership. Your attorney can explain how you can protect your spouse's interest and qualify the trust property for the marital deduction.

Marital deduction restrictions for noncitizen spouses. A marital deduction may not be claimed for property passing outright to a surviving spouse who is not a U.S. citizen. However, the marital deduction is allowed if the surviving spouse's interest is in a qualifying domestic trust

(QDOT). At least one trustee must be an individual U.S. citizen or domestic corporation with power to withhold estate tax due from distributions of trust corpus. The trust must maintain sufficient assets as required by IRS regulations. For the marital deduction to apply, the executor must make an irrevocable election on the decedent's estate tax return. On Form 706-QDT, estate tax will apply to certain distributions of trust corpus made prior to the surviving spouse's death, and to the value of the QDOT property remaining at the surviving spouse's death. You should consult an experienced tax practitioner to set up a QDOT trust and plan for distribution provisions.

The estate of a nonresident alien is subject to estate tax only to the extent that the estate is located in the United States. A marital deduction may be claimed by the estate of a nonresident alien for property passing to a surviving spouse who is a U.S. citizen. If the surviving spouse is not a U.S. citizen, then the transferred interest must be in the form of a QDOT.

Periodically review your estate plan. No estate plan is ever really final. Economic conditions and inflation constantly change values. For this reason, your plan must be reviewed periodically as changes occur in your family and business, as when a birth or death occurs; when you receive a substantial increase or decrease in income; when you enter a new business venture or resign from an old one; or when you sell, retire from, or bring new persons into business. A member of your family may no longer need any part of your estate, while others may need more. Material changes may occur in the health or life expectancy of one of your beneficiaries. Furthermore, political conditions may affect the scheduled phaseout and repeal of the federal estate tax *(39.5)*.

Caution

Get Expert Advice
Estate tax planning is not a do-it-yourself activity. You should contact experienced counsel for help in developing a plan for your future estate that will accomplish your tax and personal objectives.

39.7 Estate Tax Freeze Advisory

The object of an estate tax freeze is to reduce or eliminate estate tax on the inheritance of property by fixing the value through certain property arrangements. A complicated gift and estate tax law (IRC §§2701–2704) attempts to discourage such plans by applying special valuation rules. The rules cover not only common and preferred stock holdings within the family but also partnership interests, the deferral of dividend payments on preferred stock, life and remainder interests, and buy-sell agreements in family businesses.

The estate freeze rules impose gift tax and estate tax values for property transfers subject to the law. Because of the complexity of these rules and their effect on gift and estate values, we suggest that you seek professional advice in the following situations:

- As an owner of a family business, you plan to give common stock to family members while retaining preferred stock or recapitalize with common and preferred stock.
- You plan to give up a voting interest or liquidating rights attached to preferred stock in a family business.
- You defer payment of dividends in preferred stock in a family business.
- You plan to retain an interest for life in a transfer or purchase of property.
- You plan to give stock to a family member in a company in which you have a buy-sell agreement.

Part 6

Business Tax Planning

In this part, you will learn how to report your income from a business or profession, and how to reduce your tax liability by claiming expense deductions. Pay special attention to—

- Reporting rules for income and expenses on Schedule C (Chapter 40).
- Restrictions on deducting home office expenses. Your deduction may be limited by a restrictive income test (Chapter 40).
- Keogh, SEP, and SIMPLE retirement plan rules if you are self-employed. These plans offer tax deductions for contributions and tax-free accumulation of income within the plan. In some cases, special averaging for lump-sum distributions from a Keogh plan is allowed (Chapter 41).
- First-year expensing and depreciation write-offs for business assets (Chapter 42).
- The IRS mileage allowance as an alternative to claiming operating expenses and depreciation for your business automobile (Chapter 43).
- Computing and paying self-employment tax on self-employment earnings from a business or profession (Chapter 45).

Chapter 40

Income or Loss From Your Business or Profession

As a self-employed person, you report income and expenses from your business or profession separately from your other income, such as income from wages. On Schedule C, you report your business income and itemize your expenses. Any net profit is subject to self-employment tax, as well as regular tax. A net profit can also be the basis of deductible contributions to a SEP or Keogh retirement plan, as discussed in Chapter 41.

If you work out of your home, you may deduct home office expenses.

If you claim a loss on Schedule C, be prepared to show that you regularly and substantially participate in the business. Otherwise, your loss may be considered a passive loss deductible only from passive income, as discussed in Chapter 10.

If you have a business loss that exceeds your other income, you may carry back the loss and claim a refund. For a loss in a tax year ending in 2002, the carryback period is generally five years; *see 40.18*.

If you have no employees and business expenses of $2,500 or less, you may be able to file a simplified schedule called Schedule C-EZ; *see 40.6*.

Organizing Your Business

40.1 Forms of Doing Business

The legal form of your business determines the way you report business income and loss, the taxes you pay, the ability of the business to accumulate capital, and the extent of your personal liability. It is beyond the scope of this book to discuss the pros and cons of each form. The decision should be made with the services of a professional experienced in both the legal and tax consequences of doing business in a particular form as it applies to your current and future business prospects.

If you are going into business alone, your choices are: operating as a sole proprietor, incorporating, and forming a limited liability company (LLC). If you are going to operate with associates, you may choose to operate as a partnership, a corporation, or an LLC. If you are concerned with limiting your personal liability, your choice is between a corporation or an LLC. An LLC gives you the advantage of limited liability without having to incorporate.

As a sole proprietor, you report business profit or loss on your personal tax return, as explained in this chapter. If you are a partner, you report your share of partnership profit and loss as explained in Chapter 11. If you incorporate, the corporation pays tax on business income. You are taxable on salaries and dividends paid to you by the corporation. You may avoid this double corporate tax by making an S corporation election, which allows you to report corporate income and loss; *see 11.14.*

If you operate through an LLC as an individual, you report income and loss as a sole proprietor. If you operate an LLC with associates, the LLC reports as a partnership and you report your share of income and loss. However, under the current check-the-box rules, the LLC may elect to report as an association taxable as a corporation on Form 8832.

40.2 Reporting Self-Employed Income

You file a separate Schedule C along with Form 1040 if you are a sole proprietor of a business or a professional in your own practice. If you do freelance work as an independent contractor, you are self-employed and use Schedule C. If you are an employee with a sideline business, report the self-employment income and expenses from that business on Schedule C. Do not file Schedule C if your business is operated through a partnership or corporation. A guide to Schedule C is in *40.6.*

On Schedule C, you deduct your allowable business expenses from your business income. Net business profit (or loss) figured on Schedule C is entered on Line 12, Page 1 of Form 1040. Thus, business profit (or loss) is added to (or subtracted from) nonbusiness income on Form 1040 to compute adjusted gross income. This procedure gives you the chance to deduct your business expenses, whether you claim itemized deductions or nonbusiness deductions on Schedule A, such as charitable contributions, taxes, and medical expenses, or you claim the standard deduction where it exceeds your allowable itemized deductions; *see 13.2.*

You may be able to file a simplified schedule, Schedule C-EZ, if your income and expenses are below certain limits; *see 40.6.*

Passive loss restrictions. Pay special attention to the passive loss restrictions discussed in Chapter 10. Generally, if you do not regularly and substantially participate in your business, losses are considered passive and are deductible only against other passive income.

Accounting for Business Income

40.3 Accounting Methods for Reporting Business Income

Business income is reported on either the accrual or cash basis. If you have more than one business, you may have a different accounting method for each business.

Inventories. Unless the $10 million safe harbor discussed on page 602 applies, the IRS requires inventories at the beginning and end of every taxable year in which the production, purchase, or sale of merchandise is an income-producing factor. If you must keep inventories, you *must* use the accrual basis.

Cash method. You report income items in the taxable year in which they are received; you deduct all expenses in the taxable year in which they are paid. Under the cash method, income is also reported if it is "constructively" received. You have "constructively" received income when an amount

Filing Tip

Did You Suffer a Loss?

Business persons and professionals with a 2002 net operating loss may get a refund of taxes paid in two prior tax years. If the loss is not fully eliminated by the income of the two prior years, the balance of the loss may be used to reduce your business income for up to 20 of the following years. *See 40.18* for details.

IRS Alert

Cash Method Safe Harbor Increased

Businesses with average annual gross receipts of $10 million are now eligible to use a cash method safe harbor.

Key To Reporting Business and Professional Income and Loss

Item—	Comments—
Tax return to file	If you are self-employed, prepare Schedule C to report business or professional income. If your business expenses are $2,500 or less, and you have no employees, you may be able to file a simplified Schedule C-EZ; *see 40.6*. If you are a farmer, use Schedule F. You attach Schedule C and/or F to Form 1040. If you operate as a partnership, use Form 1065; if you operate as a corporation, use Form 1120S or Form 1120.
Method of reporting income	The cash or accrual accounting rules determine when you report income and expenses. You must use the accrual basis if you sell a product that must be inventoried. The cash-basis and accrual-basis methods are discussed at *40.3*.
Tax reporting year	There are two general tax reporting years: calendar years that end on December 31 and fiscal years that end on the last day of any month other than December. Your taxable year must be the same for both your business and nonbusiness income. Most business income must be reported on a calendar-year basis. If, as a self-employed person, you report your business income on a fiscal-year basis, you must also report your nonbusiness income on a fiscal-year basis. Use of a fiscal year is restricted for partnerships and S corporations.
Office in home	To claim home office expenses as a self-employed person, you must use the home area exclusively and on a regular basis either as a place of business to meet or deal with patients, clients, or customers in the normal course of your business or as your principal place of business. Form 8829 must be used to compute the deduction; *see 40.12*.
Social Security coverage	If you have self-employed income, you may have to pay self-employment tax, which goes to financing Social Security benefits; *see* Chapter 45.
Passive participation in a business	If you do not regularly, continuously, and substantially participate in the business, your business income or loss is subject to passive activity restrictions. A loss is deductible only against other passive activity income. The passive activity restrictions are discussed in detail in Chapter 10.
Self-employed Keogh plan	You may set up a retirement plan based on business or professional income. Individuals who are self-employed may contribute to a self-employed retirement plan, according to the rules in Chapter 41.
Depreciation	Business assets other than real estate placed in service in 2002 are depreciable over three, five, seven, 10, 15, or 20 years. Automobiles and light trucks, computers, and office equipment are in the five-year class. Property in the three-, five-, seven-, and 10-year classes is depreciable using the double declining balance method, switching to the straight-line method so as to maximize the deduction; *see* Chapter 42 for details. Automobiles are subject to special depreciation limits; *see* Chapter 43. Instead of depreciating equipment, you may claim the first-year expensing deduction. You may generally deduct up to $24,000 in 2002; *see 42.3*.
Health insurance	In 2002, you may deduct 70% of premium costs of health insurance coverage for yourself, spouse, and dependents. You may also take advantage of a medical savings account plan as explained in *17.17*.
Net operating losses	A loss incurred in your profession or business in 2002 is deducted from other income reported on Form 1040. If the 2002 loss (plus any casualty loss) exceeds income, the excess may be first carried back five years, and then forward 20 years until it is used up. A loss carried back to a prior year reduces income of that year and entitles you to a refund. A loss applied to a later year reduces income for that year. The five-year carryback for 2002 losses may be waived in favor of a two-year and in some cases a three-year carryback; *see 40.18*. You may elect to carry forward your 2002 loss for 20 years, foregoing the carryback; *see 40.22*.
Sideline business	You report business income of a sideline business following the rules that apply to full-time business. For example, if you are self-employed, you report business income on Schedule C or C-EZ. You may also have to pay self-employment tax on this income; *see* Chapter 45. You may also set up a self-employment retirement plan based on such income. If you incur losses over several years, the hobby loss rules discussed in *40.10* may limit your loss deduction.

is credited to your account, subject to your control, or set apart for you and may be drawn by you at any time. For example, in 2002 you receive a check in payment of services, but you do not cash it until 2003. You have constructively received the income in 2002, and it is taxable in 2002.

On the cash basis, you deduct expenses in the year of payment. Expenses paid by credit card are deducted in the year they are charged. Expenses paid through a "pay by phone" account with a bank are deducted in the year the bank sends the check. This date is reported by the bank on its monthly statement.

Advance payments. The IRS has generally disallowed a deduction for advance rent premiums or premium payments covering charges of a later year. However, in early 2002, the IRS announced (Announcement 2002-9) that it was planning to propose a "12-month rule" as part of proposed regulations on the capitalization of expenditures incurred in acquiring, creating, or enhancing intangible assets. Under the proposal, capitalization would not be required unless the expenditure creates or enhances intangible rights or benefits that extend beyond the earlier of: (1) 12 months after the first date on which the taxpayer realizes rights or benefits attributable to the expenditure, or (2) the end of the taxable year following the taxable year in which the expenditure is incurred.

The proposed regulations had not been released when this book went to press. *See* the *Supplement* for an update.

Cash method of accounting limited. The following may not use the cash method: a regular C corporation, a partnership with a C corporation as a partner, a tax shelter, or a tax-exempt trust with unrelated business income. Exceptions: A farming or tree-raising business may use the cash method even if it operates as a C corporation or a partnership with a C corporation as a partner. The cash method may also be used by personal service corporations in the fields of medicine, law, engineering, accounting, architecture, performing arts, actuarial science, or consulting. To qualify, substantially all of the stock must be owned directly or indirectly (through partnerships, S corporations, or personal service corporations) by employees.

If the production, purchase, or sale of merchandise is *not* an income-producing factor, the cash method may be used by a C corporation or a partnership with a C corporation as a partner if the average annual gross receipts over the prior three-year period were $5 million or less.

Cash method safe harbor for businesses with average gross receipts of $10 million or less. The IRS has finalized a cash method safe harbor for businesses with gross receipts of $10 million or less. Revenue Procedure 2002-28 allows qualifying small businesses that would otherwise have to account for inventories under the accrual method to use the cash method for taxable years ending on or after December 31, 2001. If the safe harbor applies, items that are purchased for resale to customers or used as raw materials for producing finished goods may not be deducted until the year the items are provided to customers if that is later than the year of purchase. A qualifying small business that wants to apply the safe harbor guidelines must file for an accounting method change as explained in Revenue Procedure 2002-28.

The taxpayer's average annual gross receipts must be $10 million or less for the three taxable years ending with *each* prior taxable year ending on or after December 31, 2000. A taxpayer that has not been in existence for three prior taxable years figures the average for the years it has been in existence. If a taxpayer fails to satisfy the average gross receipts test for *any* prior-year period, the cash method is not allowed for the determination year or any subsequent year.

The cash method safe harbor applies to service businesses, custom manufacturers, and any other taxpayer whose principal activity is not specifically ineligible under Revenue Procedure 2002-28. If a taxpayer's principal business activity is any of the following, Revenue Procedure 2002-28 bars the cash method safe harbor for *that* activity: retail or wholesale sales, manufacturing (other than eligible custom manufacturers), publishing, sound recording, or mining. The "principal" activity is the activity that produced the largest percentage of gross receipts in the prior year or the largest average percentage over the three prior years.

Where the taxpayer's principal activity is not in the prohibited group, the taxpayer may use the cash method for *all* of its businesses. Where the principal activity is in the prohibited group, the cash method safe harbor may not be used for *that* activity but it may be used for a separate secondary activity that does not fall within the ineligible group if a complete and separate set of books is maintained for it. For example, a plumbing contractor satisfies the prior-year principal activity test if in the prior year 60% of its gross receipts were from plumbing installations and 40% were from selling plumbing equipment at its retail store. Plumbing installation is a construction activity that is not within the prohibited group. The taxpayer may use the cash method for both the plumbing

Planning Reminder

Advantage of Cash-Basis Accounting

The cash basis has this advantage over other accounting methods: You may defer reporting income by postponing the receipt of income. But make certain that you avoid the constructive receipt rule. For example, if 2002 is a high income year or income tax rates will be lower in 2003, you might delay mailing some of your customers' bills so they do not receive them until 2003. You may also postpone the payment of presently due expenses to a year in which the deduction gives you a greater tax savings.

installation and retail businesses, subject to the timing rule for items purchased for resale and raw materials used to produce finished goods. If the principal activity had been retail sales, the cash method could not be used for that ineligible activity. However, if the taxpayer treats the two activities as separate businesses, each with it own complete set of books, the cash method could be used for the installation business assuming the $10 million gross receipts test is met.

Accrual method. On the accrual method, report income that has been earned, whether or not received, unless your right to collect the income is unsure because a substantial contingency may prevent payment; *see* the Example below.

> **EXAMPLE**
>
> You report business income as a calendar-year accrual taxpayer. You sell several products on December 27, 2002, and bill the customer in January 2003. You report the sales income on your 2002 Schedule C, even though payment is not made until 2003. Under the accrual method, you are considered to earn the income when the products are sold and delivered to the customer.

Where you are prepaid for future services that must be completed by the end of the next tax year, you report the income in the year that services are performed; *see* the following Example.

> **EXAMPLE**
>
> In 2002, you receive full payment under a one-year contract requiring you to provide 48 music lessons. In 2002, you give eight lessons, and report one-sixth ($^8/_{48}$) of the payment as income. In 2003, the remaining five-sixths of the payment must be reported, even if you do not actually give the required number of lessons.

Expenses under the accrual method are deductible in the year your liability for payment is fixed, even though payment is made in a later year. To prevent manipulation of expense deductions, there are tax law tests for fixing the timing of accrual method expense deductions. The tests generally require that *economic performance* must occur before a deduction may be claimed, but there are exceptions, such as for "recurring expenses." These rules are discussed in IRS Publication 538, which is available without charge from the IRS. Note that certain deduction timing rules are likely to be simplified by the IRS when it issues proposed regulations on the capitalization of expenditures incurred in acquiring, creating, or enhancing intangible assets. The regulations, expected by the end of 2002, had not yet been released when this book went to press; *see* the *Supplement* for an update.

Expenses owed by an accrual-method business owner to a related cash-basis taxpayer. A business expense owed to your spouse, brother, sister, parent, child, grandparent, or grandchild who reports on the cash basis may not be deducted by you until you make the payment and the relative includes it as income. The same rule applies to amounts owed to a controlled corporation (more than 50% ownership) and other related entities.

Long-term contracts. Section 460 of the Internal Revenue Code has a special percentage of completion method of accounting for long-term construction contractors.

Capitalize costs of business property you produce or buy for resale. A complicated statute (Code Section 263A) generally requires manufacturers and builders to capitalize certain indirect costs (such as administrative costs, interest expenses, storage fees, and insurance), as well as direct production expenses, by including them in inventory costs; *see* IRS Publication 538, Form 3115, and the regulations to Code Section 263A.

The IRS announced (Announcement 2002-9) that it planned to issue proposed regulations on the capitalization of expenditures incurred to acquire, create, or enhance intangible assets or benefits. The regulations, not yet released when this book went to press, are expected to provide safe harbors such as a 12-month rule, and *de minimis* rules, which would exempt specified expenditures from capitalization requirements.

Accrual deferral of service income. If, on the basis of your experience, a percentage of billings due for your services will not be collected until a later year, you do not have to report the "uncollectible" amount until the year you actually receive it. The IRS calls this the "nonaccrual-experience method."

Advantage of Accrual-Method Accounting

The accrual method has this advantage over the cash basis: It generally gives a more even and balanced financial report.

Changing Your Accounting Method

Generally, you must obtain the consent of the Internal Revenue Service prior to any change in accounting method. Apply for consent by filing Form 3115 as early as possible during the tax year for which you wish to make the change.

However, if interest or a penalty is charged for a failure to make a timely payment for the services, income is reported when the amount is billed. Furthermore, if discounts for early payments are offered, the full amount of the bill must be accrued; the discount for early payment is treated as an adjustment to income in the year payment is made.

The amount of income to be deferred is based on a percentage that considers billing and uncollectibles over the current year and the past five most recent years. The percentage is calculated by dividing the uncollectible amounts by the total billings during the six-year period. That percentage applied to the total billings during the tax year may be deferred. For example, if $200,000 was billed during the six-year period and $20,000 was uncollectible, the percentage is 10% and 10% of the current billings may be deferred. If you do not have a five-year experience, you use the period during which you were in business.

40.4 Tax Reporting Year for Self-Employed

Your taxable year must be the same for both your business and nonbusiness income. If you report your business income on a fiscal year basis, you must also report your nonbusiness income on a fiscal year basis.

Generally, you report the tax consequences of transactions that have occurred during a 12-month period. If the period ends on December 31, it is called a *calendar year*. If it ends on the last day of any month other than December, it is called a *fiscal year*. A reporting period, technically called a *taxable year*, can never be longer than 12 months unless you report on a 52-to-53-week fiscal year basis, details of which can be found in IRS Publication 538. A reporting period may be less than 12 months whenever you start or end your business in the middle of your regular taxable year, or change your taxable year.

To change from a calendar year to fiscal year reporting for self-employment income, you must ask the IRS for permission by filing Form 1128. Support your request with a business reason such as that the use of the fiscal year coincides with your business cycle. To use a fiscal year basis, you must keep your books and records following that fiscal year period.

Fiscal year restrictions. Restrictions on fiscal years for partnerships, personal service corporations, and S corporations are discussed in *11.11* and IRS Publication 538.

40.5 Reporting Business Cash Receipts to the IRS

Cash receipts of more than $10,000 in one business transaction or two or more related transactions must be reported on Form 8300. There are penalties for failure to file.

File Form 8300 with the IRS within 15 days of each cash transaction of over $10,000. Only cash payments are reported; do not report funds received by bank check or wire transfer where cash was not physically transferred. Foreign currency is considered cash. If multiple payments from a single payer (or a payer's agent) are received within a 24-hour period, the payments are aggregated, and the total must be reported if over $10,000.

The reporting requirement applies to individuals, corporations, partnerships, trusts, and estates, except for certain financial institutions that are already required to report cash transactions to the Treasury. Cash received in transactions occurring entirely outside the U.S. does not have to be reported.

The filing requirement applies to cash received for providing goods or services. Thus, an attorney, doctor, or other professional must report cash payments of over $10,000 from a client. Furthermore, cash received for setting up a trust of more than $10,000 for a client must be reported. The IRS has a program to assess penalties against attorneys who have disregarded the cash reporting rules. Courts have held that an attorney may not refuse to report large cash fees by invoking the attorney-client privilege. However, one appeals court held that disclosure of the name of a client who paid cash exceeding $10,000 was not required where disclosure would implicate the client or would reveal confidential communications made by the client to the attorney. The trial court in a closed hearing heard the attorney's claim and ruled against him, but the appeals court ruled in his favor; the circumstances were not disclosed because of their confidential nature.

On an installment sale of business property, you report each payment exceeding $10,000 within 15 days of receipt. If the initial installment is $10,000 or less, you aggregate it plus all payments received within one year of the initial payment. If the total exceeds $10,000, report the total within 15 days after the receipt of the payment that raised the total to over $10,000. In addition, if—after receiving single or aggregated reportable payments—subsequent payments within one year exceed $10,000 individually or in the aggregate, you must report the payments within 15 days.

Caution

Splitting Up a Transaction
The cash reporting requirement may not be avoided by splitting up a single transaction into separate transactions. Thus, a sale of property for $36,000 may not be broken down into four separate sales of $9,000 to avoid reporting. Similarly, an attorney who represents a client in a case must aggregate all cash payments by the client, although payments may be spread over several months. If the total exceeds $10,000, it must be reported.

EXAMPLE

On February 8, 2003, you receive an initial cash payment of $11,000. For the same transaction, you also receive cash of $4,000 on March 15, 2003; $6,000 on April 19, 2003; and $12,000 on June 13, 2003. You report the February payment by February 23, 2003. You also report the payments totaling $22,000 received from March 15, 2003, through June 13, 2003, by June 28, 2003, that is, within 15 days of the date (June 13) that the later payments, all received within a one-year period, exceeded $10,000.

Cash equivalents of $10,000 or less. Cash equivalents such as money orders, traveler's checks, cashier's checks, and bank drafts with a face value of $10,000 or less are treated as cash in sales of consumer durables, collectibles, and travel or entertainment services costing $10,000 or more. Common examples of consumer durables are autos, boats, and jewelry.

For example, if jewelry costing $12,000 is bought with $2,400 cash and traveler's checks of $9,600, the jeweler must file Form 8300 reporting the transaction. If the $2,400 were paid by personal check, the transaction would not have to be reported because personal checks are not treated as cash. Reporting exceptions are also allowed where the cash equivalent constitutes the proceeds of a bank loan, or where it is used as a down payment or promissory note payment under a payment plan used for all retail sales by the seller.

Form 8300. On Form 8300, you must provide the payer's home address and tax identification number to the IRS. You also must provide the payer with a copy of the form or a similar statement by January 31 of the following year.

A $50 penalty may be imposed for each failure to file a properly completed Form 8300 or provide the payer with a statement, unless reasonable cause is shown. The penalty may be reduced if a timely correction is made. For small businesses meeting a $5 million average gross receipts test, the maximum penalty for failure to file with the IRS is $100,000 per calendar year; otherwise, the maximum is $250,000.

If failure to file is intentional, the penalty for each failure is the *greater* of $25,000 or the cash received in the transaction, but the maximum penalty is $100,000. Criminal penalties apply for willful failure to file Form 8300 or for filing a fraudulent form.

There is an exception to the reporting requirement for persons who act as agents if they receive cash of over $10,000 from their principal and use it within 15 days in a cash transaction, provided they identify the principal to the payee in the cash transaction.

You must keep a copy of each Form 8300 you file with the IRS for five years from the date of filing.

Reporting Income and Expenses on Schedule C

40.6 Filing Schedule C

In this section are explanations of how a sole proprietor reports income and expenses on Schedule C, a sample of which is on page 606.

Schedule C-EZ. This simple form is designed for persons on the cash basis who do not have a net business loss and have:

- Business expenses of $2,500 or less;
- No inventory at any time during the year;
- Only one sole proprietorship;
- No employees;
- No home office expense deduction;
- No prior year suspended passive activity losses from this business; *and*
- No depreciation to be reported on Form 4562.

Statutory employees. Statutory employees report income and expenses on Schedule C. Thus, expenses may be deducted in full on Schedule C rather than as a miscellaneous itemized deduction *(19.1)*, subject to the 2% adjusted gross income (AGI) floor on Schedule A.

Sample Schedule C

SCHEDULE C **(Form 1040)** Department of the Treasury Internal Revenue Service (99)	**Profit or Loss From Business** (Sole Proprietorship) ▶ Partnerships, joint ventures, etc., must file Form 1065 or 1065-B. ▶ **Attach to Form 1040 or 1041.** ▶ **See Instructions for Schedule C (Form 1040).**

OMB No. 1545-0074

2002

Attachment
Sequence No. **09**

Name of proprietor

Social security number (SSN)

A Principal business or profession, including product or service (see page C-1 of the instructions)

B Enter code from pages C-7 & 8
▶

C Business name. If no separate business name, leave blank.

D Employer ID number (EIN), if any

E Business address (including suite or room no.) ▶ ....
City, town or post office, state, and ZIP code

F Accounting method: **(1)** ☐ Cash **(2)** ☐ Accrual **(3)** ☐ Other (specify) ▶ ....

G Did you "materially participate" in the operation of this business during 2002? If "No," see page C-2 for limit on losses . ☐ Yes ☐ No

H If you started or acquired this business during 2002, check here . . . . ▶ ☐

Part I **Income**

1	Gross receipts or sales. **Caution.** If this income was reported to you on Form W-2 and the "Statutory employee" box on that form was checked, see page C-2 and check here . . . . . ▶ ☐	**1**	
2	Returns and allowances	**2**	
3	Subtract line 2 from line 1	**3**	
4	Cost of goods sold (from line 42 on page 2)	**4**	
5	**Gross profit.** Subtract line 4 from line 3	**5**	
6	Other income, including Federal and state gasoline or fuel tax credit or refund (see page C-3) . . .	**6**	
7	**Gross income.** Add lines 5 and 6 . . . . ▶	**7**	

Part II **Expenses.** Enter expenses for business use of your home **only** on line 30.

8	Advertising	**8**		**19**	Pension and profit-sharing plans	**19**
9	Bad debts from sales or services (see page C-3) . .	**9**		**20**	Rent or lease (see page C-4):	
				a	Vehicles, machinery, and equipment .	**20a**
10	Car and truck expenses (see page C-3)	**10**		**b**	Other business property . .	**20b**
11	Commissions and fees . .	**11**		**21**	Repairs and maintenance . .	**21**
12	Depletion	**12**		**22**	Supplies (not included in Part III) .	**22**
				23	Taxes and licenses	**23**
13	Depreciation and section 179 expense deduction (not included in Part III) (see page C-3) . .	**13**		**24**	Travel, meals, and entertainment:	
				a	Travel	**24a**
14	Employee benefit programs (other than on line 19) . . .	**14**		**b**	Meals and entertainment	
15	Insurance (other than health) .	**15**		**c**	Enter nondeduct-ible amount in-cluded on line 24b (see page C-5) .	
16	Interest:					
a	Mortgage (paid to banks, etc.) .	**16a**		**d**	Subtract line 24c from line 24b .	**24d**
b	Other	**16b**		**25**	Utilities	**25**
17	Legal and professional services	**17**		**26**	Wages (less employment credits) .	**26**
18	Office expense	**18**		**27**	Other expenses (from line 48 on page 2)	**27**

28	**Total expenses** before expenses for business use of home. Add lines 8 through 27 in columns . ▶	**28**	
29	Tentative profit (loss). Subtract line 28 from line 7	**29**	
30	Expenses for business use of your home. Attach **Form 8829**	**30**	
31	**Net profit or (loss).** Subtract line 30 from line 29. • If a profit, enter on **Form 1040, line 12,** and **also** on **Schedule SE, line 2** (statutory employees, see page C-5). Estates and trusts, enter on Form 1041, line 3. • If a loss, you **must** go to line 32.	**31**	
32	If you have a loss, check the box that describes your investment in this activity (see page C-6). • If you checked 32a, enter the loss on **Form 1040, line 12,** and **also** on **Schedule SE, line 2** (statutory employees, see page C-5). Estates and trusts, enter on Form 1041, line 3. • If you checked 32b, you **must** attach **Form 6198.**	**32a** ☐ All investment is at risk. **32b** ☐ Some investment is not at risk.	

For Paperwork Reduction Act Notice, see Form 1040 instructions. Cat. No. 11334P **Schedule C (Form 1040) 2002**

Statutory employees are full-time life insurance salespersons, agent or commission drivers distributing certain foods and beverages, pieceworkers, and full-time traveling or city salespersons who solicit on behalf of and transmit to their principals orders from wholesalers and retailers for merchandise for resale or for supplies.

The term *full time* refers to an exclusive or principal business activity for a single company or person and not to the time spent on the job. If your principal activity is soliciting orders for one company, but you also solicit incidental orders for another company, you are a full-time salesperson for the primary company. Solicitations of orders are considered incidental to a principal business activity if you devote 20% or less of your time to the solicitation activity. A city or traveling salesperson is presumed to meet the principal business activity test in a calendar year in which he or she devotes 80% or more of working time to soliciting orders for one principal.

IRS regulations give this example: A salesman's principal activity is getting orders from retail pharmacies for a wholesale drug company called Que Company. He occasionally takes orders for two other companies. He is a statutory employee only for Que Company.

If you are a statutory employee, your company checks Box 13 on Form W-2, identifying you as a statutory employee. Although a statutory employee may treat job expenses as business expenses, the employer withholds FICA (Social Security and Medicare) taxes on wages and commissions.

You must check a box on Line 1 of Schedule C (or C-EZ) to indicate statutory employee status. If you also have self-employment earnings from another business, you must report the self-employment earnings and statutory employee income on separate Schedules C. If both types of income are earned in the same business, allocate the expenses between the two activities on the separate schedules.

Gross receipts or sales on Schedule C (Line 1). If you do not produce or sell goods, but provide only services, you do not determine cost of goods sold, but report only your receipts from services on Line 1.

Do not report as receipts on Schedule C the following items:

- Gains or losses on the sale of property used in your business or profession. These transactions are reported on Schedule D and Form 4797.
- Dividends from stock held in the ordinary course of your business. These are reported as dividends from stocks that are held for investment.

Deductions on Schedule C. Deductible business expenses are claimed in Part II; the descriptive breakdown of items is generally self-explanatory. However, note these points:

Bad debts (Line 9): Business bad debts that become totally or partially worthless during the year are deductible. *See 5.34* for determining when a debt becomes worthless. However, if you are a cash-basis taxpayer, you may not claim a bad debt deduction for amounts that are not collectible unless you have included those amounts in income. If you are an accrual-basis taxpayer, you may claim a bad debt deduction for an uncollectible receivable if the amount was included in income, either for the year the deduction is claimed or for a prior year.

Generally, you must use the specific charge-off method for deducting business bad debts. For a partially worthless debt, the deduction is limited to the amount you charge off on your books during the taxable year. You may delay the charge-off of a partially worthless bad debt until a later year when more of the debt becomes worthless or until the year in which the debt is totally worthless. In the year that a debt becomes totally worthless, you may deduct the debt to the extent that it was not previously claimed as a partially worthless debt. It is advisable to enter a charge-off on your books for a totally worthless debt. If you do not and the IRS rules that the debt was only partially worthless for that year, you would be unable to claim the deduction since a deduction for a partially worthless bad debt is limited to the amount actually charged off.

If you have not been paid for services you provided and you use the accrual method of accounting, you may use the "non-accrual-experience" method of accounting for the bad debt instead of the specific charge-off method. If you do not expect to collect an account receivable, that amount may be excluded from income. *See* IRS Publication 535 for details of the nonaccrual-experience method.

Here are some examples of business bad debt transactions:

- You sell merchandise on credit and later the buyer becomes insolvent and does not pay.
- You are in the business of making loans and a loan goes bad.
- You sell your business, but retain some accounts receivable. Later, some of these become worthless.
- You liquidate your business and are unable to collect its outstanding accounts.

 Caution

Doctor's Malpractice Insurance
A self-employed doctor may deduct the premium costs of malpractice insurance. However, a doctor who is not self-employed but employed by someone else, say a hospital, may deduct the premium costs only as a miscellaneous itemized deduction subject to the 2% of adjusted gross income floor. Whether malpractice premiums paid to a physician-owned carrier are deductible depends on how the carrier is organized. If there is a sufficient number of policyholders who are not economically related and none of whom owns a controlling interest in the insuring company, a deduction is allowed provided the premiums are reasonable and are based on sound actuarial principles.

In one case, physicians set up a physician-owned carrier that was required by state insurance authorities to set up a surplus fund. The physicians contributed to the fund and received nontransferable certificates that were redeemable only if they retired, moved out of the state, or died. The IRS and Tax Court held the contributions to the fund were nondeductible capital expenses.

In another case, a professional corporation of anesthesiologists set up a trust to pay malpractice claims, up to specified limits. The IRS and Tax Court disallowed deductions for the trust contributions on the grounds that the PC remained potentially liable. Malpractice claims within the policy limits might exceed trust funds and the PC would be liable for the difference.

Filing Tip

Health Insurance Premiums

You do not claim on Schedule C the deduction of 70% of 2002 health insurance costs for yourself, your spouse, and your dependents. You take the deduction on Line 30, Form 1040. *See also* 17.17 for the way to claim Archer MSA account contributions on Line 27 of Form 1040.

Self-employed persons may get a 100% deduction for their own coverage by covering a spouse who is an employee of the business. Coverage for the employee-spouse may include the employer-spouse and their dependents as part of the employee-spouse's family unit. The employer-spouse may deduct as a business expense (on Schedule C) the cost of medical coverage, including reimbursements, for both spouses and their dependents.

The spouse must be a bona fide employee and must meet the service requirement spelled out in the plan to be eligible for coverage. The performance of nominal or insignificant services that lack economic substance will be challenged. Further, a spouse who has a financial investment in the business may be treated as self-employed or as a joint owner. If the business is an S corporation and one spouse is a more-than-2% shareholder in the corporation, the other spouse is also treated as a more-than-2% owner and not as an employee for benefit purposes.

Caution

Interest on Business Tax Deficiency

Interest on a tax deficiency based on business income reporting is not a deductible business expense according to the IRS; interest on a tax deficiency is always nondeductible personal interest. In limited cases, the Tax Court has allowed a business expense deduction, but it has been overruled by several federal appeals courts that have upheld the IRS position denying a business expense deduction for interest on a tax deficiency.

Filing Tip

Security Trader's Operating Expenses

A security trader may deduct expenses of trading on Schedule C; for further details, *see 30.23.*

- You operate as a promoter of corporations.
- You finance your lessees, customers, or suppliers to help your business.
- You lend money to protect your professional and business reputation.
- You lend money to insure delivery of merchandise from a supplier.

Car and truck expenses (Line 10): In the year you place a car in service, you may choose between the IRS mileage allowance and deducting actual expenses, plus depreciation. You must also attach Form 4562 to support the deduction; *see* Chapter 43.

Depreciation (Line 13): Enter here the amount of your annual depreciation deduction. A complete discussion of depreciation may be found in Chapter 42. You must figure your depreciation deduction on Form 4562 for assets placed in service in 2002, or for cars, computers, or other "listed property," regardless of when the assets were placed in service.

Employee benefit programs including health insurance (Line 14): Enter your cost for the following programs you provide for your employees: accident or health plans; long-term care insurance coverage; wage continuation; self-insured medical reimbursement plans; educational assistance programs; supplemental unemployment benefits; and prepaid legal expenses. Retirement plan contributions, such as to pension and profit-sharing plans, are reported separately on Line 19.

Insurance other than health insurance (Line 15): Insurance policy premiums for the protection of your business, such as accident, burglary, embezzlement, marine risks, plate glass, public liability, workers' compensation, fire, storm, or theft, and indemnity bonds upon employees, are deductible. State unemployment insurance payments are deducted here or as taxes if they are considered taxes under state law.

Premiums paid on an insurance policy on the life of an employee or one financially interested in a business, for the purpose of protecting you from loss in the event of the death of the insured, are not deductible.

The IRS is expected to provide a "12-month" rule in proposed regulations that will allow prepaid premiums to be deducted in the year paid if the coverage term does not extend more than 12 months beyond the first date coverage is received, and also does not extend beyond the taxable year following the year in which the premium is paid. *See* the *Supplement* for an update on the proposal.

Premiums for disability insurance to cover loss of earnings when out ill or injured are nondeductible personal expenses. But you may deduct premiums covering business overhead expenses.

Interest (Line 16): Include interest on business debts, but prepaid interest that applies to future years is not deductible.

Deductible interest on an insurance loan is limited if you borrow against a life insurance policy covering yourself as an employee or the life of any other employee, officer, or other person financially interested in your business. Interest on such a loan is deductible only if the policy covers an officer or 20% owner (no more than five such "key persons" can be counted) and the loan is no more than $50,000 per person. If you own policies covering the same employees (or other persons) in more than one business, the $50,000 limit applies on an aggregate basis to all the policies. The interest deduction limit applies even if a sole proprietor borrows against a policy on his or her own life and uses the proceeds in a business; interest is not deductible to the extent the loan exceeds $50,000.

Pension and profit-sharing plans (Line 19): Keogh plan or SEP contributions made for your employees are entered here; contributions made for your account are entered directly on Form 1040 as an adjustment to income. In addition, you may have to file an information return by the last day of the seventh month following the end of the plan year; *see 41.8.*

Rent on business property (Line 20): Rent paid for the use of lofts, buildings, trucks, and other equipment is deductible. An advance rental may be deductible in the year of payment under a "12-month" rule that the IRS is expected to provide in proposed regulations, as discussed above in the discussion of prepaid premiums under Line 15.

Taxes on leased property that you pay to the lessor are deductible as additional rent.

Repairs (Line 21): The cost of repairs and maintenance is deductible provided they do not materially add to the value of the property or appreciably prolong its life. Expenses of replacements that arrest deterioration and appreciably increase the value of the property are capitalized and their cost recovered through depreciation.

Taxes (Line 23): Deduct real estate and personal property taxes on business assets here. Also deduct your share of Social Security and Medicare taxes paid on behalf of employees and payments of federal unemployment tax. Federal highway use tax is deductible. Federal import duties and excise and stamp taxes normally not deductible as itemized deductions are deductible as business taxes if incurred by the business. Taxes on business property, such as an *ad valorem* tax, must be deducted here; they are not to be treated as itemized deductions. However, the IRS holds that you may not deduct state income taxes on business income as a business expense. Its reasoning: Income taxes are personal taxes even when paid on business income. As such, you may deduct state income tax only as an itemized deduction on Schedule A. The Tax Court supports the IRS rule on the grounds that it reflects Congressional intent toward the treatment of state income taxes in figuring taxable income.

For purposes of computing a net operating loss, state income tax on business income is treated as a business deduction.

If you pay or accrue sales tax on the purchase of nondepreciable business property, the sales tax is a deductible business expense. If the property is depreciable, add the sales tax to the cost basis for purposes of computing depreciation deductions.

Travel, meals, and entertainment (Line 24): Travel expenses on overnight business trips while "away from home" *(20.6)* and 50% of meals and entertainment for business are deductible. Total meals and entertainment expenses are listed on Line 24b and then reduced by 50% on Line 24c. The total amount after figuring the 50% reduction is reported on Line 24d.

Self-employed persons may use the IRS meal allowance rates discussed at *20.4,* instead of claiming actual expenses. *See also 20.26–20.28* for record-keeping requirements for travel and entertainment expenses.

Utilities (Line 25): Deduct utilities such as gas, electric, and telephone expenses incurred in your business. However, if you have a home office *(40.12)*, you may *not* deduct the base rate (including taxes) of the first phone line into your home; *see 19.14.*

Wages (Line 26): You do not deduct wages paid to yourself. You may deduct reasonable wages paid to family members who work for you. If you have an employee who works in your office and also in your home, such as a domestic worker, you deduct that part of the salary allocated to the work in your office. If you claim a work opportunity, welfare-to-work, empowerment zone or Indian employment tax credit, the wage deduction is reduced by the credit.

Other expenses (Line 27): In Part V of Schedule C, you list deductible expenses not reported in Part II, such as amortizable business start-up costs *(40.11),* and enter the total on Line 27.

40.7 Deductions for Professionals

The following expenses incurred by self-employed professionals in the course of their work are generally allowed as deductions from income when figuring profit (or loss) from their professional practices on Schedule C:
- Dues to professional societies
- Operating expenses and repairs of car used on professional calls
- Supplies
- Subscriptions to professional journals
- Rent for office space
- Cost of fuel, light, water, and telephone used in the office
- Salaries of assistants
- Malpractice insurance; *see 40.6*
- Cost of books, information services, professional instruments, and equipment with a useful life of one year or less. Professional libraries are depreciable if their value decreases with time. Depreciation rules are discussed at *42.1.*
- Fees paid to a tax preparer for preparing Schedule C and related business forms

Professionals as employees. Professionals who are not in their own practice may not deduct professional expenses on Schedule C. Salaried professionals may deduct professional expenses only as miscellaneous itemized deductions on Schedule A, subject to the 2% adjusted gross income (AGI) floor; *see 19.1.* However, "statutory" employees may use Schedule C; *see 40.6.*

The cost of preparing for a profession. You may not deduct the cost of a professional education; *see 19.16.*

The IRS does not allow a deduction for the cost of a license to practice. However, the Tax Court has allowed attorneys to amortize over their life expectancy bar admission fees paid to state authorities; *see 19.17.*

Filing Tip

Tax Advice and Tax Preparation Costs
On Line 17 of Schedule C, you deduct the portion of tax preparation costs allocable to preparing Schedule C (or C-EZ) and related tax forms. Also deduct on Line 17 fees for tax advice related to the business.

Planning Reminder

Continuing Education Courses
The costs of courses taken to keep current with professional developments are usually deductible; *see 19.16.*

Payment of clients' expenses. An attorney may follow a practice of paying his or her clients' expenses in pending cases. The IRS will disallow a deduction claimed for these payments on the grounds that the expenses are those of the client, not the attorney. The courts agree with the IRS position where there is a net fee agreement. In a net fee agreement, expenses first reduce the recovery before the attorney takes a fee. However, where the attorney is paid under a gross fee agreement, an appeals court has reversed a Tax Court decision that disallowed the deduction of the attorney's payment of client expenses. Under a gross fee agreement, the attorney's fee is based on the gross award; the prior payment of expenses does not enter into the fee agreement and so is not reimbursed. Because he would not be reimbursed, an attorney claimed his payment of client expenses was deductible. An appeals court accepted this argument and allowed the deduction. The court allowed the deduction although California law disapproved of the practice of paying client expenses without a right of reimbursement. The court believed that there is no ethical difficulty with the practice and other jurisdictions approve of it. It is necessary for and it is the practice of personal injury firms to pay the costs of many of their clients.

If you are not allowed a current deduction for payment of clients' expenses, you may deduct your advance as a bad debt if the claim is worthless in another year; *see 40.6.*

An attorney might deduct a payment to a client reimbursing the client for a bad investment recommended by the attorney. A court upheld the deduction on the grounds that the reimbursement was required to protect the reputation of an established law practice. However, no deduction is allowed when malpractice insurance reimbursement is available but the attorney fails to make a claim.

Daily business lunches with associates have been held to lack business purpose. Courts agree with the IRS that professionals do not need to have lunch together every day to talk shop. The cost of the meals is therefore not deductible.

EXAMPLES

1. A law partnership deducted the meal costs of the staff attorneys who lunched every day at the same restaurant to discuss cases and court assignments. The deductions were disallowed as personal expenses. The Tax Court and an appeals court agreed with the IRS that daily lunches are not necessary. Co-workers generally do not need luncheons to provide social lubrication for business talk, as is true with clients.

2. A physician held luncheon meetings three or four times a week with other physicians. He argued that the purpose of the luncheons was to generate referrals. A court held that such frequent luncheons became a routine personal event not tied to specific business. The cost of the meals was not deductible.

3. A medical professional corporation (PC) deducted the cost of meals taken by its physician-stockholders at a hospital cafeteria. It argued that the doctors discussed patients and met other doctors who made referrals to them. The Tax Court agreed with the IRS that the meal costs were not deductible; doctors ate in the cafeteria for their personal convenience. Furthermore, the meal costs were taxed to the doctors as dividends. The court noted that the PC might have been able to claim a deduction had it treated the meal costs as taxable pay; however, the PC refused to take this position, unsuccessfully gambling that it could claim the costs as business deductions.

40.8 Nondeductible Expense Items

Capital expenditures may not be deducted. Generally, the cost of acquiring an asset or of prolonging its life is a capital expenditure that must be amortized over its expected life. If the useful life of an item is less than a year, its cost, including sales tax on the purchase, is deductible. Otherwise, you generally may recover your cost only through depreciation except to the extent first-year expensing applies; *see 42.3.* As discussed in *40.3*, IRS proposed regulations are expected to provide safe harbors, including a "12-month" rule, for expenditures relating to intangible assets or benefits.

EXAMPLE

A new roof is installed on your office building. If the roof increases the life of the building, its cost is a capital expenditure recovered by depreciation deductions. The cost of repairing a leak in the roof is a deductible operating expense. A deduction was allowed for the cost of a major roof renovation on evidence that the work was not designed to increase the value of the building but to correct the defect.

Caution

Penalties and Fines

Penalties or fines paid to a government agency because of a violation of any law are not deductible. You may deduct penalties imposed by a business contract for late performance or nonperformance.

Expenses while you are not in business. You are not allowed to deduct business expenses incurred during the time you are not engaged in your business or profession.

> **EXAMPLE**
>
> A lawyer continued to maintain his office while he was employed by the government. During that time he did no private law work. He only kept the office to have it ready at such time as he quit the government job and returned to practice. His costs of keeping up his office while he was working for the government were not deductible.

Bribes and kickbacks. Bribes and kickbacks are not deductible if they are illegal under a federal or a generally enforced state law that subjects the payer to a criminal penalty or provides for the loss of license or privilege to engage in business. A kickback, even if not illegal, is not deductible by a physician or other person who has furnished items or services that are payable under the Medicare or Medicaid programs. A kickback includes payments for referral of a client, patient, or customer.

In one case, the IRS, with support from the Tax Court and a federal appeals court, disallowed a deduction for legal kickbacks paid by a subcontractor. The courts held that the kickbacks were not a "necessary" business expense because the contractor had obtained nearly all of its other contracts without paying kickbacks, including contracts from the same general contractor bribed here.

40.9 How Authors and Artists May Write Off Expenses

Self-employed authors, artists, photographers, and other qualifying creative professionals may write off business expenses as they are paid. The law (Code Section 263A) that requires expenses to be amortized over the period income is received does not apply to freelancers who personally create literary manuscripts, musical or dance scores, paintings, pictures, sculptures, drawings, cartoons, graphic designs, original print editions, photographs, or photographic negatives or transparencies. Furthermore, expenses of a personal service corporation do not have to be amortized if they directly relate to expenses of a qualifying author, artist, or photographer who owns (or whose relatives own) substantially all of the corporation's stock.

Current deductions are *not* allowed for expenses relating to motion picture films, videotapes, printing, photographic plates, or similar items.

An author or artist with expenses exceeding income may be barred by the IRS from claiming a loss under a profit motive test; in that case, the profit-presumption rule discussed at *40.10* may allow a deduction of the loss.

40.10 Deducting Expenses of a Sideline Business or Hobby

There is a one-way tax rule for hobbies: Income from a hobby is taxable; expenses are deductible only to the extent you have income, and the deduction is limited on Schedule A by the 2% adjusted gross income (AGI) floor for miscellaneous itemized deductions. Hobby losses are considered nondeductible personal losses. A profitable sale of a hobby collection or activity held long term is taxable as capital gain; losses are not deductible.

How to deduct hobby expenses. If the profit presumption discussed later does *not* apply and the activity is held *not* to be engaged in for profit, business operating expenses and depreciation are deductible only as miscellaneous itemized deductions and only up to the extent of income from the activity; a deduction for expenses exceeding the income is disallowed.

A special sequence is followed in determining which expenses are deductible from income. Deducted first on Schedule A are amounts allowable without regard to whether the activity is a business engaged in for profit, such as mortgage interest and state and local taxes, as well as casualty losses (after applying the $100 and 10% of AGI casualty floors *(18.11)*). These amounts are deductible in full on the appropriate lines of Schedule A without regard to income from the activity. However, they reduce gross income from the activity for purposes of figuring whether other deductions may be claimed. If after deducting these amounts from gross income there is any income remaining, "business" operating expenses such as wages, utilities, insurance premiums, interest, advertising, repairs, and maintenance may be claimed. Then deduct depreciation and excess casualty losses not allowed in the first step to the extent of remaining income. The "business" expenses, depreciation, and excess casualty losses are allowed only as miscellaneous itemized deductions subject to the 2% AGI floor; *see 19.1*. Thus, even if the expenses offset income from the activity, none of the expenses will be deductible unless your total miscellaneous expenses (including those from the activity) exceed 2% of your adjusted gross income.

 Planning Reminder

Hobby or Sideline Business

The question of whether an activity, such as dog breeding or collecting and selling coins and stamps, is a hobby or sideline business arises when losses are incurred. As long as you show a profit, you may deduct the expenses of the activity. But when expenses exceed income and your return is examined, an agent may allow expenses only up to the amount of your income and disallow the remaining expenses that make up your loss. At this point, to claim the loss, you may be able to take advantage of a "profit presumption" discussed in *40.10*, or you may have to prove that you are engaged in the activity to make a profit.

Presumption of profit-seeking motive. You are *presumed to be* engaged in an activity for profit if you can show a profit in at least three of the last five years, including the current year. If the activity is horse breeding, training, racing, or showing, the profit presumption applies if you show profits in two of the last seven (including current) years. The presumption does not necessarily mean that losses will automatically be allowed; the IRS may try to rebut the presumption. You would then have to prove a profit motive by showing these types of facts: You spend considerable time in the activity; you keep businesslike records; you relied on expert advice; you expect the assets to appreciate in value; and losses are common in the start-up phase of your type of business.

Election postpones determination of profit presumption. If you have losses in the first few years of an activity and the IRS tries to disallow them as hobby losses, you have this option: You may make an election on Form 5213 to postpone the determination of whether the above profit presumption applies. The postponement is until after the end of the fourth taxable year (sixth year for a horse breeding, training, showing, or racing activity) following the first year of the activity. For example, if you enter a farming activity in 2002, you can elect to postpone the profit motive determination until after the end of 2006. Then, if you have realized profits in at least three of the five years (2002–2006), the profit presumption applies. When you make the election on Form 5213, you agree to waive the statute of limitations for all activity-related items in the taxable years involved. The waiver generally gives the IRS an additional two years after the filing due date for the last year in the presumption period to issue deficiencies related to the activity.

To make the election, you must file Form 5213 within three years of the due date of the return for the year you started the activity. Thus, if you started your activity during 2002, you have until April 15, 2006, to make the election. If before the end of this three-year period you receive a deficiency notice from the IRS disallowing a loss from the activity and you have not yet made the election, you can still do so within 60 days of receiving the notice. These election rules apply to individuals, partnerships, and S corporations. An election by a partnership or S corporation is binding on all partners or S corporation shareholders holding interests during the presumption period.

40.11 Deducting Expenses of Looking for a New Business

When you are planning to invest in a business, you may incur preliminary expenses for traveling to look at the property and for legal or accounting advice. Expenses incurred during a general search or preliminary investigation of a business are not deductible, including expenses related to the decision whether or not to enter a transaction. However, when you go beyond a general search and focus on acquiring a particular business, you may deduct the start-up expenses. The timing of the deduction depends on whether or not you actually go into the business.

Amortizable expenses if you go into business. When you go into a business, you may elect to amortize over at least a 60-month period the costs of investigating and setting up the business, such as expenses of surveying potential markets, products, labor supply, and transportation facilities; travel and other expenses incurred in lining up prospective distributors, suppliers, or customers; salaries or fees paid to consultants or attorneys, and fees for similar professional services. The business may be one you acquire from someone else or a new business you create. The amortization period starts when you actually begin or acquire a going business.

Organizational costs for a partnership or corporation. Costs incident to the creation of a partnership or corporation are also amortizable over a period of at least 60 months. For a partnership, qualifying expenses include legal fees for negotiating and preparing a partnership agreement, and management, consulting, or accounting fees in setting up the partnership. Amortization is not allowed for syndication costs of issuing and marketing partnership interests such as brokerage and registration fees, fees of an underwriter, and costs of preparing a prospectus.

For a corporation, amortizable expenses include the cost of organizational meetings, incorporation fees, and accounting and legal fees for drafting corporate documents. Costs of selling stock or securities, such as commissions, do not qualify.

The election to amortize is made on Part VI of Form 4562 for the first year the partnership or corporation is in business. A statement attached to the return must describe the expenses and the amortization period. The election on Form 4562 and the required statement must be filed no later than the return due date, including extensions, for the year in which the business begins.

Nonamortizable expenses. Amortizable expenses are restricted to expenses incurred in investigating the acquisition or creation of an active business, and setting up such an active business. They do not include taxes, interest, research, or experimental costs deductible under Code Section 174. Expenses of looking

Filing Tip

Start-Up Costs

The election to amortize start-up expenses is made by claiming the deduction on Part VI of Form 4562, and by attaching a statement to the return for the first year you are in business. In the statement, describe the expenses, when they were incurred, the date the business began, and the number of months (not less than 60) in the amortization period. The deduction from Form 4562 is entered in Part V of Schedule C.

for investment property may not be amortized. For rental activities to qualify as an active business, there must be significant furnishing of services incident to the rentals. For example, the operation of an apartment complex, an office building, or a shopping center would generally be considered an active business.

You may not claim any deduction for start-up expenses if you do not elect to amortize. For example, if you incur expenses prior to completion of a building to be used in an active rental business, such as rental payments for leasing the land on which the building is to be constructed, you must elect to amortize the expenses or you will lose the deduction. If you do not elect to amortize, you treat the expenses as follows:

- Costs connected with the acquisition of capital assets are capitalized and depreciated; *and*
- Costs related to assets with unlimited or indeterminable useful lives are recovered only on the future sale or liquidation of the business.

If the acquisition fails. Where you have gone beyond a general search and have focused on the acquisition of a particular business, but the acquisition falls through, you may deduct the expenses as a capital loss.

Caution

Nonamortizable Costs

You may *not* amortize the expenses incurred in acquiring or selling securities or partnership interests such as securities registration expenses or underwriters' commissions. You may *not* amortize the costs of acquiring property to be held for sale or property that may be depreciated or amortized, including expenses incident to a lease and leasehold improvements.

EXAMPLES

1. In search of a business, you place newspaper advertisements and travel to investigate various prospective ventures. You pay for audits to evaluate the potential of some of the ventures. You then decide to purchase a specific business and hire a law firm to draft necessary documents. However, you change your mind and later abandon your plan to acquire the business. According to the IRS, you may not deduct the related expenses for advertisements, travel, and audits. These are considered investigatory. You may deduct the expense of hiring the law firm.

2. Domenie left his job to invest in a business. He advertised and was contacted by a party who wished to sell. He agreed to buy, hired an attorney, transferred funds to finance the business, and worked a month with the company manager to familiarize himself with the business. Discovering misrepresentations, he refused to buy the company and deducted over $5,000 for expenses, including travel and legal fees. The IRS disallowed the deduction as incurred in a business search. The Tax Court disagreed. Domenie thought he had found a business and acted as such in transferring funds and drawing legal papers for a takeover.

Job-hunting costs. For deducting the expenses of looking for a new job, *see 19.7*.

Business Use of a Home

40.12 Exclusive and Regular Use of a Home Office

If you operate your business from your home, using a room or other space as an office or area to assemble or prepare items for sale, you may be able to deduct expenses such as utilities, insurance, repairs, and depreciation allocated to your business use of the area. To deduct home office expenses, you must prove that you use the home area *exclusively* and *on a regular basis* either as:

1. *A place of business to meet or deal with patients, clients, or customers in the normal course of your business (incidental or occasional meetings do not meet this test),* or
2. *Your principal place of business.* Your home office will qualify as your principal place of business if you spend most of your working time there and most of your business income is attributable to your activities there.

Administrative (record-keeping) activity. A home office meets the principal place of business test (Test 2) if: (1) you use it regularly and exclusively for administrative or management activities of your business and (2) you have no other fixed location where you do a substantial amount of such administrative work. Self-employed persons are the beneficiaries of this administrative/management rule. Employees usually may not take advantage of the rule because of the application of the convenience-of-the-employer test to an employee's use of a home office; *see* the Example at *19.13*. Examples of administrative and management activities include billing customers, clients, or patients; keeping books and records; ordering supplies; setting up appointments; forwarding orders; and writing reports.

Filing Tip

Using a Home Office for Administrative Tasks

A home office deduction may be claimed if you regularly and exclusively use part of your home as the only place for conducting the administrative or management activities of your business, or if only minimal administrative work is done outside your home. The home area qualifies as your principal place of business even if you spend most of your working time providing services at outside locations.

Caution

Principal Place of Business Test
The tests for deducting office expenses will generally not present problems where the home area is the principal place of business or professional activity. For example, you are a doctor and see most of your patients at an office set aside in your home. A tax dispute may arise where you have a principal place of business elsewhere and use a part of your home for occasional work or administrative paperwork. Occasional use is not sufficient. If your deduction is questioned, you must prove that the area is used regularly and exclusively to meet with customers, clients, or patients or that the home office is the only place where administrative/management activities for the business are conducted. Have evidence that you have actual office facilities. Furnish the room as an office—with a desk, files, and a phone used only for business calls. Also keep a record of work done and business visitors.

According to the IRS, performance of management or administrative activities under the following conditions do not disqualify a home office as a principal place of business:

- You have a company send out your bills from its place of business (*see* Example 1).
- You do administrative or management activities at times from a hotel or automobile (*see* Example 2).
- You occasionally conduct minimal administrative or management activities at a fixed location outside your home.
- You have suitable space to do administrative or management work outside your home but choose to use your home office for such activities (*see* Example 3).

EXAMPLES
1. A self-employed plumber does all of his repair and installation services outside of his home where he has a small office used to phone customers, order supplies, and keep his books. However, he uses a local bookkeeping service to bill his customers. He has no other fixed location for doing his administrative work. That he uses an outside billing service does not disqualify his home office as a principal place of business.
2. A self-employed sales representative for several products uses a home office to set up appointments and write up orders. When she is out of town, she writes up such orders from a hotel room. The occasional use of a hotel room to write up orders does not disqualify the home office as a principal place of business that otherwise meets the new tests.
3. A self-employed anesthesiologist spends most of his professional time at three local hospitals. One of the hospitals provides him with a small shared office where he could do administrative and management work; however, he does not use this space. He uses his home as an office to: contact patients, surgeons, and hospitals regarding schedules; prepare presentations; keep billing records and patient logs; and read medical journals and books. His use of the home office for administrative activities satisfies the principal place of business test. His choice to use his home office instead of the one provided by one hospital does not disqualify his home office as the principal place of business.

If you work at home and also outside of your home at other locations and you do not meet the administrative/management rule, deductions of home office expenses should be supported by evidence that your activities at home are relatively more important or time consuming than those outside your home.

Exclusive and regular business use of home area required. If you use a room, such as a den, both for business and family purposes, be prepared to show that a specific section of the den is used *exclusively* as office space. For example, a real estate operator was not allowed to deduct the cost of a home office, on evidence that he also used the office area for nonbusiness purposes. A partition or other physical separation of the office area is helpful but not required.

Under the regular basis test, expenses attributable to incidental or occasional trade or business use are not deductible, even if the room is used for no other purpose but business.

Even if you meet these tests, your deduction for allocable office expenses may be substantially limited or barred by a restrictive rule that limits deductions to the income from the office activity. This computation is made on Form 8829 and is illustrated in *40.15*.

Multiple business use of home office. If you use a home office for more than one business, make sure that the home office tests are met for all businesses before you claim deductions. If one business use qualifies and another use does not, the IRS will disallow deductions even for the qualifying use, *see* the following paragraph.

Employee with sideline business. Employees who use a home office for their job and for a sideline business also should be aware of this problem. Most employees are unable to show that their home office is the principal place of their work *(19.13)*. Claiming an unallowable deduction for employee home office use will jeopardize the deduction for sideline business use. This happened to Hamacher, who as a self-employed actor earned $24,600 over a two-year period from an Atlanta theater and a few radio and television commercials. He also earned $18,000 each year as the administrator of an acting school at the theater. For his job as administrator, Hamacher shared an office at the theater with other employees. He had access to this office during nonbusiness hours. He also used one of the six rooms in his apartment for an office. Because of interruptions at the theater, he used the home office to work on the school curriculum and select plays for the theater. In connection with his acting business, he used the home office to receive phone calls, to prepare for auditions, and rehearse for acting roles.

Filing Instruction

Form 8829
You must report deductible 2002 home office expenses on Form 8829. Part I is used for showing the space allocated to business use *(40.14)*; Part II for reporting deductible expenses allocated to business use *(40.14)*; Part III for figuring depreciation on the business area *(40.13)*; and Part IV for carryover to 2003 of expenses not allowed in 2002 because of income limitations applied in Part II *(40.15)*. A sample copy of Form 8829 is on page 616.

The IRS disallowed his deduction for both self-employment and employee purposes because Hamacher's office use as an employee did not qualify. The Tax Court agreed. A single-office space may be used for different business activities, but all of the uses must qualify for a deduction. Here, Hamacher's use of the home office as an employee did not qualify. He had suitable office space at the theater. He was not expected or required to do work at home. As the employee use of the home office did not qualify, the Tax Court did not have to determine if the sideline business use qualified. Even if it had qualified, no allocation of expenses between the two uses would have been made. By requiring that a home office be used "exclusively" as a principal place of business or place for seeing clients, patients, or customers, the law imposes an all-or-nothing test.

Separate structure. If in your business you use a separate structure not attached to your home, such as a studio adjacent but unattached to your home, the expenses are generally deductible if you satisfy the exclusive use and regular basis tests discussed earlier. A separate structure does not have to qualify as your principal place of business or a place for meeting patients, clients, or customers. However, the income limitation discussed at *40.15* applies. In one case, a taxpayer argued that an office located in a separate building in his backyard was not subject to the exclusive and regular business use tests and the gross income limitation. However, the IRS and Tax Court held that it was. The office building was "appurtenant" to the home and thus part of it, based on these facts: The office building was 12 feet away from the house and within the same fenced-in residential area; it did not have a separate address; it was included in the same title and subject to the same mortgage as the house; and all taxes, utilities, and insurance were paid as a unit for both buildings.

Day-care services. The exclusive-use test does not have to be met for business use of a home to provide day-care services for children and handicapped persons, or persons age 65 or older, provided certain state licensing requirements are met. If part of your home is *regularly* but not exclusively used to provide day-care services, you may deduct an allocable part of your expenses. You allocate expenses by multiplying the total costs by two fractions: (1) The total square footage in the home that is available for day-care use throughout each business day and regularly so used, divided by the total square footage for the home. (2) The total hours of operation divided by the total number of hours in a year (8,760, or 365×24).

If the area *is* exclusively used for day-care services, only fraction (1) applies.

> ### EXAMPLE
>
> Alice Jones operates a day-care center at home from 7 a.m. to 6 p.m., five days a week, 250 days a year for a total of 2,750 business-use hours during the year. Her family uses the area the rest of the time. Annual home expenses total $10,000 ($5,000 for interest and taxes; $4,000 for electricity, gas, water, trash collection, maintenance, and insurance; and $1,000 for depreciation). The total floor area of the home is 2,000 square feet; 1,500 square feet are used for day-care purposes. Alice multiplies her $10,000 of expenses by 75%, the part of the home used for day-care purposes (1,500 square feet ÷ 2,000 square feet), and also by 31.39%, the percentage of business-use time (2,750 hours ÷ 8,760 hours). Thus, she may deduct $2,354: $10,000 × 75% × 31.39%. The full $2,354 is deductible only if net income generated from the day-care facility is at least that much.

In one case, the Tax Court held that utility rooms, such as a laundry and storage room and garage, may be counted as part of the day-care business area. The IRS had argued that because the children were not allowed in these areas, the space could not be considered as used for business. The Tax Court disagreed. The laundry room was used to wash the children's clothes; the storage room and garage were used to store play items and equipment. Thus, the space was considered as used for child care even though the rooms were off limits to the children.

Storage space and inventory. If your home is the only location of a business selling products, you may deduct expenses allocated to space regularly used for inventory storage, including product samples, if the space is separately identifiable and suitable for storage.

 Filing Tip

If You Rent Your Home
If you rent rather than own your home, and you meet the home office tests in *40.12*, enter the rent you paid during the year on Line 20 (Other Expenses) of Form 8829.

40.13 What Home Office Expenses Are Deductible?

Depending on your income *(40.15)*, a deduction for home business use may include real estate taxes, mortgage interest, operating expenses (such as home insurance premiums and utility costs), and depreciation allocated to the area used for business.

Sample Form 8829 — See Brown Example in *40.15*

Form **8829**

Department of the Treasury
Internal Revenue Service   (99)

Expenses for Business Use of Your Home

▶ **File only with Schedule C (Form 1040). Use a separate Form 8829 for each home you used for business during the year.**

▶ **See separate instructions.**

OMB No. 1545-1266

20**02**

Attachment
Sequence No. **66**

Name(s) of proprietor(s) **Samuel Brown**	Your social security number **X1X : 01 : 1111**

Part I   Part of Your Home Used for Business

1	Area used regularly and exclusively for business, regularly for day care, or for storage of inventory or product samples (see instructions)	1	500 sq. ft.
2	Total area of home	2	2,500 sq. ft.
3	Divide line 1 by line 2. Enter the result as a percentage	3	20%

• **For day-care facilities not used exclusively for business, also complete lines 4–6.**

• **All others, skip lines 4–6 and enter the amount from line 3 on line 7.**

4	Multiply days used for day care during year by hours used per day	4	hr.
5	Total hours available for use during the year (365 days × 24 hours) (see instructions)	5	8,760 hr.
6	Divide line 4 by line 5. Enter the result as a decimal amount	6	.
7	Business percentage. For day-care facilities not used exclusively for business, multiply line 6 by line 3 (enter the result as a percentage). All others, enter the amount from line 3 ▶	7	20%

Part II   Figure Your Allowable Deduction

8	Enter the amount from Schedule C, line 29, **plus** any net gain or (loss) derived from the business use of your home and shown on Schedule D or Form 4797. If more than one place of business, see instructions	8	3,400

See instructions for columns (a) and (b) before completing lines 9–20.

		(a) Direct expenses	(b) Indirect expenses		
9	Casualty losses (see instructions)	9			
10	Deductible mortgage interest (see instructions)	10		10,000	
11	Real estate taxes (see instructions)	11		4,000	
12	Add lines 9, 10, and 11	12		14,000	
13	Multiply line 12, column (b) by line 7		13	2,800	
14	Add line 12, column (a) and line 13				14	2,800
15	Subtract line 14 from line 8. If zero or less, enter -0-				15	600
16	Excess mortgage interest (see instructions)	16			
17	Insurance	17		1,200	
18	Repairs and maintenance	18			
19	Utilities	19		1,800	
20	Other expenses (see instructions)	20			
21	Add lines 16 through 20	21		3,000	
22	Multiply line 21, column (b) by line 7		22	600	
23	Carryover of operating expenses from 2001 Form 8829, line 41		23		
24	Add line 21 in column (a), line 22, and line 23				24	600
25	Allowable operating expenses. Enter the **smaller** of line 15 or line 24				25	600
26	Limit on excess casualty losses and depreciation. Subtract line 25 from line 15				26	- 0 -
27	Excess casualty losses (see instructions)		27		
28	Depreciation of your home from Part III below		28	1,200	
29	Carryover of excess casualty losses and depreciation from 2001 Form 8829, line 42		29		
30	Add lines 27 through 29				30	1,200
31	Allowable excess casualty losses and depreciation. Enter the **smaller** of line 26 or line 30				31	- 0 -
32	Add lines 14, 25, and 31				32	3,400
33	Casualty loss portion, if any, from lines 14 and 31. Carry amount to **Form 4684**, Section B				33	
34	Allowable expenses for business use of your home. Subtract line 33 from line 32. Enter here and on Schedule C, line 30. If your home was used for more than one business, see instructions ▶				34	3,400

Part III   Depreciation of Your Home

35	Enter the **smaller** of your home's adjusted basis or its fair market value (see instructions)	35	238,975
36	Value of land included on line 35	36	50,000
37	Basis of building. Subtract line 36 from line 35	37	188,975
38	Business basis of building. Multiply line 37 by line 7	38	37,795
39	Depreciation percentage (see instructions)	39	3.175%
40	Depreciation allowable (see instructions). Multiply line 38 by line 39. Enter here and on line 28 above	40	1,200

Part IV   Carryover of Unallowed Expenses to 2003

41	Operating expenses. Subtract line 25 from line 24. If less than zero, enter -0-	41	- 0 -
42	Excess casualty losses and depreciation. Subtract line 31 from line 30. If less than zero, enter -0-	42	1,200

For Paperwork Reduction Act Notice, see page 4 of separate instructions.   Cat. No. 13232M   Form **8829** (2002)

The deduction is figured on Form 8829 and entered on Line 30 of Schedule C.

Expenses that affect only the business part of your home, such as repairs or painting of the home office only, are entered on Form 8829 as "direct" expenses. Expenses for running the entire home, including mortgage interest, taxes, utilities, and insurance, are deductible as "indirect" expenses to the extent of your business-use percentage; *see 40.14.*

Household expenses and repairs that do not benefit that space are not deductible. However, a pro rata share of the cost of painting the outside of a house or repairing a roof is deductible. Costs of lawn care and landscaping are not deductible.

If you install a security system for all your home's windows and doors, the portion of your monthly maintenance fee that is allocable to the office area is a deductible operating expense. Furthermore, the business portion of your cost for the system is depreciable. Thus, if the office takes up 20% of your home *(40.14)* you may deduct, subject to the income limitation in *40.15*, 20% of the maintenance fee and a depreciation deduction for 20% of the cost.

Figuring depreciation. For depreciation purposes, the cost basis of the house is the lower of the fair market value of the house at the time you started to use a part of it for business or its adjusted basis, exclusive of the land. Only that part of the cost basis allocated to the office is depreciable. Form 8829 has a special section, Part III, for making this computation.

EXAMPLE

In April 2002, you start to use one room in your house exclusively and on a regular basis to meet with clients. This room is 10% of the square footage of your home. In 1988, you bought the property for $100,000, of which $90,000 was allocated to the house. The house has a fair market value of $185,000 in April 2002. You compute depreciation on the cost basis of $90,000, which is lower than the value. You multiply $90,000 by 10% (business-use percentage), which gives you $9,000 as the depreciable basis of the business part of the house. As you started business use in the fourth month of 2002, you multiply the depreciable basis of $9,000 by 1.819%. This percentage is listed for the fourth month in the depreciation rate table for 39-year property shown below. Your depreciation deduction is $163.71 (9,000 × 1.819%).

Nonresidential Real Property (39 years—For property placed in service after May 12, 1993)

Use the column for the month of taxable year placed in service.

	1	2	3	4	5	6	7	8	9	10	11	12
Year												
1	2.461%	2.247%	2.033%	1.819%	1.605%	1.391%	1.177%	0.963%	0.749%	0.535%	0.321%	0.107%
2–39	2.564	2.564	2.564	2.564	2.564	2.564	2.564	2.564	2.564	2.564	2.564	2.564
40	0.107	0.321	0.535	0.749	0.963	1.177	1.391	1.605	1.819	2.033	2.247	2.461

40.14 Allocating Expenses to Business Use

Allocate to home office use qualifying operating expenses *(40.13)* as follows: If the rooms are not equal or approximately equal in size, compare the number of square feet of space used for business with the total number of square feet in the home and then apply the resulting percentage to the total deductible expenses.

If all rooms in your home are approximately the same size, you may base the allocation on a comparison of the number of rooms used as an office to the total number of rooms.

EXAMPLE

A doctor rents a apartment using three rooms for his office and seven rooms for his residence. The rooms are not equal in size. The apartment has 2,000 square feet; the office has 600. He allocates 30% ($^{600}/_{2,000}$) of the following expenses to his office:

	Total	Office	Residence
Rent	$7,200	$2,160	$5,040
Light	600	180	420
Heat	1,000	300	700
Wages of domestic	2,000	600	1,400
	$10,800	$3,240	$7,560

The $3,240 of office expenses are deductible as indirect interest expenses on Form 8829, subject to the income limitation in *40.15*.

Carryover Allowed

Expenses disallowed because of the income limitation may be carried forward and treated as home office expenses in a later tax year (Part IV, Form 8829). The carryover as well as the expenses of the later year are subject to the income limitation of that year. For example, tentative net profit for 2002 on Line 29 of Schedule C is $1,000. Expenses allocated to the home office are $2,000. Only $1,000 of the expenses are deductible; $1,000 is carried over to 2003.

40.15   Business Income May Limit Home Office Deductions

Even if your home business use satisfies the deduction tests in *40.12*, deductions for the business portion *(40.14)* of utilities, maintenance, and insurance costs, as well as depreciation or rent deductions, may not exceed net business income after reducing the tentative profit from Schedule C by allocable mortgage interest, real estate taxes, and casualty deductions. To make sure that deductible expenses do not exceed income, the IRS requires you to use Form 8829. If you do not realize income during the year, no deduction is allowed. For example, you are a full-time writer and use an office in your home. You do not sell any of your work this year or receive any advances or royalties. Therefore, you may not claim a home office deduction for this year. *See also 40.9* on rules for writers and artists.

Part II of Form 8829 limits the deduction of home office expenses to net income derived from office use. You start with the tentative profit from Schedule C. If you sold your home during the year, increase the tentative profit by any net gain (or decrease tentative profit by any net loss) that is allocable to the office area and reported on Schedule D or Form 4797. The following expenses are listed first in Part II of Form 8829 for purposes of applying the income limit: Casualty losses affecting the residence, deductible mortgage interest, and real estate taxes. If there is income remaining after these expenses are subtracted from the Schedule C tentative profit, then home insurance premiums, repair and maintenance expenses for the residence, utility expenses, and rent are claimed against the remaining income. Depreciation is taken into account last.

Business expenses not related to the home are deducted on the appropriate lines of Schedule C. For example, a salary paid to a secretary is deducted on Line 26 of Schedule C; the cost of depreciable business equipment used in your home is deducted on Line 13 of Schedule C.

The amount of real estate taxes, mortgage interest, or casualty losses not allocated to home office use may be claimed as itemized deductions on Schedule A.

EXAMPLE

Brown does sideline business consulting from a home office that he uses exclusively for business for all of 2002. His income in 2002 from consulting services is $12,400. He paid $3,600 for a photocopy machine and $4,000 for a computer, and had office telephone expenses of $600 and office supply costs of $800.

In addition, his home costs are:

Mortgage interest	$10,000
Real estate taxes	4,000
Insurance	1,200
Utilities	1,800

His office space took up 20% of the area of his home, and he figured depreciation allocated to business use of $1,200.

On Schedule C he claims first-year expensing *(42.3)* for the copier and the computer, and also deducts the cost of the business phone and supplies. This gives a tentative profit of $3,400 ($12,400 – $9,000) on Line 29, Schedule C.

In Part I of Form 8829, he lists the total area of the home and the area used for business, showing 20% business use.

In Part II, he enters the home costs listed above. We have taken only the relevant lines of the Form 8829 as an illustration. A sample Form 8829 is on page 616.

Form 8829 Line—

8.	Tentative profit from Schedule C, Line 29		$3,400
10b.	Mortgage interest	$10,000	
11b.	Real estate taxes	4,000	
12b.	Total	$14,000	
13 & 14.	Business portion of Line 12		2,800
15.	Remaining tentative profit		600
17b.	Insurance	1,200	
19b.	Utilities	1,800	
21b.	Total	3,000	
22, 24, & 25.	Business portion of Line 21		600
26.	Remaining tentative profit		0

No depreciation is deductible because there is no remaining business income and excess home office expenses may not generate a loss deduction. The depreciation is carried over to 2003. Home office expenses of $3,400 from Lines 14 and 25 are deducted on Line 30, Schedule C.

40.16 Home Office for Sideline Business

You may have an occupation and also run a sideline business from an office in your home. The home office expenses are deductible on Form 8829 if the office is a principal place of operating the sideline business or a place to meet with clients, customers, or patients. *See* the deduction tests at *40.12* and the income limit computation at *40.15*. Managing rental property may qualify as a business.

> **EXAMPLE**
>
> A doctor is employed full time by a hospital. He also owns six rental properties that he personally manages. He uses one bedroom in his two-bedroom home exclusively as an office to manage the properties. The room is furnished with a desk, bookcase, filing cabinet, calculators, and answering service; furnishings and other materials for preparing rental units for tenants are stored there. He may deduct expenses allocable to the home office.

Managing your own securities portfolio. Investors managing their own securities portfolios may find it difficult to convince a court that investment management is a business activity. According to Congressional committee reports, a home office deduction should be denied to an investor who uses a home office to read financial periodicals and reports, clip bond coupons, and perform similar activities. In one case, the Claims Court allowed a deduction to Moller, who spent about 40 hours a week at a home office managing a substantial stock portfolio. The Claims Court held these activities amounted to a business. However, an appeals court reversed the decision. According to the appeals court, the test is whether or not a person is a trader. A trader is in a business; an investor is not. A trader buys and sells frequently to catch daily market swings. An investor buys securities for capital appreciation and income without regard to daily market developments. Therefore, to be a trader, one's activities must be directed to short-term trading, not the long-term holding of investments. Here, Moller was an investor; he was primarily interested in the long-term growth potential of stock. He did not earn his income from the short-term turnovers of stocks. He had no significant trading profits. His interest and dividend income was 98% of his income; *see also 30.23*.

40.17 Depreciation of Office in Cooperative Apartment

If your home office meets the tests discussed in *40.12*, you may deduct depreciation on your stock interest in the cooperative. The basis for depreciation may be your share of the cooperative corporation's basis for the building or an amount computed from the price you paid for the stock. The method you use depends on whether you are the first or a later owner of the stock.

You are the first owner. In figuring your depreciation, you start with the cooperative's depreciable basis of the building. You then take your share of depreciation according to the percentage of stock interest you own. The cooperative can provide the details needed for the computation.

If space in the building is rented to commercial tenants who do not have stock interests in the corporation, the total allowable depreciation is reduced by the amount allocated to the space used by the commercial tenants.

You are a later owner of the cooperative's stock. When you buy stock from a prior owner, your depreciable basis is determined by the price of your stock and your share of the co-op's outstanding mortgage, reduced by amounts allocable to land and to commercial space.

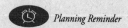 *Planning Reminder*

Substantiating the Sideline Business

In claiming home office expenses of a sideline business, it is important to be ready to prove that you are actually in business; *see 40.10*. The Tax Court has held that activities in seeking new tenants, supplying furnishings, and cleaning and preparing six units for tenants are sufficiently systematic and continuous to put a person in the rental real estate business. In some cases, the rental of even a single piece of real property may be a business if additional services are provided such as cleaning or maid service.

Figuring Net Operating Losses for Refund of Prior Taxes

40.18 Net Operating Losses for Refund of Prior Taxes

A loss incurred in your profession or unincorporated business is deducted from other income reported on Form 1040. If a loss (plus any casualty loss) exceeds income for your tax year ending in 2002, the excess may be first carried back five years, and *then* forward 20 years. You may waive the five-year carryback in favor of the regular carryback period of two years, or three years in certain cases; *see* the Law Alert on the following page. A loss carried back to a prior year reduces income of that year and entitles you to a refund. A loss applied to a later year reduces income for that year. You may elect to carry forward your 2002 loss for 20 years, foregoing the carryback; *see 40.22*.

The rules below apply not only to self-employed individuals, farmers, and professionals, but also to individuals whose casualty losses exceed income, stockholders in S corporations, and partners whose partnerships have suffered losses. Each partner claims his or her share of the partnership loss.

Carryover of loss from prior year to 2002. If you had a net operating loss in an earlier year that is being carried forward to 2002, the loss carryover is reported as a minus figure on Line 21 of Form 1040. You must attach a detailed statement showing how you figured the carryover.

Net operating losses from tax years beginning on or before August 5, 1997, expire after 15 carryforward years.

Change in marital status. If you incur a net operating loss while single but are married filing jointly in a carryback or carryforward year, the loss may be used only to offset your own income on the joint return.

If the net operating loss was claimed on a joint return and in the carryback or carryforward year you are not filing jointly with the same spouse, only your allocable share of the original loss may be claimed; *see* IRS Publication 536.

Passive activity limitation. Losses subject to passive activity rules of Chapter 10 are not deductible as net operating losses. However, losses of rental operations coming within the $25,000 allowance discussed at *10.2* may be treated as net operating loss if the loss exceeds passive and other income.

Restrictions on loss after accounting method change. You may realize a net operating loss for a short taxable year created by the accounting change. As a condition of allowing the accounting method change, the IRS may require you to forego the right to a loss carryback and agree to a six-year carryforward period; *see* Revenue Procedure 85-16.

> **EXAMPLE**
>
> You want to change from a calendar year to a fiscal year ending April 30. Assume further that May through October is your peak selling period. Thus, you may have a net operating loss for the short taxable year January 1– April 30 because of slack business. According to the IRS, if the net operating loss is $10,000 or less, you may apply the regular net operating loss carryback and carryforward rules. But if the net operating loss exceeds $10,000 and the short period is less than nine months, the operating loss must be deducted ratably over a six-year period starting with the first tax year after the short period.

40.19 Your Net Operating Loss

A net operating loss is generally the excess of deductible business expenses over business income. The net operating loss may also include the following losses and deductions:

- Casualty and theft losses, even if the property was used for personal purposes; *see* Chapter 18.
- Expenses of moving to a new job location; *see* Chapter 12.
- Deductible job expenses such as travel expenses, work clothes, costs, and union dues; *see 19.3.*
- Your share of a partnership or S corporation operating loss.
- Loss on the sale of small business investment company (SBIC) stock.
- Loss incurred on Section 1244 stock.

An operating loss may *not* include:

- Net operating loss carryback or carryover from any year.
- Capital losses that exceed capital gain.
- Excess of nonbusiness deductions over nonbusiness income plus nonbusiness net capital gain.
- Deductions for personal exemptions.
- A self-employed person's contribution to a Keogh plan.
- An IRA deduction.

Income from other sources may eliminate or reduce your net operating loss.

> **EXAMPLE**
>
> You are self-employed and incur a business loss of $10,000. Your spouse earns a salary of $10,000. When you file a joint return, your business loss will be eliminated by your spouse's salary. Similarly, if you also had salary from another position, the salary would reduce your business loss.

40.20 Form 1045

You compute your net operating loss deduction on Form 1045. You start with adjusted gross income and personal deductions shown on your tax return. As these figures include items not allowed for net operating loss purposes, you follow the line-by-line steps of Form 1045 to eliminate them. That is, you reduce the loss by the nonallowed items such as deductions for personal exemp-

Law Alert

Five-Year Carryback for 2002 Losses

The Job Creation and Worker Assistance Act of 2002 allows a five-year carryback for a net operating loss (NOL) arising in the tax year ending in 2002. The five-year carryback period may be waived by the due date (including extensions) of your return if it would be more advantageous to use the regular two-year or three-year carryback period; follow the instructions on Form 1045. The regular carryback period is generally two years, but the three-year period is allowed to qualifying small businesses with net operating losses attributable to Presidentially declared disasters. For individuals, the three-year carryback may be used for net operating losses attributable to casualty and theft losses.

An election may be made to forego any carryback and carry forward the entire NOL for 2002 for a period of up to 20 years.

tions, net capital loss, and nonbusiness deductions exceeding nonbusiness income. On the schedule, the reductions are described as adjustments. The Example at the end of this section illustrates the steps in the schedule.

Adjustment for nonbusiness deductions. Nonbusiness deductions that exceed nonbusiness income may not be included in a net operating loss deduction. Nonbusiness deductions include deductions for IRA and Keogh plans and itemized deductions such as charitable contributions, interest expense, state taxes, and medical expenses. Do not include in this non-allowed group deductible casualty and theft losses, which for net operating loss purposes are treated as business losses. If you do not claim itemized deductions in the year of the loss, you must treat the standard deduction as a nonbusiness deduction.

Nonbusiness income is income that is *not* from a trade or business—such as dividends, interest, and annuity income. The excess of nonbusiness capital gains over nonbusiness capital losses is also treated as part of nonbusiness income that offsets nonbusiness deductions.

 *Filing Instruction*

Adjustment for Capital Losses
A net nonbusiness capital loss may not be included in a net operating loss. If nonbusiness capital losses exceed nonbusiness capital gains, the excess is an adjustment that reduces your loss on Form 1045. In figuring your loss, you may take into account business capital losses only up to the total of business capital gains plus any nonbusiness capital gains remaining after the adjustment for nonbusiness deductions.

> **EXAMPLE**
>
> Income from dividends and interest is $6,000 and nonbusiness deductions are $6,500. The excess deduction of $500 is an adjustment that reduces your loss on Form 1045.

At-risk loss limitations. The loss used to figure your net operating loss deduction is subject to the at-risk rules discussed at *10.17*. If part of your investment is in nonrecourse loans or is otherwise not at risk, you must compute your deductible loss on Form 6198, which you attach to Form 1040. The deductible loss from Form 6198 is reflected in the income and deduction figures you enter on the Form 1045 schedule to compute your net operating loss deduction.

> **EXAMPLE**
>
> You are single and in 2002 you have a salary of $3,000, interest of $1,200, a net business loss of $10,000 (income of $50,000 and expenses of $60,000), itemized Schedule A deductions of $5,900, and a net nonbusiness capital gain of $1,000. After the required addbacks and adjustments are made, your net operating loss is $7,000. The following computation approximates the steps of the Form 1045 computation schedule starting from the line showing your negative adjusted gross income of $4,800.
>
> | | | |
> |---|---:|---:|
> | Salary | | $3,000 |
> | Interest | | 1,200 |
> | Capital gain income | | 1,000 |
> | Business loss | | ($10,000) |
> | Adjusted gross income | | ($4,800) |
> | Add: Exemption and itemized deductions | | (8,900) |
> | | | ($13,700) |
> | Adjustments: | | |
> | Exemption | $3,000 | |
> | Excess nonbusiness deduction * | 3,700 | 6,700 |
> | Net operating loss | | ($7,000) |
>
> *The excess nonbusiness expenses deduction was figured as follows:*
>
> | | | |
> |---|---:|---:|
> | Itemized deductions | | $5,900 |
> | Net capital gain income | $1,000 | |
> | Interest income | 1,200 | 2,200 |
> | Excess | | $3,700 |

40.21 How To Carry Back Your Net Operating Loss

As discussed in *40.18*, the carryback period for a 2002 net operating loss is generally five years, but the five-year period may be waived in favor of a two-year carryback, or three years if applicable. When you carry back the loss, you recompute your tax for the earlier year on Form 1045. After recomputing the tax on Form 1045, your refund is the difference between the tax originally paid and the lower tax figured after taking the net operating loss deduction. *See* the instructions to Form 1045 and also IRS Publication 536 for details of the recomputation calculation.

Use Form 1045 as a "quick refund" claim. The IRS will usually allow or reject your claim within 90 days from the time you file Form 1045. Do not attach Form 1045 to your 2002 Form 1040. File Form 1045 separately, together with a copy of your return. You may file Form 1045 within 12 months after the end of your tax year. If the IRS allows the refund, it may still determine later that the refund was excessive and assess additional tax.

Although using Form 1045 is the quickest way to obtain the refund, you may instead file an amended return on Form 1040X to claim the refund. You have three years after the due date (including extensions) of your 2002 tax return to file Form 1040X.

40.22 Election To Carry Forward Losses

Instead of carrying back your 2002 net operating loss under the rules in *40.21*, you may elect to forego the carryback. Instead, you just carry forward losses. The carryforward period remains 20 years under the election. The election is irrevocable.

If you are carrying forward a net operating loss from an earlier year to 2002, report the loss carryover as a minus figure on Line 21 of Form 1040 and attach a statement explaining how the carryover was computed.

Planning Reminder

Advantage of Relinquishing the Carryback

You will generally make the election to relinquish the carryback if you expect greater tax savings by carrying the loss forward. You might also make the election if you are concerned you might be audited for earlier years if you carry back a loss for a refund. You make the election by attaching a statement to this effect to your return for the year of the loss, which must be filed by the due date plus extensions. The IRS refuses to allow a late election and received court approval for its position.

Business Tax Credits

Law Alert

New York Liberty Zone Business Employee Credit

The Job Creation and Worker Assistance Act of 2002 provides a tax credit for wages paid in 2002 or 2003 to employees in the New York Liberty Zone. Employers must have on average no more than 200 employees on business days during the taxable year to qualify. The credit is claimed on Form 8884. Although the credit is an extension of the work opportunity credit, a special tax liability applies to the Liberty Zone credit, so neither Form 5884 (Work Opportunity Credit) nor Form 3800 (General Business Credit) is used.

40.23 General Business Credit

The *general business credit* includes the following credits:

- The work opportunity credit on Form 5884;
- The investment credit on Form 3468, consisting of the rehabilitation property credit *(see 31.8)*, the energy credit, and the reforestation credit;
- The alcohol fuels credit on Form 6478;
- The research credit on Form 6765;
- The low-income housing credit on Form 8586 *(see 31.8)*;
- The enhanced oil recovery credit on Form 8830;
- The disabled access credit on Form 8826;
- The welfare-to-work credit on Form 8861;
- The renewable electricity production credit on Form 8835;
- The credit for wages paid in an empowerment zone on Form 8844;
- The Indian employment credit on Form 8845;
- The orphan drug credit on Form 8820;
- The credit for employer-paid Social Security and Medicare taxes on certain tips received by employees of food and beverage establishments on Form 8846; *and*
- The credit for contributions to certain community development corporations on Form 8847.

Computing the general business credit. You compute each credit separately. If you claim only one credit, that credit is considered your *general business credit* for 2002. The credit is subject to a limitation based on tax liability that is figured on the form used to compute that particular credit. You then enter the allowable credit as your general business credit on Form 1040.

If you claim more than one credit, the credits are combined into one general business credit on Form 3800, except for the empowerment zone wages credit, which is figured on Form 8844 and not carried to Form 3800. Each of the other credits is first computed separately and then listed on Form 3800. The combined credit is subject to a limitation based on tax liability. To figure the limit, you must compute tentative alternative minimum tax (AMT) on Form 6251 even if the complete computation on Form 6251 shows that you do not have an actual AMT liability for the year. Your limit for the general business credit on Form 3800 is your regular tax liability (after tax credits other than the general business credit), *plus* actual AMT liability from Form 6251 (if any), *minus* whichever of the following is larger: either (1) tentative AMT from Form 6251 or (2) 25% of your regular income tax liability (after other credits) over $25,000.

Keep separate records of each of the component credits making up the general business credit. The credits are considered to be used up in a specific order; *see* the instructions to Form 3800.

If your full 2002 general business credit may not be claimed because of the tax liability limitation, you may be able to *carry back* the excess one year, starting with the earliest year. Check the Form 3800 instructions for restrictions on carrying back certain credits. After the carryback, any remaining credit may be *carried forward* 20 years until used up. The carrybacks and carryforwards are listed on Form 3800.

For credits arising in tax years beginning before 1998, the carryback period is three years; the carryforward period is 15 years.

If you have business credits from a passive activity under the rules discussed in Chapter 10, you must figure the credits on Form 8582-CR; generally, the credits are limited to the tax liability from passive activities.

40.24 Fuel-Related Credits

For a qualified business use, a refundable credit may be claimed for *gasoline or special fuels*. For example, a credit applies for fuel used in non-highway vehicles (other than motorboats), including generators, compressors, fork-lift trucks, and bulldozers. A credit may also be claimed for aviation fuel used for farming or commercial aviation. Different credit rates apply depending on the type of fuel. You must claim the credit on a timely filed income tax return, including extensions. You compute the credit on Form 4136, which you attach to Form 1040. For further details, *see* IRS Publication 378; farmers should *see* IRS Publication 225.

Chapter 41

Retirement Plans for Self-Employed

Self-employed persons and partners can take advantage of tax-sheltered Keogh retirement plans or simplified employee pension plans (SEPs).

Advantages flow from: (1) tax deductions allowed for contributions to the plan (a form of forced savings); (2) tax-free accumulations of income earned on assets held by the plan; and (3) in some cases, special averaging for lump-sum benefits paid from a Keogh plan on retirement.

If you have employees, you must consider the cost of covering them when setting up your plan.

If you do not have any other retirement plan and have no more than 100 employees, you may set up a salary-reduction SIMPLE IRA plan.

41.1 Who May Set Up a Keogh Plan?

You may set up a self-employed retirement plan called a *Keogh plan* if you have *net earnings* (gross business or professional income less allowable business deductions) from your sole proprietorship or partnership for which the plan is established. If you are an inactive owner, such as a limited partner, you do not qualify to set up a Keogh plan—unless you receive guaranteed payments for services that are treated as earnings from self-employment.

Partnership plans. An individual partner or partners, although self-employed, may not set up a Keogh plan. The plan must be established by the partnership. Partnership deductions for contributions to an individual partner's account are reported on the partner's Schedule K-1 (Form 1065) and deducted by the partner as an adjustment to income on Line 31 of Form 1040.

Including employees in your plan. You must include in your plan all employees who have reached age 21 with at least one year of service. An employee may be required to complete two years of service before participating if your plan provides for full and immediate vesting after no more than two years. You generally are not required to cover seasonal or part-time employees who work less than 1,000 hours during a 12-month period.

A minimum coverage rule requires that a defined benefit plan must include at least 40% of all employees, or 50 employees if that is less.

Your plan may not exclude employees who are over a certain age.

A plan may not discriminate in favor of officers or other highly compensated personnel. Benefits must be for the employees and their beneficiaries, and their plan rights may not be subject to forfeiture. A plan may not allow any of its funds to be diverted for purposes other than pension benefits. Contributions made on your behalf may not exceed the ratio of contributions made on behalf of employees.

41.2 Choosing a Keogh Plan

There are two types of Keogh plans: defined-benefit plans and defined-contribution plans, and different rules apply to each. A defined-benefit plan provides in advance for a specific retirement benefit funded by quarterly contributions based on an IRS formula and actuarial assumptions. A defined-contribution plan does not fix a specific retirement benefit, but rather sets the amount of annual contributions so that the amount of retirement benefits depends on contributions and income earned on those contributions. If contributions are geared to profits, the plan is a profit-sharing plan. A plan that requires fixed contributions regardless of profits is a money-purchase plan. If you have a profit-sharing plan, a 401(k) plan arrangement can be included to allow you (and other participants) to make elective deferral contributions of before-tax compensation to the plan.

A defined-benefit plan may prove costly if you have older employees who also must be provided with proportionate defined benefits. Furthermore, a defined-benefit plan requires you to contribute to their accounts even if you do not have profits. For 2002, the benefit limit was the lesser of (a) 100% of the participant's average compensation for the three consecutive years of highest compensation as an active participant or (b) $160,000, assuming the plan was amended to implement the $160,000 limit as allowed by the 2001 Tax Act. This dollar limit is reduced if benefits begin before age 62 and increased if benefits begin after age 65. Inflation adjustments to the $160,000 limit for years after 2002 are possible.

For defined contribution plans, the 2002 limit on annual contributions and other additions (excluding earnings) was the lesser of 100% of compensation or $40,000, assuming the plan was amended to implement these limits as allowed by the 2001 Tax Act. For years after 2002, the $40,000 limit may be adjusted for inflation.

Setting up a trust for investing in Keoghs. If you are interested in following an aggressive investment policy for funds in your Keogh plan, you will set up a trust to receive Keogh contributions. You may name yourself or an independent trustee to oversee the plan.

If you use funds to buy nontransferable annuity contracts from an insurance company, use of a trust is optional. Premium payments may be made directly to the insurance company. The annuity contract may pay a fixed monthly income for life or for a fixed period of years, or may be a variable annuity contract. Life insurance can be included only if it is incidental to retirement benefits.

If you are investing in savings certificates, you need not set up a trust; you may use a custodial account with the bank.

Planning Reminder

Employees Who Are Self-Employed on the Side

If you are an employee-member of a company retirement plan, you may set up a Keogh plan if you carry on a self-employed enterprise or profession on the side. For example, you are employed by a company that has a qualified 401(k) plan to which you make salary deferrals. At the same time, you have a sideline consulting business. You may set up a Keogh plan based on your consultant earnings. Each plan is independent of the other. As an alternative to a Keogh plan, you may contribute to a simplified employee pension plan (SEP), as discussed in *41.4*, or a SIMPLE IRA, discussed in *41.11*.

41.3 Top-Heavy Plan Restrictions

"Top-heavy" plan rules, which apply to corporate plans favoring "key employees," may also apply to a Keogh plan of a self-employed person. The top-heavy rules apply if more than 60% of the account balances or accrued benefits are for key employees; *see* below for the definition of "key employees." Even if your Keogh plan is not currently considered top heavy, your plan may be disqualified, unless it includes provisions that would automatically take effect if the plan becomes top heavy. The major top-heavy requirements are an accelerated vesting schedule and a minimum benefit (generally not less than 3% of compensation for a defined contribution plan) for non-key employees.

Vesting. A top-heavy plan must provide either 100% vesting after three years of service or graded vesting at the rate of at least 20% after two years of service, 40% after three years of service, 60% after four years of service, 80% after five years of service, and 100% after six years of service. There may be an advantage in electing three-year vesting if you have a high turnover of employees.

Who are key employees? The above top-heavy restrictions apply if more than 60% of a defined-contribution plan account balances or more than 60% of the accrued benefits of a defined-benefit plan are for key employees. For the 2002 plan year, key employees are employees who at any time during the plan year own: (1) more than a 5% interest; (2) more than a 1% interest and also earn compensation of more than $150,000; and (3) officers with compensation exceeding $130,000. The $130,000 limit is subject to increases for inflation.

41.4 Choosing a SEP

Under a SEP (simplified employee pension plan), you may contribute to a special type of IRA more than is allowed under the regular IRA rules. Contributions do not have to be made every year. When you do make contributions, they must be based on a written allocation formula and must not discriminate in favor of yourself, other owners with more than a 5% interest, or highly compensated employees. Coverage requirements for employees are at *8.15*. A salary-reduction arrangement for employees may be provided under a qualifying SEP established before 1997 or under a SIMPLE IRA plan established after 1996; *see 8.17*.

The deadline for both setting up and contributing to a SEP is the due date for your return, *including extensions*. Thus, if you have not set up a Keogh plan by the end of the taxable year *(41.1)*, you may still make a deductible retirement contribution for the year by contributing to a SEP by the due date of your return.

41.5 Deductible Keogh or SEP Contributions

The deductible limit for a Keogh plan depends on whether you have a defined-contribution plan (profit-sharing or money-purchase pension plan) or a defined-benefit plan. A SEP is treated as a profit-sharing plan subject to the defined-contribution plan deduction limits explained below.

If you have a defined-benefit plan, you generally may deduct contributions needed to produce the accrued benefits provided for by the plan. This is a complicated calculation requiring actuarial computations that call for the services of a pension expert.

Deductible contribution for 2002 to a defined-contribution Keogh Plan or a SEP. Before figuring the deductible contribution you can make for 2002 to a profit-sharing Keogh or SEP account, or to a money-purchase pension plan, you must first figure your self-employment tax liability on Schedule SE and the 50% deduction for self-employment tax to be claimed on Line 29 of Form 1040. In computing your deductible plan contribution, your net profit from Line 31 of Schedule C, Line 3 of Schedule C-EZ, or Line 36 of Schedule F is *reduced* by the deduction for 50% of self-employment tax; *see* the Example on the next page.

As a self-employed person, you are *not* allowed to figure the deductible contribution for yourself by applying the contribution rate stated in your plan. The rate must be reduced, as required by law, to reflect the reduction of net earnings by the deductible contribution itself. If your plan rate is a whole number, the reduced percentage is shown in the table below.

 Caution

Prohibited Transactions

As an owner-employee (owning more than 10% of the business), your dealings with the Keogh trust are subject to restrictions. You are generally subject to penalties if you buy property from or sell property to the trust; or charge any fees for services you render to the trust. These restrictions also apply to any member of your immediate family and any corporation in which you own more than half the voting stock, either directly or indirectly.

Before 2002, prohibited transaction penalties also applied to plan loans to owner-employees *(41.9)* but this rule has been repealed for years beginning after 2001.

Self-Employed Person's Contribution Rate Table

If plan rate is—	Self-employed person's reduced rate is—
1%	.009901
2	.019608
3	.029126
4	.038462
5	.047619
6	.056604
7	.065421
8	.074074
9	.082569
10	.090909
11	.099099
12	.107143
13	.115044
14	.122807
15	.130435
16	.137931
17	.145299
18	.152542
19	.159664
20	.166667
21	.173554
22	.180328
23	.186992
24	.193548
25*	.200000*

* *The maximum deductible percentage for contributions to your own profit-sharing Keogh, money-purchase Keogh, or SEP is 20% and for your employees, 25%.*

Fractional rates. If the plan rate is fractional and thus not listed in the table above, figure your deductible percentage this way:

1. Write the plan rate as a decimal. For example, if the plan rate is 10.5%, write .105 as the decimal amount.
2. Add 1 to the decimal rate. For example, if the rate is .105, the result is 1.105.
3. Divide Step 1 by Step 2. This gives you the deductible percentage. If the plan rate is .105, the deductible percentage is .095023 (.105 ÷ 1.105).

Figuring your maximum deductible contribution for 2002. After figuring your net earnings and reducing that amount by 50% of your self-employment tax liability, you multiply the balance by the reduced rate from the Self-Employed Person's Rate Table or the fractional rate discussed above. This is generally your maximum deductible contribution to a profit-sharing Keogh plan or SEP. However, the maximum deductible contribution cannot exceed the annual limit on additions to a defined contribution plan. If the plan was amended to implement the limits allowed by the 2001 Tax Act, the annual limit for 2002 was the lesser of (1) $40,000, or (2) $200,000 (maximum compensation that can be taken into account) multiplied by the stated plan contribution rate shown in the left column of the Self-Employed Person's Contribution Rate Table above. Step 4 of the following Example assumes the plan was amended to allow the $40,000 and $200,000 amounts to be used. Without a plan amendment, the compensation limit would be $170,000 and the overall limit would be $35,000 in Step 4.

If elective deferrals were made to the plan, extra steps are required to compute the maximum deductible contribution; *see* the Deduction Worksheet for Self-Employed in IRS Publication 560.

Caution

Deadline for Setting Up Keogh Plan or SEP

You must formally set up a Keogh plan in writing on or before the end of the taxable year in which you want the plan to be effective. For example, if you want to make a contribution for 2002, your plan must be set up on or before December 31, 2002, if you report on a calendar year basis. If a profit-sharing Keogh plan is established by the end of 2002, you have up until the due date for filing youWhat Home Office Expenses Are Deductible?What Home Office Expenses Are Deductible?r return, plus extensions, to make a deductible contribution within the limits discussed in this section.

If you miss the deadline for setting up a Keogh plan, you may contribute to a simplified employee pension plan (SEP) set up by the filing deadline for Form 1040, including extensions. *See 41.4.*

Law Alert

Higher Deductible Contribution Limits in 2002

The 2001 Tax Act increases the maximum deductible contribution rate from 15% to 25% for SEPs and profit-sharing Keogh plans starting in 2002. The compensation limit increases to $200,000 and the dollar limit to $40,000, provided the plan was amended to include the new law limits.

EXAMPLE

You are a sole proprietor with no employees and have a profit-sharing plan that provides for a 25% contribution rate. Your net self-employment earnings for 2002 from Line 31 of Schedule C are $147,000. On Schedule SE, you figure your self-employment tax liability of $14,464, and you claim a 50% deduction for self-employment taxes of $7,232 ($\frac{1}{2}$ of $14,464 self-employment tax from Schedule SE) on Line 29 of Form 1040. Your maximum deductible profit-sharing contribution for 2002 is $27,954:

Step 1.	Net earnings reduced by 50% of self-employment tax liability ($147,000 − $7,232)	$139,768
Step 2.	Self-employed person's rate in the right column of the table on the preceding page	.20
Step 3.	Step 2 rate multiplied by Step 1 reduced net earnings ($139,768 × .20)	$27,954
Step 4.	Annual limit on additions to plan for 2002: $200,000 (compensation limit) multiplied by 20% plan rate but no more than $40,000	$40,000
Step 5.	Lesser of Step 3 or Step 4. This is your maximum deductible contribution for 2002	$27,954

Contributions for your employees. The deduction complications that apply to your own contributions do not apply to contributions for employees. You make contributions for your employees at the rate specified in your plan, based upon their compensation, subject to the annual limit discussed above. Thus, in the Example above, you would contribute 25% of your employees' pay to the plan. You deduct contributions for employees when figuring your net earnings from self-employment on Schedule C or Schedule F before figuring your own deductible contribution using the steps shown in the Example above.

Contributions allowed after age 70$^1/_2$. You may continue to make contributions for yourself to a Keogh plan or SEP as long as you have self-employment income. However, you must begin to receive required minimum distributions from a SEP by April 1 of the year following the year in which you reach age 70$^1/_2$; *see 8.15.* This age 70$^1/_2$ required distribution beginning date also applies to a Keogh plan if you are a more-than-5% owner of the business; *see 7.13.*

Excess contributions. Contributions to a plan exceeding the deduction ceiling may be carried over and deducted in later years subject to the ceiling for those years. However, if contributions exceed the deductible amount, you are generally subject to a 10% penalty on nondeductible contributions that are not returned by the end of your tax year. The penalty is computed on Form 5330, which must be filed with the IRS by the end of the seventh month following the end of the tax year.

41.6 How To Claim the Keogh or SEP Deduction

Contributions made to your Keogh or SEP account as a self-employed person are deducted as an adjustment to gross income on Line 31 of Form 1040. A deduction for a contribution made for your benefit may not be part of a net operating loss.

Contributions for your employees are entered as deductions on Schedule C (or Schedule F) for purposes of computing profit or loss from your business. Trustees' fees not provided for by contributions are deductible in addition to the maximum contribution deduction.

Deductible Keogh plan contributions may generally be made at any time up to the due date of your return, including any extension of time. However, the plan itself must be set up before the close of the taxable year for which the deduction is sought. If you miss the December 31 deadline for setting up a Keogh plan, you have at least up to April 15, 2003, to set up a SEP for 2002. If you have a filing extension, you have until the extended due date to set up a SEP and make your contribution.

41.7 How To Qualify a Keogh Plan or SEP Plan

You may set up a Keogh plan and contribute to it without advance approval. But since advance approval is advisable, you may, in a determination letter, ask the IRS to review your plan. Approval requirements depend on whether you set up your own administered plan or join a master plan administered by a bank, insurance company, mutual fund, or a prototype plan sponsored by a trade or professional association. If you start your own individually designed plan, you may pay a fee and request a determination letter; *see* IRS Publication 560.

If you join a master or prototype plan, the sponsoring organization applies to the IRS for approval of its plan. You should then be given a copy of the approved plan and copies of any subsequent amendments.

To set up a SEP with a bank, broker, or other financial institution, you do not need IRS approval. If you do not maintain any other qualified retirement plan and other tests are met, a model SEP may be adopted using Form 5305-SEP.

41.8 Annual Keogh Plan Return

Partial relief from one burdensome IRS paperwork requirement may be available if your pension or profit-sharing Keogh plan covers only yourself, or you and your spouse, or you and your business partners and the spouses of the partners. Such plans are treated as one-participant plans by the IRS.

If a one-participant Keogh plan meets minimum coverage requirements, and does not cover a business that leases employees or is part of a controlled group, an annual information return for the plan may be filed on Form 5500-EZ instead of the more extensive Form 5500.

Under an exception for small one-participant plans, Form 5500-EZ does not have to be filed at all if the plan had total assets of $100,000 or less at the end of every plan year beginning on or after January 1, 1994. The exception applies if you have two or more one-participant plans that together have not exceeded the $100,000 asset threshold at the end of all post-1993 plan years. All one-participant plans must file a Form 5500-EZ for their final plan year even if the plan assets have always been below $100,000.

One-participant plans that hold more than $100,000 at the end of any plan year beginning on or after January 1, 1994, must file a Form 5500-EZ for the first year the assets exceed $100,000 and for each year thereafter, even if total plan assets are reduced to $100,000 or less. For example, if plan assets in a plan that otherwise satisfies the requirements for filing the Form 5500-EZ totaled $110,000 at the end of the 2001 plan year, and a distribution occurred in 2002 so that plan assets totaled $85,000 at the end of the 2002 plan year, a Form 5500-EZ must still be filed for the 2002 plan year and for all later plan years.

The filing deadline for Form 5500-EZ or Form 5500 is the last day of the seventh month after the end of the plan year unless an extension is obtained. Thus, for a calendar year plan, the filing deadline for the 2002 plan year will generally be July 31, 2003. A one-time extension of up to $2\frac{1}{2}$ months for filing Form 5500-EZ may be obtained by filing Form 5558 with the IRS; Form 5558 must be filed by the normal due date. Forms 5500 and 5500-EZ are filed with the U.S. Department of Labor's Pension and Welfare Benefits Administration (PWBA), rather than with the IRS. *See* the form instructions for the mailing address and the electronic filing alternative.

41.9 Restrictions on Keogh Plan Loans Repealed

For years beginning before 2002, Keogh plan loans to an owner-employee (more than 10% ownership) were subject to two prohibited transaction penalties: (1) a 15% first tier penalty and (2) a 100% penalty. However, the 2001 Tax Act eliminates the penalties for Keogh plan loans made to owner-employees after 2001.

41.10 How Keogh Plan Distributions Are Taxed

Distributions from a Keogh plan generally may not be received without penalty before age 59 ½ unless you are disabled or meet the other exceptions listed at *7.15*. If you are a more-than-5% owner you must begin to receive minimum required distributions by April 1 of the year following the year in which you reach age 70 ½; penalties may apply if an insufficient distribution is received (*see 7.13*).

A lump-sum distribution may be rolled over tax free to an IRA or other qualified plan. For participants born before 1936, 10-year averaging may be available; *see 7.2* for details. Pension dis-

Caution

Individually Designed Keogh Plans
You can set up an individually designed Keogh plan without advance IRS approval, but it is advisable to get professional assistance and request a determination letter from the IRS.

Caution

Loans From SEP Are Prohibited
Borrowing from a SEP is a prohibited transaction under the IRA rules and will result in the loss of the account's tax-exempt status. The account will be treated as if it were distributed to you on the first day of the year; *see 8.8*. The 2001 Tax Act does not change the prohibited transaction rule for IRA loans.

tributions from a Keogh are taxed under the annuity rules discussed in *7.25*, but for purposes of figuring your cost investment, include only nondeductible voluntary contributions; deductible contributions made on your behalf are not part of your investment.

If you receive amounts in excess of the benefits provided for you under the plan formula and you own more than a 5% interest in the employer, the excess benefit is subject to a 10% penalty. The penalty also applies if you were a more-than-5% owner at any time during the five plan years preceding the plan year that ends within the year of an excess distribution.

Other rules discussed at *7.1* to *7.16* apply to Keogh plans as well as qualified corporate plans.

After the death of a Keogh plan owner, distributions to beneficiaries may be spread over the periods discussed at *7.14* provided the plan covers more than one person. However, an extended payment period is not available when a one-person Keogh plan owner dies and the beneficiary is not his or her surviving spouse. This is because the plan may not be maintained following the death of the sole owner. The plan assets must be distributed to a non-spouse beneficiary by the end of the calendar year following the year of the owner's death and the beneficiary must pay the tax on the full amount at that time. This is not a problem if the beneficiary is the surviving spouse, since he or she may roll over the funds to an IRA; *see 8.14*.

SEP distributions. Distributions from a SEP are subject to the IRA rules at *8.8*.

41.11   SIMPLE IRA Plans

If you do not maintain any other retirement plan and have 100 or fewer employees, you may set up a salary-reduction type of plan for yourself and your employees. The SIMPLE IRA contribution rules are discussed at *8.18*. A SIMPLE plan may also be made as part of a 401(k) plan; *see 7.17*.

Under a SIMPLE IRA for 2002, you may contribute to your own account $7,000 of net earnings plus an additional $500 if age 50 or over by the end of the year. You may also make a "matching" contribution of up to 3% of your net earnings.

If you have employees, they generally may make elective salary-reduction contributions for 2002 up to $7,000 (plus $500 if age 50 or over). You must make a 3% matching contribution unless you choose to make a 2% non-elective contribution.

See 8.17 and *8.18* for further details on SIMPLE IRAs.

Chapter 42

Claiming Depreciation Deductions

There are three methods of claiming expense deductions for your purchases of equipment, fixtures, autos, and trucks used in your business:

- First-year expensing (Section 179 deduction), which allows a deduction of up to $24,000 in 2002.

- Bonus depreciation, which allows a first-year deduction of 30% of the adjusted basis of eligible property. This deduction is in addition to any first-year expensing.

- Regular depreciation, which allows a prorated deduction over a period of years. Most business equipment is depreciable under MACRS (modified accelerated cost recovery system) over a six-year period. MACRS applies to new and used property. The objective of MACRS is to provide rapid depreciation and to eliminate disputes over useful life, salvage value, and depreciation methods. Useful life and depreciation methods are fixed by law; salvage value is treated as zero. If you do not want to use MACRS accelerated rates, you may elect the straight-line method.

Capital investments in buildings are depreciable using the straight-line method; residential buildings are depreciated over 27.5 years; nonresidential real property placed in service after May 12, 1993, is depreciated over 39 years; *see 42.13*. Specific annual rates for each class of property are provided by IRS tables.

Land is not depreciable.

42.1 What Property May Be Depreciated?

Depreciation deductions may be claimed only for property used in your business or other income-producing activity. If the primary purpose of the property is to produce income but it fails to yield any income, the property may still be depreciated.

Depreciation may not be claimed on property held for personal purposes such as a personal residence or pleasure car. If property, such as a car, is used both for business and pleasure, only the business portion may be depreciated.

EXAMPLES

1. An anesthesiologist suspended his practice indefinitely because of malpractice premium rate increases. He continued to maintain his professional competence by taking courses and keeping up his equipment. The IRS ruled that he could not take depreciation on his equipment. Since he was no longer practicing, the depreciation did not relate to a current trade or business.

2. An electrician spent $1,325 on a trailer to carry his tools and protective clothing. Based on a useful life of three years less salvage value of $25, annual depreciation deductions came to $433. However, the IRS claimed that he could not claim depreciation during the months he was unemployed and the trailer was not used. The Tax Court disagreed. Depreciation is allowed as long as the asset is held for use in a trade or business, even though the asset is idle or its use is temporarily suspended due to business conditions.

Nondepreciable assets. Not all assets used in your business or for the production of income may be depreciable. Land is not depreciable, but the cost of landscaping business property may be depreciated if the landscaping is so closely associated with a building that it would have to be destroyed if the building were replaced. Qualifying trees and bushes are depreciable over 15 years.

Property held primarily for sale to customers or property includible in inventory is not depreciable, regardless of its useful life.

Amortization for business intangibles. The cost of goodwill, going concern value, and other intangibles including covenants not to compete, information bases, customer lists, franchises, licenses, and trademarks is amortizable over a 15-year period.

The amortization rule generally applies to property acquired after August 10, 1993. *See 42.18* for further details.

Residences. For depreciation of rented residences, *see 9.5.*

For depreciation of a sublet cooperative apartment or one used in business, *see 40.17.*

Farm property. Farmland is not depreciable; farm machinery and buildings are. Livestock acquired for work, breeding, or dairy purposes and not included in inventory may also be depreciated. For a detailed explanation of the highly technical rules for depreciating farm property and livestock, *see* IRS Publication 225, Farmer's Tax Guide.

Dispute over importance of useful life. According to the Tax Court, under ACRS (1981–86) and current MACRS law, useful life is irrelevant for claiming depreciation if you can show that an asset is subject to exhaustion, wear and tear, or obsolescence. Thus, in the case of antique musical instruments played by professional musicians, depreciation is allowable because of wear and tear, even though the instruments have an indeterminable useful life. Two federal appeals courts have agreed, allowing professional violinists to deduct ACRS depreciation for their instruments.

In a case involving exotic cars that were not used for transportation but for exhibition, MACRS depreciation was allowed because the owner showed that they were subject to obsolescence. The autos were purchased solely for exhibition. The three state-of-the-art autos were a 1987 Lotus Pantera costing $63,000, a Lotus Espirit costing $48,000, and a Ferrari Testarossa costing $290,453. Over a four-year period, the owner deducted depreciation of over $298,000 while reporting gross income from exhibition fees of $96,630. The IRS disallowed the depreciation because the cars had no determinable useful life. The Tax Court allowed the depreciation because such cars are subject to obsolescence in the car-show business when new models appear with newer designs and high-tech features. One witness testified this could occur in some cases within a year.

The Tax Court warned that such exotic cars should not be confused with museum pieces. If they had been museum pieces, such as antique cars, no depreciation would have been allowed. In the case of art objects and antiques used as business assets, the useful life requirement remains relevant because such assets are not subject to exhaustion, wear or tear, or obsolescence.

Caution

Corrections to Prior Year Returns

If you did not deduct the correct amount of depreciation for a prior year, you may be able to make a correction by filing an amended return. However, if you did not deduct the correct amount of depreciation for two or more consecutive years, you must request an accounting method change; *see* IRS Publication 946 for details. *See also 5.20* for adjustments to basis for unclaimed depreciation taken in prior years.

The IRS may continue to dispute and litigate cases in which depreciation is claimed on assets with indeterminable useful lives. For example, in a private ruling, the IRS did not allow a developer to depreciate street improvements that had been turned over to a city. The improvements were an intangible asset that improved the developer's access to its real estate projects, but this asset had an unlimited life. There was no determinable useful life because the city had agreed to maintain and replace the improvements as necessary, and there was no evidence that the city would ever assess the developer for replacement costs.

42.2 Claiming Depreciation on Your Tax Return

If you report business or professional self-employed income, use Form 4562 for assets placed in service during 2002 and enter the total deduction on Line 13, Schedule C. For claiming depreciation on "listed property" such as cars, computers, and cellular phones, you use Form 4562, regardless of the year placed in service. Listed property is explained at *42.10*. If your only depreciation deduction is for pre-2002 assets, none of which is listed property, you do not need to use Form 4562; figure the deduction on your own worksheet, and enter it on Line 13, Schedule C.

If you are an employee claiming auto expenses, you must use Form 2106 to claim depreciation on an automobile used for business purposes.

If you report rental income on Schedule E, you must use Form 4562 for claiming depreciation on buildings placed in service in 2002. For buildings placed in service before 2002, enter the depreciation deduction directly on Schedule E. If you have a rental loss on Schedule E, your deduction for depreciation and other expenses may have to be included on Form 8582 to figure net passive activity income or loss; *see* Chapter 10.

See the sample Form 4562 and Schedule E in Part 8 of this book.

42.3 First-Year Expensing Deduction

For qualifying business equipment purchased and placed in service in 2002, you may elect to deduct up to $24,000 of the cost. For equipment placed in service by a business in an "enterprise zone," the deduction may be as high as $44,000. For qualified "New York Liberty Zone property," the deduction may be as high as $59,000. For an automobile, the maximum expensing deduction in 2002 is $7,660; *see 43.4*. The portion of cost not eligible for first-year expensing may be recovered by depreciation under the regular MACRS rules *(42.4–42.5)*. The first-year expensing deduction is technically called the "Section 179 deduction."

You may *not* elect first-year expensing for property purchased before 2002, even if 2002 is the first year you use it for business.

The election is limited to tangible personal property bought in 2002 for business use, such as machinery, office equipment, a computer, car, or truck acquired from nonrelated parties. The deduction is not allowed for buildings, structural components of buildings, furniture, or refrigerators used in operating apartment buildings, property held for the production of income, or equipment previously used for personal purposes, such as an automobile bought for pleasure but later used for business.

When to elect first-year expensing. To claim the first-year expensing deduction on Form 4562, which you attach to your Form 1040, you must make the election on an *original* return for the year the property is placed in service (whether or not the return is timely filed). First-year expensing may *not* be claimed on an amended return unless it is filed within the due date for the original return (including extensions). If you fail to make the election on an original return (or on an amended return filed by the due date including extensions) the election is lost. You may not revoke the expensing election without consent from the IRS.

Partial business use. If you use the equipment for both business and personal use, business use must exceed 50% in the year the equipment is first placed into service to claim a first-year expensing deduction. The expensing deduction may be claimed for the cost allocated to business use up to the $24,000 limit; the 2002 limit for a car is $7,660 *(43.4)*.

To elect first-year expensing for "listed property" such as a computer or car *(42.10)*, business use in the first year you use it must exceed 50%. If it does, you show the amount eligible for expensing in the section for "Listed Property" on Form 4562 and then transfer the amount to the part of Form 4562 where the expensing election is claimed.

Figuring the deduction. The maximum expensing deduction in 2002 is $24,000 of the cost of qualifying property and $7,660 for a car *(43.4)*. For business use of less than 100% (but more than 50%), the expensing deduction is limited to the business portion of the cost. As discussed below, the $24,000 limit may have to be reduced because your taxable income is lower than $24,000, eligible purchases exceed $200,000, or you are married filing separately.

Caution

Losses and Low Income May Limit Deduction

The expensing deduction may not exceed the net taxable income from all businesses that you actively conduct. Net income from active businesses is figured without regard to expensing, the deduction for 50% of self-employment liability, or any net operating loss carryback or carryforward. You may include wage or salary income as active business income and if you are married filing jointly, also include your spouse's net taxable income.

If you have an overall net loss from all actively conducted businesses, you may not claim an expensing deduction for 2002. If net income is less than the cost of qualifying assets, expensing is limited to the income. However, the cost over the income limit is carried forward to 2003 on Form 4562 provided you complete the expensing section of Form 4562 for 2002. You do not get a carryover unless the deduction is claimed on the return for the first year the property is placed in service.

Planning Reminder

Year-End Purchases

Equipment placed in service on the last day of the taxable year may qualify for the entire $24,000 first-year expensing deduction. You do not have to prorate the $24,000 limit for the amount of time you held the property.

If you qualify for the full $24,000 limit, you do not have to claim the entire amount. If in 2002 you place in service more than one item of property, you may allocate the $24,000 deduction between the items. If you placed in service only one item of qualifying property that cost less than $24,000, your deduction is limited to that cost.

If you acquire property in a trade-in, the cost eligible for expensing is limited to the cash you paid. You may not include the adjusted basis of the property traded in, although your basis for the new property includes that amount.

Effect on regular depreciation. If the cost basis of the property exceeds the first-year expensing limit, you compute depreciation on the cost of the property less the amount of the first-year deduction.

> **EXAMPLE**
>
> In 2002, you placed in service a $30,000 machine and a $3,000 lathe. You elect to deduct as a first-year expense $3,000 for the lathe and $21,000 for the machine, a total of $24,000, the maximum first-year deduction. The $3,000 deduction has completely recovered the cost of the lathe. The cost of the machine is reduced by $21,000, giving a depreciable basis of $9,000 ($30,000 – $21,000).

$24,000 limit reduced if taxable income is lower. Your expensing deduction may not exceed net income from all your active businesses; *see* the Caution on this page.

$24,000 limit reduced if qualifying purchases exceed $200,000. If the total cost of qualifying property placed in service during a taxable year is over $200,000, the $24,000 expensing limit is reduced dollar for dollar by the cost of qualifying property exceeding $200,000. For example, if you place in service machinery costing $206,000, the $24,000 limit is reduced by $6,000. The reduced limit of $18,000 is shown on Form 4562 on the line labeled "Dollar limitation for tax year." If the total cost is $224,000 or more, no first-year expensing deduction is allowed.

$24,000 limit reduced if married filing separately. If you and your spouse file separate returns, the expensing limit for both of you is $24,000. Unless you agree to a different allocation, you are each allowed only a $12,000 expensing limit. The $200,000 cost threshold also applies to both of you as a unit. For example, if you place in service qualifying property costing $195,000 and your spouse places $9,000 of property in service, the total cost of $204,000 reduces the $24,000 limit by $4,000 to $20,000. The reduced limit for each of you on separate returns is $10,000.

Partners and S corporation stockholders. For property bought by a partnership or an S corporation, the $24,000 limit and taxable income limit applies to the business, as well as the owners as individual taxpayers. The partnership or S corporation determines its expensing deduction subject to the limits and allocates the deduction, if any, among the partners or shareholders. The allocated deduction may not exceed the net taxable income of the partnership or S corporation from actively conducted businesses.

An individual partner's expensing deduction may not exceed $24,000, regardless of how many partnership interests he or she has. However, the partner must reduce the basis of each partnership interest by the full allocable share of each partnership's expensing deduction, even if that amount is not deductible because of the $24,000 limit.

Disqualified acquisitions from related parties. Property does not qualify for the expense election if:

1. It is acquired from a spouse, ancestor, or lineal descendant, or from non–family-related parties subject to the loss disallowance rule, discussed in *5.6*. For purposes of the expensing election, a corporation is controlled by you and thus subject to the loss disallowance rule discussed in *5.6* if 50% or more of the stock is owned by you, your spouse, your ancestors, or your descendants.
2. The property is acquired by a member of the same controlled group (using a 50% control test).
3. The basis of the property is determined in whole or in part (a) by reference to the adjusted basis of the property of the person from whom you acquired it or (b) under the stepped-up basis rules for inherited property.

Recapture of expensing deduction. Recapture of the first-year expensing deduction may occur on a disposition of the asset or if business use falls to 50% or less. If business use falls to 50% or less after the year the property is placed in service but before the end of the depreciable recovery period *(42.4, 42.10)*, you must "recapture" the benefit from the first-year expensing deduction. The amount recaptured is the excess of the expensing deduction over the amount of depreciation that would have been claimed (through the year of recapture) without expensing; *see 42.10*. Recaptured amounts are reported as ordinary income on Form 4797.

When you sell or dispose of the property, the first-year expensing deduction is treated as depreciation for purposes of the recapture rules *(44.1)* that treat gain realized as ordinary income to the extent of depreciation claimed.

42.4 MACRS Recovery Periods

Depreciable assets other than buildings fall within a three-, five-, seven-, 10-, 15-, or 20-year recovery period under the general depreciation system (GDS). Claiming bonus depreciation *(42.20)* does not change an asset's recovery period.

Straight-line recovery for buildings is claimed over a period of 27.5 years for residential rental property or 39 years for nonresidential real property, as discussed at *42.13*.

Note: The actual write-off period of depreciation for an asset is one year longer than the class life because of the convention rules explained in *42.5–42.7*.

Three-year property. This class includes property with a class life of four years or less, other than cars and light-duty trucks, which are in the five-year class.

This class includes: special handling devices for the manufacture of food and beverages; special tools and devices for the manufacture of rubber products; special tools for the manufacture of finished plastic products, fabricated metal products, or motor vehicles; and breeding hogs. By law, racehorses more than two years old when placed in service and other horses more than 12 years old when placed in service are also in the three-year class.

Five-year property. This class includes property with a class life of more than four years and less than 10 years such as computers *(42.10)*, typewriters, copiers, duplicating equipment, heavy general-purpose trucks, trailers, cargo containers, and trailer-mounted containers. Also included by law in the five-year class are cars, light-duty trucks (actual unloaded weight less than 13,000 pounds), taxis, buses, computer-based telephone central office switching equipment, computer-related peripheral equipment, semiconductor manufacturing equipment, and property used in research and experimentation. It also includes qualified New York Liberty Zone leasehold improvements to a nonresidential building located in the New York Liberty Zone (in southern Manhattan) placed in service after September 10, 2001, and before January 1, 2007. These leasehold improvements eligible for a five-year recovery period must be depreciated using the straight-line method and are *not* eligible for bonus depreciation *(42.20)*.

Seven-year property. This class includes any property with a class life of 10 years or more but less than 16 years. This is also a catch-all category for assets with no class life that have not been assigned by law to another class. Included in the seven-year class are: office furniture and fixtures, such as desks, safes, and files; cellular phones; fax machines; refrigerators; dishwashers; and machines used to produce jewelry, musical instruments, toys, and sporting goods. Single-purpose agricultural or horticultural structures are in the 10-year class if placed in service after 1988.

Ten-year property. This includes property with a class life of 16 years or more and less than 20 years, such as vessels, barges, tugs, and water transportation equipment, and assets used in petroleum refining or in the manufacture of tobacco products and certain food products.

The 10-year class includes single-purpose agricultural and horticultural structures, and trees or vines bearing fruit or nuts, if placed in service after 1988. Under a transition rule, the seven-year period will apply to single purpose agricultural or horticultural structures under construction on July 14, 1988, or acquired pursuant to a written contract binding on that date.

Fifteen-year property. This includes land improvements such as fences, sidewalks, docks, shrubbery, roads, and bridges. It also includes other property with a class life of 20 years or more but less than 25 years, such as municipal sewage plants and telephone distribution plants. Gas station convenience stores are in the 15-year class if the property is no more than 1,400 square feet, or at least 50% of the floor space is devoted to selling petroleum products, or at least 50% of revenues are from petroleum sales. The owner of the gas station property does not have to be the operator of businesses on the property.

Twenty-year property. This class includes property with a class life of 25 years or more, such as farm buildings and municipal sewers, except that residential and nonresidential real estate is excluded; *see 42.13*.

42.5 MACRS Rates

The MACRS rate under the general depreciation system depends on the recovery period *(42.4)* for the property and whether the half-year or mid-quarter convention applies. The 200% declining balance rate applies to three-year property, five-year property, and seven-year property. *See 42.8* for the 150% declining balance rate election. These rates are adjusted for the convention rules explained below. When the 200% declining balance rate provides a lower annual deduction than the straight-

Planning Reminder

Recovery Periods
The depreciation recovery periods for different types of assets are generally fixed by law according to the rules on this page.

line rate, the 200% declining balance rate is replaced by the straight-line rate. The rates in the tables at the end of this section incorporate the applicable convention and the change from the 200% declining balance rate to a straight-line recovery. *See 42.9* for MACRS straight-line rates.

Conventions. Under the half-year convention, all property acquired during the year, regardless of when acquired during the year, is treated as acquired in the middle of the year. As a result, only one-half of the full first-year depreciation is deductible and in the year after the last class life year, the balance of the depreciation is written off. Furthermore, in the year property is sold, only half of the full depreciation for that year is deductible; *see 42.6*.

The half-year convention applies unless the total cost bases of depreciable assets placed in service during the last three months of the taxable year exceed 40% of the total bases of all property placed in service during the entire year. If this 40% test applies, you must use a mid-quarter convention to figure your annual depreciation deduction, as explained at *42.7*.

Buildings are depreciated using a mid-month convention; *see 42.13*.

Depreciation tables. The following table provides year-by-year rates for property in the three-, five-, and seven-year classes. The rates incorporate the adjustment for the half-year or mid-quarter convention and the switch from the 200% declining balance rate to the straight-line method. Use the rate shown in the table under the convention for your asset. The rate is applied to original basis, minus any first-year expensing deduction *(42.3)* and bonus depreciation *(42.20)*. You claim the deduction from the table in Form 4562, Part III, Section B labeled "General Depreciation System" (GDS).

You use the tables for the entire recovery period unless you claim a deductible casualty loss that reduces your basis in the property. For the year of the casualty loss and later years, depreciation must be based on the adjusted basis of the property at the end of the year. The tables may no longer be used; *see* IRS Publication 946 for further details.

MACRS Depreciation Rates

Year	Half-Year Convention	Mid-Quarter Convention			
		1st	2nd	3rd	4th (Quarter)
3-Year Property					
1	33.33%	58.33%	41.67%	25.00%	8.33%
2	44.45	27.78	38.89	50.00	61.11
3	14.81	12.35	14.14	16.67	20.37
4	7.41	1.54	5.30	8.33	10.19
5-Year Property					
1	20.00%	35.00%	25.00%	15.00%	5.00%
2	32.00	26.00	30.00	34.00	38.00
3	19.20	15.60	18.00	20.40	22.80
4	11.52	11.01	11.37	12.24	13.68
5	11.52	11.01	11.37	11.30	10.94
6	5.76	1.38	4.26	7.06	9.58
7-Year Property					
1	14.29%	25.00%	17.85%	10.71%	3.57%
2	24.49	21.43	23.47	25.51	27.55
3	17.49	15.31	16.76	18.22	19.68
4	12.49	10.93	11.97	13.02	14.06
5	8.93	8.75	8.87	9.30	10.04
6	8.92	8.74	8.87	8.85	8.73
7	8.93	8.75	8.87	8.86	8.73
8	4.46	1.09	3.33	5.53	7.64

EXAMPLE

During June 2002, you place in business service a machine costing $20,000. It is your only acquisition in 2002. (Assume you do not elect to expense the cost and you waive bonus depreciation.) The machine is five-year property and is subject to the half-year convention. The depreciation rate for the first year is 20% (*see* the table above for five-year property). Your 2002 depreciation deduction is $4,000 ($20,000 × 20%).

Summary of Deductions

Year	Deduction
1	$4,000
2	6,400
3	3,840
4	2,304
5	2,304
6	1,152
Total	$20,000

Planning Reminder

Half-Year Convention

The half-year convention applies unless the total cost basis of depreciable assets placed in service during the last three months of the year exceeds 40% of the total basis of all property placed in service during the year.

Under the half-year convention, all assets placed in service during the year are treated as placed in service at the midpoint of the year.

42.6 Half-Year Convention for MACRS

The half-year convention treats all business equipment placed in service during a tax year as placed in service in the midpoint of that tax year. The same rule applies in the year in which the property is disposed of. The effect of this rule is as follows: A half-year of depreciation is allowed in the first year property is placed in service, regardless of when the property is placed in service during the tax year. For each of the remaining years of the recovery period, a full year of depreciation is claimed. If you hold the property for the entire recovery period, a half-year of depreciation is claimed for the year following the end of the recovery period. If you dispose of the property before the end of the recovery period, a half-year of depreciation is allowable for the year of disposition.

See the Table of MACRS Depreciation Rates in *42.5* for year-by-year rates under the half-year convention. Apply the rate from the table to the original basis, minus any first-year expensing (*42.3*) deduction claimed.

The Example in *42.5* shows the year-by-year deduction computation for five-year property under the half-year convention. If you dispose of the property before the end of the recovery period shown in *42.5*, your deduction for the year of disposition is one-half of the deduction that would be allowed for the full year using the rate shown in the table.

Planning Reminder

Bonus Depreciation Disregarded

Bonus depreciation is *not* taken into account in determining the basis of property for purposes of the mid-quarter convention. In effect, the basis of property placed in service in the last quarter of the year is figured without a reduction for bonus depreciation when applying the 40% mid-quarter convention test.

42.7 Last Quarter Placements—Mid-Quarter Convention

A mid-quarter convention generally applies if the total cost basis of business equipment placed in service during the last three months of the tax year exceeds 40% of the total basis of all the property placed in service during the year. In applying the 40% rule, you do not count residential rental property, nonresidential realty, and assets that were placed in service and disposed of during the same year.

Under the mid-quarter convention, the first-year depreciation allowance for all property (other than nonresidential real property and residential rental property) placed in service during the year is based on the number of quarters that the asset was in service. Property placed in service at any time during a quarter is treated as having been placed in service in the middle of the quarter. The mid-quarter convention also applies to sales and disposals of property. The disposal is treated as occurring in the midpoint of the quarter.

EXAMPLE

During August 2002, you place in service office furniture costing $1,000, and in October, a computer costing $5,000. You are on the calendar year. The total basis of all property placed in service in 2002 is $6,000. As the $5,000 basis of the computer placed in service in the last quarter exceeds 40% of the total basis of all property placed in service during 2002, you must use the mid-quarter convention for the furniture and the computer. The office furniture, which is seven-year property, and the computer, which is five-year property, are depreciated using MACRS and a mid-quarter convention.

You first multiply the $1,000 basis of the furniture by 10.71%—the seven-year property mid-quarter convention rate for the third quarter (*see* the table in *42.5*). The depreciation deduction is $107. You then multiply the $5,000 basis of the computer by 5%—the five-year property mid-quarter convention rate for the fourth quarter (*see* the table in *42.5*). The deduction is $250. Total depreciation is $357.

42.8 150% Rate Election

Instead of using the 200% declining balance rate for property in the three-, five-, seven-, and 10-year classes, you may elect a 150% declining balance rate. You may prefer the 150% rate when you are subject to the alternative minimum tax (AMT). For AMT purposes, you must use the 150% rate and adjust your taxable income if the 200% rate was used for regular tax purposes; *see 23.2*. If for regular tax purposes you elect to apply the 150% rate, use the same recovery period (*see 42.4*) you would have used if you had claimed the 200% declining balance rate. Thus, the recovery period is five years for cars and computers and seven years for office furniture and fixtures. If the half-year convention applies, the first-year rate for the five-year class is 15%, and 10.71% for the seven-year class; *see* the table below. Apply the rate from the table to your original basis, minus any first-year expensing deduction claimed. If you are subject to the mid-quarter convention, *see* IRS Publication 946 for the tables showing mid-quarter convention rates.

The election to use the 150% rate must be made for all property within a given class placed in service in the same year. The election is irrevocable.

For property placed in service before 1999, the 150% rate is applied over the ADS (*42.9*) recovery periods, which in some cases are different from the GDS recovery periods.

Half-Year Convention—150% Rate

Year—	Recovery Period	
	5-Year—	7-Year—
1	15.00%	10.71%
2	25.50	19.13
3	17.85	15.03
4	16.66	12.25
5	16.66	12.25
6	8.33	12.25
7		12.25
8		6.13

42.9 Straight-Line Depreciation

You may not want an accelerated rate and may prefer to write off depreciation at an even pace. There are two straight-line methods. You may make an irrevocable election to use the straight-line method over the regular MACRS recovery period (*42.4*) under the general depreciation system (GDS). Alternatively, you may elect straight-line recovery over the designated recovery period for the class life under the alternative depreciation system (ADS). For some assets, such as cars, the GDS and ADS recovery periods are the same (five years for a car). In most cases, the ADS recovery period is longer than the GDS recovery period. For example, the recovery period for office furniture and fixtures is seven years under GDS and 10 years under ADS; for New York Liberty Zone leasehold improvement property, it is five years under GDS and nine years under ADS.

Half-year and quarter-year conventions apply to both straight-line methods; *see 42.6* and *42.7*. A mid-month convention applies under the straight-line rule for buildings; *see 42.13*.

Straight-line over regular recovery period (GDS). You make this election on Form 4562, Part III, Section B, labeled "General Depreciation System" (GDS). To elect this method for one asset, you must also use it for all other assets in the same class that are placed in service during the year. The straight-line election is irrevocable.

Straight-line under the alternative depreciation system (ADS). Under the alternative depreciation system (ADS), the straight-line recovery period is generally the same as the "class life" of the asset as determined by the IRS; the ADS recovery periods are shown in IRS Publication 946. The ADS recovery period for cars, light trucks, and computers is five years, the same as under the GDS.

 Filing Tip

Should You Elect Straight-Line Recovery?
Accelerated rates of MACRS merely give you an opportunity to advance the time of taking your deduction. This may be a decided advantage where the higher deductions in the first few years will provide you with cash for working capital or for investments in other income-producing sources. That is, by accelerating the deductions, you defer the payment of taxes that would be due if you claimed smaller depreciation deductions, using more conservative straight-line rates. The tax deferral lasts until the rapid method provides lower depreciation deductions than would the more conservative method. You are generally more likely to benefit from accelerated MACRS in an ongoing business.

If you are starting a new business in which you expect losses or low income at the start, accelerated MACRS may waste depreciation deductions that could be used in later years when your income increases. Therefore, before deciding to use accelerated MACRS rates, consider your income prospects.

For business office furniture and fixtures, the ADS straight-line recovery period is 10 years. The ADS recovery period for personal property with no class life is 12 years. For nonresidential real and residential rental property, you may elect ADS straight-line recovery over 40 years. *See* IRS Publication 946 for other ADS class lives.

Except for real estate, the ADS election applies to all property within the same class placed in service during the taxable year. For real estate, the election to use the alternative depreciation method may be made on a property-by-property basis. The election is irrevocable. The deduction is claimed on Form 4562, Part III, Section C, labeled "Alternative Depreciation System" (ADS).

Straight-line rate table. The table below shows straight-line rates for five-year, seven-year, and 10-year property under the half-year convention. As discussed earlier, the recovery period depends on whether the GDS or ADS straight-line method is used. If you are subject to the mid-quarter convention *(42.7)*, *see* IRS Publication 946 for tables showing the applicable rates.

Half-Year Convention—Straight-Line Rate			
		Recovery Period	
Year—	5-Year—	7-Year—	10-Year—
1	10.00%	7.14%	5.00%
2	20.00	14.29	10.00
3	20.00	14.29	10.00
4	20.00	14.28	10.00
5	20.00	14.29	10.00
6	10.00	14.28	10.00
7		14.29	10.00
8		7.14	10.00
9			10.00
10			10.00
11			5.00

AMT depreciation. For alternative minimum tax (AMT) purposes, depreciation is figured using the 150% declining balance rate if the 200% declining balance rate was used for regular tax purposes; *see 23.2.* If straight-line depreciation was used for regular tax purposes, AMT depreciation is figured using the straight-line alternative depreciation system (ADS) over the class life recovery period. For real estate placed in service after 1986, AMT depreciation is figured using the 40-year ADS straight-line method.

Mandatory straight-line depreciation. You are required to use the alternative depreciation system for automobiles *(43.3)* and certain computers *(42.10)* used 50% or less for business.

Alternative MACRS depreciation must also be used for:

- Figuring earnings and profits;
- Tangible property which, during the taxable year, is used predominantly outside the United States;
- Tax-exempt use property;
- Tax-exempt bond financed property; *and*
- Imported property covered by an executive order.

42.10 Computers and Other Listed Property

"Listed property" is a term applied to certain equipment that may be used for personal and business purposes. For such property, the law allows first-year expensing *(42.3)* or accelerated MACRS *(42.5)* deductions only if business use exceeds 50%. For business use of 50% or less, you must use ADS straight-line depreciation; *see 42.9.* Deductions for listed property are claimed on Form 4562. If the more-than-50%-business-use test is met in the first year and first-year expensing or accelerated MACRS is claimed, but business use of listed property falls to 50% or less during the ADS straight-line recovery period *(42.9)*, you must "recapture" first-year expensing and accelerated MACRS deductions; *see* Example 2 at the top of the following page.

What is "listed property"? Listed property includes passenger autos weighing 6,000 pounds or less, trucks *(see 43.3* for exceptions), cellular phones, computers and peripheral equipment, boats, airplanes, and any photographic, sound, or video recording equipment that could be used for en-

Caution

Depreciation Restrictions for a Computer

If you use a home computer for business but not in a qualified home office *(40.12)*, it must be used more than 50% of the time for business to claim a first-year expensing deduction. If used 50% or less for business, straight-line depreciation over the ADS recovery period is required.

tertainment or recreational purposes. However, exceptions remove some items from the listed property category for many businesses. Listed property does not include (1) any computer or peripheral equipment that you own or lease that is used exclusively at a regular business establishment, and (2) photographic, phonographic, communications, or video equipment used exclusively and regularly in your business or regular business establishment. A home office that meets the rules in *40.12* is considered a regular business establishment.

Planning Reminder

Computer Software

Software purchased "off the shelf" and used for business or investment purposes is depreciable over a three-year period provided it has a useful life exceeding one year. If the useful life does not exceed one year, the cost is immediately deductible. Also *see 42.19*.

EXAMPLES

1. You buy a computer in 2002 and use it exclusively in your regular business office. The computer is not listed property. You may claim either first-year expensing *(42.3)* or accelerated MACRS depreciation *(42.5)* and bonus depreciation *(42.20)* for your investment on Form 4562. If business use falls to 50% or less after 2002, the only deduction subject to recapture is the first-year deduction; *see 42.3*.
2. You have no regular business establishment and use a computer bought in 2002 as a freelance consultant. The computer is listed property and you may claim MACRS and/or first-year expensing only if you use the computer more than 50% for business. If business use does not exceed 50%, you may only claim ADS straight-line depreciation *(42.9)*. Your deductions are claimed in the section for "Listed Property" on Form 4562.

If business use exceeds 50% in the first year but in a later year drops to 50% or less, MACRS and any first-year expensing deduction are subject to "recapture." In the year in which business use drops to 50% or less, you recapture the excess of (1) the MACRS and first-year expensing deductions claimed in prior years over (2) the deductions that would have been allowed using ADS straight-line depreciation *(42.9)*. For the rest of the recovery period, you continue to use the alternative straight-line rate.

Recapture is figured on Form 4797. The recapture computation follows the steps shown in *43.10* for recapture of excess depreciation on an automobile.

Investor's use of a computer. For an investor who uses a home computer for managing an investment portfolio, the computer is treated as listed property. Unless the computer is also used for business, and the computer time spent on business work exceeds 50% of the total, only straight-line depreciation may be claimed; neither first-year expensing nor accelerated MACRS is allowed. Although the investment use is disregarded for purposes of the more-than-50%-business-use test, the investment use is combined with the business use for purposes of determining the percentage of depreciable cost. Depreciable investment use must relate to managing investments that produce taxable income. *See* the Examples below.

EXAMPLES

1. In 2002, Jane Adams buys a computer; she uses it 10% of the time for personal purposes, 50% of the time to manage her stock investments and 40% in a part-time research business. The more-than-50%-business-use test is not met for claiming first-year expensing or accelerated MACRS deductions. She must use ADS straight-line depreciation over five years *(42.9)*; her depreciable basis is 90% of cost.
2. Assume that Jane used the computer 60% of the time for business and 30% for investment. As business use exceeds 50%, she may claim first-year expensing under the rules discussed in *42.3*. If she instead claims accelerated MACRS, the MACRS rate is applied to 90% of her cost.

Leasing a computer or cellular phone. You may deduct the portion of your lease payments attributable to business use. However, if business use is 50% or less for any year, you must report as income an amount based on the fair market value of the unit, the percentage of business plus investment use, and percentages from two IRS tables shown in Publication 946.

42.11 Assets in Service Before 1987

Assets placed in service before 1987 were depreciated under a different recovery system called ACRS. Most of the assets have already been fully depreciated, although some assets, such as certain real estate placed in service before 1987, continue to be governed by these rules. For ACRS rates for real estate, *see 42.16*.

42.12 Straight-Line Recovery for Equipment in Service Before 1987

You may still be able to claim straight-line deductions for five-year property if a recovery period of 25 years was elected. For 10-year property, an election could have been made for straight-line depreciation over 25 or 35 years.

If you made the straight-line election, the straight-line rate to be used on your 2002 return is as follows:

Recovery Period—	Rate—
25 years	4.000%
35 years	2.857%

Because of the half-year convention, only 50% of the above percentages was allowed in the year the property was placed in service. If the property is held for the entire elected recovery period, another half-year of depreciation is allowed for the year following the end of the recovery period. If property is disposed of prior to the end of the recovery period, no cost recovery is allowable in the year of disposition. *See* IRS Publication 534 for further details.

42.13 MACRS for Real Estate Placed in Service After 1986

The recovery period for residential rental property placed in service after December 31, 1986, is 27.5 years. The recovery period for nonresidential real property is either 39 years or 31.5 years, depending on when the property was placed in service.

The method of recovery for nonresidential or residential property is the straight-line method using a mid-month convention. See the next page for rate tables for each class of property.

For nonresidential real property placed in service after December 31, 1986, but before May 13, 1993, the depreciation recovery period is 31.5 years.

For nonresidential real property placed in service after May 12, 1993, the recovery period is 39 years. Under a transition rule, the 31.5-year recovery period rather than the 39-year recovery period applies to a building placed in service before 1994 if before May 13, 1993, you had entered into a binding, written contract to buy or build it, or if, before that date, you had begun construction. The transition rule also applies if you obtained the contract or property from someone else who satisfied the pre–May 13, 1993, contract or construction requirement, provided he or she never put the building in service and you did so before 1994.

Residential rental property subject to the 27.5 year recovery period is defined as a rental building or structure for which 80% or more of the gross rental income for the tax year is rental income from dwelling units. If you occupy any part of the building, the gross rental income includes the fair rental value of the part you occupy.

A dwelling unit is a house or an apartment used to provide living accommodations in a building or structure, but not a unit in a hotel, motel, inn, or other establishment where more than one-half of the units are used on a transient basis.

Mid-month convention. Under a mid-month convention, all property placed in service or disposed of during any month is treated as placed in service or disposed of at the midpoint of that month. You may determine the first-year deduction for residential rental property by applying the percentage from the table on the following page to the original depreciable basis. In later years, use the same column of the table to figure your deduction.

> **EXAMPLE**
>
> In February 2002, you buy an apartment building for $100,000 and place it in service. You use the calendar year. The table below gives a first-year depreciation rate of 3.182% for 27.5-year residential rental property placed in service during February. Applying this rate, you get a deduction of $3,182.
>
> For 2003, the rate will be 3.636%, for a deduction of $3,636.

Additions or improvements to property. The depreciation deduction for any additions to, or improvement of, any property is figured in the same way as the deduction for the property would be figured if the property had been placed in service at the same time as the addition or improvement.

 Filing Tip

Additions and Improvements

The MACRS class for an addition or improvement is determined by the MACRS class of the property to which the addition or improvement is made. For example, if you put an addition on a rental home that you are depreciating over 27.5 years, the addition is depreciated as 27.5-year residential rental property. The period for figuring depreciation begins on the date that the addition or improvement is placed in service, or, if later, the date that the property to which the addition or improvement was made is placed in service.

Residential Rental Property (27.5 years; *see 42.13*)

USE THE COLUMN FOR THE MONTH OF TAXABLE YEAR PLACED IN SERVICE.

Month	1	2	3	4	5	6	7	8	9	10	11	12
Year
1	3.485%	3.182%	2.879%	2.576%	2.273%	1.970%	1.667%	1.364%	1.061%	0.758%	0.455%	0.152%
2–9	3.636	3.636	3.636	3.636	3.636	3.636	3.636	3.636	3.636	3.636	3.636	3.636
10	3.637	3.637	3.637	3.637	3.637	3.637	3.636	3.636	3.636	3.636	3.636	3.636
11	3.636	3.636	3.636	3.636	3.636	3.636	3.637	3.637	3.637	3.637	3.637	3.637
12	3.637	3.637	3.637	3.637	3.637	3.637	3.636	3.636	3.636	3.636	3.636	3.636
13	3.636	3.636	3.636	3.636	3.636	3.636	3.637	3.637	3.637	3.637	3.637	3.637
14	3.637	3.637	3.637	3.637	3.637	3.637	3.636	3.636	3.636	3.636	3.636	3.636
15	3.636	3.636	3.636	3.636	3.636	3.636	3.637	3.637	3.637	3.637	3.637	3.637
16	3.637	3.637	3.637	3.637	3.637	3.637	3.636	3.636	3.636	3.636	3.636	3.636
17	3.636	3.636	3.636	3.636	3.636	3.636	3.637	3.637	3.637	3.637	3.637	3.637

Nonresidential Real Property (31.5 years—placed in service before May 13, 1993; *see 42.13*)

USE THE COLUMN FOR THE MONTH OF TAXABLE YEAR PLACED IN SERVICE.

Month	1	2	3	4	5	6	7	8	9	10	11	12
Year
1	3.042%	2.778%	2.513%	2.249%	1.984%	1.720%	1.455%	1.190%	0.926%	0.661%	0.397%	0.132%
2–7	3.175	3.175	3.175	3.175	3.175	3.175	3.175	3.175	3.175	3.175	3.175	3.175
8	3.175	3.174	3.175	3.174	3.175	3.174	3.175	3.175	3.175	3.175	3.175	3.175
9	3.174	3.175	3.174	3.175	3.174	3.175	3.174	3.175	3.174	3.175	3.174	3.175
10	3.175	3.174	3.175	3.174	3.175	3.174	3.175	3.174	3.175	3.174	3.175	3.174
11	3.174	3.175	3.174	3.175	3.174	3.175	3.174	3.175	3.174	3.175	3.174	3.175
12	3.175	3.174	3.175	3.174	3.175	3.174	3.175	3.174	3.175	3.174	3.175	3.174
13	3.174	3.175	3.174	3.175	3.174	3.175	3.174	3.175	3.174	3.175	3.174	3.175
14	3.175	3.174	3.175	3.174	3.175	3.174	3.175	3.174	3.175	3.174	3.175	3.174
15	3.174	3.175	3.174	3.175	3.174	3.175	3.174	3.175	3.174	3.175	3.174	3.175
16	3.175	3.174	3.175	3.174	3.175	3.174	3.175	3.174	3.175	3.174	3.175	3.174
17	3.174	3.175	3.174	3.175	3.174	3.175	3.174	3.175	3.174	3.175	3.174	3.175

Nonresidential Real Property (39 years—placed in service on or after May 13, 1993; *see 42.13*)

USE THE COLUMN FOR THE MONTH OF TAXABLE YEAR PLACED IN SERVICE.

Month	1	2	3	4	5	6	7	8	9	10	11	12
Year
1	2.461%	2.247%	2.033%	1.819%	1.605%	1.391%	1.177%	0.963%	0.749%	0.535%	0.321%	0.107%
2–39	2.564	2.564	2.564	2.564	2.564	2.564	2.564	2.564	2.564	2.564	2.564	2.564

42.14 Demolishing a Building

When you buy improved property, the purchase price is allocated between the land and the building; only the building may be depreciated. The land may not; *see 42.1*. If you later demolish the building, you may not deduct the cost of the demolition or the undepreciated basis of the building as a loss in the year of demolition. Expenses or losses in connection with the demolition of any structure, including certified historic structures, are not deductible. They must be capitalized and added to the basis of the land on which the structure is located.

Major rehabilitation. Where you are considering a major rehabilitation of a building that involves some demolition of the building, IRS guidelines may allow you to deduct the costs of demolition and a removal of part of the structure. Under the IRS rules, the costs of structural modification may avoid capitalization if 75% or more of the existing external walls are retained as internal or external walls and 75% or more of the existing internal framework is also retained. For certified historic structures, the modification must also be part of a certified rehabilitation. The 75% tests are effective for work starting after June 5, 1995, and also for open taxable years, if an election is made for those years.

42.15 Leasehold Improvements

Improvements. Leasehold improvements are depreciated under MACRS real estate rates listed at 42.13, except for qualified New York Liberty Zone leasehold improvements to nonresidential buildings, which are depreciable over five years (42.4) under the straight-line method. You ignore the term of the lease. If the lease term is shorter than the MACRS life and you do not retain the improvements at the end of the term, the remaining undepreciated basis is a deductible loss.

Pre-1987 improvements. For leasehold improvements placed in service before 1987, the cost of improvements is deductible over the *shorter* of the following periods:

1. The useful life of the improvement if the improvement was before 1981, or the ACRS recovery period if after 1980 but before 1987, *or*

2. The remaining term of the lease.

If (1) is the shorter period, the cost of the improvement is depreciated. If (2) is the shorter period, the cost is amortized ratably.

In determining the shorter period, you must add optional lease renewals to the remaining lease term under (2) if, at the completion of the improvement, the remaining term of the original lease (excluding unexercised renewal options) is less than 60% of the useful life (or ACRS recovery period) of the improvement. Renewals do not have to be taken into account under the 60% test if the lessee can show that it is more probable that the lease would not be renewed than that it would be renewed.

If the lessee and lessor are related, the term of the lease is treated as being equal to the remaining useful life (or recovery period) of the improvement. Related parties include spouses, children, grandchildren, parents, grandparents, brothers, sisters, and certain controlled corporations, partnerships, and trusts.

42.16 Depreciating Real Estate Placed in Service After 1980 and Before 1987

The ACRS recovery period of a building that does not qualify as low-income housing depends on the year in which the building was placed in service:

- For buildings placed in service after May 8, 1985, and before 1987, the recovery period is 19 years.
- For buildings placed in service after March 15, 1984, and before May 9, 1985, the recovery period is 18 years.
- For buildings placed in service before March 16, 1984, and for all low-income housing, the recovery period is 15 years.

Mobile homes and theme parks are in the 10-year class and agricultural, horticultural, and petroleum storage structures are in the five-year class.

Under transitional rules, some 19-year buildings may be depreciated over 18 years, and some 18-year buildings over 15 years if placed in service before 1987. Specifically, recovery over 18 years is allowed for a building placed in service after May 8, 1985, provided that before May 9, 1985, (1) you began construction or had a binding contract to buy the building and (2) you placed the building in service before the end of 1986. The 18-year period also applies if construction was begun, or a contract entered into by a person who transferred the rights to you and you placed the building in service before 1987. Recovery over 15 years is allowed for a building that you (or a prior owner who transferred the right to you) began constructing or contracted for before March 16, 1984, provided you placed it in service before the end of 1986.

Planning Reminder

Abandonment of Leasehold Improvements

Upon the termination of a lease, the adjusted basis of a lessee's leasehold improvements that are abandoned may be claimed as a loss. For dispositions after June 12, 1996, a lessor may follow the rule applied to lessees if the improvements are irrevocably disposed of or abandoned at the termination of the lease. The lessor may recognize loss for the remaining adjusted basis of the improvements.

Election to use straight-line depreciation. You may have elected to use the straight-line method over the regular recovery period: 19 years for 19-year property, 18 years for 18-year property, and 15 years for 15-year property. Furthermore, for any building, a longer recovery period of either 35 or 45 years was available. An election of the straight-line method for real property had to be made on a property-by-property basis, by the return due date, plus extensions, for the year the property was placed in service.

Rate of recovery. The rate of recovery is listed in Treasury tables that are available in IRS Publication 534. The specific rates are adjusted according to the month in the first year in which a building or improvement is placed in service.

Substantial improvements. Substantial improvements made after 1986 to an ACRS building are depreciable under MACRS *(42.13)*, not ACRS.

Dispositions. If you dispose of 15-year real property, the ACRS deduction for the year of disposition is based on the number of full months in use. However, no deduction is allowed for the month of disposition.

The same full-month convention rule applies to dispositions of 18-year property placed in service before June 23, 1984.

If you dispose of other 18-year or 19-year real property, the ACRS deduction for the year of disposition is based on the number of months in use determined under a mid-month convention. Under the mid-month convention, real property disposed of any time during a month is treated as disposed of in the middle of that month. You count the month of disposition as one-half of a month of use.

See 44.1 for recapture rules on the sale of ACRS property.

Filing Instruction

Disposition of ACRS Real Estate
In the year you dispose of 15-year ACRS real property, or 18-year property placed in service before June 23, 1984, you may base a deduction on the number of full months the building was used. For other 18-year or 19-year buildings, the deduction for the year of disposition is based on full months of use plus one-half a month for the month of disposition.

42.17 When MACRS Is Not Allowed

If you place in service personal property that you previously used or that was previously owned by a related taxpayer before 1987, you may not be able to apply MACRS rules. This anti-churning restriction is designed to discourage asset transfers between related persons to take advantage of MACRS deductions that exceed the deductions allowed before 1987 under ACRS. The anti-churning restriction does not apply to personal property if, for the first full taxable year of service, the deduction allowable under ACRS would be greater than the deduction allowable under MACRS.

The anti-churning rule also does not bar MACRS rules for real estate acquired after 1986, unless you lease back the real estate to a related party who owned it before 1987.

Special rules also apply to the transfer of property in certain tax-free corporate or partnership transactions where the property was used before 1987. If you receive property in a tax-free exchange, you may have to use the method used by the transferor in computing the ACRS deduction for that part of basis that does not exceed what was the transferor's basis in the property. To the extent that basis exceeds the transferor's, the MACRS rules may apply; for example, when you paid boot in addition to transferring property.

Where property is disposed of and reacquired, the depreciation deduction is computed as if the disposition had not occurred.

42.18 Amortizing Goodwill and Other Intangibles (Section 197)

The costs of intangibles coming within Section 197 are amortized over a 15-year period. The 15-year period applies regardless of the actual useful life of "Section 197 intangibles" acquired after August 10, 1993 (or after July 25, 1991, if elected), and held in connection with a business or income-producing activity.

Generally, the amount subject to amortization is cost. Annual amortization is reported on Form 4562. The 15-year period starts with the month the intangible was acquired.

A "Section 197 intangible" is: (1) goodwill; (2) going-concern value; (3) workforce in place; (4) information base; (5) know-how, but *see* exceptions below; (6) any customer-based intangible; (7) any supplier-based intangible; (8) any license, permit, or other right granted by a governmental unit or agency; (9) any covenant not to compete made in the acquisition of a business; and (10) any franchise, trademark, or trade name.

Goodwill. Goodwill is the value of a business attributable to the expectancy of continued customer patronage, due to the name or reputation of a business or any other factor.

Franchises, trademarks, and trade names. A franchise (excluding sports franchises), trademark, or trade name is a Section 197 intangible. Amounts, whether fixed or contingent, paid on the transfer of a trademark, trade name, or franchise are chargeable to capital account and must be ratably amortized over a 15-year period. The renewal of a franchise, trademark, or trade name is treated as an acquisition of the franchise, trademark, or trade name. Renewal costs are amortized over 15 years beginning in the month of renewal.

Know-how. A patent, copyright, formula, process, design, pattern, format, or similar item may be a Section 197 intangible. However, the following interests are not Section 197 intangibles unless acquired as part of the acquisition of a business: patents, copyrights, and interests in films, sound recordings, videotapes, books, or other similar property.

Customer-based intangibles. Customer-based intangibles include the portion of an acquired trade or business attributable to a customer base, circulation base, undeveloped market or market growth, insurance in force, investment management contracts, or other relationships with customers that involve the future provision of goods or services.

Supplier-based intangibles. The portion of the purchase price of an acquired business attributable to a favorable relationship with persons who provide distribution services, such as favorable shelf or display space at a retail outlet, the existence of a favorable credit rating, or the existence of favorable supply contracts, are Section 197 intangibles.

Going-concern value. This is the additional value that attaches to property because it is an integral part of a going concern. This includes the value attributable to the ability of a trade or business to continue to operate and generate sales without interruption in spite of a change in ownership.

Workforce in place. The portion of the purchase price of an acquired business attributable to a highly skilled workforce is amortizable over 15 years. Similarly, the cost of acquiring an existing employment contract is amortizable over 15 years.

Information base. This includes the cost of acquiring customer lists; subscription lists; insurance expirations; patient or client files; lists of newspaper, magazine, radio, or television advertisers; business books and records; and operating systems. The intangible value of technical manuals, training manuals or programs, data files, and accounting or inventory control systems is also a Section 197 intangible.

Self-created intangibles. A Section 197 intangible created by a taxpayer is generally not amortizable, unless created in connection with a transaction that involves the acquisition of assets of a business. However, this deduction bar for self-created intangibles does not apply to the following: (1) any license, permit, or other right granted by a governmental unit or agency; (2) a covenant not to compete entered into on the acquisition of a business; or (3) any franchise, trademark, or trade name. For example, the 15-year amortization period may apply to the capitalized costs of registering or developing a trademark or trade name.

A person who contracts for or renews a contract for the use of a Section 197 intangible may not be considered to have created that intangible. For example, a licensee who contracts for the use of know-how may amortize capitalized costs over 15 years.

The following intangible assets are not Section 197 intangibles: (1) interests in a corporation, partnership, trust, or estate; (2) interests under certain financial contracts; (3) interests in land; (4) certain computer software; (5) certain separately acquired rights and interests; (6) interests under existing leases of tangible property; (7) interests under existing indebtedness; (8) sports franchises; (9) certain residential mortgage servicing rights; and (10) certain corporate transaction costs.

Loss limitations. A person who disposes of an amortizable Section 197 intangible at a loss and at the same time retains other Section 197 intangibles acquired in the same transaction may not deduct the loss. The disallowed loss is added to the basis of the retained Section 197 intangibles. The same rule applies if a Section 197 intangible is abandoned or becomes worthless and other Section 197 intangibles acquired in the same transaction are kept. The basis of the remaining intangibles is increased by the disallowed loss.

 *Planning Reminder*

Covenants Not To Compete

A covenant not to compete is a Section 197 intangible if paid for in connection with the acquisition of a business. Excessive compensation or rental paid to a former owner of a business for continuing to perform services or provide the use of property is considered an amount paid for a covenant not to compete if the services or property benefits the trade or business. But an amount paid under a covenant not to compete that actually represents additional consideration for corporate stock is not a Section 197 intangible and must be added to the basis of the acquired stock.

You may not treat a covenant not to compete as worthless any earlier than the disposition or worthlessness of the entire interest in a business.

Anti-churning rule. No deduction is allowed for goodwill, going-concern value, or any other Section 197 intangibles acquired by a taxpayer after August 10, 1993, if:

1. The taxpayer or a related person held or used the intangible at any time on or after July 25, 1991, and on or before August 10, 1993;
2. The taxpayer acquired the intangible from a person who held it at any time on or after July 25, 1991, and on or before August 10, 1993, and, as part of the transaction, the user of the intangible does not change; or
3. The taxpayer grants the right to use the intangible to a person or a related person who held or used the intangible at any time on or after July 25, 1991, and on or before August 10, 1993.

See IRS Publication 535 for the definition of "related persons" and exceptions to the anti-churning rule.

Dispositions. An amortizable Section 197 intangible is not a capital asset. It is treated as depreciable property, and if held for more than one year, it will generally qualify as a Section 1231 asset; *see 44.1.* Amortization claimed on a Section 197 intangible is subject to recapture under Section 1245 and gain on its sale to certain related persons is subject to ordinary income treatment under Section 1239.

42.19 Deducting the Cost of Computer Software

The cost of software installed in a computer that you buy and use in your business is not deducted separately, unless the software cost is separately stated. In most cases, the cost of software bundled with a computer is not separately stated. The cost of the computer including such software is depreciable under the rules in *42.10.*

If you buy software for business use, such as a database or spreadsheet program, the treatment of the cost depends on your use of the program. If you use it for a year or less, such as an annual tax program, you may deduct the cost as a business expense for that year. If the useful life in your business exceeds a year, you may depreciate the cost over 36 months.

Software acquired in the acquisition of a business is depreciable over 36 months if it meets tests listed in the Planning Reminder on this page; otherwise, 15-year amortization applies.

42.20 Bonus Depreciation

Bonus depreciation is an additional first-year allowance of 30% of the adjusted basis of eligible property placed in service in 2002. Bonus depreciation (also called a Section 168(k) allowance and a special depreciation allowance) can be claimed in addition to any first-year expensing. In figuring "adjusted basis" for purposes of bonus depreciation, any expensing deduction is taken into account first. Bonus depreciation is fully deductible for alternative minimum tax purposes *(see 23.2)*; no adjustment is required.

Planning Reminder

Computer Software Not Subject to Amortization

Computer software is *not* a Section 197 intangible if it: (1) is readily available to the general public; (2) is not subject to an exclusive license; and (3) has not been substantially changed. If these three tests are met, the software may be depreciated over 36 months; *see 42.19.* Computer software falling outside of this exception is considered a Section 197 intangible subject to 15-year amortization if it is acquired in the acquisition of a business.

> **EXAMPLE**
>
> In 2002, you place in service equipment costing $50,000. You elect to expense $24,000 of the cost. Your bonus depreciation deduction is $7,800, or ($50,000 − $24,000) x 30%. You can depreciate the remaining adjusted basis of the equipment ($18,200) over the property's recovery period. If the equipment is five-year property, then the depreciation allowance for 2002 is $3,640 ($18,200 x 20%). The total deductions for this equipment in 2002 equal $35,440 ($24,000 + $7,800 + 3,640).

Bonus depreciation allows the first-year dollar limit on write-offs for vehicles weighing less than 6,000 to be increased by $4,600, provided business use exceeds 50%. This increases the total dollar limit for such vehicles placed in service in 2002 to $7,660 ($4,600 bonus depreciation plus $3,060 regular dollar limit; *see 43.4).*

Eligible property. Bonus depreciation can be claimed for any property with a recovery period of 20 years or less, computer software (other than a Section 197 intangible; *see 42.18*) and qualified leasehold improvements. Qualified leasehold improvements are improvements made more than three years after the building is placed in service to an interior portion of a nonresidential building pursuant to a lease by the lessee, sublessee, or lessor; the interior of the building is occupied exclusively by the lessee or sublessee.

You must be the original user of the property. Property does *not* qualify if you entered into a written binding contract to acquire it before September 11, 2001. Bonus depreciation cannot be claimed for property that *must* be depreciated under ADS *(see 42.9)*. For example, it may not be used for listed property used 50% or less for business since such property must be depreciated under ADS.

Claiming bonus depreciation. You report bonus depreciation in Part II of Form 4562 labeled "Special Depreciation Allowance."

Election out of bonus depreciation. Unlike regular depreciation, you are not *required* to use bonus depreciation and have the option of electing out of its use. If you fail to make the election not to claim bonus depreciation, then you are deemed to have claimed it (even though you did not) and must reduce the basis of the property by the amount of bonus depreciation that could have been claimed.

The election out is made on a per-asset-class basis. Thus, for example, you can opt out of bonus depreciation for all five-year property while claiming it for seven-year property. To make the election out of claiming bonus depreciation, attach a statement to your return specifying the class of property for which the election not to claim additional depreciation is being made.

Amending 2001 return to claim bonus depreciation. If you placed qualifying property in service after September 10, 2001, and you filed your 2001 return before June 1, 2002, without claiming the special allowance, you may do so on an amended return filed by the April 15, 2003, due date for your 2002 return (without extensions). Write "Filed Pursuant to Rev. Proc. 2002-33" at the top of the amended return. Alternatively, you have until the filing due date, *including* extensions, to claim the special allowance by filing with your 2002 return a Form 3115 (Application for Change in Accounting Method). Write on the appropriate line "Automatic Change Filed Under Rev. Proc. 2002-33." You must send a copy of the Form 3115 to the IRS National Office when you file your 2002 return.

Law Alert

Bonus Depreciation for Liberty Zone Property
Qualified New York Liberty Zone property is eligible for 30% bonus depreciation. It is taken into account *before* other depreciation allowances, but *after* first-year expensing, which can be up to $59,000 under the increased expensing limit for qualified Liberty Zone property; *see* the Form 4562 instructions.

Planning Reminder

Bonus Depreciation Is Only a Timing Mechanism
Bonus depreciation enables you to deduct more of the cost of property upfront rather than over the course of the applicable recovery period (it does not affect total depreciation deductions for the property). You may wish to opt out of bonus depreciation if you expect to be in a higher tax bracket in coming years; this will allow you can obtain a greater tax benefit from depreciation deductions later on.

Chapter 43

Deducting Automobile Expenses

The costs of buying and operating a car for business are deductible under rules hedged with restrictions. Depreciation deductions for passenger autos are subject to annual ceilings. For cars placed in service in 2002, an additional first-year bonus allowance of up-to-$4,600 is generally allowed. The special allowance raises the ceiling on first-year depreciation provided business use exceeds 50%. The ceiling is $7,660, reduced for personal use. If a car placed in service in 2002 is used less than 50% for business, depreciation must be based on the straight-line method and the maximum deduction is limited to $3,060, reduced by personal use. *See 43.4* for details on the limits.

To avoid accounting for actual auto expenses and depreciation, you may claim an IRS mileage allowance. For 2002, the allowance is 36.5 cents per mile. Keep a record of business trip mileage.

If you are self-employed, you deduct your automobile expenses on Schedule C or Schedule C-EZ if eligible; *see 40.6.* Use Form 4562 to compute depreciation if you claim actual operating costs instead of the IRS mileage allowance. If you are an employee, use Form 2106 to claim unreimbursed automobile expenses, which are deductible only to the extent that together with other miscellaneous itemized deductions they exceed 2% of your adjusted gross income.

43.1 IRS Automobile Allowance

If you start to use your car for business in 2002, you have a choice of either deducting the actual operating costs of your car during business trips or deducting a flat IRS allowance of 36.5 cents per mile for business mileage during 2002.

If you placed a business car in service before 2002 and have always used the IRS mileage allowance, you may apply the 36.5-cents-per-mile rate to your 2002 business mileage or deduct your actual operating costs plus straight-line depreciation (assuming the car is not considered fully depreciated).

The mileage rate also applies to business trips in a van or pickup or panel truck as if it were a car.

The rate may not be used to deduct the costs of an automobile used for nonbusiness income-producing activities such as looking after investment property.

Allowance must be elected for the first year. The choice of the allowance must be made in the first year you place an auto in service for business travel. If you do not use the allowance in the year you first use the car for business, you may not use the allowance for that car in any other year. Thus, if you bought a car for business in 2001 and on your 2001 return you deducted actual operating costs plus depreciation, you may not use the mileage allowance on your 2002 return or in any later year.

Allowance takes the place of fixed operating costs. You may not take the allowance and deduct your actual outlays for expenses such as gasoline (including state and local taxes), oil, repairs, license tags, insurance, and depreciation. Parking fees and tolls during business trips are deductible in addition to the mileage allowance. The IRS will not disallow a deduction based on the allowance even though it exceeds your actual car costs. If you use more than one automobile in your business travel and elect the allowance, total the business mileage traveled in both cars.

EXAMPLES

1. You buy a car in 2002 and drive it on business trips. You keep a record of your business mileage. You traveled 20,000 miles on business. You may deduct $7,300 (20,000 miles × 36.5 cents). In addition, you spend $300 on tolls and parking. You may deduct a total of $7,600.

2. You use one car primarily for business and occasionally your spouse's car for business trips. In 2002, you drove your car on business trips 10,000 miles and your spouse's car 2,000 miles. Total business mileage is 12,000 miles for purposes of the 36.5-cents-per-mile allowance.

Records. You may decide to use the allowance if you do not keep accurate records of operating costs. However, you must keep a record of your business trips, dates, customers or clients visited, business purpose of the trips, your total mileage during the year, and the number of miles traveled on business. An IRS agent may attempt to verify mileage by asking for repair bills near the beginning and end of the year if the bills note mileage readings.

Mileage allowance for leased cars. The IRS mileage allowance is also available for leased vehicles. If in 2002 you leased a car for business purposes you may claim the 36.5-cents-per-mile allowance, but if you claim the allowance for 2002 you will also have to use it for the remainder of the lease period, including renewals.

Interest on a car loan and taxes. *See 43.2* for when a deduction is allowed.

Mileage allowance disallowed. You may not claim the 36.5-cents-a-mile allowance if:
- You have depreciated your car using the ACRS or MACRS method, including straight-line MACRS, or you claimed first-year expensing.
- You use in your business two or more cars simultaneously, such as in a fleet operation.
- You use your car for hire—that is, you use it as a taxicab, carrying passengers for a fare.

 *Planning Reminder*

First-Year Election Affects Later Years

In deciding whether to elect the allowance in the first year, consider not only whether you will get a bigger first-year deduction using the allowance, or deducting actual operating costs plus depreciation, but also project your mileage, operating expenses, and depreciation expenses over the years you expect to use the car. If in the first year you elect to deduct actual costs, including bonus depreciation, accelerated MACRS or straight-line MACRS depreciation, you may not use the IRS auto allowance for *that car* in a later year. On the other hand, claiming the IRS allowance in the first year you put a car in service forfeits your privilege to use bonus depreciation and MACRS and first-year expensing. If you switch from the allowance to deducting actual expenses in later years, you may claim straight-line depreciation if the car is not considered fully depreciated.

Key To Deducting Automobile Expenses

Item— | *Tax Rule—*

IRS mileage allowance

You may avoid the trouble of keeping a record of actual auto expenses and calculating depreciation by electing the IRS mileage allowance. However, to claim the allowance, you must be ready to prove business use of the auto and keep a record of your mileage. The allowance may give you a larger deduction than your actual outlays plus depreciation. You must elect the allowance in the first year you use the car for business. If you do not, you may not use the allowance for that car in any other year.

If your actual operating costs plus depreciation exceed the allowance for the first year you place the car in business service, you may claim your actual operating expenses and depreciation, but doing so will forfeit your right to elect the allowance for that car in any later year.

Depreciation

If you claim actual operating expenses for a new car, such as gasoline, repairs, and insurance costs, you may also claim depreciation. There is a cap on the annual depreciation deduction. If you placed a car in service in 2002 that was used over 50% for business, the maximum depreciation deduction is $7,660 multiplied by the percentage of business use. If business use is 50% or less, the limit is $3,060 multiplied by the business use percentage. The up-to-$7,660 limit is allowed under a new law providing a special depreciation allowance, or first-year bonus, equal to 30% of depreciable basis *(see 43.4)*. If the first-year bonus is claimed, basis for regular depreciation purposes is reduced by the special allowance. *See* the Example in *43.4*. Electing first-year expensing does not increase the $7,660 or $3,060 limit (as reduced by personal use). The total of the special allowance, first-year expensing, and regular depreciation cannot exceed the applicable limit. Electing the special allowance, first-year expensing, or regular depreciation for a car placed in service in 2002 prevents you from using the IRS mileage allowance *(43.1)* for that car in later years.

If a car placed in business service in 2002 was used 50% or less for business, the first-year bonus is not allowed and you must use straight-line depreciation subject to the regular annual ceiling; *see 43.6.* If business use is initially over 50% but declines to 50% or less in a later year, prior year depreciation deductions, including the special allowance and first-year expensing, must be recaptured as income to the extent they exceeded straight-line deductions; *see 43.10.*

For a car placed in service before 2002, *see 43.4* for the maximum depreciation you can claim for 2002.

Auto used for business and personal driving

You may deduct only the amount allocated to business mileage. For example, total mileage is 20,000 in 2002 and your business mileage is 15,000. You may claim only 75% of your deductible costs (15,000 ÷ 20,000).

Tax return reporting

If you are an *employee*, you claim actual auto expenses or the IRS allowance on Form 2106. Form 2106 requires you to list mileage for business, commuting, and other personal trips. If your auto costs are not reimbursed by your employer, you must deduct them as miscellaneous deductions subject to the 2% AGI floor on Schedule A.

If you are *self-employed*, you deduct business costs on Schedule C and use Form 4562 to compute depreciation if you claim actual operating costs. Costs deducted on Schedule C are not limited by the 2% adjusted gross income (AGI) floor.

 Law Alert

Rural Mail Carriers
U.S. Postal Service employees who use their personal vehicles on rural routes and who receive an equipment maintenance allowance figured under a collective bargaining agreement are treated as being reimbursed for their actual expenses. There is a "wash" for tax purposes. The reimbursement should not be included in the employee's income and the employee has no deduction to report on his or her return.

Employer reimbursements. If your employer reimburses your auto costs at a rate lower than the IRS allowance, you may use the IRS rate to deduct the excess over your employer's reimbursement; *see* Example 3 at *20.33*.

IRS allowance includes depreciation. When you use the IRS mileage allowance, you may not claim a separate depreciation deduction. The IRS mileage allowance includes an estimate for depreciation. However, for purposes of figuring gain or loss on a disposition, you must reduce the basis of the car according to the following rates: 12 cents per mile for 1994, 1995, 1996, 1997, 1998, and 1999, 14 cents per mile for 2000, and 15 cents per mile for 2001 and 2002.

Depreciation when switching from allowance to actual costs. If you use the IRS mileage allowance in the first year, you may switch to the actual-cost method in a later year, but depreciation must be based on the straight-line method over the remaining estimated useful life. However, no depreciation may be claimed if basis has been reduced to zero under the annual cents-per-mile reduction rule just discussed.

43.2 Auto Expense Allocations

If you do not claim the IRS mileage allowance, you may deduct car expenses on business trips such as the cost of gas and oil (including state and local taxes), repairs, parking, and tolls.

If you use your car exclusively for business, all of your operating expenses are deductible. However, if you are an employee, the deduction is limited by the 2% adjusted gross income (AGI) floor; *see 19.1.*

Apportioning car expenses between business and personal use. For a car used for business and personal purposes, deduct only the depreciation and expenses allocated to your business use of the car. Depreciation is discussed at *43.3, 43.4,* and *43.5.*

The business portion of car expenses is determined by the percentage of mileage driven on business trips during the year.

EXAMPLE

In 2002, you drove your car 15,000 miles. Of this, 12,000 miles was on business trips. The percentage of business use is 80%:

$$\frac{\text{Business Mileage}}{\text{Total Mileage}} = \frac{12,000}{15,000} = 80\%$$

Your actual car expenses (gas, oil, repairs, etc.) for the year were $1,000, of which $800 ($1,000 × 80%) is deductible. If you are an employee, the $800 is deductible as a miscellaneous itemized deduction subject to the 2% AGI floor; *see 19.1.*

Interest on car loan. If you are an *employee,* all of the interest is considered personal interest and is not deductible even if you use the car 100% of the time for your job. If you are *self-employed,* the allocated business percentage of the interest is fully deductible on Schedule C; the personal percentage is not deductible.

Taxes on purchase. Sales tax is not deductible whether you are an employee or self-employed; the tax is added to the basis of the auto for depreciation purposes; *see 43.3.* State and local property taxes are deductible as itemized deductions on Schedule A if you are an employee. If you are self-employed, deduct the business portion of the property taxes on Schedule C and the personal percentage on Schedule A if you itemize.

Leased car. If you lease a car for business use and do not claim the IRS mileage allowance *(43.1),* you deduct the lease payments plus other costs of operating the car. If the car is also used for personal driving, the lease payments must be allocated between business and personal mileage. *See also 43.12* for rules requiring the reporting of extra income attributable to the lease.

43.3 Auto Depreciation Restrictions

The law contains restrictions that limit and, in some cases, deny depreciation deductions for a business car. Employees may be unable to claim any deduction at all under an employer convenience test. Employees meeting that test and self-employed individuals must determine if they can use accelerated MACRS rates or must use straight-line rates. Finally, regardless of which depreciation method is used, the annual deduction may not exceed a ceiling set by law. For a car placed in service in 2002, the ceiling is generally $7,660; *see 43.4* for details on the annual ceilings.

Employee must satisfy employer convenience test. If you are an employee and use your own car for work, you must be ready to prove that you use a car for the *convenience of your employer* who requires you to use it in your job. If you do not meet this employer convenience test, you may not claim depreciation or first-year expensing. A letter from your employer stating you need the car for business will not meet this test.

The facts and circumstances of your use of the car may show that it is a condition of employment. For example, an inspector for a construction company uses his automobile to visit construction sites over a scattered area. The company reimburses him for his expenses. According to the IRS, the inspector's use of the car is for the convenience of the company and is a condition of the job. However, if a company car were available to the inspector, the use of his own car would not meet the condition of employment and convenience of the employer tests.

More-than-50%-business-use test for claiming expensing or accelerated MACRS depreciation. An automobile is considered "listed property," as explained in *42.10,* whether you are an employee or are self-employed. As such, you may claim first-year expensing, bonus depreciation *(43.4),* or accelerated MACRS *(43.5)* for a car placed in service during 2002 only if you use it in 2002 more than 50% of the time for business. The same annual ceiling applies to the expensing and MACRS deductions; *see 43.4.*

 Caution

Recapture of MACRS Deductions

If you meet the more-than-50% test in the year the car or other vehicle is placed in service, which entitles you to claim first-year expensing or accelerated MACRS and bonus depreciation, but business use falls to 50% or less in a later year, the recapture rules discussed at *43.10* apply.

If business use is *50% or less* in the year the auto is placed in service, first-year expensing and accelerated MACRS are barred; the auto is depreciable over a six-year period under the straight-line method. Technically, the recovery period is five years but the period is extended to six years because, in the first year, a convention rule limits the deductible percentage. *See* the straight-line rate tables at *43.6.* The straight-line method must also be used in future years, even if business use in those years exceeds 50%.

If a car is used for both business and investment purposes, only business use is considered in determining whether you meet the more-than-50%-business-use test and therefore qualify for MACRS. However, if your business use does exceed 50%, investment use is added to business use in determining your actual deduction.

> **EXAMPLE**
>
> Brown buys an automobile for $30,000 and places it in service in 2002. He uses it 40% for business and 20% for investment activity. Because he does not use his car more than 50% in his business, he may not claim first-year expensing, accelerated MACRS, or bonus depreciation. He figures depreciation using the straight-line method. The business use allocation rate for depreciation is 60% (40% for business use plus 20% investment use).

Trucks and other vehicles. The more-than-50%-business-use test generally applies to vehicles other than automobiles such as trucks, vans, boats, motorcycles, airplanes, and buses. However, the test does not apply to taxicabs and other vehicles used substantially all of the time to transport persons or property for hire. The test also does not apply to vehicles that are exempt from record-keeping requirements under *43.11,* such as a school bus, dump truck, farm tractor, or other specialized farm vehicle, delivery truck with seating only for the driver or with a folding jump seat, flat bed truck, garbage truck, passenger bus with capacity of at least 20, refrigerated truck, combine, specialized utility repair truck, unmarked law enforcement vehicle officially authorized for use, and a moving van if personal use is limited by the employer to travel from the employee's home to a move site.

A vehicle not in the exempt list is subject to the more-than-50% test for claiming accelerated MACRS depreciation or first-year expensing. If you do not satisfy the more-than-50% test, you must apply the straight-line recovery rates shown at *43.6.*

Do your employees use the car? In certain cases, an employer who provides a company car to employees as part of their compensation may be unable to count the employee's use as qualified business use, thereby preventing the employer from meeting the more-than-50%-business-use test for claiming MACRS. An employer is allowed to treat the employee's use as qualified business use only if: (1) the employee is not a relative and does not own more than 5% of the business and (2) the employer treats the fair market value of the employee's personal use of the car as wage income and withholds tax on that amount. If such income is reported, all of the employee's use, including personal use, may be counted by an employer as qualified business use.

If an employee owning more than a 5% interest is allowed use of a company car as part of his or her compensation, the employer may not count that use as qualified business use, even if the personal use is reported as income. The same strict rule applies if the car is provided to a person who is related to the employer.

43.4 Annual Ceilings on Depreciation

For cars placed in service after 1986, annual ceilings limit the amount of depreciation you may deduct. The ceilings apply both to self-employed individuals and employees. As a result of the ceilings, the actual write-off period for your car may be several years longer than the minimum recovery period of six years; *see 43.5.*

The Job Creation and Worker Assistance Act of 2002 allows a special first-year bonus allowance to be claimed for a new car bought, contracted for, and placed in service after September 10, 2001. The bonus increases the first-year limit to $7,660 for a car placed in service in 2002 and used 100% for business. A proportionate part of the $7,660 limit is allowed if business use exceeds 50% but is less than 100%. *See* below for details on the bonus allowance. If business use does not exceed 50%, the first-year bonus does not apply and the limit for a car placed in service in 2002 is $3,060, reduced by personal use.

Year-by-year ceilings for cars placed in service between 1995 and 2002 are shown in the table on page 654. These limits are also reduced for personal use.

Ceiling applies to total depreciation. The annual ceiling, reduced by personal use, limits the depreciation deduction that would otherwise be allowed, including bonus depreciation or first-year expensing. The Example below illustrates how the ceiling applies if bonus depreciation is claimed under the new law.

Bonus first-year depreciation. The Job Creation and Worker Assistance Act of 2002 allows a special first-year bonus allowance to be claimed for a new car bought, contracted for, and placed in service after September 10, 2001. The special allowance is scheduled to apply for cars bought before September 11, 2004. The bonus allowance is a deduction equal to 30% of the depreciable basis of the car. It is allowed only for cars used more than 50% for business. As discussed below, light trucks and vans weighing under 6,000 pounds (loaded) are treated as cars and are thus subject to the same rules.

The special 30% allowance is figured after any first-year expensing election (Section 179 deduction) but before regular MACRS depreciation is computed. The special allowance (as well as any first-year expensing) reduces basis for regular MACRS purposes. The total of the special allowance, first-year expensing, and regular depreciation cannot exceed the annual ceiling. If the special allowance is claimed, the ceiling for 2002 is $7,660 multiplied by the percentage of business use; *see* the Example below.

Law Alert

First-Year Bonus Depreciation for Cars Bought after September 10, 2001

A new law allows a special 30% first-year depreciation allowance for a car placed in service after September 10, 2001, provided the car is used over 50% for business. The allowance raises the depreciation limit to $7,660 multiplied by the business use percentage; *see 43.4.*

> **EXAMPLE**
>
> Theodore bought a new car on September 4, 2002, for $20,000 and for the rest of the year used it 75% for business. Theodore's car qualifies for the special allowance.
>
> Theodore chooses not to take the Section 179 deduction for the car. He does claim the new special depreciation deduction allowance. Theodore first must figure the car's depreciable basis, which is $15,000 ($20,000 × .75). He then figures the special depreciation allowance of $4,500 ($15,000 × .30).
>
> The remaining depreciable basis of $10,500 ($15,000 – $4,500) is depreciated using MACRS (200% declining balance method, half-year convention) and results in a deduction of $2,100 ($10,500 × .20). The total of the special allowance and regular MACRS depreciation is $6,600 ($4,500 + $2,100). However, Theodore's depreciation deduction is limited to $5,745 ($7,660 limit × 75% business use).

Election out of bonus depreciation. An election may be made not to claim the special allowance. You may wish to opt out in order to avoid a reduction in basis if you believe that larger depreciation deductions may provide a larger tax benefit in later years. The election must be made on a per-asset-class basis, so an election would apply to the car as well as any other five-year property placed in service during the same year. The election is made by attaching a statement to your return that you are electing not to claim the allowance for the five-year property. The election for 2002 generally must be made by April 15, 2003.

If you file your return and claim depreciation but not the special allowance, you will be deemed to have claimed it and the basis of the car will have to be reduced by the special allowance although it was not claimed.

Amended return for 2001 to claim allowance. If you filed your 2001 return before June 1, 2002, and did not claim the special allowance for a qualifying car placed in service after September 10, 2001, you can claim it on an amended return (Form 1040X) filed by April 15, 2003. Write "Filed Pursuant to Revenue Procedure 2002-33" at the top of Form 1040X. Attach a revised Form 4562 if self-employed, or Form 2106 if an employee. If the April 15, 2003, deadline is not met, the allowance for 2001 can be claimed by attaching to your 2002 return a Form 3115 (Application for Change in Accounting Method). The deadline for the Form 3115 is April 15, 2003, plus extensions for your 2002 return; *see* the tax form instructions for further details.

Light trucks and vans subject to the ceilings. The annual depreciation ceilings apply only to "passenger automobiles." For this purpose, a passenger automobile is generally considered to be any four-wheeled vehicle that is manufactured primarily for use on public streets, roads, and highways and that is weight-rated by the manufacturer at 6,000 pounds or less when unloaded (without passengers or cargo). However, an SUV, light truck, or van that is weight-rated by the manufacturer at 6,000 pounds or less when loaded (gross vehicle weight) is treated as a passenger automobile.

The following are not considered "passenger" automobiles and thus are exempt from the annual ceilings: (1) an ambulance, hearse, or combination ambulance-hearse used directly in a business and (2) a vehicle such as a taxicab used directly in the business of transporting persons or property for compensation or hire.

Filing Tip

Sport Utility Vehicles

Owners of certain sport utility vehicles (SUVs) that are used for business purposes and that have a gross vehicle weight (loaded) of more than 6,000 pounds are not subject to the ceiling on depreciation deductions. This means the owner is entitled to first-year expensing and bonus depreciation if business use exceeds 50%, as well as the full depreciation deduction using the MACRS rate shown in *43.5.*

SUV owners should check the manufacturers' specifications for their vehicles to see if the weight exceeds the 6,000 limit.

Depreciation limits on electric cars. In an effort to encourage the use of electric automobiles, a larger annual depreciation limit is allowed for electric vehicles built by an original manufacturer. In 2002, the first-year depreciation cap is set at $23,080 if the special allowance is claimed and $9,280 if it is not.

Annual Depreciation Ceiling

| | Year placed in service— | | | | | | | |
	1995	1996	1997	1998	1999	2000	2001	2002
Ceiling in—								
1995	$3,060							
1996	4,900	$3,060						
1997	2,950	4,900	3,160					
1998	1,775	2,950	5,000	3,160				
1999	1,775	1,775	3,050	5,000	3,060			
2000	1,775	1,775	1,775	2,950	5,000	3,060		
2001	1,775	1,775	1,775	1,775	2,950	4,900	3,060/7,660*	
2002	1,775	1,775	1,775	1,775	1,775	2,950	4,900	3,060/7,660*
2003	1,775	1,775	1,775	1,775	1,775	1,775	2,950	4,900
2004	1,775	1,775	1,775	1,775	1,775	1,775	1,775	2,950
2005 and later years	1,775	1,775	1,775	1,775	1,775	1,775	1,775	1,775

*Note: For cars placed in service after September 10, 2001, that are used over 50% for business, apply the $7,660 limit, reduced by personal use. The limit is $3,060 reduced by personal use if business use is 50% or less or you elect not to claim the special allowance.

43.5 MACRS Rates for Cars

Business autos placed in service in 1987 and later years are technically in a five-year MACRS class *(42.4)*, but because of the half-year or mid-quarter convention and the annual deduction ceilings *(43.3)*, the minimum depreciation period is six years.

Accelerated MACRS rate if business use in the first year exceeds 50%. To use accelerated MACRS rates, you must meet the more-than-50%-business-use test *(see 43.3)* in the year the auto is placed in business service. Generally, the accelerated MACRS rate is based on the 200% declining balance method, but a 150% declining balance rate may be elected, which may be advantageous when you are subject to the alternative minimum tax *(23.2)*.

If you meet the more-than 50% business use test, figure your first-year deduction using the rate from either the half-year convention table or the mid-quarter convention table on page 656, whichever applies. The MACRS rates from the appropriate table will be used for each year of the recovery period unless business use for a year falls to 50% or less. However, the deduction figured under the table may be claimed only to the extent that it does not exceed the annual ceiling for auto depreciation; *see* the Bill Johnston Example on page 656. *See* below for details on using the tables.

Deduction for year of disposition. If you dispose of your car before the end of the six-year MACRS recovery period, a partial-year deduction is allowed for the year of disposition under the half-year or mid-quarter convention; *see 43.7*.

Use of car after end of recovery period. If you continue to use the car for business after the end of the recovery period, and the annual deduction ceilings prevented you from deducting your full unadjusted basis during the recovery period, you generally may deduct depreciation in the succeeding years up to the annual ceiling; *see 43.8*.

Business use falls to 50% or less after the first year. What if business use exceeds 50% in the year the car is placed in service but in a later year within the recovery period business use drops to 50% or lower? In that case, the right to use accelerated MACRS (200% or 150% declining balance method) terminates. You must use the straight-line method and recapture the benefit of the accelerated deductions claimed for the prior years; *see 43.10* for the recapture rule.

Straight-line election for car if business use exceeds 50%. If business use of your car exceeds 50%, you may elect to write off your cost under the straight-line method instead of using the regular MACRS 200% declining balance method. The straight-line rates are shown in *43.6*. The straight-line deduction is limited by the annual ceilings shown in *43.4*. By electing straight-

Filing Tip

Claiming First-Year Expensing or Depreciation for Your Car

Bonus depreciation (if eligible, *see 43.4*), first-year expensing, or depreciation (under the 200% or 150% declining balance method, or the straight-line method) is claimed on Form 4562 and then entered on Schedule C of Form 1040 if you are self employed. If you are an employee, use Form 2106 to calculate your deduction, which along with your other unreimbursed job expenses is subject to the 2% AGI floor *(19.3)* for miscellaneous itemized deductions on Schedule A of Form 1040.

line depreciation, you avoid the recapture of excess MACRS deductions if business use drops to 50% or less in a later year; *see 43.10.* If the election is made, you must also use the straight-line method for all other five-year property placed in service during the same year as the car.

Electing 150% declining balance method. Depreciation rates under the half-year and mid-quarter conventions are generally based on the 200% declining balance method. You may instead make an irrevocable election to apply the 150% declining balance method. The 150% method may be advantageous when you are subject to the alternative minimum tax. For alternative minimum tax (AMT) purposes *(23.2),* auto depreciation is based on the 150% declining balance method unless you use the straight-line method for regular tax purposes. If you are subject to AMT and use the 150% declining balance method instead of the 200% declining balance method for regular tax purposes, you do not have to report an AMT adjustment on Form 6251 for auto depreciation.

An election to use the 150% declining balance method is irrevocable and must be applied to all depreciable assets placed in service in the same year, except for nonresidential real and residential rental property.

Tables Applying the Half-Year Convention or Mid-Quarter Convention

For the year you place the car in service and the year (within the recovery period) you dispose of the property, you may not claim a full year's worth of depreciation. The deduction is limited by either the half-year convention or the mid-quarter convention, depending on the month in which the car was placed in service and the other business assets, if any, placed in service during that year.

The applicable convention determines the rate table you will use to figure your depreciation deduction for the entire six-year recovery period, assuming that your business use each year exceeds 50%. The half-year and mid-quarter convention tables shown on the following page reflect the 200% or 150% declining balance method, with a switch to the straight-line method when that method provides a larger deduction; the switch to straight line is built into the tables.

For each year in the recovery period, the rate from the applicable table is applied against the business use percentage of your unadjusted basis for the car. Unadjusted basis is your cost minus any first-year expensing deduction as well as any special first-year bonus depreciation for a car placed into service after September 10, 2001 *(43.4).* The deduction figured under the table rate may be claimed to the extent that it does not exceed the annual ceiling for auto depreciation; *see* the Bill Johnston Example below.

Determining whether the half-year convention or mid-quarter convention applies. If you bought a car for your business in 2002, and it was the only business equipment placed in service during the year, then the half-year convention applies, unless you bought the car in the last quarter of 2002 (October, November, or December). Under the half-year convention, the car is treated as if it were placed in service in the middle of the year. Use the table below to determine your deduction under the half-year convention.

If the only business equipment bought in 2002 was a car bought in the last quarter (October, November, or December), the mid-quarter convention applies. Under the table for mid-quarter convention rates on the next page, a 5% rate applies for fourth-quarter property under the 200% declining balance method, subject to the $3,060 or $7,660 deduction ceiling in 2002; *see 43.4.*

If you bought other business equipment in addition to the car, you must consider the total cost basis of property placed in service during the last quarter of 2002. If the total bases of such acquisitions (other than realty) exceed 40% of the total bases of all property placed in service during the year, then a mid-quarter rate applies to *all* of the property (other than realty). The mid-quarter rate for each asset then depends on the quarter the asset was placed in service. If the 40% test is not met, then the half-year convention applies to all the property acquisitions. As shown in the mid-quarter convention table on the next page, mid-quarter rates for each year of the recovery period depend on the quarter the property is placed in service.

Deduction from table cannot exceed annual ceiling. If the deduction figured under the half-year or mid-quarter convention MACRS table exceeds the annual deduction ceiling shown in *43.4,* your deduction equals the lower annual ceiling, multiplied by the percentage of your business use. Keep in mind that if the special first-year allowance is claimed for a car placed in service after September 10, 2001, basis for MACRS purposes is reduced by the special allowance; *see* the Theodore Example in *43.4* and the second part of the Bill Johnston Example below.

 Filing Tip

Mid-Quarter Rate Limitation
If the application of the mid-quarter convention limits your deduction to less than $7,660 for a car placed in service during 2002, consider an election to claim the first-year expensing deduction at *42.3* if your business-use percentage exceeds 50%. This may allow you to deduct up to $7,660.

 Filing Tip

Capital Improvements
A capital improvement to a business auto is depreciable under MACRS in the year the improvement is made. The MACRS deductions for the improvement and the auto are considered as a unit for purposes of applying the limits on the annual MACRS depreciation deduction.

MACRS Deduction: Half-Year Convention

Year—	200% Rate	150% Rate
1	20.00%	15.00%
2	32.00	25.50
3	19.20	17.85
4	11.52	16.66
5	11.52	16.66
6	5.76	8.33

EXAMPLE

1. In May 2001, Bill Johnston placed in service a car he used 100% for business. The car cost $20,000. He did not claim first-year expensing. Here is Bill's depreciation schedule using the 200% declining balance rate, assuming the car is kept for the period shown below and is used 100% for business trips:

Year	Deduction from rate table	Annual ceiling	Allowable deduction
2001	$4,000 (20% × $20,000)	3,060	$3,060
2002	6,400 (32% × $20,000)	4,900	4,900
2003	3,840 (19.20% × $20,000)	2,950	2,950
2004	2,304 (11.52% × $20,000)	1,775	1,775
2005	2,304 (11.52% × $20,000)	1,775	1,775
2006*	1,152 (5.76% × $20,000)	1,775	1,152
2007		1,775	1,775
2008		1,775	1,775
2009		838	838

* Note that for the first five years (2001–2005), the allowable deduction is limited to the annual ceiling but in year six (2006), the deduction is based on the MACRS rate table because $1,152 (5.76% × $20,000) is less than the $1,775 annual ceiling.

2. Assume that Bill purchased the car in May 2002 instead of May 2001 and he used it 100% for business in 2002. The car qualifies for the special first-year depreciation allowance (43.4), which Bill decides to claim. The special allowance equals 30% of depreciable basis, or $6,000 (30% × $20,000). The remaining basis of $14,000 ($20,000 – $6,000) is depreciable using MACRS rates. Bill's MACRS deduction, using the 20% rate from the table, is $2,800 (20% × $14,000). The total of the special allowance plus MACRS depreciation, or $8,800 ($6,000 + $2,800), exceeds the annual limit of $7,660 that applies when the special allowance is claimed (43.4). Bill's deduction for 2002 is limited to the lower amount of $7,660. For 2003 and later years, Bill's basis for MACRS purposes is $14,000, reduced each year.

MACRS Deduction: Mid-Quarter Convention

Placed in service in—

Year—	First Quarter		Second Quarter		Third Quarter		Fourth Quarter	
	200% Rate	150% Rate	200% Rate	150% Rate	200% Rate	150% Rate	200% Rate	150% Rate
1	35.00%	26.25%	25.00%	18.75%	15.00%	11.25%	5.00%	3.75%
2	26.00	22.13	30.00	24.38	34.00	26.63	38.00	28.88
3	15.60	16.52	18.00	17.06	20.40	18.64	22.80	20.21
4	11.01	16.52	11.37	16.76	12.24	16.56	13.68	16.40
5	11.01	16.52	11.37	16.76	11.30	16.57	10.94	16.41
6	1.38	2.06	4.26	6.29	7.06	10.35	9.58	14.35

Converting a pleasure car to business use. The basis for depreciation is the lower of the market value of the car at the time of conversion or its adjusted basis, which is your original cost plus any substantial improvements and minus any deductible casualty losses or diesel fuel tax credit claimed for the car. In most cases, the value of the car will be lower than adjusted basis, and thus the value will be your depreciable basis. For a car converted to business use in 2002, the MACRS rate is applied to basis allocated to business travel. Unless you have mileage records for the entire year, you should base your business-use percentage on driving after the conversion. For example, in April 2002, you started to use your car for business and in the last nine months of the year you drove 10,000 miles, 8,000 of which were for business. This business percentage of 80% is multiplied by the fraction $^9/_{12}$ (months used for business divided by 12) to give you a business-use percentage for the year of 60% ($^9/_{12}$ of 80%).

43.6 Straight-Line Method

You may not use accelerated MACRS *(43.5)* if your business use of your car is 50% or less. Mandatory straight-line recovery rates for business use of 50% or less using the half-year or mid-quarter convention are shown below. These straight-line rates are also used if your business use exceeds 50% and you elect straight-line recovery instead of the regular MACRS method. *See 43.5* for determining whether the half-year or mid-quarter convention applies.

For each year of the six-year recovery period, apply the straight-line rate from the applicable table against your unadjusted basis, which is your cost minus any first-year expensing deduction or special depreciation allowance *(43.4)*. The deduction from the table is allowed only to the extent that it does not exceed the annual deduction ceiling *(43.4)*.

If business use initially exceeds 50% and accelerated MACRS is claimed but business use drops to 50% or less before the end of the six-year recovery period, a recapture rule applies a straight-line computation retroactively; *see 43.10.*

Straight-line year—	Half-year convention rate—
1	10%
2	20
3	20
4	20
5	20
6	10

EXAMPLE

In April 2002, you place in service an automobile which cost $24,000. You used it 40% for business. The depreciable basis is $9,600 (40% of $24,000). The depreciation deduction in 2002 is $960 (10% of $9,600) if the half-year convention applies. It is less than the annual deduction ceiling of $1,224 (40% of the $3,060 annual ceiling; *see 43.4*).

Straight-Line Mid-Quarter Convention*

Placed in service in—

Year	First Quarter	Second Quarter	Third Quarter	Fourth Quarter
1	17.50%	12.50%	7.50%	2.50%
2	20.00	20.00	20.00	20.00
3	20.00	20.00	20.00	20.00
4	20.00	20.00	20.00	20.00
5	20.00	20.00	20.00	20.00
6	2.50	7.50	12.50	17.50

The deduction may not exceed the annual deduction ceiling; see 43.4.

EXAMPLE

In 2002, you place in service a car costing $15,000 used 40% for business. Assume the mid-quarter convention applies. Depending on the applicable quarter, the deduction is listed below, figured on a basis of $6,000 ($15,000 × 40%). The first-year ceiling at 40% business use is $1,224 ($3,060 × 40%). The ceiling does not apply because the mid-quarter rates provide a lower deduction.

Quarter	Deduction
1	$1,050 ($6,000 × 17.5%)
2	750 ($6,000 × 12.5%)
3	450 ($6,000 × 7.5%)
4	150 ($6,000 × 2.5%)

43.7 Depreciation for Year in Which Car Is Disposed Of

If you dispose of your car before the end of the six-year recovery period, you are allowed a partial depreciation deduction for the year of disposition. The deduction depends on the depreciation method and convention being used.

If you were depreciating the car under the half-year convention *(43.5)*, you may claim for the year of disposition 50% of the deduction that would be allowed for the full year under the 200% or 150% declining balance method, or the straight-line method.

If you were depreciating the car under the mid-quarter convention *(43.5)*, your deduction for the year of disposition depends on the month of disposition. You deduct 87.5% of the full-year mid-quarter convention deduction *(43.5)* if the disposition occurred in October–December. If the disposition is in July–September, 62.5% of the full year's deduction is allowed. Your deduction is 37.5% of the full-year deduction if the disposition is in April–June, or 12.5% of the full-year deduction if the disposition is in January–March.

EXAMPLE

In December 2000, you bought a car costing $20,000 that you used exclusively for business until you sold it in April 2002. For 2000, you claimed a $1,000 deduction (5% fourth-quarter rate × $20,000) using the 200% declining balance rate and the mid-quarter convention *(43.5)*; this was less than the $3,060 ceiling for cars placed in service during 2000. The deduction for 2001 was $5,000. Under the fourth-quarter rate table, a deduction of $7,600 would have been allowed (38% rate for second year × $20,000) but the deduction was limited to $4,900, the ceiling *(43.4)* in the second year for a car placed in service during 2000.

For 2002, the year of disposition, the full-year deduction would be $2,950. The $2,950 annual ceiling (third-year ceiling for cars placed in service in 2000) is less than the $4,560 deduction (22.80% × $20,000) allowed under the mid-quarter convention table *(43.5)*. Since the car was disposed of in April, you may deduct 37.5% of $2,950, or $1,106, on your 2002 return.

43.8 Depreciation After Recovery Period Ends

If your business use of a car during the recovery period is 100% and your deductions are limited by the annual ceilings *(43.4)*, any remaining basis that was not deducted because of the ceilings may be depreciated in the years after the end of the recovery period.

If the car was used less than 100% for business, any unrecovered basis may be deductible, but to determine unrecovered basis, original basis must be reduced by the depreciation that would have been allowed had the car been used 100% for business.

EXAMPLE

In January 1996 you bought a car costing $28,600 that you used 100% for business every year from 1996 through 2001. Your depreciation deductions for the six-year recovery period under the 200% declining balance method were limited because of the annual deduction ceilings (*see* the ceilings at *43.4*). For 1996 through 2000, you deducted the annual ceiling

⚠ *Caution*

Basis Reduced by Depreciation

The basis of a car is reduced by the full amount of depreciation that is allowable, whether or not a full deduction is actually claimed. For example, in 2002 you place in service a car costing $25,000, used 80% for business. Assuming the half-year convention applies, the unadjusted basis of the car is reduced by $3,060, the depreciation that would have been allowed in 2002 for 100% business use, and not by the $2,448 depreciation deduction actually allowed (80% of business use × $3,060 maximum limit for 2002).

amounts. For 2001, your deduction was based on the MACRS half-year convention rate table *(43.5)* because this amount was less than the annual ceiling. Total depreciation deductions for 1996–2001 were $16,107, as shown below.

Year	200% rate deduction	Annual ceiling	Allowable deduction
1996	$5,720 (20% × $28,600)	3,060	$3,060
1997	9,152 (32% × $28,600)	4,900	4,900
1998	5,491 (19.20% × $28,600)	2,950	2,950
1999	3,295 (11.52% × $28,600)	1,775	1,775
2000	3,295 (11.52% × $28,600)	1,775	1,775
2001	1,647 (5.76% × $28,600)	1,775	1,647

At the beginning of 2002, your unrecovered basis in the car is $12,493 (the original basis of $28,600 minus the $16,107 of depreciation deductions allowed from 1996 through 2001). If you continue to use the car 100% for business in 2002 and later years, you can deduct $1,775 in 2002 and also in later years until the $12,493 of unrecovered basis is used up.

If you had *not* used the car for business 100% of the time in all prior years, your unrecovered basis would still be $12,493. That is because for purposes of figuring unrecovered basis, you must reduce original basis by the depreciation that would have been allowed based on 100% business use. For years after 2001 in which business use is 100%, deductions of $1,775 are allowed until the unrecovered basis is used up. In years of partial business use, the deduction is limited to $1,775 multiplied by the business-use percentage.

43.9 Trade-in of Business Auto

No gain or loss is recognized on a trade-in of a business auto for another business auto. Depreciation for an auto acquired in a trade-in after January 2, 2001, is generally figured as if you were still depreciating the auto that you gave up in the exchange, using the unadjusted basis and remaining recovery period of the old car. If you made an additional payment on the trade-in, the increased basis attributable to that investment is depreciated as a separate asset. *See* IRS Publication 463 for examples illustrating these rules.

43.10 Recapture of Deductions on Business Auto

If you use your car more than 50% for business in the year you place it in service, you may use MACRS accelerated rates; *see 43.5*. If business use drops to 50% or less in the second, third, fourth, fifth, or sixth year, earlier MACRS deductions must be recaptured and reported as ordinary income. In the year in which business use drops to 50% or less, you must recapture excess depreciation for all prior years. Excess depreciation is the difference between: (1) the MACRS deductions allowed in previous years, including the first-year expensing deduction and bonus first-year depreciation allowance *(43.4)*, if any, and (2) the amount of depreciation that would have been allowed if you claimed straight-line depreciation based on a six-year recovery period. *See 43.6* for straight-line rates.

The recapture rules do not apply if you elected straight-line recovery instead of applying accelerated MACRS rates.

Recapture is reported on Form 4797, which must be attached to Form 1040. The 50% business-use test and recapture rule apply to trucks and airplanes in addition to cars, but *see* the list of exceptions for taxicabs and other specialty vehicles at *43.3*.

Any recaptured amount increases the basis of the property. To compute depreciation for the year in which business use drops to 50% or less and for later years within the six-year straight-line recovery period, you apply the straight-line rates shown at *43.6*.

EXAMPLE

On June 25, 1998, you bought a car for $11,000 that you used exclusively for business in 1998, 1999, 2000, and 2001. The half-year convention applied to your MACRS deductions *(43.5)*. The deductions figured under the half-year convention table ($2,200 for 1998, $3,520 for 1999, $2,112 for 2000, and $1,267 for 2001) applied as they were less than the annual ceilings for those years ($3,160, $5,000, $2,950, and $1,775, respectively). During 2002, you used the car 40% for business and 60% for personal purposes. As you did not meet the more-than-50%-business-use test in 2002, excess depreciation of $1,399 is recaptured and reported on Form 4797 for 2002:

Total MACRS depreciation claimed (1998–2001)		$9,099
Total straight-line depreciation (43.6) allowable:		
1998—10% of $11,000	$1,100	
1999—20% of $11,000	2,200	
2000—20% of $11,000	2,200	
2001—20% of $11,000	2,200	7,700
Excess depreciation recaptured		$1,399

Your 2002 depreciation deduction is $880 ($11,000 × 20% straight-line rate in fifth year × 40% business use).

The amount of recaptured depreciation increases the adjusted basis for purposes of computing gain or loss on a disposition of the automobile.

43.11 Keeping Records of Business Use

Keep a log or diary or similar record of the business use of a car. Record the purpose of the business trips and mileage covered for business travel. In the record book, also note the odometer reading for the beginning and end of the taxable year. You need this data to prove business use. If you do not keep written records of business mileage and your return is examined, you will have to convince an IRS agent of your business mileage through oral testimony. Without written evidence, you may be unable to convince an IRS agent that you use the car for business travel or that you meet the business-use tests for claiming MACRS. You may also be subject to general negligence penalties for claiming deductions that you cannot prove you incurred.

Mileage records are not required for vehicles that are unlikely to be used for personal purposes, such as delivery trucks with seating only for the driver.

Employees using company cars are not required to keep mileage records if (1) a written company policy allows them to use the car for commuting and no other personal driving other than personal errands while commuting home or (2) a written company policy bars all personal driving except for minor stops, such as for lunch, between business travel. Owners, directors, and officers of the company generally do not qualify for exception (1).

43.12 Leased Business Autos: Deductions and Income

 Caution

Leased Auto

If in 2002 you leased for at least 30 days a car valued at over $15,500, and you deduct the lease charges as a business expense (43.12), you must reduce the deduction by an "income inclusion amount" based on an IRS table. If you claim the standard mileage allowance (43.1), the income inclusion rule does not apply. *See* IRS Publication 463 for details.

If you lease rather than purchase a car for business use, you may deduct the lease charges as a business expense deduction if you use the car exclusively for business. If you also use the car for personal driving, you may deduct only the lease payments allocated to business travel. Also keep a record of business use; *see 43.11.*

Added income. If in 2002 you lease a car for 30 days or more and the fair market value of the car at the beginning of the lease was over $15,500, you may have to report as income an amount based on an IRS table. This income rule applies if you deduct the business portion of your lease payments plus other operating costs; it does not apply if you claim the standard mileage allowance (43.1). On Schedule C (if self-employed) or Form 2106 (if an employee), the income inclusion amount reduces your deduction for lease payments so that it equals the amount that would be deductible as depreciation if you had bought the car outright. The income amount is reduced where you leased the car for less than the entire year or business use is less than 100%.

The lease tables, which are in IRS Publication 463, show income amounts for each year of the lease. Publication 463 also has tables showing income amounts for cars leased before 2002.

43.13 Deduction for Hybrid Vehicle

If you purchase a hybrid gas-electric automobile that has been certified by the IRS, you may claim a clean-burning fuel deduction even if it is used entirely for personal purposes. You must be the original owner and the deduction is allowed only for the first year of use.

The maximum deduction is $2,000 for the incremental cost of buying a car propelled by a clean-burning fuel. When this book went to press, three hybrid cars were certified for the maximum $2,000 deduction: Toyota Prius for model years 2001, 2002, and 2003; Honda Insight for model years 2000, 2001, and 2002 and Honda Civic Hybrid for model year 2003. If you bought a Honda Insight in 2000 or 2001 or Toyota Prius in 2001, you may file an amended return to claim the deduction and receive a refund.

For a personal-use car, the deduction is claimed as an adjustment to income on Line 34 of Form 1040 and so is allowed whether or not itemized deductions are claimed. Write "Clean-Fuel" next to the entry on Line 34.

Sole proprietors may claim the deduction provided the amount has not been claimed as a first-year expensing deduction (Section 179 deduction). The deduction is claimed as an "other expense" on Line 27 of Schedule C if the car is 100% used for business. If the car is only partly used for business, the business part is claimed on Line 27 of Schedule C and the personal part on Line 34 of Form 1040. For a qualifying truck or van between 10,000 and 26,000 pounds, the maximum deduction is $5,000 and for still heavier vehicles a $50,000 maximum deduction limit applies; *see* IRS Publication 535.

Gradual phaseout of deduction limit. The deduction limit is scheduled to be reduced by 25% in 2004, 50% in 2005, and 75% in 2006, and entirely eliminated in 2007.

Chapter 44

Sales of Business Property

On the sale of business assets, the tax treatment depends on the type of asset sold.

Inventory items: Profits are taxable as ordinary income; losses are fully deductible. Sales of merchandise are reported on Schedule C if you are self-employed or Schedule F if you are a farmer.

Depreciable property, such as buildings, machinery, and equipment: If you sell at a gain, the gain is taxable as ordinary income to the extent depreciation is recaptured under *44.1* and *44.2*. Any remaining gain may be treated as capital gain or ordinary income, depending on the Section 1231 computation at *44.8*. Losses may be deductible as ordinary losses; *see 44.8*. Sales are reported on Form 4797. Depreciable business equipment subject to recapture is described as a Section 1245 asset. Depreciable livestock is also a Section 1245 asset. Depreciable realty is generally described as a Section 1250 asset.

Land: If used in your business, capital gain or ordinary income may be realized under the rules of Section 1231; *see 44.8*. If land owned by your business is held for investment, gain or loss is subject to capital gain treatment. Schedule D is used to report the sale of capital assets.

44.1 Ordinary Income Recapture of Depreciation on Sale of Personal Property

On Form 4797, you report gain or loss on the sale of depreciable property. Gain realized on the sale of depreciable *personal property* (Section 1245 property) is treated as ordinary income to the extent the gain is attributed to depreciation deductions that reduced basis. In other words, the depreciation deductions are "recaptured" as ordinary income. If gain exceeds the amount of depreciation subject to recapture, the excess may be capital gain under Section 1231; *see 44.8.*

Gain on the sale of real estate placed in service before 1987 may be subject to depreciation recapture as discussed in *44.2.*

Gain subject to recapture for Section 1245 property is limited to the lower of (1) the amount realized on the sale less adjusted basis or (2) recomputed basis less the adjusted basis. Recomputed basis is adjusted basis increased by depreciation deductions allowed or allowable. Generally, the depreciation deduction taken into account for each year is the amount allowed or allowable, whichever is greater. However, for purposes of figuring what portion of the gain is treated as ordinary income under the recapture rules (but not for purposes of figuring gain or loss), the depreciation taken into account for any year will be the amount actually "allowed" on your prior returns under a proper depreciation method, rather than the amount "allowable," if the allowed deduction is smaller and you can prove its amount.

The adjusted basis of personal property depreciable under ACRS, such as business equipment and machinery, is fixed as of the beginning of the year of disposition. However, property depreciated under MACRS is subject to the convention rules so that partial depreciation under the applicable convention is allowed in the year of sale; this year of sale depreciation reduces adjusted basis.

Where basis was reduced by an investment credit for property placed in service after 1982, the basis reduction is treated as a depreciation deduction when figuring recapture; *see* Form 4797.

Caution

Dispositions Other than Sales
Exchanges of property *(6.1)* and involuntary conversions *(18.19)* may result in recapture of depreciation. For dispositions that are not sales, exchanges, or involuntary conversions, the amount of recapture is all depreciation claimed, but not in excess of the difference between adjusted basis and the smaller of fair market value at disposition or original cost.

EXAMPLE

In 2000, you placed in service equipment (five-year property) costing $10,000. In 2000 you deducted depreciation of $2,000 and in 2001 you deducted $3,200. In January 2002, you sell it for $6,000. The MACRS deduction allowed for 2002, the year of sale, is $960 (19.20% × $10,000 ÷ 2). The adjusted basis is $3,840 ($10,000 – $6,160 total depreciation). Recomputed basis is $10,000 ($3,840 + $6,160). The amount of recapture is the lower of—
1. $6,160, the recomputed basis of $10,000 less adjusted basis of $3,840; or
2. $2,160, the amount realized of $6,000 less adjusted basis of $3,840.

The lower amount of $2,160 is recaptured as ordinary income on Part III of Form 4797.

44.2 Ordinary Income Recapture on Depreciable Realty

All or part of gain on the sale of depreciable real property may be attributable to depreciation deductions that reduced the basis of the property. For example, you bought an office building for $300,000. You claimed depreciation deductions of $100,000 that reduced the basis of the building to $200,000. If you sell the building for $280,000, you will realize a gain of $80,000 ($280,000 – $200,000). The gain of $80,000 is attributable to the depreciation deductions that reduced basis to $200,000. Under the tax law, all or part of such gain may be treated as recaptured depreciation or unrecaptured Section 1250 gain.

Unrecaptured Section 1250 gain. Gain on the sale of depreciable realty held long term that is attributible to depreciation *not* subject to the ordinary income recapture rules discussed below is unrecaptured Section 1250 gain. Such gain is subject to a 25% capital gain rate where your top tax bracket exceeds 15%. Unrecaptured Section 1250 gain may be realized on the sale of depreciable property regardless of when the property was acquired. The 25% rate is applied on the Schedule D Tax Worksheet included in the Schedule D instructions.

Recaptured depreciation. Recaptured depreciation may be realized only on the sale of certain real property acquired before 1987. Gain attributed to recaptured depreciation is taxable as ordinary income. Where only part of gain attributed to depreciation is treated as recaptured depreciation, the balance is treated as unrecaptured Section 1250 gain.

Ordinary income recapture may apply to Section 1250 realty placed in service before 1987. There is no ordinary income recapture on depreciable realty placed in service after 1986 because such realty is subject to straight-line MACRS depreciation *(42.13).* Section 1250 property includes buildings and structural components, *except* for elevators and escalators or other tangible property used as an integral part of manufacturing, production, or extraction, or of furnishing transportation, electrical energy, water, gas, sewage disposal services, or communications. Property may initially be Section 1250 property and then, on a change of use, become Section 1245 property *(44.1)*. Such property may not be reconverted to Section 1250 property.

Depreciation claimed on realty during the years 1964 through 1969. Depreciation claimed during this period is not recaptured.

Depreciation claimed after 1969 for realty placed in service before 1981. For nonresidential realty, 100 percent of the depreciation claimed after 1969 in excess of straight-line recovery is subject to recapture but not in excess of the actual gain.

For residential rental property, there is no recapture of excess depreciation (over straight-line) claimed after 1969 and before 1976. Real property is considered residential rental property if 80% or more of gross income is from dwelling units. One hundred percent of the excess depreciation claimed after 1975 is subject to recapture. Part III of Form 4797 is used to compute the amount of depreciation recapture that is to be reported as ordinary income.

Depreciation claimed on realty placed in service after 1980 and before 1987. For real property placed in service after 1980 and before 1987 that was subject to ACRS, adjusted basis for computing gain or loss is the adjusted basis at the start of the year reduced by the ACRS deduction allowed for the number of months the realty is in service in the year of disposition; *see 42.16*. The recapture rules distinguish between residential and nonresidential property.

If the prescribed accelerated method is used to recover the cost of *nonresidential* property, all gain on the disposition of the realty is recaptured as ordinary income to the extent of recovery allowances previously taken. Thus, nonresidential realty will be treated in the same way as personal property *(44.1)* for purposes of recapture if the accelerated recovery allowance was claimed. If the straight-line method was elected, there is no recapture; all gain is subject to the netting rules of Section 1231 *(44.8)*.

If accelerated cost recovery is used for a *nonresidential* building and straight-line depreciation is used for a substantial improvement to that building that you are allowed to depreciate separately *(42.16)*, all gain on a disposition of the entire building is treated as ordinary income to the extent of the accelerated cost recovery claimed. Remaining gain is subject to the rules for Section 1231 assets *(44.8)*.

For *residential* real estate, there is ordinary income recapture to the extent the depreciation allowed under the prescribed accelerated method exceeds the recovery that would have been allowable if the straight-line method over the ACRS recovery period had been used. If the straight-line method was elected, there is no recapture. All gain is subject to Section 1231 netting *(44.8)*.

For *low-income rental housing,* the same rule as for residential realty applies except that recapture is phased out at the rate of one percentage point per month for property held at least 100 months, so that there is no recapture of cost recovery deductions for property held at least 200 months (16 years and 8 months).

Caution

Installment Sale

If you sell property on the installment basis, the first-year expensing deduction claimed for the property in a prior year is recaptured in the year of sale on Form 4797. An installment sale does not defer recapture of the first-year deduction; *see 44.6*.

44.3 Recapture of First-Year Expensing

On Form 4797, the first-year expensing deduction (Section 179) is treated as depreciation for purposes of recapture. When expensed property is sold or exchanged, gain is ordinary income to the extent of the first-year expense deduction plus ACRS or MACRS deductions, if any; *see 44.1*.

Expensing deductions are also subject to recapture if property placed in service after 1986 is not used more than 50% of the time for business in any year before the end of the recovery period. The amount recaptured is the excess of the first-year *expensing* deduction over the amount of depreciation that would have been claimed in prior years and in the recapture year without expensing.

Automobiles and other "listed property." If the more-than-50%-business-use test for a business automobile or other "listed property" such as certain computers *(see 42.10)* is not met in a year after the auto or other "listed property" is placed in service and before the end of the recovery period, any first-year expensing deduction is subject to recapture on Form 4797; *see* the Example at *43.10*.

44.4 Gifts and Inheritances of Depreciable Property

Gifts and charitable donations of depreciable property may be affected by the recapture rules. On the gift of depreciable property, the ordinary income potential of the depreciation carries over into the hands of the donee. When the donee later sells the property at a profit, he or she will realize ordinary income to the extent described in *44.1*. A person receiving a gift of low-income housing property includes in the holding period the period for which the donor held the property for purposes of applying the 200-month phaseout of recapture rule *(44.2)*.

On the donation of depreciable property, the amount of the contribution deduction is reduced by the amount that would be taxed as ordinary income had the donor sold the equipment at its fair market value.

The transfer of depreciable property to an heir through inheritance is not a taxable event for recapture purposes. The ordinary income potential does not carry over to the heir because his or her basis is usually fixed as of the date of the decedent's death.

Important: A gift of depreciable property subject to a mortgage may be taxed to the extent that the liability exceeds the basis of the property; *see 14.6* and *31.15*.

44.5 Involuntary Conversions and Tax-Free Exchanges

Involuntary conversions. Gain may be taxed as ordinary income in either of the following two cases: (1) you do not buy qualified replacement property or (2) you buy a qualified replacement, but the cost of the replacement is less than the amount realized on the conversion; *see 18.23*. The amount taxable as ordinary income may not exceed the amount of gain that is normally taxed under involuntary conversion rules when the replacement cost is less than the amount realized on the conversion. Also, the amount of ordinary income is increased by the value of any nondepreciable property that is bought as qualified replacement property, such as the purchase of 80% or more of stock in a company that owns property similar to the converted property.

Distributions by a partnership to a partner. A distribution of depreciable property by a partnership to a partner does not result in ordinary income to the distributee at the time of the distribution. But the partner assumes the ordinary income potential of the depreciation deduction taken by the partnership on the property. When he or she later disposes of the property, ordinary income may be realized.

44.6 Installment Sale of Depreciable Property

All depreciation recapture income (including the first-year expensing deduction) is fully taxable in the year of sale, without regard to the time of payment. This rule does not apply to installment sales made after June 6, 1984, under a contract binding on March 22, 1984, and all times thereafter.

If you are reporting on an installment basis a profitable sale of depreciable property made before June 7, 1984, "recaptured" ordinary income is reported before any of the capital gain is reported. You do not allocate the profit element of each installment payment between ordinary income and capital gain. As installments are received, you report all of the ordinary income until that amount is exhausted.

Recapture is figured on Form 4797.

44.7 Sale of a Proprietorship

The sale of a sole proprietorship is not considered as the sale of a business unit but as sales of individual business assets. Each sale is reported separately on your tax return.

A purchase of a business involves the purchase of various individual business assets of the business. To force buyers and sellers to follow the same allocation rules, current law requires both the buyer and the seller to allocate the purchase price of a business among the transferred assets using a residual method formula. Allocations are based on the proportion of sales price to an asset's fair market value and they are made in a specific order set out on Form 8594.

44.8 Property Used in a Business (Section 1231 Assets)

Form 4797 is used to report the sale or exchange of Section 1231 assets. The following properties used in a business are considered "Section 1231 assets":

- Depreciable assets such as buildings, machinery, and other equipment held more than one year. Depreciable rental property fits in this category if held more than one year.
- Land (including growing crops and water rights underlying farmland) held more than one year.
- Timber, coal, or domestic iron ore subject to special capital gain treatment.
- Leaseholds held more than one year.
- An unharvested crop on farmlands, if the crop and land are sold, exchanged, or involuntarily converted at the same time and to the same person and the land has been held more than one year. Such property is not included here if you retain an option to reacquire the land.
- Cattle and horses held for draft, breeding, dairy, or sporting purposes for at least 24 months.
- Livestock (other than cattle and horses) held for draft, breeding, dairy, or sporting purposes for at least 12 months. Poultry is not treated as livestock for purposes of Section 1231.

Caution

Tax–Free Exchanges
Ordinary income generally is not realized on a tax-free exchange or trade-in of the same type of property (unless some gain is taxed because the exchange is accompanied by "boot" *(6.3)* such as money). The ordinary income potential is assumed in the basis of the new property. However, where depreciable realty acquired before 1987 is exchanged for land, the amount of any depreciation recapture is immediately taxable in the year of the exchange.

Caution

Capital Gain or Ordinary Loss
Profitable sales and involuntary conversions of Section 1231 assets are generally treated as capital gain, except for profits on equipment *(44.1)* and real estate allocated to recaptured depreciation *(44.2)*, and losses are deducted as ordinary loss. However, the exact tax result depends on the net profit and loss realized for all sales of such property made during the tax year. Under the netting rules explained at *44.8,* the net result of these sales determines the tax treatment of each individual sale. In making the computation on Form 4797, you must also consider losses and gains from casualty, theft, and other involuntary conversions involving business and investment property held more than one year. Follow the Form 4797 instructions.

Section 1231 netting. On Form 4797, you combine all losses and gains, except gains allocated to depreciation recapture, from:

- The sale of Section 1231 assets (from the list at the beginning of this section).
- The involuntary conversion of Section 1231 assets and capital assets held for more than one year for business or investment purposes. You include casualty and theft losses incurred on business or investment property held for more than one year. However, there is an exception if losses exceed gains from casualties or thefts in one taxable year.

Involuntary conversions of capital assets held for personal purposes are not subject to a Section 1231 computation but are subject to a separate computation; *see 18.25.*

Result of netting. A net gain on Section 1231 assets from Form 4797 is entered on Schedule D as a long-term capital gain unless the recapture rule (*see* the Caution on this page) for net ordinary losses applies. A net loss on Section 1231 assets is combined on Form 4797 with ordinary income from depreciation recapture *(44.1)* and with ordinary gains and losses from the sale of business property that does not qualify for Section 1231 netting.

Installment sale. Gain realized on the installment sale of business or income-producing property held for more than a year may be capital gain one year and ordinary income another year. Actual treatment in each year depends on the net result of all sales, including installment payments received in that year; also *see 44.6.*

Losses exceed gains from casualties or thefts. On Form 4684, you must compute the net financial result from all involuntary conversions arising from fire, storm, or other casualty or theft of assets used in your business and capital assets held for business or income-producing purposes and held more than one year. The purpose of the computation is to determine whether these involuntary conversions enter into the above Section 1231 computation. If the net result is a gain, all of the assets enter into the Section 1231 computation. If the net result is a loss, then these assets do not enter into the computation; the losses are deducted separately as casualty losses, and the gains reported separately as ordinary income. If you incur only losses, the losses similarly do not enter into the Section 1231 computation.

> **EXAMPLE**
>
> You suffer an uninsured fire loss of $2,000 on business equipment and gain of $1,000 on other insured investment property damaged by a storm. All of the property was held more than one year. Because loss exceeds gain, neither transaction enters into a Section 1231 computation. The gain is reported as ordinary income and the loss is deducted as an ordinary loss. The effect is a net $1,000 loss deduction. If the figures were reversed, that is, if the gain were $2,000 and the loss $1,000, both assets would enter into the Section 1231 computation. If only the fire loss occurred, the loss would be treated as a casualty loss and would not enter into the Section 1231 computation.

44.9 Sale of Property Used for Business and Personal Purposes

One sale will be reported as two separate sales for tax purposes when you sell a car or any other equipment used for business and personal purposes, or in some cases where a sold residence (*see 29.7*) was used partly as a residence and partly as a place of business or to produce rent income.

You allocate the sales price and the basis of the property between the business portion and the personal portion. The allocation is based on use. For example, with a car, the allocation is based on mileage used in business and personal driving.

> **EXAMPLE**
>
> Two partners bought an airplane for about $54,000. They used approximately 75% of its flying time for personal flights and 25% for business flights. After using the plane for eight years, they sold it for about $35,000. Depreciation taken on the business part of the plane amounted to $13,000. The partners figured they incurred a loss of $6,000 on the sale. The IRS, allocating the proceeds and basis between business and personal use, claimed they realized a profit of $8,250 on the business part of the plane and a nondeductible loss of $14,250 on the personal part. The allocation was as follows:

 Caution

Recapture of Net Ordinary Losses
Net Section 1231 gain is not treated as capital gain but as ordinary income to the extent of net Section 1231 losses realized in the five most recent prior taxable years. Losses are recaptured in chronological order on Form 4797. Losses that have already been "recaptured" under this rule in prior years are not taken into account.

	PARTNERS' CLAIM	IRS POSITION BUSINESS (25%)	PERSONAL (75%)
Original cost	$54,000	$13,500	$40,500
Depreciation	13,000	13,000	
Adjusted basis	41,000	500	40,500
Selling price	35,000	8,750	26,250
Gain (Nondeductible loss)	($6,000)	$8,250	($14,250)

The partners argued that the IRS could not split the sale into two separate sales. They sold only one airplane and therefore there was only one sale. A federal district court and appeals court disagreed and held that the IRS method of allocation is practical and fair.

44.10 Should You Trade in Business Equipment?

The purchase of new business equipment is often partially financed by trading in old equipment. For tax purposes, a trade-in may not be a good decision. If the market value of the equipment is below its adjusted basis, it may be preferable to sell the equipment to realize an immediate deductible loss. You may not deduct a loss on a trade-in. However, if you do trade, the potential deduction reflected in the cost basis of the old equipment is not forfeited. The undepreciated basis of the old property becomes part of the basis of the new property and may be depreciated. Therefore, in deciding whether to trade or sell where a loss may be realized, determine whether you will get a greater tax reduction by taking an immediate loss on a sale or by claiming larger depreciation deductions.

If the fair market value of the old equipment exceeds its adjusted basis, you have a potential gain. To defer tax on this gain, you may want to trade the equipment in for new equipment. Your decision to sell or trade will generally be based on a comparison between (1) tax imposed on an immediate sale and larger depreciation deductions taken on the cost basis of the new property, and (2) the tax consequences of a trade-in in which the tax is deferred but reduced depreciation deductions are taken on a lower cost basis of the property. In making this comparison, you will have to estimate your future income and tax rates. Also pay attention to the possibility that gain on a sale may be taxed as ordinary income under the depreciation recapture rules; *see 44.1*.

The tax consequences of a trade-in may not be avoided by first selling the used property to the dealer who sells you the new property. The IRS will disregard the sale made to the same dealer from whom you purchase the new equipment. The two transactions will be treated as one trade-in.

44.11 Corporate Liquidation

Liquidation of a corporation and distribution of its assets for your stock is generally subject to capital gain or loss treatment. For example, on a corporate liquidation, you receive property worth $10,000 from the corporation. Assume the basis of your shares, which you have held long term, is $6,000. You have realized a long-term gain of $4,000.

If you incur legal expenses in pressing payment of a claim, you treat the fee as a capital expense, according to the IRS. The Tax Court and an appeals court hold that the fee is deductible as an expense incurred to earn income; the deduction is subject to the 2% adjusted gross income (AGI) floor discussed at *19.1*.

If you recover a judgment against the liquidator of a corporation for misuse of corporate funds, the judgment is considered part of the amount you received on liquidation and gives you capital gain, not ordinary income.

If you paid a corporate debt after liquidation, the payment reduces the gain realized on the corporate liquidation in the earlier year; thus, in effect, it is a capital loss.

If the corporation distributes liquidating payments over a period of years, gain is not reported until the distributions exceed the adjusted basis of your stock.

Chapter 45

Figuring Self-Employment Tax

Self-employment tax provides funds for Social Security and Medicare benefits. The self-employment tax is calculated on Schedule SE. You are required to prepare Schedule SE if you have self-employment net earnings of $400 or more in 2002, but you will not incur the tax unless your net self-employment earnings exceed $433.13. The tax is added to your income tax liability. When preparing your estimated tax liability, you must also include an estimate of self-employment tax; *see* Chapter 27.

On Schedule SE, self-employment income is reduced by a deduction reflected in the decimal of .9235 listed on the form. You also deduct 50% of the self-employment tax on Line 29 of Form 1040.

For 2002, the self-employment tax of 15.3% consists of the following two rates: 12.4% for Social Security and 2.9% for Medicare. After multiplying the net earnings by .9235, the combined 15.3% rate applies to a taxable earnings base of $84,900 or less; the 2.9% rate applies to all taxable earnings exceeding $84,900.

You are required to pay self-employment tax on self-employment income even after you retire and receive Social Security benefits.

45.1 What Is Self-Employment Income?

On Schedule SE, your self-employment income is generally your net profit from your business or profession whether you participate in its activities full or part time. Net profit is generally the amount shown on Line 31 of Schedule C (or Line 3 of Schedule C-EZ) if you are a sole proprietor. If you are a partner, net earnings subject to self-employment tax are taken from Line 15a, Schedule K-1 of Form 1065. If you are a farmer, net farm profit is shown on Line 36, Schedule F.

If you have more than one self-employed operation, your net profit from all the operations is combined. A loss in one self-employed business will reduce the income from another business. You file separate Schedules C for each operation and one Schedule SE showing the combined income (less losses, if any). Contributions to your own Keogh plan or SEP retirement account do not reduce the net earnings subject to self-employment tax.

Married couples. Where you and your spouse *each* have self-employment income, each spouse must figure separate self-employment income on a separate schedule. Each pays the tax on the separate self-employment income. Both schedules are attached to the joint return.

If you live in a community property state, business income is not treated as community property for self-employment tax purposes. The spouse who is actually carrying on the business is subject to self-employment tax on the earnings.

Exceptions. The following types of income or items are *not* included as self-employment income on Schedule SE:

1. Rent from real estate is generally not self-employment income. However, self-employment tax applies to the business income of a real estate dealer or income in a rental business where substantial services are rendered to the occupant, as in the leasing of—

- Rooms in a hotel or in a boarding house.
- Apartments, but only if extra services for the occupants' convenience, such as maid service or changing linens, are provided.
- Cabins or cabanas in tourist camps where you provide maid services, linens, utensils, and swimming, boating, fishing, and other facilities, for which you do not charge separately.
- Farmland in which the landlord materially participates in the actual production of the farm or in the management of production. For purposes of "material participation," the activities of a landlord's agent are not counted, only the landlord's actual participation.

2. Capital gains are not self-employment income. Self-employment income does *not* include gains from the sale of property unless it is inventory or held for sale to customers in the ordinary course of business. Thus, traders in securities *(30.23)* who buy and sell securities for their own account do not treat net gains or losses from the sales as self-employment income or loss. Dealers in commodities and options are subject to self-employment tax; *see* the chart in *45.6.*

3. Dividends and interest. Generally, dividends and interest are not self-employment income. However, dividends earned by a dealer in securities and interest on accounts receivable are treated as self-employment income if the securities are not being held for investment. A dealer is one who buys stock as inventory to sell to customers.

Net operating loss deduction. A loss carryover from past years does not reduce business income for self-employment tax purposes. Similarly, the personal exemption may not be used to reduce self-employment income.

Statutory employees. Wages of a statutory employee, such as a full-time life insurance salesperson *(40.6),* are not subject to self-employment tax, as Social Security and Medicare tax have been withheld.

Farmers. Cash or a payment in kind under the "Payment-in-Kind" program is considered earned income subject to self-employment tax.

Business interruption proceeds. The IRS and the Tax Court disagree over whether business interruption insurance proceeds must be reported as earnings subject to self-employment tax. The Tax Court held that insurance payments made to a grocer as compensation for lost earnings due to a fire were not subject to self-employment tax because the payment was not for actual services. The IRS refuses to follow the decision, holding that such payments represented income that would have been earned had business operations not been interrupted.

Filing Tip

Real Estate Investor
The owner of one office building who holds it for investment (rather than for sale in the ordinary course of business) is not a real estate dealer, but a real estate investor. If the only tenant services provided are heat, light, water, and trash collection, report the rental income and expenses on Schedule E. The activity is not a Schedule C business subject to self-employment tax.

Caution

Freelancer Fees
Fees you earn for freelance work as an independent contractor are business earnings reportable on Schedule C, and if you have a net profit, they are subject to self-employment tax on Schedule SE.

Filing Tip

Trader in Securities
If you are a trader in securities *(30.23),* gains or losses from your trading business are not subject to self-employment tax.

45.2 Partners Pay Self-Employment Tax

A general partner includes his or her share of partnership income or loss in net earnings from self-employment, including guaranteed payments. If your personal tax year is different from the partnership's tax year, you include your share of partnership income or loss for the partnership tax year ending within 2002.

A limited partner is not subject to self-employment tax on his or her share of partnership income except for guaranteed payments for services performed, which are subject to the tax.

If a general partner dies within the partnership's tax year, self-employment income includes his or her distributive share of the income earned by the partnership through the end of the month in which the death occurs. This is true even though his or her heirs or estate succeeds to the partnership rights. For this purpose, partnership income for the year is considered to be earned ratably each month.

Retirement payments from partnership. Retirement payments you receive from your partnership are *not* subject to self-employment tax if the following conditions are met:

1. The payments are made under a qualified written plan providing for periodic payments on retirement of partners with payments to continue until death.
2. You rendered no services in any business conducted by the partnership during the tax year of the partnership ending within or with your tax year.
3. By the end of the partnership's tax year, your share in the partnership's capital has been paid to you in full, and there is no obligation from the other partners to you other than with respect to the retirement payments under the plan.

45.3 Schedule SE

Schedule SE has an introductory "road map" designed to lead you to either the short or long version of Schedule SE. Once you pass through the road map, the preparation of either the short or long schedule is not difficult. In both versions, you multiply your net earnings by a decimal of .9235. Only 92.35% of net earnings is subject to the self-employment tax. The .9235 adjustment is the equivalent of a 7.65% reduction to net earnings, which, along with the income tax deduction for 50% of self-employment tax on Line 29 of Form 1040, attempts to place self-employed individuals on the same level as employees subject to FICA taxes.

The .9235 adjustment is made on Line 4 of either the short or long Schedule SE. For example, if your net profit reported on Line 31 of Schedule C is $120,000, the amount subject to self-employment tax after the adjustment is $110,820; *see* the filled-in short Schedule SE worksheet below, and *see* the next page for the long Schedule SE.

Filing Tip

50% Deduction

After you figure your self-employment tax on Schedule SE, deduct one-half of it on Line 29 of Form 1040.

Worksheet—Short Schedule SE

Section A—Short Schedule SE. Caution. Read above to see if you can use Short Schedule SE.

1	Net farm profit or (loss) from Schedule F, line 36, and farm partnerships, Schedule K-1 (Form 1065), line 15a	**1**	
2	Net profit or (loss) from Schedule C, line 31; Schedule C-EZ, line 3; Schedule K-1 (Form 1065), line 15a (other than farming); and Schedule K-1 (Form 1065-B), box 9. Ministers and members of religious orders, see page SE-1 for amounts to report on this line. See page SE-2 for other income to report	**2**	**120,000**
3	Combine lines 1 and 2	**3**	**120,000**
4	**Net earnings from self-employment.** Multiply line 3 by 92.35% (.9235). If less than $400, **do not** file this schedule; you do not owe self-employment tax . . . . ▶	**4**	**110,820**
5	**Self-employment tax.** If the amount on line 4 is: • $84,900 or less, multiply line 4 by 15.3% (.153). Enter the result here and on **Form 1040, line 56.** • More than $84,900, multiply line 4 by 2.9% (.029). Then, add $10,527.60 to the result. Enter the total here and on **Form 1040, line 56.**	**5**	**13,741**
6	**Deduction for one-half of self-employment tax.** Multiply line 5 by 50% (.5). Enter the result here and on **Form 1040, line 29** **6**	**6,871**	

For Paperwork Reduction Act Notice, see Form 1040 instructions.   Cat. No. 11358Z   **Schedule SE (Form 1040) 2002**

After the .9235 adjustment is made, net earnings are subject to the 12.4% and 2.9% rates, assuming the resulting net earnings are $400 or more. For 2002, the 12.4% Social Security rate applies to the first $84,900 of net earnings and the 2.9% Medicare rate applies to all of the net earnings.

45.4 How Wages Affect Self-Employment Tax

If you have both a net profit from self-employment and also wage and/or tip income subject to FICA taxes (Social Security and Medicare), the amount of such FICA earnings may affect your self-employment tax liability.

If your 2002 FICA wages or tips were $84,900 or over, your net self-employment profit is subject only to the 2.9% Medicare rate.

If the total of your 2002 FICA wages (and tips) plus net earnings was $84,900 or less, your entire net earnings are subject to the 12.4% Social Security rate and the 2.9% Medicare rate.

If the total of your 2002 FICA wages (and tips) plus net earnings was over the $84,900 limit for the 12.4% Social Security rate, your net self-employment earnings shown on Line 6 of long Schedule SE (after the .9235 adjustment) are subject to the 12.4% rate only to the extent of the excess of $84,900 over your FICA wages or tips. The 2.9% Medicare rate applies to the entire amount of net self-employment earnings. *See* the following Example and the filled-in long Schedule SE worksheet below.

EXAMPLE

You earn a salary of $30,000 in 2002 and have a net profit from self-employment of $60,000. As shown on the long Schedule SE worksheet below, the 12.4% rate applies to the smaller of Line 6 or Line 9. Here, the smaller amount is $54,900 shown on Line 9, the excess of $84,900 over the $30,000 of wages. The 2.9% rate applies to the total net earnings of $55,410 (after the .9235 adjustment) shown on Line 6.

12.4% × $54,900	$6,808
2.9% × $55,410	+ 1,607
	8,415

Your self-employment tax liability is $8,415. One-half of that, or $4,208, is deductible on Line 29 of Form 1040.

Worksheet—Long Schedule SE

Section B—Long Schedule SE

Part I Self-Employment Tax

Note. If your only income subject to self-employment tax is **church employee income**, skip lines 1 through 4b. Enter -0- on line 4c and go to line 5a. Income from services you performed as a minister or a member of a religious order **is not** church employee income. See page SE-1.

A	If you are a minister, member of a religious order, or Christian Science practitioner **and** you filed Form 4361, but you had $400 or more of **other** net earnings from self-employment, check here and continue with Part I . . . . . . ▶ ☐		
1	Net farm profit or (loss) from Schedule F, line 36, and farm partnerships, Schedule K-1 (Form 1065), line 15a. **Note.** Skip this line if you use the farm optional method. See page SE-3 . .	**1**	
2	Net profit or (loss) from Schedule C, line 31; Schedule C-EZ, line 3; Schedule K-1 (Form 1065), line 15a (other than farming); and Schedule K-1 (Form 1065-B), box 9. Ministers and members of religious orders, see page SE-1 for amounts to report on this line. See page SE-2 for other income to report. **Note.** Skip this line if you use the nonfarm optional method. See page SE-3.	**2**	60,000
3	Combine lines 1 and 2	**3**	60,000
4a	If line 3 is more than zero, multiply line 3 by 92.35% (.9235). Otherwise, enter amount from line 3	**4a**	55,410
b	If you elect one or both of the optional methods, enter the total of lines 15 and 17 here . .	**4b**	
c	Combine lines 4a and 4b. If less than $400, **do not** file this schedule; you do not owe self-employment tax. **Exception.** If less than $400 and you had **church employee income,** enter -0- and continue ▶	**4c**	55,410
5a	Enter your **church employee income** from Form W-2. **Caution.** See page SE-1 for definition of church employee income **5a**		
b	Multiply line 5a by 92.35% (.9235). If less than $100, enter -0-	**5b**	
6	**Net earnings from self-employment.** Add lines 4c and 5b	**6**	55,410
7	Maximum amount of combined wages and self-employment earnings subject to social security tax or the 6.2% portion of the 7.65% railroad retirement (tier 1) tax for 2002 . . .	**7**	84,900 00
8a	Total social security wages and tips (total of boxes 3 and 7 on Form(s) W-2) and railroad retirement (tier 1) compensation **8a** 30,000		
b	Unreported tips subject to social security tax (from Form 4137, line 9) **8b**		
c	Add lines 8a and 8b	**8c**	30,000
9	Subtract line 8c from line 7. If zero or less, enter -0- here and on line 10 and go to line 11 . ▶	**9**	54,900
10	Multiply the **smaller** of line 6 or line 9 by 12.4% (.124)	**10**	6,808
11	Multiply line 6 by 2.9% (.029)	**11**	1,607
12	**Self-employment tax.** Add lines 10 and 11. Enter here and on **Form 1040, line 56**	**12**	8,415
13	**Deduction for one-half of self-employment tax.** Multiply line 12 by 50% (.5). Enter the result here and on **Form 1040, line 29** **13** 4,208		

Schedule SE (Form 1040) 2002

Filing Tip

Optional Method

Electing the optional method to increase the base for Social Security coverage may also increase earned income for dependent care and earned income credit purposes.

45.5 Optional Method If 2002 Was a Low-Income or Loss Year

The law provides a small increased tax base for Social Security coverage if you have a low net profit or loss.

The increased tax base is called the optional method. One optional method is for nonfarm self-employment and another for farm income. You may not use the optional method to report an amount less than your actual net earnings from self-employment.

Nonfarm method. You may use the nonfarm optional method for 2002 if you meet all the following tests:

Test 1. Your net earnings (profit) from nonfarm self-employment on Line 31 of Schedule C, Line 3 of Schedule C-EZ, or Line 15a of Schedule K-1 (Form 1065) are less than $1,733 (.9235 × $1,733 = $1,600 maximum income subject to the optional method).

Test 2. Your net earnings from nonfarm self-employment are less than 72.189% of the total gross income you made from nonfarm self-employment.

Test 3. You had net earnings from self-employment of $400 or more in at least two of the following years: 1999, 2000, and 2001.

Test 4. You have not previously used this method for more than four years. There is a five-year lifetime limit for use of the nonfarm optional base. The years do not have to be consecutive.

Nonfarm income of $2,400 or less. If your gross income from all nonfarm trades or businesses is $2,400 or less and you meet the four tests just discussed, you may report two-thirds of the gross income from your nonfarm business as net earnings from self-employment.

EXAMPLES

1. Brown had net earnings from self-employment of $800 in 2000 and $900 in 2001 and so meets Test 3 above. In 2002, she has gross nonfarm self-employment income of $2,100 and net nonfarm self-employment earnings of $1,200. Net earnings from self-employment of $1,200 are less than $1,733 (Test 1 above) and also less than 72.189% of $2,100 gross income, or $1,516 (Test 2). Brown may figure self-employment tax on $1,400 ($\frac{2}{3}$ of $2,100).

2. Same facts as in Example 1, but Brown has a net self-employment loss of $700. She may elect to report $1,400 ($\frac{2}{3}$ of $2,100) as net earnings under the optional method.

3. Smith had gross nonfarm income of $1,000 and net nonfarm self-employment earnings of $800. He may not use the optional method because net earnings of $800 are not less than 72.189% of $1,000 gross income, or $722.

4. Jones has gross nonfarm income of $525 and net nonfarm self-employment earnings of $175. Jones may not use the optional method because two-thirds of his gross income, or $350, is less than the minimum income of $400 required to be subject to the self-employment tax.

Nonfarm income over $2,400. If your gross income from all nonfarm businesses exceeds $2,400, and you meet the four tests just discussed, you may report $1,600 as your net earnings from nonfarm self-employment.

EXAMPLES

1. White had net earnings from self-employment in 1999 of $8,500; in 2000, $10,500; and in 2001, $9,500. His 2002 gross nonfarm income is $12,000 and net nonfarm earnings are $1,200. Because his net earnings of $1,200 from self-employment are less than $1,733 and also less than 72.189% of his gross income, he may report $1,600 as his net earnings from self-employment.

2. Same facts as in Example 1, but assume net earnings for 2002 are $1,800. White may not use the optional method because his actual net earnings of $1,800 from self-employment are not less than $1,733. He reports $1,800 as net earnings using the regular method.

3. Assume White has a net loss of $700 in 2002. He may use the optional method to report $1,600 of net earnings from self-employment.

Optional farm method. If you have farming income (other than as a limited partner) you may use the farm optional method to figure your net earnings from farm self-employment.

Unlike the nonfarm optional method, the farm optional method does *not* have a two-year self-employment test (Test 3) or a requirement that actual net earnings be less than 72.189% of gross income (Test 2). There is also no limitation on the number of years you may use this method (Test 4).

If your gross income from farming is $2,400 or less, you may report two-thirds of your gross income as your net earnings from farm self-employment. If your gross income from farming exceeds $2,400 and your net earnings from farm self-employment are less than $1,733, you may report $1,600 as your net earnings from farm self-employment. If your gross income from farming exceeds $2,400 and your net earnings from farm self-employment are $1,733 or more, you may not use the optional method.

Farm income includes income from cultivating the soil or harvesting any agricultural commodities. It also includes income from the operation of a livestock, dairy, poultry, bee, fish, fruit, or truck farm, or plantation, ranch, nursery, range, orchard, or oyster bed, as well as income in the form of crop shares if you materially participate in production or management of production.

45.6 Self-Employment Tax Rules for Certain Positions

If you are—	Tax rule—
Babysitter	Where you perform services in your own home and determine the nature and manner of the services to be performed, you are considered to have self-employment income. However, where services are performed in the parent's home according to instructions by the parents, you are an employee of the parents and do not have self-employment earnings.
Clergy	If you are an ordained minister, priest, or rabbi (other than a member of a religious order who has taken a vow of poverty), you are subject to self-employment tax, unless you elect not to be covered on the grounds of conscientious or religious objection to Social Security benefits. Before 1968, a minister had to elect Social Security coverage.
	An application for exemption from Social Security coverage must be filed on or before the due date of your income tax return for the second taxable year for which you have net earnings from services as a minister of $400 or more (Form 4361). An exemption, once granted, is irrevocable. A temporary opportunity to revoke an exemption expired on April 15, 2002, plus any extension for the 2001 return.
	You must file Form 2031 to revoke the exemption.
	Self-employment tax does not apply to the rental value of any parsonage or parsonage allowance provided after retirement. Other retirement benefits from a church plan are also exempted. The exemptions are allowed retroactively for years beginning on, before, or after December 31, 1994, so a refund opportunity is available if self-employment tax was paid on such amounts in a prior year not closed by the statute of limitations.
Consultant	The IRS generally takes the position that income earned by a consultant is subject to self-employment tax. The IRS has also held that a retired executive hired as a consultant by his former firm received self-employment income, even though he was subject to an agreement prohibiting him from giving advice to competing companies. According to the IRS, consulting for one firm is a business; it makes no difference that you act as a consultant only with your former company. The IRS has also imposed self-employment tax on consulting fees, although no services were performed for them. The courts have generally approved the IRS position.
Dealer in commodities and options	Registered options dealers and commodities dealers are subject to self-employment tax on net gains from trading in Section 1256 contracts, which include regulated futures contracts, foreign currency contracts, dealer equity options, and non-equity options. Self-employment tax also applies to net gains from trading property related to such contracts, like stock used to hedge options.
Director	You are taxed as a self-employed person if you are not an employee of the company. Fees for attendance at meetings are self-employment income. If the fees are not received until after the year you provide the services, you treat the fees as self-employment earnings in the year they are received.

If you are—	Tax rule—
Employee of foreign government or international organization	If you are a U.S. citizen and you work in the United States for a foreign government or its wholly owned instrumentality, or an international organization, you pay self-employment tax if Social Security and Medicare taxes are not withheld from your pay.
Executor or guardian	If you are a professional fiduciary, you will always be treated as having self-employment income, regardless of the assets held by the estate. But if you serve as a nonprofessional executor or administrator for the estate of a deceased friend or relative, you will not be treated as having self-employment income unless all of the following tests are met: (1) the estate includes a business; (2) you actively participate in the operation of the business; and (3) all or part of your fee is related to your operation of the business. The IRS applied similar business tests to deny self-employment treatment for a guardian who was appointed by a court to care for a disabled cousin. The guardian negotiated sales of the cousin's property and invested the proceeds, but these activities were not extensive enough to be considered management of a business.
Former insurance salespersons	Termination payments by a former insurance salesperson may be exempt from self-employment tax. They must be received from an insurance company after the termination of a services agreement. No services may be performed for the company after the agreement ends and before the end of the tax year. The payments must be conditioned on the salesperson's entering into a covenant not to compete with the company for at least one year after termination. The amount of the payment must be primarily based on policies sold by (or credited to) the salesperson during the last year of the services agreement or on the period for which such policies remain in force after the termination.
Lecturer	You are not taxed as a self-employed person if you give only occasional lectures. If, however, you seek lecture engagements and get them with reasonable regularity, your lecture fees are treated as self-employment income.
Nonresident alien	You do not pay Social Security tax on your self-employment income derived from a trade, business, or profession. This is so even though you pay income tax. Your exemption from self-employment tax is not influenced by the fact that your business in the United States is carried on by an agent, employee, or partnership of which you are a member. However, if you live in Puerto Rico, the Virgin Islands, American Samoa, or Guam, you are not considered a nonresident alien and are subject to self-employment tax.
Nurse	If you are a registered nurse or licensed practical nurse who is hired directly by clients for private nursing services, you are considered self-employed. You are an employee if hired directly by a hospital or a private physician and work for a salary following a strict routine during fixed hours, or if you provide primarily domestic services in the home of a client. Where registered or licensed practical nurses are assigned nursing jobs by an agency that pays them, the IRS, in several rulings, has treated such nurses as employees of the agency. Nurses' aides, domestics, and other unlicensed individuals who classify themselves as practical nurses are treated by the IRS as employees, regardless of whether they work for a medical institution, a private physician, or a private household.
Real estate agent or door-to-door salesperson	Licensed real estate agents are considered self-employed if they have a contract specifying that they are not to be treated as employees and if substantially all of their pay is related to sales rather than number of hours worked. The same rule also applies to door-to-door salespeople with similar contracts who work on a commission basis selling products in homes or other non-retail establishments.
Technical service contractor	Consulting engineers and computer technicians who receive assignments from technical service agencies are generally treated as employees and do not pay self-employment tax. The IRS distinguishes between (1) technicians who in three-party arrangements are assigned clients by a technical services agency and (2) those who directly enter into contracts with clients. Employee status covers only technicians in Group 1. Technical specialists who contract directly with clients may be classified as independent contractors by showing that they have been consistently treated as independent contractors by the client, and that other workers in similar positions have also been treated as independent contractors. Thus, they may treat their income as self-employment income. Firms that are treated as employers of technical specialists are responsible for withholding and payroll taxes.
Writer	Royalties from writing books are self-employment income to a writer. Royalties on books by a professor employed by a university may also be self-employment income despite employment as a professor.

PART 7

Filing Your Return and What Happens After You File

This part is designed to help you —

- Organize your tax data. Whether you plan to prepare your own tax return or have someone else prepare it, you must first gather and organize your tax information.

  In Chapter 46, you will find record-keeping guides for income items and expense deductions.

- Understand how the IRS reviews your return and initiates audit procedures, including information on how the IRS matches your return with reports of distributions to you from banks, corporations, and government agencies.

- Avoid penalties for underpaying your tax. You may avoid penalties for positions taken on your tax return by making certain disclosures, obtaining authoritative support for your position, or showing reasonable cause for a tax underpayment; *see 47.5.*

- Understand the factors that might lead to an audit. Your chances of being selected for an examination depend on your income, profession, deductions claimed, and even where you live; *see 48.1.*

- Prepare for an audit. Advance preparations and knowing your rights can help support your position; *see 48.3.*

- Dispute adverse IRS determinations. You can appeal within the IRS and go to court if you disagree with the IRS audit results. If you win, you may receive attorneys' fees and other expenses; *see 48.7 and 48.8.*

- File a timely refund claim if you have overpaid your tax; *see 49.1.*

- File an amended return if you omitted income or claimed excessive deductions on your original return; *see 49.8.*

Chapter 46

Filing Your Return

Whether you prepare your return yourself or retain a professional preparer, you must first collect and organize your tax records. You cannot prepare your return unless you get your personal tax data in order. Good records will help you figure your income and deductions and will serve as a written record to present to the IRS in the event that you are audited.

Review income statements from banks, employers, brokers, and governmental agencies on their respective Forms 1099. Check for miscalculations, additions, and omissions.

Survey Chapters 12–21 of this book for deductions you can claim directly from gross income and itemized deductions you can claim on Schedule A of Form 1040.

Reviewing your tax return from prior years will help refresh your memory as to how you handled income and expenses in prior years. This review will also remind you of deductions, carryover losses, and other items you might otherwise have overlooked that you might be eligible for.

You may obtain copies of prior year tax returns by filing Form 4506 with the IRS and paying a nominal fee. In this chapter you will find a checklist of steps to take when preparing and checking your return. If you need an extension to file, *see 46.3.*

46.1 Keeping Tax Records

To maximize tax-savings opportunities, you must keep good records throughout the year. Good record-keeping makes it easier to prepare your return, reduces errors, and provides a defense to any challenge from the IRS.

- Make a habit of jotting down deductible items as they come along.
- Keep a calender or diary of expenses to record deductible items.
- Keep a file of bills. This can be an ordinary folder in which you arrange your bills and receipts alphabetically. This will remind you of deductible items and provide you with supporting evidence to present to the IRS if audited.
- Use your checkbook stubs as a record. If you own a business, you must keep a complete set of account books for it.

IRA records. If you have made nondeductible contributions to a traditional IRA, keep a record of both your nondeductible and deductible contributions. This will help you when you withdraw IRA money to figure the tax-free and taxed parts of the withdrawal *(see 8.9)*. Also keep records of contributions and conversions to Roth IRAs *(8.20–8.21)*. For these purposes, you should keep copies of Form 8606 and Form 5498; *see 8.8*.

Reinvested mutual-fund distributions. Keep annual statements that record the amount of mutual-fund distributions that you have reinvested in additional fund shares. The reinvested amounts are part of your cost basis in the fund. Unless your fund keeps track of basis for you, you need to know your basis when computing gain or loss on the redemption of fund shares; *see 32.10*.

Passive losses. If you have losses that are suspended and carried forward to future years under the passive loss restrictions *(10.13)*, keep the worksheets to Form 8582 as a record of the carryforward losses.

Home mortgage interest. Keep your bank statements and cancelled checks. If a loan secured by a first or second home is used to make substantial home improvements, keep records of the improvement costs to support your home interest deduction; *see 15.5*.

How long should you keep your records? Your records should be kept for a minimum of three years after the year to which they are applicable, since the IRS generally has three years from the date your return is filed to audit your return. Some authorities advise keeping them for six years, since in some cases where income has not been reported, the IRS may go back as far as six years to question a tax return. In cases of suspected tax fraud, there is no time limitation at all.

Keep records of transactions relating to the *basis* of property for as long as they are important in figuring the basis of the original or replacement property. For example, records of the purchase of rental property or improvements thereto must be held as long as you own the property.

As mentioned above, if you have made any nondeductible IRA contributions, records of IRA contributions and distributions must be kept until all funds have been withdrawn. Similarly, you should save mutual-fund confirmations or other records showing reinvested dividends and cash purchases of shares; these are part of your cost basis and will reduce taxable gain when you sell shares in the fund.

46.2 Getting Ready To File Your Return

You must collect your tax records before you can start the preparation of your return. Even if you employ a tax professional to prepare your return, organizing your tax data is essential. *See* the Tax Record and Return Directories at the end of this chapter for the records you need to report income and expenses and where on your return to report them. If you are using a tax return preparer, *see 46.7*. Once you have compiled all your return information and your records are complete, decide whether to use Form 1040EZ, 1040A, or 1040 with the aid of the checklist at the front of this book on page 7. After you have decided which return to file, review the form to familiarize yourself with its details.

You may use the sample forms in Part 8 to prepare a draft copy of your return. The Supplement will contain forms suitable for filing, or you can obtain forms by phone from the IRS by calling (800) 829-3676. Check the IRS instructions for obtaining forms by fax. If you have access to the Internet, you may obtain forms from the IRS website at http://www.irs.gov.

 *Planning Reminder*

Keep Copies

Photocopy your signed return and keep the copy along with copies of Form W-2 and other income statements, receipts, cancelled checks, and other items to substantiate your deductions.

Checking for possible errors. After you have completed your return, put it aside and postpone checking your completed return for several hours or even a day so that you can review it in a fresh state of mind. *See* below for common errors that might delay a refund or result in a tax deficiency and interest costs.

If mailing your return. If you are mailing your return to the IRS, first check it to ensure the following:

- Your arithmetic is correct.
- Your Social Security number, and that of your spouse if you are filing jointly, is recorded correctly on each form and schedule.
- You have filled in the proper boxes that state your filing status and exemption claims, and reported the Social Security number of each dependent; *see 21.15.*
- You have claimed the full standard deduction you are entitled to if you are age 65 or older, or blind; *see 13.4.*
- You have used the tax table or schedule applicable to your tax status; *see* Part 8 for the tax tables and the rate schedules. Use the tables if your taxable income is less than $100,000.
- You have put the refund due you or your tax payable on the correct line.
- If you owe tax and are paying by check, your check should be made out to the "United States Treasury" for the correct amount due and your Social Security number should be on the check. The IRS encourages, but does not require, that you send payment voucher Form 1040-V along with your Form 1040 payment.
- You have signed your return and, if you are filing a joint return, your spouse has also signed; *see 1.4.*
- You have attached the correct copy of your Form W-2 and all appropriate forms and schedules to your return.
- If you have elected to have your refund directly deposited into your personal account, verify that you have provided the IRS with the correct routing information on Line 71 of Form 1040, Line 45 of Form 1040A, or Line 11 of Form 1040EZ.
- You have correctly addressed the envelope and affixed proper postage.
- You use certified or registered mail or an IRS-specified private delivery service to prove that your return was postmarked on or before the filing date.

Using tax preparation software to prepare your return. If you have a personal computer, any one of the leading software programs will aid you in preparing your return by facilitating the calculation of sums, percentages, and tax liabilities. However, do not rely entirely on the computer program if you are preparing your return by yourself. You may inadvertently make an error by inputting the wrong information or there might be a quirk in the software itself. Although it may seem like a duplication of effort, preparing a return by hand and then checking it by preparing another return using the computer program will reduce the possibility of errors.

46.3 Applying for an Extension

If you cannot file your return on time, apply by the due date of the return for an extension of time to file. Send the extension request to the Internal Revenue Service office with which you file your return.

Automatic filing extension. You may get an extension without waiting for the IRS to act on your request. You receive an automatic four-month extension for your 2002 return if you file Form 4868 by April 15, 2003. The extension gives you until August 15, 2003, to file your return. A late *filing* penalty will not be imposed if you fail to submit a payment with Form 4868 provided you make a good faith estimate of your liability based upon available information at the time of filing. However, although the extension will be allowed without a payment, you will be subject to interest charges and possible penalties (discussed below) on 2002 taxes due after April 15, 2003.

You may get an extension by phone or over the Internet and use a credit card (American Express, MasterCard, Visa, or Discover Card) to make a tax payment; Form 4868 does not have to be filed if you use a credit card. Payment is made through a service provider that handles the credit card transaction and charges you a fee. *See* the Form 4868 instructions for the phone numbers and web addresses of the service providers.

If you filed a return for 2001, you may obtain an extension by phone for 2002. You can make a payment by personal check or by authorizing a direct debit from your checking or savings account; *see* Form 4868 for details. An advantage of obtaining an extension by phone is that you receive a confirmation number that can be kept with your records as proof that the extension was obtained.

Planning Reminder

Get Timely Postmark for Last Minute Mailing

Last minute filers may use specified services from *DHL, Airborne, Federal Express,* and *UPS* as well as the *U.S. Postal Service.* Do not forget to get a receipt to verify a timely postmark. If your return is postmarked before or at any time on the filing due date (April 15, 2003, for 2002 returns), it is considered timely filed under a "timely-mailing-is-timely-filing" rule, even if the IRS receives it after the due date.

The timely mailing rule also applies if you obtain a filing extension and are mailing your return on or before the extended due date.

A timely foreign postmark for a return filed from abroad will also be accepted by the IRS as proof of a timely filing.

Planning Reminder

Extension for Severe Hardship

If paying the tax due would cause you to suffer a severe hardship, you may apply for a special payment extension on Form 1127. A statement of assets and liabilities and recent expenditures and receipts must be attached. This extension is generally limited to six months. Even if the IRS allows the extension, you will still owe interest on the late payment.

When you file your return within the extension period, you enter on the appropriate line of the return any tax payment that you sent with your extension request, and include the balance of the unpaid tax, if any.

While the extension is automatically obtained by a proper filing on Form 4868, the IRS may terminate the extension by mailing you a notice at least 10 days prior to the termination date designated in the notice.

Abroad on April 15, 2003. You do not get an automatic extension for filing and paying your tax merely because you are out of the country on the filing due date. If you plan to be traveling abroad on April 15, 2003, and want to get a filing extension, you must submit a claim for the automatic four-month filing extension on Form 4868 or use a credit card (*see* above) to make a payment with an extension request.

The only exception is for U.S. citizens or residents who live and have their main place of business outside the U.S. or Puerto Rico, or military personnel stationed outside the U.S. or Puerto Rico, on April 15, 2003. Such taxpayers qualify for an automatic two-month extension, until June 16, 2003. These taxpayers may receive an additional two-month extension by filing Form 4868 by June 16 and making a proper estimate of the taxes due; as just discussed, payment of the estimated liability is not required to avoid a late *filing* penalty. However, they will still be subject to interest charges and possible penalties on taxes due after April 15, 2003.

Interest and penalty for late payment. If, on filing Form 4868, you pay less than the balance of the final tax you owe, you will be charged interest on the unpaid amount. If the tax paid with Form 4868, plus withholdings and estimated tax payments during 2002, is less than 90% of the amount due, you may also be subject to a late-payment penalty (equal to one-half of 1% of the unpaid tax per month)—unless you can show reasonable cause.

Installment arrangements. If you cannot pay the tax due for 2002 by the August 15, 2003, extension date, you should file your return and attach Form 9465 to request an installment arrangement. On Form 9465, you may request a monthly payment plan. The IRS will usually inform you within 30 days if your proposed payment plan is accepted. If it is, you will have to pay a processing fee. Even if the IRS agrees to an installment arrangement, you will have to pay interest and possibly a late-payment penalty (*see* above) on the amount not paid by the due date.

If you owe $10,000 or less and certain conditions are met, the IRS must enter into an installment arrangement if you request one. You must show that full payment cannot be currently made, and that in the previous five years you filed income tax returns and paid the tax and did not enter into an installment arrangement during that period. If the current return is a joint return, your spouse must also meet these tests for the five-year period. You must agree to pay the tax liability in full within three years.

If you are using an installment agreement to pay the tax due on a timely filed return (including extensions), the late payment penalty is reduced by half from .5% to .25% per month.

Filing extensions beyond August 15, 2003. Filing extensions beyond the automatic four-month period are allowed only if you file Form 2688 and show good cause, such as illness of yourself or a family member, or lack of information returns, such as a Form W-2 or Form 1099, needed to complete your return. Form 2688 must be filed before the end of the original four-month extension period. If the IRS agrees to your request, an additional two-month filing extension will be allowed, until October 15, 2003.

46.4 Paying Taxes Due or Getting Your Refund

If you owe tax on a return that you are mailing to the IRS, you may pay by check, money order, or credit card. Payments can also be made by direct debit from your account, either by phone or online using the IRS's Electronic Federal Tax Payment System (EFTPS).

If paying by check or money order, make it payable to the "United States Treasury." Write your Social Security number on the check or money order. The IRS encourages you to send Form 1040-V along with your payment, but the form is not required.

A credit card payment can be made by phone or over the Internet with a service provider that handles the transaction for the IRS. The service provider will impose a fee based on the amount you are paying. The tax form instruction booklet includes the toll-free number and website addresses of the service providers.

IRS online or phone option for making payments. The IRS's Electronic Federal Tax Payment System (EFTPS) now accepts online tax payments from individual as well as business taxpayers. You may use EFTPS to pay the balance due on your individual tax return or to pay estimated tax installments.

Payments are made by direct debit from an account that you designate when you enroll with EFTPS. Individual tax payments may be scheduled up to 365 days in advance and business taxes up to 120 days in advance. You can enroll online at www.eftps.gov.

Payments via EFTPS can also be made by phone after you enroll with EFTPS and set up a direct debit arrangement. Call 1-800-945-8400 for enrollment information.

Payments by electronic filers. If you file electronically, you may pay taxes by authorizing a direct debit from your checking or savings account, or by using a credit card. Check with the companies that process credit card payments for the fee that will be imposed.

Installment arrangements. If you cannot pay the full amount due on your return when you file, you may request an installment arrangement; *see 46.3.*

Refund options. If you overpaid your taxes in 2002, you can have a refund check mailed to you or have the IRS directly deposit the refund into your bank, brokerage, or mutual-fund account. For a direct deposit, provide the IRS with the correct routing information for your account as required by the IRS instructions. On Form 1040 or 1040A, you can apply all or part of the refund to your 2003 estimated tax; this is an irrevocable election.

Checking refund status by phone or online. You can call the IRS to check on the status of an expected refund. When you call the IRS automated phone service, you must provide the Social Security number shown on the return (or the first Social Security number if you filed a joint return), filing status, and the amount of the refund.

The IRS teletax phone number is 1-800-829-4477, but you may contact the IRS at 1-800-829-1040.

You can also check refund status online at www.irs.gov. The information needed to access the system is identical to that required by the phone system. Online, you can learn if the IRS has received the return, if the refund was processed, and when the direct deposit was made or the date the check was sent.

46.5 Electronic Filing

Electronic filing involves the transmission of your tax return to the IRS from the computer of a tax preparer, tax preparation software program, or online tax preparation service. To file electronically, you must use an authorized service; you cannot electronically file directly with the IRS. There is generally a fee for filing electronically, but some tax preparation websites offer free electronic filing.

Electronic filing offers a faster refund—a check mailed within three weeks or a direct deposit to your bank account. You authorize a direct deposit to a financial institution that was designated in the electronic portion of your return. On the electronic portion of the return, you provide the savings or checking account number and the "routing transit number" of your bank. The routing transit number is the electronic mailing address of your bank that directs the refund to the correct account. The number is on your checks or other account statements. Before naming a bank, first ask if it accepts direct deposits and what its conditions are for receiving a deposit.

If you must pay a fee for electronic filing, you must decide whether the faster refund is worth the fee. Keep in mind that even without electronic filing, you may instruct the IRS to directly deposit your refund to an account that you designate on your return.

If you file electronically and owe taxes, you may be able to pay by credit card or by direct debit from your checking or savings account.

Refund anticipation loans. An electronic filing service may offer a refund anticipation loan to a taxpayer who wants to receive an expected refund even sooner than the three weeks or so offered by electronic filing. The loans are received from lenders affiliated with the electronic filing service. This service is strictly an agreement between you and the filing service; the IRS is not a party to the arrangement. Before agreeing to such a loan, consider the high additional cost and whether it is worthwhile in light of the short refund payment period.

46.6 Notify the IRS of Address Changes

If the IRS does not have your current address, payment of a refund due you may be delayed. If you owe taxes, the IRS may enforce a deficiency notice sent to the address on your most recently filed tax return, even if you never receive the IRS notice.

To avoid these problems, file Form 8822 with the IRS to provide notice of an address change. Alternatively, you may send a signed written statement to the IRS Service Center covering your old residence. The statement should state the new and old address, your full name, and your Social Security or employer identification number.

If you and your spouse separate after filing a joint return, you should each notify the IRS of your current address.

If after you move you receive an IRS correspondence that has been forwarded by the Post Office, you may correct the address shown on the letter and mail it back to the IRS. Your correction is considered notice of an address change.

46.7 Choosing a Tax Return Preparer

There are two phases in preparing your tax return: (1) collecting your tax data and (2) converting that data into entries on your tax return. You must perform the first step yourself, as discussed at *46.1*. Once this is done, the second step of preparing your return may not be troublesome, especially if your return requires several entries on Form 1040A or Form 1040EZ. If you think tax return preparation is troublesome, or if you do not have the time to prepare your return, ask acquaintances about their knowledge and experience with qualified tax preparers in your area. If they are satisfied, you may want to contact their recommendations. If you cannot get recommendations, visit the offices of established franchised tax preparers.

Fees for tax return preparation depend on the complexity of the return to be filed and the preparer's professional standing. A preparer is not necessarily a trained accountant. Shop around; visit offices of preparers in your locality. This way you will get a firsthand idea of the cost of services.

If you are concerned about a possible IRS audit of your return, consider hiring a preparer who is qualified to represent taxpayers before the IRS. Only CPAs, attorneys, and enrolled agents (EAs) may represent taxpayers before the IRS, at the appeals as well as at the audit level. Attorneys or CPAs automatically qualify to practice before the IRS because of their professional licenses. An enrolled agent qualifies to practice before the IRS after passing an IRS examination or after completing five years of audit-level service as an IRS employee. Enrolled agents are also required by IRS regulations to complete continuing education courses every year. You can find an EA in your area by calling the National Association of Enrolled Agents at 1-800-424-4339.

Preparer Responsibilities

Tax preparers are subject to IRS regulations. They may be subject to penalties for understating the tax on a return or failing to keep proper records. Anyone who prepares a return or refund claim for a fee is considered a preparer under the tax law. When more than one person works on the return or claim, each schedule or entry is reviewed separately to determine the preparer of that schedule or item. A practitioner who gives advice directly relevant to a determination of the existence, characterization, or amount of an entry on a return is considered the preparer of that item.

A practitioner who prepares entries on a return that affect entries on the return of another taxpayer may also be considered the preparer of the other return if the entries are directly reflected on the other return and constitute a substantial portion of that return. For example, a practitioner preparing a partnership return may be considered the preparer of a partner's return if the entries that are picked up from the partnership return constitute a substantial portion of the partner's individual tax return. Regulations provide tests for determining whether a part of a return is considered substantial. Under the regulations, an entry is not considered substantial if it is (1) less than $2,000 or (2) less than $100,000 and also less than 20% of adjusted gross income.

You are not a preparer if you merely type or reproduce a return or claim, or prepare a return for your employer or an officer of your employer or a fellow employee.

Caution

Tax Planning Advice

Generally, do not rely on a preparer for tax planning advice. A person who can prepare a return may not have the experience or training to give tax planning advice. Consult a qualified professional, such as an accountant, CPA, tax attorney, or enrolled agent, who will charge more for tax planning services than a person who merely prepares returns during the tax season.

Preparer Penalties

A $250 penalty may be imposed on a preparer for a tax understatement if: (1) the preparer knew (or reasonably should have known) that the understatement was based on a taxpayer position that did not have a realistic possibility of being sustained on its merits and (2) the taxpayer position was frivolous or, if not frivolous, was not adequately disclosed. If the preparer can show good faith and a reasonable cause for the understatement, the $250 penalty will not be imposed. If a tax understatement is willful, or due to reckless disregard of IRS rules, a $1,000 penalty may be imposed; the penalty is $750 if the $250 penalty also applies to the return.

According to the IRS, a taxpayer position has a "realistic possibility" of being sustained on its merits if a person who is knowledgeable in the tax law would conclude, after a well-informed analysis, that there is at least a one-in-three likelihood that the position will be sustained.

For purposes of the $250 or $1,000 penalty, IRS regulations provide that only one person associated with a firm is considered to be the preparer of the return. The practitioner who signs the return is considered to be the preparer. If none of the persons considered to be preparers under IRS rules signs the return, then the person with overall supervisory responsibility is treated as the preparer for tax penalty purposes.

Note: a signing and nonsigning preparer may also be subject to a $1,000 penalty for knowingly aiding and abetting the understatement of tax liability on a return ($10,000 for corporate returns).

Preparers must satisfy the following requirements:

1. Retain a record of the name, Social Security number, and place of work of each preparer whom he or she employs. The records must be kept for three years following the close of the return period and must be made available for inspection upon request of the district director. There is a $50 penalty for each failure to keep and make available a proper record and a $50 penalty for each required item that is missing from the record. The maximum penalty for any return period is $25,000.

2. Furnish a completed copy of the return or refund claim to the taxpayer not later than when it is presented to the taxpayer for signature. There is a $50 penalty for each failure, up to a maximum of $25,000, for documents filed during any one calendar year.

3. Keep for three years and have available for inspection by the IRS a completed copy of each return or claim prepared, or a list of the names and identification numbers of taxpayers for whom returns or claims were prepared. A $50 penalty is imposed for each failure, up to a maximum of $25,000, for any return period. A preparer who sells his or her business is not relieved of the requirement of retaining these records.

4. Sign the return and include his or her identifying number or the identifying number of his or her employer. A $50 penalty is imposed for each failure, up to a maximum of $25,000, for documents filed during any calendar year. Where more than one practitioner has worked on a return, the individual with primary responsibility for overall accuracy must sign the return.

Tax preparers are subject to a $500 penalty if they endorse or negotiate a refund check issued to a taxpayer whose return they have prepared. Business managers for athletes, actors, or other professionals who prepare their clients' tax returns and handle their tax refunds may also be subject to the penalty. To avoid the penalty, the manager must act only as an agent in depositing the client's refund check.

In addition to the penalties imposed, the IRS may also seek to enjoin a preparer from engaging in fraudulent or deceptive practices or from acting as an income tax return preparer. The IRS may also seek an injunction against a preparer for "aiding and abetting" a taxpayer to underpay tax. A list of enjoined preparers is published by the IRS in the Internal Revenue Bulletin.

 Filing Tip

Alternative ID Number for Tax Preparers

On Form W-7P, a paid preparer may apply for a preparer tax identification number (PTIN). A tax preparer can use a PTIN instead of his or her Social Security number when signing returns or refund claims.

 Planning Reminder

Penalty Exception for Preparers

If you can show reasonable cause for failure to meet any of the four preparer requirements on this page, you may avoid the applicable penalty.

Tax Record and Return Directory

The following table lists tax records you need for specific items of income and expense and directs you to the return, schedule, and line on which to report the items. The items are listed in the order in which they appear on Forms 1040EZ, 1040A, and 1040.

Item	Records Needed	Reporting
Exemptions for dependents	Records of support contribution for food, lodging, medical expenses, such as cancelled checks, diary entries. Birth certificates in case age of a child is questioned. School attendance record if student status is questioned. Form 8332 allowing noncustodial parent to claim the exemption. This form must also be attached to return by noncustodial parent claiming exemption; *see 21.11.* Forms 2120 if dependent's support is shared; *see 21.10.*	Form 1040A, Line 6(c) Form 1040, Line 6(c)
Wages and salaries	Form W-2. Your employer must send your 2002 Form W-2 by January 31, 2003. Attach Copy B to your federal return. Keep Copy C for your records. If you worked for more than one employer during 2001, attach all Copy B forms to your return.	Form 1040EZ, Line 1 Form 1040A, Line 7 Form 1040, Line 7
Tip income	Form 4070 or other record showing your monthly reports of cash tips of $20 or more. Form W-2. Also *see 26.8* for reporting FICA taxes on unreported tips.	Form 1040EZ, Line 1 Form 1040A, Line 7 Form 1040, Line 7
Interest income	Form 1099-INT Form 1099-OID Deposit slips of interest received on money you loaned to others	Form 1040EZ, Line 2 ($400 or less) Form 1040A, Line 8(a); Schedule 1, Part I (over $400) Form 1040, Line 8(a); Schedule B, Part I (over $400)
Dividend income	Form 1099-DIV Company statements of dividend payments, especially if stock dividends have been paid	Form 1040A, Line 9; Schedule 1, Part II (over $400) Form 1040, Line 9; Schedule B, Part II (over $400)
Taxable refund of state and local income tax	Form 1099-G	Form 1040, Line 10
Alimony received	Deposit slips of alimony received and ex-spouse's Social Security number Copy of divorce or separation decree or agreements	Form 1040, Line 11 if taxable
Business income or loss	Business accounting records, deposit slips Business checkbook, deposit slips, invoice receipts, cancelled checks, bank statements Form 1099-MISC	Form 1040, Line 12; Schedule C or C-EZ Form 8582 if passive activity rules apply; *see* Chapter 10
Sale of stocks and bonds	Form 1099-B and broker confirmation statements	Schedule D Form 1040, Line 13
Sale of personal residence	Closing papers, records of purchase, improvements; *see 29.6.*	If taxable gain is realized, Schedule D

Tax Record and Return Directory (continued)

Item	Records Needed	Reporting
Sale of real estate	Closing statement, records of cost and improvements Records of depreciation	Form 4797 Schedule D Form 1040, Line 13
IRA distributions	Form 1099-R	Form 1040A, Line 11 Form 1040, Line 15
Pensions and annuities	Form 1099-R if you receive annuity payments or lump-sum distributions	Form 1040A, Line 12 Form 1040, Line 16
Commercial annuity income	Form 1099-R	Form 1040A, Line 12 Form 1040, Line 16
Rent income	Account records, checkbook, cancelled checks, and receipts	Schedule E Form 1040, Line 17 Form 8582 if passive activity rules apply
Royalty income	Form 1099-MISC	Schedule E Form 1040, Line 17
Partnership income	Schedule K-1, Form 1065	Schedule E Form 1040, Line 17
Beneficiary of trust or estate	Schedule K-1, Form 1041	Schedule E Form 1040, Line 17
S corporation	Schedule K-1, Form 1120S	Schedule E Form 1040, Line 17
Unemployment compensation	Form 1099-G	Form 1040A, Line 13 Form 1040, Line 19
Social Security benefits	Form SSA-1099	Form 1040A, Line 14 Form 1040, Line 20
Gambling income	Form W-2G, diary or other record showing wins and losses, losing tickets	Form 1040, Line 21
Other income	Form 1099-MISC, records of amounts received, date received	Form 1040, Line 21
Educator expenses	Records of expenses/purchase and business use	Form 1040A, Line 16 Form 1040, Line 23
IRA deductible contribution	Trustee's statements of contribution, copy of plan	Form 1040A, Line 17 Form 1040, Line 24
Student loan interest deduction	Bank statement showing interest paid	Form 1040A, Line 18 Form 1040, Line 25
Tuition and fees deduction	Student's name and taxpayer identification number, cancelled checks and statements of tuition and enrollment fees. For dependents, records of support contributions.	Form 1040A, Line 19 Form 1040, Line 26
Archer MSA (medical savings account deduction)	Trustee's statements and Form 5498-MSA, showing contributions	Form 1040, Line 27 Form 8853
Moving expenses	Cancelled checks or receipts for expenses incurred, diary or log	Form 1040, Line 28 Form 3903
Deduction for self-employment tax	Schedule SE, Form 1040	Form 1040, Line 29
Self-employed health insurance premium	Cancelled check of payment, copy of contract, insurance statement	Form 1040, Line 30
Keogh, SEP, or SIMPLE contribution for yourself	Trustee statement, copy of plan	Form 1040, Line 31
Penalty on early withdrawal of savings	Form 1099-INT	Form 1040, Line 32

Tax Record and Return Directory (continued)

Item	Records Needed	Reporting
Alimony deduction	Cancelled checks, copy of divorce or separation decree, written separation agreement, ex-spouse's Social Security number	Form 1040, Line 33
Employee expenses	Diary logs, receipts, copy of accounting to employer	Form 2106 Schedule A, Line 20
Home office expenses	Records of expenses, business use, and allocation	Form 2106 if an employee; Schedule A, Line 20 Form 8829 if self-employed; Schedule C, Line 30
Medical and dental expenses	Cancelled checks, statements, prescriptions; log of travel expenses and lodging costs	Form 1040 Schedule A, Lines 1–4
Taxes—state and local income, personal property, real estate	Form W-2 for withholding of income tax Cancelled checks Bank statements of property taxes paid by bank (mortgages) Form 1099-DIV for foreign tax Form 1099-INT or tax receipt for foreign tax withheld at source	Form 1040 Schedule A, Lines 5–9
Mortgage interest	Bank statement showing interest paid Form 1098	Form 1040 Schedule A, Lines 10 and 11
Points	Copy of bank statements, canceled checks	Form 1040 Schedule A, Lines 10 and 12
Cash donations	Cancelled checks, receipt from charity	Form 1040; Schedule A, Line 15
Volunteer expenses for charitable organizations	Log of travel, cancelled checks showing purpose	Form 1040 Schedule A, Line 15
Property donation	Description of property, records of fair market value and cost. Receipt from organization. If at least $250, a written receipt from organization to substantiate donation. Cancelled check is not sufficient. If in excess of $5,000, qualified appraisal report and statement from organization.	Form 1040 Schedule A, Line 16
Casualty and theft losses	See the "Key To Proving a Casualty Loss" on pages 354–355. For thefts, statements from witnesses, police records, or a newspaper account of the crime might help.	Form 1040 Schedule A, Line 19 Form 4684
Gambling losses	Losing tickets or receipts, diary showing daily wagers, wins, and losses	Form 1040 Schedule A, Line 27
Union dues	Wage statements showing withholding for dues or canceled checks	Form 1040 Schedule A, Line 20
Unreimbursed travel and entertainment expenses	Diary log and receipts kept according to the rules of *20.26*	Form 2106 Form 1040; Schedule A, Line 20
Earned income credit	Form W-2 if an employee, Schedule SE if self-employed, to show earnings	Form 1040 EZ, Line 8 Form 1040A, Line 41; Schedule EIC Form 1040, Line 64; Schedule EIC
Advance payment of earned income credit	Form W-2, Box 9	Form 1040A, Line 37 Form 1040, Line 59

Tax Record and Return Directory (continued)

Item	Records Needed	Reporting
Unreimbursed auto expenses if you are employed	Statement from employer requiring use of car Mileage log Receipts of expenses if actual costs are claimed Cost records of auto if depreciation is claimed	Form 2106 Form 1040 Schedule A, Line 20
Investment expenses	Cancelled checks	Form 1040; Schedule A, Line 22
Safe deposit box fee	Bank statements	Form 1040; Schedule A, Line 22
Tax preparation fees	Cancelled checks	Form 1040; Schedule A, Line 21
"Kiddie" tax	Child's Forms 1099-INT, 1099-DIV, and 1099-OID	Form 1040A, Line 28 Form 1040, Line 42 Form 8615 if income is reported on child's return Form 8814 if parent elects to report child's income on Form 1040
Child and dependent care expenses	Cancelled checks for amounts paid to care for child	Form 1040A, Line 29; Schedule 2 Form 1040, Line 46 Form 2441
Credit for the elderly or the disabled	Physician's statement of condition	Form 1040A, Line 30; Schedule 3 Form 1040, Line 47; Schedule R
Child tax credit and additional child tax credit	Records of support contribution Birth certificates in case age of a child is questioned School attendance record if student status is questioned	Form 1040A, Line 33 and Line 42 Form 1040, Line 50 and Line 66 Form 8812
Education credits	Student's name and taxpayer identification number Cancelled checks and statements of tuition and enrollment fees For dependents, records for support contributions	Form 1040A, Line 31 Form 1040, Line 48 Form 8863
Adoption credit	Adopted child's name, date of birth, and tax-payer identification number. Adoption papers showing the date the adoption became final.	Form 1040A, Line 34 Form 1040, Line 51 Form 8839
Foreign tax credit	Form 1099-DIV; foreign tax returns or statements	Form 1116 Form 1040, Line 45
Prior alternative minimum tax credit	Copy of prior year's Form 6251 Form 8801	Form 1040, Line 53
Federal taxes withheld	Form 1099 Form W-2 Form W-4V	Form 1040EZ, Line 7 Form 1040A, Line 39 Form 1040, Line 62
Estimated tax payments	Cancelled checks and copy of Form 1040-ES	Form 1040A, Line 40 Form 1040, Line 63

Chapter 47

How Tax Data Is Processed by the IRS

Data from filed tax returns and information returns is recorded in computers on magnetic tape that is sent to the National Computer Center in Martinsburg, West Virginia, for posting to the master list of taxpayers arranged by account number. Failure to file returns, duplicate or multiple filings, and other discrepancies can be detected. Data from information returns is matched with the entries on individual returns.

You are required to put your Social Security number on your tax return. Your number also appears on information returns sent to the IRS reporting the wages, interest, dividends, royalties, etc., paid to you. Your number serves as a basis for posting and cross-referencing data to your account in the master IRS file.

You may incur penalties and interest charges if you fail to comply with reporting requirements or fail to pay your taxes on time.

47.1 IRS Preliminary Review

Your return is first checked for arithmetic accuracy by the IRS. If an error is found, you receive either a refund or a bill for additional taxes. Special IRS screening also spots the following types of errors:

- Incorrectly reporting income shown on Forms W-2 or Forms 1099.
- Incorrectly applying the adjusted gross income limitations for medical expenses, casualty and theft losses, and miscellaneous itemized deductions.
- Using an auto mileage rate for business travel exceeding the IRS rate.
- Claiming of the dependent care credit by a married person filing separately; *see 25.1.*
- Using head of household rates without entering on Line 4 of Form 1040 or 1040A the name of a qualifying child who is not your dependent.
- Not supplying the Social Security number of a dependent.

If you make errors of this type, you will probably be advised by mail of the corrections and of additional tax due, or you may be asked to provide additional information to substantiate tax deductions or credits. If you disagree with an IRS assessment of additional tax, you may request an interview or submit additional information. If you file early for 2002 and the correction is made before April 15, 2003, interest is not charged.

If your return is selected for a more thorough review, you are notified by letter. This may not happen for a year or two. How to handle an audit if your return is selected for examination is discussed in Chapter 48.

Interest on refund. The IRS follows a practice of expediting refunds to avoid interest costs. If your 2002 return is filed on or before the April 15, 2003, filing deadline, the IRS does not have to pay interest if the refund is paid before May 31, 2003, which is 46 days after the April 15 filing due date. If the return is filed after April 15, 2003, with or without an extension, no interest is due on refunds paid within 45 days after the actual filing date. If the overpayment is not refunded within 45 days, interest is paid from the date the tax was overpaid up to a date determined by the IRS that can be as much as 30 days before the date of the refund check.

47.2 Information Returns Required by the IRS

The IRS matches tax returns with information returns from employers, payers of interest and dividends, brokers, and others to check whether income has been omitted from an individual's tax return. The IRS processes more than one billion information returns, primarily Forms W-2 and Forms 1099. By matching these information returns against individual tax returns, the IRS assesses billions in additional tax and penalties.

Here is a list of items for which an information return will be sent to the IRS:

Wages. Employers report wage income on Form W-2.

Dividends. Dividend payments of $10 or more during the calendar year are reported to the IRS on Form 1099-DIV. Each payer must furnish you by January 31, 2003, a statement showing the dividend payments made in 2002. Corporations, banks, and other payers, as well as persons or firms who receive such payments for you as nominee, report annually the dividend payments totaling $10 or more per person. Dividends, for reporting purposes, include dividends paid by corporations, and "dividend equivalents" paid to you while your stock is on loan for a short sale. Nontaxable distributions paid to shareholders are reported to the IRS on Form 5452.

Interest. Interest payments of $10 or more during the calendar year are reported to the IRS on Form 1099-INT. Each payer must furnish you by January 31, 2003, a statement showing the interest payments made in 2002. Interest for reporting purposes includes interest on registered corporate bonds, debentures, notes, and certificates, as well as interest on deposits with savings banks, savings and loan associations, stockbrokers, and insurance companies. No returns are required for tax-free interest.

Original issue discount (OID). The discount on time deposits and certificates maturing in more than one year is reported to the IRS on Form 1099-OID if it is at least $10. You should receive a copy of the Form 1099-OID for 2002 by January 31, 2003.

Interest and dividend income information disclosed to Social Security and other agencies. To verify your eligibility for certain government benefits, agencies such as the Social Security Administration, state unemployment compensation agencies, and state welfare agencies may obtain from the IRS information on the interest and dividend income that is shown on your tax return.

Filing Tip

Authorize Someone To Discuss Return Processing Problems
Generally, a person authorized to practice before the IRS may discuss your tax return issues with the IRS only if you sign a power of attorney on Form 2848. However, just above the signature section of your 2002 Form 1040, 1040A, or 1040EZ, you may consent to contacts between the IRS and your designee to resolve return processing issues such as mathematical errors, missing return information, or questions about refunds or payments. The designee can be a friend or relative and need not be a tax professional. A power of attorney will still be needed to handle an audit, underreported income issues, appeals within the IRS, and collection notices.

Caution

Failure To Provide a Dependent's Social Security Number
The IRS may give you an opportunity to provide the number. If the IRS disallows the exemption, it may use an immediate assessment procedure. You have 60 days to object to an immediate assessment.

Planning Reminder

Reporting Sale of Principal Residence

Sales of principal residences with a gross sales price exceeding $250,000, or $500,000 for married sellers, are reported on Form 1099-S. If the sales price does not exceed $250,000 or $500,000, the sale is not reportable provided the seller gives the person responsible for closing the sale written assurance that the full gain on the sale is excludable from income under the rules discussed at *29.1*. Although the IRS does not require a Form 1099-S for such sales, the person responsible for the closing may choose to report it.

Rents or royalties. Royalty payments of $10 or more are reported on intangible property, such as copyrights and interests in oil, gas, and other natural resources, on Form 1099-MISC. Rents collected by a real estate agent on behalf of the property owner of $600 or more also are reported on Form 1099-MISC.

State income tax refunds. States are required to report income tax refunds of $10 or more on Form 1099-G.

Unemployment compensation. Unemployment payments of $10 or more during the year are reported to the IRS on Form 1099-G, a copy of which will be furnished to unemployment benefit recipients.

Proceeds from real estate transactions. Real estate sales are generally reported on Form 1099-S to the IRS by the attorney or other party who is responsible for closing the transaction. On the sale of a home, the form must also show the portion of real property taxes imposed on the buyer. However, *see* the Planning Reminder on the left.

Proceeds from sales of securities. Brokers are required to report to the IRS on Form 1099-B gross proceeds from sales of stocks, bonds, commodities, regulated futures, and forward contracts. Commodity options are not covered by this reporting rule.

Miscellaneous income. In the course of business, persons who make payments totaling $600 or more in the calendar year must file Form 1099-MISC with the IRS if the payments are in the form of:

1. Compensation for personal services (including salaries, wages, commissions, and professional fees) from which no tax is withheld. However, no information return is required for payments to a domestic or other household employee.

2. Prizes and awards that are not for services, such as winnings on TV shows (gambling winnings are reported on Form W-2G); *or*

3. Payments of fees to physicians by insurance companies, such as Blue Cross, or by a government agency under Medicare or Medicaid. The physician or other health-care provider must receive a copy of Form 1099-MISC by January 31, 2003, for inclusion of the amount on his or her 2002 return.

Retirement plan contributions and distributions. Distributions from pension, profit-sharing and annuity plans, traditional or Roth IRAs, or simplified employee pension plans (SEPs) are reported on Form 1099-R. Contributions to a traditional IRA and conversions to a Roth IRA are reported on Form 5498.

Mortgage interest. Banks, government agencies, and businesses receiving mortgage interest and points of $600 or more for any calendar year report the payment to the IRS on Form 1098. The reporting requirement applies to interest on all obligations secured by real property. The lender must provide you with a statement of the interest reported to the IRS for 2002 by January 31, 2003.

Foreclosures and abandonments of property. If a business or government agency lends you money and later forecloses on your property or knows that you have abandoned property secured by the loan, the lender must file a report with the IRS on Form 1099-A. The purpose of the reporting requirement is to help the IRS check whether you have realized income from the discharge of indebtedness or gain on foreclosure, or whether you must recapture a previously claimed investment credit. If a report to the IRS has been made, you will be sent a statement by the lender by January 31 following the year of the foreclosure or abandonment.

Tax shelters. A new tax-shelter offering may be required to register with the IRS. If registration is required, the IRS assigns the tax shelter an identification number that must be furnished to investors. As an investor, you must report the registration number on Form 8271. Form 8271 must be attached to your tax return if you report any income or claim any deductions or credits from the shelter. Promoters of registered tax shelters and any other tax-shelter arrangements that the IRS considers potentially abusive must also keep a list of investors for seven years and provide the list to the IRS upon request. Furthermore, an investor who sells his interest in such a tax shelter to another investor must keep records identifying the buyer.

Cooperatives. Cooperatives must file annual information returns for patronage dividends totaling $10 or more during the calendar year. A statement showing the amount reported must be furnished to the patron by the end of January of the following year; *see* Form 1099-PATR.

Partnerships. A partnership does not pay income taxes, but must file an annual information return (Form 1065), stating all items of income and deductions. Also included in the return are the names and addresses of all partners, and the amount of each partner's distributive share. The return is filed at the close of the partnership's tax year, whether or not it coincides with that of its partners. Failure to file the return will result in a penalty assessable against the partnership. If a partner sells or exchanges a partnership interest and payment is partly attributable to the partner's share of unrealized receivables or substantially appreciated inventory, the partnership must be notified of the transaction and the partnership must then file an information return with the IRS, Form 8308. The purpose of the reporting requirement is to enable the IRS to verify the income attributable to the receivables and inventory, which is taxable as ordinary income. Statements to the transferor and transferee of the partnership interest must also be provided.

Barter transactions. The value of the trades by members of a barter club is subject to income tax. If you exchanged services or goods through a barter exchange during 2002, you should receive Form 1099-B from the exchange by January 31, 2003, showing the value received during 2002. The IRS also gets a copy.

Cancelled debts. If a financial institution or federal agency cancels or forgives a debt you owe of $600 or more, the cancellation will be reported to the IRS on Form 1099-C and a copy sent to you. A cancellation of a debt is generally taxable, but see exceptions in *11.8*.

47.3 When the IRS Can Assess Additional Taxes

Three-year statute of limitations. The IRS has three years after the date on which your return is filed to assess additional taxes. When you file a return before the due date, however, the three-year period starts from the due date, generally April 15.

Where the due date of a return falls on a Saturday, Sunday, or legal holiday, the due date is postponed to the next business day.

> **EXAMPLES**
> 1. You filed your 2002 return on February 5, 2003. The last day on which the IRS can make an assessment on your 2002 return is April 17, 2006.
> 2. You filed your 2000 return on May 30, 2001. The IRS has until May 30, 2004, to assess a deficiency.

Amended returns. If you file an amended return shortly before the three-year limitations period is about to expire and the return shows that you owe additional tax, the IRS has 60 days from the date it receives the return to assess the additional tax, even though the regular limitations period would expire before the 60-day period.

Six-year statute. When you fail to report an item of gross income which is more than 25% of the gross income reported on your return, the IRS has six years after the return is filed to assess additional taxes. An item that is adequately disclosed is not considered an omission.

IRS request for audit extension. If the IRS cannot complete an audit within three years, it may request that you sign Form 872 to extend the time for assessing the tax. However, where an individual was "scared" into signing such an agreement, it was held invalid. *See* the following Example.

> **EXAMPLE**
>
> Robertson, a plumber, won $30,000 in a sweepstakes. An IRS agent asked him to sign an extension agreement. Robertson never had any prior dealings with the IRS, he did not know that his return was under examination, and he was not in touch with the lawyer who prepared the return on which his sweepstakes winnings were averaged.
>
> Robertson wanted to see his lawyer before signing Form 872, but the agent pressed hard for the signature, phoning him and his wife at home and at work 20 times in a week. The agent did not tell him the amount of additional tax that might be involved, or explain that if he refused to sign he would have an opportunity before the IRS and the courts to contest any additional tax. Instead, the agent's comments gave him the impression that his home could be confiscated if he refused to sign. Robertson signed and the IRS later increased his tax.
>
> Robertson argued that the agreement was not valid. He signed under duress. The Tax Court agreed. He convinced the court that he really believed he could lose his house and property if he did not comply. No adequate explanation of the real consequences of refusal to sign was made, although Robertson asked. Since he signed Form 872 under duress, the IRS could not increase his tax after the three-year period.

Caution

No Limitation Period for Fraud

There is no limitation on when tax may be assessed where a false or fraudulent return is filed with intent to evade tax, or where no return is filed.

47.4 Interest on Deficiencies

Interest is charged on a deficiency at rates listed in the following table. The interest rate, which equals the federal short-term rate plus 3%, is determined every quarter. Interest begins to accrue from the due date of the return. Interest is compounded daily except for estimated tax penalties. Where a taxpayer has relied on IRS assistance in preparing a return, and taxes are owed because of a mathematical or clerical error, interest does not begin to accrue until 30 days from a formal demand by the IRS for the payment of additional taxes. *See 47.1* for interest on refunds and *49.6* for interest on refund claims filed on amended returns.

IRS interest rates on taxes owed are as follows:

From—	To—	Deficiency Rate—
1/1/02	12/31/02	6%
7/1/01	12/31/01	7%
4/1/01	6/30/01	8
4/1/00	3/31/01	9
4/1/99	3/31/00	8
1/1/99	3/31/99	7
4/1/98	12/31/98	8
7/1/96	3/31/98	9
4/1/96	6/30/96	8
7/1/95	3/31/96	9

47.5 Tax Penalties for Late Filing and Late Payment

Late filing. If your return is filed late without reasonable cause, the IRS may impose a penalty of 5% of the net tax due for each month the return is late, with a maximum penalty of 25%. If the return is more than 60 days late, the penalty will not be less than the smaller of $100 and 100% of the tax due. In one case, the IRS tried to impose the $100 minimum penalty on a taxpayer who did not owe any tax because her withholdings exceeded her liability. However, the Tax Court held that the minimum $100 penalty does not apply unless tax is underpaid. The IRS has agreed to follow the decision.

If failure to file is fraudulent, the monthly penalty is 15% of the net tax due, with a maximum penalty of 75%.

If you are subject to penalties for both late payment and late filing, the 0.5% penalty for late payment (but not the 1% penalty) offsets the penalty for late filing during the period that the penalties run concurrently.

Late payments. If you are late in paying your taxes, a nondeductible monthly penalty of 0.5% ($\frac{1}{2}$ of 1%) is imposed on the net amount of tax due and not paid by the due date. The maximum penalty is 25% of the tax due. The penalty is in addition to the regular interest charge. This penalty does not apply to the estimated tax; *see 27.1.* The late payment penalty does not apply if you can show that the failure to pay is due to reasonable cause and not to willful neglect.

A special reasonable cause rule applies if you obtain a filing extension. If by the original due date you paid at least 90% of your total tax liability through withholdings, estimated tax installments, or payment with your extension request, reasonable cause is presumed and the penalty does not apply for the period covered by the extension.

Unless reasonable cause is shown, the 0.5% monthly penalty also applies for failure to pay a tax deficiency within 21 calendar days of the date of notice and demand for payment if the tax due is less than $100,000. If the tax is $100,000 or more, the penalty-free payment period is 10 business days.

The monthly penalty may be doubled to 1%, if, after repeated requests to pay and a notice of levy, you do not pay. The increased penalty applies starting in the month that begins after the earlier of the following IRS notices: (1) a notice that the IRS will levy upon your assets within 10 days unless payment is made or (2) a notice demanding immediate payment where the IRS believes collection of the tax is in jeopardy. If the tax is not paid after such a demand for immediate payment, the IRS may levy upon your assets without waiting 10 days.

47.6 Tax Penalties for Inaccurate Returns

A 20% penalty generally applies to the portion of any tax underpayment attributable to (1) negligence or disregard of IRS rules and regulations; (2) substantial understatement of tax liability; (3) overvaluation of property; or (4) undervaluation of property on a gift tax or estate tax return. These penalties may be avoided by showing good faith and reasonable cause for the underpayment; a stricter version of this exception applies to charitable contribution overvaluations as discussed later in this section.

Negligence or disregard of IRS rules or regulations. The 20% penalty applies to the portion of the underpayment attributable to negligence. Negligence is defined as failing to make a reasonable attempt to comply with the law. Failure to report income shown on an information return, such as interest or dividends, is considered strong evidence of negligence.

The 20% penalty may also apply if you take a position on a return which is contrary to IRS revenue rulings, notices, or regulations. This penalty for disregarding IRS rules or regulations may be avoided if you have a reasonable basis for your position and you disclose that position on Form 8275 or on Form 8275-R in the case of a good faith position contrary to a regulation. Thus, disclosure will not avoid a penalty for a position that does not have a reasonable basis.

Substantial understatement of tax. If you understate tax liability on a return by the greater of $5,000 or 10% of the proper tax, you may be subject to a penalty equal to 20% of the underpayment attributable to the understatement.

The penalty may be avoided if you have a reasonable basis for your position and you disclose the position to the IRS on Form 8275, or on Form 8275-R in the case of a position that is contrary to an IRS regulation.

The penalty also may be avoided if you can show that your position was supported by "substantial authority" such as statutes, court decisions, final, temporary, or proposed IRS regulations, IRS revenue rulings and procedures, and press releases or notices published by the IRS in the weekly Internal Revenue Bulletin. You may also rely on IRS private letter rulings and technical advice memoranda issued after October 31, 1976, and IRS actions on decisions and general counsel memoranda issued after March 12, 1981. However, according to the IRS, such rulings and internal IRS memoranda that are more than 10 years old should be accorded very little weight. Congressional committee reports and the tax law explanations prepared by Congress's Joint Committee on Taxation, known as the "Blue Book," may be relied on as authority for your position.

However, if an understatement of tax is due to tax-shelter items, having substantial authority for your position is not enough to avoid the penalty; you must also reasonably believe that your position was "more likely than not" correct. Disclosure does not avoid a penalty for tax-shelter items.

Overvaluing property or basis. The 20% penalty for overvaluing property, such as where inflated charitable contribution deductions are claimed or where the basis of depreciable property is inflated, applies *only* if the claimed value or basis is 200% or more of the correct amount. Furthermore, there is no penalty unless the tax underpayment attributable to the overvaluation exceeds $5,000. The penalty rate is doubled to 40% if the overvaluation is 400% or more of the correct value. To avoid the penalty for donated property on the grounds that you had reasonable cause, the value must be based on a qualified appraisal *(14.12)* and your own good faith investigation of value. A potential dispute over valuation may be avoided for a donation of art with an appraised value of $50,000 or more, if you request an IRS Statement of Value (SOV); *see 14.9.*

Undervaluation on gift or estate tax return. If property is undervalued on a gift tax return or estate tax return by 50% or more, and if the tax underpayment attributed to the undervaluation exceeds $5,000, a 20% penalty applies. The penalty doubles to 40% if the undervaluation is 75% or more.

Fraud penalty. A 75% penalty applies to the portion of any tax underpayment due to fraud. If the IRS establishes that any part of an underpayment is due to fraud, the entire underpayment will be attributed to fraud, unless you prove otherwise.

Interest on penalties. A higher interest cost is imposed on individuals subject to the following penalties: failure to file a timely return, negligence or fraud, overvaluation of property, undervaluation of gift or estate tax property, *or* substantial understatement of tax liability. Interest starts to run from the due date of the return (including extensions) until the date the penalty is paid. For other penalties, interest is imposed only if the penalty is not paid within 21 calendar days of an IRS demand for payment if the penalty is less than $100,000. The interest-free period is 10 business days after the IRS demand for payment if the penalty is $100,000 or more.

Acting on wrong IRS advice. A penalty will not be imposed if you rely on erroneous advice provided in writing by IRS officials. It is necessary for you to show that you provided accurate information when asking for advice.

 Caution

Too Good to Be True
If you claim a deduction, credit, or exclusion on your return that would seem to a reasonable person to be "too good to be true" under the circumstances, the IRS is likely to consider you negligent unless you show you made an attempt to verify the correctness of the position.

Chapter 48

IRS Tax Audits

Because the IRS is unable to examine every return, it follows a policy of examining returns which, upon preliminary inspection, indicate the largest possible source of potential tax deficiency.

Returns are rated for audit according to a mathematical formula called the discriminant function system (DIF). Various weights are assigned to separate items on each tax return, thus permitting the ranking of returns for the greatest potential error. The rating method is based on data the IRS compiled from extensive audits of taxpayers conducted before 1990 under the Taxpayer Compliance Measurement Program (TCMP), which was canceled in 1994. The IRS is planning a new audit program to update its audit criteria. For business taxpayers in specific market segments, the IRS has developed detailed audit guidelines as part of its Market Segment Specialization Program (MSSP).

This chapter discusses what may trigger an audit and how you can handle an audit if your return is selected for examination.

48.1 Odds of Being Audited

The odds are low that your return will be picked for an audit. The IRS does not have the personnel and resources to examine every return, so it selects those returns which upon preliminary inspection have a high audit potential—those that are most likely to result in a substantial tax deficiency.

Audit odds vary depending on your income, profession, type of return, type of transactions reported, and where you live. Individual returns are classified by all income items on the return without regard to losses. Professional or business income reported on Schedule C and farm income reported on Schedule F is classified by total gross receipts, and corporate returns are classified by total assets.

Your return may command special IRS scrutiny because of your profession, the type of transactions reported, or the deductions claimed. The chances of being audited are greater under the following circumstances:

- Your information reported on the tax return does not match information received from third-party documentation, such as Forms 1099 and W-2.
- Your itemized deductions exceed IRS targets.
- You claim tax-shelter losses.
- You report complex investment or business transactions without clear explanations.
- You receive cash payments in your work that the IRS thinks are easy to conceal, such as cash fees received by doctors or tips received by cab drivers and waiters.
- Business expenses are large in relation to income.
- Cash contributions to charity are large in relation to income.
- You are a shareholder of a closely held corporation whose return has been examined.
- A prior audit resulted in a tax deficiency.
- An informer gives the IRS grounds to believe that you are omitting income from your return.

Itemized deductions. If your itemized deductions exceed target ranges set by the IRS, the chances of being audited increase. The IRS does not publicize its audit criteria for excessive deductions, but it does release statistics showing the average amount of deductions claimed according to reported income. Here are IRS figures based on deductions claimed on 2000 returns filed through September 2001.

Average Itemized Deductions

AGI (thousands)	Medical	Taxes	Interest	Donations
$ 15–30	$ 5,339	$ 2,175	$ 6,023	$ 1,683
30–50	4,706	3,025	6,422	1,894
50–100	6,155	4,899	7,828	2,348
100–200	12,121	9,282	11,161	3,761
200 or more	34,436	38,200	22,598	19,558

Taxpayer Bill of Rights. As a taxpayer, you have the right to be treated fairly, professionally, promptly, and courteously by the IRS and its employees. Because of many complaints of abuse in the past, Congress has passed several statutes, collectively referred to as the Taxpayer Bill of Rights, to protect taxpayers from mistreatment by IRS personnel.

One aim of the Taxpayer Bill of Rights is to have the IRS inform you of the effect of the tax action it is taking and how you can proceed and protect your rights. *See* IRS Publication 1, *Your Rights as a Taxpayer*. Thus, when the IRS starts an action against you, you should ask for an explanation of the procedural rules affecting your case, if these are not already included in the documents sent to you. For example, before the IRS may enforce a tax lien by seizing property by levy, the IRS must provide you with a notice of your right to a hearing before an appeals officer, an explanation of the levy procedures, the availability of administrative appeals and the appeals procedures, the alternatives to the proposed levy such as an installment agreement, and the rules for obtaining the release of a lien. *See* IRS Publication 556, *Examination of Returns, Appeal Rights, and Claims for Refund*; IRS Publication 594, *The IRS Collection Process;* and IRS Publication 5, *Your Appeal Rights and How to Prepare a Protest if You Don't Agree*.

Taxpayer Advocate. An important part of the Taxpayer Bill of Rights is the Taxpayer Advocate Service. The function of the Taxpayer Advocate is to assist taxpayers in resolving problems with the IRS, identify areas in which taxpayers have problems dealing with the IRS, propose changes in administrative practices of the IRS, and identify potential legislative changes that may mitigate the problems. From the Taxpayer Advocate, you can receive assistance if you have unsuccessfully tried

Caution

IRS Plans to Increase Audits
With increased funding from Congress, the IRS is planning to reverse a decade-long decline in audit rates. Increased audit coverage for high-income taxpayers will be a particular focus of the IRS over the next few years.

Planning Reminder

Taxpayer Rights Web Page
For links to IRS Publications outlining taxpayer rights, notices, examinations of tax returns, appeal rights, and collection procedures, go to the Taxpayer Rights Corner on the "Tax Info for You" page of the IRS website, www.irs.gov.

to resolve your problem with the IRS and have not had your calls or letters returned. You will be assigned a personal advocate who is in the best position to try to resolve your problem. If you face a significant hardship because of an impending IRS action or lack of IRS response to your problem, you may apply to the Taxpayer Advocate for a Taxpayer Assistance order on Form 911. Contact the Taxpayer Advocate Service by calling 1-877-777-4778, or you may write to the Advocate at the IRS office that last contacted you. Publication 1546, *The Taxpayer Advocate Service of the IRS*, has a state-by-state list of addresses and phone numbers for Advocate offices. The Taxpayer Advocate page at the IRS website has comprehensive information concerning the Taxpayer Advocate Service; go to www.irs.gov.

48.2 Types of Audits

An examination may be held by correspondence, at a local IRS office, or at the taxpayer's place of business, office, or home. An examination at an IRS office is called a desk or office examination; an examination at a place of business or home is called a field examination. When you are contacted by the IRS, you should receive an explanation of the examination process.

In a correspondence audit, the IRS sends you a letter asking for additional information about an item on your return. For example, the IRS may ask you to document a claimed deduction for charitable contributions or medical expenses. If the IRS is not satisfied with your response, you may be called in for an office audit. The IRS also notifies you by letter of mathematical or clerical errors you have made on your return, or if you have failed to report income, such as interest or dividends, that are shown by payers on information returns and matched to taxpayer returns by IRS computers.

The complexity of the transactions reported on a return generally determines whether a return will be reviewed at an office or field examination.

Most audits of individual returns, except for the self-employed, are conducted at IRS offices. An office audit usually covers only a few specific issues which the IRS specifies in its notice to you. For example, the examining agent may only be interested in seeing proof for travel expense deductions or educational expenses.

Field audits generally involve business returns; they are more extensive and time-consuming than office audits and are handled by more experienced IRS agents. For self-employed individuals, most examinations are field audits at their place of business. It is advisable to have a tax professional go over the potential weak spots in your return and represent you at the examination.

48.3 Preparing for the Audit

After an office audit is scheduled, the first thing to do is look over your return. Refresh your memory. Examine the items the IRS questioned in its notice of audit, and organize your records accordingly. Also check the rest of your return and gather proof for items you are unsure of. At this point, you should take a broad view of your return to anticipate problems you may encounter. Before the actual examination begins, consider possible settlement terms. Assume that the agent will assess additional tax, but establish the range you will consider reasonable. You can always change your mind, but giving some thought beforehand to possible settlement terms will help you later when settlements are actually discussed.

You may authorize an attorney, CPA, enrolled agent, or other individual recognized to practice before the IRS to represent you at the examination without your being there. To do so, give your representative authorization on Form 2848. An attorney or other representative authorized on Form 2848 can perform any acts that you could, including entering into a binding settlement agreement.

If you attend the audit, take only the records related to the items questioned in the IRS notice. Do not volunteer extra records; if the agent sees them, it might suggest new areas for investigation.

If you are concerned that there may be a problem of fraud, see a qualified attorney before you come into contact with an IRS official. The attorney can put your actions in perspective and help protect your legal rights. Besides, what you tell an attorney is privileged information; he or she cannot divulge or be forced to divulge data you have provided, other than data used to prepare your tax return.

A field audit of your business return is likely to involve a comprehensive examination and requires careful preparation. Together with your tax adviser, go over your return for potential areas of weakness. For example, the agent is likely to question deductions you have claimed for business travel. If you are an incorporated professional, the corporation's deductions for expenses of company-owned cars or planes will probably be reviewed. The agent may suspect that a portion of these business deductions are actually nondeductible personal travel costs; be prepared to substantiate the business portion of your total mileage and operating expenses.

Planning Reminder

Audit Scheduling

Make sure that the examination is scheduled far enough in advance for you to get ready. Do not let the IRS hurry you into an examination until you are prepared. In some localities, particularly rural areas, the IRS may give short notice in scheduling a field audit. An agent may even appear at your home or place of business and try to begin the audit immediately. Resist this pressure and reschedule the meeting at your convenience.

Under the Taxpayer Bill of Rights *(48.1)*, the IRS is generally required to hold an office audit at the office located nearest to your home. The IRS generally may not conduct a field audit at the site of a small business if the audit would essentially require the shutting down of the business, unless a direct visit is necessary to determine inventory or verify assets.

48.4 Handling the Audit

If you have authorized someone to represent you at the examination, your representative may appear at the examination without you. If the IRS wants to question you, it must issue you an administrative summons. If you are present and questioned, you may stop the examination to consult with counsel, unless the examination is pursuant to an administrative summons.

Audits conducted at an IRS office may conclude quickly because they usually involve only a few specific issues. In some cases, the audit may take less than an hour. The key to handling the audit is advance preparation. When you arrive at the IRS office, be prepared to produce your records quickly. Records should be organized by topic so that you do not waste time leafing through pages for a receipt or other document.

If the agent decides to question an item not mentioned in the notice of audit, refuse politely but firmly to answer the questions. Tell the agent that you must first review your records. If the agent insists on pursuing the matter, another meeting will have to be scheduled. The agent might decide it is not worth the time and drop the issue.

Common sense rules of courtesy should be your guide in your contacts with the agent. Avoid personality clashes; they can only interfere with a speedy and fair resolution of the examination. However, be firm in your approach and, if the agent appears to be unreasonable in his or her approach, make it clear that—if necessary—you will go all the way to court to win your point. A vacillating approach may weaken your position in reaching a settlement.

If the IRS has scheduled a field audit, ask that the examination be held at your representative's office. If you have not retained professional help and the examination takes place on your business premises, do not allow the agent free run of the area: Provide the agent with a comfortable work area for examining your records. If possible, the workplace should be isolated so that the agent can concentrate on the examination without being distracted by office operations that might spark questions. Tell your employees not to answer questions about your business or engage in small talk with the agent. As with an office audit, help speed along the field examination by having prepared your records so that requested information can be quickly produced.

Recording the examination. You have the right to make an audio recording of any interview with an IRS official. Video recordings are not permitted. No later than 10 calendar days before the interview, give written notice to the agent conducting the interview that you will make a recording. Later requests are at the discretion of the IRS. You must pay for all recording expenses and supply the equipment. The IRS may also make a recording of the interview, upon giving notice of at least 10 calendar days. However, IRS notice is not necessary if you have already submitted a request to make a recording. You have the right to obtain a transcript, at your own expense, of any recording made by the IRS. Generally, a request for a copy must be received by the IRS agent within 30 calendar days after the recording, although later requests may be honored.

48.5 Agreeing to Audit Changes

After the audit, the agent will discuss proposed changes either with you or your representative.

If you agree with the agent's proposed changes, you will be asked to sign a Form 870, which, when signed, permits an immediate assessment of a deficiency plus penalties and interest, if due. The Form 870 is called "Waiver of Restrictions on Assessment and Collection of Deficiency in Tax and Acceptance of Overassessment."

If you believe that you have done as well or better than expected regarding the proposed deficiency, you can bring the case to a close by signing the Form 870, but the agent's supervisor must also approve the assessment.

By signing the form, you limit the amount of interest charges added to the deficiency. A signed Form 870 does not prevent the IRS from reopening the case to assess an additional deficiency. If on review the deficiency is increased, you will receive a revised Form 870. You can refuse to sign the form. The signed first form has the effect of stopping the interest on the original deficiency. As a matter of practice, however, waivers of acceptances ordinarily result in closing of the case.

Caution

Waiving Your Right To Appeal
Before deciding whether to sign the Form 870, consider that, by signing, you are giving up your right of appeal to both the IRS Office of Appeals and the Tax Court. However, you may still file a refund suit in a federal district court or in the Court of Federal Claims unless you have agreed not to do so on the Form 870.

It is possible, although unlikely, that upon examining your return, the agent will determine that you are due a refund. In this situation, a signed Form 870 is considered a valid refund claim. You should file a protective refund claim even if you sign the Form 870 acknowledging the overpayment. Generally, the agent will process the refund, but if he or she fails to do so or the review staff puts it aside for some reason and the limitations period expires, the refund will be lost. The refund claim will protect you from such a mishap.

The payment of tax before the deficiency notice (90-day letter) is mailed is, in effect, a waiver of the restrictions on assessment and collection. If the payment satisfies your entire tax liability for that year, you cannot appeal to the Tax Court. You must sue for a refund in either federal district court or the Court of Federal Claims.

48.6 Disputing the Audit Changes

If you disagree with the agent and the examination takes place in an IRS office, you may ask for an immediate meeting with a supervisor to argue your side of the dispute. If an agreement is not reached at this meeting or the audit is at your office or home, the agent prepares a report of the proposed adjustments. You will receive a 30-day letter in which you are given the opportunity to request a conference. You may decide not to ask for a conference and await a formal notice of deficiency (90-day letter).

If your examination was conducted as an office audit or by correspondence, or the disputed amount does not exceed $25,000, you do not have to prepare a written protest for a conference. The written protest is a detailed presentation of your reasons for disagreeing with the agent's report. Even where a formal written protest is not required, you must provide a brief written statement indicating your reasons for disagreeing with the agent when you request an appeals conference. *See* IRS Publication 5, "Appeal Rights and Preparation of Protests for Unagreed Cases."

At the conference you may appear for yourself or be represented by an attorney or other agent, and you may bring witnesses. The conference is held in an informal manner and you are given ample opportunity to present your case.

If you cannot reach a settlement, you will receive a Notice of Deficiency, commonly called a 90-day letter. In it, you are notified that at the end of 90 days from the date it was mailed, the government will assess the additional tax.

Interest abatement. An IRS delay in completing an audit increases the interest that you have to pay when a deficiency notice is eventually issued. You may ask the IRS on Form 843 for an abatement of interest charges that are attributable to unreasonable errors or delays by IRS employees in performing a ministerial or managerial act. Interest abatement for a managerial act is allowed if the interest is on a deficiency or payment for a tax year starting after July 30, 1996.

A ministerial act is defined as a procedural or mechanical act that does not involve the exercise of an IRS employee's discretion or judgment, such as the transfer of a taxpayer's case to a different IRS office after the transfer is approved by a group manager. A managerial act refers to the exercise of discretion or judgment by an IRS employee in managing personnel. Misplacing the taxpayer's case file is also a managerial act. General IRS administrative decisions, such as prioritizing the order of processing returns, or decisions on applying the tax law, that result in delay, are not ministerial or management acts for which interest abatement is available.

Going to court. When you receive a 90-day letter, if you are still convinced that your position is correct, you may take your case to one of three courts. You may within 90 days file a petition with the Tax Court without having to pay the tax. The Tax Court has a small tax case procedure for deficiencies of $50,000 or less. Such cases are handled expeditiously and informally. Cases may be heard by appointed special trial judges. A small claim case may be discontinued at any time before a decision, but the decision when made is final. No appeal may be taken by you or the IRS.

Instead of petitioning the Tax Court, you may pay the additional tax, file a refund claim for it, and—after the refund claim is denied—sue for a refund in a federal district court or the U.S. Court of Federal Claims.

Generally, the decision to litigate should be considered by an experienced tax practitioner.

Caution

Notice of Deficiency

If you do not respond to the 30-day letter, or if you later do not reach an agreement with an appeals officer, the IRS will send you a 90-day letter, also called a "notice of deficiency." The IRS is required to specify on the notice the 90th day by which you must file your petition with the Tax Court.

Caution

Penalty for Frivolous Tax Court Action

If you bring a frivolous case to the Tax Court or unreasonably fail to pursue IRS administrative remedies, the Tax Court may impose a penalty of up to $25,000. Furthermore, if you appeal a Tax Court decision and the appeals court finds that the appeal was frivolous, the court may impose a penalty.

48.7 Recovering Costs of a Tax Dispute

In a tax dispute, you may believe that the IRS has taken an unreasonable position, forcing you to incur legal fees and other expenses to win your case. Here are highlights of the rules for recovering costs from the IRS in a case that commenced after July 30, 1996.

You may recover all or part of—
1. Reasonable administrative costs of proceedings within the IRS, and
2. Reasonable litigation costs in a court proceeding.

A judgment for reasonable litigation costs will not be awarded in any court proceeding if you did not exhaust all IRS administrative remedies. A refusal by the taxpayer to agree to an extension of time for a tax assessment is not a bar to an award, but unreasonably delaying the proceedings is.

To receive an award, you must "substantially prevail" as to the key issues in the case or the amount of tax involved. If you do, you will be entitled to a recovery unless the IRS proves that it was "substantially justified" in maintaining the position that it did. For purposes of recovering costs incurred after January 18, 1999, you are treated as the prevailing party if the IRS obtains a court judgment against you, but the judgment is equal to or less than an amount that you offered in settlement. The offer must be considered a qualified offer made during a period that begins on the date of the first letter of proposed deficiency allowing for an IRS administrative appeal and ends 30 days before the date first set for trial.

The Tax Court and other courts have interpreted "substantially justified" to be a reasonableness standard. The IRS is presumed not to be "substantially justified" if it does not follow its own published regulations, revenue rulings, procedures, notices, announcements, or a private ruling issued to the taxpayer. The IRS may try to rebut the presumption. For costs incurred after January 18, 1999, a court may also consider whether an IRS position has been rejected by federal courts of appeal of other circuits in determining whether the IRS position was substantially justified.

Reasonable administrative costs include IRS fees and expenses of attorney fees, witnesses, and experts. The IRS determines the amount of such an award, which may include costs incurred from the date the IRS sent its first letter of a proposed deficiency allowing you to ask for an administrative appeal. For an award of administrative costs, you must file an application with the IRS before the 91st day after the date on which the IRS mailed you its final decision. To appeal a denial of your application, you must petition the Tax Court within 90 days from the date the IRS mailed the denial.

Reasonable litigation costs include reasonable court costs, fees of witnesses and experts, and attorneys' fees. Fees of witnesses may not exceed the rate paid by the U.S. government. For attorneys' fees incurred in 2000 and 2001, the limit is $140 per hour. For fees incurred in 2002, the limit is $150 per hour. The $150 hourly limit may be increased for 2003 by an inflation adjustment. The court may also increase the award for attorneys' fees to account for special factors, such as the difficulty of the issues and the availability of local tax expertise.

You may *not* recover attorneys' fees if you represent yourself *(pro se)*. However, you are still entitled to recover fees for witnesses and experts. If you represent a prevailing taxpayer on a *pro bono* basis or for a nominal fee (after January 18, 1999) a court may award you or your employer reasonable attorneys' fees.

You may *not* recover costs if your net worth at the time the action begins exceeds $2 million. For proceedings commenced after August 5, 1997, the $2 million net worth limit applies separately to each spouse in determining whether a married couple filing jointly is entitled to recover legal fees. No recovery is allowed to sole proprietors, partnerships, and corporations if their net worth exceeds $7 million or they have more than 500 employees.

48.8 Suing the IRS for Unauthorized Collection

If an IRS employee or officer recklessly, intentionally, or negligently disregards the law or IRS regulations when taking a collection action, you may sue the IRS in federal district court for actual

Planning Reminder

Recovering Attorneys' Fees
Attorneys' fees include the fees paid by a taxpayer for the services of anyone who is authorized to practice before the Tax Court or IRS.

Planning Reminder

IRS Failure To Release Lien

A suit for damages may also be brought in federal district court against the IRS if IRS employees improperly fail to release a lien on your property. Before you sue, you must file an administrative claim for damages. The lawsuit must be filed within two years after your claim arose. You may sue for actual economic damages plus costs of the action; the types of damages that may be recovered are similar to those discussed for suing the IRS for unauthorized collection actions.

economic damages resulting from the IRS employee's misconduct, plus certain costs of bringing the action. The lawsuit must be filed within two years of the date your right to sue accrued.

For negligent IRS collection activities, you may sue for damages of up to $100,000, and for reckless or intentional misconduct, the maximum damage award is $1 million. Administrative remedies must be exhausted to obtain an award.

According to IRS regulations, actual economic damages that may be recovered are monetary losses you suffer as a direct result of the IRS's action. For example, a business may lose loyal customers and suffer an actual cash loss if the IRS's action damages the business's reputation. Other actual expenses could include the cost of renting a house or a car if the IRS puts a lien on or seizes your property, or loss of income due to the garnishment of your paycheck. Damages from the IRS for loss of reputation, inconvenience, or emotional distress are allowed only to the extent that they result in such actual monetary loss.

The IRS defines "costs of action" that you may recover as (1) fees of the clerk and marshall; (2) fees of the court reporter; (3) fees and disbursements for printing and witnesses; (4) copying fees; (5) docket fees; and (6) compensation for court-appointed experts and interpreters.

Litigation costs and administrative proceeding costs are not treated as "costs of the action." However, if the IRS denies your administrative claim for damages and you successfully sue in federal district court, you are considered a "prevailing party" and may recover attorneys' fees, related litigation expenses, and administrative costs before the IRS as discussed at *48.7*.

Chapter 49

Filing Refund Claims, and Amended Returns

File a refund claim on Form 1040X if you want to take advantage of a retroactive change in the law, if you have overpaid your tax because you failed to take allowable deductions or credits, or overstated your income. You may use Form 1040X to correct your return if you underreported your income or improperly claimed deductions.

File a refund claim on time. The time limits discussed at *49.2* must be strictly observed; otherwise, even if you file a valid refund claim, it will be denied because of late filing.

You do not have to file a refund claim if you have overpaid your tax due to excessive withholding of taxes on your wages or salary, or if you have overpaid your estimated tax. You get a refund on these overpayments by filing your tax return and requesting a refund for these amounts. You must file your return within three years from the time the tax was paid to get the refund; *see 49.2*.

For a refund of an overpayment of FICA taxes, *see 26.10* for how to claim a refund on your tax return. If you are not required to file a tax return, you file a refund claim on Form 843.

Earned income credit. If you are entitled to a refund due to the earned income credit for certain low-income working families, you must file your tax return to get your refund, even though your income and filing status would not otherwise require that a return be filed. *See* Chapter 25.

Caution

Time Limits Must Be Observed
Failure to file a timely refund claim is fatal, regardless of its merits. Even if you expect that your claim will have to be pursued in court, you must still file a timely refund claim. Mailing a refund claim so that it is postmarked by the due date (including extensions) qualifies as a timely filing if you use the U.S. Postal Service. The timely mailing rule also applies to refund claims that are timely deposited with private delivery services that have been designated by the IRS.

Planning Reminder

Disability Suspends Limitation
In filing a refund claim during any period in which a person is unable to manage his or her financial affairs due to a physical or mental impairment that has lasted or is expected to last for at least one year or to result in death, the law suspends the limitation period. The suspension does not apply during a period in which a guardian is authorized to handle the individual's financial affairs.

49.1 Who Should File a Refund Claim

You may file a refund claim on Form 1040X if you have overpaid your tax on your original return because you failed to take allowable deductions or credits, or overstated your income. You may also file for a refund if you wish to take advantage of a retroactive change in the law. You do not have to file a refund claim if you have overpaid your tax due to excessive withholding of taxes on your wages or salary, or if you have overpaid your estimated tax. You will receive a refund on those overpayments by filing your tax return and requesting a refund at that time.

49.2 When To File a Refund Claim

You may file a refund claim on Form 1040X within three years from the time your return was filed, or within two years from the time you paid your tax, whichever is later. However, a refund claim on a late-filed return may be barred under a three-year "look back" rule; *see* below. A return filed before its due date is treated as having been filed on the due date. The filing deadlines are suspended while you are financially disabled; *see* the Planning Reminder on this page.

A refund claim based on a bad debt or worthless securities may be made within seven years of the due date of the return for the year in which the debt or security became worthless.

The time for filing refund claims based on carrybacks of net operating losses or general business credits is within three years of the due date (including extensions) of the return for the year the loss or credit arose.

A refund claim based on your share of a joint return refund withheld by the IRS to pay your spouse's debts (49.3) may be made within six years of the date you received the IRS notice that the refund had been withheld.

If you filed an agreement giving the IRS an extended period of time in which to assess a tax against you, you are allowed an additional period in which to file a claim for refund. The claim, up to certain amounts, may be filed through the extension period and for six months afterwards.

Refund claim for withholdings and estimated tax on late-filed original return. A refund for withheld income taxes or estimated tax installments can be lost if you delay filing your original return too long. The Supreme Court agrees with the IRS that the withholdings and estimated tax are considered to be paid on the original due date of the return. To obtain a refund of these taxes, you must file the return within three years of the due date, or within three years plus any extension period if a filing extension is obtained. If the return is filed after the end of this three-year (plus extension) "look-back" period, the withholdings and estimated taxes cannot be refunded. For example, if taxes were withheld from your 1999 wages and you are due a refund but have not yet filed your 1999 return, you must do so by April 15, 2003, to obtain a refund of the withholdings. If you had obtained an extension until August 15, 2000, to file your 1999 return, the deadline for filing the refund claim would be August 15, 2003. Where such a refund is claimed on an original return mailed and postmarked (U.S. Postal Service) on or slightly before the last day of the "three years plus extension" period, the IRS at one time argued that the timely mailing/timely filing rule did not apply. But following a contrary appeals decision, the IRS will now allow a refund in this situation. Acquiescing to the court decision, the IRS now treats refund claims included on delinquent original returns as filed on the date of mailing for purposes of applying the "three years plus extension" look-back rule.

Armed Forces service members and veterans. In determining the time limits within which a refund claim may be filed, you disregard intervening periods of service in a combat zone or hazardous duty area, plus periods of continuous hospitalization outside the United States as a result of combat zone injury, and the next 180 days thereafter.

49.3 Joint Refund Claims

If a joint return was filed for a year in which a refund is due, both spouses are entitled to recover jointly and both must file a joint refund claim. Where separate returns were filed, each spouse is a separate taxpayer and may not file a claim to recover a refund based on the other spouse's return, except if that spouse becomes the fiduciary when one spouse becomes incompetent or dies. To claim a refund on behalf of a deceased spouse, you should complete Form 1310. If you are divorced and incur a net operating loss or credit that may be carried back to a year in which you were married, you may file a refund claim with your signature alone and the refund check will be made out only to you; *see* 40.18.

Injured spouse may get refund that was withheld to pay spouse's debts. If you showed a refund due on a joint return filed with a spouse who owed child support or federal student loans, the IRS may have withheld payment of the refund to cover the obligations. If you are not liable for the past-due payments, and your tax payments (withholdings or estimated tax installments) or refundable credits exceed your income reported on the joint return, you may file Form 8379 to get back your share of the refund.

49.4 Stating the Reasons for Refund Claims

The most important part of a refund claim is a statement of the "reasons" for the refund. A general claim simply noting an overpayment, without supporting facts and grounds, is not sufficient. If a claim is denied by the IRS, it may become the basis of a court suit. If you have not stated all the grounds, you may not be allowed to argue them in court. You must make a claim showing:

- All the facts that support the claim. Attach all supporting documents and tax forms supporting your claim.
- All the grounds for the claim. If you are uncertain about the exact legal grounds, alternate and even inconsistent grounds may be given. For example: "The loss was incurred from an embezzlement; if not, from a bad debt." To protect against understating the amount of the claim, you might preface the claim with this phrase: "The following or such greater amounts as may be legally refunded."

49.5 Quick Refund Claims

Form 1045 may be used for filing refunds due to carrybacks from net operating losses, and the general business credit. Form 1045 also may be used for a quick refund based on a repayment exceeding $3,000 of income reported in an earlier year. Form 1045 must be filed within 12 months after the loss year. The IRS must act on the claim within 90 days. Payment of quick refund claims is not a final settlement of your return; the IRS may still audit and then disallow the refund claim. Note that the filing of a quick refund, if rejected, may not be the basis of a suit for refund; a regular refund claim must be filed.

Tax-shelter claims. If you file a quick refund claim on Form 1045 and the IRS determines it is likely that you claimed excessive tax-shelter benefits, the IRS will offset the quick refund claim by a deficiency attributable to the tax-shelter items. You will receive the balance and receive a notice of the tax-shelter deficiency.

49.6 Interest Paid on Refunds

As discussed at *47.1*, interest is not paid by the IRS on refunds made within 45 days of the original due date or actual filing date.

If a refund claim is filed within the time limits in *49.2* and the IRS pays the refund within 45 days, interest is paid from the date of overpayment to the date the claim was filed. If the refund is not made within the 45-day period, interest is paid from the date of overpayment to a date set by the IRS that is not more than 30 days before the date of the refund check.

The IRS does not have to pay interest on overpayments resulting from net operating loss carrybacks or business credit carrybacks if a refund is paid within 45 days of the filing of the refund claim. If a refund claim based on a loss or credit carryback is filed and subsequently a quick refund claim is filed on Form 1045 for the same refund, the 45-day period starts to run on the date Form 1045 is filed.

Interest rates applied to overpayments are as follows:

Amounts outstanding between—	Rate is—
7/1/95 – 3/31/96	8 %
4/1/96 – 6/30/96	7
7/1/96 – 3/31/98	8
4/1/98 – 3/31/99	7
4/1/99 – 3/31/00	8
4/1/00 – 3/31/01	9
4/1/01 – 6/30/01	8
7/1/01 – 12/31/01	7
1/1/02 – 12/31/02	6

Caution

Refund Offset for Overdue State Taxes

If you owe state income taxes, the state can refer the debt to the Treasury Department's Financial Management Service (FMS) will offset your federal tax refund by the state tax if your address on the return is within the state seeking the offset. The state must give you written notice that the debt is being referred to the FMS and provide an opportunity for disputing the liability.

49.7 Refunds Withheld by the IRS

The Treasury Department's Financial Management Service (not the IRS) may withhold all or part of your refund if you owe child support or federal debts such as student loans or state income taxes. If you file a joint return with a spouse who owes child support or federal debts, you may be able to obtain your share of a refund due on the joint return; for further details, *see 49.3*.

49.8 Amended Returns Showing Additional Tax

If, after filing your 2002 return, you find that you did not report some income or claimed excessive deductions, you should file an amended return on Form 1040X to limit interest charges and possible tax penalties. You may also file an amended return to change the status of your return from a separate return to a joint return with your spouse. It is important to note that you may not switch from a joint return to a separate return. An amended return may also be filed if you want to change from itemized deductions to the standard deduction method, or vice versa.

If you filed early and then file an amended return by the filing due date (including any extensions) that shows additional tax due, you will not be charged interest or penalties based on the original return; the amended return is considered a substitute for the original.

You must pay the additional tax due as shown on Form 1040X. Even if you expect a refund on your original return, the IRS will not reduce the refund check to cover the additional tax. You must pay it and you will receive the original refund separately.

Part 8

2002 Tax Forms, Tax Tables, and Tax Rate Schedules

In the following pages, you will find sample tax forms for 2002 that you can use as worksheets. However, the final version of the tax forms may vary. The *Supplement* to this book will provide final blank forms suitable for filing.

Use the tax table starting on page 739 to look up your tax liability if your taxable income is less than $100,000. If your taxable income is $100,000 or more, use the tax rate schedules on page 751.

If you have long-term capital gains in excess of short-term capital losses, compute your 2002 tax liability on your taxable income, including the capital gains, on Part IV, page 2 of Schedule D. However, if your only capital gains for 2002 are mutual-fund capital gain distributions, you may be able to compute your tax using a worksheet in the instructions to Form 1040 or Form 1040A instead of having to make the Schedule D computation.

Note: All the forms in this section are based on IRS advance proofs that are subject to change. Use the IRS final version for filing your tax return. Final blank forms suitable for filing will be available in the *Supplement*. You can call the IRS for forms at 1-800-829-3676. You can download the forms from our website at www.jklasser.com, or the IRS website at www.irs.gov.

Department of the Treasury—Internal Revenue Service

Form **1040EZ**

Income Tax Return for Single and Joint Filers With No Dependents (99) 2002

OMB No. 1545-0675

Label
(See page 12.)

Use the IRS label. Otherwise, please print or type.

L A B E L H E R E

Your first name and initial	Last name	Your social security number
If a joint return, spouse's first name and initial	Last name	Spouse's social security number

Home address (number and street). If you have a P.O. box, see page 12.   Apt. no.

City, town or post office, state, and ZIP code. If you have a foreign address, see page 12.

▲ **Important!** ▲

You **must** enter your SSN(s) above.

Presidential Election Campaign (page 12) ▶

Note. Checking "Yes" will not change your tax or reduce your refund.

Do you, or your spouse if a joint return, want $3 to go to this fund? . . . . . . ▶

You ☐ Yes ☐ No   Spouse ☐ Yes ☐ No

Income

Attach Form(s) W-2 here.
Enclose, but do not attach, any payment.

1 Total wages, salaries, and tips. This should be shown in box 1 of your W-2 form(s). Attach your W-2 form(s).   **1**

2 Taxable interest. If the total is over $400, you cannot use Form 1040EZ.   **2**

3 Unemployment compensation and Alaska Permanent Fund dividends (see page 14).   **3**

4 Add lines 1, 2, and 3. This is your **adjusted gross income.**   **4**

Note. You **must** check Yes or No.

5 Can your parents (or someone else) claim you on their return?

Yes. Enter amount from ☐ worksheet on back.

No. If **single,** enter $7,700. If **married,** enter $13,850. ☐ See back for explanation.   **5**

6 Subtract line 5 from line 4. If line 5 is larger than line 4, enter -0-. This is your **taxable income.** ▶   **6**

Payments and tax

7 Federal income tax withheld from box 2 of your W-2 form(s).   **7**

8 **Earned income credit (EIC).**   **8**

9 Add lines 7 and 8. These are your **total payments.** ▶   **9**

10 **Tax.** Use the amount on **line 6 above** to find your tax in the tax table on pages 24–28 of the booklet. Then, enter the tax from the table on this line.   **10**

Refund

Have it directly deposited! See page 20 and fill in 11b, 11c, and 11d.

11a If line 9 is larger than line 10, subtract line 10 from line 9. This is your **refund.** ▶   **11a**

▶ **b** Routing number   ▶ **c** Type: ☐ Checking ☐ Savings

▶ **d** Account number

Amount you owe

12 If line 10 is larger than line 9, subtract line 9 from line 10. This is the **amount you owe.** For details on how to pay, see page 21. ▶   **12**

Third party designee

Do you want to allow another person to discuss this return with the IRS (see page 22)? ☐ **Yes.** Complete the following. ☐ **No**

Designee's name ▶   Phone no. ▶ (   )   Personal identification number (PIN) ▶

Sign here

Joint return? See page 11.

Keep a copy for your records.

Under penalties of perjury, I declare that I have examined this return, and to the best of my knowledge and belief, it is true, correct, and accurately lists all amounts and sources of income I received during the tax year. Declaration of preparer (other than the taxpayer) is based on all information of which the preparer has any knowledge.

Your signature	Date	Your occupation	Daytime phone number ( )
Spouse's signature. If a joint return, **both** must sign.	Date	Spouse's occupation	

Paid preparer's use only

Preparer's signature ▶	Date	Check if self-employed ☐	Preparer's SSN or PTIN
Firm's name (or yours if self-employed), address, and ZIP code ▶		EIN	
		Phone no.	( )

For Disclosure, Privacy Act, and Paperwork Reduction Act Notice, see page 23.   Cat. No. 11329W   Form **1040EZ** (2002)

Form	Department of the Treasury—Internal Revenue Service		
1040A	**U.S. Individual Income Tax Return** (99) **2002**	IRS Use Only—Do not write or staple in this space.	

Label
(See page 19.)

Use the IRS label.

Otherwise, please print or type.

L A B E L H E R E

Your first name and initial

Last name

If a joint return, spouse's first name and initial

Last name

Home address (number and street). If you have a P.O. box, see page 20.

Apt. no.

City, town or post office, state, and ZIP code. If you have a foreign address, see page 20.

OMB No. 1545-0085

Your social security number

Spouse's social security number

▲ **Important!** ▲

You **must** enter your SSN(s) above.

Presidential Election Campaign
(See page 20.)

▶ **Note.** Checking "Yes" will not change your tax or reduce your refund.
Do you, or your spouse if filing a joint return, want $3 to go to this fund? . . . ▶

You ☐Yes ☐No
Spouse ☐Yes ☐No

Filing status

Check only one box.

1 ☐ Single
2 ☐ Married filing jointly (even if only one had income)
3 ☐ Married filing separately. Enter spouse's SSN above and full name here. ▶ _____
4 ☐ Head of household (with qualifying person). (See page 21.) If the qualifying person is a child but not your dependent, enter this child's name here. ▶ _____
5 ☐ Qualifying widow(er) with dependent child (year spouse died ▶). (See page 22.)

Exemptions

If more than six dependents, see page 22.

6a ☐ **Yourself.** If your parent (or someone else) can claim you as a dependent on his or her tax return, **do not** check box 6a.

b ☐ **Spouse**

c **Dependents:**

(1) First name Last name	(2) Dependent's social security number	(3) Dependent's relationship to you	(4) ✓ if qualifying child for child tax credit (see page 23)
			☐
			☐
			☐
			☐
			☐
			☐

No. of boxes checked on 6a and 6b _____

No. of children on 6c who:
• lived with you _____
• did not live with you due to divorce or separation (see page 24) _____

Dependents on 6c not entered above _____

Add numbers on lines above ☐

d Total number of exemptions claimed.

Income

Attach Form(s) W-2 here. Also attach Form(s) 1099-R if tax was withheld.

If you did not get a W-2, see page 25.

Enclose, but do not attach, any payment.

7 Wages, salaries, tips, etc. Attach Form(s) W-2. | 7 |

8a **Taxable** interest. Attach Schedule 1 if required. | 8a |
b **Tax-exempt** interest. **Do not** include on line 8a. | 8b |

9 Ordinary dividends. Attach Schedule 1 if required. | 9 |

10 Capital gain distributions (see page 25). | 10 |

11a IRA distributions. | 11a | **11b** Taxable amount (see page 25). | 11b |

12a Pensions and annuities. | 12a | **12b** Taxable amount (see page 26). | 12b |

13 Unemployment compensation and Alaska Permanent Fund dividends. | 13 |

14a Social security benefits. | 14a | **14b** Taxable amount (see page 28). | 14b |

15 Add lines 7 through 14b (far right column). This is your **total income.** ▶ | 15 |

Adjusted gross income

16 Educator expenses (see page XX). | 16 |
17 IRA deduction (see page 28). | 17 |
18 Student loan interest deduction (see page 31). | 18 |
19 Tuition and fees deduction (see page XX). | 19 |
20 Add lines 16 through 19. These are your **total adjustments.** | 20 |

21 Subtract line 20 from line 15. This is your **adjusted gross income.** ▶ | 21 |

For Disclosure, Privacy Act, and Paperwork Reduction Act Notice, see page 53. Cat. No. 11327A Form **1040A** (2002)

Tax, credits, and payments	**22**	Enter the amount from line 21 (adjusted gross income).	22	

Tax, credits, and payments

23a Check if: ☐ **You** were 65 or older ☐ Blind ☐ **Spouse** was 65 or older ☐ Blind } **Enter number of boxes checked ▶** 23a [ ]

b If you are married filing separately and your spouse itemizes deductions, see page 32 and check here . . . . ▶ 23b ☐

Standard Deduction for—

• People who checked any box on line 23a or 23b **or** who can be claimed as a dependent, see page 33.

• All others:

Single, $4,700

Head of household, $6,900

Married filing jointly or Qualifying widow(er), $7,850

Married filing separately, $3,925

24 Enter your **standard deduction** (see left margin). | 24 |

25 Subtract line 24 from line 22. If line 24 is more than line 22, enter -0-. | 25 |

26 Multiply $3,000 by the total number of exemptions claimed on line 6d. | 26 |

27 Subtract line 26 from line 25. If line 26 is more than line 25, enter -0-. This is your **taxable income.** ▶ | 27 |

28 **Tax,** including any alternative minimum tax (see page 33). | 28 |

29 Credit for child and dependent care expenses. Attach Schedule 2. | 29 |

30 Credit for the elderly or the disabled. Attach Schedule 3. | 30 |

31 Education credits. Attach Form 8863. | 31 |

32 Retirement savings contributions credit. Attach Form 8880. | 32 |

33 Child tax credit (see page 36). | 33 |

34 Adoption credit. Attach Form 8839. | 34 |

35 Add lines 29 through 34. These are your **total credits.** | 35 |

36 Subtract line 35 from line 28. If line 35 is more than line 28, enter -0-. | 36 |

37 Advance earned income credit payments from Form(s) W-2. | 37 |

38 Add lines 36 and 37. This is your **total tax.** ▶ | 38 |

39 Federal income tax withheld from Forms W-2 and 1099. | 39 |

40 2002 estimated tax payments and amount applied from 2001 return. | 40 |

If you have a qualifying child, attach Schedule EIC.

41 **Earned income credit (EIC).** | 41 |

42 Additional child tax credit. Attach Form 8812. | 42 |

43 Add lines 39 through 42. These are your **total payments.** ▶ | 43 |

Refund

44 If line 43 is more than line 38, subtract line 38 from line 43. This is the amount you **overpaid.** | 44 |

Direct deposit? See page 47 and fill in 45b, 45c, and 45d.

45a Amount of line 44 you want **refunded to you.** ▶ | 45a |

▶ **b** Routing number [ ] ▶ **c** Type: ☐ Checking ☐ Savings

▶ **d** Account number [ ]

46 Amount of line 44 you want **applied to your 2003 estimated tax.** | 46 |

Amount you owe

47 **Amount you owe.** Subtract line 43 from line 38. For details on how to pay, see page 48. ▶ | 47 |

48 Estimated tax penalty (see page 48). | 48 |

Third party designee

Do you want to allow another person to discuss this return with the IRS (see page 49)? ☐ **Yes. Complete the following.** ☐ **No**

Designee's name ▶   Phone no. ▶ (   )   Personal identification number (PIN) ▶ [ ]

Sign here

Under penalties of perjury, I declare that I have examined this return and accompanying schedules and statements, and to the best of my knowledge and belief, they are true, correct, and accurately list all amounts and sources of income I received during the tax year. Declaration of preparer (other than the taxpayer) is based on all information of which the preparer has any knowledge.

Joint return? See page 20. Keep a copy for your records.

Your signature	Date	Your occupation	Daytime phone number ( )
Spouse's signature. If a joint return, **both** must sign.	Date	Spouse's occupation	

Paid preparer's use only

Preparer's signature ▶	Date	Check if self-employed ☐	Preparer's SSN or PTIN
Firm's name (or yours if self-employed), address, and ZIP code ▶		EIN	
		Phone no. ( )	

✸

Form **1040A** (2002)

Department of the Treasury—Internal Revenue Service

**Interest and Ordinary Dividends
for Form 1040A Filers** (99) **2002**

OMB No. 1545-0085

Name(s) shown on Form 1040A

Your social security number

Part I

Interest

(See page
61 and the
instructions
for Form
1040A,
line 8a.)

Note. If you received a Form 1099-INT, Form 1099-OID, or substitute statement from a brokerage firm, enter the firm's name and the total interest shown on that form.

1 List name of payer. If any interest is from a seller-financed mortgage and the buyer used the property as a personal residence, see page 61 and list this interest first. Also, show that buyer's social security number and address.

	Amount
1	

2	Add the amounts on line 1.	2
3	Excludable interest on series EE and I U.S. savings bonds issued after 1989 from Form 8815, line 14. You **must** attach Form 8815.	3
4	Subtract line 3 from line 2. Enter the result here and on Form 1040A, line 8a.	4

Part II

**Ordinary
dividends**

(See page
61 and the
instructions
for Form
1040A,
line 9.)

Note. If you received a Form 1099-DIV or substitute statement from a brokerage firm, enter the firm's name and the ordinary dividends shown on that form.

5 List name of payer. Include only ordinary dividends. If you received any capital gain distributions, see the instructions for Form 1040A, line 10.

	Amount
5	

6	Add the amounts on line 5. Enter the total here and on Form 1040A, line 9.	6

For Paperwork Reduction Act Notice, see Form 1040A instructions. Cat. No. 12075R **Schedule 1 (Form 1040A) 2002**

Schedule 2
(Form 1040A)

Department of the Treasury—Internal Revenue Service

Child and Dependent Care Expenses for Form 1040A Filers (99) 2002

OMB No. 1545-0085

Name(s) shown on Form 1040A | Your social security number

Before you begin: You need to understand the following terms. See **Definitions** on page 1 of the separate instructions.
● **Dependent Care Benefits**   ● **Qualifying Person(s)**   ● **Qualified Expenses**   ● **Earned Income**

Part I

Persons or organizations who provided the care

You **must** complete this part.

1

(a) Care provider's name	(b) Address (number, street, apt. no., city, state, and ZIP code)	(c) Identifying number (SSN or EIN)	(d) Amount paid (see instructions)

(If you need more space, use the bottom of page 2.)

Did you receive **dependent care benefits?**

— No ⟶ Complete only Part II below.

— Yes ⟶ Complete Part III on the back next.

Caution. If the care was provided in your home, you may owe employment taxes. If you do, you must use Form 1040. See **Schedule H** and its instructions for details.

Part II

Credit for child and dependent care expenses

2 Information about your **qualifying person(s).** If you have more than two qualifying persons, see the instructions.

(a) Qualifying person's name		(b) Qualifying person's social security number	(c) Qualified expenses you incurred and paid in 2002 for the person listed in column (a)
First	Last		

3 Add the amounts in column (c) of line 2. **Do not** enter more than $2,400 for one qualifying person or $4,800 for two or more persons. If you completed Part III, enter the amount from line 26. ... 3

4 Enter your **earned income.** ... 4

5 If married filing a joint return, enter your spouse's earned income (if your spouse was a student or was disabled, see the instructions); **all others,** enter the amount from line 4. ... 5

6 Enter the **smallest** of line 3, 4, or 5. ... 6

7 Enter the amount from Form 1040A, line 22. ... 7

8 Enter on line 8 the decimal amount shown below that applies to the amount on line 7.

If line 7 is:			If line 7 is:		
Over	But not over	Decimal amount is	Over	But not over	Decimal amount is
$0—10,000		.30	$20,000—22,000		.24
10,000—12,000		.29	22,000—24,000		.23
12,000—14,000		.28	24,000—26,000		.22
14,000—16,000		.27	26,000—28,000		.21
16,000—18,000		.26	28,000—No limit		.20
18,000—20,000		.25			

8   × .

9 Multiply **line 6** by the decimal amount on line 8. If you paid 2001 expenses in 2002, see the instructions. ... 9

10 Enter the amount from Form 1040A, line 28. ... 10

11 **Credit for child and dependent care expenses.** Enter the **smaller** of line 9 or line 10 here and on Form 1040A, line 29. ... 11

For Paperwork Reduction Act Notice, see Form 1040A instructions.   Cat. No. 10749I   **Schedule 2 (Form 1040A) 2002**

713

Part III

Dependent care benefits

12 Enter the total amount of **dependent care benefits** you received for 2002. This amount should be shown in box 10 of your W-2 form(s). **Do not** include amounts that were reported to you as wages in box 1 of Form(s) W-2. | **12** |

13 Enter the amount forfeited, if any. See the instructions. | **13** |

14 Subtract line 13 from line 12. | **14** |

15 Enter the total amount of **qualified expenses** incurred in 2002 for the care of the qualifying person(s). | **15** |

16 Enter the **smaller** of line 14 or 15. | **16** |

17 Enter your **earned income.** | **17** |

18 Enter the amount shown below that applies to you.
- If married filing jointly, enter your spouse's earned income (if your spouse was a student or was disabled, see the instructions for line 5).
- If married filing separately, see the instructions for the amount to enter.
- All others, enter the amount from line 17. | **18** |

19 Enter the **smallest** of line 16, 17, or 18. | **19** |

20 **Excluded benefits.** Enter here the **smaller** of the following:
- The amount from line 19 or
- $5,000 ($2,500 if married filing separately **and** you were required to enter your spouse's earned income on line 18). | **20** |

21 **Taxable benefits.** Subtract line 20 from line 14. Also, include this amount on Form 1040A, line 7. In the space to the left of line 7, enter "DCB." | **21** |

To claim the child and dependent care credit, complete lines 22–26 below.

22 Enter $2,400 ($4,800 if two or more qualifying persons). | **22** |

23 Enter the amount from line 20. | **23** |

24 Subtract line 23 from line 22. If zero or less, **stop.** You cannot take the credit. **Exception.** If you paid 2001 expenses in 2002, see the instructions for line 9. | **24** |

25 Complete line 2 on the front of this schedule. **Do not** include in column (c) any benefits shown on line 20 above. Then, add the amounts in column (c) and enter the total here. | **25** |

26 Enter the **smaller** of line 24 or 25. Also, enter this amount on line 3 on the front of this schedule and complete lines 4–11. | **26** |

Schedule 2 (Form 1040A) 2002

Form **1040**

Department of the Treasury—Internal Revenue Service

U.S. Individual Income Tax Return **2002**

(99)   IRS Use Only—Do not write or staple in this space.

For the year Jan. 1–Dec. 31, 2002, or other tax year beginning _____ , 2002, ending _____ , 20 ____

OMB No. 1545-0074

Label

(See instructions on page 19.)

Use the IRS label. Otherwise, please print or type.

Presidential Election Campaign (See page 19.)

L A B E L   H E R E

Your first name and initial | Last name | Your social security number

If a joint return, spouse's first name and initial | Last name | Spouse's social security number

Home address (number and street). If you have a P.O. box, see page 19. | Apt. no.

City, town or post office, state, and ZIP code. If you have a foreign address, see page 19.

▲ **Important!** ▲

You **must** enter your SSN(s) above.

Note. Checking "Yes" will not change your tax or reduce your refund.

Do you, or your spouse if filing a joint return, want $3 to go to this fund? . . . ▶

	You		Spouse	
	☐ Yes	☐ No	☐ Yes	☐ No

Filing Status

Check only one box.

1 ☐ Single

2 ☐ Married filing jointly (even if only one had income)

3 ☐ Married filing separately. Enter spouse's SSN above and full name here. ▶ _____

4 ☐ Head of household (with qualifying person). (See page 19.) If the qualifying person is a child but not your dependent, enter this child's name here. ▶ _____

5 ☐ Qualifying widow(er) with dependent child (year spouse died ▶ ____). (See page 19.)

Exemptions

If more than five dependents, see page 20.

6a ☐ **Yourself.** If your parent (or someone else) can claim you as a dependent on his or her tax return, **do not** check box 6a . . . .

b ☐ **Spouse** . . . .

c **Dependents:**

(1) First name Last name	(2) Dependent's social security number	(3) Dependent's relationship to you	(4) ✓ if qualifying child for child tax credit (see page 20)
_____	_____	_____	☐
_____	_____	_____	☐
_____	_____	_____	☐
_____	_____	_____	☐
_____	_____	_____	☐

No. of boxes checked on 6a and 6b ____

No. of children on 6c who:
- lived with you ____
- did not live with you due to divorce or separation (see page 20) ____

Dependents on 6c not entered above ____

Add numbers on lines above ▶ ☐

d Total number of exemptions claimed . . . .

Income

Attach Forms W-2 and W-2G here. Also attach Form(s) 1099-R if tax was withheld.

If you did not get a W-2, see page 21.

Enclose, but do not attach, any payment. Also, please use Form 1040-V.

7 Wages, salaries, tips, etc. Attach Form(s) W-2 | 7 |

8a **Taxable** interest. Attach Schedule B if required . . . | 8a |

b **Tax-exempt** interest. **Do not** include on line 8a . . . | 8b |

9 Ordinary dividends. Attach Schedule B if required . . . | 9 |

10 Taxable refunds, credits, or offsets of state and local income taxes (see page 22) . . | 10 |

11 Alimony received | 11 |

12 Business income or (loss). Attach Schedule C or C-EZ | 12 |

13 Capital gain or (loss). Attach Schedule D if required. If not required, check here ▶ ☐ | 13 |

14 Other gains or (losses). Attach Form 4797 . . . . . . | 14 |

15a IRA distributions . . | 15a | b Taxable amount (see page 23) | 15b |

16a Pensions and annuities | 16a | b Taxable amount (see page 23) | 16b |

17 Rental real estate, royalties, partnerships, S corporations, trusts, etc. Attach Schedule E | 17 |

18 Farm income or (loss). Attach Schedule F . . . . . . | 18 |

19 Unemployment compensation . . . . | 19 |

20a Social security benefits . | 20a | b Taxable amount (see page 25) | 20b |

21 Other income. List type and amount (see page 27) _____ | 21 |

22 Add the amounts in the far right column for lines 7 through 21. This is your **total income** ▶ | 22 |

Adjusted Gross Income

23 Educator expenses (see page xx) . . . . . . | 23 |

24 IRA deduction (see page 27) . . . . . . | 24 |

25 Student loan interest deduction (see page 28) . . . . | 25 |

26 Tuition and fees deduction (see page XX) . . . . . | 26 |

27 Archer MSA deduction. Attach Form 8853 . . . . | 27 |

28 Moving expenses. Attach Form 3903 . . . . . | 28 |

29 One-half of self-employment tax. Attach Schedule SE | 29 |

30 Self-employed health insurance deduction (see page 30) | 30 |

31 Self-employed SEP, SIMPLE, and qualified plans | 31 |

32 Penalty on early withdrawal of savings . . . . | 32 |

33a Alimony paid b Recipient's SSN ▶ _____ | 33a |

34 Add lines 23 through 33a . . . . | 34 |

35 Subtract line 34 from line 22. This is your **adjusted gross income** . . . . . ▶ | 35 |

For Disclosure, Privacy Act, and Paperwork Reduction Act Notice, see page 72.

Cat. No. 11320B

Form **1040** (2002)

				36	

Tax and Credits

36 Amount from line 35 (adjusted gross income) . . . . | 36 |

37a Check if: ☐ **You** were 65 or older, ☐ Blind; ☐ **Spouse** was 65 or older, ☐ Blind.
Add the number of boxes checked above and enter the total here . . . . ▶ **37a** ☐

Standard Deduction for—
● People who checked any box on line 37a or 37b **or** who can be claimed as a dependent, see page 31.
● All others:
Single, $4,700
Head of household, $6,900
Married filing jointly or Qualifying widow(er), $7,850
Married filing separately, $3,925

b If you are married filing separately and your spouse itemizes deductions, or you were a dual-status alien, see page 31 and check here . . . . . . ▶ **37b** ☐

38 **Itemized deductions** (from Schedule A) **or** your **standard deduction** (see left margin) . . | 38 |
39 Subtract line 38 from line 36 . . . . | 39 |
40 If line 36 is $103,000 or less, multiply $3,000 by the total number of exemptions claimed on line 6d. If line 36 is over $103,000, see the worksheet on page 32 . . | 40 |
41 **Taxable income.** Subtract line 40 from line 39. If line 40 is more than line 39, enter -0- | 41 |
42 **Tax** (see page 33). Check if any tax is from: **a** ☐ Form(s) 8814 **b** ☐ Form 4972 | 42 |
43 **Alternative minimum tax** (see page 34). Attach Form 6251 . . . . | 43 |
44 Add lines 42 and 43 . . . . ▶ | 44 |
45 Foreign tax credit. Attach Form 1116 if required . . . . | 45 |
46 Credit for child and dependent care expenses. Attach Form 2441 | 46 |
47 Credit for the elderly or the disabled. Attach Schedule R . | 47 |
48 Education credits. Attach Form 8863 . . . . | 48 |
49 Retirement savings contributions credit. Attach Form 8880 | 49 |
50 Child tax credit (see page XX) . . . . | 50 |
51 Adoption credit. Attach Form 8839 . . . . | 51 |
52 Credits from: **a** ☐ Form 8396 **b** ☐ Form 8859 . | 52 |
53 Other credits. Check applicable box(es): **a** ☐ Form 3800 **b** ☐ Form 8801 **c** ☐ Specify _____ | 53 |
54 Add lines 45 through 53. These are your **total credits** . . . . | 54 |
55 Subtract line 54 from line 44. If line 54 is more than line 44, enter -0- . . . . . ▶ | 55 |

Other Taxes

56 Self-employment tax. Attach Schedule SE . . . . | 56 |
57 Social security and Medicare tax on tip income not reported to employer. Attach Form 4137 . . | 57 |
58 Tax on qualified plans, including IRAs, and other tax-favored accounts. Attach Form 5329 if required . | 58 |
59 Advance earned income credit payments from Form(s) W-2 . . . . . | 59 |
60 Household employment taxes. Attach Schedule H . . . . | 60 |
61 Add lines 55 through 60. This is your **total tax** . . . . ▶ | 61 |

Payments

If you have a qualifying child, attach Schedule EIC.

62 Federal income tax withheld from Forms W-2 and 1099 . . | 62 |
63 2002 estimated tax payments and amount applied from 2001 return | 63 |
64 **Earned income credit (EIC)** . . . . | 64 |
65 Excess social security and tier 1 RRTA tax withheld (see page 51) | 65 |
66 Additional child tax credit. Attach Form 8812 . . . . | 66 |
67 Amount paid with request for extension to file (see page 51) | 67 |
68 Other payments from: **a** ☐ Form 2439 **b** ☐ Form 4136 **c** ☐ Form 8885 | 68 |
69 Add lines 62 through 68. These are your **total payments** . . . . . ▶ | 69 |

Refund

Direct deposit? See page 51 and fill in 71b, 71c, and 71d.

70 If line 69 is more than line 61, subtract line 61 from line 69. This is the amount you **overpaid** | 70 |
71a Amount of line 70 you want **refunded to you** . . . . ▶ | 71a |
▶ b Routing number |_____| ▶ c Type: ☐ Checking ☐ Savings
▶ d Account number |_____|
72 Amount of line 70 you want **applied to your 2003 estimated tax** ▶ | 72 |

Amount You Owe

73 **Amount you owe.** Subtract line 69 from line 61. For details on how to pay, see page 52 ▶ | 73 |
74 Estimated tax penalty (see page 52) . . . . . . | 74 |

Third Party Designee

Do you want to allow another person to discuss this return with the IRS (see page 53)? ☐ **Yes.** Complete the following. ☐ **No**

Designee's name ▶ _____   Phone no. ▶ ( )   Personal identification number (PIN) ▶ |____|

Sign Here

Under penalties of perjury, I declare that I have examined this return and accompanying schedules and statements, and to the best of my knowledge and belief, they are true, correct, and complete. Declaration of preparer (other than taxpayer) is based on all information of which preparer has any knowledge.

Joint return? See page 19.
Keep a copy for your records.

Your signature | Date | Your occupation | Daytime phone number ( )

Spouse's signature. If a joint return, **both** must sign. | Date | Spouse's occupation

Paid Preparer's Use Only

Preparer's signature ▶ | Date | Check if self-employed ☐ | Preparer's SSN or PTIN

Firm's name (or yours if self-employed), address, and ZIP code ▶ | EIN | Phone no. ( )

SCHEDULE C
(Form 1040)

Department of the Treasury
Internal Revenue Service   (99)

Profit or Loss From Business
(Sole Proprietorship)
▶ Partnerships, joint ventures, etc., must file Form 1065 or 1065-B.
▶ **Attach to Form 1040 or 1041.**   ▶ **See Instructions for Schedule C (Form 1040).**

OMB No. 1545-0074

2002

Attachment
Sequence No. **09**

Name of proprietor | Social security number (SSN)

A Principal business or profession, including product or service (see page C-1 of the instructions) | **B** Enter code from pages C-7 & 8 ▶

C Business name. If no separate business name, leave blank. | **D** Employer ID number (EIN), if any

E Business address (including suite or room no.) ▶ ....
City, town or post office, state, and ZIP code

F Accounting method: **(1)** ☐ Cash   **(2)** ☐ Accrual   **(3)** ☐ Other (specify) ▶ ....

G Did you "materially participate" in the operation of this business during 2002? If "No," see page C-2 for limit on losses   ☐ Yes   ☐ No

H If you started or acquired this business during 2002, check here . . . . ▶ ☐

Part I   Income

1	Gross receipts or sales. **Caution.** If this income was reported to you on Form W-2 and the "Statutory employee" box on that form was checked, see page C-2 and check here . . . . ▶ ☐	**1**
2	Returns and allowances	**2**
3	Subtract line 2 from line 1	**3**
4	Cost of goods sold (from line 42 on page 2)	**4**
5	**Gross profit.** Subtract line 4 from line 3	**5**
6	Other income, including Federal and state gasoline or fuel tax credit or refund (see page C-3) . . .	**6**
7	**Gross income.** Add lines 5 and 6 . . . . ▶	**7**

Part II   Expenses. Enter expenses for business use of your home **only** on line 30.

8	Advertising	**8**		**19**	Pension and profit-sharing plans	**19**
9	Bad debts from sales or services (see page C-3) . .	**9**		**20**	Rent or lease (see page C-4):	
				a	Vehicles, machinery, and equipment .	**20a**
10	Car and truck expenses (see page C-3)	**10**		**b**	Other business property . .	**20b**
11	Commissions and fees . . .	**11**		**21**	Repairs and maintenance . .	**21**
12	Depletion	**12**		**22**	Supplies (not included in Part III) .	**22**
13	Depreciation and section 179 expense deduction (not included in Part III) (see page C-3) . .	**13**		**23**	Taxes and licenses	**23**
				24	Travel, meals, and entertainment:	
				a	Travel	**24a**
14	Employee benefit programs (other than on line 19) . . .	**14**		**b**	Meals and entertainment	
15	Insurance (other than health) .	**15**		**c**	Enter nondeduct-ible amount in-cluded on line 24b (see page C-5) .	
16	Interest:					
a	Mortgage (paid to banks, etc.) .	**16a**		**d**	Subtract line 24c from line 24b .	**24d**
b	Other	**16b**		**25**	Utilities	**25**
17	Legal and professional services	**17**		**26**	Wages (less employment credits) .	**26**
18	Office expense	**18**		**27**	Other expenses (from line 48 on page 2)	**27**

28	**Total expenses** before expenses for business use of home. Add lines 8 through 27 in columns ▶	**28**
29	Tentative profit (loss). Subtract line 28 from line 7	**29**
30	Expenses for business use of your home. Attach **Form 8829**	**30**
31	**Net profit or (loss).** Subtract line 30 from line 29.	
	• If a profit, enter on **Form 1040, line 12,** and **also** on **Schedule SE, line 2** (statutory employees, see page C-5). Estates and trusts, enter on Form 1041, line 3.	**31**
	• If a loss, you **must** go to line 32.	
32	If you have a loss, check the box that describes your investment in this activity (see page C-6).	
	• If you checked 32a, enter the loss on **Form 1040, line 12,** and **also** on **Schedule SE, line 2** (statutory employees, see page C-5). Estates and trusts, enter on Form 1041, line 3.	**32a** ☐ All investment is at risk.
	• If you checked 32b, you **must** attach **Form 6198.**	**32b** ☐ Some investment is not at risk.

For Paperwork Reduction Act Notice, see Form 1040 instructions.   Cat. No. 11334P   Schedule C (Form 1040) 2002

Part III   **Cost of Goods Sold** (see page C-6)

33   Method(s) used to value closing inventory: **a** ☐ Cost   **b** ☐ Lower of cost or market   **c** ☐ Other (attach explanation)

34   Was there any change in determining quantities, costs, or valuations between opening and closing inventory? If "Yes," attach explanation . . . . ☐ **Yes**   ☐ **No**

35 Inventory at beginning of year. If different from last year's closing inventory, attach explanation . .	35	
36 Purchases less cost of items withdrawn for personal use	36	
37 Cost of labor. Do not include any amounts paid to yourself	37	
38 Materials and supplies	38	
39 Other costs	39	
40 Add lines 35 through 39	40	
41 Inventory at end of year	41	
42 **Cost of goods sold.** Subtract line 41 from line 40. Enter the result here and on page 1, line 4 . .	42	

Part IV   **Information on Your Vehicle.** Complete this part **only** if you are claiming car or truck expenses on line 10 and are not required to file Form 4562 for this business. See the instructions for line 13 on page C-3 to find out if you must file.

43   When did you place your vehicle in service for business purposes? (month, day, year) ▶ ..../........../........ .

44   Of the total number of miles you drove your vehicle during 2002, enter the number of miles you used your vehicle for:

   a Business ....   **b** Commuting ....   **c** Other ....

45   Do you (or your spouse) have another vehicle available for personal use? . . . . ☐ **Yes**   ☐ **No**

46   Was your vehicle available for personal use during off-duty hours? . . . . ☐ **Yes**   ☐ **No**

47a   Do you have evidence to support your deduction? . . . . ☐ **Yes**   ☐ **No**

   b   If "Yes," is the evidence written? . . . . ☐ **Yes**   ☐ **No**

Part V   **Other Expenses.** List below business expenses not included on lines 8–26 or line 30.

....		
....		
....		
....		
....		
....		
....		
....		
48 **Total other expenses.** Enter here and on page 1, line 27	48	

⊛

SCHEDULE D
(Form 1040)

Department of the Treasury
Internal Revenue Service   (99)

Capital Gains and Losses

▶ Attach to Form 1040.   ▶ See Instructions for Schedule D (Form 1040).

▶ Use Schedule D-1 to list additional transactions for lines 1 and 8.

OMB No. 1545-0074

20**02**

Attachment
Sequence No. **12**

Name(s) shown on Form 1040

Your social security number

Part I   Short-Term Capital Gains and Losses—Assets Held One Year or Less

(a) Description of property (Example: 100 sh. XYZ Co.)	(b) Date acquired (Mo., day, yr.)	(c) Date sold (Mo., day, yr.)	(d) Sales price (see page D-5 of the instructions)	(e) Cost or other basis (see page D-5 of the instructions)	(f) Gain or (loss) Subtract (e) from (d)	
1						

2 Enter your short-term totals, if any, from Schedule D-1, line 2	**2**		
3 **Total short-term sales price amounts.** Add lines 1 and 2 in column (d)	**3**		

4 Short-term gain from Form 6252 and short-term gain or (loss) from Forms 4684, 6781, and 8824 | **4** |

5 Net short-term gain or (loss) from partnerships, S corporations, estates, and trusts from Schedule(s) K-1 . . . . | **5** |

6 Short-term capital loss carryover. Enter the amount, if any, from line 8 of your 2001 Capital Loss Carryover Worksheet . . . . | **6** ( ) |

7 **Net short-term capital gain or (loss).** Combine lines 1 through 6 in column (f). | **7** |

Part II   Long-Term Capital Gains and Losses—Assets Held More Than One Year

(a) Description of property (Example: 100 sh. XYZ Co.)	(b) Date acquired (Mo., day, yr.)	(c) Date sold (Mo., day, yr.)	(d) Sales price (see page D-5 of the instructions)	(e) Cost or other basis (see page D-5 of the instructions)	(f) Gain or (loss) Subtract (e) from (d)	(g) 28% rate gain or (loss) * (see instr. below)
8						

9 Enter your long-term totals, if any, from Schedule D-1, line 9	**9**		
10 **Total long-term sales price amounts.** Add lines 8 and 9 in column (d)	**10**		

11 Gain from Form 4797, Part I; long-term gain from Forms 2439 and 6252; and long-term gain or (loss) from Forms 4684, 6781, and 8824 . . . . | **11** |

12 Net long-term gain or (loss) from partnerships, S corporations, estates, and trusts from Schedule(s) K-1. | **12** |

13 Capital gain distributions. See page D-1 of the instructions . . . . . | **13** |

14 Long-term capital loss carryover. Enter in both columns (f) and (g) the amount, if any, from line 13 of your 2001 Capital Loss Carryover Worksheet . . . . . . | **14** ( ) ( ) |

15 Combine lines 8 through 14 in column (g) . . . . | **15** |

16 **Net long-term capital gain or (loss).** Combine lines 8 through 14 in column (f)
Next: Go to Part III on the back. | **16** |

***28% rate gain or loss** includes **all** "collectibles gains and losses" (as defined on page D-6 of the instructions) and up to 50% of the eligible gain on qualified small business stock (see page D-4 of the instructions).

For Paperwork Reduction Act Notice, see Form 1040 instructions.   Cat. No. 11338H   Schedule D (Form 1040) 2002

Part III   Taxable Gain or Deductible Loss

17   Combine lines 7 and 16 and enter the result. If a loss, go to line 18. If a gain, enter the gain on Form 1040, line 13, and complete Form 1040 through line 41 . . . .   **17**

     Next: • If both lines 16 and 17 are gains **and** Form 1040, line 41, is more than zero, complete Part IV below.

          • Otherwise, skip the rest of Schedule D and complete Form 1040.

18   If line 17 is a loss, enter here and on Form 1040, line 13, the **smaller** of **(a)** that loss or **(b)** ($3,000) (or, if married filing separately, ($1,500)). Then complete Form 1040 through line 39   **18** (   )

     Next: • If the loss on line 17 is more than the loss on line 18 **or** if Form 1040, line 39, is less than zero, skip **Part IV** below and complete the **Capital Loss Carryover Worksheet** on page D-6 of the instructions before completing the rest of Form 1040.

          • Otherwise, skip **Part IV** below and complete the rest of Form 1040.

Part IV   Tax Computation Using Maximum Capital Gains Rates

19   Enter your unrecaptured section 1250 gain, if any, from line 17 of the worksheet on page D-7 of the instructions **19**

     If line 15 or line 19 is more than zero, complete the worksheet on page D-9 of the instructions to figure the amount to enter on lines 22, 29, and 40 below, and skip all other lines below. Otherwise, go to line 20.

20   Enter your taxable income from Form 1040, line 41 . . . . . .   **20**

21   Enter the **smaller** of line 16 or line 17 of Schedule D **21**

22   If you are deducting investment interest expense on Form 4952, enter the amount from Form 4952, line 4e. Otherwise, enter -0-   **22**

23   Subtract line 22 from line 21. If zero or less, enter -0- **23**

24   Subtract line 23 from line 20. If zero or less, enter -0- **24**

25   Figure the tax on the amount on line 24. Use the Tax Table or Tax Rate Schedules, whichever applies   **25**

26   Enter the **smaller** of:

     • The amount on line 20 **or**

     • $46,700 if married filing jointly or qualifying widow(er); $27,950 if single; $37,450 if head of household; or $23,350 if married filing separately   **26**

     If line 26 is greater than line 24, go to line 27. Otherwise, skip lines 27 through 33 and go to line 34.

27   Enter the amount from line 24   . . . .   **27**

28   Subtract line 27 from line 26. If zero or less, enter -0- and go to line 34   **28**

29   Enter your qualified 5-year gain, if any, from line 8 of the worksheet on page D-8   . .   **29**

30   Enter the **smaller** of line 28 or line 29 . . . .   **30**

31   Multiply line 30 by 8% (.08) **31**

32   Subtract line 30 from line 28 . . . .   **32**

33   Multiply line 32 by 10% (.10) **33**

     If the amounts on lines 23 and 28 are the same, skip lines 34 through 37 and go to line 38.

34   Enter the **smaller** of line 20 or line 23 . . . .   **34**

35   Enter the amount from line 28 (if line 28 is blank, enter -0-) . . .   **35**

36   Subtract line 35 from line 34 . . . .   **36**

37   Multiply line 36 by 20% (.20) **37**

38   Add lines 25, 31, 33, and 37 . . . .   **38**

39   Figure the tax on the amount on line 20. Use the Tax Table or Tax Rate Schedules, whichever applies   **39**

40   **Tax on all taxable income (including capital gains).** Enter the **smaller** of line 38 or line 39 here and on Form 1040, line 42   . . . .   **40**

Supplemental Income and Loss

**(From rental real estate, royalties, partnerships,
S corporations, estates, trusts, REMICs, etc.)**

▶ **Attach to Form 1040 or Form 1041.** ▶ **See Instructions for Schedule E (Form 1040).**

OMB No. 1545-0074

2002

Attachment
Sequence No. **13**

Name(s) shown on return

Your social security number

Part I   **Income or Loss From Rental Real Estate and Royalties**   **Note.** If you are in the business of renting personal property, use **Schedule C or C-EZ** (see page E-1). Report farm rental income or loss from **Form 4835** on page 2, line 39.

1 Show the kind and location of each **rental real estate property:**

A ....

B ....

C ....

2 For each rental real estate property listed on line 1, did you or your family use it during the tax year for personal purposes for more than the greater of:

- 14 days **or**
- 10% of the total days rented at fair rental value?

(See page E-1.)

	Yes	No
A		
B		
C		

Income:

		Properties			Totals (Add columns A, B, and C.)
		A	B	C	
3 Rents received	3				3
4 Royalties received	4				4

Expenses:

5 Advertising	5				
6 Auto and travel (see page E-2)	6				
7 Cleaning and maintenance	7				
8 Commissions	8				
9 Insurance	9				
10 Legal and other professional fees	10				
11 Management fees	11				
12 Mortgage interest paid to banks, etc. (see page E-2)	12				12
13 Other interest	13				
14 Repairs	14				
15 Supplies	15				
16 Taxes	16				
17 Utilities	17				
18 Other (list) ▶	18				
19 Add lines 5 through 18	19				19
20 Depreciation expense or depletion (see page E-3)	20				20
21 Total expenses. Add lines 19 and 20	21				
22 Income or (loss) from rental real estate or royalty properties. Subtract line 21 from line 3 (rents) or line 4 (royalties). If the result is a (loss), see page E-3 to find out if you must file **Form 6198**	22				
23 Deductible rental real estate loss. **Caution.** Your rental real estate loss on line 22 may be limited. See page E-3 to find out if you must file **Form 8582.** Real estate professionals must complete line 42 on page 2	23	( )	( )	( )	

24   **Income.** Add positive amounts shown on line 22. **Do not** include any losses | **24** | |

25   **Losses.** Add royalty losses from line 22 and rental real estate losses from line 23. Enter total losses here | **25** | ( ) |

26   **Total rental real estate and royalty income or (loss).** Combine lines 24 and 25. Enter the result here. If Parts II, III, IV, and line 39 on page 2 do not apply to you, also enter this amount on Form 1040, line 17. Otherwise, include this amount in the total on line 40 on page 2 | **26** | |

Name(s) shown on return. Do not enter name and social security number if shown on other side.	**Your social security number**

Note. If you report amounts from farming or fishing on Schedule E, you must enter your gross income from those activities on line 41 below. Real estate professionals must complete line 42 below.

Part II **Income or Loss From Partnerships and S Corporations** Note. If you report a loss from an at-risk activity, you **must** check either column **(e)** or **(f)** on line 27 to describe your investment in the activity. See page E-5. If you check column **(f)**, you must attach **Form 6198.**

27	(a) Name	(b) Enter P for partnership; S for S corporation	(c) Check if foreign partnership	(d) Employer identification number	Investment At Risk? (e) All is at risk	(f) Some is not at risk
A						
B						
C						
D						
E						

	Passive Income and Loss		Nonpassive Income and Loss		
	(g) Passive loss allowed (attach **Form 8582** if required)	(h) Passive income from **Schedule K–1**	(i) Nonpassive loss from **Schedule K–1**	(j) Section 179 expense deduction from **Form 4562**	(k) Nonpassive income from **Schedule K–1**
A					
B					
C					
D					
E					
28a Totals					
b Totals					

29	Add columns (h) and (k) of line 28a	29	
30	Add columns (g), (i), and (j) of line 28b	30	( )
31	**Total partnership and S corporation income or (loss).** Combine lines 29 and 30. Enter the result here and include in the total on line 40 below	31	

Part III **Income or Loss From Estates and Trusts**

32	(a) Name	(b) Employer identification number
A		
B		

	Passive Income and Loss		Nonpassive Income and Loss	
	(c) Passive deduction or loss allowed (attach **Form 8582** if required)	(d) Passive income from **Schedule K–1**	(e) Deduction or loss from **Schedule K–1**	(f) Other income from **Schedule K–1**
A				
B				
33a Totals				
b Totals				

34	Add columns (d) and (f) of line 33a	34	
35	Add columns (c) and (e) of line 33b	35	( )
36	**Total estate and trust income or (loss).** Combine lines 34 and 35. Enter the result here and include in the total on line 40 below	36	

Part IV **Income or Loss From Real Estate Mortgage Investment Conduits (REMICs)—Residual Holder**

37	(a) Name	(b) Employer identification number	(c) Excess inclusion from **Schedules Q**, line 2c (see page E-6)	(d) Taxable income (net loss) from **Schedules Q**, line 1b	(e) Income from **Schedules Q**, line 3b

38	Combine columns (d) and (e) only. Enter the result here and include in the total on line 40 below	38	

Part V **Summary**

39	Net farm rental income or (loss) from **Form 4835.** Also, complete line 41 below	39	
40	**Total income or (loss).** Combine lines 26, 31, 36, 38, and 39. Enter the result here and on Form 1040, line 17 ▶	40	
41	**Reconciliation of Farming and Fishing Income.** Enter your **gross** farming and fishing income reported on Form 4835, line 7; Schedule K-1 (Form 1065), line 15b; Schedule K-1 (Form 1120S), line 23; and Schedule K-1 (Form 1041), line 14 (see page E-6)	41	
42	**Reconciliation for Real Estate Professionals.** If you were a real estate professional (see page E-4), enter the net income or (loss) you reported anywhere on Form 1040 from all rental real estate activities in which you materially participated under the passive activity loss rules . . .	42	

Self-Employment Tax

► **Attach to Form 1040.** ► **See Instructions for Schedule SE (Form 1040).**

OMB No. 1545-0074

2002

Attachment
Sequence No. **17**

Name of person with **self-employment** income (as shown on Form 1040)

Social security number of person
with **self-employment** income ►

Who Must File Schedule SE

You must file Schedule SE if:

- You had net earnings from self-employment from **other than** church employee income (line 4 of Short Schedule SE or line 4c of Long Schedule SE) of $400 or more **or**

- You had church employee income of $108.28 or more. Income from services you performed as a minister or a member of a religious order **is not** church employee income. See page SE-1.

Note. Even if you had a loss or a small amount of income from self-employment, it may be to your benefit to file Schedule SE and use either "optional method" in Part II of Long Schedule SE. See page SE-3.

Exception. If your only self-employment income was from earnings as a minister, member of a religious order, or Christian Science practitioner **and** you filed Form 4361 and received IRS approval not to be taxed on those earnings, **do not** file Schedule SE. Instead, write "Exempt–Form 4361" on Form 1040, line 56.

May I Use Short Schedule SE or Must I Use Long Schedule SE?

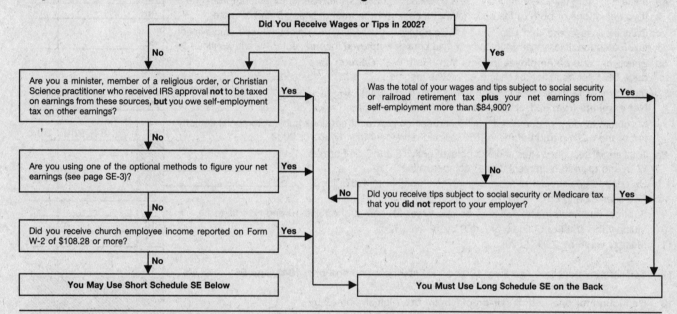

Section A—Short Schedule SE. Caution. Read above to see if you can use Short Schedule SE.

1	Net farm profit or (loss) from Schedule F, line 36, and farm partnerships, Schedule K-1 (Form 1065), line 15a	**1**
2	Net profit or (loss) from Schedule C, line 31; Schedule C-EZ, line 3; Schedule K-1 (Form 1065), line 15a (other than farming); and Schedule K-1 (Form 1065-B), box 9. Ministers and members of religious orders, see page SE-1 for amounts to report on this line. See page SE-2 for other income to report	**2**
3	Combine lines 1 and 2	**3**
4	**Net earnings from self-employment.** Multiply line 3 by 92.35% (.9235). If less than $400, **do not** file this schedule; you do not owe self-employment tax . . . . ►	**4**
5	**Self-employment tax.** If the amount on line 4 is: ● $84,900 or less, multiply line 4 by 15.3% (.153). Enter the result here and on **Form 1040, line 56.** ● More than $84,900, multiply line 4 by 2.9% (.029). Then, add $10,527.60 to the result. Enter the total here and on **Form 1040, line 56.**	**5**
6	**Deduction for one-half of self-employment tax.** Multiply line 5 by 50% (.5). Enter the result here and on **Form 1040, line 29**	**6**	

| Name of person with **self-employment** income (as shown on Form 1040) | Social security number of person with **self-employment** income ▶ | | |

Section B—Long Schedule SE

Part I   Self-Employment Tax

Note. If your only income subject to self-employment tax is **church employee income,** skip lines 1 through 4b. Enter -0- on line 4c and go to line 5a. Income from services you performed as a minister or a member of a religious order **is not** church employee income. See page SE-1.

A   If you are a minister, member of a religious order, or Christian Science practitioner **and** you filed Form 4361, but you had $400 or more of **other** net earnings from self-employment, check here and continue with Part I . . . . . . ▶ ☐

1	Net farm profit or (loss) from Schedule F, line 36, and farm partnerships, Schedule K-1 (Form 1065), line 15a. **Note.** Skip this line if you use the farm optional method. See page SE-3 . .	**1**	
2	Net profit or (loss) from Schedule C, line 31; Schedule C-EZ, line 3; Schedule K-1 (Form 1065), line 15a (other than farming); and Schedule K-1 (Form 1065-B), box 9. Ministers and members of religious orders, see page SE-1 for amounts to report on this line. See page SE-2 for other income to report. **Note.** Skip this line if you use the nonfarm optional method. See page SE-3.	**2**	
3	Combine lines 1 and 2	**3**	
4a	If line 3 is more than zero, multiply line 3 by 92.35% (.9235). Otherwise, enter amount from line 3	**4a**	
b	If you elect one or both of the optional methods, enter the total of lines 15 and 17 here . . .	**4b**	
c	Combine lines 4a and 4b. If less than $400, **do not** file this schedule; you do not owe self-employment tax. **Exception.** If less than $400 and you had **church employee income,** enter -0- and continue ▶	**4c**	
5a	Enter your **church employee income** from Form W-2. **Caution.** See page SE-1 for definition of church employee income **5a**		
b	Multiply line 5a by 92.35% (.9235). If less than $100, enter -0-	**5b**	
6	**Net earnings from self-employment.** Add lines 4c and 5b	**6**	
7	Maximum amount of combined wages and self-employment earnings subject to social security tax or the 6.2% portion of the 7.65% railroad retirement (tier 1) tax for 2002	**7**	84,900 00
8a	Total social security wages and tips (total of boxes 3 and 7 on Form(s) W-2) and railroad retirement (tier 1) compensation **8a**		
b	Unreported tips subject to social security tax (from Form 4137, line 9) **8b**		
c	Add lines 8a and 8b	**8c**	
9	Subtract line 8c from line 7. If zero or less, enter -0- here and on line 10 and go to line 11 . ▶	**9**	
10	Multiply the **smaller** of line 6 or line 9 by 12.4% (.124)	**10**	
11	Multiply line 6 by 2.9% (.029)	**11**	
12	**Self-employment tax.** Add lines 10 and 11. Enter here and on **Form 1040, line 56** . .	**12**	
13	**Deduction for one-half of self-employment tax.** Multiply line 12 by 50% (.5). Enter the result here and on **Form 1040, line 29** **13**		

Part II   Optional Methods To Figure Net Earnings (See page SE-3.)

Farm Optional Method. You may use this method **only** if:

- Your gross farm income[1] was not more than $2,400 **or**
- Your net farm profits[2] were less than $1,733.

14	Maximum income for optional methods	**14**	1,600 00
15	Enter the **smaller** of: two-thirds (⅔) of gross farm income[1] (not less than zero) or $1,600. Also include this amount on line 4b above	**15**	

Nonfarm Optional Method. You may use this method **only** if:

- Your net nonfarm profits[3] were less than $1,733 and also less than 72.189% of your gross nonfarm income[4] **and**
- You had net earnings from self-employment of at least $400 in 2 of the prior 3 years.

Caution. You may use this method no more than five times.

16	Subtract line 15 from line 14	**16**	
17	Enter the **smaller** of: two-thirds (⅔) of gross nonfarm income[4] (not less than zero) **or** the amount on line 16. Also include this amount on line 4b above	**17**	

[1]From Sch. F, line 11, and Sch. K-1 (Form 1065), line 15b.   [3]From Sch. C, line 31; Sch. C-EZ, line 3; Sch. K-1 (Form 1065), line 15a; and Sch. K-1 (Form 1065-B), box 9.
[2]From Sch. F, line 36, and Sch. K-1 (Form 1065), line 15a.   [4]From Sch. C, line 7; Sch. C-EZ, line 1; Sch. K-1 (Form 1065), line 15c; and Sch. K-1 (Form 1065-B), box 9.

                                                   Schedule SE (Form 1040) 2002

Form **2106**	**Employee Business Expenses**	OMB No. 1545-0139

Form **2106**

Department of the Treasury
Internal Revenue Service (99)

▶ See separate instructions.

▶ Attach to Form 1040.

20 02

Attachment
Sequence No. **54**

Your name	Occupation in which you incurred expenses	Social security number

Part I Employee Business Expenses and Reimbursements

Step 1 Enter Your Expenses

		Column A Other Than Meals and Entertainment	**Column B** Meals and Entertainment
1	Vehicle expense from line 22 or line 29. (Rural mail carriers: See instructions.)	**1**	
2	Parking fees, tolls, and transportation, including train, bus, etc., that **did not** involve overnight travel or commuting to and from work . .	**2**	
3	Travel expense while away from home overnight, including lodging, airplane, car rental, etc. **Do not** include meals and entertainment	**3**	
4	Business expenses not included on lines 1 through 3. **Do not** include meals and entertainment	**4**	
5	Meals and entertainment expenses (see instructions)	**5**	
6	**Total expenses.** In Column A, add lines 1 through 4 and enter the result. In Column B, enter the amount from line 5	**6**	

Note: *If you were not reimbursed for any expenses in Step 1, skip line 7 and enter the amount from line 6 on line 8.*

Step 2 Enter Reimbursements Received From Your Employer for Expenses Listed in Step 1

7	Enter reimbursements received from your employer that were **not** reported to you in box 1 of Form W-2. Include any reimbursements reported under code "L" in box 12 of your Form W-2 (see instructions)	**7**	

Step 3 Figure Expenses To Deduct on Schedule A (Form 1040)

8	Subtract line 7 from line 6. If zero or less, enter -0-. However, if line 7 is greater than line 6 in Column A, report the excess as income on Form 1040, line 7	**8**	
	Note: *If **both columns** of line 8 are zero, you cannot deduct employee business expenses. Stop here and attach Form 2106 to your return.*		
9	In Column A, enter the amount from line 8. In Column B, multiply line 8 by 50% (.50). (Employees subject to Department of Transportation (DOT) hours of service limits: Multiply meal expenses by 65% (.65) instead of 50%. For details, see instructions.)	**9**	
10	Add the amounts on line 9 of both columns and enter the total here. **Also, enter the total on Schedule A (Form 1040), line 20.** (Fee-basis state or local government officials, qualified performing artists, and individuals with disabilities: See the instructions for special rules on where to enter the total.) . . . . ▶	**10**	

For Paperwork Reduction Act Notice, see instructions.   Cat. No. 11700N   Form **2106** (2002)

Part II   Vehicle Expenses

Section A—General Information (You must complete this section if you are claiming vehicle expenses.)

		(a) Vehicle 1	(b) Vehicle 2
11	Enter the date the vehicle was placed in service **11**	/ /	/ /
12	Total miles the vehicle was driven during 2002 . . . . **12**	miles	miles
13	Business miles included on line 12 . . . . **13**	miles	miles
14	Percent of business use. Divide line 13 by line 12 . . . . **14**	%	%
15	Average daily roundtrip commuting distance **15**	miles	miles
16	Commuting miles included on line 12 . . . . **16**	miles	miles
17	Other miles. Add lines 13 and 16 and subtract the total from line 12 . . . **17**	miles	miles

18	Do you (or your spouse) have another vehicle available for personal use?	☐ Yes ☐ No
19	Was your vehicle available for personal use during off-duty hours?	☐ Yes ☐ No
20	Do you have evidence to support your deduction?	☐ Yes ☐ No
21	If "Yes," is the evidence written?	☐ Yes ☐ No

Section B—Standard Mileage Rate (See the instructions for Part II to find out whether to complete this section or Section C.)

22	Multiply line 13 by 36½¢ (.365) **22**	

Section C—Actual Expenses

		(a) Vehicle 1		(b) Vehicle 2	
23	Gasoline, oil, repairs, vehicle insurance, etc. **23**				
24a	Vehicle rentals **24a**				
b	Inclusion amount (see instructions) **24b**				
c	Subtract line 24b from line 24a **24c**				
25	Value of employer-provided vehicle (applies only if 100% of annual lease value was included on Form W-2—see instructions) **25**				
26	Add lines 23, 24c, and 25 . . **26**				
27	Multiply line 26 by the percentage on line 14 . . . **27**				
28	Depreciation. Enter amount from line 38 below **28**				
29	Add lines 27 and 28. Enter total here and on line 1 . . . . . **29**				

Section D—Depreciation of Vehicles (Use this section only if you owned the vehicle and are completing Section C for the vehicle.)

		(a) Vehicle 1		(b) Vehicle 2	
30	Enter cost or other basis (see instructions) **30**				
31	Enter section 179 deduction and special allowance (see instructions) **31**				
32	Multiply line 30 by line 14 (see instructions if you claimed the section 179 deduction or special allowance) **32**				
33	Enter depreciation method and percentage (see instructions) . **33**				
34	Multiply line 32 by the percentage on line 33 (see instructions) . . **34**				
35	Add lines 31 and 34 . . . . . **35**				
36	Enter the limit from the table in the line 36 instructions . . . **36**				
37	Multiply line 36 by the percentage on line 14 . . . **37**				
38	Enter the **smaller** of line 35 or line 37. Also enter this amount on line 28 above **38**				

Form **2106** (2002)

Form **2441**	**Child and Dependent Care Expenses**	OMB No. 1545-0068
Department of the Treasury Internal Revenue Service (99)	▶ Attach to Form 1040. ▶ See separate instructions.	**20**0**2** Attachment Sequence No. **21**

Name(s) shown on Form 1040	Your social security number

Before you begin: You need to understand the following terms. See **Definitions** on page 1 of the instructions.

● **Dependent Care Benefits**   ● **Qualifying Person(s)**   ● **Qualified Expenses**   ● **Earned Income**

Part I **Persons or Organizations Who Provided the Care—**You **must** complete this part.
(If you need more space, use the bottom of page 2.)

1	**(a)** Care provider's name	**(b)** Address (number, street, apt. no., city, state, and ZIP code)	**(c)** Identifying number (SSN or EIN)	**(d)** Amount paid (see instructions)

```
Did you receive
dependent care benefits?        No ──────▶ Complete only Part II below.

                                Yes ─────▶ Complete Part III on the back next.
```

Caution. If the care was provided in your home, you may owe employment taxes. See the instructions for Form 1040, line 60.

Part II **Credit for Child and Dependent Care Expenses**

2 Information about your **qualifying person(s).** If you have more than two qualifying persons, see the instructions.

(a) Qualifying person's name		**(b)** Qualifying person's social security number	**(c)** Qualified expenses you incurred and paid in 2002 for the person listed in column (a)
First	Last		

3 Add the amounts in column (c) of line 2. **Do not** enter more than $2,400 for one qualifying person or $4,800 for two or more persons. If you completed Part III, enter the amount from line 26 . . . . **3**

4 Enter your **earned income** **4**

5 If married filing a joint return, enter your spouse's earned income (if your spouse was a student or was disabled, see the instructions); **all others,** enter the amount from line 4 . . . . . **5**

6 Enter the **smallest** of line 3, 4, or 5 . . . . **6**

7 Enter the amount from Form 1040, line 36 . . . . . | **7** | |

8 Enter on line 8 the decimal amount shown below that applies to the amount on line 7

If line 7 is:			If line 7 is:		
Over	**But not over**	**Decimal amount is**	**Over**	**But not over**	**Decimal amount is**
$0—10,000		.30	$20,000—22,000		.24
10,000—12,000		.29	22,000—24,000		.23
12,000—14,000		.28	24,000—26,000		.22
14,000—16,000		.27	26,000—28,000		.21
16,000—18,000		.26	28,000—No limit		.20
18,000—20,000		.25			

| **8** | ✕ . |

9 Multiply line 6 by the decimal amount on line 8. If you paid 2001 expenses in 2002, see the instructions **9**

10 Enter the amount from Form 1040, line 44, minus any amount on Form 1040, line 45 . **10**

11 **Credit for child and dependent care expenses.** Enter the **smaller** of line 9 or line 10 here and on Form 1040, line 46 . . . . **11**

For Paperwork Reduction Act Notice, see page 3 of the instructions.   Cat. No. 11862M   Form **2441** (2002)

Part III Dependent Care Benefits

12 Enter the total amount of **dependent care benefits** you received for 2002. This amount should be shown in box 10 of your W-2 form(s). **Do not** include amounts that were reported to you as wages in box 1 of Form(s) W-2 . . . . | **12** |

13 Enter the amount forfeited, if any (see the instructions). . . . . | **13** |

14 Subtract line 13 from line 12 . . . . | **14** |

15 Enter the total amount of **qualified expenses** incurred in 2002 for the care of the **qualifying person(s)** . . . | **15** |

16 Enter the **smaller** of line 14 or 15 . . . . | **16** |

17 Enter your **earned income** . . . . | **17** |

18 Enter the amount shown below that applies to you.
- If married filing jointly, enter your spouse's earned income (if your spouse was a student or was disabled, see the instructions for line 5).
- If married filing separately, see the instructions for the amount to enter.
- All others, enter the amount from line 17. | **18** |

19 Enter the **smallest** of line 16, 17, or 18 . . . . . . | **19** |

20 **Excluded benefits.** Enter here the **smaller** of the following:
- The amount from line 19 or
- $5,000 ($2,500 if married filing separately **and** you were required to enter your spouse's earned income on line 18). | **20** |

21 **Taxable benefits.** Subtract line 20 from line 14. Also, include this amount on Form 1040, line 7. On the dotted line next to line 7, enter "DCB" . . . . | **21** |

To claim the child and dependent care credit, complete lines 22–26 below.

22 Enter $2,400 ($4,800 if two or more qualifying persons) . . . . | **22** |

23 Enter the amount from line 20 . . . . | **23** |

24 Subtract line 23 from line 22. If zero or less, **stop.** You cannot take the credit. **Exception.** If you paid 2001 expenses in 2002, see the instructions for line 9 . . . . | **24** |

25 Complete line 2 on the front of this form. **Do not** include in column (c) any benefits shown on line 20 above. Then, add the amounts in column (c) and enter the total here . . . | **25** |

26 Enter the **smaller** of line 24 or 25. Also, enter this amount on line 3 on the front of this form and complete lines 4–11 . . . . | **26** |

Form **2441** (2002)

Form **6251**	**Alternative Minimum Tax—Individuals**	OMB No. 1545-0227
Department of the Treasury Internal Revenue Service (99)	▶ See separate instructions. ▶ Attach to Form 1040 or Form 1040NR.	20**02** Attachment Sequence No. **32**

Name(s) shown on Form 1040 | Your social security number

Part I   Alternative Minimum Taxable Income (See instructions for how to complete each line.)

1	If filing Schedule A (Form 1040), enter the amount from Form 1040, line 39, and go to line 2. Otherwise, enter the amount from Form 1040, line 36, and go to line 7. (If zero or less, enter as a negative amount.)	**1**	
2	Medical and dental. Enter the **smaller** of Schedule A (Form 1040), line 4, **or** 2½% of Form 1040, line 36	**2**	
3	Taxes from Schedule A (Form 1040), line 9	**3**	
4	Certain interest on a home mortgage **not** used to buy, build, or improve your home	**4**	
5	Miscellaneous deductions from Schedule A (Form 1040), line 26	**5**	
6	If Form 1040, line 36, is over $137,300 (over $68,650 if married filing separately), enter the amount from line 9 of the worksheet for Schedule A (Form 1040), line 28	**6**	( )
7	Tax refund from Form 1040, line 10 or line 21	**7**	( )
8	Investment interest expense (difference between regular tax and AMT)	**8**	
9	Depletion (difference between regular tax and AMT)	**9**	
10	Net operating loss deduction from Form 1040, line 21. Enter as a positive amount	**10**	
11	Interest from specified private activity bonds exempt from the regular tax	**11**	
12	Qualified small business stock (42% of gain excluded under section 1202)	**12**	
13	Exercise of incentive stock options (excess of AMT income over regular tax income)	**13**	
14	Estates and trusts (amount from Schedule K-1 (Form 1041), line 9)	**14**	
15	Electing large partnerships (amount from Schedule K-1 (Form 1065-B), box 6)	**15**	
16	Disposition of property (difference between AMT and regular tax gain or loss)	**16**	
17	Depreciation on assets placed in service after 1986 (difference between regular tax and AMT)	**17**	
18	Passive activities (difference between AMT and regular tax income or loss)	**18**	
19	Loss limitations (difference between AMT and regular tax income or loss)	**19**	
20	Circulation costs (difference between regular tax and AMT)	**20**	
21	Long-term contracts (difference between AMT and regular tax income)	**21**	
22	Mining costs (difference between regular tax and AMT)	**22**	
23	Research and experimental costs (difference between regular tax and AMT)	**23**	
24	Income from certain installment sales before January 1, 1987	**24**	( )
25	Intangible drilling costs preference	**25**	
26	Other adjustments, including income-based related adjustments	**26**	
27	Alternative tax net operating loss deduction	**27**	( )
28	**Alternative minimum taxable income.** Combine lines 1 through 27. (If married filing separately and line 28 is more than $173,000, see page 7 of the instructions)	**28**	

Part II   Alternative Minimum Tax

29	Exemption. (If this form is for a child under age 14, see page 7 of the instructions.)	

IF your filing status is . . .	AND line 28 is not over . . .	THEN enter on line 29 . . .	
Single or head of household	$112,500	$35,750	
Married filing jointly or qualifying widow(er) . .	150,000	49,000	**29**
Married filing separately	75,000	24,500	

If line 28 is **over** the amount shown above for your filing status, see page 7 of the instructions.

30	Subtract line 29 from line 28. If zero or less, enter -0- here and on lines 33 and 35 and stop here	**30**	
31	• If you reported capital gain distributions directly on Form 1040, line 13, **or** you had a gain on both lines 16 and 17 of Schedule D (Form 1040) (as refigured for the AMT, if necessary), complete Part III on the back and enter the amount from line 57 here. • **All others:** If line 30 is $175,000 or less ($87,500 or less if married filing separately), multiply line 30 by 26% (.26). Otherwise, multiply line 30 by 28% (.28) and subtract $3,500 ($1,750 if married filing separately) from the result.	**31**	
32	Alternative minimum tax foreign tax credit (see page 7 of the instructions)	**32**	
33	Tentative minimum tax. Subtract line 32 from line 31	**33**	
34	Tax from Form 1040, line 42 (minus any tax from Form 4972 and any foreign tax credit from Form 1040, line 45)	**34**	
35	**Alternative minimum tax.** Subtract line 34 from line 33. If zero or less, enter -0-. Enter here and on Form 1040, line 43	**35**	

For Paperwork Reduction Act Notice, see page 8 of the instructions.   Cat. No. 13600G   Form **6251** (2002)

Part III   **Tax Computation Using Maximum Capital Gains Rates**

Caution: *If you **did not** complete Part IV of Schedule D (Form 1040), see page 8 of the instructions before you complete this part.*

36	Enter the amount from Form 6251, line 30	**36**
37	Enter the amount from Schedule D (Form 1040), line 23, or line 9 of the Schedule D Tax Worksheet on page D-9 of the instructions for Schedule D (Form 1040), whichever applies (as refigured for the AMT, if necessary) (see page 8 of the instructions) **37**	
38	Enter the amount from Schedule D (Form 1040), line 19 (as refigured for the AMT, if necessary) (see page 8 of the instructions) **38**	
39	Add lines 37 and 38 . . . . **39**	
40	Enter the **smaller** of line 36 or line 39.	**40**
41	Subtract line 40 from line 36	**41**
42	If line 41 is $175,000 or less ($87,500 or less if married filing separately), multiply line 41 by 26% (.26). Otherwise, multiply line 41 by 28% (.28) and subtract $3,500 ($1,750 if married filing separately) from the result	**42**
43	Enter the amount from Schedule D (Form 1040), line 28, or line 16 of the Schedule D Tax Worksheet on page D-9 of the instructions for Schedule D (Form 1040), whichever applies (as figured for the regular tax) (see page 8 of the instructions) **43**	
44	Enter the **smaller** of line 36 or line 37 . . . . **44**	
45	Enter the **smaller** of line 43 or line 44. If zero, go to line 51 . . . . . **45**	
46	Enter your qualified 5-year gain, if any, from Schedule D (Form 1040), line 29 (as refigured for the AMT, if necessary) (see page 8 of the instructions) **46**	
47	Enter the **smaller** of line 45 or line 46 . . . . **47**	
48	Multiply line 47 by 8% (.08)	**48**
49	Subtract line 47 from line 45 . . . . **49**	
50	Multiply line 49 by 10% (.10)	**50**
51	Subtract line 45 from line 44 . . . . **51**	
52	Multiply line 51 by 20% (.20)	**52**
	If line 38 is zero or blank, skip lines 53 and 54 and go to line 55. Otherwise, go to line 53.	
53	Subtract line 44 from line 40 . . . . . . **53**	
54	Multiply line 53 by 25% (.25)	**54**
55	Add lines 42, 48, 50, 52, and 54	**55**
56	If line 36 is $175,000 or less ($87,500 or less if married filing separately), multiply line 36 by 26% (.26). Otherwise, multiply line 36 by 28% (.28) and subtract $3,500 ($1,750 if married filing separately) from the result	**56**
57	Enter the **smaller** of line 55 or line 56 here and on line 31	**57**

Form **6251** (2002)

Form **8615**

Department of the Treasury
Internal Revenue Service (99)

Tax for Children Under Age 14
With Investment Income of More Than $1,500
▶ Attach only to the child's Form 1040, Form 1040A, or Form 1040NR.
▶ See separate instructions.

OMB No. 1545-0998

2002

Attachment
Sequence No. **33**

Child's name shown on return | Child's social security number

Before you begin: If the child, the parent, or any of the parent's other children under age 14 received capital gains (including capital gain distributions) or farm income, see **Pub. 929,** Tax Rules for Children and Dependents. It explains how to figure the child's tax using the **Capital Gain Tax Worksheet** in the Form 1040 or Form 1040A instructions, or **Schedule D** or **J** (Form 1040).

A Parent's name (first, initial, and last). **Caution:** See instructions before completing.

B Parent's social security number

C Parent's filing status (check one):

☐ Single ☐ Married filing jointly ☐ Married filing separately ☐ Head of household ☐ Qualifying widow(er)

Part I Child's Net Investment Income

1	Enter the child's investment income (see instructions)	**1**	
2	If the child **did not** itemize deductions on **Schedule A** (Form 1040 or Form 1040NR), enter $1,500. Otherwise, see instructions	**2**	
3	Subtract line 2 from line 1. If zero or less, **stop;** do not complete the rest of this form but **do** attach it to the child's return	**3**	
4	Enter the child's **taxable income** from Form 1040, line 41; Form 1040A, line 27; or Form 1040NR, line 39	**4**	
5	Enter the **smaller** of line 3 or line 4	**5**	

Part II Tentative Tax Based on the Tax Rate of the Parent

6	Enter the parent's **taxable income** from Form 1040, line 41; Form 1040A, line 27; Form 1040EZ, line 6; TeleFile Tax Record, line K; Form 1040NR, line 39; or Form 1040NR-EZ, line 14. If zero or less, enter -0-	**6**	
7	Enter the total, if any, from Forms 8615, line 5, of **all other** children of the parent named above. **Do not** include the amount from line 5 above	**7**	
8	Add lines 5, 6, and 7.	**8**	
9	Enter the tax on the amount on line 8 based on the **parent's** filing status above (see instructions). If the Capital Gain Tax Worksheet or Schedule D or J (Form 1040) is used, check here ▶ ☐	**9**	
10	Enter the parent's tax from Form 1040, line 42; Form 1040A, line 28, minus any alternative minimum tax; Form 1040EZ, line 10; TeleFile Tax Record, line K; Form 1040NR, line 40; or Form 1040NR-EZ, line 15. **Do not** include any tax from **Form 4972** or **8814.** If the Capital Gain Tax Worksheet or Schedule D or J (Form 1040) was used to figure the tax, check here ▶ ☐	**10**	
11	Subtract line 10 from line 9 and enter the result. If line 7 is blank, also enter this amount on line 13 and go to **Part III**	**11**	

12a	Add lines 5 and 7	**12a**		
b	Divide line 5 by line 12a. Enter the result as a decimal (rounded to at least three places)	**12b**	× .	

13	Multiply line 11 by line 12b	**13**	

Part III Child's Tax—If lines 4 and 5 above are the same, enter -0- on line 15 and go to line 16.

14	Subtract line 5 from line 4	**14**		
15	Enter the tax on the amount on line 14 based on the **child's** filing status (see instructions). If the Capital Gain Tax Worksheet or Schedule D or J (Form 1040) is used to figure the tax, check here ▶ ☐		**15**	
16	Add lines 13 and 15		**16**	
17	Enter the tax on the amount on line 4 based on the **child's** filing status (see instructions). If the Capital Gain Tax Worksheet or Schedule D or J (Form 1040) is used to figure the tax, check here ▶ ☐		**17**	
18	Enter the **larger** of line 16 or line 17 here and on the **child's** Form 1040, line 42; Form 1040A, line 28; or Form 1040NR, line 40		**18**	

For Paperwork Reduction Act Notice, see the instructions. Cat. No. 64113U Form **8615** (2002)

Form **8829**	**Expenses for Business Use of Your Home**	OMB No. 1545-1266

Form **8829**

Department of the Treasury
Internal Revenue Service   (99)

Expenses for Business Use of Your Home

▶ File only with Schedule C (Form 1040). Use a separate Form 8829 for each home you used for business during the year.

▶ See separate instructions.

OMB No. 1545-1266

2002

Attachment
Sequence No. **66**

Name(s) of proprietor(s)

Your social security number

Part I   Part of Your Home Used for Business

1	Area used regularly and exclusively for business, regularly for day care, or for storage of inventory or product samples (see instructions)	**1**	
2	Total area of home	**2**	
3	Divide line 1 by line 2. Enter the result as a percentage	**3**	%

- For day-care facilities not used exclusively for business, also complete lines 4–6.
- All others, skip lines 4–6 and enter the amount from line 3 on line 7.

4	Multiply days used for day care during year by hours used per day .	**4**	hr.
5	Total hours available for use during the year (365 days × 24 hours) (see instructions)	**5**	8,760 hr.
6	Divide line 4 by line 5. Enter the result as a decimal amount . . .	**6**	.
7	Business percentage. For day-care facilities not used exclusively for business, multiply line 6 by line 3 (enter the result as a percentage). All others, enter the amount from line 3 . . . . . ▶	**7**	%

Part II   Figure Your Allowable Deduction

8	Enter the amount from Schedule C, line 29, **plus** any net gain or (loss) derived from the business use of your home and shown on Schedule D or Form 4797. If more than one place of business, see instructions	**8**	

See instructions for columns **(a)** and **(b)** before completing lines 9–20.

		(a) Direct expenses	(b) Indirect expenses		
9	Casualty losses (see instructions)	**9**			
10	Deductible mortgage interest (see instructions) .	**10**			
11	Real estate taxes (see instructions).	**11**			
12	Add lines 9, 10, and 11.	**12**			
13	Multiply line 12, column (b) by line 7	**13**			
14	Add line 12, column (a) and line 13			**14**	
15	Subtract line 14 from line 8. If zero or less, enter -0- .			**15**	
16	Excess mortgage interest (see instructions) . .	**16**			
17	Insurance	**17**			
18	Repairs and maintenance	**18**			
19	Utilities	**19**			
20	Other expenses (see instructions)	**20**			
21	Add lines 16 through 20	**21**			
22	Multiply line 21, column (b) by line 7	**22**			
23	Carryover of operating expenses from 2001 Form 8829, line 41 . .	**23**			
24	Add line 21 in column (a), line 22, and line 23			**24**	
25	Allowable operating expenses. Enter the **smaller** of line 15 or line 24			**25**	
26	Limit on excess casualty losses and depreciation. Subtract line 25 from line 15			**26**	
27	Excess casualty losses (see instructions)	**27**			
28	Depreciation of your home from Part III below	**28**			
29	Carryover of excess casualty losses and depreciation from 2001 Form 8829, line 42	**29**			
30	Add lines 27 through 29			**30**	
31	Allowable excess casualty losses and depreciation. Enter the **smaller** of line 26 or line 30 . .			**31**	
32	Add lines 14, 25, and 31			**32**	
33	Casualty loss portion, if any, from lines 14 and 31. Carry amount to **Form 4684,** Section B .			**33**	
34	Allowable expenses for business use of your home. Subtract line 33 from line 32. Enter here and on Schedule C, line 30. If your home was used for more than one business, see instructions ▶			**34**	

Part III   Depreciation of Your Home

35	Enter the **smaller** of your home's adjusted basis or its fair market value (see instructions) . .	**35**	
36	Value of land included on line 35	**36**	
37	Basis of building. Subtract line 36 from line 35	**37**	
38	Business basis of building. Multiply line 37 by line 7	**38**	
39	Depreciation percentage (see instructions)	**39**	%
40	Depreciation allowable (see instructions). Multiply line 38 by line 39. Enter here and on line 28 above	**40**	

Part IV   Carryover of Unallowed Expenses to 2003

41	Operating expenses. Subtract line 25 from line 24. If less than zero, enter -0-	**41**	
42	Excess casualty losses and depreciation. Subtract line 31 from line 30. If less than zero, enter -0-	**42**	

For Paperwork Reduction Act Notice, see page 4 of separate instructions.   Cat. No. 13232M   Form **8829** (2002)

Form **8863**

Department of the Treasury
Internal Revenue Service

Education Credits
(Hope and Lifetime Learning Credits)

▶ See instructions. ▶ Attach to Form 1040 or Form 1040A.

OMB No. 1545-1618

2002

Attachment
Sequence No. **50**

Name(s) shown on return

Your social security number

Part I | **Hope Credit. Caution:** *The Hope credit may be claimed for no more than **2** tax years for the **same** student.*

1

(a) Student's name (as shown on page 1 of your tax return) First name / Last name	(b) Student's social security number (as shown on page 1 of your tax return)	(c) Qualified expenses (but **do not** enter more than $2,000 for each student). See instructions	(d) Enter the **smaller** of the amount in column (c) or $1,000	(e) Subtract column (d) from column (c)	(f) Enter one-half of the amount in column (e)

2 Add the amounts in columns (d) and (f) . . . . . | **2** | | ///////// | |

3 Tentative Hope credit. Add the amounts on line 2, columns (d) and (f). If you are claiming the lifetime learning credit, go to Part II; otherwise, go to Part III . . . . ▶ | **3** |

Part II | **Lifetime Learning Credit**

4

Caution: *You cannot take the Hope credit and the lifetime learning credit for the same student.*

(a) Student's name (as shown on page 1 of your tax return) First name / Last name	(b) Student's social security number (as shown on page 1 of your tax return)	(c) Qualified expenses. See instructions

5 Add the amounts on line 4, column (c), and enter the total . . . . | **5** | |

6 Enter the **smaller** of line 5 or $5,000 . . . . | **6** | |

7 Tentative lifetime learning credit. Multiply line 6 by 20% (.20) and go to Part III . . . ▶ | **7** | |

Part III | **Allowable Education Credits**

8 Tentative education credits. Add lines 3 and 7 . . . . | **8** | |

9 Enter: $102,000 if married filing jointly; $51,000 if single, head of household, or qualifying widow(er) . . . . ● | **9** | |

10 Enter the amount from Form 1040, line 36 (or Form 1040A, line 22)* | **10** | |

11 Subtract line 10 from line 9. If line 10 is equal to or more than line 9, **stop;** you cannot take any education credits . . . . . . | **11** | |

12 Enter: $20,000 if married filing jointly; $10,000 if single, head of household, or qualifying widow(er) . . . . | **12** | |

13 If line 11 is equal to or more than line 12, enter the amount from line 8 on line 14 and go to line 15. If line 11 is less than line 12, divide line 11 by line 12. Enter the result as a decimal (rounded to at least three places) . . . . | **13** | × . |

14 Multiply line 8 by line 13 . . . . ▶ | **14** | |

15 Enter the amount from Form 1040, line 44 (or Form 1040A, line 28) . . . . . . | **15** | |

16 Enter the total, if any, of your credits from Form 1040, lines 45 through 47 (or from Form 1040A, lines 29 and 30) . . . . | **16** | |

17 Subtract line 16 from line 15. If line 16 is equal to or more than line 15, **stop;** you cannot take any education credits . . . . | **17** | |

18 **Education credits.** Enter the **smaller** of line 14 or line 17 here and on Form 1040, line 48 (or Form 1040A, line 31) . . . . ▶ | **18** | |

*See Pub. 970 for the amount to enter if you are filing Form 2555, 2555-EZ, or 4563 or you are excluding income from Puerto Rico.

For Paperwork Reduction Act Notice, see page 3. | Cat. No. 25379M | Form **8863** (2002)

2002 Tax Table

Use if your taxable income is less than $100,000.
If $100,000 or more, use the Tax Rate Schedules.

Example. Mr. and Mrs. Brown are filing a joint return. Their taxable income on line 41 of Form 1040 is $25,300. First, they find the $25,300–25,350 income line. Next, they find the column for married filing jointly and read down the column. The amount shown where the income line and filing status column meet is $3,199. This is the tax amount they should enter on line 42 of their Form 1040.

Sample Table

At least	But less than	Single	Married filing jointly *	Married filing separately	Head of a household
		Your tax is—			
25,200	25,250	3,484	3,184	3,709	3,284
25,250	25,300	3,491	3,191	3,722	3,291
25,300	25,350	3,499	(3,199)	3,736	3,299
25,350	25,400	3,506	3,206	3,749	3,306

If taxable income is— At least	But less than	Single	Married filing jointly *	Married filing separately	Head of a house-hold
		Your tax is—			
0	5	0	0	0	0
5	15	1	1	1	1
15	25	2	2	2	2
25	50	4	4	4	4
50	75	6	6	6	6
75	100	9	9	9	9
100	125	11	11	11	11
125	150	14	14	14	14
150	175	16	16	16	16
175	200	19	19	19	19
200	225	21	21	21	21
225	250	24	24	24	24
250	275	26	26	26	26
275	300	29	29	29	29
300	325	31	31	31	31
325	350	34	34	34	34
350	375	36	36	36	36
375	400	39	39	39	39
400	425	41	41	41	41
425	450	44	44	44	44
450	475	46	46	46	46
475	500	49	49	49	49
500	525	51	51	51	51
525	550	54	54	54	54
550	575	56	56	56	56
575	600	59	59	59	59
600	625	61	61	61	61
625	650	64	64	64	64
650	675	66	66	66	66
675	700	69	69	69	69
700	725	71	71	71	71
725	750	74	74	74	74
750	775	76	76	76	76
775	800	79	79	79	79
800	825	81	81	81	81
825	850	84	84	84	84
850	875	86	86	86	86
875	900	89	89	89	89
900	925	91	91	91	91
925	950	94	94	94	94
950	975	96	96	96	96
975	1,000	99	99	99	99

1,000

At least	But less than	Single	Married filing jointly *	Married filing separately	Head of a house-hold
1,000	1,025	101	101	101	101
1,025	1,050	104	104	104	104
1,050	1,075	106	106	106	106
1,075	1,100	109	109	109	109
1,100	1,125	111	111	111	111
1,125	1,150	114	114	114	114
1,150	1,175	116	116	116	116
1,175	1,200	119	119	119	119
1,200	1,225	121	121	121	121
1,225	1,250	124	124	124	124
1,250	1,275	126	126	126	126
1,275	1,300	129	129	129	129

At least	But less than	Single	Married filing jointly *	Married filing separately	Head of a house-hold
1,300	1,325	131	131	131	131
1,325	1,350	134	134	134	134
1,350	1,375	136	136	136	136
1,375	1,400	139	139	139	139
1,400	1,425	141	141	141	141
1,425	1,450	144	144	144	144
1,450	1,475	146	146	146	146
1,475	1,500	149	149	149	149
1,500	1,525	151	151	151	151
1,525	1,550	154	154	154	154
1,550	1,575	156	156	156	156
1,575	1,600	159	159	159	159
1,600	1,625	161	161	161	161
1,625	1,650	164	164	164	164
1,650	1,675	166	166	166	166
1,675	1,700	169	169	169	169
1,700	1,725	171	171	171	171
1,725	1,750	174	174	174	174
1,750	1,775	176	176	176	176
1,775	1,800	179	179	179	179
1,800	1,825	181	181	181	181
1,825	1,850	184	184	184	184
1,850	1,875	186	186	186	186
1,875	1,900	189	189	189	189
1,900	1,925	191	191	191	191
1,925	1,950	194	194	194	194
1,950	1,975	196	196	196	196
1,975	2,000	199	199	199	199

2,000

At least	But less than	Single	Married filing jointly *	Married filing separately	Head of a house-hold
2,000	2,025	201	201	201	201
2,025	2,050	204	204	204	204
2,050	2,075	206	206	206	206
2,075	2,100	209	209	209	209
2,100	2,125	211	211	211	211
2,125	2,150	214	214	214	214
2,150	2,175	216	216	216	216
2,175	2,200	219	219	219	219
2,200	2,225	221	221	221	221
2,225	2,250	224	224	224	224
2,250	2,275	226	226	226	226
2,275	2,300	229	229	229	229
2,300	2,325	231	231	231	231
2,325	2,350	234	234	234	234
2,350	2,375	236	236	236	236
2,375	2,400	239	239	239	239
2,400	2,425	241	241	241	241
2,425	2,450	244	244	244	244
2,450	2,475	246	246	246	246
2,475	2,500	249	249	249	249
2,500	2,525	251	251	251	251
2,525	2,550	254	254	254	254
2,550	2,575	256	256	256	256
2,575	2,600	259	259	259	259
2,600	2,625	261	261	261	261
2,625	2,650	264	264	264	264
2,650	2,675	266	266	266	266
2,675	2,700	269	269	269	269

At least	But less than	Single	Married filing jointly *	Married filing separately	Head of a house-hold
2,700	2,725	271	271	271	271
2,725	2,750	274	274	274	274
2,750	2,775	276	276	276	276
2,775	2,800	279	279	279	279
2,800	2,825	281	281	281	281
2,825	2,850	284	284	284	284
2,850	2,875	286	286	286	286
2,875	2,900	289	289	289	289
2,900	2,925	291	291	291	291
2,925	2,950	294	294	294	294
2,950	2,975	296	296	296	296
2,975	3,000	299	299	299	299

3,000

At least	But less than	Single	Married filing jointly *	Married filing separately	Head of a house-hold
3,000	3,050	303	303	303	303
3,050	3,100	308	308	308	308
3,100	3,150	313	313	313	313
3,150	3,200	318	318	318	318
3,200	3,250	323	323	323	323
3,250	3,300	328	328	328	328
3,300	3,350	333	333	333	333
3,350	3,400	338	338	338	338
3,400	3,450	343	343	343	343
3,450	3,500	348	348	348	348
3,500	3,550	353	353	353	353
3,550	3,600	358	358	358	358
3,600	3,650	363	363	363	363
3,650	3,700	368	368	368	368
3,700	3,750	373	373	373	373
3,750	3,800	378	378	378	378
3,800	3,850	383	383	383	383
3,850	3,900	388	388	388	388
3,900	3,950	393	393	393	393
3,950	4,000	398	398	398	398

4,000

At least	But less than	Single	Married filing jointly *	Married filing separately	Head of a house-hold
4,000	4,050	403	403	403	403
4,050	4,100	408	408	408	408
4,100	4,150	413	413	413	413
4,150	4,200	418	418	418	418
4,200	4,250	423	423	423	423
4,250	4,300	428	428	428	428
4,300	4,350	433	433	433	433
4,350	4,400	438	438	438	438
4,400	4,450	443	443	443	443
4,450	4,500	448	448	448	448
4,500	4,550	453	453	453	453
4,550	4,600	458	458	458	458
4,600	4,650	463	463	463	463
4,650	4,700	468	468	468	468
4,700	4,750	473	473	473	473
4,750	4,800	478	478	478	478
4,800	4,850	483	483	483	483
4,850	4,900	488	488	488	488
4,900	4,950	493	493	493	493
4,950	5,000	498	498	498	498

* This column must also be used by a qualifying widow(er).

If taxable income is—	And you are—			
At least	But less than	Single	Married filing jointly *	Married filing separately	Head of a house-hold
		Your tax is—			

5,000

At least	But less than	Single	Married filing jointly	Married filing separately	Head of a household
5,000	5,050	503	503	503	503
5,050	5,100	508	508	508	508
5,100	5,150	513	513	513	513
5,150	5,200	518	518	518	518
5,200	5,250	523	523	523	523
5,250	5,300	528	528	528	528
5,300	5,350	533	533	533	533
5,350	5,400	538	538	538	538
5,400	5,450	543	543	543	543
5,450	5,500	548	548	548	548
5,500	5,550	553	553	553	553
5,550	5,600	558	558	558	558
5,600	5,650	563	563	563	563
5,650	5,700	568	568	568	568
5,700	5,750	573	573	573	573
5,750	5,800	578	578	578	578
5,800	5,850	583	583	583	583
5,850	5,900	588	588	588	588
5,900	5,950	593	593	593	593
5,950	6,000	598	598	598	598

6,000

At least	But less than	Single	Married filing jointly	Married filing separately	Head of a household
6,000	6,050	604	603	604	603
6,050	6,100	611	608	611	608
6,100	6,150	619	613	619	613
6,150	6,200	626	618	626	618
6,200	6,250	634	623	634	623
6,250	6,300	641	628	641	628
6,300	6,350	649	633	649	633
6,350	6,400	656	638	656	638
6,400	6,450	664	643	664	643
6,450	6,500	671	648	671	648
6,500	6,550	679	653	679	653
6,550	6,600	686	658	686	658
6,600	6,650	694	663	694	663
6,650	6,700	701	668	701	668
6,700	6,750	709	673	709	673
6,750	6,800	716	678	716	678
6,800	6,850	724	683	724	683
6,850	6,900	731	688	731	688
6,900	6,950	739	693	739	693
6,950	7,000	746	698	746	698

7,000

At least	But less than	Single	Married filing jointly	Married filing separately	Head of a household
7,000	7,050	754	703	754	703
7,050	7,100	761	708	761	708
7,100	7,150	769	713	769	713
7,150	7,200	776	718	776	718
7,200	7,250	784	723	784	723
7,250	7,300	791	728	791	728
7,300	7,350	799	733	799	733
7,350	7,400	806	738	806	738
7,400	7,450	814	743	814	743
7,450	7,500	821	748	821	748
7,500	7,550	829	753	829	753
7,550	7,600	836	758	836	758
7,600	7,650	844	763	844	763
7,650	7,700	851	768	851	768
7,700	7,750	859	773	859	773
7,750	7,800	866	778	866	778
7,800	7,850	874	783	874	783
7,850	7,900	881	788	881	788
7,900	7,950	889	793	889	793
7,950	8,000	896	798	896	798

8,000

At least	But less than	Single	Married filing jointly	Married filing separately	Head of a household
8,000	8,050	904	803	904	803
8,050	8,100	911	808	911	808
8,100	8,150	919	813	919	813
8,150	8,200	926	818	926	818
8,200	8,250	934	823	934	823
8,250	8,300	941	828	941	828
8,300	8,350	949	833	949	833
8,350	8,400	956	838	956	838
8,400	8,450	964	843	964	843
8,450	8,500	971	848	971	848
8,500	8,550	979	853	979	853
8,550	8,600	986	858	986	858
8,600	8,650	994	863	994	863
8,650	8,700	1,001	868	1,001	868
8,700	8,750	1,009	873	1,009	873
8,750	8,800	1,016	878	1,016	878
8,800	8,850	1,024	883	1,024	883
8,850	8,900	1,031	888	1,031	888
8,900	8,950	1,039	893	1,039	893
8,950	9,000	1,046	898	1,046	898

9,000

At least	But less than	Single	Married filing jointly	Married filing separately	Head of a household
9,000	9,050	1,054	903	1,054	903
9,050	9,100	1,061	908	1,061	908
9,100	9,150	1,069	913	1,069	913
9,150	9,200	1,076	918	1,076	918
9,200	9,250	1,084	923	1,084	923
9,250	9,300	1,091	928	1,091	928
9,300	9,350	1,099	933	1,099	933
9,350	9,400	1,106	938	1,106	938
9,400	9,450	1,114	943	1,114	943
9,450	9,500	1,121	948	1,121	948
9,500	9,550	1,129	953	1,129	953
9,550	9,600	1,136	958	1,136	958
9,600	9,650	1,144	963	1,144	963
9,650	9,700	1,151	968	1,151	968
9,700	9,750	1,159	973	1,159	973
9,750	9,800	1,166	978	1,166	978
9,800	9,850	1,174	983	1,174	983
9,850	9,900	1,181	988	1,181	988
9,900	9,950	1,189	993	1,189	993
9,950	10,000	1,196	998	1,196	998

10,000

At least	But less than	Single	Married filing jointly	Married filing separately	Head of a household
10,000	10,050	1,204	1,003	1,204	1,004
10,050	10,100	1,211	1,008	1,211	1,011
10,100	10,150	1,219	1,013	1,219	1,019
10,150	10,200	1,226	1,018	1,226	1,026
10,200	10,250	1,234	1,023	1,234	1,034
10,250	10,300	1,241	1,028	1,241	1,041
10,300	10,350	1,249	1,033	1,249	1,049
10,350	10,400	1,256	1,038	1,256	1,056
10,400	10,450	1,264	1,043	1,264	1,064
10,450	10,500	1,271	1,048	1,271	1,071
10,500	10,550	1,279	1,053	1,279	1,079
10,550	10,600	1,286	1,058	1,286	1,086
10,600	10,650	1,294	1,063	1,294	1,094
10,650	10,700	1,301	1,068	1,301	1,101
10,700	10,750	1,309	1,073	1,309	1,109
10,750	10,800	1,316	1,078	1,316	1,116
10,800	10,850	1,324	1,083	1,324	1,124
10,850	10,900	1,331	1,088	1,331	1,131
10,900	10,950	1,339	1,093	1,339	1,139
10,950	11,000	1,346	1,098	1,346	1,146

11,000

At least	But less than	Single	Married filing jointly	Married filing separately	Head of a household
11,000	11,050	1,354	1,103	1,354	1,154
11,050	11,100	1,361	1,108	1,361	1,161
11,100	11,150	1,369	1,113	1,369	1,169
11,150	11,200	1,376	1,118	1,376	1,176
11,200	11,250	1,384	1,123	1,384	1,184
11,250	11,300	1,391	1,128	1,391	1,191
11,300	11,350	1,399	1,133	1,399	1,199
11,350	11,400	1,406	1,138	1,406	1,206
11,400	11,450	1,414	1,143	1,414	1,214
11,450	11,500	1,421	1,148	1,421	1,221
11,500	11,550	1,429	1,153	1,429	1,229
11,550	11,600	1,436	1,158	1,436	1,236
11,600	11,650	1,444	1,163	1,444	1,244
11,650	11,700	1,451	1,168	1,451	1,251
11,700	11,750	1,459	1,173	1,459	1,259
11,750	11,800	1,466	1,178	1,466	1,266
11,800	11,850	1,474	1,183	1,474	1,274
11,850	11,900	1,481	1,188	1,481	1,281
11,900	11,950	1,489	1,193	1,489	1,289
11,950	12,000	1,496	1,198	1,496	1,296

12,000

At least	But less than	Single	Married filing jointly	Married filing separately	Head of a household
12,000	12,050	1,504	1,204	1,504	1,304
12,050	12,100	1,511	1,211	1,511	1,311
12,100	12,150	1,519	1,219	1,519	1,319
12,150	12,200	1,526	1,226	1,526	1,326
12,200	12,250	1,534	1,234	1,534	1,334
12,250	12,300	1,541	1,241	1,541	1,341
12,300	12,350	1,549	1,249	1,549	1,349
12,350	12,400	1,556	1,256	1,556	1,356
12,400	12,450	1,564	1,264	1,564	1,364
12,450	12,500	1,571	1,271	1,571	1,371
12,500	12,550	1,579	1,279	1,579	1,379
12,550	12,600	1,586	1,286	1,586	1,386
12,600	12,650	1,594	1,294	1,594	1,394
12,650	12,700	1,601	1,301	1,601	1,401
12,700	12,750	1,609	1,309	1,609	1,409
12,750	12,800	1,616	1,316	1,616	1,416
12,800	12,850	1,624	1,324	1,624	1,424
12,850	12,900	1,631	1,331	1,631	1,431
12,900	12,950	1,639	1,339	1,639	1,439
12,950	13,000	1,646	1,346	1,646	1,446

13,000

At least	But less than	Single	Married filing jointly	Married filing separately	Head of a household
13,000	13,050	1,654	1,354	1,654	1,454
13,050	13,100	1,661	1,361	1,661	1,461
13,100	13,150	1,669	1,369	1,669	1,469
13,150	13,200	1,676	1,376	1,676	1,476
13,200	13,250	1,684	1,384	1,684	1,484
13,250	13,300	1,691	1,391	1,691	1,491
13,300	13,350	1,699	1,399	1,699	1,499
13,350	13,400	1,706	1,406	1,706	1,506
13,400	13,450	1,714	1,414	1,714	1,514
13,450	13,500	1,721	1,421	1,721	1,521
13,500	13,550	1,729	1,429	1,729	1,529
13,550	13,600	1,736	1,436	1,736	1,536
13,600	13,650	1,744	1,444	1,744	1,544
13,650	13,700	1,751	1,451	1,751	1,551
13,700	13,750	1,759	1,459	1,759	1,559
13,750	13,800	1,766	1,466	1,766	1,566
13,800	13,850	1,774	1,474	1,774	1,574
13,850	13,900	1,781	1,481	1,781	1,581
13,900	13,950	1,789	1,489	1,789	1,589
13,950	14,000	1,796	1,496	1,796	1,596

* This column must also be used by a qualifying widow(er).

If taxable income is—		And you are—			
At least	But less than	Single	Married filing jointly *	Married filing separately	Head of a household
		Your tax is—			

14,000

At least	But less than	Single	Married filing jointly *	Married filing separately	Head of a household
14,000	14,050	1,804	1,504	1,804	1,604
14,050	14,100	1,811	1,511	1,811	1,611
14,100	14,150	1,819	1,519	1,819	1,619
14,150	14,200	1,826	1,526	1,826	1,626
14,200	14,250	1,834	1,534	1,834	1,634
14,250	14,300	1,841	1,541	1,841	1,641
14,300	14,350	1,849	1,549	1,849	1,649
14,350	14,400	1,856	1,556	1,856	1,656
14,400	14,450	1,864	1,564	1,864	1,664
14,450	14,500	1,871	1,571	1,871	1,671
14,500	14,550	1,879	1,579	1,879	1,679
14,550	14,600	1,886	1,586	1,886	1,686
14,600	14,650	1,894	1,594	1,894	1,694
14,650	14,700	1,901	1,601	1,901	1,701
14,700	14,750	1,909	1,609	1,909	1,709
14,750	14,800	1,916	1,616	1,916	1,716
14,800	14,850	1,924	1,624	1,924	1,724
14,850	14,900	1,931	1,631	1,931	1,731
14,900	14,950	1,939	1,639	1,939	1,739
14,950	15,000	1,946	1,646	1,946	1,746

15,000

At least	But less than	Single	Married filing jointly *	Married filing separately	Head of a household
15,000	15,050	1,954	1,654	1,954	1,754
15,050	15,100	1,961	1,661	1,961	1,761
15,100	15,150	1,969	1,669	1,969	1,769
15,150	15,200	1,976	1,676	1,976	1,776
15,200	15,250	1,984	1,684	1,984	1,784
15,250	15,300	1,991	1,691	1,991	1,791
15,300	15,350	1,999	1,699	1,999	1,799
15,350	15,400	2,006	1,706	2,006	1,806
15,400	15,450	2,014	1,714	2,014	1,814
15,450	15,500	2,021	1,721	2,021	1,821
15,500	15,550	2,029	1,729	2,029	1,829
15,550	15,600	2,036	1,736	2,036	1,836
15,600	15,650	2,044	1,744	2,044	1,844
15,650	15,700	2,051	1,751	2,051	1,851
15,700	15,750	2,059	1,759	2,059	1,859
15,750	15,800	2,066	1,766	2,066	1,866
15,800	15,850	2,074	1,774	2,074	1,874
15,850	15,900	2,081	1,781	2,081	1,881
15,900	15,950	2,089	1,789	2,089	1,889
15,950	16,000	2,096	1,796	2,096	1,896

16,000

At least	But less than	Single	Married filing jointly *	Married filing separately	Head of a household
16,000	16,050	2,104	1,804	2,104	1,904
16,050	16,100	2,111	1,811	2,111	1,911
16,100	16,150	2,119	1,819	2,119	1,919
16,150	16,200	2,126	1,826	2,126	1,926
16,200	16,250	2,134	1,834	2,134	1,934
16,250	16,300	2,141	1,841	2,141	1,941
16,300	16,350	2,149	1,849	2,149	1,949
16,350	16,400	2,156	1,856	2,156	1,956
16,400	16,450	2,164	1,864	2,164	1,964
16,450	16,500	2,171	1,871	2,171	1,971
16,500	16,550	2,179	1,879	2,179	1,979
16,550	16,600	2,186	1,886	2,186	1,986
16,600	16,650	2,194	1,894	2,194	1,994
16,650	16,700	2,201	1,901	2,201	2,001
16,700	16,750	2,209	1,909	2,209	2,009
16,750	16,800	2,216	1,916	2,216	2,016
16,800	16,850	2,224	1,924	2,224	2,024
16,850	16,900	2,231	1,931	2,231	2,031
16,900	16,950	2,239	1,939	2,239	2,039
16,950	17,000	2,246	1,946	2,246	2,046

17,000

At least	But less than	Single	Married filing jointly *	Married filing separately	Head of a household
17,000	17,050	2,254	1,954	2,254	2,054
17,050	17,100	2,261	1,961	2,261	2,061
17,100	17,150	2,269	1,969	2,269	2,069
17,150	17,200	2,276	1,976	2,276	2,076
17,200	17,250	2,284	1,984	2,284	2,084
17,250	17,300	2,291	1,991	2,291	2,091
17,300	17,350	2,299	1,999	2,299	2,099
17,350	17,400	2,306	2,006	2,306	2,106
17,400	17,450	2,314	2,014	2,314	2,114
17,450	17,500	2,321	2,021	2,321	2,121
17,500	17,550	2,329	2,029	2,329	2,129
17,550	17,600	2,336	2,036	2,336	2,136
17,600	17,650	2,344	2,044	2,344	2,144
17,650	17,700	2,351	2,051	2,351	2,151
17,700	17,750	2,359	2,059	2,359	2,159
17,750	17,800	2,366	2,066	2,366	2,166
17,800	17,850	2,374	2,074	2,374	2,174
17,850	17,900	2,381	2,081	2,381	2,181
17,900	17,950	2,389	2,089	2,389	2,189
17,950	18,000	2,396	2,096	2,396	2,196

18,000

At least	But less than	Single	Married filing jointly *	Married filing separately	Head of a household
18,000	18,050	2,404	2,104	2,404	2,204
18,050	18,100	2,411	2,111	2,411	2,211
18,100	18,150	2,419	2,119	2,419	2,219
18,150	18,200	2,426	2,126	2,426	2,226
18,200	18,250	2,434	2,134	2,434	2,234
18,250	18,300	2,441	2,141	2,441	2,241
18,300	18,350	2,449	2,149	2,449	2,249
18,350	18,400	2,456	2,156	2,456	2,256
18,400	18,450	2,464	2,164	2,464	2,264
18,450	18,500	2,471	2,171	2,471	2,271
18,500	18,550	2,479	2,179	2,479	2,279
18,550	18,600	2,486	2,186	2,486	2,286
18,600	18,650	2,494	2,194	2,494	2,294
18,650	18,700	2,501	2,201	2,501	2,301
18,700	18,750	2,509	2,209	2,509	2,309
18,750	18,800	2,516	2,216	2,516	2,316
18,800	18,850	2,524	2,224	2,524	2,324
18,850	18,900	2,531	2,231	2,531	2,331
18,900	18,950	2,539	2,239	2,539	2,339
18,950	19,000	2,546	2,246	2,546	2,346

19,000

At least	But less than	Single	Married filing jointly *	Married filing separately	Head of a household
19,000	19,050	2,554	2,254	2,554	2,354
19,050	19,100	2,561	2,261	2,561	2,361
19,100	19,150	2,569	2,269	2,569	2,369
19,150	19,200	2,576	2,276	2,576	2,376
19,200	19,250	2,584	2,284	2,584	2,384
19,250	19,300	2,591	2,291	2,591	2,391
19,300	19,350	2,599	2,299	2,599	2,399
19,350	19,400	2,606	2,306	2,606	2,406
19,400	19,450	2,614	2,314	2,614	2,414
19,450	19,500	2,621	2,321	2,621	2,421
19,500	19,550	2,629	2,329	2,629	2,429
19,550	19,600	2,636	2,336	2,636	2,436
19,600	19,650	2,644	2,344	2,644	2,444
19,650	19,700	2,651	2,351	2,651	2,451
19,700	19,750	2,659	2,359	2,659	2,459
19,750	19,800	2,666	2,366	2,666	2,466
19,800	19,850	2,674	2,374	2,674	2,474
19,850	19,900	2,681	2,381	2,681	2,481
19,900	19,950	2,689	2,389	2,689	2,489
19,950	20,000	2,696	2,396	2,696	2,496

20,000

At least	But less than	Single	Married filing jointly *	Married filing separately	Head of a household
20,000	20,050	2,704	2,404	2,704	2,504
20,050	20,100	2,711	2,411	2,711	2,511
20,100	20,150	2,719	2,419	2,719	2,519
20,150	20,200	2,726	2,426	2,726	2,526
20,200	20,250	2,734	2,434	2,734	2,534
20,250	20,300	2,741	2,441	2,741	2,541
20,300	20,350	2,749	2,449	2,749	2,549
20,350	20,400	2,756	2,456	2,756	2,556
20,400	20,450	2,764	2,464	2,764	2,564
20,450	20,500	2,771	2,471	2,771	2,571
20,500	20,550	2,779	2,479	2,779	2,579
20,550	20,600	2,786	2,486	2,786	2,586
20,600	20,650	2,794	2,494	2,794	2,594
20,650	20,700	2,801	2,501	2,801	2,601
20,700	20,750	2,809	2,509	2,809	2,609
20,750	20,800	2,816	2,516	2,816	2,616
20,800	20,850	2,824	2,524	2,824	2,624
20,850	20,900	2,831	2,531	2,831	2,631
20,900	20,950	2,839	2,539	2,839	2,639
20,950	21,000	2,846	2,546	2,846	2,646

21,000

At least	But less than	Single	Married filing jointly *	Married filing separately	Head of a household
21,000	21,050	2,854	2,554	2,854	2,654
21,050	21,100	2,861	2,561	2,861	2,661
21,100	21,150	2,869	2,569	2,869	2,669
21,150	21,200	2,876	2,576	2,876	2,676
21,200	21,250	2,884	2,584	2,884	2,684
21,250	21,300	2,891	2,591	2,891	2,691
21,300	21,350	2,899	2,599	2,899	2,699
21,350	21,400	2,906	2,606	2,906	2,706
21,400	21,450	2,914	2,614	2,914	2,714
21,450	21,500	2,921	2,621	2,921	2,721
21,500	21,550	2,929	2,629	2,929	2,729
21,550	21,600	2,936	2,636	2,936	2,736
21,600	21,650	2,944	2,644	2,944	2,744
21,650	21,700	2,951	2,651	2,951	2,751
21,700	21,750	2,959	2,659	2,959	2,759
21,750	21,800	2,966	2,666	2,966	2,766
21,800	21,850	2,974	2,674	2,974	2,774
21,850	21,900	2,981	2,681	2,981	2,781
21,900	21,950	2,989	2,689	2,989	2,789
21,950	22,000	2,996	2,696	2,996	2,796

22,000

At least	But less than	Single	Married filing jointly *	Married filing separately	Head of a household
22,000	22,050	3,004	2,704	3,004	2,804
22,050	22,100	3,011	2,711	3,011	2,811
22,100	22,150	3,019	2,719	3,019	2,819
22,150	22,200	3,026	2,726	3,026	2,826
22,200	22,250	3,034	2,734	3,034	2,834
22,250	22,300	3,041	2,741	3,041	2,841
22,300	22,350	3,049	2,749	3,049	2,849
22,350	22,400	3,056	2,756	3,056	2,856
22,400	22,450	3,064	2,764	3,064	2,864
22,450	22,500	3,071	2,771	3,071	2,871
22,500	22,550	3,079	2,779	3,079	2,879
22,550	22,600	3,086	2,786	3,086	2,886
22,600	22,650	3,094	2,794	3,094	2,894
22,650	22,700	3,101	2,801	3,101	2,901
22,700	22,750	3,109	2,809	3,109	2,909
22,750	22,800	3,116	2,816	3,116	2,916
22,800	22,850	3,124	2,824	3,124	2,924
22,850	22,900	3,131	2,831	3,131	2,931
22,900	22,950	3,139	2,839	3,139	2,939
22,950	23,000	3,146	2,846	3,146	2,946

* This column must also be used by a qualifying widow(er).

If taxable income is—		And you are—			
At least	But less than	Single	Married filing jointly *	Married filing separately	Head of a house-hold
		Your tax is—			

23,000

At least	But less than	Single	Married filing jointly *	Married filing separately	Head of a household
23,000	23,050	3,154	2,854	3,154	2,954
23,050	23,100	3,161	2,861	3,161	2,961
23,100	23,150	3,169	2,869	3,169	2,969
23,150	23,200	3,176	2,876	3,176	2,976
23,200	23,250	3,184	2,884	3,184	2,984
23,250	23,300	3,191	2,891	3,191	2,991
23,300	23,350	3,199	2,899	3,199	2,999
23,350	23,400	3,206	2,906	3,209	3,006
23,400	23,450	3,214	2,914	3,223	3,014
23,450	23,500	3,221	2,921	3,236	3,021
23,500	23,550	3,229	2,929	3,250	3,029
23,550	23,600	3,236	2,936	3,263	3,036
23,600	23,650	3,244	2,944	3,277	3,044
23,650	23,700	3,251	2,951	3,290	3,051
23,700	23,750	3,259	2,959	3,304	3,059
23,750	23,800	3,266	2,966	3,317	3,066
23,800	23,850	3,274	2,974	3,331	3,074
23,850	23,900	3,281	2,981	3,344	3,081
23,900	23,950	3,289	2,989	3,358	3,089
23,950	24,000	3,296	2,996	3,371	3,096

24,000

At least	But less than	Single	Married filing jointly *	Married filing separately	Head of a household
24,000	24,050	3,304	3,004	3,385	3,104
24,050	24,100	3,311	3,011	3,398	3,111
24,100	24,150	3,319	3,019	3,412	3,119
24,150	24,200	3,326	3,026	3,425	3,126
24,200	24,250	3,334	3,034	3,439	3,134
24,250	24,300	3,341	3,041	3,452	3,141
24,300	24,350	3,349	3,049	3,466	3,149
24,350	24,400	3,356	3,056	3,479	3,156
24,400	24,450	3,364	3,064	3,493	3,164
24,450	24,500	3,371	3,071	3,506	3,171
24,500	24,550	3,379	3,079	3,520	3,179
24,550	24,600	3,386	3,086	3,533	3,186
24,600	24,650	3,394	3,094	3,547	3,194
24,650	24,700	3,401	3,101	3,560	3,201
24,700	24,750	3,409	3,109	3,574	3,209
24,750	24,800	3,416	3,116	3,587	3,216
24,800	24,850	3,424	3,124	3,601	3,224
24,850	24,900	3,431	3,131	3,614	3,231
24,900	24,950	3,439	3,139	3,628	3,239
24,950	25,000	3,446	3,146	3,641	3,246

25,000

At least	But less than	Single	Married filing jointly *	Married filing separately	Head of a household
25,000	25,050	3,454	3,154	3,655	3,254
25,050	25,100	3,461	3,161	3,668	3,261
25,100	25,150	3,469	3,169	3,682	3,269
25,150	25,200	3,476	3,176	3,695	3,276
25,200	25,250	3,484	3,184	3,709	3,284
25,250	25,300	3,491	3,191	3,722	3,291
25,300	25,350	3,499	3,199	3,736	3,299
25,350	25,400	3,506	3,206	3,749	3,306
25,400	25,450	3,514	3,214	3,763	3,314
25,450	25,500	3,521	3,221	3,776	3,321
25,500	25,550	3,529	3,229	3,790	3,329
25,550	25,600	3,536	3,236	3,803	3,336
25,600	25,650	3,544	3,244	3,817	3,344
25,650	25,700	3,551	3,251	3,830	3,351
25,700	25,750	3,559	3,259	3,844	3,359
25,750	25,800	3,566	3,266	3,857	3,366
25,800	25,850	3,574	3,274	3,871	3,374
25,850	25,900	3,581	3,281	3,884	3,381
25,900	25,950	3,589	3,289	3,898	3,389
25,950	26,000	3,596	3,296	3,911	3,396

26,000

At least	But less than	Single	Married filing jointly *	Married filing separately	Head of a household
26,000	26,050	3,604	3,304	3,925	3,404
26,050	26,100	3,611	3,311	3,938	3,411
26,100	26,150	3,619	3,319	3,952	3,419
26,150	26,200	3,626	3,326	3,965	3,426
26,200	26,250	3,634	3,334	3,979	3,434
26,250	26,300	3,641	3,341	3,992	3,441
26,300	26,350	3,649	3,349	4,006	3,449
26,350	26,400	3,656	3,356	4,019	3,456
26,400	26,450	3,664	3,364	4,033	3,464
26,450	26,500	3,671	3,371	4,046	3,471
26,500	26,550	3,679	3,379	4,060	3,479
26,550	26,600	3,686	3,386	4,073	3,486
26,600	26,650	3,694	3,394	4,087	3,494
26,650	26,700	3,701	3,401	4,100	3,501
26,700	26,750	3,709	3,409	4,114	3,509
26,750	26,800	3,716	3,416	4,127	3,516
26,800	26,850	3,724	3,424	4,141	3,524
26,850	26,900	3,731	3,431	4,154	3,531
26,900	26,950	3,739	3,439	4,168	3,539
26,950	27,000	3,746	3,446	4,181	3,546

27,000

At least	But less than	Single	Married filing jointly *	Married filing separately	Head of a household
27,000	27,050	3,754	3,454	4,195	3,554
27,050	27,100	3,761	3,461	4,208	3,561
27,100	27,150	3,769	3,469	4,222	3,569
27,150	27,200	3,776	3,476	4,235	3,576
27,200	27,250	3,784	3,484	4,249	3,584
27,250	27,300	3,791	3,491	4,262	3,591
27,300	27,350	3,799	3,499	4,276	3,599
27,350	27,400	3,806	3,506	4,289	3,606
27,400	27,450	3,814	3,514	4,303	3,614
27,450	27,500	3,821	3,521	4,316	3,621
27,500	27,550	3,829	3,529	4,330	3,629
27,550	27,600	3,836	3,536	4,343	3,636
27,600	27,650	3,844	3,544	4,357	3,644
27,650	27,700	3,851	3,551	4,370	3,651
27,700	27,750	3,859	3,559	4,384	3,659
27,750	27,800	3,866	3,566	4,397	3,666
27,800	27,850	3,874	3,574	4,411	3,674
27,850	27,900	3,881	3,581	4,424	3,681
27,900	27,950	3,889	3,589	4,438	3,689
27,950	28,000	3,899	3,596	4,451	3,696

28,000

At least	But less than	Single	Married filing jointly *	Married filing separately	Head of a household
28,000	28,050	3,913	3,604	4,465	3,704
28,050	28,100	3,926	3,611	4,478	3,711
28,100	28,150	3,940	3,619	4,492	3,719
28,150	28,200	3,953	3,626	4,505	3,726
28,200	28,250	3,967	3,634	4,519	3,734
28,250	28,300	3,980	3,641	4,532	3,741
28,300	28,350	3,994	3,649	4,546	3,749
28,350	28,400	4,007	3,656	4,559	3,756
28,400	28,450	4,021	3,664	4,573	3,764
28,450	28,500	4,034	3,671	4,586	3,771
28,500	28,550	4,048	3,679	4,600	3,779
28,550	28,600	4,061	3,686	4,613	3,786
28,600	28,650	4,075	3,694	4,627	3,794
28,650	28,700	4,088	3,701	4,640	3,801
28,700	28,750	4,102	3,709	4,654	3,809
28,750	28,800	4,115	3,716	4,667	3,816
28,800	28,850	4,129	3,724	4,681	3,824
28,850	28,900	4,142	3,731	4,694	3,831
28,900	28,950	4,156	3,739	4,708	3,839
28,950	29,000	4,169	3,746	4,721	3,846

29,000

At least	But less than	Single	Married filing jointly *	Married filing separately	Head of a household
29,000	29,050	4,183	3,754	4,735	3,854
29,050	29,100	4,196	3,761	4,748	3,861
29,100	29,150	4,210	3,769	4,762	3,869
29,150	29,200	4,223	3,776	4,775	3,876
29,200	29,250	4,237	3,784	4,789	3,884
29,250	29,300	4,250	3,791	4,802	3,891
29,300	29,350	4,264	3,799	4,816	3,899
29,350	29,400	4,277	3,806	4,829	3,906
29,400	29,450	4,291	3,814	4,843	3,914
29,450	29,500	4,304	3,821	4,856	3,921
29,500	29,550	4,318	3,829	4,870	3,929
29,550	29,600	4,331	3,836	4,883	3,936
29,600	29,650	4,345	3,844	4,897	3,944
29,650	29,700	4,358	3,851	4,910	3,951
29,700	29,750	4,372	3,859	4,924	3,959
29,750	29,800	4,385	3,866	4,937	3,966
29,800	29,850	4,399	3,874	4,951	3,974
29,850	29,900	4,412	3,881	4,964	3,981
29,900	29,950	4,426	3,889	4,978	3,989
29,950	30,000	4,439	3,896	4,991	3,996

30,000

At least	But less than	Single	Married filing jointly *	Married filing separately	Head of a household
30,000	30,050	4,453	3,904	5,005	4,004
30,050	30,100	4,466	3,911	5,018	4,011
30,100	30,150	4,480	3,919	5,032	4,019
30,150	30,200	4,493	3,926	5,045	4,026
30,200	30,250	4,507	3,934	5,059	4,034
30,250	30,300	4,520	3,941	5,072	4,041
30,300	30,350	4,534	3,949	5,086	4,049
30,350	30,400	4,547	3,956	5,099	4,056
30,400	30,450	4,561	3,964	5,113	4,064
30,450	30,500	4,574	3,971	5,126	4,071
30,500	30,550	4,588	3,979	5,140	4,079
30,550	30,600	4,601	3,986	5,153	4,086
30,600	30,650	4,615	3,994	5,167	4,094
30,650	30,700	4,628	4,001	5,180	4,101
30,700	30,750	4,642	4,009	5,194	4,109
30,750	30,800	4,655	4,016	5,207	4,116
30,800	30,850	4,669	4,024	5,221	4,124
30,850	30,900	4,682	4,031	5,234	4,131
30,900	30,950	4,696	4,039	5,248	4,139
30,950	31,000	4,709	4,046	5,261	4,146

31,000

At least	But less than	Single	Married filing jointly *	Married filing separately	Head of a household
31,000	31,050	4,723	4,054	5,275	4,154
31,050	31,100	4,736	4,061	5,288	4,161
31,100	31,150	4,750	4,069	5,302	4,169
31,150	31,200	4,763	4,076	5,315	4,176
31,200	31,250	4,777	4,084	5,329	4,184
31,250	31,300	4,790	4,091	5,342	4,191
31,300	31,350	4,804	4,099	5,356	4,199
31,350	31,400	4,817	4,106	5,369	4,206
31,400	31,450	4,831	4,114	5,383	4,214
31,450	31,500	4,844	4,121	5,396	4,221
31,500	31,550	4,858	4,129	5,410	4,229
31,550	31,600	4,871	4,136	5,423	4,236
31,600	31,650	4,885	4,144	5,437	4,244
31,650	31,700	4,898	4,151	5,450	4,251
31,700	31,750	4,912	4,159	5,464	4,259
31,750	31,800	4,925	4,166	5,477	4,266
31,800	31,850	4,939	4,174	5,491	4,274
31,850	31,900	4,952	4,181	5,504	4,281
31,900	31,950	4,966	4,189	5,518	4,289
31,950	32,000	4,979	4,196	5,531	4,296

* This column must also be used by a qualifying widow(er).

32,000

At least	But less than	Single	Married filing jointly*	Married filing separately	Head of a household
32,000	32,050	4,993	4,204	5,545	4,304
32,050	32,100	5,006	4,211	5,558	4,311
32,100	32,150	5,020	4,219	5,572	4,319
32,150	32,200	5,033	4,226	5,585	4,326
32,200	32,250	5,047	4,234	5,599	4,334
32,250	32,300	5,060	4,241	5,612	4,341
32,300	32,350	5,074	4,249	5,626	4,349
32,350	32,400	5,087	4,256	5,639	4,356
32,400	32,450	5,101	4,264	5,653	4,364
32,450	32,500	5,114	4,271	5,666	4,371
32,500	32,550	5,128	4,279	5,680	4,379
32,550	32,600	5,141	4,286	5,693	4,386
32,600	32,650	5,155	4,294	5,707	4,394
32,650	32,700	5,168	4,301	5,720	4,401
32,700	32,750	5,182	4,309	5,734	4,409
32,750	32,800	5,195	4,316	5,747	4,416
32,800	32,850	5,209	4,324	5,761	4,424
32,850	32,900	5,222	4,331	5,774	4,431
32,900	32,950	5,236	4,339	5,788	4,439
32,950	33,000	5,249	4,346	5,801	4,446

33,000

At least	But less than	Single	Married filing jointly*	Married filing separately	Head of a household
33,000	33,050	5,263	4,354	5,815	4,454
33,050	33,100	5,276	4,361	5,828	4,461
33,100	33,150	5,290	4,369	5,842	4,469
33,150	33,200	5,303	4,376	5,855	4,476
33,200	33,250	5,317	4,384	5,869	4,484
33,250	33,300	5,330	4,391	5,882	4,491
33,300	33,350	5,344	4,399	5,896	4,499
33,350	33,400	5,357	4,406	5,909	4,506
33,400	33,450	5,371	4,414	5,923	4,514
33,450	33,500	5,384	4,421	5,936	4,521
33,500	33,550	5,398	4,429	5,950	4,529
33,550	33,600	5,411	4,436	5,963	4,536
33,600	33,650	5,425	4,444	5,977	4,544
33,650	33,700	5,438	4,451	5,990	4,551
33,700	33,750	5,452	4,459	6,004	4,559
33,750	33,800	5,465	4,466	6,017	4,566
33,800	33,850	5,479	4,474	6,031	4,574
33,850	33,900	5,492	4,481	6,044	4,581
33,900	33,950	5,506	4,489	6,058	4,589
33,950	34,000	5,519	4,496	6,071	4,596

34,000

At least	But less than	Single	Married filing jointly*	Married filing separately	Head of a household
34,000	34,050	5,533	4,504	6,085	4,604
34,050	34,100	5,546	4,511	6,098	4,611
34,100	34,150	5,560	4,519	6,112	4,619
34,150	34,200	5,573	4,526	6,125	4,626
34,200	34,250	5,587	4,534	6,139	4,634
34,250	34,300	5,600	4,541	6,152	4,641
34,300	34,350	5,614	4,549	6,166	4,649
34,350	34,400	5,627	4,556	6,179	4,656
34,400	34,450	5,641	4,564	6,193	4,664
34,450	34,500	5,654	4,571	6,206	4,671
34,500	34,550	5,668	4,579	6,220	4,679
34,550	34,600	5,681	4,586	6,233	4,686
34,600	34,650	5,695	4,594	6,247	4,694
34,650	34,700	5,708	4,601	6,260	4,701
34,700	34,750	5,722	4,609	6,274	4,709
34,750	34,800	5,735	4,616	6,287	4,716
34,800	34,850	5,749	4,624	6,301	4,724
34,850	34,900	5,762	4,631	6,314	4,731
34,900	34,950	5,776	4,639	6,328	4,739
34,950	35,000	5,789	4,646	6,341	4,746

35,000

At least	But less than	Single	Married filing jointly*	Married filing separately	Head of a household
35,000	35,050	5,803	4,654	6,355	4,754
35,050	35,100	5,816	4,661	6,368	4,761
35,100	35,150	5,830	4,669	6,382	4,769
35,150	35,200	5,843	4,676	6,395	4,776
35,200	35,250	5,857	4,684	6,409	4,784
35,250	35,300	5,870	4,691	6,422	4,791
35,300	35,350	5,884	4,699	6,436	4,799
35,350	35,400	5,897	4,706	6,449	4,806
35,400	35,450	5,911	4,714	6,463	4,814
35,450	35,500	5,924	4,721	6,476	4,821
35,500	35,550	5,938	4,729	6,490	4,829
35,550	35,600	5,951	4,736	6,503	4,836
35,600	35,650	5,965	4,744	6,517	4,844
35,650	35,700	5,978	4,751	6,530	4,851
35,700	35,750	5,992	4,759	6,544	4,859
35,750	35,800	6,005	4,766	6,557	4,866
35,800	35,850	6,019	4,774	6,571	4,874
35,850	35,900	6,032	4,781	6,584	4,881
35,900	35,950	6,046	4,789	6,598	4,889
35,950	36,000	6,059	4,796	6,611	4,896

36,000

At least	But less than	Single	Married filing jointly*	Married filing separately	Head of a household
36,000	36,050	6,073	4,804	6,625	4,904
36,050	36,100	6,086	4,811	6,638	4,911
36,100	36,150	6,100	4,819	6,652	4,919
36,150	36,200	6,113	4,826	6,665	4,926
36,200	36,250	6,127	4,834	6,679	4,934
36,250	36,300	6,140	4,841	6,692	4,941
36,300	36,350	6,154	4,849	6,706	4,949
36,350	36,400	6,167	4,856	6,719	4,956
36,400	36,450	6,181	4,864	6,733	4,964
36,450	36,500	6,194	4,871	6,746	4,971
36,500	36,550	6,208	4,879	6,760	4,979
36,550	36,600	6,221	4,886	6,773	4,986
36,600	36,650	6,235	4,894	6,787	4,994
36,650	36,700	6,248	4,901	6,800	5,001
36,700	36,750	6,262	4,909	6,814	5,009
36,750	36,800	6,275	4,916	6,827	5,016
36,800	36,850	6,289	4,924	6,841	5,024
36,850	36,900	6,302	4,931	6,854	5,031
36,900	36,950	6,316	4,939	6,868	5,039
36,950	37,000	6,329	4,946	6,881	5,046

37,000

At least	But less than	Single	Married filing jointly*	Married filing separately	Head of a household
37,000	37,050	6,343	4,954	6,895	5,054
37,050	37,100	6,356	4,961	6,908	5,061
37,100	37,150	6,370	4,969	6,922	5,069
37,150	37,200	6,383	4,976	6,935	5,076
37,200	37,250	6,397	4,984	6,949	5,084
37,250	37,300	6,410	4,991	6,962	5,091
37,300	37,350	6,424	4,999	6,976	5,099
37,350	37,400	6,437	5,006	6,989	5,106
37,400	37,450	6,451	5,014	7,003	5,114
37,450	37,500	6,464	5,021	7,016	5,124
37,500	37,550	6,478	5,029	7,030	5,138
37,550	37,600	6,491	5,036	7,043	5,151
37,600	37,650	6,505	5,044	7,057	5,165
37,650	37,700	6,518	5,051	7,070	5,178
37,700	37,750	6,532	5,059	7,084	5,192
37,750	37,800	6,545	5,066	7,097	5,205
37,800	37,850	6,559	5,074	7,111	5,219
37,850	37,900	6,572	5,081	7,124	5,232
37,900	37,950	6,586	5,089	7,138	5,246
37,950	38,000	6,599	5,096	7,151	5,259

38,000

At least	But less than	Single	Married filing jointly*	Married filing separately	Head of a household
38,000	38,050	6,613	5,104	7,165	5,273
38,050	38,100	6,626	5,111	7,178	5,286
38,100	38,150	6,640	5,119	7,192	5,300
38,150	38,200	6,653	5,126	7,205	5,313
38,200	38,250	6,667	5,134	7,219	5,327
38,250	38,300	6,680	5,141	7,232	5,340
38,300	38,350	6,694	5,149	7,246	5,354
38,350	38,400	6,707	5,156	7,259	5,367
38,400	38,450	6,721	5,164	7,273	5,381
38,450	38,500	6,734	5,171	7,286	5,394
38,500	38,550	6,748	5,179	7,300	5,408
38,550	38,600	6,761	5,186	7,313	5,421
38,600	38,650	6,775	5,194	7,327	5,435
38,650	38,700	6,788	5,201	7,340	5,448
38,700	38,750	6,802	5,209	7,354	5,462
38,750	38,800	6,815	5,216	7,367	5,475
38,800	38,850	6,829	5,224	7,381	5,489
38,850	38,900	6,842	5,231	7,394	5,502
38,900	38,950	6,856	5,239	7,408	5,516
38,950	39,000	6,869	5,246	7,421	5,529

39,000

At least	But less than	Single	Married filing jointly*	Married filing separately	Head of a household
39,000	39,050	6,883	5,254	7,435	5,543
39,050	39,100	6,896	5,261	7,448	5,556
39,100	39,150	6,910	5,269	7,462	5,570
39,150	39,200	6,923	5,276	7,475	5,583
39,200	39,250	6,937	5,284	7,489	5,597
39,250	39,300	6,950	5,291	7,502	5,610
39,300	39,350	6,964	5,299	7,516	5,624
39,350	39,400	6,977	5,306	7,529	5,637
39,400	39,450	6,991	5,314	7,543	5,651
39,450	39,500	7,004	5,321	7,556	5,664
39,500	39,550	7,018	5,329	7,570	5,678
39,550	39,600	7,031	5,336	7,583	5,691
39,600	39,650	7,045	5,344	7,597	5,705
39,650	39,700	7,058	5,351	7,610	5,718
39,700	39,750	7,072	5,359	7,624	5,732
39,750	39,800	7,085	5,366	7,637	5,745
39,800	39,850	7,099	5,374	7,651	5,759
39,850	39,900	7,112	5,381	7,664	5,772
39,900	39,950	7,126	5,389	7,678	5,786
39,950	40,000	7,139	5,396	7,691	5,799

40,000

At least	But less than	Single	Married filing jointly*	Married filing separately	Head of a household
40,000	40,050	7,153	5,404	7,705	5,813
40,050	40,100	7,166	5,411	7,718	5,826
40,100	40,150	7,180	5,419	7,732	5,840
40,150	40,200	7,193	5,426	7,745	5,853
40,200	40,250	7,207	5,434	7,759	5,867
40,250	40,300	7,220	5,441	7,772	5,880
40,300	40,350	7,234	5,449	7,786	5,894
40,350	40,400	7,247	5,456	7,799	5,907
40,400	40,450	7,261	5,464	7,813	5,921
40,450	40,500	7,274	5,471	7,826	5,934
40,500	40,550	7,288	5,479	7,840	5,948
40,550	40,600	7,301	5,486	7,853	5,961
40,600	40,650	7,315	5,494	7,867	5,975
40,650	40,700	7,328	5,501	7,880	5,988
40,700	40,750	7,342	5,509	7,894	6,002
40,750	40,800	7,355	5,516	7,907	6,015
40,800	40,850	7,369	5,524	7,921	6,029
40,850	40,900	7,382	5,531	7,934	6,042
40,900	40,950	7,396	5,539	7,948	6,056
40,950	41,000	7,409	5,546	7,961	6,069

* This column must also be used by a qualifying widow(er).

If taxable income is—		And you are—			
At least	But less than	Single	Married filing jointly *	Married filing separately	Head of a household
		Your tax is—			

41,000

At least	But less than	Single	Married filing jointly	Married filing separately	Head of household
41,000	41,050	7,423	5,554	7,975	6,083
41,050	41,100	7,436	5,561	7,988	6,096
41,100	41,150	7,450	5,569	8,002	6,110
41,150	41,200	7,463	5,576	8,015	6,123
41,200	41,250	7,477	5,584	8,029	6,137
41,250	41,300	7,490	5,591	8,042	6,150
41,300	41,350	7,504	5,599	8,056	6,164
41,350	41,400	7,517	5,606	8,069	6,177
41,400	41,450	7,531	5,614	8,083	6,191
41,450	41,500	7,544	5,621	8,096	6,204
41,500	41,550	7,558	5,629	8,110	6,218
41,550	41,600	7,571	5,636	8,123	6,231
41,600	41,650	7,585	5,644	8,137	6,245
41,650	41,700	7,598	5,651	8,150	6,258
41,700	41,750	7,612	5,659	8,164	6,272
41,750	41,800	7,625	5,666	8,177	6,285
41,800	41,850	7,639	5,674	8,191	6,299
41,850	41,900	7,652	5,681	8,204	6,312
41,900	41,950	7,666	5,689	8,218	6,326
41,950	42,000	7,679	5,696	8,231	6,339

42,000

At least	But less than	Single	Married filing jointly	Married filing separately	Head of household
42,000	42,050	7,693	5,704	8,245	6,353
42,050	42,100	7,706	5,711	8,258	6,366
42,100	42,150	7,720	5,719	8,272	6,380
42,150	42,200	7,733	5,726	8,285	6,393
42,200	42,250	7,747	5,734	8,299	6,407
42,250	42,300	7,760	5,741	8,312	6,420
42,300	42,350	7,774	5,749	8,326	6,434
42,350	42,400	7,787	5,756	8,339	6,447
42,400	42,450	7,801	5,764	8,353	6,461
42,450	42,500	7,814	5,771	8,366	6,474
42,500	42,550	7,828	5,779	8,380	6,488
42,550	42,600	7,841	5,786	8,393	6,501
42,600	42,650	7,855	5,794	8,407	6,515
42,650	42,700	7,868	5,801	8,420	6,528
42,700	42,750	7,882	5,809	8,434	6,542
42,750	42,800	7,895	5,816	8,447	6,555
42,800	42,850	7,909	5,824	8,461	6,569
42,850	42,900	7,922	5,831	8,474	6,582
42,900	42,950	7,936	5,839	8,488	6,596
42,950	43,000	7,949	5,846	8,501	6,609

43,000

At least	But less than	Single	Married filing jointly	Married filing separately	Head of household
43,000	43,050	7,963	5,854	8,515	6,623
43,050	43,100	7,976	5,861	8,528	6,636
43,100	43,150	7,990	5,869	8,542	6,650
43,150	43,200	8,003	5,876	8,555	6,663
43,200	43,250	8,017	5,884	8,569	6,677
43,250	43,300	8,030	5,891	8,582	6,690
43,300	43,350	8,044	5,899	8,596	6,704
43,350	43,400	8,057	5,906	8,609	6,717
43,400	43,450	8,071	5,914	8,623	6,731
43,450	43,500	8,084	5,921	8,636	6,744
43,500	43,550	8,098	5,929	8,650	6,758
43,550	43,600	8,111	5,936	8,663	6,771
43,600	43,650	8,125	5,944	8,677	6,785
43,650	43,700	8,138	5,951	8,690	6,798
43,700	43,750	8,152	5,959	8,704	6,812
43,750	43,800	8,165	5,966	8,717	6,825
43,800	43,850	8,179	5,974	8,731	6,839
43,850	43,900	8,192	5,981	8,744	6,852
43,900	43,950	8,206	5,989	8,758	6,866
43,950	44,000	8,219	5,996	8,771	6,879

44,000

At least	But less than	Single	Married filing jointly	Married filing separately	Head of household
44,000	44,050	8,233	6,004	8,785	6,893
44,050	44,100	8,246	6,011	8,798	6,906
44,100	44,150	8,260	6,019	8,812	6,920
44,150	44,200	8,273	6,026	8,825	6,933
44,200	44,250	8,287	6,034	8,839	6,947
44,250	44,300	8,300	6,041	8,852	6,960
44,300	44,350	8,314	6,049	8,866	6,974
44,350	44,400	8,327	6,056	8,879	6,987
44,400	44,450	8,341	6,064	8,893	7,001
44,450	44,500	8,354	6,071	8,906	7,014
44,500	44,550	8,368	6,079	8,920	7,028
44,550	44,600	8,381	6,086	8,933	7,041
44,600	44,650	8,395	6,094	8,947	7,055
44,650	44,700	8,408	6,101	8,960	7,068
44,700	44,750	8,422	6,109	8,974	7,082
44,750	44,800	8,435	6,116	8,987	7,095
44,800	44,850	8,449	6,124	9,001	7,109
44,850	44,900	8,462	6,131	9,014	7,122
44,900	44,950	8,476	6,139	9,028	7,136
44,950	45,000	8,489	6,146	9,041	7,149

45,000

At least	But less than	Single	Married filing jointly	Married filing separately	Head of household
45,000	45,050	8,503	6,154	9,055	7,163
45,050	45,100	8,516	6,161	9,068	7,176
45,100	45,150	8,530	6,169	9,082	7,190
45,150	45,200	8,543	6,176	9,095	7,203
45,200	45,250	8,557	6,184	9,109	7,217
45,250	45,300	8,570	6,191	9,122	7,230
45,300	45,350	8,584	6,199	9,136	7,244
45,350	45,400	8,597	6,206	9,149	7,257
45,400	45,450	8,611	6,214	9,163	7,271
45,450	45,500	8,624	6,221	9,176	7,284
45,500	45,550	8,638	6,229	9,190	7,298
45,550	45,600	8,651	6,236	9,203	7,311
45,600	45,650	8,665	6,244	9,217	7,325
45,650	45,700	8,678	6,251	9,230	7,338
45,700	45,750	8,692	6,259	9,244	7,352
45,750	45,800	8,705	6,266	9,257	7,365
45,800	45,850	8,719	6,274	9,271	7,379
45,850	45,900	8,732	6,281	9,284	7,392
45,900	45,950	8,746	6,289	9,298	7,406
45,950	46,000	8,759	6,296	9,311	7,419

46,000

At least	But less than	Single	Married filing jointly	Married filing separately	Head of household
46,000	46,050	8,773	6,304	9,325	7,433
46,050	46,100	8,786	6,311	9,338	7,446
46,100	46,150	8,800	6,319	9,352	7,460
46,150	46,200	8,813	6,326	9,365	7,473
46,200	46,250	8,827	6,334	9,379	7,487
46,250	46,300	8,840	6,341	9,392	7,500
46,300	46,350	8,854	6,349	9,406	7,514
46,350	46,400	8,867	6,356	9,419	7,527
46,400	46,450	8,881	6,364	9,433	7,541
46,450	46,500	8,894	6,371	9,446	7,554
46,500	46,550	8,908	6,379	9,460	7,568
46,550	46,600	8,921	6,386	9,473	7,581
46,600	46,650	8,935	6,394	9,487	7,595
46,650	46,700	8,948	6,401	9,500	7,608
46,700	46,750	8,962	6,412	9,514	7,622
46,750	46,800	8,975	6,425	9,527	7,635
46,800	46,850	8,989	6,439	9,541	7,649
46,850	46,900	9,002	6,452	9,554	7,662
46,900	46,950	9,016	6,466	9,568	7,676
46,950	47,000	9,029	6,479	9,581	7,689

47,000

At least	But less than	Single	Married filing jointly	Married filing separately	Head of household
47,000	47,050	9,043	6,493	9,595	7,703
47,050	47,100	9,056	6,506	9,608	7,716
47,100	47,150	9,070	6,520	9,622	7,730
47,150	47,200	9,083	6,533	9,635	7,743
47,200	47,250	9,097	6,547	9,649	7,757
47,250	47,300	9,110	6,560	9,662	7,770
47,300	47,350	9,124	6,574	9,676	7,784
47,350	47,400	9,137	6,587	9,689	7,797
47,400	47,450	9,151	6,601	9,703	7,811
47,450	47,500	9,164	6,614	9,716	7,824
47,500	47,550	9,178	6,628	9,730	7,838
47,550	47,600	9,191	6,641	9,743	7,851
47,600	47,650	9,205	6,655	9,757	7,865
47,650	47,700	9,218	6,668	9,770	7,878
47,700	47,750	9,232	6,682	9,784	7,892
47,750	47,800	9,245	6,695	9,797	7,905
47,800	47,850	9,259	6,709	9,811	7,919
47,850	47,900	9,272	6,722	9,824	7,932
47,900	47,950	9,286	6,736	9,838	7,946
47,950	48,000	9,299	6,749	9,851	7,959

48,000

At least	But less than	Single	Married filing jointly	Married filing separately	Head of household
48,000	48,050	9,313	6,763	9,865	7,973
48,050	48,100	9,326	6,776	9,878	7,986
48,100	48,150	9,340	6,790	9,892	8,000
48,150	48,200	9,353	6,803	9,905	8,013
48,200	48,250	9,367	6,817	9,919	8,027
48,250	48,300	9,380	6,830	9,932	8,040
48,300	48,350	9,394	6,844	9,946	8,054
48,350	48,400	9,407	6,857	9,959	8,067
48,400	48,450	9,421	6,871	9,973	8,081
48,450	48,500	9,434	6,884	9,986	8,094
48,500	48,550	9,448	6,898	10,000	8,108
48,550	48,600	9,461	6,911	10,013	8,121
48,600	48,650	9,475	6,925	10,027	8,135
48,650	48,700	9,488	6,938	10,040	8,148
48,700	48,750	9,502	6,952	10,054	8,162
48,750	48,800	9,515	6,965	10,067	8,175
48,800	48,850	9,529	6,979	10,081	8,189
48,850	48,900	9,542	6,992	10,094	8,202
48,900	48,950	9,556	7,006	10,108	8,216
48,950	49,000	9,569	7,019	10,121	8,229

49,000

At least	But less than	Single	Married filing jointly	Married filing separately	Head of household
49,000	49,050	9,583	7,033	10,135	8,243
49,050	49,100	9,596	7,046	10,148	8,256
49,100	49,150	9,610	7,060	10,162	8,270
49,150	49,200	9,623	7,073	10,175	8,283
49,200	49,250	9,637	7,087	10,189	8,297
49,250	49,300	9,650	7,100	10,202	8,310
49,300	49,350	9,664	7,114	10,216	8,324
49,350	49,400	9,677	7,127	10,229	8,337
49,400	49,450	9,691	7,141	10,243	8,351
49,450	49,500	9,704	7,154	10,256	8,364
49,500	49,550	9,718	7,168	10,270	8,378
49,550	49,600	9,731	7,181	10,283	8,391
49,600	49,650	9,745	7,195	10,297	8,405
49,650	49,700	9,758	7,208	10,310	8,418
49,700	49,750	9,772	7,222	10,324	8,432
49,750	49,800	9,785	7,235	10,337	8,445
49,800	49,850	9,799	7,249	10,351	8,459
49,850	49,900	9,812	7,262	10,364	8,472
49,900	49,950	9,826	7,276	10,378	8,486
49,950	50,000	9,839	7,289	10,391	8,499

* This column must also be used by a qualifying widow(er).

If taxable income is— At least	But less than	Single	Married filing jointly*	Married filing separately	Head of a household
50,000					
50,000	50,050	9,853	7,303	10,405	8,513
50,050	50,100	9,866	7,316	10,418	8,526
50,100	50,150	9,880	7,330	10,432	8,540
50,150	50,200	9,893	7,343	10,445	8,553
50,200	50,250	9,907	7,357	10,459	8,567
50,250	50,300	9,920	7,370	10,472	8,580
50,300	50,350	9,934	7,384	10,486	8,594
50,350	50,400	9,947	7,397	10,499	8,607
50,400	50,450	9,961	7,411	10,513	8,621
50,450	50,500	9,974	7,424	10,526	8,634
50,500	50,550	9,988	7,438	10,540	8,648
50,550	50,600	10,001	7,451	10,553	8,661
50,600	50,650	10,015	7,465	10,567	8,675
50,650	50,700	10,028	7,478	10,580	8,688
50,700	50,750	10,042	7,492	10,594	8,702
50,750	50,800	10,055	7,505	10,607	8,715
50,800	50,850	10,069	7,519	10,621	8,729
50,850	50,900	10,082	7,532	10,634	8,742
50,900	50,950	10,096	7,546	10,648	8,756
50,950	51,000	10,109	7,559	10,661	8,769
51,000					
51,000	51,050	10,123	7,573	10,675	8,783
51,050	51,100	10,136	7,586	10,688	8,796
51,100	51,150	10,150	7,600	10,702	8,810
51,150	51,200	10,163	7,613	10,715	8,823
51,200	51,250	10,177	7,627	10,729	8,837
51,250	51,300	10,190	7,640	10,742	8,850
51,300	51,350	10,204	7,654	10,756	8,864
51,350	51,400	10,217	7,667	10,769	8,877
51,400	51,450	10,231	7,681	10,783	8,891
51,450	51,500	10,244	7,694	10,796	8,904
51,500	51,550	10,258	7,708	10,810	8,918
51,550	51,600	10,271	7,721	10,823	8,931
51,600	51,650	10,285	7,735	10,837	8,945
51,650	51,700	10,298	7,748	10,850	8,958
51,700	51,750	10,312	7,762	10,864	8,972
51,750	51,800	10,325	7,775	10,877	8,985
51,800	51,850	10,339	7,789	10,891	8,999
51,850	51,900	10,352	7,802	10,904	9,012
51,900	51,950	10,366	7,816	10,918	9,026
51,950	52,000	10,379	7,829	10,931	9,039
52,000					
52,000	52,050	10,393	7,843	10,945	9,053
52,050	52,100	10,406	7,856	10,958	9,066
52,100	52,150	10,420	7,870	10,972	9,080
52,150	52,200	10,433	7,883	10,985	9,093
52,200	52,250	10,447	7,897	10,999	9,107
52,250	52,300	10,460	7,910	11,012	9,120
52,300	52,350	10,474	7,924	11,026	9,134
52,350	52,400	10,487	7,937	11,039	9,147
52,400	52,450	10,501	7,951	11,053	9,161
52,450	52,500	10,514	7,964	11,066	9,174
52,500	52,550	10,528	7,978	11,080	9,188
52,550	52,600	10,541	7,991	11,093	9,201
52,600	52,650	10,555	8,005	11,107	9,215
52,650	52,700	10,568	8,018	11,120	9,228
52,700	52,750	10,582	8,032	11,134	9,242
52,750	52,800	10,595	8,045	11,147	9,255
52,800	52,850	10,609	8,059	11,161	9,269
52,850	52,900	10,622	8,072	11,174	9,282
52,900	52,950	10,636	8,086	11,188	9,296
52,950	53,000	10,649	8,099	11,201	9,309

If taxable income is— At least	But less than	Single	Married filing jointly*	Married filing separately	Head of a household
53,000					
53,000	53,050	10,663	8,113	11,215	9,323
53,050	53,100	10,676	8,126	11,228	9,336
53,100	53,150	10,690	8,140	11,242	9,350
53,150	53,200	10,703	8,153	11,255	9,363
53,200	53,250	10,717	8,167	11,269	9,377
53,250	53,300	10,730	8,180	11,282	9,390
53,300	53,350	10,744	8,194	11,296	9,404
53,350	53,400	10,757	8,207	11,309	9,417
53,400	53,450	10,771	8,221	11,323	9,431
53,450	53,500	10,784	8,234	11,336	9,444
53,500	53,550	10,798	8,248	11,350	9,458
53,550	53,600	10,811	8,261	11,363	9,471
53,600	53,650	10,825	8,275	11,377	9,485
53,650	53,700	10,838	8,288	11,390	9,498
53,700	53,750	10,852	8,302	11,404	9,512
53,750	53,800	10,865	8,315	11,417	9,525
53,800	53,850	10,879	8,329	11,431	9,539
53,850	53,900	10,892	8,342	11,444	9,552
53,900	53,950	10,906	8,356	11,458	9,566
53,950	54,000	10,919	8,369	11,471	9,579
54,000					
54,000	54,050	10,933	8,383	11,485	9,593
54,050	54,100	10,946	8,396	11,498	9,606
54,100	54,150	10,960	8,410	11,512	9,620
54,150	54,200	10,973	8,423	11,525	9,633
54,200	54,250	10,987	8,437	11,539	9,647
54,250	54,300	11,000	8,450	11,552	9,660
54,300	54,350	11,014	8,464	11,566	9,674
54,350	54,400	11,027	8,477	11,579	9,687
54,400	54,450	11,041	8,491	11,593	9,701
54,450	54,500	11,054	8,504	11,606	9,714
54,500	54,550	11,068	8,518	11,620	9,728
54,550	54,600	11,081	8,531	11,633	9,741
54,600	54,650	11,095	8,545	11,647	9,755
54,650	54,700	11,108	8,558	11,660	9,768
54,700	54,750	11,122	8,572	11,674	9,782
54,750	54,800	11,135	8,585	11,687	9,795
54,800	54,850	11,149	8,599	11,701	9,809
54,850	54,900	11,162	8,612	11,714	9,822
54,900	54,950	11,176	8,626	11,728	9,836
54,950	55,000	11,189	8,639	11,741	9,849
55,000					
55,000	55,050	11,203	8,653	11,755	9,863
55,050	55,100	11,216	8,666	11,768	9,876
55,100	55,150	11,230	8,680	11,782	9,890
55,150	55,200	11,243	8,693	11,795	9,903
55,200	55,250	11,257	8,707	11,809	9,917
55,250	55,300	11,270	8,720	11,822	9,930
55,300	55,350	11,284	8,734	11,836	9,944
55,350	55,400	11,297	8,747	11,849	9,957
55,400	55,450	11,311	8,761	11,863	9,971
55,450	55,500	11,324	8,774	11,876	9,984
55,500	55,550	11,338	8,788	11,890	9,998
55,550	55,600	11,351	8,801	11,903	10,011
55,600	55,650	11,365	8,815	11,917	10,025
55,650	55,700	11,378	8,828	11,930	10,038
55,700	55,750	11,392	8,842	11,944	10,052
55,750	55,800	11,405	8,855	11,957	10,065
55,800	55,850	11,419	8,869	11,971	10,079
55,850	55,900	11,432	8,882	11,984	10,092
55,900	55,950	11,446	8,896	11,998	10,106
55,950	56,000	11,459	8,909	12,011	10,119

If taxable income is— At least	But less than	Single	Married filing jointly*	Married filing separately	Head of a household
56,000					
56,000	56,050	11,473	8,923	12,025	10,133
56,050	56,100	11,486	8,936	12,038	10,146
56,100	56,150	11,500	8,950	12,052	10,160
56,150	56,200	11,513	8,963	12,065	10,173
56,200	56,250	11,527	8,977	12,079	10,187
56,250	56,300	11,540	8,990	12,092	10,200
56,300	56,350	11,554	9,004	12,106	10,214
56,350	56,400	11,567	9,017	12,119	10,227
56,400	56,450	11,581	9,031	12,133	10,241
56,450	56,500	11,594	9,044	12,148	10,254
56,500	56,550	11,608	9,058	12,163	10,268
56,550	56,600	11,621	9,071	12,178	10,281
56,600	56,650	11,635	9,085	12,193	10,295
56,650	56,700	11,648	9,098	12,208	10,308
56,700	56,750	11,662	9,112	12,223	10,322
56,750	56,800	11,675	9,125	12,238	10,335
56,800	56,850	11,689	9,139	12,253	10,349
56,850	56,900	11,702	9,152	12,268	10,362
56,900	56,950	11,716	9,166	12,283	10,376
56,950	57,000	11,729	9,179	12,298	10,389
57,000					
57,000	57,050	11,743	9,193	12,313	10,403
57,050	57,100	11,756	9,206	12,328	10,416
57,100	57,150	11,770	9,220	12,343	10,430
57,150	57,200	11,783	9,233	12,358	10,443
57,200	57,250	11,797	9,247	12,373	10,457
57,250	57,300	11,810	9,260	12,388	10,470
57,300	57,350	11,824	9,274	12,403	10,484
57,350	57,400	11,837	9,287	12,418	10,497
57,400	57,450	11,851	9,301	12,433	10,511
57,450	57,500	11,864	9,314	12,448	10,524
57,500	57,550	11,878	9,328	12,463	10,538
57,550	57,600	11,891	9,341	12,478	10,551
57,600	57,650	11,905	9,355	12,493	10,565
57,650	57,700	11,918	9,368	12,508	10,578
57,700	57,750	11,932	9,382	12,523	10,592
57,750	57,800	11,945	9,395	12,538	10,605
57,800	57,850	11,959	9,409	12,553	10,619
57,850	57,900	11,972	9,422	12,568	10,632
57,900	57,950	11,986	9,436	12,583	10,646
57,950	58,000	11,999	9,449	12,598	10,659
58,000					
58,000	58,050	12,013	9,463	12,613	10,673
58,050	58,100	12,026	9,476	12,628	10,686
58,100	58,150	12,040	9,490	12,643	10,700
58,150	58,200	12,053	9,503	12,658	10,713
58,200	58,250	12,067	9,517	12,673	10,727
58,250	58,300	12,080	9,530	12,688	10,740
58,300	58,350	12,094	9,544	12,703	10,754
58,350	58,400	12,107	9,557	12,718	10,767
58,400	58,450	12,121	9,571	12,733	10,781
58,450	58,500	12,134	9,584	12,748	10,794
58,500	58,550	12,148	9,598	12,763	10,808
58,550	58,600	12,161	9,611	12,778	10,821
58,600	58,650	12,175	9,625	12,793	10,835
58,650	58,700	12,188	9,638	12,808	10,848
58,700	58,750	12,202	9,652	12,823	10,862
58,750	58,800	12,215	9,665	12,838	10,875
58,800	58,850	12,229	9,679	12,853	10,889
58,850	58,900	12,242	9,692	12,868	10,902
58,900	58,950	12,256	9,706	12,883	10,916
58,950	59,000	12,269	9,719	12,898	10,929

* This column must also be used by a qualifying widow(er).

59,000 / 60,000 / 61,000

At least	But less than	Single	Married filing jointly *	Married filing separately	Head of a house-hold
59,000					
59,000	59,050	12,283	9,733	12,913	10,943
59,050	59,100	12,296	9,746	12,928	10,956
59,100	59,150	12,310	9,760	12,943	10,970
59,150	59,200	12,323	9,773	12,958	10,983
59,200	59,250	12,337	9,787	12,973	10,997
59,250	59,300	12,350	9,800	12,988	11,010
59,300	59,350	12,364	9,814	13,003	11,024
59,350	59,400	12,377	9,827	13,018	11,037
59,400	59,450	12,391	9,841	13,033	11,051
59,450	59,500	12,404	9,854	13,048	11,064
59,500	59,550	12,418	9,868	13,063	11,078
59,550	59,600	12,431	9,881	13,078	11,091
59,600	59,650	12,445	9,895	13,093	11,105
59,650	59,700	12,458	9,908	13,108	11,118
59,700	59,750	12,472	9,922	13,123	11,132
59,750	59,800	12,485	9,935	13,138	11,145
59,800	59,850	12,499	9,949	13,153	11,159
59,850	59,900	12,512	9,962	13,168	11,172
59,900	59,950	12,526	9,976	13,183	11,186
59,950	60,000	12,539	9,989	13,198	11,199
60,000					
60,000	60,050	12,553	10,003	13,213	11,213
60,050	60,100	12,566	10,016	13,228	11,226
60,100	60,150	12,580	10,030	13,243	11,240
60,150	60,200	12,593	10,043	13,258	11,253
60,200	60,250	12,607	10,057	13,273	11,267
60,250	60,300	12,620	10,070	13,288	11,280
60,300	60,350	12,634	10,084	13,303	11,294
60,350	60,400	12,647	10,097	13,318	11,307
60,400	60,450	12,661	10,111	13,333	11,321
60,450	60,500	12,674	10,124	13,348	11,334
60,500	60,550	12,688	10,138	13,363	11,348
60,550	60,600	12,701	10,151	13,378	11,361
60,600	60,650	12,715	10,165	13,393	11,375
60,650	60,700	12,728	10,178	13,408	11,388
60,700	60,750	12,742	10,192	13,423	11,402
60,750	60,800	12,755	10,205	13,438	11,415
60,800	60,850	12,769	10,219	13,453	11,429
60,850	60,900	12,782	10,232	13,468	11,442
60,900	60,950	12,796	10,246	13,483	11,456
60,950	61,000	12,809	10,259	13,498	11,469
61,000					
61,000	61,050	12,823	10,273	13,513	11,483
61,050	61,100	12,836	10,286	13,528	11,496
61,100	61,150	12,850	10,300	13,543	11,510
61,150	61,200	12,863	10,313	13,558	11,523
61,200	61,250	12,877	10,327	13,573	11,537
61,250	61,300	12,890	10,340	13,588	11,550
61,300	61,350	12,904	10,354	13,603	11,564
61,350	61,400	12,917	10,367	13,618	11,577
61,400	61,450	12,931	10,381	13,633	11,591
61,450	61,500	12,944	10,394	13,648	11,604
61,500	61,550	12,958	10,408	13,663	11,618
61,550	61,600	12,971	10,421	13,678	11,631
61,600	61,650	12,985	10,435	13,693	11,645
61,650	61,700	12,998	10,448	13,708	11,658
61,700	61,750	13,012	10,462	13,723	11,672
61,750	61,800	13,025	10,475	13,738	11,685
61,800	61,850	13,039	10,489	13,753	11,699
61,850	61,900	13,052	10,502	13,768	11,712
61,900	61,950	13,066	10,516	13,783	11,726
61,950	62,000	13,079	10,529	13,798	11,739

62,000 / 63,000 / 64,000

At least	But less than	Single	Married filing jointly *	Married filing separately	Head of a house-hold
62,000					
62,000	62,050	13,093	10,543	13,813	11,753
62,050	62,100	13,106	10,556	13,828	11,766
62,100	62,150	13,120	10,570	13,843	11,780
62,150	62,200	13,133	10,583	13,858	11,793
62,200	62,250	13,147	10,597	13,873	11,807
62,250	62,300	13,160	10,610	13,888	11,820
62,300	62,350	13,174	10,624	13,903	11,834
62,350	62,400	13,187	10,637	13,918	11,847
62,400	62,450	13,201	10,651	13,933	11,861
62,450	62,500	13,214	10,664	13,948	11,874
62,500	62,550	13,228	10,678	13,963	11,888
62,550	62,600	13,241	10,691	13,978	11,901
62,600	62,650	13,255	10,705	13,993	11,915
62,650	62,700	13,268	10,718	14,008	11,928
62,700	62,750	13,282	10,732	14,023	11,942
62,750	62,800	13,295	10,745	14,038	11,955
62,800	62,850	13,309	10,759	14,053	11,969
62,850	62,900	13,322	10,772	14,068	11,982
62,900	62,950	13,336	10,786	14,083	11,996
62,950	63,000	13,349	10,799	14,098	12,009
63,000					
63,000	63,050	13,363	10,813	14,113	12,023
63,050	63,100	13,376	10,826	14,128	12,036
63,100	63,150	13,390	10,840	14,143	12,050
63,150	63,200	13,403	10,853	14,158	12,063
63,200	63,250	13,417	10,867	14,173	12,077
63,250	63,300	13,430	10,880	14,188	12,090
63,300	63,350	13,444	10,894	14,203	12,104
63,350	63,400	13,457	10,907	14,218	12,117
63,400	63,450	13,471	10,921	14,233	12,131
63,450	63,500	13,484	10,934	14,248	12,144
63,500	63,550	13,498	10,948	14,263	12,158
63,550	63,600	13,511	10,961	14,278	12,171
63,600	63,650	13,525	10,975	14,293	12,185
63,650	63,700	13,538	10,988	14,308	12,198
63,700	63,750	13,552	11,002	14,323	12,212
63,750	63,800	13,565	11,015	14,338	12,225
63,800	63,850	13,579	11,029	14,353	12,239
63,850	63,900	13,592	11,042	14,368	12,252
63,900	63,950	13,606	11,056	14,383	12,266
63,950	64,000	13,619	11,069	14,398	12,279
64,000					
64,000	64,050	13,633	11,083	14,413	12,293
64,050	64,100	13,646	11,096	14,428	12,306
64,100	64,150	13,660	11,110	14,443	12,320
64,150	64,200	13,673	11,123	14,458	12,333
64,200	64,250	13,687	11,137	14,473	12,347
64,250	64,300	13,700	11,150	14,488	12,360
64,300	64,350	13,714	11,164	14,503	12,374
64,350	64,400	13,727	11,177	14,518	12,387
64,400	64,450	13,741	11,191	14,533	12,401
64,450	64,500	13,754	11,204	14,548	12,414
64,500	64,550	13,768	11,218	14,563	12,428
64,550	64,600	13,781	11,231	14,578	12,441
64,600	64,650	13,795	11,245	14,593	12,455
64,650	64,700	13,808	11,258	14,608	12,468
64,700	64,750	13,822	11,272	14,623	12,482
64,750	64,800	13,835	11,285	14,638	12,495
64,800	64,850	13,849	11,299	14,653	12,509
64,850	64,900	13,862	11,312	14,668	12,522
64,900	64,950	13,876	11,326	14,683	12,536
64,950	65,000	13,889	11,339	14,698	12,549

65,000 / 66,000 / 67,000

At least	But less than	Single	Married filing jointly *	Married filing separately	Head of a house-hold
65,000					
65,000	65,050	13,903	11,353	14,713	12,563
65,050	65,100	13,916	11,366	14,728	12,576
65,100	65,150	13,930	11,380	14,743	12,590
65,150	65,200	13,943	11,393	14,758	12,603
65,200	65,250	13,957	11,407	14,773	12,617
65,250	65,300	13,970	11,420	14,788	12,630
65,300	65,350	13,984	11,434	14,803	12,644
65,350	65,400	13,997	11,447	14,818	12,657
65,400	65,450	14,011	11,461	14,833	12,671
65,450	65,500	14,024	11,474	14,848	12,684
65,500	65,550	14,038	11,488	14,863	12,698
65,550	65,600	14,051	11,501	14,878	12,711
65,600	65,650	14,065	11,515	14,893	12,725
65,650	65,700	14,078	11,528	14,908	12,738
65,700	65,750	14,092	11,542	14,923	12,752
65,750	65,800	14,105	11,555	14,938	12,765
65,800	65,850	14,119	11,569	14,953	12,779
65,850	65,900	14,132	11,582	14,968	12,792
65,900	65,950	14,146	11,596	14,983	12,806
65,950	66,000	14,159	11,609	14,998	12,819
66,000					
66,000	66,050	14,173	11,623	15,013	12,833
66,050	66,100	14,186	11,636	15,028	12,846
66,100	66,150	14,200	11,650	15,043	12,860
66,150	66,200	14,213	11,663	15,058	12,873
66,200	66,250	14,227	11,677	15,073	12,887
66,250	66,300	14,240	11,690	15,088	12,900
66,300	66,350	14,254	11,704	15,103	12,914
66,350	66,400	14,267	11,717	15,118	12,927
66,400	66,450	14,281	11,731	15,133	12,941
66,450	66,500	14,294	11,744	15,148	12,954
66,500	66,550	14,308	11,758	15,163	12,968
66,550	66,600	14,321	11,771	15,178	12,981
66,600	66,650	14,335	11,785	15,193	12,995
66,650	66,700	14,348	11,798	15,208	13,008
66,700	66,750	14,362	11,812	15,223	13,022
66,750	66,800	14,375	11,825	15,238	13,035
66,800	66,850	14,389	11,839	15,253	13,049
66,850	66,900	14,402	11,852	15,268	13,062
66,900	66,950	14,416	11,866	15,283	13,076
66,950	67,000	14,429	11,879	15,298	13,089
67,000					
67,000	67,050	14,443	11,893	15,313	13,103
67,050	67,100	14,456	11,906	15,328	13,116
67,100	67,150	14,470	11,920	15,343	13,130
67,150	67,200	14,483	11,933	15,358	13,143
67,200	67,250	14,497	11,947	15,373	13,157
67,250	67,300	14,510	11,960	15,388	13,170
67,300	67,350	14,524	11,974	15,403	13,184
67,350	67,400	14,537	11,987	15,418	13,197
67,400	67,450	14,551	12,001	15,433	13,211
67,450	67,500	14,564	12,014	15,448	13,224
67,500	67,550	14,578	12,028	15,463	13,238
67,550	67,600	14,591	12,041	15,478	13,251
67,600	67,650	14,605	12,055	15,493	13,265
67,650	67,700	14,618	12,068	15,508	13,278
67,700	67,750	14,633	12,082	15,523	13,292
67,750	67,800	14,648	12,095	15,538	13,305
67,800	67,850	14,663	12,109	15,553	13,319
67,850	67,900	14,678	12,122	15,568	13,332
67,900	67,950	14,693	12,136	15,583	13,346
67,950	68,000	14,708	12,149	15,598	13,359

* This column must also be used by a qualifying widow(er).

If taxable income is—		And you are—			
At least	But less than	Single	Married filing jointly *	Married filing separately	Head of a house-hold
		Your tax is—			

68,000

At least	But less than	Single	Married filing jointly	Married filing separately	Head of a household
68,000	68,050	14,723	12,163	15,613	13,373
68,050	68,100	14,738	12,176	15,628	13,386
68,100	68,150	14,753	12,190	15,643	13,400
68,150	68,200	14,768	12,203	15,658	13,413
68,200	68,250	14,783	12,217	15,673	13,427
68,250	68,300	14,798	12,230	15,688	13,440
68,300	68,350	14,813	12,244	15,703	13,454
68,350	68,400	14,828	12,257	15,718	13,467
68,400	68,450	14,843	12,271	15,733	13,481
68,450	68,500	14,858	12,284	15,748	13,494
68,500	68,550	14,873	12,298	15,763	13,508
68,550	68,600	14,888	12,311	15,778	13,521
68,600	68,650	14,903	12,325	15,793	13,535
68,650	68,700	14,918	12,338	15,808	13,548
68,700	68,750	14,933	12,352	15,823	13,562
68,750	68,800	14,948	12,365	15,838	13,575
68,800	68,850	14,963	12,379	15,853	13,589
68,850	68,900	14,978	12,392	15,868	13,602
68,900	68,950	14,993	12,406	15,883	13,616
68,950	69,000	15,008	12,419	15,898	13,629

69,000

At least	But less than	Single	Married filing jointly	Married filing separately	Head of a household
69,000	69,050	15,023	12,433	15,913	13,643
69,050	69,100	15,038	12,446	15,928	13,656
69,100	69,150	15,053	12,460	15,943	13,670
69,150	69,200	15,068	12,473	15,958	13,683
69,200	69,250	15,083	12,487	15,973	13,697
69,250	69,300	15,098	12,500	15,988	13,710
69,300	69,350	15,113	12,514	16,003	13,724
69,350	69,400	15,128	12,527	16,018	13,737
69,400	69,450	15,143	12,541	16,033	13,751
69,450	69,500	15,158	12,554	16,048	13,764
69,500	69,550	15,173	12,568	16,063	13,778
69,550	69,600	15,188	12,581	16,078	13,791
69,600	69,650	15,203	12,595	16,093	13,805
69,650	69,700	15,218	12,608	16,108	13,818
69,700	69,750	15,233	12,622	16,123	13,832
69,750	69,800	15,248	12,635	16,138	13,845
69,800	69,850	15,263	12,649	16,153	13,859
69,850	69,900	15,278	12,662	16,168	13,872
69,900	69,950	15,293	12,676	16,183	13,886
69,950	70,000	15,308	12,689	16,198	13,899

70,000

At least	But less than	Single	Married filing jointly	Married filing separately	Head of a household
70,000	70,050	15,323	12,703	16,213	13,913
70,050	70,100	15,338	12,716	16,228	13,926
70,100	70,150	15,353	12,730	16,243	13,940
70,150	70,200	15,368	12,743	16,258	13,953
70,200	70,250	15,383	12,757	16,273	13,967
70,250	70,300	15,398	12,770	16,288	13,980
70,300	70,350	15,413	12,784	16,303	13,994
70,350	70,400	15,428	12,797	16,318	14,007
70,400	70,450	15,443	12,811	16,333	14,021
70,450	70,500	15,458	12,824	16,348	14,034
70,500	70,550	15,473	12,838	16,363	14,048
70,550	70,600	15,488	12,851	16,378	14,061
70,600	70,650	15,503	12,865	16,393	14,075
70,650	70,700	15,518	12,878	16,408	14,088
70,700	70,750	15,533	12,892	16,423	14,102
70,750	70,800	15,548	12,905	16,438	14,115
70,800	70,850	15,563	12,919	16,453	14,129
70,850	70,900	15,578	12,932	16,468	14,142
70,900	70,950	15,593	12,946	16,483	14,156
70,950	71,000	15,608	12,959	16,498	14,169

71,000

At least	But less than	Single	Married filing jointly	Married filing separately	Head of a household
71,000	71,050	15,623	12,973	16,513	14,183
71,050	71,100	15,638	12,986	16,528	14,196
71,100	71,150	15,653	13,000	16,543	14,210
71,150	71,200	15,668	13,013	16,558	14,223
71,200	71,250	15,683	13,027	16,573	14,237
71,250	71,300	15,698	13,040	16,588	14,250
71,300	71,350	15,713	13,054	16,603	14,264
71,350	71,400	15,728	13,067	16,618	14,277
71,400	71,450	15,743	13,081	16,633	14,291
71,450	71,500	15,758	13,094	16,648	14,304
71,500	71,550	15,773	13,108	16,663	14,318
71,550	71,600	15,788	13,121	16,678	14,331
71,600	71,650	15,803	13,135	16,693	14,345
71,650	71,700	15,818	13,148	16,708	14,358
71,700	71,750	15,833	13,162	16,723	14,372
71,750	71,800	15,848	13,175	16,738	14,385
71,800	71,850	15,863	13,189	16,753	14,399
71,850	71,900	15,878	13,202	16,768	14,412
71,900	71,950	15,893	13,216	16,783	14,426
71,950	72,000	15,908	13,229	16,798	14,439

72,000

At least	But less than	Single	Married filing jointly	Married filing separately	Head of a household
72,000	72,050	15,923	13,243	16,813	14,453
72,050	72,100	15,938	13,256	16,828	14,466
72,100	72,150	15,953	13,270	16,843	14,480
72,150	72,200	15,968	13,283	16,858	14,493
72,200	72,250	15,983	13,297	16,873	14,507
72,250	72,300	15,998	13,310	16,888	14,520
72,300	72,350	16,013	13,324	16,903	14,534
72,350	72,400	16,028	13,337	16,918	14,547
72,400	72,450	16,043	13,351	16,933	14,561
72,450	72,500	16,058	13,364	16,948	14,574
72,500	72,550	16,073	13,378	16,963	14,588
72,550	72,600	16,088	13,391	16,978	14,601
72,600	72,650	16,103	13,405	16,993	14,615
72,650	72,700	16,118	13,418	17,008	14,628
72,700	72,750	16,133	13,432	17,023	14,642
72,750	72,800	16,148	13,445	17,038	14,655
72,800	72,850	16,163	13,459	17,053	14,669
72,850	72,900	16,178	13,472	17,068	14,682
72,900	72,950	16,193	13,486	17,083	14,696
72,950	73,000	16,208	13,499	17,098	14,709

73,000

At least	But less than	Single	Married filing jointly	Married filing separately	Head of a household
73,000	73,050	16,223	13,513	17,113	14,723
73,050	73,100	16,238	13,526	17,128	14,736
73,100	73,150	16,253	13,540	17,143	14,750
73,150	73,200	16,268	13,553	17,158	14,763
73,200	73,250	16,283	13,567	17,173	14,777
73,250	73,300	16,298	13,580	17,188	14,790
73,300	73,350	16,313	13,594	17,203	14,804
73,350	73,400	16,328	13,607	17,218	14,817
73,400	73,450	16,343	13,621	17,233	14,831
73,450	73,500	16,358	13,634	17,248	14,844
73,500	73,550	16,373	13,648	17,263	14,858
73,550	73,600	16,388	13,661	17,278	14,871
73,600	73,650	16,403	13,675	17,293	14,885
73,650	73,700	16,418	13,688	17,308	14,898
73,700	73,750	16,433	13,702	17,323	14,912
73,750	73,800	16,448	13,715	17,338	14,925
73,800	73,850	16,463	13,729	17,353	14,939
73,850	73,900	16,478	13,742	17,368	14,952
73,900	73,950	16,493	13,756	17,383	14,966
73,950	74,000	16,508	13,769	17,398	14,979

74,000

At least	But less than	Single	Married filing jointly	Married filing separately	Head of a household
74,000	74,050	16,523	13,783	17,413	14,993
74,050	74,100	16,538	13,796	17,428	15,006
74,100	74,150	16,553	13,810	17,443	15,020
74,150	74,200	16,568	13,823	17,458	15,033
74,200	74,250	16,583	13,837	17,473	15,047
74,250	74,300	16,598	13,850	17,488	15,060
74,300	74,350	16,613	13,864	17,503	15,074
74,350	74,400	16,628	13,877	17,518	15,087
74,400	74,450	16,643	13,891	17,533	15,101
74,450	74,500	16,658	13,904	17,548	15,114
74,500	74,550	16,673	13,918	17,563	15,128
74,550	74,600	16,688	13,931	17,578	15,141
74,600	74,650	16,703	13,945	17,593	15,155
74,650	74,700	16,718	13,958	17,608	15,168
74,700	74,750	16,733	13,972	17,623	15,182
74,750	74,800	16,748	13,985	17,638	15,195
74,800	74,850	16,763	13,999	17,653	15,209
74,850	74,900	16,778	14,012	17,668	15,222
74,900	74,950	16,793	14,026	17,683	15,236
74,950	75,000	16,808	14,039	17,698	15,249

75,000

At least	But less than	Single	Married filing jointly	Married filing separately	Head of a household
75,000	75,050	16,823	14,053	17,713	15,263
75,050	75,100	16,838	14,066	17,728	15,276
75,100	75,150	16,853	14,080	17,743	15,290
75,150	75,200	16,868	14,093	17,758	15,303
75,200	75,250	16,883	14,107	17,773	15,317
75,250	75,300	16,898	14,120	17,788	15,330
75,300	75,350	16,913	14,134	17,803	15,344
75,350	75,400	16,928	14,147	17,818	15,357
75,400	75,450	16,943	14,161	17,833	15,371
75,450	75,500	16,958	14,174	17,848	15,384
75,500	75,550	16,973	14,188	17,863	15,398
75,550	75,600	16,988	14,201	17,878	15,411
75,600	75,650	17,003	14,215	17,893	15,425
75,650	75,700	17,018	14,228	17,908	15,438
75,700	75,750	17,033	14,242	17,923	15,452
75,750	75,800	17,048	14,255	17,938	15,465
75,800	75,850	17,063	14,269	17,953	15,479
75,850	75,900	17,078	14,282	17,968	15,492
75,900	75,950	17,093	14,296	17,983	15,506
75,950	76,000	17,108	14,309	17,998	15,519

76,000

At least	But less than	Single	Married filing jointly	Married filing separately	Head of a household
76,000	76,050	17,123	14,323	18,013	15,533
76,050	76,100	17,138	14,336	18,028	15,546
76,100	76,150	17,153	14,350	18,043	15,560
76,150	76,200	17,168	14,363	18,058	15,573
76,200	76,250	17,183	14,377	18,073	15,587
76,250	76,300	17,198	14,390	18,088	15,600
76,300	76,350	17,213	14,404	18,103	15,614
76,350	76,400	17,228	14,417	18,118	15,627
76,400	76,450	17,243	14,431	18,133	15,641
76,450	76,500	17,258	14,444	18,148	15,654
76,500	76,550	17,273	14,458	18,163	15,668
76,550	76,600	17,288	14,471	18,178	15,681
76,600	76,650	17,303	14,485	18,193	15,695
76,650	76,700	17,318	14,498	18,208	15,708
76,700	76,750	17,333	14,512	18,223	15,722
76,750	76,800	17,348	14,525	18,238	15,735
76,800	76,850	17,363	14,539	18,253	15,749
76,850	76,900	17,378	14,552	18,268	15,762
76,900	76,950	17,393	14,566	18,283	15,776
76,950	77,000	17,408	14,579	18,298	15,789

* This column must also be used by a qualifying widow(er).

If taxable income is—		And you are—			
At least	But less than	Single	Married filing jointly *	Married filing separately	Head of a household
		Your tax is—			

77,000

At least	But less than	Single	Married filing jointly *	Married filing separately	Head of a household
77,000	77,050	17,423	14,593	18,313	15,803
77,050	77,100	17,438	14,606	18,328	15,816
77,100	77,150	17,453	14,620	18,343	15,830
77,150	77,200	17,468	14,633	18,358	15,843
77,200	77,250	17,483	14,647	18,373	15,857
77,250	77,300	17,498	14,660	18,388	15,870
77,300	77,350	17,513	14,674	18,403	15,884
77,350	77,400	17,528	14,687	18,418	15,897
77,400	77,450	17,543	14,701	18,433	15,911
77,450	77,500	17,558	14,714	18,448	15,924
77,500	77,550	17,573	14,728	18,463	15,938
77,550	77,600	17,588	14,741	18,478	15,951
77,600	77,650	17,603	14,755	18,493	15,965
77,650	77,700	17,618	14,768	18,508	15,978
77,700	77,750	17,633	14,782	18,523	15,992
77,750	77,800	17,648	14,795	18,538	16,005
77,800	77,850	17,663	14,809	18,553	16,019
77,850	77,900	17,678	14,822	18,568	16,032
77,900	77,950	17,693	14,836	18,583	16,046
77,950	78,000	17,708	14,849	18,598	16,059

78,000

At least	But less than	Single	Married filing jointly *	Married filing separately	Head of a household
78,000	78,050	17,723	14,863	18,613	16,073
78,050	78,100	17,738	14,876	18,628	16,086
78,100	78,150	17,753	14,890	18,643	16,100
78,150	78,200	17,768	14,903	18,658	16,113
78,200	78,250	17,783	14,917	18,673	16,127
78,250	78,300	17,798	14,930	18,688	16,140
78,300	78,350	17,813	14,944	18,703	16,154
78,350	78,400	17,828	14,957	18,718	16,167
78,400	78,450	17,843	14,971	18,733	16,181
78,450	78,500	17,858	14,984	18,748	16,194
78,500	78,550	17,873	14,998	18,763	16,208
78,550	78,600	17,888	15,011	18,778	16,221
78,600	78,650	17,903	15,025	18,793	16,235
78,650	78,700	17,918	15,038	18,808	16,248
78,700	78,750	17,933	15,052	18,823	16,262
78,750	78,800	17,948	15,065	18,838	16,275
78,800	78,850	17,963	15,079	18,853	16,289
78,850	78,900	17,978	15,092	18,868	16,302
78,900	78,950	17,993	15,106	18,883	16,316
78,950	79,000	18,008	15,119	18,898	16,329

79,000

At least	But less than	Single	Married filing jointly *	Married filing separately	Head of a household
79,000	79,050	18,023	15,133	18,913	16,343
79,050	79,100	18,038	15,146	18,928	16,356
79,100	79,150	18,053	15,160	18,943	16,370
79,150	79,200	18,068	15,173	18,958	16,383
79,200	79,250	18,083	15,187	18,973	16,397
79,250	79,300	18,098	15,200	18,988	16,410
79,300	79,350	18,113	15,214	19,003	16,424
79,350	79,400	18,128	15,227	19,018	16,437
79,400	79,450	18,143	15,241	19,033	16,451
79,450	79,500	18,158	15,254	19,048	16,464
79,500	79,550	18,173	15,268	19,063	16,478
79,550	79,600	18,188	15,281	19,078	16,491
79,600	79,650	18,203	15,295	19,093	16,505
79,650	79,700	18,218	15,308	19,108	16,518
79,700	79,750	18,233	15,322	19,123	16,532
79,750	79,800	18,248	15,335	19,138	16,545
79,800	79,850	18,263	15,349	19,153	16,559
79,850	79,900	18,278	15,362	19,168	16,572
79,900	79,950	18,293	15,376	19,183	16,586
79,950	80,000	18,308	15,389	19,198	16,599

80,000

At least	But less than	Single	Married filing jointly *	Married filing separately	Head of a household
80,000	80,050	18,323	15,403	19,213	16,613
80,050	80,100	18,338	15,416	19,228	16,626
80,100	80,150	18,353	15,430	19,243	16,640
80,150	80,200	18,368	15,443	19,258	16,653
80,200	80,250	18,383	15,457	19,273	16,667
80,250	80,300	18,398	15,470	19,288	16,680
80,300	80,350	18,413	15,484	19,303	16,694
80,350	80,400	18,428	15,497	19,318	16,707
80,400	80,450	18,443	15,511	19,333	16,721
80,450	80,500	18,458	15,524	19,348	16,734
80,500	80,550	18,473	15,538	19,363	16,748
80,550	80,600	18,488	15,551	19,378	16,761
80,600	80,650	18,503	15,565	19,393	16,775
80,650	80,700	18,518	15,578	19,408	16,788
80,700	80,750	18,533	15,592	19,423	16,802
80,750	80,800	18,548	15,605	19,438	16,815
80,800	80,850	18,563	15,619	19,453	16,829
80,850	80,900	18,578	15,632	19,468	16,842
80,900	80,950	18,593	15,646	19,483	16,856
80,950	81,000	18,608	15,659	19,498	16,869

81,000

At least	But less than	Single	Married filing jointly *	Married filing separately	Head of a household
81,000	81,050	18,623	15,673	19,513	16,883
81,050	81,100	18,638	15,686	19,528	16,896
81,100	81,150	18,653	15,700	19,543	16,910
81,150	81,200	18,668	15,713	19,558	16,923
81,200	81,250	18,683	15,727	19,573	16,937
81,250	81,300	18,698	15,740	19,588	16,950
81,300	81,350	18,713	15,754	19,603	16,964
81,350	81,400	18,728	15,767	19,618	16,977
81,400	81,450	18,743	15,781	19,633	16,991
81,450	81,500	18,758	15,794	19,648	17,004
81,500	81,550	18,773	15,808	19,663	17,018
81,550	81,600	18,788	15,821	19,678	17,031
81,600	81,650	18,803	15,835	19,693	17,045
81,650	81,700	18,818	15,848	19,708	17,058
81,700	81,750	18,833	15,862	19,723	17,072
81,750	81,800	18,848	15,875	19,738	17,085
81,800	81,850	18,863	15,889	19,753	17,099
81,850	81,900	18,878	15,902	19,768	17,112
81,900	81,950	18,893	15,916	19,783	17,126
81,950	82,000	18,908	15,929	19,798	17,139

82,000

At least	But less than	Single	Married filing jointly *	Married filing separately	Head of a household
82,000	82,050	18,923	15,943	19,813	17,153
82,050	82,100	18,938	15,956	19,828	17,166
82,100	82,150	18,953	15,970	19,843	17,180
82,150	82,200	18,968	15,983	19,858	17,193
82,200	82,250	18,983	15,997	19,873	17,207
82,250	82,300	18,998	16,010	19,888	17,220
82,300	82,350	19,013	16,024	19,903	17,234
82,350	82,400	19,028	16,037	19,918	17,247
82,400	82,450	19,043	16,051	19,933	17,261
82,450	82,500	19,058	16,064	19,948	17,274
82,500	82,550	19,073	16,078	19,963	17,288
82,550	82,600	19,088	16,091	19,978	17,301
82,600	82,650	19,103	16,105	19,993	17,315
82,650	82,700	19,118	16,118	20,008	17,328
82,700	82,750	19,133	16,132	20,023	17,342
82,750	82,800	19,148	16,145	20,038	17,355
82,800	82,850	19,163	16,159	20,053	17,369
82,850	82,900	19,178	16,172	20,068	17,382
82,900	82,950	19,193	16,186	20,083	17,396
82,950	83,000	19,208	16,199	20,098	17,409

83,000

At least	But less than	Single	Married filing jointly *	Married filing separately	Head of a household
83,000	83,050	19,223	16,213	20,113	17,423
83,050	83,100	19,238	16,226	20,128	17,436
83,100	83,150	19,253	16,240	20,143	17,450
83,150	83,200	19,268	16,253	20,158	17,463
83,200	83,250	19,283	16,267	20,173	17,477
83,250	83,300	19,298	16,280	20,188	17,490
83,300	83,350	19,313	16,294	20,203	17,504
83,350	83,400	19,328	16,307	20,218	17,517
83,400	83,450	19,343	16,321	20,233	17,531
83,450	83,500	19,358	16,334	20,248	17,544
83,500	83,550	19,373	16,348	20,263	17,558
83,550	83,600	19,388	16,361	20,278	17,571
83,600	83,650	19,403	16,375	20,293	17,585
83,650	83,700	19,418	16,388	20,308	17,598
83,700	83,750	19,433	16,402	20,323	17,612
83,750	83,800	19,448	16,415	20,338	17,625
83,800	83,850	19,463	16,429	20,353	17,639
83,850	83,900	19,478	16,442	20,368	17,652
83,900	83,950	19,493	16,456	20,383	17,666
83,950	84,000	19,508	16,469	20,398	17,679

84,000

At least	But less than	Single	Married filing jointly *	Married filing separately	Head of a household
84,000	84,050	19,523	16,483	20,413	17,693
84,050	84,100	19,538	16,496	20,428	17,706
84,100	84,150	19,553	16,510	20,443	17,720
84,150	84,200	19,568	16,523	20,458	17,733
84,200	84,250	19,583	16,537	20,473	17,747
84,250	84,300	19,598	16,550	20,488	17,760
84,300	84,350	19,613	16,564	20,503	17,774
84,350	84,400	19,628	16,577	20,518	17,787
84,400	84,450	19,643	16,591	20,533	17,801
84,450	84,500	19,658	16,604	20,548	17,814
84,500	84,550	19,673	16,618	20,563	17,828
84,550	84,600	19,688	16,631	20,578	17,841
84,600	84,650	19,703	16,645	20,593	17,855
84,650	84,700	19,718	16,658	20,608	17,868
84,700	84,750	19,733	16,672	20,623	17,882
84,750	84,800	19,748	16,685	20,638	17,895
84,800	84,850	19,763	16,699	20,653	17,909
84,850	84,900	19,778	16,712	20,668	17,922
84,900	84,950	19,793	16,726	20,683	17,936
84,950	85,000	19,808	16,739	20,698	17,949

85,000

At least	But less than	Single	Married filing jointly *	Married filing separately	Head of a household
85,000	85,050	19,823	16,753	20,713	17,963
85,050	85,100	19,838	16,766	20,728	17,976
85,100	85,150	19,853	16,780	20,743	17,990
85,150	85,200	19,868	16,793	20,758	18,003
85,200	85,250	19,883	16,807	20,773	18,017
85,250	85,300	19,898	16,820	20,788	18,030
85,300	85,350	19,913	16,834	20,803	18,044
85,350	85,400	19,928	16,847	20,818	18,057
85,400	85,450	19,943	16,861	20,833	18,071
85,450	85,500	19,958	16,874	20,848	18,084
85,500	85,550	19,973	16,888	20,863	18,098
85,550	85,600	19,988	16,901	20,878	18,111
85,600	85,650	20,003	16,915	20,893	18,125
85,650	85,700	20,018	16,928	20,908	18,138
85,700	85,750	20,033	16,942	20,923	18,152
85,750	85,800	20,048	16,955	20,938	18,165
85,800	85,850	20,063	16,969	20,953	18,179
85,850	85,900	20,078	16,982	20,968	18,192
85,900	85,950	20,093	16,996	20,983	18,206
85,950	86,000	20,108	17,009	20,998	18,219

* This column must also be used by a qualifying widow(er).

86,000

If taxable income is— At least	But less than	Single	Married filing jointly *	Married filing separately	Head of a household
86,000	86,050	20,123	17,023	21,015	18,233
86,050	86,100	20,138	17,036	21,033	18,246
86,100	86,150	20,153	17,050	21,050	18,260
86,150	86,200	20,168	17,063	21,068	18,273
86,200	86,250	20,183	17,077	21,085	18,287
86,250	86,300	20,198	17,090	21,103	18,300
86,300	86,350	20,213	17,104	21,120	18,314
86,350	86,400	20,228	17,117	21,138	18,327
86,400	86,450	20,243	17,131	21,155	18,341
86,450	86,500	20,258	17,144	21,173	18,354
86,500	86,550	20,273	17,158	21,190	18,368
86,550	86,600	20,288	17,171	21,208	18,381
86,600	86,650	20,303	17,185	21,225	18,395
86,650	86,700	20,318	17,198	21,243	18,408
86,700	86,750	20,333	17,212	21,260	18,422
86,750	86,800	20,348	17,225	21,278	18,435
86,800	86,850	20,363	17,239	21,295	18,449
86,850	86,900	20,378	17,252	21,313	18,462
86,900	86,950	20,393	17,266	21,330	18,476
86,950	87,000	20,408	17,279	21,348	18,489

87,000

If taxable income is— At least	But less than	Single	Married filing jointly *	Married filing separately	Head of a household
87,000	87,050	20,423	17,293	21,365	18,503
87,050	87,100	20,438	17,306	21,383	18,516
87,100	87,150	20,453	17,320	21,400	18,530
87,150	87,200	20,468	17,333	21,418	18,543
87,200	87,250	20,483	17,347	21,435	18,557
87,250	87,300	20,498	17,360	21,453	18,570
87,300	87,350	20,513	17,374	21,470	18,584
87,350	87,400	20,528	17,387	21,488	18,597
87,400	87,450	20,543	17,401	21,505	18,611
87,450	87,500	20,558	17,414	21,523	18,624
87,500	87,550	20,573	17,428	21,540	18,638
87,550	87,600	20,588	17,441	21,558	18,651
87,600	87,650	20,603	17,455	21,575	18,665
87,650	87,700	20,618	17,468	21,593	18,678
87,700	87,750	20,633	17,482	21,610	18,692
87,750	87,800	20,648	17,495	21,628	18,705
87,800	87,850	20,663	17,509	21,645	18,719
87,850	87,900	20,678	17,522	21,663	18,732
87,900	87,950	20,693	17,536	21,680	18,746
87,950	88,000	20,708	17,549	21,698	18,759

88,000

If taxable income is— At least	But less than	Single	Married filing jointly *	Married filing separately	Head of a household
88,000	88,050	20,723	17,563	21,715	18,773
88,050	88,100	20,738	17,576	21,733	18,786
88,100	88,150	20,753	17,590	21,750	18,800
88,150	88,200	20,768	17,603	21,768	18,813
88,200	88,250	20,783	17,617	21,785	18,827
88,250	88,300	20,798	17,630	21,803	18,840
88,300	88,350	20,813	17,644	21,820	18,854
88,350	88,400	20,828	17,657	21,838	18,867
88,400	88,450	20,843	17,671	21,855	18,881
88,450	88,500	20,858	17,684	21,873	18,894
88,500	88,550	20,873	17,698	21,890	18,908
88,550	88,600	20,888	17,711	21,908	18,921
88,600	88,650	20,903	17,725	21,925	18,935
88,650	88,700	20,918	17,738	21,943	18,948
88,700	88,750	20,933	17,752	21,960	18,962
88,750	88,800	20,948	17,765	21,978	18,975
88,800	88,850	20,963	17,779	21,995	18,989
88,850	88,900	20,978	17,792	22,013	19,002
88,900	88,950	20,993	17,806	22,030	19,016
88,950	89,000	21,008	17,819	22,048	19,029

89,000

If taxable income is— At least	But less than	Single	Married filing jointly *	Married filing separately	Head of a household
89,000	89,050	21,023	17,833	22,065	19,043
89,050	89,100	21,038	17,846	22,083	19,056
89,100	89,150	21,053	17,860	22,100	19,070
89,150	89,200	21,068	17,873	22,118	19,083
89,200	89,250	21,083	17,887	22,135	19,097
89,250	89,300	21,098	17,900	22,153	19,110
89,300	89,350	21,113	17,914	22,170	19,124
89,350	89,400	21,128	17,927	22,188	19,137
89,400	89,450	21,143	17,941	22,205	19,151
89,450	89,500	21,158	17,954	22,223	19,164
89,500	89,550	21,173	17,968	22,240	19,178
89,550	89,600	21,188	17,981	22,258	19,191
89,600	89,650	21,203	17,995	22,275	19,205
89,650	89,700	21,218	18,008	22,293	19,218
89,700	89,750	21,233	18,022	22,310	19,232
89,750	89,800	21,248	18,035	22,328	19,245
89,800	89,850	21,263	18,049	22,345	19,259
89,850	89,900	21,278	18,062	22,363	19,272
89,900	89,950	21,293	18,076	22,380	19,286
89,950	90,000	21,308	18,089	22,398	19,299

90,000

If taxable income is— At least	But less than	Single	Married filing jointly *	Married filing separately	Head of a household
90,000	90,050	21,323	18,103	22,415	19,313
90,050	90,100	21,338	18,116	22,433	19,326
90,100	90,150	21,353	18,130	22,450	19,340
90,150	90,200	21,368	18,143	22,468	19,353
90,200	90,250	21,383	18,157	22,485	19,367
90,250	90,300	21,398	18,170	22,503	19,380
90,300	90,350	21,413	18,184	22,520	19,394
90,350	90,400	21,428	18,197	22,538	19,407
90,400	90,450	21,443	18,211	22,555	19,421
90,450	90,500	21,458	18,224	22,573	19,434
90,500	90,550	21,473	18,238	22,590	19,448
90,550	90,600	21,488	18,251	22,608	19,461
90,600	90,650	21,503	18,265	22,625	19,475
90,650	90,700	21,518	18,278	22,643	19,488
90,700	90,750	21,533	18,292	22,660	19,502
90,750	90,800	21,548	18,305	22,678	19,515
90,800	90,850	21,563	18,319	22,695	19,529
90,850	90,900	21,578	18,332	22,713	19,542
90,900	90,950	21,593	18,346	22,730	19,556
90,950	91,000	21,608	18,359	22,748	19,569

91,000

If taxable income is— At least	But less than	Single	Married filing jointly *	Married filing separately	Head of a household
91,000	91,050	21,623	18,373	22,765	19,583
91,050	91,100	21,638	18,386	22,783	19,596
91,100	91,150	21,653	18,400	22,800	19,610
91,150	91,200	21,668	18,413	22,818	19,623
91,200	91,250	21,683	18,427	22,835	19,637
91,250	91,300	21,698	18,440	22,853	19,650
91,300	91,350	21,713	18,454	22,870	19,664
91,350	91,400	21,728	18,467	22,888	19,677
91,400	91,450	21,743	18,481	22,905	19,691
91,450	91,500	21,758	18,494	22,923	19,704
91,500	91,550	21,773	18,508	22,940	19,718
91,550	91,600	21,788	18,521	22,958	19,731
91,600	91,650	21,803	18,535	22,975	19,745
91,650	91,700	21,818	18,548	22,993	19,758
91,700	91,750	21,833	18,562	23,010	19,772
91,750	91,800	21,848	18,575	23,028	19,785
91,800	91,850	21,863	18,589	23,045	19,799
91,850	91,900	21,878	18,602	23,063	19,812
91,900	91,950	21,893	18,616	23,080	19,826
91,950	92,000	21,908	18,629	23,098	19,839

92,000

If taxable income is— At least	But less than	Single	Married filing jointly *	Married filing separately	Head of a household
92,000	92,050	21,923	18,643	23,115	19,853
92,050	92,100	21,938	18,656	23,133	19,866
92,100	92,150	21,953	18,670	23,150	19,880
92,150	92,200	21,968	18,683	23,168	19,893
92,200	92,250	21,983	18,697	23,185	19,907
92,250	92,300	21,998	18,710	23,203	19,920
92,300	92,350	22,013	18,724	23,220	19,934
92,350	92,400	22,028	18,737	23,238	19,947
92,400	92,450	22,043	18,751	23,255	19,961
92,450	92,500	22,058	18,764	23,273	19,974
92,500	92,550	22,073	18,778	23,290	19,988
92,550	92,600	22,088	18,791	23,308	20,001
92,600	92,650	22,103	18,805	23,325	20,015
92,650	92,700	22,118	18,818	23,343	20,028
92,700	92,750	22,133	18,832	23,360	20,042
92,750	92,800	22,148	18,845	23,378	20,055
92,800	92,850	22,163	18,859	23,395	20,069
92,850	92,900	22,178	18,872	23,413	20,082
92,900	92,950	22,193	18,886	23,430	20,096
92,950	93,000	22,208	18,899	23,448	20,109

93,000

If taxable income is— At least	But less than	Single	Married filing jointly *	Married filing separately	Head of a household
93,000	93,050	22,223	18,913	23,465	20,123
93,050	93,100	22,238	18,926	23,483	20,136
93,100	93,150	22,253	18,940	23,500	20,150
93,150	93,200	22,268	18,953	23,518	20,163
93,200	93,250	22,283	18,967	23,535	20,177
93,250	93,300	22,298	18,980	23,553	20,190
93,300	93,350	22,313	18,994	23,570	20,204
93,350	93,400	22,328	19,007	23,588	20,217
93,400	93,450	22,343	19,021	23,605	20,231
93,450	93,500	22,358	19,034	23,623	20,244
93,500	93,550	22,373	19,048	23,640	20,258
93,550	93,600	22,388	19,061	23,658	20,271
93,600	93,650	22,403	19,075	23,675	20,285
93,650	93,700	22,418	19,088	23,693	20,298
93,700	93,750	22,433	19,102	23,710	20,312
93,750	93,800	22,448	19,115	23,728	20,325
93,800	93,850	22,463	19,129	23,745	20,339
93,850	93,900	22,478	19,142	23,763	20,352
93,900	93,950	22,493	19,156	23,780	20,366
93,950	94,000	22,508	19,169	23,798	20,379

94,000

If taxable income is— At least	But less than	Single	Married filing jointly *	Married filing separately	Head of a household
94,000	94,050	22,523	19,183	23,815	20,393
94,050	94,100	22,538	19,196	23,833	20,406
94,100	94,150	22,553	19,210	23,850	20,420
94,150	94,200	22,568	19,223	23,868	20,433
94,200	94,250	22,583	19,237	23,885	20,447
94,250	94,300	22,598	19,250	23,903	20,460
94,300	94,350	22,613	19,264	23,920	20,474
94,350	94,400	22,628	19,277	23,938	20,487
94,400	94,450	22,643	19,291	23,955	20,501
94,450	94,500	22,658	19,304	23,973	20,514
94,500	94,550	22,673	19,318	23,990	20,528
94,550	94,600	22,688	19,331	24,008	20,541
94,600	94,650	22,703	19,345	24,025	20,555
94,650	94,700	22,718	19,358	24,043	20,568
94,700	94,750	22,733	19,372	24,060	20,582
94,750	94,800	22,748	19,385	24,078	20,595
94,800	94,850	22,763	19,399	24,095	20,609
94,850	94,900	22,778	19,412	24,113	20,622
94,900	94,950	22,793	19,426	24,130	20,636
94,950	95,000	22,808	19,439	24,148	20,649

* This column must also be used by a qualifying widow(er).

2002 Tax Table—Continued

If taxable income is— At least	But less than	And you are— Single	Married filing jointly *	Married filing separately	Head of a household
95,000					
95,000	95,050	22,823	19,453	24,165	20,663
95,050	95,100	22,838	19,466	24,183	20,676
95,100	95,150	22,853	19,480	24,200	20,690
95,150	95,200	22,868	19,493	24,218	20,703
95,200	95,250	22,883	19,507	24,235	20,717
95,250	95,300	22,898	19,520	24,253	20,730
95,300	95,350	22,913	19,534	24,270	20,744
95,350	95,400	22,928	19,547	24,288	20,757
95,400	95,450	22,943	19,561	24,305	20,771
95,450	95,500	22,958	19,574	24,323	20,784
95,500	95,550	22,973	19,588	24,340	20,798
95,550	95,600	22,988	19,601	24,358	20,811
95,600	95,650	23,003	19,615	24,375	20,825
95,650	95,700	23,018	19,628	24,393	20,838
95,700	95,750	23,033	19,642	24,410	20,852
95,750	95,800	23,048	19,655	24,428	20,865
95,800	95,850	23,063	19,669	24,445	20,879
95,850	95,900	23,078	19,682	24,463	20,892
95,900	95,950	23,093	19,696	24,480	20,906
95,950	96,000	23,108	19,709	24,498	20,919
96,000					
96,000	96,050	23,123	19,723	24,515	20,933
96,050	96,100	23,138	19,736	24,533	20,946
96,100	96,150	23,153	19,750	24,550	20,960
96,150	96,200	23,168	19,763	24,568	20,973
96,200	96,250	23,183	19,777	24,585	20,987
96,250	96,300	23,198	19,790	24,603	21,000
96,300	96,350	23,213	19,804	24,620	21,014
96,350	96,400	23,228	19,817	24,638	21,027
96,400	96,450	23,243	19,831	24,655	21,041
96,450	96,500	23,258	19,844	24,673	21,054
96,500	96,550	23,273	19,858	24,690	21,068
96,550	96,600	23,288	19,871	24,708	21,081
96,600	96,650	23,303	19,885	24,725	21,095
96,650	96,700	23,318	19,898	24,743	21,108
96,700	96,750	23,333	19,912	24,760	21,123
96,750	96,800	23,348	19,925	24,778	21,138
96,800	96,850	23,363	19,939	24,795	21,153
96,850	96,900	23,378	19,952	24,813	21,168
96,900	96,950	23,393	19,966	24,830	21,183
96,950	97,000	23,408	19,979	24,848	21,198
97,000					
97,000	97,050	23,423	19,993	24,865	21,213
97,050	97,100	23,438	20,006	24,883	21,228
97,100	97,150	23,453	20,020	24,900	21,243
97,150	97,200	23,468	20,033	24,918	21,258
97,200	97,250	23,483	20,047	24,935	21,273
97,250	97,300	23,498	20,060	24,953	21,288
97,300	97,350	23,513	20,074	24,970	21,303
97,350	97,400	23,528	20,087	24,988	21,318
97,400	97,450	23,543	20,101	25,005	21,333
97,450	97,500	23,558	20,114	25,023	21,348
97,500	97,550	23,573	20,128	25,040	21,363
97,550	97,600	23,588	20,141	25,058	21,378
97,600	97,650	23,603	20,155	25,075	21,393
97,650	97,700	23,618	20,168	25,093	21,408
97,700	97,750	23,633	20,182	25,110	21,423
97,750	97,800	23,648	20,195	25,128	21,438
97,800	97,850	23,663	20,209	25,145	21,453
97,850	97,900	23,678	20,222	25,163	21,468
97,900	97,950	23,693	20,236	25,180	21,483
97,950	98,000	23,708	20,249	25,198	21,498

If taxable income is— At least	But less than	And you are— Single	Married filing jointly *	Married filing separately	Head of a household
98,000					
98,000	98,050	23,723	20,263	25,215	21,513
98,050	98,100	23,738	20,276	25,233	21,528
98,100	98,150	23,753	20,290	25,250	21,543
98,150	98,200	23,768	20,303	25,268	21,558
98,200	98,250	23,783	20,317	25,285	21,573
98,250	98,300	23,798	20,330	25,303	21,588
98,300	98,350	23,813	20,344	25,320	21,603
98,350	98,400	23,828	20,357	25,338	21,618
98,400	98,450	23,843	20,371	25,355	21,633
98,450	98,500	23,858	20,384	25,373	21,648
98,500	98,550	23,873	20,398	25,390	21,663
98,550	98,600	23,888	20,411	25,408	21,678
98,600	98,650	23,903	20,425	25,425	21,693
98,650	98,700	23,918	20,438	25,443	21,708
98,700	98,750	23,933	20,452	25,460	21,723
98,750	98,800	23,948	20,465	25,478	21,738
98,800	98,850	23,963	20,479	25,495	21,753
98,850	98,900	23,978	20,492	25,513	21,768
98,900	98,950	23,993	20,506	25,530	21,783
98,950	99,000	24,008	20,519	25,548	21,798
99,000					
99,000	99,050	24,023	20,533	25,565	21,813
99,050	99,100	24,038	20,546	25,583	21,828
99,100	99,150	24,053	20,560	25,600	21,843
99,150	99,200	24,068	20,573	25,618	21,858
99,200	99,250	24,083	20,587	25,635	21,873
99,250	99,300	24,098	20,600	25,653	21,888
99,300	99,350	24,113	20,614	25,670	21,903
99,350	99,400	24,128	20,627	25,688	21,918
99,400	99,450	24,143	20,641	25,705	21,933
99,450	99,500	24,158	20,654	25,723	21,948
99,500	99,550	24,173	20,668	25,740	21,963
99,550	99,600	24,188	20,681	25,758	21,978
99,600	99,650	24,203	20,695	25,775	21,993
99,650	99,700	24,218	20,708	25,793	22,008
99,700	99,750	24,233	20,722	25,810	22,023
99,750	99,800	24,248	20,735	25,828	22,038
99,800	99,850	24,263	20,749	25,845	22,053
99,850	99,900	24,278	20,762	25,863	22,068
99,900	99,950	24,293	20,776	25,880	22,083
99,950	100,000	24,308	20,789	25,898	22,098

$100,000 or over — use the Tax Rate Schedules on page 751

* This column must also be used by a qualifying widow(er).

2002
Tax Rate
Schedules

Use **only** if your taxable income (Form 1040, line 41) is $100,000 or more. If less, use the **Tax Table**. Even though you cannot use the Tax Rate Schedules below if your taxable income is less than $100,000, all levels of taxable income are shown so taxpayers can see the tax rate that applies to each level.

Schedule X—Use if your filing status is **Single**

If the amount on Form 1040, line 41, is: Over—	But not over—	Enter on Form 1040, line 42	of the amount over—
$0	$6,000	.... 10%	$0
6,000	27,950	$600.00 + 15%	6,000
27,950	67,700	3,892.50 + 27%	27,950
67,700	141,250	14,625.00 + 30%	67,700
141,250	307,050	36,690.00 + 35%	141,250
307,050	....	94,720.00 + 38.6%	307,050

Schedule Y-1—Use if your filing status is **Married filing jointly** or **Qualifying widow(er)**

If the amount on Form 1040, line 41, is: Over—	But not over—	Enter on Form 1040, line 42	of the amount over—
$0	$12,000	.... 10%	$0
12,000	46,700	$1,200.00 + 15%	12,000
46,700	112,850	6,405.00 + 27%	46,700
112,850	171,950	24,265.50 + 30%	112,850
171,950	307,050	41,995.50 + 35%	171,950
307,050	....	89,280.50 + 38.6%	307,050

Schedule Y-2—Use if your filing status is **Married filing separately**

If the amount on Form 1040, line 41, is: Over—	But not over—	Enter on Form 1040, line 42	of the amount over—
$0	$6,000	.... 10%	$0
6,000	23,350	$600.00 + 15%	6,000
23,350	56,425	3,202.50 + 27%	23,350
56,425	85,975	12,132.75 + 30%	56,425
85,975	153,525	20,997.75 + 35%	85,975
153,525	....	44,640.25 + 38.6%	153,525

Schedule Z—Use if your filing status is **Head of household**

If the amount on Form 1040, line 41, is: Over—	But not over—	Enter on Form 1040, line 42	of the amount over—
$0	$10,000	.... 10%	$0
10,000	37,450	$1,000.00 + 15%	10,000
37,450	96,700	5,117.50 + 27%	37,450
96,700	156,600	21,115.00 + 30%	96,700
156,600	307,050	39,085.00 + 35%	156,600
307,050	....	91,742.50 + 38.6%	307,050

2002 Earned Income Credit (EIC) Table

Caution. This is not a tax table.

1. To find your credit, read down the "At least – But less than" columns and find the line that includes the amount you were told to look up from your EIC Worksheet.

2. Then, go to the column that includes your filing status and the number of qualifying children you have. Enter the credit from that column on your EIC Worksheet.

Example. If your filing status is single, you have one qualifying child, and the amount you are looking up from your EIC Worksheet is $2,455, you would enter $842.

If the amount you are looking up from the worksheet is—		And your filing status is—		
		Single, head of household, or qualifying widow(er) and you have—		
At least	But less than	No children	One child	Two children
		Your credit is—		
2,400	2,450	186	825	970
2,450	2,500	189	842	990

If the amount you are looking up from the worksheet is—		And your filing status is—					
		Single, head of household, or qualifying widow(er) and you have—			Married filing jointly and you have—		
At least	But less than	No children	One child	Two children	No children	One child	Two children
		Your credit is—			Your credit is—		
$1	$50	$2	$9	$10	$2	$9	$10
50	100	6	26	30	6	26	30
100	150	10	43	50	10	43	50
150	200	13	60	70	13	60	70
200	250	17	77	90	17	77	90
250	300	21	94	110	21	94	110
300	350	25	111	130	25	111	130
350	400	29	128	150	29	128	150
400	450	33	145	170	33	145	170
450	500	36	162	190	36	162	190
500	550	40	179	210	40	179	210
550	600	44	196	230	44	196	230
600	650	48	213	250	48	213	250
650	700	52	230	270	52	230	270
700	750	55	247	290	55	247	290
750	800	59	264	310	59	264	310
800	850	63	281	330	63	281	330
850	900	67	298	350	67	298	350
900	950	71	315	370	71	315	370
950	1,000	75	332	390	75	332	390
1,000	1,050	78	349	410	78	349	410
1,050	1,100	82	366	430	82	366	430
1,100	1,150	86	383	450	86	383	450
1,150	1,200	90	400	470	90	400	470
1,200	1,250	94	417	490	94	417	490
1,250	1,300	98	434	510	98	434	510
1,300	1,350	101	451	530	101	451	530
1,350	1,400	105	468	550	105	468	550
1,400	1,450	109	485	570	109	485	570
1,450	1,500	113	502	590	113	502	590
1,500	1,550	117	519	610	117	519	610
1,550	1,600	120	536	630	120	536	630
1,600	1,650	124	553	650	124	553	650
1,650	1,700	128	570	670	128	570	670
1,700	1,750	132	587	690	132	587	690
1,750	1,800	136	604	710	136	604	710
1,800	1,850	140	621	730	140	621	730
1,850	1,900	143	638	750	143	638	750
1,900	1,950	147	655	770	147	655	770
1,950	2,000	151	672	790	151	672	790
2,000	2,050	155	689	810	155	689	810
2,050	2,100	159	706	830	159	706	830
2,100	2,150	163	723	850	163	723	850
2,150	2,200	166	740	870	166	740	870
2,200	2,250	170	757	890	170	757	890
2,250	2,300	174	774	910	174	774	910
2,300	2,350	178	791	930	178	791	930
2,350	2,400	182	808	950	182	808	950

If the amount you are looking up from the worksheet is—		And your filing status is—					
		Single, head of household, or qualifying widow(er) and you have—			Married filing jointly and you have—		
At least	But less than	No children	One child	Two children	No children	One child	Two children
		Your credit is—			Your credit is—		
2,400	2,450	186	825	970	186	825	970
2,450	2,500	189	842	990	189	842	990
2,500	2,550	193	859	1,010	193	859	1,010
2,550	2,600	197	876	1,030	197	876	1,030
2,600	2,650	201	893	1,050	201	893	1,050
2,650	2,700	205	910	1,070	205	910	1,070
2,700	2,750	208	927	1,090	208	927	1,090
2,750	2,800	212	944	1,110	212	944	1,110
2,800	2,850	216	961	1,130	216	961	1,130
2,850	2,900	220	978	1,150	220	978	1,150
2,900	2,950	224	995	1,170	224	995	1,170
2,950	3,000	228	1,012	1,190	228	1,012	1,190
3,000	3,050	231	1,029	1,210	231	1,029	1,210
3,050	3,100	235	1,046	1,230	235	1,046	1,230
3,100	3,150	239	1,063	1,250	239	1,063	1,250
3,150	3,200	243	1,080	1,270	243	1,080	1,270
3,200	3,250	247	1,097	1,290	247	1,097	1,290
3,250	3,300	251	1,114	1,310	251	1,114	1,310
3,300	3,350	254	1,131	1,330	254	1,131	1,330
3,350	3,400	258	1,148	1,350	258	1,148	1,350
3,400	3,450	262	1,165	1,370	262	1,165	1,370
3,450	3,500	266	1,182	1,390	266	1,182	1,390
3,500	3,550	270	1,199	1,410	270	1,199	1,410
3,550	3,600	273	1,216	1,430	273	1,216	1,430
3,600	3,650	277	1,233	1,450	277	1,233	1,450
3,650	3,700	281	1,250	1,470	281	1,250	1,470
3,700	3,750	285	1,267	1,490	285	1,267	1,490
3,750	3,800	289	1,284	1,510	289	1,284	1,510
3,800	3,850	293	1,301	1,530	293	1,301	1,530
3,850	3,900	296	1,318	1,550	296	1,318	1,550
3,900	3,950	300	1,335	1,570	300	1,335	1,570
3,950	4,000	304	1,352	1,590	304	1,352	1,590
4,000	4,050	308	1,369	1,610	308	1,369	1,610
4,050	4,100	312	1,386	1,630	312	1,386	1,630
4,100	4,150	316	1,403	1,650	316	1,403	1,650
4,150	4,200	319	1,420	1,670	319	1,420	1,670
4,200	4,250	323	1,437	1,690	323	1,437	1,690
4,250	4,300	327	1,454	1,710	327	1,454	1,710
4,300	4,350	331	1,471	1,730	331	1,471	1,730
4,350	4,400	335	1,488	1,750	335	1,488	1,750
4,400	4,450	339	1,505	1,770	339	1,505	1,770
4,450	4,500	342	1,522	1,790	342	1,522	1,790
4,500	4,550	346	1,539	1,810	346	1,539	1,810
4,550	4,600	350	1,556	1,830	350	1,556	1,830
4,600	4,650	354	1,573	1,850	354	1,573	1,850
4,650	4,700	358	1,590	1,870	358	1,590	1,870
4,700	4,750	361	1,607	1,890	361	1,607	1,890
4,750	4,800	365	1,624	1,910	365	1,624	1,910

2002 Earned Income Credit (EIC) Table—*Continued* (**Caution.** This is **not** a tax table.)

If the amount you are looking up from the worksheet is—		Single, head of household, or qualifying widow(er) and you have—			Married filing jointly and you have—		
At least	But less than	No children	One child	Two children	No children	One child	Two children
		Your credit is—			Your credit is—		
4,800	4,850	369	1,641	1,930	369	1,641	1,930
4,850	4,900	373	1,658	1,950	373	1,658	1,950
4,900	4,950	376	1,675	1,970	376	1,675	1,970
4,950	5,000	376	1,692	1,990	376	1,692	1,990
5,000	5,050	376	1,709	2,010	376	1,709	2,010
5,050	5,100	376	1,726	2,030	376	1,726	2,030
5,100	5,150	376	1,743	2,050	376	1,743	2,050
5,150	5,200	376	1,760	2,070	376	1,760	2,070
5,200	5,250	376	1,777	2,090	376	1,777	2,090
5,250	5,300	376	1,794	2,110	376	1,794	2,110
5,300	5,350	376	1,811	2,130	376	1,811	2,130
5,350	5,400	376	1,828	2,150	376	1,828	2,150
5,400	5,450	376	1,845	2,170	376	1,845	2,170
5,450	5,500	376	1,862	2,190	376	1,862	2,190
5,500	5,550	376	1,879	2,210	376	1,879	2,210
5,550	5,600	376	1,896	2,230	376	1,896	2,230
5,600	5,650	376	1,913	2,250	376	1,913	2,250
5,650	5,700	376	1,930	2,270	376	1,930	2,270
5,700	5,750	376	1,947	2,290	376	1,947	2,290
5,750	5,800	376	1,964	2,310	376	1,964	2,310
5,800	5,850	376	1,981	2,330	376	1,981	2,330
5,850	5,900	376	1,998	2,350	376	1,998	2,350
5,900	5,950	376	2,015	2,370	376	2,015	2,370
5,950	6,000	376	2,032	2,390	376	2,032	2,390
6,000	6,050	376	2,049	2,410	376	2,049	2,410
6,050	6,100	376	2,066	2,430	376	2,066	2,430
6,100	6,150	376	2,083	2,450	376	2,083	2,450
6,150	6,200	374	2,100	2,470	376	2,100	2,470
6,200	6,250	370	2,117	2,490	376	2,117	2,490
6,250	6,300	366	2,134	2,510	376	2,134	2,510
6,300	6,350	362	2,151	2,530	376	2,151	2,530
6,350	6,400	358	2,168	2,550	376	2,168	2,550
6,400	6,450	355	2,185	2,570	376	2,185	2,570
6,450	6,500	351	2,202	2,590	376	2,202	2,590
6,500	6,550	347	2,219	2,610	376	2,219	2,610
6,550	6,600	343	2,236	2,630	376	2,236	2,630
6,600	6,650	339	2,253	2,650	376	2,253	2,650
6,650	6,700	335	2,270	2,670	376	2,270	2,670
6,700	6,750	332	2,287	2,690	376	2,287	2,690
6,750	6,800	328	2,304	2,710	376	2,304	2,710
6,800	6,850	324	2,321	2,730	376	2,321	2,730
6,850	6,900	320	2,338	2,750	376	2,338	2,750
6,900	6,950	316	2,355	2,770	376	2,355	2,770
6,950	7,000	313	2,372	2,790	376	2,372	2,790
7,000	7,050	309	2,389	2,810	376	2,389	2,810
7,050	7,100	305	2,406	2,830	376	2,406	2,830
7,100	7,150	301	2,423	2,850	376	2,423	2,850
7,150	7,200	297	2,440	2,870	374	2,440	2,870
7,200	7,250	293	2,457	2,890	370	2,457	2,890
7,250	7,300	290	2,474	2,910	366	2,474	2,910
7,300	7,350	286	2,491	2,930	362	2,491	2,930
7,350	7,400	282	2,506	2,950	358	2,506	2,950
7,400	7,450	278	2,506	2,970	355	2,506	2,970
7,450	7,500	274	2,506	2,990	351	2,506	2,990
7,500	7,550	270	2,506	3,010	347	2,506	3,010
7,550	7,600	267	2,506	3,030	343	2,506	3,030
7,600	7,650	263	2,506	3,050	339	2,506	3,050
7,650	7,700	259	2,506	3,070	335	2,506	3,070
7,700	7,750	255	2,506	3,090	332	2,506	3,090
7,750	7,800	251	2,506	3,110	328	2,506	3,110
7,800	7,850	247	2,506	3,130	324	2,506	3,130
7,850	7,900	244	2,506	3,150	320	2,506	3,150
7,900	7,950	240	2,506	3,170	316	2,506	3,170
7,950	8,000	236	2,506	3,190	313	2,506	3,190
8,000	8,050	232	2,506	3,210	309	2,506	3,210
8,050	8,100	228	2,506	3,230	305	2,506	3,230
8,100	8,150	225	2,506	3,250	301	2,506	3,250
8,150	8,200	221	2,506	3,270	297	2,506	3,270
8,200	8,250	217	2,506	3,290	293	2,506	3,290
8,250	8,300	213	2,506	3,310	290	2,506	3,310
8,300	8,350	209	2,506	3,330	286	2,506	3,330
8,350	8,400	205	2,506	3,350	282	2,506	3,350
8,400	8,450	202	2,506	3,370	278	2,506	3,370
8,450	8,500	198	2,506	3,390	274	2,506	3,390
8,500	8,550	194	2,506	3,410	270	2,506	3,410
8,550	8,600	190	2,506	3,430	267	2,506	3,430
8,600	8,650	186	2,506	3,450	263	2,506	3,450
8,650	8,700	182	2,506	3,470	259	2,506	3,470
8,700	8,750	179	2,506	3,490	255	2,506	3,490
8,750	8,800	175	2,506	3,510	251	2,506	3,510
8,800	8,850	171	2,506	3,530	247	2,506	3,530
8,850	8,900	167	2,506	3,550	244	2,506	3,550
8,900	8,950	163	2,506	3,570	240	2,506	3,570
8,950	9,000	160	2,506	3,590	236	2,506	3,590
9,000	9,050	156	2,506	3,610	232	2,506	3,610
9,050	9,100	152	2,506	3,630	228	2,506	3,630
9,100	9,150	148	2,506	3,650	225	2,506	3,650
9,150	9,200	144	2,506	3,670	221	2,506	3,670
9,200	9,250	140	2,506	3,690	217	2,506	3,690
9,250	9,300	137	2,506	3,710	213	2,506	3,710
9,300	9,350	133	2,506	3,730	209	2,506	3,730
9,350	9,400	129	2,506	3,750	205	2,506	3,750
9,400	9,450	125	2,506	3,770	202	2,506	3,770
9,450	9,500	121	2,506	3,790	198	2,506	3,790
9,500	9,550	117	2,506	3,810	194	2,506	3,810
9,550	9,600	114	2,506	3,830	190	2,506	3,830
9,600	9,650	110	2,506	3,850	186	2,506	3,850
9,650	9,700	106	2,506	3,870	182	2,506	3,870
9,700	9,750	102	2,506	3,890	179	2,506	3,890
9,750	9,800	98	2,506	3,910	175	2,506	3,910
9,800	9,850	94	2,506	3,930	171	2,506	3,930
9,850	9,900	91	2,506	3,950	167	2,506	3,950
9,900	9,950	87	2,506	3,970	163	2,506	3,970
9,950	10,000	83	2,506	3,990	160	2,506	3,990
10,000	10,050	79	2,506	4,010	156	2,506	4,010
10,050	10,100	75	2,506	4,030	152	2,506	4,030
10,100	10,150	72	2,506	4,050	148	2,506	4,050
10,150	10,200	68	2,506	4,070	144	2,506	4,070
10,200	10,250	64	2,506	4,090	140	2,506	4,090
10,250	10,300	60	2,506	4,110	137	2,506	4,110
10,300	10,350	56	2,506	4,130	133	2,506	4,130
10,350	10,400	52	2,506	4,140	129	2,506	4,140

2002 Earned Income Credit (EIC) Table—*Continued* (Caution. This is **not** a tax table.)

If the amount you are looking up from the worksheet is—		Single, head of household, or qualifying widow(er) and you have—			Married filing jointly and you have—		
At least	But less than	No children	One child	Two children	No children	One child	Two children
		Your credit is—			Your credit is—		
10,400	10,450	49	2,506	4,140	125	2,506	4,140
10,450	10,500	45	2,506	4,140	121	2,506	4,140
10,500	10,550	41	2,506	4,140	117	2,506	4,140
10,550	10,600	37	2,506	4,140	114	2,506	4,140
10,600	10,650	33	2,506	4,140	110	2,506	4,140
10,650	10,700	29	2,506	4,140	106	2,506	4,140
10,700	10,750	26	2,506	4,140	102	2,506	4,140
10,750	10,800	22	2,506	4,140	98	2,506	4,140
10,800	10,850	18	2,506	4,140	94	2,506	4,140
10,850	10,900	14	2,506	4,140	91	2,506	4,140
10,900	10,950	10	2,506	4,140	87	2,506	4,140
10,950	11,000	7	2,506	4,140	83	2,506	4,140
11,000	11,050	3	2,506	4,140	79	2,506	4,140
11,050	11,100	*	2,506	4,140	75	2,506	4,140
11,100	11,150	0	2,506	4,140	72	2,506	4,140
11,150	11,200	0	2,506	4,140	68	2,506	4,140
11,200	11,250	0	2,506	4,140	64	2,506	4,140
11,250	11,300	0	2,506	4,140	60	2,506	4,140
11,300	11,350	0	2,506	4,140	56	2,506	4,140
11,350	11,400	0	2,506	4,140	52	2,506	4,140
11,400	11,450	0	2,506	4,140	49	2,506	4,140
11,450	11,500	0	2,506	4,140	45	2,506	4,140
11,500	11,550	0	2,506	4,140	41	2,506	4,140
11,550	11,600	0	2,506	4,140	37	2,506	4,140
11,600	11,650	0	2,506	4,140	33	2,506	4,140
11,650	11,700	0	2,506	4,140	29	2,506	4,140
11,700	11,750	0	2,506	4,140	26	2,506	4,140
11,750	11,800	0	2,506	4,140	22	2,506	4,140
11,800	11,850	0	2,506	4,140	18	2,506	4,140
11,850	11,900	0	2,506	4,140	14	2,506	4,140
11,900	11,950	0	2,506	4,140	10	2,506	4,140
11,950	12,000	0	2,506	4,140	7	2,506	4,140
12,000	12,050	0	2,506	4,140	3	2,506	4,140
12,050	12,100	0	2,506	4,140	*	2,506	4,140
12,100	13,550	0	2,506	4,140	0	2,506	4,140
13,550	13,600	0	2,497	4,128	0	2,506	4,140
13,600	13,650	0	2,489	4,118	0	2,506	4,140
13,650	13,700	0	2,481	4,107	0	2,506	4,140
13,700	13,750	0	2,473	4,097	0	2,506	4,140
13,750	13,800	0	2,465	4,086	0	2,506	4,140
13,800	13,850	0	2,457	4,076	0	2,506	4,140
13,850	13,900	0	2,449	4,065	0	2,506	4,140
13,900	13,950	0	2,441	4,055	0	2,506	4,140
13,950	14,000	0	2,433	4,044	0	2,506	4,140
14,000	14,050	0	2,425	4,034	0	2,506	4,140
14,050	14,100	0	2,417	4,023	0	2,506	4,140
14,100	14,150	0	2,409	4,013	0	2,506	4,140
14,150	14,200	0	2,401	4,002	0	2,506	4,140
14,200	14,250	0	2,393	3,992	0	2,506	4,140
14,250	14,300	0	2,385	3,981	0	2,506	4,140
14,300	14,350	0	2,377	3,970	0	2,506	4,140
14,350	14,400	0	2,369	3,960	0	2,506	4,140
14,400	14,450	0	2,361	3,949	0	2,506	4,140
14,450	14,500	0	2,353	3,939	0	2,506	4,140
14,500	14,550	0	2,345	3,928	0	2,506	4,140
14,550	14,600	0	2,337	3,918	0	2,497	4,128

If the amount you are looking up from the worksheet is—		Single, head of household, or qualifying widow(er) and you have—			Married filing jointly and you have—		
At least	But less than	No children	One child	Two children	No children	One child	Two children
		Your credit is—			Your credit is—		
14,600	14,650	0	2,329	3,907	0	2,489	4,118
14,650	14,700	0	2,321	3,897	0	2,481	4,107
14,700	14,750	0	2,313	3,886	0	2,473	4,097
14,750	14,800	0	2,305	3,876	0	2,465	4,086
14,800	14,850	0	2,297	3,865	0	2,457	4,076
14,850	14,900	0	2,289	3,855	0	2,449	4,065
14,900	14,950	0	2,281	3,844	0	2,441	4,055
14,950	15,000	0	2,273	3,834	0	2,433	4,044
15,000	15,050	0	2,265	3,823	0	2,425	4,034
15,050	15,100	0	2,257	3,813	0	2,417	4,023
15,100	15,150	0	2,249	3,802	0	2,409	4,013
15,150	15,200	0	2,241	3,791	0	2,401	4,002
15,200	15,250	0	2,233	3,781	0	2,393	3,992
15,250	15,300	0	2,225	3,770	0	2,385	3,981
15,300	15,350	0	2,217	3,760	0	2,377	3,970
15,350	15,400	0	2,209	3,749	0	2,369	3,960
15,400	15,450	0	2,201	3,739	0	2,361	3,949
15,450	15,500	0	2,193	3,728	0	2,353	3,939
15,500	15,550	0	2,185	3,718	0	2,345	3,928
15,550	15,600	0	2,177	3,707	0	2,337	3,918
15,600	15,650	0	2,169	3,697	0	2,329	3,907
15,650	15,700	0	2,161	3,686	0	2,321	3,897
15,700	15,750	0	2,153	3,676	0	2,313	3,886
15,750	15,800	0	2,145	3,665	0	2,305	3,876
15,800	15,850	0	2,137	3,655	0	2,297	3,865
15,850	15,900	0	2,129	3,644	0	2,289	3,855
15,900	15,950	0	2,121	3,634	0	2,281	3,844
15,950	16,000	0	2,113	3,623	0	2,273	3,834
16,000	16,050	0	2,106	3,612	0	2,265	3,823
16,050	16,100	0	2,098	3,602	0	2,257	3,813
16,100	16,150	0	2,090	3,591	0	2,249	3,802
16,150	16,200	0	2,082	3,581	0	2,241	3,791
16,200	16,250	0	2,074	3,570	0	2,233	3,781
16,250	16,300	0	2,066	3,560	0	2,225	3,770
16,300	16,350	0	2,058	3,549	0	2,217	3,760
16,350	16,400	0	2,050	3,539	0	2,209	3,749
16,400	16,450	0	2,042	3,528	0	2,201	3,739
16,450	16,500	0	2,034	3,518	0	2,193	3,728
16,500	16,550	0	2,026	3,507	0	2,185	3,718
16,550	16,600	0	2,018	3,497	0	2,177	3,707
16,600	16,650	0	2,010	3,486	0	2,169	3,697
16,650	16,700	0	2,002	3,476	0	2,161	3,686
16,700	16,750	0	1,994	3,465	0	2,153	3,676
16,750	16,800	0	1,986	3,454	0	2,145	3,665
16,800	16,850	0	1,978	3,444	0	2,137	3,655
16,850	16,900	0	1,970	3,433	0	2,129	3,644
16,900	16,950	0	1,962	3,423	0	2,121	3,634
16,950	17,000	0	1,954	3,412	0	2,113	3,623
17,000	17,050	0	1,946	3,402	0	2,106	3,612
17,050	17,100	0	1,938	3,391	0	2,098	3,602
17,100	17,150	0	1,930	3,381	0	2,090	3,591
17,150	17,200	0	1,922	3,370	0	2,082	3,581
17,200	17,250	0	1,914	3,360	0	2,074	3,570
17,250	17,300	0	1,906	3,349	0	2,066	3,560
17,300	17,350	0	1,898	3,339	0	2,058	3,549
17,350	17,400	0	1,890	3,328	0	2,050	3,539

*If the amount you are looking up from the worksheet is at least $11,050 ($12,050 if married filing jointly) but less than $11,060 ($12,060 if married filing jointly), your credit is $1. Otherwise, you cannot take the credit.

If the amount you are looking up from the worksheet is—		Single, head of household, or qualifying widow(er) and you have—			Married filing jointly and you have—		
At least	But less than	No children	One child	Two children	No children	One child	Two children
		Your credit is—			Your credit is—		
17,400	17,450	0	1,882	3,318	0	2,042	3,528
17,450	17,500	0	1,874	3,307	0	2,034	3,518
17,500	17,550	0	1,866	3,297	0	2,026	3,507
17,550	17,600	0	1,858	3,286	0	2,018	3,497
17,600	17,650	0	1,850	3,275	0	2,010	3,486
17,650	17,700	0	1,842	3,265	0	2,002	3,476
17,700	17,750	0	1,834	3,254	0	1,994	3,465
17,750	17,800	0	1,826	3,244	0	1,986	3,454
17,800	17,850	0	1,818	3,233	0	1,978	3,444
17,850	17,900	0	1,810	3,223	0	1,970	3,433
17,900	17,950	0	1,802	3,212	0	1,962	3,423
17,950	18,000	0	1,794	3,202	0	1,954	3,412
18,000	18,050	0	1,786	3,191	0	1,946	3,402
18,050	18,100	0	1,778	3,181	0	1,938	3,391
18,100	18,150	0	1,770	3,170	0	1,930	3,381
18,150	18,200	0	1,762	3,160	0	1,922	3,370
18,200	18,250	0	1,754	3,149	0	1,914	3,360
18,250	18,300	0	1,746	3,139	0	1,906	3,349
18,300	18,350	0	1,738	3,128	0	1,898	3,339
18,350	18,400	0	1,730	3,118	0	1,890	3,328
18,400	18,450	0	1,722	3,107	0	1,882	3,318
18,450	18,500	0	1,714	3,096	0	1,874	3,307
18,500	18,550	0	1,706	3,086	0	1,866	3,297
18,550	18,600	0	1,698	3,075	0	1,858	3,286
18,600	18,650	0	1,690	3,065	0	1,850	3,275
18,650	18,700	0	1,682	3,054	0	1,842	3,265
18,700	18,750	0	1,674	3,044	0	1,834	3,254
18,750	18,800	0	1,666	3,033	0	1,826	3,244
18,800	18,850	0	1,658	3,023	0	1,818	3,233
18,850	18,900	0	1,650	3,012	0	1,810	3,223
18,900	18,950	0	1,642	3,002	0	1,802	3,212
18,950	19,000	0	1,634	2,991	0	1,794	3,202
19,000	19,050	0	1,626	2,981	0	1,786	3,191
19,050	19,100	0	1,618	2,970	0	1,778	3,181
19,100	19,150	0	1,610	2,960	0	1,770	3,170
19,150	19,200	0	1,602	2,949	0	1,762	3,160
19,200	19,250	0	1,594	2,939	0	1,754	3,149
19,250	19,300	0	1,586	2,928	0	1,746	3,139
19,300	19,350	0	1,578	2,917	0	1,738	3,128
19,350	19,400	0	1,570	2,907	0	1,730	3,118
19,400	19,450	0	1,562	2,896	0	1,722	3,107
19,450	19,500	0	1,554	2,886	0	1,714	3,096
19,500	19,550	0	1,546	2,875	0	1,706	3,086
19,550	19,600	0	1,538	2,865	0	1,698	3,075
19,600	19,650	0	1,530	2,854	0	1,690	3,065
19,650	19,700	0	1,522	2,844	0	1,682	3,054
19,700	19,750	0	1,514	2,833	0	1,674	3,044
19,750	19,800	0	1,506	2,823	0	1,666	3,033
19,800	19,850	0	1,498	2,812	0	1,658	3,023
19,850	19,900	0	1,490	2,802	0	1,650	3,012
19,900	19,950	0	1,482	2,791	0	1,642	3,002
19,950	20,000	0	1,474	2,781	0	1,634	2,991
20,000	20,050	0	1,466	2,770	0	1,626	2,981
20,050	20,100	0	1,458	2,760	0	1,618	2,970
20,100	20,150	0	1,450	2,749	0	1,610	2,960
20,150	20,200	0	1,442	2,738	0	1,602	2,949
20,200	20,250	0	1,434	2,728	0	1,594	2,939
20,250	20,300	0	1,426	2,717	0	1,586	2,928
20,300	20,350	0	1,418	2,707	0	1,578	2,917
20,350	20,400	0	1,410	2,696	0	1,570	2,907
20,400	20,450	0	1,402	2,686	0	1,562	2,896
20,450	20,500	0	1,394	2,675	0	1,554	2,886
20,500	20,550	0	1,386	2,665	0	1,546	2,875
20,550	20,600	0	1,378	2,654	0	1,538	2,865
20,600	20,650	0	1,370	2,644	0	1,530	2,854
20,650	20,700	0	1,362	2,633	0	1,522	2,844
20,700	20,750	0	1,354	2,623	0	1,514	2,833
20,750	20,800	0	1,346	2,612	0	1,506	2,823
20,800	20,850	0	1,338	2,602	0	1,498	2,812
20,850	20,900	0	1,330	2,591	0	1,490	2,802
20,900	20,950	0	1,322	2,581	0	1,482	2,791
20,950	21,000	0	1,314	2,570	0	1,474	2,781
21,000	21,050	0	1,307	2,559	0	1,466	2,770
21,050	21,100	0	1,299	2,549	0	1,458	2,760
21,100	21,150	0	1,291	2,538	0	1,450	2,749
21,150	21,200	0	1,283	2,528	0	1,442	2,738
21,200	21,250	0	1,275	2,517	0	1,434	2,728
21,250	21,300	0	1,267	2,507	0	1,426	2,717
21,300	21,350	0	1,259	2,496	0	1,418	2,707
21,350	21,400	0	1,251	2,486	0	1,410	2,696
21,400	21,450	0	1,243	2,475	0	1,402	2,686
21,450	21,500	0	1,235	2,465	0	1,394	2,675
21,500	21,550	0	1,227	2,454	0	1,386	2,665
21,550	21,600	0	1,219	2,444	0	1,378	2,654
21,600	21,650	0	1,211	2,433	0	1,370	2,644
21,650	21,700	0	1,203	2,423	0	1,362	2,633
21,700	21,750	0	1,195	2,412	0	1,354	2,623
21,750	21,800	0	1,187	2,401	0	1,346	2,612
21,800	21,850	0	1,179	2,391	0	1,338	2,602
21,850	21,900	0	1,171	2,380	0	1,330	2,591
21,900	21,950	0	1,163	2,370	0	1,322	2,581
21,950	22,000	0	1,155	2,359	0	1,314	2,570
22,000	22,050	0	1,147	2,349	0	1,307	2,559
22,050	22,100	0	1,139	2,338	0	1,299	2,549
22,100	22,150	0	1,131	2,328	0	1,291	2,538
22,150	22,200	0	1,123	2,317	0	1,283	2,528
22,200	22,250	0	1,115	2,307	0	1,275	2,517
22,250	22,300	0	1,107	2,296	0	1,267	2,507
22,300	22,350	0	1,099	2,286	0	1,259	2,496
22,350	22,400	0	1,091	2,275	0	1,251	2,486
22,400	22,450	0	1,083	2,265	0	1,243	2,475
22,450	22,500	0	1,075	2,254	0	1,235	2,465
22,500	22,550	0	1,067	2,244	0	1,227	2,454
22,550	22,600	0	1,059	2,233	0	1,219	2,444
22,600	22,650	0	1,051	2,222	0	1,211	2,433
22,650	22,700	0	1,043	2,212	0	1,203	2,423
22,700	22,750	0	1,035	2,201	0	1,195	2,412
22,750	22,800	0	1,027	2,191	0	1,187	2,401
22,800	22,850	0	1,019	2,180	0	1,179	2,391
22,850	22,900	0	1,011	2,170	0	1,171	2,380
22,900	22,950	0	1,003	2,159	0	1,163	2,370
22,950	23,000	0	995	2,149	0	1,155	2,359

2002 Earned Income Credit (EIC) Table—Continued   (Caution. This is **not** a tax table.)

If the amount you are looking up from the worksheet is—		Single, head of household, or qualifying widow(er) and you have—			Married filing jointly and you have—		
At least	But less than	No children	One child	Two children	No children	One child	Two children
		Your credit is—			Your credit is—		
23,000	23,050	0	987	2,138	0	1,147	2,349
23,050	23,100	0	979	2,128	0	1,139	2,338
23,100	23,150	0	971	2,117	0	1,131	2,328
23,150	23,200	0	963	2,107	0	1,123	2,317
23,200	23,250	0	955	2,096	0	1,115	2,307
23,250	23,300	0	947	2,086	0	1,107	2,296
23,300	23,350	0	939	2,075	0	1,099	2,286
23,350	23,400	0	931	2,065	0	1,091	2,275
23,400	23,450	0	923	2,054	0	1,083	2,265
23,450	23,500	0	915	2,043	0	1,075	2,254
23,500	23,550	0	907	2,033	0	1,067	2,244
23,550	23,600	0	899	2,022	0	1,059	2,233
23,600	23,650	0	891	2,012	0	1,051	2,222
23,650	23,700	0	883	2,001	0	1,043	2,212
23,700	23,750	0	875	1,991	0	1,035	2,201
23,750	23,800	0	867	1,980	0	1,027	2,191
23,800	23,850	0	859	1,970	0	1,019	2,180
23,850	23,900	0	851	1,959	0	1,011	2,170
23,900	23,950	0	843	1,949	0	1,003	2,159
23,950	24,000	0	835	1,938	0	995	2,149
24,000	24,050	0	827	1,928	0	987	2,138
24,050	24,100	0	819	1,917	0	979	2,128
24,100	24,150	0	811	1,907	0	971	2,117
24,150	24,200	0	803	1,896	0	963	2,107
24,200	24,250	0	795	1,886	0	955	2,096
24,250	24,300	0	787	1,875	0	947	2,086
24,300	24,350	0	779	1,864	0	939	2,075
24,350	24,400	0	771	1,854	0	931	2,065
24,400	24,450	0	763	1,843	0	923	2,054
24,450	24,500	0	755	1,833	0	915	2,043
24,500	24,550	0	747	1,822	0	907	2,033
24,550	24,600	0	739	1,812	0	899	2,022
24,600	24,650	0	731	1,801	0	891	2,012
24,650	24,700	0	723	1,791	0	883	2,001
24,700	24,750	0	715	1,780	0	875	1,991
24,750	24,800	0	707	1,770	0	867	1,980
24,800	24,850	0	699	1,759	0	859	1,970
24,850	24,900	0	691	1,749	0	851	1,959
24,900	24,950	0	683	1,738	0	843	1,949
24,950	25,000	0	675	1,728	0	835	1,938
25,000	25,050	0	667	1,717	0	827	1,928
25,050	25,100	0	659	1,707	0	819	1,917
25,100	25,150	0	651	1,696	0	811	1,907
25,150	25,200	0	643	1,685	0	803	1,896
25,200	25,250	0	635	1,675	0	795	1,886
25,250	25,300	0	627	1,664	0	787	1,875
25,300	25,350	0	619	1,654	0	779	1,864
25,350	25,400	0	611	1,643	0	771	1,854
25,400	25,450	0	603	1,633	0	763	1,843
25,450	25,500	0	595	1,622	0	755	1,833
25,500	25,550	0	587	1,612	0	747	1,822
25,550	25,600	0	579	1,601	0	739	1,812
25,600	25,650	0	571	1,591	0	731	1,801
25,650	25,700	0	563	1,580	0	723	1,791
25,700	25,750	0	555	1,570	0	715	1,780
25,750	25,800	0	547	1,559	0	707	1,770

If the amount you are looking up from the worksheet is—		Single, head of household, or qualifying widow(er) and you have—			Married filing jointly and you have—		
At least	But less than	No children	One child	Two children	No children	One child	Two children
		Your credit is—			Your credit is—		
25,800	25,850	0	539	1,549	0	699	1,759
25,850	25,900	0	531	1,538	0	691	1,749
25,900	25,950	0	523	1,528	0	683	1,738
25,950	26,000	0	515	1,517	0	675	1,728
26,000	26,050	0	508	1,506	0	667	1,717
26,050	26,100	0	500	1,496	0	659	1,707
26,100	26,150	0	492	1,485	0	651	1,696
26,150	26,200	0	484	1,475	0	643	1,685
26,200	26,250	0	476	1,464	0	635	1,675
26,250	26,300	0	468	1,454	0	627	1,664
26,300	26,350	0	460	1,443	0	619	1,654
26,350	26,400	0	452	1,433	0	611	1,643
26,400	26,450	0	444	1,422	0	603	1,633
26,450	26,500	0	436	1,412	0	595	1,622
26,500	26,550	0	428	1,401	0	587	1,612
26,550	26,600	0	420	1,391	0	579	1,601
26,600	26,650	0	412	1,380	0	571	1,591
26,650	26,700	0	404	1,370	0	563	1,580
26,700	26,750	0	396	1,359	0	555	1,570
26,750	26,800	0	388	1,348	0	547	1,559
26,800	26,850	0	380	1,338	0	539	1,549
26,850	26,900	0	372	1,327	0	531	1,538
26,900	26,950	0	364	1,317	0	523	1,528
26,950	27,000	0	356	1,306	0	515	1,517
27,000	27,050	0	348	1,296	0	508	1,506
27,050	27,100	0	340	1,285	0	500	1,496
27,100	27,150	0	332	1,275	0	492	1,485
27,150	27,200	0	324	1,264	0	484	1,475
27,200	27,250	0	316	1,254	0	476	1,464
27,250	27,300	0	308	1,243	0	468	1,454
27,300	27,350	0	300	1,233	0	460	1,443
27,350	27,400	0	292	1,222	0	452	1,433
27,400	27,450	0	284	1,212	0	444	1,422
27,450	27,500	0	276	1,201	0	436	1,412
27,500	27,550	0	268	1,191	0	428	1,401
27,550	27,600	0	260	1,180	0	420	1,391
27,600	27,650	0	252	1,169	0	412	1,380
27,650	27,700	0	244	1,159	0	404	1,370
27,700	27,750	0	236	1,148	0	396	1,359
27,750	27,800	0	228	1,138	0	388	1,348
27,800	27,850	0	220	1,127	0	380	1,338
27,850	27,900	0	212	1,117	0	372	1,327
27,900	27,950	0	204	1,106	0	364	1,317
27,950	28,000	0	196	1,096	0	356	1,306
28,000	28,050	0	188	1,085	0	348	1,296
28,050	28,100	0	180	1,075	0	340	1,285
28,100	28,150	0	172	1,064	0	332	1,275
28,150	28,200	0	164	1,054	0	324	1,264
28,200	28,250	0	156	1,043	0	316	1,254
28,250	28,300	0	148	1,033	0	308	1,243
28,300	28,350	0	140	1,022	0	300	1,233
28,350	28,400	0	132	1,012	0	292	1,222
28,400	28,450	0	124	1,001	0	284	1,212
28,450	28,500	0	116	990	0	276	1,201
28,500	28,550	0	108	980	0	268	1,191
28,550	28,600	0	100	969	0	260	1,180

If the amount you are looking up from the worksheet is—		Single, head of household, or qualifying widow(er) and you have—			Married filing jointly and you have—			If the amount you are looking up from the worksheet is—		Single, head of household, or qualifying widow(er) and you have—			Married filing jointly and you have—		
At least	But less than	No children	One child	Two children	No children	One child	Two children	At least	But less than	No children	One child	Two children	No children	One child	Two children
		Your credit is—			Your credit is—					Your credit is—			Your credit is—		
28,600	28,650	0	92	959	0	252	1,169	31,400	31,450	0	0	369	0	0	580
28,650	28,700	0	84	948	0	244	1,159	31,450	31,500	0	0	359	0	0	569
28,700	28,750	0	76	938	0	236	1,148	31,500	31,550	0	0	348	0	0	559
28,750	28,800	0	68	927	0	228	1,138	31,550	31,600	0	0	338	0	0	548
28,800	28,850	0	60	917	0	220	1,127	31,600	31,650	0	0	327	0	0	538
28,850	28,900	0	52	906	0	212	1,117	31,650	31,700	0	0	317	0	0	527
28,900	28,950	0	44	896	0	204	1,106	31,700	31,750	0	0	306	0	0	517
28,950	29,000	0	36	885	0	196	1,096	31,750	31,800	0	0	295	0	0	506
29,000	29,050	0	28	875	0	188	1,085	31,800	31,850	0	0	285	0	0	496
29,050	29,100	0	20	864	0	180	1,075	31,850	31,900	0	0	274	0	0	485
29,100	29,150	0	12	854	0	172	1,064	31,900	31,950	0	0	264	0	0	475
29,150	29,200	0	4	843	0	164	1,054	31,950	32,000	0	0	253	0	0	464
29,200	29,250	0	**	833	0	156	1,043	32,000	32,050	0	0	243	0	0	453
29,250	29,300	0	0	822	0	148	1,033	32,050	32,100	0	0	232	0	0	443
29,300	29,350	0	0	811	0	140	1,022	32,100	32,150	0	0	222	0	0	432
29,350	29,400	0	0	801	0	132	1,012	32,150	32,200	0	0	211	0	0	422
29,400	29,450	0	0	790	0	124	1,001	32,200	32,250	0	0	201	0	0	411
29,450	29,500	0	0	780	0	116	990	32,250	32,300	0	0	190	0	0	401
29,500	29,550	0	0	769	0	108	980	32,300	32,350	0	0	180	0	0	390
29,550	29,600	0	0	759	0	100	969	32,350	32,400	0	0	169	0	0	380
29,600	29,650	0	0	748	0	92	959	32,400	32,450	0	0	159	0	0	369
29,650	29,700	0	0	738	0	84	948	32,450	32,500	0	0	148	0	0	359
29,700	29,750	0	0	727	0	76	938	32,500	32,550	0	0	138	0	0	348
29,750	29,800	0	0	717	0	68	927	32,550	32,600	0	0	127	0	0	338
29,800	29,850	0	0	706	0	60	917	32,600	32,650	0	0	116	0	0	327
29,850	29,900	0	0	696	0	52	906	32,650	32,700	0	0	106	0	0	317
29,900	29,950	0	0	685	0	44	896	32,700	32,750	0	0	95	0	0	306
29,950	30,000	0	0	675	0	36	885	32,750	32,800	0	0	85	0	0	295
30,000	30,050	0	0	664	0	28	875	32,800	32,850	0	0	74	0	0	285
30,050	30,100	0	0	654	0	20	864	32,850	32,900	0	0	64	0	0	274
30,100	30,150	0	0	643	0	12	854	32,900	32,950	0	0	53	0	0	264
30,150	30,200	0	0	632	0	4	843	32,950	33,000	0	0	43	0	0	253
30,200	30,250	0	0	622	0	**	833	33,000	33,050	0	0	32	0	0	243
30,250	30,300	0	0	611	0	0	822	33,050	33,100	0	0	22	0	0	232
30,300	30,350	0	0	601	0	0	811	33,100	33,150	0	0	11	0	0	222
30,350	30,400	0	0	590	0	0	801	33,150	33,200	0	0	***	0	0	211
30,400	30,450	0	0	580	0	0	790	33,200	33,250	0	0	0	0	0	201
30,450	30,500	0	0	569	0	0	780	33,250	33,300	0	0	0	0	0	190
30,500	30,550	0	0	559	0	0	769	33,300	33,350	0	0	0	0	0	180
30,550	30,600	0	0	548	0	0	759	33,350	33,400	0	0	0	0	0	169
30,600	30,650	0	0	538	0	0	748	33,400	33,450	0	0	0	0	0	159
30,650	30,700	0	0	527	0	0	738	33,450	33,500	0	0	0	0	0	148
30,700	30,750	0	0	517	0	0	727	33,500	33,550	0	0	0	0	0	138
30,750	30,800	0	0	506	0	0	717	33,550	33,600	0	0	0	0	0	127
30,800	30,850	0	0	496	0	0	706	33,600	33,650	0	0	0	0	0	116
30,850	30,900	0	0	485	0	0	696	33,650	33,700	0	0	0	0	0	106
30,900	30,950	0	0	475	0	0	685	33,700	33,750	0	0	0	0	0	95
30,950	31,000	0	0	464	0	0	675	33,750	33,800	0	0	0	0	0	85
31,000	31,050	0	0	453	0	0	664	33,800	33,850	0	0	0	0	0	74
31,050	31,100	0	0	443	0	0	654	33,850	33,900	0	0	0	0	0	64
31,100	31,150	0	0	432	0	0	643	33,900	33,950	0	0	0	0	0	53
31,150	31,200	0	0	422	0	0	632	33,950	34,000	0	0	0	0	0	43
31,200	31,250	0	0	411	0	0	622	34,000	34,050	0	0	0	0	0	32
31,250	31,300	0	0	401	0	0	611	34,050	34,100	0	0	0	0	0	22
31,300	31,350	0	0	390	0	0	601	34,100	34,150	0	0	0	0	0	11
31,350	31,400	0	0	380	0	0	590	34,150	34,178	0	0	0	0	0	3
								34,178 or more		0	0	0	0	0	0

**If the amount you are looking up from the worksheet is at least $29,200 ($30,200 if married filing jointly) but less than $29,201 ($30,201 if married filing jointly), your credit is $1. Otherwise, you cannot take the credit.

***If the amount you are looking up from the worksheet is at least $33,150 but less than $33,178, your credit is $3. Otherwise, you cannot take the credit.

Part 9

Glossary & Index

The following glossary and index will help you quickly find answers to your specific tax questions.

Glossary: The glossary explains technical tax terms in plain, easy-to-understand language.

Index: The index directs you to the exact page and section where an item you are interested in is discussed.

Glossary of Tax Terms

A

Accelerated cost recovery system (ACRS). A statutory method of depreciation allowing accelerated rates for most types of property used in business and income-producing activities during the years 1981 through 1986. It has been superseded by the modified accelerated cost recovery system (MACRS) for assets placed in service after 1986; *see 42.4* and *42.11*.

Accelerated depreciation. Depreciation methods that allow faster write-offs than straight-line rates in the earlier periods of the useful life of an asset. For example, in the first few years of recovery, MACRS allows a 200% double declining balance write-off, twice the straight-line rate; *see 42.5–42.8*.

Accountable reimbursement plan. An employer reimbursement or allowance arrangement that requires you to adequately substantiate business expenses to your employer, and to return any excess reimbursement; *see 20.31*.

Accrual method of accounting. A business method of accounting requiring income to be reported when earned and expenses to be deducted when incurred. However, deductions generally may not be claimed until economic performance has occurred; *see 40.3*.

Acquisition debt. Debt used to buy, build, or construct a principal residence or second home and that generally qualifies for a full interest expense deduction; *see 15.2*.

Active participation. Test for determining deductibility of IRA deductions. Active participants in employer retirement plans are subject to IRA deduction phase-out rules if adjusted gross income exceeds certain thresholds; *see 8.4*.

Adjusted basis. A statutory term describing the cost used to determine your profit or loss from a sale or exchange of property. It is generally your original cost, increased by capital improvements, and decreased by depreciation, depletion, and other capital write-offs; *see 5.20*.

Adjusted gross income (AGI). Important tax term representing gross income less allowable adjustments, such as IRA, alimony, and Keogh deductions. AGI determines whether various tax benefits are phased out, such as personal exemptions, itemized deductions, and the rental loss allowance; *see 12.1* and modified adjusted gross income (MAGI).

Alimony. Payments made to a separated or divorced spouse as required by a decree or agreement. Qualifying payments are deductible by the payor and taxable to the payee; *see Chapter 37*.

Alternative minimum tax (AMT). A tax triggered if certain tax benefits reduce your regular income tax below the tax computed on Form 6251 for AMT purposes; *see Chapter 23*.

Amended return. On Form 1040X, you may file an amended return within a three-year period to correct a mistake made on an original or previously amended return; *see 49.2*.

Amortizable bond premium. The additional amount paid over the face amount of an obligation that may be deducted under the rules in *4.17*.

Amortization of intangibles. Writing off an investment in intangible assets over the projected life of the assets, *see 42.18*.

Amount realized. A statutory term used to figure your profit or loss on a sale or exchange. Generally, it is sales proceeds plus mortgages assumed or taken subject to, less transaction expenses, such as commissions and legal costs; *see 5.14*.

Amount recognized. The amount of gain reportable and subject to tax. On certain tax-free exchanges of property, gain is not recognized in the year it is realized; *see 6.1*.

Annualized rate. A rate for a period of less than a year computed as though for a full year.

Annuity. An annual payment of money by a company or individual to a person called the annuitant. Payment is for a fixed period or the life of the annuitant. Tax consequences depend on the type of contract and funding; *see 7.22–7.30*.

Applicable federal rate. Interest rate fixed by the Treasury for determining imputed interest; *see 4.31* and *4.32*.

Appreciation in value. Increase in value of property due to market conditions. When you sell appreciated property, you pay tax on the appreciation since the date of purchase. When you donate appreciated property held long term, you may generally deduct the appreciated value; *see 14.6*.

Archer Medical Savings Account (MSA). A type of medical plan combining high deductible medical insurance protection with an IRA-type savings account fund to pay unreimbursed medical expenses; *see 17.17*.

Assessment. The IRS action of fixing tax liability that sets in motion collection procedures, such as charging interest, imposing penalties, and, if necessary, seizing property; *see 47.3*.

Asset. Anything owned that has cash or exchange value.

Assignment. The legal transfer of property, rights, or interest to another person called an assignee. You cannot avoid tax on income by assigning the income to another person.

At-risk rules. Rules limiting loss deductions to cash investments and personal liability notes. An exception for real estate treats certain nonrecourse commercial loans as amounts "at risk"; *see 10.18*.

Attorneys' fee awards. Taxpayers who prevail in the Tax Court or other federal court may recover up to a certain amount for attorneys' fees, plus other litigation expenses, by showing that the IRS position was unreasonable; *see 48.7*.

Audit. An IRS examination of your tax return, generally limited to a three-year period after you file; *see Chapter 48*.

Averaging. Some retirees may use favorable averaging methods to compute tax on a lump-sum distribution if they were born before 1936, *see 7.2–7.7*.

Away from home. A tax requirement for deducting travel expenses on a business trip. Sleeping arrangements are required for at least one night before returning home; *see 20.3* and *20.5–20.6*.

B

Balloon. A final payment on a loan in one lump sum.

Basis. Generally, the amount paid for property. You need to know your basis to figure gain or loss on a sale; *see 5.16*.

Bonus depreciation. A special first-year depreciation deduction of 30% of basis for qualifying business equipment and leasehold improvements purchased after September 10, 2001, but before September 10,

2004; *see 42.3.* For automobiles bought after September 10, 2001, and used over 50% for business, the bonus depreciation deduction increases the regular first-year deduction ceiling by $4,600; *see 43.4.*

Boot. Generally, the receipt of cash or its equivalent accompanying an exchange of property. In a tax-free exchange, boot is subject to immediate tax; *see 6.3.*

C

Calendar year. A year that begins on January 1 and ends on December 31.

Cancellation of debt. Release of a debt without consideration by a creditor. Cancellations of debt are generally taxable; *see 11.8.*

Capital. The excess of assets over liabilities.

Capital asset. Property subject to capital gain or loss treatment. Almost all assets you own are considered capital assets except for certain business assets or works you created; *see 5.2.*

Capital expenses. Costs that are not currently deductible and that are added to the basis of property. A capital expense generally increases the value of property. When added to depreciable property, the cost is deductible over the life of the asset.

Capital gain or loss. The difference between amount realized and adjusted basis on the sale or exchange of capital assets. Long-term capital gains are taxed favorably, as explained in Chapter 5. Capital losses are deducted first against capital gains, and then again up to $3,000 of other income; *see 5.1–5.5.*

Capital gain distribution. A mutual-fund distribution allocated to gains realized on the sale of fund portfolio assets. You report the distribution as long-term capital gain even if you held the fund shares short term; *see 32.5–32.6.*

Capital loss carryover. A capital loss that is not deductible because it exceeds the annual $3,000 capital loss ceiling. A carryover loss may be deducted from capital gains of later years plus up to $3,000 of ordinary income; *see 5.4.*

Capitalization. Adding a cost or expense to the basis of the property.

Carryback. A tax technique for receiving a refund of back taxes by applying a deduction or credit from a current tax year to a prior tax year. For example, a business net operating loss may be carried back for two years.

Carryforward. A tax technique of applying a loss or credit from a current year to a later year. For example, a business net operating loss may be carried forward 20 years instead of being carried back; *see 40.18.*

Cash method of accounting. Reporting income when actually or constructively received and deducting expenses when paid. Certain businesses may not use the cash method; *see 40.3.*

Casualty loss. Loss from an unforeseen and sudden event that is deductible, subject to a 10% income floor and $100 reduction for personal losses; *see 18.11.*

Charitable contributions. An itemized deduction is allowed for donations to qualifying charities. For property donations, the deductible amount depends on the type of property and donee organization, your holding period, and in some cases how the property is used; *see Chapter 14.*

Check the box. A term describing a classification rule that provides automatic partnership pass-through treatment for most businesses with two or more members unless the members elect on Form 8832 to be taxed as a corporation.

Child and dependent care credit. A credit of up to 30% based on certain care expenses incurred to allow you to work; *see 25.3.*

Child support. Payments to support a minor child generally to a custodial parent under a divorce or separation decree or agreement. The payments are not deductible; *see 37.5.*

Community income. Income earned by persons domiciled in community property states and treated as belonging equally to husband and wife; *see 1.6.*

Condemnation. The seizure of property by a public authority for a public purpose. Tax on gain realized on many conversions may be deferred; *see 18.18–18.19 and 18.25.*

Constructive receipt. A tax rule that taxes income that is not received by you but that you may draw upon; *see 2.2.*

Consumer interest. Interest incurred on personal debt and consumer credit. Consumer interest is not deductible.

Convention. Rule for determining MACRS depreciation in the year property is placed in service. Either a half-year convention or mid-quarter convention applies; *see 42.5–42.7.*

Corporation. An entity organized under state law and generally treated as a separate taxpayer unless an S election is made.

Coverdell Education Savings Account. A special account set up to fund education expenses of a student; *see 38.11–38.12.*

Credit. A tax credit directly reduces tax liability, as opposed to a deduction that reduces income subject to tax.

D

Declining balance method. A rapid depreciation method determined by a constant percentage based on useful life and applied to the adjusted basis of the property; *see 42.5 and 42.8.*

Deductions. Items directly reducing income. Personal deductions such as for mortgage interest, state and local taxes, and charitable contributions are allowed only if deductions are itemized on Schedule A, but deductions such as for alimony, capital losses, moving expenses to a new job location, business losses, student loan interest, and IRA and Keogh deductions are deducted from gross income even if itemized deductions are not claimed; *see Chapter 12.*

Deferred compensation. A portion of earnings withheld by an employer or put into a retirement plan for distribution to the employee at a later date. If certain legal requirements are met, the deferred amount is not taxable until actually paid, for example, after retirement; *see 2.8.*

Deficiency. The excess of the tax assessed by the IRS over the amount reported on your return; *see 48.6.*

Defined benefit plan. A retirement plan that pays fixed benefits based on actuarial projections; *see 41.2.*

Defined contribution plan. A retirement plan that pays benefits based on contributions to individual accounts, plus accumulated earnings. Contributions are generally based on a percentage of salary or earned income; *see 41.2.*

Dependency exemption. A fixed deduction allowed to every taxpayer, except those who may be claimed as a dependent by another person. Extra exemption deductions are allowed for a spouse on a joint return and for each qualifying dependent. A deduction of $3,000 is allowed for each exemption claimed on 2002 returns, but the deduction is phased out for certain high income individuals; *see 21.16.*

Dependent. A person supported by another person. If certain tests are met, a dependency exemption may be claimed for the dependent; *see Chapter 21.*

Depletion. Deduction claimed for the use of mineral resources; *see 9.15.*

Depreciable property. A business or income-producing asset with a useful life exceeding one year; see 42.1.

Depreciation. Writing off the cost of depreciable property over a period of years, usually its class life or recovery period specified in the tax law; see 42.4.

Depreciation recapture. An amount of gain on the sale of certain depreciable property that is treated as ordinary income in the case of personal property. Recapture is computed on Form 4797; see 44.1. For recapture on the sale of realty, see 44.2.

Disaster losses. Casualty losses such as from a storm, in areas declared by the President to warrant federal assistance. An election may be made to deduct the loss in the year before the loss or the year of the loss; see 18.3.

Dividend. A distribution made by a corporation to its shareholders generally of company earnings or surplus. Most dividends are taxable but exceptions are explained in Chapter 4.

E

Earned income. Compensation for performing personal services. You must have earned income for a deductible IRA; see 8.2, or to claim the earned income credit, see 25.13.

Earned income credit. A credit allowed to taxpayers with earned income or adjusted gross income (AGI) below certain thresholds; see 25.12.

Education credits. There are two education credits: the Hope credit and the lifetime learning credit; see 38.7.

Education IRA. See Coverdell Education Savings Account and 38.11–38.12.

Estate tax. A tax imposed on the value of a decedent's taxable estate, after deductions and credits; see 39.4.

Estimated tax. Advance payment of current tax liability based either on wage withholdings or installment payments of your estimated tax liability. To avoid penalties, you generally must pay to the IRS either 90% of your final tax liability, or either 100% or 110% of the prior year's tax liability, depending on your adjusted gross income; see Chapter 27.

Exemption. *See* Dependency exemption.

F

Fair market value. What a willing buyer would pay to a willing seller when neither is under any compulsion to buy or sell.

Fiduciary. A person or corporation such as a trustee, executor, or guardian who manages property for another person.

First-year expensing (or Section 179 deduction). In 2002, a deduction of up to $24,000 (or $44,000 for qualifying businesses in an enterprise zone or $59,000 for qualifying businesses in the New York Liberty Zone) of the cost of business equipment in the year placed in service; see 42.3.

Fiscal year. A 12-month period ending on the last day of any month other than December. Partnerships, S corporations, and personal service corporations are limited in their choice of fiscal years and face special restrictions.

Flexible spending arrangements. A salary reduction plan that allows employees to pay for enhanced medical coverage or dependent care expenses on a tax-free basis; see 3.14.

Foreign earned income exclusion. In 2002, up to $80,000 of foreign earned income is exempt from tax if a foreign residence or physical presence test is met; see 36.1–36.2.

Foreign tax credit. A credit for income taxes paid to a foreign country or U.S. possession; see 36.14.

401(k) plan. A deferred pay plan, authorized by Section 401(k) of the Internal Revenue Code, under which a percentage of an employee's salary is withheld and placed in a savings account or the company's profit-sharing plan. Income accumulates on the deferred amount until withdrawn by the employee at age $59\frac{1}{2}$ or when the employee retires or leaves the company; see 7.17.

G

Gift tax. Gifts in excess of a $11,000 per donee annual exclusion are subject to gift tax, but the tax may be offset by a unified gift and estate tax credit; see 33.1.

Grantor trust rules. Tax rules that tax the grantor of a trust on the trust income; see 33.3.

Gross income. The total amount of income received from all sources before exclusions and deductions.

Gross receipts. Total business receipts reported on Schedule C or Schedule C-EZ before deducting adjustments for returns and allowances and cost of goods sold; see 40.6.

Group-term life insurance. Employees are not taxed on up to $50,000 of group-term coverage; see 3.3.

H

Head of household. Generally, an unmarried person who maintains a household for dependents and is allowed to compute his or her tax based on head of household rates, which are more favorable than single person rates; see 1.12.

Health Reimbursement Account (HRA). Employer established account that provides tax-free reimbursements to employees for deductibles and other expenses that could be taken as itemized deductions; see 3.2.

Hobby loss. Hobby expenses are deductible only up to income from the activity; loss deductions are not allowed; see 40.10.

Holding period. The length of time that an asset is owned and that generally determines long- or short-term capital gain treatment; see 5.3 and 5.9–5.12.

Home equity debt. Debt secured by a principal residence or second home to the extent of the excess of fair market value over acquisition debt. An interest deduction is generally allowed for home equity debt up to $100,000 ($50,000 if married filing separately); see 15.3.

I

Imputed interest. Interest deemed earned on seller-financed sales or low-interest loans, where the parties' stated interest rate is below the applicable IRS federal rate; see 4.31 and 4.32.

Incentive stock option. Options meeting tax law tests that defer tax on the option transaction until the obtained stock is sold; see 2.17.

Inclusion amount for leased cars. Based on an IRS table, an amount that reduces a business deduction taken for payments on an auto leased for a minimum of 30 days and valued at over $15,500; see 43.12.

Income in respect of a decedent. Income earned by a person before death but taxable to an estate or heir who receives it; see 1.14 and 11.4.

Independent contractor. One who controls his or her own work and reports as a self-employed person; see Chapters 40 and 45.

Individual retirement account (IRA). A retirement account to which up to $3,000 (or up to $3,500 if you are 50 or over) may be contributed annually, but deductions for the contribution are restricted if you are covered by a company retirement plan. Earnings accumulate tax free; see Chapter 8.

Innocent spouse. A spouse who claims that he or she should not be liable on a joint return; *see 1.7.*

Installment sale. A sale of property that allows for tax deferment if at least one payment is received after the end of the tax year in which the sale occurs. The installment method does not apply to year-end sales of publicly traded securities. Dealers may not use the installment method. Investors with very large installment balances could face a special tax; *see 5.21.*

Intangible assets. Intangible assets that come within Section 197, such as goodwill, are amortizable over a 15-year period; *see 42.18.*

Inter vivos or lifetime trust. A trust created during the lifetime of the person who created the trust. If irrevocable, income on the trust principal is generally shifted to the trust beneficiaries; *see 33.3.*

Investment in the contract. The total cost investment in an annuity. When annuity payments are made, the portion allocable to the cost investment is tax free; *see 7.22 and 7.27.*

Investment interest. Interest on debt used to carry investments, but not including interest expense from a passive activity. Deductions are limited to net investment income; *see 15.10.*

Involuntary conversion. Forced disposition of property due to condemnation, theft, or casualty. Tax on gain from involuntary conversions may be deferred if replacement property is purchased; *see 18.19.*

Itemized deductions. Items, such as interest, state and local taxes, charitable contributions, and medical deductions, claimed on Schedule A of Form 1040. Itemized deductions are subtracted from adjusted gross income to arrive at taxable income; *see* Chapter 13. The amount of itemized deductions is also subject to a reduction when adjusted gross income exceeds certain limits; *see 13.7.*

J

Joint return. A return filed by a married couple reporting their combined income and deductions. Joint return status provides tax savings to many couples; *see 1.4.*

Joint tenants. Ownership of property by two persons. When one dies, the decedent's interest passes to the survivor; *see 5.18.*

K

Keogh plan. Retirement plan set up by a self-employed person, providing tax-deductible contributions, tax-free income accumulations until withdrawal, and favorable averaging for qualifying lump-sum distributions; *see* Chapter 41.

Kiddie tax. The tax on the investment income in excess of $1,500 (may change after 2002) of a dependent child under age 14, based on the parents' marginal tax rate and computed on Form 8615; *see 24.3.*

L

Legally separated. A husband and wife who are required to live apart from each other by the terms of a decree of separate maintenance. Payments under the decree are deductible by the payor and taxable to the payee as alimony; *see 37.2.*

Like-kind exchange. An exchange of similar assets used in a business or held for investment on which gain may be deferred; *see 6.1.*

Lump-sum distribution. Payments within one tax year of the entire amount due to a participant in a qualified retirement plan. Qualifying lump sums may be directly rolled over tax free, or, in some cases, are eligible for current tax under a favorable averaging method; *see 7.2.*

M

Marital deduction. An estate tax and gift tax deduction for assets passing to a spouse. It allows estate and gift transfers completely free of tax; *see 39.6.*

Market discount. The difference between face value of bond and lower market price, attributable to rising interest rates. On a sale, gain on the bond is generally taxed as ordinary income to the extent of the discount; *see 4.20.*

Material participation tests. Rules for determining whether a person is active in a business activity for passive activity rule purposes. Unless the tests are met, passive loss limits apply; *see 10.6.*

Medical Savings Account (MSA). *See* Archer Medical Savings Account and *17.17.*

Miscellaneous itemized deductions. Generally, itemized deductions for job and investment expenses subject to a 2% of adjusted gross income floor; *see* Chapter 19.

Modified ACRS (MACRS). Depreciation methods applied to assets placed in service after 1986.

Modified adjusted gross income (MAGI). This is generally adjusted gross income increased by certain items such as tax-free foreign earned income. MAGI usually is used to determine phaseouts of certain deductions and credits.

Mortgage interest. Fully deductible interest on up to two residences if acquisition debt secured by a home is $1 million or less, and home equity debt is $100,000 or less; *see 15.1.*

Moving expenses. Certain expenses of moving to a new job location are deductible if distance and time tests are met; *see 12.3–12.8.*

N

Net operating loss. A business loss that exceeds current income may be carried back against income of prior years and carried forward as a deduction from future income until eliminated. The carryback and carryforward periods are discussed in *40.18–40.22.*

New York Liberty Zone. The area in lower Manhattan located on or south of Canal Street, and on or South of East Broadway and Grand Street where these intersect with Canal Street. In the wake of the September 11, 2001, terrorist attacks, special tax benefits are provided to businesses and property owners in the Liberty Zone.

Nonperiodic distributions. A 20% withholding rule applies to nonperiodic distributions, such as lump-sum distributions, paid directly to employees from an employer plan; *see 7.8* and *26.11.*

Nonrecourse financing. Debt on which a person is not personally liable. In case of nonpayment, the creditor must foreclose on property securing the debt. At-risk rules generally bar losses where there is nonrecourse financing, but an exception applies to certain nonrecourse financing for real estate; *see 10.18.*

Nonresident alien. A person who is not a United States citizen or a permanent resident. Tax is generally limited to income from U.S. sources; *see 1.16.*

O

Ordinary and necessary. A statutory requirement for the deductibility of a business expense.

Ordinary income. Income other than capital gains.

Glossary

Ordinary loss. A loss other than a capital loss.

Original issue discount (OID). The difference between the face value of a bond and its original issue price. OID is reported on an annual basis as interest income; *see 4.19.*

P

Partnership. An unincorporated business or income-producing entity organized by two or more persons. A partnership is not subject to tax but passes through to the partners all income, deductions, and credits, according to the terms of the partnership agreement; *see 11.9–11.14.*

Passive activity loss rules. Rules that limit the deduction of losses from passive activities to income from other passive activities. Passive activities include investment rental operations or businesses in which you do not materially participate; *see 10.1.*

Patronage dividend. A taxable distribution made by a cooperative to its members or patrons.

Pension. Payments to employees from an employer-funded retirement plan for past services; *see 7.25–7.27.*

Percentage depletion. A deduction method that applies a fixed percentage to the gross income generated by mineral property; *see 9.15.*

Personal exemption. An automatic exemption given to a taxpayer unless he or she may be claimed as a dependent by another taxpayer. For 2002, the exemption amount is $3,000. Exemptions are phased out for certain high income taxpayers; *see 21.16.*

Personal interest. Tax term for interest on personal loans and consumer purchases. Such interest is not deductible.

Placed in service. The time when a depreciable asset is ready to be used. The date fixes the beginning of the depreciation period.

Points. Charges to the homeowner at the time of the loan. A point is equal to 1 percent. Depending on the type of loan, points may be currently deductible or amortized over the life of the loan; *see 15.8.*

Premature distributions. Withdrawals before age 59$^1/_2$ from qualified retirement plans are subject to penalties unless specific exceptions are met; *see 7.15 and 8.12.*

Principal residence. On a sale of a principal residence, you may avoid tax under the rules explained in Chapter 29.

Probate estate. Property held in a decedent's name passing by will; *see 39.1.*

Profit-sharing plan. A defined contribution plan under which the amount contributed to the employees' accounts is based on a percentage of the employer's profits; *see 8.5 and 41.2.*

Provisional income. If your provisional income exceeds a base amount, part of your Social Security benefits may be subject to tax. To figure provisional income, *see 34.3.*

Q

Qualified charitable organization. A nonprofit philanthropic organization that is approved by the U.S. Treasury to receive charitable contribution deductions; *see 14.1.*

Qualified plan. A retirement plan that meets tax law tests and allows for tax deferment and tax-free accumulation of income until benefits are withdrawn. Pension, profit-sharing, stock bonus, employee stock ownership, and Keogh plans and IRAs may be qualified plans; *see Chapters 7, 8, and 41.*

Qualified tuition program (QTP). A state-sponsored college savings plan or prepayment plan, or a prepayment plan established by a private college; *see 38.5.*

Qualifying widow or widower. A filing status entitling the taxpayer with dependents to use joint tax rates for up to two tax years after the death of a spouse; *see 1.11.*

R

Real estate investment trust (REIT). An entity that invests primarily in real estate and mortgages and passes through income to investors; *see 31.1.*

Real estate professional. An individual who, because of his or her real estate activity, qualifies to deduct rental losses from nonpassive income; *see 10.3.*

Real property. Land and the buildings on land. Buildings are depreciable; *see 42.13 and 42.16.*

Recognized gain or loss. The amount of gain or loss to be reported on a tax return. Gain may not be recognized on certain exchanges of property; *see 6.1.*

Recovery property. Tangible depreciable property placed in service after 1980 and before 1987 and depreciable under ACRS; *see 42.11 and 42.16.*

Refundable tax credit. A credit that entitles you to a refund even if you owe no tax for the year.

Required Minimum Distributions (RMDs). Distributions that must be taken annually to avoid a 50% IRS penalty by a traditional IRA account holder starting with the year age 70$^1/_2$ is reached. For qualified plan participants the starting date may be delayed for employees working beyond age 70$^1/_2$. Minimum distribution rules also apply to beneficiaries of qualified plans, traditional IRAs and Roth IRAs. *See 7.13–7.14, 8.13–8.14, and 8.24.*

Residence interest. Term for deductible mortgage interest on a principal residence and a second home; *see 15.1–15.2.*

Residential rental property. Real property in which 80% or more of the gross income is from dwelling units. Under MACRS, depreciation is claimed over 27.5 years under the straight-line method; *see 42.13.*

Return of capital. A distribution of your investment that is not subject to tax unless the distribution exceeds your investment; *see 4.11.*

Revocable trust. A trust that may be changed or terminated by its creator or another person. Such trusts do not provide an income tax savings to the creator; *see 33.3.*

Rollover. A tax-free reinvestment of a distribution from a qualified retirement plan into an IRA or other qualified plan within 60 days; *see 7.3, 7.8, and 8.10.*

Roth IRA. A nondeductible contributory IRA that allows for tax-free accumulation of income. Qualifying distributions are completely tax free. *See 8.19–8.24.*

Royalty income. Amounts received for the use of property such as mineral property, a book, a movie, or a patent; *see 9.11.*

S

Salvage value. The estimated value of an asset at the end of its useful life. Salvage value is ignored by ACRS and MACRS rules.

S corporation. A corporation that elects S status in order to receive tax treatment similar to a partnership; *see Chapter 11.*

Scholarships. Grants to degree candidates receive tax-free treatment if awarded after August 16, 1986, and used for tuition and course-related expenses, but not room and board; *see 38.1.*

Section 179 deduction (or First-year expensing). Expensing deduction, in 2002 up to $24,000, allowed for investments in depreciable business equipment in the year the property is placed in service. The deduction may be as high as $44,000 for quali-

Glossary

fying businesses in an enterprise zone or $59,000 for qualifying businesses in the New York Liberty Zone; *see 42.3.*

Section 457 plan. Deferred compensation plan set up by a state or local government, or tax-exempt organization, which allows tax-free deferrals of salary; *see 7.21.*

Section 1231 property. Depreciable property used in a trade or business and held for more than a year. All Section 1231 gains and losses are netted; a net gain is treated as capital gain, a net loss as an ordinary loss; *see 44.8.*

Self-employed person. An individual who operates a business or profession as a proprietor or independent contractor and reports self-employment income on Schedule C; *see* Chapters 40 and 45.

Self-employment tax. Tax paid by self-employed persons to finance Social Security coverage. In 2002, there are two rates. A 12.4% rate applies to a taxable earnings base of $84,900 or less and a 2.9% rate applies to all net earnings; *see* Chapter 45.

Separate return. Return filed by a married person who does not file a joint return. Filing separately may save taxes where each spouse has separate deductions, but certain tax benefits require a joint return; *see 1.3.*

Short sale. Sale of borrowed securities made to freeze a paper profit or to gain from a declining market; *see 30.5.*

Short tax year. A tax year of less than 12 months. May occur with the startup of a business or change in accounting method.

Short-term capital gain or loss. Gain or loss on the sale or exchange of a capital asset held one year or less; *see 5.1, 5.2,* and *5.10.*

Simplified employee plan (SEP). IRA-type plan set up by an employer, rather than the employee. Salary-reduction contributions may be allowed to plans of small employers set up before 1997; *see 8.15-8.16.*

Single. The filing status of an individual who is not married on December 31 of the year for which a return is filed; *see 1.1.*

Standard deduction. A fixed deduction allowed to taxpayers who do not itemize deductions. The amount depends on filing status, age, and blindness; *see 13.1.*

Standard mileage rate. A fixed rate allowed by the IRS for business auto expenses in place of deducting actual expenses; *see 43.1.*

Statutory employees. Certain employees, such as full-time life insurance salespersons, who may report income and deductions on Schedule C, rather than on Schedule A as miscellaneous itemized deductions; *see 40.6.*

Stock dividend. A distribution of additional shares of a corporation's stock to its shareholders; *see 4.6.*

Stock option. A right to buy stock at a fixed price.

Straddle. Taking an offsetting investment position to reduce the risk of loss in a similar investment; *see 30.9.*

Straight-line method. A method of depreciating the cost of a depreciable asset on a pro rata basis over its cost recovery period; *see 42.9, 42.12.*

T

Tangible personal property. Movable property, such as desks, computers, machinery, and autos, depreciable over a five-year or seven-year period; *see 42.4.*

Taxable income. Net income after claiming all deductions from gross income and adjusted gross income, such as IRA deductions, itemized deductions, or the standard deduction, and personal exemptions; *see 22.1.*

Tax attributes. When debts are cancelled in bankruptcy cases, the cancelled amount is excluded from gross income. Tax attributes are certain losses, credits, and property basis that must be reduced to the extent of the exclusion; *see 11.8.*

Tax deferral. Shifting income to a later year, such as where you defer taxable interest to the following year by purchasing a T-bill or savings certificate maturing after the end of the current year; *see* Chapter 4. Investments in qualified retirement plans provide tax deferral (*see* Chapters 7, 8, and 41).

Tax home. The area of your principal place of business or employment. You must be away from your tax home on a business trip to deduct travel expenses; *see 20.6-20.9.*

Tax identification number. For an individual, his or her Social Security number; for businesses, fiduciaries, and other nonindividual taxpayers, the employer identification number.

Tax preference items. Items that may subject a taxpayer to the alternative minimum tax (AMT); *see 23.3.*

Tax rate schedules. Used by taxpayers with taxable incomes of $100,000 or more; *see* Part 8.

Tax-sheltered annuity. A type of retirement annuity offered to employees of charitable organizations and educational systems, generally funded by employee salary-reduction contributions; *see 7.20.*

Tax tables. Used by taxpayers with taxable incomes of less than $100,000 to look up their tax; *see* Part 8.

Tax year. A period (generally 12 months) for reporting income and expenses; *see 40.4.*

Tenancy by the entireties. A joint tenancy in real property in the name of both husband and wife. On the death of one tenant, the survivor receives entire interest.

Tenants in common. Two or more persons who have undivided ownership rights in property. Upon death of a tenant, his or her share passes to his or her estate, rather than to the surviving tenants.

Testamentary trust. A trust established under a will.

Trust. An arrangement under which one person transfers legal ownership of assets to another person or corporation (the trustee) for the benefit of one or more third persons (beneficiaries).

U

Unrecaptured Section 1250 gain. Long-term gain realized on the sale of depreciable realty attributed to depreciation deductions and subject to a 25% capital gain rate; *see 5.3 and 44.2.*

Useful life. For property not depreciated under ACRS or MACRS, the estimate of time in which a depreciable asset will be used.

V

Vacation homes. The tax law limits deductions for vacation homes, broadly defined as any dwelling unit used by the owner or the owner's relatives for more than a specified period; *see 9.7.*

W

Wash sales. Sales on which losses are disallowed because you recover your market position within a 61-day period; *see 30.6.*

Withholding. An amount taken from income as a pre-payment of an individual's tax liability for the year. In the case of wages, the employer withholds part of every wage payment. Backup withholding from dividend or interest income is required if you do not provide the payer with a correct taxpayer identification number. Withholding on pensions and IRAs is automatic unless you elect to waive withholding; *see* Chapter 26.

Index

Index

Amortization
 adjusted basis and, 5.20:117–18
 of bond premium, 4.17:82–83
 business intangibles, 42.1:632–33
 expenses in new business, 40.11:612
 of goodwill and other intangibles, 42.18:644–46
 method, for annuity schedule payments, 8.12:194
Amount realized, 29.5:484, 5.14:111
AMT. *See* Alternative Minimum Tax
Annualized income installment method for estimated taxes, 27.1:468
Annuities (annuity income). *See also* Retirement plans
 commercial
  endowment policies, conversion of, 7.24:172–73
  figuring taxable part of, 7.22:167–70
  life expectancy tables, 7.22:168, 7.23:170–72
  penalty on premature withdrawals, 7.22:170
  refund feature, 7.22:168
  variable annuities, 7.22:169
 contracts
  exchanges of, 6.12:144
  from insurance company, and Keogh plan, 41.2:625
 employee
  changing cost recovery methods, 7.25:173
  Civil Service retirement fund, 7.29:176
  cost of, 7.27:175
  of tax-exempt and schools (403(b) Plans), 7.20:165–66
  reporting, 7.25:173
  retired military personnel, 7.30:177
  simplified method for calculating recovery amount, 7.26:173–75
  withdrawals before annuity starting date, 7.28:175–76
 schedule payments of IRAs, 8.12:193–94
 for surviving spouse, 7.11:158
 switching, 7.20:166
 tax-sheltered, distributions from, 7.20:166
Annulment degree, 37.2:576
Antarctic region, not meeting foreign residence, 36.5:567
Anthrax attacks, 555, 35.9:561. *See also* Victims of Terrorism Tax Relief Act of 2001
Anti-churning rule, Section 197, 42.17:644, 42.18:645
Applicable federal rate (AFR), for seller-financed sales, 4.32:97
Appraisals
 of art objects, 14.6:293, 14.9:297–98
 for disaster relief, 18.12:358
 fees, as miscellaneous expense, 14.12:300, 19.25:383
 of home, 9.5:219
 penalty for substantial overvaluation of property, 14.12:300, 14.16:302
Appreciated financial position, constructive sales of, 30.8:499–500
Arbitrage bonds, 4.25:90
Arbitrage transactions of short sales, 30.5:496
Archer MSAs, 17.17:343–44
 eligibility for, 3.1:54–55
 tax-free benefits from, 3.2:58

Armed forces, members of. *See also* Foreign service officers; Veterans Administration
 automatic extension to file return if on duty outside the U.S. or Puerto Rico on April 15, 2002, 35.7:560
 benefits not subject to tax, 35.2:556–57
 combat zone death, tax forgiveness for, 35.6:559–60
 combat zone duty, 2.15:47, 555, 35.4:557–58, 35.5:559
 deductions for, 35.3:557
 disability pensions for, 2.15:47
 disability retirement pay, 35.2:557
 estate tax rate reduction for personnel killed in action while serving in combat zone, 35.6:559
 extension to pay tax when entering service, 35.7:560
 income taxes withheld on pay to, 26.2:461
 IRS e-mail address to ask about returns, taxes, and combat zone status, 35.5:559
 missing status, 35.6:559
 moving expenses, 12.4:275
 permanent duty station of, 20.6:392
 reservists, tax information for, 35.8:560–61
 retired, annuity election, 7.30:177
 support test for dependents and, 21.7:417
 taxable pay and benefits, 35.1:556
 tax deadlines for support personnel, 35.5:559
 tax-free benefits, 35.2:556–57
 tax savings for, Chapter 35 (555–61)
 Vietnam MIAs, 35.6:560
 when to file, 49.2:702
Artists
 reporting royalty income, 9.11:226, 9.12:226
 self-employed, 9.12:226, 40.9:611
Art objects, 14.9:297–98, 14.17:304
Assessments, 16.5:322–23
Assets, intangible business property, amortization for, 42.18:644–46
At-risk loss limitations, 40.20:620–21
At risk rules
 amounts considered at risk, 10.18:251
 amounts not at risk, 10.19:251–53
 carryover of disallowed losses, 10.21:253
 Form 6198, 10.17:250–51
 passive loss rules and, 10.17:251
 recapture of losses where at risk is less than zero, 10.22:253
 several activities, investment in, 10.20:253
Athletes, professional
 alien, temporarily in U.S., 1.18:28–30
 tax home for travel expense purposes, 20.7:393
At-the-money call option, 30.11:503
Attorney
 contingent fee paid from taxable award, 11.7:260
 estate tax planning, 39.6:595
 fees, deductibility of, 19.26:383–85
 fees, itemizing, 19.26:383–85
 fees, of marital settlements, 37.4:578, 37.8:580
 fees, recovering from, 48.7:699
 law school costs, 19.15:376, 19.17:378
 material participation tests for, 10.6:240
Audits
 about, Chapter 48 (684–90)
 agreeing to audit changes, 48.5:697–98

 cost of preparing for, 19.25:382–83
 disputing changes of, 48.6:698
 handling, 48.4:697
 interest abatement, 48.6:698
 IRS request for extension, 47.3:691
 odds of being audited, 48.1:695–96
 preparing for, 48.3:696–97
 recording IRS examination, 48.4:697
 recovering costs from, 48.7:699
 scheduling, 48.3:696
 types of, 48.2:696
 unified, for partnerships, 11.13:265
 waiving right to appeal, 48.5:697–98
Aunts, relationship test for claiming an exemption, 21.3:413
Authors, self-employed, 9.12:226, 40.9:611
Automobile. *See also* Travel and transportation expenses; Vehicles
 allocations of expenses between business and personal use, 43.2:651
 basis reduced by depreciation, 43.8:658–59
 business use, deducting expenses, 43.1:649–50
 company cars as fringe benefit, 3.7:62–64
 converting pleasure car to business use, 43.5:657
 damage to, deducting, 18.1:346–47, 18.7:352–53
 deducting expenses, Chapter 43 (648–61)
 deducting on Schedule C, 40.6:608, 648
 demonstration cars as fringe benefit, 3.7:62
 depreciation of
  after recovery period ends, 43.8:658–59
  annual ceilings on, 43.4:652–54
  business use of 50% or less, 43.6:657–58
  for year in which car is disposed of, 43.7:658
 donations, 14.6:294, 14.7:296
 electric cars, 43.4:654
 employee deduction limit of 2% AGI, 43.2:651
 employer convenience test, 43.3:651
 exotic cars, 42.1:632
 IRS mileage allowance, 19.8:372–73, 43.1:649–50
 leased business autos, 43.2:651, 43.12:660
 license fees, 16.10:326
 loans for, interest on, 43.2:651
 loans on, 43.1:649, 43.2:651
 local transportation costs for job-related travel, 19.8:372–73
 MACRS accelerated rates, 43.1:649–50, 43.3:651–52, 43.5:654
 MACRS deductions for capital improvements, 43.5:655
 MACRS recovery periods, 42.4:635
 mileage allowances, 19.8:372–73, 20.33:409
 more-than-50% business-use test, 43.3:651–52, 43.5:654–55
 "passenger" types exempt from annual ceilings on depreciation, 43.4:653
 placed in service after September 10, 2001, 43.4:652–54, 43.5:655
 recapture of deductions, 43.10:659
 recapture of first-year expensing, 44.3:664
 recordkeeping, 43.11:660
 reporting taxable benefits, 3.7:62
 school, transportation to, 19.22:380
 as support item, 21.7:416
 trade-in of, 43.9:659, 44.10:667

Index

Construction to residence, figuring gain or loss on sale of, 29.5:484

Constructive sales of appreciated financial positions, 30.8:499–500

Consultants
material participation tests for, 10.6:240
self-employment tax rules for, 45.6:673

Contingent fees
paid out of taxable awards, 19.27:385
salary or wage income (compensation), 2.1:39–40

Contingent payment sales
fixed payment period, 5.25:123–24
maximum selling price, 5.25:123
rent/royalty income agreement, 5.25:123–24

Continuing care facilities
deductibility of payments to, 17.11:338–39
imputed interest on payments to, 34.11:554
loans to, 4.31:96
payment to, as support item, 21.8:417
tax effects of moving to, 34.10:553–54

Contract cancellations, 30.9:501

Contract price, 5.22:120

CONUS meals and incidental expenses, 20.4:390–91

CONUS federal travel rates, 20.32:408

Convenience of employer test for employer-furnished meals or lodging, 3.11:65

Convention travel
nondeductible, 19.24:382
outside North American area, deducting expenses at, 20.14:398–99
travel and entertainment deductions for, 20.1:388

Conventions and seminars, deducting expenses of, 20.12:397–98

Conversion transaction, capital gain restricted on, 30.9:501, 30.10:501–2

Convertible bonds, 4.17:83, 30.7:498–99

Convertible securities, tax-free exchanges of, 6.8:143, 30.7:498–99

Convertible stocks, 30.7:498–99

Cooperative housing unit
basis for gain or loss, 29.5:485
capital loss of stock in, 29.9:488
deductions on, 15.9:314, 16.6:323, 16.9:325
depreciation of office in, 40.17:619, 42.1:632
depreciation on, 9.4:218
home acquisition loans for, 15.2:308
information returns required by the IRS, 47.2:690
residence ownership requirement, 29.1:480

Co-owners, shared-equity financing agreements for, 9.8:221

Copiers, 19.11:375, 42.4:635

Copyrights. See also Intangible personal property; Royalty income and deductions
depreciation of costs over life of, 9.13:226–27
information returns required by the IRS, 47.2:690

Corporate bonds, 30.16:506–8
issuing and trading, 30.16:507

Corporate liquidation, 44.11:667

Corporation. See also S corporation
benefits to shareholder-employee, 4.7:75

closely held
passive activity rules, 10.15:248
tax-free exchanges with, 6.10:143–44
earnings and profits of, 4.5:74–75
form of doing business, 40.1:600
organizational costs, 40.11:612
reorganizations or mergers, exchanging market discount bonds in, 4.20:85–87

Cosmetic surgery
as job expense, 19.9:374
reimbursed, 3.2:57
when deductible, 17.3:329

Cost basis of home, decreases to, 29.6:485

Cost depletion, 9.15:227–28

Counselor of elementary and secondary school. See Educator expenses

Coupon bonds
stripped, 4.22:88
zero, 4.22:88

Covenant not to compete, Section 197, 42.18:645

Coverdell Education Savings Accounts, 38.4:582–83, 38.11:588, 38.12:589.
contributing to, 38.11:588
contribution limits for 2002, 38.11:588
coordination with education credits, 38.12:589
distributions from, 38.12:589, 38.13:590
effect on education tax credits, 38.7:586

Credit card
fees not deductible, 19.25:383
paying taxes with, 46.2:679, 46.4:680–81
statements, as record, 20.27:404

Crop damage payments, voluntary withholding on, 26.7:463

Cruise ships
business trips on, 20.5:392
conventions on, deductions for, 20.14:399

Custodial parents, exemption for child and, 21.11:421

Custodial accounts, 33.2:538–40

D

Daily meal allowance for 2002, 20.4:390–91

Damages, receipts in court actions for, 11.7:259–60

Day care center, dependent care credit and, 25.6:451–52

Day care services, 3.4:60
home used to provide, 40.12:615

Deadline
for Coverdell ESAs, 38.11:588
for donation receipts in 2002, 14.15:302
for filing returns, 6
for Form 3115 (Application for Change in Accounting Method), 43.4:653
for estimated tax installments for 2003, 27.3:470
for gains on publicly traded securities, 30.1:492
Keogh plans, 41.6:628
for Roth IRA, 8.20:207–8
for setting up SEP or Keogh plan, 41.4:626, 41.5:627
for SIMPLE IRAs, 8.17:205

Dealer in commodities and options, self-employment tax rules for, 45.1:669, 45.6:673

Dealer of securities, 30.23:514, 40.6:608, 45.1:669

Dealer sales, installment, 5.21:119

Death. See also Decedent (deceased person)
of Armed Forces personnel, 35.6:559–60
of dependent, 21.3:412–13
of investor in a passive interest, 10.13:247
in terroristic or military actions, 35.6:559–60

Death benefits, separate payment of, 7.28:175–76

Death of spouse. See also Surviving spouse
before sale of home, 29.3:482
claiming any unused loss carryover, 5.5:103
community property rules and, 1.6:16
estimated taxes, 27.4:470
exemption claim, 21.2:412
filing new Form W-4, 26.6:463
IRA transfer upon, 8.11:191
in 2001 or 2000, qualifying widow(er) rates, 1.11:23
in 2002, 1.10:21–22

Debt obligations, 4.23:88–89. See also Bonds

Debts. See also Bad debt deductions; Interest (paid or owed); Loans
cancellation of, 11.8:260–62, 11.14:265
cancellation of debts you owe, as taxable income, 2.3:40
consumer, home equity loan to pay, 15.3:309
home equity, 15.1:307, 15.3:309
owed to you, interest income on, 4.14:79
Partnerships, 11.8:262
S corporation, 11.8:262, 11.14:265

Decedent (deceased person). See also Executor or administrator; Surviving spouse
capital loss carryover and, 5.4:102
distribution of Roth IRAs to beneficiaries, 8.24:213
filing returns for, 1.14:26–27
final return of, 1.14:26–27
income in respect of (IRD), 11.16:267
joint tenancy basis rules for surviving tenants, 5.18:115–16
medical expenses of, 1.14:26–27, 17.8:336
partnership income, 1.14:26–27
promptly closing estate, 1.14:26–27
refund due to, 1.14:26–27
reporting income of deceased spouse, 1.10:21–22
Series E or EE bonds transferred at death, 4.29:94
survivors of workers abroad returning to U.S., 36.6:569
transfer of depreciable property, 44.4:664–65
transfer of installment notes, 5.28:125–26

Declining balance method for automobile depreciation, 43.7:658

Deductible contribution to Keogh or SEP, 41.4:626, 41.5:626–28
self-employed's rate table for figuring, 41.5:627

Deductible medical expenses, 17.4:329–33

Deductions. See also Itemized deductions; Standard deduction
accelerating, 28.1:476
claiming, 269–424
of deceased person, 1.14:26–27
expenses of looking for new business, 40.11:612
first-year expensing, 40.8:610, 42.3:633–35
from gross income, 12.2:272–74
limited by losses and low income, 42.3:633–35

Deemed sale for 2001 and suspended losses, 10.13:247

Index

Index

Index

Index

Losses disallowed on sales to related persons, capital gains (or losses), 5.6:**103**–4
Lost deposits, 4.13:**79**
Lottery winnings, 11.2:**255**
Low-income housing credit, 31.8:**522**, 40.23:**622**
Lump-sum distributions from retirement plans. *See* Retirement plans
  distributions that may not be rolled over, 7.7:**154**
  of employer securities, 7.10:**157**–58
  of endowment policy, 7.24:**172**–73
  once in a lifetime election, 7.3:**150**
  options if you were born before 1936, 7.3:**149**–50
  prior rollover caution, 7.2:**149**
  from qualified retirement plans, 11.16:**267**
  rollovers, 7.2:**149**, 7.3:**150**, 7.7:**153**–54

M

M+C MSAs (Medicare + Choice Medical Savings Accounts), 3.1:**55**
M&IE rate (meals and incidental expenses), 20.4:**390**
MACRS (modified accelerated cost recovery system)
  additions and improvements to property, 42.13:**641**–42, 42.16:**643**–44
  alternative depreciation system (ADS) vs., 42.9:**638**–39
  AMT and, 23.2:**435**–36, 23.3:**437**–38
  for automobiles, 43.1:**649**–50, 43.3:**651**–52, 43.10:**659**
    half-year convention, 43.5:**655**–56
    mid-quarter conversion, 43.5:**655**–56
  class lives under, 42.4:**635**
  deductions, 44.3:**664**
  depreciation rate, 19.10:**374**–75, 42.5:**635**–37, 42.7:**637**
  half-year convention for, 42.6:**637**
  mid-quarter convention for, 42.7:**637**–38
  150% rate election, 42.8:**638**
  for real estate placed in service after 1986, 42.13:**641**–42
  recovery periods, 42.4:**635**
  straight-line depreciation vs., 42.9:**638**–39
  when not allowed, 42.17:**644**
MAGI (modified adjusted gross income)
  AGI and, 38.10:**588**
  eligibility for deductible higher education expenses, 38.13:**590**
  IRA deductions and, 8.3:**181**–82, 8.4:**182**–85
  $100,000 MAGI limit for converting traditional IRA to Roth IRA, 8.21:**208**–9
  phase-out, education credits and, 38.10:**587**–88
  phase-out limits to Roth IRA, 8.20:**207**, 8.21:**208**–9
  student loan interest deduction, 38.6:**584**–85, 38.10:**587**–88
Maintenance expenses, as rental income deduction, 9.2:**216**, 9.9:**223**. *See also* Household expenses
Malpractice insurance, 40.6:**607**, 40.7:**609**
Management fees, 31.1:**517**
Margin account with a broker, interest deduction, 15.13:**318**

Marginal production, higher depletion for, 9.16:**229**
Marginal tax rate, phaseout increases of, 21.16:**423**–24
Marital actions
  deducting legal fees for recovered taxable damages, 19.26:**383**–85
  key to settlement issues, **577**
Marital deduction
  estate tax and, 39.6:**594**–95
  for noncitizen spouses, 39.6:**594**–95
Marital status, about, **3**
  change in, and net operating loss, 40.18:**619**–20
  determined at end of year, 1.1:**10**
Marked-to-market rules for Section 1256 contracts, 30.9:**501**
Market discount bonds, 4.18:**84**
  interest on loans to buy, 4.20:**85**–87, 15.10:**314**–15
  reporting income on, 4.20:**85**–87
  tax-exempts, 4.26:**90**
Mark-to-mark election, 30.24:**515**
Marriage (married persons)
  capital losses of, 5.5:**103**
  common law, filing status and, 1.1:**10**
  earned income test for dependent care credit, 25.5:**451**
  estimated taxes by, 27.4:**470**
  filing jointly
    moving expenses, 12.6:**277**
    Social Security benefits, 34.7:**552**
  filing separately
    ineligible for deduction for higher education expenses in 2002–2005, 38.13:**590**
    rental real estate loss allowance, 10.2:**233**
    and Social Security benefits, 34.3:**549**, 34.7:**552**
    $24,000 limit reduced if, 42.3:**634**
    versus jointly, 1.3:**11**–13
  IRAs, spousal, 8.3:**181**–82
  married IRA owners, 8.21:**209**
  self-employment income and, 45.1:**669**
  separate property and, 1.6:**15**
  separate residences and, 29.3:**483**
  switching to joint return, 1.3:**13**
  working in different cities, tax home of, 20.8:**393**–94
Marriage penalty relief, delayed, 1.1:**10**
Material participation, 10.15:**248**, 31.2:**518**
  IRS tests for, 10.6:**239**–40
  limited partners, 10.11:**245**
  proof of, 10.6:**238**
  recharacterization, 10.9:**242**–44
  rental real estate activity, 10.3:**235**
  self-employment income and, 45.1:**669**
  tests, 10.3:**235**–36, 10.4:**237**, 10.6:**238**–40
MBA courses, deductibility of, 19.15:**377**
Meal allowance, per diem travel allowance, 20.32:**408**–9
Meal costs
  nondeductible, 12.3:**274**–75
  at nursing home, 17.11:**338**

Meal expenses. *See also* Entertainment and meal expenses
  cash allowances for, 3.11:**66**
  to employees on employer premises, 20.24:**401**–3
  employer charges for, 3.11:**65**–67
  employer-furnished meals, 3.11:**65**–67
  IRS meal allowance, 20.4:**390**–91
  overnight-sleep test, 20.2:**390**
  overtime meal money as de minimis fringe benefit, 3.9:**64**
  record-keeping, 20.4:**391**
Medical or dental expenses, Ch. 17
  about, **280**
  AGI income and deductions, 17.4:**331**
  Archer MSAs, 3.1:**54**–55, 12.2:**273**, 17.17:**343**–44
  business expenses, deductible as, 17.14:**341**–42
  care costs qualifying as, 25.7:**452**–54
  conferences, 17.9:**337**
  for continuing care facilities, 34.10:**553**–54
  deductible, 17.2:**328**–29, 17.4:**330**
  employees on leave, 3.14:**69**–70
  flexible spending arrangements (FSAs) and, 3.14:**69**–70
  exception to IRA early-withdrawal penalty, 8.12:**192**
  home improvements as, 17.13:**340**–41
  long-term care insurance, 17.15:**342**
  nondeductible, 17.3:**329**, 17.4:**331**
  nurses' wages, 17.12:**339**–40
  of decedent, 1.14:**26**–27, 17.8:**336**
  of terminally ill, 17.16:**343**
  premiums of medical care policies, 17.5:**333**–34
  reduction of, 17.4:**329**–33
  reimbursements for, 11.6:**258**, 17.4:**329**–33
  reimbursements for, 3.2:**56**–58
  schooling for mentally or physically handicapped, 17.10:**338**
  self-employed and, 17.5:**334**
  senior citizen care facilities/nursing homes, 17.11:**338**–39
  as support item, 21.7:**416**
  travel costs as deductions, 17.9:**336**–38
Medical savings accounts (MSAs), 3.1:**54**–56. *See* Archer MSAs
Medicare tax. *See also* FICA tax
  child tax credit and, 25.1:**448**
  deducting on Schedule C, 40.6:**608**
  employer health and accident plans and, 3.1:**54**–56
  for household employees, 25.9:**454**, 25.10:**454**–56
  not a support item, 21.7:**417**
  self-employment tax and, 45.4:**671**
  uncollected taxes, 3.3:**59**, 26.8:**463**–64
  withholdings, 26.8:**463**–64, 26.10:**464**–65
Mexico, aliens who commute from, 183-day test and, 1.18:**29**
Mileage allowance, by IRS, 19.8:**372**–73, 43.1:**649**–50
Mileage test, for moving expenses, 12.4:**275**
Military personnel. *See* Armed forces
Minimum interest rules, 4.30:**94**
Minimum distribution rules, 7.13:**160**, 8.13:**195**–99

Index

Index

Index

Index

Index

Index

Index: Tax Forms, Schedules, and Tables

If you like your money, you'll love ours.

Using Microsoft® Money 2003 Deluxe throughout the year makes tax time easier!

Ease into Money 2003

It's easy to start using Money. Begin with your most common transactions: paycheck, bills, and checks. Enter your information into Money 2003 instead of your checkbook register. Or, even better, Money 2003 can download your information automatically from your financial institution. Your information can be automatically filtered for tax line-items, potential deductions and much more!

Monitor your tax liabilities

Throughout the year, Money 2003 gives you easy access to your personalized tax information, allowing you to quickly review your withholding and potential tax liabilities. The home page Advisor FYI™ alerts remind you of important tax deadlines to help you stay on top of your taxes.

Manage your deductions

Every time you enter information into Money 2003, the Deduction Finder can spot potential tax deductions you may be eligible for. You can use Money's Capital Gains Estimator to see how a mid-year investment sell-off might change your tax situation.

File it and forget it

Relevant information in Money 2003 can be easily exported into popular tax software or even sent to your accountant. Or, you can use the Money 2003 Tax Time To-Do List to gather the information you need for filing by hand. **Money 2003 Deluxe comes with over $160 worth of financial services, including FREE online tax preparation and filing from H&R Block.**

Microsoft Money 2003 is the personal finance software that works for you every day. Download a trial version of Money 2003 Deluxe FREE at:
http://www.microsoft.com/money/promo/trial

Good in the 50 United States and the District of Columbia.

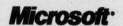